Lecture Notes in Computer Science 5850

Commenced Publication in 1973
Founding and Former Series Editors:
Gerhard Goos, Juris Hartmanis, and Jan van Leeuwen

Ana Cavalcanti Dennis Dams (Eds.)

FM 2009: Formal Methods

Second World Congress
Eindhoven, The Netherlands, November 2-6, 2009
Proceedings

Springer

Volume Editors

Ana Cavalcanti
University of York
Department of Computer Science
Heslington
York Y010 5DD, UK
E-mail: ana.cavalcanti@cs.york.ac.uk

Dennis Dams
Bell Laboratories
600 Mountain Ave.
Murray Hill
NJ 07974, USA
E-mail: dennis@research.bell-labs.com

Library of Congress Control Number: 2009936485

CR Subject Classification (1998): D.2, F.3, D.3, D.1, J.1, K.6, F.4

LNCS Sublibrary: SL 2 – Programming and Software Engineering

ISSN 0302-9743
ISBN-10 3-642-05088-3 Springer Berlin Heidelberg New York
ISBN-13 978-3-642-05088-6 Springer Berlin Heidelberg New York

springer.com

Typesetting: Camera-ready by author, data conversion by Scientific Publishing Services, Chennai, India
Printed on acid-free paper SPIN: 12778379 06/3180 5 4 3 2 1 0

Preface

FM 2009, the 16th International Symposium on Formal Methods, marked the 10th anniversary of the First World Congress on Formal Methods that was held in 1999 in Toulouse, France. We wished to celebrate this by advertising and organizing FM 2009 as the Second World Congress in the FM series, aiming to once again bring together the formal methods communities from all over the world. The statistics displayed in the table on the next page include the number of countries represented by the Programme Committee members, as well as of the authors of submitted and accepted papers.

Novel this year was a special track on tools and industrial applications. Submissions of papers on these topics were especially encouraged, but not given any special treatment. (It was just as hard to get a special track paper accepted as any other paper.) What we did promote, however, was a discussion of how originality, contribution, and soundness should be judged for these papers. The following questions were used by our Programme Committee.

- Does the tool provide a proof of concept, or solve an important problem?
- Is there an interesting algorithm implemented in the tool?
- Were new techniques used to implement the tool?
- If it is an industrial application, does it clearly present the lessons learned in relation to the use of formal methods?
- Is the tool available (not necessarily for free) to the community?
- Are there (measured or significant) experiments that support the claims?
- How does the tool scale to larger problems?
- What is the (potential) impact of the tool or case study?
- What is the complexity of the tool or application?

We believe these questions can help future authors and reviewers of such papers.

The authors of a selection of the papers included here will be invited to submit extended versions of their papers to special anniversary issues of two reputable journals: *Formal Aspects of Computing* and *Formal Methods in System Design*.

An event of this scale is only possible when many put their energy and passion together. We have attempted to thank all those people. If you feel you should have been included but are not, rest assured that this is not intentional, and please accept our apologies.

For the first time, a number of scientific events dedicated to Formal Methods and their application decided to co-locate under the heading of *Formal Methods Week (FMweek)*. We hope that you enjoyed FM 2009, as well as several of the other events. Or, did you miss it? Maybe next time then!

August 2009

Ana Cavalcanti
Dennis Dams

Statistics

number of PC members	83
number of countries of PC members	46
number of submissions	139
number of countries of submissions' authors	38
number of reviews per paper**	4
number of papers accepted*	45
number of countries of accepted papers' authors	23
number of invited papers	5

* There are 3 additional papers included from Industry Day
** with a few exceptions in both directions

Organization

Chairs

General	Jos Baeten
Workshop	Erik de Vink
Tutorial	Jan Friso Groote
Publicity	Arend Rensink
Tool Exhibition	Alexander Serebrenik
Doctoral Symposium	Mohammad Mousavi Emil Sekerinski
Industry Day	Jozef Hooman Andreas Roth Marcel Verhoef
Local Organization	Tijn Borghuis Christine van Gils Heleen de Morrée

Programme Committee

Ralph-Johan Back
Jos Baeten
Sergey Baranov
Gilles Barthe
Rahma Ben-Ayed
Mohamed Bettaz
Dines Bjørner
Michael Butler
Rodrigo Cardoso
Ana Cavalcanti (Chair)
Flavio Corradini
Jorge Cuellar
Dennis Dams (Chair)
Van Hung Dang
Jim Davies
Susanna Donatelli
Jin Song Dong
Cindy Eisner
Lars-Henrik Eriksson
Juhan-P. Ernits
Jasmin Fisher
John Fitzgerald
Limor Fix
Marc Frappier
Marcelo Frias
Masahiro Fujita
Marie-Claude Gaudel
Stefania Gnesi
Lindsay Groves
Anthony Hall
Anne Haxthausen
Ian Hayes
Matthew Hennessy
Leszek Holenderski
Ralf Huuck
Predrag Janicic
Cliff Jones
Rajeev Joshi
Shmuel Katz
Moonzoo Kim
Nils Klarlund
Jens Knoop
Bob Kurshan
Peter Gorm Larsen
Yves Ledru
Insup Lee
Huimin Lin
Zhiming Liu
Nancy Lynch
Tom Maibaum
Dino Mandrioli
Annabelle McIver
Dominique Mery
Marius Minea
Sjouke Mauw
Peter Mueller
Tobias Nipkow
Manuel Nunez
Jose Nuno Oliveira
Gordon Pace

Paritosh Pandya
Alberto Pardo
Frantisek Plasil
Jaco van de Pol
Ingrid Rewitzky
Leila Ribeiro
Augusto Sampaio
Steve Schneider
Christel Seguin
Emil Sekerinski
Kaisa Sere
Natalia Sidorova
Marjan Sirjani
Ketil Stolen
Andrzej Tarlecki
Axel van Lamsweerde
Daniel Varro
Marcel Verhoef
Jurgen Vinju
Willem Visser
Farn Wang
Jim Woodcock
Husnu Yenigun

Additional Reviewers

Nazareno Aguirre
Bijan Alizadeh
José Almeida
David Arney
Vlastimil Babka
Ezio Bartocci
Nazim Benaissa
Josh Berdine
Pierre Bieber
Jean-Paul Bodeveix
Reinder Bril
Lukas Bulwahn
Andrew Butterfield
Diletta Cacciagrano
Cristiano Calcagno
Jian Chang
Jia-Fu Chen
Chen Chunqing
Manuel Clavel
Robert Colvin
Pieter Cuijpers
Kriangsak Damchoom
Francesco De Angelis
Nikhil Dinesh
Simon Doherty
Brijesh Dongol
Andrew Edmunds
Michel Embe-Jiague
Gabriel Erzse
Alessandro Fantechi
Yuzhang Feng
Pietro Ferrara
Miguel Ferreira
Pascal Fontaine
Benoît Fraikin
Adrian Francalanza
David Frutos-Escrig
Carlo Furia
Rohit Gheyi
Mike Gordon
Bogdan Groza
Tormod Haavaldsrud
Daniel Hedin
Rolf Hennicker
Hsi-Min Ho
Shin Hong
Andras Horvath
Chung-Hao Huang
Guo-Chiao Huang
Marieke Huisman
Juliano Iyoda
Mohammad-Javad Izadi
Bart Jacobs
Tomasz Janowski
Pavel Jezek
Sun Jun
Amir Kantor
Ehsan Khamespanah
Ramtin Khosravi
Jan Kofron
Natallia Kokash
Pierre Konopacki
Barbara Kordy
Daniel Kroening
Ruurd Kuiper
Cesar Kunz
Ralf Laemmel
Linas Laibinis
Jaewoo Lee
Hermann Lehner
David Lester
Yang Liu
Luis Llana
Kamal Lodaya
Carlos Luna
Mass Lund
Yi Lv
Issam Maamria
Pasquale Malacaria
Petra Malik
Filip Maric
Mieke Massink
Franco Mazzanti
Mercedes Merayo
Stephan Merz
Dale Miller
Charles Morisset
Alexandre Mota
MohammadReza Mousavi
Ned Nedialkov
Truong Nguyen
Van Nguyen
Rotem Oshman
Olga Pacheco
Hong Pan
Jun Pang
Pavel Parizek
David Parker
Luigia Petre
Jorge Pinto
Nir Piterman
Tomas Poch
Andrea Polini
Vinayak Prabhu
Matteo Pradella

Viorel Preoteasa
Niloofar Razavi
Barbara Re
Joris Rehm
Abdolbaghi Rezazadeh
Tamara Rezk
Oliviero Riganelli
Mauno Rönkkö
Fernando Rosa-Velardo
Matteo Rossi
Ragnhild Runde
Mar Yah Said
Cesar Sanchez
Stefan Schwoon
Fredrik Seehusen
Alexander Serebrenik
Ondrej Sery
Sharon Shoham
Luis Sierra
Francois Siewe
Neeraj Singh
Bjornar Solhaug
Paola Spoletini
Ofer Shtrichman
Jeremy Sproston
Volker Stolz
Sayantan Surs
Dejvuth Suwimonteerabuth
Andras Telcs
Mark Timmer
Nikola Trcka
Helen Treharne
Carmela Troncoso
Hoang Truong
Ninh Truong
Edward Turner
Shinya Umeno
Jan-Martijn van der Werf
Ton van Deursen
Szilvia Varro-Gyapay
Ha Viet
Marc Voorhoeve
Shaohui Wang
Shuling Wang
Michael Weber
James Welch
Kirsten Winter
Simon Winwood
Hong-Hsin Wu
Rong-Shuan Wu
Hsuen-Chin Yang
Lv Yi
Eduardo Zambon
Santiago Zanella
Chenyi Zhang
Xian Zhang
Jianjun Zhao

FM Steering Committee

Dines Bjørner
John Fitzgerald
Marie-Claude Gaudel
Stefania Gnesi
Ian Hayes
Jim Woodcock
Pamela Zave

Workshops

FMIS - Formal Methods for Interactive Systems
Organizers: Michael Harrison and Mieke Massink

CompMod - Computational Models for Cell Processes
Organizers: Ralph-Johan Back, Ion Petre and Erik de Vink

FMA - Formal Methods for Aeronautics
Organizers: Manuela Bujorianu, Michael Fisher, and Corina Pasareanu

QFM - Quantitative Formal Methods: Theory and Applications
Organizers: Suzana Andova and Annabelle McIver

VDM and Overture
Organizers: Peter Gorm Larsen and Jeremy Bryans

FAVO - Formal Aspects of Virtual Organizations
Organizers: John Fitzgerald and Jeremy Bryans

FOPARA - Foundational and Practical Aspects of Resource Analysis
Organizers: Marko van Eekelen and Olha Shkaravska

Tutorials

Analyzing UML/OCL Models with HOL-OCL
Tutors: Achim Brucker and Burkhart Wolff

Practical MPI and Pthread Dynamic Verification
Tutors: Ganesh Gopalakrishnan and Robert Kirby

Behavioral Analysis Using mCRL2
Tutors: Aad Mathijssen, Michel Reniers, and Tim Willemse

Constraint-Based Validation of Imperative Programs
Tutors: Michel Rueher and Arnaud Gotlieb

Bounded Model-Checking and Satisfiability-Checking: A Flexible Approach for System Modeling and Verification
Tutors: Angelo Morzenti, Matteo Pradella, Matteo Rossi

Computational Systems Biology
Tutors: Ion Petre and Ralph-Johan Back

Rely/Guarantee-Thinking
Tutors: Joey Coleman and Cliff Jones

Doctoral Symposium Programme Committee

S. Arun-Kumar
Paulo Borba
Michael Butler
Jin Song Dong
Wan Fokkink
Ichiro Hasuo
Anna Ingolfsdottir
Joost-Pieter Katoen
Ian Mackie
MohammadReza Mousavi
Mila Dalla Preda
Emil Sekerinski
Sandeep Shukla
Bernd-Holger Schlingloff
Elena Troubitsyna
Tarmo Uustalu
Frits Vaandrager
Husnu Yenigun

Best Paper Awards to

Raymond Boute
Andre Platzer and Edmund Clarke

Special Thanks to

The local organizers
EasyChair, Andrei Voronkov, Tatiana Rybina
Congress Office TU/e
Formal Techniques Industrial Association (ForTIA)
Ursula Barth, Alfred Hofmann, Anna Kramer, Christine Reiss, Jessica Wengzik, and Gokula Prakash at Springer
Van Abbemuseum
The city of Eindhoven
FMweek 2009

Sponsored by

SAP
Springer

Table of Contents

Invited Papers

Formal Methods for Privacy 1
Michael Carl Tschantz and Jeannette M. Wing

What Can Formal Methods Bring to Systems Biology? 16
Nicola Bonzanni, K. Anton Feenstra, Wan Fokkink, and Elzbieta Krepska

Guess and Verify – Back to the Future 23
Colin O'Halloran

Verification, Testing and Statistics 33
Sriram K. Rajamani

Security, Probability and Nearly Fair Coins in the Cryptographers' Café 41
Annabelle McIver, Larissa Meinicke, and Carroll Morgan

Model Checking I

Recursive Abstractions for Parameterized Systems 72
Joxan Jaffar and Andrew E. Santosa

Abstract Model Checking without Computing the Abstraction 89
Stefano Tonetta

Three-Valued Spotlight Abstractions 106
Jonas Schrieb, Heike Wehrheim, and Daniel Wonisch

Fair Model Checking with Process Counter Abstraction 123
Jun Sun, Yang Liu, Abhik Roychoudhury, Shanshan Liu, and Jin Song Dong

Compositionality

Systematic Development of Trustworthy Component Systems 140
Rodrigo Ramos, Augusto Sampaio, and Alexandre Mota

Partial Order Reductions Using Compositional Confluence Detection ... 157
Frédéric Lang and Radu Mateescu

A Formal Method for Developing Provably Correct Fault-Tolerant Systems Using Partial Refinement and Composition 173
Ralph Jeffords, Constance Heitmeyer, Myla Archer, and Elizabeth Leonard

Verification

Abstract Specification of the UBIFS File System for Flash Memory 190
Andreas Schierl, Gerhard Schellhorn, Dominik Haneberg, and Wolfgang Reif

Inferring Mealy Machines 207
Muzammil Shahbaz and Roland Groz

Formal Management of CAD/CAM Processes 223
Michael Kohlhase, Johannes Lemburg, Lutz Schröder, and Ewaryst Schulz

Concurrency

Translating Safe Petri Nets to Statecharts in a Structure-Preserving Way 239
Rik Eshuis

Symbolic Predictive Analysis for Concurrent Programs 256
Chao Wang, Sudipta Kundu, Malay Ganai, and Aarti Gupta

On the Difficulties of Concurrent-System Design, Illustrated with a 2×2 Switch Case Study 273
Edgar G. Daylight and Sandeep K. Shukla

Refinement

Sums and Lovers: Case Studies in Security, Compositionality and Refinement 289
Annabelle K. McIver and Carroll C. Morgan

Iterative Refinement of Reverse-Engineered Models by Model-Based Testing 305
Neil Walkinshaw, John Derrick, and Qiang Guo

Model Checking Linearizability via Refinement 321
Yang Liu, Wei Chen, Yanhong A. Liu, and Jun Sun

Static Analysis

It's Doomed; We Can Prove It 338
Jochen Hoenicke, K. Rustan M. Leino, Andreas Podelski, Martin Schäf, and Thomas Wies

"Carbon Credits" for Resource-Bounded Computations Using Amortised Analysis 354
Steffen Jost, Hans-Wolfgang Loidl, Kevin Hammond, Norman Scaife, and Martin Hofmann

Field-Sensitive Value Analysis by Field-Insensitive Analysis 370
Elvira Albert, Puri Arenas, Samir Genaim, and Germán Puebla

Theorem Proving

Making Temporal Logic Calculational: A Tool for Unification and Discovery 387
Raymond Boute

A Tableau for CTL* 403
Mark Reynolds

Certifiable Specification and Verification of C Programs 419
Christoph Lüth and Dennis Walter

Formal Reasoning about Expectation Properties for Continuous Random Variables 435
Osman Hasan, Naeem Abbasi, Behzad Akbarpour, Sofiène Tahar, and Reza Akbarpour

Semantics

The Denotational Semantics of *slotted-Circus* 451
Paweł Gancarski and Andrew Butterfield

Unifying Probability with Nondeterminism 467
Yifeng Chen and J.W. Sanders

Towards an Operational Semantics for Alloy 483
Theophilos Giannakopoulos, Daniel J. Dougherty, Kathi Fisler, and Shriram Krishnamurthi

A Robust Semantics Hides Fewer Errors 499
Steve Reeves and David Streader

Special Track: Industrial Applications I

Analysis of a Clock Synchronization Protocol for Wireless Sensor Networks 516
Faranak Heidarian, Julien Schmaltz, and Frits Vaandrager

Formal Verification of Avionics Software Products 532
Jean Souyris, Virginie Wiels, David Delmas, and Hervé Delseny

Formal Verification of Curved Flight Collision Avoidance Maneuvers: A Case Study 547
André Platzer and Edmund M. Clarke

Object-Orientation

Connecting UML and VDM++ with Open Tool Support 563
Kenneth Lausdahl, Hans Kristian Agerlund Lintrup, and Peter Gorm Larsen

Language and Tool Support for Class and State Machine Refinement in UML-B 579
Mar Yah Said, Michael Butler, and Colin Snook

Dynamic Classes: Modular Asynchronous Evolution of Distributed Concurrent Objects 596
Einar Broch Johnsen, Marcel Kyas, and Ingrid Chieh Yu

Abstract Object Creation in Dynamic Logic: To Be or Not to Be Created 612
Wolfgang Ahrendt, Frank S. de Boer, and Immo Grabe

Pointers

Reasoning about Memory Layouts 628
Holger Gast

A Smooth Combination of Linear and Herbrand Equalities for Polynomial Time Must-Alias Analysis 644
Helmut Seidl, Vesal Vojdani, and Varmo Vene

Real-Time

On the Complexity of Synthesizing Relaxed and Graceful Bounded-Time 2-Phase Recovery 660
Borzoo Bonakdarpour and Sandeep S. Kulkarni

Verifying Real-Time Systems against Scenario-Based Requirements 676
Kim G. Larsen, Shuhao Li, Brian Nielsen, and Saulius Pusinskas

Special Track: Tools and Industrial Applications II

Formal Specification of a Cardiac Pacing System 692
Artur Oliveira Gomes and Marcel Vinícius Medeiros Oliveira

Automated Property Verification for Large Scale B Models 708
Michael Leuschel, Jérôme Falampin, Fabian Fritz, and Daniel Plagge

Reduced Execution Semantics of MPI: From Theory to Practice 724
Sarvani Vakkalanka, Anh Vo, Ganesh Gopalakrishnan, and Robert M. Kirby

Model Checking II

A Metric Encoding for Bounded Model Checking 741
Matteo Pradella, Angelo Morzenti, and Pierluigi San Pietro

An Incremental Approach to Scope-Bounded Checking Using a Lightweight Formal Method 757
Danhua Shao, Sarfraz Khurshid, and Dewayne E. Perry

Verifying Information Flow Control over Unbounded Processes 773
William R. Harris, Nicholas A. Kidd, Sagar Chaki, Somesh Jha, and Thomas Reps

Specification and Verification of Web Applications in Rewriting Logic 790
María Alpuente, Demis Ballis, and Daniel Romero

Industry-Day Abstracts

Verifying the Microsoft Hyper-V Hypervisor with VCC 806
Dirk Leinenbach and Thomas Santen

Industrial Practice in Formal Methods: A Review 810
J.C. Bicarregui, J.S Fitzgerald, P.G. Larsen, and J.C.P. Woodcock

Model-Based GUI Testing Using UPPAAL at Novo Nordisk 814
Ulrik H. Hjort, Jacob Illum, Kim G. Larsen, Michael A. Petersen, and Arne Skou

Author Index 819

Formal Methods for Privacy

Michael Carl Tschantz and Jeannette M. Wing

Computer Science Department
Carnegie Mellon University
5000 Forbes Avenue
Pittsburgh, PA 15213
mtschant@cs.cmu.edu, wing@cs.cmu.edu

Abstract. Privacy means something different to everyone. Against a vast and rich canvas of diverse types of privacy rights and violations, we argue technology's dual role in privacy: new technologies raise new threats to privacy rights and new technologies can help preserve privacy. Formal methods, as just one class of technology, can be applied to privacy, but privacy raises new challenges, and thus new research opportunities, for the formal methods community.

1 Introduction

What is privacy? Today, the answer seems to be "It all depends on whom you ask." There are philosophical, legal, societal, and technical notions of privacy. Cultures differ in their expectations regarding privacy. In some cultures, it is impolite to ask someone's age or someone's salary. Governments differ in their citizens' rights to privacy; just witness the difference in privacy among the United States, the European Union, and China. What an adult thinks as private differs from what a teenager thinks, and vice versa [1].

New technologies give rise to new privacy concerns. Warren and Brandeis's 1890 seminal paper, "The Right to Privacy," was written after photographic and printing technologies made it easier to share and spread images and text in public [2]. Skipping ahead a century, with the explosion of the Internet, privacy is finally getting serious attention by the scientific community. More and more personal information about us is available online. It is by our choice that we give our credit card numbers to on-line retailers for the convenience of on-line shopping. Companies like Google, Yahoo, and Microsoft track our search queries to personalize the ads we see alongside the response to a query. With cloud computing, we further entrust in third parties the storage and management of private information in places unknown to us. We are making it easier for others to find out about our personal habits, tastes, and history. In some cases it is deliberate. The rise of social networks like Facebook, on-line community sites like Flickr, and communication tools like Twitter raises new questions about privacy, as people willingly give up some privacy to enhance social relationships or to share information easily with friends. At the same time, cyberattacks have increased

A. Cavalcanti and D. Dams (Eds.): FM 2009, LNCS 5850, pp. 1–15, 2009.

in number and sophistication, making it more likely that unintentionally or not, personal information will fall into the wrong hands.

The National Academies study *Engaging Privacy and Information Technology in a Digital Age* [3] presents a compelling argument for the need for technology and policy experts to work together in addressing privacy, especially as new technology raises new privacy concerns. It is our responsibility as scientists and engineers to understand what can or cannot be done from a technical point of view on privacy: what is provably possible or impossible and what is practically possible or impossible. Otherwise, society may end up in a situation where privacy regulations put into place are technically infeasible to meet.

In this paper, we start in Section 2 by painting a broad picture of the diverse types of privacy. Against this canvas, we discuss the dual role of technology: how new technologies pose new threats to privacy (Section 3) and how technologies can help preserve privacy (Section 4). Finally, focusing on formal methods, as a specific class of technology, we identify some opportunities and challenges in using formal methods to protect privacy (Section 5).

2 Types of Privacy Rights and Violations

Philosophers justify the importance of privacy in different ways. Bloustein defends privacy as necessary for human dignity [4]. Others focus on privacy's role in enabling intimate relations [5,6,7,8] or interpersonal relations in general [9]. Gavison views privacy as a means of controlling access to the person [10].

Given the numerous philosophical justifications, legal scholars, starting with Prosser [11], have generally viewed privacy as a collection of related rights rather than a single concept. Solove in 2006 provided a taxonomy of possible privacy violations [12]. He collects these related violations into four groups: *invasions*, *information collection*, *information processing*, and *information dissemination*.

Invasions represent interference in what is traditionally considered the private sphere of life. Solove identifies two forms of invasions. The first involves physical *intrusions* either upon private property (such as trespassing in the home) or upon the body (such as blocking one's passage). The second is *decisional interference*, which is interfering with personal decisions. For example, the Supreme Court of the United States has used the right to privacy to justify limiting the government's ability to regulate contraceptives [13,14], abortion [15], and sodomy [16] (cf. [17]). However, some view invasions as violations of other rights such as property and security rights in the case of intrusions [18], or the rights to autonomy and liberty in the case of decisional interference [19].

Solove's remaining three groupings of privacy rights are more difficult to reduce to other rights. They all involve a *data subject* about whom a *data holder* has information. The data holder may commit privacy violations in how he collects the information, how he processes it, or how he disseminates it to others.

Information collection includes making observations through *surveillance* and seeking information through *interrogation*. Information collection affects privacy by making people uneasy in how the collected information could be used. Thus, it is a violation of privacy even if the collected information is never used. Furthermore, interrogation can place people in the awkward position of having to refuse to answer questions. Even in the absence of these violations *per se*, information collection should be controlled to prevent other violations of privacy such as blackmail.

Even if information is collected in privacy-respecting ways, it can be processed in ways that violate privacy. Such information processing violations have the following forms. *Aggregation* is similar to surveillance in that it makes information available, but aggregation does so by combining diffuse pieces of information rather than collecting new information. Aggregation enables inferences that would be unavailable otherwise. *Identification*, linking information with a person by way of an identifier, also makes information more available and may alter how a person is treated. *Insecurity* makes information more available to those who should not be granted access such as identity thieves and can also lead to distortion of data if false data is entered. *Secondary uses* make information available for purposes for which it was not originally intended. *Exclusion* is the inability of a data subject to know what records are kept, to view them, to know how they are used, or to correct them. All these forms of information processing create uncertainty on the part of the data subject. Exclusion directly causes this uncertainty by keeping information about the information kept on the data subject secret. The other forms of information processing create this uncertainty by making information available in new, possibly unanticipated ways. Even in the absence of more material misuse of the information, such uncertainty can be a harm in of itself as it forces the data subject to live in fear of how his information may be used.

After information is processed, the data holder will typically disseminate it to others for use. Some forms of information dissemination can violate privacy by providing information to inappropriate entities. A breach of *confidentiality* occurs when a trusted data holder provides information about a data subject. An example would be a violation of patient-physician confidentiality. *Disclosure* involves not a violation of trust as with confidentiality, but rather the making of private information known outside the group of individuals who are expected to know it. *Exposure* occurs when embarrassing but trivial information is shared stripping the data subject of his dignity. *Distortion* is the presentation of false information about a person. Distortion harms not only the subject, whose reputation is damaged, but also third parties who are no longer able to accurately judge the subject's character. *Appropriation* is related to distortion. Appropriation associates a person with a cause or product that he did not agree to endorse. Appropriation adversely affects the ability of the person to present himself as he chooses. *Increased accessibility* occurs when a data holder makes previously available information more easily acquirable. It is a threat to privacy as it makes possible uses of the information that were previously too inefficient, and furthermore, potentially encourage unintended secondary uses. Rather than disseminating information, *blackmail* involves the threat of disseminating information unless some demand is met. It uses private information to create an inappropriate power relation with no social benefits.

These types of violations exist independent of technologies. However, technology plays a dual role in privacy. On the one hand, new technologies can create new ways of infringing upon privacy rights. On the other hand, new technologies can create new ways of preserving privacy.

3 Technology Raises New Privacy Concerns

Technological advances normally represent progress. The utility of these advances, however, must be balanced against any new privacy concerns they create. This tension forces society to examine how a new technology could affect privacy and how to mitigate any ill effects.

The courts often lead this examination. The first important U.S. law review article on privacy, Warren and Brandeis's "The Right to Privacy," was written in response to the ability of new cameras to take pictures quickly enough to capture images of unwilling subjects [2]. The advent of wire tapping technology led first to its acceptance [20] and then to its rejection [21] by the U.S. Supreme Court as its understanding of the technology, people's uses of phones, and government's obligations to privacy changed. Other new forms of surveillance including aerial observation [22,23], tracking devices [24,25], hidden video cameras [26], and thermal imaging [27] have all also been studied by courts in the U.S.

New technology has driven governments to create new regulations. The rise of large computer databases with new aggregation abilities led to the U.S. Federal Trade Commission's Fair Information Practice Principles requiring security and limiting secondary uses and exclusion [28]. In France, the public outcry over a proposal to create an aggregate government database, the System for Administrative Files Automation and the Registration of Individuals (SAFARI), forced the government to create the National Data Processing and Liberties Commission (CNIL), an independent regulatory agency. The rise of electronic commerce and the privacy concerns it created resulted in Canada's Personal Information Protection and Electronic Documents Act. Privacy concerns about electronic health records lead to the Privacy Rule under the Health Insurance Portability and Accountability Act (HIPPA) in the U.S. to mixed results [29]. Each of these regulations is designed to allow new technologies to be used, but not in ways that could violate privacy.

Society is still forming its response to some new technologies. For example, data mining, one technique used for aggregation, has received a mixed reaction. In the U.S., the Total Information Awareness data mining program was largely shut down by Congress, only to be followed by the Analysis, Dissemination, Visualization, Insight and Semantic Enhancement (ADVISE) system, also shut down. However, rather then banning the practice, the Federal Agency Data Mining Reporting Act of 2007 requires agencies to report on their uses of data mining to Congress. Apparently, Congress has not come to a consensus on how to limit data mining and is still studying the concern on a case by case basis.

4 Technology Helps Preserve Privacy

Some of the new threats to privacy created by technology cannot efficiently or effectively be addressed by government action alone. Further technological advances can in some cases provide ways to mitigate these new threats.

In this section, we first give a quick tour through many different technical approaches used to complement or to reinforce non-technical approaches to preserving privacy (Section 4.1), and then focus in detail on two related classes of privacy violations, *disclosure and aggregation*, which have garnered the most attention recently from the computer science community (Section 4.2). We save till Section 5 our discussion of the role that formal methods, as a class of technology, can play in privacy.

4.1 A Diversity of Technical Approaches

While a government may legislate punishment for breaching the security of computer systems storing private records, such punishments can at best only dissuade criminals; they do not prevent privacy violations in any absolute sense. Cryptographic-based technologies with provably secure properties (e.g., one-time pads that guarantee perfect secrecy) or systems that have been formally verified with respect to a given security property (e.g., secure operating systems kernels [30,31,32]) can actually make some violations impossible. Likewise, identity theft laws might discourage the practice, but digital signatures can prevent appropriation [33,34]. Even security technologies, such as intrusion detection systems and spam filters, which may not have provably secure properties, are indispensable in practice for mitigating attacks of intrusion.

In some cases, a data subject might not trust the government or third-party data holders to prevent a violation. For example, political bosses or coercive agents might attempt to learn for which candidate someone voted. In such cases, voting schemes that inherently prevent the disclosure of this information, even to election officials, would be more trustworthy; such schemes have been developed using cryptography (e.g., [35,36]) or paper methods inspired by cryptography [37]. Political dissidents who wish to hide their online activities can use onion routing, based on repeated encryption, for anonymous Internet use [38]. Privacy preserving data mining (e.g., [39]) offers the government a way of finding suspicious activities without giving it access to private information [40,41]. *Vanishing data* guarantees data subjects that their private data stored in the "cloud" be permanently unreadable at a specific time; this recent work by Geambasu et al. [42] relies on public-key cryptography, Shamir's secret sharing scheme, and the natural churn of distributed hash tables in the Internet.

Mathematical formulations of different notions of privacy are also useful for guiding the development of privacy preserving technologies and making it easier to identify privacy violations. Halpern and O'Neill formalize privacy relevant concepts such as secrecy and anonymity using logics of knowledge [43]. In response to Gavison's desire for "protection from being brought to the attention of others" [10], Chawla et al. formalize a notion of an individual's record being conspicuously different from the other records in a set [44]; they characterize this notion in terms of high-dimensional spaces over the reals.

4.2 A Heightened Focus on Disclosure and Aggregation

As Solove notes, aggregation can violate privacy [12]. The form of aggregation Solove describes is when the data holder combines data from multiple sources. Another form of aggregation occurs when the data holder publishes a seemingly harmless data set and an adversary combines this data set with others to find out information that the data holder did not intend to be learned. In this case, the adversary commits the violation of aggregation, but the data holder inadvertently commits the violation of disclosure. Thus, a responsible data holder must ensure that any data he releases cannot be aggregated by others to learn private information.

In the context of databases and anonymization, researchers have studied a special case of the above attack, called *linkage attacks*. In its simplest form, a collection of records, each about an individual, is anonymized by removing any explicit identifiers, such as names or IP addresses. After a data holder releases the anonymized database, an adversary compares it to another database that is not anonymized but holds information about some of the same people in the anonymized database. If one database holds a record r_1 and the second database holds a record r_2 such that r_1 and r_2 agree on values of attributes tracked by both databases, then the adversary can infer that the two records, r_1 and r_2, refer to the same person with some probability. For example, suppose we know a person, Leslie, is in two databases: one lists him as the only person who has the zip code 15217 and who is male; the anonymized one contains only one person who has the zip code 15217 and is male, and furthermore this person has AIDS. We may conclude that Leslie has AIDS. This attack works despite the first database listing no private information (presuming that one's zip code and gender are not private) and the second attempting to protect privacy by anonymization.

In light of the 2006 release of AOL search data, attempts to anonymize search query logs have shown they are prone to linkage and other attacks as well (e.g., see [45,46]). In the same year Netflix released an anonymized database of rented movies for its Netflix Prize competition; Narayanan and Shmatikov showed how to use a linkage-based attack to identify subscriber records in the database, and thus discover people's political preferences and other sensitive information [47].

A variety of attempts have been made to come up with anonymization approaches not subject to this weakness. One such approach, k-Anonymity, places additional syntactic requirements on the anonymized database [48]. However, for some databases, this approach failed to protect against slightly more complicated versions of the linkage attack. While further work has ruled out some of these attacks (e.g., [49,50,51]), no robust, compositional approach has been found.

A different approach comes from the statistics community. *Statistical disclosure limitation* attempts to preserve privacy despite releasing statistics. (For an overview see [52].) Two methods in this line of work are based on releasing tables of data, where entries in the table are either frequencies (counts), e.g., the number of respondents with the same combination of attributes, or magnitudes, the aggregate of individual counts. A third method uses microdata, a sanitization of individual responses. The public is most familiar with these statistical approaches since they are the basis for publishing census data, performing medical studies, and conducting consumer surveys. Surveyors collect information on a large number of individuals and only release aggregations of responses. These aggregations provide statistically significant results about the problem at hand (e.g., the efficacy of a new pharmaceutical) while not including information that an adversary may use to determine the responses of any of the individual respondents.

A more semantic approach originates with Dalenius. He proposed the requirement that an adversary with the aggregate information learns nothing about any of the data subjects that he could not have known without the aggregate information [53]. Unfortunately, Dwork proves that if a data holder provides the exact value of a "useful" aggregate (where "useful" is measured in terms of a utility function), it is impossible for Dalenius's requirement to hold [54]. Fortunately, she with others showed that by adding noise to the value of the statistic, an adversary could be kept from learning much information about any one individual, leading to the formal definition of *differential privacy* [55]. This formal work on differential privacy inspired practical applications such as the Privacy Integrated Queries (PINQ) system, an API for querying SQL-like databases [56], and an algorithm for releasing query click graphs [57].

Differential privacy is theoretical work, complete with formal definitions, theorems explaining its power, and provable guarantees for systems developed to satisfy it [54]. While PINQ was developed with the specification of differential privacy in mind, the development exemplifies "formal methods light" with no attempt to verify formally that the resulting system satisfies the specification. This line of work on differential privacy could benefit from formal methods that enables such verification.

5 Opportunitics and Challenges for Formal Methods

Formal methods can and should be applied to privacy; however, the nature of privacy offers new challenges, and thus new research opportunities, for the formal methods community.

We start in Section 5.1 with our traditional tools of the trade, and for each, hint at some new problems privacy raises. We then point out in Section 5.2 privacy-specific needs, exposing new territory for the formal methods community to explore.

5.1 Formal Methods Technology

All the machinery of the formal methods community can help us gain a more rigorous understanding of privacy rights, threats, and violations. We can use formal models, from state machines to process algebras to game theory, to model the behavior of the system and its threat environment. We can use formal logics and formal languages to state different aspects of privacy, to state desired properties of these systems, to state privacy policies, to reason about when a model satisfies a property or policy, and to detect inconsistencies between different privacy policies. Automated analyses and tools enable us to scale the applicability of these foundational models and logics to realistic systems. Privacy does pose new challenges, requiring possibly new models, logics, languages, analyses, and tools.

Models
In formal methods, we traditionally model a system and its environment and the interactions between the two. Many methods may simply make assumptions about the environment in which the system operates, thus focusing primarily on modeling the system. To model failures, for example, due to natural disasters or unforeseen events, we usually can get away with abstracting from the different classes of failures and model a single failure action (that could occur at any state) or a single failure state.

Security already challenges this simplicity in modeling. We cannot make assumptions about an adversary the way we might about hardware failures or extreme events like hurricanes. On the other hand, it often suffices to include the adversary as part of the system's environment, and assume the worst case (e.g., treating an adversary's action as a Byzantine failure).

Privacy may require yet a new approach to or at least a new outlook on modeling. Privacy involves three entities: the data holder (system), an adversary (part of the environment), and the data subject. Consider this difference between security and privacy: In security, the entity in control of the system also has an inherent interest in its security. In privacy, the system is controlled by the data holder, but it is the data subject that benefits from privacy. Formal methods akin to proof-carrying code [58], which requires the data holder to provide an easy-to-check certificate to the data subject, might be one way to address this kind of difference.

Privacy requires modeling different relationships among the (minimally) three entities. Complications arise because relationships do not necessarily enjoy simple algebraic properties and because relationships change over time. For example if person X *trusts* Y and Y *trusts* Z that does not mean X *trusts* Z. X needs to trust that Y will not pass on any information about X to Z. Moreover, if X eventually breaks his trust relation with Y then X would like Y to forget all the information Y had about X. This problem is similar to revoking access rights in security except that instead of removing the right to access information (knowledge about X), it is the information itself that is removed.

Logics
The success of many formal methods rests on decades of work on defining and applying logics (e.g., temporal logics) for specifying and reasoning about system behavior. Properties of interest, which drive the underlying logics needed to express them, are often formulated as assertions over traces (e.g., sequences

of states, sequences of state transitions, or sequences of alternating states and transitions).

McLean, however, shows that a class of information-flow properties cannot be expressed as trace properties [59]. In particular, *non-interference*, which characterizes when no information flows from a high-level (e.g., top secret) subject to a low-level (e.g., public) subject [60], cannot be expressed as a property over a single trace. Non-interference formalizes the notion of keeping secure information secret from an adversary. Since secrecy is often a starting point for thinking about privacy, we will likely need new logics for specifying and reasoning about such non-trace properties and other privacy properties more generally.

Formal Policy Languages

The privacy right of exclusion requires that data subjects know how their information will be used. Thus, data holders must codify their practices into publicly available privacy policies. While most of these policies are written in natural language, some attempts have been made to express them in machine readable formats. For example, EPAL is a language for expressing policies with the intention of allowing automated enforcement [61]. Other policy languages such as P3P [62], which has a formal notation, inform website visitors of the site's privacy practices and enable automated methods for finding privacy-conscientious sites [63]. These languages, however, lack formal semantics.

Barth et al. do provide a formal language for specifying notions expressed in privacy policies such as HIPAA, the Children's Online Privacy Protection Act, and the Gramm-Leach-Bliley Act (about financial disclosures) [64]. Their language uses traditional linear temporal logic and its semantics is based on a formal model of *contextual integrity*, Nissenbaum's philosophical theory of information dissemination [65]. Much work remains in extending such formal languages to handle more forms of privacy.

Abstraction and Refinement

Formal methods have been particularly successful at reasoning above the level of code. That success, however, relies fundamentally on abstraction and/or refinement. Commuting diagrams allow us to abstract from the code and do formal reasoning at higher levels of description, but these diagrams rely on well-defined abstraction functions or refinement relations. Similarly, methods that successively refine a high-level specification to a lower-level one, until executable code is reached, rely on well-defined correctness-preserving transformations.

As discussed above, some privacy relevant properties, such as secrecy, are not trace properties. Furthermore, while a specification may satisfy a secrecy property, a refinement of the specification might not. Mantel [66], Jürjens [67], and Alur et al. [68] define specialized forms of refinement that preserve such secrecy properties. Similarly, Clarkson and Schneider [69] develop a theory of *hyperproperties* (sets of properties), which can express information-flow properties, and characterize a set of hyperproperties for which refinement is valid. These works just begin to address aspects of privacy; attention to other aspects may require new abstraction and/or refinement methods.

Policy Composition
Given that different components of a system might be governed by different policies or that one system might be governed by more than one policy, we must also provide methods of compositional reasoning: Given two components, A and B, and privacy policies, P_1 and P_2, if A satisfies P_1 and B satisfies P_2, what does that say about the composition of A and B with respect to P_1, P_2, and $P_1 \wedge P_2$? Privacy policies are likely in practice not to be compositional. For example, the National Science Foundation has a privacy policy that says reviewers of each grant proposal must remain anonymous to the grant proposers; the National Institutes of Health has a different review policy where the names of the study (review) group members are known to the grant proposers. For NSF and NIH to have a joint program, therefore, some compromise between the policies needs to be made, while still preserving "to some degree" the spirit of both policies. This general challenge of composition already exists for other properties such as serializability in databases, feature interaction in telephone services, and noninterference in security. Privacy adds to this challenge.

Code-level Analysis
Formal methods, especially when combined with static analysis techniques, have been successful at finding correctness bugs (e.g., [70]) and security vulnerabilities (e.g., [71,72]) at the code level. What kind of code-level reasoning could we do for privacy, either to prove that a privacy policy is preserved or to discover a privacy violation?

Automated Tools
One of the advantages of formal methods is that formal specifications are amenable to machine manipulation and machine analysis (e.g., finding bugs or proving properties). Automation not just helps us catch human errors, but also enables us to scale up pencil-and-paper techniques.

We need to explore the use of and extensions required for formal methods tools, such as theorem provers and models checkers, for verifying privacy policies or discovering privacy violations. While much foundational work in terms of models, logics, and languages remain, none will become of practical import unless our automated analysis tools scale to work for realistic systems.

5.2 Privacy-Specific Needs

Statistical/Quantitative Reasoning
The statistical nature of privacy raises a new challenge for formal methods. For example, aggregating the weights of a large number of individuals into the average weight is expected to make it difficult for an adversary to learn much about any one of the individuals. Thus, this form of aggregation can protect the private information (individual weights) while still providing a useful statistic (the average weight). In security, information flow is viewed as black and white: if a flow occurs from high to low, a violation has occurred. In privacy, a "small" amount of flow may be acceptable since we are unlikely to learn a lot about the weight of any one person from learning the average of many. While some work has

been done on *quantitative* information flow (e.g., [73,74,75,76]), even the tools developed from this work would consider the system as violating security (see [77] for why and an approach that does not), and thus would be inappropriate for a statistical notion of privacy.

More generally, formal methods may need to be extended to assure statistical guarantees rather than our traditional black-and-white correctness guarantees. A hybrid approach would be to combine traditional formal models with statistical models or formal methods with statistical methods.

Trustworthy Computing: Conflicting Requirements
While trade-offs are hardly new to computer science, privacy raises a new set of such trade-offs. Trustworthy computing requires balancing privacy with security, reliability, and usability. It would be good to have a formal understanding of the relationships among these properties. For example, we want auditability for security, to determine the source of a security breach. However, auditability is at odds with anonymity, a desired aspect of privacy. Thus, to what degree can we provide auditability while providing some degree of anonymity? (This is not suggest that security and privacy are opposites: security is necessary for privacy.) To achieve reliability, especially availability, we often replicate data at different locations; replicas increase the likelihood that an attacker can access private data and make it harder for users to track and manage (e.g., delete) their data. Trade-offs between privacy and usability are similar to those between security and usability. We want to allow users to control how much of their information is released to others, but we want to make it easy for them to specify this control, and even more challenging, to understand the implications of what they specify and to be able to change the specifications over time.

6 Summary

Privacy touches the philosophy, legal, political, social science, and technical communities. Technical approaches to privacy must be part of the basis in creating privacy laws and in designing privacy regulations. Laws and policies need to be technically feasible to implement.

In this paper we focused on the dual role of technology in this vast privacy space: new technologies cause us to revisit old laws or create new ones; at the same time, advances in technology can help preserve privacy rights or mitigate consequences of privacy violations.

Formal methods is a technology that can help by providing everything from foundational formalizations of privacy to practical tools for checking for privacy violations. However, we have barely begun to use formal methods to study privacy in depth; we hope the community is ready to rise to the challenge.

Acknowledgments. Our understanding of privacy has benefited from conversations with Anupam Datta, Dilsun Kaynar, and Jennifer Tam. This research was sponsored in part by the US Army Research Office under contract no. DAAD19-02-1-0389 ("Perpetually Available and Secure Information Systems") at Carnegie

Mellon University's CyLab. It was also partially supported by the National Science Foundation, while the second author was working at the Foundation. The views and conclusions contained in this document are those of the authors and should not be interpreted as representing the official policies, either expressed or implied, of any sponsoring institution, the U.S. government, or any other entity.

References

1. Boyd, D.: Why youth (heart) social network sites: The role of networked publics in teenage social life. In: Buckingham, D. (ed.) MacArthur Foundation Series on Digital Learning–Youth, Identity, Digital Media Volume. MIT Press, Cambridge (2007)
2. Warren, B.: The right to privacy. Harvard Law Review IV(5) (1890)
3. National Research Council: Engaging privacy and information technology in a digital age. In: Waldo, J., Lin, H.S., Millett, L.I. (eds.) National Research Council of the National Academies. The National Academies Press, Washington (2007)
4. Bloustein, E.: Privacy as an aspect of human dignity: An answer to dean prosser. New York University Law Review 39, 962 (1964)
5. Fried, C.: An Anatomy of Values. Harvard University Press, Cambridge (1970)
6. Gerety, T.: Redefining privacy. Harvard Civil Rights-Civil Liberties Law Review 12, 233–296 (1977)
7. Gerstein, R.: Intimacy and privacy. Ethics 89, 76–81 (1978)
8. Cohen, J.: Regulating Intimacy: A New Legal Paradigm. Princeton University Press, Princeton (2002)
9. Rachels, J.: Why privacy is important. Philosophy and Public Affairs 4, 323–333 (1975)
10. Gavison, R.: Privacy and the limits of law. Yale Law Journal 89(3), 421–471 (1980)
11. Prosser, W.L.: Privacy. California Law Review 48, 383 (1960)
12. Solove, D.J.: A taxonomy of privacy. University of Pennsylvania Law Review 154(3), 477–560 (2006)
13. Supreme Court of the United States: Griswold v. Connecticut. United States Reports 381, 479 (1965)
14. Supreme Court of the United States: Eisenstadt v. Baird. United States Reports 405, 438 (1972)
15. Supreme Court of the United States: Roe v. Wade. United States Reports 410, 113 (1973)
16. Supreme Court of the United States: Lawrence v. Texas. United States Reports 538, 918 (2003)
17. Supreme Court of the United States: Bowers v. Hardwick. United States Reports 478, 186 (1986)
18. Thomson, J.: The right to privacy. Philosophy and Public Affairs 4, 295–314 (1975)
19. Parent, W.: Privacy, morality and the law. Philosophy and Public Affairs 12, 269–288 (1983)
20. Supreme Court of the United States: Olmstead v. United States. United States Reports 277, 438 (1928)
21. Supreme Court of the United States: Katz v. United States. United States Reports 389, 347 (1967)
22. Supreme Court of the United States: Dow Chemical Co. v. United States. United States Reports 476, 227 (1986)

23. Supreme Court of the United States: Florida v. Riley. United States Reports 488, 455 (1989)
24. Supreme Court of the United States: United States v. Knotts. United States Reports 460, 276 (1983)
25. Supreme Court of the United States: United States v. Karo. United States Reports 468, 705 (1984)
26. New Hampshire Supreme Court: Hamberger v. Eastman. Atlantic Reporter 206, 239 (1964)
27. Supreme Court of the United States: Kyllo v. United States. United States Reports 533, 27 (2001)
28. Secretary's Advisory Committee on Automated Personal Data Systems: Records, computers, and the rights of citizens. Technical report, U.S. Department of Health, Education, and Welfare (July 1973)
29. Francis, T.: Spread of records stirs fears of privacy erosion. The Wall Street Journal, December 28 (2006)
30. Benzel, T.V.: Analysis of a kemel verification. In: Proceedings of the IEEE Symposium on Security and Privacy (1984)
31. Silverman, J.: Reflections on the verification of the security of an operating system kernel. In: Proceedings of the Ninth ACM Symposium on Operating Systems Principles, Bretton Woods, New Hampshire (1983)
32. Klein, G., Elphinstone, K., Heiser, G., Andronick, J., Cock, D., Derrin, P., Elkaduwe, D., Engelhardt, K., Kolanski, R., Norrish, M., Sewell, T., Tuch, H., Winwood, S.: sel4: Formal verification of an os kernel. In: Proceedings of the 22nd ACM Symposium on Operating Systems Principles, Big Sky, Montana (October 2009)
33. Diffie, W., Hellman, M.: New directions in cryptography. IEEE Transactions on Information Theory 22(6), 644–654 (1976)
34. Rivest, R.L., Shamir, A., Adleman, L.: A method for obtaining digital signatures and public-key cryptosystems. Commun. ACM 21(2), 120–126 (1978)
35. Chaum, D.: Secret ballot receipts: True voter-verifiable elections. IEEE J. Security and Privacy, 38–47 (2004)
36. Benaloh, J., Tuinstra, D.: Receipt-free secret ballot elections. In: Proceedings of the 26th Annual ACM symposium on Theory of Computing, Montreal, Canada (1994)
37. Rivest, R.L., Smith, W.D.: Three voting protocols: Threeballot, vav, and twin. In: EVT 2007: Proceedings of the USENIX Workshop on Accurate Electronic Voting Technology, Berkeley, CA, USA, p. 16. USENIX Association (2007)
38. Goldschlag, D.M., Reed, M.G., Syverson, P.F.: Onion routing. Commun. ACM 42(2), 39–41 (1999)
39. Verykios, V.S., Bertino, E., Fovino, I.N., Provenza, L.P., Saygin, Y., Theodoridis, Y.: State-of-the-art in privacy preserving data mining. ACM SIGMOD Record 3(1), 50–57 (2004)
40. National Research Council: Protecting Individual Privacy in the Struggle Against Terrorists. The National Academies Press, Washington (2008)
41. Bergstein, B.: Research explores data mining, privacy. USA Today, June 18 (2008)
42. Geambasu, R., Kohno, T., Levy, A., Levy, H.M.: Vanish: Increasing data privacy with self-destructing data. In: Proceedings of the USENIX Security Symposium, Montreal, Canada (August 2009)
43. Halpern, J., O'Neill, K.: Secrecy in multiagent systems. In: CSFW 2002: Proceedings of the 15th IEEE workshop on Computer Security Foundations, Washington, DC, USA, pp. 32–46. IEEE Computer Society, Los Alamitos (2002), `http://www.kevinoneill.org/papers/secrecy.pdf`

44. Chawla, S., Dwork, C., McSherry, F., Smith, A., Wee, H.: Toward privacy in public databases. In: Kilian, J. (ed.) TCC 2005. LNCS, vol. 3378, pp. 363–385. Springer, Heidelberg (2005)
45. Jones, R., Kumar, R., Pang, B., Tomkins, A.: I Know What You Did Last Summer: Query Logs and User Privacy. In: Proceedings of the Sixteenth ACM Conference on Information and Knowledge Management, Lisbon, Portugal (2007)
46. Kumar, R., Novak, J., Pang, B., Tomkins, A.: On anonymizing query logs via token-based hashing. In: Proceedings of the 16th International Conference on World Wide Web, Banff, Alberta, Canada (2007)
47. Narayanan, A., Shmatikov, V.: Robust de-anonymization of large sparse datasets. In: SP 2008: Proceedings of the 2008 IEEE Symposium on Security and Privacy, Washington, DC, USA, pp. 111–125. IEEE Computer Society, Los Alamitos (2008)
48. Sweeney, L.: k-Anonymity: A model for protecting privacy. Int. J. Uncertain. Fuzziness Knowl.-Based Syst. 10(5), 557–570 (2002)
49. Machanavajjhala, A., Kifer, D., Gehrke, J., Venkitasubramaniam, M.: ℓ-Diversity: Privacy beyond k-anonymity. ACM Trans. Knowl. Discov. Data 1(1), 3 (2007)
50. Li, N., Li, T., Venkatasubramanian, S.: t-closeness: Privacy beyond k-anonymity and l-diversity. In: IEEE 23rd International Conference on Data Engineering. ICDE 2007, April 15-20, pp. 106–115 (2007)
51. Xiao, X., Tao, Y.: m-Invariance: Towards privacy preserving re-publication of dynamic datasets. In: SIGMOD 2007: Proceedings of the 2007 ACM SIGMOD international conference on Management of data, pp. 689–700. ACM Press, New York (2007)
52. Federal Committee on Statistical Methodology: Statistical disclosure limitation methodology. Statistical Policy Working Paper 22 (2005)
53. Dalenius, T.: Towards a methodology for statistical disclosure control. Statistik Tidskrift 15, 429–444 (1977)
54. Dwork, C.: Differential privacy. In: Bugliesi, M., Preneel, B., Sassone, V., Wegener, I. (eds.) ICALP 2006. LNCS, vol. 4052, pp. 1–12. Springer, Heidelberg (2006)
55. Dwork, C., McSherry, F., Nissim, K., Smith, A.: Calibrating noise to sensitivity in private data analysis. In: Halevi, S., Rabin, T. (eds.) TCC 2006. LNCS, vol. 3876, pp. 265–284. Springer, Heidelberg (2006)
56. McSherry, F.: Privacy integrated queries: An extensible platform for privacy-preserving data analysis. In: SIGMOD 2009: Proceedings of the 2009 ACM SIGMOD international conference on Management of data. ACM, New York (to appear, 2009), `http://research.microsoft.com/apps/pubs/?id=80218`
57. Korolova, A., Kenthapadi, K., Mishra, N., Ntoulas, A.: Releasing search queries and clicks privately. In: Proceedings of the 2009 International World Wide Web Conference, Madrid, Spain (2009)
58. Necula, G.C., Lee, P.: Safe kernel extensions without run-time checking. SIGOPS Oper. Syst. Rev. 30(SI), 229–243 (1996)
59. McLean, J.: A general theory of composition for trace sets closed under selective interleaving functions. In: SP 1994: Proceedings of the 1994 IEEE Symposium on Security and Privacy, Washington, DC, USA, p. 79. IEEE Computer Society, Los Alamitos (1994)
60. Goguen, J.A., Meseguer, J.: Security policies and security models. In: Proceedings of the IEEE Symposium on Security and Privacy (1982)
61. Powers, C., Schunter, M.: Enterprise privacy authorization language (EPAL 1.2). W3C Member Submission (November 2003)
62. Cranor, L.F.: Web Privacy with P3P. O'Reilly, Sebastopol (2002)

63. Cranor, L.F., Guduru, P., Arjula, M.: User interfaces for privacy agents. ACM Trans. Comput.-Hum. Interact. 13(2), 135–178 (2006)
64. Barth, A., Datta, A., Mitchell, J.C., Nissenbaum, H.: Privacy and contextual integrity: Framework and applications. In: SP 2006: Proceedings of the 2006 IEEE Symposium on Security and Privacy, Washington, DC, USA, pp. 184–198. IEEE Computer Society, Los Alamitos (2006)
65. Nissenbaum, H.: Privacy as contextual integrity. Washington Law Review 79(1) (2004)
66. Mantel, H.: Preserving information flow properties under refinement. In: SP 2001: Proceedings of the 2001 IEEE Symposium on Security and Privacy, Washington, DC, USA, p. 78. IEEE Computer Society, Los Alamitos (2001)
67. Jürjens, J.: Secrecy-preserving refinement. In: Oliveira, J.N., Zave, P. (eds.) FME 2001. LNCS, vol. 2021, pp. 135–152. Springer, Heidelberg (2001)
68. Alur, R., Černý, P., Zdancewic, S.: Preserving secrecy under refinement. In: Bugliesi, M., Preneel, B., Sassone, V., Wegener, I. (eds.) ICALP 2006. LNCS, vol. 4052, pp. 107–118. Springer, Heidelberg (2006)
69. Clarkson, M.R., Schneider, F.B.: Hyperproperties. In: Proceedings of IEEE Computer Security Foundations Symposium (June 2008)
70. Ball, T., Rajamani, S.: Automatically validating temporal safety properties of interfaces. In: Dwyer, M.B. (ed.) SPIN 2001. LNCS, vol. 2057, p. 103. Springer, Heidelberg (2001)
71. Cowan, C., Wagle, P., Pu, C., Beattie, S., Walpole, J.: Buffer overflows: Attacks and defenses for the vulnerability of the decade. In: SANS 2000 (1999)
72. Newsome, J., Song, D.: Dynamic taint analysis: Automatic detection, analysis, and signature generation of exploit attacks on commodity software. In: Network and Distributed Systems Security Symposium (February 2005)
73. Clarkson, M.R., Myers, A.C., Schneider, F.B.: Belief in information flow. In: CSFW 2005: Proceedings of the 18th IEEE workshop on Computer Security Foundations, Washington, DC, USA, pp. 31–45. IEEE Computer Society, Los Alamitos (2005)
74. Clark, D., Hunt, S., Malacaria, P.: A static analysis for quantifying information flow in a simple imperative language. Journal of Computer Security 15, 321–371 (2007)
75. McCamant, S., Ernst, M.D.: A simulation-based proof technique for dynamic information flow. In: PLAS 2007: Proceedings of the 2007 workshop on Programming languages and analysis for security, pp. 41–46. ACM, New York (2007)
76. Newsome, J., Song, D.: Influence: A quantitative approach for data integrity. Technical Report CMU-CyLab-08-005, CyLab, Carnegie Mellon University (February 2008)
77. Tschantz, M.C., Nori, A.V.: Measuring the loss of privacy from statistics. In: Gulwani, S., Seshia, S.A. (eds.) Proceedings of the 1st Workshop on Quantitative Analysis of Software (QA 2009), Technical Report UCB/EECS-2009-93, Electrical Engineering and Computer Sciences, University of California at Berkeley, pp. 27–36 (June 2009)

What Can Formal Methods Bring to Systems Biology?

Nicola Bonzanni, K. Anton Feenstra, Wan Fokkink, and Elzbieta Krepska

Vrije Universiteit Amsterdam, Department of Computer Science
De Boelelaan 1081a, 1081 HV Amsterdam, The Netherlands
{bonzanni,feenstra,wanf,ekr}@few.vu.nl

Abstract. This position paper argues that the operational modelling approaches from the formal methods community can be applied fruitfully within the systems biology domain. The results can be complementary to the traditional mathematical descriptive modelling approaches used in systems biology. We discuss one example: a recent Petri net analysis of *C. elegans* vulval development.

1 Systems Biology

Systems biology studies complex interactions in biological systems, with the aim to understand better the entirety of processes that happen in such a system, as well as to grasp the emergent properties of such a system as a whole. This can for instance be at the level of metabolic or interaction networks, signal transduction, genetic regulatory networks, multi-cellular development, or social behaviour of insects.

The last decade has seen a rapid and successful development in the collaboration between biologists and computer scientists in the area of systems biology and bioinformatics. It has turned out that formal modelling and analysis techniques that have been developed for distributed computer systems, are applicable to biological systems as well. Namely, both kinds of systems have a lot in common. Biological systems are built from separate components that communicate with each other and thus influence each other's behaviour. Notably, signal transduction within a cell consists of cascades of biochemical reactions, by which for instance genes are activated or down-regulated. The genes themselves produce the proteins that drive signal transduction, and cells can be connected in a multicellular organism, making this basically one large, complex distributed system. Another, very different, example at the organism level is how ants in one colony send stimuli to each other in the form of pheromones.

Biological systems are reactive systems, as they continuously interact with their environment. In November 2002, David Harel [11] put forward a grand challenge to computer science, to build a fully animated model of a multi-cellular organism as a reactive system; specifically, he suggested to build such a model of the *C. elegans* nematode worm, which serves as a one of the model organisms in developmental biology.

Open questions in biology that could be addressed in such a modelling framework include the following, listed in order from a detailed, molecular viewpoint to a more global view of whole organisms:

- How complete is our knowledge of metabolic, signalling and regulatory processes at a molecular level?

A. Cavalcanti and D. Dams (Eds.): FM 2009, LNCS 5850, pp. 16–22, 2009.

- How is the interplay between different pathways or network modules organized and regulated?
- How is the interaction between intra-cellular processes and inter/extra-cellular processes organized?
- How do cells self-organize?
- How do cells differentiate?
- How are self-organization and differentiation of cells connected?
- How does self-organization and differentiation lead to the formation of complex structures like organs (e.g. the eye, brain, kidney)?

One grand open question that pervades the whole of biological research is, how could all of this *evolve*? This is exemplified by the title of the 1973 essay by Theodosius Dobzhansky [4] that "Nothing in biology makes sense except in the light of evolution". Some recent theoretical work [5] highlights an interesting possibility, that flexibility in regulation is a necessary component of evolution, but has itself been evolved in biological systems.

2 Formal Models of Biological Systems

Why would a biologist want to use formal models? First of all, formal models can be an excellent way to store and share knowledge on biological systems, and to reason about such systems. Furthermore, in vivo experiments in the lab tend to take an awfully long time, and are labour intensive. In comparison, in silico experiments (i.e. computer experiments) can take relatively little time and effort. And for instance genetic perturbations can be difficult (or unethical) to perform in the lab, while they may require trivial adaptations of a formal model.

The time is ripe for exploiting the synergy between (systems) biology and formal methods. First of all we have reached the point where biological knowledge of for instance signal transduction has become so detailed, that enough information is available to start building sensible formal models. Second, the development of analysis techniques for formal methods, and the power of the underlying computer hardware, has made it possible to apply formal methods to very complex systems. Although we are certainly not (and possibly never will be) at a level where a full-fledged formal analysis of the entire genetic regulatory network of one cell is within reach, we can definitely already study interesting, and challenging, fragments of such networks.

It is important to realise that biology (like e.g. physics, chemistry, sociology, economics) is an empirical science. This is basically orthogonal to the standard application of formal methods in computer science, where a formal analysis is used to design and prove properties of a computer system. If a desired property of a computer system turns out to fail, then we can in principle adapt the system at hand. In contrast, biological systems are simply (and quite literally) a fact of life, and formal models 'only' serve to better understand the inner workings and emergent properties of such systems. So while in computer science model validation typically leads to a redesign of the corresponding computer system, in systems biology it leads to a redesign of the model itself, if in silico experiments on the model do not correspond with in vivo experiments on the real-life biological system. A nice comparison between these two approaches can be found in the introduction of [18].

Fisher and Henzinger [6] distinguish two kinds of models for biological systems: operational versus denotational (or, as they phrase it, computational versus mathematical). On the one hand, operational models (such as Petri nets) are executable and mimic biological processes. On the other hand, denotational models (such as differential equations) express mathematical relationships between quantities and how they change over time. Denotational models are in general quantitative, and in systems biology tend to require a lot of computation power to simulate, let alone to solve mathematically. Also it is often practically impossible to obtain the precise quantitative information needed for such models. Operational models are in general qualitative, and are thus at a higher abstraction level and easier to analyse. Moreover, Fisher and Henzinger, as well as Regev and Shapiro [17], make a convincing case that a good operational model may explain the mechanisms behind a biological system in a more intuitive fashion than a denotational model.

Metaphorically one can ask the question whether molecules in a cell, or cells themselves, solve differential equations to decide what to do in a particular situation, or rather when they encounter one another follow simple sets of rules derived from their physical interactions. In that respect, one may consider the continuous, mathematical models as an approximation of the discrete molecular processes, rather than viewing the qualitative model as a course-grained abstraction of a continuous reality.

An operational model progresses from state to state, where an event at a local component gives rise to a state transition at the global system level. Fisher et al. [7] argue that (unbounded) asynchrony does not mimic real-life biological behaviour properly. Typically, asynchrony allows that one component keeps on executing events, while another component is frozen out, or executes only few events. While in real life, all components are able to execute at a certain rate. Bounded asynchrony, a phrase coined by Fisher et al. [7], lets components proceed in an asynchronous fashion, while making sure that they all can proceed at their own rate. A good example of bounded asynchrony is the maximally parallel execution semantics of Petri nets; we will return to this semantics in Section 3.

We briefly mention the three modelling paradigms from the formal methods community that are used most frequently for building operational models of biological systems.

Petri nets are well-suited for modelling biochemical networks such as genetic regulatory pathways. The places in a Petri net can represent genes, protein species and complexes. Transitions represent reactions or transfer of a signal. Arcs represent reaction substrates and products. Firing of a transition is execution of a reaction: consuming substrates and creating products. Cell Illustrator [15] is an example of a Petri net tool that targets biological mechanisms and pathways.

Process calculi, such as process algebra and the π-calculus, extended with probabilities or stochastics, can be used to model the interaction between organisms. Early ground-breaking work in this direction was done by Tofts [21] in the context of process algebra, with regard to ant behaviour. The Bioambients calculus [16], which is based on the π-calculus, targets various aspects of molecular localisation and compartmentalization.

Live sequence charts are an extension of the graphical specification language message sequence charts; notably, they allow a distinction between mandatory and possible behaviour. They have been used successfully by Harel and his co-workers to build visual models of reactive biological systems, see e.g. [12].

Model checking is in principle an excellent methodology to verify interesting properties of specifications in any of these three formalisms. And as is well-known, abstraction techniques and distributed model checking (see e.g. [1]) can help to alleviate the state explosion problem. However, in view of the very large scale and complexity of biological systems, so far even these optimisation techniques cannot push model checking applications in this area beyond toy examples. Simulations methods are commonly used to evaluate complex and high-dimensional models, and are applicable in principle to both operational and denotational models. Well-known drawbacks, compared to model checking, are that this approach can suffer from limited sampling due to the high-dimensional state space, and that there may be corners of the state space that have a biological relevance but that are very hard to reach with simulations. Still, in spite of these drawbacks, for the moment Monte Carlo simulations are currently the best method to analyse formal specifications of real-life biological systems.

In our view, for the successful application of formal methods in the systems biology domain, it is expedient to use a simple modelling framework, and analysis techniques that take relatively little computation power. This may at first sound paradoxical, but simplicity in modelling and analysis methods will make it easier to master the enormous complexity of real-life biological systems. Moreover, it will help to communicate with biologists on the basis of formal models, and in the hopefully not too far future will make it attractive for biologists to start using formal modelling tools.

3 A Petri Net Analysis of *C. elegans* Vulval Development

Petri nets representing regulatory and signalling networks We recall that a Petri net is a bipartite directed graph consisting of two kinds of nodes: places that indicate the local availability of resources, and transitions which are active components that can change the state of the resources. Each place can hold one or more tokens. Weighted arcs connect places and transitions. In [13] we explained a method to represent biological knowledge as a Petri net. As explained before, places represent genes and protein species, i.e., bound and unbound, active and inactive, or at different locations, while transitions represent biological processes. Firing of a transition is execution of a process, e.g. consuming substrates or creating products. The number of tokens in a place is interpreted as follows. For genes as a boolean value, 0 means not present and 1 present. For proteins, there are abstract concentration levels 0-6, going from not present, via low, medium, and high concentration to saturated level. The rationale behind this approach is to abstract away from unknown absolute molecule concentration levels, as we intend to represent relative concentrations and rates. If desired, a modeller could fine-tune the granularity of the model by adjusting the number of available concentration levels.

Biological systems are highly concurrent, as in cells all reactions can happen in parallel and most are independent of each other. Therefore, in [13] we advocate to use what is called maximal parallelism [3]. A fully asynchronous approach would allow one part of the network to deploy prolonged activity, while another part of the network shows no activity at all. In real life, all parts can progress at roughly the same rate. Maximal parallelism promotes activity throughout the network. The maximal parallel execution semantics can be summarised informally as execute greedily as many transitions as possible in one step. A maximally parallel step leaves no enabled transitions in the net, and, in principle, should be developed in such a way that it corresponds to one time step in the evolution of the biological system. This is possible because the modeller can capture relative rates and concentration levels using appropriate weights on arcs. Typically, if in one time unit a protein A is produced four times more than a protein B, then the transition that captures production of A should have a weight that is four times as large as the weight of the one that captures B production.

In nature a cell tends to saturate with a product, and as a result the reaction slows down or stops. To mimic this behaviour, each place in the Petri net has a predefined maximum capacity of six. To guarantee that the highest concentration level can be attained, we introduced bounded execution with overshooting. A transition can only fire if each output place holds fewer than six tokens. Since each transition can possibly move more than one token at once into its output places, each transition can overshoot the pre-given capacity at most once.

C. elegans vulval development *C. elegans* is a round worm, about 1mm in length, living in soil. In order to lay eggs, the *C. elegans* hermaphrodites grow an organ called vulva. The complexity and universality of the biological mechanisms underlying the vulval development (e.g. cell-cell interactions, cell differentiation, cross-talk between pathways, gene regulation), and the intensive biological investigations undertaken during the last 20 years [19] make this process an extremely appealing case study [8,9,10,14,20]. In particular, the considerable amount of descriptive biological knowledge about the process joint with the lack of precise biochemical parameters, and the large number of genetic perturbations tested in vivo, welcome the research of alternative modelling procedures. These approaches should be able to express the descriptive knowledge in a formal way, abstract the processes enough to overcome the absence of fine-grained biochemical parameters, and check the behaviour of the system with a sound methodology.

Recently we developed a Petri net model of the process that leads to the formation of the vulva during *C. elegans* development [2], using the Petri net framework described above. It comprises 600 nodes (places and transitions) and 1000 arcs. In this network we could identify different modules. These correspond to different biological functions, such as gene expression, protein activation, and protein degradation. It is possible to reuse modules corresponding to a function, like small building blocks, to compose more complex modules, and eventually build a full cell. The cell itself is a module that can be reused, as can other modules like pathways or cascades.

To analyse the Petri net model, we applied Monte Carlo simulations. We simulated 64 different genetic perturbations. Twenty-two experiments previously selected in [9] were used for model calibration. Thirty perturbations were used for validation: 26 from [9], three from [19], and one from [22]. The remaining twelve simulations constitute new predictions that invite further in vivo experiments.

This case study shows that the basic Petri net formalism can be used effectively to mimic and comprehend complex biological processes.

4 Conclusions

Transforming 'data' into 'knowledge' is a holy grail in Life Sciences. Sometimes we have much data but relatively little descriptive knowledge, e.g. a whole genome sequenced and protein interaction data, but little information about the single genes and their functions. At other times we have excellent descriptive knowledge about a biological process but lack the biochemical details to simulate or explain accurately the phenomenon. For instance, we may know the response of an organism to a certain stimulus but we do not know which molecules are responsible, or we may know the molecules but not all the biochemical parameters to reproduce the behaviour of the organism in silico.

Reaching the sweet spot in between abstraction and biological significance is one of the big challenges in applying formal methods to biology. On the one hand, a fine-grained approach potentially gives more detailed predictions and a better approximation of the observed behaviour, but it has to cope with a huge number of parameters that are largely unknown and could not be effectively handled by, for instance, model checking techniques. On the other hand, a coarse-grained approach developed at a higher level of abstraction needs fewer detailed parameters and is computationally cheaper, but it might have to be tailored to answering a single question, lowering the overall biological significance of the model. Therefore, it is crucial to choose the appropriate abstraction level and formalism in respect to the biological questions that the modeller wants to address.

To pick up the right questions is a pivotal choice, and to understand their biological significance is essential. In order to accomplish these two goals, it is necessary to establish a clear and unambiguous communication channel between 'biologists' and 'computer scientists'. Furthermore, it is necessary to expand the application of formal methods beyond the manageable but only moderately interesting collection of the toy examples. Although several different formal methods can achieve such objectives, in our experience the intuitiveness of its graphical representation, tied with the strict formal definition of Petri net, contributed greatly to establish a common ground for 'biologists' and 'computer scientists'.

References

1. Barnat, J., Brim, L., Cerná, I., Drazan, S., Šafránek, D.: Parallel model checking large-scale genetic regulatory networks with DiVinE. In: Proc. FBTC 2007. ENTCS, vol. 194(3), pp. 35–50. Elsevier, Amsterdam (2008)
2. Bonzanni, N., Krepska, E., Feenstra, A., Fokkink, W., Kielmann, T., Bal, H., Heringa, J.: Executing multicellular differentiation: Quantitative predictive modelling of *C. elegans* vulval development. Bioinformatics (in press)
3. Burkhard, H.-D.: On priorities of parallelism. In: Salwicki, A. (ed.) Logic of Programs 1980. LNCS, vol. 148, pp. 86–97. Springer, Heidelberg (1983)
4. Dobzhansky, T.: Nothing in Biology Makes Sense Except in the Light of Evolution. American Biology Teacher 35, 125–129 (1973)
5. Crombach, A., Hogeweg, P.: Evolution of evolvability in gene regulatory networks. PLoS Comput. Biol. 4, e1000112 (2008), doi:10.1371/journal.pcbi.1000112

6. Fisher, J., Henzinger, T.: Executable cell biology. Nature Biotechnology 25(11), 1239–1249 (2007)
7. Fisher, J., Henzinger, T., Mateescu, M., Piterman, N.: Bounded Asynchrony: Concurrency for Modeling Cell-Cell Interactions. In: Fisher, J. (ed.) FMSB 2008. LNCS (LNBI), vol. 5054, pp. 17–32. Springer, Heidelberg (2008)
8. Fisher, J., Piterman, N., Hajnal, A., Henzinger, T.A.: Predictive modeling of signaling crosstalk during *C. elegans* vulval development. PLoS Comput. Biol. 3, e92 (2007)
9. Fisher, J., Piterman, N., Jane Albert Hubbard, E., Stern, M.J., Harel, D.: Computational insights into Caenorhabditis elegans vulval development. P. Natl. Acad. Sci. USA 102, 1951–1956 (2005)
10. Giurumescu, C.A., Sternberg, P.W., Asthagiri, A.R.: Intercellular coupling amplifies fate segregation during *Caenorhabditis elegans* vulval development. P. Natl. Acad. Sci. USA 103, 1331–1336 (2006)
11. Harel, D.: A grand challenge for computing: Towards full reactive modeling of a multicellular animal. Bulletin of the EATCS 81, 226–235 (2003)
12. Kam, N., Harel, D., Kugler, H., Marelly, R., Pnueli, A., Jane Albert Hubbard, E., Stern, M.: Formal modeling of *C. elegans* development: A scenario-based approach. In: Priami, C. (ed.) CMSB 2003. LNCS, vol. 2602, pp. 4–20. Springer, Heidelberg (2003)
13. Krepska, E., Bonzanni, N., Feenstra, A., Fokkink, W., Kielmann, T., Bal, H., Heringa, J.: Design issues for qualitative modelling of biological cells with Petri nets. In: Fisher, J. (ed.) FMSB 2008. LNCS (LNBI), vol. 5054, pp. 48–62. Springer, Heidelberg (2008)
14. Li, C., Nagasaki, M., Ueno, K., Miyano, S.: Simulation-based model checking approach to cell fate specification during *Caenorhabditis elegans* vulval development by hybrid functional Petri net with extension. BMC Syst. Biol. 3, 42 (2009)
15. Nagasaki, M., Saito, A., Doi, A., Matsuno, H., Miyano, S.: Using Cell Illustrator and Pathway Databases. Springer, Heidelberg (2009)
16. Regev, A., Panina, E., Silverman, W., Cardelli, L., Shapiro, E.: BioAmbients: An abstraction for biological compartments. Theoretical Computer Science 325(1), 141–167 (2004)
17. Regev, A., Shapiro, E.: Cellular abstractions: Cells as computation. Nature 419, 343 (2002)
18. Sadot, A., Fisher, J., Barak, D., Admanit, Y., Stern, M., Hubbard, J.A., Harel, D.: Toward verified biological models. IEEE/ACM Transactions on Computational Biology and Bioinformatics 5(2), 223–234 (2008)
19. Sternberg, P.W.: Chapter on vulval development in *Wormbook* (June 2005), `http://www.wormbook.org/chapters/www_vulvaldev/vulvaldev.html`
20. Sun, X., Hong, P.: Computational modeling of *Caenorhabditis elegans* vulval induction. Bioinformatics 507, i499–i507 (2007)
21. Tofts, C.: Describing social insect behaviour using process algebra. Transactions of the Society for Computer Simulation 9(4), 227–283 (1992)
22. Yoo, A.S., Greenwald, I.: LIN-12/Notch activation leads to microRNA-mediated downregulation of Vav in *C. elegans*. Science 310, 1330–1333 (2005)

Guess and Verify – Back to the Future

Colin O'Halloran

QinetiQ Ltd, Malvern Technology Park, Worcestershire WR14 3PS, UK
cmohalloran@qinetiq.com

Abstract. The problem addressed in this paper is the increasing time and cost of developing critical software. In particular the tried and trusted software development processes for safety critical software are becoming untenable because of the costs involved. Model Based Development, in the general, offers a solution to reducing time and cost in software development. Unfortunately the requirement of independence of verification can negate any gains and indeed lead to more cost. The approach advocated in this paper is to employ the "guess and verify" paradigm in the context of automatic code generation to enable automated verification that is independent of the code generation. The approach is illustrated by the development of an automated verification capability for a commercial automatic code generator. A research topic on metadata for automatic code generators is suggested.

Keywords: Verification, Cost, Automation, Software, Models, Proof, Simulink.

1 Introduction

In Boehm and Basili's paper on the top 10 list for software defect reduction [1] they state:

> "All other things being equal, it costs 50 percent more per source instruction to develop high-dependability software products than to develop low-dependability software products. ..."

To understand why this is the case it is worth considering safety critical embedded systems. Such software systems go through rigorous verification processes before being put into service. Verification is a major source of cost in the development process because of the importance placed on achieving independence from software developers. It is also the case that most designs are subject to frequent change during development, even up to flight trials. This greatly increases the cost of the development as the complete system may need to be re-verified to the same level of rigour several times before release to service.

1.1 Verification Costs and Complexity

There is a clear trend towards greater complexity in software systems. This growing complexity in terms of size and distribution is making the cost of verification

A. Cavalcanti and D. Dams (Eds.): FM 2009, LNCS 5850, pp. 23–32, 2009.

(using current methods) grow in a non-linear fashion with respect to the cost of just writing the software. The non-linear relationship between writing software and verifying it using current methods has severe implications for software projects and the risk of them being cancelled. Consider fig 1. below:

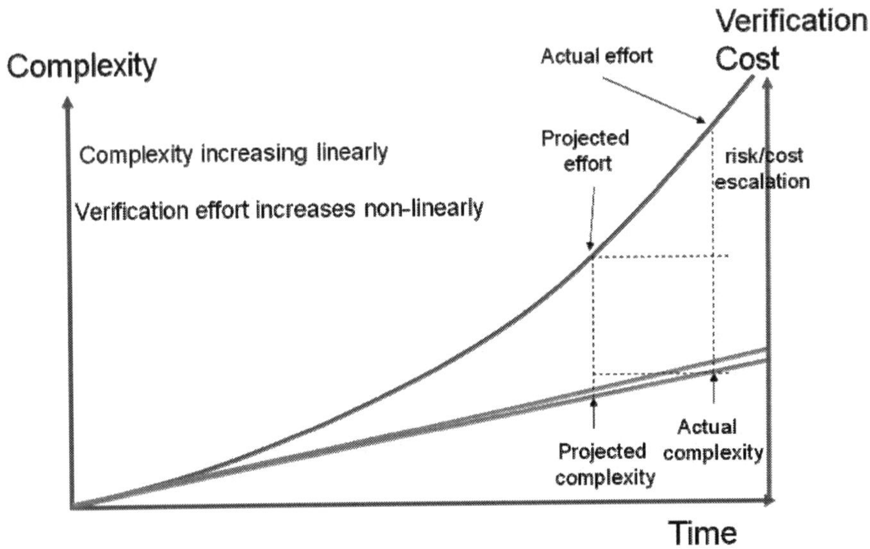

Fig. 1. Assuming verification effort is non-linear with respect to a linear increase in complexity, this figure illustrates how a small error in estimating the actual complexity of software would cause significant time and cost overruns in a project

A small error in estimating the complexity of the software system leads to a disproportionate increase in verification costs. For the kinds of capability demanded by the market, this means that small estimation errors can lead to a significant risk of project cancellation because of time and cost overruns. The cost implications mean that financial directors are playing an increasing role in software development policy. The currently favoured tool of the financial director to mitigate the risks of cost escalation is that of off-shore development.

Currently the typical way cost savings are achieved is to outsource software development and its verification to countries with significantly cheaper labour costs. However, significant concerns with this strategy are emerging. The first concern is possible loss of Intellectual Property. Even if this is not the case there is the concern that potential competitors are being trained in developing key software systems. The logical next step would be to integrate these systems and move up the value chain, thus competing with the tier 1 or 2 system developers who originally outsourced the software development. In the United States there is also a particular concern about security with the threat of malicious code being inserted into outsourced software. Therefore if the major cost driver of verification can be solved then there would be adoption of a solution in key areas.

1.2 The Importance of Independence

RTCA document DO-178B and EUROCAE document ED-12B, "Software Considerations in Airborne Systems and Equipment Certification," proposes verification independence as a means of achieving additional assurance for the quality and safety of software installed in airborne systems and equipment. Specifically, DO-178B/ED-12B recommends verification independence. The desire for independence of verification also occurs in other areas such as the nuclear industry.

The reason independence is desirable is that it is a basic strategy for lowering the impact of human error. For example, to achieve a target of 10^{-6} it might be possible to disaggregate this using an independence argument into two targets of 10^{-2} and 10^{-4}. The problem is that unless independence is "obvious" it can be difficult to demonstrate it [2]. For example the notion of diverse software implementing the same functionality does not stand up to scrutiny. However the use of diverse fault removing techniques has been found to be useful in detecting errors [3].

The correctness by construction approach without independent verification means that the burden of demonstrating freedom from error can be too difficult to empirically demonstrate. Even the use of mathematical proof is not immune to this criticism since it is ultimately a human endeavour and therefore vulnerable to human error. For example the presence of errors in the implementation of proof tools is well known. The independence of one approach from another approach means that an error in one has to exactly mask an error in the other.

There are still wrinkles that need to be ironed out, the main ones being that there might be a common misunderstanding of the semantics of the specification/model or of the target language. However even if independence of diverse approaches cannot be claimed, it may still be possible to make a conservative claim for the conditional probability of the failure of independence [4].

In summary there is a technical case for employing the "guess and verify" approach to software verification. The adoption of commercial automatic code generators means that the few times they do fail can be sufficiently mitigated by a diverse verification approach. This paper will also argue that the "guess and verify" approach can in general be made automatic through automatic code generators supplying meta-data on the code generation itself.

2 An Architecture for Independent Verification

In fig. 2 a representation of the architecture used by QinetiQ is presented. Above the dotted line the independent development of the code occurs. Below the dotted line the independent verification consists of three tools: a Refinement Script Generator; a Refinement Checker; and a Theorem Prover. There is a fourth tool that automatically generates a formal specification based upon the formal semantics of the modelling language [5]; it is elided to concentrate on the most important parts. A particular instance of the architecture is described in detail in [6]. The Refinement Checker and the Refinement Script Generator are described in more detail in subsections below.

The Refinement Script Generator takes information from various sources to generate a refinement argument that may or may not be true. As the name implies the

Refinement Checker determines the validity of the refinement argument by generating verification conditions that are discharged using the Theorem Prover. The simplification theory used by the Theorem Prover is specialised for the code language and the modelling language. By sufficiently constraining the code generated, the generation of the refinement argument and taking the structure of the formal specification into account then the simplification theory can in principle discharge all the verification conditions – assuming the refinement argument is correct.

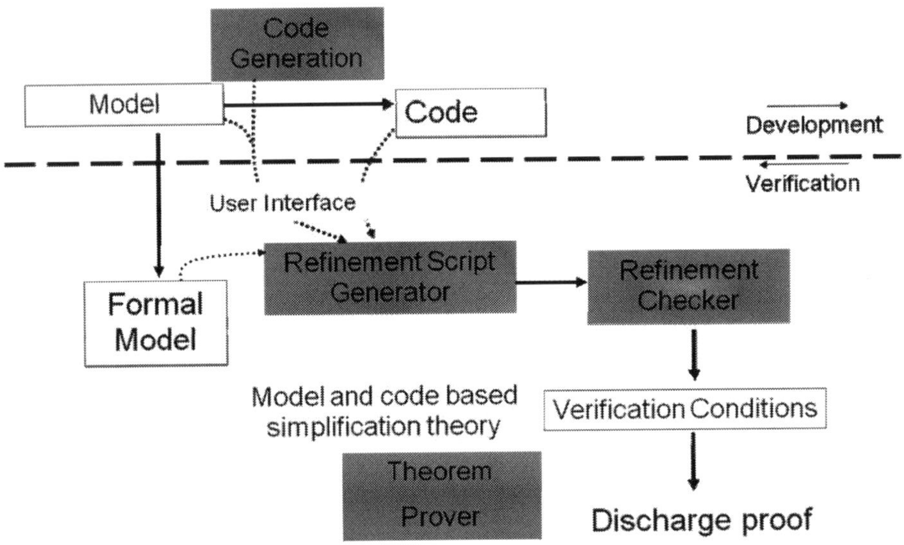

Fig. 2. An architecture for independent verification

2.1 A Refinement Checker

QinetiQ's refinement checker developed in the early 1990s for Ada programs is called the DAZ tool [7]. The form of refinement supported by DAZ is loosely based upon Carroll Morgan's refinement calculus [8]. Superficially it looks very much like Morgan's refinement calculus, but it is not a calculus and the executable code is a predictable subset of Ada.

A formal refinement starts with a specification statement that has a frame for the variables that can change and uses the Z notation to express the precondition and post condition. The refinement statement can then be refined to source code via a series of refinement steps. Each refinement step results in verification conditions generated by DAZ to establish the validity of the refinement.

A refinement checker, called QCZ, for a predictable subset of C is currently under development at QinetiQ. Analogous verification tools have been produced elsewhere, for example the Caduceus tool [9] and the verification tool for C0 developed by the Verisoft Project [10]. Both DAZ and QCZ take refinement conjectures and verify the correctness of the refinement within the guess and verify paradigm.

2.2 A Refinement Script Generator

QinetiQ's refinement checker takes a refinement conjecture as input. In general it takes considerable effort and some skill to produce a refinement argument. However the Simulink language has a limited number of ways of constructing a model and this constrains the form of the refinement. There are also many ways in which a refinement might be constructed, for example large steps leading to fewer and more complex verification conditions as opposed to smaller steps with consequently simpler but more verification conditions.

If a canonical form of refinement is conformed with then this leads to a canonical set of verification conditions. The canonical verification conditions can in turn be simplified by a limited number of proof tactics. To get closer to such a canonical form a tool is required that links parts of the Simulink diagram with the corresponding parts of the Ada program subunit. The process is called witnessing and the tool that supports it is the Refinement Script Generator, RSG. The witnessing language processed by the tool identifies correspondences between wires (also known as signals) in the Simulink diagram and the values of Ada variables at specific points in the program unit.

RSG ensures that witnessing is done by maintaining a wave front of wires in the Simulink diagram, prompting the user to supply a witness for any wire on the wave front. When a wire's witness has been supplied the wave front advances along that wire. The witness script is complete when the wave front has crossed the entire diagram.

A witness script for a typical 80 line program unit will be around 100 to 150 lines long. For manually developed code requiring manual witnessing this will take around 2 to 3 hours to construct, but might require re-work if an error is made. Note an error in the witness script will result in a verification failure when the refinement check takes place.

3 Metadata for Automated Code Generation

Automatic code generators typically produce information that allows the code generated to be traced back to that part of the model it was generated from. In some instances this informal textual relationship is formalized and used as an input to tools. For example one of the key enabling technologies of IBM's Rational Rhapsody [11] product is that it provides direct model code associativity. In essence this means that a change in code brings a change in the model, and a change in the model changes the code. The existence of such technology means that the basis for generating a refinement conjecture also exists. Such a refinement conjecture would enable verification by tools that were *independent* from the code generation.

Unfortunately it is unlikely that commercial vendors would be willing to expose the details of their code generation technology. For example The Mathworks have moved from an open template based approach for code generation to the use of opaque code generation steps. However QinetiQ's technology for generating refinement conjectures from abstract witnessing information suggested that the traceability information, which is already exposed by commercial automatic code generators, would be sufficient to generate a refinement conjecture. Further this refinement conjecture could be only one possible route for the development of the code, not necessarily the actual code generation path.

3.1 The B4S Automatic Code Generator

The requirement for independence led QinetiQ to approach Applied Dynamics International, ADI [12]. ADI develop and market a graphical design tool, code generator and automated tester. This graphical tool has been in use for over a decade, generating production quality safety critical application code for jet engine controllers. It was their code generator, called B4S, and its capability to take Simulink models as input that interested QinetiQ.

ADI were also interested in QinetiQ's technology to the extent that they quickly invested their own time and money in collaboration with QinetiQ. The purpose of the collaboration was to determine whether ADI could generate the witnessing information for automatically generating a refinement conjecture. As discussed this was previously generated manually with tool support.

The conjecture that traceability information, which is a customer requirement for automatic code generators, would be sufficient to generate witnessing information proved to be correct. Within weeks ADI were able to produce the required witness information as annotations in the generated code that could be processed by QinetiQ. The witnessing information is an example of metadata that provides sufficient information for a refinement conjecture to be automatically generated and automatically verified – assuming the code generated actually does satisfy the original model.

3.2 Harnessing the B4S Metadata

The metadata is used within a tool based process that must be set up by a person through a user interface. The specification directory needs to be defined; this is where the formal specifications automatically generated from the Simulink model will be placed. Next the analysis directory, where the results of the verification will be put, needs to be defined.

The results of the verification will be a record of all the verification conditions and their proof. If a verification condition is unproven then the simplified verification condition will also be placed there for examination within the ProofPower tool. In practice QinetiQ have found that unproven verification conditions contain sufficient information to diagnose an error in the automatically generated code.

The next step is to define the directory where the automatically generated code will be placed by the B4S automatic code generator. The Simulink from which the formal specification will be independently generated must also be specified through the user interface. In particular the parts of the Simulink model that correspond to program units needs to be given. QinetiQ use this facility to set up the verification of manually developed code that is being analyzed for errors. For the B4S tool this information is automatically available because the automatic code generator selects those parts of the model specified in Simulink's underlying .mdl file to generate the program unit. Finally which subprograms that require verification need to be defined; this is because changes to the Simulink model will not necessarily lead to re-generation of all the program units.

The next stage is to perform the verification. During this stage the metadata is used to define the formal relation between Simulink signals in the model and the variables in the code that implement those signals. The definition of the formal relation is done automatically because of the metadata. For manually developed code the metadata has to be generated by a tool that is manually driven. Although the tool is simple enough for undergraduates to use, it can be a tedious error prone activity that used to lead to verification failures that required re-work.

At this point the verification can actually proceed and, depending upon the size of an individual program unit, the time can range from a few minutes (for tens of lines of code per unit) to hours (for hundreds of lines of code per unit).

The verification stage is illustrated by an annotated snapshot of the user interface in fig. 3.

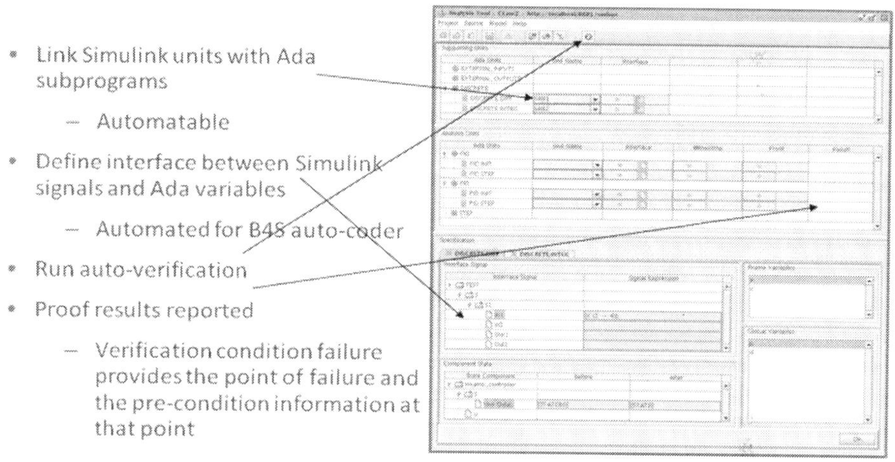

Fig. 3. An annotated snapshot of the user interface for the verification stage

3.3 A Research Challenge

Much work already exists on formalising modelling languages such as UML. As already discussed there are a number of verification tools that can be used to check refinement conjectures. Commercially available automatic code generators are readily available for many modelling languages. The challenge is to bring these together to provide completely automated verification processes that are independent from these automatic code generators.

The advantage of independent verification has been discussed, but it is worth repeating. The advantage of independent verification is essentially the clear diversity of software tools that means that lower levels of reliability need to be *claimed* in order to meet an overall reliability figure. In practice the actual level of reliability of, for example, QinetiQ's verification tools will be higher than required for, other reasons.

The requirement of a fully automated process is necessary for widespread adoption for commercial use. Without full automation the cost reductions will be insufficient for adoption except for the most expensive projects and there will be significant resistance to doing something novel that requires manual input beyond current practices.

The key to achieving full automation for a range of models and automatic code generators is the generation of the kind of metadata described in this paper. QinetiQ's research has demonstrated that it is possible for a commercially available automatic code generator and the Simulink modelling language. The conjecture is that there is a family of languages, or even a single unified language, that defines a set of possible refinement conjectures that have to be true if automatically generated code correctly implements the model it was generated from. Clearly there will need to be constraints on the automated code generator, the target language and the modelling language. Part of the research will be to explore and trade-off these constraints to develop a theory that underpins a metadata language.

One reason for believing that there is a general theory for such metadata is the observation that the target languages for commercially available automatic code generators share many of the same control flow and data representation concepts. The same seems to be true of many modelling languages, or at least those subsets of the modelling language that are used for automatic code generation.

4 Conclusions

It is widely accepted that the complexity of software is increasing and that the corresponding verification costs are rising in a non-linear fashion. This is not sustainable meaning that there will have to be large trade-offs between cost, capability and integrity.

High reliability or high consequence systems tend to require independence of verification. The approach advocated in this paper is to employ the "guess and verify" paradigm in the context of automatic code generation to enable automated verification that is independent of the code generation. The approach is illustrated by the development of an automated verification capability for a commercial automatic code generator called B4S.

A technical argument has been made that the diversity provided by the "guess and verify" approach leads to higher assurance of freedom from errors than just relying upon a single fault removal procedure. In addition to this argument there is a commercial imperative to adopting a "guess and verify" approach that can be automated. This is that commercial automatic code generators will tend to change frequently in response to their market. The reason for this is that the adoption of modelling languages is driven by the capability to model systems, simulate them and analyse them.

New capability tends to be added to modelling languages and tools in order to differentiate them from the competition. This means that change in automatic code generators is inevitable and if they do not adapt to new modelling opportunities then they will be relegated to niche uses. QinetiQ's experience is that a "guess and verify" framework can be readily adapted to evolution of the semantics of a modelling language. Further the only aspect that requires requalification is the generation of the formal specification since the rest of the tools are independent of the code generator. This independence also means that such an automated verification framework is only dependent on the metadata generated by an automatic code generator; therefore it could be used with any other automatic code generator that generated semantically equivalent metadata.

QinetiQ's experience of implementing an automated procedure for Simulink relies upon metadata generated from B4S and suggests that it could be generalised. The conjecture is that there is a family of languages, or even a single unified language, that defines a set of possible refinement conjectures that have to be true if automatically generated code correctly implements the model it was generated from. If a theory could be developed to underpin the semantic basis for such metadata then an open standard could be developed that could be adopted by commercial developers of automatic code generators. Offering such a capability would be a significant differentiator from competitors.

The paper started with a quote from Boehm and Basili, the full quote is:

"All other things being equal, it costs 50 percent more per source instruction to develop high-dependability software products than to develop low-dependability software products. However, the investment is more than worth it if the project involves significant operations and maintenance costs."

Coupling automatic code generation with independent automated verification promises to reduce the cost of developing high-dependability software from 50% to 15% more than that of low-dependability software. This could be achieved by, for example, stripping out unit testing and repeated re-work. Hence the old paradigm of "guess and verify" does have a future.

Acknowledgments. The source of this paper is due to many of my QinetiQ colleagues. Nick Tudor's work on the Formal Methods supplement of DO178C has informed the argument of independence and the commercial aspects of it. The concept of witnessing and the Refinement Script Generator were born out of necessity to deal with the post verification of thousands of lines of code. Mark Adams developed the idea of a refinement argument that could be automatically generated and be amenable to automated proof from work done by Alf Smith. Hazel Duncan has taken over and built upon the significant proof automation of Mark Adams. The concept of a witnessing approach and the Refinement Script Generator was developed and implemented by Phil Clayton. Richard Harrison developed the architecture for controlling the interactions between the tools. Mark Teasdale developed the Z producer tool, previously called ClawZ, that automatically generates a formal specification in a scalable and evolvable manner. The original work on producing the Z model was done under contract by Roger Jones and Rob Arthan, of Lemma1, who along with Dave King was responsible for the implementation of DAZ from a formal specification provided by DRA. All of the individuals named above also worked with each other to make the whole work together. The automatic generation of a witnessing script by B4S was joint work between Phil Clayton and Mike Senneff.

References

1. Boehm, B., Basili, V.R.: Software Defect Reduction Top 10 List. Computer 34(1), 135–137 (2001)
2. Littlewood, B.: On Diversity, and the Elusiveness of Independence. In: Anderson, S., Bologna, S., Felici, M. (eds.) SAFECOMP 2002. LNCS, vol. 2434, pp. 249–973. Springer, Heidelberg (2002)
3. Littlewood, B., Popov, P., Strigini, L., Shryane, N.: Modeling the Effects of Combining Diverse Software Fault Detection Techniques. IEEE Transactions on Software Engineering archive 26(12), 1157–1167 (2000)
4. Littlewood, B.: The Use of Proof in Diversity Arguments. IEEE Trans. Software Eng. 26(10), 1022–1023 (2000)
5. Arthan, R.D., Caseley, P., O'Halloran, C., Smith, A.: Control Laws in Z. In: ICFEM 2000, pp. 169–176 (2000)
6. Adams, M.M., Clayton, P.B.: ClawZ: Cost-Effective Formal Verification for Control Systems. In: Lau, K.-K., Banach, R. (eds.) ICFEM 2005. LNCS, vol. 3785, pp. 465–479. Springer, Heidelberg (2005)
7. O'Halloran, C., Arthan, R.D., King, D.: Using a Formal Specification Contractually. Formal Aspects of Computing 9(4), 349–358 (1997)
8. Morgan, C.: Programming from Specifications. Prentice Hall Series in Computer Science (1990)
9. Filliâtre, J.-C., Marché, C.: Multi-prover Verification of C Programs. In: Davies, J., Schulte, W., Barnett, M. (eds.) ICFEM 2004. LNCS, vol. 3308, pp. 15–29. Springer, Heidelberg (2004)
10. `http://www.verisoft.de`
11. `http://www.telelogic.com/products/rhapsody/index.cfm`
12. `http://www.adi.com`

Verification, Testing and Statistics

Sriram K. Rajamani

Microsoft Research India
sriram@microsoft.com

Abstract. Programming tools have expanded both in scope of the problems they solve, and in the kinds of techniques they use. Traditionally, programming tools have focused on detecting errors in programs. Recently, this scope has broadened to help with other programming tasks, including inferring specifications, helping diagnose root cause of errors during debugging, and managing knowledge in large projects. Also, traditionally programming tools have been based on either static or dynamic program analysis. Modern programming tools combine static and dynamic program analysis together with techniques from other disciplines such as statistical and probabilistic inference, and information retrieval. This paper reports on some such tools built by the Rigorous Software Engineering group at Microsoft Research India.

Large scale software development is an enormous engineering and scientific challenge. Over the past several decades several tools and techniques have been proposed to aid programmers and testers in the complex tasks associated with designing, implementing, testing and maintaining large software.

The "formal methods" community has been traditionally focusing on building tools to automatically check if the program, or some abstraction or model of the program satisfies a set of specifications. Such tools are classified as "program verification tools" or "static analysis tools". Though program verification has been the holy grail of the formal methods community, practical applications of verification run into major challenges. It is difficult to write detailed specifications, and it is hard to scale verification algorithms to large software. In spite of these difficulties, several tools have been successful in finding bugs and establishing certain weak specifications of programs (see for example [2,7,6]). However, bug finding is only one aspect of software development. Other software development activities such as design, maintenance and debugging have received relatively less attention from the formal methods community.

Traditionally, programming tools have been based either on static analysis or dynamic analysis. Static analysis involves analyzing a program by inspecting its text and reasoning about all possible behaviors without running the program, and dynamic analysis involves running the program. We believe that by combining static analysis and dynamic analysis together with techniques from other disciplines such as probabilistic and statistical techniques, and information retrieval techniques, we can solve a broader range of problems.

A. Cavalcanti and D. Dams (Eds.): FM 2009, LNCS 5850, pp. 33–40, 2009.

In this paper we report on both these trends using three projects:

- YOGI, a tool for finding bugs and proving safety properties of programs, by combining verification and testing,
- MERLIN, a tool to infer security specifications of software by combining static analysis with probabilistic inference,
- DEBUGADVISOR, a tool to find relevant information during debugging by combining domain specific knowledge about programs with information retrieval.

1 Combining Verification and Testing

Software validation is the task of determining if the software meets the expectations of its users. For the most part, industrial practice of software engineering uses *testing* to validate software. That is, we execute the software using test inputs that mimic how the user is expected to interact with the software, and declare success if the outcomes of the executions satisfy our expectations. There are various granularities in which testing is performed, ranging from unit testing that tests small portions of the system, to system-wide tests.

Testing is incomplete in the sense that it validates the software only for the test inputs that we execute. The software might exhibit undesired behavior with test inputs we do not have. Verification has a more ambitious goal —to formally prove that the software meets its expectations for all possible test inputs, and for all possible executions.

Testing and verification have complementary strengths in solving this problem. Testing typically suffers from low coverage. Thus, even if a software has been tested by a group of testers and found satisfactory as far as the desired specification is considered, a customer might well exercise a behavior that violates the specification, and expose a bug that was not detected during testing. However, every violation found using testing is a true error that can happen on the field, and this is one of the biggest strengths of testing. Verification, on the other hand, offers the promise of full behavioral coverage. Thus, when we use a verification tool to establish that a program satisfies the specification, we can be certain that the specification holds for all possible behaviors of the system. However, if a verification tool says that the program does *not* satisfy the specification, it might very well be due to the tool's inability to carry out the proof.

Suppose a specification is given to us, and we are interested in finding either a test input that violates the specification, or prove that the specification is satisfied for all inputs. For simplicity, let us consider assertional specifications that are expressed as assert statements of the form **assert**(e), where e is a predicate on the state of the program. Such a specification fails if an execution reaches an assert statement **assert**(e) in a state S such that predicate e does not hold in state S.

For the past few years, we have been investigating methods for combining static analysis in the style of counter-example driven refinement à la SLAM [3], with dynamic analysis in the style of concolic execution à la DART [8]. Our first attempt in this direction was the SYNERGY algorithm [10], which handled single procedure programs with only integer variables. Then, we proposed DASH [4], which had new ideas to handle pointer aliasing and procedure calls in programs.

The DASH algorithm simultaneously maintains a set of test runs and a region-graph abstraction of the program. The region-graph is the usual existential abstraction used by tools based on predicate abstraction [3,11]. Tests are used to find bugs and abstractions are used to prove their absence. During every iteration, if a concrete test has managed to reach the error region, a bug has been found. If no path in the abstract region graph exists from the initial region to the error region, a proof of correctness has been found. If neither of the above two cases are true, then we have an abstract counterexample, which is a sequence of regions in the abstract region graph, along which a test can be potentially driven to reveal a bug. The DASH algorithm crucially relies on the notion of a frontier [10,4], which is the boundary between tested and untested regions along an abstract counterexample that a concrete test has managed to reach. In every iteration, the algorithm first attempts to extend the frontier using test case generation techniques similar to DART. If test case generation fails, then the algorithm refines the abstract region graph so as to eliminate the abstract counterexample. For doing refinement, the DASH algorithm uses a new refinement operator WP_α which is the usual weakest precondition operator parameterized to handle only aliasing situations that arise in the tests that are executed [4].

The DASH algorithm is related to the Lee-Yannakakis algorithm [14], with the main difference being that the Lee-Yannakakis algorithm computes bisimulations, whereas the DASH algorithm computes simulations, which are coarser. See [10] for a more detailed comparison with the Lee-Yannakakis algorithm.

Most program analyses scale to large programs by building so called "summaries" at procedure boundaries. Summaries memoize analysis findings at procedure boundaries, and enable reusing these findings at other appropriate calling contexts of a procedure. Recently, we have proposed a new algorithm, called SMASH, to combine so-called "may-summaries" used in verification tools like SLAM with so-called "must-summaries" used in testing tools like DART [9].

A may-summary of a procedure is used to denote the absence of paths in the state space of the procedure, and a must-summary is used to denote presence of paths in the state space of the procedure. One of the most interesting aspects of the SMASH algorithm is the *interplay* between may-summaries and must-summaries. Suppose we want to ask if a path exists (that is, does a must-summary exist that shows the presence of such a path) between a set of states A that are input states to a procedure P_1, to a set of output states B of procedure P_1. Procedure P_1 could have several paths, and suppose one of these paths calls procedure P_2. Suppose there is a may-summary of P_2 that can be used to prove the absence of paths from set A to set B, then this information can be used to prune the search to avoid exploring the path that calls procedure P_2 (including all the paths inside the body of P_2 and its transitive callees) and explore other paths in P_1 to build the desired must-summary. Dually, suppose we want to ask if no path exists (that is, does a may-summary exist that shows the absence of such a path) between a set of states C that are input states to a procedure P_1, to a set of output states D of procedure P_1. Again, procedure P_1 could have several paths, and suppose one of these paths calls procedure P_2. The presence of certain kinds of must-summaries in P_2 can be used to avoid potentially expensive may analysis of procedure P_2 and still build the desired may-summary for P_1. More details can be found in [9], where we also quantify the amount of interplay between may-summaries and must-summaries empirically by running the tool over a large number of programs.

All of the above ideas have been implemented in a tool called YOGI, and empirical results from running and using the tool have been very promising [17].

2 Inferring Specifications Using Statistics

One of the difficulties with writing specifications is that they are very detailed — sometimes as detailed as the code itself. It would be useful if general guidelines could be given by the user at a high level, and tools would automatically infer detailed specifications from these guidelines.

As an example, consider the problem of detecting information flow vulnerabilities in programs. Here, certain data elements in the software (such as ones entered by the user, or passed from some untrusted program) are deemed to be "tainted", and the software is required to inspect the data and "sanitize" it before using it in a trusted context such as a database query. A formal specification of information flow security consists of classifying methods in a program into (a)*sources*: these nodes originate taint or lack of trust, (b)*sinks*: these nodes have the property that it is erroneous to pass tainted data to them, (c)*sanitizers*: these nodes cleanse or untaint the input (even if input is tainted, output is not tainted), (d)*regular nodes*: these nodes simply propagate taint information from inputs to outputs without any modification. In this setting an *information flow vulnerability* is a path from a source to a sink that is not sanitized.

Since typical applications have tens of thousands of methods, it takes intensive (and error-prone) manual effort to give a detailed specification that classifies each method into a source, sanitizer, sink or regular node. Consider a data propagation graph of the program, whose nodes are methods and whose edges indicate flow of information. That is, an edge exists from node (method) m_1 to node (method) m_2 iff data flows from m_1 to m_2 either using an argument or return value of a procedure call, or using global variables.

We do not know which nodes in the propagation graph are sources, sinks or sanitizers. We propose to use Bayesian inference to determine this. We associate a random variable with each node in the propagation graph, where each such random variable can take one of four values— source, sink, sanitizer or regular node. If such random variables are chosen from independent probability distributions (for instance, a binomial distribution for each random variable), the outcome of such an experiment is unlikely to be useful, since we are ignoring the structure of the program and our intuitions about likely specifications. However, we have a lot of information about the desired outcome of such an experiment. These beliefs can be used to constrain the probability distributions of each of the random variables using Bayesian reasoning.

In particular, let us consider some beliefs about the desired outcome in our example. It is reasonable to believe that errors are rare and that most paths in propagation graphs are secure. That is, the probability that a path goes from a source to a sink with no intervening sanitizer is very low. Also, it is unlikely that a path between a source and a sink contains two or more sanitizers. If information flows from method m_1 to m_2, then m_1 is more likely to be a source than m_2, and m_2 is more likely to be a sink than m_1.

All the above beliefs are not absolute. If we were to treat them as boolean constraints which all need to be satisfied, they could even be mutually contradictory. Thus, we represent all these beliefs as probabilistic constraints, and desire to compute the marginal probability distributions associated with each individual random variable. Computing marginal distributions naïvely does not scale, since the naïve computation is exponential. However, if the joint probability distribution can be written as a product of factors, where each factor is a distribution over a small number of random variables, there are very efficient algorithms such as the sum-product algorithm [13] to compute the desired marginal distributions.

We have built a tool called MERLIN to automatically infer sources, sinks and sanitizers using this approach. MERLIN first builds a propagation graph of the program using static analysis, and uses the above beliefs to build a factor graph from the propagation graph. Probabilistic inference is then performed on the factor graph, and thresholding over the computed marginal distributions is used to compute the desired specifications. Our implementation of MERLIN uses the INFER.NET tool [16] to perform probabilistic inference.

We believe that this general recipe can be used to infer specifications in several situations: model the specification associated with each component as a random variable, model the beliefs we have about the outcome of the inference as a set of probabilistic constraints, perform probabilistic inference to obtain marginal probabilities for each of the random variables, and perform thresholding on the marginals to obtain the specifications.

3 Finding Related Information during Debugging

In large software development projects, when a programmer is assigned a bug to fix, she typically spends a lot of time searching (in an ad-hoc manner) for instances from the past where similar bugs have been debugged, analyzed and resolved. We have built a tool called DEBUGADVISOR [1] to automate this search process. We first describe the major challenges associated with this problem, and then our approach.

The first challenge involves understanding what constitutes a search query. In principle, we would like to leverage all of the context the user has on the current problem, including the state of the machine being debugged, information in the current bug report, information obtained from the user's interaction with the debugger, etc. This context contains several objects such as call stacks, image names, semaphores, mutexes, memory dumps, exceptions etc. Each of them have their own domain specific notions of similarity to be used when two instances of such objects are compared. The second challenge involves dealing with the diversity of information sources that contain potentially useful information for the user. These include past bug reports, logs of interactive debugger sessions, information on related source code changes, and information about people in the organization. These information sources are variegated, and the data is of varied type —a mixture of structured and unstructured data.

We approach the first challenge (capturing the context of the user) by allowing a *fat query* —a query which could be kilobytes of structured and unstructured data containing all contextual information for the issue being debugged, including natural language text, textual rendering of core dumps, debugger output etc. DebugAdvisor allows users to search through all our software repositories (version control, bug database, logs of debugger sessions, etc) using a fat query interface. The fat query interface is quite different when compared with short query strings commonly used in information retrieval systems. Previously, our users had to search through each data repository separately using several queries, each of which was restricted to a short query string, and they had no automatic mechanism to combine these search results. DebugAdvisor's fat query interface allows users to query all these diverse data repositories with a single query.

We approach the second challenge (diversity of information sources) by partitioning the search problem into two phases. The first "search" phase takes a fat query as input and returns a ranked list of bug descriptions that match the query. These bug descriptions contain a mix of structured and unstructured data. The second "link analysis" phase uses the output of the first phase to retrieve a set of related recommendations such as people, source files and functions.

The key idea in the search phase is to uniformly represent both queries and information sources as a collection of *features*, which are formalized as *typed documents*. Typed documents have a recursive type structure with four type constructors:(1) unordered bag of terms, (2) ordered list of terms, (3) weighted terms, and (4) key-value pairs. Features with arbitrary structure are expressed by combining these type constructors. Representing features as typed documents leads to an important advantage —it separates the process of defining and extracting domain specific structure from the process of indexing and searching. The former needs to be done by a domain expert, but the latter can be done generically from the type structure.

The link analysis phase of DebugAdvisor retrieves recommendations about people, source files, binaries, and source functions that are relevant to the current query, by analyzing relationships between these entities. We are inspired by link-analysis algorithms such as Page Rank [5] and HITS [12] to compute these recommendations. Unlike the world-wide web, where explicit URL pointers between pages provide the link structure, there are no explicit links between these data sources. For fixed bugs, it is possible to discover the version control revision that was made to fix the bug. We can then find out which lines of code were changed to fix the bug, which functions and which binaries were changed, and who made the change. The output of such an analysis is a relationship graph, which relates elements in bug descriptions, source files, functions, binaries and people. Starting with a "seed" set of bug descriptions from the search phase, the link analysis phase performs probabilistic inference and retrieves a ranked list of people, files, binaries and functions related to the seed set.

We have deployed DebugAdvisor to several hundred users internally within Microsoft, and the feedback has been very positive [1].

4 Summary

Large scale software development is a difficult engineering endeavor. So far, formal methods have been primarily associated with program verification, and bug detection in programs or models. In this paper we have taken a broader view of programming tools, used to aid various tasks performed during the software development life cycle including specification inference and knowledge management. We have also illustrated the power obtained by combining various analysis techniques such as verification, testing, statistical and probabilistic inference, and information retrieval. We believe that such hybrid tools that exploit synergies between various techniques and solve a broad set of programming tasks will become more widely used by programmers, testers and other stakeholders in the software development life cycle.

Acknowledgement

We thank our collaborators B. Ashok, Anindya Banerjee, Nels Beckman, Bhargav Gulavani, Patrice Godefroid, Tom Henzinger, Joseph Joy, Yamini Kannan, Ben Livshits, Aditya Nori, Rob Simmons, Gopal Srinivasa, Sai Tetali, Aditya Thakur and Vipindeep Vangala. We thank the anonymous reviewers for their comments on a draft of this paper.

References

1. Ashok, B., Joy, J., Liang, H., Rajamani, S.K., Srinivasa, G., Vangala, V.: DebugAdvisor: A recommendation system for debugging. In: ESEC/FSE 2009: Foundations of Software Engineering (to appear, 2009)
2. Ball, T., Bounimova, E., Cook, B., Levin, V., Lichtenberg, J., McGarvey, C., Ondrusek, B., Rajamani, S.K., Ustuner, A.: Thorough static analysis of device drivers. In: EuroSys 2006: European Systems Conference, pp. 73–85. ACM Press, New York (2006)
3. Ball, T., Rajamani, S.K.: Automatically validating temporal safety properties of interfaces. In: Dwyer, M.B. (ed.) SPIN 2001. LNCS, vol. 2057, pp. 103–122. Springer, Heidelberg (2001)

4. Beckman, N.E., Nori, A.V., Rajamani, S.K., Simmons, R.J.: Proofs from tests. In: ISSTA 2008: International Symposium on Software Testing and Analysis, pp. 3–14. ACM Press, New York (2008)
5. Brin, S., Page, L.: The anatomy of a large-scale hypertextual web search engine. Comput. Netw. ISDN Syst. 30(1-7), 107–117 (1998)
6. Engler, D., Chelf, B., Chou, A., Hallem, S.: Checking system rules using system-specific, programmer-written compiler extensions. In: OSDI 2000: Operating System Design and Implementation, pp. 1–16. Usenix Association (2008)
7. Hackett, B., Das, M., Wang, D., Yang, Z.: Modular checking for buffer overflows in the large. In: ICSE 2006: International Conference on Software Engineering, pp. 232–241. ACM Press, New York (2006)
8. Godefroid, P., Klarlund, N., Sen, K.: DART: Directed automated random testing. In: PLDI 2005: Programming Language Design and Implementation, pp. 213–223. ACM Press, New York (2005)
9. Godefroid, P., Nori, A.V., Rajamani, S.K., Tetali, S.: Compositional may-must program analysis: Unleashing the power of alternation. Microsoft Research Technical Report MSR-TR-2009-2. Microsoft Research (2009)
10. Gulavani, B.S., Henzinger, T.A., Kannan, Y., Nori, A.V., Rajamani, S.K.: SYNERGY: A new algorithm for property checking. In: FSE 2006: Foundations of Software Engineering, pp. 117–127. ACM Press, New York (2006)
11. Henzinger, T.A., Jhala, R., Majumdar, R., Sutre, G.: Lazy abstraction. In: POPL 2002: Principles of Programming Languages, pp. 58–70. ACM Press, New York (2002)
12. Kleinberg, J.M.: Hubs, authorities, and communities. ACM Computing Surveys 31, 4es, 5 (1999)
13. Kschischang, F.R., Frey, B.J., Loeliger, H.A.: Factor graphs and the sum-product algorithm. IEEE Trans. Information Theory 47(2), 498–519 (2001)
14. Lee, D., Yannakakis, M.: On-line minimization of transition systems. In: Theory of Computing (STOC), pp. 264–274. ACM, New York (1992)
15. Livshits, B., Nori, A.V., Rajamani, S.K., Banerjee, A.: Merlin: Specification inference for explicit information flow problems. In: PLDI 2009: Programming Language Design and Implementation, ACM Press, New York (to appear, 2009)
16. Minka, T., Winn, J., Guiver, J., Kannan, A.: Infer.NET 2.2, Microsoft Research Cambridge (2009), `http://research.microsoft.com/infernet`
17. Nori, A.V., Rajamani, S.K., Tetali, S., Thakur, A.V.: The Yogi project: Software property checking via static analysis and testing. In: Kowalewski, S., Philippou, A. (eds.) TACAS 2009. LNCS, vol. 5505, pp. 178–181. Springer, Heidelberg (2009)

Security, Probability and Nearly Fair Coins in the Cryptographers' Café

Annabelle McIver[1], Larissa Meinicke[1], and Carroll Morgan[2,⋆]

[1] Dept. Computer Science, Macquarie University, NSW 2109 Australia
[2] School of Comp. Sci. and Eng., Univ. New South Wales, NSW 2052 Australia

Abstract. Security and probability are both artefacts that we hope to bring increasingly within the reach of refinement-based Formal Methods; although we have worked on them separately, in the past, the goal has always been to bring them together.

In this report we describe our ongoing work in that direction: we relate it to a well known problem in security, Chaum's *Dining Cryptographers*, where the various criteria of correctness that might apply to it expose precisely the issues we have found to be significant in our efforts to deal with security, probability and abstraction all at once.

Taking our conviction into this unfamiliar and demanding territory, that abstraction and refinement are the key tools of software development, has turned out to be an exciting challenge.

1 Introduction

When I took office, only high-energy physicists had ever heard of what is called the World Wide Web... Now even my cat has its own page.

More than 10 years later, the internet is the playground of far stranger things than White-House pets,[1] and some estimates place its size upwards of tens of billions of websites: everybody and every thing seems to be at it. There has been a boom not only in science and business but also in private transactions, so that where once decisions were based on "rules of thumb" and inter-personal relationships, now we increasingly defer to automation — even when it is our security and privacy that is at stake.

The movement towards "transactions at a distance" has spawned a huge number of ingenious algorithms and protocols to make computers do for us what we used to do for ourselves, using "gut feeling" and the full repertoire of body language and other out-of-band channels. The reliance on machines has blurred the distinction between the real world –with all its uncertainties– and software, with its inescapable reliance on an exact unforgiving model — one that its designers hope has some connection to its environment and purpose. As users thus we place an increasingly heavy burden on those designers: once they could assume

⋆ We acknowledge the support of the Australian Research Council Grant DP0879529.

[1] The quote is attributed to Bill Clinton in 1996 (but unconfirmed).

A. Cavalcanti and D. Dams (Eds.): FM 2009, LNCS 5850, pp. 41–71, 2009.

absolute regularity; and now they must decide just what exactly *can* be assumed in an uncertain world, and what guarantees can be given with any confidence about the software they create.

The answer–we believe in Formal Methods– is to create rigorous models of the phenomena with which the software must contend, as far as is possible. As we do so, we are misunderstood by the wider Computer Science community when they accuse us of believing that the real world can be captured entirely in mathematics, or that the only way to write programs is to calculate them by hand with a quill pen.

> *It is as if planning a household budget using decimals for dollars, and a computer for calculation, were somehow evidence of one's belief that all of family life can be reduced to arithmetic. The truth –as everyone knows– is that using arithmetic for what can be quantified leaves more time to enjoy what can't be.*

Similarly, formalising and automating what can be captured in semantics, models and calculi for computer applications leaves more time for concentrating on the aspects that require intuition, common sense and good taste. Thus our aim is always to expand our formalisations so that we can capture more.[2]

In this paper we concentrate on capturing more aspects of software systems for which security is an issue and whose operational envorinment is only partially predictable. Specifically, our goal is a mathematical model of probability, security and modularity: they are –we will argue– closely linked phenomena, and (we do not need to argue) they are all relevant to the design of computer systems and the control and understanding of their behaviour and their applications.

Crucial to getting a grip on slippery concepts is to setting up a framework within which one can pose precise questions and draw rigorous conclusions. If the conclusions agree with our intuitions, or nearly so, then we proceed, elaborating the framework; if not, we backtrack and try a different angle. Constructing a framework requires, in turn, a repertoire of small, compelling examples that can serve as targets for the construction.

Our compelling example is Chaum's well known exemplary problem of the Dining Cryptographers: we stretch it and twist it in order to illustrate the intricacies that arise when we mix the above concepts. From there we discuss a number of models which attempt to tame those intricacies, and finally we pose some further intriguing lines of research.

---

[2] Assailed on both sides, Formal Methods is sometimes thought to be trying to reinvent or trivialise the long-established work of mathematicians. It's not so. Nobody for example worries about the correctness of Bubble Sort *in principle*; but because source-level reasoning about array segments remains difficult for many people, every day new and incorrect sorting programs are written by accident... and propagated: that's bad *practice*. Finding better ways to reason about array segments at the source level would therefore be an improvement for everyone.

2 The Cryptographers' Café

In this section we introduce Chaum's *Dining Cryptographers* protocol, and we outline the point of view that will allow us to use it to explore refinement and nondeterminism as well as the security and probability it already contains. Here is the original abstract, which sketches the problem domain:

> *Keeping confidential who sends which messages, in a world where any physical transmission can be traced to its origin, seems impossible. The solution presented here is unconditionally or cryptographically secure, depending on whether it is based on one-time-use keys or on public keys, respectively. It can be adapted to address efficiently a wide variety of practical considerations.* [8]

Now we look at the solution, and see where it leads.

2.1 Chaum's Solution: The Dining Cryptographers' Protocol

Chaum's protocol for anonymity is built around the following story:

> Three cryptographers have finished their lunch, and ask the waiter for their bill; the waiter says it's already been paid. But by whom? The cryptographers do the following to find out.
>
> Each pair of cryptographers flips a fair coin privately between the two of them, concealed from the third; then each announces whether she paid, but lies if the two flipped coins she sees show different faces. (1)
>
> If the number of "I paid" utterances is odd, then indeed one of the cryptographers paid; but only she knows which one that was (i.e. herself). If the number is even, then the bill was paid by a fourth party.

Chaum gives a rigorous mathematical proof that, no matter what an individual cryptographer observes, because the coins are fair (50%) the chance she can guess which other cryptographer paid *after* the protocol (50%) is the same as it was before (50%).

His proof does not refer to a specific program text, and so makes no use of anything that could be called a program logic. Our contribution is *not* however to increase the rigour of Chaum's argument. It is rigorous already. Rather we want to find a way of capturing that style of argument in a programming-language context so that we can be more confident when we confront larger, more complex examples of it in actual applications, and so that we have some chance of automating it.

As a first step, we separate concerns by dealing with the hiding and the probability separately. We name the cryptographers A, B and C; then

> Cryptographer A's utterance does not reveal whether she paid, since neither of the other two cryptographers B, C knows both of the coins A consulted when deciding whether to lie or not: Cryptographer B sees one but not the other; and Cryptographer C sees the other but not the one. The same applies from Cryptographers' B, C points of view.
>
> Yet when the parity of the three utterances is calculated, each coin is tallied twice and so cancels out. Thus the parity of "I paid" *claims* is the same as the parity of "I paid" *acts*. That number of acts is either zero or one (because the bill is paid at most once, no matter by whom) — and so it is determined by the parity. (2)

The attractiveness of this formulation is that it reduces the problem to Boolean algebra, a domain much closer to programming logic. But it raises some intriguing questions, as we now see.

2.2 What Is the Relevance of the Fair Coins?

Given that the statement of the protocol (1) refers to "fair coins," and our version of the correctness argument (2) does not, it's reasonable to ask where in our framework the fairness should fit in. Clearly the coins' bias has *some* bearing, since in the extreme case –returning always heads, or always tails– the cryptographer's utterances won't be encrypted at all: with each coin's outcome known in advance, whether or not the coin can be seen, a cryptographer's utterance will reveal her act. In that case the protocol is clearly incorrect.

But what if the coins are biased only a little bit? At what point of bias does the protocol become incorrect? If it's correct only when the coins are exactly fair, and incorrect otherwise, is the protocol therefore unimplementable? Or does it become "increasingly incorrect" as the bias increases? After all, there are no exactly fair coins in nature.

And worse — what about the case where the coins *are* extremely biased, but no-one knows beforehand what that bias is? Furthermore, does it make a difference if the bias is not fixed and is able to change with time?

2.3 The Café

The key to the questions of Sec. 2.2 –and our point of departure– is *time* in the sense that it implies repeated trials. We elaborate the example of Sec. 2.1 by imagining that the cryptographers meet in the same café every day, and that the protocol (1) is carried out on each occasion. Suppose that the waitress, observing this, notes that Cryptographer A *always* says "I paid."[3] What does she conclude?

[3] More precisely, she serves a statistically significant number of lunches, say a whole year's worth, and Cryptographer A says "I paid" on all of them. This is discussed further in Sec. 8.10.

She concludes quite a lot. Given that the coins are independent of each other (irrespective of whether they are fair), and that Cryptographer A follows the protocol properly (whether she believes she paid is not influenced *post hoc* by the coin-flips), the waitress concludes that Cryptographer A either pays every time, or never pays. Moreover, she knows also that both of the coins Cryptographer A sees are completely unfair. For this is the only way, given independence (and in the absence of magic) that the utterance of A can be the same every time. Note that the waitress does *not* learn whether A is a philanthropist or a miser; she learns only that A is resolutely one or the other. Thus –in spite of (2)– without an explicit appeal to fairness the protocol seems insecure.

Let's push this example further, and examine its dependence on the coins' bias when that bias is not extreme. For simplicity, we consider just one hidden coin c and a secret h: the coin is flipped, and $c{=}h$ is revealed.[4] What do we learn about c and h if this is done repeatedly?

From now on, for uniformity, our coins show `true` and `false` (sometimes abbreviated `T` and `F`). Over many runs, there will be some proportion p_c of c's being `T`; similarly there will have been some proportion p_h of h's being `T`. The resulting proportion of $c{=}h$'s being `true` will then be

$$p_t \quad := \quad p_c p_h + (1{-}p_c)(1{-}p_h) \ , \tag{3}$$

and arithmetic shows that p_t is $1/2$ just when one or both of $p_{\{c,h\}}$ is $1/2$.

If p_t is *not* $1/2$, then it will be some distance away so that $2p_t$ is $1{+}\varepsilon_t$, say, and for $\varepsilon{\geq}0$ we could say that an ε-biased coin has a probability range of ε, the interval $[(1{-}\varepsilon)/2, (1{+}\varepsilon)/2]$, an interval which we abbreviate as just $[\varepsilon]$. Defining $\varepsilon_c, \varepsilon_h$ similarly, we can bring (3) into a much neater form, that

$$\varepsilon_t \quad = \quad \varepsilon_c \varepsilon_h \ . \tag{4}$$

Then, since $|\varepsilon_{\{t,c,h\}}| \leq 1$, we can see immediately that $|\varepsilon_t| \leq |\varepsilon_{\{c,h\}}|$. That is, the observed bias $|\varepsilon_t|$ is a lower bound for the hidden biases $|\varepsilon_c|$ and $|\varepsilon_h|$. Note particularly that whatever $|\varepsilon_t|$ we observe we can infer a *no lesser* bias $|\varepsilon_h|$ in the hidden h without knowing anything about the bias (or not) of the coin c.

That last sentence gives us a glimpse of the continuum we were looking for: if there is no observed bias, i.e. ε_t is zero, then one of $\varepsilon_{\{c,h\}}$ must be zero also and we learn nothing about the other one. On the other hand, if $c{=}h$ always or never, so that ε_t is one, then *both* $\varepsilon_{\{c,h\}}$ must be one as well.

Between the extremes of exactly fair ($\varepsilon{=}0$) and wholly nondeterministic ($\varepsilon{=}1$), however, we have coins of varying quality. What can we conclude about those?

2.4 The Challenge

The series of examples and questions above are intended to reveal what we consider to be important and significant challenges for any formal method operating in the domain of probability, nondeterminism and security. In Sec. 8 to come we

[4] This is an example of what elsewhere we call the Encryption Lemma.

will return to the Café and say more about what outcomes we expect from a formal analysis built on a model that is practical enough to use in the construction of actual software. Between now and then, we (re-)visit the underlying themes that have led us to this point.

3 Underlying Themes: A Trio of Features and Their History

Program models and logics applicable to problems like those above will include demonic choice, probabilistic choice and hidden variables. Rather than attempting to integrate these features at once we have approached the problem in smaller, overlapping steps. A benefit is a thorough and incremental exploration of the different modelling issues; another benefit is that some of the less feature-rich models are adequate for modelling certain classes of problems, and so it has been worthwhile to explore these models in their own right.

One of the first steps taken towards the integration of demonic choice, probabilistic choice and hidden variables was to build a framework [41,59] combining the first two of these three features. Another has been the development of the *Shadow Model* [37,44,49,54,55,56] for programs with demonic choices and hidden state (but not probability).

A third development, which we report in this paper, may be seen as a hybrid of the above two models in which the value of the hidden variables may be unknown, but must vary according to a known distribution. This model, the *Quantum Model*, does contain nondeterminism; but this nondeterminism is "visible," whereas uncertainty about the value of the hidden state can only be probabilistic and not nondeterministic.

In the following sections we start by giving an overview of all of those frameworks: the basic model, the Shadow Model and the Quantum Model. We conclude with a discussion of the challenges posed by integrating the three and, on that basis, we suggest another incremental way to move forward.

4 The Basics: Probability and Demonic Choice[5]

Demonic choice in sequential programming was conspicuously popularised by Dijkstra [14]: it was perhaps the first elementary appearance of nondeterminism at the source-code level, and was intended to express abstraction in the design process.[6] As its importance and relevance increased, it acquired an operator of its own, so that nowadays we simply write $\mathit{this} \sqcap \mathit{that}$ for pure demonic choice, whereas Dijkstra would have written

$$\begin{array}{ll} \textbf{if} & \mathsf{true} \rightarrow \mathit{this} \\ [\!] & \mathsf{true} \rightarrow \mathit{that} \\ \textbf{fi}\ . & \end{array}$$

[5] This section is very brief, given the availability of other literature [6,7,17,21,23,24,25,26,27,29,39,40,41,42,21,45,46,47,48,52,53,58,59,64,65].

[6] And it was often misunderstood to be advocating nondeterminism at run-time.

A natural refinement of the qualitative unpredictable choice $\sqcap$ is the *quantitatively* unpredictable choice ${}_p\oplus$, so that *this*${}_p\oplus$*that* chooses *this* with probability p and (therefore) *that* with probability $1-p$. This *replacement* of $\sqcap$ by ${}_p\oplus$ was given a Dijkstra-like semantics by Kozen [34,35] and, later, put in a more general setting by Jones [32,31].

Our own contribution was to treat both forms of nondeterminism –demonic and probabilistic– within the same framework, thus simultaneously generalising the two approaches above [41,59]. With this in place, we can describe a "nearly fair choice" by using both forms of nondeterminism together. For example, the behaviour of a program *this* ${}_{[\varepsilon]}\oplus$ *that* which describes a coin "within ε of being fair" may be represented by

$$(\mathit{this}\ {}_{\frac{1-\varepsilon}{2}}\oplus\ \mathit{that}) \quad \sqcap \quad (\mathit{this}\ {}_{\frac{1+\varepsilon}{2}}\oplus\ \mathit{that})\ .$$

This begins to address the issue of nearly fair coins that was first raised in Sec. 2.2 and to which we return in Sec. 8.

5 The Shadow: Hidden Nondeterministic State[7]

5.1 The Shadow in Essence

The Shadow Model arose in order to allow development of non-interference - style protocols by refinement. A long-standing problem in the area was that nondeterminism in a specification usually is an invitation to the developer (or the run-time system) to pick one alternative out of many presented: the intention of offering the choice is to indicate that any of the alternatives is acceptable.

In security however nondeterminism indicates instead a hidden, or high-security value known only to be in a set; and an implementation's picking just one of those values is exactly what the specification is not allowing. Rather it is specifying exactly the opposite, that the "ignorance" of the unknown value should *not* be decreased.

In the Shadow Model these two conflicting uses of nondeterminism are dealt with by partitioning the state space into *visible* variables $v{:}\,\mathcal{V}$, say, and *hidden* variables $h{:}\,\mathcal{H}$ and storing the hidden part as a set of the possible values it could be, rather than as a single definitive value — that is, the state space is $\mathcal{V}{\times}\mathbb{P}\mathcal{H}$ rather than the conventional $\mathcal{V}{\times}\mathcal{H}$.[8] Then (informally) conventional refinement allows whole sets of hidden variables' values to be discarded; but it does not allow the sets themselves to be reduced.

For example, for the program

$$v{:}{\in}\,\{0,1\};\ \ h{:}{\in}\,\{v{+}1, v{+}2\} \tag{5}$$

the denotation in the style $\mathcal{V}{\times}\mathbb{P}\mathcal{H}$ as above of the final states would be the set of pairs $\{(0,\{0,1\}),(1,\{1,2\})\}$; and a possible refinement then would be to throw

[7] Also this section is brief: there are two other detailed papers at this venue on The Shadow [44,55].

[8] We write $\mathbb{P}\cdot$ for powerset.

the whole first pair away, leaving just the $\{(1,\{1,2\})\}$ which is the denotation of the program $v{:=}1; h{:\in}\{v{+}1, v{+}2\}$. On the other hand, it is not a refinement simply to remove values from the h-sets: the denotation $\{(0,\{1\}),(1,\{2\})\}$ of the program $v{:\in}\{0,1\}; h{:=}v{+}1$ is not a refinement of (5).

With this Shadow Model one can prove that the Dining Cryptographers Protocol is secure for a single run, in the sense that it is a secure refinement of the specification "reveal whether a cryptographer paid, and nothing else." (See Sec. 8.1 for a more detailed discussion of this and, in particular, for the significance of "single run.")

5.2 The Shadow's Abstraction of Probability

The Shadow is a *qualitative* semantics for security and hiding, indicating only what is hidden and what its possible values are. In practice, hidden values are chosen *quantitatively* according to distributions that are intended to minimise the probability that an attacker can determine what the actual hidden variables are.

In the cases where a quantitative analysis is necessary, an obvious step is to replace the encapsulated set $\mathbb{P}\mathcal{H}$ of hidden values by instead an encapsulated distribution $\mathbb{D}\mathcal{H}$ over the same base type, so that the state space becomes $\mathcal{V}\times\mathbb{D}\mathcal{H}$. That leads conceptually to what we call The Quantum Model, explained in the next section.

6 The Quantum Model:[9] Hidden Probabilistic State and Ignorant Nondeterminism

6.1 Motivation

Our work on probabilistic/demonic semantics, summarised above in Sec. 4, achieved a natural generalisation of its antecedents: its operational (relational) model was $S{\to}\mathbb{P}\mathbb{D}S$, generalising both the purely demonic model $S{\to}\mathbb{P}S$ and the purely probabilistic model $S \to \mathbb{D}S$;[10] and its corresponding "expectation transformer" model $(S{\to}\mathbb{R}) \to (S{\to}\mathbb{R})$ generalised the predicate-transformer model $(S{\to}\{0,1\}) \to (S{\to}\{0,1\})$,[11] including the discovery of the quantitative form of conjunctivity, called sublinearity [41, p.146].

Much of that work was achieved by "playing out" the initial insights of Kozen and Jones [34,35,32,31] along the the familiar trajectory that Dijkstra [14] and

[9] Initial experiments with this are described in unpublished notes [57,38].
We said "conceptually" above because in fact the Quantum Model was developed ten years before The Shadow, in response to issues to do with data refinement as explained in Sec. 6.2 below. Because of the model's complexity, however, it was decided to "put it on ice" and seek an intermediate, simpler step in the hope that it would make the issues clearer. We alter the fossil record by placing the Shadow before the Quantum in this presentation.

[10] We write $\mathbb{D}\cdot$ for "distributions over."

[11] The predicate-transformer model is usually described as $\mathbb{P}S{\to}\mathbb{P}S$. We used the above equivalent formulation to make the connection clear with the more general model.

```
module Fork {
// No data.
  public Flip { g:= T ⊓ F }
}
```
(a) The Demonic Fork

```
module Spade {
  private h:= T ⊓ F;
  public Flip { g:= h; h:= T ⊓ F }
}
```
(b) The Demonic Spade

Fig. 1. *The Fork* has no data. *The Spade* has a local variable h initialised demonically.

others had established for purely probabilistic and purely demonic programs respectively. An unexpected obstacle arose however when we attempted to continue that trajectory along the path of data refinement [33,4,19]. We found that the modular probabilistic programs require the same program features –such as the ability to hide information– as security applications do.

We explain the data-refinement problem in the following section; it leads directly to the Quantum Model.

6.2 The Fork and the Spade[12]

Consider the two modules shown in Fig. 1. It is well known that the left-hand module *Fork* can be transformed via data-refinement into the right-hand module *Spade*; we just use the representation transformer $h{:=}\,\mathsf{T} \sqcap \mathsf{F}$.[13]

The algebraic inequality (actually identity) that justifies this is

$$g{:=}\,\mathsf{T} \sqcap \mathsf{F};\ h{:=}\,\mathsf{T} \sqcap \mathsf{F} \quad \sqsubseteq \quad h{:=}\,\mathsf{T} \sqcap \mathsf{F};\ g{:=}\,h;\ h{:=}\,\mathsf{T} \sqcap \mathsf{F}\ ,$$

that is that $Op_F; rep \sqsubseteq rep; Op_S$ where Op_F is the Fork's operation and Op_S is the Spade's operation and *rep* is the representation transformer [4,19,5]. Now we can carry out the same transformation (structurally) if we replace demonic choice $\sqcap$ by probabilistic choice ${}_p\oplus$ throughout, as in Fig. 2. This time the justifying inequality is

$$g{:=}\,\mathsf{T}\ {}_p\!\oplus \mathsf{F};\ h{:=}\,\mathsf{T}\ {}_p\!\oplus \mathsf{F} \quad \sqsubseteq \quad h{:=}\,\mathsf{T}\ {}_p\!\oplus \mathsf{F};\ g{:=}\,h;\ h{:=}\,\mathsf{T}\ {}_p\!\oplus \mathsf{F}\ . \qquad (6)$$

Unfortunately, in the probabilistic case the (6)-like inequality fails in general for statements in the *rest* of the program, whatever they might be. For example, consider a statement $g'{:=}\,\mathsf{T} \sqcap \mathsf{F}$ in the surrounding program, for some second global variable g' distinct from g. The justifying (6)-like inequation here is the requirement

$$g'{:=}\,\mathsf{T} \sqcap \mathsf{F};\ h{:=}\,\mathsf{T}\ {}_p\!\oplus \mathsf{F} \qquad (7)$$

$$\sqsubseteq \quad h{:=}\,\mathsf{T}\ {}_p\!\oplus \mathsf{F};\ g'{:=}\,\mathsf{T} \sqcap \mathsf{F}\ . \qquad (8)$$

---

[12] These two examples were prominent players in the Oxford-Manchester "football matches" on data-refinement in 1986 [2].

[13] We are using the formulation of data-refinement in which the "coupling invariant" is given by a program rather than a predicate [4,19]: here we call it the *representation transformer*.

module *Fork* {
// No data.
public *Flip* { $g{:=}\,\mathsf{T}\ {}_p\!\oplus \mathsf{F}$ }
}

(a) The Probabilistic Fork

module *Spade* {
private $h{:=}\,\mathsf{T}\ {}_p\!\oplus \mathsf{F}$;
public *Flip* { $g{:=}\,h; h{:=}\,\mathsf{T}\ {}_p\!\oplus \mathsf{F}$ }
}

(b) The Probabilistic Spade

Fig. 2. This time *The Spade* has a local variable h initialised probabilistically

And this putative refinement fails, for for the following reasons.

In our basic semantics of Sec. 4, on the right-hand side (8) we can have g' and h finally equal on every run, since the demonic assignment to g' can be resolved to $g{:=}\,h$. But leaving g', h equal every time is *not* a possible behaviour of the left-hand side (7), since the demon's assignment to g' occurs before h's final value has been chosen.

This failure is not acceptable. It would mean that altering the interior of a module could not be done without checking every statement in the surrounding program, however large that program might be. The point of having modules is to avoid precisely that.

6.3 Encapsulated Distributions, and the Quantum Model

The key idea for solving the data-transformation problems exemplified by the failed refinement (7)$\not\sqsubseteq$(8) is to "encapsulate" the local variable h in a distribution, one to which nondeterminism related to the visible variable v does not have access. Thus where the state-space normally would be $\mathcal{V}{\times}\mathcal{H}$, the encapsulated state-space would be $S{:=}\,\mathcal{V}{\times}\mathbb{D}\mathcal{H}$. On top of this we introduce the basic construction for probability and nondeterminism Sec. 4, which then gives $S \rightarrow \mathbb{PD}S$ as our model: putting them together therefore gives $(\mathcal{V}{\times}\mathbb{D}\mathcal{H}){\rightarrow}\mathbb{PD}(\mathcal{V}{\times}\mathbb{D}\mathcal{H})$ overall as the semantic type of a program with visible- and local variables.

From now on local variables will be called *hidden* variables. Here is an example of how the above could work.

In the classical model $(\mathcal{V}{\times}\mathcal{H}) \rightarrow \mathbb{PD}(\mathcal{V}{\times}\mathcal{H})$ the program $h{:=}\,\mathsf{T}\ {}_p\!\oplus h{:=}\,\mathsf{F}$ produces from initial state (v_0, h_0) the singleton-set outcome $\{(v_0, \mathsf{T})\ {}_p\!\oplus (v_0, \mathsf{F})\}$, i.e. a set containing exactly one distribution; it's a singleton set because there's no demonic choice. A subsequent program $v{:=}\,\mathsf{T} \sqcap v{:=}\,\mathsf{F}$ then acts first on the distribution's two points (v_0, T) and (v_0, F) separately, producing for each a further pair of point distributions: we get $\{\overline{(\mathsf{T},\mathsf{T})}, \overline{(\mathsf{F},\mathsf{T})}\}$ in the first case and $\{\overline{(\mathsf{T},\mathsf{F})}, \overline{(\mathsf{F},\mathsf{F})}\}$ in the second.[14] Those two sets are then interpolated Cartesian-wise, after the fact, using the same ${}_p\!\oplus$ that acted originally between the two initial points. That gives finally the four-element set

$$\{\overline{(\mathsf{T},\mathsf{T})}\ {}_p\!\oplus \overline{(\mathsf{T},\mathsf{F})}, \overline{(\mathsf{T},\mathsf{T})}\ {}_p\!\oplus \overline{(\mathsf{F},\mathsf{F})}, \overline{(\mathsf{F},\mathsf{T})}\ {}_p\!\oplus \overline{(\mathsf{T},\mathsf{F})}, \overline{(\mathsf{F},\mathsf{T})}\ {}_p\!\oplus \overline{(\mathsf{F},\mathsf{F})}\}\ ,$$

[14] We use $\overline{x}$ for the *point distribution* assigning probability one to x and (therefore) zero to everything else.

that is a four-way demonic choice between particular distributions.[15] The third of those four demonic choices is the distribution $(\mathsf{F},\mathsf{T})\ {}_p\oplus\ (\mathsf{T},\mathsf{F})$ in which the final values of v, h are guaranteed to be different; the second on the other hand is $(\mathsf{T},\mathsf{T})\ {}_p\oplus\ (\mathsf{F},\mathsf{F})$ where they are guaranteed to be the same. The demon has access to both choices (as well as the other two remaining), and in this way can treat a testing-inspired postcondition $v{=}h$ with complete contempt, forcing the equality to yield true or false exactly as it pleases. The operational explanation we give (have given) for this is that the demon, acting second, "can see" the value of h produced first and than can target, or avoid it at will.

Now we contrast this with the encapsulated "quantum" view. This time the model is $(\mathcal{V}\times\mathbb{D}\mathcal{H})\rightarrow\mathbb{PD}(\mathcal{V}\times\mathbb{D}\mathcal{H})$ and the program $h{:=}\,\mathsf{T}\ {}_p\oplus h{:=}\,\mathsf{F}$ produces from initial state $(v_0,\overline{h_0})$ the singleton-set outcome $\{\overline{(v_0,\mathsf{T}\ {}_p\oplus\ \mathsf{F})}\}$ again containing just one distribution: but crucially this time it is a *point* distribution: the proper (non-point) probabilistic choice over h is still "suspended" further inside. Given a point distribution, the subsequent program $v{:=}\,\mathsf{T}\sqcap v{:=}\,\mathsf{F}$ has only one point to act on, giving the set $\{\overline{(\mathsf{T},\mathsf{T}\ {}_p\oplus\ \mathsf{F})},\overline{(\mathsf{F},\mathsf{T}\ {}_p\oplus\ \mathsf{F})}\}$ and with no Cartesian-wise interpolation. Now if the postcondition is again $v{=}h$, then the demon's attempt to minimise its probability of being true is limited to just two choices (no longer four), that is in deciding which of p and $1{-}p$ is the lesser and acting appropriately. For example if p were $3/4$, i.e. it is more likely that h is T, then the demon would choose the second pair (corresponding to having executed $v{:=}\,\mathsf{F}$), and the probability of $v{=}h$ would be only $1/4$. The demon can do this because, although it cannot see h, it can still see the program code and thus knows the value of p. In spite of that, it cannot make the $v{=}h$ -probability lower than $1/4$ and, in particular, it cannot make it zero as it did above.

With that prologue, we can now explain why we think of this as the "quantum model."[16]

6.4 The Act of Observing Collapses the Distribution

We take $h{:=}\,\mathsf{T}\ {}_p\oplus h{:=}\,\mathsf{F}$ again as our first step, and in the quantum model (which we now call the above) we reach outcome $\{\overline{(v_0,\mathsf{T}\ {}_p\oplus\ \mathsf{F})}\}$. But now we take as our second step the command $v{:=}\,h$ whereby the suspended "quantum state" $\mathsf{T}\ {}_p\oplus\ \mathsf{F}$ of h is "observed" by an assignment to the visible v. What happens?

In this model, the assignment $v{:=}\,h$ "collapses" the quantum state, forcing it to resolve its suspended probabilistic choice one way or the other: the outcome overall is $\{(\mathsf{T},\overline{\mathsf{T}})\ {}_p\oplus\ (\mathsf{F},\overline{\mathsf{F}})\}$, now a *visible* probabilistic choice ${}_p\oplus$ in both of whose branches the value of h is completely determined: it's given by the point distribution $\overline{\mathsf{T}}$ or by the point distribution $\overline{\mathsf{F}}$.

---

[15] In the basic model this includes as well, by convention, all interpolations of those four distributions.

[16] And we must say right away that it is not at all (in our view) a real contender for a model of quantum computation, because for a start our probabilities are real-valued: for *qbits* they would instead have to be complex numbers. It does however have some features reminiscent of popular-science accounts of quantum mechanics, as we now see.

As a second example of quantum collapse, we consider the program

$$h{:=}\,(0 \oplus 1 \oplus 2 \oplus 3);\;\; v{:=}\,h \,\mathbf{mod}\, 2$$

in which the repeated $\oplus$'s indicate a uniform choice, in this case between four alternatives and so 1/4 for each. Here the first command produces a fully encapsulated state as before; but the second statement collapses it only partially. The final outcome has denotation $\{(0, 0\,{}_{1/2}{\oplus}\, 2)\,{}_{1/2}{\oplus}\,(1, 1\,{}_{1/2}{\oplus}\, 3)\}$, representing a program we could write

$$v{:=}\,0;\;\; h{:=}\,0\,{}_{1/2}{\oplus}\,2 \quad {}_{1/2}{\oplus} \quad v{:=}\,1;\;\; h{:=}\,1\,{}_{1/2}{\oplus}\,3$$

in which a visible probabilistic choice ${}_{1/2}{\oplus}$ occurs between the two possibilities for the low-order bit of h (0 or 1), but the value of the high-order bit is still suspended in the hidden, internal probabilistic choice.

For this program you can be sure that afterwards you will know the parity of h, but you cannot predict beforehand what that parity will be. And –either way– you still know nothing about the high-order bit.

7 The Generalised Quantum Model

However compelling (or not) the Quantum Model of Sec. 6.3 might be, it can only be a step on the way: in general, hidden variable h could be the subject of nondeterministic assignments as well as probabilistic ones; and the model $(\mathcal{V}{\times}\mathbb{D}\mathcal{H}){\rightarrow}\mathbb{P}\mathbb{D}(\mathcal{V}{\times}\mathbb{D}\mathcal{H})$ is not rich enough to include that, since the encapsulated state for h is only $\mathbb{D}\mathcal{H}$.

The ability to specify nondeterministic and probabilistic assignments to h is especially important for real applications in which the source of randomness, used to conceal a hidden value, is not perfect. For example, the coins used by the Dining Cryptographers of Sec. 2 will probably be both demonic and probabilistic, since as we noted "fair coins" are ideal objects that do not exist in nature. Not only will a typical coin have a heads-probability of "nearly" (but not exactly) 50%, that probability could vary slightly depending on environmental conditions (e.g. ambient temperature): thus we must ultimately deal with not only accuracy but stability. The abstraction $coin{:=}\,\mathsf{T}\;{}_{[\varepsilon]}{\oplus}\,\mathsf{F}$, introduced in Secs. 2.3 & 4, describes that nicely: it's a coin whose total deviation is ε, centred on being fair. The value ε, which represents the stability of the coin, may be treated as a parameter of the problem.

7.1 Preliminary Investigations

Early investigations led us to suppose that the type of a Generalised Quantum model might be

$$(\mathcal{V}{\times}\mathbb{P}\mathbb{D}\mathcal{H}) \rightarrow \overset{\downarrow\, outer}{\mathbb{P}}\mathbb{D}(\mathcal{V}{\times}\underset{\uparrow\, inner}{\mathbb{P}}\mathbb{D}\mathcal{H})\;, \tag{9}$$

in which hidden assignments, such as $h := A\ {}_{[\varepsilon]}{\oplus}\ B$ would be recorded in the "inner" $\mathbb{PD}$, and visible assignments, $v := A\ {}_{[\varepsilon]}{\oplus}\ B$, would be captured in the "outer" $\mathbb{PD}$. In this model interactions between nondeterminism and probability in such visible (or hidden assignments) would be treated as before: a statement $v{:=}\mathsf{T}\ {}_{[\varepsilon]}{\oplus}\ \mathsf{F}$, for example, is the nondeterministic choice over all probabilities $p{\in}[\varepsilon]$, that is $|2p{-}1| \leq \varepsilon$, of the pure probabilistic choice $v{:=}\mathsf{T}\ {}_p{\oplus}\ \mathsf{F}$. If all this were to be done successfully, we would be able to observe continuous range of behaviours as ε varies from 0 up to is maximum value 1: when ε is zero, as small as it can be, we have $({}_{[0]}{\oplus}) = ({}_{1/2}{\oplus})$, i.e. pure probabilistic choice. And when ε is 1, as large as it can be, we have $({}_{[1]}{\oplus}) = (\sqcap)$, pure demonic choice.

In spite of this promising beginning, the proposed fully generalised model (9) stretched our expertise: calculations in it were quite complex, and its logic was elusive [57,38]. As a strategic move, therefore, we put that path aside and (eventually) decided to address a simpler, but related problem: with a final goal of encapsulated demonic/probabilistic state in mind, and a tentative model of encapsulated probability (alone, as above), it seemed reasonable to attempt a model of encapsulated demonic nondeterminism (alone). That became the Shadow Model of Sec. 5.[17]

In this remainder of this section we outline some of the challenges we face in generalising the Quantum model so that the encapsulated hidden state may be both probabilistic and nondeterministic.

7.2 The Observers' View: A Difficulty

In a typical security application there may be multiple agents with different views of the system (that is, different partitions into visible and hidden). For example, in the Dining Cryptographers, the waitress has one perspective of the system, and Cryptographer A has another. Similarly, a system comprising many modules, each with different visibility requirements, may be thought of as being composed of multiple agents each one with her own view.

Both the Shadow and Quantum models may be used to model such applications from the perspective of any one of the agents, or *observers*, in the system. In these program models, the state space describes not just the visible state from that observer's perspective, but what is known about the visible/hidden -state partition. How might we represent an observer's perspective of the state in a model in which hidden variables may be set probabilistically *and* nondeterministically?

Unfortunately, our earlier guess (9) is too simplistic to specify some programs that we might be interested in. Take for example a system that is to be modelled from the perspective of an onlooker who can see variable v, but not h. What can that observer see, and deduce, after the operation

[17] This is a revisionist history in a further sense, since the full encapsulated model –as a goal– was sitting happily on the shelf until Engelhardt and Moses, independently, encouraged us to look at their achievements –with van der Meyden– in dealing simultaneously with refinement and knowledge [16,15].

$$v := \mathsf{T}\ {}_{1/2}\oplus\ \mathsf{F}; h{:=}\, v \quad \sqcap \quad v := \mathsf{T}\ {}_{1/2}\oplus\ \mathsf{F}; h{:=} \neg v \tag{10}$$

in which both the $\sqcap$ and the ${}_{1/2}\oplus$'s are hidden?

Since the $\sqcap$ in particular is hidden and the outcome of the visible variable v is indistinguishable in both alternatives, the denotation of the program's result cannot use the outer $\mathbb{P}$ to express that choice: we are limited to denotations of the form $\mathbb{D}(\mathcal{V} \times \mathbb{PD}\mathcal{H})$. In fact (abusing notation) it must be of the form

$$\mathcal{V} \times \mathbb{PD}\mathcal{H} \quad {}_{1/2}\oplus \quad \mathcal{V} \times \mathbb{PD}\mathcal{H}$$

since the observed distribution of v between T and F will be 50% no matter which branch is taken. What then are the candidates for the left- and the right $\mathbb{PD}\mathcal{H}$? It can't be $\{\overline{\mathsf{T}}, \overline{\mathsf{F}}\}$ on both sides, since that loses the property of (10) that the h-values are also 50% distributed.

But how else might the observer describe what he can and cannot see about that operation within the program model proposed? It doesn't seem as though it can be done without either revealing too much about the value of the hidden variable, or retaining too little information about its distribution.

This suggests that a state space richer than $\mathcal{V} \times \mathbb{PD}\mathcal{H}$ is going to be needed to describe an observer's view of the program state. That is one aspect of our current research.

7.3 Multiple Agents: Who Makes the Choice?

In The Shadow- and in The Quantum Model the state space is used to describe the behaviour of a program from the perspective of *one* of the agents in the system. Systems with multiple agents may thus be analysed by considering the system view of each agent separately. (The Quantum Model is limited in this respect since it cannot be used to model the perspective of any agent for which the hidden state is subject to nondeterminism.)

For example, take a system with Agent A, who can see variable a only, Agent B that can see variable b only and (implicitly) an anonymous observer who can't see either. Suppose A sets a nondeterministically, and then B does the same with b as in the program

$$\mathbf{vis}_A\ a; \mathbf{vis}_B\ b; \quad a{:\in_A} \{\mathsf{T}, \mathsf{F}\};\ b{:\in_B} \{\mathsf{T}, \mathsf{F}\}\ ,$$

where "$\mathbf{vis}_A$" means visible only to Agent A (and similar), and "$:\in_A$" means chosen according to what Agent A can see.

With the Shadow Model, we see that from the point of view of Agent A the system is $\mathbf{vis}\ a; \mathbf{hid}\ b \cdots$, i.e. with a visible and b hidden. To Agent B it is complementary, that is as if declared $\mathbf{hid}\ a; \mathbf{vis}\ b \cdots$ — and for the anonymous observer it is $\mathbf{hid}\ a, b \cdots$.

The reason that each agent may be treated separately in the Shadow semantics (which is defined using a "one-test run testing regime" — see Sec. 8.3 to come) is that we do not care (and cannot tell) whether nondeterministic choices are made independently or not. For example, when the Shadow is used to model the system from Agent A's perspective, we cannot tell whether the choice $b{:\in_B}\,\{\mathsf{T},\mathsf{F}\}$ can be influenced by the value of a, and so as Agent A we do not need to know what Agent B's view of the system is. (The Quantum model avoids these issues altogether by dissallowing hidden-state nondeterminism.)

Unfortunately, the situation is unlikely to be as simple in the Generalised Quantum model. Consider the similar system

$$\mathbf{vis}_A\ a; \mathbf{vis}_B\ b; \quad a{:=}\,\mathsf{T}\ _{1/2}{\oplus}\ \mathsf{F};\ b{:\in_B}\,\{\mathsf{T},\mathsf{F}\}$$

in which the first choice is probabilistic. From A's point of view it is still **vis** a; **hid** b but, in spite of the fact that A cannot see b it is still important to A whether the choice $b{:\in_B}\,\{\mathsf{T},\mathsf{F}\}$ can depend on a. This is because the outcome of a subsequent code fragment **vis** $a'; a'{:=}\,a{\oplus}b$ is affected by that question.[18] That is, even from A's point of view it has become important what B can see, and that B makes the choice $b{:\in_B}\,\{\mathsf{T},\mathsf{F}\}$ rather than for example $b{:\in_A}\,\{\mathsf{T},\mathsf{F}\}$. For this reason it might not be possible to split our analysis neatly into separate views as we do in The Shadow. That is, if we would like to model probabilistic programs with multiple agents, and have so-called "nuanced" nondeterministic choices as above, controlled by different agents, then we will require a semantics that retains information about the different agent's views of the system.

Instead of working directly on such a feature-rich program model, we suggest that a next step forward would be to build a model where hidden nondeterministic choices must be made with either total ignorance, *oblivious* choice, or knowledge of the entire state (*omniscient* choice). It would be sufficient in the dining cryptographers problem, for example, to model all the choices as being oblivious.

8 The Cryptographers' Café: Reprise

Long ago (it must seem) in Sec. 2 we posed the problem of an accurate analysis of the Cryptographers' Café; in the meantime we have examined a number of potential program models and background issues. We can note immediately that the basic probabilistic/demonic model of Sec. 4 is not rich enough to formalise our problem, because the coins must be hidden. And since the cryptographers' coins involve both probability (because we suspect they must be fair coins) and demonic choice (because we cannot expect to find physical coins that are exactly fair), neither the technique of Sec. 5 (for hidden demonic choice) nor of Sec. 6 (for hidden probability) is sufficient on its own. In Sec. 7 just above we investigated therefore some of the issues to be faced when joining hidden probability and hidden nondeterminism together. In this section, we speculate on what we might find once we have done so.

[18] We write $\oplus$ for exclusive-or.

(a) Specification

$$
\begin{array}{l}
\textbf{hid } y_A, y_B, y_C; \\
\textbf{reveal } y_A \oplus y_B \oplus y_C
\end{array}
$$

(b) Implementation

$$
\begin{array}{l}
\textbf{hid } y_A, y_B, y_C; \\
[\![\ \textbf{hid } c_A, c_B, c_C \colon \mathsf{Bool}; \\
\quad c_A {:\in} \mathsf{Bool}; \\
\quad c_B {:\in} \mathsf{Bool}; \\
\quad c_C {:\in} \mathsf{Bool}; \\
\quad \textbf{reveal } y_A \oplus c_B \oplus y_C; \\
\quad \textbf{reveal } y_B \oplus c_C \oplus y_A; \\
\quad \textbf{reveal } y_C \oplus c_A \oplus y_B; \\
]\!]
\end{array}
$$

The three cryptographers' choices are $y_{\{A,B,C\}}$; the three coins are $c_{\{A,B,C\}}$ with c_A being opposite y_A etc. and so hidden from her. We assume the cryptographer's choices are made before the protocol begins; the coins, which are local variables, are flipped during the protocol.

The statement **reveal** E publishes to everyone the value of E but does not expose explicitly any of E's constituent sub-expressions [43,49,37].

Thus the specification reveals (to everyone) the exclusive-or of the cryptographers' actions. The implementation reveals three separate Booleans whose exclusive-or equals the value revealed by the specification. The key question is whether the implementation reveals *more* than that.

Fig. 3. The Dining Cryptographers: Specification and Implementation

8.1 The Shadow Suffices for One-Off Lunches

We must remember right at the start that the Dining Cryptographers Protocol is not itself under suspicion. Rather we are using it –in various formulations– to test our approaches to capturing the essential features of protocols of the kind it exemplifies. We have already showed elsewhere [54,49] that the Shadow Model can prove the refinement (a) $\sqsubseteq$ (b) in Fig. 3.

Yet we argued in Sec. 2 that Fig. 3(b) is *not* a correct implementation in the case that the cyptographers are observed over many trials. What exactly then did our purported proofs show? The answer depends crucially on the notion of what tests we are allowed to perform on the implementation.[19]

8.2 Testing Standard Classical Sequential Programs

By *standard* programs we mean "non-probabilistic," and by *classical* we mean "without hiding."

[19] This is true when assessing the suitability of any notion of computer-system correctness: one must know exactly what tests it is expected to pass.

A test for a standard classical program Q is a context $\mathbb{C}$ into which the program Q can be put. The combination $\mathbb{C}(Q)$ is then run *a single time*, and it's observed whether $\mathbb{C}(Q)$ diverges or not. We have $P \sqsubseteq Q$ *for testing* just when, for all $\mathbb{C}$, if $\mathbb{C}(Q)$ fails the test by diverging, on any single run, then $\mathbb{C}(P)$ can fail also.[20]

How does this fit in with *wp*-style refinement? There we have the definition $P \sqsubseteq_{wp} Q$ just when for all postconditions ψ the implication $wp.P.\psi \Rightarrow wp.Q.\psi$ holds [3,61,50,51,5], where a postcondition is a subset of the state space (equivalently a predicate over the program variables).

Now if $P \sqsubseteq_{wp} Q$ then by monotonicity of programs and the permissible program operators we have that $\mathbb{C}(P) \sqsubseteq_{wp} \mathbb{C}(Q)$, and so we have as a consequence the implication $wp.\mathbb{C}(P).\mathsf{true} \Rightarrow wp.\mathbb{C}(Q).\mathsf{true}$ — that is, if $\mathbb{C}(Q)$ can diverge ($\neg wp.\mathbb{C}(Q).\mathsf{true}$) then so can $\mathbb{C}(P)$ diverge ($\neg wp.\mathbb{C}(P).\mathsf{true}$). That establishes that *wp*-refinement implies testing refinement as we defined it above.

For the opposite direction, we suppose that $P \not\sqsubseteq_{wp} Q$ so that for some state s_0 and postcondition ψ we have $wp.P.\psi.s_0 \wedge \neg wp.Q.\psi.s_0$. Choose context $\mathbb{C}$ so that $\mathbb{C}(X)$ is $s{:=}\, s_0; X; \{\psi\}$, where the assumption $\{\psi\}$ acts as **skip** in states satisfying (belonging to) ψ and diverges otherwise [51, Sec. 1.8]. Then $\mathbb{C}(P)$ does not diverge but $\mathbb{C}(Q)$ can diverge, so that we have $P \not\sqsubseteq Q$ for testing also, and have established that in fact $\sqsubseteq_{wp}$ and single-time-testing refinement are exactly the same.

8.3 Testing Standard Programs with Hiding

To capture hiding, our tests are extended: they now include *as well as the above* (Sec. 8.2) an attacker's *guess* of the value of h within its type $\mathcal{H}$: it's expressed as a subset H of $\mathcal{H}$ of the value the hidden variable h might have. A program-in-context $\mathbb{C}(Q)$ is deemed to fail the test H if either it diverges (as before) or it converges but in that latter case the attacker can prove conclusively on the basis of his observations that $h{\in}H$.

With these richer tests we can see more structure in their outcomes. Whereas in Sec. 8.2 there were just two outcomes *diverge* and *converge*, now there are many: we have *diverge* as before, but now also *converge with h provably in H* for any $H{\subseteq}\mathcal{H}$. The two-outcome case Sec. 8.2 is just the special case in which we fix $H{:=}\,\emptyset$. Clearly there is a refinement order on these outcomes, too: divergence is at bottom, and larger guesses are above smaller ones — we could call this order $\sqsubseteq_{obs}$.

With the differing detail but unifying theme of this section and the previous, the use of the context, and the general idea behind it, should now be clear: given two programs P, Q whose refinement status might be complex, we define $P \sqsubseteq Q$ just when for all contexts $\mathbb{C}$ we have $\mathbb{C}(P) \sqsubseteq_{obs} \mathbb{C}(Q)$. The point of that is the

[20] Here we borrow notions best known from process algebra [10]; those ideas featured prominently in the football matches [2].

simplicity of $\sqsubseteq_{obs}$ — it is necessarily a subjective definition, and so must be one that the community generally can accept as self-evidently reasonable.[21]

8.4 The "single-test" Convention Applies to The Shadow

In both Sec. 8.2 and Sec. 8.3 above we stipulated "single tests," and this is surprisingly important. Its consequence is that an implementation cannot be invalidated on the basis of considering two or more testing outcomes at the same time: each test must be considered on its own. This is not a theorem, or even a necessity: rather it is an explicit choice we make about how we define "is implemented by."

It's this single-time definition of test that prevents our telling the difference between "cold" nondeterminism that is unknown but fixed (like having either a heads-only or tails-only coin, but not being able to predict which it will be), and "hot" nondeterminism that can vary (like an ordinary coin that can reveal a different face on each flip, even though we know it's either heads or tails). We do not judge this distinction either as worthwhile, or worthless: it depends on the circumstances. Nevertheless if one adopts the single-time testing regime, then there is no point in having a semantics that distinguishes hot- from cold nondeterminism. Given the style of computing that was dominant at the time of flow-charts [18], and the introduction of Hoare logic [28] and weakest preconditions [14], it's no wonder that single-time testing was assumed: most programs were sequential, and ran on mainframes. That assumption is one of the reasons that the relational calculus —so simple— is sufficient for that kind of sequential program: it need not (cannot) distinguish hot and cold.

The Shadow too, in that tradition, is based on single tests — as are many other formal approaches to non-interference [20,9,36,63]: and that is why it does not *necessarily* apply to the Café in which, effectively, many tests are made.

It is also the reason that The Shadow does not stipulate whether later hidden nondeterministic choices can be influenced by earlier hidden nondeterministic outcomes. (Recall Sec. 7.3.) It seems a reasonable question: given that the hidden choice $h_0{:}{\in}\{\mathsf{T},\mathsf{F}\}$ cannot be seen by the attacker, can it be seen by a subsequent hidden choice $h_1{:}{\in}\{\mathsf{T},\mathsf{F}\}$ to a different variable? The surprising answer, as we saw, is that it doesn't matter, since in single-time testing you cannot determine whether the h_1-choice was influenced by the h_0-choice or not.

8.5 Proving (in-)correctness in the Café

Having addressed the question posed at the end of Sec. 8.1, the next step is to ask how the purported refinement of Fig. 3 would fare in a probabilistic/demonic-

[21] A particularly good example of this is found in probabilistic/demonic process algebras [1], where the notion of refinement is very complex and not generally agreed. Research there concentrates on finding a testing regime that uses contexts to reduce refinement to something as simple as decreasing the probability of divergence, or increasing the probability of performing some single distinguished "success action" [10].

with-hiding semantics if we constructed one along the lines suggested in Sec. 7. The answer is that *we expect it to fail.* In this section we sketch speculatively just how the as-yet-to-be-constructed model would signal that failure.

Rather than address the whole protocol, we concentrate on the *Encryption Lemma*, a key part of its qualitative proof [54,43,49]. That lemma states that in the context of a global hidden Boolean h the following refinement holds:

$$\mathbf{skip} \quad \sqsubseteq \quad [\![\ \mathbf{hid}\ h';\ \ h' {:}{\in}\ \mathsf{Bool}; \mathbf{reveal}\ h {\oplus} h' \ ]\!] \ .^{22} \tag{11}$$

This via refinement states that the right-hide side reveals nothing about h, since clearly the left-hand side does not.

Now suppose that the global h has been set previously via an assignment $h{:=}\,\mathsf{true}\ {}_p{\oplus}\ \mathsf{false}$. (In so doing, we leave the world of single-time testing, since probabilities cannot be expressed or detected there.) Does (11) still hold?

In our semantics we might expect that the denotation of the right-hand side of (11) is a set of behaviours that may be observed by an onlooker, in which each of those observable behaviours is associated with a set of "hidden" probabilistic states that could actually have produced it. In this program an onlooker can see the outcome of the reveal statement, and so an observable behaviour is the distribution of true and false values shown by the reveal. Given that the demonic choice $h'{:}{\in}\ \mathsf{Bool}$ is interpreted as "choose h' with some unknown probability q" [41,59], where $0{\leq}q{\leq}1$, for each observable behaviour of the reveal statement we can calculate that what h' must have been from the fact that h was set deterministically using probability p. This means that there can only be one "hidden" probabilistic state associated with every visible outcome. For all visible outcomes other than that created by choosing h' to be 1/2, there will be a correlation between the outcome of the reveal statement and the hidden distribution of h-values: that means that our knowledge of h's value will not have been left unchanged by the operation. And this is not something that our mathematical definition of refinement would accept as a refinement of **skip** since, that would –of course– have left h's distribution unchanged.

8.6 Testing Probabilistic Programs with Hiding

Given the conceptual programme established by our discussion of testing, the guesswork of Sec. 8.5 must be accompanied by a discussion of the testing regime we have in mind. As remarked there, it cannot any longer be single-time.

Here we expect to be using *single-tabulation* testing: the program Q under test is run repeatedly in come context $\mathbb{C}$, and we tabulate the outcomes and their frequencies. What we are not allowed to do is to run the program repeatedly on two separate occasions and then to draw conclusions from the two separate tabulations that result.

Such a regime is implicit in our earlier probabilistic work where however we do not model hiding [41,59]. We would therefore –without hiding– be dealing

[22] We use brackets $[\![\cdot]\!]$ to delimit the scope of local declarations.

with a quantitative version of the tests of Sec. 8.2 where the refinement criterion for $P\sqsubseteq Q$ would be "if program-in-context $\mathbb{C}(Q)$ can diverge with a probability at least p, then so can $\mathbb{C}(P)$." Note that this single-tabulation restriction again makes the issue of hot- vs. cold nondeterminism irrelevant: if you are restricted to a single tabulation of outcomes, there is no way in which you can tell the difference with respect to a demonic coin-choice $h{:\in}\,\mathsf{Bool}$ whether this is implemented via a number of different coins with (therefore) varying bias, or whether it is a single one whose bias is unknown.[23]

In our speculative semantics –with hiding– our single-tabulation testing could be a simple probabilistic powerdomain [32,31] built over the underlying order on H-guesses sketched in Sec. 8.3.

8.7 The Importance of Fair Coins

We saw in Sec. 2.1 that the Dining Cryptographers' Protocol, and others like it, is described in terms of fair coins (1) even though the fairness was not explicitly used in our correctness argument (2). One reason for this (we think) is that the correctness relies crucially on the independence of the coins from other phenomena (such as the cryptographers' already-made decisions) and indeed from each other. That independence in its abstract *demonic* form is very difficult to formalise, and so an easy route to ensuring it is realised is to make the choices with a fair-coin -flip since –barring sophisticated nanotechnology within the coin itself– it is going to implement precisely the kind of independence we mean but which we cannot pin-down with a precise mathematical description.[24]

In spite of that, we saw in Sec. 8.5 that the fairness really does matter; and in Chaum's original presentation it mattered too. That is, in our speculative semantics it matters because we would expect the refinement

$$\textbf{skip} \quad \sqsubseteq \quad [\![\ \textbf{hid}\ h';\ h'{:=}\,\mathsf{true}\ {}_{1/2}{\oplus}\ \mathsf{false};\ \textbf{reveal}\ h{\oplus}h'\ ]\!] \qquad (12)$$

[23] Imagine watching a single referee throughout a football season. Could you tell with a single tabulation for the whole season whether he decides the kickoff using one coin or several? A multiple-tabulation testing regime would allow you to compare one season with another, and then (only then) you would be able to distinguish the two cases.

[24] There are many examples of this "abstraction aversion" in everyday life. For example, in a two-battery torch (flashlight) the batteries must be inserted in the same direction; but either way will do. (We ignore issues of the shape of the contacts, and concentrate on electricity.) A picture describing this abstraction is hard to imagine, however: if both alternatives were shown, would people think they needed four batteries? The usual solution is to replace the specification (either way, but consistent) with an implementation (both facing inwards) and then cynically to present that as the specification. Most people won't even notice that the abstraction has been stolen.

Similarly, what ideally would be an abstract description ("independent mutually ignorant demonic choices") is replaced pragmatically by a concrete one ("separate fair coins") — that's the best we can do with our current tools.

to go through even though (11) does not. Firstly, the denotation of the right-hand side would no longer be a demonic choice, since the choice of h' is deterministic (i.e. no longer demonic, although still probabilistic). Secondly, if one asks the Bayesian question "What is the *a posteriori* distribution of h after the right-hand side of (12)?" the answer will be that it is the same as the *a priori*, because the distribution of h' is fair. (That is exactly the key point of Chaum's proof.) With any other distribution of h', however, the *a priori* and *a posteriori* distributions of h would differ. Thus in this case only –an exactly fair coin– the refinement is accepted.[25]

8.8 The Non-existence of Fair Coins

Our conclusion –generalised from the discussion of Sec. 8.7– seems to be that the Dining Cryptographers' Protocol suffices for use in the Café just when the coins are exactly fair, and not otherwise. But they never are exactly fair, and so with a definition of refinement as "yes or no," we seems to be stranded: our refinement proofs apply only to *ideal* situations, ones that never occur in reality. That is, the semantics we are hoping to develop (Sec. 7) seems to be running the risk of becoming "ideal" in a similar sense: pejorative.

There are two complementary steps possible to avoid, at this point, being relegated to the Platonic School of Formal Methods. One is to introduce *approximate refinement*, where we would say (intuitively) that $P \sqsubseteq_p Q$ means that P is refined by Q with probability p, with a special case being probabilistic equivalence [66,67,30,13,11,12]. The "with probability p" applied to refinement can be made precise in various ways, and the first thing one would prove is that $\sqsubseteq_1$ coincides with ordinary, certain refinement; similarly $\sqsubseteq_0$ would be the universal relation.

The reason we don't take this approach is that we cannot see how to couple it with a notion of testing in the case that the probability p of refinement is intermediate, not equal to zero or one. And we think the testing connection

[25] The usual example of this is a nearly reliable test for a disease: say with 99% reliability if the test detects the disease, the patient really is diseased; the remaining 1% is called a "false positive." We assume 1% for false negatives also. Now we suppose that in the population just 1% of the people have the disease, so that if a person is selected at random, then this is the *a priori* probability that she has it. If she tests positive, what now is the probability that she really does have the disease?

The probability of her testing positive is $0.99 \times 0.01 + 0.01 \times 0.99 = 0.0198$, and the (conditional) probability she has the disease, i.e. *given* that she tested positive, is then $0.01 \times 0.99/0.0198 = 50\%$. This is the *a posteriori* probability, and it has changed from the *a priori* probability (which was 1%): the test is not equivalent to **skip**.

Now finally suppose that the test is only 50% reliable, either way. The calculation becomes $0.99 \times 0.5 + 0.5 \times 0.99 = 0.5$, i.e. the probability of testing positive is 0.5 (and in fact would be that no matter what the distribution of the disease in the population); and the *a posteriori* probability is $0.99 \times 0.5/0.5 = 99\%$, just the same as the *a priori*. This 50%-reliable test *is* equivalent to **skip**.

is essential. There are other more technical questions that loom as well: for example, if we have $P \sqsubseteq_p Q \sqsubseteq_q R$, what then is the refinement relation between P and R? Is it $\sqsubseteq_{pq}$ perhaps? But what if the fact that p and q are not both one is due to the same cause, that they are "common-mode" failures? Then we would expect a composite probability higher than pq — but how mathematically and quantitatively do we capture the common-mode dependence?

Thus we take a different approach: we use our ability to combine nondeterminism and probability to reflect the implementation's inadequacy back into a corresponding inadequacy, a weakening of the specification. An example of this technique is the probabilistic steam boiler [48,41] and the tank monitor [64] in which probabilistically unreliable sensors in the implementation force, via a yes-or-no refinement relation, a probabilistically unreliable *specification*. The refinement relation remains definite.

In applying that idea to our current examples (11 & 12) we would postulate a refinement

$$\text{“not-quite-}\mathbf{skip}\text{”} \quad \sqsubseteq \quad [\![\ \mathbf{hid}\ h';\ h' := \mathsf{true}\ {}_{[\varepsilon]}\!\oplus \mathsf{false};\ \mathbf{reveal}\ h \oplus h'\ ]\!] \tag{13}$$

in which we have to figure out what "not-quite-**skip**" is. (Recall Secs. 2.3 & 4: the subscript $[\varepsilon]$ abbreviates $[(1-\varepsilon)/2, (1+\varepsilon)/2]$.)

In fact a good candidate for the definition of "not-quite-**skip**" is provided by (13) itself. The statement **reveal** E, where E is an expression possibly containing hidden variables, publishes E to the world at large — but any calculations done to determine E are *not* published [43,49]. Thus for example **reveal** $h \oplus h'$ publishes whether h and h' are equal but, beyond that, says nothing about either of them.

The Shadow definition of **reveal** E was chosen so that it was equal to the program fragment

$$[\![\ \mathbf{vis}\ v;\ v := E\ ]\!]\ , \tag{14}$$

where a local visible variable v is introduced temporarily to receive E's value. Because v is visible, everyone can see its final value (thus publishing E); but because it is local, it does not affect the rest of the program in any other way. We extend the revelation command so that the expression can be probabilistic and even nondeterministic, postulating that its definition will still respect (14). Thus we would have

$$\mathbf{reveal}\ h\ {}_p\!\oplus \neg h \quad = \quad [\![\ \mathbf{vis}\ v;\ v := (h\ {}_p\!\oplus \neg h)\ ]\!]\ ,$$

in which the assignment to v is atomic.[26] That suggests our weakened specification, and respects our (still) definite refinement, in fact equality:

$$\mathbf{reveal}\ (h\ {}_{[\varepsilon]}\!\oplus \neg h) \quad = \quad [\![\ \mathbf{hid}\ h';\ h' := \mathsf{true}\ {}_{[\varepsilon]}\!\oplus \mathsf{false};\ \mathbf{reveal}\ h \oplus h'\ ]\!]\ . \tag{15}$$

[26] For those with some familiarity with The Shadow: the atomicity requirement distinguishes the command from the composite (non-atomic) fragment $v := h\ {}_p\!\oplus v := \neg h$ in which the branch taken –left, or right– would be visible to the attacker. The composite fragment is in fact for any p equal to the simpler **reveal** h since, after its execution and knowing which assignment was executed, an attacker would also know whether to "un-negate" the revelation or not in order to deduce h's value.

hid y_A, y_B, y_C;

reveal $y_A \;{}_{[\delta]}\!\oplus \neg y_A$;
reveal $y_B \;{}_{[\delta]}\!\oplus \neg y_B$;
reveal $y_C \;{}_{[\delta]}\!\oplus \neg y_C$;

reveal $y_A \oplus y_B \oplus y_C$

(a) Specification

hid y_A, y_B, y_C;
$[\![$ **hid** c_A, c_B, c_C: Bool;
$c_A := (\mathsf{true}\;{}_{[\varepsilon]}\!\oplus \mathsf{false})$;
$c_B := (\mathsf{true}\;{}_{[\varepsilon]}\!\oplus \mathsf{false})$;
$c_C := (\mathsf{true}\;{}_{[\varepsilon]}\!\oplus \mathsf{false})$;

reveal $y_A \oplus c_B \oplus y_C$;
reveal $y_B \oplus c_C \oplus y_A$;
reveal $y_C \oplus c_A \oplus y_B$;
$]\!]$

(b) Implementation

Here the coins, which are local variables, are flipped during the protocol and are within ε of being fair.

The specification reveals to everyone the exclusive-or of the cryptographers' actions collectively, and a little bit about the cryptographers' actions individually. The δ depends on ε: it should tends to zero as ε tends to zero and to 1 as ε tends to 1.

Below we argue informally that $\delta := \varepsilon^2$ is correct, though perhaps not the best we can do.

Fig. 4. The Dining Cryptographers: Specification and Implementation revisited

8.9 Weakening the Café's Specification

In Fig. 4(a) we have modified the Café's specification along the lines suggested in Sec. 8.8. Our informal justification for the suggested choice $\delta := \varepsilon^2$ of specification tolerance is as follows.

Each cryptographer's act –say y_A for example– is exclusive-or'd with a composite Boolean: it is $c_B \oplus c_C$ in the case of y_A. From our earlier calculation (4) we know that if $c_{\{B,C\}}$ are at most ε-biased then the composite $c_B \oplus c_C$ is at most $\varepsilon\varepsilon$ -biased. The postulated reveal statements are then by definition (of the extended **reveal**) biased by that value, that is by ε^2.

The reason we are not sure whether this is as good as it could be is that the three composite values (the other two being $c_C \oplus c_A$ and $c_A \oplus c_B$) are not independent: it might be that revealing a lot about one cryptographer has a limiting effect on what can be revealed about another.[27]

We now discuss the importance of the δ parameter from the specifier's, that is the customer's point of view: we have gone to a lot of trouble to formulate it; we should now explore how to use it. We'll look at three cases.

Exactly fair coins. In this case $\varepsilon = 0$ and so $\delta = 0$ also. Thus in the specification we find **reveal** $y_{A\,[0]}\!\oplus \neg y_A$ etc., that is **reveal** $y_{A\,1/2}\!\oplus \neg y_A$ which is equivalent to **skip**. Thus all three revelations of $y_{\{A,B,C\}}$ can be removed, and we are

[27] In fact we should recall that this whole construction is speculative, since we do not yet have a finalised semantics in which to prove it.

left with the original specification of Fig. 3. The refinement then establishes that using fair coins results in no leaks at all.

Coins of completely unknown bias. In this case ε=1 and so δ=1 also. Thus in the specification we find **reveal** $y_A \;_{[1]}\!\oplus \neg y_A$, that is by definition the command **reveal** $y_A \sqcap \neg y_A$. This, by definition again (14), is equal to

$$[\![\ \mathbf{vis}\ v;\ \ v{:=}\,(y_A \sqcap \neg y_A)\ ]\!]\ .^{28} \tag{16}$$

Interpreting Program (16) throws into relief one of the major issues in the construction of our sophisticated model: what can the nondeterminism "see"? We are assuming –speculatively– that it can see nothing, and so (16) is describing an experiment where a cryptographer chooses an act (y_A), and it is decided *independently of that choice* whether to reveal the act or its complement. Once that decision is made, the value (or its complement) is revealed *but we still do not know whether the complement was taken.* What can we deduce about the cryptographer's bias in her actions? We reason as follows.

Suppose the revealed value has distribution $\mathsf{true}\ _{1/4}\!\oplus \mathsf{false}$. If the cryptographer is sufficiently biased, it is possible since the nondeterminism in (16) could have been resolved e.g. to just **reveal** y_A . Then, from our earlier arithmetic, we would know that in fact the cryptographer has bias at least 1/2, and we know that *without* being told anything about how (16) was resolved. Thus we *can* deduce something in this case: the *specification* **reveal** $y_A \sqcap \neg y_A$ expresses an insecurity, as it should — for the implementation is insecure also.

It's instructive also to look at the situation from the cryptographer's point of view: suppose she is indeed 1/2 -biased but, embarrassed about that, she wants to keep her bias secret. Should she risk dining with the others, according to the implementation given in Fig. 4(b)? Rather than study the implementation, she studies the specification (having been well schooled in Formal Methods). She sees that from the specification an observer could learn that her bias is *at least* 1/2, since that is what would be deduced if the $\sqcap$ were always taken the same way, as we saw above. (The reason for the "at least" is that a $\mathsf{true}\ _{1/4}\!\oplus \mathsf{false}$ outcome in the reported result could also result from a greater bias in the cryptographer which is masked by some lesser bias in the $\sqcap$.)

Coins that are nearly fair. Finally, in this last case, we examine whether being able to limit the bias really does give us access to a continuum of

---

[28] In the standard Shadow (non-probabilistic) this would reveal nothing, since we could reason

$$v{:=}\,(y_A \sqcap \neg y_A) \quad = \quad v{:\in}\,\{y_A, \neg y_A\} \quad = \quad v{:\in}\,\{\mathsf{true}, \mathsf{false}\}\ .$$

And indeed in a single-run testing scenario it does not reveal anything. It's important therefore that we remember here that our scenario is more general.

insecurity: so far, we have seen either "all" or "nothing." We continue with the embarrassed cryptographer of the previous case: can she deduce that in the current case her potential for embarrassment is smaller than before? Yes she can; and to explain that we return one final time, in the next section, to the issue of testing.

8.10 Hypothesis Testing

If a cryptographer is exactly fair, then also her utterances will be exactly fair no matter what the bias of the coins. Given that, we can reason that over 100 lunches, say, with probability 95% she will say she paid for between 40 and 60 of them.[29]

However, just as there are no exactly fair coins, neither are there going to be exactly fair cryptographers: let's say that a cryptographer is *reasonable* if her bias is no more than 10%. In this case it does make a difference to her utterances whether the coins she faces are biased, and indeed her most biased utterances will result from the most biased coins. What range of utterances should we expect?

If the cryptographer is only just reasonable, and *wlog* is on the miserly side, then she is described by $y{:=}\,\mathsf{T}_{\,0.45}{\oplus}\,\mathsf{F}$. With completely biased coins –the worst case– then *wlog* this will be the description of her utterances too.[30] Given that, we can reason that over 100 lunches with probability 95% she will say "I paid" at least 36 times.[31] Thus –undoing our *wlog*'s– a reasonable cryptographer will in 100 trials with 95% probability say "I paid" between 36 and 64 times.

Now let's look at the case of the unreasonable, indeed miserly 50%-biased cryptographer $y{:=}\,\mathsf{T}_{\,0.25}{\oplus}\,\mathsf{F}$. Using fully biased coins, with what probability will

[29] With -1 assigned to F and 1 to T, the mean of her outcomes y is 0 and the variance is 1; over 100 independent trials the distribution of the sum y_{100} will therefore have mean 0 and variance 100. From the Central Limit Theorem [22] the derived variable $\hat{y} := y_{100}/\sqrt{100}$ will be approximately normally distributed, and so we have $-1.96 \leq \hat{y} \leq -1.96$ with probability 95% (from tables of the Normal Distribution). Thus $-19.6 \leq y_{100} \leq 19.6$, so that out of 100 lunches she is slightly more than 95% certain to say "I paid" for between 40 and 60 of them.

Note this is *not* the same as saying "If the frequency of I-paid utterances is between 40 and 60 out of 100, then with 95% probability the cryptographer is fair." That kind of statement requires a prior distribution on the cryptographers, which we are not assuming.

[30] The "without loss of generality"'s mean that we could have taken the complementary $y{:=}\,\mathsf{T}_{\,0.55}{\oplus}\,\mathsf{F}$ for the cryptographer, and that we could have allowed the biased coins always to invert her outcome. But none of that makes any difference to the analysis to come.

[31] The mean of her utterances y is -0.1 and the variance is 0.99; the distribution of the sum y_{100} has mean -10 and variance 99. The derived variable is $\hat{y} := (y_{100}+10)/\sqrt{99}$ and will satisfy $-1.65 \leq \hat{y}$ with probability 95%. Thus $-1.65 \times \sqrt{99} - 10 = -26.4 \leq y_{100}$, so that she is slightly more than 95% certain to say "I paid" for at least $(100 - 26.4)/2 \approx 36$ lunches.

her utterances fall *outside* of the range 36–64 that we with confidence 95% would expect of a reasonable cryptographer? That probability turns out to be 99.7%.[32]

Thus if we set 36–64 "I paid"'s in 100 trials as our "reasonableness" criterion in the case of potentially fully biased coins, a reasonable cryptographer will be unfairly judged as biased only 5% of the time while a 50%-biased cryptographer will escape detection only 0.3% of the time.

All the above was prelude to our discussion of *partially* biased coins: we now assume for argument's sake that the coins' (composite) bias is no more than 50%, and we re-do the above calculations to see how it affects the miserly cryptographer's chance of escaping detection.

As before, we determine our criteria by considering how a reasonable cryptographer would be likely to behave: facing a 50%-biased coin, she will *wlog* have utterances with distribution at worst $y{:=}\,\mathsf{T}\,_{0.475}{\oplus}\,\mathsf{F}$. Over 100 lunches with probability 95% she will say "I paid" between 39 and 61 times.[33]

The miserly cryptographer will *wlog* have utterances at worst $y{:=}\,\mathsf{T}\,_{0.375}{\oplus}\,\mathsf{F}$ — in both cases, the coins' bias mitigates the cryptographer's intrinsic bias to give a smaller bias in her utterances. With what probability will the miser's utterances fall *outside* of the range 39–61 that we might expect of a reasonable cryptographer facing a 50%-biased coin? It turns out to be 64.8%, which though still high is a much less rigorous test than the 99.7% she faced before.[34]

Thus if we set 39–61 "I paid"'s in 100 trials as our "reasonableness" criterion in the case of 50%-biased coins, so that as before a reasonable cryptographer will be unfairly judged as biased only 5% of the time, a 50%-biased cryptographer will now escape judgement 35.6% of the time (in fact roughly 100 times as often as she did in the fully biased case). The miser is being (partially) protected by the (partial) secrecy implemented by the (partially) secure protocol.

It is interesting to speculate whether our model will have

$$\textbf{reveal}\ h\ _{[\varepsilon_1]}{\oplus}\ \neg h \quad\sqsubseteq\quad \textbf{reveal}\ h\ _{[\varepsilon_0]}{\oplus}\ \neg h$$

whenever $\varepsilon_1 \geq \varepsilon_0$.

---

32 The mean of her utterances y is -0.5 and the variance is 0.75; the distribution of the sum y_{100} has mean -50 and variance 75. The derived variable is $\hat{y} := (y_{100}+50)/\sqrt{75}$ which, to appear reasonable, from Footnote 31 must satisfy $(-26.4+50)/\sqrt{75} = 2.72 \leq \hat{y}$. It does that with probability 0.3%.

33 The mean of her utterances y is -0.05 and the variance is 0.9975; the distribution of the sum y_{100} has mean -5 and variance 99.75. The derived variable is $\hat{y} := (y_{100} + 5)/\sqrt{99.75}$ and will (as before) satisfy $-1.65 \leq \hat{y}$ with probability 95%. Thus $-1.65\times\sqrt{99.75} - 5 = -21.5 \leq y_{100}$, so that she is slightly more than 95% certain to say "I paid" for at least 39 lunches.

34 The mean of her outcomes y is -0.25 and the variance is 0.875; the distribution of the sum y_{100} has mean -25 and variance 87.5. The derived variable is $\hat{y} := (y_{100} + 25)/\sqrt{87.5}$ which to appear reasonable must satisfy $(-21.5+25)/\sqrt{87.5} = 0.37 \leq \hat{y}$. It does that with probability 35.6%.

9 Conclusions

In this paper we have explored the abstract phenomena underpinning secure software systems which operate in partially predictable environments; we have suggested a number of models and investigated how they measure up to the problems software designers face. Yet however successful a mathematical model is at capturing the underlying phenomena, we understand that its impact may be limited and its results marginalised if the formal techniques it can support cannot be made accessible to actual program developers.

We say that a formal technique is *usable* only if it can be practically applied, and *relevant* only if it delivers accurate results. Unfortunately usability and relevance can normally coexist only if the theoretical basis for the technique is both simple enough to be supported by automated tools[35] *and yet* complicated enough to yield accurate results. As the examples of this paper show it is unlikely that there is such a *one model to fit all* for any problem domain which includes all the features of hiding, probability and multiple agents. That's is not to say that there is no solution at all — but as formal methods researchers the challenge is to find accurate models with usable abstractions, models whose relationships to each other are well enough understood to support tool-based analyses and to apply after all to generic and relevant scenarios.

10 Epilogue: A Café-Strength Proof of the Cryptographers' Protocol

The Shadow Model captures the qualitative correlation between hidden and visible state. It is simple enough to support an algebra which is amenable to routine calculation: we have twice earlier published refinement-style proofs of the Cryptographers' Protocol [54,49], the novelty being of course not in the protocol (published long ago) nor in its correctness (established by its inventor) but in the style of proof (program algebra and refinement). In doing so we hoped to encourage Formal Methods to expand further into these application areas.

Our earlier proofs –as for the other approaches based on qualitative noninterference [20,9,36,63]– abstracted from probability, from the fairness of the coins, and as we explained at length above that left open the question of their validity when repeated trials of the protocol are carried out — which is its usual environment, after all. And we proposed several methods *in spe* that might legitimise a fully quantitative proof. What would that proof look like?

There is a good chance that the café-strength proof of the Cryptographers' Protocol, thus valid for repeated trials, will have exactly *the same structure as our original qualitative proof.*

That is because the original proof's use of the "qualitative" Encryption Lemma (11) seems to be its only point of vulnerability in the more general context; and

[35] This is rather a stark definition, as it ignores the huge benefits to be gained in a Formal-Methods education, which might not be based on tool support.

the less-abstract "uniform" Encryption Lemma (12) is *not* similarly vulnerable. All the other algebraic properties appear to carry through. If we are right, then there will be a large class of security protocols which, if proven correct with a carefully chosen *qualititative* repertoire of algebraic laws, will retain their correctness in the more general context of repeated runs — provided certain crucial demonic choices (the ones that play a part in uses of the Encryption Lemma) are replaced by uniform probabilistic choices. No other changes should be required.

As we have seen elsewhere, with purely qualitative treatments of probabilistic fairness [46,23], that would have a significant impact on the applicability of tools, by allowing them to remain Boolean rather than having to deal with proper probabilities.

Watch this space...

References

1. A large literature on probabilistic process algebras from 1990 or before
2. A series of meetings between Oxford and Manchester over the general principles of data refinement (reification) and its completeness, Participants included Jifeng He, Tony Hoare, Cliff Jones, Peter Lupton, Carroll Morgan, Tobias Nipkow, Ken Robinson, Bill Roscoe, Jeff Sanders, Ib Sørensen and Mike Spivey (1986)
3. Back, R.-J.R.: On the correctness of refinement steps in program development. Report A-1978-4, Dept. Comp. Sci., Univ. Helsinki (1978)
4. Back, R.-J.R.: Data refinement in the refinement calculus. In: Proceedings 22nd Hawaii International Conference of System Sciences, Kailua-Kona (January 1989)
5. Back, R.-J.R., von Wright, J.: Refinement Calculus: A Systematic Introduction. Springer, Heidelberg (1998)
6. Butler, M.J., Hartel, P.H.: Reasoning about Grover's quantum search algorithm using probabilistic WP. ACM Trans. Prog. Lang. Sys. 21(3), 417–430 (1999)
7. Celiku, O., McIver, A.: Cost-based analysis of probabilistic programs mechanised in HOL. Nordic. Jnl. Comp. 11(2), 102–128 (2004)
8. Chaum, D.: The Dining Cryptographers problem: Unconditional sender and recipient untraceability. J. Cryptol. 1(1), 65–75 (1988)
9. Cohen, E.S.: Information transmission in sequential programs. ACM SIGOPS Operatings Systems Review 11(5), 133–139 (1977)
10. de Nicola, M., Hennessy, M.: Testing equivalence for processes. Theo. Comp. Sci. 34 (1984)
11. Deng, Y., Chothia, T., Palamidessi, C., Pang, J.: Metrics for action-labelled quantitative transition systems. Electronic Notes in Theoretical Computer Science 153(2), 79–96 (2006)
12. Deng, Y., Du, W.: Kantorovich metric in computer science: A brief survey. In: Proceedings of the 7th Workshop on Quantitative Aspects of Programming Languages (to appear, 2009)
13. Desharnais, J., Jagadeesan, R., Gupta, V., Panangaden, P.: The metric analogue of weak bisimulation for probabilistic processes. In: Proc. of the 17th Annual IEEE Symp. Logic in Computer Science, pp. 413–422. IEEE, Los Alamitos (2002)
14. Dijkstra, E.W.: A Discipline of Programming. Prentice-Hall, Englewood Cliffs (1976)
15. Engelhardt, K., Moses, Y., van der Meyden, R.: Unpublished report, Univ. NSW (2005)

16. Engelhardt, K., van der Meyden, R., Moses, Y.: A refinement theory that supports reasoning about knowledge and time. In: Nieuwenhuis, R., Voronkov, A. (eds.) LPAR 2001. LNCS (LNAI), vol. 2250, pp. 125–141. Springer, Heidelberg (2001)
17. Fidge, C., Shankland, C.: But what if I don't want to wait forever? Formal Aspects of Computing 14(3), 281–294 (2003)
18. Floyd, R.W.: Assigning meanings to programs. In: Schwartz, J.T. (ed.) Mathematical Aspects of Computer Science. Proc. Symp. Appl. Math., vol. 19, pp. 19–32. American Mathematical Society, Providence (1967)
19. Gardiner, P.H.B., Morgan, C.C.: Data refinement of predicate transformers. Theo. Comp. Sci. 87, 143–162 (1991); Reprinted in [60]
20. Goguen, J.A., Meseguer, J.: Unwinding and inference control. In: Proc. IEEE Symp. on Security and Privacy, pp. 75–86 (1984)
21. Gonzalia, C., McIver, A.K.: Automating refinement checking in probabilistic system design. In: Butler, M., Hinchey, M.G., Larrondo-Petrie, M.M. (eds.) ICFEM 2007. LNCS, vol. 4789, pp. 212–231. Springer, Heidelberg (2007)
22. Grimmett, G.R., Welsh, D.: Probability: an Introduction. Oxford Science Publications (1986)
23. Hallerstede, S., Hoang, T.S.: Qualitative probabilistic modelling in Event-B. In: Davies, J., Gibbons, J. (eds.) IFM 2007. LNCS, vol. 4591, pp. 293–312. Springer, Heidelberg (2007)
24. He, J., Seidel, K., McIver, A.K.: Probabilistic models for the guarded command language. Science of Computer Programming 28, 171–192 (1997)
25. Hoang, T.S.: The Development of a Probabilistic B-Method and a Supporting Toolkit. PhD thesis, Computer Science and Engineering (2005)
26. Hoang, T.S., McIver, A.K., Morgan, C.C., Robinson, K.A., Jin, Z.D.: Probabilistic invariants for probabilistic machines. In: Bert, D., Bowen, J.P., King, S. (eds.) ZB 2003. LNCS, vol. 2651, pp. 240–259. Springer, Heidelberg (2003)
27. Hoang, T.S., Morgan, C.C., Robinson, K.A., Jin, Z.D.: Refinement in probabilistic *B*: Foundation and case study. In: Treharne, H., King, S., Henson, M.C., Schneider, S. (eds.) ZB 2005. LNCS, vol. 3455. Springer, Heidelberg (2005)
28. Hoare, C.A.R.: An axiomatic basis for computer programming. Comm. ACM 12(10), 576–580 (1969)
29. Hurd, J., McIver, A.K., Morgan, C.C.: Probabilistic guarded commands mechanised in HOL. Theo. Comp. Sci. 346(1), 96–112 (2005)
30. de Vink, E.P., den Hartog, J.I., de Bakker, J.W.: Metric semantics and full abstractness for action refinement and probabilistic choice. Electronic Notes in Theo. Comp. Sci. 40 (2001)
31. Jones, C.: Probabilistic nondeterminism. Monograph ECS-LFCS-90-105, Edinburgh University, Ph.D. Thesis (1990)
32. Jones, C., Plotkin, G.: A probabilistic powerdomain of evaluations. In: Proceedings of the IEEE 4th Annual Symposium on Logic in Computer Science, pp. 186–195. IEEE Computer Society Press, Los Alamitos (1989)
33. Jones, C.B.: Systematic Software Development using VDM. Prentice-Hall, Englewood Cliffs (1986)
34. Kozen, D.: Semantics of probabilistic programs. Jnl. Comp. Sys. Sci. 22, 328–350 (1981)
35. Kozen, D.: A probabilistic PDL. Jnl. Comp. Sys. Sci. 30(2), 162–178 (1985)
36. Leino, K.R.M., Joshi, R.: A semantic approach to secure information flow. Science of Computer Programming 37(1–3), 113–138 (2000)
37. McIver, A.K.: The secure art of computer programming. In: Proc. ICTAC 2009 (2009) (invited presentation)

38. McIver, A.K., Morgan, C.C.: A quantified measure of security 2: A programming logic. Available at [62, key McIver:98A] (1998)
39. McIver, A.K., Morgan, C.C.: Demonic, angelic and unbounded probabilistic choices in sequential programs. Acta. Inf. 37(4/5), 329–354 (2001)
40. McIver, A.K., Morgan, C.C.: Abstraction and refinement of probabilistic systems. In: Katoen, J.-P. (ed.) ACM SIGMetrics Performance Evaluation Review, vol. 32. ACM, New York (2005)
41. McIver, A.K., Morgan, C.C.: Abstraction, Refinement and Proof for Probabilistic Systems. Tech. Mono. Comp. Sci. (2005)
42. McIver, A.K., Morgan, C.C.: Developing and reasoning about probabilistic programs in pGCL. In: Cavalcanti, A., Sampaio, A., Woodcock, J. (eds.) PSSE 2004. LNCS, vol. 3167, pp. 123–155. Springer, Heidelberg (2006)
43. McIver, A.K., Morgan, C.C.: A calculus of revelations. In: Presented at VSTTE Theories Workshop (October 2008), `http://www.cs.york.ac.uk/vstte08/`
44. McIver, A.K., Morgan, C.C.: Sums and lovers: Case studies in security, compositionality and refinement. In: Cavalcanti, A., Dams, D. (eds.) FM 2009. LNCS. Springer, Heidelberg (2009)
45. McIver, A.K., Morgan, C.C., Gonzalia, C.: Proofs and refutations for probabilistic systems. In: Cuellar, J., Maibaum, T., Sere, K. (eds.) FM 2008. LNCS, vol. 5014, pp. 100–115. Springer, Heidelberg (2008)
46. McIver, A.K., Morgan, C.C., Hoang, T.S.: Probabilistic termination in B. In: Bert, D., Bowen, J.P., King, S. (eds.) ZB 2003. LNCS, vol. 2651, pp. 216–239. Springer, Heidelberg (2003)
47. McIver, A.K., Morgan, C.C., Sanders, J.W.: Probably Hoare? Hoare probably! In: Davies, J.W., Roscoe, A.W., Woodcock, J.C.P. (eds.) Millennial Perspectives in Computer Science, Cornerstones of Computing, pp. 271–282. Palgrave, Oxford (2000)
48. McIver, A.K., Morgan, C.C., Troubitsyna, E.: The probabilistic steam boiler: a case study in probabilistic data refinement. In: Bert, D. (ed.) B 1998. LNCS, vol. 1393, pp. 250–265. Springer, Heidelberg (1998); Also [41, ch. 4]
49. McIver, A., Morgan, C.: The thousand-and-one cryptographers. In: Festschrift in Honour of Tony Hoare (to appear, 2009)
50. Morgan, C.C.: The specification statement. ACM Trans. Prog. Lang. Sys. 10(3), 403–419 (1988); Reprinted in [60]
51. Morgan, C.C.: Programming from Specifications, 2nd edn. Prentice-Hall, Englewood Cliffs (1994), `web.comlab.ox.ac.uk/oucl/publications/books/PfS/`
52. Morgan, C.C.: Proof rules for probabilistic loops. In: Jifeng, H., Cooke, J., Wallis, P. (eds.) Proc. BCS-FACS 7th Refinement Workshop, Workshops in Computing. Springer, Heidelberg (1996), `ewic.bcs.org/conferences/1996/refinement/papers/paper10.htm`
53. Morgan, C.C.: The generalised substitution language extended to probabilistic programs. In: Bert, D. (ed.) B 1998. LNCS, vol. 1393, pp. 9–25. Springer, Heidelberg (1998)
54. Morgan, C.C.: The Shadow Knows: Refinement of ignorance in sequential programs. In: Uustalu, T. (ed.) MPC 2006. LNCS, vol. 4014, pp. 359–378. Springer, Heidelberg (2006)
55. Morgan, C.C.: How to brew-up a refinement ordering. In: Boiten, E., Derrick, J., Reeves, S. (eds.) Proc. 2009 Refine Workshop, Eindhoven (2009)
56. Morgan, C.C.: The Shadow Knows: Refinement of ignorance in sequential programs. Science of Computer Programming 74(8) (2009); Treats Oblivious Transfer

57. Morgan, C.C., McIver, A.K.: A quantified measure of security 1: a relational model. Available at [62, key Morgan:98a] (1998)
58. Morgan, C.C., McIver, A.K.: pGCL: Formal reasoning for random algorithms. South African Comp. Jnl. 22, 14–27 (1999)
59. Morgan, C.C., McIver, A.K., Seidel, K.: Probabilistic predicate transformers. ACM Trans. Prog. Lang. Sys. 18(3), 325–353 (1996), `doi.acm.org/10.1145/229542.229547`
60. Morgan, C.C., Vickers, T.N. (eds.): On the Refinement Calculus. FACIT Series in Computer Science. Springer, Berlin (1994)
61. Morris, J.M.: A theoretical basis for stepwise refinement and the programming calculus. Science of Computer Programming 9(3), 287–306 (1987)
62. Probabilistic Systems Group. Publications, `http://www.cse.unsw.edu.au/~carrollm/probs`
63. Sabelfeld, A., Sands, D.: A PER model of secure information flow. Higher-Order and Symbolic Computation 14(1), 59–91 (2001)
64. Schneider, S., Hoang, T.S., Robinson, K.A., Treharne, H.: Tank monitoring: a pAMN case study. Formal Aspects of Computing 18(3), 308–328 (2006)
65. Tix, R., Keimel, K., Plotkin, G.D.: Semantic domains for combining probability and non-determinism. ENTCS 129, 1–104 (2005)
66. van Breugel, F.: Comparative Metric Semantics of Programming Languages: Nondeterminism and Recursion. Theoretical Computer Science (1997)
67. Ying, M., Wirsing, M.: Approximate Bisimilarity. In: Rus, T. (ed.) AMAST 2000. LNCS, vol. 1816, pp. 309–322. Springer, Heidelberg (2000)

Recursive Abstractions for Parameterized Systems

Joxan Jaffar and Andrew E. Santosa

Department of Computer Science, National University of Singapore
Singapore 117590
{joxan,andrews}@comp.nus.edu.sg

Abstract. We consider a language of recursively defined formulas about arrays of variables, suitable for specifying safety properties of parameterized systems. We then present an abstract interpretation framework which translates a paramerized system as a symbolic transition system which propagates such formulas as abstractions of underlying concrete states. The main contribution is a proof method for implications between the formulas, which then provides for an implementation of this abstract interpreter.

1 Introduction

Automation of verification of parameterized systems are an active area of research [1, 2, 3, 4, 5, 6, 7]. One essential challenge is to reason about the unbounded parameter n representing the number of processes in the system. This usually entails the provision of an induction hypothesis, a step that is often limited to manual intervention. This challenge adds to the standard one when the domain of discourse of the processes are infinite-state.

In this paper, we present an abstract interpretation [8] approach for the verification of infinite-state parameterized systems.

First, we present a language for the general specification of properties of arrays of variables, each of whom has length equal to the parameter n. The expressive power of this language stems from its ability to specify complex properties on these arrays. In particular, these complex properties are just those that arise from a language which allows *recursive definitions* of properties of interest.

Second, we present a symbolic transition framework for obtaining a symbolic execution tree which (a) is finite, and (b) represents all possible concrete traces of the system. This is achieved, as in standard abstract interpretation, by computing a symbolic execution tree but using a process of abstraction on the symbolic states so that the total number of abstract states encountered is bounded. Verification of a particular (safety) property of the system is then obtained simply by inspection of the tree.

Third, the key step therefore is to compute two things: (a) given an abstract state and a transition of the parameterized system, compute the new abstract state, and (b) determine if a computed abstract state is subsumed by the previously computed abstract states (so that no further action is required on this state). The main contribution of this paper is an algorithm to determine both.

Consider a driving example of a parameterized system of $n \geq 2$ process where each process simply increments the value of shared variable x (see Figure 1 (left)). The idea is to prove, given an initial state where $x = 0$, that $x = n$ at termination.

A. Cavalcanti and D. Dams (Eds.): FM 2009, LNCS 5850, pp. 72–88, 2009.

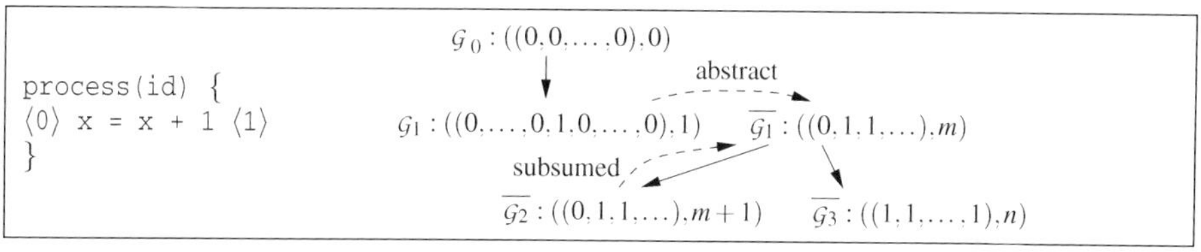

Fig. 1. Abstract Computation Tree of Counting Ones

Figure 1 (right) outlines the steps in generating the symbolic execution tree for this example. The tree is constructed by letting each process proceed from an initial program point $\langle 0 \rangle$ to its final point $\langle 1 \rangle$.

We start with a program state of $\mathcal{G}_0 = ((0,0,\cdots,0),0)$ where the first element is a sequence of n bits representing the program counter, and the second element represents the value of x. A first transition would bring the system to a state $\mathcal{G}_1 = ((0, \cdots, 0, 1, 0, \cdots, 0), 1)$, where the position of the "1" is anywhere in the range 1 to n, and the value of x is now 1. At this point, we would like to abstract this state to a state $\overline{\mathcal{G}_1}$ where the counter has, not exactly one numeral 1, but some $1 \leq m < n$ copies of the numeral 1. Further, the value of x is not 1, but instead is equal to m. Let us denote this state $((0,1,1,\cdots),m)$.

There are now two possible transitions: first, corresponding to the case where $\overline{\mathcal{G}_1}$ has at least two 0's, we get a new state $\overline{\mathcal{G}_2}$ whose counter has a mixture of 0's and 1's. But this new state is already covered by $\overline{\mathcal{G}_1}$ and hence need not be considered further. The second case is where $\overline{\mathcal{G}_1}$ has exactly one 0, in which the final transition results in the final state $\overline{\mathcal{G}_3} = ((1,1,\cdots,1),x)$ where the counter has all 1's. Since the value of x in $\overline{\mathcal{G}_3}$ equals the number of 1's, it follows that $x = n$ in this final state.

The key points in this proof are as follow. First, we employed the notion of an abstract state $\overline{\mathcal{G}_1}$ where the counter has $1 \leq m < n$ copies of 1 (the rest are 0), and $x = m$. We then show that the concrete state $\mathcal{G}_1$ emanating from the initial state is in fact an instance of $\overline{\mathcal{G}_1}$. We then showed that the state $\overline{\mathcal{G}_2}$ emanating from $\overline{\mathcal{G}_1}$ is either (a) itself $\overline{\mathcal{G}_1}$ (which therefore requires no further consideration), or (b) the final state $\overline{\mathcal{G}_3} : ((1,1,\cdots,1),x)$, and where $x = n$. Thus the proof that $x = n$ at the end is established.

The main result in this paper, in terms of this example, is first to construct the computation tree, but more importantly to provide an automatic proof of the conditions that make the tree a true representation of all the traces of the underlying parameterized system. In our example, our algorithm proves the entailments $\mathcal{G}_1 \models \overline{\mathcal{G}_1}$ and $\overline{\mathcal{G}_2} \models \overline{\mathcal{G}_1}$. Although not exemplified, all states in discussed here are written in our constraint language using arrays and recursive definitions, which is to be discussed in Section 2. For instance, the state $\mathcal{G}_0$ is represented using n-element array of zeroes which is defined using a recursive definition. We provide an algorithm to prove entailments in verification conditions which involve integer arrays and the recursive definitions.

In summary, our contributions are threefold:

- We present a language for defining recursive abstractions consisting of recursive definitions and integer arrays. Such abstractions are to be used to represent core properties of the parameterized system that are invariant over the parameter n of the system. The provision of these abstractions is generally restricted to be manual.

- Then we provide a symbolic traversal mechanism to construct a symbolic execution tree which exhibits the behavior of the parameterized system, which is exemplified in Figure 1 (left). In constructing the tree we abstract the states encountered using the recursive abstractions. In the above example, this is exemplified with the abstraction of $\mathcal{G}_1$ to $\overline{\mathcal{G}_1}$. Our objective is to produce a closed tree, where all the paths in the tree reaches the end of the program's execution (the case of $\overline{\mathcal{G}_3}$ above) or ends in a state that is subsumed by some other state in the tree (the case of $\overline{\mathcal{G}_2}$, which is subsumed by $\overline{\mathcal{G}_1}$).

  Now, there are two kinds of proofs needed: one is for the correctness of the abstraction step (represented as the *entailment* $\mathcal{G}_1 \models \overline{\mathcal{G}_1}$ of two formulas). Similarly, we need a proof of entailment of formulas defining the subsumption of one state over another (eg. $\overline{\mathcal{G}_2} \models \overline{\mathcal{G}_1}$ above).
- Finally we devise a proof method where the recursive definitions and the arrays work together in the entailment proof. In this way, the *only* manual intervention required is to provide the abstraction of a state (in our example, the provision of the abstraction $\overline{\mathcal{G}_1}$ to abstract $\mathcal{G}_1$). Dispensing with this kind of manual intervention is, in general, clearly as challenging as discovering loop invariants in regular programs. However, it is essentially dependent on knowledge about the *algorithm* underpinning the system, and not about the *proof system* itself.

1.1 Related Work

Central to the present paper is the prior work [9] which presented a general method for the proof of (entailment between) recursively defined predicates. This method is a proof reduction strategy augmented with a principle of *coinduction*, the primary means to obtain a terminating proof. In the present paper, the earlier work is extended first by a symbolic transition system which models the behavior of the underlying parameterized system. A more important extension is the consideration of array formulas. These array formulas are particularly useful for specifying abstract properties of states of a parameterized systems.

Recent work by [3] concerns a class of formulas, environment predicates, in a way that systems can be abstracted into a finite number of such formulas. The essence of the formula is a universally quantified expression relating the local variable of a reference process to all other processes. For example, a formula of the form $\forall j \neq i : x[i] < x[j]$ could be used to state that the local variable x of the reference process i is less than the corresponding variable in *all other* processes. A separate method is used to ensure that the relationships inside the quantification fall into a finite set eg. predicate abstraction. An important advantage of these works is the possibility of automatically deriving the abstract formulas from a system.

The *indexed predicates* method [4] is somewhat similar to environment predicates in that the formula describes universally quantified statements over indices which range over all processes. Determining which indexed predicates are appropriate is however not completely automatic. Further, these methods are not accompanied by an abstract transition relation.

The paper [1] presents safety verification technique of parameterized systems using abstraction and constraints. Key ideas include the handling of existentially and universally-quantified transition guards), and the use of *gap-order constraints*. Abstraction is done by weakening the gap-order constraints.

Our method differs from the above three works because we present a general language for the specification of *any* abstraction, and not a restricted class. We further provide a transition relation which can work with the abstraction language in order to generate lemmas sufficient for a correctness proof. The proof method, while not decidable, is general and can dispense with a large class of applications.

Earlier work on counter abstraction [7] clearly is relevant to our abstractions which is centrally concerned with describing abstract properties of program counters. Later works on *invisible invariants* [6] show that by proving properties of systems with a fixed (and small) parameter, that the properties indeed hold when the parameter is not restricted. In both these classes of works, however, the system is assumed to be finite state.

There are some other works using inductive, as opposed to abstraction, methods for example [5]. While these methods address a large class of formulas, they often depend on significant manual intervention.

We finally mention the work of [2] which, in one aspect, is closest in philosophy to our work. The main idea is to represent both the system and the property (including liveness properties) as *logic programs*. In this sense, they are using recursive definitions as we do. The main method involves proving a predicate by a process of folding/unfolding of the logic programs until the proof is obvious from the syntactic structure of the resulting programs. They do not consider array formulas or abstract interpretation.

2 The Language

In this section we provide a short description of constraint language allowed by the underlying constraint solver assumed in all our examples.

2.1 Basic Constraints

We first consider *basic constraints* which are constructed from two kinds of terms: integer terms and *array expressions*. Integer terms are constructed in the usual way, with one addition: the array element. The latter is defined recursively to be of the form $a[i]$ where a is an array expression and i an integer term. An array expression is either an array variable or of the form $\langle a,i,j\rangle$ where a is an array expression and i,j are integer terms.

The meaning of an array expression is simply a map from integers into integers, and the meaning of an array expression $a' = \langle a,i,j\rangle$ is a map just like a except that $a'[i] = j$. The meaning of array elements is governed by the classic McCarthy [10] axioms:

$$i = k \rightarrow \langle a,i,j\rangle[k] = j$$
$$i \neq k \rightarrow \langle a,i,j\rangle[k] = a[k]$$

A basic constraint is either an integer equality or inequality, or an equation between array expressions. The meaning of a constraint is defined in the obvious way.

```
sys(N,K,X) :- 1 ≤ Id ≤ N, K[Id] = 0, K'=<K,Id,1>, X'=X+1, sys(N,K',X').
```

Fig. 2. Transitions of Counting Ones

In what follows, we use constraint to mean either an atomic constraint or a conjunction of constraints. We shall use the symbol ψ or Ψ, with or without subscripts, to denote a constraint.

2.2 Recursive Constraints

We now formalize *recursive constraints* using the framework of Constraint Logic Programming (CLP) [11]. To keep this paper self-contained, we now provide a brief background on CLP.

An *atom* is of the form $p(\tilde{t})$ where p is a user-defined predicate symbol and $\tilde{t}$ a tuple of terms, written in the language of an underlying constraint solver. A *rule* is of the form A:-$\Psi,\tilde{B}$ where the atom A is the *head* of the rule, and the sequence of atoms $\tilde{B}$ and constraint Ψ constitute the *body* of the rule. The body of the rule represents a conjunction of the atoms and constraints within. The constraint Ψ is also written in the language of the underlying constraint solver, which is assumed to be able to decide (at least reasonably frequently) whether Ψ is satisfiable or not. A rule represents implication with the body as antecedent and the head as the conclusion. A *program* is a finite set of rules, which represents a conjunction of those rules. The semantics of a program is the smallest set of (variable-free) atoms that satisfy the program. Given a CLP program, recursive constraints are constructed using recursive predicates defined in the program.

Example 1 (Count Ones). The following program formalizes the states described in the "counting ones" example (note that _ denotes "any" value). In the predicates below, the number `N` represents the parameter, the array `K` represents the counter, and `X` represents the shared variable. `Allzeroes(N,K,X)` holds for any `N`, `K`, and `X` when `K` is an array of length `N` with all elements zero and `X` is zero. `Allones(N,K,X)` holds when all elements of `K` are one, and `X=N`. Finally, the meaning of `abs(N, K, M)` is that `K` is a bit vector and `M` is the number of 1's in `K`.

```
allzeroes(0, _, 0).
allzeroes(N, ⟨K,N,0⟩, 0) :- N > 0, allzeroes(N-1, K, 0).
allones(0, _, 0).
allones(N, ⟨K,N,1⟩, N) :- N > 0, allones(N-1, K, N-1).
bit(0).
bit(1).
abs(0, _, 0).
abs(N, ⟨K,N,B⟩, M+B) :- N > 0, bit(B), abs(N-1, K, M).
```

3 Formalization of a Parameterized System

We now formalize a parameterized system as a transition system. We assume interleaving execution of the concurrent processes, where a transition that is executed by a process is considered atomic, that is, no other process can observe the system state when another process is executing a transition. Similar to the definition of recursive constraints in the previous section, the transition systems here are also defined using CLP, where a CLP rule models a state transition of the system.

3.1 Abstract Computation Trees

Before proceeding, we require a few more definitions on CLP. A *substitution* θ simultaneously replaces each variable in a term or constraint e into some expression, and we write $e\theta$ to denote the result. We sometimes write θ more specificly as $[e_1/t_1,\ldots,e_n/t_n]$ to denote substitution of t_i by e_i for $1 \leq i \leq n$. A *renaming* is a substitution which maps each variable in the expression into a variable distinct from other variables. A *grounding* is a substitution which maps each integer or array variable into its intended universe of discourse: an integer or an array. Where Ψ is a constraint, a grounding of Ψ results in *true* or *false* in the usual way.

A *grounding* θ of an atom $p(\tilde{t})$ is an object of the form $p(\tilde{t}\theta)$ having no variables. A grounding of a goal $\mathcal{G} \equiv (p(\tilde{t}),\Psi)$ is a grounding θ of $p(\tilde{t})$ where $\Psi\theta$ is *true*. We write $[\![\mathcal{G}]\!]$ to denote the set of groundings of $\mathcal{G}$. We say that a goal $\mathcal{G}$ *entails* another goal $\mathcal{G}'$, written $\mathcal{G} \models \mathcal{G}'$, if $[\![\mathcal{G}]\!] \subseteq [\![\mathcal{G}']\!]$.

From now on we speak about *goals* which have exactly the same format as the body of a rule. A goal that contains only constraints and no atoms is called *final*.

Let $\mathcal{G} \equiv (B_1,\cdots,B_n,\Psi)$ and P denote a goal and program respectively. Let $R \equiv A\,\text{:-}\,\Psi_1,C_1,\cdots,C_m$ denote a rule in P, written so that none of its variables appear in $\mathcal{G}$. Let the equation $A = B$ be shorthand for the pairwise equation of the corresponding arguments of A and B. A *reduct* of $\mathcal{G}$ using a rule R which head matches an atom B_i in $\mathcal{G}$, denoted $\text{REDUCT}_{B_i}(\mathcal{G},R)$, is of the form

$(B_1,\cdots,B_{i-1},C_1,\cdots,C_m,B_{i+1},\cdots,B_n,(B_i = A),\Psi,\Psi_1)$

provided the constraint $(B_i = A) \wedge \Psi \wedge \Psi_1$ is satisfiable.

Definition 1 (Unfold). *Given a program P and a goal $\mathcal{G}$,* $\text{UNFOLD}_B(\mathcal{G})$ *is* $\{\mathcal{G}' | \exists R \in P : \mathcal{G}' = \text{REDUCT}_B(\mathcal{G},R)\}$. □

A *derivation sequence* for a goal $\mathcal{G}_0$ is a possibly infinite sequence of goals $\mathcal{G}_0$, $\mathcal{G}_1$, $\cdots$ where $\mathcal{G}_i$, $i > 0$ is a reduct of $\mathcal{G}_{i-1}$. If the last goal $\mathcal{G}_n$ is a final (hence no rule R of the program can be applied to generate a reduct of $\mathcal{G}_n$), we say that the derivation is *successful*. Since a goal can be unfolded to a number of other goals (reducts), we can identify the *derivation tree* of a goal.

Definition 2 (Abstract Computation Tree). *An* abstract computation tree *is defined just like a derivation tree with one exception: the use of a derivation step may produce not the reduct goal $\mathcal{G}$ as originally defined, but a* generalization $\overline{\mathcal{G}}$ *of this reduct goal. Whenever such a generalization is performed in the tree construction, we say that an* abstraction step *is performed on $\mathcal{G}$ obtaining $\overline{\mathcal{G}}$.* □

Our concern in this paper is primarily to compute an abstract computation tree which represents all the concrete traces of the underlying parameterized system. The following property of abstract trees ensures this.

Definition 3 (Closure). *An abstract computation tree is* closed *if each leaf node represents a goal $\mathcal{G}$ which is either terminal, ie. no transition is possible from $\mathcal{G}$, or which is entailed by a goal labelling another node in the tree.* □

3.2 Symbolic Transitions

Next we describe how to represent a parameterized system as a CLP program. In doing so, we inherit a framework of abstract computation trees of parameterized systems. More specifically, the safety property that we seek can then be obtained by inspection of a closed abstract computation tree that we can generate from the system.

We start with a predicate of the form **sys**(N,K,T,X) where the number N represents the parameter, the N-element array K represents the program counter, the N-element array T represents each *local* variable of each process, and finally, X represents a shared/global variable. Multiple copies of T and/or X may be used as appropriate.

We then write symbolic transitions of a parameterized systems using the following general format:

```
sys(N, K, T, X) :- K[Id] = α, K' = <K, Id, β>,
    Ψ(N, K, T, X, K', T', X'), sys(N, K', T', X').
```

This describes a transition from a program point α to a point β in a process. The variable Id symbolically represents a (nondeterministic) choice of which process is being executed. We call such variables *index* variables. The formula Ψ denotes a (basic or recursive) constraint relating the current values K,T,X and future values K',T',X' of the key variables.

Consider again the example of Figure 1, and consider its transition system in Figure 2. The transition system consists of transitions from program counter $\langle 0 \rangle$ to $\langle 1 \rangle$ of a parameterized system, where each process simply increments its local variable X and terminates[1]. The system terminates when the program counter contains only 1's, ie. when all processes are at point $\langle 1 \rangle$.

3.3 The Top-Level Verification Process

In this section we outline the verification process. The process starts with a goal representing the initial state of the system. Reduction and abstraction steps are then successively applied to the goal resulting in a number of verification conditions (obligations), which are proved using our proof method.

We now exemplify using the Counting Ones example of Section 1. This goal representing the initial state is $\mathcal{G}_0$ in Figure 1. Recall that we formalize the transitions of the Counting Ones example in Figure 2. In our formalization, we represent the goal $\mathcal{G}_0$ as follows **sys**$(N,K,X), allzeroes(N,K,X)$ denoting a state where all the elements of the array K are zero.

We apply the transition of Figure 2 by reducing $\mathcal{G}_0$ into the goal $\mathcal{G}_1$, which in our formalism is the goal **sys**$(N,K',X'), allzeroes(N,K,X), 1 \leq Id_1 \leq N, K[Id_1] = 0, K' = \langle K, Id_1, 1 \rangle, X' = X+1$. The goal represents a state where only one of the elements of the array K is set to 1. Note that this reduction step is akin to strongest postcondition

[1] *Termination* here means that no further execution is defined.

propagation [12] since given the precondition $allzeroes(N,K,X)$, the postcondition is exactly $(\exists K,X,Id_1 : allzeroes(N,K,X), 1 \leq Id_1 \leq N, K[Id_1] = 0, K' = \langle K, Id_1, 1\rangle, X' = X+1)[K/K', X/X']$.

We now abstract the goal $\mathcal{G}_1$ into $\overline{\mathcal{G}_1}$, which in our formalism is represented as $\textbf{sys}(N,K',X'), abs(N,K',X')$. Here one verification condition in the form of an entailment is generated:

$$allzeroes(N,K,X), 1 \leq Id_1 \leq N, K[Id_1] = 0, K' = \langle K, Id_1, 1\rangle, X' = X+1 \\ \models abs(N,K',X').$$

The proof this obligation guarantess that the abstraction is an over approximation.

Now, the propagation from $\overline{\mathcal{G}_1}$ to $\overline{\mathcal{G}_2}$ is again done by applying unfold (reduction) to the predicate **sys** based on its definition (Figure 2). As the result, we obtain the goal $\overline{\mathcal{G}_2}$ as follows:

$$\textbf{sys}(N,K'',X''), abs(N,K',X'), 1 \leq Id_2 \leq N, K'[Id_2] = 0, K'' = \langle K', Id_2, 1\rangle, X'' = X'+1$$

Proving of subsumption of $\overline{\mathcal{G}_2}$ by $\overline{\mathcal{G}_1}$ is now equivalent to the proof of the verification condition

$$abs(N,K',X'), 1 \leq Id_2 \leq N, K'[Id_2] = 0, K'' = \langle K', Id_2, 1\rangle, X'' = X'+1 \\ \models abs(N,K',X')[K''/K', X''/X'].$$

The purpose of renaming in the above example is to match the system variables of $\overline{\mathcal{G}_2}$ with those of $\overline{\mathcal{G}_1}$.

4 The Proof Method

In this key section, we consider proof obligations of the form $\mathcal{G} \models \mathcal{H}$ for goals $\mathcal{G}$ and $\mathcal{H}$ possibly containing recursive constraints.

Intuitively, we proceed as follows: unfold the recursive predicates in $\mathcal{G}$ *completely* a finite number of steps in order to obtain a "frontier" containing the goals $\mathcal{G}_1, \ldots, \mathcal{G}_n$. We note that "completely" here means that $\{\mathcal{G}_1, \ldots, \mathcal{G}_n\} = \text{UNFOLD}_A(\mathcal{G})$. We then unfold $\mathcal{H}$ obtaining goals $\mathcal{H}_1, \ldots, \mathcal{H}_m$, but this time not necessarily completely, that is, we only require that $\{\mathcal{H}_1, \ldots, \mathcal{H}_m\} \subseteq \text{UN-FOLD}_B(\mathcal{H})$. This situation is depicted in Figure 3. Then, the proof holds if

$$\mathcal{G}_1 \vee \ldots \vee \mathcal{G}_n \models \mathcal{H}_1 \vee \ldots \vee \mathcal{H}_m$$

or alternatively, $\mathcal{G}_i \models \mathcal{H}_1 \vee \ldots \vee \mathcal{H}_m$ for all $1 \leq i \leq n$. This follows from the fact that $\mathcal{G} \models \mathcal{G}_1 \vee \ldots \vee \mathcal{G}_n$, (which is not true in general, but true in the least-model semantics of CLP), and the fact $\mathcal{H}_j \models \mathcal{H}$ for all j such that

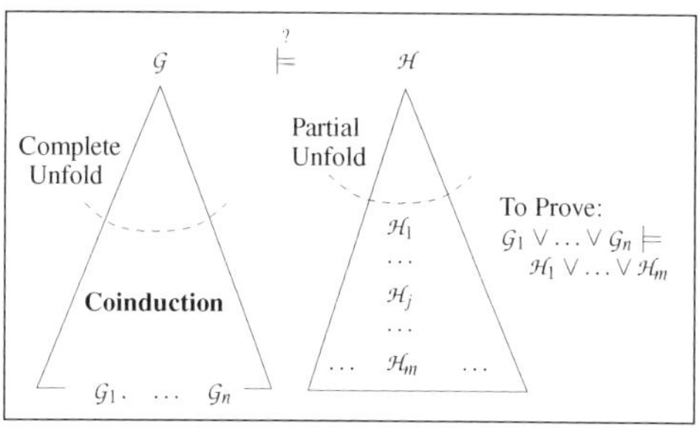

Fig. 3. Informal Structure of Proof Process

$1 \leq j \leq m$. If all variables in $\mathcal{H}$ appear in $\mathcal{G}$, we can reduce the proof to $\forall i : 1 \leq i \leq n, \exists j : 1 \leq j \leq m : \mathcal{G}_i \models \mathcal{H}_j$. Finally, we seek to eliminate the predicates in $\mathcal{H}_j$ so the remaining proof is one about basic constraints.

In this paper we do not go further with the proof of basic constraints. We instead assume the use of a standard black-box solver, such as the SMT solvers [13, 14, 15]. In our own experiments, we use a method from [16] to convert constraints on array segments into constraints on integers, and then dispatch the integer constraints using the real-number solver of CLP($\mathcal{R}$) .

In addition to this overall idea of using left and right unfolds, there are a few more rules, as detailed below.

4.1 The Coinduction Rule

Before presenting our collection of proof rules, one of them, the coinduction rule, deserves preliminary explanation. Let us illustrate this rule on a small example. Consider the definition of the following two recursive predicates

```
m4(0).                 even(0).
m4(X+4) :- m4(X).      even(X+2) :- even(X).
```

whose domain is the set of non-negative integers. The predicate `m4` defines the set of multiples of four, whereas the predicate `even` defines the set of even numbers. We shall attempt to prove that `m4(X)`$\models$`even(X)`, which in fact states that every multiple of four is even. We start the proof process by performing a *complete* unfolding on the lhs goal (see definition in Section 4). We note that `m4(X)` has two possible unfoldings, one leading to the empty goal with the answer `X=0`, and another one leading to the goal `m4(X'),X'=X-4`. The two unfolding operations, applied to the original proof obligation result in the following two new proof obligations, both of which need to be discharged in order to prove the original one.

`X=0` $\models$ `even(X)` (1)   `m4(X'),X'=X-4` $\models$ `even(X)` (2)

The proof obligation (1) can be easily discharged. Since unfolding on the lhs is no longer possible, we can only unfold on the rhs. We choose[1] to unfold with rule `even(0)`, which results in a new proof obligation which is trivially true, since its lhs and rhs are identical.

For proof obligation (2), before attempting any further unfolding, we note that the lhs `m4(X')` of the current proof obligation, and the lhs `m4(X)` of the original proof obligation, are unifiable (as long as we consider `X'` a fresh variable), which enables the application of the coinduction principle. First, we "discover" the *induction hypothesis* `m4(X')`$\models$`even(X')`, as a variant of the original proof obligation. Then, we use this induction hypothesis to replace `m4(X')` in (2) by `even(X')`. This yields the new proof obligation

`even(X'),X'=X-4` $\models$ `even(X)` (3)

To discharge (3), we unfold twice on the rhs, using the `even(X+2) :- even(X)` rule. The resulting proof obligation is

`even(X'),X'=X-4` $\models$ `even(X'''),X'''=X''-2,X''=X-2` (3)

$$\text{(LU+I)}\quad \frac{\Pi \uplus \{\tilde{A} \vdash \mathcal{G} \models \mathcal{H}\}}{\Pi \cup \bigcup_{i=1}^{n} \{\tilde{A} \cup \{\mathcal{G} \models \mathcal{H}\} \vdash \mathcal{G}_i \models \mathcal{H}\}} \quad \begin{array}{l}\text{UNFOLD}(\mathcal{G}) = \\ \{\mathcal{G}_1, \ldots, \mathcal{G}_n\}\end{array}$$

$$\text{(RU)}\quad \frac{\Pi \uplus \{\tilde{A} \vdash \mathcal{G} \models \mathcal{H}\}}{\Pi \cup \{\tilde{A} \vdash \mathcal{G} \models \mathcal{H}'\}} \quad \mathcal{H}' \in \text{UNFOLD}(\mathcal{H})$$

$$\text{(CO)}\quad \frac{\Pi \uplus \{\tilde{A} \vdash \mathcal{G} \models \mathcal{H}\}}{\Pi \cup \{\tilde{A} \vdash \mathcal{H}'\theta \models \mathcal{H}\}} \quad \begin{array}{l}\mathcal{G}' \models \mathcal{H}' \in \tilde{A} \text{ and there} \\ \text{exists a substitution } \theta \text{ s.t. } \mathcal{G} \models \mathcal{G}'\theta\end{array}$$

$$\text{(CP)}\quad \frac{\Pi \uplus \{\tilde{A} \vdash \mathcal{G} \wedge p(\tilde{x}) \models \mathcal{H} \wedge p(\tilde{y})\}}{\Pi \uplus \{\tilde{A} \vdash \mathcal{G} \models \mathcal{H} \wedge \tilde{x} = \tilde{y}\}}$$

$$\text{(SPL)}\quad \frac{\Pi \uplus \{\tilde{A} \vdash \mathcal{G} \models \mathcal{H}\}}{\Pi \cup \bigcup_{i=1}^{k} \{\tilde{A} \vdash \mathcal{G} \wedge \psi_i \models \mathcal{H}\}} \quad \psi_1 \vee \ldots \vee \psi_k \text{ is valid}$$

$$\text{(EXR)}\quad \frac{\Pi \uplus \{\tilde{A} \vdash \mathcal{G} \models \mathcal{H}(z)\}}{\Pi \uplus \{\tilde{A} \vdash \mathcal{G} \wedge z = e \models \mathcal{H}(z)\}} \quad z \text{ is existential}$$

Fig. 4. Proof Rules for Recursive Constraints

where variables `X''` and `X'''` are existentially quantified[2]. Using constraint simplification, we reduce this proof obligation to `even(X-4)`$\models$`even(X-4)`, which is obviously true.

In the above example, `m4(X)` is unfolded to a goal with answer `X=0`, however, in general the proof method does not require a base case. We could remove the fact `m4(0)` from the definition of `m4`, and still obtain a successful proof. We call our technique "coinduction" from the fact that it does not require any base case.

4.2 The Proof Rules

We now present a formal calculus for the proof of assertions $\mathcal{G} \models \mathcal{H}$. To handle the possibly infinite unfoldings of $\mathcal{G}$ and $\mathcal{H}$, we shall depend on coinduction, which allows the assumption of a *previous* obligation. The proof proceeds by manipulating a set of *proof obligations* until it finally becomes empty or a counterexample is found. Formally, a *proof obligation* is of the form $\tilde{A} \vdash \mathcal{G} \models \mathcal{H}$ where the $\mathcal{G}$ and $\mathcal{H}$ are goals and $\tilde{A}$ is a set of *assumption* goals whose assumption (coinductively) can be used to discharge the proof obligation at hand. This set is implemented in our algorithm as a memo table.

Our proof rules are presented in Figure 4. The $\uplus$ symbol represents the disjoint union of two sets, and emphasizes the fact that in an expression of the form $A \uplus B$, we have that $A \cap B = \emptyset$. Each rule operates on the (possibly empty) set of proof obligations Π, by selecting one of its proof obligations and attempting to discharge it. In this process, new proof obligations may be produced. We note that our proof rules are presented in

[2] For clarity, we sometimes prefix such variables with '?'.

REDUCE($\mathcal{G} \models \mathcal{H}$) **returns boolean**

choose one of the following:

- Constraint Proof: (CP) + Constraint Solving
  Apply a constraint proof to $\mathcal{G} \models \mathcal{H}$.
  If successful, **return** *true*, otherwise **return** *false*
- Memoize ($\mathcal{G} \models \mathcal{H}$) as an assumption
- Coinduction: (CO)
  if there is an assumption $\mathcal{G}' \models \mathcal{H}'$ such that
  REDUCE($\mathcal{G} \models \mathcal{G}'\theta$) = *true* $\wedge$ REDUCE($\mathcal{H}'\theta \models \mathcal{H}$) = *true*
  then return *true*.
- Unfold:
  choose left or right
  case: Left: (LU+I)
  choose an atom A in $\mathcal{G}$ to reduce
  for all reducts $\mathcal{G}_L$ of $\mathcal{G}$ using A: if REDUCE($\mathcal{G}_L \models \mathcal{H}$) = *false* **return** *false*
  return *true*
  case: Right: (RU)
  choose an atom A in $\mathcal{H}$ to reduce, obtaining $\mathcal{G}_R$
  return REDUCE($\mathcal{G} \models \mathcal{G}_R$)
- Split:
  Find an index variable Id and a parameter variable N and apply the split rule using $Id \neq N \vee Id = N$ to split $\mathcal{G}$ into $\mathcal{G}_1$ and $\mathcal{G}_2$.
  return REDUCE($\mathcal{G}_1 \models \mathcal{H}$) $\wedge$ REDUCE($\mathcal{G}_2 \models \mathcal{H}$)
- Existential Variable Removal:
  If an existential array variable z appears in the form $z = \langle x, i, e \rangle$, then simply substitute z by $\langle x, i, e \rangle$ everywhere (in $\mathcal{H}$). If however z appears in the form $x = \langle z, i, e \rangle$ where x is not existential, then find an expression in $\mathcal{G}$ of the form $x = \langle x', i, e \rangle$ and replace z by x'. Let the result be $\mathcal{H}'$.
  return REDUCE($\mathcal{G} \models \mathcal{H}'$)

Fig. 5. Search Algorithm for Recursive Constraints

the "reverse" manner than usual, where the conclusions to be proven is written above the horizontal line and the premise to achieve the conclusion is written below the line. Our proof rules can be considered as a system of production of premises whose proofs establish the desired conclusion.

The *left unfold with new induction hypothesis* (LU+I) (or simply "left unfold") rule performs a complete unfold on the lhs of a proof obligation, producing a new set of proof obligations. The original formula, while removed from Π, is added as an assumption to every newly produced proof obligation, opening the door to using coinduction later in the proof.

The rule *right unfold* (RU) performs an unfold operation on the rhs of a proof obligation. In general, the two unfold rules will be systematically interleaved. The resulting proof obligations are then discharged either coinductively or directly, using the (CO) and (CP) rules, respectively.

The rule *coinduction application* (CO) transforms an obligation by using an assumption, and thus opens the door to discharging that obligation via the direct proof (CP) rule. Since assumptions can only be created using the (LU+I) rule, the (CO) rule realizes the coinduction principle. The underlying principle behind the (CO) rule is that a "similar" assertion $\mathcal{G}' \models \mathcal{H}'$ has been previously encountered in the proof process, and assumed as true.

Note that this test for coinduction applicability is itself of the form $\mathcal{G} \models \mathcal{H}$. However, the important point here is that this test can only be carried out using basic constraints, in the manner prescribed for the CP rule described below. In other words, this test does not use the definitions of (recursive) predicates.

The rule *constraint proof* (CP), when used repeatedly, discharges a proof obligation by reducing it to a form which contains no recursive predicates. The intended use of this rule is in case the recursive predicates of the rhs is the subset of the recursive predicates of the lhs such that repeated applications of the rule results in rhs containing no recursive predicates. We then simply ignore the lhs predicates and attempt to establish the remaining obligation using our basic constraint solver.

The rule *split* (SPL) rule is straightforward: to break up the proof into pieces. The rule *existential removal* (EXR) rule is similarly straightforward: to remove one instance of an *existential* variable, one that appears only in the rhs. What is not straightforward however is precisely how we use the SPL and EXR rules: in the former case, how do we choose the constraints ψ_i? And in the latter, how do we choose the expression e? We present answers to this in the search algorithm below.

4.3 The Search Algorithm

Given a proof obligation $\mathcal{G} \models \mathcal{H}$, a proof shall start with $\Pi = \{\emptyset \vdash \mathcal{G} \models \mathcal{H}\}$, and proceed by repeatedly applying the rules in Figure 4 to it. We now describe a strategy so as to make the application of the rules automated. Here we propose systematic interleaving of the left-unfold (LU+I) and right-unfold (RU) rules, attempting a constraint proof along the way. As CLP can be executed by resolution, we can also execute our proof rules, based on an algorithm which has some resemblance to tabled resolution.

We present our algorithm in pseudocode in Figure 5. Note that the presentation is in the form of a nondeterministic algorithm, and the order executing each choice of the nondeterministic operator **choose** needs to be implemented by some form of systematic strategy, for example, by a breadth-first strategy. Clearly there is a combinatorial explosion here, but in practice the number of steps required for a proof is not large. Even so, the matter of efficiently choosing which order to apply the rules is beyond the scope of this paper.

In Figure 5, by a *constraint proof* of a obligation, we mean to repeatedly apply the CP rule in order to remove all occurrences of predicates in the obligation, in an obvious way. Then the basic constraint solver is applied to the resulting obligation.

Next consider the split rule in Figure 5. Note that we have specified the rather specific instance of the SPL rule in which we replace a constraint of the form $Id \leq N$, where Id is an index variable and N represents the parameter, by (a disjunction of) two constraints $Id \leq N, Id = N$ ($Id = N$) and $Id \leq N, Id \neq N$ ($Id < N$). The reason for this is purely technical; it is essentially because our recursive assertions depend on $Id \leq N$ and since

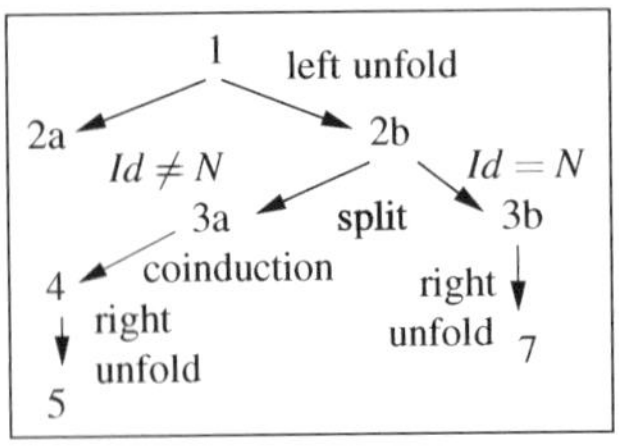

Fig. 6. Proof Tree

they are recursive on N, a recursive state may end up with the situation where $Id > N-1$, a situation which is not similar to the parent state.

Finally consider the existential variable elimination rule in Figure 5. The essential idea here is simply that an existential variable is most likely to correspond to some array expression on the lhs. Once again, this choice of existential variable elimination is purely technical and was created because it works in practice.

Lemma 1 (Soundness of Rules). *$\mathcal{G} \models \mathcal{H}$ if, starting with the proof obligation $\emptyset \vdash \mathcal{G} \models \mathcal{H}$, there exists a sequence of applications of proof rules that results in proof obligations $\tilde{A} \vdash \mathcal{G}' \models \mathcal{H}'$ such that (a) $\mathcal{H}'$ contains only constraints, and (b) $\mathcal{G}' \models \mathcal{H}'$ can be discharged by the basic constraint solver.* □

5 Examples

5.1 Counting Ones

In Figure 1, the tree is closed is due to state subsumption formalized as $\overline{\mathcal{G}_2} \models \overline{\mathcal{G}_1}$:
1: $1 \leq Id_2 \leq N, K'[Id_2] = 0 \models abs(N, \langle K', id_2, 1\rangle, X'+1)$

A complete proof tree is outlined in Figure 6. The algorithm left unfolds Obligation 1 into 2a and 2b (not shown). Obligation 2a can be proved directly. Obligation 2b is now split into 3a and 3b. For 3a, we add the constraint $Id \neq N$, and for 3b we add the complementary constraint $Id = N$. We omit detailing 3b, and we proceed with explaining the proof of 3a. Obligation 3a is as follows:
3a: $abs(N-1, K'', X'-B), bit(B), K''[Id_2] = 0, 1 \leq Id_2 < N$
$\models abs(N, \langle\langle K'', N, B\rangle, Id_2, 1\rangle, X'+1)$

We now perform the crucial step of applying coinduction to Obligation 3a. This is permitted because the lhs of 1 is entailed by the lhs goal 3a. To see this, perform the substitutions $[N-1/N, X'-B/X']$ on Obligation 1. The result of applying coinduction is:
4: $abs(N-1, \langle K'', Id_2, 1\rangle, X'-B+1), bit(B), K''[Id_2] = 0, 1 \leq Id_2 < N$
$\models abs(N, \langle\langle K'', N, B\rangle, Id_2, 1\rangle, X'+1)$

We now right unfold this into Obligation 5, and prove Obligation 5 by constraint reasoning, which is omitted.

5.2 Bakery Algorithm (Atomic Version)

To show a more substantial example, consider the bakery mutual exclusion algorithm [17]. Here we consider, somewhat unrealistically, a simplified presentation where the test for entry into the critical section, which considers the collection of all processes, is assumed to be performed atomically.

```
process(id) {
⟨0⟩ t[id] = max(t[1],...,t[N]) + 1;
⟨1⟩ await(forall j!=id : t[id]==0 ∨ t[id]<t[j]);
⟨2⟩ t[id] = 0; goto ⟨0⟩ }

sys(K,T,N) :- K[Id]=0, 1≤Id≤N, max(T,N,X), sys(⟨K,Id,1⟩, ⟨T,Id,X+1⟩, N).
sys(K,T,N) :- K[Id]=1, 1≤Id≤N, crit(T,N,Id), sys(⟨K,Id,2⟩,T,N).
sys(K,T,N) :- K[Id]=2, 1≤Id≤N, sys(⟨K,Id,0⟩, ⟨T,Id,0⟩,N).
```

$$abs(K,T,1) \text{ :- } (K[1]=0, T[1]=0) \vee (K[1]=1, T[1]>0).$$
$$abs(K,T,N) \text{ :- } N>1, ((K[N]=0, T[N]=) \vee (K[N]=1, T[N]>0)), abs(K,T,N-1).$$

$$max(T,1,X) \text{ :- } X \geq T[1].$$
$$max(T,N,X) \text{ :- } N>1, X \geq T[N], max(T,N-1,X).$$

$$crit(T,1,Id) \text{ :- } Id=1 \vee T[1]=0 \vee T[1]>T[Id].$$
$$crit(T,N,Id) \text{ :- } N>1, (Id=N \vee T[N]=0 \vee T[N]>T[Id]), crit(T,N-1,Id).$$

Fig. 7. Transitions and Predicates for Bakery

We represent the transitions and the recursive abstractions used in Figure 7.

A closed computation tree is depicted in Figure 8. The initial state $\mathcal{G}_0$ is where the counter is all zeroes, and the local variables $T[]$ (the "tickets") are also all zero. The state $\mathcal{G}_1$ denotes one transition of one process, symbolically denoted by Id, from point $\langle 0\rangle$ to $\langle 1\rangle$. At this point we perform an abstraction to obtain a state $\overline{\mathcal{G}_1}$ which contains not one but a number of program points at 1. This abstraction also constrains the tickets so that if a counter is zero, then the corresponding ticket is also zero.

No further abstraction is needed. That is, the computation tree under $\overline{\mathcal{G}_1}$ is in fact closed, as indicated. Note that mutual exclusion then follows from the fact that from state $\mathcal{G}_{2b}$ or $\mathcal{G}_{3a}$, the only states in which a process is in the critical section, there is no possible transition by a different process to enter the section. This is emphasized by the the notation "infeasible" in Figure 8.

One of the conditions to show closure is that the (leaf) state $\mathcal{G}_{3a}$ is subsumed by $\mathcal{G}_{2b}$. (There are several others, eg. that $\mathcal{G}_{3c}$ is subsumed by $\overline{\mathcal{G}_1}$. We shall omit considering these.) This is formalized as:

$$\begin{aligned}\text{D.1}: \; & abs(K',T',N), crit(T',N,Id_1), max(T',N,X), 1 \leq Id_1 \leq N,\\ & K'[Id_1]=1, 1 \leq Id_2 \leq N, \langle K',Id_1,2\rangle[Id_2]=0\\ & \models abs(?S,\langle T',Id_2,X+1\rangle,N), crit(\langle T',Id_2,X+1\rangle,N,?Id_3),\\ & 1 \leq ?Id_3 \leq N, ?S[?Id_3]=1, \langle\langle K',Id_1,2\rangle,Id_2,1\rangle = \langle ?S,?Id_3,2\rangle\end{aligned}$$

In the above, the prefix '?' denotes existentially-quantified variables. For space reasons, we omit the detailed proof. Instead, we depict in the proof tree of Figure 8 the major steps that can be used in the proof.

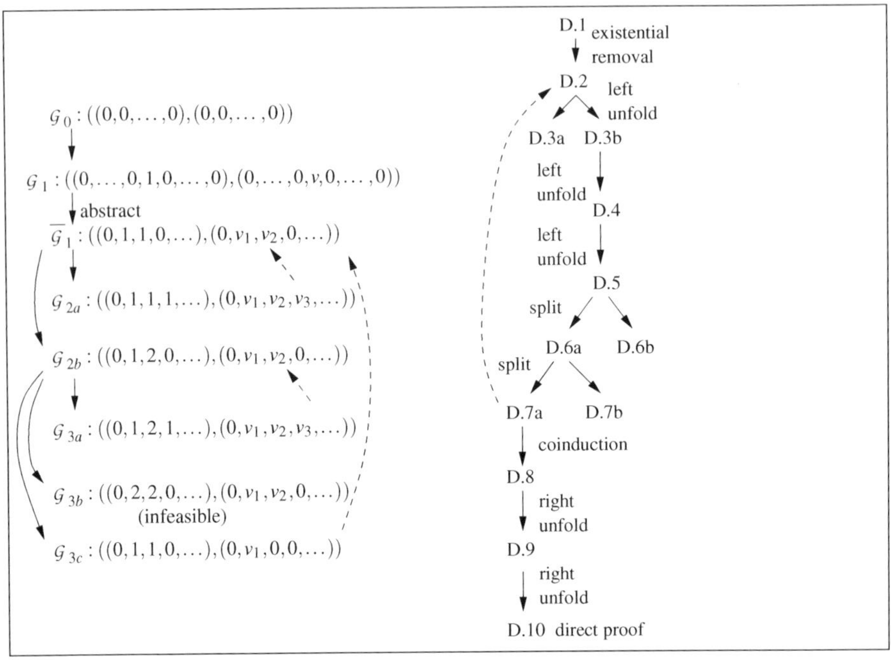

Fig. 8. Computation and Proof Trees of Bakery Algorithm

5.3 Original Bakery Algorithm

We finally discuss the original version of the bakery algorithm [17]. Our purpose here is to demonstrate abstraction beyond an array of variables. Here, abstraction is needed because there is an additional loop implementing the incremental request for entry into the critical section. To our knowledge, we provide the first systematic proof of the original bakery algorithm. Our proof technique is semiautomatic, where the user only provide the declarative specification of loop invariants.

We show the program in Figure 9. We focus on the replacement of the *await* blocking primitive in Figure 7 by a loop from $\langle 3 \rangle$ to $\langle 8 \rangle$, which itself contains two internal busy-waiting loops. Figure 9 also shows the transition system of the loop, and the predicate that is used. In the program and elsewhere, the operator $\prec$ is defined as follows: when $(a,b) \prec (c,d)$ holds, then either $a < b$ or when $a = b$, then $b < d$.

Figure 10 depicts an abstract computation tree. The state $\mathcal{G}_2$ represents entry into the outerloop, and $\overline{\mathcal{G}_2}$ its abstraction. $\mathcal{G}_{3a}$ is its exit. The states $\mathcal{G}_{3b}$ and $\mathcal{G}_{ba}$ represent the two inner loops. The interesting aspect is the abstraction indicated. It alone is sufficient to produce a closed tree. More specifically, we abstract $\mathcal{G}_2$: $\mathbf{sys}(K',C,T,J',N), K[Id_1] = 3, K' = \langle K, Id_1, 4\rangle, J' = \langle J, Id_1, 1\rangle$ into $\overline{\mathcal{G}_2}$: $\mathbf{sys}(K',C,T,J',N), K'[Id_1] = 4, crit(C,T,J',Id_1), 1 \leq J'[Id_1] \leq N+1$.

```
    process(id) {
⟨0⟩     c[id] = 1;
⟨1⟩     t[id] = 1 + maximum(t[1],...,t[n]);
⟨2⟩     c[id] = 0;
⟨3⟩     j[id] = 1;
⟨4⟩     while (j ≤ N) {
⟨5⟩         if (c[j]!=0) goto ⟨5⟩;
⟨6⟩         if (t[j]!=0 && (t[j],j) ≺ (t[i],i)) goto ⟨6⟩;
⟨7⟩         j = j+1; }
⟨8⟩     goto ⟨0⟩; }

sys(K,C,T,J,N) :- K[Id]=3, sys(⟨K,Id,4⟩,C,T,⟨J,Id,1⟩,N)
sys(K,C,T,J,N) :- K[Id]=4, J[Id]≤ N, sys(⟨K,Id,5⟩,C,T,J,N)
sys(K,C,T,J,N) :- K[Id]=4, J[Id]>N, sys(⟨K,Id,8⟩,C,T,J,N)
sys(K,C,T,J,N) :- K[Id]=5, C[J]≠ 0, sys(K,C,T,J,N)
sys(K,C,T,J,N) :- K[Id]=5, C[J]=0, sys(⟨K,Id,6⟩,C,T,J,N)
sys(K,C,T,J,N) :- K[Id]=6, T[J]≠0, ((T[J],J)≺(T[Id],Id)), sys(K,C,T,J,N)
sys(K,C,T,J,N) :- K[Id]=6, (T[J]=0∨((T[Id],Id)≺(T[J],J)),
        sys(⟨K,Id,7⟩,C,T,J,N)
sys(K,C,T,J,N) :- K[Id]=7, sys(⟨K,Id,4⟩,C,T,⟨J,Id,J[Id]+1⟩,N)
```

$crit(C,T,1,Id)$:- $Id = 1 \vee (C[1] = 0, (T[Id], Id) \prec (T[1], 1))$
$crit(C,T,N,Id)$:- $Id = N \vee (C[N] = 0, (T[Id], Id) \prec (T[N], N)), crit(C,T,N-1,Id)$.

Fig. 9. Original Bakery with Transitions of the Entry Loop and Predicate

The state subsumption is formalized as the entailment $\mathcal{G}_6 \models \overline{\mathcal{G}}_2$ as follows:

$$K'[Id_1] = 4, crit(C,T,J',Id_1), 1 \leq J'[Id_1] \leq N+1, K'[Id_2] = 4,$$
$$K'' = \langle K', Id_2, 5\rangle, K''[Id_3] = 5, K''' = \langle K', Id_3, 6\rangle, C[J'[Id_3]] = 3,$$
$$T[J'] = 0 \vee (T[Id_4], Id_4) \prec (T[J'[Id_4]], J'[Id_4]), K'''[Id_4] = 6, K^{iv} = \langle K''', Id_4, 7\rangle,$$
$$K^{iv}[Id_5] = 7, K^{v} = \langle K^{iv}, Id_5, 4\rangle, J'' = \langle J', Id, J'[Id_5]+1\rangle$$
$$\models crit(C,T,J'',?Id_6), K^{v}[Id_1] = 4, 1 \leq J''[?Id_6] \leq N+1$$

which can be proven along the lines indicated above. We omit the details.

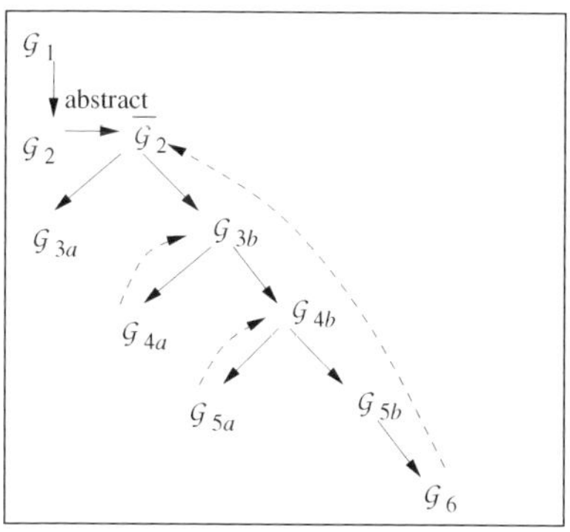

Fig. 10. Abstract Computation Tree for Entry Loop

6 Concluding Remarks

We presented a language of recursively defined formulas about arrays of variables for the purpose of specifying abstract states of parameterized systems. We then present a symbolic transition framework for these formulas. This can produce a finite representation of the behaviour of the system from which safety properties can be ascertained. The main result is a two step algorithm for proving entailment of these formulas. In the first step, we employ a key concept of coindunction in order to reduce the recursive definitions to formulas about arrays and integers. In the second, we reduced these formulas to integer formulas.

Though we considered only safety properties in this paper, it is easy to see that our notion of closed abstract tree does in fact contain the key information needed to argue about termination and liveness. Essentially, this is because our framework is equiped with symbolic transitions. What is needed is to show that in every path ending in a subsumed state, that the execution from the parent state decreases a well founded measure.

References

1. Abdulla, P.A., Delzanno, G., Rezine, A.: Parameterized verification of infinite-state processes with global constraints. In: Damm, W., Hermanns, H. (eds.) CAV 2007. LNCS, vol. 4590, pp. 145–157. Springer, Heidelberg (2007)
2. Roychoudhury, A., Ramakrishnan, I.V.: Automated inductive verification of parameterized protocols. In: Berry, G., Comon, H., Finkel, A. (eds.) CAV 2001. LNCS, vol. 2102, pp. 25–37. Springer, Heidelberg (2001)
3. Clarke, E.M., Talupur, M., Veith, H.: Environment abstraction for parameterized verification. In: Emerson, E.A., Namjoshi, K.S. (eds.) VMCAI 2006. LNCS, vol. 3855, pp. 126–141. Springer, Heidelberg (2006)
4. Lahiri, S., Bryant, R.: Indexed predicate discovery for unbounded system verification. In: Alur, R., Peled, D.A. (eds.) CAV 2004. LNCS, vol. 3114, pp. 135–147. Springer, Heidelberg (2004)
5. McMillan, K.L.: Induction in compositional model checking. In: Emerson, E.A., Sistla, A.P. (eds.) CAV 2000. LNCS, vol. 1855, pp. 312–327. Springer, Heidelberg (2000)
6. Pnueli, A., Ruah, S., Zuck, L.: Automatic deductive verification with invisible invariants. In: Margaria, T., Yi, W. (eds.) TACAS 2001. LNCS, vol. 2031, p. 82. Springer, Heidelberg (2001)
7. Pnueli, A., Xu, J., Zuck, L.: Liveness with $(0, 1, \infty)$ counter abstraction. In: Brinksma, E., Larsen, K.G. (eds.) CAV 2002. LNCS, vol. 2404, p. 107. Springer, Heidelberg (2002)
8. Cousot, P., Cousot, R.: Abstract interpretation: A unified lattice model for static analysis. In: 4th POPL, pp. 238–252. ACM Press, New York (1977)
9. Jaffar, J., Santosa, A.E., Voicu, R.: A coinduction rule for entailment of recursively defined properties. In: Stuckey, P.J. (ed.) CP 2008. LNCS, vol. 5202, pp. 493–508. Springer, Heidelberg (2008)
10. McCarthy, J.: Towards a mathematical science of computation. In: Popplewell, C.M. (ed.) IFIP Congress 1962. North-Holland, Amsterdam (1983)
11. Jaffar, J., Maher, M.J.: Constraint logic programming: A survey. J. LP 19/20, 503–581 (1994)
12. Dijkstra, E.W., Scholten, C.S.: Predicate Calculus and Program Semantics. Springer, Heidelberg (1989)
13. Barrett, C., Dill, D.L., Levitt, J.R.: Validity checking for combinations of theories with equality. In: Srivas, M., Camilleri, A. (eds.) FMCAD 1996. LNCS, vol. 1166, pp. 187–201. Springer, Heidelberg (1996)
14. Barrett, C., Berezin, S.: CVC Lite: A new implementation of the cooperating validity checker. In: Alur, R., Peled, D.A. (eds.) CAV 2004. LNCS, vol. 3114, pp. 515–518. Springer, Heidelberg (2004)
15. Nelson, G., Oppen, D.C.: Simplification by cooperating decision procedures. ACM Transactions on Programming Languages and Systems 1(2), 245–257 (1979)
16. Jaffar, J., Lassez, J.L.: Reasoning about array segments. In: ECAI 1982, pp. 62–66 (1982)
17. Lamport, L.: A new solution of Dijkstra's concurrent programming problem. Comm. ACM 17(8), 453–455 (1974)

Abstract Model Checking without Computing the Abstraction

Stefano Tonetta*

FBK-Irst
tonettas@fbk.eu

Abstract. Abstraction is a fundamental technique that enables the verification of large systems. In symbolic model checking, abstractions are defined by formulas that relate concrete and abstract variables. In predicate abstraction, the abstract variables are equivalent to some predicates over the concrete variables.

In order to apply model checking on the abstract state space, it is usually necessary to compute a quantifier-free formula that is equivalent to the abstract transition relation. In predicate abstraction, the quantifier elimination can be obtained by solving an ALLSAT problem. In many practical cases, this computation results into a bottleneck.

In this paper, we propose a new algorithm that combines abstraction with bounded model checking and k-induction. The algorithm does not rely on quantifier elimination, but encodes the model checking problem over the abstract state space into SAT problems. The algorithm is a novelty in the state-of-the-art of abstract model checking because it avoids computing the abstraction. An experimental evaluation with case studies taken from an industrial project shows that the new algorithm is more efficient and reaches in some cases a time improvement that is exponential in the number of predicates.

1 Introduction

Model Checking (MC) [14,26] is an automatic technique to verify if a system satisfies a property. The main problem of MC is the state-space explosion, i.e., the system is often too large to be verified. *Abstraction* [8] and symbolic representation [3] are two major classes of techniques broadly adopted to tackle the problem.

Abstraction defines a relationship between the states of the concrete system and the states of a smaller system, which is more amenable for the verification. Typically, abstraction over-approximates the semantics of the system so that if a property holds in the abstract system, then it holds also in the concrete one. A particular abstraction technique widely used with MC is *predicate abstraction*

* The author would like to thank the Provincia Autonoma di Trento for the support with the project ANACONDA, and A. Cimatti, M. Roveri, and V. Schuppan for helpful discussions and feedback.

A. Cavalcanti and D. Dams (Eds.): FM 2009, LNCS 5850, pp. 89–105, 2009.

[15,11], where a set of predicates is chosen so that the abstract state space observes only the evolution of these predicates in the original system.

Symbolic model checking [3] represents sets of states and transitions with formulas. Symbolic algorithms manipulate formulas exploiting BDD-based or SAT-based techniques. SMT solvers, which combine SAT techniques with solvers for decidable first-order theories, are used when the system is described with first-order formulas. Bounded Model Checking (BMC) [2] is a symbolic technique that looks for counterexamples only with a bounded length k. BMC problems are encoded into SAT problems, which are then solved using either a SAT solver or an SMT solver, depending on the language used to describe the system. k-induction [27] is a technique used to prove that, if there is no counterexample of length up to k, then we can conclude that the property holds. The conditions to prove that k is sufficiently large are encoded into SAT problems.

In order to combine symbolic model checking with abstraction, it is necessary to compute a quantifier-free formula representing the transition relation of the abstract system. This is typically obtained by eliminating the quantifiers in the definition of the abstraction. When the abstract state space is finite, as in the case of predicate abstraction, the abstract transition relation can be obtained by solving an ALLSAT problem, i.e., by enumerating the models satisfying the formula that defines the abstraction. In some cases, however, quantifier elimination is not possible, and in practice, also for predicate abstraction, results to be a bottleneck (see, e.g., [10,19,4]).

In this paper, we propose a new algorithm for solving the problem of model checking an abstract system. The idea is to embed the definition of the abstraction in the BMC and k-induction encodings. This way, we can verify the correctness of the abstract system without computing the abstraction. The algorithm can be applied to predicate abstraction, but also to infinite-state abstraction such as abstraction obtained by projection. We extend the abstract BMC and k-induction to check the language emptiness of infinite-state fair transition systems.

With regard to the standard approach to abstract model checking which computes the abstraction upfront, the new algorithm considers only the parts of the abstract state space that are relevant to the search. The solver is used to solve a satisfiability problem rather than to enumerate all possible solutions. With regard to model checking the concrete state space, the new algorithm exploits the abstraction and solves more problems. When the abstract state space is finite as in the case of predicate abstraction, k-induction is guaranteed to terminate, which is not the case for the concrete infinite-state space.

We performed an experimental evaluation on benchmarks extracted from an industrial project on requirements validation. The results show that the new algorithm can solve problems where the computation of the abstraction is not feasible, while in general is more efficient and can yield a time improvement that is exponential in the number of predicates.

The paper is structured as follows: in Sec. 2, we describe the project that motivated our research; in Sec. 3, we overview the background of symbolic model checking and abstraction; in Sec. 4, we present the new algorithm for model checking an abstract system; in Sec. 5, we present the experimental evaluation; in Sec. 6, we discuss the related work; finally, in Sec. 7, we conclude and hint some future directions.

2 Motivations

2.1 Requirements Validation

Our work is motivated by a project funded by the European Railway Agency (`http://www.era.europa.eu`). The aim of the project was to develop a methodology supported by a tool for the validation of the System Requirement Specification of the European Train Control System (ETCS). The ETCS specification is a set of requirements related to the automatic supervision of the location and speed performed by the train on-board system. Building on emerging formal methods for requirements validation, the requirements are formalized in first-order temporal formulas and the analysis is based on a series of satisfiability problems [5]. The satisfiability of the formulas is reduced to the problem of language emptiness of fair transition systems. We use a BMC encoding with loops to find accepting paths in the transition systems. When the problem cannot be solved with BMC, we use predicate abstraction to check if the language of the transition system is empty.

The systems generated by the process of requirements validation are very large including hundreds of Boolean variables and tens of real variables. Unlike in the standard setting of MC, there is no property that can guide the abstraction and the source of inconsistency is not known a priori. Even when a set of predicates of the abstraction is manually defined, proving the language emptiness of such systems is challenging, because the computation of the abstraction becomes prohibitive with a dozen of predicates.

3 Background

3.1 Fair Transition Systems

Fair Transition Systems (FTSs) [21] are a symbolic representation of infinite-state automata. In symbolic model checking [3], FTSs are used to represent both the system and the property. Set of states are expressed by means of logical formulas over a given set $\mathcal{V}$ of variables, while set of transitions are represented by formulas over $\mathcal{V}$ and the set $\mathcal{V}'$ of next variables $\{v'\}_{v\in\mathcal{V}}$, where v' represents the next value of v. Symbolic algorithms manipulate such formulas in order to check if the system satisfies the property. We assume that the formulas belong to a decidable fragment of first-order logic for which we have a satisfiability solver. We use the abbreviations sat and unsat for satisfiable and unsatisfiable, resp.

Definition 1. *A Fair Transition System (FTS) is a tuple* $\langle \mathcal{V}, I, T, \mathcal{F} \rangle$, *where*

- $\mathcal{V}$ *is the set of variables,*
- $I(\mathcal{V})$ *is a formula that represents the initial condition,*
- $T(\mathcal{V}, \mathcal{V}')$ *is a formula that represents the transition relation,*
- $\mathcal{F} = \{F_1, ..., F_n\}$ *is a set of formulas representing the fairness conditions.*

The set $\mathcal{S}_\mathcal{V}$ of states is given by all truth assignments to the variables $\mathcal{V}$. Given a state s, we use s' to denote the corresponding truth assignment to the next state variables, i.e. $s' = s[\mathcal{V}'/\mathcal{V}]$. A state s is initial iff $s \models I(\mathcal{V})$. Given two states s_1 and s_2, there exists a transition between s_1 and s_2 iff $s_1, s_2' \models T(\mathcal{V}, \mathcal{V}')$. If π is a sequence of states we denote with π_i the i-th state of the sequence. If π is finite we denote with $|\pi|$ the length of π. A finite [resp. infinite] path of an FTS is a finite [resp. infinite] sequence of states π such that, for all i, $1 \leq i < |\pi|$ [resp. $i \geq 1$], there exists a transition between π_i and π_{i+1} ($\pi_i, \pi_{i+1}' \models T$). A path π is initial iff π_1 is an initial state ($\pi_1 \models I$). An infinite path π is fair iff, for all $F \in \mathcal{F}$, for infinitely many i, $\pi_i \models F$.

Given an FTS M and a formula $\varphi(\mathcal{V})$, the reachability problem is the problem of finding an initial finite path $s_0, ..., s_k$ of M such that $s_k \models \varphi$. Model checking of invariant properties can be reduced to a reachability problem.

The language of an FTS is given by the set of all initial fair paths. Given an FTS M, the language emptiness problem is the problem of finding an initial fair path of M. Model checking and satisfiability of linear-time temporal formulas are typically reduced to the emptiness language problem of equivalent FTSs [28]. Thus, also the validation of requirements expressed in temporal logic is typically solved by looking for an initial fair path in the FTS equivalent to. the conjunction of the requirements.

Example 1. Consider a system $\langle \{\delta_t, t, e\}, \mathit{true}, T_c \wedge T_d \wedge T_e, \{F_d, F_e\} \rangle$ where:

- δ_t is a non-negative real variable representing the time elapsed at every step.
- t is a timer (real variable) that progresses when $\delta_t > 0$ and can be reset when $\delta_t = 0$.
- e is a Boolean variable that can change only when $\delta_t = 0$.
- $T_c := \delta_t > 0 \rightarrow (e' = e \wedge t' - t = \delta_t)$ represents the constraint of a step with elapsing time.
- $T_d := \delta_t = 0 \rightarrow (t' = t \vee t' = 0)$ represents the constraint of a discrete step.
- $T_e := e \rightarrow (e' \wedge t' = t)$ states that when e becomes (non-deterministically) true both e and t do not change anymore.
- $F_d := \delta_t > 0$ forces the progress of time.
- $F_e := e$ forces the Boolean variable e to become eventually true.

The system has an infinite number of initial paths that reach the formula e, but no infinite fair path, because when e becomes true the time is forced to freeze. For example, the path shown in Fig. 1 is an initial path of the system, but cannot be extended to any fair path.

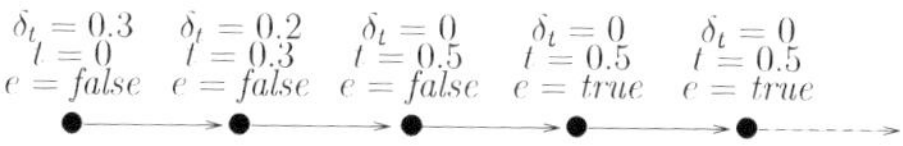

Fig. 1. Example of path

3.2 Abstraction

Abstraction [8] is used to reduce the search space while preserving the satisfaction of some properties. In MC, the abstraction is usually obtained by means of a surjective function $\alpha : \mathcal{S}_{\mathcal{V}} \to \mathcal{S}_{\hat{\mathcal{V}}}$, called abstraction function, that maps states of an FTS M into states of a smaller FTS $\hat{M}$. The concretization function $\gamma : \mathcal{S}_{\hat{\mathcal{V}}} \to 2^{\mathcal{S}_{\mathcal{V}}}$ is defined as $\gamma(\hat{s}) = \{s \in \mathcal{S}_{\mathcal{V}} \mid \alpha(s) = \hat{s}\}$. The abstraction function α is symbolically represented by a formula $H_\alpha(\mathcal{V}, \hat{\mathcal{V}})$ such that $s, \hat{s} \models H_\alpha$ iff $\alpha(s) = \hat{s}$.

Once the set $\hat{\mathcal{V}}$ of abstract variables and the relation H_α are given, the abstraction $\hat{M}_\alpha$ is obtained by existentially quantifying the variables of M.

Definition 2. *Given an FTS M, a set $\hat{\mathcal{V}}$ of abstract variables and the relation H_α, the abstract FTS $\hat{M}_\alpha = \langle \hat{\mathcal{V}}, \hat{I}_\alpha, \hat{T}_\alpha, \hat{\mathcal{F}}_\alpha \rangle$ is defined as follows:*

- $\hat{I}_\alpha(\hat{\mathcal{V}}) := \exists \mathcal{V}(I(\mathcal{V}) \wedge H_\alpha(\mathcal{V}, \hat{\mathcal{V}}))$,
- $\hat{T}_\alpha(\hat{\mathcal{V}}, \hat{\mathcal{V}}') := \exists \mathcal{V} \exists \mathcal{V}'(T(\mathcal{V}, \mathcal{V}') \wedge H_\alpha(\mathcal{V}, \hat{\mathcal{V}}) \wedge H_\alpha(\mathcal{V}', \hat{\mathcal{V}}'))$.
- $\hat{\mathcal{F}}_\alpha = \{\hat{F}_\alpha\}_{F \in \mathcal{F}}$ *where* $\hat{F}_\alpha(\hat{\mathcal{V}}) := \exists \mathcal{V}(F(\mathcal{V}) \wedge H_\alpha(\mathcal{V}, \hat{\mathcal{V}}))$.

Given a formula φ, we define its abstract version $\hat{\varphi}_\alpha$ as $\exists \mathcal{V}(\varphi(\mathcal{V}) \wedge H_\alpha(\mathcal{V}, \hat{\mathcal{V}}))$.

The abstraction over-approximates the reachability of an FTS M, in the sense that if a condition is reachable in M, then also its abstract version is reachable in $\hat{M}_\alpha$. Similarly, if M has an initial fair path, the same holds for $\hat{M}_\alpha$. Thus, if we prove that a set of states is not reachable in $\hat{M}_\alpha$, or that $\hat{M}_\alpha$ does not have any initial fair path, the same can be concluded for the concrete FTS M.

Predicate abstraction. In Predicate Abstraction [15], the abstract state-space is described with a set of predicates; each predicate is represented by an abstract variable. Given an FTS M, we select a set $\mathbb{P}$ of predicates, such that each predicate $P \in \mathbb{P}$ is a formula over the variables $\mathcal{V}$ that characterizes relevant facts of the system. For every $P \in \mathbb{P}$, we introduce a new abstract variable v_P and define $\mathcal{V}_{\mathbb{P}}$ as $\{v_P\}_{P \in \mathbb{P}}$.

The abstraction function $\alpha_{\mathbb{P}}$ is defined as $\alpha_{\mathbb{P}}(s) := \{v_P \in \mathcal{V}_{\mathbb{P}} \mid s \models P\}$, while $H_{\mathbb{P}}$ is defined as follows:

$$H_{\mathbb{P}}(\mathcal{V}, \mathcal{V}_{\mathbb{P}}) := \bigwedge_{P \in \mathbb{P}} v_P \leftrightarrow P(\mathcal{V}) \tag{1}$$

Example 2. Consider the system of Ex. 1 and the predicates $\delta_t > 0$ and e. If we eliminate the quantifiers in the definition of abstraction, we obtain the FTS $\langle \{v_{\delta_t}, v_e\}, true, v_e \to (v_e \wedge \neg v_{\delta_t}), \{v_{\delta_t}, v_e\} \rangle$. This abstract system has finite states and it is easy to see that it does not have fair paths.

3.3 Bounded Model Checking

Bounded Model Checking (BMC) ([2]) considers only initial paths of length up to a certain bound. Given a bound k, an FTS M and a formula $\varphi(\mathcal{V})$, the bounded reachability problem is the problem of finding, for some $j \leq k$ an initial finite path $s_0, ..., s_j$ of M such that $s_j \models \varphi$. The problem is usually reduced to a satisfiability problem.

In the following, given a set X of variables, we use several copies of X, one for each state of the path we are looking for. We will denote with X_i the i-th copy of X. Thus, $V_i = \{v_i\}_{v \in \mathcal{V}}$, where v_i represents the i-th copy of v.

Definition 3. *Given an FTS M, and a bound k, the formula $PATH_{M,k}$ is defined as follows:*

$$PATH_{M,k} := \bigwedge_{1 \leq h \leq k} T(\mathcal{V}_{h-1}, \mathcal{V}_h) \tag{2}$$

Definition 4. *Given an FTS M, a bound k, and a formula φ, the formula $BMC_{M,k,\varphi}$ is defined as follows:*

$$BMC_{M,k,\varphi} := I(\mathcal{V}_0) \wedge PATH_{M,k} \wedge \varphi(\mathcal{V}_k) \tag{3}$$

The formula $BMC_{M,k,\varphi}$ encodes the bounded reachability problem.

Theorem 1. *$BMC_{M,k,\varphi}$ is sat iff there exists an initial path of length k reaching φ.*

Bounded model checking with fair paths. A similar encoding is often used to find lasso-shape initial fair paths of length up to k.

Definition 5. *Given an FTS M, and a bound k, the formula $BMC^{loop}_{M,k}$ is defined as follows:*

$$BMC^{loop}_{M,k} := I(\mathcal{V}_0) \wedge PATH_{M,k} \wedge \bigvee_{0 \leq l < k,\, v \in V} \bigwedge v_l = v_k \wedge \bigwedge_{F \in \mathcal{F},\, l \leq h < k} \bigvee F(\mathcal{V}_h) \tag{4}$$

As $BMC_{M,k,\varphi}$ is an approximation of the reachability problem, $BMC^{loop}_{M,k}$ is an approximation of the language emptiness problem: if the formula is sat, the language is not empty; otherwise, we have to increase the bound. However, if the state space is not finite, it is not guaranteed that there exists a bound sufficient to solve the problem.

3.4 K-Induction

K-induction [27] is a technique that proves that if a set of states is not reachable in k steps, then it is not reachable at all. On the lines of the induction principle, it consists of a base step, which solves the bounded reachability problem with a given bound k of steps, and an inductive step, which concludes that k is sufficient

input : FTS $M = \langle \mathcal{V}, I, T \rangle$ and formula φ
output : YES if φ is reachable in M, NO otherwise
begin
    k:=0;
    if $BMC_{M,k,\varphi}$ *is sat* **then**
        return YES
    else if $KINDFW_{M,k+1}$ *or* $KINDBW_{M,k+1,\varphi}$ *is unsat* **then**
        return NO
    else
        k++;
end

Algorithm 1. K-induction(KIND)

to solve the (unbounded) reachability problem. The idea of the inductive step is to check either if the initial states cannot reach new (non-visited) states in $k+1$ steps, or the target set of states cannot be reached in $k+1$ steps. These checks can be solved by means of satisfiability.

Definition 6. *Given an FTS M, and a bound k, the formula $SIMPLEPATH_{M,k}$ is defined as follows:*

$$SIMPLEPATH_{M,k} := PATH_{M,k} \wedge \bigwedge_{0 \le i < j \le k} \neg \bigwedge_{v \in \mathcal{V}} v_i = v_j \tag{5}$$

Definition 7. *Given an FTS M, and a bound k, the formula $KINDFW_{M,k}$ is defined as follows:*

$$KINDFW_{M,k} := I(\mathcal{V}_0) \wedge SIMPLEPATH_{M,k} \tag{6}$$

Theorem 2. *If $KINDFW_{M,k+1}$ is unsat, then M does not have an initial simple path with more than k states.*

Definition 8. *Given an FTS M, a formula φ, and a bound k, the formula $KINDBW_{M,k,\varphi}$ is defined as follows:*

$$KINDBW_{M,k,\varphi} := SIMPLEPATH_{M,k} \wedge \varphi(\mathcal{V}_k) \tag{7}$$

Theorem 3. *If $KINDBW_{M,k+1,\varphi}$ is unsat, M does not have a simple path reaching φ with more than k states.*

Corollary 1. *If, for all $i \le k$, $BMC_{M,i,\varphi}$ is unsat and, either $KINDFW_{M,k+1}$ or $KINDBW_{M,k+1,\varphi}$ is unsat as well, then φ is not reachable in M.*

Corollary 1 gives rise to Algorithm 3.4, where the formulas are iteratively checked for increasing values of k. In case M is finite-state, Algorithm 3.4 is guaranteed to terminate. The works in [27] and [13] exploit stronger version of $KINDFW_{M,k}$ and $KINDBW_{M,k,\varphi}$ that consider the negation of the initial condition I and the target condition φ respectively.

3.5 Abstract Model Checking with Abstraction

The standard way to solve the reachability problem or the emptiness problem on the abstraction of an FTS M is first to compute the FTS $\hat{M}$ and then to apply model checking techniques on the abstract state space. We denote with AMC_{reach} such procedure when it solves the reachability problem, while with AMC_{loop} the similar procedure that checks the language emptiness of the abstraction of M.

4 Abstract Model Checking without Abstraction

4.1 General Idea

The key idea of the paper is to embed the definition of the abstraction in the encoding of BMC. This highlights the possibility of pre-computing the quantification of the abstract variables. Let us consider the abstract version of the formula 3, namely:

$$\hat{I}_\alpha(\hat{\mathcal{V}}_0) \wedge \bigwedge_{1 \leq h \leq k} \hat{T}_\alpha(\hat{\mathcal{V}}_{h-1}, \hat{\mathcal{V}}_h) \wedge \hat{\varphi}_\alpha(\hat{\mathcal{V}}_k) \equiv$$
$$\hat{I}_\alpha(\hat{\mathcal{V}}_0) \wedge \hat{T}_\alpha(\hat{\mathcal{V}}_0, \hat{\mathcal{V}}_1) \ldots \wedge \hat{T}_\alpha(\hat{\mathcal{V}}_{k-1}, \hat{\mathcal{V}}_k) \wedge \hat{\varphi}_\alpha(\hat{\mathcal{V}}_k)$$

If we substitute $\hat{I}_\alpha$, $\hat{T}_\alpha$, and $\hat{\varphi}_\alpha$ with their definitions, we obtain:

$$I(\mathcal{V}_0) \wedge H_\alpha(\mathcal{V}_0, \hat{\mathcal{V}}_0) \wedge H_\alpha(\overline{\mathcal{V}}_0, \hat{\mathcal{V}}_0) \wedge T(\overline{\mathcal{V}}_0, \mathcal{V}_1) \wedge H_\alpha(\mathcal{V}_1, \hat{\mathcal{V}}_1) \wedge \ldots \wedge$$
$$H_\alpha(\overline{\mathcal{V}}_{k-1}, \hat{\mathcal{V}}_{k-1}) \wedge T(\overline{\mathcal{V}}_{k-1}, \mathcal{V}_k) \wedge H_\alpha(\mathcal{V}_k, \hat{\mathcal{V}}_k) \wedge H_\alpha(\overline{\mathcal{V}}_k, \hat{\mathcal{V}}_k) \wedge \varphi(\overline{\mathcal{V}}_k)$$

where quantifiers have been lifted at top level by renaming some bound variables.

Note that the scope of abstract variables $\hat{\mathcal{V}}_i$ is limited to two copies of the abstraction relation. Let us define the formula $EQ_\alpha(\mathcal{V}, \overline{\mathcal{V}})$ as

$$EQ_\alpha(\mathcal{V}, \overline{\mathcal{V}}) := \exists \hat{\mathcal{V}}(H_\alpha(\mathcal{V}, \hat{\mathcal{V}}) \wedge H_\alpha(\overline{\mathcal{V}}, \hat{\mathcal{V}})) \tag{8}$$

EQ_α encodes the fact that two concrete states correspond to the same abstract state. Formally, $s, \overline{s} \models EQ_\alpha$ iff $\alpha(s) = \alpha(\overline{s})$. We can use EQ_α to provide abstract versions of the formulas used for BMC and k-induction. Intuitively, instead of having a contiguous sequence of transitions, the encoding represents a sequence of disconnected transitions where every gap between two transitions is forced to lay in the same abstract state (see Fig. 2).

In most of abstraction, the quantifier in EQ_α can be easily eliminated. For example in predicate abstraction:

$$EQ_\alpha \equiv EQ_{\mathbb{P}}(\mathcal{V}, \overline{\mathcal{V}}) := \bigwedge_{P \in \mathbb{P}} P(\mathcal{V}) \leftrightarrow P(\overline{\mathcal{V}}) \tag{9}$$

Another interesting case is the abstraction by projection where the abstract variables are a subset $\tilde{\mathcal{V}}$ of the concrete variables and the non-abstract variables are quantified out. In this case,

$$EQ_\alpha \equiv EQ_{\tilde{\mathcal{V}}}(\mathcal{V}, \overline{\mathcal{V}}) := \bigwedge_{v \in \tilde{\mathcal{V}}} v = \overline{v} \tag{10}$$

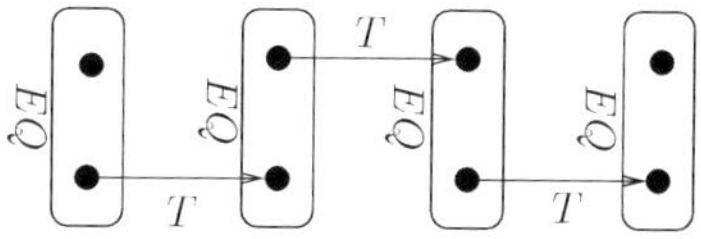

Fig. 2. Abstract path

4.2 Paths and Simple Paths

We first define the abstract version of the $PATH_{M,k}$ and $SIMPLEPATH_{M,k}$ used in the encoding of BMC and k-induction.

Definition 9. *Given an FTS $M = \langle \mathcal{V}, I, T \rangle$, an abstraction function α, and a bound k, the formula $\widehat{PATH}_{M,\alpha,k}$ is defined as follows:*

$$\widehat{PATH}_{M,\alpha,k} := \bigwedge_{1 \leq h < k} (T(\mathcal{V}_{h-1}, \overline{\mathcal{V}}_h) \wedge EQ_\alpha(\overline{\mathcal{V}}_h, \mathcal{V}_h)) \wedge T(\mathcal{V}_{k-1}, \mathcal{V}_k) \quad (11)$$

Theorem 4. *$\widehat{PATH}_{M,\alpha,k}$ is sat iff $PATH_{\hat{M}_\alpha,k}$ is sat.*

Definition 10. *Given an FTS $M = \langle \mathcal{V}, I, T \rangle$, an abstraction function α, and a bound k, the formula $\widehat{SIMPLEPATH}_{M,\alpha,k}$ is defined as follows:*

$$\widehat{SIMPLEPATH}_{M,\alpha,k} := \widehat{PATH}_{M,\alpha,k} \wedge \bigwedge_{0 \leq i < j \leq k} \neg EQ_\alpha(\mathcal{V}_i, \mathcal{V}_j) \quad (12)$$

Theorem 5. *$\widehat{SIMPLEPATH}_{M,\alpha,k}$ is sat iff $SIMPLEPATH_{\hat{M}_\alpha,k}$ is sat.*

4.3 Abstract Bounded Model Checking

We define the abstract version of the BMC encoding. The formula $\widehat{BMC}_{M,\alpha,k,\varphi}$ is sat iff $BMC_{\hat{M}_\alpha,k,\varphi}$ is sat. Therefore, if $\widehat{BMC}_{M,\alpha,k,\varphi}$ is unsat then we can deduce that there are no initial paths reaching $\hat{\varphi}_\alpha$ in k steps in $\hat{M}_\alpha$. If $\widehat{BMC}_{M,\alpha,k,\varphi}$ is sat, we can extract from its model a satisfying assignment for $BMC_{\hat{M}_\alpha,k,\varphi}$.

Definition 11. *Given an FTS $M = \langle \mathcal{V}, I, T \rangle$, a formula φ, an abstraction function α, and a bound k, the formula $\widehat{BMC}_{M,\alpha,k,\varphi}$ is defined as follows:*

$$\widehat{BMC}_{M,\alpha,k,\varphi} := I(\overline{\mathcal{V}}_0) \wedge EQ_\alpha(\overline{\mathcal{V}}_0, \mathcal{V}_0) \wedge \widehat{PATH}_{M,\alpha,k} \wedge EQ_\alpha(\mathcal{V}_k, \overline{\mathcal{V}}_k) \wedge \varphi(\overline{\mathcal{V}}_k) \quad (13)$$

Theorem 6. *$\widehat{BMC}_{M,\alpha,k,\varphi}$ is sat iff $BMC_{\hat{M}_\alpha,k,\varphi}$ is sat.*

Similarly, we can define the abstract version of $BMC^{loop}_{M,k}$.

Definition 12. *Given an FTS M, a bound k, and an abstraction function α, the formula $\widehat{BMC}^{loop}_{M,\alpha,k}$ is defined as follows:*

$$\widehat{BMC}^{loop}_{M,\alpha,k} := I(\overline{\mathcal{V}}_0) \wedge EQ_\alpha(\overline{\mathcal{V}}_0, \mathcal{V}_0) \wedge \widehat{PATH}_{M,\alpha,k} \wedge \bigvee_{0 \leq l < k,\, v \in V} \bigwedge EQ_\alpha(\mathcal{V}_l, \mathcal{V}_k) \wedge \bigwedge_{F \in \mathcal{F},\, l \leq h < k} \bigvee F(V_h) \tag{14}$$

Theorem 7. *$\widehat{BMC}^{loop}_{M,\alpha,k}$ is sat iff $BMC^{loop}_{\hat{M}_\alpha,k}$ is sat.*

4.4 Abstract k-Induction

We define the abstract version of the k-induction conditions. The formulas $\widehat{KINDFW}_{M,\alpha,k}$ and $\widehat{KINDBW}_{M,\alpha,k,\varphi}$ are sat iff respectively $KINDFW_{\hat{M}_\alpha,k}$ and $KINDBW_{\hat{M}_\alpha,k,\varphi}$ are sat. Therefore, if $\widehat{BMC}_{M,\alpha,k,\varphi}$ is unsat and, either $\widehat{KINDFW}_{M,\alpha,k}$ or $\widehat{KINDBW}_{M,\alpha,k,\varphi}$ is unsat then we can conclude that $\hat{\varphi}_\alpha$ is not reachable.

Notice that we do not use the stronger version of $KINDFW_{\hat{M}_\alpha,k}$ and $KINDBW_{\hat{M}_\alpha,k,\varphi}$ defined in [27], because they require to express the negation of $\hat{I}_\alpha$ and $\hat{\varphi}_\alpha$. In fact, the definitions of $\hat{I}_\alpha$ and $\hat{\varphi}_\alpha$ involve an existential quantification, and their negation cannot be handled by the satisfiability solver.

Definition 13. *Given an FTS $M = \langle \mathcal{V}, I, T \rangle$, an abstraction function α, and a bound k, the formula $\widehat{KINDFW}_{M,\alpha,k}$ is defined as follows:*

$$\widehat{KINDFW}_{M,\alpha,k} := I(\overline{\mathcal{V}}_0) \wedge EQ_\alpha(\overline{\mathcal{V}}_0, \mathcal{V}_0) \wedge \widehat{SIMPLEPATH}_{M,\alpha,k} \tag{15}$$

Theorem 8. *$\widehat{KINDFW}_{M,\alpha,k}$ is sat iff $KINDFW_{\hat{M}_\alpha,k}$ is sat.*

Definition 14. *Given an FTS $M = \langle \mathcal{V}, I, T \rangle$, a formula φ, an abstraction function α, and a bound k, the formula $\widehat{KINDBW}_{M,\alpha,k,\varphi}$ is defined as follows:*

$$\widehat{KINDBW}_{M,\alpha,k,\varphi} := \widehat{SIMPLEPATH}_{M,\alpha,k} \wedge EQ_\alpha(\mathcal{V}_k, \overline{\mathcal{V}}_k) \wedge \varphi(\overline{\mathcal{V}}_k) \tag{16}$$

Theorem 9. *$\widehat{KINDBW}_{M,\alpha,k,\varphi}$ is sat iff $KINDBW_{\hat{M}_\alpha,k,\varphi}$ is sat.*

Corollary 2. *If, for all $i \leq k$, $\widehat{BMC}_{M,\alpha,i,\varphi}$ is unsat and, either $\widehat{KINDFW}_{M,\alpha,k+1}$ or $\widehat{KINDBW}_{M,\alpha,k+1,\varphi}$ is unsat, then $\hat{\varphi}_\alpha$ is not reachable in $\hat{M}_\alpha$.*

4.5 Abstract Model Checking

The formulas $\widehat{BMC}_{M,\alpha,k,\varphi}$, $\widehat{BMC}^{loop}_{M,\alpha,k}$, $\widehat{KINDFW}_{M,\alpha,k}$, and $\widehat{KINDBW}_{M,\alpha,k,\varphi}$ can be used to define different procedures for solving reachability and language

input : concrete FTS $M = \langle \mathcal{V}, I, T \rangle$ and formula φ
output : YES if $\hat{\varphi}_\alpha$ is reachable in $\hat{M}_\alpha$, NO otherwise
begin
  $k{:=}0$;
  if $\widehat{BMC}_{M,\alpha,k,\varphi}$ *is sat* **then**
    return YES
  else if $\widehat{KINDFW}_{M,\alpha,k+1}$ *or* $\widehat{KINDBW}_{M,\alpha,k+1,\varphi}$ *is unsat* **then**
    return NO
  else
    k++;
end

Algorithm 2. Abstract model checking without abstraction

emptiness of an abstraction of an FTS. We denote such procedures with AMCWA$_{reach}$ and AMCWA$_{loop}$ respectively. AMCWA$_{reach}$ is shown in Algorithm 2. On the lines of k-induction, it iteratively increases the bound k till either it finds a counterexample or it proves the property correct. Unlike Algorithm 1, the path found by BMC is abstract and the bound used by k-induction to conclude is related to the abstract state space. In particular, when the abstract state space is finite, such bound is guaranteed to exist.

AMCWA$_{loop}$ is similar to AMCWA$_{reach}$, but $\widehat{BMC}^{loop}_{M,\alpha,k}$ is used instead of $\widehat{BMC}_{M,\alpha,k,\varphi}$, and only $\widehat{KINDFW}_{M,\alpha,k}$ is used to prove the absence of initial fair paths. In principle, we can add further induction conditions based on fairness, but in practice we experienced that they do not manage to conclude and solve the problem, and therefore we can save the related overhead.

When predicate abstraction is adopted, both AMC and AMCWA are exponential in the number of predicates. However, AMC must find all solutions of the abstraction formula, while AMCWA delegates the blow up to the search. The computation of the abstraction in AMC is orthogonal to the search and is computed upfront, while AMCWA considers only the parts of the abstract state space that are relevant to the search. The solver is used to solve a satisfiability problem rather than to enumerate all possible solutions.

Example 3. Consider the FTS of Ex. 1 and the predicates of Ex. 2. AMCWA proves that the FTS has an empty language by checking that $\widehat{BMC}^{loop}_{M,\alpha,k}$ is unsat for $k = 1, 2, 3, 4$ and that $KINDFW_{M,k}$ is unsat for $k = 4$. Note that k-induction on the concrete FTS cannot prove the same.

5 Experimental Evaluation

5.1 Implementation

We implemented AMCWA$_{reach}$ and AMCWA$_{loop}$ in CEGAR [4], and we evaluated the performance of the two algorithms on an Intel 2.2GHz Laptop equipped with 2GB of memory running Linux. We set a timeout of one hour and the space limit of 2GB. BMC and k-induction problems have been solved with the MathSAT SMT solver without incrementality. The same solver has been used to solve the ALLSAT problem for the computation of the abstraction, as already implemented in CEGAR. All the data and binaries necessary to reproduce the presented results are available at `http://es.fbk.eu/people/tonetta/tests/fm09/`

5.2 Emptiness Checking for Requirements Validation

In a project funded by ERA, we investigated the feasibility of the formalization and validation of ETCS functions (see `http://www.era.europa.eu/`). The requirements have been formalized in a fragment of first-order temporal logic [21]. The techniques used to validate the requirements were based on a series of checks for the language emptiness of large transition systems, which encode the consistency of different sets of requirements. The systems had around 300 Boolean variables, 50 real variables, and few integers. Most of times, the requirements were consistent and we used BMC to generate paths as witnesses. Inconsistencies found during the project were mainly due to unfeasible scenarios considered on purpose to test the formalization of the requirements.

We consider the fragment of the ETCS specification analyzed in [6], and we add unfeasible scenarios on the lines of those proposed in the ETCS project. For each problem, we consider a set of predicates that is sufficient to prove the inconsistency. We ran the abstract model checking algorithms with and without the computation of the abstraction for increasing number of predicates.

We obtained the results reported in Fig. 3. The time is plotted in log-scale against the number of predicates. The vertical line highlights the number N which is sufficient to prove the language emptiness of the FTS. Thus, for $i < N$ the algorithm find an abstract (spurious) path, while for $i \geq N$ the algorithm conclude that the language is empty. The tables reports the k at which k-induction stopped with N predicates. The other columns of the table report the size, in terms of number of variables and number of fairness conditions of the FTS. We use $\#r$,$\#b$,$\#f$ with the meaning, r real variables, b Boolean variables, and f fairness conditions.

In ETCS2 and ETCS4, the new algorithm outperforms the computation of the abstraction. In ETCS7 and ETCS8, the improvement scales up exponentially. Note that in ETCS7 and ETCS8, for $i \geq N$, the AMC reaches the timeout. Thus the computation of the abstraction prevents to prove the inconsistency, and the new algorithm manages to prove problems that were not previously solved. Finally, in ETCS9 we have some points were the new algorithm performs worse. However, as the number of predicates scales up the new algorithm is definitely the winner. The data regarding memory consumption have similar plots. As for AMC, the time is almost totally spent in the computation of the abstraction, while the search in the abstract state space is negligible.

Note that, unlike the computation of the predicate abstraction which seems a regular exponential function over the number of predicates, the performance

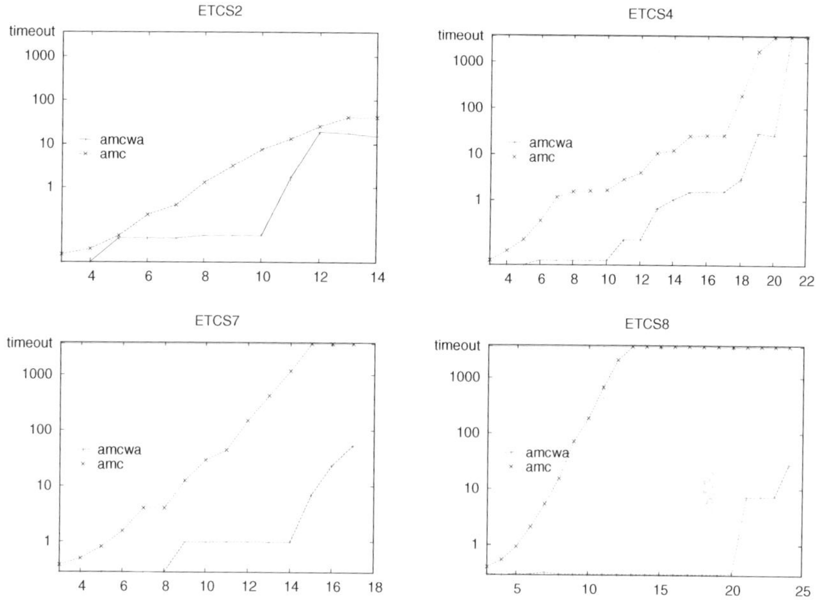

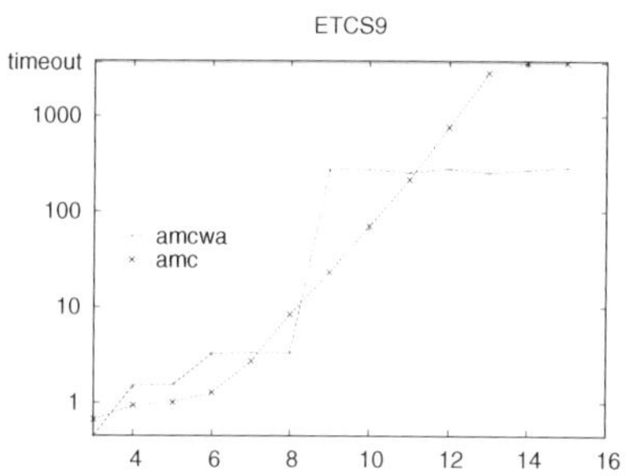

Name:	N	K	$\#r$	$\#b$	$\#f$
ETCS2	11	8	4	12	2
ETCS4	13	4	7	21	2
ETCS7	15	5	50	182	11
ETCS8	21	5	51	184	12
ETCS9	10	18	66	262	19

Fig. 3. The results of the experimental evaluation

of the new algorithm seems a step function. This is due to the dependency on the depth necessary to use k-induction, and on the fact that some predicates increase such depth, while others do not affect it.

5.3 Number of Predicates vs. Search Depth

We now consider a scalable system manually crafted to investigate the dependency on the number N of predicates and the bound K that is necessary to solve the problem. The system has N Boolean variables P_i, with $1 \leq i \leq N$, and N bounded integers v_i, $1 \leq i \leq N$. The variables P_i are initially *false* and non-deterministically become *true*. For $1 \leq i < N$, the variable P_i can become *true* only if P_{i+1} is *true*. Besides, the variable P_{N-K} can become *true* only if P_1 is *true*. Therefore the property $\neg P_1$ is an invariant of the concrete system, and,

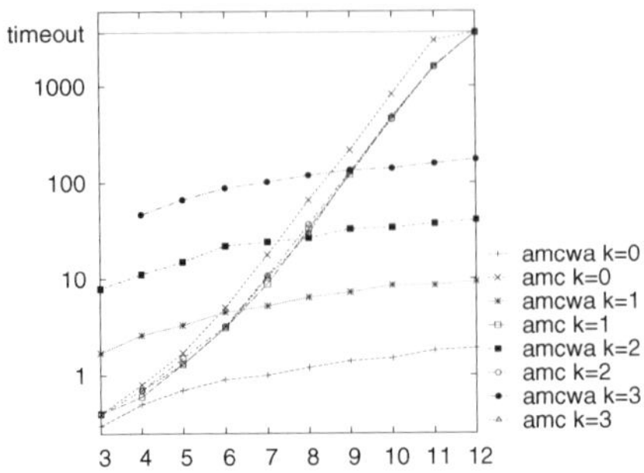

Fig. 4. Results for case study. X axis: parameter N. Y axis: time in seconds.

if we choose $\mathbb{P} = \{P_i\}_{1 \leq i \leq N}$, it is an invariant also of the abstract system. The relationships among the variables P_i involve the variables v_i so that the abstraction does not result straightforward. Moreover, fixed a value for the variables P_i, the variable v_i can range over the whole domain. This makes k-induction of the concrete system infeasible because it would require a too large bound. Note instead that the initial simple paths have at most K steps (basically, the paths that change the variables P_i for $N - K + 1 \leq i \leq N$). This allows us to prove the property on the abstract system by means of k-induction with bound K.

The results are plotted in Fig. 4 in log-scale for increasing values of N. As expected, the time spent in the computation of the abstraction grows exponentially with the number of involved predicates. The search done by AMC_{reach} results to be polynomial in the number of predicates, and strongly depends on the necessary inductive depth.

6 Related Work

Combinations of predicate abstraction with SAT-based techniques are numerous in the literature. As discussed in the introduction, a SAT or SMT solver is typically used to compute the abstraction. The problem of verifying if an abstract path can be simulated on the concrete system is encoded into a BMC problem [9]. Many works on abstraction refinement use also BMC as a model checking procedure. The CEGAR loop described in [20] uses SAT as the only decision procedure. The model checking of the abstract state space is based on BMC and k-induction. Unlike this paper, the abstraction computation and the abstract model checking are distinct steps of the loop.

In [24], BMC is used on the concrete system, the proof of unsatisfiability of the abstract path simulation is used to build the abstraction, and the result of the abstract model checking is used to increase the bound of the search. The work in [16] improves [24] by applying BMC to both the concrete and the abstract system. Also in [22,23], predicates are not used and the abstract system is built by extracting interpolants from the unsatisfiability proof of some path conditions. The efficiency of these works is based on the capability of the refinement to find constraints that are on one hand strong enough to prove the property, on the other hand weak enough to keep the verification complexity low. As the mentioned approaches, this paper aims at avoiding the computation of the abstract state space, but remains in the framework of abstraction precisely defined by a function (rather than computed by the refinement procedure).

In [17], the abstraction is computed on demand along the search. The algorithm exploits the control-flow graph of programs to localize the search to control locations, and avoids building the abstraction for unreachable location. Nevertheless, also this approach needs a quantifier elimination to compute the abstract image of reachable locations.

The work presented in [18] combines symbolic execution with abstraction, but differently from this paper, the abstraction is based on induction and is computed separately from the search. Notably, the counterexamples (which are called *leaping* because they leap due to the abstraction) are used for diagnosis.

A common way to tackle the complexity of predicate abstraction is to approximate the computation by allowing more transitions (see, e.g., [7,12,1]). The complexity is shifted to the refinement that must take care of removing spurious transitions, resulting in an increased number of refinement iterations. This paper focuses only on minimal abstraction, although the technique can be modified in order to search approximated abstract state space.

The definition of $EQ_{\mathbb{P}}$ can be found already in [29], but is used only to compare predicate abstraction with localization reduction.

7 Conclusions

In this paper, we proposed a new algorithm to model check an abstract system without computing the abstraction. While the classic paradigm performs a quantifier elimination to build the abstraction, we encode the model checking problem into satisfiability problems over the concrete variables. We adapted the algorithm based on k-induction to look for finite and infinite fair paths in the abstract system. We showed that the new algorithm can obtain an exponentially better scalability and solved real world problems that were beyond the reach of standard predicate abstraction.

The improvement is of course affected by many parameters. In particular, the abstract state must be amenable for proving the invariant with k-induction. K-induction may be a very effective technique, but, since it is based on the induction principle, it does not manage to prove always an invariant: in the finite-state case, the technique is complete, but the bound necessary to prove the property may become too large; in the infinite-state case, the loop is not guaranteed to terminate. In practice, one has to exploit invariants as in [25].

We plan to integrate the abstract model checking technique into a full abstraction refinement loop. We can exploit the search done by the solver to extract useful information such as abstract transitions, and reachability results on the concrete state space. We can use the obtained leaping counterexamples for diagnosis as suggested in [18]. We can exploit the incrementality of the solver, to boost the search by exploiting the clauses learned by previous iterations and to check the satisfiability of the inductive condition in an incremental way as described in [13].

References

1. Ball, T., Podelski, A., Rajamani, S.K.: Boolean and Cartesian abstraction for model checking C programs. STTT 5(1), 49–58 (2003)
2. Biere, A., Cimatti, A., Clarke, E.M., Zhu, Y.: Symbolic Model Checking without BDDs. In: Cleaveland, W.R. (ed.) TACAS 1999. LNCS, vol. 1579, pp. 193–207. Springer, Heidelberg (1999)
3. Burch, J.R., Clarke, E.M., McMillan, K.L., Dill, D.L., Hwang, L.J.: Symbolic Model Checking: 10^{20} States and Beyond. Inf. and Comp. 98(2), 142–170 (1992)
4. Cavada, R., Cimatti, A., Franzén, A., Kalyanasundaram, K., Roveri, M., Shyamasundar, R.K.: Computing predicate abstractions by integrating BDDs and SMT solvers. In: FMCAD, pp. 69–76. IEEE, Los Alamitos (2007)
5. Cimatti, A., Roveri, M., Susi, A., Tonetta, S.: Object models with temporal constraints. Journal of Software and Systems Modeling (SoSyM), `http://www.springerlink.com/content/46244553v2769511/`, doi: 10.1007/s10270-009-0130-7
6. Cimatti, A., Roveri, M., Tonetta, S.: Requirements Validation for Hybrid Systems. In: Bouajjani, A., Maler, O. (eds.) CAV 2009. LNCS, vol. 5643, pp. 188–203. Springer, Heidelberg (2009)
7. Clarke, E.M., Grumberg, O., Jha, S., Lu, Y., Veith, H.: Counterexample-Guided Abstraction Refinement. In: Emerson, E.A., Sistla, A.P. (eds.) CAV 2000. LNCS, vol. 1855, pp. 154–169. Springer, Heidelberg (2000)
8. Clarke, E.M., Grumberg, O., Long, D.E.: Model Checking and Abstraction. ACM Trans. Program. Lang. Syst. 16(5), 1512–1542 (1994)
9. Clarke, E.M., Gupta, A., Kukula, J.H., Strichman, O.: SAT Based Abstraction-Refinement Using ILP and Machine Learning Techniques. In: Brinksma, E., Larsen, K.G. (eds.) CAV 2002. LNCS, vol. 2404, pp. 265–279. Springer, Heidelberg (2002)
10. Clarke, E.M., Kroening, D., Sharygina, N., Yorav, K.: Predicate Abstraction of ANSI-C Programs Using SAT. FMSD 25(2-3), 105–127 (2004)
11. Colón, M., Uribe, T.E.: Generating Finite-State Abstractions of Reactive Systems Using Decision Procedures. In: Y. Vardi, M. (ed.) CAV 1998. LNCS, vol. 1427, pp. 293–304. Springer, Heidelberg (1998)
12. Das, S., Dill, D.L.: Successive Approximation of Abstract Transition Relations. In: LICS, pp. 51–60 (2001)
13. Eén, N., Sörensson, N.: Temporal induction by incremental SAT solving. Electr. Notes Theor. Comput. Sci. 89(4) (2003)
14. Emerson, E.A., Clarke, E.M.: Using Branching Time Temporal Logic to Synthesize Synchronization Skeletons. Sci. Comput. Program 2(3), 241–266 (1982)
15. Graf, S., Saïdi, H.: Construction of Abstract State Graphs with PVS. In: Grumberg, O. (ed.) CAV 1997. LNCS, vol. 1254, pp. 72–83. Springer, Heidelberg (1997)
16. Gupta, A., Strichman, O.: Abstraction Refinement for Bounded Model Checking. In: Etessami, K., Rajamani, S.K. (eds.) CAV 2005. LNCS, vol. 3576, pp. 112–124. Springer, Heidelberg (2005)
17. Henzinger, T.A., Jhala, R., Majumdar, R., Sutre, G.: Lazy abstraction. In: POPL, pp. 58–70 (2002)

18. Kroening, D., Sharygina, N., Tonetta, S., Tsitovich, A., Wintersteiger, C.M.: Loop Summarization Using Abstract Transformers. In: Cha, S(S.), Choi, J.-Y., Kim, M., Lee, I., Viswanathan, M. (eds.) ATVA 2008. LNCS, vol. 5311, pp. 111–125. Springer, Heidelberg (2008)
19. Lahiri, S.K., Bryant, R.E., Cook, B.: A Symbolic Approach to Predicate Abstraction. In: Hunt Jr., W.A., Somenzi, F. (eds.) CAV 2003. LNCS, vol. 2725, pp. 141–153. Springer, Heidelberg (2003)
20. Li, B., Wang, C., Somenzi, F.: Abstraction refinement in symbolic model checking using satisfiability as the only decision procedure. STTT 7(2), 143–155 (2005)
21. Manna, Z., Pnueli, A.: The Temporal Logic of Reactive and Concurrent Systems: Specification. Springer, Heidelberg (1992)
22. McMillan, K.L.: Interpolation and SAT-Based Model Checking. In: Hunt Jr., W.A., Somenzi, F. (eds.) CAV 2003. LNCS, vol. 2725, pp. 1–13. Springer, Heidelberg (2003)
23. McMillan, K.L.: Lazy Abstraction with Interpolants. In: Ball, T., Jones, R.B. (eds.) CAV 2006. LNCS, vol. 4144, pp. 123–136. Springer, Heidelberg (2006)
24. McMillan, K.L., Amla, N.: Automatic Abstraction without Counterexamples. In: Garavel, H., Hatcliff, J. (eds.) TACAS 2003. LNCS, vol. 2619, pp. 2–17. Springer, Heidelberg (2003)
25. Pike, L.: Real-time system verification by k-induction. Technical Report TM-2005-213751, NASA Langley Research Center (May 2005)
26. Queille, J.-P., Sifakis, J.: Specification and verification of concurrent systems in CESAR. In: Dezani-Ciancaglini, M., Montanari, U. (eds.) Programming 1982. LNCS, vol. 137, pp. 337–351. Springer, Heidelberg (1982)
27. Sheeran, M., Singh, S., Stålmarck, G.: Checking Safety Properties Using Induction and a SAT-Solver. In: Johnson, S.D., Hunt Jr., W.A. (eds.) FMCAD 2000. LNCS, vol. 1954, pp. 108–125. Springer, Heidelberg (2000)
28. Vardi, M.Y., Wolper, P.: An Automata-Theoretic Approach to Automatic Program Verification. In: LICS, pp. 332–344 (1986)
29. Wang, C., Kim, H., Gupta, A.: Hybrid CEGAR: combining variable hiding and predicate abstraction. In: ICCAD, pp. 310–317 (2007)

Three-Valued Spotlight Abstractions

Jonas Schrieb, Heike Wehrheim, and Daniel Wonisch

Universität Paderborn, Institut für Informatik
33098 Paderborn, Germany
jonas@upb.de, wehrheim@upb.de, dwonisch@mail.upb.de

Abstract. Spotlight abstractions in verification focus on one specific component in a parallel system while disregarding most information about the rest. Existing spotlight abstractions are either based on over- or on underapproximations of the parallel system, thus either preserving existential or universal properties. In this paper we present three-valued spotlight abstractions for parallel systems which preserve both existential and universal properties. We show correctness of the abstraction technique as well as present a procedure for abstraction refinement. The technique has been implemented on top of an existing three-valued model checker. Experimental results show that our technique can outperform existing predicate abstraction tools on certain classes of parallel systems.

1 Introduction

Abstraction techniques in verification have long been studied as a means for reducing the complexity of model checking [1]. While early work focused on basically transferring the idea of abstract interpretation from program analysis [2] to model checking [3], today predicate abstractions, elaborate means for finding predicates and refining abstractions are in the focus of research. Several tools implement such abstraction and abstraction refinement techniques (e.g. Blast [4], SLAM [5], MAGIC [6], ARMC [7], SATABS [8]).

Spotlight abstractions are specific abstraction techniques for parallel systems, where a "spotlight" is set on certain processes and the remaining ones are kept in the "shade", i.e. are only considered to a small degree. Spotlight abstractions are usually applied to parametrized systems, consisting of an unknown number (encoded by a parameter) of almost identical components, a typical representative being a mutual exclusion algorithm for n processes. Counter abstraction [9] keeps one process precise while only "counting" the number of processes which are at particular program locations (counting being cut off at 2). Environment abstraction [10] in addition keeps predicates in the abstraction relating variables of the one component to those of other components. The term "spotlight" has recently been coined by Wachter and Westphal [11], who show that all these abstractions can be seen as an instance of *canonical abstractions* which have been employed as an abstraction technique in shape analysis [12]. They apply their canonical abstractions on car platoons with an unknown number of (identical) cars.

In this paper, we apply the spotlight principle to a different class of parallel systems. Instead of assuming (almost) identity of parallel components, we allow for arbitrary compositions (but fixed, not parametric), and instead of treating properties talking about

A. Cavalcanti and D. Dams (Eds.): FM 2009, LNCS 5850, pp. 106–122, 2009.

all processes, we specialize to *local* properties of individual processes. Starting with a given parallel system (with shared variables) and a temporal logic property for a specific component C_i, we try to verify the property by considering as few other components as possible. Thus our first abstraction only contains an abstracted version of C_i. Once we find that the property cannot be proven on this abstraction of C_i alone, we gradually refine the abstraction by either adding new predicates to the abstraction of C_i, or adding a new component possibly influencing C_i. As a first example, consider the simple parallel program of Figure 1.

```
              int x1 = 1; int x2 = 1; int x3 = 1;
while (x1 > 0)      || while (x2 > 0) {  || while (x3 > 0) {
   x1 = x1 - 1;     ||     x1 = x1 - 1;  ||     x2 = x2 - 1;
END:                ||     x2 = x2 - 1;  ||     x3 = x3 - 1;
                    || }                 || }
      (1)                   (2)                  (3)
```

Fig. 1. Program CHAIN_3

In this program we have a chain of dependencies among the processes due to the three variables. When checking for a property like $AF\ (pc_1 = \texttt{END})$ (i.e., check whether the program location END in component 1 is always reached, assuming fairness), our approach constructs the following abstractions (given in Figure 2). The first abstraction (a) would consider component (1) alone with no predicates. Components (2) and (3) are summarized into one component, infinitely passing through a loop. A first analysis reveals that we need to add the predicate $(x1 > 0)$ to the abstraction of component (1) as to determine termination of the loop (giving abstraction (b)). Since $x1$ is a shared variable, the abstraction of (2) and (3) is changed as to incorporate a possible but unknown change (denoted by *) of predicate $(x1 > 0)$. On this abstraction we still cannot determine termination of the loop, since it is not clear whether $x1 > 0$ eventually becomes *false*. The next two abstractions thus first add another predicate $(x1 > 1)$ and then component (2) (steps (c) and (d)). On this final abstraction we are able to prove validity of the above property (under the reasonable fairness assumption that every process eventually makes progress), even without determining whether the loop in (2) is actually executed. Thus variables $x2$ and $x3$ as well as component (3) never have to be considered. The same effect happens for all programs CHAIN_n (with n components and n variables xi), i.e. independent of the number of processes, property $AF(pc_1 = END)$ can be proven with two components in the spotlight and two predicates only.

In contrast to almost all other spotlight abstractions, we use three-valued abstractions for our approach, thereby being able to preserve both existential and universal properties. Many-valued model checking techniques [13, 14] verify properties of *partial Kripke structures*. Partiality may refer to both transitions and atomic propositions. In a three-valued setting, transitions can be present (*true*), not present (*false*) or simply unknown ($\perp$), the same principle applies to atomic propositions. Such partiality may arise out of inconsistent specifications, unknown sub-components in systems or - as in

```
while (*)   || while (true)
  { }       ||   { }
END:        ||
```

(*a*) (1) (2, 3)

```
                                              (x1>0) = true;
while (x1>0)                                || while (true)
  {(x1>0) = (x1>0)?*:false;}                ||   {(x1>0)=*;}
END:                                        ||
```

(*b*) (1) (2, 3)

```
                    (x1>0) = true; (x1>1) = false;
while (x1>0)                                 || while (true)
   {(x1>0) = (x1>1) ? true : false,          ||    {(x1>0),(x1>1) = *,*;}
    (x1>1) = (x1>1) ? * : false;}            ||
END:                                         ||
```

(*c*) (1) (2, 3)

```
                      (x1>0) = true; (x1>1) = false;
while(x1>0)                          ||while(*)                             ||while(true)
 {(x1>0) = (x1>1)?true:false,        || {(x1>0) = (x1>1)?true:false,        || { }
  (x1>1) = (x1>1)?*:false;}          ||  (x1>1) = (x1>1)?*:false;}          ||
END:                                 ||                                     ||
```

(*d*) (1) (2) (3)

Fig. 2. Abstractions (a) to (d)

our case and alike [15] - imprecisions due to abstraction. Model checking techniques for partial Kripke structures have already intensively been studied, a BDD- (MDD-)based model checker for arbitrary many-valued Kripke structures is χChek [16]. The use of partial Kripke structures as abstractions has the advantage of preserving both existential and universal properties (given an appropriate abstraction): The outcome of a model checking run on a partial Kripke structure can be *true*, *false* or $\perp$. In three-valued abstractions both *true* and *false* results can be transferred to the original system, only the $\perp$ result necessitates abstraction refinement.

In this paper, we employ three-valued Kripke structures for our spotlight abstractions. We show that our abstractions give us a completeness preorder relation [17] between full and abstracted system (preserving fairness), thus guaranteeing the preservation of full CTL properties. We furthermore develop a technique for abstraction refinement which either adds further predicates to the components currently in the abstraction, or a new component. The approach has been implemented on top of the model checker χChek and we report on promising results.

2 Basic Definitions

We start with a brief introduction to partial Kripke structures and the interpretation of temporal logic formulae on them. Partial Kripke structures will be the semantic domain of our abstracted programs. For the abstractions that we present here, we only need *three-valued* Kripke structures; extension to arbitrary many values can be found in [14].

In a three-valued Kripke structure an atomic proposition or transition can not only be present or absent, but also unknown (Fig. 3(b)). The logical basis for this is *Kleene logic* [18]. Kleene logic $\mathbf{3} := \{true, false, \bot\}$ extends classical logic $\mathbf{2} := \{true, false\}$ by a value $\bot$ standing for "unknown". A *truth order* "$\sqsubseteq$" (with $false \sqsubseteq \bot \sqsubseteq true$) and an *information order* "$\leq$" (with $\bot \leq true$, $\bot \leq false$ and $true, false$ incomparable) are defined on $\mathbf{3}$ and shown in Fig. 3(a). Conjunction is defined by $a \wedge b := min(a, b)$ and disjunction by $a \vee b := max(a, b)$ where min and max apply to the truth order $\sqsubseteq$. The negation is defined as $\neg true := false$, $\neg false := true$ and $\neg\bot := \bot$. Note that the operations $\vee, \wedge, \neg$ applied to $true$ and $false$ have the same meaning as in $\mathbf{2}$.

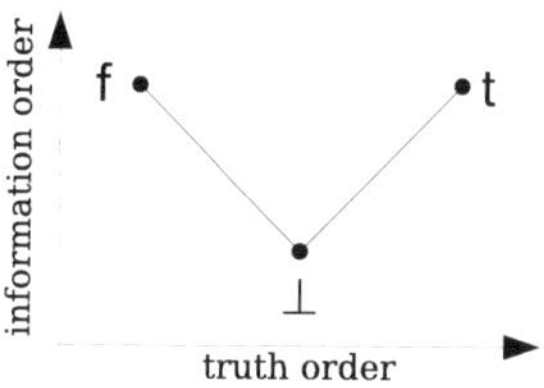

(a) Three-valued Kleene logic

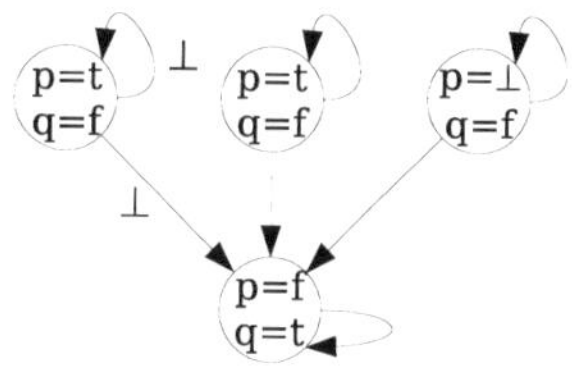

(b) Three-valued Kripke structure with atomic propositions $\mathsf{AP} = \{p, q\}$

$$[\![EGp]\!](\ldots) = \bot, t, \bot$$
$$[\![AGp]\!](\ldots) = \bot, f, f$$
$$[\![E[pUq]]\!](\ldots) = \bot, t, \bot$$
$$[\![A[pUq]]\!](\ldots) = \bot, f, f$$

(c) CTL formulae valuated in the upper 3 states of the structure in Fig. 3(b)

Fig. 3.

A three-valued Kripke structure is a classical Kripke structure where all occurrences of classical logic $\mathbf{2}$ are replaced by $\mathbf{3}$. The other way round, a classical Kripke structure is a three-valued Kripke structure where no $\bot$ occurs. In the following, whenever we just talk about Kripke structures, the three-valued case is meant.

Definition 1 (Three-Valued Kripke Structure). *Given a nonempty finite set of atomic propositions* AP*, a three-valued Kripke structure is a 3-tuple* (S, R, L) *where*

- S *is a set of states,*
- $R : S \times S \rightarrow \mathbf{3}$ *is a total*[1] *three-valued transition relation and*
- $L : \mathsf{AP} \times S \rightarrow \mathbf{3}$ *is a three-valued function labeling states with atomic propositions.*

For specifying properties of programs we use computation-tree logic (CTL) [19].

Definition 2 (Syntax of CTL). *Let* AP *be a set of atomic propositions. The syntax of CTL is given by the following grammar:*

$$\varphi ::= p \mid \varphi \vee \varphi \mid \varphi \wedge \varphi \mid \neg\varphi \mid EX\varphi \mid AX\varphi \mid EF\varphi \mid AF\varphi \mid EG\varphi \mid AG\varphi \mid E[\varphi U \varphi] \mid A[\varphi U \varphi]$$

where p *is an atomic proposition of* AP.

[1] Here *total* means that for any $s \in S$ there is an outgoing transition, i.e. there exist $t \in S$ with $R(s, t) \neq false$.

In the classical setting, a function $[\![\cdot]\!](\cdot) : CTL \times S \rightarrow \mathbf{2}$ tells us whether a formula holds in a given state or not, and is defined inductively over the structure of a formula. Let $\Pi_s = \{(s_0, s_1, s_2, \ldots) \in S^{\mathbb{N}} \mid s_0 = s \text{ and } \forall_{i \geq 0}: R(s_i, s_{i+1}) \neq false\}$ be the set of *all paths starting in* $s \in S$, and for a path π, the i-th state is denoted as π_i. Then for instance "there exists a path such that φ holds until ψ" is formally defined as:

$$[\![E[\varphi U \psi]]\!](s) \quad := \quad \exists \pi \in \Pi_s \colon \exists k \geq 0 \colon \quad [\![\psi]\!](\pi_k) \ \wedge \ \forall i < k \colon [\![\varphi]\!](\pi_i)$$

For three-valued structures, the interpretation is extended in such a way that it stays consistent with the classical setting if no $\perp$ is used. This is achieved by replacing universal quantifiers with conjunction and existential quantifiers with disjunction. Furthermore, the truth values of the transitions on the path have to be taken into account[2].

Informally, an E-formula is *true* if the subformula holds on at least one path without $\perp$-transitions. The reason for excluding paths with $\perp$-transitions is that it is unclear whether they really exist. Therefore paths with $\perp$-transitions may only contribute *false* or $\perp$ to the truth value. Analogously, for an A-formula paths with $\perp$-transitions may only contribute *true* or $\perp$. To achieve this, one needs the *transition value on the path from* π_0 *to* π_k, i.e. $R^k(\pi) := \bigwedge_{0 \leq i < k} R(\pi_i, \pi_{i+1})$. In the following we define the interpretation only for a subset of CTL, the remaining operators can be derived by the usual dualities.

Definition 3 (Three-Valued Interpretation of CTL). *Let* AP *be a set of atomic propositions and* $K = (S, R, L)$ *a three-valued Kripke structure over* AP. *The interpretation function* $[\![\cdot]\!](\cdot) : CTL \times S \rightarrow \mathbf{3}$ *with respect to* K *is inductively defined on the grammar of a CTL-formula:*

$$[\![p]\!](s) := L(p, s) \text{ for } p \in AP \qquad [\![\varphi \wedge \psi]\!](s) := [\![\varphi]\!](s) \wedge [\![\psi]\!](s) \qquad [\![\neg\varphi]\!](s) := \neg[\![\varphi]\!](s)$$

$$[\![EX\varphi]\!](s) := \bigvee_{\pi \in \Pi_s} \left(R^1(\pi) \ \wedge \ [\![\varphi]\!](\pi_1)\right) \qquad [\![EG\varphi]\!](s) := \bigvee_{\pi \in \Pi_s} \bigwedge_{k \geq 0} \left(R^k(\pi) \ \wedge \ [\![\varphi]\!](\pi_k)\right)$$

$$[\![E[\varphi U \psi]]\!](s) := \bigvee_{\pi \in \Pi_s} \bigvee_{k \geq 0} \left(R^k(\pi) \ \wedge \ \left([\![\psi]\!](\pi_k) \wedge \bigwedge_{0 \leq i < k} [\![\varphi]\!](\pi_i)\right)\right)$$

If K *is not clear from the context, the interpretation function is denoted as* $[\![\cdot]\!]_K(\cdot)$

For some properties it will be necessary to assume some kind of fairness between parallel processes, e.g. that every process will eventually progress. To this end, we extend the definition of three-valued Kripke structures with fairness and adapt the interpretation of CTL formulae to fair Kripke structures.

Definition 4 (Fair Three-Valued Kripke Structures). *A* fair *three-valued Kripke structure is a 4-tuple* $(S, R, L, \mathcal{F})$ *where* S, L *and* R *are as before and additionally a set of fairness constraints* $\mathcal{F} \subseteq \mathcal{P}(R^{-1}(\{true, \perp\}))$ *is given, where each constraint is a set of non-false transitions.*

---

[2] Using the classical logic for any $\pi \in \Pi_s$ we have that $R(\pi_i, \pi_{i+1}) = true$, and therefore all requirements for R in Def. 3 are consistent with but also redundant for the two-valued case. Also, notice that with Def. 3 the condition $R(s_i, s_{i+1}) \neq false$ is no longer needed in Π_s.

The fair interpretation of CTL formulas then requires all considered paths to be fair, i.e. to infinitely often take a transition from every set in $\mathcal{F}$.

Next, we take a look at our programs. We model programs as control flow graphs with operations similar to Dijkstra's guarded commands. In most cases we also give the programs as pseudocode (like in the introduction) assuming the translation to a control flow graph is clear. The definitions are taken with slight changes from [15] but extended with parallel composition.

Definition 5 (Operations). *Let $Var = \{v_1, \ldots, v_n\}$ be a set of variables. The set of all operations Ops on these variables consists of all statements "$assume(e) : v_1 := e_1, \ldots, v_n := e_n$", where $e, e_1, \ldots, e_n$ are expressions over Var.*

The "assume"-part is often omitted, namely when the guard is true. As an example, x1=x1-1 stands for $assume(true) : x1 := x1 - 1$. Operations appear as labels of transitions in control flow graphs, often only either as guard or as variable assignments. CFGs for the parallel components from the program of the introduction are given in Fig. 4.

Definition 6 (Programs as Control Flow Graphs (CFG)). *A CFG is a structure $G = (Loc, \delta)$ where Loc is a finite set of locations, and $\delta : Loc \times Loc \rightarrow \mathbf{2}$ is a transition relation. A program is modeled by a labeled CFG $Prg = (Loc, \delta, \tau)$, where τ labels each edge of the CFG G with one operation of Ops.*

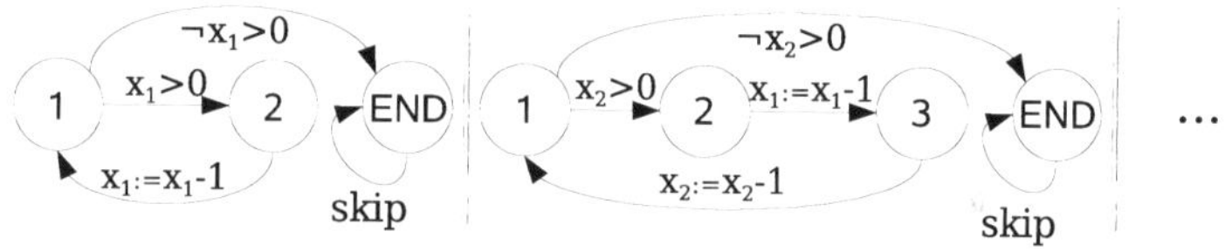

Fig. 4. CFGs for CHAIN$_n$. The numbering of nodes is according to line numbers in the programs. Hereby "END" (and later also "E") denotes the last line. "$x_i > 0$" is short for "$assume(x_i > 0)$".

We denote by $Var(Prg)$ the set of all program variables, and by $LVar(Prg) \subseteq Var(Prg)$ the set of all variables that occur on the left-hand-side in an operation of Prg, i.e. all variables that might be changed by a program. If several programs Prg_i, i from some index set I, are composed into a parallel program $||_{i \in I} Prg_i$, this simply results in the product graph of all CFGs (PCFG), where at each combined location $(l_1, \ldots, l_n) \in \times_{i \in I} Loc_i$ one transition from a component is non-deterministically chosen and taken. Each transition is furthermore labeled with the component program it belongs to, i.e. the transition relation δ is a function $Loc \times I \times Loc \rightarrow \mathbf{2}$ and the operations given by τ function $Loc \times I \times Loc \rightarrow Ops$. The definition is straightforward and due to lack of space omitted.

The programs, viz. PCFGs, are next equipped with a semantics in terms of (so far) two-valued Kripke structures. To this end, we have to define valuations of variables. For any set of typed variables Var, let S_{Var} be the set of all possible states, i.e. the set of all type-correct valuations of variables. For any state $s \in S_{Var}$ and any expression e over Var, $s(e)$ denotes the valuation of the expression in state s. The Kripke structure corresponding to a program is the result of combining the PCFG with program states. There is a transition between two states if we have a transition between the corresponding locations in the PCFG and the corresponding operation is consistent with the change of program state. The fairness constraint consists of sets each one containing all transitions caused by the same program component, i.e. a path is fair if all components eventually progress. Note that we explicitly add atomic propositions of the form $pc_i = k$, for k a location in a component CFG.

Definition 7 ((Parallel) Programs as Kripke Structures). *Let Prg be the parallel program given by* $\langle Loc, \delta, \tau\rangle := \|_{i\in I} Prg_i$, *and P a set of quantifier free predicates over the program variables. The corresponding Kripke structure is* $K_P(Prg)$ *over* $\mathsf{AP} = P \cup \{\text{“}pc_i = x\text{”} \mid i \in I, x \in Loc_i\}$ *with:*

- $S \quad := Loc \times S_{Var(Prg)}$
- $R(\langle l,s\rangle, \langle k,t\rangle) \quad := \bigvee_{i\in I} \Big(\underbrace{\delta(l,i,k) \ \wedge\ s(e) \ \wedge\ t(v_1) = s(e_1) \ \wedge \ldots \wedge\ t(v_n) = s(e_n)}_{=:R_i(\langle l,s\rangle,\langle k,t\rangle)}\Big)$
  assuming that $\tau(l,i,k)$ *is “*$assume(e)$*:* $v_1 := e_1, \ldots, v_n := e_n$*”*
- $L(p, \langle l,s\rangle) \quad := s(p)$ *for any* $p \in P$
- $L(pc_i = x, \langle l,s\rangle) := \begin{cases} true & \text{if } l_i = x \\ false & \text{else} \end{cases}$ *where* l_i *is the location of* Prg_i *in tuple* l
- $\mathcal{F} \quad := \left\{R_i^{-1}(\{true, \bot\})\right\}_{i\in I}$ *for each* Prg_i*: one constraint that contains all transitions caused by* Prg_i

Last, we need to define syntax and semantics of abstracted programs. Here, we also follow standard approaches for predicate abstraction (e.g. [15, 20] using *boolean programs*. Boolean programs are very much alike normal programs, viz. CFGs, except that instead of variables we have predicates (over variables) and thus assignments are not to variables but to predicates. In a program state, a predicate can be true, false or - in our case - $\bot$. For a given set of predicates P, the state space is thus $\mathbf{3}^P$. The *boolean operations BOps* appearing as labels of the CFG thus naturally are of the form

$$assume(pe) : p_1 := pe_1, \ldots, p_m := pe_m$$

where $p_i \in P$. The expressions on the right-hand-side often take the form *choice*(a,b) for boolean expressions a, b with the following semantics:

$$s(choice(a,b)) = \begin{cases} true & \text{if } s(a) \text{ is } true \\ false & \text{if } s(b) \text{ is } true \\ \bot & \text{else} \end{cases}$$

The same abbreviations as for non-boolean operations are allowed. Additionally, $\bot$ is short for *choice*(f,f), $\neg$*choice*(a,b) means *choice*(b,a) and any boolean expression e can be written instead of *choice*$(e,\neg e)$. The expression “`(x1>0) ? *:false`” in the introduction for instance is translated into *choice*$(false, \neg(x1 > 0))$, as it becomes $false$ if and only if $\neg(x1 > 0)$ is $true$ and its value is unknown in any other case. Particularly, there is no case where the expression may become definitely $true$ and therefore the first argument of the *choice* operator is $false$.

(Parallel) boolean programs are thus simply (P)CFGs labeled with operations from $BOps$. We will denote boolean programs by $BPrg_i$ instead of Prg and the index set for parallel processes by BI instead of I. The Kripke structure semantics for boolean programs follows those for ordinary programs except for the fact that we might now both have $\bot$ as value for predicates as well as as a label for transitions, i.e. states are from $Loc \times \mathbf{3}^P$ and transitions get $\bot$-labels if the assume-condition evaluates to $\bot$.

Boolean operations are used to approximate the operations of non-boolean programs. This is the basis of predicate abstraction and will shortly be explained next. Predicate abstraction is then combined with spotlight abstraction which in addition abstracts away from components in the parallel composition.

As an example for approximation of operations, take from our concrete program of the introduction the assignment `x1 := x1 - 1`.

- For $P = \{p_1 \equiv x1 > 0, p_2 \equiv x1 - 1 > 0\}$ we have that p_2 is a weakest precondition of p_1 with respect to the assignment, i.e. if p_2 was *true* beforehand, then afterward p_1 is *true*, and if $\neg p_2$ was *true* beforehand, then p_1 becomes *false*. Thus the operation can be approximated by "$p_1 := choice(p_2, \neg p_2)$".
- Another situation already occurred in the introduction where we had the case that $P = \{p_1 \equiv x1 > 0\}$. With predicates only from P, there is no possibility to express a condition for p_1 to become *true* after the assignment, but if $\neg p_1$ was *true* beforehand, then p_1 stays *false*. Here we thus need to approximate the assignment by "$p_1 := choice(false, \neg p_1)$".

A partial boolean expression $pe = choice(a, b)$ approximates a boolean expression e (denoted as $pe \preceq e$), if a logically implies e, and b logically implies $\neg e$. The approximation is extended to operations by: "$assume(pe) : p_1 := pe_1, \ldots, p_m := pe_m$" $\preceq$ "$assume(e) : v_1 := e_1, \ldots, v_n := e_n$" iff $pe \preceq e$ and $pe_i \preceq wp_{op}(p_i)$, where $wp_{op}(p_i)$ is the weakest precondition of the predicate p_i with respect to the parallel assignment $v_1 := e_1, \ldots, v_n := e_n$ (abbreviated as op). A sequential boolean program $BPrg$ then approximates a program Prg if they have isomorphic CFGs and the operations in $BPrg$ approximate the corresponding ones in Prg.

3 Spotlight Abstractions

Boolean programs are helpful in cutting down the state space by reducing the information about program data in each state. Spotlight abstraction tackles another issue specifically occurring in parallel programs: the behavior of a large number of processes may be irrelevant for the property to be checked yet they might appear in the abstraction if they influence the value of predicates. The idea behind spotlight abstraction is to divide processes into two groups. The ones in the spotlight are examined in detail – each of these processes will be abstracted by its own boolean program. The others are almost left out: together, they are all summarized into *one* "shade" process $BPrg_\bot$ consisting of only one continuously executed operation that approximates all operations from the left-out processes simultaneously. This operation simply sets all predicates which depend on variables that might be changed by left-out processes to "unknown".

The parallel composition of processes in spotlight and $BPrg_\bot$ will then be model-checked. If in this model-checking run a left-out process turns out to be necessary, it joins the processes in the spotlight (by means of abstraction refinement). Alike other approaches, we use the counterexample generated by the model checking run to refine our abstraction. Similar to the work in [17, 15] on multi-valued abstractions, we are able to transfer *both* definite results ($true$ and $false$) from the abstraction to the original system for *any* CTL-formula.

Given a parallel program $Prg := ||_{i\in I}\, Prg_i$, a CTL-property φ and an initial set of processes $Init \subset I$ (e.g. all processes occurring in φ), we proceed as follows:

1. $spotlight := \{Prg_i\}_{i\in Init}$, $P :=$ { all predicates over $Var(Prg)$ occurring in φ }
2. While no definite answer is found:
   3. Build the spotlight abstraction with focus only on processes in *spotlight*.
   4. Model-check φ in the (much smaller) abstraction.
   5. If φ is $true$ or $false$ in the abstraction, output this as result for Prg and stop,
   6. else, use a counter-example for refinement resulting in either an additional predicate $p \notin P$ or an additional component $Prg_i \notin spotlight$
   7. $spotlight := spotlight \cup \{Prg_i\}$, $P := P \cup \{p\}$

For the program CHAIN$_3$ of the introduction, we let $Init := \{1\}$ since the property $AF(pc_1 = END)$ is local for process 1. The set of predicates is $P = \emptyset$. The spotlight abstraction in the above procedure is constructed according to the following definition.

Definition 8 (Spotlight Abstraction of Parallel Programs). *Let $Prg := ||_{i\in I}\, Prg_i$ be a parallel program and $BPrg := ||_{i\in BI}\, BPrg_i$ a parallel boolean program with predicates $P = \{p_1, \dots, p_m\}$ and $BI \subset I \,\dot\cup\, \{\bot\}$ the set of processes in the spotlight plus possibly the shade process. BPrg approximates Prg iff*

- *for every $i \in BI \setminus \{\bot\}$: $BPrg_i$ approximates Prg_i.*
- *$BI = I$ or $I \setminus BI \neq \emptyset$, $\bot \in BI$ and $BPrg_\bot$ is a CFG with $Loc_\bot = \{\bot\}$ and a single loop labeled with $p'_1 := \bot, \dots, p'_s := \bot$ where $\{p'_1, \dots, p'_s\} \subseteq P$ is the subset of all predicates depending on variables from $\bigcup_{i\in I\setminus BI} LVar(Prg_i)$, i.e. depending on variables that might be changed by parallel components not in spotlight.*

The PCFG of the spotlight abstraction of program CHAIN$_3$ with $spotlight = \{Prg_1\}$ (i.e. $BI = \{1, \bot\}$) and predicates P either $\emptyset$, $\{(x_1 > 0)\}$ or $\{(x_1 > 0), (x_1 > 1)\}$, is given in the left of Figure 5 (see page 116), its Kripke semantics can be found in the right part.

The Kripke structure semantics for spotlight abstractions follows those of boolean programs except for one point: besides the predicates in P we also have atomic propositions of the form $pc_i = k$ (component i is at location k). For processes not in the spotlight, i.e. $i \in I \setminus BI$, the valuation of $pc_i = k$ is always $\bot$. This reflects the fact that we do not know at which location processes not in the spotlight might be.

Of course, we would like to transfer model-checking results from spotlight abstractions to the original program. In [17], a *completeness preorder* is defined between three-valued Kripke structures, and it is proven that if some property is $true/false$ in some Kripke structure, then this also holds in any corresponding state of any more complete Kripke structure. In our proof, we establish a completeness relation between a concrete program and its spotlight abstraction that satisfies some slightly stronger properties than required by [17]. Unfortunately, we cannot apply their theorem, as it does not consider fair semantics as needed here. Instead, we give a direct proof which is however close to their work. In this proof we use the strengthened properties in our completeness relation to preserve our specific fairness constraints from definition 7.

The following theorem relates the model checking results of concrete and abstracted program for *corresponding* states. A concrete state $\langle l_c, s_c \rangle$ and an abstract state $\langle l_a, s_a \rangle$ are said to correspond to each other if the labeling of the concrete state is always "more definitive" than that one of the abstract state. If L_A and L_C are two labeling functions over the same atomic propositions AP, we write $L_A(q_a) \leq L_C(q_c)$ for being "more definitive" if $\forall p \in \mathsf{AP} : L_A(p, q_a) \leq L_C(p, q_c)$[3].

Theorem 1. *Let $Prg = \|_{i \in I} Prg_i$ be a parallel program and $BPrg = \|_{i \in BI} BPrg_i$ a boolean abstraction using predicates $P = \{p_1, \ldots, p_m\}$. Furthermore, let $K_P(Prg) = (S_C, R_C, L_C, \mathcal{F}_C)$ be the concrete Kripke structure and $K_P(BPrg) = (S_A, R_A, L_A, \mathcal{F}_A)$ the abstract one. Then for any two states $\langle l_c, s_c \rangle \in S_C$ and $\langle l_a, s_a \rangle \in S_A$ with $L_A(\langle l_a, s_a \rangle) \leq L_C(\langle l_c, s_c \rangle)$ and for any CTL-formula φ over the predicates in P or program locations the following holds with respect to (fair) interpretation:*

$$[\![\varphi]\!]_{K_P(BPrg)}(q_a) \leq [\![\varphi]\!]_{K_P(Prg)}(q_c)$$

Proof. The proof is omitted due to space constraints (see [21]).

Hence any "definite" result (true or false) obtained on the abstraction holds for the concrete program as well.

4 Abstraction Refinement

In this section we present our approach to refining the abstraction based on a given counterexample. For some state s and a CTL-formula φ with $[\![\varphi]\!](s) =: \perp$, a three-valued counterexample is a finite subtree of the computation tree that explains why $\perp$ holds [22]. In practice, a model-checker like χChek [16] outputs only a single branch in this counterexample representing an execution path on which φ is $\perp$. In this branch, there must exist at least one $\perp$-transition or a state with an atomic proposition labeled with $\perp$ causing[4] the $\perp$-value of the path. If there exist several, then an arbitrary (e.g. the first that is found) may be chosen. To extract a new predicate or a new component for spotlight, we proceed as follows:

1. One reason for the path to become $\perp$ might be a $\perp$-transition from some state s to s'. This can only be due to the *assume* condition of the corresponding boolean operation being $\perp$ in s. There are two cases to distinguish:

[3] Since the program counters are part of the atomic propositions and are either *true* or *false* for all processes in spotlight, in corresponding abstract and concrete states these processes are always at the same program location.

[4] We do without a formal definition for *causing the $\perp$-value*. Instead, we give a brief example. Consider a Kripke structure with two states $(p = \perp, q = true) \xrightarrow{\perp} (p = true, q = \perp)$ and the CTL formula $\varphi = EX(p \wedge q)$ which is evaluated in the first state. Clearly, the $\perp$-transition as well as $q = \perp$ in the second state cause the $\perp$, but $p = \perp$ in the first state doesn't.

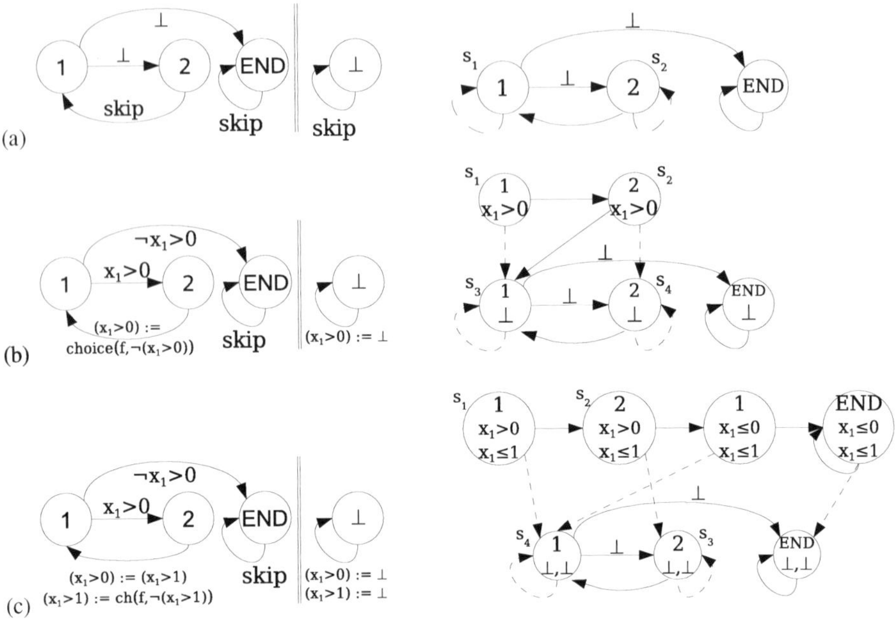

Fig. 5. PCFGs and Kripke semantics for the abstractions (a) to (c) of the example program (for those of (d) see [21]). Transitions caused by $BPrg_{\bot}$ are indicated by dashed lines.

   (a) If the *assume* condition e of the corresponding concrete operation is already contained in the set of predicates, then e is $\bot$ in s and we continue with step 2.
   (b) Else we use e as new predicate.
2. The other reason might be a predicate p that is $\bot$ in some state s. Let $\tilde{s}$ be the last predecessor of s, where p was *true* or *false* and $\tilde{s}'$ the direct successor of $\tilde{s}$. There are three cases to distinguish:
   (a) The transition between $\tilde{s}$ and $\tilde{s}'$ is due to an operation op of a process in spotlight, and the weakest precondition $wp_{op}(p)$ is already contained in the set of predicates. Then $wp_{op}(p)$ is $\bot$ in $\tilde{s}$ and we further backtrack with step 2.
   (b) The same, but $wp_{op}(p)$ is not yet contained in the set of predicates. Then we use $wp_{op}(p)$ as new predicate.
   (c) If the transition is due to an operation of $BPrg_{\bot}$, then output one arbitrary (e.g., the first that has been found) process writing on variables occurring in p. This process will be added to the spotlight.

After every such step we reach an abstraction for which Theorem 1 holds. To illustrate the strategy we consider our example (see Fig. 1) and the CTL-formula $\varphi \equiv (AF\ pc_1 = \texttt{END})$. The four steps are already given in pseudocode in figure 2. Here we will show their Kripke semantics (see Fig. 5) and how the refinement works on it.

(a) φ only contains an atomic proposition concerning the program counter of the first process and no predicates over any variables. So we start with $spotlight = \{1\}$ and

$P = \emptyset$. The corresponding Kripke structure is shown in figure 5a. If we examine the counterexample $s_1 \to s_2 \to s_1 \to \ldots$, the cause for $\perp$ is the transition from s_1 to s_2. Via step 1.b we get the new predicate $p_1 \equiv x_1 > 0$.

(b) The Kripke structure for *spotlight* $= \{1\}$ and $P = \{p_1 \equiv x_1 > 0\}$ is shown in figure 5b. If we examine the counter-example $s_1 \to s_2 \to s_3 \to s_4 \to s_3 \to \ldots$, the cause for $\perp$ is the transition from s_3 to s_4. Since the corresponding *assume* condition is already a predicate (step 1.a) we go on with step 2. With $\tilde{s} = s_2$ and $\tilde{s}' = s_3$, we get the new predicate $p_2 \equiv x1 - 1 > 0$ via step 2.b.

(c) The Kripke structure for *spotlight* $= \{1\}$ and $P = \{p_1 \equiv x_1 > 0, p_2 \equiv x_1 - 1 > 0\}$ is shown in figure 5c. If we examine the counter-example $s_1 \to s_2 \to s_3 \to s_4 \to s_3 \to \ldots$, the cause for $\perp$ is the transition from s_4 to s_3. Since the corresponding *assume* condition is already a predicate (step 1.a), we go on with step 2. With $\tilde{s} = s_2$ and $\tilde{s}' = s_3$, we add process 2 to the spotlight because of step 2.c.

(d) The Kripke structure for *spotlight* $= \{1, 2\}$ and P as in (c) still has several $\perp$-transitions due to the abstraction (see [21]). Nonetheless, under fair semantics the model-checker returns $[\![AF pc_1 = \texttt{END}]\!](s_1) = \mathit{true}$. Due to theorem 1, we can transfer this property to the original program and stop refinement.

5 Experimental Results

We have a prototype implementation of our spotlight abstraction and abstraction refinement technique, called 3Spot, which works on top of the multi-valued model checker χChek [16]. Our tool reads in a parallel program (in a simple C-like syntax), constructs its abstraction (using Z3 as prover) and builds an MDD of the partial Kripke structure which is given to χChek. The model checker then returns true or false (which is immediately reported to the user) or a counter-example as a witness for a $\perp$ result. The counter-example is next analyzed and abstraction refinement proceeds as explained before. While supporting almost all control structures of the C language, we currently only support `int`, `bool`, and `mutex` as data types (i.e. no arrays, no pointers).

We have experimented with a number of case studies to test our approach. As expected, on sequential programs our tool cannot compete with other abstraction refinement model checkers like BLAST [4], SATABS [8], and ARMC [7] since we so far have spent no effort at all in optimizations. The difference becomes visible when checking parallel programs with respect to local properties.

In the following we compare our implementation 3Spot with SATABS and ARMC using different case studies. While SATABS does provide built-in functionality to check parallel programs, we simulate parallel programs in ARMC by adding program counter variables for all processes and simply treating them as data. Another option would have been to compute the product CFG and then use the single special program counter variable that ARMC allows. Our conjecture is, however, that ARMC would then run much slower on our examples. For our comparison we have preferred ARMC over – for instance – BLAST because the input format used in ARMC (transition constraints) allows us to easily encode program counters as data[5].

[5] The data race checker of BLAST [23] is no longer available in the current releases.

Table 1 shows the results of our benchmark. We ran the tests on a 3GHz Pentium 4 Linux system (Debian etch) with 1GB memory (Satabs, ARMC) and on a 3GHZ Pentium 4 Windows system (Windows XP) with 1GB memory (3Spot) respectively. Since some test runs took very long we stopped them after at most 2.5 hours.

As first case study we used CHAIN$_n$, the generalized version of the introductory program CHAIN$_3$, and tried to verify $AG\ (pc_1 = \texttt{END} \Rightarrow (x1 \leq 0))$[6]. Although our implementation only needs to take two processes into the spotlight, ARMC's performance is almost as good as the performance of 3Spot. Interestingly, the technique to model program counters as data allows ARMC to pick only the program counters of interest as predicates. So in this case ARMC only considers the program counters of process 1 and process 2 while ignoring all the other processes. This allows ARMC to be as fast as 3Spot for small n and to be significantly faster than SATABS in this example. Still, when using large values for n like e.g. $n = 100$ (last row) 3Spot can take advantage of the fact that it can ignore whole processes, while ARMC has to consider each operation separately and in particular has to compute the abstraction of the operation.

In addition to heterogeneous programs like CHAIN$_n$, we have looked at uniform parallel programs, in particular those using semaphores for synchronization. To be able to efficiently treat such programs without needing to incorporate all components, we have developed a specific abstraction technique for semaphores.

A semaphore is modeled as an integer variable $v \in \{-1, \ldots, n\}$ indicating which process locks it ($v = -1$ if none). Process i may *acquire* v by "$assume(v = -1) : v := i$" and *release* v via "$assume(v = i) : v := -1$". Using the technique described above, processes not in spotlight could "maybe" release locks of processes in spotlight, as the $\perp$-process repeatedly sets "$(v = -1) := \perp$". We avoid this problem by changing this assignment to "$(v = -1) := choice(false, \neg(v = -1))$". This means, if a semaphore is free or "maybe" locked the $\perp$-process can do anything with it (i.e. $(v = -1)$ is set to $\perp$), but a definitely locked semaphore will never be released (i.e. $(v = -1)$ remains $false$). One can prove a modified version of theorem 1, where the possible initial states q_a and q_c are slightly restricted (see [21]). This enables us to get model checking results without having to look at all processes only because they share a semaphore.

As an example consider the following program MUTEX$_n$: n processes all consisting of the code "`while(true){NC:skip; acquire v; CS:skip; release v}`". For simplicity in this example, all processes are uniform, switching between a non-critical section `NC` and a critical section `CS`, where the latter is guarded by a semaphore v. Of course, the sections `NC` and `CS` may look very different in real-world programs, making this example also heterogeneous.

We used MUTEX$_n$ as second case study in our benchmark and checked the CTL-formula $AG\neg(pc_1 = \texttt{CS} \wedge pc_2 = \texttt{CS})$. Thus, in this case study we try to verify that our use of semaphores indeed ensures that process one and process two may not enter the critical section at the very same time. The idea behind this is that process one and process two may share a resource r we are interested in, while the other processes may share other resources with process one and two we are not interested in at this moment, but that cause the need of a semaphore for *all* processes instead of only one and two.

[6] We did not check the liveness property $AF\ (pc_1 = \texttt{END})$ because it can not be (directly) expressed in SATABS and ARMC.

As for the results, 3Spot clearly outperforms ARMC in number of predicates generated and time needed (see table 1). Unfortunately, we were not able to verify this program with SATABS because the pthread library used for semaphores in SATABS and that provided with the Linux distribution on our test system were different and thus we could not test the semaphore feature in SATABS.

For our last case study we implemented Dijkstra's mutual exclusion algorithm [24] and tried to verify $AG\neg(pc_1 = \mathsf{CS} \wedge pc_2 = \mathsf{CS})$, i.e. the same property as for MUTEX$_n$ but using a mutual exclusion *algorithm* rather than a build-in semaphore. Although we are not able to take advantage of our specific abstraction technique for semaphores in this case we still only need to take the first two processes into the spotlight. This allows us to again be faster than both SATABS and ARMC, even though the overall performance is worse than for MUTEX$_n$ (see table 1).

Table 1. Benchmark results of 3SPOT in comparison to SATABS and ARMC. (*): No results, because the built-in semaphores used by SATABS were not available on our test system.

		3SPOT			SATABS		ARMC	
	n	processes	predicates	time	predicates	time	predicates	time
CHAIN	2	2	2	$0.53s$	9	$7.02s$	5	$0.09s$
	3	2	2	$0.55s$	21	$66.6s$	5	$0.11s$
	4	2	2	$0.56s$	32	$17.8m$	5	$0.15s$
	5	2	2	$0.56s$	?	$> 2.5h$	5	$0.18s$
	100	2	2	$0.66s$	?	out of memory	5	$22.1s$
MUTEX	7	2	1	$0.50s$	(*)	(*)	17	$1.71s$
	12	2	1	$0.50s$	(*)	(*)	27	$9.31s$
	17	2	1	$0.52s$	(*)	(*)	37	$32.6s$
	50	2	1	$0.56s$	(*)	(*)	103	$29.0m$
	100	2	1	$0.59s$	(*)	(*)	?	$> 2.5h$
DIJKSTRA	2	2	2	$0.88s$	5	$3.35s$	50	$29.9s$
	3	2	3	$1.44s$	6	$43.6s$	59	$350s$
	4	2	4	$2.51s$	6	$252s$	66	$20.5m$
	5	2	5	$5.50s$	8	$65.8m$	72	$53.0m$
	6	2	6	$16.4s$	?	$> 2.5h$	?	$> 2.5h$
	7	2	7	$190s$	?	$> 2.5h$	?	$> 2.5h$

6 Conclusion

In this paper we have introduced a specific predicate abstraction technique for parallel programs. We have been interested in verifying *local* properties of components, which can - because of shared variables of components - however be influenced by other components. This gave rise to particular spotlight abstractions, focusing on a set of components while completely omitting others. Due to the use of a three-valued setting, we obtain abstractions that preserve both existential and universal properties thus only necessitating abstraction refinement when the result of a verification run is "unknown". While using CTL as a logic for specifying properties here, we conjecture that – similar to [17] – the same result also holds for the mu-calculus. We have furthermore shown how abstraction refinement for spotlight abstractions proceeds, either adding new predicates or further components. The technique has been implemented on top of an existing three-valued model checker and shows promising results.

Related work. Our work is connected to other approaches in a number of ways. The work closest to us is that in [15] and [17] which introduce *many-valued abstractions*. From [17] we have taken the idea of showing a completeness order (here extended with fairness) between original and abstracted system as to preserve full CTL properties. From [15] (and from [20]) we have taken most of our notations for describing programs and their abstractions. The particular definition of abstraction differs from [15]: Gurfinkel and Chechik discuss three different kinds of approximations, the most precise one (called *exact approximation*) employs four different truth values. The main difference however lies in the class of programs treated: neither of the two above cited approaches consider abstractions for parallel programs. Our focus has been on the development of a specific spotlight abstraction for parallel programs. Abstraction refinement for spotlight abstractions for the verification of dynamic systems is treated in [25]. Similar to us, counterexamples are inspected as to determine the processes which need to be moved into the spotlight. The choice between a new process and a new predicate however has not to be taken as no predicate abstraction is used.

Two-valued abstraction techniques for parallel programs are treated in e.g. [9], [10, 11, 6]. The canonical abstractions of [11] also employ a third value $\perp$, but do not make use of this additional information, $\perp$ is treated as *false*. These approaches mainly tackle parametrized systems, consisting of an unknown number of (almost) identical components. This is different from our approach since we do not assume identity of components, however a fixed number. Furthermore, we allow for full CTL model checking while some of the above approaches only treat safety properties.

Finally, our approach is related to other analysis techniques which construct abstractions of different parts of a program with different degrees. Examples for this are *lazy abstractions* [26] (predicate abstraction with different number of predicates for different program parts), *thread-modular abstractions* [23] (employing assume-guarantee reasoning to show absence of data races in parallel programs, however not allowing for full CTL model checking) or *heterogeneous abstractions* [27] (program heap abstracted in different degrees).

Future work. As future work we intend to experiment further with abstraction refinement techniques. It is possible to find both examples for which the addition of a predicate is to be preferred over the addition of a component and vice versa. Further experimentation would allow us to find heuristics for determining when to prefer which kind of refinement. A decisive factor for this is also the counterexample generated by the model checker: some counterexamples hint to an addition of a predicate although this might necessitate more refinement steps than an addition of a component would yield (and again vice versa). A heuristic for a targeted search during model checking might supply us with better counterexamples leading to a smaller number of refinement steps.

References

1. Clarke, E., Grumberg, O., Peled, D.: Model checking. MIT Press, Cambridge (1999)
2. Cousot, P., Cousot, R.: Abstract interpretation: A unified lattice model for static analysis of programs by construction or approximation of fixpoints. In: POPL (1977)
3. Clarke, E.M., Grumberg, O., Long, D.E.: Model checking and abstraction. In: 19th ACM POPL (1992)
4. Beyer, D., Henzinger, T.A., Jhala, R., Majumdar, R.: The Software Model Checker Blast: Applications to Software Engineering. In: STTT (2007)
5. Ball, T., Cook, B., Levin, V., Rajamani, S.K.: SLAM and Static Driver Verifier: Technology Transfer of Formal Methods inside Microsoft. In: Boiten, E.A., Derrick, J., Smith, G.P. (eds.) IFM 2004. LNCS, vol. 2999, pp. 1–20. Springer, Heidelberg (2004)
6. Chaki, S., Clarke, E., Groce, A., Jha, S., Veith, H.: Modular Verification of Software Components in C. IEEE Trans. on Software Engineering (TSE) 30(6), 388–402 (2004)
7. Podelski, A., Rybalchenko, A.: ARMC: The logical choice for software model checking with abstraction refinement. In: Hanus, M. (ed.) PADL 2007. LNCS, vol. 4354, pp. 245–259. Springer, Heidelberg (2007)
8. Clarke, E., Kroening, D., Sharygina, N., Yorav, K.: SATABS: SAT-Based Predicate Abstraction for ANSI-C. In: Halbwachs, N., Zuck, L.D. (eds.) TACAS 2005. LNCS, vol. 3440, pp. 570–574. Springer, Heidelberg (2005)
9. Pnueli, A., Xu, J., Zuck, L.D.: Liveness with (0, 1, infty)-counter abstraction. In: Brinksma, E., Larsen, K.G. (eds.) CAV 2002. LNCS, vol. 2404, pp. 107–122. Springer, Heidelberg (2002)
10. Clarke, E.M., Talupur, M., Veith, H.: Environment abstraction for parameterized verification. In: Emerson, E.A., Namjoshi, K.S. (eds.) VMCAI 2006. LNCS, vol. 3855, pp. 126–141. Springer, Heidelberg (2006)
11. Wachter, B., Westphal, B.: The Spotlight Principle: On Process-Summarizing State Abstractions. In: Cook, B., Podelski, A. (eds.) VMCAI 2007. LNCS, vol. 4349, pp. 182–198. Springer, Heidelberg (2007)
12. Sagiv, S., Reps, T.W., Wilhelm, R.: Parametric shape analysis via 3-valued logic. In: Symposium on Principles of Programming Languages, pp. 105–118 (1999)
13. Bruns, G., Godefroid, P.: Model checking with multi-valued logics. In: Díaz, J., Karhumäki, J., Lepistö, A., Sannella, D. (eds.) ICALP 2004. LNCS, vol. 3142, pp. 281–293. Springer, Heidelberg (2004)
14. Chechik, M., Devereux, B., Easterbrook, S.M., Gurfinkel, A.: Multi-valued symbolic model-checking. ACM Trans. Softw. Eng. Methodol. 12(4), 371–408 (2003)
15. Gurfinkel, A., Chechik, M.: Why waste a perfectly good abstraction? In: Hermanns, H., Palsberg, J. (eds.) TACAS 2006. LNCS, vol. 3920, pp. 212–226. Springer, Heidelberg (2006)
16. Easterbrook, S.M., Chechik, M., Devereux, B., et al.: χchek: A model checker for multi-valued reasoning. In: ICSE, pp. 804–805. IEEE Computer Society, Los Alamitos (2003)
17. Godefroid, P., Jagadeesan, R.: Automatic abstraction using generalized model checking. In: Brinksma, E., Larsen, K.G. (eds.) CAV 2002. LNCS, vol. 2404, pp. 137–150. Springer, Heidelberg (2002)
18. Fitting, M.: Kleene's three valued logics and their children. FI 20, 113–131 (1994)
19. Clarke, E.M., Emerson, E.A., Sistla, A.P.: Automatic verification of finite-state concurrent systems using temporal logic specifications. ACM TPLS 8, 244–263 (1986)
20. Ball, T., Podelski, A., Rajamani, S.K.: Boolean and cartesian abstraction for model checking C programs. STTT 5(1), 49–58 (2003)
21. Schrieb, J., Wehrheim, H., Wonisch, D.: Three-valued spotlight abstractions (2009), `http://www.cs.upb.de/en/ag-bloemer/people/jonas`

22. Gurfinkel, A., Chechik, M.: Generating counterexamples for multi-valued model-checking. In: Araki, K., Gnesi, S., Mandrioli, D. (eds.) FME 2003. LNCS, vol. 2805, pp. 503–521. Springer, Heidelberg (2003)
23. Henzinger, T., Jhala, R., Majumdar, R., Qadeer, S.: Thread-modular abstraction refinement. In: Hunt Jr., W.A., Somenzi, F. (eds.) CAV 2003. LNCS, vol. 2725, pp. 262–274. Springer, Heidelberg (2003)
24. Dijkstra, E.W.: Solution of a problem in concurrent programming control. Commun. ACM 8(9), 569 (1965)
25. Toben, T.: Counterexample guided spotlight abstraction refinement. In: Suzuki, K., Higashino, T., Yasumoto, K., El-Fakih, K. (eds.) FORTE 2008. LNCS, vol. 5048, pp. 21–36. Springer, Heidelberg (2008)
26. Henzinger, T.A., Jhala, R., Majumdar, R., Sutre, G.: Lazy abstraction. In: POPL, pp. 58–70 (2002)
27. Yahav, E., Ramalingam, G.: Verifying safety properties using separation and heterogeneous abstractions. In: PLDI, pp. 25–34. ACM, New York (2004)

Fair Model Checking with Process Counter Abstraction*

Jun Sun, Yang Liu, Abhik Roychoudhury, Shanshan Liu, and Jin Song Dong

School of Computing, National University of Singapore
{sunj, liuyang, abhik, liushans, dongjs}@comp.nus.edu.sg

Abstract. Parameterized systems are characterized by the presence of a large (or even unbounded) number of behaviorally similar processes, and they often appear in distributed/concurrent systems. A common state space abstraction for checking parameterized systems involves not keeping track of process identifiers by grouping behaviorally similar processes. Such an abstraction, while useful, conflicts with the notion of fairness. Because process identifiers are lost in the abstraction, it is difficult to ensure fairness (in terms of progress in executions) among the processes. In this work, we study the problem of fair model checking with process counter abstraction. Even without maintaining the process identifiers, our on-the-fly checking algorithm enforces fairness by keeping track of the local states from where actions are enabled / executed within an execution trace. We enhance our home-grown PAT model checker with the technique and show its usability via the automated verification of several real-life protocols.

1 Introduction

Parameterized concurrent systems consist of a large (or even unbounded) number of behaviorally similar processes of the same type. Such systems frequently arise in distributed algorithms and protocols (*e.g.*, cache coherence protocols, control software in automotive / avionics) — where the number of behaviorally similar processes is unbounded during system design, but is fixed later during system deployment. Thus, the deployed system contains fixed, finite number of behaviorally similar processes. However during system modeling/verification it is convenient to not fix the number of processes in the system for the sake for achieving more general verification results. A parameterized system represents an infinite family of instances, each instance being finite-state. Property verification of a parameterized system involves verifying that *every finite state instance of the system* satisfies the property in question. In general, verification of parameterized systems is undecidable [2].

A common practice for analyzing parameterized systems can be to fix the number of processes to a constant. To avoid state space explosion, the constant is often small, compared to the size of the real applications. Model checking is then performed in the hope of finding a bug which is exhibited by a fixed (and small) number of processes. This practice can be incorrect because the real size of the systems is often unknown during system design (but fixed later during system deployment). It is also difficult to

* This research has been supported in part by National University of Singapore FRC grant R-252-000-385-112 and R-252-000-320-112.

A. Cavalcanti and D. Dams (Eds.): FM 2009, LNCS 5850, pp. 123–139, 2009.

fix the number of processes to a "large enough" constant such that the restricted system with fixed number of processes is observationally equivalent to the parameterized system with unboundedly many processes. Computing such a *large enough constant* is undecidable after all, since the parameterized verification problem is undecidable.

Since parameterized systems contain process types with large number of behaviorally similar processes (whose behavior follows a local finite state machine or FSM), a natural state space abstraction is to group the processes based on which state of the local FSM they reside in [23, 7, 24]. Thus, instead of saying "process 1 is in state s, process 2 is in state t and process 3 is in state s" — we simply say "2 processes are in state s and 1 is in state t". Such an abstraction reduces the state space by exploiting a powerful state space symmetry (concrete global states with different process identifiers but the same count of the processes in the individual local states get grouped into the same abstract global state), as often evidenced in real-life concurrent systems such as a caches, memories, mutual exclusion protocols and network protocols. Verification by traversing the abstract state space here produces a sound and complete verification procedure. However, if the total number of processes is unbounded, the aforementioned counter abstraction still does not produce a finite state abstract system. The count of processes in a local state can still be ω (unbounded number), if the total number of processes is ω. To achieve a finite state abstract system, we can adopt a *cutoff number*, so that any count greater than the *cutoff* number is abstracted to ω. This yields a finite state abstract system, model checking which we get a sound but incomplete verification procedure — any linear time Temporal Logic (LTL) property verified in the abstract system holds for all concrete finite-state instances of the system, but not vice-versa.

Contributions. In this paper, we study the problem of fair model checking with process counter abstraction. Imagine a bus protocol where a large / unbounded number of processors are contending for bus access. If we do not assume any fairness in the bus arbitration policy, we cannot prove the non-starvation property, that is, bus accesses by processors are eventually granted. In general, fairness constraints are often needed for verification of such liveness properties — ignoring fairness constraints results in unrealistic counterexamples (e.g. where a processor requesting for bus access is persistently ignored by the bus arbiter for example) being reported. These counterexamples are of no interest to the protocol designer. To systematically rule out such unrealistic counterexamples (which never happen in a real implementation), it is important to verify the abstract system produced by our process counter abstraction under fairness. We do so in this paper. However, this constitutes a significant *technical challenge* — since we do not even keep track of the process identifiers, how can we ensure a fair scheduling among the individual processes!

In this work, we develop a novel technique for model checking parameterized systems under (weak or strong) fairness, against linear temporal logic (LTL) formulae. We show that model checking under fairness is feasible, even without the knowledge of process identifiers. This is done by systematically keeping track of the local states from which actions are enabled / executed within any infinite loop of the abstract state space. We develop necessary theorems to prove the soundness of our technique, and also present efficient on-the-fly model checking algorithms. Our method is realized within our home-grown PAT model checker [26]. The usability / scalability of PAT is demonstrated via (i) automated verification of several real-life parameterized systems and (ii) a quantitative comparison with the SPIN model checker [17].

2 Preliminaries

We begin by formally defining our system model.

Definition 1 (System Model). *A system model is a structure* $\mathcal{S} = (Var_G, init_G, Proc)$ *where* Var_G *is a finite set of global variables,* $init_G$ *is their initial valuation and* $Proc$ *is a parallel composition of multiple processes* $Proc = P_1 \parallel P_2 \parallel \cdots$ *such that each process* $P_i = (S_i, init_i, \rightarrow_i)$ *is a transition system.*

We assume that all global variables have finite domains and each P_i has finitely many local states. A local state represents a program text together with its local context (e.g. valuation of the local variables). Two local states are equivalent if and only if they represent the same program text and the same local context. Let $State$ be the set of all local states. We assume that $State$ has finitely many elements. This disallows unbounded non-tail recursion which results in infinite different local states. $Proc$ may be composed of infinitely many processes. Each process has a unique identifier. In an abuse of notation, we use P_i to represent the identifier of process P_i when the context is clear. Notice that two local states from different processes are equivalent only if the process identifiers are irrelevant to the program texts they represent. Processes may communicate through global variables, (multi-party) barrier synchronization or synchronous/asynchronous message passing. It can be shown that parallel composition $\parallel$ is symmetric and associative.

Example 1. Fig. 1 shows a model of the readers/writers problem, which is a simple protocol for the coordination of readers and writers accessing a shared resource. The protocol, which we refer to as RW, is designed for arbitrary number of readers and writers. Several readers can read concurrently, whereas writers require exclusive access. Global variable $counter$ records the number of readers which are currently accessing the resource; $writing$ is true if and only if a writer is updating the resource. A transition is of the form $[guard]name\{assignments\}$, where $guard$ is a guard condition which must be true for the transition to be taken and $assignments$ is a simple sequential program which updates global variables. The following are properties which are to be verified.

$$\Box !(counter > 0 \land writing) \qquad - Prop_1$$
$$\Box \Diamond counter > 0 \qquad - Prop_2$$

Property $Prop_1$ is a safety property which states that writing and reading cannot occur simultaneously. Property $Prop_2$ is a liveness property which states that always eventually the resource can be accessed by some reader.

In order to define the operational semantics of a system model, we define the notion of a configuration to capture the global system state during the execution, which is referred to as *concrete configurations*. This terminology distinguishes the notion from the state space abstraction and the abstract configurations which will be introduced later.

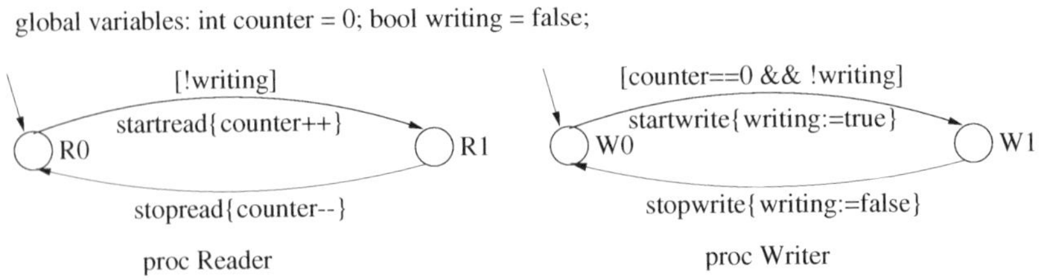

Fig. 1. Readers/writers model

Definition 2 (Concrete Configuration). *Let S be a system model. A concrete configuration of S is a pair $(v, \langle s_1, s_2, \cdots \rangle)$ where v is the valuation of the global variables (channel buffers may be viewed as global variables), and $s_i \in S_i$ is the local state in which process P_i is residing.*

A system transition is of the form $(v, \langle s_1, s_2, \cdots \rangle) \rightarrow_{Ag} (v', \langle s_1', s_2', \cdots \rangle)$ where the system configuration after the transition is $(v', \langle s_1', s_2', \cdots \rangle)$ and Ag is a set of participating processes. For simplicity, set Ag (short for *agent*) is often omitted if irreverent. A system transition could be one of the following forms:

(i) a local transition of P_i which updates its local state (from s_i to s_i') and possibly updating global variables (from v to v'). An example is the transition from $R0$ to $R1$ of a reader. In such a case, P_i is the participating process, i.e., $Ag = \{P_i\}$.

(ii) a multi-party synchronous transition among processes $P_i, \cdots, P_j$. Examples are message sending/receiving through channels with buffer size 0 (e.g., as in Promela [17]) and alphabetized barrier synchronization in the classic CSP. In such a case, local states of the participating processes are updated simultaneously. The participating processes are $P_i, \cdots, P_j$.

(iii) process creation of P_m by P_i. In such a case, an additional local state is appended to the sequence $\langle s_1, s_2, \cdots \rangle$, and the state of P_i is changed at the same time. Assume for now that the sequence $\langle s_1, s_2, \cdots \rangle$ is always finite before process creation. It becomes clear in Section 5 that this assumption is not necessary. In such a case, the participating processes are P_i and P_m.

(iv) process deletion of P_i. In such case, the local state of P_i is removed from the sequence $(\langle s_1, s_2, \cdots \rangle)$. The participating process is P_i.

Definition 3 (Concrete Transition System). *Let $S = (Var_G, init_G, Proc)$ be a system model, where $Proc = P_1 \parallel P_2 \parallel \cdots$ such that each process $P_i = (S_i, init_i, \rightarrow_i)$ is a local transition system. The concrete transition system corresponding to S is a 3-tuple $T_S = (C, init, \hookrightarrow)$ where C is the set of all reachable system configurations, $init$ is the initial concrete configuration $(init_G, \langle init_1, init_2, \cdots \rangle)$ and $\hookrightarrow$ is the global transition relation obtained by composing the local transition relations $\rightarrow_i$ in parallel.*

An execution of S is an infinite sequence of configurations $E = \langle c_0, c_1, \cdots, c_i, \cdots \rangle$ where $c_0 = init$ and $c_i \hookrightarrow c_{i+1}$ for all $i \geq 0$. Given a model S and a system configuration c, let $enabled_S(c)$ (or $enabled(c)$ when the context is clear) be the set of processes which is ready to make some progress, i.e., $enabled(c) = \{P_i \mid \exists c', c \hookrightarrow_{Ag} c' \wedge P_i \in Ag\}$. The following defines two common notions of fairness in system executions, i.e., weak fairness and strong fairness.

Definition 4 (Weak Fairness). *Let $\mathcal{S}$ be a system model. An execution $\langle c_1, c_2, \cdots \rangle$ of $T_{\mathcal{S}}$ is weakly fair, if and only if, for every P_i there are infinitely many k such that $c_k \rightarrow_{Ag} c_{k+1}$ and $P_i \in Ag$ if there exists n so that $P_i \in enabled(c_m)$ for all $m > n$.*

Weak fairness states that if a process becomes enabled forever after some steps, then it must be engaged infinitely often. From another point of view, weak fairness guarantees that each process is only finitely faster than the others.

Definition 5 (Strong Fairness). *Let $\mathcal{S}$ be a system model. An execution $\langle c_1, c_2, \cdots \rangle$ of $T_{\mathcal{S}}$ is strongly fair, if and only if, for every P_i there are infinitely many k such that $c_k \rightarrow_{Ag} c_{k+1}$ and $P_i \in Ag$ if there are infinitely many n such that $P_i \in enabled(c_n)$.*

Strong fairness states that if a process is infinitely often enabled, it must be infinitely often engaged. This type of fairness is particularly useful in the analysis of systems that use semaphores, synchronous communication, and other special coordination primitives. Clearly, strong fairness guarantees weak fairness.

In this work, we assume that system properties are expressed as *LTL formulae constituted by propositions on global variables*. One way to state property of a single process is to migrate part of its local context to global variables. Let ϕ be a property. $\mathcal{S}$ satisfies ϕ, written as $\mathcal{S} \vDash \phi$, if and only if every execution of $T_{\mathcal{S}}$ satisfies ϕ. $\mathcal{S}$ satisfies ϕ under weak fairness, written as $\mathcal{S} \vDash_{wf} \phi$, if and only if, every weakly fair execution of $T_{\mathcal{S}}$ satisfies ϕ. T satisfies ϕ under strong fairness, written as $T \vDash_{sf} \phi$, if and only if, every strongly fair execution of T satisfies ϕ.

Given the RW model presented in Fig. 1, it can be shown that $RW \vDash Prop_1$. It is, however, not easy to prove it using standard model checking techniques. The challenge is that many or unbounded number of readers and writers cause state space explosion. Also, RW fails $Prop_2$ without fairness constraint. For instance, a counterexample is $\langle startwrite, stopwrite \rangle^{\infty}$, i.e., a writer keeps updating the resource without any reader ever accessing it. This is unreasonable if the system scheduler is well-designed or the processors that the readers/writers execute on have comparable speed. To avoid such counterexamples, we need to perform model checking under fairness.

3 Process Counter Representation

Parameterized systems contain behaviorally similar or even identical processes. Given a configuration $(v, \langle \cdots, s_i, \cdots, s_j, \cdots \rangle)$, multiple local states[1] may be equivalent. A natural "abstraction" is to record only how many copies of a local state are there.

Let $\mathcal{S}$ be a system model. An alternative representation of a concrete configuration is a pair (v, f) where v is the valuation of the global variables and f is a total function from a local state to the set of processes residing at the state. For instance, given that $R0$ is a local state in Fig. 1, $f(R0) = \{P_i, P_j, P_k\}$ if and only if reader processes P_i, P_j and P_k

[1] The processes residing at the local states may or may not have the same process type.

are residing at state $R0$. This representation is sound and complete because processes at equivalent local states are behavioral equivalent and $\|$ composition is symmetric and associative (so that processes ordering is irrelevant).

Furthermore, given a local state s and processes residing at s, we may consider the processes indistinguishable (as the process identifiers must be irrelevant given the local states are equivalent) and abstract the process identifiers. That is, instead of associating a set of process identifiers with a local state, we only keep track of the number of processes. Instead of setting $f(R0) = \{P_i, P_j, P_k\}$, we now set $f(R0) = 3$. *In this and the next section, we assume that the total number of processes is bounded.*

Definition 6 (Abstract Configuration). *Let $\mathcal{S}$ be a system model. An abstract configuration of $\mathcal{S}$ is a pair (v, f) where v is a valuation of the global variables and $f : State \rightarrow \mathbb{N}$ is a total function[2] such that $f(s) = n$ if and only if n processes are residing at s.*

Given a concrete configuration $cc = (v, \langle s_0, s_1, \cdots \rangle)$, let $\mathcal{F}(\langle s_0, s_1, \cdots \rangle)$ returns the function f (refer to Definition 6) — that is, $f(s) = n$ if and only if there are n states in $\langle s_0, s_1, \cdots \rangle$ which are equivalent to s. Further, we write $\mathcal{F}(cc)$ to denote $(v, \mathcal{F}(\langle s_0, s_1, \cdots \rangle))$. Given a concrete transition $c \rightarrow_{Ag} c'$, the corresponding abstraction transition is written as $a \hookrightarrow_{Ls} a'$ where $a = \mathcal{F}(c)$ and $a' = \mathcal{F}(c')$ and Ls (short for local-states) is the local states at which processes in Ag are. That is, Ls is the set of local states from which there is a process leaving during the transition. We remark that Ls is obtained similarly as Ag is.

Given a local state s and an abstract configuration a, we define $enabled(s, a)$ *to be true if and only if* $\exists\, a',\ a \hookrightarrow_{Ls} a' \wedge s \in Ls$, i.e., a process is enabled to leave s in a. For instance, given the transition system in Fig. 2, $Ls = \{R0\}$ for the transition from $A0$ to $A1$ and $enabled(R0, A1)$ is true.

Definition 7 (Abstract Transition System). *Let $\mathcal{S} = (Var_G, init_G, Proc)$ be a system model, where $Proc = P_1 \parallel P_2 \parallel \cdots$ such that each process $P_i = (S_i, init_i, \rightarrow_i)$ is a local transition system. An abstract transition system of $\mathcal{S}$ is a 3-tuple $A_{\mathcal{S}} = (C, init, \hookrightarrow)$ where C is the set of all reachable abstract system configurations, $init \in C$ is $(init_G, \mathcal{F}(init_G, \langle init_1, init_2, \cdots \rangle))$ and $\hookrightarrow$ is the abstract global transition relation.*

We remark that the abstract transition relation can be constructed *without* constructing the concrete transition relation, which is essential to avoid state space explosion. Given the model presented in Fig. 1, if there are 2 readers and 2 writers, then the abstract transition system is shown in Fig. 2.

A concrete execution of $T_{\mathcal{S}}$ can be uniquely mapped to an execution of $A_{\mathcal{S}}$ by applying $\mathcal{F}$ to every configuration in the sequence. For instance, let $X = \langle c_0, c_1, \cdots, c_i, \cdots \rangle$ be an execution of $T_{\mathcal{S}}$ (i.e., a concrete execution), the corresponding execution of $A_{\mathcal{S}}$ is $L = \langle \mathcal{F}(c_0), \mathcal{F}(c_1), \cdots, \mathcal{F}(c_i), \cdots \rangle$ (i.e., the abstract execution). In an abuse of notation, we write $\mathcal{F}(X)$ to denote L. Notice that the valuation of the global variables are preserved. Essentially, no information is lost during the abstraction. It can be shown that $A_{\mathcal{S}} \vDash \phi$ if and only if $T_{\mathcal{S}} \vDash \phi$.

[2] In PAT, the mapping from a local state to 0 is always omitted for memory saving.

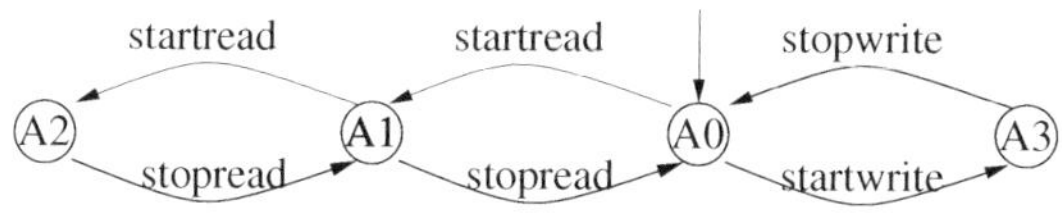

A0: ((writing,false),(counter,0),(R0,2),(R1,0),(W0,2),(W1,0))
A1: ((writing,false),(counter,1),(R0,1),(R1,1),(W0,2),(W1,0))
A2: ((writing,false),(counter,2),(R0,0),(R1,2),(W0,2),(W1,0))
A3: ((writing,true),(counter,0),(R0,2),(R1,0),(W0,1),(W1,1))

Fig. 2. Readers/writers model

4 Fair Model Checking Method

Process counter abstraction may significantly reduce the number of states. It is useful for verification of safety properties. However, it conflicts with the notion of fairness. A counterexample to a liveness property under fairness must be a fair execution of the system. By Definition 4 and 5, the knowledge of which processes are enabled or engaged is necessary in order to check whether an execution is fair or not. In this section, we develop the necessary theorems and algorithms to show that model checking under fairness constraints is feasible even without the knowledge of process identifiers.

By assumption the total number of processes is finite, the abstract transition system A_S has finitely many states. An infinite execution of A_S must form a loop (with a finite prefix to the loop). Assume that the loop starts with index i and ends with k, written as $L_i^k = \langle c_0, \cdots, c_i, c_{i+1}, \cdots, c_{i+k}, c_{i+k+1} \rangle$ where $c_{i+k+1} = c_i$. We define the following functions to collect loop properties and use them to define fairness later.

$$
\begin{aligned}
always(L_i^k) &= \{s : State \mid \forall j : \{i, \cdots, i+k\},\ enabled(s, c_j)\} \\
once(L_i^k) &= \{s : State \mid \exists j : \{i, \cdots, i+k\},\ enabled(s, c_j)\} \\
leave(L_i^k) &= \{s : State \mid \exists j : \{i, \cdots, i+k\},\ c_j \hookrightarrow_{Ls} c_{j+1} \wedge s \in Ls\}
\end{aligned}
$$

Intuitively, $always(L_i^k)$ is the set of local states from where there are processes, which are ready to make some progress, throughout the execution of the loop; $once(L_i^k)$ is the set of local states where there is a process which is ready to make some progress, at least once during the execution of the loop; $leave(L_i^k)$ is the set of local states from which processes leave during the loop. For instance, given the abstract transition system in Fig. 2, $X = \langle A0, A1, A2 \rangle^\infty$ is a loop starting with index 0 and ending with index 2. $always(X) = \varnothing$; $once(X) = \{R0, R1, W0\}$; $leave(X) = \{R0, R1\}$.

The following lemma allows us to check whether an execution is fair by only looking at the abstract execution.

Lemma 1. *Let S be a system model; X be an execution of T_S; $L_i^k = \mathcal{F}(X)$ be the respective abstract execution of A_S. (1). $always(L_i^k) \subseteq leave(L_i^k)$ if X is weakly fair; (2). $once(L_i^k) \subseteq leave(L_i^k)$ if X is strongly fair.*

Proof. (1). Assume X is weakly fair. By definition, if state s is in $always(L_i^k)$, there must be a process residing at s which is enabled to leave during every step of the loop. If it is the same process P, P is always enabled during the loop and therefore, by definition 4, P must participate in a transition infinitely often because X is weakly fair. Therefore, P must leave s during the loop. By definition, s must be in $leave(L_i^k)$. If there are different processes enabled at s during the loop, there must be a process leaving s, so that $s \in leave(L_i^k)$. Thus, $always(L_i^k) \subseteq leave(L_i^k)$.

(2). Assume X is strongly fair. By definition, if state s is in $once(L_i^k)$, there must be a process residing at s which is enabled to leave during one step of the loop. Let P be the process. Because P is infinitely often enabled, by Definition 4, P must participate in a transition infinitely often because X is strongly fair. Therefore, P must leave s during the loop. By definition, s must be in $leave(L_i^k)$. □

The following lemma allows us to generate a concrete fair execution if an abstract *fair* execution is identified.

Lemma 2. *Let $\mathcal{S}$ be a model; L_i^k be an execution of $A_\mathcal{S}$. (1). There exists a weakly fair execution X of $T_\mathcal{S}$ such that $\mathcal{F}(X) = L_i^k$ if $always(L_i^k) \subseteq leave(L_i^k)$; (2). If $once(L_i^k) \subseteq leave(L_i^k)$, there exists a strongly fair execution X of $T_\mathcal{S}$ such that $\mathcal{F}(X) = L_i^k$.*

Proof. (1). By a simple argument, there must exist an execution X of $T_\mathcal{S}$ such that $\mathcal{F}(X) = L_i^k$. Next, we show that we can unfold the loop (of the abstract fair execution) as many times as necessary to let all processes make some progress, so as to generate a weakly fair concrete execution. Assume P is the set of processes residing at a state s during the loop. Because $always(L_i^k) \subseteq leave(L_i^k)$, if $s \in always(L_i^k)$, there must be a transition during which a process leaves s. We repeat the loop multiple times and choose a different process from P to leave each time. The generated execution must be weakly fair.

(2). Similarly as above. □

The following theorem shows that we can perform model checking under fairness by examining the abstract transition system only.

Theorem 1. *Let $\mathcal{S}$ be a system model. Let ϕ be an LTL property. (1). $\mathcal{S} \vDash_{wf} \phi$ if and only if for all executions L_i^k of $A_\mathcal{S}$ we have $always(L_i^k) \subseteq leave(L_i^k) \Rightarrow L_i^k \vDash \phi$; (2). $\mathcal{S} \vDash_{sf} \phi$ if and only if for all execution L_i^k of $A_\mathcal{S}$ we have $once(L_i^k) \subseteq leave(L_i^k) \Rightarrow L_i^k \vDash \phi$.*

Proof. (1). **if** part: Assume that for all L_i^k of $A_\mathcal{S}$ we have $L_i^k \vDash \phi$ if $always(L_i^k) \subseteq leave(L_i^k)$, and $\mathcal{S} \nvDash_{wf} \phi$. By definition, there exists a weakly fair execution X of $T_\mathcal{S}$ such that $X \nvDash \phi$. Let L_i^k be $\mathcal{F}(X)$. By lemma 1, $always(L_i^k) \subseteq leave(L_i^k)$ and hence $L_i^k \vDash \phi$. Because our abstraction preserves valuation of global variables, $L_i^k \nvDash \phi$ as $X \nvDash \phi$. We reach a contradiction.
only if part: Assume that $\mathcal{S} \vDash_{wf} \phi$ and there exists L_i^k of $A_\mathcal{S}$ such that $always(L_i^k) \subseteq leave(L_i^k)$, and $L_i^k \nvDash_{wf} \phi$. By lemma 2, there must exist X of $T_\mathcal{S}$ such that X is weakly fair. Because process counter abstraction preserves valuations of global variables, $X \nvDash \phi$. Hence, we reach contradiction.

(2). Similarly as above. □

Thus, in order to prove that $\mathcal{S}$ satisfies ϕ under fairness, we need to show that there is no execution L_i^k of $A_\mathcal{S}$ such that $L_i^k \nvDash \phi$ and the execution satisfies an additional constraint for fairness, i.e., $always(L_i^k) \subseteq leave(L_i^k)$ for weak fairness or $once(L_i^k) \subseteq leave(L_i^k)$ for strong fairness. Or, if $\mathcal{S} \not\models_{wf} \phi$, then there must be an execution L_i^k of $A_\mathcal{S}$ such that L_i^k satisfies the fairness condition and $L_i^k \not\models \phi$. In such a case, we can generate a concrete execution.

Following the above discussion, fair model checking parameterized systems is reduced to searching for particular loops in $A_\mathcal{S}$. There are two groups of methods for loop searching. One is based on nested depth-first-search (DFS) [17] and the other is based on identifying strongly connected components (SCC) [12]. It has been shown that the nested DFS is not suitable for model checking under fairness assumptions, as whether an execution is fair depends on the path instead of one state [17]. In this work, we extend the approaches presented in [12, 27] to cope with weak or strong fairness and process counter abstraction. Given $A_\mathcal{S}$ and a property ϕ, model checking involves searching for an execution of $A_\mathcal{S}$ which fails ϕ. In automata-based model checking, the negation of ϕ is translated to an equivalent Büchi automaton $\mathcal{B}_{\neg\phi}$, which is then composed with $A_\mathcal{S}$. Notice that a state in the produce of $A_\mathcal{S}$ and $\mathcal{B}_{\neg\phi}$ is a pair (a, b) where a is an abstract configuration of $A_\mathcal{S}$ and b is a state of $\mathcal{B}_{\neg\phi}$. Model checking under fairness involves searching for a fair execution which is accepted by the Büchi automaton.

Given a transition system, a strongly connected subgraph is a subgraph such that there is a path connecting any two states in the subgraph. An MSCC is a maximal strongly connected subgraph. Given the product of $A_\mathcal{S}$ and $\mathcal{B}_{\neg\phi}$, let scg be a set of states which, together with the transitions among them, forms a strongly connected subgraph. We say scg is accepting if and only if there exists one state (a, b) in scg such that b is an accepting state of $\mathcal{B}_{\neg\phi}$. In an abuse of notation, we refer to scg as the strongly connected subgraph in the following. The following lifts the previously defined functions on loops to strongly connected subgraphs.

$$
\begin{aligned}
always(scg) &= \{y : State \mid \forall\, x : scg,\ enabled(y, x)\} \\
once(scg) &= \{y : State \mid \exists\, x : scg,\ enabled(y, x)\} \\
leave(scg) &= \{z : State \mid \exists\, x, y : scg,\ z \in leave(x, y)\}
\end{aligned}
$$

$always(scg)$ is the set of local states such that for any local state in $always(scg)$, there is a process ready to leave the local state for every state in scg; $once(scg)$ is the set of local states such that for some local state in $once(scg)$, there is a process ready to leave the local state for some state in scg; and $leave(scg)$ is the set of local states such that there is a transition in scg during which there is a process leaving the local state. Given the abstract transition system in Fig. 2, $scg = \{A0, A1, A2, A3\}$ constitutes a strongly connected subgraph. $always(scg) =$ nil; $once(scg) = \{R0, R1, W0, W1\}$; $leave(scg) = \{R0, R1, W0, W1\}$.

Lemma 3. *Let $\mathcal{S}$ be a system model. There exists an execution L_i^k of $A_\mathcal{S}$ such that $always(L_i^k) \subseteq leave(L_i^k)$ if and only if there exists an MSCC scc of $A_\mathcal{S}$ such that $always(scc) \subseteq leave(scc)$.*

Proof. The **if** part is trivially true. The **only if** part is proved as follows. Assume there exists execution L_i^k of $A_\mathcal{S}$ such that $always(L_i^k) \subseteq leave(L_i^k)$, there must exist a strongly connected subgraph scg which satisfies $always(scg) \subseteq leave(scg)$. Let scc

procedure $checkingUnderWeakFairness(A_{\mathcal{S}}, \mathcal{B}_{\neg\phi})$
while there are un-visited states in $A_{\mathcal{S}} \otimes \mathcal{B}_{\neg\phi}$
  use the improved Tarjan's algorithm to identify one SCC, say scg;
  if scg is accepting to $\mathcal{B}_{\neg\phi}$ and $always(scg) \subseteq leave(scg)$
    generate a counterexample and **return** false;
  endif
endwhile
return $true$;

Fig. 3. Model checking algorithm under weak fairness

be the MSCC which contains scg. We have $always(scc) \subseteq always(scg)$, therefore, the MSCC scc satisfies $always(scc) \subseteq always(scg) \subseteq leave(scg) \subseteq leave(scc)$. □

The above lemma allows us to use MSCC detection algorithms for model checking under weak fairness. Fig. 3 presents an on-the-fly model checking algorithm based on Tarjan's algorithm for identifying MSCCs. The idea is to search for an MSCC scg such that $always(scg) \subseteq leave(scg)$ and scg is accepting. The algorithm terminates in two ways, either one such MSCC is found or all MSCCs have been examined (and it returns true). In the former case, an abstract counterexample is generated. In the latter case, we successfully prove the property. Given the system presented in Fig. 2, $\{A0, A1, A2, A3\}$ constitutes the only MSCC, which satisfies $always(scg) \subseteq leave(scg)$. The complexity of the algorithm is linear in the number of transitions of $A_{\mathcal{S}}$.

Lemma 4. *Let $\mathcal{S}$ be a system model. There exists an execution L_i^k of $A_{\mathcal{S}}$ such that $once(L_i^k) \subseteq leave(L_i^k)$ if and only if there exists a strongly connected subgraph scg of $A_{\mathcal{S}}$ such that $once(scg) \subseteq leave(scg)$.*

We skip the proof of the lemma as it is straightforward. The lemma allows us to extend the algorithm proposed in [27] for model checking under strong fairness. Fig. 4 presents the modified algorithm. The idea is to search for a strongly connected subgraph scg such that $once(scg) \subseteq leave(scg)$ and scg is accepting. Notice that a strongly connected subgraph must be contained in one and only one MSCC. The algorithm searches for MSCCs using Tarjan's algorithm. Once an MSCC scg is found (at line 2), if scg is accepting and satisfies $once(scg) \subseteq leave(scg)$, then we generate an abstract counterexample. If scg is accepting but fails $once(scg) \subseteq leave(scg)$, instead of throwing away the MSCC, we prune a set of *bad states* from the SCC and then examinate the remaining states (at line 6) for strongly connected subgraphs. Intuitively, *bad states* are the reasons why the SCC fails the condition $once(scg) \subseteq leave(scg)$. Formally,

$$bad(scg) = \{x : scg \mid \exists\, y,\ y \notin leave(scg) \wedge y \in enabled(y, x)\}$$

That is, a state s is bad if and only if there exists a local state y such that a process may leave y at state s and yet there is no process leaving y given all transitions in scg. By pruning all bad states, there might be a strongly connected subgraph in the remaining states which satisfies the fairness constraint.

```
procedure checkingUnderStrongFairness(A_S, B_¬φ, states)
while there are un-visited states in states
    use Tarjan's algorithm to identify a subset of states which forms an SCC, say scg;
    if scg is accepting to B_¬φ
        if once(scg) ⊆ leave(scg)
            generate a counterexample and return false;
        else if checkingUnderStrongFairness(A_S, B_¬φ, scg \ bad(scg)) is false
            return false;
        endif
    endif
endwhile
return true;
```

Fig. 4. Model checking algorithm under strong fairness

The algorithm is partly inspired by the one presented in [16] for checking emptiness of Streett automata. Soundness of the algorithm follows the discussion in [27, 16]. It can be shown that any state of a strongly connected subgraph which satisfies the constraints is never pruned. As a result, if there exists such a strongly connected subgraph scg, a strongly connected subgraph which contains scg or scg itself must be found eventually. Termination of the algorithm is guaranteed because the number of visited states and pruned states are monotonically increasing. The complexity of the algorithm is linear in $\#states \times \#trans$ where $\#states$ and $\#trans$ are the number of states and transitions of $A_{\mathcal{S}}$ respectively. A tighter bound on the complexity can be found in [16].

5 Counter Abstraction for Infinitely Many Processes

In the previous sections, we assume that the number of processes (and hence the size of the abstract transition system) is finite and bounded. If the number of processes is unbounded, there might be unbounded number of processes residing at a local state, e.g., the number of reader processes residing at $R0$ in Fig. 1 might be infinite. In such a case, we choose a *cutoff* number and then apply further abstraction. In the following, we *modify* the definition of abstract configurations and abstract transition systems to handle unbounded number of processes.

Definition 8. *Let $\mathcal{S}$ be a system model with unboundedly many processes. Let K be a positive natural number (i.e., the cutoff number). An abstract configuration of $\mathcal{S}$ is a pair (v, g) where v is the valuation of the global variables and $g : State \rightarrow \mathbb{N} \cup \{\omega\}$ is a total function such that $g(s) = n$ if and only if $n (\leq K)$ processes are residing at s and $g(s) = \omega$ if and only if more than K processes are at s.*

Given a configuration $(v, \langle s_0, s_1, \cdots \rangle)$, we define a function $\mathcal{G}$ similar to function $\mathcal{F}$, i.e., $\mathcal{G}(\langle s_0, s_1, \cdots \rangle))$ returns function g (refer to Definition 8) such that given any state s, $g(s) = n$ if and only if there are n states in $\langle s_0, s_1, \cdots \rangle$ which are equivalent to s and $g(s) = \omega$ if and only if there are more than K states in $\langle s_0, s_1, \cdots \rangle$ which are equivalent to s. Furthermore, $\mathcal{G}(c) = (v, \mathcal{G}(\langle s_0, s_1, \cdots \rangle))$.

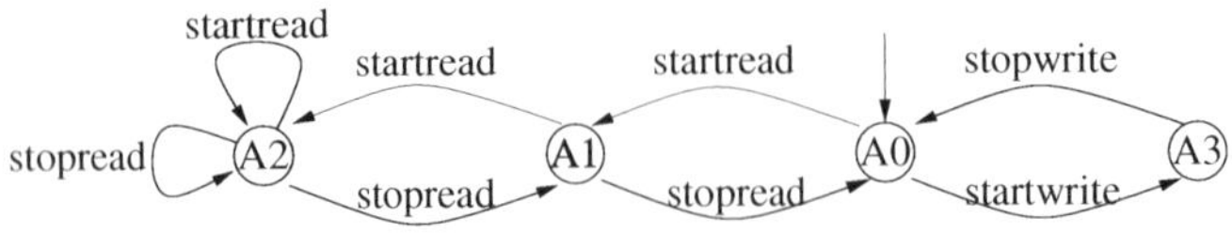

A0: ((writing,false),(counter,0),(R0,inf),(R1,0),(W0,inf),(W1,0))
A1: ((writing,false),(counter,1),(R0,inf),(R1,1),(W0,inf),(W1,0))
A2: ((writing,false),(counter,inf),(R0,inf),(R1,inf),(W0,inf),(W1,0))
A3: ((writing,true),(counter,0),(R0,inf),(R1,0),(W0,inf),(W1,1))

Fig. 5. Abstract readers/writers model

The abstract transition relation of $\mathcal{S}$ (as per the above abstraction) can be constructed without constructing the concrete transition relation. We illustrate how to generate an abstract transition in the following. Given an abstract configuration (v, g), if $g(s) > 0$, a *local transition* from state s to state s', creating a process with initial state $init$ may result in different abstract configurations (v, g') depending on g. In particular, g' equals g except that $g'(s) = g(s) - 1$ and $g'(s') = g(s') + 1$ and $g'(init) = g(init) + 1$ assuming $\omega + 1 = \omega$, $K + 1 = \omega$ and $\omega - 1$ is either ω or K. We remark that by assumption $State$ is a finite set and therefore the domain of g is always finite. This allows us to drop the assumption that the number of processes must be finite before process creation. Similarly, we abstract synchronous transitions and process termination.

The *abstract transition system* for a system model $\mathcal{S}$ with unboundedly many processes, written as $R_{\mathcal{S}}$ (to distinguish from $A_{\mathcal{S}}$), is now obtained by applying the aforementioned abstract transition relation from the initial abstract configuration.

Example 2. Assume that the cutoff number is 1 and there are infinitely many readers and writers in the readers/writers model. Because $counter$ is potentially unbounded and, we mark $counter$ as a special process counter variable which dynamically counts the number of processes which are reading (at state $R1$). If the number of *reading* processes is larger than the cutoff number, $counter$ is set to ω too. The abstract transition system A_{RW} is shown in Fig. 5. The abstract transition system may contain spurious traces. For instance, the trace $\langle start, (stopread)^{\infty}\rangle$ is spurious. It is straightforward to prove that $A_{RW} \models Prop_1$ based on the abstract transition system.

The abstract transition system now has only finitely many states even if there are unbounded number of processes and, therefore, is subject to model checking. As illustrated in the preceding example, the abstraction is sound but incomplete in the presence of unboundedly many processes. Given an execution X of $T_{\mathcal{S}}$, let $\mathcal{G}(X)$ be the corresponding execution of the abstract transition system. An execution L of $R_{\mathcal{S}}$ is spurious if and only if there does not exist an execution X of $T_{\mathcal{S}}$ such that $\mathcal{G}(X) = L$. Because the abstraction only introduces execution traces (but does not remove any), we can formally establish a simulation relation (but not a bisimulation) between the abstract and concrete transition systems, that is, $R_{\mathcal{S}}$ simulates $T_{\mathcal{S}}$. Thus, while verifying an LTL property ϕ we can conclude $T_{\mathcal{S}} \models \phi$ if we can show that $R_{\mathcal{S}} \models \phi$. Of course, $R_{\mathcal{S}} \models \phi$ will be accomplished by model checking under fairness.

The following re-establishes Lemma 1 and (part of) Theorem 1 in the setting of $R_{\mathcal{S}}$. We skip the proof as they are similar to that of Lemma 1 and Theorem 1 respectively.

Lemma 5. *Let $\mathcal{S}$ be a system model, X be an execution of $T_{\mathcal{S}}$ and $L_i^k = \mathcal{G}(X)$ be the corresponding execution of $R_{\mathcal{S}}$. We have (1). $always(L_i^k) \subseteq leave(L_i^k)$ if X is weakly fair; (2). $once(L_i^k) \subseteq leave(L_i^k)$ if X is strongly fair.*

Theorem 2. *Let $\mathcal{S}$ be a system model and ϕ be an LTL property. (1). $\mathcal{S} \models_{wf} \phi$ if for all execution traces L_i^k of $R_{\mathcal{S}}$ we have $always(L_i^k) \subseteq leave(L_i^k) \Rightarrow L_i^k \models \phi$; (2). $\mathcal{S} \models_{sf} \phi$ if for all execution traces L_i^k of $R_{\mathcal{S}}$ we have $once(L_i^k) \subseteq leave(L_i^k) \Rightarrow L_i^k \models \phi$;*

The reverse of Theorem 2 is not true because of spurious traces. We remark that the model checking algorithms presented in Section 4 are applicable to $R_{\mathcal{S}}$ (as the abstraction function is irrelevant to the algorithm). By Theorem 2, if model checking of $R_{\mathcal{S}}$ (using the algorithms presented in Section 4 under weak/fairness constraint) returns true, we conclude that the system satisfies the property (under the respective fairness).

6 Case Studies

Our method has been realized in the *Process Analysis Toolkit* (PAT) [26]. PAT is designed for systematic validation of distributed/concurrent systems using state-of-the-art model checking techniques. In the following, we show the usability/scalability of our method via the automated verification of several real-life parameterized systems. All the models are embedded in the PAT package and available online. The experimental results are summarized in the following table, where NA means not applicable (hence not tried, due to limit of the tool); NF means not feasible (out of 2GB memory or running for more than 4 hours). The data is obtained with Intel Core 2 Quad 9550 CPU at 2.83GHz and 2GB RAM. We compared PAT with SPIN [17] on model checking under no fairness or weak fairness. Notice that SPIN does not support strong fairness and is limited to 255 processes.

Model	#Proc	Property	No Fairness			Weak Fairness			Strong Fairness		
			Result	PAT	SPIN	Result	PAT	SPIN	Result	PAT	Spin
LE	10	$\Diamond\Box$ *one leader*	false	0.04	0.015	true	0.06	320	true	0.06	NA
LE	100	$\Diamond\Box$ *one leader*	false	0.04	0.015	true	0.27	NF	true	0.28	NA
LE	1000	$\Diamond\Box$ *one leader*	false	0.04	NA	true	2.26	NA	true	2.75	NA
LE	10000	$\Diamond\Box$ *one leader*	false	0.04	NA	true	23.89	NA	true	68.78	NA
LE	∞	$\Diamond\Box$ *one leader*	false	0.06	NA	true	264.78	NA	true	463.9	NA
KV	2	$Prop_{Kvalue}$	false	0.05	0	true	0.6	1.14	true	0.6	NA
KV	3	$Prop_{Kvalue}$	false	0.05	0	true	4.56	61.2	true	4.59	NA
KV	4	$Prop_{Kvalue}$	false	0.05	0.015	true	29.2	NF	true	30.24	NA
KV	5	$Prop_{Kvalue}$	false	0.06	0.015	true	174.5	NF	true	187.1	NA
KV	∞	$Prop_{Kvalue}$	false	0.12	NA	?	NF	NA	?	NF	NA
Stack	5	$Prop_{stack}$	false	0.06	0.015	false	0.78	NF	false	0.74	NA
Stack	7	$Prop_{stack}$	false	0.06	0.015	false	11.3	NF	false	12.1	NA
Stack	9	$Prop_{stack}$	false	0.06	0.015	false	158.6	NF	false	191.8	NA
Stack	10	$Prop_{stack}$	false	0.05	0.015	false	596.1	NF	false	780.3	NA
ML	10	$\Box\Diamond$ *access*	true	0.11	21.5	true	0.11	107	true	0.11	NA
ML	100	$\Box\Diamond$ *access*	true	1.04	NF	true	1.04	NF	true	1.04	NA
ML	1000	$\Box\Diamond$ *access*	true	11.04	NA	true	11.08	NA	true	11.08	NA
ML	∞	$\Box\Diamond$ *access*	true	13.8	NA	true	13.8	NA	true	13.8	NA

The first model (LE) is a self-stabilizing leader election protocol for complete networks [11]. Mobile ad hoc networks consist of multiple mobile nodes which interact with each other. The interactions among the nodes are subject to fairness constraints. One essential property of a self-stabilizing population protocols is that all nodes must eventually converge to the correct configurations. We verify the self-stabilizing leader election algorithm for complete network graphs (i.e., any pair of nodes are connected). The property is that eventually always there is one and only one leader in the network, i.e., $\Diamond\Box$ $one\ leader$. PAT successfully proved the property under weak or strong fairness for many or unbounded number of network nodes (with cutoff number 2). SPIN took much more time to prove the property under weak fairness. The reason is that the fair model checking algorithm in SPIN copies the global state machine $n+2$ times (for n processes) so as to give each process a fair chance to progress, which increases the verification time by a factor that is linear in the number of network nodes.

The second model (KV) is a K-valued register [3]. A shared K-valued multi-reader single-writer register R can be simulated by an array of K binary registers. When the single writer process wants to write v into R, it will set the v-th element of B to 1 and then set all the values before v-th element to 0. When a reader wants to read the value, it will do an upwards scan first from 0 to the first element u whose value is 1, then do a downwards scan from u to 0 and remember the index of the last element with value 1, which is the return value of the reading operation. A *progress* property is that $Prop_{Kvalue} = \Box(read\_inv \rightarrow \Diamond read\_res)$, i.e., a reading operation ($read\_inv$) eventually returns some valid value ($read\_res$). With no fairness, both PAT and SPIN identified a counterexample quickly. Because the model contains many local states, the size of A_S increases rapidly. PAT proved the property under weak/strong fairness for 5 processes, whereas SPIN was limited to 3 processes with weak fairness.

The third model ($Stack$) is a lock-free stack [28]. In concurrent systems, in order to improve the performance, the stack can be implemented by a linked list, which is shared by arbitrary number of processes. Each push or pop operation keeps trying to update the stack until no other process interrupts. The property of interest is that a process must eventually be able to update the stack, which can be expressed as the LTL $Prop_{stack} = \Box(push\_inv \rightarrow \Diamond push\_res)$ where event $push\_inv$ ($push\_res$) marks the starting (ending) of $push$ operation. The property is false even under strong fairness.

The fourth model (ML) is the Java meta-lock algorithm [1]. In Java language, any object can be synchronized by different threads via synchronized methods or statements. The Java meta-locking algorithm is designed to ensure the mutually exclusive access to an object. A synchronized method first acquires a lock on the object, executes the method and then releases the lock. The property is that always eventually some thread is accessing the object, i.e., $\Box\Diamond$ $access$, which is true without fairness. This example shows that the computational overhead due to fairness is negligible in PAT.

In another experiment, we use a model in which processes all behave differently (so that counter abstraction results in no reduction) and each process has many local states. We then compare the verification results with or without process counter abstraction. The result shows the computational and memory overhead for applying the abstraction is negligible. In summary, the enhanced PAT model checker complements existing model checkers in terms of not only performance but also the ability to perform model checking under weak or strong fairness with process counter abstraction.

7 Discussion and Related Work

We studied model checking under fairness with process counter abstraction. The contribution of our work is twofold. First, we presented a fully automatic method for property checking of under fairness with process counter abstraction. We showed that fairness can be achieved without the knowledge of process identifiers. Secondly, we enhanced our home-grown PAT model checker to support our method and applied it on large scale parameterized systems to demonstrate its scalability. As for future work, we plan to investigate methods to combine well-known state space reduction techniques (such as partial order reduction, data abstraction for infinite domain data variables) with the process counter abstraction so as to extend the applicability of our model checker.

Verification of parameterized systems is undecidable [2]. There are two possible remedies to this problem: either we look for restricted subsets of parameterized systems for which the verification problem becomes decidable, or we look for sound but not necessarily complete methods. The first approach tries to identify a *restricted subset* of parameterized systems and temporal properties, such that if a property holds for a system with up to a certain number of processes, then it holds for any number of processes in the system. Moreover, the verification for the reduced system can be accomplished by using model checking. This approach can be used to verify a number of systems [13,18,8]. The sound but incomplete approaches include methods based on synthesis of invisible invariant (*e.g.*, [10]); methods based on network invariant (*e.g.*, [21]) that relies on the effectiveness of a generated invariant and the invariant refinement techniques; regular model checking [19] that requires acceleration techniques. Verification of liveness properties under fairness constraints have been studied in [15,17,20]. These works are based on SCC-related algorithms and decide the existence of an accepting run of the product of the transition system and Büchi automata, Streett automata or linear weak alternating automaton.

The works closest to ours are the methods based on *counter abstraction* (*e.g.*, [7,24, 23]). In particular, verification of liveness properties under fairness is addressed in [23]. In [23], the fairness constraints for the abstract system are generated manually (or via heuristics) from the fairness constraints for the concrete system. Different from the above work, our method handles one (possibly large) instance of parameterized systems at a time and uses counter abstraction to improve verification effectiveness. In addition, fairness conditions are integrated into the on-the-fly model checking algorithm which proceeds on the abstract state representation — making our method fully automated.

Our method is related to work on symmetry reduction [9,5]. A solution for applying symmetry reduction under fairness is discussed in [9]. Their method works by finding a candidate fair path in the abstract transition system and then using special annotations to resolve the abstract path to a threaded structure which then determines whether there is a corresponding fair path in the concrete transition system. A similar approach was presented in [14]. Different from the above, our method employs a specialized form of symmetry reduction and deals with the abstract transition system only and requires no annotations. Additionally, a number of works on combining abstraction and fairness, were presented in [6,22,29,4,25]. Our work explores one particular kind of abstraction and shows that it works with fairness with a simple twist.

References

1. Agesen, O., Detlefs, D., Garthwaite, A., Knippel, R., Ramakrishna, Y.S., White, D.: An Efficient Meta-Lock for Implementing Ubiquitous Synchronization. In: OOPSLA, pp. 207–222 (1999)
2. Apt, K.R., Kozen, D.: Limits for automatic verification of finite-state concurrent systems. Inf. Process. Lett. 22(6), 307–309 (1986)
3. Attiya, H., Welch, J.: Distributed Computing: Fundamentals, Simulations, and Advanced Topics, 2nd edn. John Wiley & Sons, Inc., Publication, Chichester (2004)
4. Bosnacki, D., Ioustinova, N., Sidorova, N.: Using Fairness to Make Abstractions Work. In: Graf, S., Mounier, L. (eds.) SPIN 2004. LNCS, vol. 2989, pp. 198–215. Springer, Heidelberg (2004)
5. Clarke, E.M., Filkorn, T., Jha, S.: Exploiting Symmetry In Temporal Logic Model Checking. In: Courcoubetis, C. (ed.) CAV 1993. LNCS, vol. 697, pp. 450–462. Springer, Heidelberg (1993)
6. Dams, D., Gerth, R., Grumberg, O.: Fair Model Checking of Abstractions. In: VCL 2000 (2000)
7. Delzanno, G.: Automatic Verification of Parameterized Cache Coherence Protocols. In: Emerson, E.A., Sistla, A.P. (eds.) CAV 2000. LNCS, vol. 1855, pp. 53–68. Springer, Heidelberg (2000)
8. Emerson, E.A., Namjoshi, K.S.: On Reasoning About Rings. Int. J. Found. Comput. Sci. 14(4), 527–550 (2003)
9. Emerson, E.A., Sistla, A.P.: Utilizing Symmetry when Model-Checking under Fairness Assumptions: An Automata-Theoretic Approach. ACM Trans. Program. Lang. Syst. 19(4), 617–638 (1997)
10. Fang, Y., McMillan, K.L., Pnueli, A., Zuck, L.D.: Liveness by Invisible Invariants. In: Najm, E., Pradat-Peyre, J.-F., Donzeau-Gouge, V.V. (eds.) FORTE 2006. LNCS, vol. 4229, pp. 356–371. Springer, Heidelberg (2006)
11. Fischer, M.J., Jiang, H.: Self-stabilizing Leader Election in Networks of Finite-state Anonymous Agents. In: Shvartsman, M.M.A.A. (ed.) OPODIS 2006. LNCS, vol. 4305, pp. 395–409. Springer, Heidelberg (2006)
12. Geldenhuys, J., Valmari, A.: More efficient on-the-fly LTL verification with Tarjan's algorithm. Theoretical Computer Science 345(1), 60–82 (2005)
13. German, S.M., Sistla, A.P.: Reasoning about Systems with Many Processes. J. ACM 39(3), 675–735 (1992)
14. Gyuris, V., Sistla, A.P.: On-the-Fly Model Checking Under Fairness That Exploits Symmetry. In: Grumberg, O. (ed.) CAV 1997. LNCS, vol. 1254, pp. 232–243. Springer, Heidelberg (1997)
15. Hammer, M., Knapp, A., Merz, S.: Truly On-the-Fly LTL Model Checking. In: Halbwachs, N., Zuck, L.D. (eds.) TACAS 2005. LNCS, vol. 3440, pp. 191–205. Springer, Heidelberg (2005)
16. Henzinger, M.R., Telle, J.A.: Faster Algorithms for the Nonemptiness of Streett Automata and for Communication Protocol Pruning. In: Karlsson, R., Lingas, A. (eds.) SWAT 1996. LNCS, vol. 1097, pp. 16–27. Springer, Heidelberg (1996)

17. Holzmann, G.J.: The SPIN Model Checker: Primer and Reference Manual. Addison Wesley, Reading (2003)
18. Ip, C.N., Dill, D.L.: Verifying Systems with Replicated Components in Mur&b.phiv. Formal Methods in System Design 14(3), 273–310 (1999)
19. Jonsson, B., Saksena, M.: Systematic Acceleration in Regular Model Checking. In: Damm, W., Hermanns, H. (eds.) CAV 2007. LNCS, vol. 4590, pp. 131–144. Springer, Heidelberg (2007)
20. Kesten, Y., Pnueli, A., Raviv, L., Shahar, E.: Model Checking with Strong Fairness. Formal Methods and System Design 28(1), 57–84 (2006)
21. Lesens, D., Halbwachs, N., Raymond, P.: Automatic Verification of Parameterized Linear Networks of Processes. In: POPL, pp. 346–357 (1997)
22. Nitsche, U., Wolper, P.: Relative Liveness and Behavior Abstraction (Extended Abstract). In: PODC 1997, pp. 45–52 (1997)
23. Pnueli, A., Xu, J., Zuck, L.D.: Liveness with (0, 1, infty)-Counter Abstraction. In: Brinksma, E., Larsen, K.G. (eds.) CAV 2002. LNCS, vol. 2404, pp. 107–122. Springer, Heidelberg (2002)
24. Pong, F., Dubois, M.: A New Approach for the Verification of Cache Coherence Protocols. IEEE Trans. Parallel Distrib. Syst. 6(8), 773–787 (1995)
25. Pong, F., Dubois, M.: Verification Techniques for Cache Coherence Protocols. ACM Comput. Surv. 29(1), 82–126 (1996)
26. Sun, J., Liu, Y., Dong, J.S., Pang, J.: PAT: Towards Flexible Verification under Fairness. In: Bouajjani, A., Maler, O. (eds.) CAV 2009. LNCS, vol. 5643, pp. 709–714. Springer, Heidelberg (2009)
27. Sun, J., Liu, Y., Dong, J.S., Wang, H.H.: Specifying and verifying event-based fairness enhanced systems. In: Liu, S., Maibaum, T., Araki, K. (eds.) ICFEM 2008. LNCS, vol. 5256, pp. 318–337. Springer, Heidelberg (2008)
28. Treiber, R.K.: Systems programming: Coping with parallelism. Technical report (1986)
29. Ultes-Nitsche, U., St. James, S.: Improved Verification of Linear-time Properties within Fairness: Weakly Continuation-closed Behaviour Abstractions Computed from Trace Reductions. Softw. Test., Verif. Reliab. 13(4), 241–255 (2003)

Systematic Development of Trustworthy Component Systems

Rodrigo Ramos, Augusto Sampaio, and Alexandre Mota

Centro de Informática, Universidade Federal de Pernambuco
P.O. Box 7851, CEP 50732970, Recife, Brazil
{rtr,acas,acm}@cin.ufpe.br

Abstract. In this paper, we propose a systematic approach, based on the CSP process algebra, to preserve deadlock- and livelock-freedom by construction in I/O component composition. In contrast to existing classical approaches, we allow components to have complex behaviour, protocols and contracts. As a consequence, it is possible to predict the behaviour of a wide range of component-based systems prior to their implementation, based on known properties of the system components.

1 Introduction

Because software failures can cause extensive, even disastrous, damage, the successful deployment of systems depends on the extent to which we can justifiably trust on them. Accidents are caused by failures of individual components and by dysfunctional interactions between non-failed components. In fact, most dysfunctional interactions are originated by classical problems in concurrent systems.

Much effort is devoted to the correctness of component-based systems (CBS) using formal notations and techniques, after such systems are built [1,2,3,4]. However, instead of bringing guidance to the engineer (like suggesting how to avoid such failures *a priori*), they hide the expertise needed to understand, and predict, the quality of the developed systems. In a previous effort [5], we have investigated patterns and compatibility notions in the integration of heterogeneous software components. These notions have been used to guarantee that the behaviour of original components are preserved for a specific architectural style.

Here, we propose three basic composition rules for components and connectors, which can be regarded as safe steps to form a wide variety of trustworthy component systems. The systematic use of these rules guarantees, by construction, the absence of the classical deadlock and livelock problems.

We use the CSP process algebra [6] to formalise our entire approach. CSP allows the description of system components in terms of synchronous processes that operate independently, and interact with each other through message-passing communication. The relationship between processes is described using process algebraic operators from which elaborate concurrency and distributed patterns can be constructed. Moreover, CSP offers rich semantic models that support a wide range of process verification, and comparisons, which have shown to be useful to support the rigorous development of CBS [7,8].

A. Cavalcanti and D. Dams (Eds.): FM 2009, LNCS 5850, pp. 140–156, 2009.

Our contributions can be summarised as follows: we first formalise I/O components and connectors as distinguished design entities (Sect. 2). Then, in Sect. 3, we propose three composition rules for these entities that guarantee deadlock- and livelock-freedom by construction. Finally, we present a example in Sect. 4, which illustrates how the composition rules are applied. Related work, and our conclusions and future work are presented in Sect. 5.

2 Component Driven Architectures in CSP

We formalise several concepts in CBS: *interfaces*, *components*, and *connectors*. We focus on interaction points of black box components and their observable behaviour. To illustrate the proposed notions, we use an example: the communication between a *CLIENT* and a *SERVER* component in an ATM system.

Fig. 1 shows the entire system as a component, which is hierarchically composed of other components (*CLIENT* and *SERVER*) and a connector (*CON*). In summary, the system behaves as follows: after the user identification, *CLIENT* offers to the user a choice between withdrawing money and checking the account balance. In our example, both withdraw and balance operations are expected to be performed by another component: *SERVER*. The connector *CON* helps to sort out communication issues between these components, such as alphabet heterogeneity. Further details are shown in the next sections.

In our approach, components and connectors are basically represented by a process in CSP. When reasoning in CSP, we consider the failures/divergence semantic model [6] that allows us to explain whether a system deadlock or livelock. In the failures/divergenge model, a process is represented by its traces, failures and divergences. A trace is a set of finite sequences of communications a process can perform. A failure is a pair (s, X), where s is a trace of the process and X is the set of events the process can refuse to perform after s is performed. A divergence is basically a trace which indicates when the process starts to perform infinite sequences of consecutive internal actions.

2.1 Component Model

Component capabilities are usually described by means of interfaces, which define component provided or required services. In this work, we assume that interfaces simply consist of input and output events in CSP. At this level of abstraction, a pair with an input and an output event might be understood as representing, for instance, the invocation of a method.

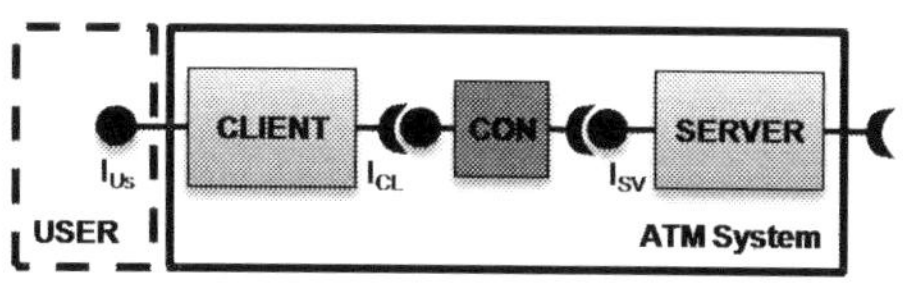

Fig. 1. An example of a simple ATM System

Before we define the interfaces, we present the definition of I/O types that represent communications with distinct events for input and output.

Definition 1 (I/O Types). *Let T and U be two disjoint sets of values. Then, we define an I/O type as a type parameterised by these two sets, as follows:*

$$IOT_{T,U} = in.T \mid out.U$$

In a communication between a pair of components, typically T and U will be the sets of input and output values for one component and, conversely, the set of output and input values for the other component. Therefore, $IOT_{T,U}$ would be the I/O type of one component and $IOT_{U,T}$ the I/O type of the other component. To ease readability, we use the following abbreviations.

Definition 2 (Interface). *Let T_{IN} and T_{OUT} be sets of values for input and output communication of a given component. We call the types that represent the interface of such a component a regular interface and a conjugate interface (namely I and $\sim I$, respectively), and define them as follows:*

$$I = IOT_{T_{IN},T_{OUT}} \qquad \sim I = IOT_{T_{OUT},T_{IN}}$$

We also introduce the projection functions *inputs* and *outputs* as follows:

$$inputs(I) = ran(in) \cap I \qquad inputs(\sim I) = ran(out) \cap \sim I$$
$$outputs(I) = ran(out) \cap I \qquad outputs(\sim I) = ran(in) \cap \sim I$$

As a consequence of Def. 2, a regular interface is a type whose input and output events are tagged by *in* and *out*, respectively, whereas a conjugated interface has input and output tagged by *out* and *in*, respectively. The modifiers *in* and *out* behave in CSP as functions that take an arbitrary value and yields the same value prefixed by those modifiers; the intersection with the whole interface restricts the range of *in* and *out* ($ran(in)$ and $ran(out)$) to the values within the interface. For instance, for $T_{IN} = \{a, b\}$ and $T_{OUT} = \{w, z\}$, $inputs(I) = outputs(\sim I) = \{in.a, in.b\}$ and $outputs(I) = inputs(\sim I) = \{out.w, out.z\}$. For the sake of brevity, we use $\sim$ as an operator that takes a regular interface and yields a conjugate interface, and vice-versa. So that $\sim\sim I = I$.

Apart from a static representation provided by interfaces, design entities are also expressed by their dynamic behaviour. In this work, we focus on components that repeatedly present the same behaviour to the environment, which is itself defined in terms of *interaction patterns* [9]. Each interaction pattern consists of a finite sequence of events that, when performed, leads the component back to its initial state. In this manner, the component repeatedly offers these sequences of events, similar to possible transactions performed against a database management system. These patterns cover a wide range of applications, found in several technologies such as, for instance, session Enterprise JavaBeans^{TM} and transactional conversational services. Moreover, it is aligned with a common practice, *transaction-based reduction*, to alleviate state space explosion.

To present the interaction patterns of a process P, $InteractionPatterns(P)$, we use the CSP operator P/s. If $s \in traces(P)$ then P/s (pronounced 'P after s') represents the behaviour of P after the trace s is performed. So, $InteractionPatterns(P)$ is the set of traces that lead the process to its initial state.

Definition 3 (Interaction Patterns). *Let P be a CSP process.*

$$InteractionPatterns(P) = \{s : traces(P) \mid P \sqsubseteq_{FD} (P/s)\}$$

Def. 3 is characterised in terms of the CSP failures/divergence semantic model. It defines the set of traces after which the process presents the same failures and divergences; these are precisely the interaction patterns of P.

We define a component contract in terms of its behaviour, interaction points and respective interfaces. The dynamic behaviour presents the observable communication of a component through its interaction points. Each interaction point is represented in CSP by a communication channel.

Definition 4 (Interaction Component Contract). *A component contract Ctr comprises an observational behaviour $\mathcal{B}$, a set of channels $\mathcal{C}$, a set of interfaces $\mathcal{I}$, and a function $\mathcal{R} : \mathcal{C} \rightarrow \mathcal{I}$ between channels and interfaces:*

$$Ctr : \langle \mathcal{B}, \mathcal{R}, \mathcal{I}, \mathcal{C} \rangle$$

such that

- $\mathrm{dom}\,\mathcal{R} = \mathcal{C} \wedge \mathrm{ran}\,\mathcal{R} = \mathcal{I} \wedge \alpha\mathcal{B} \subseteq \bigcup_{c:\,\mathcal{C}} \{\!|\ c\ |\!\}$
- $\forall\, s \in traces(\mathcal{B}) \bullet \exists\, p : InteractionPatterns(\mathcal{B}) \bullet s \preceq p$
- $\forall\, t\hat{\ }\langle c.a \rangle : traces(\mathcal{B}) \mid c \in \mathcal{C} \wedge a \in outputs(\mathcal{R}(c)) \bullet (t, \{\!|\ c\ |\!\} - \{c.a\}) \in failures(\mathcal{B})$

The operator $\{\!|\ ch\ |\!\}$ stands for all events represented by a channel ch; for instance, if ch communicates values of the set $\{1, 2\}$, $\{\!|\ ch\ |\!\} = \{ch.1, ch.2\}$. The notation αP stands for the alphabet of a process P. They are used in the definition above to state that the behaviour $\mathcal{B}$ of Ctr (denoted by $\mathcal{B}_{Ctr}$) performs only events defined in channels of $\mathcal{C}_{Ctr}$. Each of these channels is typed by an interface within $\mathcal{I}_{Ctr}$, according to the function $\mathcal{R}$.

The first proviso of Def. 4 states that component elements are consistent with each other. All channels are typed by an interface, and the component only communicates through such channels. The second proviso requires that the component continuously repeats the same behaviour, through recursion; this is defined in terms of interaction patterns. Its traces must be a prefix ($\preceq$) of an interaction pattern or of a combination of them; in either case they belong to $InteractionPatterns(P)$. The last proviso defines a component as an autonomous entity and, furthermore, only it can choose which event is enabled from a choice involving output events, whenever a trace (t) enables an output event ($c.a$), the component does not offer any guarantee of communicating any other possible enabled event (after t). In CSP, this means that whenever there exists a trace $t\hat{\ }\langle c.a \rangle$ (concatenating t and $\langle c.a \rangle$), the tuple $(t, \{\!|\ c\ |\!\} - \{c.a\})$ belongs to $failures(\mathcal{B})$. Def. 4 observes a component in isolation; other constructive constraints are defined in Sect. 3 to forbid undesirable synchronism with the environment.

To exemplify contracts, we show them in the CSP syntax. In our example, the *CLIENT* and *SERVER* components have their contracts defined by Ctr_{CL} and Ctr_{SV}, respectively. As we focus on the interaction of these two components, we restrict their contracts to the information that pertains this interaction.

$$Ctr_{CL} = \langle CLIENT, \{us \mapsto I_{US}, cl \mapsto I_{CL}\}, \{I_{US}, I_{CL}\}, \{us, cl\}\rangle$$
$$Ctr_{SV} = \langle SERVER, \{sv \mapsto I_{SV}\}, \{I_{SV}\}, \{sv\}\rangle$$

Ctr_{CL} has two channels: *us* and *cl*, which are typed by I_{US} and I_{CL}, respectively. The former channel provides services to the user, and the latter delegates the computation of such services to the *SERVER* component. Ctr_{SV} provides bank services to the *CLIENT* component trough a channel *sv*, which is typed by I_{SV}. Syntactically, the elements of Ctr_{CL} are written in CSP as follows.

$$
\begin{array}{l}
I_{CL} = IOT_{CL_{IN}, CL_{OUT}} \\
CL_{OUT} = wd.Int \mid resBal.Int \\
CL_{IN} = ackWd..Bool \mid reqBal \\
\textbf{channel}\ \ cl : I_{CL} \\
CLIENT = us.in.insertCard?num \rightarrow us.in.enterPin?pin \rightarrow \\
\qquad\qquad (WDRAW(us, cl) \,\Box\, BAL(us, cl)) \,;\, us.out!takeCard \rightarrow CLIENT \\
WDRAW = us.in.withdraw?val \rightarrow cl.out!wd.val \rightarrow cl.in.ackWd \rightarrow \\
\qquad\qquad us.out!takeCash \rightarrow SKIP \\
BAL = us.in.balance \rightarrow cl.out!reqBal \rightarrow cl.in.resBal?x \rightarrow \\
\qquad\quad us.out!takeSlip.x \rightarrow SKIP
\end{array}
$$

In the example, the events in I_{CL} are those used by *CLIENT* to interact with *SERVER*. I_{CL} contains the events for withdrawing money (tagged with *wd*) and for requiring and receiving an account balance (tagged with *reqBal* and *resBal*, respectively). These events use the (assumed) built-in data types *Bool* and *Int* to represent boolean and integer values, respectively.

The process *CLIENT* is the specification of the component dynamic behaviour in CSP. To help readability in our specification, we assume that a request event with an input parameter takes the form *ch.in.tag?x*, where *ch* is the name of a channel and *x* acts as an input pattern, which can be empty (as in *balance*) or with a variable (as in *insertCard?num*). The notation *ch.out!v* is used for response events, where *v* is an expression. The data processing starts by acquiring the card number from the environment using the channel *us*. Next, the prefix operator ($\rightarrow$) states that the event *us.in.enterPin?pin* takes place, representing the validation of the user token and password. Then, *CLIENT* offers two choices deterministically ($\Box$): it engages either on the events *withdraw* or *balance*, to withdraw money or to check the account balance, respectively. The operation is started by the occurrence of the *cl.out!wd* or the *cl.out!reqBal* event, and can be completed by the *cl.in.ackWd?a* and *cl.in.resBal?x* events. The events *us.out!takeCash*, *us.out!takeCard* and *us.out!takeSlip* inform the user about the operation finalisation. *SKIP* is a primitive process that stands for a successful termination. The sequential composition operator $;$ composes two processes: $P ; Q$ behaves like P until it terminates successfully, when it behaves like Q.

Syntactically, the elements of Ctr_{SV} are written in CSP as follows.

$$I_{SV} = IOT_{CL_{OUT}, CL_{IN}}$$
$$\textbf{channel} \;\; sv : I_{SV}$$
$$\begin{aligned} SERVER = {} & sv.in.wd?x \to (\sqcap a : Bool \bullet sv.out!ackWd.a) \to SERVER \\ & \square\; sv.in.reqBal \to (\sqcap y : Int \bullet sv.out!resBal.y) \to SERVER \end{aligned}$$

The *SERVER* component has a provided interface I_{SV} whose values for input and output communication are defined in the opposite direction of those in I_{CL}. We have defined I_{SV} as a regular interface in order to ease the understanding of the communication direction in the *SERVER* behaviour. The way the communication between *CLIENT* and *SERVER* is bridged is presented afterwards.

The process *SERVER* offers a deterministic choice ($\square$) between a withdraw and a balance request, which is represented by the occurrence of the communications $sv.in.wd?x$ and $sv.in.reqBal$. After receiving a withdraw or balance request, it internally decides (nondeterministic choice $\sqcap$) the value of the withdraw acknowledgement ($ackWd!a$) and that of the balance response ($resBal.y$); the nondeterministic choice is usually associated to internal actions of the component, which decides the value that is output.

Naturally, specifications of the component behaviour at different abstraction levels are desirable. For instance, it is convenient to express communications using protocols that specify allowed execution traces of the component services, with an exclusive focus on events communicated via a specific channel.

Definition 5 (Protocol). *Let Ctr be a component contract and ch a channel, such that $ch \in \mathcal{C}_{Ctr}$. The protocol over the channel ch (denoted by $Prot(Ctr, ch)$) is defined as:*

$$Prot(Ctr, ch) = \mathcal{B}_{Ctr} \upharpoonright \{\mid ch \mid\}[^{x}/_{ch.x}]$$

The restriction operator $P \upharpoonright X$ can be defined in terms of the CSP operator $P \setminus Y$, where all events within Y are hidden from P, and $Y = \alpha P - X$; only events within the alphabet of the process P (αP) and not in Y are visible in $P \setminus Y$. For instance, the process $Q = (a \to b \to SKIP) \setminus \{a\}$ is the same as $Q = b \to SKIP$, which is also the same as $Q = (a \to b \to SKIP) \upharpoonright \{b\}$. ($[^{x}/_{ch.x}]$) is a forgetful renaming that makes the protocol behaviour independent of the channel ch; $[^{x}/_{ch.x}]$ represents a bijection from an event $ch.x$, which comprises a channel name (ch) and a value (x), to an event x. In this manner, it is easier to check if two communications on two channels have the same behaviour.

In our example, the protocol of *CLIENT* over cl is expressed as follows.

$$\begin{aligned} Prot(Ctr_{CL}, cl) = {} & cl.out.wd!val \to cl.in.ackWd \to Prot(Ctr_{CL}, us) \\ & \square\; cl.out.reqBal \to cl.in.resBal?x \to Prot(Ctr_{CL}, us) \end{aligned}$$

A protocol is a projection of the component behaviour over a channel.

The direct composition of two components is described by the synchronisation of their events in CSP, such that an output is only transmitted when the other component is enabled to input it, and vice-versa.

Definition 6 (Direct Composition). *Let P and Q be two component contracts, such that $CC = \mathcal{C}_P \cap \mathcal{C}_Q$, and $\forall\, c : CC \bullet \mathcal{R}_P(c) = \sim\mathcal{R}_Q(c)$. Then, the direct* *composition of P and Q (namely $P \curlyeqsucc Q$) is given by:*

$$P \curlyeqsucc Q = \langle (\mathcal{B}_P \parallel_{\{|CC|\}} \mathcal{B}_Q), R_{PQ}, \operatorname{ran} R_{PQ}, \operatorname{dom} R_{PQ} \rangle$$

where $R_{PQ} = CC \lhd (\mathcal{R}_P \cup \mathcal{R}_Q)$

In the definition above, the behaviour of the composition is defined by the synchronisation of the behaviour of P and Q in all interactions of the channels in CC (this is expressed through the parallel CSP operator $\parallel$). Any communication related to CC is hidden from the environment (using the operator $\backslash$), and is not considered in the mapping of channels. The operator $\lhd$ stands for domain subtraction; it is used to restrict the mapping from channels into interfaces and, furthermore, to restrict the set of channels and interfaces in the composition.

By definition, components are regarded as reusable units of composition. However, the direct composition excludes a wide variety of components, which would be eligible for composition but present mismatch problems. An alternative approach is to use connectors to mediate interaction.

Connectors establish coordination rules that govern component interaction and specify any auxiliary mechanisms required [1], such as mapping between heterogeneous communications. They are regarded more broadly as *exogenous coordinators*, intended to mean 'coordination from outside' the components.

To increase the range of components they integrate, connectors are abstractly defined at the design level to serve needs of unspecified components. They become components only later in the life-cycle, on the assembly with the components, by relying on the component contracts [10].

We represent the dynamic behaviour of abstract connectors as parameterised CSP processes, whose parameters represent component channels and protocols.

Definition 7 (Abstract Connector). *An abstract connector $AC(S_C, S_I, S_P)$ is described by a behaviour parameterised by a sequence of distinct channels S_C, a sequence of arbitrary interfaces S_I and a sequence of processes S_P, such that $\#S_C = \#S_P = \#S_I \wedge \forall i : 0..\#S_I \bullet \alpha S_P(i) = \{S_I(i)\}$.*

A connector is formed of similar elements to a component, but its behaviour is parameterised. Instead of sets of channels and interfaces, we use sequences, which are more suitable to parametrise the connector specification. We consider the sequence of processes as protocols over the channels that parametrise the connector. For consistence among these parameter sequences, we establish that they have the same size, and that all processes only communicate values on their associated interfaces. When the connector parameters are instantiated, it becomes a component that behaves according to the connector behaviour.

Definition 8 (Connection Instantiation). *Let AC be an abstract connector, SC a sequence of channels, SP a sequence of processes, and SI a sequence of interfaces, such that SC, SP and SI satisfy the constraints to be parameters of AC. Then $\mathcal{F}(AC, S_C, S_I, S_P)$ is a component contract defined by:*

$$\mathcal{F}(AC, S_C, S_I, S_P) = \langle AC(S_C, S_I, S_P), \{i : 0..\#S_C \bullet (S_C(i) \mapsto S_I(i))\}, \\ \operatorname{ran} S_I, \operatorname{ran} S_C \rangle$$

The definition above bridges the gap between two abstraction levels: an abstract connector at design stage and its instantiation at component integration and deployment level. We say that the function $\mathfrak{F}$ has an *instantiation role*. It takes an abstract connector AC and its list of parameters (S_C, S_I and S_P) and constructs a component, which is a concrete version of AC.

One of the simplest, and most common, connectors is the one presented below. It aims at copying values from one channel to another. It does not perform any verification concerning protocols, so they are not referenced in the definition.

$$Con_{copy}(\langle c_1, c_2\rangle, \langle I_1, I_2\rangle, SEQP) = \mu\, X \bullet \quad \begin{array}{l} c_1?x : inputs(I_1) \rightarrow c_2.reverse(x) \rightarrow X \\ \Box\ c_2?y : inputs(I_2) \rightarrow c_1.reverse(y) \rightarrow X \end{array}$$

where $reverse(in.x) = out.x$, $reverse(out.x) = in.x$

This connector intermediates the communication between two components, so that an output of one is transmitted to the other, and vice-versa. Every event value is transmitted with a tag direction; *in* becomes *out*, and *out* becomes *in*.

The composition of two components using a connector can be performed through two direct composition steps. We first assemble a component ($CLIENT$, in our example) to the connector (CON). Then, the second step is to assemble the resulting composition to the other component ($SERVER$). Substituting CON by a concrete connector that uses Con_{copy} in our example, the resulting process is obtained from the (two-steps) composition of $CLIENT$ and $SERVER$:

$$ATM_{system} = Ctr_{CL} \asymp CON \asymp Ctr_{SV}$$

where $CON = \mathfrak{F}(Con_{copy}, \langle cl, sv\rangle, \langle I_{CL}, I_{SV}\rangle, \langle Prot(Ctr_{CL}, cl), Prot(Ctr_{SV}, sv)\rangle)$.

However, the naive use of direct compositions (even through a connector), without checking their compatibilities, can easily introduce problems in the composition. In order to safely compose components, some provisos must be checked.

3 Composition Rules

In this section we present three basic rules for the composition of components (and connectors): *interleave*, *communication* and *feedback* composition. They aim at guiding the developer in component integration guaranteeing, by construction, preservation of deadlock- and livelock-freedom in elaborate systems.

All composition rules (see Fig. 2) specialise the direct composition (Def. 6) with the relevant provisos. The interleave composition is the simplest one. It captures compositions where no communication is performed. The communication composition allows components to interact without introducing deadlocks and livelocks in a system with a simple tree topology. In such a topology, the pairwise verification of component communication guarantees deadlock-freedom in the entire system. The absence of livelock is guaranteed by the analysis of the interaction patterns. The last composition rule, feedback, allows the developer to construct deadlock- and livelock-free systems with an elaborate graph topology. These are basic composition rules that can be used together to design a wide variety of systems. More elaborate rules can be derived from these basic ones.

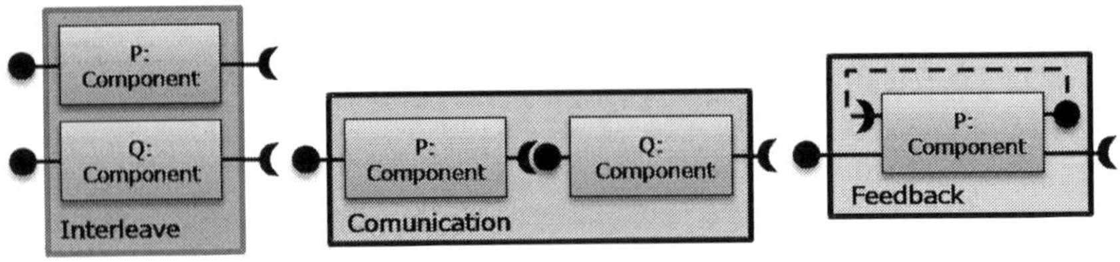

Fig. 2. The three composition rules proposed in this work

The simplest form of composition is to aggregate two independent entities such that, after composition, these entities still do not communicate between themselves. They directly communicate with the environment as before, with no interference from each other. To perform this composition, there is a proviso that they do not share any communication channel.

Definition 9 (Interleave Composition). *Let P and Q be two component contracts, such that P and Q have disjoint channels, $\mathcal{C}_P \cap \mathcal{C}_Q = \emptyset$. Then, the interleave composition of P and Q (namely $P\,[|||]\,Q$) is given by:*

$$P\,[|||]\,Q = P \curlyeqsucc Q$$

The above composition form is, by definition, a particular kind of *direct composition* that involves no communication, resulting in an entity that performs all events defined in the original entities without any interference from each other.

Lemma 1 (Deadlock-free and Livelock-free Interleave Composition) *The interleave composition of two deadlock-free and livelock-free component contracts is also deadlock-free and livelock-free.*

Proof It follows direct from the condition that the components do not share any channel and no communication is hidden. Furthermore, $\mathcal{B}_{P\,[|||]\,Q} = \mathcal{B}_P \mid\mid\mid \mathcal{B}_Q$. As, $\mathcal{B}_P$ and $\mathcal{B}_Q$ are deadlock- and livelock-free, then so is $\mathcal{B}_{P\,[|||]\,Q}$. □

The second form of composition states the most common way for assembling complementary channels of two entities. It links channels of one entity to channels of the other, as in a direct composition (Def. 6).

In order to allow property preservation by construction in CBS, we require that the channels obey compatible protocols. Compatibility is achieved by checking that all possible sequences of output values in one channel are accepted by the corresponding input channel. Moreover, a component must never deadlock waiting for an input event that does not come. Such complementarity precludes the two common errors: message refused and message not understood.

Definition 10 (Protocol Compatibility). *Let P_1 and P_2 be two protocols for channels c_1 and c_2, such that $P_1 = Prot(Ctr_1, c_1)$ and $P_2 = Prot(Ctr_2, c_2)$, $I_1 = \mathcal{R}_{Ctr_1}(c_1)$ and $I_2 = \mathcal{R}_{Ctr_2}(c_2)$, and $\sim I_1 = I_2$. Then, the protocols P_1 and P_2 are compatible (denoted by $P_1 \approx P_2$) if, and only if:*

$$\forall\, i, j : \{1,2\} \mid i \neq j \bullet \forall\, t^\frown\langle out.a\rangle : traces(P_i) \bullet (t, \{in.a\}) \notin failures(P_j)) \wedge \\ \forall\, t^\frown\langle in.a\rangle : traces(P_i) \bullet (t, \{out.x \mid out.x \in I_j\}) \notin failures(P_j))$$

This is an effective way of ensuring that the communication between two components is deadlock-free. This notion is related to stuck-freedom conformance [11], concerning events in Ii and Ij, but we consider only synchronous communication.

Another important requirement is to avoid the compositions to livelock. It happens when a component infinitely performs internal actions, refusing any external communication. This might be introduced, for instance, when we hide the channels involved in a composition (see Def. 6). An interesting observation is that an infinite trace is formed of the concatenation of several interaction patterns in an interaction component contract. So, in order to avoid livelocks, we must track the channels used by the interaction patterns of a component.

Definition 11 (Interaction Channels). *Let Ctr be an interaction component contract. Then its interaction channels are:*

$$IntChannels\, Ctr = \{U \mid \exists\, t \in InteractionPatterns(\mathcal{B}_{Ctr}) \wedge U = chans(t)\}$$

where $chans(t)$ *are the channels used in the trace* t, $chans(\langle\rangle) = \emptyset$, $chans(\langle c.x \rangle) = \{c \mid \exists\, c.x \in \operatorname{ran} t\}$.

Based on the definition of protocol compatibility and interaction channels, we define communication composition as follows:

Definition 12 (Communication Composition). *Let P and Q be two component contracts such that* $ic \in \mathcal{C}_P \wedge oc \in \mathcal{C}_Q$, $\{ic\} \notin IntChannels(P) \wedge \{ic\} \notin IntChannels\ (Q)$, *and* $Prot(P, ic) \approx Prot(Q, oc)$. *Then, the communication composition of P and Q (namely* $P[ic \leftrightarrow oc]Q$*) via ic and oc is defined as follows:*

$$P[ic \leftrightarrow oc]Q = P \stackrel{\smile}{\asymp} CON \stackrel{\smile}{\asymp} Q$$

where $CON = \mathcal{F}(Con_{copy}, \langle ic, oc \rangle, \langle \mathcal{R}_P(ic), \mathcal{R}_Q(oc) \rangle, \langle Prot(P, ic), Prot(Q, oc) \rangle)$

In the composition $P[ic \leftrightarrow oc]Q$, values of P are forwarded to Q through the channel connector Con_{copy}, which are confined in the composition (see Def. 6); the abstract connector Con_{copy} is instantiated by the function $\mathcal{F}$.

Lemma 2 (Deadlock-free and Livelock-free Communication Composition). *The communication composition of two deadlock-free and livelock-free component contracts is also deadlock-free and livelock-free.*

Proof. The *communication composition* is formed of two direct compositions. The Con_{copy} behaves as an one place buffer that always accepts communications from P or Q. As consequence, the proof that the communication with Con_{copy} does not deadlock is straightforward. All communications from Con_{copy} to P and Q are, in fact, originated from Q and P, respectively. As the proviso requires that their protocols be compatible, Q always accepts communications from P, and vice-versa. Livelock-freedom is obtained from the fact that new traces, resulted from the synchronisation, does not have any of their events hidden. □

The last form of composition shows how we can build cyclic topologies. In particular, we focus on binding two channels of the same component, namely feedback composition. Since we build systems by composing entities pairwisely, a system can always be taken as a single large grain entity. In doing so, composing channels of this large grain component allows introducing cycles in the system.

Due to the existence of cycles, new conditions have to be taken in account to preserve behavioural properties in the composition. This topic is closely related to the study of more general approaches to ensure deadlock freedom [12,6]. According to [6], in any deadlock state of the system, there is a cycle of ungranted requests with respect to its vocabulary. The system deadlocks when it gets into a state where each process of a cycle is waiting to output to the next and has no external communication. So, to avoid deadlock we simply have to avoid cycles of ungranted requests.

In order to avoid such cycles, we base our approach on a notion of *independent channels.* This concept is used to analyse the communication performed between two communication channels, checking whether desirable scenarios for their assembly exist. We define that a channel c_1 is independent of a channel c_2 in a process when any synchronism with c_2 does not interfere with the order of events communicated by c_1.

Definition 13 (Independent Channels). *Let c_1 and c_2 be two channels used by a component contract Q. Then, c_1 is independent of c_2 (denoted by $c_1 \mathcal{K}\, c_2$) iff:*

$$Prot(Q, c_1) \sqsubseteq_F Prot(Q \curlyeqsucc CHAOSCOMP, c_1)$$

where:

- $CHAOSCOMP = \langle CHAOS(c_2), \{(c_2 \mapsto \mathcal{R}_Q(c_2))\}, \{\mathcal{R}_Q(c_2)\}, \{c_2\}\rangle$
- $CHAOS(c) = Stop \sqcap (c?x \rightarrow CHAOS(c))$.

In the definition above, the component *CHAOSCOMP* represents the worst possible interferences through the channel c_2. So, if the protocol of c_1 is still the same after these interferences, then c_1 is independent of c_2. *Channel independency* is a transitive relation. Therefore, if a channel c_1 is independent of another channel c_2, it is independent of all the channels that c_2 is independent of.

As a consequence, the simplest way to avoid ungranted request cycles is to forbid the feedback composition of a channel c with a channel that is not independent of c. The intuition here is in accordance with the notion of independence between parallel I/O processes proposed in [12] to avoid deadlocks.

Definition 14 (FeedBack Composition). *Let P be a component contract, and ic and oc two channels, such that $\{ic, oc\} \subseteq \mathcal{C}_P$, $\{ic, oc\} \notin IntChannels(P)$, $Prot(P, ic) \approx Prot(P, oc)$, and $ic\, \mathcal{K}\, oc$. Then, the feedback composition P (namely $P[oc \hookrightarrow ic]$) hooking oc to ic is defined as follows:*

$$P[oc \hookrightarrow ic] = P \curlyeqsucc CON$$

where $CON = \mathcal{F}(Con_{copy}, \langle ic, oc\rangle, \langle \mathcal{R}_P(ic), \mathcal{R}_Q(oc)\rangle, \langle Prot(P, ic), Prot(P, oc)\rangle)$

In the resulting composition, $P[oc \hookrightarrow ic]$, values of P through oc are communicated to the feedback channel ic. Both channels oc and ic are then confined in the composition and are not available to the environment.

Lemma 3 (Deadlock-free and Livelock-free Feedback Composition) *The feedback composition of a deadlock-free and livelock-free component contract is also deadlock-free and livelock-free.*

Proof The proof is similar to the one for Lemma 2. However, in addition, we must check that no cycle of ungranted requests is introduced in the composition. In other words, that there is no cycle in which all components are willing to communicate with the next component. As the two channels involved in the composition are independent, no cycle of ungranted requests is introduced. □

From our proposed building block constructors (composition rules), any system S can be structured as follows.

$$S ::= P \mid S \, [|||] \, S \mid S[c_1 \leftrightarrow c_2]S \mid S[c_1 \hookrightarrow c_2]$$

where P is a component contract whose behaviour is deadlock- and livelock-free. We say that any component system that follows this grammar is in *normal form.*

Theorem 1 (Trustworthy Component Systems). *Any system S in normal form, built from deadlock-free and livelock-free components, is also deadlock-free and livelock-free.*

Proof. Direct from lemmas 1, 2, and 3. □

4 Example

In order to illustrate the application of the composition rules proposed in the precious section, we refine the scenario of the ATM system initially presented in Sect 2. This more elaborate scenario consists mainly of two *CLIENT* and two *SERVER* instances that run concurrently (see Fig. 3.a). No component instance knows each other; each *CLIENT* (*Client*1 or *Client*2) interacts with an arbitrary *SERVER* (*Server*1 or *Server*2) to request services, without knowing the identity of each other. The consistent interaction of *CLIENT*'s and *SERVER*'s must be carefully coordinated by the system. In order to achieve that, we design an elaborate connector (called *Connector Network* in Fig. 3.a) composed of other connector instances (see its structure in Fig. 3.b).

The *Connector Network* consists of instances of two kinds of connectors: *LBC* and *CCM*. Together, they efficiently route all communications of a *CLIENT* to

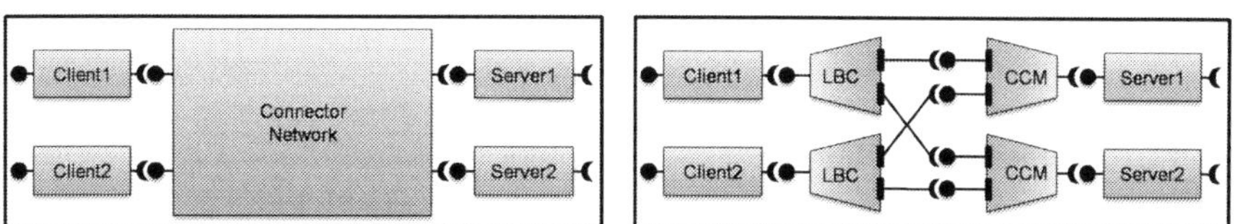

(a) Black box view of the System (b) Structure of the Connector Network

Fig. 3. Case Study: A more elaborate ATM System

a *SERVER*, establishing a safe communication path between both components until they finish their interaction. The *LBC* is a load balance connector, which verifies which *SERVER* is available at the moment. The *CCM* formalises a component communication manager, which identifies whether a *SERVER* is able to interact with a new *CLIENT* or whether it is busy with an existing interaction. To coordinate the information routing, these connectors communicate data and control events. The control events are used to provide feedback on how the communication is been performed. The following *CCM* and *LBC* processes represent the equally named connectors.

$$CCM(\langle c_o, c_1, c_2, f_1, f_2\rangle, SI, \langle P_{[c_o]}, P_2, P_3, P_4, P_5\rangle) = CCM'(c_1, c_2, f_1, f_2, c_o, P_{[c_o]})$$
$$LBC(\langle c_1, c_2, c_i, f_1, f_2\rangle, SI, \langle P_{[c_1]}, P_{[c_2]}, P_3, P_4, P_5\rangle) = LBC'(c_i, f_1, f_2, c_1, c_2, P_{[c_1]}, P_{[c_2]})$$

The channels of both connectors are distinguished between control and data information. In fact, to help understanding, we only show data channels in our illustration (Fig. 3). As observed in the expressions above, some protocol and interface information are immaterial in the definition of the connectors. Bellow, we define the auxiliary processes *CCM'* and *LBC'*.

channel *free*

$$\begin{aligned}
CCM'(c_1, c_2, f_1, f_2, c_o, P_{[c_o]}) = \mu X \bullet \quad & Copy(c_1, c_o, \langle\rangle, P_{[c_o]}) \fatsemi free \rightarrow X \\
& \Box\ Copy(c_2, c_o, \langle\rangle, P_{[c_o]}) \fatsemi free \rightarrow X \\
& \parallel_{\{|c_1, c_2, free|\}} (Avail(f_1, c_2, idle) \interleave Avail(f_2, c_1, idle))
\end{aligned}$$

$$\begin{aligned}
Avail(f, c, status) = \quad & f.in?isbusy \rightarrow f.out!status \rightarrow Avail(f, c, status) \\
& \Box\ c \rightarrow Avail(f, c, busy) \\
& \Box\ free \rightarrow Avail(f, c, idle)
\end{aligned}$$

$$\begin{aligned}
Copy(c_i, c_o, s, P_{[c_o]}) = \quad & c_i.in?x \rightarrow c_o.out!x \rightarrow Copy'(c_i, c_o, s\hat{}\langle x\rangle, P_{[c_o]}) \\
& \Box\ c_o.in?y \rightarrow c_i.out!y \rightarrow Copy'(c_i, c_o, s\hat{}\langle y\rangle, P_{[c_o]})
\end{aligned}$$

$$Copy'(c_i, c_o, s, P_{[c_o]}) = SKIP \not< P_{[c_o]} \sqsubseteq_F (P_{[c_o]}/s) \not> Copy(c_i, c_o, s, P_{[c_o]})$$

$$\begin{aligned}
LBC'(c_i, f_1, f_2, c_1, c_2, P_{[c_1]}, P_{[c_2]}) = \mu X \bullet\ & f_1.out!isbusy \rightarrow f_2.out!isbusy \rightarrow \\
(\quad & f_1.in?idle \rightarrow f_2.in?x \rightarrow Copy(c_i, c_1, \langle\rangle, P_{[c_1]}) \fatsemi X \\
\Box\ & f_1.in?busy \rightarrow (\quad f_2.in?idle \rightarrow Copy(c_i, c_2, \langle\rangle, P_{[c_2]}) \fatsemi X \\
& \qquad \Box\ f_2.in?busy \rightarrow X))
\end{aligned}$$

In the CSP processes above, c_i, c_1, c_2, and c_o are channels used for communicating data. The channels c_1 and c_2 are used to communicate data between the connectors *LBC* and *CCM*, whereas c_i and c_o represent channels for communication with the environment. The channels f_1 and f_2 are used to communicate control data between the connectors. The channel *free* is used for internal synchronisation in the *CCM*. To ease the definitions of the connectors, we use protocol $P_{[c_j]}$, where c_j stands for the channel associated to the protocol. In fact, these protocols represent the behaviour of the *SERVER* component over these channels when the connector is instantiated.

The *CCM* repeatedly behaves as a connector that copies events either from c_1 or c_2 to c_o. It chooses between the two behaviours depending on which channel has first enabled an event to be performed. It continuously transfers values between such channels until it concludes an interaction (a trace that leads the process to its initial state). At any time, the process can receive an event $f_j.isbusy$

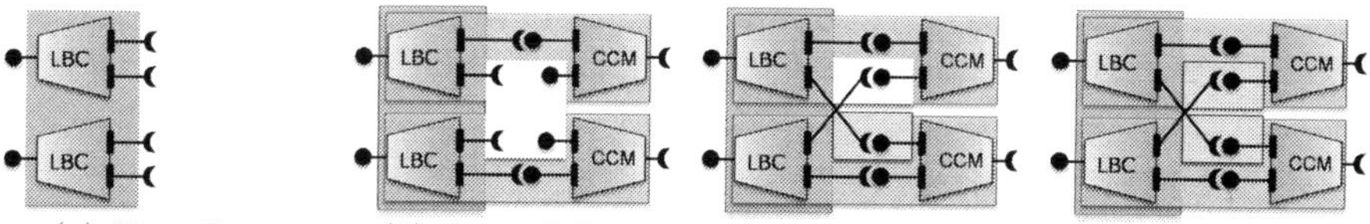

(a) First Step (b) Second Step (c) Third Step (d) Fourth Step

Fig. 4. The composition of basic connectors to form the network of connectors

asking if the connector is already engaged in an interaction. If so, it communicates $f_j.busy$; otherwise, it communicates $f_j.idle$. The *LBC* starts by sending an event $f_j.isbusy$ to each connector assembled to c_1 and c_2. The first to answer $f_j.idle$ enables a communication. It continuously copies data from a channel c_i to this connector until it finishes an interaction.

To build the *Connector Network*, we compose instances of these connectors using our composition rules. This guarantees that the resulting component is deadlock-free and livelock-free. Due to space restrictions, we do not show their instantiation. *LBC* and *CCM* depend on the coordinated component contracts. In our example, we assume they are used to mediate the communication between *CLIENT* and *SERVER*, previously described in Sect. 2.1. So, data channels have same interfaces as those components, and the protocols are based on the *SERVER* protocol ($P_{[c_j]} = Prot(Ctr_{SV}, sv)$).

Based on these component contracts, we are able to incrementally construct the *Connector Network*. Fig. 4 summarises our strategy to compose such concrete connectors. To build the coordinator, we first perform an *interleave composition* of the two instances of *LBC* using (see Fig. 4.a). Then, we perform a *communication composition* with each *CCM* connector to the result of the previous composition (see Fig. 4.b). Subsequently, we use the *feedback composition* to assembly the inner instances of the *LBC* to instances of the *CCM* (see Fig. 4.c and 4.d). Control channels are assembled afterwards using similar feedback compositions. All these transformations have been conducted based on the CSP descriptions of the processes.

5 Conclusion

We have proposed a systematic approach for building trustworthy component-based systems (CBS) (see Theo. 1). The approach relies on three rules for composing components (including concrete connectors): *interleave*, *communication* and *feedback* compositions. They guarantee deadlock- and livelock-freedom in the compositions based on the assumptions that the original components hold these properties. The entire approach is underpinned by the CSP process algebra, which offers rich semantic models that support a wide range of process verification, and comparisons. In fact, CSP has shown to be very useful to support the rigorous development of component based systems, as a hidden formalism for modelling languages used in practise [7,8].

To guarantee deadlock-freedom, the composition rules include side conditions that require the compatibility between communication protocols and the independence of channels. The former ensures compatibility between component communications, and the latter avoids undesirable architectural configurations, such as *cycles of ungranted requests* [6]. To guarantee livelock-freedom, the composition rules include side conditions which require that no *interaction pattern* (recurring behaviour) of the original component be entirely hidden in the black-box composition. Each composition results in a software component, whose properties are directly derived from the components involved in the composition. These properties are called $\mathcal{B}$, $\mathcal{R}$, $\mathcal{I}$, $\mathcal{C}$, $\mathcal{K}$, and represent the behaviour, channel types, interfaces, channels, and derivable metadata, such as independence relationship among channels, of the component, and protocols.

Even though there are many approaches to formally model CBS [2,13,14,15], to our knowledge the question of preserving behavioural properties by construction has not yet been fully systematised as we have done in this work. Despite the fact that our notions are compatible with most component-based approaches, especially those based on CSP [1,3], these approaches aim at verifying the entire system before implementation, but not at predicting behavioural properties by construction during design. We can ensure deadlock- and livelock-freedom in a constructive way, as a result of applying composition rules, as opposed to performing model checking verification after the system has been built.

The work reported in [13] presents an extensive study of the verification of important quality properties in CBS. It discusses the verification of liveness, local progress, local and global deadlock, and fairness. We implicitly discuss these properties, except fairness. Local progress and deadlock are addressed altogether in our *protocol compatibility* notions. Liveness is addressed in each composition rule by the guarantee of livelock-freedom. Global deadlock freedom is obtained in the entire system by construction. Our approach is also similar to others in some respects. For instance, similar verifications for *protocol compatibility* are found in rCOS [3], SOFA [4] and Interface Automata [14]. Side conditions of our composition rules have the same intention as the assumption to remove *potential deadlocks* in [15]. Similar to our work, [2,6] analyse deadlock scenarios in several network topologies. Although they cover a wide range of topologies, some verifications are not amenable for an approach by constructions, like ours. Livelock verification by construction is not addressed in such works.

Some approaches [12,16] do predict some system properties based on the properties of its constituting components. These works focus on different properties. The work reported in [16] does not focus on behavioural properties; rather, it presents some results on performance. The approach presented in [12] proposes rules to guarantee the absence of deadlocks by construction. These rules impose that CBS should satisfy specific architectural styles, which prevent deadlock scenarios. Despite the fact that it is presented a comprehensive set of styles, such as resource sharing and client-server, these are restrictive in some situations; for instance, a component must always accept any input data value. In our work, we allow components to have arbitrary protocols, with distinct input and output communication. Moreover, we also use connectors as an important part of our composition approach, and present them at two different abstraction levels, which are aligned with practical approaches [10,17] to model connectors.

A distinguishing feature of our approach is that each of the proposed composition rules is intentionally simple to capture a particular communication pattern with the relevant side conditions to preserve behavioural properties. Complex interactions can be progressively built from these very simple rules, as illustrated by our case study. As future work we intend to investigate other composition rules, or derivations of those proposed here, and build tool support for the design of trustworthy component systems.

References

1. Allen, R., Garlan, D.: A formal basis for architectural connection. ACM Transactions 6(3), 213–249 (1997)
2. Aldini, A., Bernardo, M.: A general approach to deadlock freedom verification for software architectures. In: Araki, K., Gnesi, S., Mandrioli, D. (eds.) FME 2003. LNCS, vol. 2805, pp. 658–677. Springer, Heidelberg (2003)
3. He, J., Li, X., Liu, Z.: A Theory of Reactive Components. Elsevier 160, 173–195 (2006)
4. Plasil, F., Visnovsky, S.: Behavior protocols for software components. IEEE Transactions on Software Engineering 28(11), 1056–1076 (2002)
5. Ramos, R., Sampaio, A., Mota, A.: Framework composition conformance via refinement checking. In: SAC, pp. 119–125. ACM, New York (2008)
6. Roscoe, A.W.: Theory and Practice of Concurrency. The Prentice-Hall Series in Computer Science. Prentice-Hall, Englewood Cliffs (1998)
7. Ramos, R., Sampaio, A., Mota, A.: A Semantics for UML-RT Active Classes via Mapping into Circus. In: Steffen, M., Zavattaro, G. (eds.) FMOODS 2005. LNCS, vol. 3535, pp. 99–114. Springer, Heidelberg (2005)
8. Ramos, R., Sampaio, A., Mota, A.: Transformation Laws for UML-RT. In: Gorrieri, R., Wehrheim, H. (eds.) FMOODS 2006. LNCS, vol. 4037, pp. 123–137. Springer, Heidelberg (2006)
9. Bracciali, A., Brogi, A., Turini, F.: Coordinating interaction patterns. In: ACM Symposium on Applied Computing, pp. 159–165. ACM, New York (2001)
10. Matougui, S., Beugnard, A.: How to Implement Software Connectors? In: Kutvonen, L., Alonistioti, N. (eds.) DAIS 2005. LNCS, vol. 3543, pp. 83–94. Springer, Heidelberg (2005)
11. Fournet, C., Hoare, T., Rajamani, S.K., Rehof, J.: Stuck-Free Conformance. In: Alur, R., Peled, D.A. (eds.) CAV 2004. LNCS, vol. 3114, pp. 242–254. Springer, Heidelberg (2004)
12. Martin, J.M.R., Jassim, S.A.: A tool for proving deadlock freedom. In: 20th World Occam and Transputer User Group Technical Meeting, Wotug-20. IOS Press, Amsterdam (1997)

13. Gößler, G., Graf, S., Majster-Cederbaum, M., Martens, M., Sifakis, J.: An approach to modelling and verification of component based systems. In: van Leeuwen, J., Italiano, G.F., van der Hoek, W., Meinel, C., Sack, H., Plášil, F. (eds.) SOFSEM 2007. LNCS, vol. 4362, pp. 295–308. Springer, Heidelberg (2007)
14. Alfaro, L., Henzinger, T.: Interface-based design. In: Engineering Theories of Software-intensive Systems. NATO, vol. 195, pp. 83–104. Springer, Heidelberg (2005)
15. Giannakopoulou, D., Pasareanu, C.S., Barringer, H.: Component verification with automatically generated assumptions. Autom. Softw. Eng. 12(3), 297–320 (2005)
16. Ivers, J., Moreno, G.A.: PACC starter kit: developing software with predictable behavior. In: ICSE Companion, pp. 949–950. ACM, New York (2008)
17. Arbab, F.: Reo: a channel-based coordination model for component composition. Mathematical. Structures in Comp. Sci. 14(3), 329–366 (2004)

Partial Order Reductions Using Compositional Confluence Detection

Frédéric Lang and Radu Mateescu

VASY project-team, INRIA Grenoble Rhône-Alpes/LIG, Montbonnot, France
{Frederic.Lang,Radu.Mateescu}@inria.fr

Abstract. Explicit state methods have proven useful in verifying safety-critical systems containing concurrent processes that run asynchronously and communicate. Such methods consist of inspecting the states and transitions of a graph representation of the system. Their main limitation is state explosion, which happens when the graph is too large to be stored in the available computer memory. Several techniques can be used to palliate state explosion, such as on-the-fly verification, compositional verification, and partial order reductions. In this paper, we propose a new technique of partial order reductions based on compositional confluence detection (CCD), which can be combined with the techniques mentioned above. CCD is based upon a generalization of the notion of confluence defined by Milner and exploits the fact that synchronizing transitions that are confluent in the individual processes yield a confluent transition in the system graph. It thus consists of analysing the transitions of the individual process graphs and the synchronization structure to identify such confluent transitions compositionally. Under some additional conditions, the confluent transitions can be given priority over the other transitions, thus enabling graph reductions. We propose two such additional conditions: one ensuring that the generated graph is equivalent to the original system graph modulo branching bisimulation, and one ensuring that the generated graph contains the same deadlock states as the original system graph. We also describe how CCD-based reductions were implemented in the CADP toolbox, and present examples and a case study in which adding CCD improves reductions with respect to compositional verification and other partial order reductions.

1 Introduction

This paper deals with systems, hereafter called *asynchronous systems*, which can be modeled by a composition of individual processes that execute in parallel at independent speeds and communicate. Asynchronous systems can be found in many application domains, such as communication protocols, embedded software, hardware architectures, distributed systems, etc.

Industrial asynchronous systems are often subject to strong constraints in terms of development cost and/or reliability. A way to address these constraints is to use methods allowing the identification of bugs as early as possible in the

A. Cavalcanti and D. Dams (Eds.): FM 2009, LNCS 5850, pp. 157–172, 2009.

development cycle. Explicit state verification is such a method, and consists of verifying properties by systematic exploration of the states and transitions of an abstract model of the system.

Although appropriate for verifying asynchronous systems, explicit state verification may be limited by the combinatorial explosion of the number of states and transitions (called *state explosion*). Among the numerous techniques that have been proposed to palliate state explosion, the following have proved to be effective:

- *On-the-fly verification* (see e.g., [9,8,21,31,29]) consists of enumerating the states and transitions in an order determined by a property of interest, thus enabling one to find property violations before the whole system graph has been generated.
- *Compositional verification* (see e.g., [7,28,41,44,46,6,38,16,24,39,14,11]) consists of replacing individual processes by property-preserving abstractions of limited size.
- *Partial order reductions* (see e.g., [15,42,35,20,43,36,37,19,33,3,34]) consist of choosing not to explore interleavings of actions that are not relevant with respect to either the properties or the graph equivalence of interest.

Regarding partial order reductions, two lines of work coexist. The first addresses the identification of a subset called *persistent* [15] (or *ample* [35], or *stubborn* [42], see [36] for a survey[1]) of the operations that define the transitions of the system, such that all operations outside this subset are independent of all operations inside this subset. This allows the operations outside the persistent subset to be ignored in the current state. Depending on additional conditions, persistent subsets may preserve various classes of properties (e.g., deadlocks, LTL-X, CTL-X, etc.) and/or graph equivalence relations (e.g., branching equivalence [45], weak trace equivalence [5], etc). Other methods based on the identification of independent transitions, such as *sleep sets* [15], can be combined with persistent sets to obtain more reductions.

The second line of work addresses the detection of particular non-observable transitions (non-observable transitions are also called τ-transitions) that satisfy the property of confluence [32,20,19,47,2,3,34], using either symbolic or explicit-state techniques. Such transitions can be given priority over the rest of the transitions of the system, thus avoiding exploration of useless states and transitions while preserving branching (and observational) equivalence. Among the symbolic detection techniques, the proof-theoretic technique of [3] statically generates a formula encoding the confluence condition from a μCRL program, and then solves it using a separate theorem prover. Among the explicit-state techniques, the global technique of [19] computes the maximal set of strongly confluent τ-transitions and reduces the graph with respect to this set. A local technique was proposed in [2], which computes on-the-fly a representation map associating a single state to each connected subgraph of confluent τ-transitions. Another

[1] In this paper, the term *persistent* will refer equally to persistent, ample, or stubborn.

technique was proposed in [34], which reformulates the detection as the resolution of a BES (*Boolean Equation System*) and prioritizes confluent τ-transitions in the individual processes before composing them, using the fact that branching equivalence is a congruence for the parallel composition of processes. Compared to persistent subset methods, whose practical effectiveness depends on the accuracy of identifying independent operations (by analyzing the system description), confluence detection methods are able to detect all confluent transitions (by exploring the system graph), potentially leading to better reductions.

In this paper, we present a new compositional partial order reduction method for systems described as networks of communicating automata. This method, named CCD (*Compositional Confluence Detection*), exploits the confluence of individual process transitions that are not necessarily labeled by τ and thus cannot be prioritized in the individual processes. CCD relies on the fact that synchronizing such transitions always yields a confluent transition in the graph of the composition. As an immediate consequence, if the latter transition is labeled by τ (i.e., hidden after synchronization), then giving it priority preserves branching equivalence. We also describe conditions to ensure that even transitions that are not labeled by τ can be prioritized, while still preserving the deadlocks of the system.

The aim of CCD is to use compositionality to detect confluence more efficiently than explicit-state techniques applied directly to the graph of the composition, the counterpart being that not all confluent transitions are necessarily detected (as in persistent subset methods). Nevertheless, CCD and persistent subset methods are orthogonal, meaning that neither method applied individually performs better than both methods applied together. Thus, CCD can be freely added in order to improve the reductions achieved by persistent subset methods. Moreover, the definition of confluent transitions is language-independent (i.e., it does not rely upon the description language — in our case EXP.OPEN 2.0 [25] — but only upon the system graph), making CCD suitable for networks of communicating automata produced from any description language equipped with interleaving semantics.

CCD was implemented in the CADP toolbox [12] and more particularly in the existing EXP.OPEN 2.0 tool for compositional verification, which provides on-the-fly verification of compositions of processes. A new procedure was developed, which searches and annotates the confluent (or strictly confluent) transitions of a graph, using a BES to encode the confluence property. This procedure is invoked on the individual processes so that EXP.OPEN 2.0 can then generate a reduced graph for the composition, possibly combined with already available persistent subset methods.

Experimental results show that adding CCD may improve reductions with respect to compositional verification and persistent subset methods.

Paper outline. Section 2 gives preliminary definitions and theorems. Section 3 formally presents the semantic model that we use to represent asynchronous systems. Section 4 presents the main result of the paper. Section 5 describes how the CCD technique is implemented in the CADP toolbox. Section 6 presents several experimental results. Section 7 reports about the application of CCD in an industrial case-study. Finally, Section 8 gives concluding remarks.

2 Preliminaries

We consider the standard LTS (*Labeled Transition System*) semantic model [32], which is a graph consisting of a set of *states*, an *initial state*, and a set of *transitions* between states, each transition being labeled by an action of the system.

Definition 1 (Labeled Transition System). Let $\mathcal{A}$ be a set of symbols called *labels*, which contains a special symbol τ, called the *unobservable label*. An LTS is a quadruple $(Q, A, \rightarrow, q_0)$, where Q is the set of *states*, $A \subseteq \mathcal{A}$ is the set of *labels*, $\rightarrow \subseteq Q \times A \times Q$ is the *transition relation*, and $q_0 \in Q$ is the *initial state* of the LTS. As usual, we may write $q_1 \xrightarrow{a} q_2$ instead of $(q_1, a, q_2) \in \rightarrow$. Any sequence of the form $q_1 \xrightarrow{a_1} q_2 \xrightarrow{a_2} \dots q_n \xrightarrow{a_n} q_{n+1}$ is called a *path of length n* from q_1 to q_{n+1} ($n \geq 0$). We write $q_1 \longrightarrow^n q_{n+1}$ if there exists such a path. The transition relation is acyclic if every path from a state to itself has length 0. □

Branching equivalence [45] is a weak bisimulation relation between states of an LTS that removes some τ-transitions while preserving the branching structure of the LTS. Therefore, branching equivalence is of interest when verifying branching-time temporal logic properties that concern only observable labels.

Definition 2 (Branching equivalence [45]). As usual, we write $\xrightarrow{\tau*}$ the reflexive and transitive closure of $\xrightarrow{\tau}$. Two states $q_1, q_2 \in Q$ are *branching equivalent* if and only if there exists a relation $R \subseteq Q \times Q$ such that $R(q_1, q_2)$ and (1) for each transition $q_1 \xrightarrow{a} q_1'$, either $a = \tau$ and $R(q_1', q_2)$ or there is a path $q_2 \xrightarrow{\tau*} q_2' \xrightarrow{a} q_2''$ such that $R(q_1, q_2')$ and $R(q_1', q_2'')$, and (2) for each transition $q_2 \xrightarrow{a} q_2'$, either $a = \tau$ and $R(q_1, q_2')$, or there is a path $q_1 \xrightarrow{\tau*} q_1' \xrightarrow{a} q_1''$ such that $R(q_1', q_2)$ and $R(q_1'', q_2')$. □

The following definition of *strong confluence* is a synthesis of the definitions of *confluence* by Milner [32], which is a property of processes, and *partial strong τ-confluence* by Groote and van de Pol [19], which is a property of τ-transitions. We thus generalize Groote and van de Pol's definition to transitions labeled by arbitrary symbols, as was the case of Milner's original definition. In addition, we distinguish between the property of strong confluence, and a slightly more constrained property, named *strict* strong confluence.

Definition 3 (Strong confluence). Let $(Q, A, \rightarrow, q_0)$ be an LTS and $T \subseteq \rightarrow$. We write $q \xrightarrow{a}_T q'$ if $(q, a, q') \in T$. We write $q \xrightarrow{\overline{a}} q'$ if either $q \xrightarrow{a} q'$ or $q = q'$ and $a = \tau$, and similarly for $q \xrightarrow{\overline{a}}_T q'$. T is *strongly confluent* if for every pair of distinct transitions $q_1 \xrightarrow{a}_T q_2$ and $q_1 \xrightarrow{b} q_3$, there exists a state q_4 such that $q_3 \xrightarrow{\overline{a}}_T q_4$ and $q_2 \xrightarrow{\overline{b}} q_4$. T is *strictly strongly confluent* if for every pair of distinct transitions $q_1 \xrightarrow{a}_T q_2$ and $q_1 \xrightarrow{b} q_3$, there exists a state q_4 such that

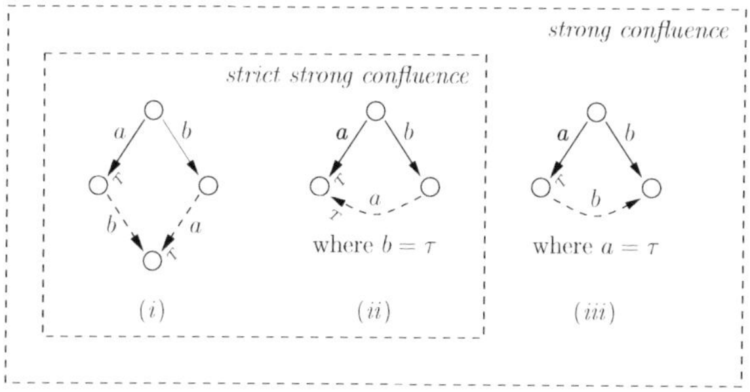

Fig. 1. Graphical definition of *strong confluence* and *strict strong confluence*

$q_3 \xrightarrow{a}_T q_4$ and $q_2 \xrightarrow{\bar{b}} q_4$. A transition is *strongly confluent* (respectively *strictly strongly confluent*) if there exists a strongly confluent set (respectively strictly strongly confluent set) $T \subseteq \rightarrow$ containing that transition. □

Figure 1 gives a graphical picture of strong confluence. Plain arrows denote transitions quantified universally, whereas dotted arrows denote transitions quantified existentially. For strict strong confluence, case (*iii*) is excluded.

Strong τ-confluence is strong confluence of τ-transitions. Weaker notions of τ-confluence have been defined [20,47], but are out of the scope of this paper. For brevity, we use below the terms confluent and strictly confluent instead of strongly confluent and strictly strongly confluent, respectively.

Prioritization consists of giving priority to some transitions. Definition 4 below generalizes the definition of [19], which was restricted to τ-transitions.

Definition 4 (Prioritization [19]). Let $(Q, A, \rightarrow_1, q_0)$ be an LTS and $T \subseteq \rightarrow_1$. A *prioritization* of $(Q, A, \rightarrow_1, q_0)$ with respect to T is any LTS of the form $(Q, A, \rightarrow_2, q_0)$, where $\rightarrow_2 \subseteq \rightarrow_1$ and for all $q_1, q_2 \in Q, a \in A$, if $q_1 \xrightarrow{a}_1 q_2$ then (1) $q_1 \xrightarrow{a}_2 q_2$ or (2) there exists $q_3 \in Q$ and $b \in A$ such that $q_1 \xrightarrow{b}_2 q_3 \in T$. □

In [19], Groote and van de Pol proved that branching bisimulation is preserved by prioritization of τ-confluent transitions, provided the LTS does not contain cycles of τ-transitions. Theorem 1 below relaxes this constraint by only requiring that the set of prioritized τ-confluent transitions does not contain cycles (which is similar to the cycle-closing condition for ample sets [35]).

Theorem 1. Let $(Q, A, \rightarrow, q_0)$ be an LTS and $T \subseteq \rightarrow$ such that T is acyclic and contains only τ-confluent transitions. Any prioritization of $(Q, A, \rightarrow, q_0)$ with respect to T yields an LTS that is branching equivalent to $(Q, A, \rightarrow, q_0)$. □

Theorem 2 below states that deadlock states can always be reached without following transitions that are in choice with strictly confluent transitions. This allows prioritization of strictly confluent transitions, while ensuring that at least one (minimal) diagnostic path can be found for each deadlock state. The detailed proof can be found in [27].

Theorem 2. Let $(Q, A, \rightarrow, q_0)$ be an LTS, $T \subseteq \rightarrow$ a strictly confluent set of transitions, and $q_\delta \in Q$ be a deadlock state. If $q_1 \longrightarrow^n q_\delta$ and $q_1 \xrightarrow{a}_T q_2$, then $q_2 \longrightarrow^m q_\delta$ with $m < n$. □

Therefore, any prioritization of $(Q, A, \rightarrow, q_0)$ with respect to T yields an LTS that has the same deadlock states as $(Q, A, \rightarrow, q_0)$.

Note. Theorem 2 is not true for non-strict confluence, as illustrated by the LTS consisting of the transition $q_1 \xrightarrow{a} q_\delta$ and the (non-strictly) confluent transition $q_1 \xrightarrow{\tau} q_1$.

3 Networks of LTSs

This section introduces networks of LTSs [25,26], a concurrent model close to MEC [1] and FC2 [4], which consists of a set of LTSs composed in parallel and synchronizing following general synchronization rules.

Definition 5 (Vector). A *vector* of *length* n over a set T is an element of T^n. Let $\boldsymbol{v}$, also written $(v_1, \ldots, v_n)$, be a vector of length n. The elements of $1..n$ are called the *indices* of $\boldsymbol{v}$. For each $i \in 1..n$, $\boldsymbol{v}[i]$ denotes the ith element v_i of $\boldsymbol{v}$. □

Definition 6 (Network of LTSs). Let $\bullet \notin \mathcal{A}$ be a special symbol denoting *inaction*. A *synchronization vector* is a vector over $\mathcal{A} \cup \{\bullet\}$. Let $\boldsymbol{t}$ be a synchronization vector of length n. The *active components* of $\boldsymbol{t}$, written $\text{act}(\boldsymbol{t})$, are defined as the set $\{i \in 1..n \mid \boldsymbol{t}[i] \neq \bullet\}$. The *inactive components* of $\boldsymbol{t}$, written $\text{inact}(\boldsymbol{t})$, are defined as the set $1..n \setminus \text{act}(\boldsymbol{t})$. A *synchronization rule* of length n is a pair $(\boldsymbol{t}, a)$, where $\boldsymbol{t}$ is a synchronization vector of length n and $a \in \mathcal{A}$. The elements $\boldsymbol{t}$ and a are called respectively the *left-* and *right-hand sides* of the synchronization rule. A *network of* LTSs N of length n is a pair $(\boldsymbol{S}, V)$ where $\boldsymbol{S}$ is a vector of length n over LTSs and V is a set of synchronization rules of length n. □

In the sequel, we may use the term network instead of network of LTSs. A network $(\boldsymbol{S}, V)$ therefore denotes a product of LTSs, where each rule expresses a constraint on the vector of LTSs $\boldsymbol{S}$. In a given state of the product, each rule $(\boldsymbol{t}, a) \in V$ yields a transition labeled by a under the condition that, assuming $\text{act}(\boldsymbol{t}) = \{i_0, \ldots, i_m\}$, the LTSs $\boldsymbol{S}[i_0], \ldots, \boldsymbol{S}[i_m]$ may synchronize altogether on transitions labeled respectively by $\boldsymbol{t}[i_0], \ldots, \boldsymbol{t}[i_m]$. This is described formally by the following definition.

Definition 7 (Network semantics). Let N be a network of length n defined as a couple $(\boldsymbol{S}, V)$ and for each $i \in 1..n$, let $\boldsymbol{S}[i]$ be the LTS $(Q_i, A_i, \rightarrow_i, q_{0i})$. The *semantics* of N, written $lts(N)$ or $lts(\boldsymbol{S}, V)$, is an LTS $(Q, A, \rightarrow, \boldsymbol{q}_0)$ where $Q \subseteq Q_1 \times \ldots \times Q_n$, $\boldsymbol{q}_0 = (q_{01}, \ldots, q_{0n})$ and $A = \{a \mid (\boldsymbol{t}, a) \in V\}$. Given a synchronization rule $(\boldsymbol{t}, a) \in V$ and a state $\boldsymbol{q} \in Q_1 \times \ldots \times Q_n$, we define the *successors* of $\boldsymbol{q}$ by rule $(\boldsymbol{t}, a)$, written $\text{succ}(\boldsymbol{q}, (\boldsymbol{t}, a))$, as follows:

$$\begin{aligned}\text{succ}(\boldsymbol{q}, (\boldsymbol{t}, a)) = \{\boldsymbol{q}' \in Q_1 \times \ldots \times Q_n \mid\ & (\forall i \in \text{act}(\boldsymbol{t}))\ \boldsymbol{q}[i] \xrightarrow{\boldsymbol{t}[i]}_i \boldsymbol{q}'[i] \wedge \\ & (\forall i \in \text{inact}(\boldsymbol{t}))\ \boldsymbol{q}[i] = \boldsymbol{q}'[i]\}\end{aligned}$$

The state set Q and the transition relation $\rightarrow$ of $lts(N)$ are the smallest set and the smallest relation such that $\boldsymbol{q_0} \in Q$ and:
$q \in Q \wedge (\boldsymbol{t}, a) \in V \wedge \boldsymbol{q'} \in \text{succ}(\boldsymbol{q}, (\boldsymbol{t}, a)) \Rightarrow \boldsymbol{q'} \in Q \wedge \boldsymbol{q} \xrightarrow{a} \boldsymbol{q'}$. □

Synchronization rules must obey the following admissibility condition, which forbids cutting, synchronization and renaming of the τ transitions present in the individual LTSs. This is suitable for a process algebraic framework, most parallel composition, hiding, renaming, and cutting operators of which can be translated into rules obeying these conditions. This also ensures that weak trace equivalence and stronger relations (e.g., safety, observational, branching, and strong equivalences) are congruences for synchronization rules [25].

Definition 8 (Network admissibility). The network $(\boldsymbol{S}, V)$ is *admissible* if for each q, q', i such that $q \xrightarrow{\tau}_i q'$ there exists a rule $(\boldsymbol{t}_i, \tau) \in V$ where $\boldsymbol{t}_i[i] = \tau$, $(\forall j \neq i)\ \boldsymbol{t}_i[j] = \bullet$, and $(\forall (t, a) \in V \setminus \{(\boldsymbol{t}_i, \tau)\})\ t[i] \neq \tau$. Below, every network will be assumed to be admissible. □

Example 1. We consider the simple network of LTSs consisting of the vector of LTSs $(Sender_1, Bag, Sender_2)$ depicted in Figure 2 (the topmost node being the initial state of each LTS), and of the following four synchronization rules: $((s_1, s_1, \bullet), \tau)$, $((\bullet, s_2, s_2), \tau)$, $((\bullet, r_1, \bullet), r_1)$, $((\bullet, r_2, \bullet), r_2)$.

This network represents two processes $Sender_1$ and $Sender_2$, which send their respective messages s_1 and s_2 via a communication buffer that contains one place for each sender and uses a *bag* policy (received messages can be delivered in any order). Every transition in the individual LTSs of this network is strictly confluent. The LTS (*i*) depicted in Figure 3, page 165, represents the semantics of this network.

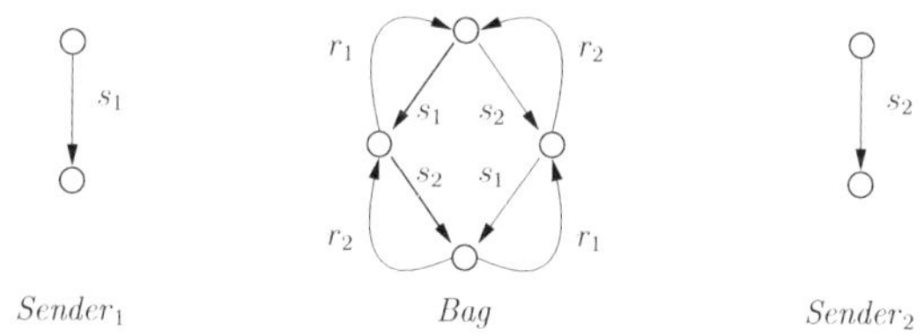

Fig. 2. Individual LTSs of the network defined in Example 1

4 Compositional Confluence Detection

Although prioritizing confluent transitions yields LTS reductions, finding confluent transitions in large LTSs such as those obtained by parallel composition of smaller LTSs can be quite expensive in practice. Instead, the aim of CCD is to infer confluence in the large LTS from the (much cheaper to find) confluence present in the smaller LTSs that are composed.

Definition 9. Let $(\boldsymbol{S}, V)$ be a network, $(\boldsymbol{t}, a) \in V$, and $\boldsymbol{q}$, $\boldsymbol{q}'$ be states of $lts(\boldsymbol{S}, V)$. We write all_conf$(\boldsymbol{q}, (\boldsymbol{t}, a), \boldsymbol{q}')$ for the predicate "$\boldsymbol{q}' \in \text{succ}(\boldsymbol{q}, (\boldsymbol{t}, a)) \wedge (\forall i \in \text{act}(\boldsymbol{t}))\ \boldsymbol{q}[i] \xrightarrow{\boldsymbol{t}[i]}_i \boldsymbol{q}'[i]$ is confluent". We write all_conf_strict for the same predicate, where "*strictly confluent*" replaces "*confluent*". □

Theorem 3 below presents the main result of this paper: synchronizations involving only confluent (resp. strictly confluent) transitions in the individual LTSs produce confluent (resp. strictly confluent) transitions in the LTS of the network.

Theorem 3 (Compositional confluence detection). Let $(\boldsymbol{S}, V)$ be a network, $(\boldsymbol{t}, a) \in V$, and $\boldsymbol{q}$, $\boldsymbol{q}'$ be states of $lts(\boldsymbol{S}, V)$. (1) If all_conf$(\boldsymbol{q}, (\boldsymbol{t}, a), \boldsymbol{q}')$, then $\boldsymbol{q} \xrightarrow{a} \boldsymbol{q}'$ is confluent and (2) if all_conf_strict$(\boldsymbol{q}, (\boldsymbol{t}, a), \boldsymbol{q}')$, then $\boldsymbol{q} \xrightarrow{a} \boldsymbol{q}'$ is strictly confluent. □

The proof [27] consists of showing that the set $\{\boldsymbol{p} \xrightarrow{a} \boldsymbol{p}' \mid \text{all\_conf}(\boldsymbol{p}, (\boldsymbol{t}, a), \boldsymbol{p}')\}$ is indeed a confluent set (and similarly for the strictly confluent case).

We call *deadlock preserving reduction using* CCD a prioritization of transitions obtained from synchronization of strictly confluent transitions (which indeed preserves the deadlocks of the system following Theorems 2 and 3), and *branching preserving reduction using* CCD a prioritization of τ-transitions obtained from synchronization of confluent transitions, provided they are acyclic (which indeed preserves branching bisimulation following Theorems 1 and 3). The major differences between both reductions are thus the following: (1) branching preserving reduction does not require strict confluence; (2) deadlock preserving reduction does not require any acyclicity condition; and (3) deadlock preserving reduction does not require the prioritized transitions to be labeled by τ, which preserves the labels of diagnostic paths leading to deadlock states.

Example 2. Figure 3 depicts three LTSs corresponding to the network presented in Example 1, page 163. LTS (*i*) corresponds to the semantics of the network, generated without reduction. LTS (*ii*) is the same generated with branching preserving reduction using CCD and thus is branching equivalent to LTS (*i*). LTS (*iii*) is the same generated with deadlock preserving reduction using CCD and thus has the same deadlock state as LTS (*i*).

As persistent subset methods, CCD is able to detect commuting transitions by a local analysis of the network. For persistent subsets, a relation of independence between the transitions enabled in the current state is computed dynamically by inspection of the transitions enabled in the individual LTSs and of their interactions (defined here as synchronization rules). By contrast, CCD performs a static analysis of the individual LTSs to detect which transitions are locally confluent, the dynamic part being limited to checking whether a transition of the network can be obtained by synchronizing only locally confluent transitions.

Branching preserving reduction using CCD does not require detection of all confluent transitions in the individual LTSs of the network, but can be restricted to those active in a synchronization rule of the form $(\boldsymbol{t}, \tau)$. In a network $(\boldsymbol{S}, V)$ of length n, we thus compute for each $i \in 1..n$ a subset $C_i \subseteq A_i$ of labels

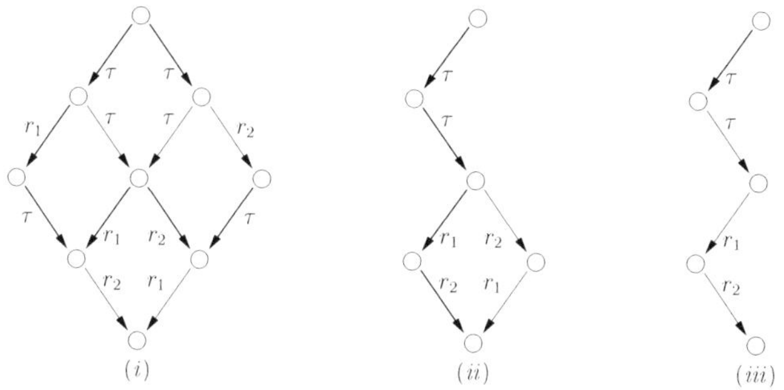

Fig. 3. Three LTSs corresponding to the semantics of the network of Example 1, one generated without CCD (i) and two generated using CCD preserving respectively branching equivalence (ii) and deadlocks (iii)

that contains all labels $\boldsymbol{t}[i] \neq \bullet$ such that there exists $(\boldsymbol{t}, \tau) \in V$. For deadlock preserving reduction, the subset C_i is defined as A_i.

The problem of detecting confluence in the individual LTSs is reformulated in terms of the local resolution of a BES (*Boolean Equation System*), following the scheme we proposed in [34]. Given an LTS $(Q_i, A_i, \rightarrow_i, {q_0}_i)$ and a subset $C_i \subseteq A_i$ of labels, the BES encoding the detection of confluent transitions labeled by actions in C_i is defined as follows:

$$\left\{X_{q_1 a q_2} \stackrel{\nu}{=} \bigwedge_{q_1 \xrightarrow{b}_i q_3} \bigvee_{q_2 \xrightarrow{\overline{b}}_i q_4} \Big(\bigvee_{q_3 \xrightarrow{\overline{a}}_i q_4'} (q_4 = q_4' \wedge X_{q_3 a q_4}) \vee (a = \tau \wedge q_3 = q_4)\Big)\right\}$$

Each boolean variable $X_{q_1 a q_2}$, where $q_1, q_2 \in Q_i$ and $a \in C_i$, evaluates to true if and only if $q_1 \xrightarrow{a}_i q_2$ is confluent. The BES has maximal fixed point semantics because we seek to determine the maximal set of confluent transitions contained in an LTS. For strict confluence, $\bigvee_{q_3 \xrightarrow{\overline{a}}_i q_4'}$ must be merely replaced by $\bigvee_{q_3 \xrightarrow{a}_i q_4'}$.

The correctness of this encoding [27] is based upon a bijection between the fixed point solutions of the BES and the sets of confluent transitions labeled by actions in C_i; thus, the maximal fixed point solution gives the whole set of such confluent transitions.

5 Implementation

CCD was implemented in CADP[2] (*Construction and Analysis of Distributed Processes*) [12], a toolbox for the design of communication protocols and distributed systems, which offers a wide set of functionalities, ranging from step-by-step simulation to massively-parallel model checking. CADP is designed in a modular way and puts the emphasis on intermediate formats and programming interfaces. CADP provides the BCG compact graph format for storing explicit LTSs and the OPEN/CÆSAR [10] application programming interface for representing and manipulating implicit LTSs in the form of an initial state and a successor

[2] `http://www.inrialpes.fr/vasy/cadp`

state function. The GENERATOR tool converts an OPEN/CÆSAR implicit LTS into an explicit BCG graph. The BCG_MIN tool allows minimization of BCG graphs modulo strong and branching bisimulation.

EXP.OPEN 2.0 (an extension of the previous version EXP.OPEN 1.0 of Bozga, Fernandez, and Mounier) is a compiler into OPEN/CÆSAR implicit LTSs of systems made of BCG graphs composed using synchronization vectors and parallel composition, hiding, renaming, and cutting operators taken from the CCS [32], CSP [39], LOTOS [22], E-LOTOS [23], and μCRL [18] process algebras. As an intermediate step, those systems are translated into the network of LTSs model presented in Definition 6. EXP.OPEN 2.0 has several partial order reduction options that allow standard persistent set methods (generalizations of Ramakrishna and Smolka's method presented in [37]) to be applied on-the-fly, among which **-branching** preserves branching bisimulation, **-ratebranching** preserves stochastic branching bisimulation[3], **-deadpreserving** preserves deadlocks, and **-weaktrace** preserves weak trace equivalence (i.e., observable traces).

We developed in the EXP.OPEN 2.0 tool a new procedure that takes as input a BCG graph, a file that contains a set of labels represented using a list of regular expressions, and a boolean parameter for strictness. For each transition whose label matches one of the regular expressions, this procedure checks whether this transition is confluent (or strictly confluent if the boolean parameter is set to true). The BES encoding the confluence detection problem is solved using a global algorithm similar to those in [30]. This produces as output an LTS in the BCG format, the transition labels of which are prefixed by a special tag indicating confluence when appropriate.

We also added to EXP.OPEN 2.0 a new **-confluence** option, which can only be used in combination with one of the partial order reduction options already available (**-branching**, **-deadpreserving**, **-ratebranching**, **-weaktrace**[4]). In this case, EXP.OPEN 2.0 first computes the labels for which confluence detection is useful, and then calls the above procedure (setting the boolean parameter to true if EXP.OPEN was called with the **-deadpreserving** option) on the individual LTSs, providing these labels as input. Finally, it uses the information collected in the individual LTSs to prioritize the confluent transitions on the fly.

6 Experimental Results

We applied partial order reductions using CCD to several examples. To this aim, we used a 2 GHz, 16 GB RAM, dual core AMD Opteron 64-bit computer running 64-bit Linux. Examples identified by a two digit number xy (01, 10, 11, etc.) correspond to LTS compositions extracted from an official CADP demo available at `ftp://ftp.inrialpes.fr/pub/vasy/demos/demo_`xy. These include telecommunication protocols (01, 10, 11, 18, 20, 27), distributed systems

[3] This option is similar to **-branching** and additionally gives priority to τ-transitions over stochastic transitions.

[4] Note that branching preserving reduction using CCD also preserves weaker relations such as weak trace equivalence.

(25, 28, 35, 36, 37), and asynchronous circuits (38). Examples $st(1)$, $st(2)$, and $st(3)$ correspond to process compositions provided to us by the STMicroelectronics company, which uses Cadp to verify critical parts of their future-generation multiprocessor systems on chip.

In each example, the individual Ltss were first minimized (compositionally) modulo branching bisimulation using Bcg_Min. This already achieves more reduction than the compositional τ-confluence technique presented in [34], since minimization modulo branching bisimulation subsumes τ-confluence reduction. The Lts of their composition was then generated using Exp.Open 2.0 and Generator following different strategies: (1) using no partial order reduction at all, (2) using persistent sets, and (3) using both persistent sets and Ccd. Figure 4 reports the size (in states/transitions) of the resulting Lts obtained when using option **-branching** (top) or **-deadpreserving** (bottom). The symbol "–" indicates that the number of states and/or transitions is the same as in the column immediately to the left.

These experiments show that Ccd may improve the reductions obtained using persistent sets and compositional verification, most particularly in examples 37, 38, $st(1)$, $st(2)$, and $st(3)$. Indeed, in these examples the individual Ltss are themselves obtained by parallel compositions of smaller processes. This tends to generate confluent transitions, which are detected locally by Ccd. On the other hand, it is not a surprise that neither Ccd nor persistent sets methods preserving branching bisimulation reduce examples 25, 27(1), 27(2) and 28, since the resulting Ltss corresponding to these examples contain no confluent transitions.

One might be amazed by the reduction of $st(1)$ to an Lts with only one state and one transition in the deadlock preserving case. The reason is that one Lts of the network has a strictly confluent self looping transition that is independent from the other Ltss. Therefore, the network cannot have a deadlock and is reduced by Ccd to this trivial, deadlock-free Lts.

For $st(1)$, $st(2)$, and $st(3)$, we also compared the total time and peak memory needed to generate the product Lts (using Exp.Open 2.0/Generator) and then minimize it modulo branching bisimulation (using Bcg_Min), without using any partial order reduction and with persistent sets combined with Ccd. This includes time and memory used by the tools Exp.Open 2.0, Generator and Bcg_Min. Figure 5 shows that Ccd may significantly reduce the total time and peak memory (for $st(3)$, 30% and 40%, respectively) needed to generate a minimal Lts.

7 Case Study

We present here in more detail the use of Ccd in the context of the Multival project[5], which aims at the formal specification, verification, and performance evaluation of multiprocessor multithreaded architectures developed by Bull, the Cea/Leti, and STMicroelectronics. The case-study below concerns xStream, a multiprocessor dataflow architecture designed by STMicroelectronics for high performance embedded multimedia streaming applications. In this architecture,

[5] `http://www.inrialpes.fr/vasy/multival`

Branching preserving reduction

Example	No partial order reduction	Persistent sets	Persistent sets + CCD
01	112/380	–/328	–/–
10	688/2,540	–/2,200	–/–
11	2,995/9,228	–/–	–/9,200
18	129,728/749,312	–/746,880	–/–
20	504,920/5,341,821	–/–	–/5,340,117
25	11,031/34,728	–/–	–/–
27(1)	1,530/5,021	–/–	–/–
27(2)	6,315/22,703	–/–	–/–
28	600/1,925	–/–	–/–
35	156,957/767,211	–/–	–/–
36	23,627/84,707	21/20	–/–
37	22,545/158,318	–/–	541/2,809
38	1,404/3,510	–/3,504	390/591
st(1)	6,993/100,566	–/–	–/79,803
st(2)	1,109,025/7,448,719	–/–	–/6,163,259
st(3)	5,419,575/37,639,782	–/–	5,172,660/24,792,525

Deadlock preserving reduction

Example	No partial order reduction	Persistent sets	Persistent sets + CCD
01	112/380	92/194	–/–
10	688/2,540	568/1,332	–/–
11	2,995/9,228	2,018/4,688	–/4,670
18	129,728/749,312	124,304/689,760	90,248/431,232
20	504,920/5,341,821	481,406/4,193,022	481,397/4,191,555
25	11,031/34,728	6,414/11,625	–/–
27(1)	1,530/5,021	1,524/4,811	–/–
27(2)	6,315/22,703	6,298/22,185	–/–
28	600/1,925	375/902	–/–
35	156,957/767,211	–/–	–/–
36	23,627/84,707	171/170	–/–
37	22,545/158,318	–/–	76/128
38	1,404/3,510	–/3,474	492/673
st(1)	6,993/100,566	6,864/96,394	1/1
st(2)	1,109,025/7,448,719	–/7,138,844	101,575/346,534
st(3)	5,419,575/37,639,782	5,289,255/34,202,947	397,360/1,333,014

Fig. 4. LTS sizes in states/transitions for branching and deadlock preserving reductions

computation nodes (e.g., filters) communicate using xSTREAM queues connected by a NoC (*Network on Chip*) composed of routers connected by direct communication links.

We used as input the network of communicating LTSs produced from a LOTOS specification of two xSTREAM queues connected via a NoC with four routers. The architecture of the system is depicted below, where the components `N0` and `N1` denote the routers involved in the communication between `PUSHQ` and `POPQ`, the behaviour of which incorporates perturbations induced by the other two routers of the NoC.

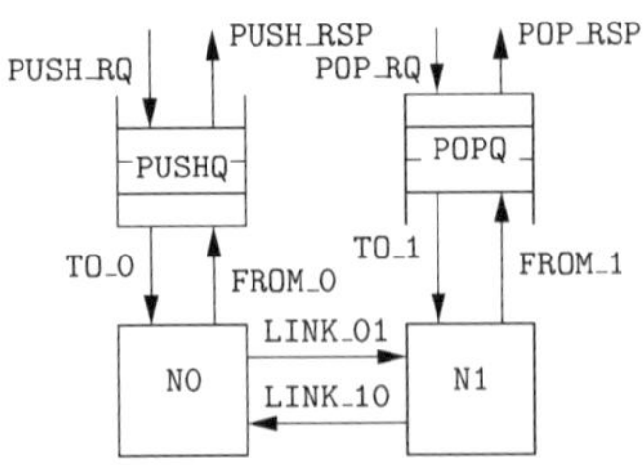

	No partial order reduction		Persistent sets + CCD	
	total time (s)	peak memory (MB)	total time (s)	peak memory (MB)
$st(1)$	0.72	5.6	0.91	5.6
$st(2)$	271	312	287	271
$st(3)$	2,116	1,390	1,588	981

Fig. 5. Resources used to generate and reduce LTSs modulo branching bisimulation

	without CCD			with CCD		
	intermediate	time (s)	mem. (MB)	intermediate	time (s)	mem. (MB)
itf_POPQ+N1	244,569/1,320,644	18.56	51	179,706/587,187	9.66	26
N0+PUSHQ	22,674/120,222	1.35	17	22,674/86,528	1.12	17
N0+N1+PUSHQ	140,364/828,930	12.62	32	95,208/444,972	6.40	22
NOC4	324,261/2,549,399	11.32	93	310,026/1,073,316	9.77	46

Fig. 6. Performance of LTS generation and minimization with and without CCD

The LTS of the system can be generated and minimized compositionally using the SVL [11] language of CADP. The generation was done first with CCD deactivated, then with CCD activated. For each case, Figure 6 gives the following information: The "*intermediate*" column indicates the size (in states/transitions) of the intermediate LTS generated by the EXP.OPEN tool, before minimization modulo branching bisimulation; The "*time*" and "*mem.*" columns indicate respectively the cumulative time (in seconds) and memory peak (in megabytes) taken by LTS generation (including confluence detection when relevant) and minimization modulo branching bisimulation.

Figure 6 shows that CCD may reduce both the time (the LTSs `"itf_POPQ+NI.bcg"` and `"NO+N1+PUSHQ.bcg"` were generated and minimized twice faster with CCD than without CCD) and memory (`"itf_POPQ+NI.bcg"` and `"NOC4.bcg"` were generated using about half as much memory with CCD as without CCD).

8 Conclusion

CCD (*Compositional Confluence Detection*) is a partial order reduction method that applies to systems of communicating automata. It detects confluent transitions in the product graph, by first detecting the confluent transitions in the individual automata and then analysing their synchronizations. Confluent transitions of the product graph can be given priority over the other transitions, thus yielding graph reductions. We detailed two variants of CCD: one that preserves branching bisimilarity with the product graph, and one that preserves its deadlocks.

CCD was implemented in the CADP toolbox. An encoding of the confluence property using a BES (*Boolean Equation System*) allows the detection of all confluent transitions in an automaton. The existing tool EXP.OPEN 2.0, which supports modeling and verification of systems of communicating automata, was extended to exploit on-the-fly the confluence detected in the individual automata.

CCD can be combined with both compositional verification and other partial order reductions, such as persistent sets. We presented experimental results showing that CCD may significantly reduce both the size of the system graph and the total time and peak memory needed to generate a minimal graph.

As future work, we plan to combine CCD reductions with distributed graph generation [13] in order to further scale up its capabilities. This distribution can be done both at automata level (by launching distributed instances of confluence detection for each automaton in the network or by performing the confluence detection during the distributed generation of each automaton) and at network level (by coupling CCD with the distributed generation of the product graph).

Acknowledgements. We are grateful to W. Serwe (INRIA/VASY) and to E. Lantreibecq (STMicroelectronics) for providing the specifications of the xSTREAM NoC. We also warmly thank the anonymous referees for their useful remarks.

References

1. Arnold, A.: MEC: A System for Constructing and Analysing Transition Systems. In: Sifakis, J. (ed.) CAV 1989. LNCS, vol. 407. Springer, Heidelberg (1990)
2. Blom, S.C.C.: Partial τ-Confluence for Efficient State Space Generation. Technical Report SEN–R0123, CWI (2001)
3. Blom, S., van de Pol, J.: State Space Reduction by Proving Confluence. In: Brinksma, E., Larsen, K.G. (eds.) CAV 2002. LNCS, vol. 2404, p. 596. Springer, Heidelberg (2002)
4. Bouali, A., Ressouche, A., Roy, V., de Simone, R.: The Fc2Tools set: a Toolset for the Verification of Concurrent Systems. In: Alur, R., Henzinger, T.A. (eds.) CAV 1996. LNCS, vol. 1102. Springer, Heidelberg (1996)
5. Brookes, S.D., Hoare, C.A.R., Roscoe, A.W.: A Theory of Communicating Sequential Processes. Journal of the ACM 31(3), 560–599 (1984)
6. Cheung, S.C., Kramer, J.: Enhancing Compositional Reachability Analysis with Context Constraints. In: Foundations of Software Engineering (1993)
7. Fernandez, J.-C.: ALDEBARAN : un système de vérification par réduction de processus communicants. Thèse de Doctorat, Univ. J. Fourier, Grenoble (1988)
8. Fernandez, J.-C., Jard, C., Jéron, T., Mounier, L.: On the Fly Verification of Finite Transition Systems. In: FMSD (1992)
9. Fernandez, J.-C., Mounier, L.: Verifying Bisimulations "On the Fly". In: FDT (1990)
10. Garavel, H.: OPEN/CÆSAR: An Open Software Architecture for Verification, Simulation, and Testing. In: Steffen, B. (ed.) TACAS 1998. LNCS, vol. 1384, p. 68. Springer, Heidelberg (1998)
11. Garavel, H., Lang, F.: SVL: a Scripting Language for Compositional Verification. In: FORTE. Kluwer, Dordrecht (2001)
12. Garavel, H., Lang, F., Mateescu, R., Serwe, W.: CADP 2006: A Toolbox for the Construction and Analysis of Distributed Processes. In: Damm, W., Hermanns, H. (eds.) CAV 2007. LNCS, vol. 4590, pp. 158–163. Springer, Heidelberg (2007)
13. Garavel, H., Mateescu, R., Bergamini, D., Curic, A., Descoubes, N., Joubert, C., Smarandache-Sturm, I., Stragier, G.: DISTRIBUTOR and BCG_MERGE: Tools for Distributed Explicit State Space Generation. In: Hermanns, H., Palsberg, J. (eds.) TACAS 2006. LNCS, vol. 3920, pp. 445–449. Springer, Heidelberg (2006)

14. Giannakopoulou, D.: Model Checking for Concurrent Software Architectures. PhD thesis, Imperial College, Univ. of London, Dept. of Computer Science (1999)
15. Godefroid, P.: Using Partial Orders to Improve Automatic Verification Methods. In: Computer-Aided Verification. DIMACS Series, vol. 3 (1990)
16. Graf, S., Steffen, B., Lüttgen, G.: Compositional Minimization of Finite State Systems using Interface Specifications. FAC 8(5), 607–616 (1996)
17. Graf, S., Steffen, B.: Compositional Minimization of Finite State Systems. In: Clarke, E., Kurshan, R.P. (eds.) CAV 1990. LNCS, vol. 531. Springer, Heidelberg (1991)
18. Groote, J.F., Ponse, A.: The Syntax and Semantics of μCRL. In: Algebra of Communicating Processes, Workshops in Computing Series (1995)
19. Groote, J.F., van de Pol, J.: State Space Reduction using Partial τ-Confluence. In: Nielsen, M., Rovan, B. (eds.) MFCS 2000. LNCS, vol. 1893, p. 383. Springer, Heidelberg (2000)
20. Groote, J.F., Sellink, M.P.A.: Confluence for process verification. TCS 170(1–2), 47–81 (1996)
21. Holzmann, G.J.: On-The-Fly Model Checking. ACM Comp. Surveys 28(4) (1996)
22. ISO/IEC. LOTOS — A Formal Description Technique Based on the Temporal Ordering of Observational Behaviour. International Standard 8807, ISO (1989)
23. ISO/IEC. Enhancements to LOTOS (E-LOTOS). International Standard 15437:2001, ISO (2001)
24. Krimm, J.-P., Mounier, L.: Compositional State Space Generation from LOTOS Programs. In: Brinksma, E. (ed.) TACAS 1997. LNCS, vol. 1217. Springer, Heidelberg (1997)
25. Lang, F.: EXP.OPEN 2.0: A Flexible Tool Integrating Partial Order, Compositional, and On-the-fly Verification Methods. In: Romijn, J.M.T., Smith, G.P., van de Pol, J. (eds.) IFM 2005. LNCS, vol. 3771, pp. 70–88. Springer, Heidelberg (2005)
26. Lang, F.: Refined Interfaces for Compositional Verification. In: Najm, E., Pradat-Peyre, J.-F., Donzeau-Gouge, V.V. (eds.) FORTE 2006. LNCS, vol. 4229, pp. 159–174. Springer, Heidelberg (2006)
27. Lang, F., Mateescu, R.: Partial Order Reductions using Compositional Confluence Detection. In: Extended version of FM 2009, INRIA (2009)
28. Malhotra, J., Smolka, S.A., Giacalone, A., Shapiro, R.: A Tool for Hierarchical Design and Simulation of Concurrent Systems. In: Specification and Verification of Concurrent Systems (1988)
29. Mateescu, R.: A Generic On-the-Fly Solver for Alternation-Free Boolean Equation Systems. In: Garavel, H., Hatcliff, J. (eds.) TACAS 2003. LNCS, vol. 2619, pp. 81–96. Springer, Heidelberg (2003)
30. Mateescu, R.: CAESAR_SOLVE: A Generic Library for On-the-Fly Resolution of Alternation-Free Boolean Equation Systems. STTT 8(1), 37–56 (2006)
31. Mateescu, R., Sighireanu, M.: Efficient On-the-Fly Model-Checking for Regular Alternation-Free Mu-Calculus. SCP 46(3), 255–281 (2003)
32. Milner, R.: Communication and Concurrency. Prentice-Hall, Englewood Cliffs (1989)
33. Nalumasu, R., Gopalakrishnan, G.: An Efficient Partial Order Reduction Algorithm with an Alternative Proviso Implementation. FMSD 20(3) (2002)
34. Pace, G., Lang, F., Mateescu, R.: Calculating τ-Confluence Compositionally. In: Hunt Jr., W.A., Somenzi, F. (eds.) CAV 2003. LNCS, vol. 2725, pp. 446–459. Springer, Heidelberg (2003)
35. Peled, D.A.: Combining partial order reduction with on-the-fly model-checking. In: Dill, D.L. (ed.) CAV 1994. LNCS, vol. 818. Springer, Heidelberg (1994)

36. Peled, D.A., Pratt, V.R., Holzmann, G.J. (eds.): Partial Order Methods in Verification. DIMACS Series, vol. 29 (1997)
37. Ramakrishna, Y.S., Smolka, S.A.: Partial-Order Reduction in the Weak Modal Mu-Calculus. In: Mazurkiewicz, A., Winkowski, J. (eds.) CONCUR 1997. LNCS, vol. 1243, pp. 5–24. Springer, Heidelberg (1997)
38. Roscoe, A.W., Gardiner, P.H.B., Goldsmith, M.H., Hulance, J.R., Jackson, D.M., Scattergood, J.B.: Hierarchical compression for model-checking CSP *or* how to check 10^{20} dining philosophers for deadlock. In: Brinksma, E., Steffen, B., Cleaveland, W.R., Larsen, K.G., Margaria, T. (eds.) TACAS 1995. LNCS, vol. 1019, pp. 133–152. Springer, Heidelberg (1995)
39. Roscoe, A.W.: The Theory and Practice of Concurrency. Prentice Hall, Englewood Cliffs (1998)
40. Sabnani, K., Lapone, A., Uyar, M.: An Algorithmic Procedure for Checking Safety Properties of Protocols. IEEE Trans. on Communications 37(9), 940–948 (1989)
41. Tai, K.C., Koppol, V.: Hierarchy-Based Incremental Reachability Analysis of Communication Protocols. In: Network Protocols. IEEE Press, Los Alamitos (1993)
42. Valmari, A.: A Stubborn Attack on State Explosion. In: Computer-Aided Verification. DIMACS Series, vol. 3 (1990)
43. Valmari, A.: Stubborn Set Methods for Process Algebras. In: Partial Order Methods in Verification. DIMACS Series, vol. 29. AMS, Providence (1997)
44. Valmari, A.: Compositional State Space Generation. In: Rozenberg, G. (ed.) APN 1993. LNCS, vol. 674, pp. 427–457. Springer, Heidelberg (1993)
45. van Glabbeek, R.J., Weijland, W.P.: Branching-Time and Abstraction in Bisimulation Semantics. In: IFIP World Computer Congress (1989)
46. Yeh, W.J.: Controlling State Explosion in Reachability Analysis. PhD thesis, Software Engineering Research Center (SERC) Laboratory, Purdue Univ. (1993)
47. Ying, M.: Weak confluence and τ-inertness. TCS 238(1–2), 465–475 (2000)

A Formal Method for Developing Provably Correct Fault-Tolerant Systems Using Partial Refinement and Composition

Ralph Jeffords, Constance Heitmeyer, Myla Archer, and Elizabeth Leonard

Naval Research Laboratory
Washington, DC 20375
{jeffords,heitmeyer,archer,leonard}@itd.nrl.navy.mil

Abstract. It is widely agreed that building correct fault-tolerant systems is very difficult. To address this problem, this paper introduces a new model-based approach for developing *masking fault-tolerant systems*. As in component-based software development, two (or more) component specifications are developed, one implementing the required normal behavior and the other(s) the required fault-handling behavior. The specification of the required normal behavior is verified to satisfy system properties, whereas each specification of the required fault-handling behavior is shown to satisfy both system properties, typically weakened, and fault-tolerance properties, both of which can then be inferred of the composed fault-tolerant system. The paper presents the formal foundations of our approach, including a new notion of *partial refinement* and two compositional proof rules. To demonstrate and validate the approach, the paper applies it to a real-world avionics example.

1 Introduction

It is widely agreed that building a correct fault-tolerant system is very difficult. One promising approach, proposed by us and others, for obtaining a high-assurance fault-tolerant system is to specify the system requirements in two phases [4, 18, 7, 19]. In the first phase, the *normal* (also called *ideal*) system behavior, the system behavior when no faults can occur, is specified. In the second phase, the no-faults assumption is removed, and the system's required fault-tolerant behavior is specified. Such an approach has many advantages. First, a specification of the normal behavior known to be correct can be reused if the design of fault-tolerance changes. Second, if the fault-tolerant system can be expressed as an extension of a system with normal behavior by adding a set of fault-handling components, the specification is easier to understand and easier to construct than a fault-tolerant system specified as a single component. Third, by applying formal specification during two separate phases, errors may be uncovered—e.g., by applying formal verification—that might otherwise be overlooked. For example, our application of two-phase specification and verification to a real-world avionics device [7] uncovered modeling errors previously unnoticed (see Section 5). Finally, specifications of the fault-handling components may be reused in other systems.

The model-based approach proposed in this paper has attributes of two other popular approaches for developing software systems. As in aspect-oriented programming

A. Cavalcanti and D. Dams (Eds.): FM 2009, LNCS 5850, pp. 173–189, 2009.

[17, 16], the approach weaves certain aspects, specifically, the "fault-tolerant" aspects, into the original program. Moreover, as in component-based software development, two (or more) components are developed separately, and later composed to produce the final implementation. This paper makes three contributions; it presents: 1) a component-based approach for developing a special class of fault-tolerant systems, called "masking" fault-tolerant systems, which uses formal specification and formal verification to obtain high confidence of system correctness; 2) a formal foundation, including a set of sound compositional proof rules, a formal notion of *fault-tolerant extension*, and a formal notion of *partial refinement* with an associated notion of *partial property inheritance*; and 3) a complete example of applying the approach to a real-world system.

The paper's organization is as follows. After defining *masking* fault-tolerance, Section 2 briefly reviews the SCR (Software Cost Reduction) method used in our example. Section 3 introduces our formal method for developing fault-tolerant systems, an extension of the approach to software development presented in [7]. To establish a formal foundation for the method, Section 4, inspired by the theory of fault tolerance in [18] and the theory of retrenchment applied to fault-tolerant systems in [5], presents our new notions of partial refinement and fault-tolerant extension, and two compositional proof rules. To demonstrate and validate our approach and to show how formal methods can be used to support the approach, Section 5 applies the method to a device controller in an avionics system [20]. Finally, Sections 6 and 7 discuss related work and present some conclusions. Although SCR is used in Section 5 to demonstrate our approach, the method and theory presented in this paper are basically applicable in any software development which specifies components as state machine models.

2 Background

2.1 Masking Fault-Tolerance

This paper focuses on *masking fault-tolerance*, a form of fault-tolerance in which the system always recovers to normal behavior after a fault occurs, so that the occurrence of faults is rendered mostly invisible, i.e., "masked." We consider two variants of masking fault tolerance. In the first variant, *transparent* masking, all safety properties [2] of the system are preserved even in the presence of faults, and the effect of faults on the system behavior is completely invisible. In the second variant, *eventual* masking, some critical subset of the set of safety properties is preserved during fault handling, though other safety properties guaranteed during normal behavior may be violated. When masking is transparent, the system's fault-tolerant behavior is a refinement of its normal behavior. For eventual masking, system behavior during fault-handling is a *degraded* version of normal behavior, and the relationship of the full fault-tolerant system behavior to normal system behavior is captured by the notions of fault-tolerant extension and partial refinement presented in Section 4.[1] The Altitude Switch (ASW) example in Section 5 illustrates both variants of masking fault-tolerance.

[1] Many use "masking fault-tolerance" to refer only to what we call "transparent masking."

2.2 The SCR Requirements Method

The SCR (Software Cost Reduction) [13, 12] method uses a special tabular notation and a set of tools for formally specifying, validating, and verifying software and system requirements. See [12, 11] for a review of the SCR tabular notation, the state machine model which defines the SCR semantics, and the SCR tools.

An important construct in SCR, the *mode class*, can be very useful in specifying the required behavior of fault-tolerant systems. Conceptually, each mode in a mode class corresponds to a "mode of operation" of the system. Thus, for example, in flight software, pilot-visible modes determine how the software reacts to a given pilot input. As shown in Section 5, modes similarly have a special role in SCR specifications of fault-tolerant systems.

3 A Formal Method for Building Fault-Tolerant Systems

This section introduces a new method for building a fault-tolerant system. Based on concepts in Parnas' Four Variable Model [21], the method is applied in two phases. In the first phase, the normal system behavior is specified and shown to satisfy a set of critical properties, most commonly, safety properties [2]. In the second phase, I/O devices, e.g., sensors and actuators, are selected, hardware and other faults which may occur are identified, and the system's *fault-tolerant* behavior is designed and specified. The fault-tolerant specification formulated in this phase is shown to satisfy 1) the critical system properties, typically weakened, which were verified in the first phase and 2) new properties specifying fault detection and fault recovery. While each phase is described below as a sequence of steps, the precise ordering of the steps may vary, and some steps may occur in parallel.

3.1 Specify the Normal System Behavior

In the first phase, the system behavior is specified under the assumption that no faults can occur, and essential system properties are formulated and verified. The "normal" behavior omits any mention of I/O devices, or of hardware faults and other system malfunctions.

Specify NAT and REQ. To represent the system's normal behavior, a state machine model of the system requirements is formulated in terms of two sets of environmental variables—monitored and controlled variables—and two relations—REQ and NAT—from Parnas' Four Variable Model [21]. Both NAT and REQ are defined on the monitored and controlled variables. NAT specifies the natural constraints on monitored and controlled variables, such as constraints imposed by physical laws and the system environment. REQ specifies the required relation the system must maintain between the monitored and controlled variables under the assumptions defined by NAT. In the first phase, an assumption is that the system can obtain perfect values of the monitored quantities and compute perfect values of the controlled variables. During this phase, the system tolerances are also defined; these may include the required precision of values of controlled variables, timing constraints imposed by REQ on the controlled variables, and timing constraints imposed by NAT.

Formulate the System Properties. In this step, the critical system properties are formulated as properties of the state machine model. If possible, these properties should be safety properties, since the second phase produces a refinement (i.e., when the system is operating normally), and safety properties are preserved under refinement [1].

Verify the System Properties. In the final step, the properties are verified to hold in the state machine model, using, for example, a model checker or theorem prover.

3.2 Specify the Fault-Tolerant Behavior

In the second phase, the assumption that the system can perfectly measure values of monitored quantities and perfectly compute values of controlled quantities is removed, and I/O devices are selected to estimate values of monitored quantities and to set values of controlled quantities. Also removed is the assumption that no faults occur. Possible faults are identified, and the system is designed to tolerate some of these faults. Finally, the fault-tolerant behavior is specified as a fault-tolerant extension (see Section 4) which adds extra behavior to handle faults and which may include new externally visible behavior, e.g., operator notification of a sensor failure.

Select I/O Devices and Identify Likely Faults. In the second phase, the first step is to select a set of I/O devices and to document the device characteristics, including identification of possible faults. Among the possible faults are faults that invalidate either sensor inputs or actuator outputs and faults that corrupt the program's computations. Examples of faults include the failure of a single sensor, the simultaneous failure of all system sensors, and the failure of a monitored variable to change value within some time interval. For practical reasons, the system is designed to respond to only some possible faults. An example of an extremely unlikely fault is simultaneous failure of all system sensors—recovery from such a massive failure is likely to be impossible. Once a set of faults is selected, a design is developed that either makes the system tolerant of a fault or reports a fault so that action may be taken to correct or mitigate the fault.

Design and Specify the Fault-Tolerant Behavior. A wide range of fault-tolerance techniques have been proposed. One example is hardware redundancy, where two or more versions of a single sensor are available, but only one is operational at a time. If the operational sensor fails, the system switches control to a back-up sensor. In another version of hardware redundancy, three (or any odd number of) sensors each sample a monitored quantity's value, and a majority vote determines the value of the quantity. Some fault-tolerance techniques make faults transparent. For example, if three sensors measure aircraft altitude, a majority vote may produce estimates of the altitude satisfying the system's tolerance requirements and do so in a transparent manner. Other techniques do not make faults transparent—for example, techniques which report a fault to an operator, who then takes some corrective action.

Verify Properties of the Fault-Tolerant Specification. In this step, the critical properties verified to hold for the normal system behavior must be shown to hold for the fault-tolerant behavior. In some cases, properties of the normal system will not hold throughout the fault-tolerant system but may remain true for only some behavior (e.g., for only the normal behavior). A new notion of partial refinement, defined in Section 4, describes the conditions which must be established for the fault-tolerant system to partially inherit properties of the normal system. In addition, new properties are formulated to describe the required behavior when a fault is detected and when the system recovers from a fault. It must then be shown that the fault-tolerant specification satisfies these new properties, which can be established as invariants with the aid of compositional proof rules, such as those presented in Section 4.2.

4 Formal Foundations

This section presents formal definitions, theoretical results, and formal techniques that support our approach to developing provably correct fault-tolerant systems. The most important concepts and results include our notions of *partial refinement* and *fault-tolerant extension*, and two proof methods for establishing properties of a fault-tolerant extension based on properties of the normal (fault-free) system behavior it extends. The first proof method is based on Theorem 1 concerning property inheritance under partial refinement; the second is based on compositional proof rules for invariants, two of which are shown in Figure 2. The section begins with general notions concerning state machines, then introduces fault-tolerance concepts, and finally, discusses additional concepts and results that apply as additional assumptions about state machines are added—first, that states are determined by the values of a set of state variables, and second, that the state machines are specified in SCR. Each concept or result presented is introduced at the highest level of generality possible. The definitions, results, and techniques of this section are illustrated in the ASW example presented in Section 5.

4.1 General Definitions

To establish some terminology, we begin with the (well-known) definitions of *state machine* and *invariant property* (*invariant*, for short). As is often customary, we consider predicates to be synonymous with sets; thus, "P is a predicate on set S" $\equiv$ "$P \subseteq S$", "$P(s)$ holds" $\equiv$ "$s \in P$", etc.

Definition 1. State machine. *A* state machine **A** *is a triple* (S_A, Θ_A, ρ_A), *where* S_A *is a nonempty set of states,* $\Theta_A \subseteq S_A$ *is a nonempty set of* initial *states, and* $\rho_A \subseteq S_A \times S_A$ *is a set of* transitions *that contains the stutter step* (s_A, s_A) *for every* s_A *in* S_A. *A state* $s_A \in S_A$ *is* reachable *if there is a sequence* $(s_0, s_1), (s_1, s_2), \ldots (s_{n-1}, s_n)$ *of transitions in* ρ_A *such that* s_0 *is an initial state and* $s_n = s_A$. *A transition* $(s_A, s'_A) \in \rho_A$ *is a* reachable transition *if* s_A *is a reachable state. Reachable states/transitions of* **A** *are also called* A-reachable states/transitions.

Definition 2. One-state and two-state predicates/invariants. *Let* $\mathbf{A} = (S_A, \Theta_A, \rho_A)$ *be a state machine. Then a* one-state predicate *of* **A** *is a predicate* $P \subseteq S_A$, *and a* two-state predicate *of* **A** *is a predicate* $P \subseteq S_A \times S_A$. *A one-state (two-state) predicate* P *is a state (transition)* invariant *of* **A** *if all reachable states (transitions) of* **A** *are in* P.

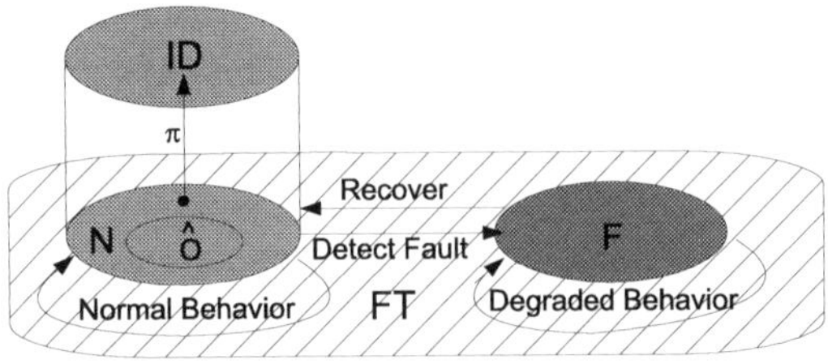

Fig. 1. Transitions in the fault-tolerant system **FT**

We next define two notions that describe how two state machines (e.g., two models of a system) may be related. The well known notion of *refinement* is especially useful in the context of software development because the existence of a refinement mapping from a state machine **C** to a state machine **A** at a more abstract level permits important properties—including all safety properties (and hence all one-state and two-state invariants)—proved of **A** to be inferred of **C**. A new notion, which we call *partial refinement*, is a generalization of refinement useful in situations where the approximation by a detailed system model to a model of normal system behavior is inexact.

Definition 3. Refinement. *Let* **A** = (S_A, Θ_A, ρ_A) *and* **C** = (S_C, Θ_C, ρ_C) *be two state machines, and let* $\alpha : S_C \rightarrow S_A$ *be a mapping from the states of* **C** *to the states of* **A**. *Then* α *is a* refinement mapping *if 1) for every* s_C *in* Θ_C, $\alpha(s_C)$ *is in* Θ_A, *and 2)* $\rho_A(\alpha(s_C), \alpha(s'_C))$ *for every pair of states* s_C, s'_C *in* S_C *such that* $\rho_C(s_C, s'_C)$.

Definition 4. Partial Refinement. *Let* **A** = (S_A, Θ_A, ρ_A) *and* **C** = (S_C, Θ_C, ρ_C) *be two state machines and* $\alpha : S_C \overset{\circ}{\rightarrow} S_A$ *be a partial mapping from states of* **C** *to states of* **A**. *Then* α *is a* partial refinement mapping *if 1) for every* s_C *in* Θ_C, $\alpha(s_C)$ *is defined and in* Θ_A, *and 2)* $\rho_A(\alpha(s_C), \alpha(s'_C))$ *for every pair of states* s_C, s'_C *in the domain* $\alpha^{-1}(S_A)$ *of* α *such that* $\rho_C(s_C, s'_C)$. *When a partial refinement mapping* α *exists from* **C** *to* **A**, *we say that* **C** *is a* partial refinement *of* **A** *(with respect to* α*).*

The notions of *vulnerable state* and *vulnerable transition* are useful (see Theorem 1) in describing the circumstances under which properties proved of a state machine **A** can be partially inferred for a state machine **C** that is a partial refinement of **A**.

Definition 5. Vulnerable states and vulnerable transitions. *Let* **A** = (S_A, Θ_A, ρ_A) *and* **C** = (S_C, Θ_C, ρ_C) *be two state machines, and let* $\alpha : S_C \overset{\circ}{\rightarrow} S_A$ *be a partial refinement. Then a state* s_C *in the domain of* α *is* vulnerable *if there exists a state* s'_C *in* S_C *such that* $\rho_C(s_C, s'_C)$ *but the transition* (s_C, s'_C) *does not map under* α *to a transition in* **A** *(in which case we refer to* (s_C, s'_C) *as a* vulnerable transition*).*

4.2 Concepts for Fault Tolerance

Our method for including fault tolerance in the software development process described in Section 3 begins with a model **ID** of the normal (software) system behavior. In the next phase, **ID** is used as a basis for constructing a model **FT** of the system that is a *fault-tolerant extension* of **ID** in the following sense:

Definition 6. Fault-tolerant extension. *Given a state machine model* **ID** *of a system, a second state machine model* **FT** *of the system is a* fault-tolerant extension *of* **ID** *if:*

- *the state set S_{FT} of* **FT** *partitions naturally into two sets: 1) N, the set of normal states, which includes Θ_{FT} and 2) F, the set of fault-handling states that represent the system state after a fault has occurred, and*
- *there is a map $\pi : N \rightarrow S_{ID}$ and a two-state predicate $O \subseteq N \times N$ for* **FT** *such that $\pi(\Theta_{FT}) \subseteq \Theta_{ID}$ and $s_1, s_2 \in N \wedge O(s_1, s_2) \ \wedge \ \rho_{FT}(s_1, s_2) \Rightarrow \rho_{ID}(\pi(s_1), \pi(s_2))$.*

The map π and predicate O are, respectively, the normal state map *and* normal transition predicate *for* **FT**.

Figure 1 illustrates the structure of **FT** and its relationship to **ID**. There are five classes of transitions in **FT**:

1. transitions from N to N that map to transitions in **ID** (Normal Behavior),
2. transitions from N to N that do not map to transitions in **ID** (not shown),
3. transitions from N to F (Fault Detection),
4. transitions from F to F (Degraded Behavior), and
5. transitions from F to N (Fault Recovery).

Remark 1. When **FT** is a fault-tolerant extension of **ID**, π is a partial refinement mapping from the state machine $(S_{FT}, \Theta_{FT}, O \cap \rho_{FT})$ to **ID**. Further, if **FT** has no transitions of class 2, class 3 represents all vulnerable transitions in **FT**, and $\pi : S_{FT} \overset{\circ}{\rightarrow} S_{ID}$ is a partial refinement mapping from **FT** to **ID**.

Even when π is not a partial refinement from **FT** to **ID**, there is still guaranteed to be a partial refinement from **FT** to **ID** whose domain can be defined in terms of the normal transition predicate O in Definition 6. In particular, given O, let $\hat{O}$ be the one-state predicate for **FT** defined by:

$$\hat{O}(s_1) \triangleq (\forall s_2 \in S_{FT} : \rho(s_1, s_2) \Rightarrow O(s_1, s_2))$$

(It is easily seen, as indicated in Figure 1, that $\hat{O} \subseteq N$.) Then, for any state $s \in S_{\mathbf{FT}}$, $\hat{O}(s)$ implies that all transitions in **FT** from s map to transitions in **ID**. Therefore, restricted to the set $\hat{O}$, the map π is a partial refinement map from **FT** to **ID**.

If (s_1, s_2) is a transition in **FT** of class 5, we refer to s_2 as a *reentry state*. Further, if (s_1, s_2) is of class 2, we refer to s_2 as an *exceptional target state*. By a simple inductive argument, we have:

Lemma 1. *If every reentry state and every exceptional target state in N maps under π to a reachable state in* **ID**, *then every* **FT**-*reachable state in N maps under π to a reachable state in* **ID**, *and every* **FT**-*reachable transition in $\hat{O} \subseteq N$ maps under π to a reachable transition in* **ID**.

$$
\begin{array}{ll}
(1) & Q \text{ is a one-state predicate for } \mathbf{FT} \text{ such that } Q \text{ respects } \pi \\
(2) & \pi(\Theta_{FT}) \subseteq \Theta_{ID} \subseteq \pi(Q) \\
(3) & s_1, s_2 \in S_{ID} \ \wedge \ \pi(Q)(s_1) \ \wedge \ \rho_{ID}(s_1, s_2) \quad \Rightarrow \quad \pi(Q)(s_2) \\
(4) & s_1, s_2 \in S_{FT} \ \wedge \ \rho_{FT}(s_1, s_2) \quad \Rightarrow \quad [(Q(s_1) \ \wedge \ \neg O(s_1, s_2)) \ \Rightarrow \ Q(s_2)] \\
(5) & s_1, s_2 \in N \subset S_{FT} \wedge \rho_{FT}(s_1, s_2) \quad \Rightarrow \quad [O(s_1, s_2) \ \Rightarrow \ \rho_{ID}(\pi(s_1), \pi(s_2))] \\
\hline
 & Q \text{ is a state invariant of } \mathbf{FT}
\end{array}
$$

$$
\begin{array}{ll}
(1) & P \text{ and } Q \text{ are two-state predicates for } \mathbf{FT} \text{ such that } P \Rightarrow Q \ \wedge \ P \text{ respects } \pi \\
(2) & s_1, s_2 \in S_{ID} \ \wedge \ \rho_{ID}(s_1, s_2) \quad \Rightarrow \quad ((\pi \times \pi)(P))(s_1, s_2) \\
(3) & s_1, s_2 \in S_{FT} \ \wedge \ \rho_{FT}(s_1, s_2) \quad \Rightarrow \quad [\neg O(s_1, s_2) \Rightarrow Q(s_1, s_2)] \\
(4) & s_1, s_2 \in N \subset S_{FT} \wedge \rho_{FT}(s_1, s_2) \quad \Rightarrow \quad [O(s_1, s_2) \ \Rightarrow \ \rho_{ID}(\pi(s_1), \pi(s_2))] \\
\hline
 & Q \text{ is a transition invariant of } \mathbf{FT}
\end{array}
$$

Fig. 2. Proof rules for state and transition invariants of **FT**

Using the notation above, we can now state:

Theorem 1. Property inheritance under partial refinement. *Let* **FT** *be a fault-tolerant extension of* **ID** *in which every reentry or exceptional target state maps under* π *to a reachable state in* **ID**. *Then 1) for every one-state invariant* P *of* **ID**, $\Phi(P) \triangleq P \circ \pi$ *holds for every* **FT**-*reachable state in* N, *and 2) for every two-state invariant* P *of* **ID**, $\Phi(P) \triangleq P \circ (\pi \times \pi)$ *holds for every non-vulnerable reachable transition of* **FT** *from a state in* N *(thus, in particular, for every reachable transition of* **FT** *from a state in* $\hat{O}$*).*

As shown below, the fault-tolerant ASW behavior is a fault-tolerant extension of the normal ASW behavior with natural definitions for N and F (see Section 5), π (see Section 4.3), and O (see Section 4.4) such that all transitions from N to N are of class 1. Further, we have proven formally that all reentry states in the fault-tolerant version of the ASW are reachable, and there are no exceptional target states. Hence, for the ASW, Theorem 1 can be used to deduce properties of **FT** from properties of **ID**.

In general, however, to supplement Theorem 1, a method is needed for establishing properties of **FT** in the case when it is difficult or impossible to establish that all reentry states and exceptional target states in **FT** map under π to reachable states of **ID**. For this purpose, we provide *compositional proof rules* analogous to those in [15]. We first define what it means for a predicate to *respect* a mapping:

Definition 7. *Let* $\pi : S_1 \rightarrow S_2$ *be a mapping from set* S_1 *to set* S_2. *Then 1) a predicate* Q *on* S_1 respects π *if for all* $s, \hat{s}$ *in* S_1, $Q(s) \wedge (\pi(s) = \pi(\hat{s})) \Rightarrow Q(\hat{s})$, *and 2) a predicate* Q *on* $S_1 \times S_1$ respects π *if for all* $s, \hat{s}, s', \hat{s}'$ *in* S_1, $Q(s, s') \wedge (\pi(s) = \pi(\hat{s})) \wedge (\pi(s') = \pi(\hat{s}')) \Rightarrow Q(\hat{s}, \hat{s}')$.

Figure 2 gives proof rules for establishing that a one-state (two-state) predicate Q on **FT** is a state (transition) invariant of **FT**. Note that line (5) of the first proof rule and line (4) in the second proof rule are part of the definition of fault-tolerant extension.

4.3 Fault Tolerance Concepts in Terms of State Variables

When the states of a state machine are defined by a vector of values associated with a set of state variables (as is true, for example, in SCR specifications), it is possible to interpret the concepts in Section 4.2 more explicitly. In particular, constructing a fault tolerant system model **FT** from a normal system model **ID** is usually done by adding any new variables, new values of types of existing variables, and new transitions needed to describe the triggering and subsequent handling of faults. We will refer to the original variables as *normal* variables, and the added variables as *fault-tolerance* variables; for any normal variable, we will refer to its possible values in **ID** as *normal* values, and any new possible values added in **FT** as *extended* values. In this terminology, the states in $N \subseteq S_{FT}$ are those for which all normal variables have normal values. The map $\pi : N \rightarrow S_{ID}$ can then simply be chosen to be the projection map with respect to the normal variables.

Although Definition 2 represents predicates abstractly as sets when states are determined by the values assigned to state variables, most predicates of interest can be represented syntactically as relations among state variables and constants. Further, on a syntactic level, the map(s) Φ defined in Theorem 1 will be the identity.

4.4 Modeling Fault Tolerance in SCR

As shown in Section 5.2 below, several aspects of an SCR specification can be used to advantage in defining **FT** as a fault-tolerant extension of a normal system specification **ID** in the sense of Definition 6. These aspects include mode classes, tables to define the behavior of individual variables, and the description of transitions in terms of events.

We call a fault-tolerant extension **FT** of **ID** obtained by the technique of Section 5.2 *simple* if any row splits in the table of any normal variable result in new rows defining updated values of the variable that are either the same as in the original row for **ID** or are among the extended values for that variable. (For example, row 3 of Table 1 is split into rows 3a and 3b of Table 6.) In the terminology of Definition 6, in a simple fault-tolerant extension, every transition from N in **FT** either maps under π to a normal transition in **ID** or is a transition from N to F (class 3). It is not difficult to prove the following:

Theorem 2. *For any simple fault-tolerant extension* **FT** *of* **ID**, *the normal state map* π *is a partial refinement mapping and one can choose the normal transition predicate to be*

$$O(s_1, s_2) \triangleq N(s_1) \wedge N(s_2).$$

Thus, since the predicate N can be expressed simply as an assertion that no normal variable has an extended value, it is possible in the context of SCR to compute O for any **FT** defined as a simple fault-tolerant extension of **ID**.[2]

---

[2] We have also shown that O can be automatically computed for some examples in which **FT** is not a simple fault-tolerant extension of **ID**.

5 Example: Altitude Switch (ASW)

This section shows how the method presented in Section 3 can be applied using SCR to a practical system, the Altitude Switch (ASW) controller in an avionics system [20]. The goal of the ASW example is to demonstrate the specification of a system's normal behavior **ID** and the separate specification of its fault-tolerant behavior **FT** as a simple fault-tolerant extension. This is in contrast to [7], which presents an earlier SCR specification of the ASW behavior, whose goal was to demonstrate the application of Parnas' Four Variable Model to software development using SCR.

The primary function of the ASW is to power on a generic Device of Interest (DOI) when an aircraft descends below a threshold altitude. In some cases, the pilot can set an inhibitor button to prevent the powering on of the DOI. The pilot can also press a reset button to reinitialize the ASW. Fault-tolerance is supported by three sensors and the system clock. If certain events occur (e.g., all three sensors fail for some time period), the system enters a fault mode and may take some action (e.g., turn on a fault indicator lamp). Recovery from a fault occurs when the pilot resets the system.

Sections 5.1 and 5.2 describe the results of applying our method to the specification and verification of both the normal and the fault-tolerant ASW behavior. Section 5.2 also shows how the theoretical results in Section 4 can be used to prove properties of the ASW's fault-tolerant behavior **FT**. Starting from property P_2 of the normal ASW behavior, our results about property inheritance allow us to derive $\tilde{P}_2$, a weakening of P_2, which holds in **FT**, while our compositional proof rules can be used to show that $\hat{P}_2$, a different weakening of P_2, also holds in **FT**. Table 4 defines both P_2 and $\hat{P}_2$. Property $\tilde{P}_2$ is defined in Section 5.2.

5.1 Specify and Verify the Normal Behavior of the ASW

To characterize the normal behavior **ID** of the ASW, this section presents a state machine model of the ASW's normal behavior expressed in terms of NAT and REQ, and a set of critical system properties which are expected to hold in the model.

Specify NAT and REQ. The normal ASW behavior is specified in terms of 1) controlled and monitored variables, 2) environmental assumptions, 3) system modes and how they change in response to monitored variable changes, and 4) the required relation between the monitored and controlled variables. The relation NAT is defined by 1) and 2) and the relation REQ by 3) and 4).

The ASW has a single controlled variable `cWakeUpDOI`, a boolean, initially false, which signals the DOI to power on, and six monitored variables: 1) `mAltBelow`, true if the aircraft's altitude is below a threshold; 2) `mDOIStatus`, which indicates whether the DOI is on; 3) `mInitializing`, true if the DOI is initializing; 4) `mInhibit`, which indicates whether powering on the DOI is inhibited; 5) `mReset`, true when the pilot has pressed the reset button; and 6) `mTime`, the time measured by the system clock. The ASW also has a single mode class `mcStatus` containing three system modes: 1) `init` (system is initializing), 2) `awaitDOIon` (system has requested power to the DOI and is awaiting a signal that the DOI is operational), and 3) `standby` (all other cases).

Table 1. Mode transition table for `mcStatus`

Row No.	Old Mode	Event	New Mode
1	init	@F(mInitializing)	standby
2	standby	@T(mReset)	init
3	standby	@T(mAltBelow) WHEN (NOT mInhibit AND mDOIStatus = off)	awaitDOIon
4	awaitDOIon	@T(mDOIStatus = on)	standby
5	awaitDOIon	@T(mReset)	init

Table 2. `cWakeUpDOI` cond. table

Mode in mcStatus	cWakeUpDOI
init, standby	*False*
awaitDOIon	*True*

Table 1 defines the ASW mode transitions. Once initialization is complete (event @F(`mInitializing`) occurs), the system moves from `init` to `standby`. It returns to `init` when the pilot pushes the reset button (@T(`mReset`) occurs). The system moves from `standby` to `awaitDOIon` when the aircraft descends below the threshold altitude (@T(`mAltBelow`) occurs), but only when powering on is not inhibited, and the DOI is not powered on. Once the DOI signals that it is powered on (@T(`mDOIStatus` = `on`) occurs), the system goes from `awaitDOIon` to `standby`. Table 2 defines the value of the controlled variable `cWakeUpDOI` as a function of the mode class `mcStatus`. If `mcStatus` = `awaitDOIon`, then `cWakeUpDOI` is *True*; otherwise, it is *False*.

Table 3. ASW Assumptions

Name	System	Formal Statement
A_1	**ID, FT**	$(\texttt{mTime}' - \texttt{mTime}) \in \{0, 1\}$
A_2	**ID**	$\texttt{DUR(mcStatus} = \texttt{init)} \leq \texttt{InitDur}$
A_3	**ID**	$\texttt{DUR(mcStatus} = \texttt{awaitDOIon)} \leq \texttt{FaultDur}$
A_4	**FT**	$\texttt{DUR(cFaultIndicator} = \texttt{on)} \leq \texttt{FaultDur}$

The relation NAT for ASW contains three assumptions, A_1, A_2, and A_3, each a constraint on the system timing (see Table 3).[3] The first assumption, A_1, states that time never decreases and, if time increases, it increases by one time unit.[4] Assumptions A_2 and A_3 define constraints on the time that the system remains in specified modes. To represent these constraints, we require SCR's `DUR` operator. Informally, if c is a condition and k is a positive integer, the predicate $\texttt{DUR}(c) = k$ holds at step i if in step i condition c is true and has been true for exactly k time units. A_2 requires that the ASW

[3] In Tables 3-5, assumptions and properties of *both* the normal (**ID**) and fault-tolerant (**FT**) systems are presented. Any row in these tables that applies only to **FT** is described in Section 5.2.

[4] The primed variable `mTime'` in Table 3 and other primed expressions refer to the expression's value in the new state; any unprimed expression refers to the expression's value in the old state.

spend no more than InitDur time units initializing, while A_3 requires the system to power on the DOI in no more than FaultDur time units.

Specify the ASW Properties. Table 4 defines two required properties, P_1 and P_2, of the ASW's normal behavior. P_1, a safety property, states that pressing the reset button always causes the system to return to the initial mode. P_2, another safety property, specifies the event and conditions that must hold to wake up the DOI. A user can execute the SCR invariant generator [14] to derive a set of state invariants from an SCR specification. Such invariants may be used as auxiliary properties in proving other properties, such as P_1 and P_2. Applying the invariant generator to the specification of the normal ASW behavior (defined by Table 1, Table 2, and assumptions A_1-A_3) automatically constructs the state invariant H_1, which is defined in Table 5.

Verify the ASW Properties. The property checker Salsa [8] easily verifies that the specification of the ASW's normal behavior satisfies P_1 and P_2. Completing the proof of P_2 requires the auxiliary H_1; proving P_1 requires no auxiliaries.

Table 4. ASW Properties

Name	System	Formal Statement
P_1	ID, FT	$\texttt{@T(mReset)} \Rightarrow \texttt{mcStatus}' = \texttt{init}$
P_2	ID	$\texttt{mcStatus} = \texttt{standby} \land \texttt{@T(mAltBelow)} \land \neg\texttt{mInhibit}$ $\land\ \texttt{mDOIStatus} = \texttt{off} \Rightarrow \texttt{cWakeUpDOI}'$
$\hat{P}_2$	FT	$\texttt{mcStatus} = \texttt{standby} \land \texttt{@T(mAltBelow)} \land \neg\texttt{mInhibit}$ $\land\ \texttt{mDOIStatus} = \texttt{off} \land \neg\texttt{mAltimeterFail} \Rightarrow \texttt{cWakeUpDOI}'$
G_1	FT	$\texttt{mAltimeterFail} \land \texttt{mcStatus} = \texttt{standby} \Rightarrow \texttt{mcStatus}' \neq \texttt{awaitDOIon}$
G_2	FT	$\texttt{mcStatus} = \texttt{fault} \Rightarrow \texttt{mcStatus}' = \texttt{init} \lor \texttt{mcStatus}' = \texttt{fault}$

Table 5. ASW State Invariants

Name	System	Formal Statement
H_1	ID, FT	$(\texttt{mcStatus} = \texttt{awaitDOIon}) \Leftrightarrow \texttt{cWakeUpDOI}$
J_2	FT	$\texttt{cFaultIndicator} = \texttt{on} \Leftrightarrow \texttt{mcStatus} = \texttt{fault}$
J_3	FT	$\texttt{DUR(cFaultIndicator} = \texttt{on)} \neq 0 \Rightarrow \texttt{cFaultIndicator} = \texttt{on}$

5.2 Specify and Verify the Fault-Tolerant Behavior of the ASW

This section describes how the normal behavior of the ASW can be refined to handle faults. First, the I/O devices are selected. Next, the faults that the ASW system will be designed to handle are identified, and the fault-tolerant and failure notification behavior of the ASW are specified. Finally, new ASW properties are formulated to capture the required fault-tolerant behavior, and these new properties as well as the ASW properties proven for the normal behavior, possibly reformulated, are proven to hold in the fault-tolerant specification.

Select the ASW I/O Devices. To estimate whether the aircraft is below the threshold altitude, three altimeters are selected, one analog and the other two digital. For a description of the other I/O devices selected for the ASW, see [7].

Identify Likely ASW Faults. The ASW is designed to tolerate three faults: 1) the failure of all three altimeters, 2) remaining in the initialization mode too long, and 3) failure to power on the DOI on request within some time limit. All three faults are examples of eventual masking—the system enters a fault handling state but eventually recovers to normal behavior. To notify the pilot when a fault occurs, the ASW turns on a Fault Indicator lamp. The ASW is also designed to handle a single altimeter failure; it uses the remaining two altimeters to determine whether the aircraft is below the threshold altitude. This is an example of masking where the fault is transparent at the system level—the system never enters a fault handling state when only one altimeter fails.

Specify ASW Fault-Tolerant Behavior. Generally, adding behavior related to fault detection, notification, and handling to the specification of normal system behavior requires new monitored variables to detect faults, new controlled variable to report the occurrence of faults, and new values for any variable, and, in particular, new fault modes in mode classes. To define the additional behavior in SCR, tables defining the new variables are added, and tables defining the existing variables are modified and extended.

Adding fault-handling and fault notification to the normal ASW specification **ID** requires 1) a new monitored variable `mAltimeterFail` to signal the failure of all three altimeters,[5] 2) a new controlled variable `cFaultIndicator` to notify the pilot of a fault by turning on a lamp, 3) a new mode `fault` to indicate the detection of a fault, 4) a new table defining `cFaultIndicator`, and 5) the modification and extension of two tables: the table defining the controlled variable `cWakeUpDOI` and the mode transition table defining the mode class `mcStatus`. The final step removes assumptions A_2 and A_3, thus allowing the fault-tolerant system to suffer from these faults.

To define a new mode transition table capturing fault detection and recovery, the mode transition table for the ASW normal behavior, Table 1, is replaced with a new mode transition table, containing rows 1, 2, 4, and 5 of Table 1 and rows 6, 7, and 8 of Table 6, and replacing row 3 of Table 1 with rows 3a and 3b of Table 6. In the new table, a fault is detected 1) if the system takes more than `InitDur` time units to initialize (replaces the deleted A_2), 2) if the DOI takes more than `FaultDur` time units to power up (replaces the deleted A_3), or 3) if all three altimeters have failed for more than `FaultDur` time units. Three rows of Table 6 (rows 3b, 6, and 7), each marked by a simple arrow, indicate the detection of the three faults. The system recovers from a fault when the pilot presses `mReset` in response to the Fault Indicator lamp turning on. To represent recovery, a new transition from `fault` to `init`, triggered by `@T(mReset)`, is added (row 8, marked by a squiggly arrow). To force the system to recover within some bounded time, a new assumption A_4 (see Table 3) is that the pilot always responds to a failure notification by pushing reset within some time limit. To complete the new table, row 3 of Table 1 is split into row 3a and row 3b based on whether `mAltimeterFail` is

[5] Because this paper focuses on the fault-tolerance aspects of the ASW, the details of how `mAltimeterFail` is computed are omitted. For these details, see [7].

Table 6. Fault Handling Modifications for Mode Transition Table in Table 1

	Row No.	Old Mode	Event	New Mode
†	3a	`standby`	`@T(mAltBelow) WHEN (NOT mInhibit AND mDOIStatus = off)` AND NOT mAltimeterFail	`awaitDOIon`
→	3b	`standby`	`@T(mAltBelow) WHEN (NOT mInhibit AND mDOIStatus = off)` AND mAltimeterFail	`fault`
→	6	`init`	`@T(DUR(mcStatus = init) > InitDur)`	`fault`
→	7	`awaitDOIon`	`@T(DUR(mcStatus = awaitDOIon) > FaultDur) OR @T(DUR(mAltimeterFail) > FaultDur)`	`fault`
⇝	8	`fault`	`@T(mReset)`	`init`

Table 7. New table defining `cFaultIndicator`

Mode in `mcStatus`	`cFaultIndicator`
`init, standby, awaitDOIon`	`off`
`fault`	`on`

Table 8. Revised table for `cWakeUpDOI`

Mode in `mcStatus`	`cWakeUpDOI`
`init, standby, fault`	*False*
`awaitDOIon`	*True*

true. If true, the system goes to `fault` (row 3b); otherwise, it goes to `awaitDOIon` as in the normal specification **ID** (row 3a, marked by a dagger).

To indicate when the Fault Indicator lamp is on, a new table, Table 7, is defined to indicate that `cFaultIndicator` is on when the system is in the `fault` mode and off otherwise. The last step is to add the `fault` mode to the set of modes which assign the value *false* to the table defining `cWakeUpDOI` (see Table 8).

Adding the new mode `fault` to the specification allows a normal state in the ASW to be distinguished from a fault handling state. In particular, we define a state predicate N, where N : `mcStatus` $\neq$ `fault`, and a second state predicate F, where F : `mcStatus` = `fault`.

Verify the ASW Fault-Tolerance Properties. The safety properties, P_1 and P_2, properties of the specification **ID** of normal behavior, are also included as candidate properties of the fault-tolerant version **FT** of the ASW. In addition, safety properties, G_1 and G_2, defined in Table 4, represent part of the required fault-tolerant behavior of the ASW [9]. To support the proofs of the properties P_1, P_2, G_1, and G_2, the SCR invariant generator is applied to the fault-tolerant specification. Of the two invariants generated, the first corresponds exactly to H_1, the invariant generated previously from the normal specification **ID**; the second invariant J_2 is defined in Table 5. The third invariant J_3, also defined in Table 5, is a property of the `DUR` operator. Using J_2 and J_3 as auxiliary invariants, we used Salsa to check the fault-tolerant specification **FT** for all properties listed in Table 4. All but P_2 were shown to be invariants. Thus the required behavior represented by P_2 fails in **FT** (that is, when all altimeters fail). Applying Theorem 1 from Section 4, we can show that **FT** inherits the weakened property $\tilde{P}_2 \triangleq N' \Rightarrow P_2$ from property P_2 of **ID**. In addition, the second compositional proof rule from Section 4 with $P = P_2$ provides an alternate way to show that $\hat{P}_2$, a weakened version of P_2, holds in **FT**. (See Table 4 for the definition of $\hat{P}_2$.)

To further evaluate the ASW specifications, we checked additional properties, e.g., the property $\texttt{DUR}(\texttt{mcStatus} = \texttt{standby} \wedge \texttt{mAltimeterFail}) \leq \texttt{FaultDur}$, whose invariance guarantees that the ASW never remains in $\texttt{mcStatus} = \texttt{standby}$ too long. Failure to prove this property led to the discovery (via simulation) that the ASW could remain in mode `standby` forever—not a desired behavior. Although our specification does not fix this problem, the example shows how checking properties is a useful technique for discovering errors in specifications.

6 Related Work

Our model fits the formal notion of masking fault-tolerance of [18], but rather than expressing recovery as a liveness property, we use bounded liveness, which is more practical. Other compositional approaches to fault-tolerance describe the design of fault-tolerant detectors and correctors [4] and the automatic generation of fault-tolerant systems [18, 3]. Our notion of fault-tolerant extension is most closely related to the notion of retrenchment formulated by Banach et al. [6] and the application of retrenchment to fault-tolerant systems [5]. General retrenchment is a means of formally expressing normal and exceptional behavior as a formula of the form $A \Rightarrow B \vee C$, where $A \Rightarrow B$ is true for the normal cases, and $A \Rightarrow C$ is true for the exceptional cases. Our concept of the relation of fault-tolerant behavior to normal behavior can also be described in this form: $\rho_{\mathrm{FT}}(s_1, s_2) \Rightarrow (O(s_1, s_2) \wedge \rho_{\mathrm{ID}}(\pi(s_1), \pi(s_2)) \vee \neg O(s_1, s_2) \wedge \gamma(s_1, s_2))$, where γ is derived from the transitions of classes 2–5. The novelty of our approach is recognition that this disjunction may be expressed equivalently as the conjunction of two implications, $\rho_{\mathrm{FT}}(s_1, s_2) \wedge O(s_1, s_2) \Rightarrow \rho_{\mathrm{ID}}(\pi(s_1), \pi(s_2))$ and $\rho_{\mathrm{FT}}(s_1, s_2) \wedge \neg O(s_1, s_2) \Rightarrow \gamma(s_1, s_2)$, thus providing the basis for our theory of partial refinement and the development of compositional proof rules.

In [19], Liu and Joseph describe *classical refinement* of fault-tolerant systems as well as refinement of timing and scheduling requirements. Classical refinement is well-suited to implementation of "transparent masking fault-tolerance," often using redundancy, and contrasts with eventual masking fault-tolerance, which tolerates weaker invariant properties when the system is faulty (i.e., has degraded performance), and thus requires a different approach such as partial refinement.

Our extension of "normal" behavior with added fault-tolerant behavior may be viewed as a transformation of the normal system. A number of researchers, e.g. [19, 10], apply the transformational approach to the development of fault-tolerant systems. This approach is also found in Katz' formal treatment of aspect-oriented programming [16]. In addition, Katz describes how various aspects affect temporal logic properties of a system and defines a "weakly invasive" aspect as one implemented as code which always returns to some state of the underlying system. The relationship of a "weakly invasive" aspect to the underlying system is analogous to the relationship of F to N in

Figure 1 when there are no exceptional target states and every entry state maps under π to a reachable state in **ID**. In this case, an analog of our Theorem 1 would hold for the augmented system.

7 Conclusions

This paper has presented a new method, based on Parnas' Four Variable Model, for specifying and verifying the required behavior of a fault-tolerant system; provided a theory of partial refinement and fault-tolerant extension, and a set of compositional proof rules, as a foundation for the method; and demonstrated how the SCR language and tools can be used to support the new method as a structured alternative to the ad hoc construction and monolithic verification of fault-tolerant systems. Like Banach's theory of retrenchment, our theory of partial refinement and fault-tolerant extension applies not only to fault-tolerant systems, but more generally to all systems with both normal and exceptional behavior.

One major benefit of the compositional approach presented here is that it separates the task of specifying the normal system behavior from the task of specifying the fault-tolerant behavior, thus simplifying the specification of such systems and making their specifications both easier to understand and easier to change. The theory in Section 4 provides the basis for formulating additional compositional proof rules and vulnerability analyses, both topics for future research. We also plan to explore the utility of our approach for fault-tolerance techniques other than masking. For example, omitting recovery results in a method which applies to fail-safe fault-tolerance.

Formal proofs of state and transition invariants capturing desired system behavior, together with properties derived from partial refinement and verified using our compositional proof rules, should lead to high confidence that the specification of a given fault-tolerant system is correct. Our new approach is supported by the SCR toolset, where increasing confidence of correctness is supported by simulation, model-checking, and proofs of invariants. In future research, we plan to explore the automatic construction of efficient source code from the **FT** specification using the SCR code generator [22] and other code synthesis techniques.

Acknowledgments

The authors thank the anonymous referees for their helpful comments as well as Sandeep Kulkarni for useful discussions on applying SCR to fault-tolerant systems. This research was funded by the Office of Naval Research.

References

1. Abadi, M., Lamport, L.: The existence of refinement mappings. Theoretical Computer Science 82(2), 253–284 (1991)
2. Alpern, B., Schneider, F.B.: Defining liveness. Inf. Process. Lett. 21(4), 181–185 (1985)
3. Arora, A., Attie, P.C., Emerson, E.A.: Synthesis of fault-tolerant concurrent programs. In: Proc. PODC 1998, pp. 173–182 (1998)

4. Arora, A., Kulkarni, S.S.: Component based design of multitolerant systems. IEEE Trans. Softw. Eng. 24(1), 63–78 (1998)
5. Banach, R., Cross, R.: Safety requirements and fault trees using retrenchment. In: Heisel, M., Liggesmeyer, P., Wittmann, S. (eds.) SAFECOMP 2004. LNCS, vol. 3219, pp. 210–223. Springer, Heidelberg (2004)
6. Banach, R., Poppleton, M., Jeske, C., Stepney, S.: Engineering and theoretical underpinnings of retrenchment. Sci. Comput. Prog. 67, 301–329 (2007)
7. Bharadwaj, R., Heitmeyer, C.: Developing high assurance avionics systems with the SCR requirements method. In: Proc. 19th Digital Avionics Sys. Conf. (2000)
8. Bharadwaj, R., Sims, S.: Salsa: Combining constraint solvers with BDDs for automatic invariant checking. In: Schwartzbach, M.I., Graf, S. (eds.) TACAS 2000. LNCS, vol. 1785, p. 378. Springer, Heidelberg (2000)
9. Ebnenasir, A.: Automatic Synthesis of Fault-Tolerance. PhD thesis, Michigan State Univ., East Lansing, MI (2005)
10. Gärtner, F.C.: Transformational approaches to the specification and verification of fault-tolerant systems: Formal background and classification. J. Univ. Comput. Sci. 5(10) (1999)
11. Heitmeyer, C., Archer, M., Bharadwaj, R., Jeffords, R.: Tools for constructing requirements specifications: The SCR toolset at the age of ten. Computer Systems Science and Engineering 20(1), 19–35 (2005)
12. Heitmeyer, C.L., Jeffords, R.D., Labaw, B.G.: Automated consistency checking of requirements specifications. ACM Transactions on Software Engineering and Methodology 5(3), 231–261 (1996)
13. Heninger, K.L.: Specifying software requirements for complex systems: New techniques and their application. IEEE Trans. Softw. Eng. SE-6 (1980)
14. Jeffords, R., Heitmeyer, C.: Automatic generation of state invariants from requirements specifications. In: Proc. Sixth ACM SIGSOFT Symp. on Foundations of Software Eng. (1998)
15. Jeffords, R.D., Heitmeyer, C.L.: A strategy for efficiently verifying requirements. In: ESEC/FSE-11: Proc. 9th Euro. Softw. Eng. Conf./11th ACM SIGSOFT Int. Symp. on Foundations of Softw. Eng., pp. 28–37 (2003)
16. Katz, S.: Aspect categories and classes of temporal properties. In: Rashid, A., Aksit, M. (eds.) Transactions on Aspect-Oriented Software Development I. LNCS, vol. 3880, pp. 106–134. Springer, Heidelberg (2006)
17. Kiczales, G., Lamping, J., Medhekar, A., Maeda, C., Lopes, C.V., Loingtier, J.-M., Irwin, J.: Aspect-oriented programming. In: Aksit, M., Matsuoka, S. (eds.) ECOOP 1997. LNCS, vol. 1241, pp. 220–242. Springer, Heidelberg (1997)
18. Kulkarni, S.S., Arora, A.: Automating the addition of fault-tolerance. In: Joseph, M. (ed.) FTRTFT 2000. LNCS, vol. 1926, pp. 82–93. Springer, Heidelberg (2000)
19. Liu, Z., Joseph, M.: Specification and verification of fault-tolerance, timing, and scheduling. ACM Trans. Program. Lang. Syst. 21(1), 46–89 (1999)
20. Miller, S.P., Tribble, A.: Extending the four-variable model to bridge the system-software gap. In: Proc. 20th Digital Avionics Sys. Conf. (October 2001)
21. Parnas, D.L., Madey, J.: Functional documentation for computer systems. Science of Computer Programming 25(1), 41–61 (1995)
22. Rothamel, T., Heitmeyer, C., Leonard, E., Liu, A.: Generating optimized code from SCR specifications. In: Proceedings, ACM SIGPLAN/SIGBED Conference on Languages, Compilers, and Tools for Embedded Systems (LCTES 2006) (June 2006)

Abstract Specification of the UBIFS File System for Flash Memory

Andreas Schierl, Gerhard Schellhorn, Dominik Haneberg, and Wolfgang Reif

Lehrstuhl für Softwaretechnik und Programmiersprachen,
Universität Augsburg, D-86135 Augsburg, Germany
{schierl,schellhorn,haneberg,reif}@informatik.uni-augsburg.de

Abstract. Today we see an increasing demand for flash memory because it has certain advantages like resistance against kinetic shock. However, reliable data storage also requires a specialized file system knowing and handling the limitations of flash memory. This paper develops a formal, abstract model for the UBIFS flash file system, which has recently been included in the Linux kernel. We develop formal specifications for the core components of the file system: the inode-based file store, the flash index, its cached copy in the RAM and the journal to save the differences. Based on these data structures we give an abstract specification of the interface operations of UBIFS and prove some of the most important properties using the interactive verification system KIV.

1 Introduction

Flash memory has become popular in recent years as a robust medium to store data. Its main advantage compared to traditional hard disks is that it has no moving parts and is therefore much less susceptible to mechanical shocks or vibration. Therefore it is popular in digital audio players, digital cameras and mobile phones.

Flash memory is also getting more and more important in embedded systems (e.g. automotive [28]) where space restrictions rule out magnetic drives, as well as in mass storage systems (solid state disk storage systems like the RamSan-5000 from Texas Memory Systems) since it has shorter access times than hard disks.

Flash memory has different characteristics when compared to a traditional hard disk. These are explained in Section 2. In brief, flash memory cannot be overwritten, but only erased in blocks and erasing should be done evenly ("wear leveling"). These properties imply that standard file systems cannot be used with flash memory directly.

Two solutions are possible: either a flash translation layer is implemented (typically in hardware), translating standard file system operations into flash operations. This is the standard solution used e.g. in USB flash drives. It has the advantage that any file system can be used on top (e.g. NTFS or ext2). On the other hand, the characteristics of file systems (e.g. partitioning of the data

A. Cavalcanti and D. Dams (Eds.): FM 2009, LNCS 5850, pp. 190–206, 2009.

into the content of files, directory trees, or other meta data like journals etc.) cannot be effectively exploited using this solution.

Therefore a number of flash file systems (abbreviated FFS in the following) has been developed, that optimize the file system structure to be used with flash memory. Many of these FFS are proprietary (see [9] for an overview). A very recent development is UBIFS [14], which was added to the Linux kernel last year.

Increased use of flash memory in safety-critical applications has led Joshi and Holzmann [16] from the NASA Jet Propulsion Laboratory in 2007 to propose the verification of a FFS as a new challenge in Hoare's verification Grand Challenge [13]. Their goal was a verified FFS for use in future missions. NASA already uses flash memory in spacecraft, e.g. on the Mars Exploration Rovers. This already had nearly disastrous consequences as the Mars Rover Spirit was almost lost due to an anomaly in the software access to the flash store [22].

A roadmap to solving the challenge has been published by Freitas, Woodcock and Butterfield [8]. This paper presents our first steps towards solving this challenge.

There has been other work on the formal specification of file systems. First, some papers exist which start top-down by specifying directory trees and POSIX like file operations, e.g. the specifications of [20] of a UNIX-like file system, or our own specification of a mandatory security model for file systems on smart cards [26]. More recently and targeted towards the Grand Challenge, Damchoom, Butler and Abrial [5] have given a high-level model of directory trees and some refinements. An abstract specification of POSIX is also given in [7] (some results are also in [21]). Butterfield and Woodcock [4] have started bottom-up with a formal specification of the ONFI standard of flash memory itself. The most elaborate work we are aware of is the one by Kang and Jackson [17] using Alloy. Its relation to our work will be discussed in Section 7. Our approach is middle-out, since our main goal was to understand the critical requirements of an efficient, real implementation. Therefore we have analyzed the code of UBIFS (ca. 35.000 loc), and developed an abstract, formal model from it. Although the resulting model is still *very* abstract and leaves out a lot of relevant details, it already covers some of the important aspects of any FFS implementation. These are:

1. Updates on flash are out-of-place because overwriting is impossible.
2. Like most traditional file systems the FFS is structured as a graph of inodes.
3. For efficiency, the main index data structure is cached in RAM.
4. Due to e.g. a system crash the RAM index can always get lost. The FFS stores a *journal* to recover from such a crash with a *replay* operation.
5. Care has been taken that the elementary assignments in the file system operations will map to atomic updates in the final implementation, to ensure that all intermediate states will be recoverable.

The paper is organized as follows. Section 2 gives an overview over the data structures and how the implementation works. Section 3 gives details of the structure of inodes, and how they represent directory trees. The formal specifications we have set up in our interactive theorem prover KIV are explained. Section 4 explains how the journal works. Section 5 lists the specified file system operations and gives the code specifying the 'create file' operation as an example. Section 6 lists the properties we have verified with KIV and discusses the effort needed. Full specifications and proofs are available from the Web [18].

Section 7 presents a number of topics which still require future work to bring our abstract model close to a verified implementation. In particular, our model, just as UBIFS, does not consider wear leveling, but relegates it to a separate, lower level, called UBI ("unsorted block images"). Finally, Section 8 concludes.

2 Flash Memory and UBIFS

Flash memory has certain special characteristics that require a treatment that is substantially different from magnetic storage. The crucial difference is that in-place update of data, i.e. overwriting stored data, is not possible. To write new data on a currently used part of the flash memory, that part must first be erased, i.e. set back to an unwritten state. Flash media are organized in so-called erase blocks, which are the smallest data units that can be erased (typically 64 KB). Simulating in-place updates by reading a complete erase block, resetting it and writing back the modified erase block is not viable for two reasons. First, it is about 100 times slower than writing the modified data to a free erase block and second, it wears out the media. This is due to the second great difference between magnetic and flash storage. Flash memory gets destroyed by erasing. Depending on the used flash technology, the flash storage is destroyed after 10.000 to 2.000.000 erase cycles. This requires special FFS treatment, because the FFS must deal with the problem of deterioration of parts of the media that are erased often and with the fact that in-place changes of already written data are not possible. Therefore data is updated out-of-place instead, i.e. the new version of the data is written somewhere else on the media. This entails the need for *garbage collection* because sooner or later the different erase blocks all contain parts with valid data and parts with obsolete data. Garbage collection must be able to efficiently decide if an entry in an erase block still belongs to a valid file or directory. This is done by storing additional metadata with the actual data. The combination of metadata and data is called a *node*.

A node records which file (or to be precise which *inode*) the node belongs to, what kind of data is stored in the node and the data themselves. The structure of the nodes in UBIFS and our resulting specification are described in Sect. 3. In our model, the nodes that are stored on the flash are contained in the flash store. The flash store is modeled as a finite mapping of *addresses* to nodes. Figure 1 shows the 4 central data structures of UBIFS (one of them the flash store) and explains what impacts the different operations have on them. The flash store is represented by the third column in Fig. 1, initially containing some data *FS* and some empty areas ($\emptyset$). In step ① of the figure, a regular operation (*OP*) is

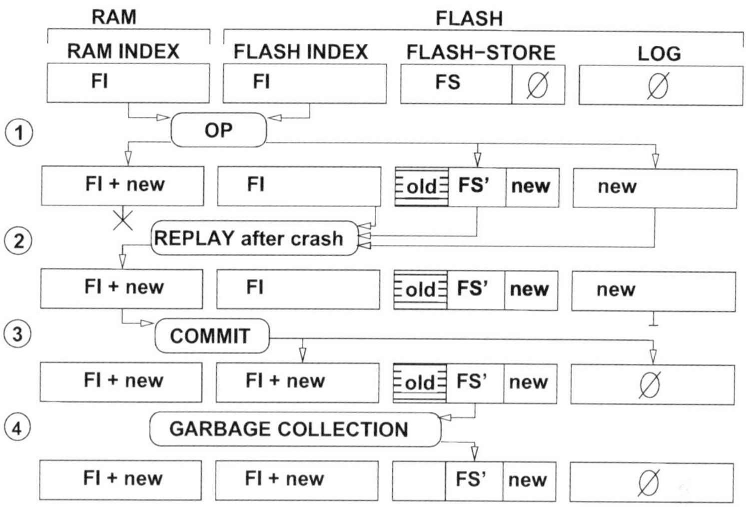

Fig. 1. Impact of UBIFS operations on the data structures

performed, e.g. overwriting data in a file. The second line shows the new state: The flash store has some new data (*new*), some unchanged parts (FS') and some obsolete data (*old*) due to the out-of-place updates. These obsolete data can be collected by garbage collection as shown in step (4).

A problem that is crucial for the efficiency of the FFS is indexing. Without an index that allows searching for a specific node efficiently, the whole media would have to be scanned. Therefore UBIFS uses an index that maps so-called *keys* (which are, roughly speaking, unique identifiers of nodes) to the address of the node on the flash media. The index in UBIFS is organized as a B^+-tree and stored in memory (later on called *RAM index*). For efficiency reasons, the index should be stored on flash as well, because rebuilding the index by scanning the complete media (as JFFS2 [29] does) takes up a lot of time at mount time. Therefore UBIFS also stores the index on flash (later on *flash index*). The RAM index and the flash index are shown as the two leftmost columns in Fig. 1. Having an index on flash poses some difficulties as

- the index must be updated out-of-place on the flash media (this is done by using a wandering tree).
- the index has to be changed every time old data is changed or new data is written (because the new data must be added to the index and the position of the modified data changes due to out-of-place updates).

To limit the number of changes to the flash index, UBIFS does not update the flash index immediately, but uses a *journal* (also called *log*) of recent changes instead. Section 4 gives details on our model of the UBIFS journal. The log can be seen in the rightmost column of Fig. 1. Its use is illustrated in the second line of Fig. 1: The log contains references to the new data written to the flash store in step (1) and the RAM index was updated accordingly ($FI + new$) while the flash index remained unchanged.

At certain points in time, the flash index is synchronized with the RAM index by the *commit* operation. This can be seen as step (3) in Fig. 1: The flash index is replaced with the current RAM index and the log is emptied[1]. One problem remains: What happens when the system crashes (e.g. power-failure) before the RAM index is written to flash? In this case, the flash index is out-of-date, compared to the data in the flash store. This problem is solved by the journal, because it records all changes to the data on flash that have not yet been added to the flash index. A special operation, *replay*, is done after a system crash to recover an up-to-date RAM index (step (2) in Fig. 1): First, the flash index is read as preliminary RAM index. Then all changes that were recorded in the log are applied to this preliminary RAM index. After the replay, the correct RAM index has been rebuilt.

3 Data Layout for UBIFS

The data layout used in UBIFS follows the file system representation used in the Linux virtual file system switch (VFS). The Linux kernel implements POSIX file system functions [15] as calls to VFS functions that provide a common interface for all implemented file systems.

Inodes (index nodes) are the primary data structure used in VFS[2]. They represent objects in the file system (such as files, directories, symlinks or devices) and are identified by an inode number. Inodes store information about objects, such as size, link count, modification date or permissions, but do not contain the name of the object. Mapping between names and objects is done using *dentries* (directory entries) which say that a certain object can be found in a certain directory under a certain name[3]. This separation is required as a single inode can be referred to in multiple directories (used for hard links). The directory tree can be viewed as an edge-labeled, directed graph consisting of inodes as vertices and dentries as edges. Furthermore negative dentries are used in memory to express that no object with the given name exists in a directory. These are used as a response when looking for nonexistent files, or as parameters for the file name when creating new files or directories. File contents are stored as fixed-size data blocks, called *pages*, belonging to file inodes. When opening a file or directory to access its contents, a *file* data structure (called file handle in user space) is used in memory to manage the inode number and the current position within the inode.

---

[1] This can be performed atomically, because all changes are stored out-of-place and the effective replace is executed by writing one block containing all the pointers to the data structures.

[2] See `struct inode` in `include/linux/fs.h`, [19]

[3] See `struct dentry` in `include/linux/dcache.h`, [19]

We thus define inodes, dentries and file handles as free data types generated by constructors mkinode, mkdentry, negdentry and mkfile.

inode = mkinode (. .ino : nat; . .directory : bool; . .nlink : nat; . .size : nat)
dentry = mkdentry (. .name : string; . .ino : nat) **with** . .dentry?
| negdentry (. .name : string) **with** . .negdentry?
file = mkfile (. .ino : nat; . .pos : nat)

This definition includes selector functions `.ino`, `.directory`, `.nlink`, `.size`, `.name` and `.pos` for accessing the constructor arguments, as well as type predicates `.dentry?` and `.negdentry?` to decide between the two types of dentries (the dot before predicates and functions indicates postfix notation).

UBIFS stores these data structures (except for file handles and negative dentries which are never stored) as nodes as described in the previous section. These nodes contain meta data (called *key*) to uniquely identify the corresponding node, and data containing the remaining information. For inodes, the inode number is sufficient as a key, whereas dentries require the parent inode number and the file name. Pages are referred to by the inode number and the position within the file.

Figure 2 shows the representation of a sample directory tree as UBIFS nodes. It contains two files, `test.txt` and `empty.txt` and a directory `temp` containing a hard link to `test.txt` named `test2.txt`.

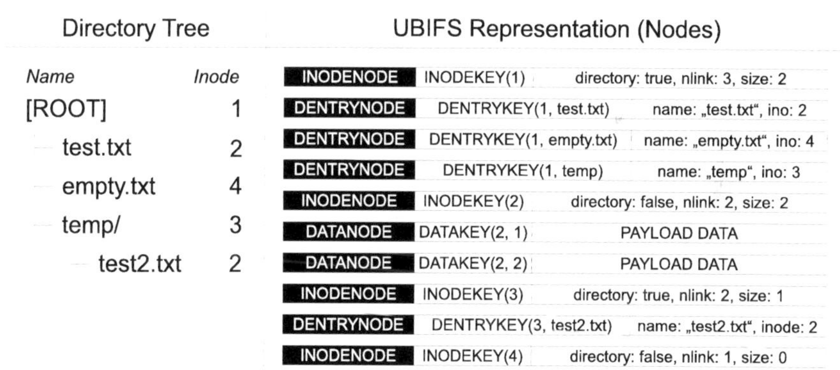

Fig. 2. Directory tree representation in UBIFS

Nodes for inodes in this abstraction contain extra information about size and link count. For files, the size gives the file size, measured in number of pages, and links gives the number of dentries (hard links) referencing the inode. Directories use the number of contained objects as size, and the number of links is calculated as (2 + number of subdirectories)[4].

[4] Directories may not appear as hard links, so this number is the result of counting the one allowed link, the "virtual" hard link "." of the directory to itself and the ".." link to the parent in each subdirectory.

For nodes and keys, we use the following specification[5]:

$$
\begin{aligned}
\textbf{node} = {} & \text{inodenode}\ (. .\text{key} : \text{key};\ . .\text{directory} : \text{bool};\\
& \quad . .\text{nlink} : \text{nat};\ . .\text{size} : \text{nat})\ \textbf{with}\ . .\text{inode?}\\
& \mid \text{dentrynode}\ (. .\text{key} : \text{key};\ . .\text{name} : \text{string};\\
& \quad . .\text{ino} : \text{nat})\ \textbf{with}\ . .\text{dentry?}\\
& \mid \text{datanode}\ (. .\text{key} : \text{key};\ . .\text{data} : \text{page})\ \textbf{with}\ . .\text{data?}\\
\textbf{key} = {} & \text{inodekey}\ (. .\text{ino} : \text{nat})\ \textbf{with}\ . .\text{inode?}\\
& \mid \text{datakey}\ (. .\text{ino} : \text{nat};\ . .\text{part} : \text{nat})\ \textbf{with}\ . .\text{data?}\\
& \mid \text{dentrykey}\ (. .\text{ino} : \text{nat};\ . .\text{name} : \text{string})\ \textbf{with}\ . .\text{dentry?}
\end{aligned}
$$

Information about inode 1 can be found in a node with inode key 1. To list all objects contained in this directory, all (valid) nodes with a dentry key containing 1 as a first argument have to be enumerated. The same goes for reading contents of a file, by scanning for corresponding data keys (their first parameter denotes the inode number, the second states the position inside the file).

File system data cannot directly be indexed and accessed using flash memory locations, as this would require overwriting flash memory on data change. Instead, data is referred to by its unique key. Finding matching nodes for a given key by sequentially scanning the entire flash memory however is very slow. UBIFS holds an index datastructure mapping keys to flash memory addresses in the RAM (called *RAM index*). It allows to quickly access nodes with a given key, or to enumerate all existing dentry or data keys for a given inode. When writing a new version of an existing node, the new copy is written to the flash store, and the address for its key is updated in the RAM index.

Formally, both the flash store and the two indexes (in RAM and on flash) are an instance of the abstract data type *store(elem,data)*.

$$\textbf{flashstore} = \text{store(address,node)} \qquad\qquad \textbf{index} = \text{store(key,address)}$$

A store is a partial function with a finite domain of elements with type *elem* and codomain *data*. In a set-theory based language such as Z [27] stores would be represented as a relation (set of pairs) for the function graph, and the update operation would be written as $st \oplus \{k \mapsto d\}$. In KIV stores are directly specified as an abstract, non-free data type generated from the empty store and an update operation *st[k,d]*, which allocates k if necessary, and overwrites the value at k with *d*. This avoids the need for a left-uniqueness constraint as an invariant.

4 The UBIFS Journal

This section describes how the journal operates and how it is linked to flash and RAM index. The correlation between flash store, journal and the indices is shown in Fig. 3.

[5] See `struct ubifs_data_node`, `struct ubifs_ino_node` and `struct ubifs_data_node` in `fs/ubifs/ubifs-media.h` for nodes, and `struct ubifs_key` in `fs/ubifs/ubifs.h` as well as `ino_key_init`, `dent_key_init` and `data_key_init` in `fs/ubifs/key.h`, [19].

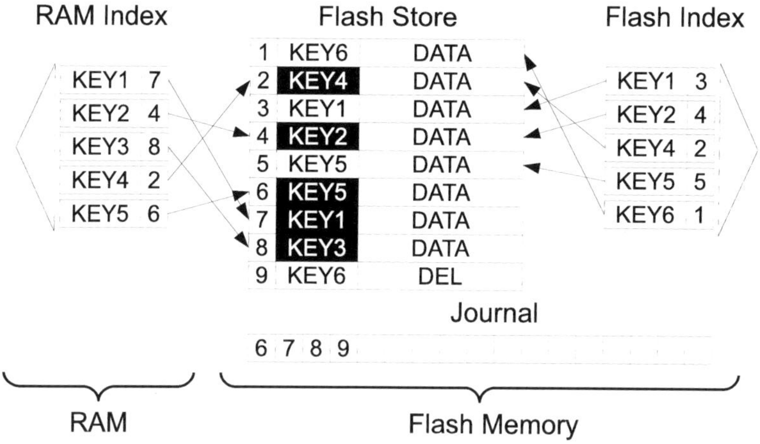

Fig. 3. RAM index, flash index, flash store and journal

To create a new node, this is written to an unused address in the flash store and simultaneously[6] added to the log. Afterwards, its address is stored in the RAM index for further access to its key. This way, the data is safe, even if the RAM index gets lost without a commit e. g. caused by a power failure, because the correct state of the RAM index can be restored by information from flash index, flash store and log.

This method allows for creating new and overwriting existing nodes. However, deleting nodes is not possible because it would require pure index operations (delete a key from the index). Therefore, UBIFS uses specialized delete nodes which are written to the flash store, but cause deletion from the RAM index when replayed (marked as DEL[7] in Fig. 3).

When performing a replay in the situation of Fig. 3, the contents of the flash index are copied to the RAM index. When replaying address `6`, the `6` is stored in the RAM index as new address for key `KEY5`. The same goes for address `7`, while `8` adds `KEY3` to the index. Address `9` contains a deletion entry that causes `KEY6` to be deleted from the index.

The figure also shows the need for garbage collection: addresses `1`, `3` and `5` store data which are no longer in the index and therefore can be reused.

5 File System Operations

For applying changes to the contents of the file system, the Linux VFS provides file system operations. These can be grouped into inode operations, file

[6] This is possible because UBIFS does not use an explicit list for the log, but treats all nodes in certain erase blocks as log entries.

[7] UBIFS uses inode nodes with link count 0 or dentry nodes with destination inode number 0 to delete the corresponding keys.

operations, and address space operations. Inode operations allow creating, renaming or deleting inodes, whereas file operations allow for working with inode contents (data stored in files or directory entries). Address space operations include all operations that work with pages, and are used in the Linux kernel to implement file operations accessing file contents. They are included here to allow for using abstract pages when handling file contents.

We will start with an inode operation called *create*[8], used for creating new files. It expects the inode number of the containing directory (`P_INO`), and a negative dentry specifying the file name (`DENT`) as input. `DENT` is overwritten with the newly created dentry.

create#(P_INO; DENT, FS, RI, LOG) {
  choose INO **with** $\neg$ inodekey(INO) $\in$ RI $\wedge$ INO $>$ 0 **in** {
    let INODE = getinode(P_INO, FS, RI) **in**
    choose ADR_1, ADR_2, ADR_3 **with** new(ADR_1, ADR_2, ADR_3, FS) **in** {
      FS := FS
        [ADR_1, inodenode(inodekey(INO), false, 1, 0)]
        [ADR_2, dentrynode(dentrykey(P_INO, DENT.name), DENT.name, INO)]
        [ADR_3, inodenode(inodekey(INODE.ino),
          INODE.directory, INODE.nlink, INODE.size + 1)],
      LOG := LOG + ADR_1 + ADR_2 + ADR_3;
      RI := RI[inodekey(INO), ADR_1];
      RI := RI[dentrykey(P_INO, DENT.name), ADR_2];
      RI := RI[inodekey(INODE.ino), ADR_3] };
    DENT := mkdentry(DENT.name, INO) }};

The notation used to describe the rule is similar to that of ASM rules [11], [3], but it should be noted that only parallel assignment, denoted with a comma, is executed atomically, while sequential composition (with semicolon) is not. **choose** binds new local variables (here e.g. INO) to values that satisfy the **with** clause.

The operation writes a new inode node for the created file (link count `1`, size `0`) and a dentry node for a dentry pointing from the parent directory `P_INO` to the new inode, named as given in `DENT`. It increases the parent directory size by 1 to reflect the increased number of objects contained in the directory.

To correctly perform these changes, it first selects an unused inode number and three new addresses (predicate new) from the flash store, and loads the inode given by `P_INO`. It then atomically writes three new nodes into new locations of the flash store `FS`, simultaneously adding the locations to the journal `LOG`. Afterwards it updates the RAM index `RI` with the new addresses, and changes the reference parameter `DENT` to return the newly created dentry.

The following inode operations also change the directory structure. Their informal description leaves out standard parameters FS, RI and LOG. Full details can be found on the Web [18].

unlink(P_INO, DENT) Removes the file referred to by `DENT` from the directory `P_INO`. If the dentry was the last link to the referred file, the inode and file

[8] See `ubifs_create` in `fs/ubifs/dir.c`, [19].

contents are also deleted, otherwise only the dentry is removed. `DENT` is returned as a negative dentry.

link(OLD_DENT, NEW_INO, NEW_DENT) Creates a hard link to the file referred to by `OLD_DENT`, placed in the directory `NEW_INO` and named as given by the negative dentry `NEW_DENT`. Returns the newly created dentry in `NEW_DENT`.

mkdir(P_INO, DENT) Creates a new directory in `P_INO`, with the name given in the negative dentry `DENT`. The newly created dentry is returned in `DENT`.

rmdir(P_INO, DENT) Removes the (empty) directory referred to by the dentry `DENT` located in the parent directory `P_INO`. `DENT` is changed into a negative dentry.

rename(OLD_INO, OLD_DENT, NEW_INO, NEW_DENT) Moves the object (file or directory) referred to by `OLD_DENT` from directory `OLD_INO` to directory `NEW_INO`, changing its name to `NEW_DENT.name`. If the object referred to by `NEW_DENT` exists, it has to be of the same type (file or directory) as `OLD_DENT`, and it is overwritten (i. e. deleted).

lookup(P_INO, DENT) Checks for the existence of a object named `DENT.name` in the directory `P_INO`. If it exists, the dentry is returned in `DENT`, otherwise a negative dentry is returned.

For inode contents, the following file and address space operations exist:

open(INO, FILE) Opens the file or directory given in `INO`, and returns a new file handle in `FILE`.

release(INO, FILE) Called when the last process closes an inode (file or directory), to clean up temporary data. Unused in the given specification.

readpage(FILE, PAGENO, PAGE) Reads the page with number `PAGENO` from the file referred to in `FILE`, and returns it in `PAGE`.

writepage(FILE, PAGENO, PAGE) Writes the data from `PAGE` as new page numbered `PAGENO` to file `FILE`.

truncate(FILE, PAGENO) Sets the file size of the file referred to in `FILE` to `PAGENO`, deleting all pages beyond.

readdir(FILE, DENT) Returns the next object of the directory referred to in `FILE`, or a negative dentry if no further file or directory exists. The (positive or negative) dentry is returned in `DENT`, and the position stored in `FILE` is increased to return the next object at the next call.

Finally, our model defines garbage collection, commit and replay as described in Sect. 2.

6 Verification

Our verification efforts have focused on three properties, described in the following paragraphs. The last paragraph gives a summary of the effort involved.

Functional Correctness of the Operations. We proved that all specified operations terminate and fulfill postconditions about their results. As most operations and all supporting functions are non-recursive and only use loops over the elements of finite lists, termination is quite obvious, and proving does not pose great complexity – even regardless whether any preconditions hold or not.

Only garbage collection has a precondition for termination, as it is specified as a non-deterministic choice of a new, isomorphic state, which only terminates if such a state exists.

For the other inode and file operations, we give and prove total correctness assertions that describe their behavior. We write $wp(\alpha,\varphi)$ to denote the weakest precondition of program α with respect to a postcondition φ[9]. Proofs in KIV are done using sequent calculus and symbolic execution of programs, see [23] for details.

For the create operation described in the previous section we demand[10]:

$$\begin{aligned}&\text{valid-dir-ino(P)} \wedge \text{valid-negdentry(P, DENT)}\\ \rightarrow\ &wp(\text{create(P; DENT), valid-dentry(P, DENT)} \wedge \text{valid-file-ino(DENT.ino)})\end{aligned}$$

When called with a valid directory inode (i. e. the inode exists, is of type directory and has a link count of 2 or higher) and a valid negative dentry (i. e. no dentry with the given name exists in the given directory) as parameters, the operation yields a dentry (ideally with the same name, but we do not demand that here) that exists in the given directory and references a valid file (i. e. the inode referred to exists, is a file and has a link count of at least 1).

Giving postconditions for readpage or writepage individually turned out to be rather hard when trying to remain implementation independent, so we decided to use the combined postcondition that reading data after writing returns exactly the data written:

$$wp(\text{writepage(file, pageno, pg) ; readpage(file, pageno; pg2), pg} = \text{pg2})$$

Furthermore, file contents of a file remain unchanged when writing to another file or to another position inside the file:

$$\begin{aligned}&\text{valid-file(f1)} \wedge \text{valid-file(f2)} \wedge (\text{f1.ino} \neq \text{f2.ino} \vee \text{n1} \neq \text{n2}) \wedge \text{store-cons(fs,ri,fi,log)}\\ \rightarrow\ &wp(\text{readpage\#(f1,n1;p1);writepage\#(f2,n2,p);readpage\#(f1,n1;p2), p1=p2})\end{aligned}$$

The pre- and postconditions for the other operations as well as their proofs can be found on the Web [18].

Consistency of the File System. Another basic requirement is that the file system is always consistent. We formally define a predicate *fs-cons(fs,ri)* for the file store *fs* and the RAM index *ri* (flash index and log are irrelevant as they are only required for replay), and prove that it is an invariant of all operations.

For each key stored in the RAM index, *fs-cons* requires that its address must be allocated in the flash store, and that the key is stored as that node's key. Further requirements depend on the type of key.

Dentry keys must belong to a valid directory and reference a valid inode. The name stored in the key must be equal to the copy of the name stored in the node. Data keys have to belong to a valid file inode, and the requirements for inode keys are differentiated between files and directories. For files, the link count has to be equal to the number of dentries referencing the file, and for each data key

9 In KIV $wp(\alpha,\varphi)$ is written as $\langle\!|\alpha|\!\rangle\varphi$.

10 We suppress standard parameters FS, RI and LOG in all predicates and procedure calls for better readability.

belonging to the file, the page number (*part*) has to be less than the file's size. Directories have to have 2 + number of subdirectories as their link count, and the number of contained dentries as size. Furthermore, no directory may have more than 1 (stored) dentry referencing it[11].

The formal proof obligation for invariance is

$$\text{fs-cons(fs, ri)} \rightarrow wp(op, \text{fs-cons(fs, ri)})$$

where *op* stands for any of the operations defined in the previous section. As this property describes correlations between the different types of keys, it cannot be proven step by step for each individual update of flash store and RAM index; the property is not restored until all steps of an operation are completed. So the proofs have to take the operation as a whole, complicating the definition and application of reusable lemmata.

Correctness of the Replay Process. The replay operation should be able to restore a consistent state after a crash, losing as little data as possible. We therefore define a predicate *log-cons* claiming that a replay in the current situation will correctly restore the RAM index to a state isomorphic to the one with current RAM index contents. The formal definition is

$$\text{log-cons(fs, ri, fi, log)} \leftrightarrow wp(\text{replay(fs, fi, log; ri2), (fs, ri)} \cong \text{(fs, ri2)})$$

If this predicate is true, we will not lose data at a crash (except maybe for the changes of the current operation). A reliable file system should always preserve this predicate, even in the middle of an operation. For verification we have taken the weaker approach to prove that this predicate is invariant

$$\begin{aligned}&\text{log-cons(fs,ri,fi,log)} \wedge \text{store-cons(fs,ri,log)} \wedge \text{datanode-cons(fs,ri)}\\ \rightarrow\ & wp(op, \text{log-cons(fs,ri,fi,log)} \wedge \text{store-cons(fs,ri,log)} \wedge \text{datanode-cons(fs,ri))}\end{aligned}$$

Note that *log-cons* used in the pre- and postcondition is defined using a wp-formula itself, so the formula is not a total correctness formula in the usual sense, where pre- and postcondition are defined using predicate logic only. Nevertheless KIV's logic can prove this formula using symbolic execution for formulas in preconditions too.

The invariance above ensures the file system robust wrt. crashes *between* operations. Still, the implementation of the operations is designed in a way such that a similar property also holds anytime during the execution of operations. As one of the next steps we plan to prove this fact using KIV's temporal logic [1], [2] which is able to express and prove the full property[12].

Proving the invariance of *log-cons* required two auxiliary invariants, *store-cons* and *datanode-cons*. The predicate store-cons requires that each address referred to in the RAM index or log has to be allocated in the flash store, and datanode-cons demands that each data key belongs to a valid file inode and describes a page within the file length. The former is needed to avoid accessing addresses in

[11] The root directory has no link, all other directories have one, as further hard links to directories are not allowed.

[12] An alternative would be to encode the operations as a sequence of small steps using a program counter, as is often done for model checking. Then the property would have to be proved to be invariant in every small step.

the flash store that are not yet allocated, whereas the latter is needed as replaying some operations causes data keys beyond the file size to be deleted.

Statistics about our Specification and Verification. Developing and verifying our specification mainly consisted of four steps. We first collected and analyzed material about UBIFS, mainly from the UBIFS whitepaper [14] and the UBIFS source code in the Linux kernel. During four weeks, we developed a basic understanding of the mechanisms and found a suitable abstraction level for the specification. In the following two weeks, the required data structures and operations were specified, as well as the invariants we wanted to prove. Proving the correctness of the replay operation (log-cons) took another two weeks, during which we corrected minor errors in the specification and found the additional preconditions needed for log consistency. Our last steps were to prove the total correctness assertions and the file system consistency. This took about as long as the log consistency, though the resulting proofs for fs-cons were a lot larger than the ones for log-cons – especially for the *rename* operation which contains many case distinctions (file vs. directory, rename vs. overwrite).

7 Outlook

The work of this paper defines a first abstract model of the essential data structures needed in a FFS. We intend to use it as an intermediate layer in the development of a sequence of refinements, which starts with an abstract POSIX specification such as the ones of [5], [7] and ends with an implementation based on a specification of flash memory, like the one of [4]. There will be many obstacles deriving such refinements, and we discuss these problems briefly in the following paragraphs on future work.

A rather different approach has been taken by Kang and Jackson [17]. This work builds a vertical prototype by focussing on the read/write operations for files, ignoring issues such as directory structure, indexes and journals (their file system roughly corresponds to the file store component of our model). They define an abstract level, where reading/writing a file is atomic. These are refined to reading and writing pages, which is done on a model that is closer to implementation than ours, since it already considers a mapping from logical to physical blocks. To check properties of the model, Alloy (and the Kodkod engine) is used to check that finite approximations of the model do not have counter examples. This approach is weaker than verification, but gives excellent results for debugging specifications. Our current work is on attaching Kodkod as a pre-checker to validate KIV theorems before proof attempts [6], similar to the proposal in [7]. The Alloy model also includes an interesting analysis of a high-level recovery mechanism for failed write attempts. UBIFS delegates recovery mechanism mainly to UBI (see below). Two high-level mechanisms for recovery exist in UBIFS: one for log entries, which may not have been completely written; another for the root node of the B^+-tree of the file index, see [14]. Both are very different from the one analyzed in [17]. Since our model is still too abstract (no B^+-trees and no concrete layout of the journal as data in erase blocks), these will only show up in refinements.

From POSIX to our UBIFS Model. Our abstract model is based on the interface that UBIFS offers to the general Linux virtual file system switch (VFS). It assumes that our operations are protected by locks and will therefore not be executed concurrently.[13] However, above our specification this is no longer true. As an example, writing a full file can no longer be assumed to be atomic: it will consist of several pages being written (it is possible that several processes concurrently read and write a file!). In reality, these page writes will even be cached. Even if a write operation has finished, the data may not yet be on the flash (only calling the Linux flush command ensures that caches are emptied). We therefore expect the theoretical question of how concurrency should be handled to dominate the question of a correct refinement.

As a first step, it is of course possible to ignore the concurrency problem (as has been done in [17]). Then implementing POSIX operations correctly using our abstract interface should be possible using standard data refinement. Of course, for such a refinement, some additional data such as modification dates and access rights would have to be added.

From our Model to Flash Memory. Our model has abstracted from many details of a real flash file system. First, and most important we have abstracted from wear leveling. Since wear leveling is not dealt within UBIFS, but in a separate UBI layer that maps logical to physical erase blocks, this seemed natural. We expect the correctness of this layer not to pose too difficult theoretical questions. The challenging question for this refinement is whether it is possible to prove something about the quality of wear leveling. This looks possible for UBI, since its wear leveling strategy is based on counting erase cycles.

Second, we have abstracted index structures, which are B^+-trees in reality. The lower level representation allows two optimizations: first, only those parts of the flash index which are currently needed, must be loaded into RAM. Second, the commit operation does not simply copy the full B^+-tree from RAM to the flash memory as in our simple specification. Instead it copies only those parts that have changed since the last commit. This means that the flash index becomes a "wandering tree". Parts of it move with every commit.

Third, all three data structures, the flash store, the flash index and the journal will be represented uniformly by pieces of memory in logical erase blocks (LEBs). The challenging problem here is to verify garbage collection, which we only specified to give some isomorphic file system. This algorithm is rather complex. It uses an auxiliary data structure to find out efficiently how much room is left in each LEB. This data structure, the LPT ("LEB property tree") is also implemented as a wandering tree.

Finally, there are several more issues we have ignored: on the fly compression (using zlib or LZO), the handling of orphan nodes, which are needed to handle still open files that have been deleted, and hashing of index keys are three examples.

[13] This is mostly true in the implementation, with one notable exception: the commit operation may be executed in parallel with regular operations.

In summary, we think that the development of a verified flash file system will need a lot more effort than our previous contribution to the Grand Challenge with the Mondex case study ([12], [25], [24], [10]).

8 Conclusion

We have given an abstract specification of a flash file system which was derived by abstracting as much as possible from the details of the UBIFS system. We have specified the four central data structures: the file store which stores node-structured data, the flash index, its cached copy in the RAM and the journal. Based on these, we have specified the most relevant interface operations.

We have verified that the operations keep the file system in a consistent state, and that they satisfy some total correctness assertions. We have also verified that the journal is used correctly and enables recovery at every time.

Our model should be of general interest for the development of a correct flash file system, since variants of the data structures and operations we describe should be relevant for every realistic, efficient implementation.

Nevertheless the model given in this paper is only our first step towards the development of a verified flash file system implementation. We plan to use the model as an intermediate layer of a series of refinements, which starts with an abstract model of POSIX-like operations and leads down to to an efficient implementation like UBIFS based on a specification of flash memory.

References

1. Balser, M., Bäumler, S., Reif, W., Schellhorn, G.: Interactive verification of concurrent systems using symbolic execution. In: Proceedings of 7th International Workshop of Implementation of Logics, IWIL 2008 (2008)
2. Bäumler, S., Nafz, F., Balser, M., Reif, W.: Compositional proofs with symbolic execution. In: Beckert, B., Klein, G. (eds.) Proceedings of the 5th International Verification Workshop. Ceur Workshop Proceedings, vol. 372 (2008)
3. Börger, E., Stärk, R.F.: Abstract State Machines—A Method for High-Level System Design and Analysis. Springer, Heidelberg (2003)
4. Butterfield, A., Woodcock, J.: Formalising flash memory: First steps. In: Proc. of the 12th IEEE Int. Conf. on Engineering Complex Computer Systems (ICECCS), Washington DC, USA, pp. 251–260. IEEE Comp. Soc., Los Alamitos (2007)
5. Damchoom, K., Butler, M., Abrial, J.-R.: Modelling and proof of a tree-structured file system in Event-B and Rodin. In: Liu, S., Maibaum, T., Araki, K. (eds.) ICFEM 2008. LNCS, vol. 5256, pp. 25–44. Springer, Heidelberg (2008)
6. Dunets, A., Schellhorn, G., Reif, W.: Automating Algebraic Specifications of Non-freely Generated Data Types. In: Cha, S(S.), Choi, J.-Y., Kim, M., Lee, I., Viswanathan, M. (eds.) ATVA 2008. LNCS, vol. 5311, pp. 141–155. Springer, Heidelberg (2008)

7. Ferreira, M.A., Silva, S.S., Oliveira, J.N.: Verifying Intel flash file system core specification. In: Modelling and Analysis in VDM: Proceedings of the Fourth VDM/Overture Workshop. School of Computing Science, Newcastle University (2008) Technical Report CS-TR-1099
8. Freitas, L., Woodcock, J., Butterfield, A.: Posix and the verification grand challenge: A roadmap. In: ICECCS 2008: Proc. of the 13th IEEE Int. Conf. on Eng. of Complex Computer Systems, Washington, DC, USA, pp. 153–162 (2008)
9. Gal, E., Toledo, S.: Algorithms and data structures for flash memory. ACM computing surveys, 138–163 (2005)
10. Grandy, H., Bischof, M., Schellhorn, G., Reif, W., Stenzel, K.: Verification of Mondex Electronic Purses with KIV: From a Security Protocol to Verified Code. In: Cuellar, J., Maibaum, T., Sere, K. (eds.) FM 2008. LNCS, vol. 5014, pp. 165–180. Springer, Heidelberg (2008)
11. Gurevich, Y.: Evolving algebras 1993: Lipari guide. In: Börger, E. (ed.) Specification and Validation Methods, pp. 9–36. Oxford Univ. Press, Oxford (1995)
12. Haneberg, D., Schellhorn, G., Grandy, H., Reif, W.: Verification of Mondex Electronic Purses with KIV: From Transactions to a Security Protocol. Formal Aspects of Computing 20(1) (January 2008)
13. Hoare, C.A.R.: The verifying compiler: A grand challenge for computing research. J. ACM 50(1), 63–69 (2003)
14. Hunter, A.: A brief introduction to the design of UBIFS (2008), `http://www.linux-mtd.infradead.org/doc/ubifs_whitepaper.pdf`
15. The Open Group Base Specifications Issue 6, IEEE Std 1003.1, 2004 Edition (2004), `http://www.unix.org/version3/online.html` (login required)
16. Joshi, R., Holzmann, G.J.: A mini challenge: build a verifiable filesystem. Formal Aspects of Computing 19(2) (June 2007)
17. Kang, E., Jackson, D.: Formal modelling and analysis of a flash filesystem in Alloy. In: Börger, E., Butler, M., Bowen, J.P., Boca, P. (eds.) ABZ 2008. LNCS, vol. 5238, pp. 294–308. Springer, Heidelberg (2008)
18. Web presentation of the Flash File System Case Study in KIV (2009), `http://www.informatik.uni-augsburg.de/swt/projects/flash.html`
19. LXR - the Linux cross reference, `http://lxr.linux.no/`
20. Morgan, C., Sufrin, B.: Specification of the UNIX filing system. In: Specification case studies, pp. 91–140. Prentice Hall (UK) Ltd., Hertfordshire (1987)
21. Oliveira, J.N.: Extended Static Checking by Calculation Using the Pointfree Transform. In: Bove, A., et al. (eds.) LerNet ALFA Summer School 2008. LNCS, vol. 5520, pp. 195–251. Springer, Heidelberg (2009)
22. Reeves, G., Neilson, T.: The Mars Rover Spirit FLASH anomaly. In: Aerospace Conference, pp. 4186–4199. IEEE, Los Alamitos (2005)
23. Reif, W., Schellhorn, G., Stenzel, K., Balser, M.: Structured specifications and interactive proofs with KIV. In: Bibel, W., Schmitt, P. (eds.) Automated Deduction—A Basis for Applications, ch. 1, vol. II, pp. 13–39. Kluwer Academic Publishers, Dordrecht (1998)
24. Schellhorn, G., Banach, R.: A concept-driven construction of the mondex protocol using three refinements. In: Börger, E., Butler, M., Bowen, J.P., Boca, P. (eds.) ABZ 2008. LNCS, vol. 5238, pp. 39–41. Springer, Heidelberg (2008)

25. Schellhorn, G., Grandy, H., Haneberg, D., Moebius, N., Reif, W.: A Systematic Verification Approach for Mondex Electronic Purses using ASMs. In: Glässer, U., Abrial, J.-R. (eds.) Dagstuhl Seminar on Rigorous Methods for Software Construction and Analysis. LNCS, vol. 5115. Springer, Heidelberg (2008)
26. Schellhorn, G., Reif, W., Schairer, A., Karger, P., Austel, V., Toll, D.: Verified Formal Security Models for Multiapplicative Smart Cards. Special issue of the Journal of Computer Security 10(4), 339–367 (2002)
27. Spivey, J.M.: The Z Notation: A Reference Manual. Prentice Hall, Englewood Cliffs (1992)
28. STMicroelectronics. SPC56xB/C/D Automotive 32-bit Flash microcontrollers for car body applications (February 2009), `http://www.st.com/stonline/products/promlit/a_automotive.htm`
29. Woodhouse, D.: JFFS: The Journalling Flash File System (2001), `http://sources.redhat.com/jffs2/jffs2.pdf`

Inferring Mealy Machines

Muzammil Shahbaz and Roland Groz

Grenoble Universities,
F-38402 St Martin d'Hères Cedex, France
{muzammil,groz}@imag.fr

Abstract. Automata learning techniques are getting significant importance for their applications in a wide variety of software engineering problems, especially in the analysis and testing of complex systems. In recent studies, a previous learning approach [1] has been extended to synthesize Mealy machine models which are specifically tailored for I/O based systems. In this paper, we discuss the inference of Mealy machines and propose improvements that reduces the worst-time learning complexity of the existing algorithm. The gain over the complexity of the proposed algorithm has also been confirmed by experimentation on a large set of finite state machines.

1 Introduction

The field of automata learning has made a significant impact on a wide area of software engineering problems. For example, the learning techniques have been used to study the unknown behaviors of the system [2], testing the system [3], verifying interesting properties [4], building specification and maintaining the applications [5]. The use of such techniques actually ease the traditional practice of model driven engineering for the systems that consist of third-party components. The fact that these components come from different sources and have gone through various revisions before they are actually used, the components usually do not come with the formal and up-to-date specifications. Normally, the users of the components have to confront with their informal or insufficient information that hinders the direct applications of formal validation approaches. The application of automata learning techniques is a solution to synthesize the behavior models of the components, so that they could be used to analyze, test and validate the overall system using formal approaches.

Among various learning approaches, a well-known approach which has remained a major focus of the applied research in learning is the classical procedure, called L^* (aka Angluin's algorithm) [1]. Under this view, a component is assumed to be an unknown regular language whose alphabet is known. Then, the algorithm is applied to infer a Deterministic Finite Automaton (DFA) that models the unknown language in polynomial time (under certain assumptions).

Recent studies on reactive systems, e.g, telecom services, web-based applications, data acquisition modules, embedded system controllers etc, advocate the need of learning other forms of automata. This is due to the fact that complex

A. Cavalcanti and D. Dams (Eds.): FM 2009, LNCS 5850, pp. 207–222, 2009.

systems characterize their behaviors in terms of input/output (i/o). Typically, such systems receive inputs from the environment, take decisions on internal transitions, perform computations and finally produce the corresponding outputs to the environment. Arguably, DFA models are not appropriate for modeling such systems since they lack the structure of i/o based behavior modeling. The more natural modeling of such systems is through Mealy machines that is much more concise compared to DFA models. Moreover, it is observed that a DFA model normally contains far more states than a Mealy machine if they model the same problem [6] [7]. Thus, efforts of learning Mealy machines are beneficial in terms of learning the state space of the problem to cater the complexity. We refer to the previous studies [7][5][6] for a detailed comparison of DFA and Mealy machine modeling of reactive systems.

In this paper, we discuss the learning of Mealy machines using the settings from Angluin's algorithm. There are many works which formally and informally present the adaptation of Angluin's algorithm to learn Mealy machines. However, we propose here some modifications in the adapted algorithm that brings down the complexity of learning Mealy machines significantly in some contexts.

The paper is organized as follows. Section 2 provides the basics of Angluin's algorithm informally. Section 3 discusses how Angluin's algorithm can be adapted for Mealy machine inference and how the adaptation can further be improved. Section 4 presents the adapted algorithm to learn Mealy machines, its complexity and its illustration on an example. Section 5 presents our improvements on the adapted algorithm, its complexity and its illustration on an example. Section 6 compares the complexity of the two algorithms on a finite state machine workbench experimentally. Section 7 concludes the paper.

2 Overview of Angluin's Algorithm

We refer to the original paper [1] for the complete discussion on learning DFA using Angluin's algorithm L^*. Here, we describe the algorithm informally.

The learning algorithm L^* starts by asking *membership queries* over the known alphabet Σ of the language to check whether certain strings from Σ^* are accepted or rejected by the language. The result of each such query in terms of "1" (accepted) or "0" (rejected) is recorded as an observation in a table. These queries are asked iteratively until the conditions on the observation table, i.e., it must be *closed* and *consistent*, are satisfied. The algorithm then conjectures a DFA based upon the observations recorded in the table. It then asks an *equivalence query* to a so called *oracle*, that knows the unknown language, to verify whether the conjecture is equivalent to the target DFA. The oracle validates the conjecture if it is correct or replies with a counterexample otherwise. A counterexample is a sequence that distinguishes the conjecture with the target DFA. The algorithm processes the counterexample in the table and performs another run of asking membership queries to construct a "better" conjecture. The algorithm iterates in this fashion until it produces a correct conjecture that is isomorphic to the target DFA.

Let $|\Sigma|$ be the size of the alphabet Σ, n be the total number of states in the target DFA and m be the length of the longest counterexample provided by the oracle, then the worst case complexity of Angluin's algorithm is $O(|\Sigma|mn^2)$.

3 From DFA to Mealy Machine

It is observed that Angluin's algorithm L^* can be used to learn Mealy machines through model transformation techniques. A simple way is to define a mapping from inputs and outputs of the machine to letters in a DFA's alphabet Σ. This can be done either by taking inputs and outputs as letters, i.e., $\Sigma = I \cup O$ [5] or by considering couples of inputs and outputs as letters, i.e., $\Sigma = I \times O$ [8]. But these methods increase the size of Σ and thus raise complexity problems because the algorithm is polynomial on these factors. However, there is a straightforward implication of L^* on learning Mealy machines by slightly modifying the structure of the observation table. The idea is to record the behaviors of the system as output strings in the table instead of recording just "1" and "0", as in the case of language inference. Similarly, we can modify the related concepts, such as making the table closed and consistent and making a conjecture from the table etc. For processing counterexamples in the table, we can also easily adapt the corresponding method from L^*. This adaptation of L^* to learn Mealy machines has already been discussed, formally [7] [9] [10] [3], and informally [6] [11].

However, our contribution in the inference of Mealy machines is the proposal of a new method for processing counterexamples that consequently reduces the complexity of the algorithm. The complexity analysis shows that by using our method for processing counterexamples, the algorithm for learning Mealy machines requires less number of queries, compared to the adapted method.

4 Inferring Mealy Machines

Definition 1. *A Mealy Machine is a sextuple $(Q, I, O, \delta, \lambda, q_0)$, where Q is the non-empty finite set of states, $q_0 \in Q$ is the initial state, I is the finite set of input symbols, O is the finite set of output symbols, $\delta : Q \times I \rightarrow Q$ is the transition function, $\lambda : Q \times I \rightarrow O$ is the output function.*

Definition 1 provides the formal definition of (deterministic) Mealy machines. When a Mealy machine is in the current (source) state $q \in Q$ and receives $i \in I$, it moves to the target state specified by $\delta(q, i)$ and produces an output given by $\lambda(q, i)$. The functions δ and λ are extended from symbols to strings in the standard way. We consider that the Mealy machines are input-enabled, i.e., $dom(\delta) = dom(\lambda) = Q \times I$. We denote by $suff^k(\omega)$, the suffix of a string ω of length k. Let $\omega = a \cdot b \cdots x \cdot y \cdot z$, then $suff^3(\omega) = x \cdot y \cdot z$. An example of a Mealy machine over the sets $I = \{a, b\}$ and $O = \{x, y\}$ is shown in Figure 1.

Now, we detail the learning of Mealy machines using the settings from Angluin's algorithm L^*, that has also been mentioned in the existing works. As for

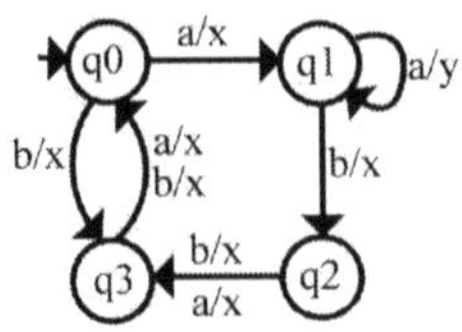

Fig. 1. Example of a Mealy Machine

DFA learning, the two main assumptions in learning Mealy machines are i) The basic input set I is known, and ii) The machine can be reset before each query.

The algorithm asks *output queries* [3] that are strings from I^+ and obtain the corresponding output strings from the machine. This is similar to the concept of membership queries in L^*. The difference is that instead of 1 or 0, the machine replies with the complete output string. Let $\omega \in I^+$, i.e., an input string of the query, then the machine replies to the query with $\lambda(q_0, \omega)$. The response to each query is recorded in the observation table. The queries are asked iteratively until the conditions on the observation table, i.e., it must be *closed* and *consistent*, are satisfied. This follows by making the Mealy machine conjecture from the table. The algorithm then asks equivalence query to the oracle. If the oracle says "yes", i.e., the conjecture is correct, then the algorithm terminates the procedure by outputting the conjecture. If the oracle replies with a counterexample, then the algorithm processes the counterexample in the table and refines the conjecture.

The formal description of learning Mealy machines is given in the subsequent sections. We denote by $\mathcal{M} = \{Q_\mathcal{M}, I, O, \delta_\mathcal{M}, \lambda_\mathcal{M}, q_{0\mathcal{M}}\}$ the unknown Mealy machine model that has a minimum number of states. We assume that the input/output interfaces of the machines are accessible, i.e., the input interface from where an input can be sent and the output interface from where an output can be observed.

4.1 Observation Table

We denote by ${L_M}^*$ the learning algorithm for Mealy machines. At any given time, ${L_M}^*$ has information about a finite collection of input strings from I^+ and their corresponding output strings from O^+. This information is organized into an observation table, denoted by (S_M, E_M, T_M). The structure of the table is directly imported from Angluin's algorithm L^*. Let S_M and E_M be non-empty finite sets of finite strings over I. S_M is a prefix-closed set that always contains an empty string ϵ. E_M is a suffix-closed set (except $\epsilon \notin E_M$). Let T_M be a finite function that maps $(S_M \cup S_M \cdot I) \times E_M$ to O^+. If $s \in S_M \cup S_M \cdot I$ and $e \in E_M$, then $T_M(s, e)$ contains the output string from $\lambda_\mathcal{M}(q_{0\mathcal{M}}, s \cdot e)$. The rows of the table consist of the elements of $S_M \cup S_M \cdot I$ and the columns consist of the elements of E_M.

Since S_M and E_M are non-empty sets, the table is initialized by $S_M = \{\epsilon\}$ and $E_M = I$, i.e., every input symbol makes one column in the table, with the entry for a row $s \in S_M \cup S_M \cdot I$ and a column $e \in E_M$ equals to $T_M(s, e)$. The equivalence of rows is defined with respect to the strings in E_M. Suppose $s, t \in S_M \cup S_M \cdot I$ are two rows, then s and t are equivalent, denoted by $s \cong_{E_M} t$, if and only if $T_M(s, e) = T_M(t, e)$, for all $e \in E_M$. We denote by $[s]$ the equivalence class of rows that also includes s. An example of the observation table (S_M, E_M, T_M) for learning the Mealy machine in Figure 1 is given in Table 1.

Table 1. Example of the Observation Table (S_M, E_M, T_M)

		E_M	
		a	b
S_M	ϵ	x	x
$S_M \cdot I$	a	y	x
	b	x	x

The algorithm $L_M{}^*$ eventually uses the observation table (S_M, E_M, T_M) to build a Mealy machine conjecture. The strings or prefixes in S_M are the potential states of the conjecture, and the strings or suffixes in E_M distinguish these states from each other.

To build a valid Mealy machine conjecture from the observations, the table must satisfy two conditions. The first condition is that the table must be *closed*, i.e., for each $t \in S_M \cdot I$, there exists an $s \in S_M$, such that $s \cong_{E_M} t$. If the table is not closed, then a potential state that can be observed in the table would not appear in the conjecture. The second condition is that the table must be *consistent*, i.e., for each $s, t \in S_M$ such that $s \cong_{E_M} t$, it holds that $s \cdot i \cong_{E_M} t \cdot i$, for all $i \in I$. If the table is not consistent then two seemingly equivalent states in the conjecture may point to different target states for the same input.

When the observation table (S_M, E_M, T_M) is closed and consistent, then a Mealy machine conjecture can be constructed as follows:

Definition 2. *Let (S_M, E_M, T_M) be a closed and consistent observation table, then the Mealy machine conjecture $M_M = (Q_M, I, O, \delta_M, \lambda_M, q_{0M})$ is defined, where*

- $Q_M = \{[s] | s \in S_M\}$
- $q_{0M} = [\epsilon]$
- $\delta_M([s], i) = [s \cdot i], \forall s \in S_M, i \in I$
- $\lambda_M([s], i) = T_M(s, i), \forall i \in I$

To see that M_M is well defined, note that S_M is a non-empty prefix-closed set and it contains at least one row ϵ, hence Q_M and q_{0M} are well-defined. For all $s, t \in S_M$ such that $s \cong_{E_M} t$, we have $[s] = [t]$. Since the table is consistent, for all $i \in I$, $[s \cdot i] = [t \cdot i]$ holds. Since the table is closed, there exists $u \in S_M$ such that $[u] = [s \cdot i] = [t \cdot i]$ holds. Hence δ_M is well defined. Since E_M is non-empty and $E_M \supseteq I$ always hold. If there exists $s, t \in S_M$ such that $s \cong_{E_M} t$, then for all $i \in I$, $T_M(s, i) = T_M(t, i)$. Hence, λ_M is well defined.

Theorem 1. *If (S_M, E_M, T_M) is a closed and consistent observation table, then the Mealy machine conjecture M_M from (S_M, E_M, T_M) is consistent with the finite function T_M. That is, for every $s \in S_M \cup S_M \cdot I$ and $e \in E_M$, $\lambda_M(\delta_M(q_{0M}, s), e) = T_M(s, e)$. Any other Mealy machine consistent with T_M but inequivalent to M_M must have more states.*

Theorem 1 claims the correctness of the conjecture. Niese [7] has given a formal proof of the correctness, which is a simple adaptation of the proofs in Angluin's algorithm, in which the range of the output function is replaced by O^+. Note that the conjecture is proved to be consistent with the observation table by exhibiting the prefix-closed and suffix-closed properties of S_M and E_M respectively. Moreover, the conjecture is the minimum machine by construction.

4.2 The Algorithm $L_M{}^*$

The algorithm $L_M{}^*$ starts by initializing (S_M, E_M, T_M) with $S_M = \{\epsilon\}$ and $E_M = I$. To determine T_M, it asks output queries constructed from the table. For each $s \in S_M \cup S_M \cdot I$ and $e \in E_M$, a query is constructed as $s \cdot e$. The corresponding output string of the machine, i.e., $\lambda_{\mathcal{M}}(q_{0\mathcal{M}}, s \cdot e)$, is recorded with the help of the function T_M. Note that the table is prefix-closed which means that $\lambda_{\mathcal{M}}(q_{0\mathcal{M}}, s)$ can be derived from the observations already recorded in the table. Therefore, $L_M{}^*$ records only the suffix of the output string of the length of e in the table as $T_M(s, e) = \mathit{suff}^{|e|}(\lambda_{\mathcal{M}}(q_{0\mathcal{M}}, s \cdot e))$.

After filling the table with the result of the queries, $L_M{}^*$ checks if the table is closed and consistent. If it is not closed, then $L_M{}^*$ finds $t \in S_M \cdot I$ such that $t \not\cong_{E_M} s$, for all $s \in S_M$. Then, it moves t to S_M and $T_M(t \cdot i, e)$ is determined for all $i \in I, e \in E_M$ in $S_M \cdot I$. If the table is not consistent, then $L_M{}^*$ finds $s, t \in S_M, e \in E_M$ and $i \in I$ such that $s \cong_{E_M} t$, but $T_M(s \cdot i, e) \neq T_M(t \cdot i, e)$. Then, it adds the string $i \cdot e$ to E_M and extends the table by asking output queries for the missing elements.

When the table is closed and consistent, $L_M{}^*$ makes a Mealy machine conjecture M_M from the table according to Definition 2.

4.3 Example

We illustrate the algorithm $L_M{}^*$ on the Mealy machine $\mathcal{M}$ given in Figure 1. The algorithm initializes (S_M, E_M, T_M) with $S_M = \{\epsilon\}$ and $S_M \cdot I = E_M = \{a, b\}$. Then, it asks the output queries to fill the table, as shown in Table 1. When the table is filled, $L_M{}^*$ checks if it is closed and consistent.

Table 1 is not closed since the row a in $S_M \cdot I$ is not equivalent to any row in S_M. Therefore, $L_M{}^*$ moves the row a to S_M and extends the table accordingly. Then, $L_M{}^*$ asks the output queries for the missing elements of the table. Table 2 shows the resulting observation table.

The new table is closed and consistent, so $L_M{}^*$ makes the conjecture $M_M{}^{(1)} = (Q_{M_M{}^{(1)}}, I, O, \delta_{M_M{}^{(1)}}, \lambda_{M_M{}^{(1)}}, q_{0M_M{}^{(1)}})$ from Table 2. The conjecture $M_M{}^{(1)}$ is shown in Figure 2.

Table 2. Closed and Consistent Observation Table (S_M, E_M, T_M) for learning $\mathcal{M}$ in Figure 1

	a	b
ϵ	x	x
a	y	x
b	x	x
$a \cdot a$	y	x
$a \cdot b$	x	x

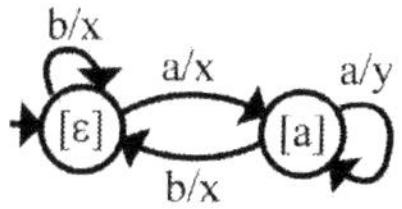

Fig. 2. The conjecture $M_M{}^{(1)}$ from Table 2

Now, $L_M{}^*$ asks an equivalence query to the oracle. Since, the conjecture $M_M{}^{(1)}$ is not correct, the oracle replies with a counterexample. The methods for processing counterexamples are discussed in the following sections. We shall illustrate the methods with the help of the same example. We provide here a counterexample that will be used in their illustrations.

Let $a \cdot b \cdot a \cdot b \cdot b \cdot a \cdot a$ be a counterexample for $M_M{}^{(1)}$, since

- $\lambda_{M_M{}^{(1)}}(q_{0M_M{}^{(1)}}, a \cdot b \cdot a \cdot b \cdot b \cdot a \cdot a) = x \cdot x \cdot x \cdot x \cdot x \cdot x \cdot y$ and
- $\lambda_{\mathcal{M}}(q_{0\mathcal{M}}, a \cdot b \cdot a \cdot b \cdot b \cdot a \cdot a) = x \cdot x \cdot x \cdot x \cdot x \cdot x \cdot x$.

We choose a long counterexample to better illustrate the methods and to realize how they work when the counterexamples of arbitrary lengths are provided. In practice[1], it is not sure whether we obtain always the shortest counterexample.

4.4 Processing Counterexamples in $L_M{}^*$

Angluin's algorithm L^* provides a method for processing a counterexample in the observation table, so that the conjecture is refined with at least one more state. For the algorithm $L_M{}^*$, we can adapt Angluin's method straightforwardly. The adapted method is described as follows.

Directly Adapted Method from L^*. Let $M_M = (Q_M, I, O, \delta_M, \lambda_M, q_{0M})$ be the conjecture from a closed and consistent observation table (S_M, E_M, T_M) for learning the machine $\mathcal{M}$. Let ν be a string from I^+ as a counterexample such that $\lambda_M(q_{0M}, \nu) \neq \lambda_{\mathcal{M}}(q_{0\mathcal{M}}, \nu)$. Then, $L_M{}^*$ adds all the prefixes of ν to S_M and extends (S_M, E_M, T_M) accordingly. The algorithm makes another run of output queries until (S_M, E_M, T_M) is closed and consistent, followed by making a new conjecture.

4.5 Complexity

We analyze the total number of output queries asked by $L_M{}^*$ in the worst case by the factors $|I|$, i.e., the size of I, n, i.e., the number of states of the minimum

[1] There are many frameworks that have been proposed to replace the oracle in Angluin's settings. The interested reader is referred to the works [12] [4] [13] for the comprehensive discussions on the limits of learning without oracles.

Table 3. The Observation Tables (S_M, E_M, T_M) for processing the counterexample $a \cdot b \cdot a \cdot b \cdot b \cdot a \cdot a$ for $M_M{}^{(1)}$ using the adapted method from L^*. The boxes in the tables show the rows which make the tables inconsistent.

	a	b
[ϵ]	x	x
a	y	x
[$a \cdot b$]	x	x
$a \cdot b \cdot a$	x	x
$a \cdot b \cdot a \cdot b$	x	x
$a \cdot b \cdot a \cdot b \cdot b$	x	x
$a \cdot b \cdot a \cdot b \cdot b \cdot a$	x	x
$a \cdot b \cdot a \cdot b \cdot b \cdot a \cdot a$	y	x
b	x	x
$a \cdot a$	y	x
$a \cdot b \cdot b$	x	x
$a \cdot b \cdot a \cdot a$	x	x
$a \cdot b \cdot a \cdot b \cdot a$	y	x
$a \cdot b \cdot a \cdot b \cdot b \cdot b$	x	x
$a \cdot b \cdot a \cdot b \cdot b \cdot a \cdot b$	x	x
$a \cdot b \cdot a \cdot b \cdot b \cdot a \cdot a \cdot a$	y	x
$a \cdot b \cdot a \cdot b \cdot b \cdot a \cdot a \cdot b$	x	x

(i) Adding the prefixes of $a \cdot b \cdot a \cdot b \cdot b \cdot a \cdot a$ to S_M

	a	b	$a \cdot a$
ϵ	x	x	$x \cdot y$
a	y	x	$y \cdot y$
[$a \cdot b$]	x	x	$x \cdot x$
[$a \cdot b \cdot a$]	x	x	$x \cdot x$
$a \cdot b \cdot a \cdot b$	x	x	$x \cdot y$
$a \cdot b \cdot a \cdot b \cdot b$	x	x	$x \cdot x$
$a \cdot b \cdot a \cdot b \cdot b \cdot a$	x	x	$x \cdot y$
$a \cdot b \cdot a \cdot b \cdot b \cdot a \cdot a$	y	x	$y \cdot y$
b	x	x	$x \cdot x$
$a \cdot a$	y	x	$y \cdot y$
$a \cdot b \cdot b$	x	x	$x \cdot x$
$a \cdot b \cdot a \cdot a$	x	x	$x \cdot y$
$a \cdot b \cdot a \cdot b \cdot a$	y	x	$y \cdot y$
$a \cdot b \cdot a \cdot b \cdot b \cdot b$	x	x	$x \cdot y$
$a \cdot b \cdot a \cdot b \cdot b \cdot a \cdot b$	x	x	$x \cdot x$
$a \cdot b \cdot a \cdot b \cdot b \cdot a \cdot a \cdot a$	y	x	$y \cdot y$
$a \cdot b \cdot a \cdot b \cdot b \cdot a \cdot a \cdot b$	x	x	$x \cdot x$

(ii) Adding $a \cdot a$ to E_M

	a	b	$a \cdot a$	$a \cdot a \cdot a$	$b \cdot a \cdot a$
ϵ	x	x	$x \cdot y$	$x \cdot y \cdot y$	$x \cdot x \cdot x$
a	y	x	$y \cdot y$	$y \cdot y \cdot y$	$x \cdot x \cdot x$
$a \cdot b$	x	x	$x \cdot x$	$x \cdot x \cdot x$	$x \cdot x \cdot x$
$a \cdot b \cdot a$	x	x	$x \cdot x$	$x \cdot x \cdot y$	$x \cdot x \cdot y$
$a \cdot b \cdot a \cdot b$	x	x	$x \cdot y$	$x \cdot y \cdot y$	$x \cdot x \cdot x$
$a \cdot b \cdot a \cdot b \cdot b$	x	x	$x \cdot x$	$x \cdot x \cdot y$	$x \cdot x \cdot y$
$a \cdot b \cdot a \cdot b \cdot b \cdot a$	x	x	$x \cdot y$	$x \cdot y \cdot y$	$x \cdot x \cdot x$
$a \cdot b \cdot a \cdot b \cdot b \cdot a \cdot a$	y	x	$y \cdot y$	$y \cdot y \cdot y$	$x \cdot x \cdot x$
b	x	x	$x \cdot x$	$x \cdot x \cdot y$	$x \cdot x \cdot y$
$a \cdot a$	y	x	$y \cdot y$	$y \cdot y \cdot y$	$x \cdot x \cdot x$
$a \cdot b \cdot b$	x	x	$x \cdot x$	$x \cdot x \cdot y$	$x \cdot x \cdot y$
$a \cdot b \cdot a \cdot a$	x	x	$x \cdot y$	$x \cdot y \cdot y$	$x \cdot x \cdot x$
$a \cdot b \cdot a \cdot b \cdot a$	y	x	$y \cdot y$	$y \cdot y \cdot y$	$x \cdot x \cdot x$
$a \cdot b \cdot a \cdot b \cdot b \cdot b$	x	x	$x \cdot y$	$x \cdot y \cdot y$	$x \cdot x \cdot x$
$a \cdot b \cdot a \cdot b \cdot b \cdot a \cdot b$	x	x	$x \cdot x$	$x \cdot x \cdot y$	$x \cdot x \cdot y$
$a \cdot b \cdot a \cdot b \cdot b \cdot a \cdot a \cdot a$	y	x	$y \cdot y$	$y \cdot y \cdot y$	$x \cdot x \cdot x$
$a \cdot b \cdot a \cdot b \cdot b \cdot a \cdot a \cdot b$	x	x	$x \cdot x$	$x \cdot x \cdot x$	$x \cdot x \cdot x$

(iii) Adding $a \cdot a \cdot a$ and $b \cdot a \cdot a$ to E_M

machine $\mathcal{M}$ and m, i.e., the maximum length of any counterexample provided for learning $\mathcal{M}$.

Initially, S_M contains one element. Each time (S_M, E_M, T_M) is found not closed, one element is added to S_M. This introduces a new row to S_M, so a new state in the conjecture. This can happen for at most $n-1$ times. For each counterexample of length at most m, there can be at most m strings that are added to S_M, and there can be at most $n-1$ counterexamples to distinguish n states. Thus, the size of S_M cannot exceed $n + m(n-1)$.

Initially, E_M contains $|I|$ elements. Each time (S_M, E_M, T_M) is found not consistent, one element is added to E_M. This can happen for at most $n-1$ times to distinguish n states. Thus, the size of E_M cannot exceed $|I| + n - 1$.

Thus, $L_M{}^*$ produces a correct conjecture by asking maximum $(S_M \cup S_M \cdot I) \times E_M = O(|I|^2nm + |I|mn^2)$ output queries.

4.6 Example

For the conjecture $M_M{}^{(1)}$ in Figure 2 for learning the Mealy machine $\mathcal{M}$ in Figure 1, we have a counterexample as $\nu = a \cdot b \cdot a \cdot b \cdot b \cdot a \cdot a$. According to the adapted method for processing counterexample, $L_M{}^*$ adds all the prefixes of ν, i.e., a, $a \cdot b$, $a \cdot b \cdot a$, $a \cdot b \cdot a \cdot b$, $a \cdot b \cdot a \cdot b \cdot b$, $a \cdot b \cdot a \cdot b \cdot b \cdot a$, and $a \cdot b \cdot a \cdot b \cdot b \cdot a \cdot a$ to S_M and extends $S_M \cdot I$ accordingly. The table is then filled with the missing elements by asking output queries. Table 3 (i) shows the resulting observation table. Then, $L_M{}^*$ checks if the table is closed and consistent.

Table 3 (i) is closed but not consistent since $\epsilon \cong_{E_M} a \cdot b$, but $T_M(\epsilon \cdot a, a) \neq T_M(a \cdot b \cdot a, a)$. To make the table consistent, the string $a \cdot a$ is added to E_M and the table is filled accordingly. Table 3 (ii) shows the resulting observation table, in which the rows ϵ and $a \cdot b$ have become different. Now, $L_M{}^*$ checks if Table 3 (ii) is closed and consistent.

Table 3 (ii) is closed but not consistent since $a \cdot b \cong_{E_M} a \cdot b \cdot a$ but $T_M(a \cdot b \cdot a, a \cdot a) \neq T_M(a \cdot b \cdot a \cdot a, a \cdot a)$. To make the table consistent, the string $a \cdot a \cdot a$

is added to E_M. For the same rows, the other reason for inconsistency is due to $T_M(a \cdot b \cdot b, a \cdot a) \neq T_M(a \cdot b \cdot a \cdot b, a \cdot a)$. Therefore, the string $b \cdot a \cdot a$ is also added to E_M and the table is filled accordingly. Table 3 (iii) shows the resulting observation table, in which the rows $a \cdot b$ and $a \cdot b \cdot a$ have become different.

Table 3 (iii) is closed and consistent, and thus ${L_M}^*$ terminates by making a conjecture isomorphic to $\mathcal{M}$. The total number of output queries asked by ${L_M}^*$ is 85.

5 Improvements to Mealy Machine Inference

We propose improvements to the algorithm of learning Mealy machines by providing a new method for processing counterexamples in the observation table (S_M, E_M, T_M). The complexity calculations and the experimental results of our proposal show a significant reduction in the output queries that the algorithm asks during the learning procedure. We denote the algorithm with the improved method for processing counterexamples by ${L_M}^+$. In this section, we describe the idea of our improvements and the complete algorithm with its complexity, correctness and example illustration.

5.1 Motivation

Rivest & Schapire [14] observed that the basic Angluin's algorithm L^* can be improved by removing consistency check of the observation table. Consistency is checked only when two rows in the upper part of the table are found equivalent. That means, if the rows of the table remain inequivalent, then inconsistency will never occur and the condition will always hold trivially. They observed that the rows become equivalent in the table due to the improper handling of counterexamples. A counterexample is an experiment that distinguishes two or more equivalent rows (or states) in the table and thereby causes an increase in the size of the column. However, L^* does not follow this scheme directly, rather it adds a new row for each prefix of the counterexample in the table, assuming that all are potential states of the conjecture. Later, the rows are filled with the help of membership queries (no new column is added yet). This is where an inconsistency can occur in the table if the two rows become equivalent but their future behaviors are not equivalent. Thus, the two rows must be distinguished by adding a distinguishing sequence as a column in the table.

Rivest & Schapire proposed a method for processing counterexamples, which does not add the prefixes in the table. Thus, the rows remain inequivalent during the whole learning process. Their method consists in finding a distinguishing sequence from the counterexample and directly add the sequence in the columns. However, their method requires a relaxation on the prefix-closed and suffix-closed properties of the table, which are in fact the vital properties for having a consistent conjecture from the table [1]. If the table does not have such properties then the new conjecture might not be consistent with the table, and therefore, might still classify the previous counterexamples incorrectly. Balcazar et al. [15]

argued that by using the method of Rivest & Schapire, one can obtain the same counterexample to answer several equivalence queries in L^*. In addition, Berg & Raffelt [16] compiled the results from Balcazar et al. [15] and explained the complete method of Rivest & Schapire.

Our improvement in the algorithm for learning Mealy machines is inspired by Rivest & Schapire's idea. We also suggest to keep only inequivalent rows in S_M so that inconsistencies can never occur. However, we propose a new method for processing counterexamples such that it does not import the same problem as in the case of Rivest & Schapire. Our method for processing counterexample keeps (S_M, E_M, T_M) prefix-closed and suffix-closed, and therefore, the new conjecture is always consistent with the observations in (S_M, E_M, T_M), according to Theorem 1.

5.2 The Algorithm ${L_M}^+$

In the algorithm ${L_M}^+$, the definition of the observation table (S_M, E_M, T_M), described in Section 4.1, and the basic flow of the algorithm, described in Section 4.2, remain unchanged. However, the additional property of (S_M, E_M, T_M) is that all the rows in S_M are inequivalent, i.e., for all $s, t \in S_M$, $s \not\cong_{E_M} t$. This means ${L_M}^+$ does not need to check for consistency because it always trivially holds. However, ${L_M}^+$ processes counterexamples according to the new method, which is described in the following.

5.3 Processing Counterexamples in ${L_M}^+$

Let $M_M = (Q_M, I, O, \delta_M, \lambda_M, q_{0M})$ be the conjecture from the closed (and consistent) observation table (S_M, E_M, T_M) for learning the machine $\mathcal{M}$. Let ν be a string from I^+ as a counterexample such that $\lambda_M(q_{0M}, \nu) \neq \lambda_{\mathcal{M}}(q_{0\mathcal{M}}, \nu)$. The main objective of a counterexample is to distinguish the conjecture from the unknown machine. That means, the counterexample must contain a distinguishing sequence to distinguish at least two seemingly equivalent states of the conjecture; so that when applying the distinguishing sequence on these states, they become different.

In our method of processing counterexample, we look for the distinguishing sequence in the counterexample and add the sequence directly to E_M. Then, the two seemingly equivalent rows[2] in S_M become different. For this purpose, we divide ν into its appropriate prefix and suffix such that the suffix contains the distinguishing sequence. The division occurs in the following way.

We divide ν by looking at its longest prefix in $S_M \cup S_M \cdot I$ and take the remaining string as the suffix. Let $\nu = u \cdot v$ such that $u \in S_M \cup S_M \cdot I$. If there exists $u' \in S_M \cup S_M \cdot I$ another prefix of ν then $|u| > |u'|$, i.e., u is the longest prefix of ν in $S_M \cup S_M \cdot I$. The idea of selecting u from the observation table is that u is the access string that is already known such that $\lambda_M(q_{0M}, u) = \lambda_{\mathcal{M}}(q_{0\mathcal{M}}, u)$. The fact that ν is a counterexample then $\lambda_M(q_{0M}, u \cdot v) \neq \lambda_{\mathcal{M}}(q_{0\mathcal{M}}, u \cdot v)$ must

[2] Recall that the rows in S_M represent the states of the conjecture.

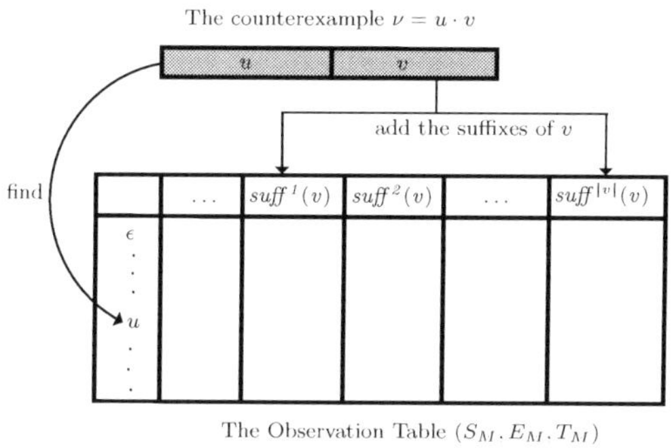

Fig. 3. Conceptual view of the method for processing counterexamples in $L_M{}^+$

hold. That means, v contains the distinguishing sequence to distinguish two rows in S_M. So, it is sufficient to add v to E_M. In fact, we add all the suffixes of v such that E_M remains suffix-closed.

Figure 3 provides a conceptual view of the method for processing a counterexample ν. It shows that ν is divided into the prefix u and the suffix v, such that $u \in S_M \cup S_M \cdot I$. Then, ν is processed by adding all the suffixes of v to E_M. The correctness proof of the method is given in the following section.

5.4 Correctness

Let $M_M = (Q_M, I, O, \delta_M, \lambda_M, q_{0M})$ be the conjecture from the closed (and consistent) observation table (S_M, E_M, T_M). Let $\nu = u \cdot i \cdot v$ be the counterexample for M_M such that $\lambda_M(q_{0M}, u \cdot i \cdot v) \neq \lambda_{\mathcal{M}}(q_{0\mathcal{M}}, u \cdot i \cdot v)$. Let $u \cdot i$ be the longest prefix of ν in $S_M \cup S_M \cdot I$ and v be the corresponding suffix of ν. If ν is a counterexample then it must distinguish $[u \cdot i]$ from a seemingly equivalent state, i.e., $\lambda_{\mathcal{M}}(q_{0\mathcal{M}}, u \cdot i \cdot v) \neq \lambda_{\mathcal{M}}(q_{0\mathcal{M}}, t \cdot v)$, for some $t \in S_M$ such that $[t] = [u \cdot i]$. Thus, v contains a distinguishing sequence for the rows $u \cdot i$ and t.

Suppose we process ν in (S_M, E_M, T_M) by adding all the suffixes of v to E_M. Let us name the table as (S'_M, E'_M, T'_M) after this addition. Later, we ask output queries to fill the missing elements of the table (S'_M, E'_M, T'_M). Then, E'_M contains the distinguishing sequence that distinguishes the rows t and $u \cdot i$ in (S'_M, E'_M, T'_M). That is, there must exist some experiment $e \in E'_M$ such that $T'_M(t, e) \neq T'_M(u \cdot i, e)$. This implies that $u \cdot i \not\cong_{E'_M} t$. In fact, $u \cdot i \in S'_M \cdot I$, since $t \in S'_M$ and there cannot be two equivalent rows in S'_M. If $u \cdot i \in S'_M \cdot I$ then trivially $u \in S'_M$. Moreover, in the table (S_M, E_M, T_M), if $u \cdot i \not\cong_{E_M} s$, for $s \in S_M$, then in the extended table (S'_M, E'_M, T'_M), $u \cdot i \not\cong_{E'_M} s$ also holds, for $s \in S'_M$. Therefore, $u \cdot i$ is a row in (S'_M, E'_M, T'_M) that is inequivalent to any row in S'_M. This makes the table not closed. Thus, making the table closed will move $u \cdot i$ to S'_M. Since, u is already in S'_M, this operation keeps (S'_M, E'_M, T'_M) prefix-closed. Since, S'_M is extended by one row, the new conjecture M'_M from the closed (S'_M, E'_M, T'_M) will contain at least one more state than M_M.

It is simple to check whether (S'_M, E'_M, T'_M) is suffix-closed, since E'_M is extended from E_M, which is suffix-closed, and E'_M contains the suffixes of v. Thus, (S'_M, E'_M, T'_M) is suffix-closed.

This proves the correctness of the method, since (S'_M, E'_M, T'_M) is a closed (and consistent) observation table that is prefix-closed and suffix-closed and contains the prefix $u \cdot i$ and the suffix v of the counterexample ν. Therefore, the conjecture M'_M from (S'_M, E'_M, T'_M) will be consistent with the function T'_M (Theorem 1) that will find at least one more state. □

Theorem 2. *Let (S_M, E_M, T_M) be a closed (and consistent) observation table and M_M be the conjecture from (S_M, E_M, T_M). Let $\nu = u \cdot i \cdot v$ be the counterexample for M_M, where $u \cdot i$ is in $S_M \cup S_M \cdot I$. Let the table be extended as (S'_M, E'_M, T'_M) by adding all the suffixes of v to E_M, then the closed (and consistent) observation table (S'_M, E'_M, T'_M) is prefix-closed and suffix-closed. The conjecture M'_M from (S'_M, E'_M, T'_M) will be consistent with T'_M and must have at least one more state than M_M.*

5.5 Complexity

We analyze the total number of output queries asked by ${L_M}^+$ in the worst case by the factors $|I|$, i.e., the size of I, n, i.e., the number of states of the minimum machine $\mathcal{M}$ and m, i.e., the maximum length of any counterexample provided for learning $\mathcal{M}$.

The size of S_M increases monotonically up to the limit of n as the algorithm runs. The only operation that extends S_M is making the table *closed*. Every time (S_M, E_M, T_M) is not closed, one element is added to S_M. This introduces a new row to S_M, so a new state in the conjecture. This can happen at most $n-1$ times, since it keeps one element initially. Hence, the size of S_M is at most n.

E_M contains $|I|$ elements initially. If a counterexample is provided then at most m suffixes are added to E_M. There can be provided at most $n-1$ counterexamples to distinguish n states, thus the maximum size of E_M cannot exceed $|I| + m(n-1)$.

Thus, ${L_M}^+$ produces a correct conjecture by asking maximum $(S_M \cup S_M \cdot I) \times E_M = O(|I|^2 n + |I| m n^2)$ output queries.

5.6 Example

We illustrate the algorithm ${L_M}^+$ on the Mealy machine $\mathcal{M}$ given in Figure 1. Since, ${L_M}^+$ is only different from ${L_M}^*$ with respect to the method for processing counterexamples, the initial run of ${L_M}^+$ is same as described in Section 4.3. So, ${L_M}^+$ finds a closed (and consistent) table as Table 2 and draws the conjecture ${M_M}^{(1)}$, shown in Figure 2, from Table 2. Here, we illustrate how ${L_M}^+$ processes counterexamples to refine the conjecture.

For the conjecture ${M_M}^{(1)}$, we have a counterexample as $\nu = a \cdot b \cdot a \cdot b \cdot b \cdot a \cdot a$. According to the improved method for processing counterexample, ${L_M}^+$ finds the longest prefix u of the counterexample in $S_M \cup S_M \cdot I$ in Table 2. The prefix

Table 4. The Observation Tables (S_M, E_M, T_M) for processing the counterexample $a \cdot b \cdot a \cdot b \cdot b \cdot a \cdot a$ for ${M_M}^{(1)}$ using the improved method. The boxes in the tables show the rows which make the tables not closed.

	a	b	$a \cdot a$	$b \cdot a \cdot a$	$b \cdot b \cdot a \cdot a$	$a \cdot b \cdot b \cdot a \cdot a$
ϵ	x	x	$x \cdot y$	$x \cdot x \cdot x$	$x \cdot x \cdot x \cdot y$	$x \cdot x \cdot x \cdot x \cdot x$
a	y	x	$y \cdot y$	$x \cdot x \cdot x$	$x \cdot x \cdot x \cdot x$	$y \cdot x \cdot x \cdot x \cdot x$
$\boxed{b}$	x	x	$x \cdot x$	$x \cdot x \cdot y$	$x \cdot x \cdot x \cdot x$	$x \cdot x \cdot x \cdot x \cdot y$
$a \cdot a$	y	x	$y \cdot y$	$x \cdot x \cdot x$	$x \cdot x \cdot x \cdot x$	$y \cdot x \cdot x \cdot x \cdot x$
$\boxed{a \cdot b}$	x	x	$x \cdot x$	$x \cdot x \cdot x$	$x \cdot x \cdot x \cdot y$	$x \cdot x \cdot x \cdot x \cdot x$

(i) Adding the suffixes of $a \cdot b \cdot b \cdot a \cdot a$ to E_M

	a	b	$a \cdot a$	$b \cdot a \cdot a$	$b \cdot b \cdot a \cdot a$	$a \cdot b \cdot b \cdot a \cdot a$
ϵ	x	x	$x \cdot y$	$x \cdot x \cdot x$	$x \cdot x \cdot x \cdot y$	$x \cdot x \cdot x \cdot x \cdot x$
a	y	x	$y \cdot y$	$x \cdot x \cdot x$	$x \cdot x \cdot x \cdot x$	$y \cdot x \cdot x \cdot x \cdot x$
b	x	x	$x \cdot x$	$x \cdot x \cdot y$	$x \cdot x \cdot x \cdot x$	$x \cdot x \cdot x \cdot x \cdot y$
$a \cdot b$	x	x	$x \cdot x$	$x \cdot x \cdot x$	$x \cdot x \cdot x \cdot y$	$x \cdot x \cdot x \cdot x \cdot x$
$a \cdot a$	y	x	$y \cdot y$	$x \cdot x \cdot x$	$x \cdot x \cdot x \cdot x$	$y \cdot x \cdot x \cdot x \cdot x$
$b \cdot a$	x	x	$x \cdot y$	$x \cdot x \cdot x$	$x \cdot x \cdot x \cdot y$	$x \cdot x \cdot x \cdot x \cdot x$
$b \cdot b$	x	x	$x \cdot y$	$x \cdot x \cdot x$	$x \cdot x \cdot x \cdot y$	$x \cdot x \cdot x \cdot x \cdot x$
$a \cdot b \cdot a$	x	x	$x \cdot x$	$x \cdot x \cdot y$	$x \cdot x \cdot x \cdot x$	$x \cdot x \cdot x \cdot x \cdot y$
$a \cdot b \cdot b$	x	x	$x \cdot x$	$x \cdot x \cdot y$	$x \cdot x \cdot x \cdot x$	$x \cdot x \cdot x \cdot x \cdot y$

(ii) Moving the rows b and $a \cdot b$ to S_M

$u = a \cdot b$ is the longest prefix found, so the remaining suffix is $v = a \cdot b \cdot b \cdot a \cdot a$. The algorithm adds all the suffixes of v, i.e., a, $a \cdot a$, $b \cdot a \cdot a$, $b \cdot b \cdot a \cdot a$ and $a \cdot b \cdot b \cdot a \cdot a$ to E_M. The table is filled by asking output queries for the missing elements. Table 4 (i) is the resulting observation table. Then, ${L_M}^+$ checks if the table is closed.

Table 4 (i) is not closed since the rows b and $a \cdot b$ are not equivalent to any rows in S_M. Hence, the rows b and $a \cdot b$ are moved to S_M and the table is extended accordingly. The table is filled by asking output queries for the missing elements. Table 4 (ii) is the resulting observation table. Now, ${L_M}^+$ checks whether Table 4 (ii) is closed.

Table 4 (ii) is closed, and thus ${L_M}^+$ terminates by making a conjecture isomorphic to $\mathcal{M}$. The total number of output queries asked by ${L_M}^+$ is 54.

6 Experimentation

We have performed an experimental evaluation to compare the adaptation of Angluin's algorithm for learning Mealy machines ${L_M}^*$ with our improved algorithm ${L_M}^+$. The worst case theoretical complexity analysis has shown that ${L_M}^+$ outperforms ${L_M}^*$ in terms of number of output queries. It is interesting to evaluate the average case complexity of the algorithms when the input sets, the number of states and the length of counterexamples are of arbitrary sizes.

The examples in the experiments are the synthetic finite state models of real world systems (e.g., Vending machine, ATM and ABP protocols, Mailing Systems etc) that are shipped with *Edinburgh Concurrency Workbench (CWB)* [17]. CWB is a tool for manipulating, analyzing and verifying concurrent systems. The examples in the workbench have also been used to investigate the applicability of Angluin's algorithm in learning reactive systems [18]. These examples were originally modeled as Non-Deterministic Finite Automata (NFA), with partial transition relations, in which every state is a final state. Therefore, we have transferred first each example to its corresponding DFA. The resulting DFA contains every state as final, plus one non-final (sink) state which loops itself for all inputs.

All inputs from a state that are invalid (missing transitions in the original NFA) are directed to the sink state. Then, we learn the Mealy machines models of the CWB examples using both algorithms one by one. We have also simulated an oracle so that the algorithms could ask equivalence queries for conjectures until they find correct models. The oracle obtains a counterexample by calculating a symmetric difference between the original example and the provided conjecture.

The number of output queries asked by the algorithms are given in Table 5. The first column labels the example. The second column shows the size of the input set I. The third column shows the minimum number of states in the example when modeled as DFA and Mealy machines. The fourth and fifth columns show the number of output queries asked by $L_M{}^*$ and $L_M{}^+$, respectively. The last column shows the reduction factor in queries asked by $L_M{}^+$ against $L_M{}^*$, i.e., $\frac{no.\ of\ output\ queries\ in\ L_M{}^*}{no.\ of\ output\ queries\ in\ L_M{}^+} - 1$.

Table 5. Comparison of $L_M{}^*$ with $L_M{}^+$ on the examples of CWB workbench. The examples are listed in ascending order with respect to the number of states.

Examples	$\|I\|$	No. of States	No. of Output Queries		Reduction Factor
		DFA / Mealy (min)	$L_M{}^*$	$L_M{}^+$	
ABP-Lossy	3	11	754	340	1.22
Peterson2	3	11	910	374	1.43
Small	5	11	462	392	0.18
VM	5	11	836	392	1.13
Buff3	3	12	580	259	1.24
Shed2	6	13	824	790	0.04
ABP-Safe	3	19	2336	754	2.1
TMR1	5	19	1396	1728	-0.2
VMnew	4	29	2595	1404	0.85
CSPROT	5	44	4864	3094	0.57

The experiments have been conducted on 10 CWB examples. All examples are of different sizes in terms of number of states and input set size. The results show that $L_M{}^+$ outperformed $L_M{}^*$ in almost all the examples. The greatest reduction factor achieved is 2.1 on the example *ABP-Safe*. However, there is only one example *TMR1* in which $L_M{}^+$ has performed negatively. This is because the implementation of our oracle provides arbitrary counterexamples that could influence the number of output queries in few cases.

Apart from the CWB workbench, we have also experimented on arbitrary random Mealy machines. We generated a set of 1500 machines with sizes ranging between 1 and 500 states and input size up to 15. The average reduction factor we achieved on this set is 1.32. We also studied the query complexity with respect to the relation of input size with the number of states. Up to 1250 machines were generated with larger inputs and relatively fewer states. We achieved the best result on this set with the average reduction factor of 1.66.

As we know from our worst case complexity analysis, $L_M{}^+$ performs better than $L_M{}^*$. We have experimentally confirmed the difference in complexity of the two algorithms on the finite state machine workbench, as well as on a large set of arbitrary random Mealy machines.

7 Conclusion and Perspectives

We have presented two algorithms for inferring Mealy machines, namely ${L_M}^*$ and ${L_M}^+$. The algorithm ${L_M}^*$ is a straightforward adaptation from the algorithm L^*. The algorithm ${L_M}^+$ is our proposal that contains a new method for processing counterexamples. The complexity calculations of the two algorithms shows that ${L_M}^+$ has a gain on the number of output queries over ${L_M}^*$.

The crux of the complexity comparison comes from the fact that when we deal with real systems, they work on huge data sets as their possible inputs. When these systems are learned, the size of the input set I becomes large enough to cripple the learning procedure. In most cases, $|I|$ is a dominant factor over the number of the states n. Therefore, when we look on the parts of the complexity calculations which exhibit a difference, i.e., $|I|^2nm$ for ${L_M}^*$ and $|I|^2n$ for ${L_M}^+$, then it is obvious that ${L_M}^+$ has a clear gain over ${L_M}^*$ as $|I|$ grows[3].

Another aspect of the complexity gain of ${L_M}^+$ comes from the fact that it is not easy to obtain always "smart" counterexamples that are short and yet can find the difference between the black box machine and the conjecture. Normally, we obtain counterexamples of arbitrary lengths in practice (without assuming a perfect oracle). They are usually long input strings that run over the same states of the black box machine many times to exhibit the difference. When ${L_M}^*$ processes such counterexamples in the observation table by adding all the prefixes of the counterexample to S_M, it adds unnecessarily as many states as the length of the counterexample. This follows the extension of the table due to $S_M \cdot I$. However, after filling the table with output queries, it is realized that only few prefixes in S_M are the potential states. On the contrary, the method for processing counterexample in ${L_M}^+$ consists in adding the suffixes of only a part of the counterexample to E_M. Then, ${L_M}^+$ finds the exact rows through output queries which must be the potential states and then moves the rows to S_M (see Section 5.4). So, the length of a counterexample m is less worrisome when applying ${L_M}^+$. As m becomes large, ${L_M}^+$ has more gain over ${L_M}^*$.

From the above discussion, we conclude that ${L_M}^+$ outperforms ${L_M}^*$, notably when the size of the input set I and the length of the counterexamples m are large. We have also confirmed the gain of ${L_M}^+$ over ${L_M}^*$ by experimentation on *CWB* [17] workbench of synthetic finite state models of real world systems, as well as on the random machines, where m, I and n are of different sizes.

The research in the approach of combining learning and testing has remained our major focus in the recent past [13]. We intend to continue our research in these directions to explore the benefits of our approach in disciplines, such as learning other forms of automata and its application on the integrated systems of black box components.

[3] Contrary to CWB examples which are small enough to realize the impact of the input size on the complexity, the experiments with random machines with large input sizes provides a good confidence on the gain.

References

1. Angluin, D.: Learning regular sets from queries and counterexamples. Information and Computation 2, 87–106 (1987)
2. Muccini, H., Polini, A., Ricci, F., Bertolino, A.: Monitoring architectural properties in dynamic component-based systems. In: Schmidt, H.W., Crnković, I., Heineman, G.T., Stafford, J.A. (eds.) CBSE 2007. LNCS, vol. 4608, pp. 124–139. Springer, Heidelberg (2007)
3. Shu, G., Lee, D.: Testing security properties of protocol implementations-a machine learning based approach. In: ICDCS, p. 25. IEEE Computer Society, Los Alamitos (2007)
4. Peled, D., Vardi, M.Y., Yannakakis, M.: Black box checking. In: Proceedings of FORTE 1999, Beijing, China (1999)
5. Hungar, H., Niese, O., Steffen, B.: Domain-specific optimization in automata learning. In: Hunt Jr., W.A., Somenzi, F. (eds.) CAV 2003. LNCS, vol. 2725, pp. 315–327. Springer, Heidelberg (2003)
6. Margaria, T., Niese, O., Raffelt, H., Steffen, B.: Efficient test-based model generation for legacy reactive systems. In: HLDVT, pp. 95–100. IEEE Computer Society, Los Alamitos (2004)
7. Niese, O.: An Integrated Approach to Testing Complex Systems. PhD thesis, University of Dortmund (2003)
8. Mäkinen, E., Systä, T.: MAS - an interactive synthesizer to support behavioral modelling in UML. In: ICSE 2001, pp. 15–24. IEEE Computer Society, Los Alamitos (2001)
9. Berg, T., Grinchtein, O., Jonsson, B., Leucker, M., Raffelt, H., Steffen, B.: On the correspondence between conformance testing and regular inference. In: Cerioli, M. (ed.) FASE 2005. LNCS, vol. 3442, pp. 175–189. Springer, Heidelberg (2005)
10. Li, K., Groz, R., Shahbaz, M.: Integration testing of components guided by incremental state machine learning. In: TAIC PART, pp. 59–70. IEEE Computer Society, Los Alamitos (2006)
11. Pena, J.M., Oliveira, A.L.: A new algorithm for the reduction of incompletely specified finite state machines. In: ICCAD, pp. 482–489. ACM, New York (1998)
12. Frazier, M., Goldman, S., Mishra, N., Pitt, L.: Learning from a consistently ignorant teacher. J. Comput. Syst. Sci. 52(3), 471–492 (1996)
13. Shahbaz, M.: Reverse Engineering Enhanced State Models of Black Box Components to support Integration Testing. PhD thesis, Grenoble Universities (2008)
14. Rivest, R.L., Schapire, R.E.: Inference of finite automata using homing sequences. In: Machine Learning: From Theory to Applications, pp. 51–73 (1993)
15. Balcazar, J.L., Diaz, J., Gavalda, R.: Algorithms for learning finite automata from queries: A unified view. In: AALC, pp. 53–72 (1997)
16. Berg, T., Raffelt, H.: Model checking. In: Broy, M., Jonsson, B., Katoen, J.-P., Leucker, M., Pretschner, A. (eds.) Model-Based Testing of Reactive Systems. LNCS, vol. 3472, pp. 557–603. Springer, Heidelberg (2005)
17. Moller, F., Stevens, P.: Edinburgh Concurrency Workbench User Manual, Version 7.1 (2004), `http://homepages.inf.ed.ac.uk/perdita/cwb/`
18. Berg, T., Jonsson, B., Leucker, M., Saksena, M.: Insights to angluin's learning. Electr. Notes Theor. Comput. Sci. 118, 3–18 (2005)

Formal Management of CAD/CAM Processes*

Michael Kohlhase, Johannes Lemburg, Lutz Schröder, and Ewaryst Schulz

DFKI Bremen, Germany
<firstname>.<lastname>@dfki.de

Abstract. Systematic engineering design processes have many aspects in common with software engineering, with CAD/CAM objects replacing program code as the implementation stage of the development. They are, however, currently considerably less formal. We propose to draw on the mentioned similarities and transfer methods from software engineering to engineering design in order to enhance in particular the reliability and reusability of engineering processes. We lay out a vision of a document-oriented design process that integrates CAD/CAM documents with requirement specifications; as a first step towards supporting such a process, we present a tool that interfaces a CAD system with program verification workflows, thus allowing for completely formalised development strands within a semi-formal methodology.

1 Introduction

Much of our life is shaped by technical artifacts, ranging in terms of intrinsic complexity from ball point pens to autonomous robots. These artifacts are the result of *engineering design processes* that determine their quality, safety, and suitability for their intended purposes and are governed by best practices, norms, and regulations. The systematic development of products is guided by descriptions of problems and their solutions on different levels of abstraction, such as the requirements list, the function structure, the principle solution, and eventually the embodiment design. The elements of these representations are linked by dependencies within and across the different levels of abstraction. The present state of the art in computer-aided design and manufacture of industrial artifacts (CAD/CAM) does not support this cross-linking of dependencies. Consequently, e.g. non-embodied principle solutions are still often shared and stored in the form of hand-made sketches and oral explanations. In other words, large parts of the engineering process are not completely representable in current CAD/CAM systems, which are focused primarily on the embodiment level.

In contrast, software engineers have long acknowledged the need for a formal mathematical representation of the software development process. In particular, formal specification and verification of software and hardware systems are essential in safety-critical or security areas where one cannot take the risk of failure. Formal method success stories include the verification of the Pentium IV arithmetic, the Traffic Collision Avoidance System TCAS, and various security protocols. In many cases, only the use of

* Work performed as part of the project FormalSafe funded by the German Federal Ministry of Education and Research (FKZ 01IW07002).

A. Cavalcanti and D. Dams (Eds.): FM 2009, LNCS 5850, pp. 223–238, 2009.

logic-based techniques has been able to reveal serious bugs in software and hardware systems; in other cases, spectacular and costly failures such as the loss of the Mars Climate Orbiter could have been avoided by formal techniques. Norms such as IEC 61508 make the use of formal methods mandatory for software of the highest safety integrity level (SIL 3). Thus, formal methods will form an integral part of any systematic methodology for safe system design.

The main goal of the present work is to outline how formal methods, hitherto used predominantly in areas such as software development and circuit design that are inherently dominated by logic-oriented thinking anyway, can be transferred to the domain of CAD/CAM, which is more closely tied to the physical world. In particular, we wish to tie formal specification documents in with a semi-formal engineering design process. Potential benefits for the CAD/CAM process include

- formal verification of physical properties of the objects designed
- tracing of (formalized) requirements across the development process
- improved control over the coherence of designs
- semantically founded change management.

We lay out this vision in some more detail, relating it to an extended discussion of current best practice in engineering design (Section 2), before we proceed to report a first step towards enabling the use of formal methods in engineering design: we describe a tool that extracts formal descriptions of geometric objects from CAD/CAM designs (Section 3). Specifically, the tool exports designs in the CAD/CAM system SolidWorks into a syntactic representation in the wide-spectrum language HasCasl [12], thereby making the connection to a formal semantics of CAD/CAM objects in terms of standard three-dimensional affine geometry as defined in a corresponding specification library. We apply the tool in a case study (Section 4) involving a toy but pioneering example where we prove that a simple CAD drawing implements an abstractly described geometric object, using the semi-automatic theorem prover Isabelle/HOL, interaction with which is via logic translations implemented in the Bremen heterogeneous tool set Hets [9].

2 A Document-Oriented Process for CAD/CAM

Best practices for designing technical artifacts are typically standardised by professional societies. In our exposition here, we will follow the German VDI 2221 [14], which postulates that the design process proceeds in well-defined phases, in which an initial idea is refined step-by-step to a fully specified product documentation. We observe that the process is similar to the software engineering process and that the stages in the design process result in specification documents, as they are e.g. found in the V-model

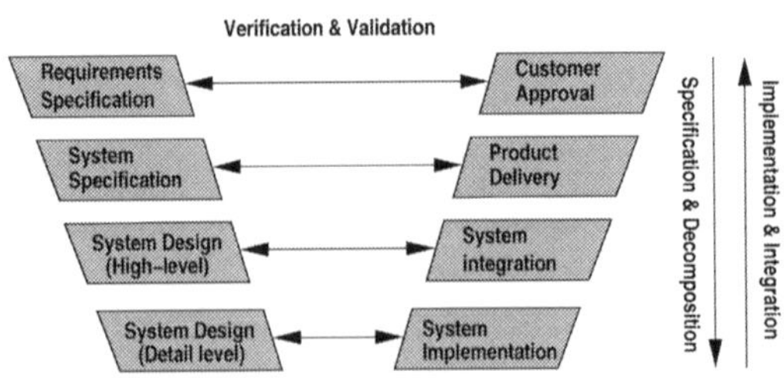

Fig. 1. The V-model of Software Engineering

(see Fig. 1). In contrast to software engineering approaches like the V-model, however, VDI 2221 (and actual current practice in engineering design) does not provide a mechanism to ensure consistency between the design stages, or methods for verifying that products actually meet requirements specified in preceding phases of the development. In fact, the VDI 2221 process corresponds only to the left leg of the process depicted in Fig. 1, while the quality control process (the right leg in Fig. 1 and the main contribution of the V-model) is left unspecified.

2.1 The Engineering Design Process

To make the correspondence between VDI 2221 and the V-model explicit we review the six stages of VDI 2221[1] and relate them to the V-model before we illustrate them with a simple example.

S1 **Purpose/Problem:** a concise formulation of the purpose of the product to be designed.
S2 **Requirements List:** a list of explicit named properties of the envisioned product. It is developed in cooperation between designer and client and corresponds to the user specification document in the V-model.
S3 **Functional Structure:** A document that identifies the functional components of the envisioned product and puts them into relation with each other.
S4 **Solution in Principle:** a specification of the most salient aspects of the design. It can either be a CAD design like the one in Fig. 2 below or a hand drawing [8].
S5 **Embodiment Design/"Gestalt":** a CAD design which specifies the exact shape of the finished product.
S6 **Documentation:** accompanies all steps of the design process.

Note that most of these design steps result in informal text documents, with step S5 being the notable exception. In the envisioned document-oriented engineering design process we will concentrate on these documents, enhance them with semantic annotations and link them to background specifications to enable machine support: e.g. requirements tracing, management of change, or verification of physical properties. Before discussing this vision in more detail, let us set up an example.

2.2 The Design of a Hammer

A rational reconstruction of the design process of a machinist's hammer according to the German industrial norm DIN 1041 would proceed as follows.

The Purpose of a Hammer. The first and most important step in setting up a requirements list is the specification of the purpose of the product. The purpose describes the intended use of the product solution-neutrally. This is the highest level of abstraction within the design process. In the case of a hammering tool, the purpose can be in the form of a very simple definition:

[1] In fact, [14] specifies additional stages for determining modular structures and developing their embodiments, which we will subsume in steps S3 and S5.

> A **hammer** is an apparatus for transmitting an impulse to an object, e.g. for driving a nail into a wall.

In reference to a hand-tool in contrast to e.g. a hammer mill, the purpose can be narrowed to:

> A **hammer** is an apparatus for the manual generation and transmission of a defined impulse to an object, e.g. for driving a nail into a wall.

Ideally, the list of requirements of a product should be unambiguous, clear and complete. However, this is rarely the case in a real life design process, e.g. due to implicit customer wishes, which in fact are often more important to the market-success of a product than the explicitly named requirements. In the case of the hammer, the requirements might include the following.

Explicit Requirements

E1 The hammer has to fulfil the standard DIN 1041 and all related subsequent standards, namely: DIN 1193, DIN 1195, DIN 5111, DIN 68340 and DIN ISO 2786-1.
E2 The handle has to be painted with a clear lacquer over all and with colour RAL 7011 (iron grey) at 10 cm from the lower end.
E3 A company logo of 20mm length is placed on each of the two sides of the handle.

Implicit Requirements

I1 The hammer must be usable for right-handed and left-handed persons.
I2 The hammer should be ergonomic.
I3 The hammer must fit into a standard tool chest.
I4 The hammer shall look strong and matter-of-fact.

Functional Specification of a Hammer. Within the design process, the functional specification is done by setting up the function structure that breaks down the complex problem into manageable smaller sub-functions and represents the logical interrelationships of the given tasks. As in the previous design steps, the function structure is still solution neutral. The aim is to open up a preferably broad solution field, which will be narrowed by explicit named criteria within further steps of the design process.

The function structure is intended to explain interrelationships within the future embodied product; therefore, the connection between function structure and the given product has to be clear. Every sub-function can be found within the product, or the product is not a suitable solution. On the other hand, function structures are not appropriate as a tool for reverse engineering, because the relation between the embodied product and the underlying functions is ambiguous. On the right, we depict one possible functional structure for

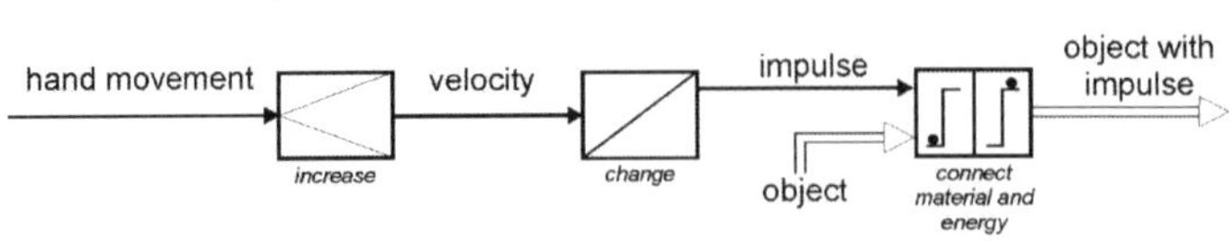

the hammer as an apparatus for the manual generation and transmission of a defined impulse to an object.

The Principle Solution for a Hammer. From the functional specification, we develop a *principle solution* (see Fig. 2). This solution abstracts from the physical traits of the eventual product and identifies the functional parts. For a hammer, one of these is the handle, here a cylindrical part of the hammer shaft used for gripping. The fact that it is symmetric/cylindrical is a response to the requirement E1. The handle is connected to an inert mass (depicted by a solid ball in Fig. 2) which is again connected to an *active surface* that delivers the impact on the object. The size and form of the active surface will be determined by the requirement I2. In fact, the principle solution reveals that there is a second possible active area of the hammer, opposite to the primary one; Fig. 2 shows three variants of the principle solution with differing secondary active surfaces.

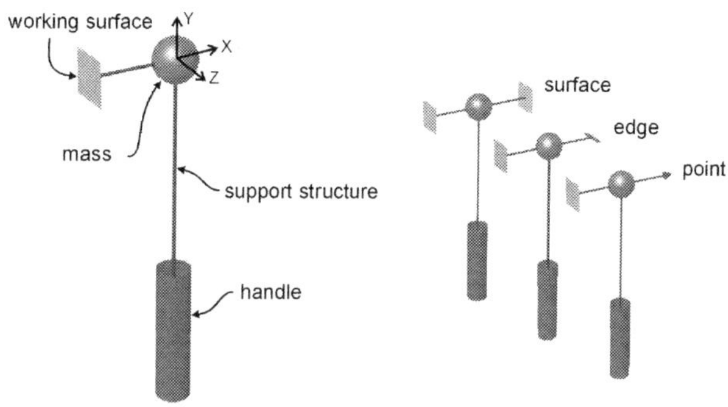

Fig. 2. A principle solution for a Hammer

The Embodiment of a Hammer. Note that the principle solution is not a finished design yet, since it abstracts from most of the physical traits of a hammer, e.g. the dimensions of the shaft and the form of the head, which will be specified in the embodiment design step. Here, the ultimate three-dimensional shape and the materials of the product are derived, taking into account material properties, manufacturability constraints, specialised purposes, and aesthetic factors. These can lead to the widely differing final designs we see in use today.

2.3 A Document-Oriented Design Process

We propose to reinforce the systematic engineering design process laid out above with technologies and practices from software engineering and Formal Methods to obtain a document-oriented process where designs are semantically enhanced and linked to formal and semi-formal specifications. It is crucial to note that the various design documents necessarily have differing levels of rigour, ranging from informal and hard-to-quantify requirements like I2 to mathematical proofs of security-relevant properties, e.g. in aerospace applications. Additionally, different product parts and aspects underlie differing economic and security-related constraints, so that design quality control must be supported at various levels of formality (going beyond strictly ontological annotation as e.g. in the EXPRESS language that forms part of the STEP *Standard for product data exchange*, ISO 10303 [6,11]). As a consequence, design documents need to be encoded in a document format that supports *flexible degrees of formality*, such as OMDoc (Open Mathematical Documents [7]). The OMDoc format concentrates on structural aspects of the knowledge embedded in documents and provides a markup infrastructure to make it explicit by annotation. Crucially, the format supports a fine-granular mixture of formal and informal elements and thus supports, e.g., the stepwise migration from informal user requirements to specifications expressed in formal logics supported by verification environments like the Bremen heterogeneous tool set HETS [9]. The format itself is *semi-formal*, i.e. focuses on explicitly structured documents where relevant concepts are annotated by references to *content dictionaries* that specify the meaning of the terms used in design documents. Semi-formal design documents already bring added value to the engineering process by enabling machine support for many common quality control tasks like *requirements tracing* and *management of change* which are based on an explicitly given dependency relation (see [1] for details). Fully formal development strands embedded in a semi-formal process additionally allow for the rigorous verification of critical properties in a design, thus providing a reliable link between various stages of the engineering design process. It is this aspect that we concentrate on in the following.

3 Invading SOLIDWORKS

We now illustrate how the document-oriented formal/semi-formal methodology in engineering design processes laid out in the last section can be supported by means of an integration of formal methods tools with the widely used CAD system SOLIDWORKS [13]. The latter serves mainly as a demonstration platform; our overall approach is sufficiently general to apply equally well to any other CAD system that provides suitable interfaces.

Our approach to interfacing with SOLIDWORKS is *invasive*, i.e. we implement semantic services through direct access to the data structures of the CAD system. At present, we provide a SOLIDWORKS plug-in[2] that extracts designs as formal specifications, i.e. as lists of terms denoting sketches and features, and as formulas expressing constraints relating these sketches and features. These data are obtained using the SOLIDWORKS API, and are output as a HASCASL [12] specification encoded in an OMDOC file [7].

Overview of HASCASL. HASCASL is a higher order extension of the standard algebraic specification language CASL (Common Algebraic Specification Language) [2,10] with partial higher order functions and type-class based shallow polymorphism. The HASCASL syntax appearing in the specifications shown in the following is largely self-explanatory; we briefly recall the meaning of some keywords, referring to [12] for the full language definition. Variables for individuals, functions and types are declared using the keyword **var**. The keyword **type** declares, possibly polymorphic, types. Types are, a priori, loose; a **free type**, however, is an algebraic data type built from constructor operations following the standard no-junk-no-confusion principle. Types are used in the profiles of operations, declared and, optionally, defined using the keyword **op**.

[2] Available as a Visual Basic macro for SOLIDWORKS 2008, SP1 or higher, from: `http://www.informatik.uni-bremen.de/~lschrode/SolidWorks/SWExtractor.swp`

Operations may be used to state axioms in standard higher order syntax, with some additional features necessitated through the presence of partial functions, which however will not play a major role in the specifications shown here (although they do show up in the geometric libraries under discussion). Names of axioms are declared in the form %(axiom_name)%.

Beyond these *basic specification* constructs, HASCASL inherits mechanisms for structured specification from CASL. In particular, *named* specifications are introduced by the keyword **spec**; specification *extensions* that use previously defined syntactic material in new declarations are indicated by the keyword **then**; and unions of syntactically independent specifications are constructed using the keyword **and**. Annotation of extensions in the form **then %implies** indicates that the extension consists purely of theorems that follow from the axioms declared previously. Named specifications may be parameterized over arbitrary specifications. They may be imported using the given name. Named morphisms between two specifications can be defined using the keyword **view** to express that modulo a specified symbol translation, the source specification is a logical consequence of the target specification. HASCASL is connected to the Isabelle/HOL theorem prover via HETS [9].

The SOLIDWORKS Object Model. In order to obtain a formal representation of CAD designs, we define the SOLIDWORKS object types as algebraic data types in a HASCASL specification[3] following the SOLIDWORKS object hierarchy, using a predefined polymorphic data type $List\ a$ of lists over a. (All specifications shown below are abridged.)

spec SOLIDWORKS = AFFINEREALSPACE3DWITHSETS
then free types
  SWPlane ::= *SWPlane* (*SpacePoint* : *Point*; *NormalVector* : *VectorStar*;
            InnerCS : *Vector*);
  SWArc ::= *SWArc* (*Center* : *Point*; *Start* : *Point*; *End* : *Point*);
  SWLine ::= *SWLine* (*From* : *Point*; *To* : *Point*);
  SWSpline ::= *SWSpline* (*Points* : *List Point*);
  SWSketchObject ::= *type SWArc* | *type SWLine* | *type SWSpline*;
  SWSketch ::= *SWSketch* (*Objects* : *List SWSketchObject*;
            Plane : *SWPlane*);
  SWExtrusion ::= *SWExtrusion* (*Sketch* : *SWSketch*; *Depth* : *Real*);
  ...
  SWFeature ::= *type SWExtrusion* | ...

This provides a formal *syntax* of CAD designs, which we then underpin with a formal geometric *semantics*. The constructs are classified as follows.

– *Base objects* are *real numbers*, *vectors*, *points*, and *planes*, the latter given by a point on the plane, the normal vector and a vector in the plane to indicate an inner coordinate system.

[3] All mentioned HASCASL specifications can be obtained under `https://svn-agbkb.informatik.uni-bremen.de/Hets-lib/trunk/HasCASL/Real3D/`

- *Sketch objects:* From base objects, we can construct *sketch objects* which are *lines* defined by a start and an end point, *arcs* also given by start and end, and additionally a center point, and *splines* given by a list of anchor points.
- *Sketch:* A plane together with a list of sketch objects contained in it constitutes a *sketch*.
- *Features* represent three dimensional solid objects. They can be constructed from one or more sketches by several *feature constructors*, which may take additional parameters.

We will focus in the following on the *extrusion* feature constructor which represents the figure that results as the space covered by a sketch when moved orthogonally to the plane of the sketch for a given distance.

In order to reason formally about SolidWorks designs, we equip them with a semantics in terms of point sets in three-dimensional affine space (i.e. in $\mathbb{R}^3$ equipped with the standard affine structure). For example, the term $SWLine(A, B)$ is interpreted as a line segment from point A to point B in $\mathbb{R}^3$. Formally, the semantics is based on point set constructors that correspond to the syntax constructors, specified as follows.

spec SolidWorksSemanticConstructors =
    AffineRealSpace3DWithSets
then ops
    $VWithLength(v : Vector; s : Real) : Vector =$
        $v \; when \; v = 0 \; else \; (s \, / \, (|| \, v \, || \; as \; NonZero)) * v;$
    $VPlane(normal : Vector) : VectorSet = \lambda \, y : Vector \bullet orth \, (y, normal);$
    $VBall(r : Real) : VectorSet = \lambda \, y : Vector \bullet || \, y \, || \leq r;$
    $ActAttach(p : Point; vs : VectorSet) : PointSet = p + vs;$
    $ActExtrude(ax : Vector; ps : PointSet) : PointSet =$
    $\lambda \, x : Point \bullet \exists \, l : Real; y : Point$
        $\bullet \, l \; isIn \; closedinterval \, (0, 1) \wedge y \; isIn \; ps \wedge x = y + l * ax;$

Using these semantic constructors, the point set interpretation of, e.g., planes and features is given by the specification below. Note that the semantics of sketch objects additionally depends on a plane, which is specified only at the level of the enclosing sketch. We give a simplified version of the semantics where we ignore the fact that one has to distinguish between open and closed sketches — open sketches are implicitly equipped with a default wall thickness, while closed sketches are understood as filled objects. In particular, we elide the full definition of the semantics of arcs; we are, for purposes of the case study of Section 4, only interested in the case of closed arcs, which define discs.

spec SolidWorksWithSemantics = SolidWorks
and SolidWorksSemanticConstructors
then ops
    $i : SWExtrusion \rightarrow PointSet;$
    $i : SWPlane \rightarrow PointSet$
    $i : SWSketch \rightarrow PointSet;$

$is : SWSketchObject \times SWPlane \rightarrow PointSet;$
$is : (List\ SWSketchObject) \times SWPlane \rightarrow PointSet;$
vars $o, x, y, z : Point; n : VectorStar; ics : Vector; l : Real;$
$sk : SWSketch; plane : SWPlane;$
$sko : SWSketchObject; skos : List\ SWSketchObject$
• $i\ (SWPlane\ (o, n, ics)) = ActAttach\ (o, VPlane\ n);$
• $is\ ([\,], plane) = emptySet;$
• $is\ (sko :: skos, plane) = is\ (sko, plane)\ union\ is\ (skos, plane);$
• $is\ (SWArc\ (x, y, z), plane) = \ldots$
• $i\ (SWSketch\ (skos, plane)) = is\ (skos, plane);$
• $i\ (SWPlane\ (o, n, ics)) = ActAttach\ (o, VPlane\ n);$
• $i\ (SWExtrusion\ (sk, l))$
$= ActExtrude(VWithLength\ (NormalVector\ (Plane\ sk), l), i\ sk);$

In the case study of the next section, we will show a concrete example which illustrates the use of the plug-in in the context of our envisioned development process. Here, the tool chain connects SOLIDWORKS to HASCASL via the plug-in, and the heterogeneous tool set HETS then allows for the automatic generation of proof obligations to be discharged in a semiautomatic theorem prover such as Isabelle/HOL. The case study is mainly concerned with the verification of designs against abstract requirements. Further potential uses of the invasive approach include *semantic preloading*, i.e. automated rapid prototyping of designs from abstract specifications, as well as requirements tracing and a closer general integration of specifications and designs, e.g. by user-accessible links between specifications and parts in the SOLIDWORKS design.

4 Case Study: Simple Geometric Objects

We will now illustrate what form a formal strand of the integrated formal/semi-formal development process advocated above might take on a very basic case study: we construct a simple object in the CAD/CAM system, specifically a cylinder, export its formal description using our tool, and then formally verify that it implements a prescribed abstract geometric shape, i.e., that it really is a cylinder; here, we use the standard concept of specification refinement made available in HETS via the syntactic construct of views as exemplified below.

In practice it turns out that, rather than verify the correctness of a particular design directly, it is more convenient to develop a library of common design patterns. Given a formal export of a CAD/CAM object and an abstract specification for this object, we then only have to match the object term against the patterns in our pattern library, for which correctness has already been verified once and for all. In Section 4.1 we will show a sample proof of a design pattern.

Naively, one would imagine that there is really nothing to verify about a geometric object: a cylinder is a cylinder is a cylinder. But as soon as one starts using a real CAD system, it becomes clear that the situation is actually more complex. The mathematical concept of a three-dimensional geometric object is a set of points in three-dimensional euclidean space, typically described by a general formation principle and a number of parameters. E.g. in the case of a (solid) cylinder, the parameters are

- the coordinates of some anchor point, say the centre of the cylinder,
- the spatial direction of the axis,
- the height h and the radius r,

and the formation principle for cylinders prescribes that these parameters describe the set of points p such that

- p has distance at most r from the axis (regarded as an infinite straight line);
- the orthogonal projection of p onto the axis has distance at most h from the centre point, and
- p lies in the positive half space determined by the base plane.

On the other hand, the design that we extract from our CAD construction[4] takes a totally different form: instead of defining a point set using the above-mentioned parameters, we construct the cylinder as a *feature* by applying a suitable *feature constructor* to more basic two-dimensional objects called *sketches* as laid out in Section 3. Additionally, we may impose *constraints* on the dimensions involved, e.g. equality of two sides in a triangle, a point which we have not explicitly treated in Section 3. Specifically, the construction of a cylinder in SolidWorks would typically proceed as follows.

- Create a plane.
- Insert a circle into the plane, described as a circular arc with coincident start and end points.
- Extrude the circle to a certain depth.

Thus, the cylinder is constructed as a feature stemming from the extrusion feature constructor which is anchored in a sketch consisting of one sketch object, a circle. We shall generally refer to a combination of features as described above as a *concrete design*, while a definition via mathematical point sets will be called an *abstract design*.

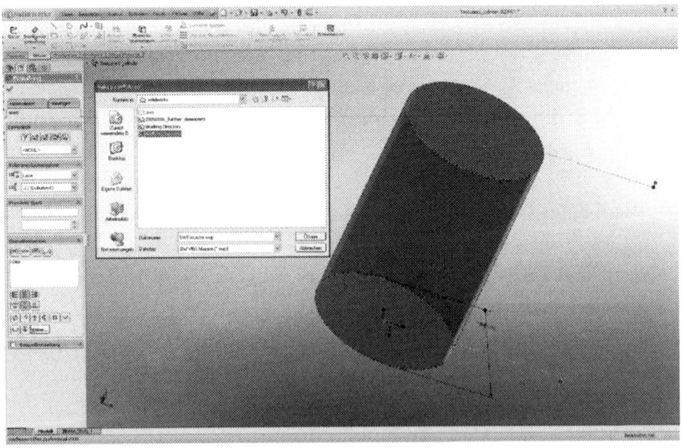

Fig. 3. Call to the SolidWorks plug-in to export a cylinder

[4] The CAD design of the cylinder is available under `http://www.informatik.uni-bremen.de/~lschrode/SolidWorks/CylinderTestCase.SLDPRT`

While in the above case it is easy to see intuitively that the concrete design matches the abstract design, i.e. that extruding a circle really yields a cylinder, the formalisation of this intuition is by no means an entirely trivial enterprise, and more complex objects quickly lead to quite challenging verification tasks – imagine e.g. having to check that two given circular extrusions of two circles yield two interlocking chain links. Additional complexity arises from the above-mentioned constraints – e.g. one may initially leave the height of the cylinder open, cut part of the cylinder off using a skewed plane placed at a defined angle to the base plane and touching the perimeter of the bottom circle, and then impose that the height of the short side of the arising cut cylinder is half that of the long side, thus completely determining the height.

It is therefore desirable to have machine support for checking that an abstract design is actually implemented by a given concrete design. Besides the mere fact that one can verify geometric shapes, added benefits include

- Easy proofs of physical and geometric properties of the objects involved – e.g. once one has matched the abstract cylinder to the concrete cylinder, one can now prove *on the abstract side* (much more easily than on the concrete side) that the cylinder adheres to a prescribed surface area, volume, or mass (if the density is known).
- Better control over the cohesion and consistency of the design – e.g. if it turns out that the design fails to match the abstract object, this may mean that the designer has accidentally left extraneous degrees of freedom. Such errors may later lead to blocked designs that cannot be completed due to unsatisfiability of their constraints, a notorious problem in computer-aided construction; verification against abstract designs may help in detecting such errors at an early stage of the development process.
- The abstract design may in fact properly abstract from the concrete shape of the final object, e.g. by leaving less relevant dimensions open (within certain ranges) or omitting features that do not play a central role in the present stage of the design process, thus providing for a property-centered approach to evolutionary design.

Further possible semantic services enabled by the connection between abstract and concrete designs within HETS include semantic annotation and requirements tracing as discussed in Section 2. A more visionary potential application of abstract designs is the automated derivation of concrete designs, i.e. rapid prototyping by compilation of abstract designs into preliminary *formally verified* CAD documents.

A collection of geometry libraries. The basis of the proposed formal geometric verification framework is a collection of HASCASL specification libraries, structured as follows. The abstract specification of three dimensional basic geometry is contained in a library which provides the fundamental types and objects such as the data types *Point* and *Vector* for points and vectors in $\mathbb{R}^3$, types for point sets and vector sets, and operations on these types. These specifications import parametrised specifications from a library of abstract linear algebra and affine geometry, which provides the basic notions of a Euclidean vector space such as linear dependency, norm and distance, the inner product and orthogonality, and the operations which relate points and vectors in affine geometry. For instance, the basic definition of an affine space, i.e. intuitively a vector space without origin, is given as follows.

spec AFFINESPACE[VECTORSPACE[FIELD]] =
  type *Point*
  op $\_\_+\_\_ : Point \times Space \rightarrow Point$ %(point space map)%
  vars $p, q : Point; v, w : Space$
  $\bullet\ p + v = p + w \Rightarrow v = w$ %(plus injective)%
  $\bullet\ \exists\, y : Space \bullet p + y = q$ %(plus surjective)%
  $\bullet\ p + (v + w) = p + v + w;$ %(point vector plus associative)%
then %**implies**
  $\forall\, p : Point; v, w : Space$
  $\bullet\ p + v + w = p + w + v;$ %(point vector plus commutative)%
end

spec EXTAFFINESPACE [AFFINESPACE[VECTORSPACE[FIELD]]] = %**def**
  op $vec : Point \times Point \rightarrow Space$
  $\forall\, p, q : Point \bullet p + vec\ (p, q) = q;$ %(vec def)%
then %**implies**
  vars $p, q, r : Point; v, w : Space$
  $\bullet\ vec\ (p, q) + vec\ (q, r) = vec\ (p, r)$ %(transitivity of vec plus)%
  $\bullet\ vec\ (p, q) = -\ vec\ (q, p)$ %(antisymmetry of vec)%
  $\bullet\ p + v = q \Rightarrow v = vec\ (p, q);$ %(plus vec identity)%
end

(Here, we employ a pattern where specifications are separated into a base part containing only the bare definitions and an extended part containing derived operations, marked as such by the semantic annotation %**def**.)

The libraries for SOLIDWORKS consist of the data types and semantics introduced in Section 3 and common concrete design patterns such as, e.g., the construction of a cylinder described earlier in this section. They also contain views stating the correctness of these patterns, as exemplified next. Constructions exported from SOLIDWORKS using our tool can then be matched with design patterns in the library via (trivial) views, thus inheriting the correctness w.r.t. the abstract design from the design pattern.

4.1 A Proof of a Refinement View

We illustrate the verification of concrete design patterns against abstract designs on our running example, the cylinder. The abstract design is specified as follows.

spec CYLINDER = AFFINEREALSPACE3DWITHSETS
then op $Cylinder(offset : Point; r : RealPos; ax : VectorStar) : PointSet =$
  $\lambda\, x : Point \bullet let\ v = vec\ (offset, x)\ in$
    $\|\ proj\ (v, ax)\ \| \leq \|\ ax\ \|$
    $\wedge\ \|\ orthcomp\ (v, ax)\ \| \leq r$
    $\wedge\ (v * ax) \geq 0;$

We wish to match this with the concrete design pattern modelling the CAD construction process outlined above (importing the previously established fact that planes in SOLIDWORKS are really affine planes):

spec SOLIDWORKSCYLBYARCEXTRUSION =
    SOLIDWORKSPLANE_IS_AFFINEPLANE
then op
    SWCylinder(center, boundarypt : Point; axis : VectorStar): SWFeature =
    let plane = SWPlane (center, axis, V (0, 0, 0));
        arc = SWArc (center, boundarypt, boundarypt);
        height = || *axis* ||
    in SWExtrusion (SWSketch ([*arc*], *plane), height);*

view SWCYLBYAE_ISCYLINDER : CYLINDER **to**
    {SOLIDWORKSCYLBYARCEXTRUSION
    then op
        Cylinder(offset : Point; r : RealPos; axis : VectorStar): PointSet =
        let boundary = λ *p : Point* • *let v = vec (offset, p)*
                                        in orth (*v*, *axis*) $\wedge$ || *v* || = *r*;
            boundarypt = choose boundary
        in i (SWCylinder (offset, boundarypt, axis));
    }

The above view expresses that every affine cylinder can be realized by our concrete design pattern. It induces a proof obligation stating that the operation $Cylinder$ defined in the view by means of $i \circ SWCylinder$ is equal to the operation $Cylinder$ defined in the specification *Cylinder*, the source of the view. Translated into an Isabelle/HOL assertion via HETS, the proof obligation takes the following sh

```
theorem def_of_Cylinder :
"ALL axis offset r.
 Cylinder (( offset , r ), axis ) =
 (% x. let v = vec( offset , x)
       in ( || proj (v, gn_inj (axis )) || <=' || gn_inj (axis ) || &
            || orthcomp(v, gn_inj (axis )) || <=' gn_inj(r )) &
          v *_4 gn_inj (axis ) >=' 0'')"
```

We will sketch the corresponding proof in Isabelle/HOL, using a slightly more readable notation than those in the original Isabelle source code[5]. After the unfolding of function definitions such as $SWCylinder$, $SWExtrusion$, i, $ActExtrude$ and some bookkeeping steps involving let-environments, conditionals, and function equality, we arrive at an equivalence of the form

```
(1) Exists l:Real , y:Point .
   (1.1) l in [0..1] /\ (1.2) y in (ball intersection plane) /\ (1.3) x = y + l * axis
<=> (2)
   (2.1) ||vp|| <= ||axis|| /\ (2.2) ||vo|| <= r /\ (2.3) v * axis >= 0
```

s `x`, `offset`, `r` and `axis` and a local environment containing the following variable bindings (function symbols are explained in Table 1).

[5] The Isabelle source code for this proof can be obtained under `https://svn-agbkb.informatik.uni-bremen.de/Hets-lib/trunk/HasCASL/Real3D/SolidWorks/CylinderView.thy`

```
(0.1) boundary = \p. let v=vec( offset , p) in orth(v, axis) /\ ||v|| = r
(0.2) bp = choose(boundary)
(0.3) r1 = vec( offset , bp)
(0.4) pln = SWPlane offset axis 0
(0.5) arc = SWArc offset bp bp
(0.6) ht = || axis ||
(0.7) ball = ActAttach( offset , VBall(||r1 ||))
(0.8) plane = i(pln)
(0.9) v = vec( offset , x)
(0.10) vp = proj(v, axis)
(0.11) vo = orthcomp(v, axis)
```

Function symbols and their meaning

FUNCTION	DESCRIPTION
`[0..1]`	closed unit interval
`intersection`	binary set intersection
`*`	overloaded binary operator (inner product, scalar multiplication, ...)
`||-||`	norm of a vector
`vec`	the vector connecting two points
`orth`	the orthogonality predicate for two vectors
`choose`	usual choice operator for a predicate
`SWPlane`	SOLIDWORKS constructor for a plane (see Section 3)
`SWArc`	SOLIDWORKS constructor for an arc (see Section 3)
`VBall`	vector set constructor for a ball (see Section 3)
`ActAttach`	point set constructor adding a vector set to a point (see Section 3)
`i`	interpretation function (see Section 3)
`proj`	orthogonal projection of a vector onto another
`orthcomp`	the orthogonal component of an orthogonal decomposition

The key to the proof is the relation between `v`, `y` and `l` and the orthogonal decomposition of `v` along the `axis`: `v = vp + vo`. From `(0.8)` together with `(0.4)` and the semantics definition for a plane, we obtain `plane = offset + VPlane(axis) = offset +` {`z` | `orth(z,axis)`}, and with (1.2), which gives us `y in plane`, we have `y = offset + y'` with `y'` satisfying `orth(y',axis)`. Similarly we obtain from `(0.7)` that `y = offset + y''` with `y'' <= ||r1||` and of course `y' = y''` by injectivity of the addition of vectors to points in affine space. Substituting `y` into `(1.3)` gives us `x = offset + y' + l * axis`.

On the other hand, from `(0.9)` we have `x = offset + v = offset + vo + vp` with `vp` a multiple of `axis` and `vo` orthogonal to it. Hence we obtain `offset + y' + l * axis = offset + vo + vp` and thus `y' + l * axis = vo + vp`. As `l * axis` and `vp` are linearly dependent and each side of the equation is the unique orthogonal decomposition of `v`, we obtain finally our relation as `y' = vo` and `l * axis = vp`. To show `(1) => (2)` using this relation it remains to establish the following.

```
(1') l in [0..1] /\ (1.2') y in ball
=> (2)
   (2.1') ||l * axis|| <=||axis|| /\ (2.2') ||y'|| <=r
/\ (2.3') (vo + l * axis) * axis >=0
```

The rest is now real arithmetic together with the distributive law of the inner product and some basic facts concerning the inner product and the norm, thus concluding the correctness proof of the concrete design pattern for cylinders.

5 Conclusion and Further Work

We have argued that systematic engineering design processes (as laid down e.g. in VDI 2221) have many commonalities with software engineering. To transfer methods from software engineering to engineering design we have to deal with the fact that engineering design processes are considerably less formal and are geared towards producing CAD/CAM objects instead of program code. We have formulated a semi-formal, document-oriented design process that integrates CAD/CAM documents with specification documents of various degrees of formalisation, up to and including fully formal specification and verification. To support the CAD/CAM parts of this design process, we have extended a widely used CAD system with an interface for exporting CAD objects to the Bremen heterogeneous tool set HETS, specifically to translate them into specifications in the wide-spectrum language HASCASL. Thereby, we turn CAD designs into fully formal documents, as the export mechanism defines a rigorous geometric semantics for them. Moreover, we have illustrated the formal proof obligations that may arise in this process, and as a proof of concept, we have presented a sample proof that verifies the implementation of a simple abstract geometric object by a CAD design. One of the lessons to be learned from even such a basic case study is that the matching of concrete CAD designs with geometric concepts should be via a library of pre-established design and construction patterns. Together with the modularisation facilities afforded by the use of HASCASL within HETS, such a library will also play an important role in eventually making formal approaches to engineering design scale to realistic systems.

The present work forms part of a long-term endeavor where we want to rethink the systematic engineering design process as a whole. Further steps in this program include improved automated proof support for geometric proofs possibly using an integration of computer algebra systems into the HETS framework, rapid prototyping of CAD/CAM objects from abstract specifications, and verification of CAD/CAM designs against formalised industrial standards. The immediate next stage in this process is to go one step further up the ladder, proceeding from the specification and verification of simple shapes to simple artifacts such as the hammer. Besides being technically more complex, this leads to a conceptually higher level of abstraction as one will wish to specify abstract *properties* rather than the *shape* of the artifact. The reasoning support for formalised geometry may eventually profit from existing results on automated theorem proving in geometry including [3,15,4,5], either by reuse of concepts or by importing existing theorems using the heterogeneous mechanisms provided by HETS.

Acknowledgements

We gratefully acknowledge discussions with Bernd Krieg-Brückner, Dieter Hutter, Christoph Lüth, and Till Mossakowski, and thank Tanmay Pradhan for his work on the SolidWorks plug-in. Erwin R. Catesbeiana has contributed his known opinions on fundamental matters of logic.

References

1. Autexier, S., Hutter, D., Mossakowski, T., Schairer, A.: Maya: Maintaining structured documents, ch. 26.12 of [7]
2. Bidoit, M., Mosses, P.D.: CASL User Manual. LNCS, vol. 2900. Springer, Heidelberg (2004)
3. Chou, S.-C.: Mechanical Geometry Theorem Proving. Reidel, Dordrecht (1988)
4. Gräbe, H.-G.: The SymbolicData GEO records - a public repository of geometry theorem proof schemes. In: Winkler, F. (ed.) ADG 2002. LNCS (LNAI), vol. 2930, pp. 67–86. Springer, Heidelberg (2004)
5. Hales, T.C.: Introduction to the Flyspeck project. In: Mathematics, Algorithms, Proofs. Schloss Dagstuhl, Germany. Dagstuhl Seminar Proceedings. Internationales Begegnungs- und Forschungszentrum fuer Informatik (IBFI), vol. 05021 (2006)
6. ISO 10303-1, Industrial automation systems and integration — Product data representation and exchange, Part 1: Overview and fundamental principles. International Organization for Standardization (1994)
7. Kohlhase, M.: OMDoc – An Open Markup Format for Mathematical Documents [version 1.2]. LNCS (LNAI), vol. 4180. Springer, Heidelberg (2006)
8. Lemburg, J.P.: Methodik der schrittweisen Gestaltsynthese. PhD thesis, Fakultät für Maschinenwesen, RWTH Aachen (2008)
9. Mossakowski, T., Maeder, C., Lüttich, K.: The heterogeneous tool set. In: Grumberg, O., Huth, M. (eds.) TACAS 2007. LNCS, vol. 4424, pp. 519–522. Springer, Heidelberg (2007)
10. Mosses, P.D. (ed.): CASL Reference Manual. LNCS, vol. 2960. Springer, Heidelberg (2004)
11. Pratt, M.J.: Introduction to ISO 10303 - the STEP standard for product data exchange. J. Comput. Inf. Sci. Eng. 1, 102–103 (2001)
12. Schröder, L., Mossakowski, T.: HasCasl: Integrated higher-order specification and program development. Theoret. Comput. Sci. 410, 1217–1260 (2009)
13. Introducing SolidWorks. SolidWorks Corporation, Concord, MA (2002)
14. VDI-Gesellschaft Entwicklung Konstruktion Vertrieb. Methodik zum Entwickeln und Konstruieren technischer Systeme und Produkte (1995), English title: Systematic approach to the development and design of technical systems and products
15. Wu, W.-T.: *Mechanical Theorem Proving in Geometries*. Texts and Monographs in Symbolic Computation, vol. 1. Springer, Heidelberg (1994)

Translating Safe Petri Nets to Statecharts in a Structure-Preserving Way

Rik Eshuis

Eindhoven University of Technology, School of Industrial Engineering
P.O. Box 513, 5600 MB Eindhoven, The Netherlands
h.eshuis@tue.nl

Abstract. Statecharts and Petri nets are two popular visual formalisms for modelling complex systems that exhibit concurrency. Both formalisms are supported by various design tools. To enable the automated exchange of models between Petri net and statechart tools, we present a structural, polynomial algorithm that translates safe Petri nets into statecharts. The translation algorithm preserves both the structure and the behaviour of the input net. The algorithm can fail, since not every safe net has a statechart translation that preserves both its structure and behaviour. The class of safe nets for which the algorithm succeeds is formally characterised. Some statechart translations are not constructible by the algorithm, but this does not seem to be a severe limitation in practice.

1 Introduction

While finite state machines are a popular technique for formally modelling the control flow of simple systems, it has long been recognised that for complex concurrent systems more powerful techniques are needed. Petri nets [15] and statecharts [8] are two visual formalisms that extend finite state machines with constructs for modelling concurrency in succinct way. In practice, both formalisms are used side by side. For instance, UML [16] contains both activity diagrams, which have been inspired by Petri nets, and statecharts.

Both formalisms are supported by various tools, such as GreatSPN [1] and PEP [6] for Petri nets, and Statemate [10], Stateflow [14], and several UML tools such as Rational Rose [12] for statecharts. Tools supporting Petri nets, like GreatSPN and PEP, are strongly focused on analysis of functional and stochastic properties, while tools supporting statecharts, like Statemate and UML tools, are usually more focused on interactive simulation and on software code generation.

To allow designers to use both Petri net and statechart tools, it is useful to have formally defined translations between the two formalisms. Such formal translations enable the automated exchange of models between different tools [6,7,17]. For instance, a designer can first use a Petri net tool to analyse functional properties of a net design, next use an automated translation to transform the net into a statechart, and then use a statechart tool to generate software code.

A. Cavalcanti and D. Dams (Eds.): FM 2009, LNCS 5850, pp. 239–255, 2009.

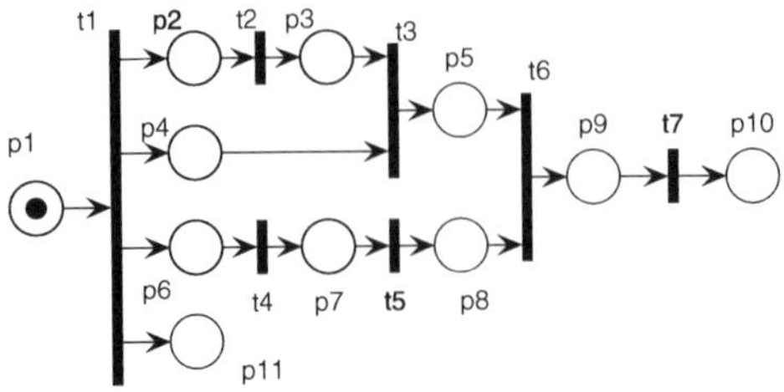

Fig. 1. Example Petri net

Ideally, such translations preserve the behaviour of the original model [7], neither reducing nor adding behaviour. Moreover, such translations should preserve the syntactic structure of the input models as much as possible, to support roundtrip engineering and to make it easier for designers to understand the produced translations. Without the requirement of structure preservation, for each model with finite behavior a trivial translation exists: compute the transition system of a model in formalism A, which resembles a finite state machine, and translate this transition system into formalism B. However, the syntactic structure of the two models would then be completely different, as the input model is concurrent but the output model sequential. Moreover, such a translation is prohibitively expensive for large models due to the state explosion problem.

While structure-preserving translations from statecharts to Petri nets exist [11,18], translations for the reverse direction are lacking. This paper defines a structure/behaviour-preserving translation from Petri nets to statecharts, i.e. a translation that preserves both the structure and the behaviour of the input nets. To introduce the translation, Fig. 1 shows a Petri net and Fig. 2 its structure/behaviour-preserving statechart translation (the syntax of Petri nets and statecharts is explained in Sect. 2). To show the correspondence between both models, statechart BASIC nodes and hyperedges are labelled with the names of the corresponding Petri net constructs.

As the example shows, the key difficulty in defining the translation algorithm is constructing the statechart AND/OR tree, which has no counterpart in Petri net syntax. Still, the translation algorithm we define in this paper is structural: it maps Petri net syntax to statechart syntax, without using any Petri net analysis technique like place invariants or reachability graphs. The time complexity of the algorithm is polynomial, so it scales to large Petri net models.

Not every net has a structure/behaviour-preserving statechart translation, so the algorithm can fail. For example, in statecharts each node is either present or not present in the current state, while in Petri nets a place can be present multiple times in the current state, i.e. a place can contain multiple tokens. In that case, the place and the Petri net are called unsafe. Therefore, an unsafe Petri net like Fig. 3(a) has no structure/behaviour-preserving statechart translation, since an unsafe place cannot map to one BASIC node. Still, by using a

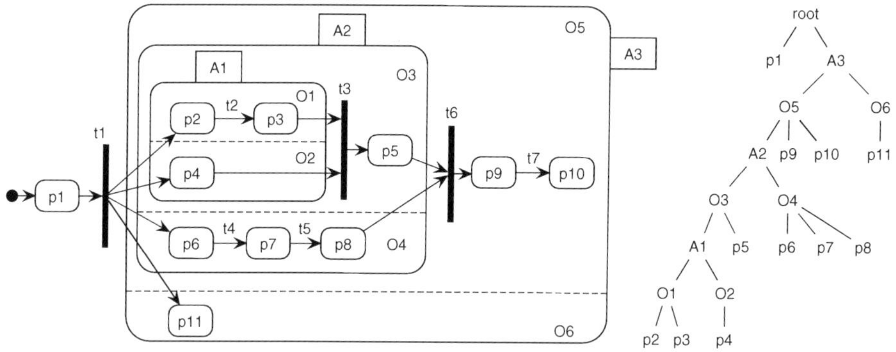

Fig. 2. Statechart translation and its AND/OR tree for the Petri net in Fig. 1

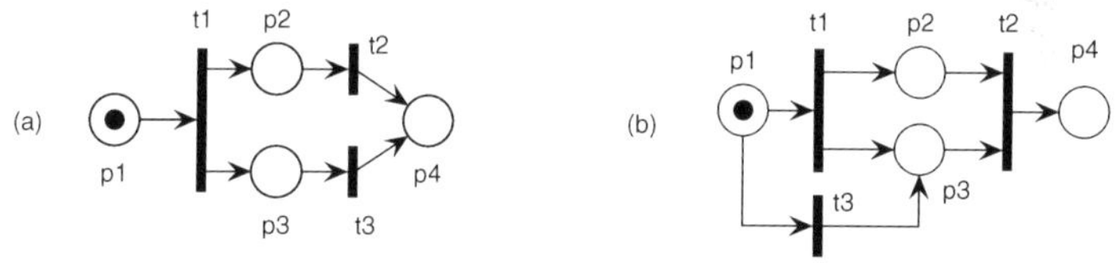

Fig. 3. Two Petri nets without structure/behaviour-preserving statechart translations

behaviour-preserving translation from unsafe nets to safe nets [2], also an unsafe net can be translated to a statechart using the translation algorithm defined this paper.

However, there do exist safe Petri nets like Fig. 3(b) that have no structure/ behaviour-preserving statechart translation, as we explain in Sect. 5. There we also show that there are safe nets for which the algorithm does not construct a statechart even though a structure/behaviour-preserving statechart translation does exist. Since these statecharts are not constructible by the algorithm, the algorithm is incomplete. However, such statecharts are not likely to be drawn in practice, so this does not seem to be a severe limitation. In Sect. 5, we also formally characterise the subclass of safe nets for which the algorithm returns a statechart, so the algorithm is sound and complete for this class of Petri nets.

To simplify the exposition, we do not consider transition labels for statecharts and Petri nets in this paper. This implies we use a generic, abstract statechart semantics in which a transition is not triggered by an event, but is taken when its input state nodes are in the current state. The translation defined in this paper can provide the basis for more advanced translations which deal with events and data, for example. Moreover, we do not consider weights on Petri net arcs, since these are only useful for unsafe nets.

The remainder of this paper is structured as follows. Section 2 provides background on Petri nets and statecharts. Section 3 explains the basics of the translation, including two reduction steps on Petri nets. These steps are used in Sect. 4 in a polynomial translation algorithm. The algorithm preserves the structure and the behaviour of the input net. Section 5 discusses the expressiveness and completeness of the translation. Section 6 presents related work. Section 7 winds up with conclusions and further work.

2 Background

We informally present the basics of Petri nets and statecharts. More formal introductions can be found in an accompanying technical report [5] and in [15] for Petri nets, and [4] for statecharts.

2.1 Petri Nets

A Petri net (Place/Transition net) consists of places, represented by circles, transitions, represented by bars, and directed arcs connecting places to transitions and vice versa. The preset of an element $x \in P \cup T$, denoted $\bullet x$, is the set of elements that have an outgoing arc that enters x, while the postset of x, denoted $x\bullet$, is the set of elements that have an incoming arc that leaves x. For example, in Fig. 1, for t1 we have $\bullet\mathtt{t1} = \{\mathtt{p1}\}$ and $\mathtt{t1}\bullet = \{\mathtt{p2}, \mathtt{p4}, \mathtt{p6}, \mathtt{p11}\}$. We require that each transition has a non-empty preset and a non-empty postset. If a place is in the preset(postset) of t, then it is input(output) to t.

As explained in the introduction, we are concerned here with safe nets, which are nets in which each place contains at most one token, visualised as a black dot. Places marked with a token belong to the current state (also called marking). A transition t is enabled in a state if all its input places have a token, so are in the state. In Fig. 1, transition t1 is enabled. Upon firing, from each input place a token is removed, and to each output place a token is added.

We require that each net has a single start place ι, like p1 in Fig. 1. For each place in the net, there must be a path from ι to that place. The initial state of each net will be $\{\iota\}$. Standard definitions of Petri nets do not enforce a single start place, but we use it here to simplify the translation. Furthermore, each safe net having an initial marking in which set of places $X \subseteq P$ is marked can be extended into a net with from a conceptual modelling point of view equivalent behaviour, by adding a single start place ι and a new transition t_ι with preset $\{\iota\}$ and postset X.

Formally, a Petri net is a tuple (P, T, F, ι) where P is the set of places, T the set of transitions such that $P \cap T = \emptyset$, $F \subseteq (P \times T) \cup (T \times P)$ the set of arcs, and $\iota \in P$ the start place. Standard definitions of Petri nets also use weights on arcs, but since weights are only useful for unsafe nets, we do not consider these.

2.2 Statecharts

Statecharts extend finite state machines with AND/OR decomposition of state nodes and event broadcasting. As explained in the introduction, we do not focus on events, and therefore statechart transitions do not carry any label here. State nodes are arranged in an AND/OR tree. Visually, the parent-child relation is represented by nesting the child inside the parent node. Leaves of the tree are BASIC nodes, while internal nodes are either AND nodes or OR nodes. An AND node specifies parallel decomposition, while an OR node specifies exclusive-or decomposition. For technical reasons, the root rt of the tree is always an OR node. The root is never shown in a statechart diagram. A node x is a descendant of node y if $x = y$ or x is (indirectly) contained inside y; node y is then ancestor of x. For example, p2 is descendant of A3 in Fig. 2.

A state C of a statechart, called a configuration, is a maximal set of nodes that the system can be in simultaneously. Configurations for the statechart in Fig. 2 are for example $\{\mathsf{p1}, rt\}$ and $\{\mathsf{p5}, \mathsf{p8}, \mathsf{p11}, \mathsf{O3}, \mathsf{O4}, \mathsf{O5}, \mathsf{O6}, \mathsf{A2}, \mathsf{A3}, rt\}$. Each configuration C has to satisfy the following three constraints:

- if a non-root node is in C, its parent is in C too,
- if an AND node is in C, all its children are in C too,
- if an OR node is in C, then one of its children is in C too.

Like Petri nets, nodes in a statechart can be connected by transitions, which we call hyperedges from now on to avoid confusion with transitions in a Petri net. Hyperedges can have input nodes (called source nodes) and output nodes (called target nodes). A hyperedge can have a non-BASIC node as source or target node. For hyperedge h, set $source(h)$ denotes the set of source nodes of h while $target(h)$ the set of target nodes. It is required that each pair of nodes in $source(h)$ and each pair of nodes in $target(h)$ are *orthogonal*, that is, given two different sources (targets), the smallest node containing both sources (targets) is an AND node, so the sources (targets) can be in the same configuration. In Fig. 4, n2 and n4 are orthogonal since the smallest node containing both is AND node A. We adopt the UML notation for statecharts: a hyperedge with a single source node and a single target node is visualised as a simple directed edge, while a hyperedge having more than one source or target node is visualised as a bar having incoming and outgoing edges.

A hyperedge is enabled if all its source nodes are in the current configuration. However, the computation of the state reached after taking the hyperedge is more involved than for Petri nets, since the next state has to satisfy the constraints for configurations. First, all nodes below the scope of h are left, so they are removed from the current configuration. The scope of h is the smallest OR node that contains all the input and output nodes of h, i.e., all other OR node that contain all the input and output nodes also contain the scope of h. For example, the scope of hyperedge t6 in Fig. 2 is O5.

Next, the targets of h (and their ancestors below the scope of h) are added to the state. If the resulting state is not a configuration, then $target(h)$ is not complete. For instance, in Fig. 4, the target set of h4 is incomplete, since $\{\mathsf{n5},\mathsf{O2},\mathsf{A},rt\}$ is not a configuration, as it contains AND node A, but not all children of A. Harel and Naamad [10] explain a static procedure for normalising statecharts, in which each incomplete target set X of a hyperedge is extended into a complete target set. The resulting hyperedges with complete target sets are called full compound

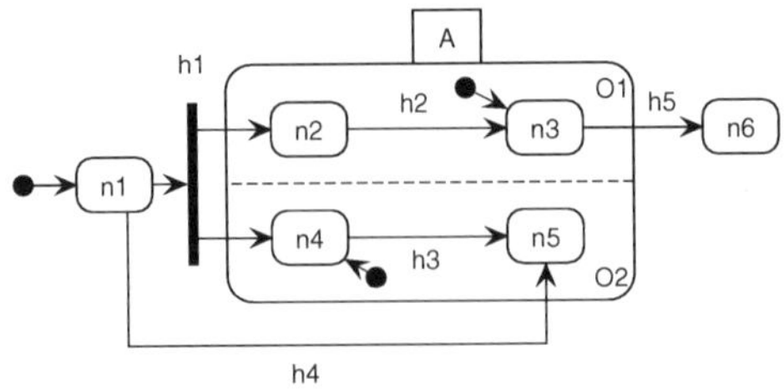

Fig. 4. Non-normalised statechart

transitions [10]. A complete description of the procedure is out of scope here, but an important element is the use of the default child node (pointed to by an arrow leaving a black dot) for each OR node that causes incompletion of X. For example, the default node of O1 in Fig. 4 is BASIC node n3, and therefore the complete target set for h4 is $\{n3, n5\}$.

Our translation maps Petri nets to normalised statecharts, such as the one in Fig. 2. Note that a normalised statechart is like an ordinary statechart, except that default nodes are superfluous, since each hyperedge already has a complete target set. Therefore, we omit default nodes from the statechart definition.

Formally, a (normalised) statechart is a tuple $(N,H,source,target,child,type,I)$. Set N contains the nodes, set H the hyperedges, where $N \cap H = \emptyset$. Functions $source, target : H \rightarrow \mathcal{P}(N)$ specify for each hyperedge the non-empty sets of input nodes and output nodes, respectively. Predicate $child \subseteq N \times N$ relates a node to its parent node, so $(n, n') \in child$ means n is child of n'. There should be one node rt that has no parent, so rt is the root of the tree. Function $type : N \rightarrow \{\text{BASIC,AND,OR}\}$ assigns to each node from N its type. A node is BASIC if and only if it has no children. Set $I \subseteq N$ is the initial configuration. For non-normalised statecharts, I can be computed by taking the default completion of OR root rt [4], similar to the way target sets are completed [10]. Our translation will construct I explicitly.

3 Translation Basics

In this section, we explain the basics of the translation algorithm defined in the next section.

Preserving structure. To ensure that the constructed translation is structure-preserving, the algorithm maps each place to a BASIC node and each transition t with preset X and postset Y to a hyperedge h having source set X and target set Y. Both mappings are bijective. Thus, the translation algorithm embeds the Petri net structure in the statechart structure.

Building the AND/OR tree. The AND/OR nodes of the statechart have no counterpart in the Petri net, but are constructed by the translation algorithm. These nodes have to be arranged in a tree, the leaves of which are the BASIC nodes. To construct the internal nodes of the tree, of type AND and OR, transitions are processed. For each transition t, an OR node o must be created which acts as the scope of hyperedge t in the statechart. Moreover, if t has a non-singleton preset (postset), then the places in the preset (postset) are active in parallel, so an AND node, child of o, needs to be constructed that contains all BASIC nodes in $\bullet t$ ($t\bullet$). For example, for transition t3 in Fig. 1, in the corresponding statechart in Fig. 2 AND node A1 has been created.

Nesting nodes. Complicating issue is that an AND node can be nested inside another AND node. For example, in Fig. 2, AND node A1 is nested inside A2 and A3. Thus, the translation algorithm cannot create for the postset of t1 an AND node a with four OR children that have the output places of t1 as BASIC children; instead, it needs to create an AND node with two OR children, in one of which AND nodes A2 and A1 are nested. To create a proper nesting, we construct the AND/OR tree bottom-up. So, when creating the AND/OR tree for the Petri net in Fig. 1, first AND node A1 and its OR children is constructed, then A2 and its OR children, and finally A3 and its OR children.

Ordering of transitions. To ensure that the tree is constructed bottom-up, transitions need to be processed in a certain order. For example, we see that in Fig. 2 the scope of hyperedge t2 (OR node O1) is more nested than that of t1 (root rt). Therefore, the transition t2 needs to be processed before t1.

The ordering constraint we use is that a transition t_1 should be processed before a transition t_2, written $t_1 \prec t_2$, if either $\bullet t_1 \subset t_2\bullet$ or $t_1\bullet \subset \bullet t_2$. In both cases, in the resulting statechart the scope of hyperedge t_1 is nested inside the scope of t_2. Therefore t_1 needs to be processed before t_2. A transition t can only be processed if there exists no other transition t' such that $t' \prec t$.

Processing of transitions. Conceptually, the actual construction of the AND/OR tree is done by letting each place link to a partial AND/OR tree that has an OR root. A transition is processed by reducing it, as well as its preset and postset, to a single place. The AND/OR tree of this new place is constructed by aggregating the AND/OR trees of the places in the pre- and postset of t.

To simplify the presentation, we let each place be the root of the corresponding tree, rather than annotating a place with a tree. Initially, for each place p a corresponding tree, consisting of OR root o_p and its child p is constructed. Place o_p replaces p in the original input net. Figure 5 shows for the example Petri net in Fig. 1 the initial net and the initially constructed AND/OR trees.

Next, we explain the reduction steps, in which the AND/OR trees get merged, in detail.

Reduction step 1. The first reduction step consists of two substeps that are symmetrical, one reducing the preset of a transition, the other its postset. In step 1a, the non-singleton preset $Q = \{q_1, .., q_n\}$ of transition t is reduced to a place p that becomes the single input place of t. If t already has a singe input

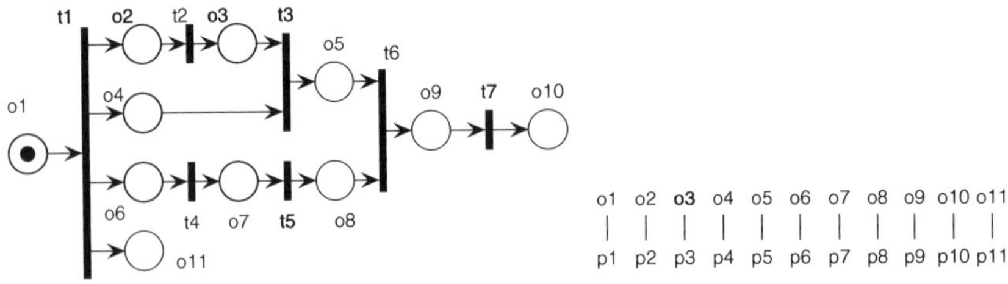

Fig. 5. Initial Petri net and initially constructed AND/OR trees for Fig. 1

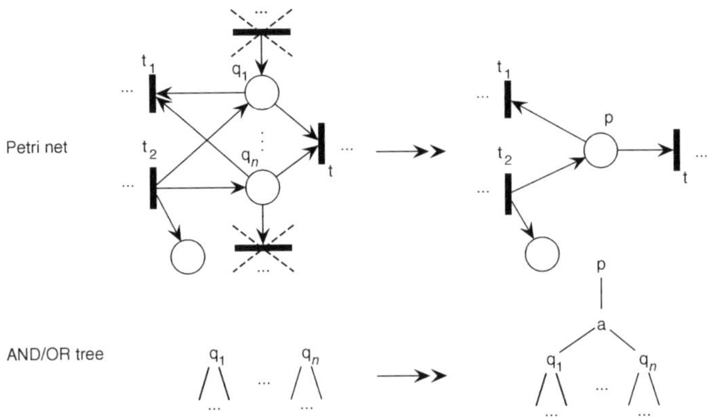

Fig. 6. Reduction step 1a; a dotted cross indicates absence of a transition

place, step 1a is skipped. Otherwise, each transition in T that has a place in Q as input or output place, instead gets p as input or output place. If such a neighbouring transition has multiple places in Q in its preset or postset, these are all removed and replaced by single place p. The AND/OR tree for p is constructed by creating an AND node a which becomes child of new OR root p. Children of a are the places in Q, which are the roots of the corresponding trees. Figure 6 specifies reduction step 1a graphically.

However, step 1a is only allowed if each place in Q has the same input and output transitions, and skipped otherwise. If the condition were dropped, this reduction step would violate the statechart syntax or not preserve behaviour:

- Statechart syntax is violated if a transition t' has some places of Q in its postset, but not all. To see why, suppose that step 1a is executed, so an AND node a is created that is parent of all places in Q. Let $q \in Q$ be a place that is not in the postset of t'. Then each BASIC node in the AND/OR tree linked to q is orthogonal to each of the BASIC nodes in Q. So t' maps to a hyperedge that has an incomplete target set Q. But normalised statecharts only allow hyperedges with complete target sets.

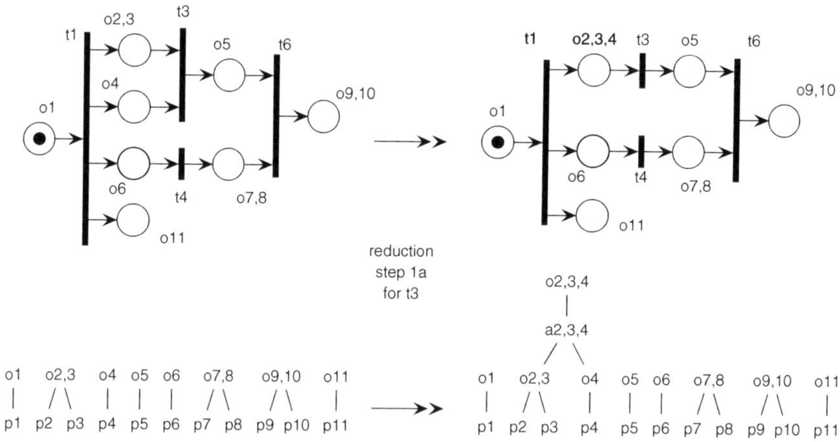

Fig. 7. Applying reduction step 1a for t3 in Fig. 1 (t2, t5, t7 have been processed)

To illustrate this: the net in Fig. 3(b) violates the condition for t = t2 due to t' = t3. Executing step 1a for t2 would create an AND node for the preset of t2, but then the target set of t3 is incomplete (BASIC node p2 is lacking).

- Behaviour is not preserved if a transition t' leaves some places in Q but not all. By similar reasoning as in the previous case, executing step 1a would map t to a hyperedge that has an incomplete source set, i.e., there is a BASIC node outside the source set that is orthogonal to each state in the source set. Taking such a hyperedge implies that a BASIC node is left that is not a source of the hyperedge. For instance, if in Fig. 4 hyperedge h5 is taken in configuration $\{\mathsf{n3}, \mathsf{n4}, \mathsf{O1}, \mathsf{O2}, \mathsf{A}, rt\}$, then the next configuration will be $\{\mathsf{n6}, rt\}$. So BASIC node n4 is left even though it was not a source of h5. In Petri nets, such behaviour is impossible due the locality principle [3], which states that each transition can only consume tokens from places that are in its preset. Thus, mapping a transition to a hyperedge with an incomplete source set does not preserve behaviour.

To illustrate reduction step 1a, we show how t3 from Fig. 5 is reduced. The reduced net in the top-left of Fig. 7 has been obtained after processing transitions t2, t5 and t7. Note that t6 $\not<$ t7, so t7 can reduced before t6. Next, the preset of transition t3 in Fig. 7 can be reduced. The resulting Petri net and AND/OR trees are shown on the right.

In step 1b, step 1a is repeated but then for the postset of t. Again, step 1b is skipped if the postset is a singleton or if not each place in Q has the same input and output transitions. Reduction step 1b can be specified graphically by reversing all arrows between places $q_1, .., q_n, p$ and transition t in Fig. 6.

Reduction step 2. The second step reduces a transition t with a single input place q and a single output place r to a new place p. If the preset or postset of t is not a singleton, step 2 is skipped. Otherwise, all transitions in T that

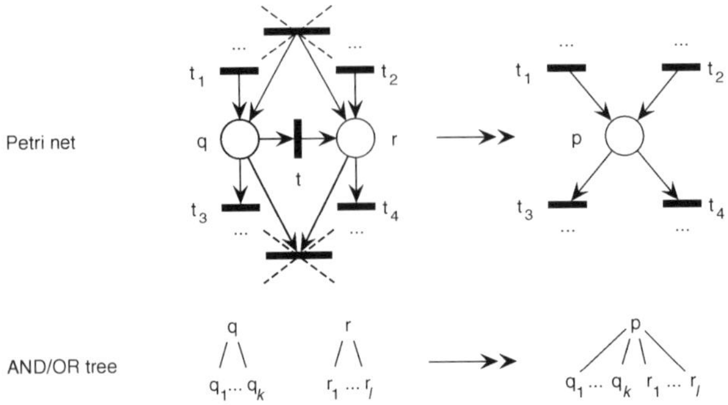

Fig. 8. Reduction step 2; a dotted cross indicates absence of a transition

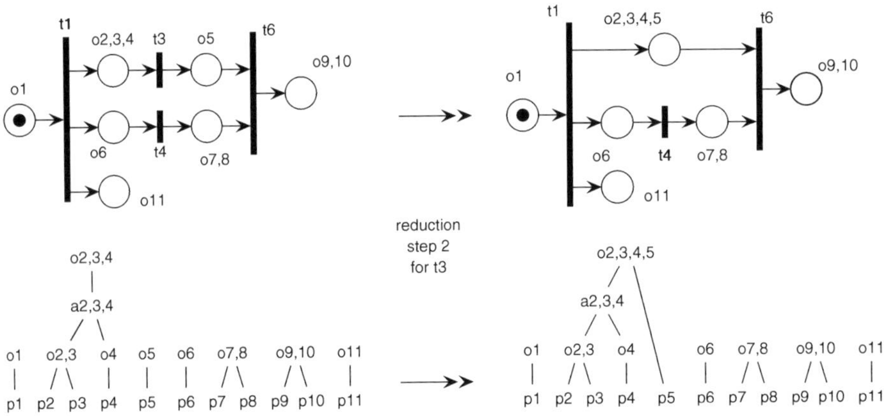

Fig. 9. Applying reduction step 2 for t3 in Fig. 1

have q or r as input or output place, instead get p as input or output place. The AND/OR tree of p is constructed by merging the roots of the two trees of q and r. Figure 8 specifies the reduction step graphically.

However, this reduction is only allowed if there is not a transition t' that has both q and r in its preset or both q and r in its postset. If the condition were dropped, this reduction step would result in BASIC nodes q, r not being orthogonal, since they have the same OR parent, namely p, while they are both source or target node of hyperedge t', which violates the statechart syntax. For instance, in Fig. 3(a), if transition t2 has been reduced and replaced by a place p that is output place of t1 and p3, then t3 cannot be reduced next in step 2, since t1 has both the input place (p3) and output place (p) of t3 in its postset.

Continuing with the processing of t3, the reduced net on the righthand side in Fig. 7 can be further reduced since t3 has a single input place o2,3,4 and a single output place o5. Figure 9 shows the resulting net and the node hierarchies.

Failure. If one the steps cannot be applied since its condition is not met, then the translation algorithm fails. In some peculiar cases, a structure/behaviour-preserving statechart translation may exist; see the detailed discussion in Sect. 5.

4 Algorithm

We now explain the actual translation algorithm PETRINETTOSTATECHART in detail. The algorithm expects as input a Petri net (P, T, F, ι) and returns a statechart. If the translation fails, the returned statechart is empty. Due to space limitations, formal definitions of the reduction steps and the updates of variables *child* and *type* have been omitted; they can be found in a technical report [5]. A prototype tool implementing the algorithm is available for download from `http://is.ieis.tue.nl/staff/heshuis/pn2sc`.

The algorithm uses three variables, *child*, *type*, and *root*, that will be used as part of the returned statechart structure. Variable *child* models the child-of relation of the statechart nodes, which are places from the Petri net *plus* the new places created by the reduction steps. We use U to denote the universe of all possible places, where $P \subseteq U$. Variable *type* is a function assigning to each node its type. Variable *root* is the root node of the constructed statechart.

In the actual procedure, first a copy of the input Petri net is created. This copy is passed as parameter to the algorithm CONSTRUCTTREE, which computes *child*, *type* and *root*. A copy is passed and not the original net, since at l. 10 the presets and postsets of the original net are used, not the ones of the reduced net. If CONSTRUCTTREE has computed a non-empty relation *child*, a statechart SC is constructed and returned. Nodes of SC are all places in P plus the places created by CONSTRUCTTREE, which equals the domain of function *type*. The initial configuration is the initial place of the input net, which is a child of *root*. Otherwise, if *child* is empty, then no AND/OR tree could be constructed and therefore the empty statechart is returned.

1: **procedure** PETRINETTOSTATECHART((P, T, F, ι))
2:     **var** $child : \mathcal{P}(U \times U)$
3:     **var** $type : U \rightarrow \{\text{BASIC}, \text{AND}, \text{OR}\}$
4:     **var** $root : U$
5:     **begin**
6:         $(P', T', F', \iota') := (P, T, F, \iota)$
7:         $child := \emptyset$; $type := \emptyset$
8:         CONSTRUCTTREE((P', T', F', ι'))
9:         **if** $child \neq \emptyset$ **then**
10:             $SC := (dom(type), T, \{t \mapsto \bullet t \mid t \in T\}, \{t \mapsto t\bullet \mid t \in T\}, child, type, \{\iota, root\})$
11:         **else**
12:             $SC := (\emptyset, \emptyset, \emptyset, \emptyset, \emptyset, \emptyset, \emptyset)$
13:         **end if**
14:         **return** SC
15:     **end**

We now detail the most important procedure, CONSTRUCTTREE, which is a subprocedure of the main procedure. First, for each place p a new place o_p is constructed, which acts as OR parent of p in the constructed node hierarchy. Place o_p replaces p in the net. Next, each transition from T is processed in a while loop. A transition $t \in T$ is selected for processing if it is a lower bound according to $\prec$, i.e., there is no other transition $t' \in T$ such that $\bullet t' \subset t\bullet$ or $\bullet t' \subset t\bullet$. For the example net in Fig. 5, the lower bound transitions are t2, t4, t5, and t7. Note that by definition of $\prec$, for example t3 $\not\prec$ t1 and t4 $\not\prec$ t5.

```
16:     procedure CONSTRUCTTREE((P, T, F, ι))
17:         for p ∈ P do
18:             replace p with new place o_p; let o_p be OR parent of p (upd. child, type)
19:         end for
20:         while T ≠ ∅ do
21:             t := a lower bound of T using ≺
```

During the processing of t, the two reduction steps specified in Sect. 3 are applied if their preconditions are met. If step 2 cannot be applied, then either step 1a or 1b could not be applied. Consequently, the procedure can stop, reset *child*, and return (l. 34), since no structure/behaviour-preserving statechart can be constructed. If one the places q or r is the initial place ι, then ι must be updated with the new place p (l. 31).

If the while loop is finished, so there are no more transitions in T, then single place ι remains. This place is root of the constructed AND/OR tree. Therefore, *root* is updated with ι (l. 37).

```
22:             if each pair q1, q2 ∈ •t has equal pre- and postsets then
23:                 apply reduction step 1a (upd. child, type)
24:             end if
25:             if each pair r1, r2 ∈ t• has equal pre- and postsets then
26:                 apply reduction step 1b (upd. child, type)
27:             end if
28:             if •t = {q} and t• = {r} and ∄t' ∈ T : q, r ∈ •t' ∨ q, r ∈ t'• then
29:                 apply reduction step 2 (upd. child, type)
30:                 if ι = q ∨ ι = r then
31:                     ι := the new place p
32:                 end if
33:             else
34:                 child := ∅; return
35:             end if
36:         end while
37:         root := ι
38:     end procedure
39: end procedure
```

In an accompanying technical report [5], the algorithm is proven correct, i.e., if a non-empty statechart is returned, the translation is behaviour-preserving: the behaviour of the statechart is isomorphic to the behaviour of the input net. Also in [5], the worst-case time complexity is shown to be quadratic in the size of the input Petri net.

5 Analysis

We analyse the expressiveness and completeness of the translation algorithm.

Expressiveness. To characterise the class of nets for which the algorithm returns a non-empty statechart, we first need the auxiliary notion of an area, which is a new concept in Petri net theory. Let $PN = (P, T, F, \iota)$ be a Petri net and $X \subseteq P$ be a nonempty set of places. Then X is an *area* if and only if for every $t \in T$, $\bullet t \subseteq X \Leftrightarrow t\bullet \subseteq X$. For example, in Fig. 1, sets $\{\mathsf{p2}, \mathsf{p3}\}$ and $\{\mathsf{p2}, \mathsf{p3}, \mathsf{p4}, \mathsf{p5}\}$ are areas, but $\{\mathsf{p5}\}$ is not. Given a set of places $X \subseteq P$, the minimal area of X, denoted $minArea(X)$, is the minimal set of places $Y \subseteq P$ such that $X \subseteq Y$ and Y is an area. For example, $minArea(\{\mathsf{p3}, \mathsf{p4}\}) = \{\mathsf{p2}, \mathsf{p3}, \mathsf{p4}, \mathsf{p5}\}$.

We use the notion of area to define the notion of cover. Let X be the preset or postset of some transition t. Then the *cover* of X, written $cover(X)$ is defined to be $\bigcup_{x \in X} minArea(\{x\})$. If the translation succeeds, then the AND node created for X contains all places in $cover(X)$ as BASIC nodes. For example, in Fig. 1, $cover(\{\mathsf{p3}, \mathsf{p4}\}) = \{\mathsf{p2}, \mathsf{p3}, \mathsf{p4}\}$. The places in this set are BASIC descendants of A1 in Fig. 2. Note that p5 is not included in $cover(\{\mathsf{p3}, \mathsf{p4}\})$.

A Petri net PN has *nestable covers* if and only if for every $X, Y \subseteq P$ such that X and Y are preset or postset of some transitions in T, $cover(X) \cap cover(Y) \neq \emptyset$ implies $cover(X) \subseteq cover(Y)$ or $cover(Y) \subseteq cover(X)$. The net in Fig. 10 does not have nestable covers, since $cover(\mathsf{t2}\bullet)$ and $cover(\bullet\mathsf{t5})$ are not nestable. But both unsafe nets in Fig. 3 do have nestable covers, so we need an additional criterion to rule out those nets.

A transition t has *consistent areas* if and only if for every set $X, Y \subseteq P$ such that $X \cup Y \subseteq \bullet t$ or $X \cup Y \subseteq t\bullet$, if $X \cap Y = \emptyset$ then $minArea(X) \cap minArea(Y) = \emptyset$. A Petri net PN has consistent areas if each transition has consistent areas. The nets in Fig. 3 do not have consistent areas: in both nets, $minArea(\{\mathsf{p2}\}) \cap minArea(\{\mathsf{p3}\}) \neq \emptyset$. In Fig. 3(b), $minArea(\{\mathsf{p3}\}) = \{\mathsf{p1}, \mathsf{p2}, \mathsf{p3}, \mathsf{p4}\}$.

In the technical report [5], we prove that the algorithm returns a non-empty statechart if and only if the input Petri net has nestable covers and consistent areas. Thus, the algorithm is sound and complete for this class of Petri nets.

This result implies that for Fig. 10 no structure-preserving statechart translation exists, due to place p5 which synchronises two parallel branches. However, in statecharts cross-synchronisation is typically expressed with event broadcasting. For example, Fig. 10 can map to a statechart in which there is no BASIC node corresponding to p5 and in which hyperedge t2 generates an event that triggers hyperedge t5. Thus, there does exist a statechart translation with similar behaviour as the Petri net, but the translation is not structure-preserving. Extending our translation to handle safe nets with cross-synchronisation by using statecharts with event broadcasting is part of future work.

As a final note on the expressiveness of the translation, consider the example net in Fig. 1. It exhibits a high degree of (block-)structuredness, since it does not contain choices or loops. In the corresponding statechart in Fig. 2, no goto-like constructs are used: for example OR nodes O1, O2, O4, and O6 each have a single entry and a single exit point. However, the example in Fig. 11 shows

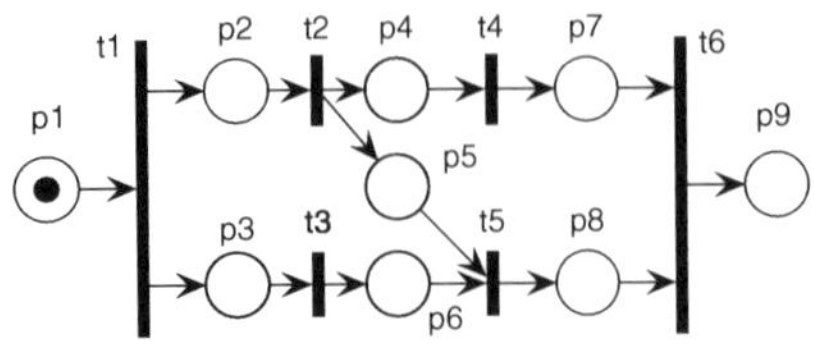

Fig. 10. Safe Petri net with cross-synchronisation which has no structure-preserving statechart translation

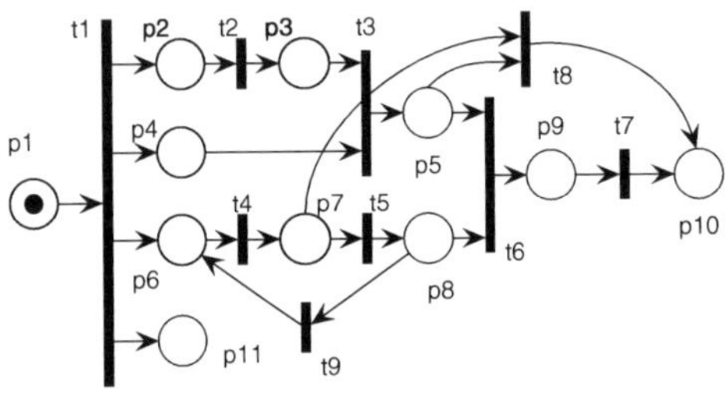

Fig. 11. Unstructured Petri net for which the algorithm constructs the same AND/OR tree as in Fig. 2

that the algorithm can also deal with unstructured nets that have a mixture of choices and loops: transition t8 leaves the loop headed by p6 in a goto-like way. The AND/OR tree constructed for this example by the algorithm is the same as in Fig. 2, but now for instance O4 has two exit points: p7 (for t8) and p8 (for t6).

Incompleteness. Still there are Petri nets that are outside the class defined above, but for which structure/behaviour-preserving statechart translations do exist. In this sense, the algorithm is incomplete. Statecharts which the algorithm fails to construct contain OR nodes with unconnected BASIC descendants. For instance, the algorithm cannot construct a statechart for the Petri net in Fig. 12(b), since the non-singleton presets and postsets {p1,p2} and {p2,p3} cannot be reduced. A structure/behaviour-preserving statechart translation does exist, as shown in the same figure. Note that the BASIC descendants p1 and p3 of the OR node are not connected by any hyperedge with a scope lower than or equal to O1.

In practice, this incompleteness does not seem to be a severe limitation. Statecharts in which some OR nodes contain unconnected BASIC children do not occur in practice, since a common though unwritten rule of thumb is to group only related (connected) BASIC nodes in an OR node, as can be inferred from the many statechart examples in the literature, e.g. [4,8]. A much more obvious translation for the Petri net in Fig. 12(b) is to use statecharts with overlapping [9] and to construct a statechart with two overlapping AND nodes, one for {p1,p2} and one for {p2,p3}.

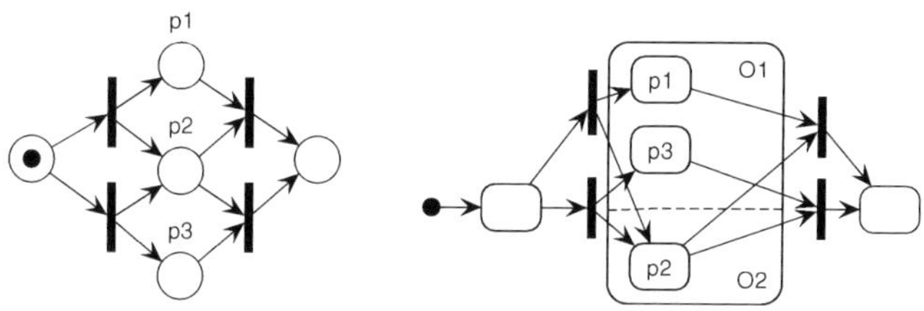

Fig. 12. Petri net and corresponding structure/behaviour-preserving statechart translation that the algorithm cannot construct

6 Related Work

Only a few papers consider translations from Petri nets to statecharts. The only published work with a considerable amount of detail is a paper by Schnabel et al. [19]. They outline an interactive method to translate a safe Petri net into a statechart. A place invariant is a set of places for which the sum of tokens in these places remains constant during any execution. Roughly speaking, each invariant maps to a parallel OR node o of a statechart, and each place in the invariant to a BASIC node in o. Since the same place can occur in several place invariants, it can translate into several BASIC nodes. Schnabel et al. outline some ways to prevent such duplications, but sometimes duplications cannot be avoided, for example for the net in Fig. 11. Our approach does not duplicate places and is fully automated.

For UML 1.x activity diagrams, whose syntax resembles Petri net syntax, a syntactic constraint was defined to give them a semantics in terms of UML statecharts [16]. For Petri nets, the constraint states that each transition having more than two output places is followed by a matching transition having the same number of input places, and that different pairs of transitions are properly nested, so a transition can only match one other transition. Each pair of matching transitions translates into an AND node. Our translation does not impose such a constraint on input nets (cf. the nets in Fig. 1 and 11), so it is more general.

As stated in the introduction, translations for the reverse direction, from statecharts to Petri nets, appear quite frequently in the literature (e.g. [11,18]). Main difference with our approach is that our translation constructs the AND/OR tree, while these other translations remove the AND/OR tree by omitting composite nodes. So our translation is more complex than these reverse translations.

Finally, Kishinevsky et al. [13] define a Petri net variant that incorporates some statechart features. The variant, called place chart net, uses hierarchy on places and preemptive transitions: a transition does not only empty its input places but also all descendant places of the input places. However, the relation between place chart nets and Petri nets is not formally analysed.

7 Conclusion

We have defined a polynomial algorithm that translates a subclass of safe Petri nets to statecharts in a structure-preserving way, so constructed statecharts resemble the input nets. The algorithm is structural and does not use any Petri net analysis technique. Moreover, it preserves the behaviour of the input net. Since the algorithm is polynomial, it is also efficient for large Petri nets.

There are several directions for further work. First, by considering statecharts with event broadcasting, the translation can be extended to deal with a broader class of safe nets. Also, the algorithm can be extended to statecharts with overlapping [9]. On the more applied side, the algorithm can be used as a foundation for implementing model transformations between UML activity diagrams, which resemble Petri nets, and UML statecharts [16]. Activity diagrams can specify the stateful behaviour of objects, whose lifecycles are independently specified in UML statecharts. The translation algorithm can be used to transform object behaviour specified in UML activity diagrams into UML statecharts, either to check consistency with an existing object lifecycle or to synthesise an object lifecycle from scratch.

References

1. Ajmone Marsan, M., Balbo, G., Conte, G., Donatelli, S., Franceschinis, G.: Modelling with Generalized Stochastic Petri Nets. J. Wiley, Chichester (1995)
2. Best, E., Darondeau, P., Wimmel, H.: Making Petri nets safe and free of internal transitions. Fundamenta Informaticae 80(1-3), 75–90 (2007)
3. Desel, J., Juhás, G.: What is a Petri net? Informal answers for the informed reader. In: Ehrig, H., Juhás, G., Padberg, J., Rozenberg, G. (eds.) APN 2001. LNCS, vol. 2128, pp. 1–27. Springer, Heidelberg (2001)
4. Eshuis, R.: Reconciling statechart semantics. Science of Computer Programming 74(3), 65–99 (2009)
5. Eshuis, R.: Translating safe Petri nets to statecharts in a structure-preserving way. Beta Working Paper Series, WP 282, Eindhoven University of Technology (2009)
6. Grahlmann, B.: The PEP tool. In: Grumberg, O. (ed.) CAV 1997. LNCS, vol. 1254, pp. 440–443. Springer, Heidelberg (1997)
7. Grumberg, O., Katz, S.: Veritech: a framework for translating among model description notations. STTT 9(2), 119–132 (2007)
8. Harel, D.: Statecharts: A visual formalism for complex systems. Science of Computer Programming 8(3), 231–274 (1987)
9. Harel, D., Kahana, C.-A.: On statecharts with overlapping. ACM Transactions on Software Engineering and Methodology 1(4), 399–421 (1992)
10. Harel, D., Naamad, A.: The STATEMATE semantics of statecharts. ACM Transactions on Software Engineering and Methodology 5(4), 293–333 (1996)
11. Huszerl, G., Majzik, I., Pataricza, A., Kosmidis, K., Dal Cin, M.: Quantitative analysis of UML statechart models of dependable systems. Computer Journal 45(3), 260–277 (2002)
12. IBM Rational Software. Rose (2009), `http://www.ibm.com/software/rational`

13. Kishinevsky, M., Cortadella, J., Kondratyev, A., Lavagno, L., Taubin, A., Yakovlev, A.: Coupling asynchrony and interrupts: Place chart nets. In: Azéma, P., Balbo, G. (eds.) ICATPN 1997. LNCS, vol. 1248, pp. 328–347. Springer, Heidelberg (1997)
14. The Mathworks. Stateflow user's guide (2009), http://www.mathworks.com
15. Murata, T.: Petri nets: Properties, analysis, and applications. Proc. of the IEEE 77(4), 541–580 (1989)
16. Object Management Group. UML specification (2009), http://www.uml.org
17. Rausch, M., Krogh, B.: Transformations between different model forms in discrete event systems. In: Proc. IEEE SMC 1997, vol. 3, pp. 2841–2846 (1997)
18. Saldhana, J.A., Shatz, S.M., Hu, Z.: Formalization of object behavior and interactions from UML models. International Journal of Software Engineering and Knowledge Engineering 11(6), 643–673 (2001)
19. Schnabel, M., Nenninger, G., Krebs, V.: Konvertierung sicherer Petri-netze in statecharts (in German). Automatisierungstechnik 47(12), 571–580 (1999)

Symbolic Predictive Analysis for Concurrent Programs

Chao Wang[1], Sudipta Kundu[2], Malay Ganai[1], and Aarti Gupta[1]

[1] NEC Laboratories America, Princeton, NJ, USA
[2] University of California, San Diego, La Jolla, CA, USA

Abstract. Predictive analysis aims at detecting concurrency errors during runtime by monitoring a concrete execution trace of a concurrent program. In recent years, various models based on happens-before causality relations have been proposed for predictive analysis to improve the interleaving coverage while ensuring the absence of false alarms. However, these models are based on only the observed events, and typically do not utilize source code. Furthermore, the enumerative algorithms they use for verifying safety properties in the predicted execution traces often suffer from the interleaving explosion problem. In this paper, we introduce a new symbolic causal model based on source code and the observed events, and propose a symbolic algorithm to check whether a safety property holds in all feasible permutations of events in the given execution trace. Rather than explicitly enumerating the interleavings, our algorithm conducts the verification using a novel encoding of the causal model and symbolic reasoning with a satisfiability modulo theory (SMT) solver. Our algorithm has a larger interleaving coverage than known causal models in the literature. We also propose a method to *symbolically bound* the number of context switches allowed in an interleaving, to further improve the scalability of the algorithm.

1 Introduction

Predictive analysis aims at detecting concurrency errors by observing execution traces of a concurrent program which themselves may be non-erroneous. Due to the inherent nondeterminism in scheduling concurrent processes/threads, executing a program with the same test input may lead to different program behaviors. This poses a significant challenge in testing—even if a test input may cause a failure, the erroneous interleaving manifesting the failure may not be executed during testing. Furthermore, merely executing the same test multiple times does not always increase the interleaving coverage. In predictive analysis, a concrete execution trace is given, together with a correctness property in the form of assertions embedded in the trace. The given execution trace need not violate the property, but there may exist an alternative trace, i.e., a feasible permutation of events of the given trace, that violates the property. The goal of predictive analysis is to detect such erroneous traces by *statically* analyzing the given execution trace without re-executing the program.

Existing predictive analysis algorithms can be classified into two categories based on the quality of reported bugs. The first category consists of methods that do not miss real errors but may report bogus errors. Historically, algorithms based on lockset analysis [1,2,3] fall into the first category. They strive to cover all possible interleavings that are feasible permutations of events of the given trace, but at the same time may

A. Cavalcanti and D. Dams (Eds.): FM 2009, LNCS 5850, pp. 256–272, 2009.

introduce some interleavings that can never appear in the actual program execution. The second category consists of methods that do not report bogus errors but may miss some real errors. In these methods [4,5,6], various causal models have been used, with many inspired by Lamport's happens-before causality [7]. They provide the *feasibility guarantee*–that all the reported erroneous interleavings are actual program executions, but they may not cover all interleavings allowed by the program source code.

This paper also focuses on predictive analysis algorithms with the feasibility guarantee. In this context, one can view the given execution trace as a total order of events appearing in the trace, and view the causal model as a partial order of events, which admits the given trace as well as many alternative interleavings. However, two significant problems remain to be solved. First, checking all the feasible interleavings allowed by a causal model for property violations is a bottleneck. Despite the long quest for more coverage in causal models, little has been done to improve the underlying checking algorithms. Existing methods [4,5,6] often rely on explicit enumeration of interleavings, which does not scale when the number of interleavings is large. In reality, the more general a causal model is, the larger the number of interleavings it admits. Second, these causal models often do not assume that source code is available, and therefore rely on observing only the *concrete events* during execution. In a concrete event, typically the values read from or written to shared memory locations are available, whereas the actual program code that produces the event is not known. Consequently, often unnecessarily strong happens-before causality is imposed to achieve the desired feasibility guarantee.

In this paper, we propose a *symbolic* predictive analysis algorithm to address these two problems. We assume that the source code is available for instrumentation to obtain *symbolic events* at runtime. We introduce a symbolic causal model based on program source code and observed events in a trace. The new model is designed to achieve the goal of covering more interleavings; it also facilitates a constraint-based modeling where various concurrency primitives or semantics (locks, semaphores, happens-before, sequential consistency, etc.) are handled easily and uniformly. More specifically, we make the following contributions:

- We introduce a *concurrent trace program* as a symbolic predictive model to capture feasible interleavings that can be predicted from a given execution trace.
- We propose a safety property checking algorithm using a concurrent static single assignment (CSSA) based encoding and symbolic reasoning with a SMT solver. The symbolic search automatically captures property- or goal-directed pruning, through conflict analysis and learning features in modern SMT solvers.
- We propose a simple method to symbolically bound the number of context switches in an interleaving, which further improves the scalability of our algorithm.

If desired, our symbolic algorithm can be further constrained to match the interleaving coverage of known causal models in the literature. In effect, our new model has a larger interleaving coverage than the existing models.

The remainder of this paper is organized as follows. In Section 2, we provide a motivating example and illustrate our ideas. In Section 3, we formally define execution traces and our predictive model. In Section 4, we present the SMT-based symbolic property checking algorithm. In Section 5, we present the symbolic encoding to enforce context-bounding. In Section 6, we demonstrate how our algorithm can be constrained to match a more restrictive causal model [6]. We present our experimental results in Section 7. We review related work in Section 8 and give our conclusions in Section 9.

2 Motivating Example

Fig. 1 shows a multithreaded program execution trace, modified from an example in [6]. There are two concurrent threads T_1 and T_2, three shared variables x, y and z, two thread-local variables a and b, and a counting semaphore l. The semaphore l can be viewed as an integer variable initialized to 1. $acq(l)$ acquires the semaphore when $(l > 0)$ and decreases l by one, while $rel(l)$ releases the semaphore and increases l by one. The initial program state is $x = y = 0$. The sequence $\rho = t_1–t_{11}t_{13}$ of statements denotes the execution order of the given trace. The correctness property is specified as an assertion in t_{12}. The given trace ρ does not violate this assertion. However, a *feasible permutation* of this trace, $\rho' = (t_1–t_4)t_9t_{10}t_{11}t_{12}t_{13}(t_5–t_8)$, exposes the error.

To our knowledge, none of the *sound* causal models in the literature, including [7,4,5,6], can predict this error. By sound, we mean that the predictive technique does not generate false alarms (most of the lockset based algorithms are not sound). For instance, if Lamport's happens-before causality is used to define the feasible trace permutations of ρ, the execution order of all *read-after-write* event pairs in ρ, which are over the same shared variable, must be respected. It means that event t_8 must be executed before t_{10} and event t_7 must be executed before t_{11}. These *happens-before* constraints are sufficient but often not necessary to ensure that the admitted traces are feasible—many other feasible interleavings are left out.

Various causal models proposed subsequently aimed at lifting some of these happens-before constraints without jeopardizing the feasibility guarantee [4,5,6]. However, when applied to the example in Fig. 1, none of them can predict the erroneous trace $\rho' = (t_1–t_4)t_9t_{10}t_{11}t_{12}t_{13}(t_5–t_8)$. Consider, for example, the *maximal causal model* in [6]. The model relies on the axioms of semaphore and sequential consistency and is general enough to subsume other known causal models. This model allows all the classic happens-before constraints to be lifted, except for the one stating that event t_7 must happen before t_{11}. Changing their execution order may lead to a different program state. As a result, the model in [6] cannot be used to predict the error in ρ'.

The reason these sound models cannot predict the error in Fig. 1 is that they model events in ρ as the concrete values read from or written to shared variables. Such *concrete events* are tied closely to the given trace. Consider t_{11} `:if(x>b)`, for instance; it is regarded as *an event that reads value* 1 *from variable* x. This is a partial interpretation because other program statements, such as `if(b>x)`, `if(x>1)`, and even assignment `b:=x`, may produce the same event. Consequently, unnecessarily strong happens-before constraints are imposed over event t_{11} to ensure the feasibility of all admitted traces, regardless of what statement produces the event.

In contrast, we model the execution trace as a sequence of *symbolic events* by considering the program statements that produce ρ and capturing abstract values (e.g. relevant predicates). For instance, we model event t_{11} as assume$(x > b)$, where assume(c) means the condition c holds when the event is executed, indicating that t_{11} is produced by a branching statement and $(x > b)$ is the condition taken. We do not use the happens-before causality to define the set of admitted traces. Instead, we allow all possible interleavings of these symbolic events as long as the sequential consistency semantics of a concurrent program execution is respected. In the running example, it is possible to move symbolic events t_9–t_{12} ahead of t_5–t_8 while still maintaining the sequential consistency. As a result, our new algorithm, while maintaining the feasibility guarantee, is capable of predicting the erroneous behavior in ρ'.

Thread T_1	Thread T_2
$t_1 : a := x$	
$t_2 : acq(l)$	
$t_3 : x := 2 + a$	
$t_4 : rel(l)$	
$t_5 : y := 1 + a$	
$t_6 : acq(l)$	
$t_7 : x := 1 + a$	
$t_8 : rel(l)$	
	$t_9 : b := 0$
	$t_{10} : acq(l)$
	$t_{11} : if(x > b)$
	$t_{12} :$ assert$(y == 1)$
	$t_{13} : rel(l)$

Fig. 1. The sequence of executed program statements (x=y=0 initially)

$t_1 : \langle 1, (\mathsf{assume}(\mathsf{true}), \{a := x\}) \rangle$
$t_2 : \langle 1, (\mathsf{assume}(l > 0), \{l := l - 1\}) \rangle$
$t_3 : \langle 1, (\mathsf{assume}(\mathsf{true}), \{x := 2 + a\}) \rangle$
$t_4 : \langle 1, (\mathsf{assume}(\mathsf{true}), \{l := l + 1\}) \rangle$
$t_5 : \langle 1, (\mathsf{assume}(\mathsf{true}), \{y := 1 + a\}) \rangle$
$t_6 : \langle 1, (\mathsf{assume}(l > 0), \{l := l - 1\}) \rangle$
$t_7 : \langle 1, (\mathsf{assume}(\mathsf{true}), \{x := 1 + a\}) \rangle$
$t_8 : \langle 1, (\mathsf{assume}(\mathsf{true}), \{l := l + 1\}) \rangle$

$t_9 : \langle 2, (\mathsf{assume}(\mathsf{true}), \{b := 0\}) \rangle$
$t_{10} : \langle 2, (\mathsf{assume}(l > 0), \{l := l - 1\}) \rangle$
$t_{11} : \langle 2, (\mathsf{assume}(x > b), \{\ \}) \rangle$
$t_{12} : \langle 2, (\mathsf{assert}(y = 1)) \rangle$
$t_{13} : \langle 2, (\mathsf{assume}(\mathsf{true}), \{l := l + 1\}) \rangle$

Fig. 2. The symbolic representation of the execution trace (x=y=0 initially)

3 Preliminaries

In this section, we define programs, execution traces, and concurrent trace programs. Concurrent trace programs are our models for symbolic predictive analysis.

3.1 Programs and Execution Traces

A *concurrent program* has a finite set of *threads* and a finite set SV of *shared variables*. Each thread T_i, where $1 \le i \le k$, has a finite set of *local variables* LV_i.

- Let $Tid = \{1, \ldots, k\}$ be the set of thread indices.
- Let $V_i = SV \cup LV_i$, where $1 \le i \le k$, be the set of variables accessible in T_i.

The remaining aspects of a concurrent program, including the control flow and the expression syntax, are intentionally left unspecified in order to be more general. Instead, we directly define the symbolic execution traces.

A *symbolic execution trace* of a program is a finite sequence of events $\rho = t_1 \ldots t_n$. An *event* $t \in \rho$ is a tuple $\langle tid, action \rangle$, where $tid \in Tid$ is a thread index and $action$ is an atomic computation. An action in thread T_i may be one of the following:

- $(\mathsf{assume}(c), asgn)$ is the atomic *guarded assignment* action, where
  - $asgn$ is a set of assignments, each of the form $v := exp$, where $v \in V_i$ is a variable and exp is an expression over V_i.

  - assume(c) means the conditional expression c over V_i must be true for the assignments in $asgn$ to execute.
- assert(c) is the assertion action. The conditional expression c over V_i must be true when the event is executed; otherwise, an error is raised.

Each event in the execution trace is unique. If a statement in the textual representation of the program is executed again, e.g., when it is inside a loop or a routine called by multiple threads, a new event will be generated at run time [8].

By defining the expression syntax suitably, the symbolic trace representation can model the execution of any shared-memory multithreaded program. Details on modeling generic C/C++ language constructs are not directly related to concurrency; for more information refer to recent efforts in [9,10].

The guarded assignment action has the following three variants: (1) when the guard $c =$ true, it can model normal assignments in a basic block; (2) when the assignment set $asgn$ is empty, assume(c) or assume($\neg c$) can model the execution of a branching statement `if(c)-else`; and (3) with both the guard and the assignment set, it can model the atomic *check-and-set* operation, which is the foundation of all types of concurrency primitives. For example, acquiring a counting semaphore l can be modeled as the action (assume($l > 0$), $\{l := l - 1\}$).

Example. Fig. 2 shows an example symbolic execution trace representation, which corresponds to ρ in Fig. 1. Note that the synchronization primitive $acq(l)$ in t_2 is modeled as an atomic guarded assignment action. The normal assignment in t_1 is modeled with assume(true). The if-statement in t_{11} is modeled with $asgn$ being an empty set.

3.2 Concurrent Trace Programs

The semantics of a symbolic execution trace is defined using a state transition system. Let $V = SV \cup \bigcup_i LV_i$, $1 \leq i \leq k$, be the set of all program variables and Val be a set of values of variables in V. A *state* is a map $s : V \rightarrow Val$ assigning a value to each variable. We also use $s[v]$ and $s[exp]$ to denote the values of $v \in V$ and expression exp in state s. We say that a *state transition* $s \xrightarrow{t} s'$ exists, where s, s' are states and t is an event in thread T_i, $1 \leq i \leq k$, iff one of the following conditions holds:

- $t = \langle i, (\text{assume}(c), asgn)\rangle$, $s[c]$ is true, and for each assignment $v := exp$ in $asgn$, $s'[v] = s[exp]$ holds; states s and s' agree on all other variables.
- $t = \langle i, \text{assert}(c)\rangle$ and $s[c]$ is true. When $s[c]$ is false, an attempt to execute event t raises an error.

Let $\rho = t_1 \dots t_n$ be a symbolic execution trace of a concurrent program P. It defines a total order on the symbolic events. From ρ we can derive a partial order called the concurrent trace program (CTP).

Definition 1. *The* concurrent trace program *of ρ is a partially ordered set $CTP_\rho = (T, \sqsubseteq)$ such that,*

- *$T = \{t \mid t \in \rho\}$ is the set of events, and*
- *$\sqsubseteq$ is a partial order such that, for any $t_i, t_j \in T$, $t_i \sqsubseteq t_j$ iff $tid(t_i) = tid(t_j)$ and $i < j$ (in ρ, event t_i appears before t_j).*

In the sequel, we will say a transition $t \in CTP_\rho$ to mean that $t \in T$ is associated with the CTP. Intuitively, CTP_ρ orders events from the same thread by their execution order in ρ; events from different threads are not *explicitly* ordered with each other. Keeping events symbolic and allowing events from different threads to remain un-ordered with each other is the crucial difference from existing sound causal models [7,4,5,6].

We guarantee the feasibility of predicted traces through the notion of *feasible linearizations* of CTP_ρ. A linearization of this partial order is an alternative interleaving of events in ρ. Let $\rho' = t'_1 \dots t'_n$ be a linearization of CTP_ρ. We say that ρ' is a *feasible linearization* iff there exist states $s_0, \dots, s_n$ such that, s_0 is the initial state of the program and for all $i = 1, \dots, n$, there exists a transition $s_{i-1} \xrightarrow{t'_i} s_i$. Note that this definition captures the standard sequential consistency semantics for concurrent programs, where we modeled concurrency primitives such as locks by using auxiliary shared variables in atomic guarded assignment events.

4 Symbolic Predictive Analysis Algorithm

Given an execution trace ρ, we derive the model CTP_ρ and *symbolically* check all its feasible linearizations for property violations. For this, we create a formula Φ_{CTP_ρ} such that Φ_{CTP_ρ} is satisfiable iff there exists a feasible linearization of CTP_ρ that violates the property. Specifically, we use an encoding that creates the formula in a quantifier-free first-order logic to facilitate the application of off-the-shelf SMT solvers [11].

4.1 Concurrent Static Single Assignment

Our encoding is based on transforming the concurrent trace program into a concurrent static single assignment (CSSA) form, inspired by [12]. The CSSA form has the property that each variable is defined exactly once. Here a *definition* of variable $v \in V$ is an event that modifies v, and a *use* of v is an event where it appears in an expression. In our case, an event defines v iff v appears in the left-hand-side of an assignment; an event uses v iff v appears in a condition (an assume or the assert) or the right-hand-side of an assignment.

Unlike in the classic sequential SSA form, we need not add ϕ-functions to model the confluence of multiple if-else branches because in a concurrent trace program, each thread has a single control path. The branching decisions have already been made during program execution resulting in the trace ρ.

We differentiate shared variables in SV from local variables in LV_i, $1 \leq i \leq k$. Each use of variable $v \in LV_i$ corresponds to a unique definition, a preceding event in the same thread T_i that defines v. For shared variables, however, each use of variable $v \in SV$ may map to multiple definitions due to thread interleaving. A π-function is added to model the confluence of these possible definitions.

Definition 2. *A π-function, introduced for a shared variable v immediately before its use, has the form $\pi(v_1, \dots, v_l)$, where each v_i, $1 \leq i \leq l$, is either the most recent definition of v in the same thread as the use, or a definition of v in another concurrent thread.*

Therefore, the construction of CSSA consists of the following steps:

1. Create unique names for local/shared variables in their definitions.
2. For each use of a local variable $v \in LV_i$, $1 \leq i \leq k$, replace v with the most recent (unique) definition v'.
3. For each use of a shared variable $v \in SV$, create a unique name v' and add the definition $v' \leftarrow \pi(v_1, \ldots, v_l)$. Then replace v with the new definition v'.

Example. Fig. 3 shows the CSSA form of the CTP in Fig. 2. We add new names π^1–π^9 and π-functions for the shared variable uses. The condition $(x > b)$ in t_{11} becomes $(\pi^7 > b_1)$ where $\pi^7 \leftarrow \pi(x_0, x_1, x_2)$ denotes the current value of shared variable x and b_1 denotes the value of local variable b defined in t_9. The names x_0, x_1, x_2 denote the values of x defined in t_0, t_3 and t_7, respectively. Event t_0 is added to model the initial values of the variables.

t_0 : $\langle 1, (\mathsf{assume}(true), \{x_0 := 0, y_0 := 0, l_0 := 1\}) \rangle$
t_1 : $\langle 1, (\mathsf{assume}(true), \{a_1 := \pi^1\}) \rangle$ where $\pi^1 \leftarrow \pi(x_0)$
t_2 : $\langle 1, (\mathsf{assume}(\pi^2 > 0), \{l_1 := \pi^2 - 1\}) \rangle$ where $\pi^2 \leftarrow \pi(l_0, l_5, l_6)$
t_3 : $\langle 1, (\mathsf{assume}(true), \{x_1 := 2 + a_1\}) \rangle$
t_4 : $\langle 1, (\mathsf{assume}(true), \{l_2 := \pi^3 + 1\}) \rangle$ where $\pi^3 \leftarrow \pi(l_1, l_5, l_6)$
t_5 : $\langle 1, (\mathsf{assume}(true), \{y_1 := 1 + a_1\}) \rangle$
t_6 : $\langle 1, (\mathsf{assume}(\pi^4 > 0), \{l_3 := \pi^4 - 1\}) \rangle$ where $\pi^4 \leftarrow \pi(l_2, l_5, l_6)$
t_7 : $\langle 1, (\mathsf{assume}(true), \{x_2 := 1 + a_1\}) \rangle$
t_8 : $\langle 1, (\mathsf{assume}(true), \{l_4 := \pi^5 + 1\}) \rangle$ where $\pi^5 \leftarrow \pi(l_3, l_5, l_6)$

t_9 : $\langle 2, (\mathsf{assume}(true), \{b_1 := 0\}) \rangle$
t_{10} : $\langle 2, (\mathsf{assume}(\pi^6 > 0), \{l_5 := \pi^6 - 1\}) \rangle$ where $\pi^6 \leftarrow \pi(l_0, l_1, l_2, l_3, l_4)$
t_{11} : $\langle 2, (\mathsf{assume}(\pi^7 > b_1), \{\ \}) \rangle$ where $\pi^7 \leftarrow \pi(x_0, x_1, x_2)$
t_{12} : $\langle 2, (\mathsf{assert}(\pi^8 = 1)) \rangle$ where $\pi^8 \leftarrow \pi(y_0, y_1)$
t_{13} : $\langle 2, (\mathsf{assume}(true), \{l_6 := \pi^9 + 1\}) \rangle$ where $\pi^9 \leftarrow \pi(l_0, l_1, l_2, l_3, l_4, l_5)$

Fig. 3. The CSSA form of the concurrent trace program

Semantics of π-Functions. Let $v' \leftarrow \pi(v_1, \ldots, v_l)$ be defined in event t, and each v_i, $1 \leq i \leq l$, be defined in event t_i. The π-function may return any of the parameters as the result depending on the write-read consistency in a particular interleaving. Intuitively, $(v' = v_i)$ in an interleaving iff v_i is the most recent definition before event t. More formally, $(v' = v_i)$, $1 \leq i \leq l$, holds iff the following conditions hold,

– event t_i, which defines v_i, is executed before event t; and
– any event t_j that defines v_j, $1 \leq i \leq l$ and $j \neq i$, is executed either before the definition t_i or after the use t.

4.2 CSSA-Based SAT Encoding

We construct the quantifier-free first-order logic formula Φ_{CTP}[1] based on the notion of feasible linearizations of CTP (in Section 3.2) and the π-function semantics (in Section 4.1). The construction is straightforward and follows their definitions. The entire

[1] We omit the subscript ρ in CTP_ρ where it is understood from the context.

formula Φ_{CTP} consists of the following four subformulas:

$$\Phi_{CTP} := \Phi_{PO} \wedge \Phi_{VD} \wedge \Phi_{PI} \wedge \neg\Phi_{PRP}$$

where Φ_{PO} encodes the program order, Φ_{VD} encodes the variable definitions, Φ_{PI} encodes the π-functions, and Φ_{PRP} encodes the property.

To help present the encoding algorithm, we use the following notations:

- **first event t_{first}:** we add a dummy event t_{first} to be the first executed event in the CTP. That is, $\forall t \in CTP$ and $t \neq t_{\mathsf{first}}$, event t must be executed after t_{first};
- **last event t_{last}:** we add a dummy event t_{last} to be the last executed event in the CTP. That is, $\forall t \in CTP$ and $t \neq t_{\mathsf{last}}$, event t must be executed before t_{last};
- **first event t^i_{first} of thread T_i:** for each $i \in Tid$, this is the first event of the thread;
- **last event t^i_{last} of thread T_i:** for each $i \in Tid$, this is the last event of the thread;
- **thread-local preceding event:** for each event t, we define its thread-local preceding event t' as follows: $tid(t') = tid(t)$ and for any other event $t'' \in CTP$ such that $tid(t'') = tid(t)$, either $t'' \sqsubseteq t'$ or $t \sqsubseteq t''$.
- **HB-constraint:** we use $HB(t, t')$ to denote that event t is executed before event t'. The actual constraint comprising $HB(t, t')$ is described in the next section.

Path Conditions. For each event $t \in CTP$, we define path condition $g(t)$ such that t is executed iff $g(t)$ is true. The path conditions are computed as follows:

1. If $t = t_{\mathsf{first}}$, or $t = t^i_{\mathsf{first}}$ where $i \in Tid$, let $g(t) :=$ true.
2. Otherwise, t has a thread-local preceding event t'.
   - if t' has action (assume(c), $asgn$), let $g(t) := c \wedge g(t')$;
   - if t' has action assert(c), let $g(t) := g(t')$.

   Note that an assert event does not contribute to the path condition.

Program Order (Φ_{PO}). Formula Φ_{PO} captures the event order within each thread. *It does not impose any inter-thread constraint.* Let $\Phi_{PO} :=$ true initially. For each event $t \in CTP$,

1. If $t = t_{\mathsf{first}}$, do nothing;
2. If $t = t^i_{\mathsf{first}}$, where $i \in Tid$, let $\Phi_{PO} := \Phi_{PO} \wedge HB(t_{\mathsf{first}}, t^i_{\mathsf{first}})$;
3. If $t = t_{\mathsf{last}}$, let $\Phi_{PO} := \Phi_{PO} \wedge \bigwedge_{\forall i \in Tid} HB(t^i_{\mathsf{last}}, t_{\mathsf{last}})$;
4. Otherwise, t has a thread-local preceding event t'; let $\Phi_{PO} := \Phi_{PO} \wedge HB(t', t)$.

Variable Definition (Φ_{VD}). Formula Φ_{VD} is the conjunction of all variable definitions. Let $\Phi_{VD} :=$ true initially. For each event $t \in CTP$,

1. If t has action (assume(c), $asgn$), for each assignment $v := exp$ in $asgn$, let $\Phi_{VD} := \Phi_{VD} \wedge (v = exp)$;
2. Otherwise, do nothing.

The π-Function (Φ_{PI}). Each π-function defines a new variable v', and Φ_{PI} is a conjunction of all these variable definitions. Let $\Phi_{PI} :=$ true initially. For each

$v' \leftarrow \pi(v_1, \ldots, v_l)$ defined in event t, where v' is used; also assume that each v_i, $1 \leq i \leq l$, is defined in event t_i. Let

$$\Phi_{PI} := \Phi_{PI} \wedge \bigvee_{i=1}^{l} (v' = v_i) \wedge g(t_i) \wedge HB(t_i, t) \wedge \bigwedge_{j=1, j \neq i}^{l} (HB(t_j, t_i) \vee HB(t, t_j))$$

Intuitively, the π-function evaluates to v_i iff it chooses the i-th definition in the π-set (indicated by $g(t_i) \wedge HB(t_i, t)$), such that any other definition v_j, $1 \leq j \leq l$ and $j \neq i$, is either before t_i, or after this use of v_i in t.

Assertion Property (Φ_{PRP}). Let $t \in CTP$ be the event with action $\mathsf{assert}(c)$, which specifies the correctness property.

$$\Phi_{PRP} := (g(t) \rightarrow c)$$

Intuitively, the assertion condition c must hold if t is executed. Recall that Φ_{PRP} is negated in Φ_{CTP_ρ} to search for property violations.

Example. Fig. 4 illustrates the CSSA-based encoding of the example in Fig. 3, where the subformulas that form Φ_{PO} and Φ_{VD} are listed. In the figure, t_0, t_{14} are the dummy entry and exit events. Φ_{PRP} (at t_{12}) is defined as $\neg g_{12} \vee (\pi^8 = 1)$. The subformula in Φ_{PI} for $\pi^7 \leftarrow \pi(x_0, x_1, x_2)$ in t_{11} is defined as follows:

$$\begin{array}{llll} t_{11}: & (\ \pi^7 = x_0 \wedge (\mathsf{true}) & \wedge HB(t_{11}, t_3) & \wedge HB(t_{11}, t_7) \\ & \vee \pi^7 = x_1 \wedge g_3 \wedge HB(t_3, t_{11}) & \wedge \mathsf{true} & \wedge HB(t_{11}, t_7) \\ & \vee \pi^7 = x_2 \wedge g_7 \wedge HB(t_7, t_{11}) & \wedge \mathsf{true} & \wedge \mathsf{true}) \end{array}$$

Note that some HB-constraints evaluate to constant false and true—such simplification is frequent and is performed in our implementation to reduce the formula size.

Let n be the number of events in a CTP, n_π be the number of shared variable uses, and l_π be the maximal number of parameters in any π-function. Our encoding produces a formula of size $O(n + n_\pi \times l_\pi^2)$. Although in the worst case—when each event *reads and writes all* shared variables—$(n_\pi \times l_\pi^2)$ becomes $O(n^3)$, it is rare in realistic applications. The reason is that shared variable accesses in a concurrent program are often kept few and far in between, especially when compared to computations within threads, to minimize the synchronization overhead. In contrast, conventional bounded model checking (BMC) algorithms, e.g. [13,14], often generate significantly larger formulas. To cover all feasible interleavings in a CTP, the BMC unrolling depth needs to be n, and within each time frame all the n events need to be modeled. Furthermore, the BMC formula size cannot be easily reduced even though l_π and n_π are significantly smaller than n. In Section 7, we will present experimental comparison of our CSSA-based encoding with the BMC algorithm in [13].

4.3 Proof of Correctness

Recall that for two arbitrary events t and t', the constraint $HB(t, t')$ denote that t must be executed before t'. Consider a model where we introduce for each event $t \in CTP$ a fresh integer variable $\mathcal{O}(t)$ denoting its execution time[2]. A satisfiable solution for

[2] The execution time is an integer denoting its position in the linearization.

Path Conditions:		Program Order:	Variable Definitions:
t_0 :			$x_0 = 0 \wedge y_0 = 0 \wedge l_0 = 1$
t_1 :	$g_1 = \text{true}$	$HB(t_0, t_1)$	$a_1 = \pi^1$
t_2 :	$g_2 = g_1 \wedge (\pi^2 > 0)$	$HB(t_1, t_2)$	$l_1 = \pi^2 - 1$
t_3 :	$g_3 = g_2$	$HB(t_2, t_3)$	$x_1 = 2 + a_1$
t_4 :	$g_4 = g_3$	$HB(t_3, t_4)$	$l_2 = \pi^3 + 1$
t_5 :	$g_5 = g_4$	$HB(t_4, t_5)$	$y_1 = 1 + a_1$
t_6 :	$g_6 = g_5 \wedge (\pi^4 > 0)$	$HB(t_5, t_6)$	$l_3 = \pi^4 - 1$
t_7 :	$g_7 = g_6$	$HB(t_6, t_7)$	$x_2 = 1 + a_1$
t_8 :	$g_8 = g_7$	$HB(t_7, t_8)$	$l_4 = \pi^5 + 1$
t_9 :	$g_9 = \text{true}$	$HB(t_0, t_9)$	
t_{10} :	$g_{10} = g_9 \wedge (\pi^6 > 0)$	$HB(t_9, t_{10})$	$b_1 = 0$
t_{11} :	$g_{11} = g_{10} \wedge (\pi^7 > b_1)$	$HB(t_{10}, t_{11})$	$l_5 = \pi^6 - 1$
t_{12} :	$g_{12} = g_{11}$	$HB(t_{11}, t_{12})$	
t_{13} :	$g_{13} = g_{13}$	$HB(t_{12}, t_{13})$	$l_6 = \pi^9 + 1$
t_{14} :		$HB(t_8, t_{14}) \wedge HB(t_{13}, t_{14})$	

Fig. 4. The CSSA-based symbolic encoding of the CTP in Fig. 3

Φ_{CTP_ρ} therefore induces values of $\mathcal{O}(t)$, i.e., times of all events in the linearization. The constraint $HB(t, t')$ is captured as follows:

$$HB(t, t') := \mathcal{O}(t) < \mathcal{O}(t')$$

We now state the correctness of our encoding.

Theorem 1. *Formula Φ_{CTP} is satisfiable iff there exists a feasible linearization of the CTP that violates the assertion property.*

Proof. The encoding closely follows our definitions of CTP, feasible linearizations, and the semantics of π-functions. The proof is straightforward and is omitted for brevity.

5 Symbolic Context Bounding

In this section, we present a symbolic encoding that effectively bounds the number of context switches allowed by an interleaving.

Traditionally, a *context switch* is defined as the computing process of storing and restoring the CPU state (context) when executing a concurrent program, such that multiple processes or threads can share a single CPU resource. The idea of using context bounding to reduce complexity in verifying concurrent programs was introduced by Qadeer and Rehof [15]. Several subsequent studies have confirmed [16,17] that concurrency bugs in practice can often be exposed in interleavings with a surprisingly small number of context switches.

Example. Consider the running example in Fig. 1. If we restrict the number of context switches of an interleaving to 1, there are only two possibilities:

$$\rho' = (t_1 t_2 \ldots t_8)(t_9 t_{10} \ldots t_{13})$$
$$\rho'' = (t_9 t_{10} \ldots t_{13})(t_1 t_2 \ldots t_8)$$

In both cases the context switch happens when one thread completes its execution. However, none of the two traces is erroneous; and ρ'' is not even feasible. When we increase the context bound to 2, the number of admitted interleavings remains small but now the following trace is included:

$$\rho''' = (t_1 t_2 t_3)(t_9 t_{10} t_{11} t_{12})(t_4 \ldots t_8)$$

The trace has two context switches and exposes the error in t_{12} (where $y = 0$).

5.1 Revisiting the HB-Constraints

We defined $HB(t, t')$ as $\mathcal{O}(t) < \mathcal{O}(t')$ earlier. However, the *strictly-less-than* constraint is sufficient, but not necessary, to ensure the correctness of our encoding. To facilitate context bounding, we modify the definition of $HB(t, t')$ as follows:

1. $HB(t, t') := \mathcal{O}(t) \leq \mathcal{O}(t')$ if one of the following conditions hold: $tid(t) = tid(t')$, or $t = t_{\text{first}}$, or $t' = t_{\text{last}}$.
2. $HB(t, t') := \mathcal{O}(t) < \mathcal{O}(t')$ otherwise.

Note first that, if two events t, t' are from the same thread, the execution time $\mathcal{O}(t)$ need not be strictly less than $\mathcal{O}(t')$ to enforce $HB(t, t')$. This is because the CSSA form, through the renaming of definitions and uses of thread-local variables, already guarantees the *flow-sensitivity* within each thread; that is, implicitly, a definition always happens before the subsequent uses. Therefore, when $tid(t) = tid(t')$, we relax the definition of $HB(t, t')$ by using *less than or equal to*[3].

Second, if events t, t' are from two different threads (and $t \neq t_{\text{first}}$, $t \neq t_{\text{last}}$), according to our encoding rules, the constraint $HB(t, t')$ must have been introduced by the subformula Φ_{PI} encoding π-functions. In such case, $HB(t, t')$ means that there is *at least one context switch* between the execution of t and t'. Therefore, when $tid(t) \neq tid(t')$, we force event t to happen *strictly before* event t' in time.

5.2 Adding the Context Bound

Let b be the maximal number of context switches allowed in an interleaving. Given the formula Φ_{CTP_ρ} as defined in the previous section, we construct the context-bounded formula $\Phi_{CTP_\rho}(b)$ as follows:

$$\Phi_{CTP_\rho}(b) := \Phi_{CTP_\rho} \wedge (\mathcal{O}(t_{\text{last}}) - \mathcal{O}(t_{\text{first}}) \leq b)$$

The additional constraint states that t_{last}, the unique exit event, must be executed no more than b steps later than t_{first}, the unique entry event.

The execution times of the events in a trace always form a non-decreasing sequence. Furthermore, the execution time is forced to increase whenever a context switch happens, i.e., as a result of $HB(t, t')$ when $tid(t) \neq tid(t')$. In the above constraint, such increases of execution time is limited to less than or equal to b[4].

---

[3] When $HB(t, t')$ is a constant, we replace it with true or false.

[4] In CHESS [16], whose exploration algorithm is purely explicit rather than symbolic, a variant is used to count only the *preemptive* context switches.

Theorem 2. *Let ρ' be a feasible linearization of CTP_ρ. Let $CB(\rho')$ be the number of context switches in ρ'. If $CB(\rho') \leq b$ and ρ' violates the correctness property, then $\Phi_{CTP_\rho}(b)$ is satisfiable.*

Proof. Let $m = CB(\rho')$. We partition ρ' into $m+1$ segments $seg_0\ seg_1 \ldots seg_m$ such that each segment is a subsequence of events without context switch. Now we assign an execution time (integer) for all $t \in \rho'$ as follows: $\mathcal{O}(t) = i$ iff $t \in seg_i$, where $0 \leq i \leq m$. In our encoding, only the HB-constraints in Φ_{PO} and Φ_{PI} and the context-bound constraint refer to the $\mathcal{O}(t)$ variables. The above variable assignment is guaranteed to satisfy these constraints. Therefore, if ρ' violates the correctness property, then $\Phi_{CTP_\rho}(b)$ is satisfiable. □

By the same reasoning, if $CB(\rho') > b$, trace ρ' is excluded by formula $\Phi_{CTP_\rho}(b)$.

5.3 Lifting the CB Constraint

In the context bounded analysis, one can empirically choose a bound b_{max} and check the satisfiability of formula $\Phi_{CTP_\rho}(b_{max})$. Alternatively, one can iteratively set $b = 1, 2, \ldots, b_{max}$; and for each b, check the satisfiability of the formula

$$\Phi_{CTP_\rho} \wedge (\mathcal{O}(t_{\mathsf{last}}) - \mathcal{O}(t_{\mathsf{first}}) = b)$$

In both cases, if the formula is satisfiable, an error has been found. Otherwise, the SMT solver used to decide the formula can return a subset of the given formula as a *proof of unsatisfiability*. More formally, the proof of unsatisfiability of a formula f, which is unsatisfiable, is a subformula f_{unsat} of f such that f_{unsat} itself is also unsatisfiable.

The proof of unsatisfiability f_{unsat} can be viewed as a generalization of the given formula f; it is more general because some of the constraints of f may not be needed to prove unsatisfiability. In our method, we can check whether the context-bound constraint appears in f_{unsat}. If the context-bound constraint does not appear in f_{unsat}, it means that, even without context bounding, the formula Φ_{CTP_ρ} itself is unsatisfiable. In other words, we have generalized the context-bounded proof into a proof of the general case—that the property holds in all the feasible interleavings.

6 Relating to Other Causal Models

In this section, we show that our symbolic algorithm can be further constrained to match known causal models in the literature. By doing this exercise, we also demonstrate that our algorithm has a larger interleaving coverage. Since the maximal causal model [6], proposed recently by Serbănută, Chen and Rosu, has the capability of capturing more feasible interleavings than prior sound causal models, we will use it as an example. In this case, our algorithm provides a symbolic property checking algorithm, in contrast to their model checking algorithm based on explicit enumeration.

We assume that during the program execution, only events involving shared objects are monitored, and except for synchronization primitives, the program code that produces the events are not available. Therefore, an event is in one of the following forms:

- A concurrency synchronization/communication primitive;
- Reading value val from a shared variable $v \in SV$;
- Writing value val to a shared variable $v \in SV$.
- An assertion event (the property);

Example. We slightly modify the example in Fig. 1 as follows: *we always replace* $t_3 : x := 2 + a$ *with* $t'_3 : x := 1 + a$. The sequence of concrete events in ρ is shown in Fig. 5. There still exists an erroneous trace that violates the assertion in t_{12}. The difference between the two examples is subtle: in the original example, the erroneous trace ρ' in Section 2 cannot be predicted by the maximal causal model; whereas in the modified example, the erroneous trace can be predicted by the maximal causal model. The reason is that in the modified example, the program code in t'_3 and t_7 produce identical events in ρ: *Writing value 1 to the shared variable* x. Therefore, t_{11} can be moved ahead of t_5 but after t_4 (the permutation satisfies the sequential consistency axioms used in the maximal causal model).

Thread T_1	Thread T_2
t_1 : reading 0 from x	
t_2 : $acq(l)$	
t'_3 : writing 1 to x	
t_4 : $rel(l)$	
t_5 : writing 1 to y	
t_6 : $acq(l)$	
t_7 : writing 1 to x	
t_8 : $rel(l)$	
	t_9 : nop
	t_{10} : $acq(l)$
	t_{11} : reading 1 from x
	t_{12} : assert($y == 1$)
	t_{13} : $rel(l)$

Fig. 5. The concrete event sequence

$\star\star\, t_1$:	$\langle\, 1, (\mathsf{assume}(x = 0), \{\ \})\,\rangle$
t_2 :	$\langle\, 1, (\mathsf{assume}(l > 0), \{l := l - 1\})\,\rangle$
$\star\star\, t'_3$:	$\langle\, 1, (\mathsf{assume}(\mathsf{true}), \{x := 1\})\,\rangle$
t_4 :	$\langle\, 1, (\mathsf{assume}(\mathsf{true}), \{l := l + 1\})\,\rangle$
$\star\star\, t_5$:	$\langle\, 1, (\mathsf{assume}(\mathsf{true}), \{y := 1\})\,\rangle$
t_6 :	$\langle\, 1, (\mathsf{assume}(l > 0), \{l := l - 1\})\,\rangle$
$\star\star\, t_7$:	$\langle\, 1, (\mathsf{assume}(\mathsf{true}), \{x := 1\})\,\rangle$
t_8 :	$\langle\, 1, (\mathsf{assume}(\mathsf{true}), \{l := l + 1\})\,\rangle$
$\star\star\, t_9$:	$\langle\, 2, (\mathsf{assume}(\mathsf{true}), \{\ \})\,\rangle$
t_{10} :	$\langle\, 2, (\mathsf{assume}(l > 0), \{l := l - 1\})\,\rangle$
$\star\star\, t_{11}$:	$\langle\, 2, (\mathsf{assume}(x = 1), \{\ \})\,\rangle$
t_{12} :	$\langle\, 2, (\mathsf{assert}(y = 1))\,\rangle$
t_{13} :	$\langle\, 2, (\mathsf{assume}(\mathsf{true}), \{l := l + 1\})\,\rangle$

Fig. 6. The reduced causal model

Let $CTP_\rho = (T, \sqsubseteq)$ be the model as in Definition 1. We derive the constrained model CM_ρ as shown in Fig. 6. Whenever an event has a different form in CM_ρ from the one in CTP_ρ (Fig. 2), we mark it with the symbol $\star\star$. Note that all the semaphore events remain symbolic, whereas the rest are underapproximated into concrete values. For instance, event t_1 is reduced from $\langle 1, (\mathsf{assume}(\mathsf{true}), \{a := x\})\rangle$ to $\langle 1, (\mathsf{assume}(x = 0), \{\ \})\rangle$, because value 0 is being read from the shared variable x in the given trace ρ. Similarly, event t'_3 is reduced from $\langle 1, (\mathsf{assume}(\mathsf{true}), \{x := 1 + a\})\rangle$ to $\langle 1, (\mathsf{assume}(\mathsf{true}), \{x := 1\})\rangle$, because the right-hand-side expression evaluates to 1 in ρ. These events are no longer symbolic. Note that concrete events correspond to constant values, which can be propagated to further simplify the constraints in our encoding. However, these also result in less coverage in CM_ρ than CTP_ρ.

Semantics of the Constrained CTP. Since CM_ρ shares the same symbolic representation as CTP_ρ, the notion of *feasible linearizations* of a CTP, defined in Section 3.2, and the symbolic algorithm in Section 4 remain applicable. In the running example, the erroneous trace $\rho' = (t_1 t_2 t'_3 t_4) t_9 t_{10} t_{11} t_{12} t_{13} (t_5\text{–}t_8)$ is admitted by CM_ρ.

Table 1. Experimental results of symbolic predictive analysis (MO–memory out 800 MB)

The Test Program			The Given Trace		Run Time (s)			Run Time (s)	
program name	threads	shared / vars	property	length	slicing	predict	predict-cb	BMC[13]	Explicit
banking-2	2	97 / 264	passed	843	1.4	0.1	0.1	0.3	36.5
banking-2a	2	97 / 264	error	843	1.4	0.1	0.1	7.2	1.2
banking-5	5	104 / 331	passed	1622	1.7	0.3	0.1	2.7	>600
banking-5a	5	104 / 331	error	1622	1.7	0.1	0.1	>600	1.8
banking-10	10	114 / 441	passed	2725	7.0	1.6	0.6	31.8	>600
banking-10a	10	114 / 441	error	2725	7.0	0.1	0.1	MO	2.8
indexer-10	10	285 / 539	passed	3000	1.1	0.1	0.1	0.1	12.8
indexer-15	15	305 / 669	passed	4277	2.3	0.1	0.1	>600	>600
indexer-15a	15	305 / 669	error	4277	2.2	0.4	0.2	>600	>600
indexer-20	20	325 / 799	passed	5647	4.0	0.4	0.1	MO	>600
indexer-20a	20	325 / 799	error	5647	4.1	3.2	0.7	MO	>600
indexer-25	25	345 / 829	passed	7482	6.0	0.9	0.1	MO	>600
indexer-25a	25	345 / 829	error	7482	6.1	26.1	9.8	MO	>600

7 Experiments

We have implemented the proposed symbolic predictive analysis algorithm in a tool called *Fusion*. Our tool is capable of handling symbolic execution traces generated by arbitrary multi-threaded C programs using the Linux *PThreads* library. We use the *Yices* SMT solver [11] to solve the satisfiability formulas.

We have conducted preliminary experiments using the following benchmarks. The first set consists of C variants of the *banking* example [18] with known bugs due to atomicity violations. Unlike previous work [3,5,6], we directly check the functional correctness property, stating the consistency of all bank accounts at the end of the execution; this is a significantly harder problem than detecting data races [5,6] or atomicity violations [3] (which may not cause a violation of the functional property). The second set of benchmarks are the *indexer* examples from [19], which we implemented using C and the Linux *PThreads* library. In these examples, multiple threads share a hash table with 128 entries. With less than 12 threads, there is no hash table collision among different threads—although this fact cannot be easily inferred by purely static analysis. With more than 12 threads, the number of irredundant interleavings (after partial order reduction) quickly explodes. In our experiments, we set the number of threads to 15, 20, and 25, respectively. Our properties are assertions stating that no collision has happened on a particular hash table entry. The experiments[5] were conducted on a PC with 1.6 GHz Intel processor and 2GB memory running Fedora 8.

Table 1 shows the results. The first three columns show the statistics of the test cases, including the name, the number of threads, and the number of shared and total variables (that are accessed in the trace). The next two columns show whether the given (non-erroneous) trace has an erroneous permutation, and the trace length after slicing. The next three columns show the run times of trace capturing and slicing, our symbolic analysis, and our context-bounded symbolic analysis (with bound 2). The final two

[5] Examples're available at http://www.nec-labs.com/~chaowang/pubDOC/predict-example.tar

columns show the run times of a BMC algorithm [13] with the unrolling depth set to the trace length and an explicit search algorithm enhanced by DPOR [19].

The slicing in our experiments is thread-sensitive and the traces after slicing consist of mostly irreducible shared variable accesses—for each access, there exists at least one conflicting access from a concurrent thread. The number of equivalence classes of interleavings is directly related to the number of such shared accesses (worst-case double-exponential [15]). In the *indexer* examples, for instance, since there is no hash table collision with fewer than 12 threads, the problem is easier to solve. (In [19], such cases were used to showcase the power of the DPOR algorithm in dynamically detecting these non-conflicting variable accesses). However, when the number of threads is set to 15, 20, and 25, the number of collisions increases rapidly. Our results show that purely explicit algorithms, even with DPOR, do not scale well in such cases. This is likely a bottleneck for other explicit enumeration based approaches as well. The BMC algorithm did not perform well because of its large formula sizes as a result of explicitly unrolling the transition relation. In contrast, our symbolic algorithm remains efficient in navigating the large search space.

8 Related Work

The fundamental concept used in this paper is the partial order over the events in an execution trace. This is related to the *happens-before* causality introduced by Lamport in [7]. However, Lamport's happens-before causality, as well as the various subsequent causal models [4,5,6], has a strictly less interleaving coverage than our model. Our use of the HB constraints to specify the execution order among events is related to, but is more abstract than, the logical clocks [7] and the vector clocks [20].

Our symbolic encoding is related to, but is different from, the SSA-based SAT encoding [9], which is popular for *sequential* programs. We use *difference logic* to directly capture the partial order. This differs from CheckFence [21], which explicitly encodes ordering between all pairs of relevant events (shared variable accesses) in pure Boolean logic. Our context-bounded analysis differs from the work in [17], since they do not use SAT, but reduce concurrent programs to sequential programs and then use SMV. TCBMC [22] also uses context-bounding in their symbolic encoding. However, it has to *a priori* fix the number of bounded context switches. In contrast, our method in Section 4 is for the unbounded case—the context-bounding constraint in Section 5 is optional and is used to further improve performance. Furthermore, all the aforementioned methods were applied to whole programs and not to trace programs.

At a high level, our work also relates to dynamic model checking [23,16,24,13]. However, these algorithms need to re-execute the program when exploring different interleavings, and in general, they are not property-directed. Our goal is to detect errors *without re-executing the program.* In our previous work [8], we have used the notion of concurrent trace program but the goal was to prune the search space in dynamic model checking. In this work, we use the CTP and the CSSA-based encoding for predictive analysis. To our knowledge, this is the first attempt at symbolic predictive analysis.

9 Conclusions

In this paper, we propose a symbolic algorithm for detecting concurrency errors in all feasible permutations of events in a give execution trace. The new algorithm uses a succinct concurrent static single assignment (CSSA) based encoding to generate an SMT formula such that the violation of an assertion property exists iff the SMT formula is satisfiable. We also propose a symbolic method to bound the number of context switches in an interleaving. The new algorithm can achieve a better interleaving coverage, and at the same time is more scalable than the explicit enumeration algorithms used by the various existing methods for predictive analysis. Besides predictive analysis, we believe that our CSSA-based encoding can be useful in many other contexts, since it is general enough to handle any bounded straight-line concurrent program.

Acknowledgements

We would like to thank Fang Yu for his help with implementing the CSSA-based encoding. We would also like to thank Sriram Sankaranarayanan, Rajeev Alur, and Nishant Sinha for their critique of the draft.

References

1. Savage, S., Burrows, M., Nelson, G., Sobalvarro, P., Anderson, T.: Eraser: A dynamic data race detector for multithreaded programs. ACM Trans. Comput. Syst. 15(4), 391–411 (1997)
2. Flanagan, C., Freund, S.N.: Atomizer: A dynamic atomicity checker for multithreaded programs. In: Parallel and Distributed Processing Symposium (IPDPS). IEEE, Los Alamitos (2004)
3. Wang, L., Stoller, S.D.: Runtime analysis of atomicity for multithreaded programs. IEEE Trans. Software Eng. 32(2), 93–110 (2006)
4. Sen, K., Rosu, G., Agha, G.: Detecting errors in multithreaded programs by generalized predictive analysis of executions. In: Steffen, M., Zavattaro, G. (eds.) FMOODS 2005. LNCS, vol. 3535, pp. 211–226. Springer, Heidelberg (2005)
5. Chen, F., Rosu, G.: Parametric and sliced causality. In: Damm, W., Hermanns, H. (eds.) CAV 2007. LNCS, vol. 4590, pp. 240–253. Springer, Heidelberg (2007)
6. Serbănută, T.F., Chen, F., Rosu, G.: Maximal causal models for multithreaded systems. Technical Report UIUCDCS-R-2008-3017, University of Illinois at Urbana-Champaign (2008)
7. Lamport, L.: Time, clocks, and the ordering of events in a distributed system. Commun. ACM 21(7), 558–565 (1978)
8. Wang, C., Chaudhuri, S., Gupta, A., Yang, Y.: Symbolic pruning of concurrent program executions. In: Foundations of Software Engineering. ACM, New York (2009)
9. Clarke, E., Kroening, D., Lerda, F.: A tool for checking ANSI-C programs. In: Jensen, K., Podelski, A. (eds.) TACAS 2004. LNCS, vol. 2988, pp. 168–176. Springer, Heidelberg (2004)
10. Lahiri, S., Qadeer, S.: Back to the future: revisiting precise program verification using SMT solvers. In: Principles of Programming Languages, pp. 171–182. ACM, New York (2008)
11. Dutertre, B., de Moura, L.: A fast linear-arithmetic solver for DPLL(T). In: Ball, T., Jones, R.B. (eds.) CAV 2006. LNCS, vol. 4144, pp. 81–94. Springer, Heidelberg (2006)

12. Lee, J., Padua, D., Midkiff, S.: Basic compiler algorithms for parallel programs. In: Principles and Practice of Parallel Programming, pp. 1–12 (1999)
13. Wang, C., Yang, Z., Kahlon, V., Gupta, A.: Peephole partial order reduction. In: Ramakrishnan, C.R., Rehof, J. (eds.) TACAS 2008. LNCS, vol. 4963, pp. 382–396. Springer, Heidelberg (2008)
14. Kahlon, V., Wang, C., Gupta, A.: Monotonic partial order reduction: An optimal symbolic partial order reduction technique. In: Bouajjani, A., Maler, O. (eds.) CAV 2009. LNCS, vol. 5643, pp. 398–413. Springer, Heidelberg (2009)
15. Qadeer, S., Rehof, J.: Context-bounded model checking of concurrent software. In: Halbwachs, N., Zuck, L.D. (eds.) TACAS 2005. LNCS, vol. 3440, pp. 93–107. Springer, Heidelberg (2005)
16. Musuvathi, M., Qadeer, S.: CHESS: Systematic stress testing of concurrent software. In: Puebla, G. (ed.) LOPSTR 2006. LNCS, vol. 4407, pp. 15–16. Springer, Heidelberg (2007)
17. Lal, A., Reps, T.W.: Reducing concurrent analysis under a context bound to sequential analysis. In: Gupta, A., Malik, S. (eds.) CAV 2008. LNCS, vol. 5123, pp. 37–51. Springer, Heidelberg (2008)
18. Farchi, E., Nir, Y., Ur, S.: Concurrent bug patterns and how to test them. In: Guo, M. (ed.) ISPA 2003. LNCS, vol. 2745, p. 286. Springer, Heidelberg (2003)
19. Flanagan, C., Godefroid, P.: Dynamic partial-order reduction for model checking software. In: Principles of programming languages, pp. 110–121 (2005)
20. Fidge, C.J.: Logical time in distributed computing systems. IEEE Computer 24(8), 28–33 (1991)
21. Burckhardt, S., Alur, R., Martin, M.: CheckFence: checking consistency of concurrent data types on relaxed memory models. In: Programming Language Design and Implementation, pp. 12–21. ACM, New York (2007)
22. Rabinovitz, I., Grumberg, O.: Bounded model checking of concurrent programs. In: Etessami, K., Rajamani, S.K. (eds.) CAV 2005. LNCS, vol. 3576, pp. 82–97. Springer, Heidelberg (2005)
23. Godefroid, P.: Software model checking: The VeriSoft approach. Formal Methods in System Design 26(2), 77–101 (2005)
24. Yang, Y., Chen, X., Gopalakrishnan, G.: Inspect: A Runtime Model Checker for Multithreaded C Programs. Technical Report UUCS-08-004, University of Utah (2008)

On the Difficulties of Concurrent-System Design, Illustrated with a 2×2 Switch Case Study

Edgar G. Daylight[1] and Sandeep K. Shukla[2]

[1] a.k.a. Karel Van Oudheusden,
Institute of Logic, Language, and Computation,
University of Amsterdam, The Netherlands
egdaylight@yahoo.com

[2] Department of Electrical & Computer Engineering,
Virginia Tech., USA
shukla@vt.edu

Abstract. While various specification languages for concurrent-system design exist today, it is often not clear which specification language is more suitable than another for a particular case study. To address this problem, we study four different specification languages for the same 2×2 Switch case study: $\texttt{TLA}^+$, `Bluespec`, Statecharts, and the Algebra of Communicating Processes (`ACP`). By slightly altering the design intent of the Switch, we obtain more complicated behaviors of the Switch. For each design intent, we investigate how each specification, in each of the specification languages, captures the corresponding behavior. By using three different criteria, we judge each specification and specification language. For our case study, however, all four specification languages perform poorly in at least two criteria! Hence, this paper illustrates, on a seemingly simple case study, some of the prevailing difficulties of concurrent-system design.

Keywords: formal specification languages, local reasoning, adaptability, non-functional requirements.

1 Introduction

Many papers on concurrent-system design introduce a specification language, backed up by multiple case studies. This paper, in contrast, studies various specification languages for a particular case study, i.e. a 2×2 Switch. In fact, we will examine three different behaviors of the Switch by means of the same specification language, and do this for four different languages: $\texttt{TLA}^+$, `Bluespec`, Statecharts, and the Algebra of Communicating Processes (`ACP`).

To compare specifications, we introduce three criteria in Sections 1.1-1.3. The importance of each criterion depends primarily on the designer's purpose to use the specification language.

A. Cavalcanti and D. Dams (Eds.): FM 2009, LNCS 5850, pp. 273–288, 2009.

1.1 Local Reasoning

In order to introduce our first criterion, we present the following line of thought. The complexity encountered when specifying a concurrent system is proportional to the degree of global spatial and temporal reasoning that is required on behalf of the designer. *Global spatial reasoning* is synonymous for reasoning across relatively many spatial elements of the system under investigation (i.e., the Switch). For example, a designer who reasons across four different buffers of the Switch applies more global spatial reasoning than a designer who only has to reason across a maximum of two buffers while specifying the Switch's behavior. *Global temporal reasoning* is synonymous for reasoning across relatively many states of the system. A designer who reasons across five consecutive states of the Switch's underlying Finite State Machine applies more global temporal reasoning than a designer who only has to reason across a maximum of two consecutive states.

Global (spatial and temporal) reasoning may depend on either the case study, the chosen specification language, or both. An important remark is, that, if global reasoning for the Switch is not influenced by the chosen specification language, then there is little to gain from our subsequent discussions in terms of global reasoning. Our analysis, however, will show that the chosen specification language does in fact matter. For instance, global reasoning about a $\texttt{TLA}^+$ specification generally differs from that of an `ACP` specification, even though the amount of global reasoning can be the same in both cases.

Our first criterion, therefore, is the *local* (as opposed to global) reasoning that is required by the designer in order to specify the Switch's behavior.

Local Reasoning as an Ideal. It should be noted, however, that since each system is built from localized components that work together by means of some form of communication, we view local reasoning more as an ideal than as a realistic attribute of a specification language. We also stress that it is a subjective matter as to whether a specification language should avoid global reasoning as much as possible or not.

The ideal of local reasoning is best illustrated by means of a Kahn Process Network (KPN). In his 1974 paper [7], Kahn showed that if (i) each component process in a KPN is monotonic and continuous, and if (ii) the communications between such processes are infinitely buffered, then (iii) the entire system is deterministic and deadlock-free. Proving (i) and (ii) only requires local reasoning, while the result (iii) is a global property of the system under investigation. However, when confronted with a realistic (i.e. implementable) system, property (ii) does not hold. This, in turn, results in global reasoning when proving correctness claims, such as deadlock-freedom.

1.2 Adaptability

A second criterion is adaptability to variations in design intent. A specification language is adaptable for the Switch case study if it is capable of coping well with variations in the design intent of the Switch. For instance, consider two specifications in the same language of a simple 2×2 Switch and a more complicated

2×2 Switch, respectively. Is the second specification, relative to the complicated Switch's behavior, as "clear" as the original specification relative to the simple Switch's behavior?

Unfortunately, we currently lack a practically applicable metric for "clarity". However, instead of ignoring the second criterion altogether, we shall attempt to improve our understanding of what it is that makes a specification "clear". We will make claims about adaptability in this paper, but then primarily based on intuition instead of on a rigorous definition. The reader is, of course, free to use his or her own notion of "clarity" when studying the presented specifications.

1.3 Capturing the Design Intent

Our third criterion amounts to checking whether each specification captures the corresponding design intent of the Switch. In particular, since each of the Switch's design intents, presented later, contains a constraint of maximum throughput, we will check whether this constraint is met by each specification.

Two important remarks are, however, in order. First, it is a subjective matter as to whether a "high-level" specification should be able to capture a non-functional requirement, such as maximal throughput, or not. Second, many variations of the presented specification languages exist, such as timed process algebras, which we do not cover in this paper. These variations are explicitly designed to capture such non-functional requirements.

Outline. After presenting three different design intents of the 2×2 Switch in Section 2, we start off with two guarded-command languages in Section 3: `TLA`$^+$ and `Bluespec`. The short intermezzo in Section 4 then distinguishes between `TLA`$^+$ and `Bluespec` on the one hand and Statecharts and `ACP` on the other hand. Afterwards, we discuss Statecharts in Section 5 and `ACP` in Section 6. Finally, conclusions and future work are presented in Section 7.

2 Design Intent

We distinguish between a Simplified Switch, the Original Switch initially presented in [1], and a Modified Switch.

The Simplified 2×2 Switch. Figure 1(i) depicts the Simplified Switch. Its design intent can be described as follows. The Switch contains two input `FIFO`s (`i0` and `i1`) and two output `FIFO`s (`o0` and `o1`). A packet can arrive on `i0` or `i1`. If the first bit of the packet has the value 0, then it is routed to `o0`, else to `o1`. Each `FIFO` has the same finite capacity of $cap \geq 1$ packets. Each packet contains 32 bits. A packet can only move if the output `FIFO` is not full. Maximum throughput is required: a packet should move if it can. A shared resource collision can occur when the packets at the head of both input `FIFO`s have the same destination. In this case, `i0` is given priority and `i1`'s packet is delayed.

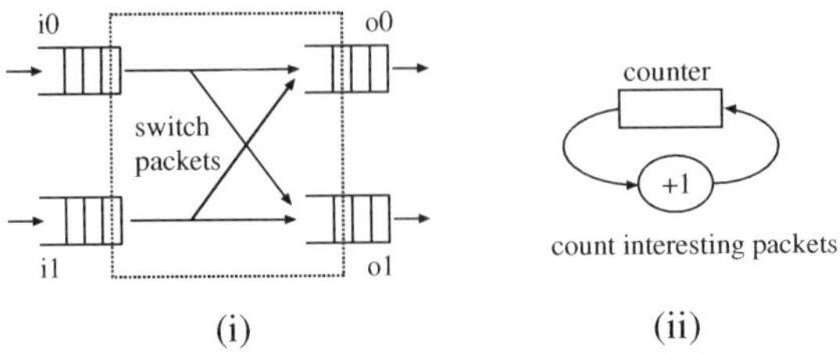

Fig. 1. A 2×2 Switch (i) and a counter (ii)

The Original 2×2 Switch. The Original Switch is the Simplified Switch in Figure 1(i) together with a counter shown in Figure 1(ii). The counter counts all "interesting" packets that are routed from the input to the output buffers. A packet is "interesting" if its second, third, and fourth bit are all equal to zero; else, the packet is "boring". The counter is intentionally restricted: it can only be incremented by one value at each clock cycle. Therefore, a shared resource collision can occur when both head packets (of the input `FIFOs`) are interesting. In this case, again, `i0` is given priority and `i1`'s head packet is delayed.

The Modified 2×2 Switch. Based on the design intent of the Original Switch, we define ($\triangleq$) two conditions $C1$ and $C2$ as follows:

$C1 \triangleq$ both head packets have the same destination

$C2 \triangleq$ both head packets are interesting

These definitions allow us to distinguish between the following three disjoint cases in which a shared resource collision can occur:

Case 1:	$C1 \wedge C2$	`i0`
Case 2:	$C1 \wedge \neg C2$	`i0`
Case 3:	$\neg C1 \wedge C2$	`i1`

So far we have, in all three cases, given priority to `i0`'s head packet. Now, however, we alter the design intent by giving priority to `i1`'s head packet in the third case, as is shown in the third column above. I.e., if both head packets have a different destination and are interesting, then `i0`'s head packet is delayed and `i1`'s is routed. The latter, of course, only occurs if the destination buffer is not full. Note also that a shared collision can not occur when $\neg(C1 \vee C2)$ holds. The corresponding Switch is called the Modified Switch in the sequel.

3 Two Guarded-Command Languages

The guarded-command languages `TLA`$^+$ and `Bluespec` are addressed in this section. By specifying the Simplified Switch in `TLA`$^+$ (Section 3.1) and the Original Switch in `Bluespec` (Section 3.2), we show that both languages are syntactically very similar and, hence, do not differ much in terms of the first and second criterion. That is, local reasoning and adaptability are not affected when using `TLA`$^+$ instead of `Bluespec` or vice versa. In terms of implementation, however, both languages do differ greatly and this has implications for the third criterion (Section 3.3). Finally, by continuing with `Bluespec` and specifying the Modified Switch (Section 3.4), we show that `Bluespec` is not as adaptable as we[1] would like, thereby addressing the second criterion. The first criterion of local reasoning is addressed throughout the following sections.

3.1 TLA$^+$ and the Simplified Switch

Lamport's TLA$^+$ is a specification language for systems, ranging from program interfaces to distributed systems. A TLA$^+$ specification of the Simplified Switch is presented in Table 1 and discussed below.

Lamport's objective with TLA$^+$ is to specify a complete system in a single formula [8, p.16]. For the Simplified Switch, this single formula corresponds to line 7 in Table 1. It will be discussed later.

Lines 1 to 2 in Table 1 can be described as follows. Line 1 introduces the four variables of the TLA$^+$ specification. Each variable represents a buffer (i.e. a list of packets). Line 2 specifies that all buffers are initially empty.

A TLA$^+$ specification contains actions such as action R_0 in line 3 and action R_1 in line 5. Action R_0 describes the transfer of a packet from input buffer `i0` to output buffer `o0` or `o1`. Similarly, action R_1 describes the transfer of a packet from `i1` to `o0` or `o1`.

Each action is a logical implication ($\rightarrow$). For instance, action R_0 contains premises, an implication in line 4, and state changes as conclusions. Action R_0 can be described in greater detail as follows. First, an abbreviation is introduced: *pack* denotes the head packet of input buffer `i0` (if there is a head packet). Second, the three premises state that (a) input buffer `i0` is not empty, (b) if *pack*'s first bit is equal to zero, then output buffer `o0` is not full, and (c) if *pack*'s first bit is equal to one, then output buffer `o1` is not full. Third, if all premises hold, then the conclusions need to hold as well. The conclusions state that (d) the new value of input buffer `i0` (i.e. $i0'$) is obtained by dequeuing $i0$'s head packet, (e) output buffer $o0'$ is obtained either by appending *pack* to $o0$ or by leaving $o0$ unchanged, and (f) output buffer $o1'$ is obtained either by leaving $o1$ unchanged or by appending *pack* to $o1$. An important remark here is, that, if *pack* is routed to `o0`, then `o1` remains unchanged: $o1' = o1$. That is, it is *not* possible that a packet from `i1` is *simultaneously* routed to `o1`. A similar remark holds for the scenario in which *pack* is routed from `i0` to `o1` and `o0` has to remain unchanged: $o0' = o0$.

Action R_1 describes the routing of a packet $pack_2$ from `i1` to `o0` or `o1`. The specification of the logical implication is more complicated (in comparison to that of R_0) because it captures `i0`'s priority over `i1`: when the head packets of both `i0` (i.e. $pack_1$) and `i1` (i.e. $pack_2$) have the same destination, then $pack_2$

[1] "we" refers here to the authors and *other* readers. Of course, due to the subjective nature of this exposition, which we can not completely avoid, `Bluespec` advocates and others may disagree with our stated point of view. Similar remarks hold for some of the other statements in this paper.

has to be delayed and $pack_1$ is given priority. This behaviour is captured by the last premise. The rest of R_1, however, is similar to R_0.

Either action R_0 or R_1 suffices to illustrate global spatial reasoning. Action R_1, for instance, relies on the head packets of both `i0` and `i1` and on the status of both output buffers `o0` and `o1`. That is, the designer has to reason across all four state elements of the Simplified Switch.

To illustrate global temporal reasoning, we refer to the "single-formula specification" of the Simplified Switch in line 7. It expresses that, at every moment, either R_0 is executed, or R_1 is executed, or nothing is executed (due to the subscript $\langle i0,\ i1,\ o0,\ o1\rangle$ which expresses the potential for stuttering). To understand line 7, the designer has to reason across both actions R_0 and R_1 and mentally simulate the Switch's behaviour across multiple (e.g. three) clock cycles.

Table 1. The Simplified 2×2 Switch in TLA$^+$

(1) variables: $i0,\ i1,\ o0,\ o1$ $i0,\ i1,\ o0,\ o1 \in$ List of Packets	(5) Act R_1: let $pack_1 = i0.first$ let $pack_2 = i1.first$ $i1 \not\equiv \langle\,\rangle$ $\wedge\ (pack_2\,[0] = 0) \rightarrow (\neg\, o0.full)$ $\wedge\ (pack_2\,[0] = 1) \rightarrow (\neg\, o1.full)$ $\wedge\ \neg\,(pack_1\,[0] = pack_2\,[0])$
(2) Init: $i0 = i1 = o0 = o1 = \langle\,\rangle$,	
(3) Act R_0: let $pack = i0.first$ $i0 \not\equiv \langle\,\rangle$ $\wedge\ (pack\,[0] = 0) \rightarrow (\neg\, o0.full)$ $\wedge\ (pack\,[0] = 1) \rightarrow (\neg\, o1.full)$	(6) $\rightarrow$ $\langle$ $i1' = i1.deq;$ $o0' = ((pack_2\,[0] = 0)\ ?\ o0.enq\,(pack_2)\ :\ o0)\,;$ $o1' = ((pack_2\,[0] = 0)\ ?\ o1\ :\ o1.enq\,(pack_2))\,;$ $\rangle$
(4) $\rightarrow$ $\langle$ $i0' = i0.deq;$ $o0' = ((pack\,[0] = 0)\ ?\ o0.enq\,(pack)\ :\ o0)\,;$ $o1' = ((pack\,[0] = 0)\ ?\ o1\ :\ o1.enq\,(pack))\,;$ $\rangle$	(7) $[\text{Act } R_0\ \vee\ \text{Act } R_1\,]_{\langle i0,\ i1,\ o0,\ o1\rangle}$

3.2 Bluespec and the Original Switch

The guarded command language `Bluespec` [6] can be used to 'elegantly' specify the Original Switch's behavior. Indeed, this is accomplished by just two rules (i.e. guarded commands) `r0` and `r1` in Table 2.

Rule `r0` describes the behaviour of `i0` with respect to `o0`, `o1`, and the counter `c`. Line 3 presents a trivially true guard. Lines 4-6 contain `let` statements and lines 7-9 constitute the main body of the rule. Note that lines 7-9 are all executed in the same clock cycle. That is, a semicolon denotes parallel composition.

Lines 4-6 can be clarified as follows. Line 4 assigns to `x` the head packet of buffer `i0`. This assignment can only occur if `i0` is not empty. We discuss later what happens if `i0` actually is empty. Line 5 is a comment for line 6 which, in turn, assigns the appropriate output buffer (`o0` or `o1`) to `out`, depending on the first bit of packet `x`.

Table 2. The Original 2×2 Switch in Bluespec, as defined in [1]

```
(1) (* descending_urgency = "r0, r1" *)

(2) // Rule for moving packets from i0:
(3) rule r0; // Trivially true guard.
(4)  let x = i0.first;
(5)  // Pick destination FIFO, called out:
(6)  let out = ( (x[0]==0) ? o0 : o1 );
(7)  i0.deq;
(8)  out.enq(x);
(9)  if (x[3:1]==0) c<=c+1;
(10) endrule

(11) // Rule for moving packets from i1:
(12) rule r1; // Trivially true guard.
(13)  let x = i1.first;
(14)  let out = ( (x[0]==0) ? o0 : o1 );
(15)  i1.deq;
(16)  out.enq(x);
(17)  if (x[3:1]==0) c<=c+1;
(18) endrule
```

Lines 7-9 can be clarified as follows. Line 7 describes the dequeuing (of the head packet) from `i0`. Line 8 describes the enqueueing of that packet (i.e. `x`) into the appropriate output buffer `out`. Line 9 describes the incrementation of the counter if packet `x` is interesting.

Rule `r1`, on the other hand, describes the behaviour of `i1` with respect to `o0`, `o1`, and `c`. It is very similar to rule `r0`.

Table 2's meaning relies on three hidden assumptions which need to be made explicit (at least mentally) when reasoning about the correctness of the specification. First, the descending urgency, expressed in line 1, specifies rule `r0`'s priority over rule `r1`. This means that, if the execution of both rules were to result in the access of a shared state element (e.g. counter `c`), then only `r0` is actually executed and `r1`'s execution is postponed. Second, since rule `r0` relies on the head packet of `i0` (in line 4), the guard of `r0` implicitly contains a test to check whether `i0` actually contains at least one packet. In other words, even though line 3 presents a trivially true guard; the actual guard, behind the scenes, is not trivially true at all. The designer can, of course, according to his preference, specify this guard explicitly as we have done with TLA$^+$ in Table 1 –but it is considered elegant practice not to do so [1]. Third, since rule `r0` relies on output buffers `o0` and `o1` (in line 6), the guard of `r0` implicitly contains a test to check whether these buffers aren't full. This assumption is very similar to the previous one and has also been made explicit with TLA$^+$ in Table 1.

Bluespec requires global spatial reasoning. For instance, rule `r1` in Table 2 relies on at least four state elements: the head packet of `i1`, the output buffers `o0` and `o1`, and the counter `c`. To illustrate global temporal reasoning, we refer to the Bluespec specification of the Modified Switch in Section 3.4.

3.3 Comparison: TLA$^+$ vs. Bluespec

A difference between TLA$^+$ and Bluespec is that the semantics of the former does not rely on a run-time scheduler while that of the latter does. The implication is that at most one rule in Table 1 is executed during each cycle, while Bluespec's compiler will implement a greedy run-time scheduler that *guarantees* that all the non conflicting rules in Table 2 execute[2]. Therefore, in terms of the third criterion in Section 1, it is tempting to state that $\mathtt{TLA}^+$ does not meet the requirement of maximum throughput while `Bluespec` does. In retrospect, however, it should be noted that the $\mathtt{TLA}^+$ specification by no means excludes the possibility that the final implementation (i.e. hardware) will respect the maximum throughput requirement as well. A guarantee, however, can not be made in this case.

It is also interesting to note that the $\mathtt{TLA}^+$ and `Bluespec` specifications differ in how they express the priority that `i0` has over `i1`. In the $\mathtt{TLA}^+$ specification in Table 1, the priority constraint is made explicit in the two actions R_0 and R_1. In the `Bluespec` specification in Table 2, a priority operator is used in Line 1. This operator is, however, merely syntactic sugar and therefore does not reduce the amount of global reasoning that is required on behalf of the designer (in comparison to the $\mathtt{TLA}^+$ specification).

3.4 `Bluespec` and the Modified Switch

For the Modified Switch, we present our own `Bluespec` specification in Table 3. To clarify, we first refer to Section 2 where we introduced three cases in which a shared-resource collision can occur. Cases 1 and 2 can be dealt with in one rule, called `rule r1`. Case 3 can be dealt with in another rule, called `rule r2`. The guards of each rule are:

`rule r1` $C1$
`rule r2` $\neg C1 \wedge C2$

Clearly, `rule r1` and `rule r2` are mutually exclusive. That is, `Bluespec`'s run-time scheduler will never select both rules to execute in parallel.

To specify the Modified Switch we also have to take into account when a shared collision can not occur, i.e. when $\neg(C1 \vee C2)$ holds. We accomplish this in two rules `rule r3A` and `rule r3B` (very similar to those in Table 2).

The specification in Table 3 is self explanatory. It has been criticized by others because all four rules contain very similar statements. For instance, the incrementation of counter `c` is expressed in all four rules. (The same remark holds for the two rules in Table 2.) The criticism is understandable but due to lack of an alternative, we (currently) think Table 3 is representative for a `Bluespec` design of the Modified Switch. In other words, Table 2 and Table 3, together, illustrate that the `Bluespec` language is not as adaptable as we would like.

Table 3 also suffers from global reasoning. First, global spatial reasoning is required for each of the four rules. For instance, `rule r2` requires the designer to reason in terms of four state elements `i1`, `o0`, `o1`, and `c` –not to mention the bits of `i0` and `i1`'s head packets when writing down the guard $\neg C1 \wedge C2$. Second,

---

[2] Maximum throughput is achieved by our two presented `Bluespec` specifications (Table 2 and also Table 3, discussed later). But, it should be noted that, in general, this may not be the case, even though all conflict-free rules are selected at every cycle (by a greedy run-time scheduler). In other words, maximum throughput is, in general, not so easily obtainable. See e.g. [9] for details concerning `Bluespec`'s semantics and run-time scheduler.

global temporal reasoning is more apparent here, in comparison to the Original Switch, since the designer has to reason across four rules (instead of two) in order to convince himself that all rules, together, exhibit the desired behavior.

Table 3. The Modified 2×2 Switch in Bluespec

`rule r1 when` $C1$	`rule r3A when` $\neg(C1 \vee C2)$
`let x = i0.first;`	`let x = i0.first;`
`let out = ( (x[0]==0) ? o0 : o1 );`	`let out = ( (x[0]==0) ? o0 : o1 );`
`i0.deq;`	`i0.deq;`
`out.enq(x);`	`out.enq(x);`
`if (x[3:1]==0) c<=c+1;`	`if (x[3:1]==0) c<=c+1;`
`endrule`	`endrule`
`rule r2 when` $\neg C1 \wedge C2$	`rule r3B when` $\neg(C1 \vee C2)$
`let x = i1.first;`	`let x = i1.first;`
`let out = ( (x[0]==0) ? o0 : o1 );`	`let out = ( (x[0]==0) ? o0 : o1 );`
`i1.deq;`	`i1.deq;`
`out.enq(x);`	`out.enq(x);`
`if (x[3:1]==0) c<=c+1;`	`if (x[3:1]==0) c<=c+1;`
`endrule`	`endrule`

4 Intermezzo: TLA+ and Bluespec vs. Statecharts and ACP

Having presented TLA+ and Bluespec in the previous section, we address Statecharts [5] and ACP [4] in the next two sections. At this point, however, we describe a major difference between TLA+ & Bluespec on the one hand and Statecharts & ACP on the other hand.

TLA+ & Bluespec do not partition their state space. I.e., TLA+ & Bluespec are global state models, where guards (of guarded actions) are evaluated on the global state. When an action in TLA+ (or a rule in Bluespec) is executed, it can affect any part of the global state. For this reason, each such action is atomic. In TLA+, actions are ensured to be atomic by interleaving. Hence, no explicit synchronization is needed. In Bluespec, rules are made atomic by ensuring that (i) they do not conflict each other when executed in the same clock cycle, and (ii) the changes they make to the global state only become visible at the synchronization points of a global clock tick.

Statecharts & ACP, on the other hand, do partition their state space. That is, in Statecharts & ACP, there is no global state visible to each action. In Statecharts, for instance, the state is partitioned into smaller Statecharts and each such Statechart changes its corresponding local state. Only when synchronous communication takes place between two Statecharts, can common (partially global) state be modified. A similar remark holds for ACP where each process acts on its own local state.

5 Statecharts

Statecharts can be used to model the design intent of the Original Switch, as shown in Figure 2. After describing this figure, an important discussion follows.

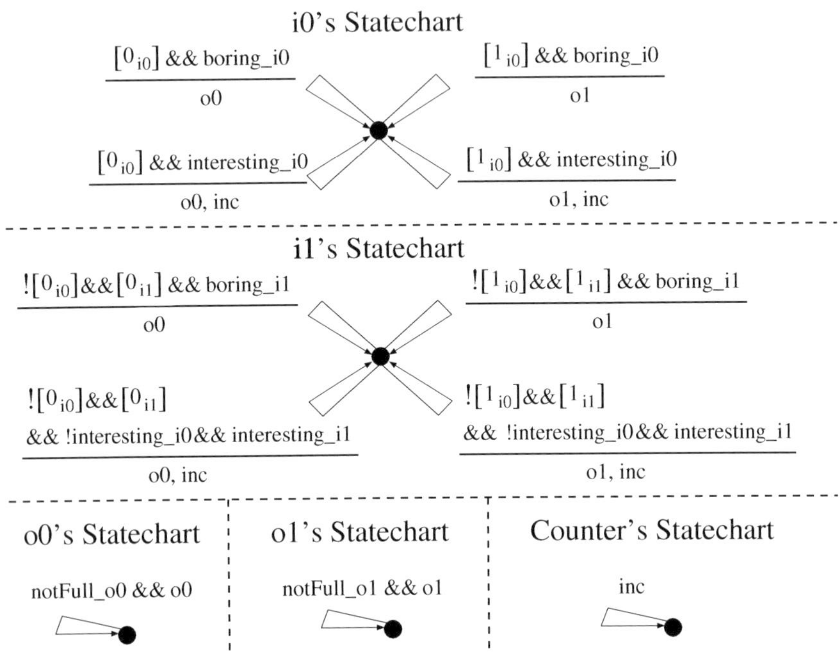

Fig. 2. The Statechart design of the Original 2×2 Switch

The behavior of the Original Switch is captured in Figure 2. It consists of five smaller concurrent Statecharts[3], one for each of the following five spatial elements: `i0`, `i1`, `o0`, `o1`, and the counter. Statechart `i0` can be clarified as follows. It consists of one state and four transitions. The top leftmost transition, for instance, amounts to checking whether `i0`'s head packet has a leading bit 0 and is boring: $[0_{i0}]$ && boring_`i0`. If so, then `i0`'s Statechart synchronizes with `o0`'s Statechart by means of $o0$, signifying the transfer of `i0`'s head packet to `o0`. Note, however, that `o0`'s Statechart tests whether `o0` is not full, as desired, and that this functionality does *not* belong to `i0`'s Statechart. The other transitions in `i0`'s Statechart are self explanatory.

An interesting observation is that each Statechart contains just a single state. This does not, however, imply that one can solely reason about each smaller Statechart's state in isolation in order to convince oneself that the complete

[3] We received this design from an anonymous reviewer in the Spring of 2008. It is much simpler than our own original Statechart design in [3].

specification is correct. For instance, to understand i0's Statechart, we are required to study o0's Statechart's transition as well in order to then visualize the transfer of a packet from i0 to o0. Likewise, in order to visualize the simultaneous transfer of two packets, we are required to reason across (at least) four different Statecharts: i0, i1, o0, and o1. This amounts to global spatial reasoning. Likewise, to capture the priority that i0 has over i1, we are required to visualize the sequentialized transfer of head packets from i0 and i1. This amounts to global temporal reasoning.

To specify the Simplified Switch, the reader merely needs to remove the boring_X, interesting_X, and *inc* notation from Figure 2 along with the small Statechart of the counter.

Discussion. After (a previous version of) this paper was accepted, we, the authors, found a serious error in Figure 2, which we illustrate by means of the following scenario. Input buffers i0 and i1 have interesting head packets that have to be routed to o0 and o1, respectively. Assume also that buffer o0 is full and o1 is not full. Then, in accordance to the design intent, it should be the case that i0's head packet is delayed while i1's head packet is routed (and the counter is incremented by one). But this scenario, amongst other similar ones, is *not* specified in Figure 2. To resolve this problem, i1's Statechart needs to be modified such that it also contains functionality that checks whether output buffer o0 is full or not (likewise for o1). Hence, more global reasoning is required to correctly capture the Switch's behavior.

Lack of space and relevance prevents us from presenting an improved, yet more complicated, Statechart diagram of the Original Switch. The lack of relevance is due to two reasons. First, we are unable to convince ourselves that the "improved" specification *is* correct with respect to the design intent. This remark essentially holds for *all* specifications in this paper and embodies our main message in Section 7. Second, many readers of (previous versions of) this paper, including ourselves, have mistakingly approved of Figure 2. It is exactly *this* incorrect approval that illustrates the difficulty of concurrent-system design; presenting improved Statechart diagrams would only obscure this important observation.

6 The Algebra of Communicating Processes

The Algebra of Communicating Processes (ACP) is used below to specify the behavior of the Original Switch. The corresponding specification is called Spec. It is based on priorities from [2] to capture i0's dominance over i1 and is similar to the previous specifications in the sense that it abstracts[4] away the behavior of the buffers.

The outline of this section can be described as follows. Section 6.1 presents short but important definitions in order to obtain Spec. In Section 6.2 we explain

[4] This abstraction is an essential difference between Spec and the ACP specifications presented in [4] where buffers are typically *not* abstracted away.

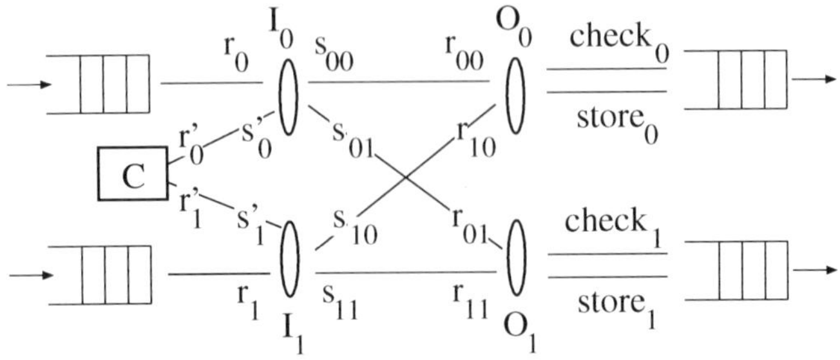

Fig. 3. Input (I_0 and I_1), output (O_0 and O_1), and counter (C) processes

how Spec can be modified in order to obtain specifications of the Simple and Modified Switches. Finally, Section 6.3 addresses the three criteria for ACP.

6.1 The ACP Specification Spec

Let D denote a finite set of data elements where each element $d \in D$ is a packet of 32 bits; i.e., $D = \{0, 1\}^{32}$. We write $d0$ to denote a packet whose first bit has the value zero appended by the 31 bits in d; i.e. $d \in \{0, 1\}^{31}$. Likewise for $d1$ where the first bit has the value one.

In the sequel, we denote the input-buffer processes by I_0 and I_1, the output-buffer processes by O_0 and O_1, and the counter by C. Figure 3 presents names for the input- and output channels. For instance, I_0 has one input channel r_0 (where r abbreviates "read") and three output channels s_{00}, s_{01}, and s'_0 (where s abbreviates "send"). Similarly for I_1. Process O_0 has two input channels r_{00} and r_{10} and two output channels $check_0$ and $store_0$. Channel $check_0$ is used to check whether the corresponding output buffer is not full, and $store_0$ is used to store a data packet in that buffer. Likewise for O_1, $check_1$, and $store_1$.

Communications. Concerning I_0, we want its output channels s_{00}, s_{01}, and s'_0 to communicate with r_{00}, r_{01}, and r'_0, respectively. We capture these requirements in the left-hand column below with $x \equiv y$ denoting that x is syntactic sugar for y:

$c_{00}(d) \equiv \gamma(s_{00}(d), r_{00}(d))$ $\quad$ $c_{10}(d) \equiv \gamma(s_{10}(d), r_{10}(d))$
$c_{01}(d) \equiv \gamma(s_{01}(d), r_{01}(d))$ $\quad$ $c_{11}(d) \equiv \gamma(s_{11}(d), r_{11}(d))$
$c'_0 \equiv \gamma(s'_0, r'_0)$ $\quad$ $c'_1 \equiv \gamma(s'_1, r'_1)$

where d is an arbitrary element of D. The γ notation is defined in [4]. Likewise for I_1, we want its output channels s_{10}, s_{11}, and s'_1 to communicate with r_{10}, r_{11}, and r'_1, respectively, as is shown in the right-hand column above.

Specification Spec **- Encapsulation - Priorities**
To capture the behavior of the Original Switch, we define:
Spec $= \Theta\,(\partial_H\,(\,I_0 \,\|\, I_1 \,\|\, O_0 \,\|\, O_1 \,\|\, C(0)))$
The five processes are placed in parallel ($\|$) and the counter is initialized to 0. The encapsulation operator ∂_H and priority operator Θ are addressed next.

The encapsulation operator ∂_H is defined by means of the encapsulation set:
$H = \{s_{00}(d),\ s_{01}(d),\ s_{10}(d),\ s_{11}(d) \mid d \in D\} \cup$
$\{r_{00}(d),\ r_{01}(d),\ r_{10}(d),\ r_{11}(d) \mid d \in D\} \cup \{r'_0,\ s'_0,\ r'_1,\ s'_1\}$
Based on this definition, ∂_H in `Spec` forces the send processes to synchronize with the read processes.

The priority operator Θ is defined by expressing the precedence ($>$) that I_0 has over I_1 as follows:
$\forall d, d' \in \{0,1\}^{31}.\ \ c_{00}(d0) > c_{10}(d'0)\ \ \&\ \ c_{01}(d1) > c_{11}(d'1)\ \ \&\ \ c'_0 > c'_1$

Spatial *or* Temporal Reasoning. At this stage of our exposition, we make the following interesting observation. The specifications, presented so far, mainly require reasoning in one dimension, i.e. in terms of either space or time but typically not both. For instance, to specify each communication (γ), we only need to reason across two processes and do not require any temporal reasoning. Likewise, to specify `Spec`, we combine the terms I_0, I_1, O_0, O_1, and C. This is a spatial decomposition (global spatial reasoning) in which we do not need to reason in time. While a similar remark holds for the set H, we note that this is not the case for the $>$ order[5].

In short, the reasoning has been relatively local so far, especially when compared to the specifications presented in previous sections. However, as expected, global reasoning can not be completely avoided, as the following process definitions illustrate.

The Processes. The two input processes are defined as follows:
$I_0 = r_0(d\,000\,0) \,.\, s'_0 \,.\, s_{00}(d\,000\,0) \,.\, I_0 \,+\, r_0(d\,cba\,0) \,.\, s_{00}(d\,cba\,0) \,.\, I_0 \,+$
$r_0(d\,000\,1) \,.\, s'_0 \,.\, s_{01}(d\,000\,1) \,.\, I_0 \,+\, r_0(d\,cba\,1) \,.\, s_{01}(d\,cba\,1) \,.\, I_0$
$I_1 = r_1(d\,000\,0) \,.\, s'_1 \,.\, s_{10}(d\,000\,0) \,.\, I_1 \,+\, r_1(d\,cba\,0) \,.\, s_{10}(d\,cba\,0) \,.\, I_1 \,+$
$r_1(d\,000\,1) \,.\, s'_1 \,.\, s_{11}(d\,000\,1) \,.\, I_1 \,+\, r_1(d\,cba\,1) \,.\, s_{11}(d\,cba\,1) \,.\, I_1$
with $cba \in \{0,1\}^3 \setminus \{000\}$ and $d \in \{0,1\}^{28}$.

The notation $r_0(d\,cba\,1)$ expresses the arrival of a data packet on channel r_0 whose first bit is 1, its second bit is a, third bit is b, fourth bit is c, and all other 28 bits, together, constitute d.

The four terms of I_0's definition are separated by a $+$ sign, expressing disjunction. For further clarification, consider the first term of I_0 which is: $r_0(d\,000\,0) \,.\, s'_0 \,.\, s_{00}(d\,000\,0) \,.\, I_0$. It states that if an interesting data packet with destination `o0` arrives on input channel r_0, then the counter has to be incremented (by means of s'_0) and the packet has to be send to `o0` (by means of s_{00}). After these actions have taken place, the state I_0 is re-entered.

The two output processes and the counter process are defined as:
$O_0 = check_0 \,.\, (\, r_{00}(d0) + r_{10}(d0)\,) \,.\, store_0(d0) \,.\, O_0$
$O_1 = check_1 \,.\, (\, r_{01}(d1) + r_{11}(d1)\,) \,.\, store_1(d1) \,.\, O_1$ with $d \in \{0,1\}^{31}$
$C(n) = r'_0 \,.\, C(n+1) \,+\, r'_1 \,.\, C(n+1)$ with $n \in \mathbb{N}$

[5] As pointed out by an anonymous referee, the $>$ order is merely another way to reason about time and, hence, does not decrease the global reasoning.

To understand each process definition (e.g. I_0), one has to reason across multiple clock cycles (i.e. data packets) and across multiple channels. On the one hand, the reasoning is still relatively local in the sense that the four process terms are separated from each other by means of the channels. On the other hand, to convince oneself that the specification is correct, a designer will typically derive (part of) the specification's underlying state-transition graph and reason about it's correctness with respect to the original design intent. This reasoning *is* global (in both space and time).

6.2 The Simplified and Modified Switches

We briefly explain how the previous ACP-based definitions need to be modified in order to obtain specifications of the Simplified and the Modified Switches.

To specify the Simplified Switch, apply the following six steps. First, remove the counter C and r'_0, s'_0, r'_1, and s'_1 from Figure 3. Second, remove the communications c'_0 and c'_1. Third, remove $C(0)$ from Spec. Fourth, remove $\{r'_0, s'_0, r'_1, s'_1\}$ from H. Fifth, remove the last conjunct from the priorities. Sixth, redefine the two input process terms as follows:

$I_0 = r_0(d0) \cdot s_{00}(d0) \cdot I_0 + r_0(d1) \cdot s_{01}(d1) \cdot I_0$

$I_1 = r_1(d0) \cdot s_{10}(d0) \cdot I_1 + r_1(d1) \cdot s_{11}(d1) \cdot I_1 \qquad$ with $d \in \{0,1\}^{31}$.

To specify the Modified Switch, recall conditions $C1$ and $C2$ in Section 2. The formal definitions of $C1(d,d')$ and $C2(d,d')$ –where d and d' denote the two head data packets under consideration– are straightforward and hence omitted. Given these conditions, we need to modify the priorities of Spec as follows[6]:

$\forall d, d' \in \{0,1\}^{32}$.

$$C1(d,d') \wedge C2(d,d') \Rightarrow c_{00}(d) > c_{10}(d') \;\&\; c_{01}(d) > c_{11}(d') \;\&\; c'_0(d) > c'_1(d')$$
$$C1(d,d') \wedge \neg C2(d,d') \Rightarrow c_{00}(d) > c_{10}(d') \;\&\; c_{01}(d) > c_{11}(d')$$
$$\neg C1(d,d') \wedge C2(d,d') \Rightarrow c'_0(d) < c'_1(d')$$

All of the extensions, described in the previous two paragraphs, are straightforward[7]. We are therefore tempted to conclude that: the ACP language fares well in terms of adaptability for the 2×2 Switch case study.

6.3 Three Criteria

The three criteria of Section 1 for ACP are addressed as follows. First, ACP requires global reasoning in order to convince oneself that the specification is correct. Second, ACP fares well in terms of adaptability for the presented case study. Third, ACP is similar to TLA$^+$ in the sense that it can not guarantee that the final implementation respects the maximum-throughput requirement (i.e. ACP has an interleaving semantics).

6 The critical reader will note the difference between $c'_0(d)$ and $c'_1(d')$ from c'_0 and c'_1. Hence, the communications and encapsulation set H need to be modified accordingly.

7 For the first author. And, not so for at least one ACP expert (an anonymous referee). This suggests that we are using ACP in a non-standard way in this paper.

Table 4. Results of our comparative study

	local reasoning	adaptability	maximum throughput
TLA^{+}	–	–	–
Bluespec	–	–	+
Statecharts	–	–	
ACP	–	+	–

(i)

Informal Design Intent
↓ ?
Formal Specification
↓ ok
Formal Implementation

(ii)

7 Conclusions and Future Work

We have compared four specification languages on the same case study (i.e. the Switch), as opposed to promoting one language by selectively choosing 'suitable' case studies. Our comparisons, based on three criteria, are summarized in Table 4(i), where a plus is preferable over a minus. The blank entry for the maximum-throughput criterion for Statecharts denotes that, in this (short) paper, we have not been able to show that either a plus or a minus sign is warranted.

On the one hand, the presented results in Table 4(i) are of course debatable: they are based on our level of expertise in each of the specification languages and on only one concurrent system (the Switch). In particular, Table 4(i) states that Statecharts don't fare well for adaptability but this is primarily due to our unsuccessful attempt to correctly capture the behavior of the Original Switch.

On the other hand, it is interesting to note that two of the four anonymous reviewers of this paper have championed our incorrect Statechart design. Both reviewers also disfavored the ACP specification while at least one of them claimed to be experienced in ACP. These comments merely serve the purpose of backing up our main conclusion:

> The seemingly simple design intents of the Switch case study are extremely difficult to formalize correctly.

Table 4(ii) captures this message graphically: the first refinement step, labelled with a question mark, is far more problematic than the second, labelled with 'ok'. But, it is the second step that is heavily researched today and not the first.

Since we have been unable to adequately capture the Switches' behaviors in this paper, further investigations are warranted. With respect to the question mark in Table 4(ii), it seems desirable to have a concurrent specification framework, endowed with a tool for formal verification or theorem proving to verify that design intents are correctly captured. But then the question arises: How does one even formulate the properties to verify, if capturing the design intent is hard? We hope the reader will join us in our quest to address this problem and inform us if relevant work along these lines has already been conducted.

Acknowledgements. Thanks go to Alban Ponse for helping the first author understand the Algebra of Communicating Processes. This work was partially supported by an AFOSR grant, and NSF grant CCF-0702316.

References

1. Automatic Generation of Control Logic with Bluespec SystemVerilog, Bluespec, Inc., Initially (February 2005), `bluespec.com/products/Papers.htm`
2. Bergstra, J.A., Ponse, A., van der Zwaag, M.B.: Branching time and orthogonal bisimulation equivalence. Theoretical Computer Science 309, 313–355 (2003)
3. Daylight, E.G.: The Difficulty of Correctly Designing a 2×2 Switch, Technical Report No. 2007-16, Virginia Tech. (May 2007), `http://fermat.ece.vt.edu/Publications/pubs/techrep/techrep0716.pdf`
4. Fokkink, W.J.: Introduction to Process Algebra. In: Texts in Theoretical Computer Science. Springer, Heidelberg (2000)
5. Harel, D.: Statecharts: A visual Formalism for complex systems. Sc. of Comp. Prog. 8, 231–274 (1987)
6. Hoe, J.C., Arvind: Operation-Centric Hardware Description and Synthesis. IEEE Trans. on Computer-Aided Design of Integrated Circuits and Systems 23(9), 1277–1288 (2004)
7. Kahn, G.: The Semantics of a Simple Language for Parallel Programming. Information Processing, 471–475 (1974)
8. Lamport, L.: Specifying Systems: The $\texttt{TLA}^+$ Language and Tools for Hardware and Software Engineers. Addison-Wesley Professional, Reading (2002)
9. Singh, G., Shukla, S.K.: Verifying Compiler Based Refinement of Bluespec^{TM} Specifications Using the SPIN Model Checker. In: Havelund, K., Majumdar, R., Palsberg, J. (eds.) SPIN 2008. LNCS, vol. 5156, pp. 250–269. Springer, Heidelberg (2008)

Sums and Lovers: Case Studies in Security, Compositionality and Refinement

Annabelle K. McIver[1,⋆] and Carroll C. Morgan[2,⋆]

[1] Dept. Computer Science, Macquarie University, NSW 2109 Australia
[2] School of Comp. Sci. and Eng., Univ. New South Wales, NSW 2052 Australia

Abstract. A truly secure protocol is one which *never* violates its security requirements, no matter how bizarre the circumstances, provided those circumstances are within its terms of reference. Such cast-iron guarantees, as far as they are possible, require formal techniques: proof or model-checking. Informally, they are difficult or impossible to achieve.

Our technique is *refinement*, until recently not much applied to security. We argue its benefits by giving rigorous formal developments, in refinement-based program algebra, of several security case studies.

A conspicuous feature of our studies is their layers of abstraction and –for the main study, in particular– that the protocol is unbounded in state, placing its verification beyond the reach of model checkers.

Correctness in all contexts is crucial for our goal of layered, refinement-based developments. This is ensured by our semantics in which the program constructors are monotonic with respect to "security-aware" refinement, which is in turn a generalisation of compositionality.

Keywords: Refinement of security; formalised secrecy; hierarchical security reasoning; compositional semantics.

1 Introduction

This paper is about verifying computer programs that have security- as well as functional requirements; in particular it is about developing them in a layered, refinement-oriented way. To do that we use the novel *Shadow Semantics* [14,15] that supports security refinement.

Security refinement is a variation of (classical) refinement that preserves non-interference properties (as well as classical, functional ones), and features compositionality and hierarchical proof with an emphasis unusual for security-protocol development. Those features are emphasised because they are essential for scale-up and deployment into arbitrary contexts: in security protocols, the influence of the deployment environment can be particularly subtle.

In relation to other approaches, such as model checking, ours is dual. We begin with a specification rather than an implementation, one so simple that its security and functional properties are self-evident — or are at least small enough to be subjected to rigorous algorithmic checking [19]. Then secure refinement

⋆ We acknowledge the support of the Australian Research Council Grant DP0879529.

A. Cavalcanti and D. Dams (Eds.): FM 2009, LNCS 5850, pp. 289–304, 2009.

ensures that non-interference -style flaws in the implementation code, no matter how many refinement steps are taken to reach it, must have already been present in that specification. Because the code of course is probably too large and complicated to understand directly, that property is especially beneficial.

Our main contribution, in summary, is to argue by example that the secure-refinement paradigm [14,15], including its compositionality and layers of abstraction, can greatly extend the size and complexity of security applications that can be verified. The principal case study is a protocol for Yao's Millionaraires' Problem [23], especially suitable because it includes four (sub-) protocols nested like dolls within it: our paradigm allows them to be treated separately, so that each can be understood in isolation. That contrasts with the Millionaires' code "flattened" in Fig. 4 to the second-from-bottom level of abstraction: at face value it is impenetrable.

In §3 we set out the semantics for secure refinement; and in §4 we begin our series of case studies, in increasing order of complexity; but before any of that, in §2 we introduce multi-party computations. Throughout we use left-associating dot for function application, so that $f.x.y$ means $(f(x))(y)$ or $f(x,y)$, and we take (un-)Currying for granted where necessary. Comprehensions/quantifications are written uniformly, as $(\mathsf{Q}x{:}\,T|R{\cdot}E)$ for quantifier Q, bound variable(s) x of type(s) T, range-predicate R (probably) constraining x and element-constructor E in which x (probably) appears free: for sets the opening "(Q" is "{" and the closing ")" is "}" so that e.g. the comprehension $\{x,y{:}\,\mathbb{N} \mid y{=}x^2 \cdot z{+}y\}$ is the set of numbers $z, z{+}1, z{+}4, \cdots$ that exceed z by a perfect square exactly.

In the conclusions §8 we set out our **strategic goals** for the whole approach.

2 Secure Multi-party Computation: An Overview

In *Multi-party computations* (*MPC*'s) separate agents hold their own shares of a shared computation, as illustrated in Fig. 1. Only at the end are the shares combined; and the computation is *secure* if no information is released until that point. We specify a typical two-party *MPC* as

$$\mathbf{vis}_A\ a; \mathbf{vis}_B\ b; \mathbf{vis}\ x; \quad x{:=}\,a \otimes b\ , \tag{1}$$

in which two agents A and B, with their respective variables a and b visible only to them separately, *somehow collaboratively calculate* the result $a{\otimes}b$ and publish it in the variable

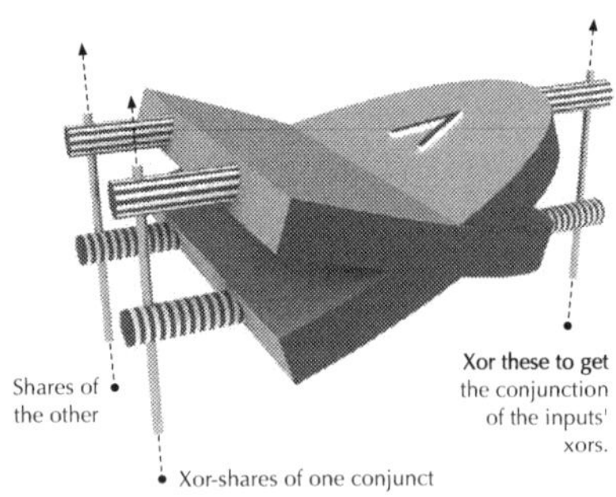

Agent A sees the upper shares, the two inputs and one output; B sees the lower . The upper/lower exclusive-or of the two outputs is the conjunction of the left- and right inputs' separate upper/lower xor's.

Fig. 1. ⊕-shared conjunction: §6.2

x; but they reveal nothing (more) about a, b in the process, either to each other or to a third party. Our declaration $\mathbf{vis}_A\ a$ means that only A can observe the value of a (similarly for B); and the undecorated **vis** means x is observable to all, in this case both A, B and third parties. For example, if $\otimes$ were conjunction then (1) specifies that A (knowing a) learns b when a holds, but not otherwise; and a third party learns the exact values a, b only when they are both true. Although the assignment (1) cannot be executed directly when A and B are physically distributed, nevertheless the security and functionality properties it *specifies* are indeed self-evident once $\otimes$ is fixed. But the "somehow collaboratively calculate" above is a matter of *implementing* the specification, using local variables of limited visibility and exchange of messages between the agents. We will see much of that in §5ff; and it is not self-evident at all.

An *unsatisfactory* implementation of (1) involves a real-time *trusted third party* ($rTTP$): both A, B submit their values to an agent C which performs the computation privately and announces only the result. But this Agent C is a corruptible bottleneck and, worse, it would learn a, b in the process. The $rTTP$ can be avoided by appealing to the sub-protocol *Oblivious Transfer* [17,18] in which a TTP (no "r") participates only off-line and before the computation proper begins: his Agent C is not a bottleneck, and it does not learn a or b.

Our main case study is Yao's millionaires A, B of §7 who compare their fortunes a, b without revealing either: only the Boolean $a<b$ is published. For us it is a showcase exemplar, because it makes our point of layered development so well: it uses the Lovers' II protocol (§6.2), using Lovers' I (§6.1), using Oblivious Transfer (§5), using the Encryption Lemma (§4); moreover our treatment of the main loop (§7.3, unbounded riches) abstracts from the loop body (§7.1, the two-bit millionaires). Layering and compositionality are conspicuous, our technique's specialty; and our dealing easily with unbounded state is another innovation.

Our contribution in detail is thus to formalise and prove a number of exemplary non-interference -style security protocols *while moving through layers of abstraction* and *in some cases with unbounded state.* We aim for a method with the potential to scale, and to be automated, and moreover one which would guide a designer to an understanding of the implications of his proposed design, a paramount criterion for critical software. The Millionaires illustrate the hierarchical approach: when written out in full, the code comprises roughly 30 intricate lines (Fig. 4); only abstraction controls this complexity. Finally, the proofs are lengthy; but crucially *they are boring*, comprising many tiny steps similar to those already automated in probabilistic program algebra [12], and thus easily checked.

3 The Shadow Model of Security and Refinement

The Shadow Model extends the *non-interference model* of security [7] to determine an attacker's inferred knowledge of hidden (high-security) variables at each point in the computation; we then require that the inferred knowledge *is not increased* by secure refinement.

In its original form, non-interference partitions variables into high-security- and low-security classes: we call them *hidden* and *visible*. A "non-interference -secure" program is then one where our attacker cannot infer *hidden* variables' initial values from *visible* variables' values (initial or final). With just two variables v, h of class visible, hidden resp. a possibly nondeterministic program r thus takes initial states (v, h) to sets of final visible states v' and is of type $\mathcal{V} \to \mathcal{H} \to \mathbb{P}\mathcal{V}$, where $\mathcal{V}, \mathcal{H}$ are the value sets corresponding to the types of v, h. Such a program r is *non-interference -secure* just when for any initial visible the set of possible final visibles is independent of the initial hidden [9,20], that is for any $v{:}\,\mathcal{V}$ we have $(\forall h_0, h_1{:}\,\mathcal{H} \cdot r.v.h_0 = r.v.h_1)$.

In our approach [14] we extended this view, in several stages. The first was to concentrate on final- (rather than initial) hidden values and therefore to model programs as $\mathcal{V}\to\mathcal{H}\to\mathbb{P}(\mathcal{V}\times\mathcal{H})$. For two such programs $r_{\{1,2\}}$ we say that $r_1 \sqsubseteq r_2$, that r_1 "is securely refined by" r_2, whenever both the following hold:

(i) For any initial state v, h each possible r_2 outcome v', h' is also a possible r_1 outcome, that is for all $v{:}\,\mathcal{V}$ and $h{:}\,\mathcal{H}$ we have $r_1.v.h \supseteq r_2.v.h$.
This is the classical "can reduce nondeterminism" form of refinement.

(ii) For all $v{:}\,\mathcal{V}, h{:}\,\mathcal{H}$, and $v'{:}\,\mathcal{V}$ satisfying $(\exists h'_2{:}\,\mathcal{H} \cdot (v', h'_2) \in r_2.v.h)$, we have for all $h'{:}\,\mathcal{H}$ that $(v', h') \in r_1.v.h$ implies $(v', h') \in r_2.v.h$.
This second condition says that for any observed visibles v, v' and any initial h the attacker's "deductive powers" w.r.t. final h''s cannot be improved by refinement: there can only be more possibilities for h', never fewer.

In this simple setting the two conditions together do not yet allow an attacker's ignorance of h strictly to increase: secure refinement seems to boil down to allowing decrease of nondeterminism in v but not in h. But strict increase of hidden nondeterminism *is* possible: we meet it later, in §3.3.

Still in the simple setting, as an example restrict all our variables' types so that $\mathcal{V}{=}\mathcal{H}{=}\{0,1\}$, and let r_1 be the program that can produce from any initial values (v, h) any one of the four possible (v', h') final values in $\mathcal{V} \times \mathcal{H}$ (so that the final values of v and h are uncorrelated). Then the program r_2 that can produce only the two final values $\{(0,0),(0,1)\}$ is a secure refinement of r_1; but the program r_3 that produces only the two final values $\{(0,0),(1,1)\}$ is not a secure refinement (although it is a classical one).

This is because r_2 reduces r_1's visible nondeterminism, but does not affect the hidden nondeterminism in h'. In r_3, however, variables v' and h' are correlated.

3.1 The Shadow *H* of *h* Records *h*'s Inferred Values

In r_1 above the set of possible final values of h' was $\{0,1\}$ for each v' separately. This set is called "The Shadow," and represents explicitly an attacker's ignorance of h': it is the smallest set of possibilities he must consider possible, by inference. In r_2 that shadow was the same; but in r_3 the shadow was smaller, just $\{v'\}$ for each v', and that is why r_3 was not a secure refinement of r_1.

In the shadow semantics we track this inference, so that our program state becomes a triple (v, h, H) with H a subset of $\mathcal{H}$ — and in each triple the H

contains exactly those (other) values that h might have. The (extended) output triples of the three example programs are then respectively

$$\begin{array}{ll} r_1 \text{ — } & \{(0,0,\{0,1\}),\ (0,1,\{0,1\}),\ (1,0,\{0,1\}),\ (1,1,\{0,1\})\} \\ r_2 \text{ — } & \{(0,0,\{0,1\}),\ (0,1,\{0,1\})\} \\ r_3 \text{ — } & \{(0,0,\{0\}),\ (1,1,\{1\})\}\ , \end{array}$$

and we have $r_1 \sqsubseteq r_2$ because r_1's set of outcomes includes all of r_2's. But for r_3 we find that its outcome $(0,0,\{0\})$ does not occur among r_1's outcomes, nor is there even an r_1-outcome $(0,0,H')$ with $H' \subseteq \{0\}$ that would satisfy (ii). That, again, is why $r_1 \not\sqsubseteq r_3$.

For sequential composition of shadow-enhanced programs, not only final- but also initial triples (v,h,H) must be dealt with: the final triples of a first component become initial triples for a second. We now define the shadow semantics exactly, in four stages, by showing how those triples are generated.

3.2 Step 1: The Shadow Semantics of Atomic Programs

A classical program r is an input-output relation between $\mathcal{V} \times \mathcal{H}$ -pairs. Considered as a single, atomic action its shadow-enhanced semantics addShadow.r is a relation between $\mathcal{V} \times \mathcal{H} \times \mathbb{P}\mathcal{H}$ -triples and is defined as follows:

Definition 1. *Atomic shadow semantics* Given a classical program $r\colon \mathcal{V} \to \mathcal{H} \to \mathbb{P}(\mathcal{V} \times \mathcal{H})$ we define its *shadow enhancement* addShadow.r of type $\mathcal{V} \to \mathcal{H} \to \mathbb{P}\mathcal{H} \to \mathbb{P}(\mathcal{V} \times \mathcal{H} \times \mathbb{P}\mathcal{H})$ so that addShadow.$r.v.h.H \ni (v',h',H')$ just when both

(i) $\quad r.v.h \ni (v',h')$ — *classical*

(ii) and $\quad H' = \{h'\colon \mathcal{H} \mid (\exists h''\colon H \cdot r.v.h'' \ni (v',h'))\}$. — *shadow*

□

Clause (i) says that the classical projection of addShadow.r's behaviour is the same as the classical behaviour of just r itself. Clause (ii) says that the final shadow H' contains all those values h' compatible with allowing the original hidden value to range as h'' over the initial shadow H.

As a first example, let the syntax $x{:\in}\, S$ denote the standard program that chooses variable x's value from a non-empty set S. Assume here only that S is constant, not depending on v, h. Then from Def. 1 we have that

(i) Choosing v affects only v because
$$\text{addShadow}.(v{:\in}\, S).v.h.H = \{v'\colon S \cdot (v',h,H)\}$$
(ii) Choosing h affects both h *and* H, possibly introducing ignorance because
$$\text{addShadow}.(h{:\in}\, S).v.h.H = \{h'\colon S \cdot (v,h',S)\}$$
(iii) An assignment of hidden to visible "collapses" ignorance because
$$\text{addShadow}.(v{:=}\, h).v.h.H = \{(h,h,\{h\}\}$$

From (ii) and (iii) the composition addShadow.$(h{:\in}\, S)$; addShadow.$(v{:=}\, h)$ first introduces ignorance: we do not know h's exact value "at the semicolon." But then the ignorance is removed: we deduce h's value, at the end, by observing v. The composition (ii); (iii) as a whole is nondeterministic, and it yields $\{x\colon S \cdot (x,x,\{x\})\}$ with v,h's common final value x drawn arbitrarily from S; but whatever that value is, it is known that h has it because H is a singleton.

3.3 Step 2: The Shadow Semantics of Straight-Line Programs

General (non-atomic) programs gain their shadows by repeated application of §3.2 as implied by induction over their syntax, as shown in Fig. 2. The only non-traditional command is **reveal** that publishes an expression but changes no program variables; note it does change the shadow.

3.4 Step 3: Refinement's Properties via Gedanken Experiments

Our definition of refinement is based on scale-up experiments with program algebra [14,15]. Our first observation is that the semantics enforces *perfect recall*, that visible variables reveal information even if subsequently overwritten. This is because refinement must be *monotonic*, i.e. (A) that refinement of a program portion must refine the whole program; and (B) that conventional refinements involving v only must remain valid. Both principles (A,B) are required in order to be able to develop large programs via local reasoning over small portions.

Without perfect recall, overwriting v would prevent program $v{:=}\,h; v{:\in}\,\{0,1\}$ from revealing h. Yet from (B) we have $v{:\in}\,\{0,1\} \sqsubseteq v{:=}\,v$; and then from (A) we have $(v{:=}\,h; v{:\in}\,\{0,1\}) \sqsubseteq (v{:=}\,h; v{:=}\,v)$ — and it would be a violation of secure refinement for the *rhs* to reveal h while the *lhs* does not. Thus the premise –imperfect recall– is false.

A similar experiment applies to conditionals: because (A,B) validates

$$\textbf{if } h{=}0 \textbf{ then } v{:\in}\,\{0,1\} \textbf{ else } v{:\in}\,\{0,1\} \textbf{ fi} \quad \sqsubseteq \quad \textbf{if } h{=}0 \textbf{ then } v{:=}\,0 \textbf{ else } v{:=}\,1 \textbf{ fi}$$

we must accept that the **if**-test reveals its outcome, in this case whether $h{=}0$ holds initially. And nondeterministic choice $P_1 \sqcap P_2$ is visible to the attacker because each of the two branches $P_{\{1,2\}}$ can be refined separately.

Equality of programs is a special case of refinement, whence compositionality is a special case of monotonicity: two programs with equal semantics in isolation must remain equal in all contexts. With those ideas in place, we define refinement as follows:

Definition 2. *Refinement* For programs $P_{\{1,2\}}$ we say that P_1 *is securely refined by* P_2 and write $P_1 \sqsubseteq P_2$ just when for all v, h, H we have

$$(\forall\,(v', h', H'_2){:}\, [\![P_2]\!].v.h.H \cdot \\ (\,\exists H'_1{:}\,\mathbb{P}\mathcal{H} \mid H'_1 \subseteq H'_2 \cdot \quad (v', h', H'_1) \in [\![P_1]\!].v.h.H\,)\ )\ ,$$

with $[\![\cdot]\!]$ as defined in Fig. 2.

This means that for each initial triple (v, h, H) every final triple (v', h', H'_2) produced by P_2 must be "justified" by the existence of a triple (v', h', H'_1), with equal or smaller ignorance, produced by P_1 under the same circumstances. □

From Fig. 2 we have e.g. that $[\![h{:=}\,0 \sqcap h{:=}\,1]\!].v.h.H$ is $\{(v,0,\{0\}), (v,1,\{1\})\}$, yet the strictly more refined $[\![h{:\in}\,\{0,1\}]\!].v.h.H$ is $\{(v,0,\{0,1\}), (v,1,\{0,1\})\}$. This is thus an example of a strict refinement where the two commands differ only by an increase of ignorance: they have equal nondeterminism classically, but in one case ($\sqcap$) it can be observed by the attacker and in the other case ($:\in$) it cannot. The "more ignorant" triple $(v,0,\{0,1\})$ is strictly justified by the "less ignorant" triple $(v,0,\{0\})$, where we say "strictly" because $\{0\} \subset \{0,1\}$.

	Program P	Semantics $[\![P]\!].v.h.H$	
Publish a value	**reveal** $E.v.h$	$\{\ (v,\ h,\ \{h'\!:H \mid E.v.h' = E.v.h\})\ \}$	
Assign to visible	$v{:=}\ E.v.h$	$\{\ (E.v.h,\ h,\ \{h'\!:H \mid E.v.h' = E.v.h\})\ \}$	$\star$
Assign to hidden	$h{:=}\ E.v.h$	$\{\ (v,\ E.v.h,\ \{h'\!:H \cdot E.v.h'\})\ \}$	$\star$
Choose visible	$v{:\in}\ S.v.h$	$\{v'\!:S.v.h \cdot\ (v',\ h,\ \{h'\!:H \mid v' \in S.v.h'\})\ \}$	$\star$
Choose hidden	$h{:\in}\ S.v.h$	$\{h'\!:S.v.h \cdot\ (v,\ h',\ \{h'\!:H; h''\!:S.v.h' \cdot h''\})\ \}$	$\star$
Execute atomically	$\langle\!\langle P \rangle\!\rangle$	addShadow.("classical semantics of P")	
Sequential composition	$P_1; P_2$	lift.$[\![P_2]\!]$.($[\![P_1]\!].v.h.H$)	
Demonic choice	$P_1 \sqcap P_2$	$[\![P_1]\!].v.h.H \cup [\![P_2]\!].v.h.H$	
Conditional	**if** $E.v.h$ **then** P_t **else** P_f **fi**	$[\![P_t]\!].v.h.\{h'\!:H \mid E.v.h' = \textbf{true}\}$ $\lhd\ E.v.h\ \rhd$ $[\![P_f]\!].v.h.\{h'\!:H \mid E.v.h' = \textbf{false}\}$ (We write *if* $\lhd$ *cond* $\rhd$ *else* [8] $\longrightarrow$)	

The syntactically atomic commands A marked $\star$ have the property that $A = \langle\!\langle A \rangle\!\rangle$. This is deliberate: syntactic atoms execute atomically. The function lift.$[\![P_2]\!]$ applies $[\![P_2]\!]$ to all triples in its set-valued argument, un-Currying each time, and then takes the union of all results.
The extension to many variables $v_1, v_2, \cdots$ and $h_1, h_2, \cdots$, including local declarations, is straightforward [14,15].

Fig. 2. Semantics of non-looping commands

3.5 Step 4: Properties –and Utility– of Atomicity Brackets $\langle\!\langle\cdot\rangle\!\rangle$

The atomicity brackets $\langle\!\langle\cdot\rangle\!\rangle$ treat their contents as a single classical command, and thus classical *equality* (although not classical refinement) can be used within them. In simple cases atomicity is preserved by composition, but not in general:

Lemma 1. *atomicity and composition* Given two programs $P_{\{1,2\}}$ over v, h we have $\langle\!\langle P_1; P_2 \rangle\!\rangle = \langle\!\langle P_1 \rangle\!\rangle; \langle\!\langle P_2 \rangle\!\rangle$ just when v's *intermediate* value, i.e. "at the semicolon," can be deduced from its *endpoint* values, i.e. initial and final, possibly in combination. The semicolon is interpreted classically on the left, and as in Fig. 2 on the right.

Proof. Given in [1, App. A]. □

This lemma is as significant when its conditions are *not* met as when they are. It means for example that we cannot conclude from Lem. 1 that $\langle\!\langle v{:=}\ h; v{:=}\ 0 \rangle\!\rangle = \langle\!\langle v{:=}\ h \rangle\!\rangle; \langle\!\langle v{:=}\ 0 \rangle\!\rangle$, since on the left the intermediate value of v cannot be deduced from its endpoint values: for h is not visible at the beginning and v itself has been "erased" at the end. And indeed from Def. 1

(i) On the left we have $\langle\!\langle v{:=}\,h; v{:=}\,0\rangle\!\rangle.v.h.H = \{(0, h, H)\}$
(ii) Whereas on the right we have $(\langle\!\langle v{:=}\,h\rangle\!\rangle; \langle\!\langle v{:=}\,0\rangle\!\rangle).v.h.H = \{(0, h, \{h\})\}$

This is perfect recall again. More interesting is the utility of introducing atomicity temporarily in a derivation, as illustrated in §4 below: when applicable, we can infer security properties via (simpler) classical equalities within $\langle\!\langle\cdot\rangle\!\rangle$.

3.6 Multiple Agents, and the Attacker'S Capabilities

In a multi-agent system each agent has a limited knowledge of the system state, determined by his *point of view*; and different agents have different views. The above simple semantics reflects A's viewpoint, say, by interpreting variables declared to be $\mathbf{vis}_{list}$ as visible (v) variables if A is in *list* and as hidden (h) variables otherwise. More precisely,

- **var** means the associated variable's visibility is unknown or irrelevant.
- **vis** means the associated variable is visible to all agents.
- **hid** means the associated variable is hidden from all agents.
- $\mathbf{vis}_{list}$ means the associated variable is visible to all agents in the (non-empty) list, and is hidden from all others (including third parties).
- $\mathbf{hid}_{list}$ means the associated variable is hidden from all agents in the list, and is visible to all others (including third parties).

For example in (1), from A's viewpoint the specification would be interpreted with a and x visible and b hidden; for B the interpretation hides a instead of b. For a third party X, say, both a, b are hidden but x is still visible.

From Agent A's point of view (say) an attacker uses a run-time debugger to single-step through an execution of the program. Each step's size is determined by atomicity, either implied syntactically or given by $\langle\!\langle\cdot\rangle\!\rangle$; when the program is paused, the current point in the program source-code is indicated; and hovering over a variable reveals its value provided its annotation (in this case) makes it visible to A: e.g. "yes" for $\mathbf{vis}_A$ or $\mathbf{hid}_B$, and "no" for $\mathbf{hid}_A$ or $\mathbf{vis}_B$.

Conventionally, a successful attack is one that "breaks the security." For us, however, a successful attack is one that *breaks the refinement*: if we claim that $P \sqsubseteq Q$, and yet an attacker subjects Q to hostile tests that reveal something P cannot reveal, then our claimed refinement must be false (and we'd better review the reasoning that seemed to prove it). Crucially however we will have suffered a failure of calculation, not of guesswork: only the former can be audited.

The conventional view is a special case of ours: if P reveals nothing, then $P \sqsubseteq Q$ means that also Q must reveal nothing. Thus a successful attack with such a specification P is one in which Q is forced to reveal anything at all.

Finally, if a refinement is valid yet an insecurity is discovered (relative to some informal requirement), then the security-preservation property of refinement means that the insecurity *was already present* in the specification.

4 First Case Study: The Encryption Lemma (*EL*)

For Booleans x, y we write $(x \oplus y) := E$ to abbreviate the specification statement $x, y{:}[x \oplus y = E]$, thus an atomic command that sets x, y nondeterministically so that their exclusive-or equals E [13]. By making the command atomic, we have $(x \oplus y := E) \;=\; \langle\!\langle x, y{:}[x \oplus y = E] \rangle\!\rangle$ by definition.

A very common pattern in non-interference -style protocols is the idiom $[\![$ **vis** $v;$ **hid** $h' \cdot (v \oplus h') := h$ $]\!]$ in the context of a declaration **hid** h; it is equivalent classically to **skip** because it assigns only to local variables, whose scope is indicated by $[\![\cdots]\!]$. As our first example of secure refinement (actually equality) we show it is *security*-equivalent to **skip** also, in spite of its assigning a hidden *rhs* (variable h) to a partly visible *lhs* (includes v). We have via Shadow-secure program algebra the equalities

$$
\begin{array}{lll}
 & [\![\ \textbf{vis}\ v; \textbf{hid}\ h' \cdot\ v \oplus h' := h\ ]\!] & \\
= & [\![\ \textbf{vis}\ v; \textbf{hid}\ h' \cdot\ \langle\!\langle v, h'{:}[v \oplus h' = h] \rangle\!\rangle\ ]\!] & \text{“defined above”} \\
= & [\![\ \textbf{vis}\ v; \textbf{hid}\ h' \cdot\ \langle\!\langle v{:}\in \{0,1\}; h' := h \oplus v \rangle\!\rangle\ ]\!] & \text{“classical reasoning within } \langle\!\langle \cdot \rangle\!\rangle\text{”} \\
= & [\![\ \textbf{vis}\ v; \textbf{hid}\ h' \cdot\ \langle\!\langle v{:}\in \{0,1\} \rangle\!\rangle; \langle\!\langle h' := h \oplus v \rangle\!\rangle\ ]\!] & \text{“Lem. 1”} \\
= & [\![\ \textbf{vis}\ v; \textbf{hid}\ h' \cdot\ v{:}\in \{0,1\}; h' := h \oplus v\ ]\!] & \text{“syntactic atoms”} \\
= & [\![\ \textbf{vis}\ v \cdot\ v{:}\in \{0,1\}; [\![\ \textbf{hid}\ h' \cdot\ h' := h \oplus v\ ]\!]]\!] & \text{“}h' \text{ not free } \heartsuit\text{”} \\
= & [\![\ \textbf{vis}\ v \cdot\ v{:}\in \{0,1\}]\!] & \text{“assignment of anything to local hidden is } \textbf{skip}\ \heartsuit\text{”} \\
= & \textbf{skip}\ , & \text{“assignment of visibles to local visible is } \textbf{skip}\ \heartsuit\text{”}
\end{array}
$$

where at $\heartsuit$ we appeal to manipulations of scope, and more primitive **skip**-equivalences, that because of space we must justify elsewhere [14,15]. That is, each step can be justified by the semantics of §3, and the overall chain of equalities establishes our Encryption Lemma: we will see it often.

5 Second Case Study: §4⇒ Oblivious Transfer (*OT*)

The *Oblivious Transfer Protocol* builds on §4: an agent A transfers to Agent B one of two secrets, as B chooses: but A does not learn which secret B chose; and B does not learn the other secret. The protocol is originally due to Rabin [17]; we use Rivest's specialisation of it [18]. Its specification is

$$
\begin{array}{ll}
\textbf{vis}_A\ m_0, m_1; & \text{“Oblivious Transfer specification”} \\
\textbf{vis}_B\ c{:}\,\mathsf{Bool}, m; & \\
\quad m := (m_1 \lhd c \rhd m_0)\ , & \Leftarrow \text{We write } (\textit{left} \text{ if } \textit{condition} \text{ else } \textit{right})\ [8].
\end{array}
$$

where the variables without scope brackets are global, and are assumed subsequently. It is implemented via a third, trusted party C who contributes *before* the protocol begins, and indeed before A, B need even have decided what their variables' values are to be. A complete derivation is published elsewhere [15], and it relies on the Encryption Lemma of §4.

In brief (and approximately), Agent C gives two secret keys $k_{\{x,y\}}$ to A; and as well C gives one of those keys to B, telling him which one it is; Agent C then leaves. When the protocol proper begins, Agent B instructs A to encrypt $m_{\{0,1\}}$ either with $k_{\{x,y\}}$ or $k_{\{y,x\}}$ resp. so as to ensure B holds the correct key for the value he wants to decode. Agent A sends both encrypted values to B. Because A sends both, he cannot tell which B really wants; because B holds only one key, he can decrypt only his choice. The derivation is also given in [1, App. C].

6 Third Case Study: The Lovers' Protocols

The Lovers' Protocols (see for example "Dating without embarrassment" [21]) in this section are our first examples of two-party computations, and form the backbone of the later derivation of the Millionaires' Protocol. Throughout we assume two agents A, B.

6.1 §5⇒ Lovers' Protocol I (*LP1*)

In this simple protocol Agent A knows a Boolean a and Agent B knows a Boolean b; they construct two Boolean outcomes a', b' known by A, B resp. so that

1. neither agent learns anything more about $a \wedge b$ as a result of learning its own a' or b' (as well as knowing its own a, b); and
2. the exclusive-or $a' \oplus b'$ reveals $a \wedge b$ without revealing anything more about either of a, b to any agent, whether A, B or some third party.

Here is the derivation; remember that each step has to be valid from both A and B's point of view. We have

$$\begin{array}{lll} & \mathbf{vis}_A\ a, a'; \mathbf{vis}_B\ b, b'; \quad \Leftarrow \text{Global variables: assumed below.} & \text{"specification"} \\ & (a' \oplus b') := a \wedge b & \\ & & \\ = & \langle\!\langle\ a' :\in \{0,1\};\ \ b' := (a \wedge b) \oplus a'\ \rangle\!\rangle & \text{"atomicity reasoning: compare } EL\text{"} \\ = & a' :\in \{0,1\};\ \ b' := (a \wedge b) \oplus a' & \text{"Lem. 1: compare } EL\text{"} \\ = & a' :\in \{0,1\};\ \ b' := (a \lhd b \rhd 0) \oplus a' & \text{"Boolean algebra: } \mathbf{true} \text{ is 1, } \mathbf{false} \text{ is 0"} \\ & & \\ = & a' :\in \{0,1\}; & \text{"Boolean algebra"} \\ & b' := (a \oplus a' \lhd b \rhd a')\ . \quad \Leftarrow \text{Implemented by } \textit{Oblivious Transfer}. & \end{array}$$

Our semantics §3 plays two roles here, in the background: it legitimises the manipulations immediately above that introduced OT into the implementation, which in §8 we call *horizontal* reasoning. And it assures us (compositionality/monotonicity) that when OT is in its turn replaced by a still lower-level implementation *derived elsewhere, but in the same semantics*, the validity will be preserved: that is *vertical* reasoning.

6.2 §4, §6.1⇒ Lovers' Protocol II (*LP2*) from Fig. 1

The second Lovers' Protocol extends the first: here even the incoming values a, b are available only as "$\oplus$-shares" so that $a = a_A \oplus a_B$ and $b = b_A \oplus b_B$, just as they might have been constructed by an *LP1*. That is Agent A knows a_A and b_A; Agent B knows a_B and b_B; but neither knows a or b. We want to construct a', b' known by A, B resp. so that $a' \oplus b' = (a_A \oplus a_B) \wedge (b_B \oplus b_A) = a \wedge b$. We have

$$
\begin{array}{lll}
& \textbf{vis}_A\ a', a_A, b_A; \quad \Leftarrow \text{These globals assumed below.} & \text{“specification”} \\
& \textbf{vis}_B\ b', a_B, b_B; & \\
& \quad (a' \oplus b') := (a_A \oplus a_B) \wedge (b_A \oplus b_B) & \\
= & \quad (a' \oplus b') := a_A \wedge b_A \ \oplus\ a_A \wedge b_B \ \oplus\ a_B \wedge b_A \ \oplus\ a_B \wedge b_B & \text{“Boolean algebra”} \\
= & \llbracket\ \textbf{vis}_A\ r_A;\ \textbf{vis}_B\ w_B; & \text{“}EL\text{ for } A\text{, and for } B \text{ (different visibilities),} \\
& \quad (r_A \oplus w_B) := a_A \wedge b_B; & \text{where } h \text{ is the expression } a_A \wedge b_B; \\
& \quad (a' \oplus b') := a_A \wedge b_A \ \oplus\ a_A \wedge b_B \ \oplus\ a_B \wedge b_A \ \oplus\ a_B \wedge b_B\ \rrbracket & \text{then scope”} \\
= & \llbracket\ \textbf{vis}_A\ r_A, w_A;\ \textbf{vis}_B\ r_B, w_B; & \text{“}EL\text{ for } A\text{, and for } B; \\
& \quad (r_A \oplus w_B) := a_A \wedge b_B;\ (r_B \oplus w_A) := a_B \wedge b_A; & \text{then scope”} \\
& \quad (a' \oplus b') := a_A \wedge b_A \ \oplus\ a_A \wedge b_B \ \oplus\ a_B \wedge b_A \ \oplus\ a_B \wedge b_B\ \rrbracket & \\
= & \llbracket\ \textbf{vis}_A\ r_A, w_A;\ \textbf{vis}_B\ r_B, w_B; & \text{“Program- and Boolean algebra”} \\
& \quad (r_A \oplus w_B) := a_A \wedge b_B;\ (r_B \oplus w_A) := a_B \wedge b_A; & \\
& \quad (a' \oplus b') := a_A \wedge b_A \oplus r_A \oplus w_A \quad \oplus \quad w_B \oplus r_B \oplus a_B \wedge b_B\ \rrbracket & \\
\sqsubseteq & \llbracket\ \textbf{vis}_A\ r_A, w_A;\ \textbf{vis}_B\ r_B, w_B; & \text{“see below”} \\
& \quad (r_A \oplus w_B) := a_A \wedge b_B;\ (r_B \oplus w_A) := a_B \wedge b_A; \quad \Leftarrow \text{Implemented by } \mathit{LP1}. & \\
& \quad a' := a_A \wedge b_A \ \oplus\ r_A \oplus w_A; & \\
& \quad b' := w_B \oplus r_B \ \oplus\ a_B \wedge b_B\ \rrbracket\ . &
\end{array}
$$

The last step is clearly a classical refinement; it is secure (as well) because A, B already know the values revealed to them by the individual assignments to a', b'. Note that it is a proper refinement, not an equality.[1]

7 Main Case Study: The Millionaires Do Their Sums

This, our main example, sets us apart from validation of straight-line protocols over finite state-spaces: we develop a (secure) loop; and the state-space can be arbitrarily large. Two millionaires want to find which has the bigger fortune without either revealing to the other how big their fortunes actually are. Since two-bit millionaires expose the main issues of the protocol, we will start with them — and then we generalise to "-aires" of arbitrary wealth.

[1] Other proper classical refinements of $(a' \oplus b') := E_A \oplus E_B$ include $a', b' := \neg E_A, \neg E_B$ and $a', b' := E_B, E_A$. In the former case the extra $\neg$'s are pointless; and the latter case would not be a *secure* refinement, since e.g. it would reveal E_B to A.

7.1 §6⇒ The Two-Bit Millionaires (MP_2)

We compare a pair of two-bit numbers without revealing either: two integers $0 \le a, b < 4$ with $a{=}\langle a_1, a_0\rangle$ and $b{=}\langle b_1, b_0\rangle$ are given in binary, and we reveal $(2a_1{+}a_0 < 2b_1{+}b_0)$ by calculating $a_1{<}b_1 \oplus (a_1{=}b_1 \wedge a_0{<}b_0)$.[2] Thus we have a formula in which only conjunctions, negations and exclusive-or appear, and the implementation is simply a stitching together of what we did earlier in §6. Its derivation is given in [1, App. B]; the result is

$$
\begin{array}{ll}
\mathbf{vis}_A\ a', a_{\{0,1\}};\ \mathbf{vis}_B\ b', b_{\{0,1\}} & \text{“specification”} \\
\quad (a' \oplus b'){:=}\,(2a_1{+}a_0 < 2b_1{+}b_0) &
\end{array}
$$

$$
\begin{array}{lll}
\sqsubseteq & [\![\ \mathbf{vis}_A\ a_A, b_A, w_A;\ \mathbf{vis}_B\ a_B, b_B, w_B; & \text{“from [1, App. B]”} \\
& \quad (a_A \oplus a_B){:=}\,\neg a_1 \wedge b_1; \quad \Leftarrow \text{Lovers' Protocol I.} & \\
& \quad (w_A \oplus w_B){:=}\,\neg a_0 \wedge b_0; \quad \Leftarrow \text{Lovers' Protocol I.} & \\
& \quad (b_A \oplus b_B){:=}\,(\neg a_1 \oplus b_1) \wedge (w_A \oplus w_B); \quad \Leftarrow \text{Lovers' Protocol II.} & \\
& \quad a', b'{:=}\,(a_A \oplus b_A), (a_B \oplus b_B)\ ]\!] \ . &
\end{array}
\qquad (2)
$$

7.2 §7.1, §7.3 (to Come)⇒ The Unbounded Millionaires (MP_N)

Now we imagine more generally that we have two N-bit numbers $a(N..0]$ and $b(N..0]$ and we want to compare them in the same oblivious way as in the two-bit case. There we moved from least- to most-significant bit: that suggests as the “effect so far” invariant that some Boolean l always indicates whether $a(n..0]$ is strictly less than $b(n..0]$ as n increases from 0 to N; obviously for security we split that l into two shares $l_{\{a,b\}}$. At the end the shares' exclusive-or gives the Boolean $a{<}b$ the millionaries seek; but the shares are not directly combined until then. Thus the specification is

$$
\begin{array}{ll}
\mathbf{vis}_A\ a(N..0], l_a; & \text{“specification”} \\
\mathbf{vis}_B\ b(N..0], l_b; & \\
\quad (l_a \oplus l_b){:=}\ a_{(N..0]} < b_{(N..0]} &
\end{array}
\qquad (3)
$$

and, because of our comments above, we aim at the implementation

$$
\begin{array}{ll}
[\![\ \mathbf{vis}\ n; & \text{“implementation guess”} \\
\quad n{:=}\,0; & \\
\quad (l_a \oplus l_b){:=}\,0; & \\
\quad \mathbf{while}\ n{<}N\ \mathbf{do} & \\
\qquad (l_a \oplus l_b){:=}\ a_n{<}b_n \oplus (a_n{=}b_n \wedge l_a{\oplus}l_b); & \Leftarrow MP_2 \text{ modified:} \\
\qquad n{:=}\,n+1 & \quad \text{maintains the invariant.} \\
\quad \mathbf{od} & \\
]\!] \ . &
\end{array}
\qquad (4)
$$

[2] We thank Berry Schoenmakers for this suggestion of using $\oplus$ rather than $\vee$ here.

7.3 How Do We Deal with Loops?

Moving to an unbounded state-space leads consequentially away from straight-line programs: for arbitrarily rich millionaires our comparison requires a loop. We extend our semantics with fixed points in the usual way: thus a terminating loop **while** B **do** *body* **od** equals some other program fragment P just when via secure program algebra we can manipulate **if** B **then** (*body*;P) **fi** to become P again. For our case we hypothesise that our **while**-loop at (4) implements the straight-line code fragment P as follows:

$$\begin{array}{ll} \textbf{if } n{<}N \textbf{ then} & \text{“postulated effect} \\ \quad (l_a \oplus l_b){:=}\ a_{(N..n]}{<}b_{(N..n]} \oplus (a_{(N..n]}{=}b_{(N..n]} \wedge l_a \oplus l_b); & \text{of loop”} \\ \quad n{:=}\ N & \\ \textbf{fi}\ . & \end{array} \tag{5}$$

We check this program-algebraically in [1, App. D]. Most of the manipulations are routine (i.e. would be the same steps even if one were reasoning carefully with only functional properties in mind); but a crucial step (marked $\star$ in the appendix) uses EL to establish that the individual calculations within each iteration do not leak any information as the loop proceeds.

Thus in our proposed implementation (4) we can again rely on compositional semantics to replace the loop by its equivalent straight-line code (5). That gives

$$\begin{array}{lll}
& [\![\ \textbf{vis } n; & \text{“loop within (4) replaced by} \\
& \quad n{:=}\ 0; & \text{equivalent straight-line code (5)”} \\
& \quad (l_a \oplus l_b){:=}\ 0; & \\
& \quad \textbf{if } n{<}N \textbf{ then} & \\
& \qquad (l_a \oplus l_b){:=}\ a_{(N..n]}{<}b_{(N..n]} \oplus (a_{(N..n]}{=}b_{(N..n]} \wedge l_a \oplus l_b); & \\
& \qquad n{:=}\ N & \\
& \quad \textbf{fi}\ ]\!] & \\
= & [\![\ \textbf{vis } n; & \text{“program algebra”} \\
& \quad n{:=}\ 0; & \\
& \quad (l_a \oplus l_b){:=}\ 0; & \\
& \quad \textbf{if } 0{<}N \textbf{ then} & \\
& \qquad (l_a \oplus l_b){:=}\ a_{(N..0]}{<}b_{(N..0]} \oplus (a_{(N..0]}{=}b_{(N..0]} \wedge 0); & \\
& \qquad n{:=}\ N & \\
& \quad \textbf{fi}\ ]\!] & \\
= & (l_a \oplus l_b){:=}\ 0; & \text{“Eliminate local } n \\
& \textbf{if } 0{<}N \textbf{ then } (l_a \oplus l_b){:=}\ a_{(N..0]} < b_{(N..0]} \textbf{ fi} & \text{and simplify } \wedge 0\text{”} \\
= & (l_a \oplus l_b){:=}\ a_{(N..0]} < b_{(N..0]}\ , & \text{“}0{\le}N \text{ assumed, and } a_{(0..0]}{<}b_{(0..0]} = 0\text{”}
\end{array}$$

thus establishing that (3) is indeed implemented by (4).

The interior assignment of the loop (4, MP_2 modified) is based on the two-bit protocol MP_2, a small difference being that the final sub-expression is $l_a \oplus l_b$

rather than a comparison of two data-bits $a_0 < b_0$ as it was in §7.1 above. By analogy with the derivation of (2) in [1, App. B], we complete our verified implementation as shown in Fig. 4, where the appeals to *LP1,2* have been expanded.

8 Conclusions and Strategy

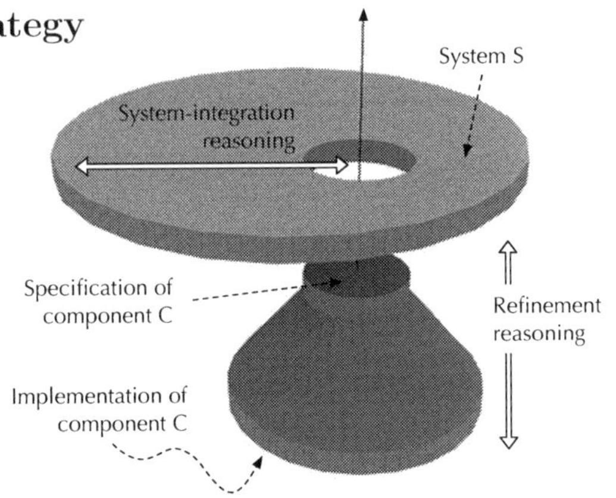

The compositionality of the security semantics is necessary for the correctness of the two types of reasoning separately...

... and for their mutual consistency.

Fig. 3. Horizontal- and vertical reasoning

"Horizontal" reasoning across the disc of Fig. 3 (recall §6.1) uses the specification of Component C to establish that it plays its proper role in the context of system S; this is done (1) without referring to the implementation of C at all. "Vertical" reasoning, down the cone, establishes that C's implementation has properties no worse than its specification; this is done (2) in isolation, without referring to any contextual system S at all. Then compositionality (3) ensures that these two separate activities (1,2) are consistent when combined. These basic features (1,2,3) of refinement are well known, but in each case require a semantics appropriate to the application domain: **our overall strategy** is to formulate such a semantics [14,15] for the non-interference -style security domain, and thus to make the rigorous development of security applications more accessible to our (refinement) community.

Our specific aim in this paper, for which we chose the Millionaires' problem, was to demonstrate scalability within a topical application domain. (See for example the recent practical application of two-party secure computation [4], and the current interest in the use of the oblivious transfer as a cryptographic primitive [10].) We used both vertical reasoning (from specification to implementation of components) and horizontal reasoning (use of components' specifications only) in doing so. To our knowledge our proof here is the first (formally) for the full Millionaires' problem. More generally our goal is to verify security-critical software, hence our particular focus on source-level reasoning and proofs which apply in all contexts; within those specific confines we are amongst the first to prove a (randomised) security protocol with unbounded state. Paulson [16] and Coble [5] also have general proofs relating to specific security properties over computations with unbounded resources.

The Shadow has been extended to deal semantically with *loops* §7.3 and syntactically with labelled *views* §3.6, the latter to enable the uniform treatment of the complementary security goals of multiple agents. The relationship to other

$(l_a \oplus l_b) := \; (a_{(N..0]} < b_{(N..0]})$ $\Leftarrow$ Exclusive-or $l_{\{a,b\}}$ finally, for the outcome $a{<}b$.

$$
\begin{array}{ll}
\sqsubseteq & [\![\ \textbf{vis}\ n; \\
& \quad n{:=}0; \\
& \quad (l_a \oplus l_b){:=}0; \\
& \quad \textbf{while}\ n{<}N\ \textbf{do} \\
& \quad\quad \textbf{vis}_A\ a_A, b_A, w_A, x_A, r_A;\ \ \textbf{vis}_B\ a_B, b_B, w_B, x_B, r_B; \\
& \quad\quad \left.\begin{array}{l}
a_A{:\in}\{0,1\};\ a_B{:=}(a_n{\equiv}a_A \lhd b_n \rhd a_A); \\
w_A{:\in}\{0,1\};\ w_B{:=}(l_a{\equiv}w_A \lhd l_b \rhd w_A); \\
r_A{:\in}\{0,1\};\ x_B{:=}(r_A{\equiv}a_n \lhd w_B \rhd r_A); \\
r_B{:\in}\{0,1\};\ x_A{:=}(r_B{\oplus}b_n \lhd w_A \rhd r_B);
\end{array}\right\}\ \text{Each of these expands to six statements and four further pre-distributed bits.} \\
& \quad\quad b_A, b_B{:=}(\neg a_n{\wedge}w_A \oplus r_A \oplus x_A), (x_B \oplus r_B \oplus b_n{\wedge}w_B); \\
& \quad\quad l_a, l_b{:=}(a_A \oplus b_A), (a_B \oplus b_B); \\
& \quad\quad n{:=}n+1 \\
& \quad \textbf{od}\ ]\!] .
\end{array}
$$

Each of the four transfers abstracts from six elementary statements, making over thirty elementary statements in all. Ten local variables are declared in the loop body, at this level. The *TTP* acts within the Oblivious Transfers, supplying four random bits for each: thus $24N$ further random bits are used in total.

Fig. 4. Millionaires: The complete code at the level of Oblivious Transfers

formal semantics of non-intereference has been summarised in detail elsewhere [14,15]; it is comparable to Leino [9] and Sabelfeld [20], but differs in details; and it shares the goals of the pioneering work of Mantel [11] and Engelhardt [6].

We believe that three prominent features of our approach make it suitable for practical verification: (a) secure refinement preserves (non-interference) security properties; (b) refinement is monotonic (implying compositionality); and (c) we exploit a simple source-level program algebra.

Features (a,b) allow layering of design; and (c) allows proofs to be constructed from many small (algebraic) steps, of the kind suited to automation [12]. This distinguishes us from other refinement-oriented approaches that do not so much emphasise code-level algebraic reasoning [9,20,11,6], on the one hand, or appear not to be compositional [3,2], on the other.

Our plans include constructing/extending computer-based tools to prove the small algebraic steps, based on theorem-proving over the Shadow semantics, and thus to form a library of allowed transformations. At the same time we hope to integrate Shadow-style reasoning, based on such a library, into industrial-strength refinement-based developments [22].

References

1. Appendices are available at,
`www.cse.unsw.edu.au/~carrollm/probs/bibliographyBody.html#McIver:09`
2. Černý, P.: Private communication (February 2009)

3. Alur, R., Černý, P., Zdancewic, S.: Preserving secrecy under refinement. In: Bugliesi, M., Preneel, B., Sassone, V., Wegener, I. (eds.) ICALP 2006. LNCS, vol. 4052, pp. 107–118. Springer, Heidelberg (2006)
4. Bogetoft, P., Christensen, D.L., Damgård, I., Geisler, M., Jakobsen, T., Krøigaard, M., Nielsen, J.D., Nielsen, J.B., Nielsen, K., Pagter, J., Schwartzbach, M., Toft, T.: Secure multiparty computation goes live, `http://eprint.iacr.org/2008/068`
5. Coble, A.: Formalized information-theoretic proofs of privacy using the HOL-4 theorem-prover. In: Borisov, N., Goldberg, I. (eds.) PETS 2008. LNCS, vol. 5134, pp. 77–98. Springer, Heidelberg (2008)
6. Engelhardt, K., van der Meyden, R., Moses, Y.: A refinement theory that supports reasoning about knowledge and time. In: Nieuwenhuis, R., Voronkov, A. (eds.) LPAR 2001. LNCS (LNAI), vol. 2250, pp. 125–141. Springer, Heidelberg (2001)
7. Goguen, J.A., Meseguer, J.: Unwinding and inference control. In: Proc. IEEE Symp. on Security and Privacy, pp. 75–86 (1984)
8. Hoare, C.A.R.: A couple of novelties in the propositional calculus. Zeitschr für Math. Logik und Grundlagen der Math. 31(2), 173–178 (1985)
9. Leino, K.R.M., Joshi, R.: A semantic approach to secure information flow. Science of Computer Programming 37(1–3), 113–138 (2000)
10. Malkhi, D., Nisan, N., Pinkas, B., Sella, Y.: Fairplay — A secure two-party computation system. In: Proc. 13th Conf. on USENIX Security Symposium. USENIX Association (2004)
11. Mantel, H.: Preserving information flow properties under refinement. In: Proc. IEEE Symp. Security and Privacy, pp. 78–91 (2001)
12. McIver, A.K., Cohen, E., Morgan, C., Gonzalia, C.: Using probabilistic Kleene algebra pKA for protocol verification. Journal of Logic and Algebraic Programming 76(1), 90–111 (2008)
13. Morgan, C.C.: Programming from Specifications, 2nd edn. Prentice-Hall, Englewood Cliffs (1994), `web.comlab.ox.ac.uk/oucl/publications/books/PfS/`
14. Morgan, C.C.: The Shadow Knows: Refinement of ignorance in sequential programs. In: Uustalu, T. (ed.) Math. Prog. Construction. LNCS, vol. 4014, pp. 359–378. Springer, Heidelberg (2006) Treats Dining Cryptographers
15. Morgan, C.C.: The Shadow Knows: Refinement of ignorance in sequential programs. Science of Computer Programming 74(8) (2009) Treats Oblivious Transfer
16. Paulson, L.: Proving properties of security protocols by induction, `http://www.cl.cam.ac.uk/techreports/UCAM-CL-TR-409.pdf`
17. Rabin, M.O.: How to exchange secrets by oblivious transfer. Technical Report TR-81, Harvard University (1981), `http://eprint.iacr.org/2005/187`
18. Rivest, R.: Unconditionally secure commitment and oblivious transfer schemes using private channels and a trusted initialiser. Technical report, M.I.T (1999), `http://theory.lcs.mit.edu/~rivest/Rivest-commitment.pdf`
19. Ryan, P., Schneider, S., Goldsmith, M., Lowe, G., Roscoe, B.: Modelling and Analysis of Security Protocols. Addison-Wesley, Reading (2000)
20. Sabelfeld, A., Sands, D.: A PER model of secure information flow. Higher-Order and Symbolic Computation 14(1), 59–91 (2001)
21. Schoenmakers, B.: Cryptography lecture notes, `http://www.win.tue.nl/~berry/2WC13/LectureNotes.pdf`
22. `http://www.deploy-project.eu`
23. Yao, A.C.-C.: Protocols for secure computations (extended abstract). In: Annual Symposium on Foundations of Computer Science (FOCS 1982), pp. 160–164 (1982)

Iterative Refinement of Reverse-Engineered Models by Model-Based Testing

Neil Walkinshaw, John Derrick, and Qiang Guo

Department of Computer Science, The University of Sheffield, Sheffield, UK

Abstract. This paper presents an iterative technique to accurately reverse engineer models of the behaviour of software systems. A key novelty of the approach is the fact that it uses model-based testing to refine the hypothesised model. The process can in principle be entirely automated, and only requires a very small amount of manually generated information to begin with. We have implemented the technique for use in the development of Erlang systems and describe both the methodology as well as our implementation.

Keywords: Reverse engineering; model-based testing; Erlang.

1 Introduction

Several important software verification and validation techniques rely on the availability of models that describe the software behaviour, models which should be accurate, and capture every relevant requirement of the system. In practice this requirement is unrealistic. The manual process of developing a specification can be error-prone and expensive. Moreover, software is commonly developed under restrictive time constraints; developers tend to concentrate on developing the implementation and do not have time to generate and maintain accurate specifications in tandem. The notion of a fully accurate model being maintained (or even existing to begin with) is unfortunately at present largely a myth.

An alternative approach is to *generate* models, or specifications, of a system from the implementation itself, and this paper is concerned with the challenge of reverse-engineering *state machine models* from an implementation. Ideally, such a reverse-engineering technique can be run at any point during the development of an implementation to provide a snapshot of system behaviour. The use of reverse-engineered models is that they can be inspected by developers to give an understanding of how the system behaves in practice. If they are correct (with respect to the developer's requirements), they can be used for core software maintenance tasks such as documentation and regression-testing. If, upon inspection, they are found to be out of step with system requirements, they can be used to identify which parts of the system are faulty.

In reality, reverse-engineering techniques tend to be less straightforward. They tend to require an extensive sample of program execution traces, which can be difficult to identify and collect. Consequently, the models can be inaccurate, and are therefore less useful to the developer.

A. Cavalcanti and D. Dams (Eds.): FM 2009, LNCS 5850, pp. 305–320, 2009.

In this paper we introduce an iterative reverse-engineering method that will ensure an adequate sample of execution traces by incorporating a model-based testing technique. Unlike most other existing techniques, no initial traces or models are required at all. Instead, a model-based testing framework is used to iteratively populate the set of traces that are used to infer the model, the inference being performed with our StateChum model inference tool [1]. One nice aspect of the approach is that the inference technique uses heuristics that have been shown to be effective for sparse samples of traces, meaning that it does not rely on systematic, expensive testing techniques. In this paper we demonstrate its effectiveness with respect to the QuickCheck testing framework and the Erlang programming language.

Implementation of the technique for use in Erlang development. This work has been carried out in the context of the EU ProTest project[1], which aims to improve the model-based testing of concurrent and distributed telecoms systems.

Erlang [2] was, along with its Open Telecoms Platform (OTP), originally developed by Ericsson for the rapid development of network applications. However, its usage has now spread beyond that domain to a number of sectors. Erlang has been designed to provide a paradigm for the development of distributed soft real-time systems, where multiple processes can be spread across many nodes in a network. Consequently, a lot of the development effort involved in implementing an Erlang system is concerned with how these processes interact with each other and their environment. The protocol an Erlang process follows when communicating with other processes or responds to internal events is often implemented in terms of finite state machines, which is why they play a particularly important role and our technique is particularly appropriate.

The rapid development that is facilitated by Erlang means that formal specifications are, however, often neglected. It is often perceived to be more expedient to verify and document the system on an ad-hoc basis, and it is unrealistic to expect a developer in a commercial environment to provide an accurate and complete formal specification that can be used for more rigorous verification techniques. Producing an accurate specification that captures all of the necessary functionality can be a challenging and time-consuming task, particularly for complex systems. Furthermore, as the requirements change and the system is modified, keeping complex specifications up to date can be overwhelming, even with the best of intentions.

It is this problem that the technique presented in this paper aims to solve. The technique we develop iteratively reverse-engineers a state-machine from the implementation by using program tests, with only a small amount of manual input required. The result is a model that closely conforms to the actual system behaviour. The intention is that this final model can be validated and, if necessary, refined by the developer, and then used as a reference model for

[1] `http://www.protest-project.eu/`

subsequent program development tasks such as regression testing, and as a basis for communication amongst developers.

The paper is structured as follows. Section 2 provides some background on Erlang and QuickCheck, and the challenge of reverse-engineering finite state machines from software implementations. Section 3 introduces our iterative process that adopts model-based testing techniques to drive the inference and provides details of our implementation. The process is illustrated with a case study in Section 4, and Section 5 concludes.

2 Background

2.1 Erlang and QuickCheck

Erlang is a concurrent functional language with specific support for the development of distributed, fault-tolerant systems with soft real-time requirements [2]. It was designed from the start to support a concurrency-oriented programming paradigm and large distributed implementations that this supports. It was developed initially by Ericsson as a platform for rapid development of network-applications, but its applications have now expanded to include computer telephony, banking, TCP/IP programming (HTTP, SSL, Email, Instant messaging, etc) and 3D-modelling. It is increasingly used to develop applications that are business-critical, for example, its use in Ericsson's AXD-301 switch that provides British Telecom's internet backbone.

However, verification and validation of Erlang systems is to-date a largely ad-hoc, manual process. Consequently there is an inherent danger that important functionality remains untested and undocumented. Thus along with its recent growth in popularity, there has been a concerted drive to develop more automated and systematic techniques.

QuickCheck. One of these techniques is QuickCheck [3], an automated model-based testing tool for Erlang. It has become one of the standard testing tools used by Erlang developers. The 'model' is conventionally provided by the developer, as a set of simple properties that must hold for the program to behave correctly, and these are expressed as temporal logic properties in Erlang itself. For example, the following property would check that the reverse function for lists behaves as expected:

```
prop\_reverse() ->
      ?FORALL(Xs,list(int()),
      lists:reverse(lists:reverse(Xs)) == Xs).
```

Given such a property, QuickCheck uses random data generators to produce inputs that will exercise the system, with the aim of producing counter-examples. Once a counter-example is found, QuickCheck attempts to use successive tests to home in on the precise reason for the failure, with the aim of producing the smallest possible counter-example.

QuickCheck has recently been extended to so that one can test an implementation against a model given as a finite state machine (rather than just a predicate). The use of a finite state machine allows one to specify the permitted sequences of program functions, along with their effect on the data-state of the system. As well as selecting random data-inputs for the functions, QuickCheck also selects random paths through the state machine, with the aim of verifying the existence of state transitions. The key fact for our reverse-engineering technique is that *for a given state-machine model, QuickCheck can produce the requisite sequences of inputs (with the necessary data parameters) to automatically test any path in the model against the actual software system.*

2.2 Reverse-Engineering State Machines

Reverse-engineering techniques aim to address this problem. Broadly speaking, these approaches can be separated into two categories: Those based on source-code analysis (c.f. [4]), and those based on analysis of execution traces. Here we focus on the latter (dynamic) approaches. They are based on the analysis of program traces [5,6] which are sequences of events (e.g. function calls, message-passing events etc.), that may optionally be annotated with variable values. The traces can be recorded by instrumenting the source code, or by using one of the trace tools, e.g. for Erlang those that are included in the OTP framework. Traces that lead to a program failure (i.e. an exception) are annotated as such, so that the last recorded trace event corresponds to the point of failure.

From a given set of traces, the challenge for reverse-engineering techniques is to produce a candidate state machine that conforms to the provided set of traces. This is akin to the challenge of inferring a regular grammar, which is conventionally represented as a state machine from a given set of strings (a problem originally posed in 1967 [7]). In fact, most reverse-engineering techniques are inspired by techniques that were initially devised as grammar-inference techniques [8,1,6].

It is unrealistic to expect an inference technique to be able to infer a machine that exactly represents the underlying software system from any arbitrary set of traces. An inference technique will only produce an accurate result if the provided set of traces is *characteristic* of the behaviour of the underlying software system [8,6]. In terms of state machines, this must include enough information about what the program can and cannot do to enable the inference technique to identify every state transition, and to distinguish between every pair of non-equivalent states. Thus the key challenges lie in (a) *identifying* the relevant subset of executions and (b) *collecting* them - a potentially expensive and time-consuming process.

Most reverse-engineering inference techniques are *passive* [9,10], in that they presume that the necessary traces have already been identified and collected prior to inferring the candidate model. However, given that the initial set of traces is unlikely to contain all of the necessary information, the resulting model is often only poor approximation of the real implementation.

In an effort to address this, a number of *active* techniques have been developed. Active techniques are augmented with the ability to pose questions about the target model, to help the developer to identify the set of required traces. Such techniques come in two flavours: those based on Angluin's L^* algorithm [11], and those based on state-merging techniques [8]. Both techniques are iterative; they construct a hypothesis model, and use it as a basis for posing questions to some oracle. The essential difference between the two techniques comes down to expense. Techniques based on Angluin's algorithm rely on asking a large number of questions in order to produce an accurate model - and such an approach is infeasible in the setting our work is placed. Thus here we use state-merging techniques which place a greater emphasis on heuristics. These are less demanding in terms of the number of questions asked, but have nonetheless been shown to produce models that are reasonably accurate [8,6].

In our previous work we have applied active state-merging to the challenge of reverse-engineering [1,12], however, this has relied on a substantial amount of human intervention, where each query posed by the technique either had to be answered directly by the human or had to be executed manually. Expecting a human to be able to directly answer every query is unrealistic; the amount of knowledge required would undermine the whole purpose of reverse engineering the model in the first place. Expecting a human to manually execute each query is a tedious and time-consuming process, requiring the generation of suitable data parameters for each execution as well.

Here we describe an extension of this approach, that leverages the strengths of model-based testing techniques with the powerful heuristic inference abilities of state-merging techniques. The resulting process removes the human bottleneck. Instead of being driven by a built-in question-generator, which can be very expensive, it will be up to the model-based tester to select the tests and to execute them. This means that the developer can choose the testing technique, and determine the expense (and resulting accuracy) of the technique. In our implementation of the technique we use the QuickCheck framework, but this can be substituted according to circumstance.

3 Iteratively Testing Reverse-Engineered Models

This paper introduces a technique to remove the human bottle-neck that arises with conventional dynamic model inference techniques. Instead of requiring a human to identify relevant program executions and collect the ensuing traces, model-based testing techniques are used to automate the process. The amount of a-priori knowledge of the program under analysis is minimal, although there are a number of optional mechanisms that can be used to add this information if it is available.

To explain the technique we use a simple example of a text editor, the LTS for which is shown in Figure 1(a), where as usual we take an LTS is a quadruple $A = (Q, \Sigma, \delta, q_0)$, where Q is a finite set of states, Σ is a finite alphabet, $\delta : Q \times \Sigma \rightarrow Q$ is a partial function and $q_0 \in Q$.

Our technique builds up a sequence of candidate models, each one being a bit more accurate than the last, these models can be viewed as partial LTS's, defined as follows [13], which allow us to distinguish between model transitions that are known to be invalid, and transitions that are simply not known to exist at all.

Definition 1 (Partial LTS (PLTS)). *A PLTS is a tuple* $A = (Q, \Sigma, \delta, q_0, \Psi)$*. This is defined as a LTS, but it is assumed to be only partial. To make the explicit distinction between unknown and invalid behaviour,* Ψ *makes the set of invalid labels from a given state explicit –* $\Psi \subseteq Q \times \Sigma$ *where* $(q, \sigma) \in \Psi$ *implies that* $\delta(q, \sigma) \notin Q$*.*

To define the language of a PLTS, we draw on the inductive definition for an extended transition function $\hat{\delta}$ used by Hopcroft *et al.* [14] to define two notions of language: prescribed and proscribed which are used below.

Definition 2 (Prescribed and Proscribed Languages of a PLTS). *For a state* p *and a string* w*, the extended transition function* $\hat{\delta}$ *returns the state* p *that is reached when starting in state* p *and processing sequence* w*. For the base case* $\hat{\delta}(q, \epsilon) = q$*. For the inductive case, let* w *be of the form* xa*, where* a *is the last element, and* x *is the prefix. Then* $\hat{\delta}(q, w) = \delta(\hat{\delta}(q, x), a)$*.*

Given the extended transition function, the prescribed *language of a PLTS A can be defined as follows:* $PreL(A) = \{w | \hat{\delta}(q_0, w) \in Q\}$*.*

The proscribed *language of a PLTS can be defined as:* $ProL(A)\{xa | (\hat{\delta}(q_0, x), a) \in \psi\}$*. By construction* $PreL(A) \cap ProL(A) = \emptyset$*.*

3.1 The Basic Process

The basic technique is straightforward. A human user provides the program of interest, along with a small initial set of traces, these are required to identify the set of functions of the program that are of interest (i.e. the alphabet of the target machine). From this an initial hypothesis model is constructed - a single state, with transitions for each element of the alphabet that loop back to that state. This is provided as input to a state-machine testing framework, which generates tests from the model. These tests are executed in the program, and a tracing mechanism is used to record the executions. As soon as a test is found that contradicts the expected behaviour as described by the model, the process is restarted, but this time the model is inferred from the test traces. This process iterates until no further discrepancies can be found by testing.

The basic process is captured by algorithm 1. It takes as input the program under analysis $Prog$, along with a valid trace (or several if necessary) that contains every element in the alphabet of the target machine. It uses four external functions: $inferPLTS$, sub, $generateTests$ and $runTest$. $inferPLTS$ will be described in more detail below. sub simply returns a substring of a string $String$ up to some index i. $generateTests$ and $runTest$ represent the functionality of the model-based testing framework. $generateTests$ is responsible for generating tests from a PLTS, which may be achieved by a number of standard state machine testing algorithms. $runTest$ executes a test $test$ on a program $Prog$, and returns a zero if the test passes, or a number pointing to the index of $test$ where the failure happened.

```
Input: Prog, Pos
Data: Neg, test, fail, failedPLTS
Uses: inferPLTS(T+, T−), generateTests(PLTS), runTest(t, Prog), sub(String, i)
Result: PLTS
1  Neg ← ∅;
2  PLTS ← inferPLTS(Pos, Neg);
3  while test ← generateTests(PLTS) do
4      fail ← runTest(test, Prog);
5      if fail = 0 then
6          Pos ← Pos ∪ {test};
7          if test ∈ ProL(PLTS) then
8              PLTS ← inferPLTS(Pos, Neg);
9
10     else
11         failed ← sub(test, fail);
12         Neg ← Neg ∪ {failed};
13         if failed ∈ PreL(PLTS) then
14             PLTS ← inferPLTS(Pos, Neg);
15
16     end
17 end
18 return PLTS
```

Algorithm 1. Basic iterative algorithm

An initial PLTS is generated by calling the $inferPLTS$ function with $Neg = \emptyset$ and Pos to contain one possible initial trace: the only requirement for the initial trace is that it contains every function in the alphabet of the target machine at least once. For our editor example, the initial sequence could simply be $< load, edit, save, close, exit >$, but any sequence in Σ^* is valid. $inferPLTS$ returns the most general model possible and in this initial iteration will always consist of a single state, with one looping transition that is labelled by the transitions from the trace in Pos. Formally, the resulting PLTS is defined as $A = (Q, \Sigma, \Delta, q_0, \Psi)$ where: $Q = \{q_0\}$, $\forall \sigma \in \Sigma$, $\delta(q_0, \sigma) \rightarrow q_0$ and $\Psi = \emptyset$. The purpose of the ensuing process is to refine this model - to ensure that the behaviour represented by the final PLTS accurately reflects that of the actual implementation. In our example, this initial model is shown in Figure 1(a).

Thus the algorithm iterates. To illustrate this suppose that we have chosen to use the QuickCheck testing framework (i.e. this will provide the functionality of the external functions $generateTests(PLTS)$ and $runTest(test, Prog)$). Being a model-based testing framework, QuickCheck needs a model to generate tests from. For this we use our initial model, the one in Figure 1 (b).

QuickCheck chooses a random test - and may choose to try to execute the sequence $< load, close, close, edit >$ (line 3). This fails, so the variable $fail$, which stores the point of failure in the $test$ is set to the index returned by $runTest$, which is 3. The failing sub-sequence $failed$ is identified by taking the first three elements of the test: $< load, close, close >$ (line 11). This is added to the set of impossible sequences Neg (line 12). Because the sequence $failed$ *is* possible in the current candidate model (belongs to the *prescribed* language), a discrepancy has been identified (line 13). Consequently a new model is inferred, taking the updated set Neg into account, which results in the model shown in Figure 1(c).

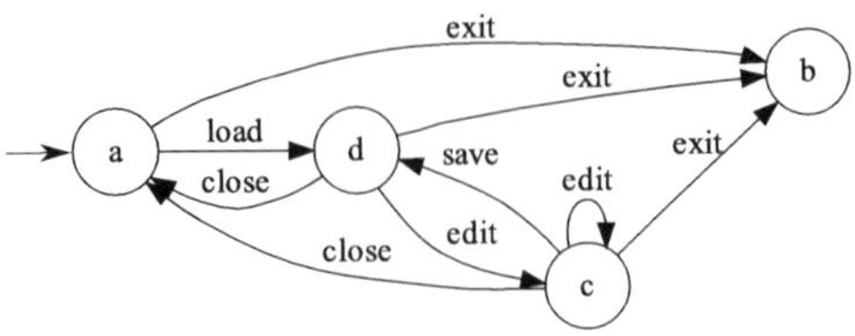

(a) correct model

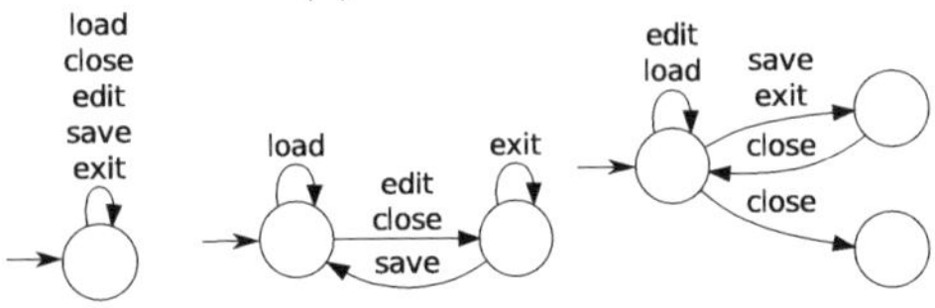

(b) (c) (d)

Fig. 1. Inference iterations on editor example

In the next iteration, the updated model is used as a basis for $generateTests$. Suppose that this time it returns the test $< load, edit, exit >$, which when executed does not fail. $fail$ is thus set to 0 (line 4), and the test is added to the set of valid traces Pos (line 6). Since the test has passed, and this is prescribed by the model, there is no disagreement between the test outcome and the model, so another test can be executed. It is important to note that QuickCheck, our tester of choice, will never generate tests that *should* fail according to the provided model, so in our case the branch in line 8 will not occur. Nevertheless, more systematic testing techniques such as the W-Method [15] do attempt tests that should fail; in this case, if a test does not fail when it should according to the current model, a new model has to be generated.

3.2 Model Inference

The inference process, which is called by the $inferPLTS$ function in the algorithm, is based upon the EDSM / blue-fringe state-merging method [16,8,1]. A brief illustration will be provided with respect to the editor example. As described above, the algorithm gradually gathers a set of traces that are either valid, or invalid. The purpose of $inferPLTS$ is to infer a state machine from these, that is a suitable generalisation - i.e. will correctly classify previously unseen traces as either valid or invalid.

To do this, the two sets of traces Pos and Neg are aggregated into a single tree - referred to as an *augmented prefix tree acceptor (APTA)*. This tree represents the most specific and precise machine possible, that exactly corresponds to the provided sets of traces. For example, suppose the model-based tester has selected the test $< load, edit, edit, save, load >$ for the next iteration from the model in Figure 1 (c). This test fails, because only one file can be opened at a time. $InferPTA$ is called to build a new model, incorporating this test. Figure 2 (a) shows the corresponding APTA (valid traces are listed under S^+, and invalid

Initial traces
S^+:
$< load, edit, save, close, exit >$
$< load, edit, exit >$
S^-:
$< load, close, close >$
$< load, edit, edit, save, load >$

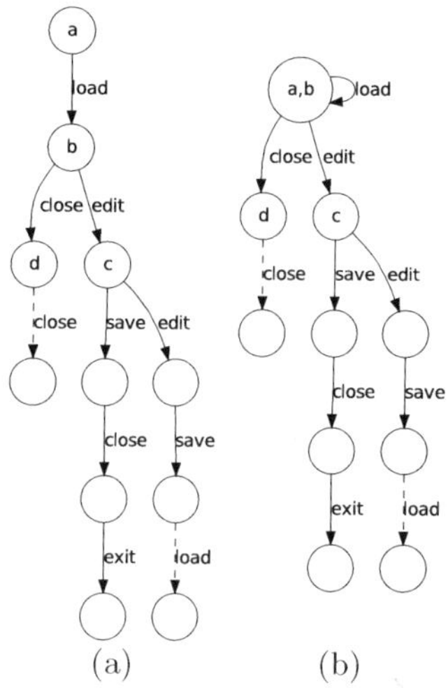

Fig. 2. Augmented Prefix Tree Acceptor and illustration of merging

traces are listed under S^-). Dashed lines in this tree represent paths in the tree that are invalid.

The goal of the inference is to identify states in this tree that are actually equivalent, and to merge them. In doing so, this will collapse the machine down to a minimal machine that is a generalisation of the set of traces. The merging process is iterative - lots of subsequent merges are required to reach the final machine. At each iteration, a set of state-pairs is selected using the Blue-Fringe algorithm [16], a colour-based breadth-first traversal algorithm (a description of this is beyond the scope of this paper). Each candidate pair is assigned a score, which indicates the likelihood that the states are equivalent. The score is computed by comparing the extent to which the suffixes of each state overlap with each other[2]. Any pairs with non-negative scores can potentially be merged. A pair of states is incompatible if a sequence is possible from one state, but impossible from the other - this leads to a score of -1. Once the scores have been computed, the pair with the highest score is merged, and the entire process starts afresh, until no further pairs can be merged.

To illustrate the scoring process, we refer back to the example prefix-tree in Figure 2 (a). Initially, the Blue-Fringe algorithm suggests only one pair of states (a,b). They have a score of zero, so they can be merged. The result is shown in Figure 2 (b). In the next iteration, we are given the option of selecting to merge either pairs ((ab),c) or ((ab),d). This is where the scoring comes into play - we want to select the pair that are most likely to be equivalent. In this case it is straightforward because the score for ((ab),d) is -1; a close is possible from state ab, but not from state d, ruling out that merge. The score for ((ab),c) is 2; both

[2] The Blue-Fringe algorithm ensures that the suffixes of one state are guaranteed to be a tree without loops, which facilitates this score computation.

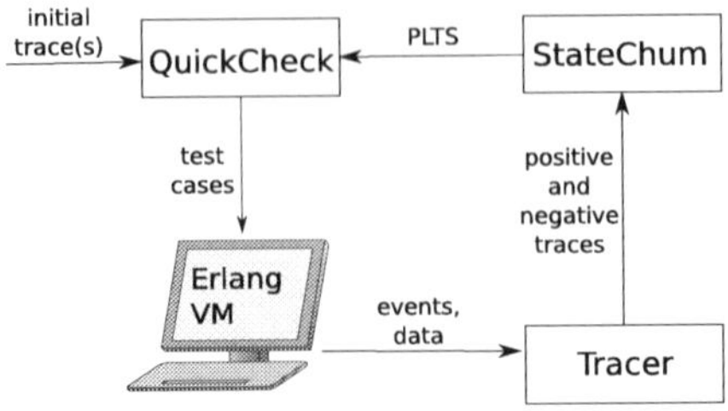

Fig. 3. Schematic overview of implementation

states share the suffix $< edit, save >$, so this is chosen to be merged. This is how the merging process continues until no more merges can be carried out. The resulting machine is shown in Figure 1(d).

3.3 Implementation of the Technique

We have implemented the technique for use on programs written in Erlang. However, the approach is essentially a black-box one, and is not tied to a specific language or paradigm. A schematic overview of the key components is given in Figure 3, and the tools that are used for the inference, testing and tracing are briefly described below.

Model Inference: StateChum[3] is an open-source model inference framework that has been developed by the authors [1]. It implements a state-merging approach as described in the previous section. The tracing mechanism (described below) has been augmented with a small script that translates traces into suitable input files.

Tracing: Erlang has a wide array of tracing tools, many of which are included in the standard Erlang OTP libraries. The traces used in this work are however laid out in a particular format, to facilitate the application of other trace-analysis tools such as Daikon [17]. To this end, a small Erlang tracing module was developed[4], which runs as an independent Erlang process. The source code is instrumented at the exit points of functions that are of interest, such that every time an instrumented point is executed, it sends the relevant details (function name and variable values) to the trace process. The tracing process produces an output in the form of a Daikon trace file. It is optionally possible to add abstractions, which map the traces from lower level events to sequences of higher-level program functions.

Testing: As discussed earlier QuickCheck is particularly suited to this work because it can incorporate finite state machine (FSM) specifications[5]. The

[3] `http://statechum.sourceforge.net/`
[4] `http://www.dcs.shef.ac.uk/~nw/Files/FM2009/dtraceGenerator.erl`
[5] `http://quviq.com/eqc_fsm%20example/index.htm`

```
-record(state,{openfile}).
% openfile stores the name of
% the open file
%===== initial state =====
initial_state() -> a.
initial_state_data() ->
  #state{openfile=[]}.
%===== data generator =====
filename() -> elements([''test1'',
  ''test2'',''test3'']).
% data transformations
%===== state transition system =====
```

```
a(S) [{b,{call,editor,exit,[]}},
 {d,{call,editor,load,[filename()]}}].
b(S) [].
c(S) [{c,{call,editor,edit,[chars(4)]}},
 {a,{call,editor,close,[S#state.openfile]}},
 {b,{call,editor,exit,[]}},
 {d,{call,editor,save,[]}}].
d(S) [{c,{call,editor,edit,[chars(4)]}},
 {a,{call,editor,close,[S#state.openfile]}},
 {b,{call,editor,exit,[]}}].
```

Fig. 4. Example QuickCheck FSM specification of text-editor

specification of an FSM is essentially divided into four parts: The initial state specification, the state transition system, the data transformations and the data generators. A small example specification is shown in Figure 4. It should be noted that this example only contains the essential information for a FSM construction; QuickCheck supports a variety of other constructs (such as pre/post-conditions), which are omitted here.

Currently, all of the steps in Figure 3 are automated. With our implementation the user to provide an initial trace, along with a parameter stating the number of tests that should be executed for each candidate model. This will cause the entire process to iterate, terminating once it has produced a model that does not disagree with any tests.

4 Case Study

The case study revolves around a simple FTP-client that is a modified version of the `ssh_sftp`, which is part of the Erlang OTP ssh libraries (version 1.0.2) released by Ericsson[6]. For reference the main files involved in the tracing and testing are available on the web[7].

Subject system and set-up. The main functions of the FTP client are presented in Table 1. In this model we will only consider the operation of the FTP client with respect to a single file. The client has been deliberately designed to incorporate some reasonably intricate state-based rules. Only one file-handle can exist at a given time. Since a file has to be opened in either 'read' or 'write' mode, this means that a file can not be written to and read from at the same time. We have added the constraint that it is impossible to read from an empty file, and it is impossible to write to, or read from, a specific position in the file without having explicitly obtained the position using the *write_position* / *read_position* files first.

We start off by identifying the instrumentation points in the source code. This consists of identifying the points in the source code that correspond to exit

[6] `http://www3.erlang.org/documentation/doc-5.6.5/lib/ssh-1.0.2/doc/html/`

[7] `http://www.dcs.shef.ac.uk/~nw/Files/FM2009/`

Table 1. Functions of the FTP client (Σ in the PLTS)

Function	Description
connect	connect to server, only one connection permitted at a time
disconnect	disconnect from server
open_writable, open_readable	open file in 'write' or 'read' mode
close_writable, close_readable	close file in 'write' or 'read' mode
write, read	write data to or read data from beginning of the file
write_position, read_position	obtain a specific position for writing to or reading from the file
pwrite, pread	write to or read from a specific position in the file
delete	delete the file

points for the abstract functions. In our case this is straightforward, as the abstract functions all correspond to actual function definitions in `ssh_sftp`. As an example, at the end point of `ssh_sftp.open` we insert a statement to add the name of the function "open", its arguments and the output of the function (see accompanying website for sample files). Depending on the arguments, the tracer either records an execution of the function as "open_new" or "open_existing". Having set up the tracer, all that remains is to set up the QuickCheck tester. StateChum has been augmented to automatically generate the QuickCheck model files from the inferred transition systems.

The inferred models. Figure 5 contains two snapshots from the inference process, which consisted of 57 iterations in total when run using the implementation of our technique described above. The process terminated when the testing process yielded no further tests that revealed faults in the hypothesis. The entire set of iterations is available on the accompanying website. For the sake of readability, proscribed transitions are not shown. Figure 5 (a) shows the model produced after 28 iterations. This model contains a number of errors (e.g., it permits the file to be opened in 'read' mode while it is still open in 'write' mode). The final candidate specification, which is produced after 57 iterations has 9 states, and is the most accurate version produced. Every state transition that is permitted in the model is also possible in the actual implementation (i.e., the inference process has made no over-generalisations).

Degree of accuracy. The key question is: how useful is the technique? One aspect of this is to what extent the inferred model is the actual behaviour of the implementation, although it should be noted that even a partial model will be of use to a developer in increasing their understanding of the system.

Figure 6 shows a "diff" between the final inferred model and the target. The technique used to compute this is defined in [18]. From this comparison it can be established that 19 transitions were correctly inferred by the machine, that 16 transitions are missing, and that 6 superfluous transitions have been added. Most of the missing transitions are of a particular nature: they are events that should be possible from every state in the system and would consequently require a very large number of tests to capture. The events "disconnect" and "delete" should be possible from most states, and account for 9 of the 16 transitions. The remaining missing transitions represent relatively minor differences in behaviour.

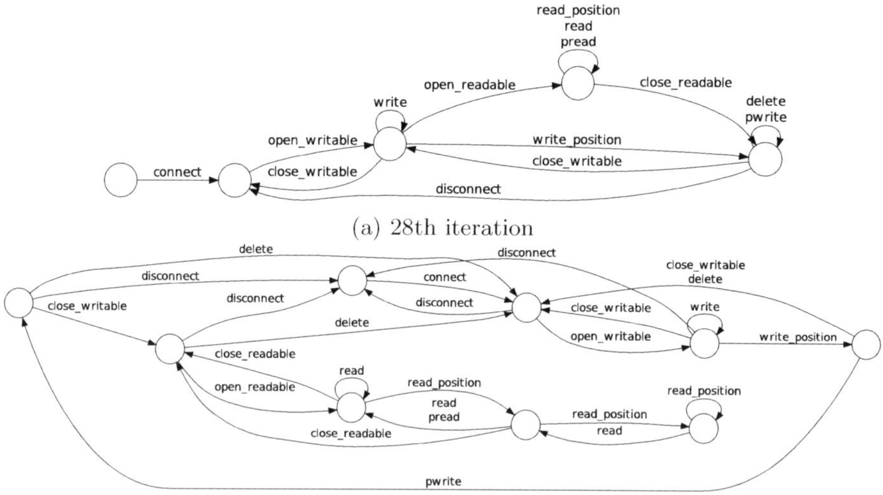

(a) 28th iteration

(b) 57th (final) iteration

Fig. 5. Inferred models

The correctly inferred transitions produce a reasonably accurate overview of how the system behaves; the system has its three well defined phases of operation - connection, writing to a file, and reading from that file. The requirement that a file can only be open either in "write" or "read" mode is correctly captured, and a file must be written to before it can be read.

To compare the language of the inferred model with its intended target precision, we adopt a technique that is defined in [19]. Precision denotes the extent to which the language that is represented by the inferred machine represents the language of the target state machine of the actual software system. Recall denotes the extent to which the language that is represented by the target machine is covered by the inferred machine. These measures have been applied to the inferred machine to separately assess the accuracy in terms of both valid and invalid languages. In terms of the valid language of the two machines, the precision is 96.2%, with a recall of 41%. The low positive recall tallies with the large number of missing transitions; a large number of sequences that should be accepted by the inferred machine are missing. In terms of negative precision and recall, the machine has a precision of 85%, and a recall of 99.5%.

In summary, both methods of comparison indicate that the model is precise, and that it captures the essential functionality of the system. Inaccuracies are primarily due to the fact that the model is inferred model can end up missing certain transitions, especially those that are possible from every state (such as "disconnect"). In practice, this can be explained by the choice of testing technique. Current versions of QuickCheck explore the model randomly, and only choose transitions that are in the model - they do not attempt to explore unspecified behaviour. This inevitably leads to some transitions potentially being missed out.

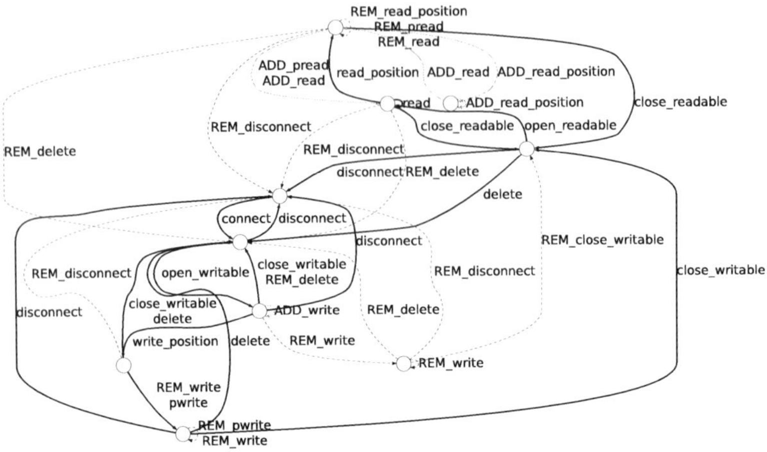

Fig. 6. Difference between final inferred model and reference model - Bold transitions are correct, thin (green) lines are added, dashed (red) lines are missing

A major strength of the technique demonstrated above is that it is based on an inference technique (the EDSM-bluefringe state-merging technique) that excels at dealing with *sparse* samples of program traces or tests. It can arrive at a reasonable hypothesis of how the program behaves, without requiring an exhaustive or impractically large number of traces or tests. One potential weakness of the implementation here is that, if errors are made early on in the state-merging process, they are compounded by future merges, so it relies on a sufficient base of traces to prevent invalid merges from happening. The iterative testing process is responsible for gathering this base of traces in the form of tests.

As a result, the accuracy of the final result is highly dependent on the testing technique that is used - in the name of efficiency we have used a simple random testing approach in QuickCheck. There are however a number of systematic testing techniques, such as the W-method mentioned above [15], and evaluation of how these can be integrated into the process is a key area of future work that we wish to undertake.

5 Conclusions and Future Work

This paper has presented an iterative approach to reverse-engineering labelled transition systems. The approach has been implemented and demonstrated with respect to and Erlang system, but can in princple be applied to any system regardless of the underlying language. The inference engine, along with the various illustratory resources are openly available.

The approach was demonstrated with respect to a small model of a real Erlang implementation of a FTP client. The resulting model is shown to be very precise, both in terms of the graph structure and the language that this represents.

There are a number of ways by which the authors intend to extend this work. A more extensive case-study will be used, to ensure that the approach scales reasonably to larger systems. There is already a lot of experimental evidence from the grammar inference community [16] to suggest that this will be the case. Previous work by the authors has involved the manual provision of selected LTL constraints to increase the efficiency and accuracy of the inference process. It is our intention to integrate these techniques with the current testing infrastructure.

As mentioned in Section 3.3, the traces are produced in the Daikon format [17]. Daikon can infer data constraints on variables from execution traces. We are currently investigating the use of Daikon to infer pre/post-conditions from Erlang executions, which can then be used to annotate the reverse-engineered state machines.

There are a number of QuickCheck features that could be used to increase the efficacy of the testing process. As mentioned previously, it is our intention to use the transition-weighting feature to coax the tester towards certain states that would otherwise be in danger of being left unexplored by random tests. It is envisaged that Uchitel's PLTS formalism could be particularly useful in this respect, helping to identify those states with lots of 'unknown' transitions, to automate the assignment of weights in the hypothesis machine.

Acknowledgements. This work is supported by the EU FP7 ProTest project. Walkinshaw is also supported by the EPSRC REGI grant (EP/F065825/1). The authors would like to thank Thomas Arts, John Hughes, Koen Claessen and Hans Svensson at ITU / Chalmers, Gothenburg for their valuable suggestions and comments.

References

1. Walkinshaw, N., Bogdanov, K., Holcombe, M., Salahuddin, S.: Reverse Engineering State Machines by Interactive Grammar Inference. In: 14th IEEE International Working Conference on Reverse Engineering, WCRE (2007)
2. Armstrong, J.: Programming Erlang: Software for a Concurrent World. Pragmatic Bookshelf (July 2007)
3. Claessen, K., Hughes, J.: Quickcheck: A Lightweight Tool for Random Testing of Haskell Programs. In: Proceedings of the International Conference on Functional Programming (ICFP), pp. 268–279 (2000)
4. Walkinshaw, N., Bogdanov, K., Ali, S., Holcombe, M.: Automated discovery of state transitions and their functions in source code. Software Testing, Verification and Reliability 18(2) (2008)
5. Ernst, M.: Static and Dynamic Analysis: Synergy and Duality. In: Proceedings of the International Workshop on Dynamic Analysis, WODA (2003)
6. Walkinshaw, N., Bogdanov, K., Holcombe, M., Salahuddin, S.: Improving Dynamic Software Analysis by Applying Grammar Inference Principles. Journal of Software Maintenance and Evolution: Research and Practice (2008)
7. Gold, E.: Language Identification in the Limit. Information and Control 10, 447–474 (1967)

8. Dupont, P., Lambeau, B., Damas, C., van Lamsweerde, A.: The QSM Algorithm and its Application to Software Behavior Model Induction. Applied Artificial Intelligence 22, 77–115 (2008)
9. Biermann, A., Feldman, J.: On the Synthesis of Finite-State Machines from Samples of their Behavior. IEEE Transactions on Computers 21, 592–597 (1972)
10. Cook, J., Wolf, A.: Discovering Models of Software Processes from Event-Based Data. ACM Transactions on Software Engineering and Methodology 7(3), 215–249 (1998)
11. Angluin, D.: Learning Regular Sets from Queries and Counterexamples. Information and Computation 75, 87–106 (1987)
12. Walkinshaw, N., Bogdanov, K.: Inferring Finite-State Models with Temporal Constraints. In: Proceedings of the 23rd International Conference on Automated Software Engineering, ASE (2008)
13. Uchitel, S., Kramer, J., Magee, J.: Behaviour Model Elaboration using Partial Labelled Transition Systems. In: 4th joint meeting of the European Software Engineering Conference and ACM SIGSOFT Symposium on the Foundations of Software Engineering (ESEC/FSE), pp. 19–27 (2003)
14. Hopcroft, J., Motwani, R., Ullman, J.: Introduction to Automata Theory, Languages, and Computation, 3rd edn. Addison-Wesley, Reading (2007)
15. Chow, T.: Testing Software Design Modelled by Finite State Machines. IEEE Transactions on Software Engineering 4(3), 178–187 (1978)
16. Lang, K., Pearlmutter, B., Price, R.: Results of the Abbadingo One DFA Learning Competition and a New Evidence-Driven State Merging Algorithm. In: Honavar, V.G., Slutzki, G. (eds.) ICGI 1998. LNCS (LNAI), vol. 1433, pp. 1–12. Springer, Heidelberg (1998)
17. Ernst, M., Cockrell, J., Griswold, W., Notkin, D.: Dynamically Discovering Likely Program Invariants to Support Program Evolution. Transactions on Software Engineering 27(2), 1–25 (2001)
18. Bogdanov, K., Walkinshaw, N.: Computing the Structural Difference between State-Based Models. In: 16th IEEE Working Conference on Reverse Engineering, WCRE (2009)
19. Walkinshaw, N., Bogdanov, K., Johnson, K.: Evaluation and Comparison of Inferred Regular Grammars. In: Proceedings of the International Colloquium on Grammar Inference (ICGI), St. Malo, France (2008)

Model Checking Linearizability via Refinement

Yang Liu[1], Wei Chen[2], Yanhong A. Liu[3], and Jun Sun[1]

[1] School of Computing, National University of Singapore
{liuyang,sunj}@comp.nus.edu.sg
[2] Microsoft Research Asia
weic@microsoft.com
[3] Computer Science Department
State University of New York at Stony Brook
liu@cs.sunysb.edu

Abstract. Linearizability is an important correctness criterion for implementations of concurrent objects. Automatic checking of linearizability is challenging because it requires checking that 1) all executions of concurrent operations be serializable, and 2) the serialized executions be correct with respect to the sequential semantics. This paper describes a new method to automatically check linearizability based on refinement relations from abstract specifications to concrete implementations. Our method avoids the often difficult task of determining linearization points in implementations, but can also take advantage of linearization points if they are given. The method exploits model checking of finite state systems specified as concurrent processes with shared variables. Partial order reduction is used to effectively reduce the search space. The approach is built into a toolset that supports a rich set of concurrent operators. The tool has been used to automatically check a variety of implementations of concurrent objects, including the first algorithms for the mailbox problem and scalable NonZero indicators. Our system was able to find all known and injected bugs in these implementations.

1 Introduction

Linearizability [13] is an important correctness criterion for implementations of objects shared by concurrent processes, where each process performs a sequence of operations on the shared objects. Informally, a shared object is *linearizable* if each operation on the object can be understood as occurring instantaneously at some point, called the *linearization point*, between its invocation and its response, and its behavior at that point is consistent with the specification for the corresponding sequential execution of the operation.

One common strategy for proving linearizability of an implementation (used in manual proofs or automatic verification) is to determine linearization points in the implementation of all operations and then show that these operations are executed atomically at the linearization points [11,2,29]. However, for many concurrent algorithms, it is difficult or even impossible to statically determine all linearization points. For example, in the K-valued register algorithm (Section 10.2.1 of [4]), linearization points differ depending on the execution history. Furthermore, the linearization points determined

A. Cavalcanti and D. Dams (Eds.): FM 2009, LNCS 5850, pp. 321–337, 2009.

might be incorrect, which can give wrong results of linearizability. Therefore, it is desirable to have automatic solutions to verifying these algorithms without knowing linearization points. However, existing methods for automatic verification without using linearization points either apply to limited kinds of concurrent algorithms [30] or are inefficient [29].

Contribution. This paper describes a new method for automatically checking linearizability based on refinement relations from abstract specifications to concrete implementations. Our method does not rely on knowing linearization points, but can take advantage of them if given. The method exploits model checking of finite state systems specified as concurrent processes with shared variables, and is not limited to any particular kinds of concurrent algorithms. We exploit powerful optimizations to improve the efficiency and scalability of our checking method.

Refinement requires that the set of execution traces of a concrete implementation be a subset of that of an abstract specification. Thus, we express linearizability as trace refinement of operation invocations and responses from the abstract specification to the concrete implementation, where the abstract specification is correct with respect to sequential semantics. The idea of refinement has been explored before: Alur et al. [1] showed that linearizability can be cast as containment of two regular languages, and Derrick et al. [8] expressed linearizability as non-atomic refinement of Object-Z and CSP models. Some similar approaches [6,10,16] prove linearizability using trace simulation. In this work, we give a general and rigorous definition of linearizability, regardless of the modeling language used, using refinement.

Our model checking method exploits on-the-fly refinement checking (so that counterexamples, if any, can be produced without generating the entire search space, as in FDR [20]), partial order reduction (to effectively reduce the search space), symmetry reduction (to handel large or even unbounded number of processes) and other optimizations. If linearization points are known and can be marked in the implementation, our approach constructs an even smaller search space. Some of the optimizations are specialized for linearizability checking while others are general. The result is a powerful linearizability checking method that is much more efficient than prior work. A model checking tool, PAT [24] (*http://pat.comp.nus.edu.sg*), is developed to provide automated support for this approach. PAT supports an event-based modeling language that has a rich set of concurrent operators. Our engineering effort realizes all these optimizations in PAT. We have used PAT to automatically check not only established algorithms, such as concurrent stack and queue algorithms, but also larger and more sophisticated algorithms that were not formally verified before—the first algorithms for the mailbox problem [3] and scalable NonZero indicators [11]. Both algorithms use sophisticated data structures and control structures, so the linearization points are difficulty to determine. The verification details of the two algorithms can be found in [15] and [32] respectively. Counterexamples were reported quickly for incorrect algorithms, such as an incorrect implementation of concurrent queues [21]. Experimental results show that our solution is much more efficient and scalable than prior work [29].

The rest of the paper is structured as follows. Section 2 gives the standard definition of linearizability. Section 3 shows how to express linearizability using refinement relations in general. Section 4 describes verification and optimization methods. Section 5 presents experimental results. Section 6 discusses related work and concludes.

2 Linearizability

Linearizability [13] is a safety property of concurrent systems, over sequences of events corresponding to the invocations and responses of the operations on shared objects. It is formalized as follows.

In a shared memory model $\mathcal{M}$, $O = \{o_1, \ldots, o_k\}$ denotes the set of k shared objects, $P = \{p_1, \ldots, p_n\}$ denotes the set of n processes accessing the objects. Shared objects support a set of *operations*, which are pairs of invocations and matching responses. Every shared object has a set of states that it could be in. A *sequential specification* of a (deterministic) shared object[1] is a function that maps every pair of invocation and object state to a pair of response and a new object state.

The behavior of $\mathcal{M}$ is defined as H, the set of all possible sequences of invocations and responses together with the initial states of the objects. A history $\sigma \in H$ induces an irreflexive partial order $<_\sigma$ on operations such that $op_1 <_\sigma op_2$ if the response of operation op_1 occurs in σ before the invocation of operation op_2. Operations in σ that are not related by $<_\sigma$ are concurrent. σ is sequential iff $<_\sigma$ is a strict total order. Let $\sigma|_i$ be the projection of σ on process p_i, which is the subsequence of σ consisting of all invocations and responses that are performed by p_i. Let $\sigma|_{o_i}$ be the projection of σ on object o_i, which is the subsequence of σ consisting of all invocations and responses of operations that are performed on object o_i.

A sequential history σ is *legal* if it respects the sequential specifications of the objects. More specifically, for each object o_i, if s_j is the state of o_i before the invocation of the j-th operation op_j in $\sigma|_{o_i}$, then response of op_j and the resulting new state s_{j+1} of o_i follow the sequential specification of o_i. For example, a sequence of read and write operations of an object is legal if each read returns the value of the preceding write if there is one, and otherwise it returns the initial value. Every history σ of a shared memory model $\mathcal{M}$ must satisfy the following basic properties:

Correct interaction. For each process p_i, $\sigma|_i$ consists of alternating invocations and matching responses, starting with an invocation. This property prevents *pipelining* operations.

Closeness. Every invocation has a matching response. This property prevents *pending* operations.

In addition to these two, liveness property is also important for some critical systems, which guarantees the progress of the systems. Even if the model satisfies linearizability, it may not progress as desired. For instance, even under a fair scheduler Treiber's push/pop [25] might never terminate if there is always another concurrent push/pop. We remark that liveness properties can be formulated as Linear Temporal Logic (LTL) formulae (an example is given at the end of Example 1) and checked using standard LTL model checkers (with or without the assumption of a fair scheduler).

[1] More rigorously, the sequential specification is for a *type* of shared objects. For simplicity, however, we refer to both actual shared objects and their types interchangeably in this paper.

Given a history σ, a *sequential permutation* π of σ is a sequential history in which the set of operations as well as the initial states of the objects are the same as in σ. The formal definition of linearizability is given as follows.

Linearizability. There exists a sequential permutation π of σ such that

1. for each object o_i, $\pi|_{o_i}$ is a legal sequential history (i.e. π respects the sequential specification of the objects), and
2. if $op_1 <_\sigma op_2$, then $op_1 <_\pi op_2$ (i.e., π respects the run-time ordering of operations).

Linearizability can be equivalently defined as follows: In every history σ, if we assign increasing time values to all invocations and responses, then every operation can be shrunk to a single time point between its invocation time and response time such that the operation appears to be completed instantaneously at this time point [16,4]. This time point for each operation is called its *linearization point*. Linearizability is a safety property [16], so its violation can be detected in a finite prefix of the execution history.

Linearizability is defined in terms of the interface (invocations and responses) of high-level operations. In a real concurrent program, the high-level operations are implemented by algorithms on concrete shared data structures, e.g., using a linked list to implement a shared stack object. Therefore, the execution of high-level operations may have complicated interleaving of low-level actions. Linearizability of a concrete concurrent algorithm requires that, despite complicated low-level interleaving, the history of high-level invocation and response events still has a sequential permutation that respects both the run-time ordering among operations and the sequential specification of the objects. This idea is formally presented in the next section using refinement relations in a process algebra extended with shared variables.

3 Linearizability as Refinement Relations

We model concurrent systems using a process algebra extended with shared variables. The behavior of a model is described using a labeled transition system generated from the model. We define linearizability as a refinement relation from an implementation model to a specification model.

3.1 Modeling Language

We introduce the relevant subset of syntax of CSP (Communicating Sequential Processes) [14] extended with shared variables and give its operational semantics. Note that our approach is not limited to process algebra like CSP; it is also applicable to any programming language with formal operational semantics. We chose this language because of its rich set of operators for concurrent communications.

Definition 1 (Process). *A process P is defined using the grammar*[2]*:*

$$\begin{aligned} P ::= &\ Stop \mid Skip \mid e\{assignments\} \rightarrow P \mid P \setminus X \mid P_1;\ P_2 \mid P_1 \Box P_2 \\ &\mid P_1 \lhd b \rhd P_2 \mid P_1 \mid\mid\mid P_2 \mid\mid\mid \cdots \mid\mid\mid P_n \end{aligned}$$

[2] Parallel composition $(P_1 \parallel P_2 \parallel \cdots \parallel P_n)$ is omitted in the paper since it is irrelevant to our discussion. We include it in our technical report [15].

where $P, P_1, P_2, \ldots, P_n$ are processes, e is a name representing an event with an optionally attached sequence of assignments to shared variables, X is a set of names, and b is a Boolean expression.

Stop is the process that communicates nothing, also called deadlock. $Skip = \checkmark \rightarrow Stop$, where $\checkmark$ is the termination event. Event prefixing $e \rightarrow P$ performs e and afterwards behaves as process P. If e is attached with assignments, the valuation of the shared variables is updated accordingly. For simplicity, assignments are restricted to update only shared variables. Process $P \setminus X$ hides all occurrences of events in X. An event is invisible iff it is explicitly hidden by the hiding operator $P \setminus X$. Sequential composition, $P_1; P_2$, behaves as P_1 until its termination and then behaves as P_2. External choice $P_1 \Box P_2$ is solved only by the occurrence of a visible event. Conditional choice $P_1 \lhd b \rhd P_2$ behaves as P_1 if the Boolean expression b evaluates to true, and behaves as P_2 otherwise. Indexed interleaving $P_1 \mid\mid\mid P_2 \mid\mid\mid \cdots \mid\mid\mid P_n$ runs all processes independently except for communication through shared variables. Processes may be recursively defined, and may have parameters (see examples later).

The most noticeable extension to CSP is the use of shared variables. It has long been known [14] that one can model a variable as a process parallel to the processes that use it. Nevertheless, direct support of variables allows concise modeling and efficient verification. The shared memory contains integer/Boolean variables and arrays, which can be read/written atomically by all processes. Nonblocking algorithms use synchronization primitives such as *compare and swap (CAS)* and *load linked (LL)/store-conditional (SC)*. Our language provides strong support for these synchronization primitives by using conditional choices, which is elaborated in [32]. The complete syntax and formal operational semantics of our language is presented in [23].

The semantics of a model is defined with a labeled transition system (LTS). Let Σ denote the set of all visible events and τ denote the set of all invisible events. Since invisible events are indistinguishable, we sometimes also use τ to represent an arbitrary invisible event. Let Σ^* be the set of finite traces. Let Σ_τ be $\Sigma \cup \tau$.

Definition 2 (LTS). *A LTS is a 3-tuple $L = (S, init, T)$ where S is a set of states, $init \in S$ is the initial state, and $T \subseteq S \times \Sigma_\tau \times S$ is a labeled transition relation.*

For states $s, s' \in S$ and $e \in \Sigma_\tau$, we write $s \xrightarrow{e} s'$ to denote $(s, e, s') \in T$. The set of enabled events at s is $enabled(s) = \{e : \Sigma_\tau \mid \exists\, s' \in S, s \xrightarrow{e} s'\}$. We write $s \xrightarrow{e_1, e_2, \cdots, e_n} s'$ iff there exist $s_1, \cdots, s_{n+1} \in S$ such that $s_i \xrightarrow{e_i} s_{i+1}$ for all $1 \leq i \leq n$, $s_1 = s$ and $s_{n+1} = s'$, and $s \xrightarrow{\tau *} s'$ iff $s = s'$ or $s \xrightarrow{\tau, \cdots, \tau} s'$. The set of states reachable from s by performing zero or more τ transitions is $\tau^*(s) = \{s' : S \mid s \xrightarrow{\tau *} s'\}$. Let $tr : \Sigma^*$ be a sequence of visible events. $s \stackrel{tr}{\Rightarrow} s'$ if and only if there exist $e_1, e_2, \cdots, e_n \in \Sigma_\tau$ such that $s \xrightarrow{e_1, e_2, \cdots, e_n} s'$ and $tr = \langle e_1, e_2, \cdots, e_n \rangle \upharpoonright \tau$ is the trace with invisible events removed. The set of traces of L is $traces(L) = \{tr : \Sigma^* \mid \exists\, s' \in S, init \stackrel{tr}{\Rightarrow} s'\}$.

For example, Fig. 1 shows a LTS[3] generated from *ReaderA* process in Example 1, where τ labels are omitted for simplicity. Due to the use of shared variables, a state of the system is a pair (P, V), where P is the current process expression, and V is the

[3] The dotted circles will be explained in Section 4 and should be ignored for now.

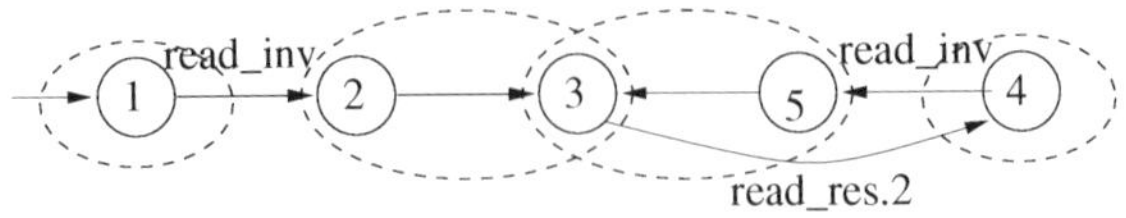

Fig. 1. A LTS Example

current valuation of the shared variables represented as a mapping from names to values. Given a LTS $(S, init, T)$, the size of S can be infinite for two reasons. First, variables may have infinite domains. Second, processes may allow unbounded replication by recursion, e.g., $P = (a \to P;\ c \to Skip) \,\Box\, b \to Skip$, or $P = a \to P \mathbin{|||} P$. In this paper, we consider only LTSs with a finite number of states. In particular, we bound the sizes of value domains and the number of processes by constants. In our examples, bounding the sizes of value domains also bounds the depths of recursions.

Definition 3 (Refinement). *Let $L_{im} = (S_{im}, init_{im}, T_{im})$ be a LTS for an implementation. Let $L_{sp} = (S_{sp}, init_{sp}, T_{sp})$ be a LTS for a specification. L_{im} refines L_{sp}, written as $L_{im} \sqsupseteq_T L_{sp}$, iff $traces(L_{im}) \subseteq traces(L_{sp})$.*

3.2 Linearizability

This section shows how to create high-level linearizable specifications and how to use a refinement relation to define linearizability of concurrent implementations.

To create a high-level linearizable specification for a shared object, we rely on the idea that in any linearizable history, any operation can be thought of as occurring at some linearization point. We define the specification LTS $L_{sp} = (S_{sp}, init_{sp}, T_{sp})$ for a shared object o in the following way. Every execution of an operation op of o on a process p_i includes three atomic steps: the invocation action $inv(op)_i$, the linearization action $lin(op)_i$, and the response action $res(op, resp)_i$. The linearization action $lin(op)_i$ performs the computation based on the sequential specification of the object. In particular, it maps the invocation and the object state before the operation to a new object state and a response, changes the object to the new state, and buffers the response $resp$ locally. The response action $res(op, resp)_i$ generates the actual response $resp$ using the buffered result from the linearization action. Each of the three actions is executed atomically without being interfered by any other action, but the three actions of one operation may be interleaved with the actions of other operations. In L_{sp}, all $inv(op)_i$ and $res(op, resp)_i$ are visible events, while $lin(op)_i$ are invisible events.

In a LTS $L_{sp} = (S_{sp}, init_{sp}, T_{sp})$, each process p_i has (a) an idle state $s_{p_i,0}$, (b) a state $s(op)_{p_i,1}$ for every operation op of object o, representing the state after the invocation of op but before the linearization action of op, and (c) $s(op, resp)_{p_i,2}$ for every operation op and every possible response $resp$ of this operation, representing the state after the linearization action of op but before the response of op. Then S_{sp} is the cross product of all object values and all process states. $init_{sp}$ is the combination of the initial value of object o and $s_{p_i,0}$'s for all processes p_i. For $s \in S_{sp}$, let s_{v_o} be the value of object o encoded in s, s_{p_i} be the state of p_i in s, and s_{-p_i} and $s_{-p_i,-v_o}$ be the state s excluding s_{p_i} and excluding s_{p_i} and s_{v_o}, respectively. The labeled transition relation T_{sp} is such that for $(s, e, s') \in T$, (a) if $e = inv(op)_i$, then $s_{-p_i} = s'_{-p_i}$, $s_{p_i} = s_{p_i,0}$, and $s'_{p_i} = s(op)_{p_i,1}$; (b) if $e = lin(op)_i$, then $s_{-p_i,-v_o} = s'_{-p_i,-v_o}$, $s_{p_i} = s(op)_{p_i,1}$, and $s'_{p_i} = s(op, resp)_{p_i,2}$, such that s'_{v_o} and $resp$ are the new object value and the response, respectively, based on the sequential specification of object o as well as the old object state s_{v_o} and the state $s_{p_i} = s(op)_{p_i,1}$ of process p_i; (c) if $e = res(op, resp)_i$, then $s_{-p_i} = s'_{-p_i}$, $s_{p_i} = s(op, resp)_{p_i,2}$, and $s'_{p_i} = s_{p_i,0}$.

Example 1 (K-valued register). We use a shared K-valued single-reader single-writer register algorithm (Section 10.2.1 of [4]) to demonstrate the ideas above. The linearizable abstract model is defined as follows, where R is the shared register with initial value K, and M is a local variable to store the value read from R.

$$
\begin{aligned}
&ReaderA() &&= read\_inv \rightarrow read\{M = R;\ \} \rightarrow read\_res.M \rightarrow ReaderA();\\
&WriteA(v) &&= write\_inv.v \rightarrow write\{R = v;\ \} \rightarrow write\_res \rightarrow Skip;\\
&WriterA() &&= (WriteA(0)\ \Box\ WriteA(1)\ \Box \ldots \Box\ WriteA(K-1));\ WriterA();\\
&RegisterA() &&= (ReaderA()\ |||\ WriterA()) \backslash \{read, write\};
\end{aligned}
$$

The $ReaderA$ process repeatedly reads the value of register R and stores the value in local variable M. Event $read\_res.M$ returns the value in M. $WriteA(v)$ writes the given value v into R. Event $write\_inv.v$ stores the value v to be written into the register. The $WriterA$ process repeatedly writes a value in the range of 0 to $K - 1$. External choices are used here to enumerate all possible values. $RegisterA$ interleaves the reader and writer processes and hides the $read$ and $write$ events (linearization actions). The only visible events are the invocation and response of the read and write operations. This model generates all the possible linearizable traces.

We now consider a LTS $L_{im} = (S_{im}, init_{im}, T_{im})$ that supposedly implements object o. The visible events of L_{im} are also those $inv(op)_i$'s and $res(op, resp)_i$'s. For example, the following models an implementation of a K-valued register using an array B of K binary registers (storing only 0 and 1).

$$
\begin{aligned}
&Reader() &&= read\_inv \rightarrow UpScan(0);\\
&UpScan(i) &&= DownScan(i-1, i) \lhd B[i] = 1 \rhd UpScan(i+1);\\
&DownScan(i, v) &&= (read\_res.v \rightarrow Reader()) \lhd i < 0 \rhd\\
& &&\qquad (DownScan(i-1, i) \lhd B[i] = 1 \rhd DownScan(i-1, v));\\
&Write(v) &&= write\_inv.v \rightarrow \tau\{B[v] = 1;\ \} \rightarrow WriterScan(v-1);\\
&WriterScan(i) &&= (write\_res \rightarrow Skip) \lhd i < 0 \rhd\\
& &&\qquad (\tau\{B[i] = 0;\ \} \rightarrow WriterScan(i-1));\\
&Writer() &&= (Write(0)\ \Box\ Write(1)\ \Box \ldots \Box\ Write(K));\ Writer();\\
&Register() &&= Reader()\ |||\ Writer();
\end{aligned}
$$

The $Reader$ process first does a upward scan from element 0 to the first non-zero element i, and then does a downward scan from element $i - 1$ to element 0 and returns the index of last element whose value is 1. Event $read\_res.v$ returns this index as the return value of the read operation. The $Write(v)$ process first sets the v-th element of B to 1, and then does a downward scan to set all elements before i to 0. Note that in this implementation, the linearization point for $Reader$ is the last point where the parameter v in $DownScan$ process is assigned in the execution. Therefore, the linearization point can not be statically determined. Instead, it can be in either $UpScan$ or $DownScan$. We remark that one liveness property can be verified by model checking $\Box read\_inv \Rightarrow \Diamond read\_res$ where $\Box$ and $\Diamond$ are modal operators which read as 'always' and 'eventually' respectively. □

Theorem 1 characterizes linearizability of the implementation through a refinement relation and thus establishes our approach to verifying linearizability. Different versions of this result appeared in distributed computing literature, for example, in Lynch's book [16], Theorems 13.3-13.5.

Theorem 1. *All traces of L_{im} are linearizable iff $L_{im} \sqsupseteq_T L_{sp}$.*

Proof (sketch). Sufficient condition: For any trace $\sigma \in traces(L_{im})$, because $L_{im} \sqsupseteq_T L_{sp}$, σ is also a trace of L_{sp}. Let ρ be the execution history of L_{sp} that generates the trace σ. We define the sequential permutation π of σ as the reordering of operations in σ in the same order as the linearization actions $lin(op)_i$'s of all operations op and all processes p_i in ρ. If $op_1 <_\sigma op_2$, the linearization action of op_1 must be ordered before the linearization action of op_2 in ρ, and thus $op_1 <_\pi op_2$. It is also easy to verify that π is a legal sequential history of object o, since the linearization action of every operation in ρ is the only action in the operation that affects the object state based on its sequential specification, and the order of operations in π respects the order of linearization actions in ρ.

Necessary condition: Let σ be a trace of L_{im}. By assumption σ is linearizable. We need to show that σ is also a trace of L_{sp}. Since σ is linearizable, there is a sequential permutation π of σ such that π respects both the sequential specification of object o and the run-time ordering of the operations in σ. We construct an execution history ρ of L_{sp} from σ and π as follows. Starting from the first event of σ, for any event e in σ, (a) if it is an invocation event, append it to ρ; (b) if it is a response event $res(op, resp)_i$, locate the operation op in π, and for each unprocessed operation op' by a process j before op in π, process op' by appending a linearization action $lin(op')_j$ to ρ, following the order of π; finally append $lin(op)_i$ and $res(op, resp)_i$ to ρ. It is not difficult to show that the execution history ρ constructed this way is indeed a history of L_{sp}. Moreover, obviously the trace of ρ is σ. Therefore, σ is also a trace of L_{sp}. □

The above theorem shows that to verify linearizability of an implementation, it is necessary and sufficient to show that the implementation LTS is a refinement of the specification LTS as we defined above. This provides the theoretical foundation of our verification of linearizability. Notice that the verification by refinement given above does not require identifying low-level actions in the implementation as linearization points, which is a difficult (and sometimes even impossible) task. In fact, the verification can be automatically carried out without any special knowledge about the implementation beyond knowing the implementation code.

In some cases, one may be able to identify certain events in an implementation as linearization points. We call these linearization events. For example, three linearization events have been identified in the stack algorithm [2]. In these cases, we can make these events visible and hide other events (including the invocation and response events) and verify refinement relation only for these events. More specifically, we obtain a specification LTS L'_{sp} by the following two modifications to L_{sp}: (a) for each linearization action $lin(op)_i$, we change it to $lin(op, resp)_i$ so that the response $resp$ computed by this linearization action is included; and (b) all linearization actions are visible while all $inv(op)_i$ and $res(op, resp)_i$ are invisible. Let L'_{im} be an implementation LTS such that its linearization events are visible and all other events are invisible, and its linearization events are also specified as $lin(op, resp)_i$.

Theorem 2. *Let L'_{sp} and L'_{im} be the specification and implementation LTSs such that linearization events are specified as $lin(op, resp)_i$ and are the only visible events. If $L'_{im} \sqsupseteq_T L'_{sp}$, then the implementation is linearizable. Conversely, if the implementation is linearizable, and* it can be shown that no other actions in the implementation can be linearization actions, *then $L'_{im} \sqsupseteq_T L'_{sp}$.*

The proof of the theorem can be found [15]. With this theorem, the verification of linearizability could be more efficient based on only linearization events. However, one important remark is that, as stated in the theorem, to make refinement a necessary condition of linearizability in this case, one has to show that no other actions in the implementation can be linearization points. In other words, the determined linearization points have to be complete. Otherwise, even if the verification finds a counterexample for the refinement relation, we cannot conclude that the implementation is not linearizable since we may have failed in determining all possible linearization events. Examples of implementations modeled using linearization points can be found in [15].

4 Verification of Linearizability

This section presents a general algorithm for refinement checking, which is further extended with partial order reduction and other optimizations.

4.1 Refinement Checking Algorithm

To establish a refinement relationship, every reachable state of the implementation must be compared with every state of the specification reachable via the same trace. Because of nondeterminism caused by interleaving of multiple clients and invisible events, there may be many such states in the specification. Thus, the specification is normalized, by standard subset construction. A *normalized* state is a set of states that can be reached by the same trace from a given state.

Definition 4 (Normalized LTS). *Let $(S, init, T)$ be a LTS. The normalized LTS is $(NS, Ninit, NT)$ where NS is the set of subsets of S, $Ninit = \tau^*(init)$, and $NT = \{(P, e, Q) \mid P \in NS \wedge Q = \{s : S \mid \exists v_1 : P,\ \exists v_2 : S,\ (v_1, e, v_2) \in T \wedge s \in \tau^*(v_2)\}\}$.*

Given a normalized state $s \in NS$, $enabled(s)$ is $\bigcup_{x \in s} enabled(x)$. Given a LTS constructed from a process, the normalized LTS corresponds to the normalized process. A state in the normalized LTS groups a set of states in the original LTS which are all connected by τ-transitions. For instance, the dotted circles in Fig. 1 shows the normalized

```
procedure linearizability(Impl, Spec)
1. checked := ∅; pending.push((init_im, τ*(init_sp)));
2. while pending is not empty do
3.     (Im, NSp) := pending.pop();
4.     checked := checked ∪ {(Im, NSp)};
5.     if enabled(Im) ⊈ (enabled(NSp) ∪ {τ}) then        – C1
6.         return false;
7.     endif
8.     foreach (Im', NSp') ∈ next(Im, NSp)
9.         if (Im', NSp') ∉ checked then
10.            pending.push((Im', NSp'));
11.        endif
12.    endfor
13. endwhile
14. return true;
```

Fig. 2. Algorithm: *linearizability*(*Impl*, *Spec*)

states. Notice that, given a trace, the normalized transition relation NT is deterministic, i.e., for any normalized state P and any event e, there is at most one normalized state Q such that $(P, e, Q) \in NT$.

Based on the refinement checking algorithms in FDR [19], we present a modified on-the-fly refinement checking algorithm that applies partial order reduction. We remark that partial order reduction is an effective reduction method due to the nature of concurrent algorithms. Let $Spec = (S_{sp}, init_{sp}, T_{sp})$ be a specification and $Impl = (S_{im}, init_{im}, T_{im})$ be an implementation. Refinement checking is reduced to reachability analysis of the product of *Impl* and normalized *Spec*. Because normalization in general is computationally expensive, our checking algorithm in Fig. 2 performs normalization on-the-fly, whilst searching for a counterexample.

The algorithm in Fig. 2 performs a depth-first search for a pair (Im, NSp) where Im is a state of the implementation and NSp is a normalized state of the specification such that, the set of enabled events of Im is not a subset of those of NSp (C1). The algorithm returns true if no such pair is found. If C1 is satisfied, a counterexample violating trace refinement is found. The procedure for producing a counterexample is straightforward and hence omitted. Lines 8 to 12 proceed to explore new states of the product of *Impl* and *Spec* and push them onto the stack *pending*. Function $next(Im, NSp)$ returns the children of state (Im, NSp) in the product, which is the following set,

$$\{(Im', NSp) \mid (Im, \tau, Im') \in T_{im}\} \cup \{(Im', NSp') \mid \exists\, e,\ (Im, e, Im') \in T_{im} \land \\ \forall\, s : NSp',\ \exists\, s_1 : NSp,\ \exists\, s_2 : NSp',\ (s_1, e, s_2) \in T_{sp} \land s \in \tau^*(s_2)\}$$

A new state of the product is obtained by either the implementation taking a τ transition (and the specification remains unchanged) or the implementation and the specification engaging the same event simultaneously. To compute $next(Im, NSp)$ (e.g., calculating $\tau^*(s_2)$), it is necessary to compute the set of states reached by a τ-transition from a

procedure $tau(S)$

foreach P_i

  $por := enabled_{P_i}(S) \subseteq \tau \cup X \wedge enabled_{P_i}(S) = current(P_i);$

  foreach $e \in enabled_{P_i}(S)$

    $por := por \wedge \neg\, onstack(e) \wedge \forall\, e' : \Sigma_j,\ j \neq i \Rightarrow \neg\, dep(e, e');$

  endfor

  if por **then return** $\{(((\cdots \mid\mid\mid P_i' \mid\mid\mid \cdots) \setminus X), V) \mid (P_i, V) \xrightarrow{e} (P_i', V)\};$

endfor

return $\{S' \mid S \xrightarrow{\tau} S'\};$

Fig. 3. Algorithm: $tau(S)$

given state. This function is implemented by procedure $tau(S)$ (Fig. 3), which explores all outgoing transitions of S and returns the set of states reachable from S via one τ-transition. It uses partial order reduction and is explained in the next section.

The *linearizability* algorithm is linear in the number of transitions in the product. Assume both *Impl* and *Spec* have finite states. The algorithm terminates because *checked* is monotonically increasing. The soundness of the algorithm follows from [19]. Because normalization is done on-the-fly, it is possible to find a counterexample before the specification is completely normalized.

4.2 Optimizations

Like any model checking algorithm, linearizability checking suffers from state space explosion. This section describes several optimization techniques to solve this problem.

Partial order reduction (POR) is effective for checking linearizability. Our reduction realizes and extends early works on POR for process algebras [28] and refinement checking [31]. The idea of the reduction is that events may be independent, e.g., $read\_inv$ of different readers are independent of each other. Given $P = P_1 \mid\mid\mid \cdots \mid\mid\mid P_n$ and two enabled events e_1 and e_2, e_1 depends on e_2, written as $dep(e_1, e_2)$, if e_1 and e_2 are from the same process or e_1 updates a variable to be accessed by e_2, or vice versa. Notice that $dep(e_1, e_2) \Leftrightarrow dep(e_2, e_1)$. Two events are independent if neither depends on the other. Because the ordering of independent events is irrelevant to the correctness of linearizability checking, we may ignore some of the ordering so as to reduce the search space. Since interleaving composition is the main source of state space explosion, we consider that *Im* is in the form of $((P_1 \mid\mid\mid P_2 \mid\mid\mid \cdots \mid\mid\mid P_n) \setminus X, V)$, where P_i is a process, X is a set of events and V is the valuation of the variables. We show how to explore only a subset of enabled transitions and yet preserve soundness.

Function $next(Im, NSp)$, which depends on function $tau(S)$, is used to expand the search tree. POR is mainly applied to function $tau(S)$. Because tau is applied to the specification or implementation independently, as long as we guarantee that the reduced state graph (of either *Impl* or *Spec*) is trace-equivalent to the full state graph, there is a refinement relationship in the reduced state space if and only if there is one in the full state space. Fig. 3 shows function $tau(S)$. The idea is to identify one process P_i

such that all τ-transitions from P_i are independent of those from other processes, by checking a set of heuristic conditions. Intuitively, a process P_i is chosen if and only if,

- $enabled_{P_i}(S) \subseteq \tau \cup X$, i.e., events enabled in process P_i are all invisible,
- $enabled_{P_i}(S) = current(P_i)$, i.e., given P_i and any valuation of the global variables, all events that could be enabled in process P_i (denoted by $current(P_i)$) are enabled (denoted by $enabled_{P_i}(S)$). This is a sufficient condition to guarantee that an event that is dependent on a transition from P_i cannot be executed without a transition from P_i occurring first,
- $\neg\, onstack(e)$, i.e., executing e does not result in a state on the search stack,
- $\forall\, e' : \Sigma_j,\ j \neq i \Rightarrow \neg\, dep(e, e')$, i.e., all enabled events are independent of events from other process P_j (denoted as Σ_j).

If no such P_i is found, we expand the node with all enabled events (line 8). Following the arguments of [28] and [31], it can be shown that the reduced state graph is trace-equivalent to the full graph.

The above applies POR to τ-transitions only. PAT is capable of applying POR to visible events. Because both *Impl* and *Spec* must make corresponding transitions for a visible event, reduction for visible events is complicated. Fig. 4 presents the algorithm, i.e., the refined $next$. If *Im* is not stable (i.e., $tau(Im) \neq Im$), we apply the algorithm tau' (tau' is same as tau in Fig. 3 except that line 8 returns $\varnothing$) to identify a subset of τ-transitions (line 2). If no such subset exists, the pair (Im, NSp) is fully expanded (line 10). An algorithm $visible$ similar to tau' is used to check if a given visible event e is a candidate for POR. Function $processes(e)$ returns all process components (of the composition) whose alphabet contains e. Firstly, we choose a possible candidate from *Im* using the algorithm $visible$. Event e is chosen if and only if, for each process in $processes(e)$, e is the only event from the process that can be enabled, all other enabled events are independent of e, and performing e does not result in a state on the stack. Next, we check if e satisfies the same set of conditions for each state in the normalized state of the specification. If it does, e is used to expand the search tree at line 9 (and all other enabled events are ignored). In order to find such e efficiently, the candidate events are selected in a pre-defined order, i.e., events that have the least number of associated processes are chosen first. The soundness proof of the algorithm can be found in our technical report [15].

Our approach works without knowledge of linearization points. Nonetheless, having the knowledge would allow us to take full advantage of POR. Because the linearization points are the only places where data consistency must be checked, we may amend the above algorithm to perform data consistency check at the linearization points. As a result, encoding relevant data as part of the event is not necessary and the model contains fewer events, which translates to fewer traces. Furthermore, because only the linearization points need to be synchronized, we may hide all other events, and turn visible transitions into τ-transitions that are subject to POR.

Besides partial order reduction, our approach is compatible with other state space reduction techniques or abstract interpretation techniques. Distributed algorithms and protocols are usually designed for a large (or even unbounded) number of similar processes. They are therefore subject to symmetric reduction [12]. For instance, different

procedure $next'(Im, NSp)$
if $\tau \in enabled(Im)$ **then**
    $nextmoves := tau'(Im)$;
    if $(nextmoves \neq \emptyset)$ **then return** $nextmoves$;
else
    foreach $e \in enabled(Im)$
        $por := visible(Im, e)$;
        foreach $S \in NSp$
            $por := por \wedge visible(S, e)$;
        if por **then return** $\{(Im', \tau^*(NSp')) \mid Im \xrightarrow{e} Im' \wedge NSp \xrightarrow{e} NSp'\}$;
return $next(Im, NSp)$;

procedure $visible(Im, e)$
$por := \neg\, onstack(e) \wedge \forall\, e' : \Sigma_j,\ e' \neq e \Rightarrow \neg\, dep(e, e')$;
foreach $P_i \in processes(e)$
    $por := por \wedge enabled_{P_i}(Im) = current(P_i) = \{e\}$;
return por;

Fig. 4. Algorithm: $next'(Im, NSp)$ and $visible(Im, e)$

writers (i.e., $WriterA(i)$) in Example 1 are symmetric and therefore, it is sound (subject to property-specific conditions) to only explore one writer and conclude the same for all other writers. If the processes are identical, then it is subject to process counter abstraction. For example, in the concurrent stack algorithm, the processes invoking push and pop are symmetric and therefore, we only keep track of the number of processes, instead of the exact processes. In this way, we may prove the property for arbitrary number of processes. We skip the details due to space constraints.

5 Experiments

Our method has been implemented and applied to a number of concurrent algorithms, including *register*—the K-valued register algorithm[4] in Section 3, *stack*—a concurrent stack algorithm [25], *queue*—a concurrent non-blocking queue algorithm in Fig. 3 of [18], *buggy queue*—an incorrect queue algorithm [21], and *mailbox* and *SNZI*—the first algorithms for the mailbox problem [3] and scalable Non-Zero indicators [11], respectively. Details for verifying these examples can be found in our technical report [15]. Table 1 summarizes part of our experiments, where '-' means out of memory or more than 4 hours, and '(points)' means that linearization points are given.

The number of states and running time increase rapidly with data size and the number of processes, e.g., 3 processes for *register*, *stack*, *queue*, and *SNZI* vs. 2 processes. The results conform to theoretical results [1]: model checking linearizability is in EXPSPACE for both time and space. When linearization points are known, the complexity

[4] We extend this example with 2 readers and 1 writer. The correctness is verified using PAT.

Table 1. Experiment results on a PC with 2.83 GHz Intel Q9550 CPU and 2 GB memory

Algorithm	**#Proc.**	**Linear-izable**	**Time(sec)** w/o POR	**#States** w/o POR	**Time(sec)** with POR	**#States** with POR
4-valued *register*	2	true	6.14	50893	5.72	43977
5-valued *register*	2	true	44.9	349333	60.4	307155
6-valued *register*	2	true	297	2062437	789	1838177
3-valued *register* with 2 readers and 1 writer	3	true	294	479859	393	361255
stack of size 12	2	true	138	540769	65.9	395345
stack of size 14	2	true	411	763401	99.4	599077
stack of size 2	3	true	-	-	4321	4767519
stack of size 12 (points)	2	true	0.62	9677	0.82	9677
stack of size 14 (points)	2	true	0.82	12963	1.11	12963
stack of size 2 (points)	3	true	1.14	10385	1.56	10385
stack of size 2 (points)	4	true	37.6	219471	49.4	219471
queue of size 6	2	true	134	432511	86.2	343446
queue of size 8	2	true	256	104582	218	938542
buggy queue of size 10	2	false	10.9	32126	6.87	32126
buggy queue of size 20	2	false	52.73	105326	41.1	105326
mailbox of 3 operations	2	true	71.6	272608	27.8	120166
mailbox of 4 operations	2	true	2904	9928706	954	3696700
SNZI of size 2	2	true	1298	712857	322	341845
SNZI of size 3	3	true	-	-	6214	8451568

is still EXPSPACE, but the state space reduces significantly since the state spaces of implementation and specification are smaller. We show that the speedup of knowing linearization points is in the order of $O(2^{k \cdot 2^n \cdot (k^{2n} - k^n)})$, where k is the size of the shared object and n is the number of processes [15]. Use of partial order reduction effectively reduces the search space and running time in most cases, including *stack* and *queue*, and especially *mailbox* and *SNZI* because their algorithms have multiple internal transitions. For *register*, the state space is reduced but running time increases because of computational overhead. For *buggy queue* [21], the counterexamples (discovered firstly in [7]) are produced quickly after exploring only part of the state space.

Vechev and Yahav [29] also provided automated verification. Their approach needs to find a linearizable sequence for each history, whose worst-case time is exponential in the length of the history, as it may have to try all possible permutations of the history. As a result, the number of operations they can check is only 2 or 3. In contrast, our approach handles all possible interleaving of operations given sizes of the shared objects. Because of partial order reduction and other optimizations, our approach is more scalable than theirs. For instance, we can verify stacks of size 14, which means any number of stack operations that contain up to 14 consecutive push operations.

Experiments suggest that PAT is faster than FDR for systems without variables [22]. Modeling variables using processes and lack of partial order reduction will make FDR even slower. Therefore we skip comparison with FDR on these examples.

6 Discussions

In terms of modeling of linearizability, our approach is based on the trace refinement of LTSs, which is similar to [1]. Our refinement checking algorithm is related to existing on-the-fly behavioral equivalence and pre-order checking algorithms (e.g., [19,9]). The non-atomic refinement defined in [8] separates the data explicitly as state-based formalism Object-Z. This modeling requires to have the knowledge of linearization points, and also prevents automatic verification techniques such as model checking to be used.

Formal verification of linearizability is a much studied research area, since linearizability is a central property for the correctness of concurrent algorithms. There are various approaches in the literature, as discussed below.

Manual proving. Herlihy and Wing [13] present a methodology for verifying linearizability by defining a function that maps every state of an concurrent object to the set of all possible abstract values representing it. Vafeiadis et. al. [27] use rely-guarantee reasoning to verify linearizability for a family of implementations for linked lists. Neither of them requires statically determined linearization points, but they are manual.

Using theorem provers. Verification using theorem provers (e.g., PVS) is another approach [10,6]. In these works, algorithms are proved to be linearizable by using simulation between input/output automata modeling the behavior of an abstract set and the implementation. However, theorem prover based approach is not automatic. Conversion to IO automata and use of PVS require strong expertise.

Static analysis. Wang and Stoller [30] present a static analysis that verifies linearizability for an unbounded number of threads. Their approach detects certain coding patterns, which are known to be atomic regardless of the environment. This solution is not complete (i.e., not applicable to all algorithms).

Model checking. Amit et al. [2] presented a shape difference abstraction that tracks the difference between two heaps. This approach works well if the concrete heap and the abstract heap have almost identical shapes. Recently, Manevich et al. [17] and Berdine et al. [5] extended it to handle larger number and unbounded number of threads, respectively. Vafeiadis [26] further improved this solution to allow linearization points in different threads. The main limitation of these approaches is that users need to provide linearization points, which are unknown for some algorithms. In [29], Vechev and Yahav provided two methods for linearizability checking. The first method is a fully automatic, but inefficient as discussed in Section 5. The second method requires algorithm-specific user annotations for linearization points, which is not generic.

In this work, we expressed linearizability using a refinement relation. A fully automatic model checking algorithm for linearizability verification is developed and built in a practical tool PAT. Several case studies show that our approach is capable of verifying practical algorithms and identifying bugs inX faulty implementations. Several future directions are possible. Algorithms that accept an infinite number of threads or unbound data structures make model checking impossible. Symmetric properties among threads can reduce infinite number of threads to a small number. Shape analysis can also be incorporated into the model checking to handle unbounded data size.

References

1. Alur, R., Mcmillan, K., Peled, D.: Model-checking of Correctness Conditions for Concurrent Objects. In: LICS 1996, pp. 219–228. IEEE, Los Alamitos (1996)
2. Amit, D., Rinetzky, N., Reps, T., Sagiv, M., Yahav, E.: Comparison under Abstraction for Verifying Linearizability. In: Damm, W., Hermanns, H. (eds.) CAV 2007. LNCS, vol. 4590, pp. 477–490. Springer, Heidelberg (2007)
3. Arguilera, M.K., Gafni, E., Lamport, L.: The Mailbox Problem. In: Taubenfeld, G. (ed.) DISC 2008. LNCS, vol. 5218, pp. 1–15. Springer, Heidelberg (2008)
4. Attiya, H., Welch, J.: Distributed Computing: Fundamentals, Simulations, and Advanced Topics, 2nd edn. John Wiley & Sons, Inc., Publication, Chichester (2004)
5. Berdine, J., Lev-Ami, T., Manevich, R., Ramalingam, G., Sagiv, S.: Thread Quantification for Concurrent Shape Analysis. In: Gupta, A., Malik, S. (eds.) CAV 2008. LNCS, vol. 5123, pp. 399–413. Springer, Heidelberg (2008)
6. Colvin, R., Doherty, S., Groves, L.: Verifying Concurrent Data Structures by Simulation. Electronic Notes in Theoretical Computer Science 137(2), 93–110 (2005)
7. Colvin, R., Groves, L.: Formal Verification of an Array-Based Nonblocking Queue. In: ICECCS 2005, pp. 507–516. IEEE, Los Alamitos (2005)
8. Derrick, J., Schellhorn, G., Wehrheim, H.: Proving Linearizability Via Non-atomic Refinement. In: Davies, J., Gibbons, J. (eds.) IFM 2007. LNCS, vol. 4591, pp. 195–214. Springer, Heidelberg (2007)
9. Dill, D.L., Hu, A.J., Wong-Toi, H.: Checking for Language Inclusion Using Simulation Preorders. In: Larsen, K.G., Skou, A. (eds.) CAV 1991. LNCS, vol. 575, pp. 255–265. Springer, Heidelberg (1992)
10. Doherty, S., Groves, L., Luchangco, V., Moir, M.: Formal Verification of a Practical Lock-free Queue Algorithm. In: de Frutos-Escrig, D., Núñez, M. (eds.) FORTE 2004. LNCS, vol. 3235, pp. 97–114. Springer, Heidelberg (2004)
11. Ellen, F., Lev, Y., Luchangco, V., Moir, M.: SNZI: Scalable NonZero Indicators. In: PODC 2007, pp. 13–22. ACM, New York (2007)
12. Emerson, E.A., Trefler, R.J.: From Asymmetry to Full Symmetry: New Techniques for Symmetry Reduction in Model Checking. In: Pierre, L., Kropf, T. (eds.) CHARME 1999. LNCS, vol. 1703, pp. 142–157. Springer, Heidelberg (1999)
13. Herlihy, M., Wing, J.M.: Linearizability: A Correctness Condition for Concurrent Objects. ACM Transactions on Programming Language and Systems 12(3), 463–492 (1990)
14. Hoare, C.A.R.: Communicating Sequential Processes. International Series in Computer Science. Prentice-Hall, Englewood Cliffs (1985), `www.usingcsp.com/cspbook.pdf`
15. Liu, Y., Chen, W., Liu, Y.A., Sun, J.: Model Checking Linearizability via Refinement. Technical Report TR08c, National Univ. of Singapore (May 2009), `http://www.comp.nus.edu.sg/~pat/report.pdf`
16. Lynch, N.: Distributed Algorithms. Morgan Kaufmann, San Francisco (1997)
17. Manevich, R., Lev-Ami, T., Sagiv, M., Ramalingam, G., Berdine, J.: Heap Decomposition for Concurrent Shape Analysis. In: Alpuente, M., Vidal, G. (eds.) SAS 2008. LNCS, vol. 5079, pp. 363–377. Springer, Heidelberg (2008)
18. Michael, M.M., Scott, M.L.: Nonblocking Algorithms and Preemption-Safe Locking on Multiprogrammed Shared Memory Multiprocessors. Journal of Parallel and Distributed Computing 51, 1–26 (1998)
19. Roscoe, A.W.: Model-checking CSP. In: A classical mind: essays in honour of C. A. R. Hoare, pp. 353–378 (1994)
20. Roscoe, A.W.: The Theory and Practice of Concurrency. Prentice-Hall, Englewood Cliffs (1997)

21. Shann, C.H., Huang, T.L., Chen, C.: A Practical Nonblocking Queue Algorithm Using Compare-and-Swap. In: ICPADS 2000, pp. 470–475. IEEE, Los Alamitos (2000)
22. Sun, J., Liu, Y., Dong, J.S.: Model Checking CSP Revisited: Introducing a Process Analysis Toolkit. In: ISoLA 2008, pp. 307–322. Springer, Heidelberg (2008)
23. Sun, J., Liu, Y., Dong, J.S., Chen, C.Q.: Integrating Specification and Programs for System Modeling and Verification. In: TASE 2009, pp. 127–135. IEEE, Los Alamitos (2009)
24. Sun, J., Liu, Y., Dong, J.S., Pang, J.: PAT: Towards Flexible Verification under Fairness. In: Bouajjani, A., Maler, O. (eds.) CAV 2009. LNCS, vol. 5643, pp. 702–708. Springer, Heidelberg (2009)
25. Treiber, R.K.: Systems Programming: Coping with Parallelism. Technical Report RJ 5118, IBM Almaden Research Center (1986)
26. Vafeiadis, V.: Shape-Value Abstraction for Verifying Linearizability. In: Jones, N.D., Müller-Olm, M. (eds.) VMCAI 2009. LNCS, vol. 5403, pp. 335–348. Springer, Heidelberg (2009)
27. Vafeiadis, V., Herlihy, M., Hoare, T., Shapiro, M.: Proving Correctness of Highly-concurrent Linearisable Objects. In: PPoPP 2006, pp. 129–136. ACM, New York (2006)
28. Valmari, A.: Stubborn Set Methods for Process Algebras. In: PMIV 1996. DIMACS Series in Discrete Mathematics and Theoretical Computer Science, vol. 29, pp. 213–231 (1996)
29. Vechev, M., Yahav, E.: Deriving Linearizable Fine-grained Concurrent Objects. In: PLDI 2008, pp. 125–135. ACM, New York (2008)
30. Wang, L., Stoller, S.: Static Analysis of Atomicity for Programs with Non-blocking Synchronization. In: PPoPP 2005, pp. 61–71. ACM, New York (2005)
31. Wehrheim, H.: Partial Order Reductions for Failures Refinement. Electronic Notes in Theoretical Computer Science 27 (1999)
32. Zhang, S.J., Liu, Y., Sun, J., Dong, J.S., Chen, W., Liu, Y.A.: Formal Verification of Scalable NonZero Indicators. In: SEKE 2009, pp. 406–411. Knowledge Systems Institute Graduate School (2009)

It's Doomed; We Can Prove It

Jochen Hoenicke[1], K. Rustan M. Leino[2], Andreas Podelski[1], Martin Schäf[1], and Thomas Wies[1,3]

[1] University of Freiburg
[2] Microsoft Research, Redmond
[3] EPFL, Switzerland

Abstract. Programming errors found early are the cheapest. Tools applying to the early stage of code development exist but either they suffer from false positives ("noise") or they require strong user interaction. We propose to avoid this deficiency by defining a new class of errors. A program fragment is *doomed* if its execution will inevitably fail, in whatever state it is started. We use a formal verification method to identify such errors fully automatically and, most significantly, without producing noise. We report on preliminary experiments with a prototype tool.

1 Introduction

Software engineers agree on that bugs found early are the cheapest. Tools applying to this stage of development, however, usually suffer from false positives or require strong user interaction. Perhaps the only "cheap" bugs are those found by the compiler. Fixing them is cheap since they are fixed by the programmer as they appear. We note that no programmer would doubt the relevance of a compiling error in a program fragment because this is an error regardless of the intended use of the program fragment, i.e., there is no way it can be dismissed (there is no "noise").

In this paper, we propose the definition of a class of program errors that can be detected as early (i.e., for a possibly isolated program fragment), as automatically (i.e., by a tool, without user input and without user interaction) and as precisely (no noise) as, e.g., a missing semicolon.

We define that a program fragment is *doomed* if an execution that reaches it will inevitably fail, i.e., executing the program fragment will never lead to a normal termination of the program.

We present a formal verification method (on top of an existing static checker) to identify such errors fully automatically and, most significantly, without producing noise. We report on a prototype implementation on top of Boogie [2, 4] that can be used in combination with Spec# or VCC [6] to either analyze C# or C programs. Preliminary experimental results indicate its practical potential.

A. Cavalcanti and D. Dams (Eds.): FM 2009, LNCS 5850, pp. 338–353, 2009.

Related Work. We first want to point out that the class of errors our approach finds is subsumed by almost every bug detection tool and that most tools will find even more real bugs. However, the increased error detection rate comes at a price: these tools either produce a lot of noise or they require heavy user interaction. For instance, a set of unit tests that executes every statement in the program at least once will detect all errors related to doomed program points but one has to write or generate the test cases.

Our work can best be compared to Findbugs [1], which tries to find a reasonable amount of bugs using different control and dataflow analysis approaches while having in mind that flooding the user with false positives would ruin everything. With Findbugs, we share the idea of searching for contradictions in the dataflow. For this purpose, Findbugs uses a special pattern detection mechanism which is very fast but can miss errors and produce false positives. We give an experimental comparison of our approach and Findbugs in Section 7.

Other static analysis tools like e.g., Splint [9] are less comparable since they focus on finding as many bugs as possible and therefore produce noise or require special code annotations.

The results produced by our tool could be reproduced using full fledged automatic verifiers such as BLAST [12] by first trying to prove the program, collecting all unverified assertions, negating them and rerunning the verification. If the verifier is able to prove such a negated assertion then, the corresponding statement will fail under any circumstances. However, this would be a rather convoluted and costly way to find doomed program points. Also, tools such as BLAST are meant to be applied to the whole program, i.e., at a rather late stage of development when the errors we are targeting have probably already been fixed.

From the algorithmic point of view, our approach is strongly related to extended static checkers such as ESC/Java [10] and modular program verifiers such as Spec# [4, 2]. While these tools issue warnings whenever they cannot prove the absence of an error, as opposed to issuing warnings only for definite errors, we share their approach of transforming the program and the idea of using predicate transformers to obtain a representation that can be checked by a theorem prover [17]. These tools use special annotations such as invariants to prove certain properties. For the purpose of error detection, though, these annotations are not required. As we show later on, the user can still provide such information in order to increase the error detection rate.

Proving the existence of bad states, as done by Rümmer and Shah [21], differs from our approach in that they prove the existence of inputs for which something bad might happen while a doomed program point guarantees that nothing good can happen when reaching it. Their approach will find more errors, but requires a specification of the desired inputs or will otherwise be imprecise. Doomed points are errors regardless of the desired program behavior.

There is also previous work on refinement and noise reduction techniques for existing error detection and verification approaches. That work has the effect of reducing false positives, but we instead take a new approach.

2 Examples

In the following, we present a collection of examples that demonstrate what kinds of errors our approach is able to find and, more importantly, what kinds of vulnerabilities it does not report.

Example 1. Our first example is given in Figure 1. It demonstrates a trivial, yet common error that can happen during development. In fact, the example is inspired by an error that was found in an old version of Eclipse [14].

If our algorithm identifies an error in a program, then it will report not just the statement that crashes, but also the statements that actually lead to the crash. This provides additional hints to the developer that help him to fix the error. If we apply our algorithm to the example program, then it will report lines 5 and 6 as a guaranteed error. It reports line 6 because whenever the expression `*ptr` is evaluated, this will cause a null pointer dereference. It further reports line 5 because if the else branch of the conditional is taken, `ptr==0` has been evaluated to true, which guarantees the error in line 6.

```
1 int access(int *ptr)
2 {
3   if (ptr)
4     *ptr = 0;
5   else
6     printf ("%d", *ptr);
7
8   return 0;
9 }
```

Fig. 1. TRIVIAL

```
1  int getMin(int *a, int x) {
2    int i, j, temp;
3    for (i= x-1; i >= 0; i--) {
4      for (j= 1; j <= i; j++) {
5        if (a[j-1] > a[j]) {
6          temp = a[j-1];
7          a[j-1] = a[j];
8          a[j] = temp;
9        }
10     }
11   }
12   return a[i];
13 }
```

Fig. 2. LOOP

Example 2. Our second example is less trivial, yet contains a common error. The function `getMin` in Figure 2 returns the minimal element of an array. For this purpose, it first sorts the array and then returns the first element. However, there is a mistake in the loop bound of the *for* loop in line 3. The loop will decrease the variable `i` until it has a negative value. This leads to an out-of-bounds array access in line 12. Our algorithm detects that the out-of-bounds access is inevitable. It reports lines 3 and 12 as what leads to the error. This is the only warning emitted by our algorithm. Since there is no precondition saying that array `a` is allocated and its size is given by `x`, any attempt to verify that the procedure is safe without taking into account its calling context would generate additional warnings of potential boundary errors.

```
1  /* Sorted tree */
2
3  typedef void* T;
4  typedef struct
5     entry *Entry;
6  struct entry
7  {
8        Entry left ;
9        Entry right ;
10       int key ;
11       T data ;
12 };
```

```
12 void update(Entry root,
13              int key, T dat) {
14   Entry x = root;
15   while (x->key != key) {
16     if (key < x->key)
17       x = x->left;
18     else
19       x = x->right;
20   }
21   x->data = dat;
22 }
```

Fig. 3. COMPLEX

Example 3. Our last example demonstrates how the user of our tool benefits from the fact that it detects guaranteed errors rather than arbitrary errors. The program fragment in Figure 3 is taken from a library that implements a map data structure using a sorted binary tree. The function `update` takes three parameters: the root of the data structure, a key to an entry in the data structure, and a data value. It then traverses the tree to find the entry for the given key and updates the data value associated with this key. The function works correctly if the calling context guarantees that there is already an entry for the given key in the data structure. If this assumption is violated, the function crashes. Note that there is no null pointer check that guards the dereference of variable `x` in the while condition at line 16. The fact that there is an entry for the given key guarantees that `x` is not null.

It is a real challenge for any bug finding tool to prove that line 15 does not cause a null pointer dereference and, thus, not report this line as a potential error. For extended static checking or a modular program verifier, the user needs to specify the precondition saying that there exists an entry in the tree for the given key. However, this is not sufficient to prove the absence of a null pointer dereference. The user further needs to specify a data structure invariant that expresses the fact that the tree is sorted. This information is required in the loop invariant of the while loop. Even if all necessary specifications are given, automatically proving that the loop invariant implies the absence of null pointer dereferences is still tricky. Extended static checkers use theorem provers to automate this task. The theorem prover needs to conclude from the sortedness property and the existence of an entry for the given key that this entry is located in the subtree that the while loop traverses into. Modern theorem provers still require proof hints from the user to accomplish such proofs. All these tasks are time consuming and require the expertise of a verification engineer.

If, on the other hand, one attempts to use abstraction based program analyses to automatically infer the necessary preconditions, then only the use of a very sophisticated shape analysis would leave any hope for success. However, such analyses are expensive and do not yet scale well to large programs. Using them online while coding is unrealistic.

In contrast, our algorithm will not report any errors, simply because there exist executions that never dereference any null pointers.

3 Doomed Program Points

We now formally define the new class of errors that we consider in this paper.

In order to abstract away from the details of a concrete programming language, we only assume that a program defines a set of possibly infinite *executions* (sequences of states).

We assume that executions are divided into two types: admissible executions and inadmissible executions. An execution is inadmissible if it causes some undesirable behavior; in particular, it is inadmissible if it diverges or violates an assertion. Syntactically, we only assume that a program comes with a finite set of *program points*.
Each state in an execution belongs to a unique *program point*. We say that an execution passes through a program point ℓ if one of its states belongs to ℓ.

Definition 1. *A program point ℓ is called* doomed *if all executions that pass through ℓ are inadmissible.*

In particular, a program containing a doomed program point has an inadmissible execution, or no execution passes through it (i.e., it is part of *dead code*). Once a doomed program point is reached in an execution, this execution is guaranteed to fail. In this sense, doomed program points are the witnesses of guaranteed errors.

We define the problem of *error verification* as the problem of identifying all doomed program points in a given program. We say that an algorithm for this problem is sound if, for any given program, it identifies only doomed program points. We say that it is complete if it identifies all doomed program points.

4 Preliminaries

We define our algorithm with respect to a subset of the Boogie language [2,18]. Boogie is an intermediate verification language designed for program analysis. It provides a small set of control constructs that, yet, allows the encoding of full-fledged programming languages such as C, C#, and Java (see, e.g., [2,5,6]).

The syntax of our simple language is defined in Figure 4. A program consists of a sequence of blocks. Each block consists of a unique program point, a sequential statement, and a goto statement that connects the block with a non-empty set of successor blocks. The atomic statements of our language are assignments, non-deterministic assignments (**havoc**) of program variables, assert statements, and assume statements. We do not specify the concrete syntax of expressions that are used in these statements. In principle, they can be arbitrarily complex

$$
\begin{aligned}
\mathit{Program} &::= \mathit{Block}^{+} \\
\mathit{Block} &::= \mathit{PPId} : \ \mathit{Stmt};\ \textbf{goto}\ \mathit{PPId}^{+} \\
\mathit{Stmt} &::= \mathit{VarId} := \mathit{Expr} \mid \textbf{havoc}\ \mathit{VarId}^{+} \\
&\quad \mid \textbf{assert}\ \mathit{Expr} \mid \textbf{assume}\ \mathit{Expr} \\
&\quad \mid \mathit{Stmt};\ \mathit{Stmt}
\end{aligned}
$$

Fig. 4. Simple Language

logical formulae. Each block either has a transition to other blocks or goes to a unique program point called *Term* which means that the program has terminated normally.

A program state is a valuation of the program variables and a program counter that evaluates to a program point *id*. A program gives rise to a set of executions. An execution consists of a sequence of states describing the successive execution of the program blocks starting from some block in the program. An execution terminates normally if it reaches the block *Term*, it ends in an error if an **assert** in some block evaluates to *false*, and it is infinite if the program does not terminate. A sequence of states where an **assume** in a block evaluates to *false* models an infeasible computation. The admissible executions are the feasible executions that terminate normally.

If we translate a real program into our simple language, we can model arrays and the program's heap using function-valued program variables that map indices or memory addresses to values. The concrete representation of the heap depends on the semantics of the translated language. For example, one way to model a Java-like language is to use a function-valued program variable per field in a class; other possible memory models are discussed, e.g., in [6,16,18,19]. For brevity of exposition, our simple language does not support procedures (although BOOGIE does).

5 Error Verification Algorithm

Outline. We now give the outline of our algorithm for error verification. It is implemented by the procedure Exorcise given in Figure 5. Procedure Exorcise takes a program as input and returns a set of doomed program points. The procedure first transforms the input program P into a program P' in loop-free passive form. This means, that (1) program P' has no cycle in the graph formed by its blocks and goto statements and (2) blocks in P' consist only of assume and assert statements. The transformation is such that the set of doomed program points in P' is a subset of the set of doomed program points of P.

After the transformation, procedure Exorcise iterates over all program points in program P'. For each program point ℓ, it generates a logical formula $\mathsf{EVC}(\ell, P')$. We call $\mathsf{EVC}(\ell, P')$ an *error verification condition.* The error verification condition is valid if and only if program point ℓ is doomed in P'. The

```
proc Exorcise(P : program)
   var Doomed : set of doomed program points
   var P' : program
   var φ : formula

   begin
      P' := Transform(P)
      for each program point ℓ in P' do
         φ := EVC(ℓ, P')
         if Valid(φ) then
            add ℓ to Doomed
      od
      return Doomed
   end
```

Fig. 5. Error verification algorithm

procedure then calls the subroutine Valid, which checks whether the error verification condition is valid. We assume that Valid is a sound test for logical validity, e.g., implemented by a theorem prover. If the error verification condition is valid, then the program point ℓ is added to the set of doomed program points.

For exposition purposes, we will present simplified versions of subroutines Transform and EVC, and argue that procedure Exorcise is sound. Afterwards, we discuss improvements of these subroutines that are crucial for scalability of the algorithm and increased error detection rate.

Program transformation. In the following, we describe a simple version of subroutine Transform that transforms a program into loop-free passive form [11,3]. Note that the transformation described below is by now standard and is used in several extended static checkers and program verifiers (e.g.,, [10,2]). We therefore provide only a brief description. For a more detailed discussion, see [3].

The first step in Transform(P) is to transform program P into a loop-free program. We now think of our program P as a control flow graph where each block is a single node labeled with the program point associated with the block. We assume that each cycle in the graph has a unique entry point, the *loop header* (if not, one can first apply node splitting, see e.g., [15]). Edges from nodes inside a cycle back to the loop header are called *back edges*. We assume without loss of generality that a loop header is a block that consists of just one goto statement that either goes to the first block of the loop body or skips the loop, jumping to a block that we call the *loop exit*. The variables that are modified by a statement in the loop are called *loop targets*. We can now over-approximate any number of loop iterations as follows: first, wipe out all information about the loop targets by inserting appropriate havoc statements on entry to the loop body; then, replace each back edge of the loop with an edge to the loop exit. We can think of this transformation as eliminating loops using trivial loop invariants. In fact, if the user or some preceding analysis provides loop invariants, they can be incorporated into the transformation to increase precision (see [3]).

Once our program is loop free, procedure Transform(P) transforms it to passive form. First, we apply a *single assignment* transformation [7] where auxiliary variables are introduced to ensure that each program variable is assigned at most once per execution path [11]. The general idea is to replace each read of a variable by the auxiliary variable that represents its value at that point in the program, and to introduce a new auxiliary variable for every write. For example, an assignment $x := x + 1$ may be transformed into $x_{k+1} := x_k + 1$, where k is some sequence number (see [11, 3] for details). Second, since no assignment of an auxiliary variable is preceded by a use of that variable, we can replace each assignment $x_k := e$ by an assume statement **assume**($x_k = e$).

The following proposition states soundness of the transformation into loop-free passive form.

Proposition 1. *For any program P, the set of doomed program points of program* Transform(P) *is a subset of the doomed program points of program P.*

The proof relies on the fact that the program obtained from loop elimination preserves all admissible executions of the original program. Furthermore, there is a mapping from executions of the loop-free program to executions of the passive program that preserves admissibility.

Error Verification Conditions. We now describe how we generate an error verification condition for a given program point in a loop-free passive program.

Recall that the *weakest precondition* $wp.S.Q$ of a statement S with respect to predicate Q describes the pre-states of S from which every execution of S terminates normally in a state satisfying Q [8]. Thus, if the weakest precondition $wp.S.true$ is universally valid, then all executions of statement S are admissible. Therefore, weakest preconditions are used for generating verification conditions that prove program correctness.

We can use a similar approach to check for doomed program points. The *weakest liberal precondition* of a statement S with respect to a predicate Q describes the pre-states of S from which every terminating execution of S ends in Q [8]. Thus, $wlp.S.false$ is the set of all states such that any normally terminating execution of S ends in a state satisfying *false*, which means that there are no executions of S that terminate normally. Thus, weakest liberal preconditions allow us to precisely characterize statements with guaranteed errors.

Proposition 2. *Let S be a passive loop-free program. If $wlp.S.false$ is universally valid, then all executions of S are inadmissible.*

The proof of Proposition 2 goes by structural induction over S using the predicate transformer semantics of passive loop-free programs from [20] that is given in Table 1. Hereby, the statement $S \square T$ stands for non-deterministic choice between statements S and T. Since our program is in passive form, the statements of the program do not affect the program state. The only effect of a passive

Table 1. Semantics of predicate transformers

Stmt	$wp.Stmt.Q$	$wlp.Stmt.Q$
assert E	$E \wedge Q$	$E \implies Q$
assume E	$E \implies Q$	$E \implies Q$
$S;T$	$wp.S.(wp.T.Q)$	$wlp.S.(wlp.T.Q)$
$S \,\square\, T$	$wp.S.Q \wedge wp.T.Q$	$wlp.S.Q \wedge wlp.T.Q$

statement is to choose whether the execution is admissible. As described in [11], this allows us to capture the semantics of a passive program in terms of so called *outcome predicates*. Given a statement S, the predicate $N.S$ denotes the pre-states of S from which the execution of S may be admissible, while predicate $W.S$ denotes the pre-states from which the execution of S may be inadmissible. The formal semantics of these two outcome predicates is given in Table 2. Using

Table 2. Semantics of outcome predicates

Stmt	$N.Stmt$	$W.Stmt$
assert E	E	$\neg E$
assume E	E	*false*
$S;T$	$N.S \wedge N.T$	$W.S \vee (N.S \wedge W.T)$
$S \,\square\, T$	$N.S \vee N.T$	$W.S \vee W.T$

these outcome predicates, it is shown in [17] that weakest preconditions can be characterized as

$$wp.S.Q \equiv \neg(W.S) \wedge (N.S \implies Q) \ .$$

Similarly, we can characterize weakest liberal preconditions as follows.

Proposition 3. *Let S be a program in passive form and Q a predicate. Then the following equivalence holds:*

$$wlp.S.Q \equiv (N.S \implies Q) \ .$$

The size of predicate $N.S$ is linear in the size of statement S. We can, thus, conclude that the size of the weakest liberal precondition $wlp.S.false$ is also linear in S. In contrast, the weakest precondition is worst-case quadratic.

For a program point ℓ in a loop-free passive program P we denote by $st(\ell, P)$ the statement that corresponds to the subprogram following this program point. The statement $st(\ell, P)$ can be computed from the control-flow structure of the program as follows: given the block

$$\ell : \ S; \, \mathbf{goto}\, \ell_1, \ldots, \ell_n$$

for a program point ℓ in P, the corresponding statement $st(\ell, P)$ is defined recursively as

$$st(\ell, P) \stackrel{\text{def}}{=} S; (st(\ell_1, P) \,\square \cdots \square\, st(\ell_n, P)) \ .$$

For the terminating program point *Term*, the statement $st(Term, P)$ is the empty statement. Since program P is loop-free, statement $st(\ell, P)$ is well-defined for all program points.

We can now define the error verification condition $\mathsf{EVC}(\ell, P)$ as follows:

$$\mathsf{EVC}(\ell, P) \stackrel{\text{def}}{=} wlp.st(\ell, P).false \ .$$

Hereby, $wlp.st(\ell, P)$ is computed according to Proposition 3. From Proposition 2 we conclude that error verification condition generation is sound.

Proposition 4. *Let P be a program in loop-free passive form and ℓ a program point in P. Then, ℓ is doomed if the error verification condition* $\mathsf{EVC}(\ell, P)$ *is valid.*

Soundness. From Proposition 1 and 4 we can now conclude the soundness of our algorithm.

Theorem 1. *Procedure* Exorcise *is a sound algorithm for the error verification problem.*

Avoiding exponential blow-up. The weakest liberal precondition for statement $st(\ell, P)$ and a predicate Q can be computed recursively as follows:

$$wlp.st(\ell, P).Q = wlp.S. \begin{pmatrix} \quad wlp.st(\ell_1, P).Q \\ \wedge \ \ldots \\ \wedge \ wlp.st(\ell_n, P).Q \end{pmatrix} \tag{1}$$

However, there is a crucial problem when one computes $wlp.st(\ell, P).false$ using Equation 1. If a program point ℓ' is reachable from ℓ then $wlp.st(\ell', P).false$ occurs as a subformula in $wlp.st(\ell, P).false$ as many times as there are paths in the control-flow graph from ℓ to ℓ'. This can lead to an exponential blow-up in the size of the resulting verification condition. We follow the idea of [3] and [17] and avoid this blow-up by defining Equation 1 in the underlying logic. For this purpose, we introduce auxiliary Boolean variables B_ℓ for $wlp.st(\ell, P).false$ and build the formula

$$\begin{aligned} F_{Bdef} : & \bigwedge_{\ell \in P} (B_\ell \equiv wlp.S.(B_{\ell_1} \wedge \cdots \wedge B_{\ell_n}) \\ & \wedge (B_{Term} \equiv false) \end{aligned}$$

Using this definition we redefine our EVC as follows.

$$\mathsf{EVC}(\ell, P) \stackrel{\text{def}}{=} F_{Bdef} \implies \neg B_\ell \, .$$

6 Extended EVC Generation

Until now, our algorithm only detects errors that occur in every path that starts in a program point ℓ. Code that precedes the program point is not taken into account when checking $\mathsf{EVC}(\ell, P)$. An example is given in Figure 6. The program point in line 3 is doomed, since the value of i is never a valid pointer at this program point. To prove this, one needs to consider the assignment in line 1. It is not enough to just consider every conditional block by itself. We detect program points in conditional blocks by introducing a new variable R_ℓ that indicates that the block B_ℓ was reached. The variable is initially false; an assignment that sets the variable to true is added to the block and we change the post-condition from *false* to $R_\ell \implies \mathit{false}$.

```
1 int *i = 0;
2 if (k != 0)
3       *i = 3;
```

Fig. 6. PATHPROG

We introduce all reachability variables at the same time but set only one R_ℓ to false in the precondition. Thus, we do the following transformation of the program (before passifying the program). The Block $\ell : S; \mathbf{goto}\, \ell_1, \ldots, \ell_n$ is transformed to

$$\ell : R_\ell := \mathit{true}; S; \mathbf{goto}\, \ell_1, \ldots, \ell_n$$

and in the block Term we add the assertion

$$\mathbf{assert}(\bigwedge_{\ell \in P} R_\ell)$$

We compute F_{Bdef} for this annotated program as described in the previous section.

We now redefine our EVC. To check if there is a doomed program point in block B_ℓ we check the validity of

$$\mathsf{EVC}(\ell, P) \stackrel{\text{def}}{=} \neg R_\ell \wedge F_{Bdef} \implies \neg B_{start}\,.$$

Proposition 5. *Let P be a program in loop-free passive form and ℓ a program point in P. Then, ℓ is doomed if and only if the error verification condition $\mathsf{EVC}(\ell, P)$ is valid.*

As for the weaker Proposition 4, we can conclude from Proposition 1 and 5, that our algorithm is sound.

Completeness. Our algorithm is not complete for unrestricted programs because the error verification problem is in general undecidable[1]. However, if we start from a loop-free program then the algorithm is complete under the assumption that the generated verification conditions are expressible in some logical theory for which validity checking is decidable.

[1] An instance of the error verification problem is to decide whether a given program never terminates.

Faster Theorem Prover Interaction. Instead of checking validity of EVC, we check the unsatisfiability of its negation

$$\neg R_\ell \wedge F_{Bdef} \wedge B_{start} .$$

Since the part $F_{Bdef} \wedge B_{start}$ does not change, we can push it as axiom and then just check unsatisfiability of $\neg R_\ell$ for each Block B_ℓ. This way the theorem prover has to parse the main part of the verification condition only once and can reuse lemmas that are derived from this formula.

7 Implementation and Experiments

We have built a prototype implementation of algorithm Exorcise on top of Boogie [2] and applied it to a C# version of the Findbugs Null Pointer Microbenchmark [13] and the examples in Figures 1, 2, and 3. For our prototype, we have used heuristics for dealing with loops and function calls. We describe these heuristics in the following.

Loops: In order to increase detection rate we unroll each loop body three times. One unrolling for the first, the last, and an arbitrary iteration. For the arbitrary iteration, we set all variables modified inside the loop body to havoc at the beginning and at the end of the unrolled iteration. The back edges of the original loop are replaced. For the first iteration, the back edges are changed to the first block of the arbitrary and the last iteration. For the arbitrary iteration, the back edge is changed to the last iteration. The last iteration will always leave the loop. This simple unrolling allows us e.g., to find doomed program points caused by iteration across array bounds as in Figure 2 as well as simple cases of non-termination where an iterator is not iterated inside the loop body.

By unrolling the first and last iteration, we might have introduced unreachable control flow (e.g., there is a condition in the loop body that is satisfied only in the third iteration). We are not allowed to check these program points since they might be false positives. Thus we only check the first block of the unrolled iterations. Most guaranteed errors inside the loop body will propagate to this point.

Function Calls: We handle functions calls by simple inlining. As for loops, we have to be careful that we do not introduce additional control flow paths. Thus, we check only the first block of an inlined function.

Obviously, inlining will not scale, since we still have to check all functions separately. Therefore, we inline only up to a certain depth and use trivial contracts for any further calls. So far, we have experienced that this is not as bad as it would seem, since doomed program points tend to have a local scope, i.e., in practice there are only few guaranteed errors that involve multiple function calls.

Experiments: The results of our experiments are shown in Table 3. The result columns show whether the respective tool detects an existing error (true positive), a non-existing error (false positive), misses an error (false negative), or does not produce a warning on correct code (true negative). The benchmark contains nine functions with one null pointer error and five without. Our algorithm is able to detect all nine null pointer errors without producing false positives. Findbugs misses three errors, but does not produce false positives either. Spec# misses true positives and produces false positives if no further information is provided. More benchmarks on the Findbugs Null Pointer Micro Benchmark can be found in [13].

All benchmarks were executed several times on a 2.4 GHz machine with 2 GB of RAM running Windows XP. Our approach is slower than Spec#. While Spec# checks each function once, our tool has to check each block of a function separately in the worst case. We are working on optimizations concerning the size and construction of the formula and the interaction with the theorem prover, but for the worst case our algorithm will always be slower than Spec#.

Table 3. Comparison of Exorcise, Findbugs and Spec# on the Findbugs Null Pointer Micro Benchmark and the example from Figures 1, 2, and 3. The columns list the analyzed function, whether it contains a bug, the running time and result of Exorcise, the result of Findbugs, and running time and result of Spec#. Results can either be true positives if an error is found, true negatives if no error is reported on correct programs, false positives if a non-existing error is reported, or false negatives if an existing error is overlooked.

		Exorcise		Findbugs [13]	Spec# [2]	
program	incorrect?	time (in ms)	result	result	time (in ms)	result
fp1	no	156	true neg	true neg	39	true neg
tp1	yes	171	true pos	false neg	27	true pos
fp2	no	160	true neg	true neg	35	true neg
tp2	yes	160	true pos	false neg	27	true pos
fp3	no	175	true neg	true neg	50	true neg
tp3	yes	187.5	true pos	true pos	58.5	true pos
tp4	yes	109.2	true pos	true pos	35	true pos
fp4	no	171	true neg	true neg	43	true neg
tp5	yes	152	true pos	true pos	15.5	true pos
tp6	yes	144	true pos	true pos	31	true pos
itp1	yes	109.2	true pos	false neg	15.6	false neg
ifp1	no	93.6	true neg	true neg	46.8	true neg
itp2	yes	15.6	true pos	true pos	0	false neg
itp3	yes	46.8	true pos	true pos	15.6	false neg
TRIVIAL	yes	179.5	true pos	true pos	54.5	true pos
LOOP	yes	699	true pos	false neg	129	true pos, 3 false pos
COMPLEX	no	246	true neg	true neg	43	2 false pos
Total Time		3.2 s		4.53 s	0.67 s	

The times measured for Findbugs are not directly comparable to those for our analysis, since Findbugs computes many pieces of additional information. For larger programs, Findbugs should be faster than Spec# and Exorcise, but so far we have not found a good benchmark that is available in both C# and Java.

The big bottleneck of this approach is that our algorithm has to check for each block if it contains a doomed program point. Using the insight that a block that has only one successor will be doomed if the successor is doomed, we can reduce the number of checked blocks. Furthermore, using the optimization from the previous section, we observe that the theorem prover, after checking the first block, can reuse large parts of its work for the remaining blocks. Table 4 shows how much time our implementation spends on constructing the EVC, checking the first block, and checking all further blocks. Looking at e.g., the function Loop, we observe that the time spent on checking all blocks but the first one is less then checking the first block.

Table 4. Number of total blocks checked and the time (in ms) consumed for constructing the EVC, checking the first block, and the average time for all further blocks

program	# queries	EVC construction (ms)	1st block (ms)	avg ms/block
tp1	5	17	134	2
Trivial	3	17	150	2
Loop	7	62	391	23
Complex	5	18	166	5

8 Conclusion

The main contribution of this work is the idea of error verification and the demonstration that this idea can be realized in practice. We have shown that error verification can easily be integrated in extended static checkers or program verifiers that provide the infrastructure for generating verification conditions and automatic theorem provers to check them. We therefore believe that this idea can now be adopted and extended by many others. We see a huge potential in this work as this can be a formal method which is applicable by every programmer. Using the fact that it can be built on top of e.g., Spec#, it also allows the programmer to annotate his program using e.g., pre- and postconditions to see if certain properties are always violated. This allows a smooth learning curve towards the use of full program verification.

We see much room for further improvements of our method. For instance, we want to optimize error verification by developing specialized techniques for finding *correct* executions, so that error verification conditions are quickly recognized as invalid. Doomed program points are sparse; i.e., almost all generated error verification conditions are not valid in practice (this is in contrast with the usual verification conditions, for correctness). Every programmer's experience confirms the intuition that it is easier to find a correct execution (for a program fragment that has no guaranteed error) than to find an incorrect one (for a program fragment that may lead to an error). This gives an interesting potential for optimization.

Maybe the best reason to use our approach is that there is no argument against it: our method is fully automatic and it remains invisible to the user as long as no doomed program point is found. If a warning is emitted, then this is a definite indication that the program is incorrect.

References

1. Ayewah, N., Pugh, W., David Morgenthaler, J., Penix, J., Zhou, Y.: Evaluating static analysis defect warnings on production software. In: Workshop on Program Analysis for Software Tools and Engineering, PASTE, pp. 1–8. ACM, New York (2007)
2. Barnett, M., Chang, B.-Y.E., DeLine, R., Jacobs, B., Leino, K.R.M.: Boogie: A modular reusable verifier for object-oriented programs. In: de Boer, F.S., Bonsangue, M.M., Graf, S., de Roever, W.-P. (eds.) FMCO 2005. LNCS, vol. 4111, pp. 364–387. Springer, Heidelberg (2006)
3. Barnett, M., Leino, K.R.M.: Weakest-precondition of unstructured programs. In: Workshop on Program Analysis for Software Tools and Engineering, PASTE, pp. 82–87. ACM, New York (2005)
4. Barnett, M., Leino, K.R.M., Schulte, W.: The Spec# programming system: An overview. In: Barthe, G., Burdy, L., Huisman, M., Lanet, J.-L., Muntean, T. (eds.) CASSIS 2004. LNCS, vol. 3362, pp. 49–69. Springer, Heidelberg (2005)
5. Chatterjee, S., Lahiri, S., Qadeer, S., Rakamaric, Z.: A reachability predicate for analyzing low-level software. In: Grumberg, O., Huth, M. (eds.) TACAS 2007. LNCS, vol. 4424, pp. 19–33. Springer, Heidelberg (2007)
6. Cohen, E., Moskal, M., Schulte, W., Tobies, S.: A practical verification methodology for concurrent programs. Technical Report MSR-TR-2009-15, Microsoft Research (February 2009)
7. Cytron, R., Ferrante, J., Rosen, B.K., Wegman, M.N., Kenneth Zadeck, F.: Efficiently computing static single assignment form and the control dependence graph. ACM Transactions on Programming Languages and Systems, TOPLAS 13(4), 451–490 (1991)
8. Dijkstra, E.W.: A Discipline of Programming. Prentice Hall, Englewood Cliffs (1976)
9. Evans, D., Larochelle, D.: Improving security using extensible lightweight static analysis. IEEE Software 19(1), 42–51 (2002)
10. Flanagan, C., Leino, K.R.M., Lillibridge, M., Nelson, G., Saxe, J.B., Stata, R.: Extended static checking for Java. In: ACM Conference on Programming Language Design and Implementation, PLDI, pp. 234–245. ACM, New York (2002)
11. Flanagan, C., Saxe, J.B.: Avoiding exponential explosion: generating compact verification conditions. In: Annual ACM Symposium on the Principles of Programming Languages, POPL, pp. 193–205. ACM, New York (2001)
12. Henzinger, T.A., Jhala, R., Majumdar, R., Sutre, G.: Software verification with BLAST. In: Ball, T., Rajamani, S.K. (eds.) SPIN 2003. LNCS, vol. 2648, pp. 235–239. Springer, Heidelberg (2003)

13. Hovemeyer, D., Pugh, W.: Finding more null pointer bugs, but not too many. In: Workshop on Program Analysis for Software Tools and Engineering, PASTE, pp. 9–14. ACM, New York (2007)
14. Hovemeyer, D., Spacco, J., Pugh, W.: Evaluating and tuning a static analysis to find null pointer bugs. ACM SIGSOFT Software Engineering Notes 31(1), 13–19 (2006)
15. Janssen, J., Corporaal, H.: Making graphs reducible with controlled node splitting. ACM Transactions on Programming Languages and Systems, TOPLAS 19(6), 1031–1052 (1997)
16. Kuncak, V.: Modular Data Structure Verification. PhD thesis, EECS Department, Massachusetts Institute of Technology (February 2007)
17. Rustan, K., Leino, M.: Efficient weakest preconditions. Information Processing Letters, IPL 93(6), 281–288 (2005)
18. Rustan, K., Leino, M.: This is Boogie 2. Manuscript KRML 178 (June 2008), `http://research.microsoft.com/~leino/papers.html`
19. Luckham, D.C., Suzuki, N.: Verification of array, record, and pointer operations in Pascal. ACM Transactions on Programming Languages and Systems, TOPLAS 1(2), 226–244 (1979)
20. Nelson, G.: A generalization of Dijkstra's calculus. ACM Transactions on Programming Languages and Systems, TOPLAS 11(4), 517–561 (1989)
21. Rümmer, P., Shah, M.A.: Proving programs incorrect using a sequent calculus for Java Dynamic Logic. In: Gurevich, Y., Meyer, B. (eds.) TAP 2007. LNCS, vol. 4454, pp. 41–60. Springer, Heidelberg (2007)

"Carbon Credits" for Resource-Bounded Computations Using Amortised Analysis

Steffen Jost[1], Hans-Wolfgang Loidl[2], Kevin Hammond[1], Norman Scaife[3], and Martin Hofmann[2]

[1] St Andrews University, St Andrews, Scotland, UK
{jost,kh}@cs.st-andrews.ac.uk
[2] Ludwig-Maximilians University, Munich, Germany
{hwloidl,mhofmann}@tcs.ifi.lmu.de
[3] Université Blaise-Pascal, Clermont-Ferrand, France
Norman.Scaife@univ-bpclermont.fr

Abstract. Bounding resource usage is important for a number of areas, notably real-time embedded systems and safety-critical systems. In this paper, we present a fully automatic static type-based analysis for inferring upper bounds on resource usage for programs involving general algebraic datatypes and full recursion. Our method can easily be used to bound any countable resource, without needing to revisit proofs. We apply the analysis to the important metrics of worst-case execution time, stack- and heap-space usage. Our results from several realistic embedded control applications demonstrate good matches between our inferred bounds and measured worst-case costs for heap and stack usage. For time usage we infer good bounds for one application. Where we obtain less tight bounds, this is due to the use of software floating-point libraries.

1 Introduction

Programs often produce undesirable "emissions", such as littering the memory with garbage. Our work is aimed at predicting limits on such emissions in advance of execution. "Emissions" here refer to any quantifiable resource that is used by the program. In this paper, we will focus on the key resources of worst-case execution time, heap allocations, and stack usage. Predicting emissions limits is clearly desirable in general, and can be vital in safety-critical, embedded systems.

Our method can be explained by analogy to an attempted countermeasure to global warming: some governments are attempting to reduce industrial pollution by issuing tradable carbon credits. The law then dictates that each CO_2 emission must be offset by expending an appropriate number of carbon credits. It follows that the total amount of emissions is *a priori* bounded by the number of carbon credits that have been previously issued by the authorities. Following this analogy, we will similarly issue credits for computer programs. The "emissions" of each program operation must then be *immediately* justified by spending a corresponding number of credits. The use of "carbon credits" for software analysis does, however, have several advantages over the political situation: i) we can

A. Cavalcanti and D. Dams (Eds.): FM 2009, LNCS 5850, pp. 354–369, 2009.

prove that each and every emission that occurs is legitimate and that it has been properly paid for by spending credits; ii) we have zero bureaucratic overhead, since we use an efficient *compile-time* analysis, there need be no modifications whatever to the original program, and we therefore do not change actual execution costs; and iii) we provide an *automatic static analysis* that, when successful, provides a *guaranteed* upper bound on the number of credits that must be issued initially to ensure that a program can run to completion, rather than using a heuristic to determine the requirements. The amount of credits a program is allowed to spend is specified as part of its type. This allows the absolute number of credits to vary in relation to the actual input, as shown below.

Example: Tree Processing. Consider a tree-processing function *mill*, whose argument has been determined by our analysis to have type $\mathsf{tree}(\mathsf{Node}\langle 7\rangle \mid \mathsf{Leaf}\langle 0.5\rangle)$. Given this type, we can determine that processing the first tree below requires at most $23 = \lfloor 23.5 \rfloor$ credits[1]: 7 credits per node and 0.5 credits for each leaf reference; and that processing either of the other trees requires at most $\lfloor 15.5 \rfloor$ credits, regardless of aliasing.

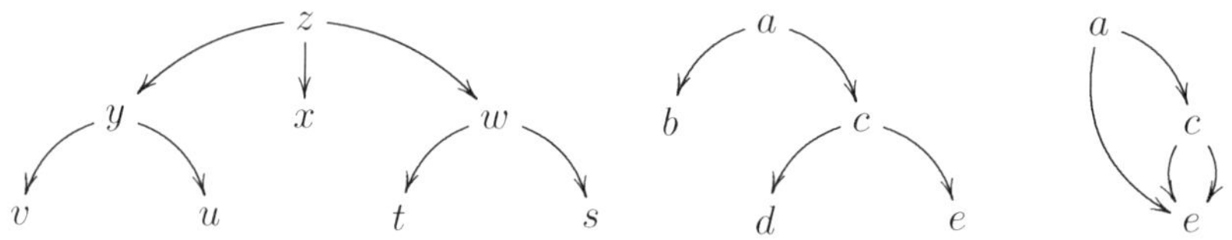

In fact, the type given by our analysis allows us to easily determine an upper bound on the cost of *mill* for any input tree. For example, for a tree of 27 nodes and 75 leaves, we can compute the credit quota from the type as $7 \cdot 27 + 0.5 \cdot 75 = 226.5$, without needing to consider the actual node or leaf values. The crucial point is that while we are analysing *mill*, our analysis only needs to keep track of this single number. Indeed, the entire dynamic state of the program at any time during its execution *could* be abstracted into such a number, representing the total unspent credits at that point in its execution. Because the number of credits must always be non-negative, this then establishes an upper bound on the total future execution costs (time or space, etc.) of the program. Note that since this includes the cost incurred by all subsequent function calls, recursive or otherwise, it follows that our analysis will also deal with outsourced emissions.

Novel contributions made by this paper: We present a fully automatic compile-time analysis for inferring upper bounds on generic program execution costs, in the form of a new resource-aware type system. The underlying principle used in our automatic analysis is a modified version of Tarjan's *amortised cost analysis* [17], as previously applied to heap allocation by Hofmann and Jost [11]. We prove that the annotated type of terms describes its maximal resource requirement with respect to a given operational semantics. Our analysis becomes automatic by providing type inference for this system and solving any constraints that are generated by using an external linear programming solver.

[1] Note while only whole credits may be spent, fractional credits can be accumulated.

Moreover, we extend previous work:

a) by dealing with arbitrary (recursive) algebraic datatypes;
b) by providing a unified generic approach that presents a soundness proof that holds for arbitrary cost metrics and for many different operational models;
c) by applying the approach to real-world examples, notably worst-case execution time on the Renesas M32C/85U processor.

Section 2 introduces a simple functional language that exhibits our analysis. We consider the soundness of our analysis in Section 5, discuss several example programs in Section 6 and cover related work in Section 7. Section 8 concludes.

2 The Schopenhauer Notation

We illustrate our approach using a simple, strict, purely functional programming language Schopenhauer (named after the German philosopher), which includes recursive datatypes and full recursion, and which is intended as a simple core language for richer notations, such as our own Hume language [9]. Schopenhauer programs comprise a set of one or more (possibly mutually recursive) function declarations. For simplicity, functions and datatypes are monomorphic (we are currently investigating the extension to polymorphic definitions).

$$
\begin{array}{lcll}
\textit{prog} & ::= & \textit{varid}_1\ \textit{vars}_1\ \texttt{=}\ \textit{expr}_1\ \texttt{;}\ \ldots\ \texttt{;}\ \textit{varid}_n\ \textit{vars}_n\ \texttt{=}\ \textit{expr}_n & n \geq 1 \\
\textit{vars} & ::= & \langle\ \textit{varid}_1\ \texttt{,}\ \ldots\ \texttt{,}\ \textit{varid}_n\ \rangle & n \geq 0 \\
\textit{expr} & ::= & \textit{const} \mid \textit{varid} \mid \textit{varid}\ \textit{vars} \mid \textit{conid}\ \textit{vars} & \\
 & \mid & \texttt{case}\ \textit{varid}\ \texttt{of}\ \textit{conid}\ \textit{vars}\ \texttt{->}\ \textit{expr}_1\ \texttt{|}\ \textit{expr}_2 & \\
 & \mid & \texttt{let}\ \textit{varid}\ \texttt{=}\ \textit{expr}_1\ \texttt{in}\ \textit{expr}_2 & \\
 & \mid & \texttt{LET}\ \textit{varid}\ \texttt{=}\ \textit{expr}_1\ \texttt{IN}\ \textit{expr}_2 &
\end{array}
$$

The Schopenhauer syntax is fairly conventional, except that: i) we distinguish variable and constructor identifiers; ii) pattern matches are not nested and only allow two branches; iii) we have two forms of let-expression; and iv) function calls are in let-normal form, i.e. arguments are always simple variables. The latter restriction is purely for convenience, since it simplifies the construction of our soundness proof in Section 5 by removing some tedious redundancies. There is no drawback to this since Schopenhauer features two kinds of let-expressions, `let` and `LET`, the former appearing in source programs, and the latter introduced as a result of internal translation. Both forms have identical semantics but they may have differing operational costs, depending on the desired operational model and on the translation into let-normal form. Since the ordinary let-expression usually incurs some overhead for managing the created reference, it cannot be used to transform expressions into let-normal form in a cost-preserving manner.

3 Schopenhauer Operational Semantics

Our operational semantics (Figure 1) is fairly standard, using a program signature Σ to map function identifiers to their defining bodies. The interesting

$$\frac{n \in \mathbb{Z} \qquad \ell \notin \mathrm{dom}(\mathcal{H})}{\mathcal{V}, \mathcal{H} \vdash^{q' + \texttt{KmkInt}}_{q'} n \rightsquigarrow \ell, \mathcal{H}[\ell \mapsto (\mathsf{int}, \mathsf{n})]} \qquad \frac{\mathcal{V}(x) = \ell}{\mathcal{V}, \mathcal{H} \vdash^{q' + \texttt{KpushVar}}_{q'} x \rightsquigarrow \ell, \mathcal{H}}$$

$$\frac{\Sigma(\mathit{fid}) = (e_f; y_1, \ldots, y_k; C; \psi) \qquad [y_1 \mapsto \mathcal{V}(x_1), \ldots, y_k \mapsto \mathcal{V}(x_k)], \mathcal{H} \vdash^{q - \texttt{Kcall}(k)}_{q' + \texttt{Kcall'}(k)} e_f \rightsquigarrow \ell, \mathcal{H}'}{\mathcal{V}, \mathcal{H} \vdash^{q}_{q'} \mathit{fid}\ \langle x_1, \cdots, x_k \rangle \rightsquigarrow \ell, \mathcal{H}'}$$

$$\frac{c \in \mathsf{Constrs} \qquad \ell \notin \mathrm{dom}(\mathcal{H}) \qquad k \geq 0 \qquad w = (\mathsf{constr}_c, \mathcal{V}(x_1), \ldots, \mathcal{V}(x_k))}{\mathcal{V}, \mathcal{H} \vdash^{q' + \texttt{KCons}(k)}_{q'} c\ \langle x_1, \ldots, x_k \rangle \rightsquigarrow \ell, \mathcal{H}[\ell \mapsto w]}$$

$$\frac{\mathcal{H}(\ell) = (c, \ell_1, \ldots, \ell_k) \qquad \mathcal{V}[y_1 \mapsto \ell_1, \ldots, y_k \mapsto \ell_k], \mathcal{H} \vdash^{q - \texttt{KCaseT}(k)}_{q' + \texttt{KCaseT'}(k)} e_1 \rightsquigarrow \ell, \mathcal{H}'}{\mathcal{V}[x \mapsto \ell], \mathcal{H} \vdash^{q}_{q'} \texttt{case}\ x\ \texttt{of}\ c\ \langle y_1, \ldots, y_k \rangle\ \texttt{->}\ e_1 \,|\, e_2 \rightsquigarrow \ell, \mathcal{H}'}$$

$$\frac{\mathcal{H}(\mathcal{V}(x)) \neq (c, \ell_1, \ldots, \ell_k) \qquad \mathcal{V}, \mathcal{H} \vdash^{q - \texttt{KCaseF}(k)}_{q' + \texttt{KCaseF'}(k)} e_2 \rightsquigarrow \ell, \mathcal{H}'}{\mathcal{V}, \mathcal{H} \vdash^{q}_{q'} \texttt{case}\ x\ \texttt{of}\ c\ \langle y_1, \ldots, y_k \rangle\ \texttt{->}\ e_1 \,|\, e_2 \rightsquigarrow \ell, \mathcal{H}'}$$

$$\frac{\mathcal{V}, \mathcal{H} \vdash^{q_1 - \texttt{KLet1}}_{q_2} e_1 \rightsquigarrow \ell_1, \mathcal{H}_1 \qquad \mathcal{V}[x \mapsto \ell_1], \mathcal{H}_1 \vdash^{q_2 - \texttt{KLet2}}_{q' + \texttt{KLet3}} e_2 \rightsquigarrow \ell_2, \mathcal{H}_2}{\mathcal{V}, \mathcal{H} \vdash^{q_1}_{q'} \texttt{let}\ x\ \texttt{=}\ e_1\ \texttt{in}\ e_2 \rightsquigarrow \ell_2, \mathcal{H}_2}$$

Note that the rule for `LET ... IN` *is identical to that for* `let ... in` *above, except in replacing constants* `KLet1`, `KLet2` *and* `KLet3` *with* `KLET1`, `KLET2` *and* `KLET3`, *respectively.*

Fig. 1. Schopenhauer Operational Semantics

feature of our semantics is that it is instrumented by a (non-negative) resource counter, which *defines* the cost of each operation. This counter is intended to *measure* execution costs, with the execution being stuck if the counter becomes negative. We will prove later that our analysis determines an upper bound on the smallest starting value for this counter, and so prevents this from happening.

An environment, $\mathcal{V}$, is a mapping from variables to locations, denoted by ℓ. A heap, $\mathcal{H}$, is a partial map from locations to values w. $\mathcal{H}[\ell \mapsto w]$ denotes a heap that maps ℓ to value w and otherwise acts as $\mathcal{H}$. Values are simple tuples whose first component is a flag that indicates the kind of the value, e.g. $(\mathsf{bool}, \mathtt{tt})$ for the boolean constant *true*, $(\mathsf{int}, 42)$ for the integer 42, etc. The judgement

$$\mathcal{V}, \mathcal{H} \vdash^{n}_{n'} e \rightsquigarrow \ell, \mathcal{H}'$$

then means that under the initial environment $\mathcal{V}$ and heap $\mathcal{H}$, the expression e evaluates to location ℓ (all values are boxed) and post-heap $\mathcal{H}'$, provided at least n units of the selected resource are available before the computation. Furthermore, n' units are available after the computation. Hence, for example, $\mathcal{V}, \mathcal{H} \vdash^{3}_{1} e \rightsquigarrow \ell, \mathcal{H}'$ simply means that 3 resource units are sufficient for evaluating e, and that exactly one is unused after the computation. This one unit might, or might not, have been used temporarily. We will simply write $\mathcal{V}, \mathcal{H} \vdash e \rightsquigarrow \ell, \mathcal{H}'$ if there exists n, n' such that $\mathcal{V}, \mathcal{H} \vdash^{n}_{n'} e \rightsquigarrow \ell, \mathcal{H}'$.

Cost Parameters. The operational rules involve a number of constants which serve as parameters for an arbitrary cost model. For example, the constant `KmkInt` denotes the cost for an integer constant. If an integer occupies two heap units, and we are interested in heap usage, we set this constant to two; if each pointer occupies a single stack unit, and we are interested in stack usage, we set this value to one; and so on. Some cost parameters are parametrised to allow better precision to be obtained, e.g. for execution time, the cost of matching a constructor may vary according to the number of arguments it has.

It is important to note that our soundness proof does not rely on any specific values for these constants. Any suitable values may be used according to the required operational cost model. While it would be possible to expand the cost parameters to vectors, in order to deal with several simultaneous metrics, for example, this would require similar vector annotations in our type systems, requiring a high notational overhead, without making a new contribution.

4 Schopenhauer Type Rules

The *annotated types* of Schopenhauer are given by the following grammar:

$$T ::= \mathsf{int} \mid X \mid \mu X.\{\ c_1{:}(q_1, \overrightarrow{T_1}) \mid \ldots \mid c_k{:}(q_k, \overrightarrow{T_k})\ \} \mid \overrightarrow{T} \xrightarrow[p']{p} T'$$

where X is a type variable, $c_i \in \mathsf{Constrs}$ are constructor labels; p, p', q_i are either non-negative rational constants or resource variables belonging to the infinite set of *resource variables* CV ranging over $\mathbb{Q}^+$; and we write $\overrightarrow{T}$ for $\langle\ T_1\ \ldots\ T_n\ \rangle$ where $n \geq 0$. For convenience, we extend all operators pointwise when used in conjunction with the vector notation i.e. $\overrightarrow{A} = \overrightarrow{B}$ stands for $\forall i\,.\,A_i = B_i$. Let ψ, ϕ, ξ range over sets of linear inequalities over resource variables. We write $\psi \Rightarrow \phi$ to denote that ψ entails ϕ, i.e. all valuations $v{:}\,\mathsf{CV} \to \mathbb{Q}^+$ which satisfy ψ also satisfy all constraints in ϕ. We write $v \Rightarrow \phi$ if the valuations satisfies all constraints. We extend valuations to types and type contexts in the obvious way. Valuations using non-negative real numbers are permissible, but rational annotations are of most interest since they allow the use of in-place update, as described in [11].

Algebraic datatypes are defined as usual, except that the type carries a resource variable for each constructor. The type rules for Schopenhauer then govern how credits are associated with runtime values of an annotated type. The number of credits associated with a runtime value w of type A is denoted by $\Phi^{v}_{\mathcal{H}}(w : A)$, formalised in Definition 2 in Section 5. Intuitively, it is the sum over all constructor nodes reachable from w, where the weight of each constructor in the sum is determined by the type A. As we have seen in the tree/mill example in the introduction, a single constructor node may contribute many times to this sum, possibly each time with a different weight, determined by the type of the reference used to access it. While this definition is paramount to our soundness proof, any practical application only requires the computation of this number for the initial memory configuration, for which it can always be easily computed. It is easy to see, for example, that the number of credits associated with a list of integers having the type $\mu X.\{\texttt{Nil} : (z_0, \langle\rangle)|\texttt{Cons} : (z, \langle \mathsf{int}, X\rangle)\}$ is simply $z_0 + n \cdot z$, where n is the length of the list. We naturally extend this definition to environments and type contexts by summation over the domain of the context.

We can now formulate the type rules for Schopenhauer (which are standard apart from the references to cost and resource variables). Let Γ denote a typing context mapping identifiers to annotated Schopenhauer types. The Schopenhauer typing judgement $\Gamma \vdash^{q}_{q'} e : A \mid \phi$ then reads "for all valuations v that satisfy all constraints in ϕ, the expression e has Schopenhauer type $v(A)$ under context $v(\Gamma)$; moreover evaluating e under environment $\mathcal{V}$ and heap $\mathcal{H}$ requires at most $v(q) + \Phi^{v}_{\mathcal{H}}(\mathcal{V} : \Gamma)$ credits and leaves at least $v(q') + \Phi^{v}_{\mathcal{H}}(\mathcal{V} : \Gamma)$ credits available afterwards". The types thus bound resource usage and we will formalise the above statement as our main theorem (Theorem 1), which requires as a precondition that the context, environment and heap are all mutually consistent.

A Schopenhauer program is a mapping Σ, called the *signature* of the program, which maps function identifiers *fid* belonging to the set Var to a quadruple consisting of: i) a term defining the function's body; ii) an ordered list of argument variables; iii) a type; and iv) a set of constraints involving the annotations of the type. Since the signature Σ is fixed for each program to be analysed, for simplicity, we omit it from the premises of each type rule. A Schopenhauer program is *well-typed* if and only if for each identifier *fid*

$$\Sigma(\mathit{fid}) = (e_{\mathit{fid}}; y_1, \ldots, y_a; \langle A_1, \ldots, A_a\rangle \xrightarrow[p']{p} C; \psi) \quad \Longrightarrow \quad y_1{:}A_1, \ldots, y_a{:}A_a \vdash^{p - \texttt{Kcall}(a)}_{p' + \texttt{Kcall}'(a)} e_{\mathit{fid}} : C \mid \psi$$

Basic Expressions. Primitive terms have fixed costs. Requiring all available credits to be spent simplifies proofs, without imposing any restrictions, since a substructural rule allows costs to be relaxed where required.

$$\frac{n \in \mathbb{Z}}{\varnothing \vdash^{\texttt{KmkInt}}_{0} n : \mathsf{int} \mid \emptyset}\ (\textsc{Int}) \qquad \frac{}{x{:}A \vdash^{\texttt{KpushVar}}_{0} x : A \mid \emptyset}\ (\textsc{Var})$$

Function Call. The cost of function application is represented by the constants $\texttt{Kcall}(k)$ and $\texttt{Kcall}'(k)$, which specify, respectively, the absolute costs of setting up before the call and clearing up after the call. In addition, each argument may carry further credits, depending on its type, to pay for the function's execution. For simplicity, we have prohibited zero-arity function calls.

$$\frac{\Sigma(\mathit{fid}) = \left(e_{\mathit{fid}}; y_1, \ldots, y_k; \langle A_1, \ldots, A_k\rangle \xrightarrow[p']{p} C; \psi\right) \qquad k \geq 1}{y_1{:}A_1, \ldots, y_k{:}A_k \vdash^{p + \texttt{Kcall}(k)}_{p' - \texttt{Kcall}'(k)} \mathit{fid}\ \langle y_1, \cdots, y_k\rangle : C \mid \psi}\ (\textsc{App})$$

Algebraic Datatypes. The Constr rule plays a crucial role in our annotated type system, since this is where available credits may be associated with a new data structure. Credits cannot be used while they are associated with data.

$$\frac{c \in \mathsf{Constrs} \qquad C = \mu X.\{\cdots \mid c : (p, \langle B_1, \ldots, B_k\rangle) \mid \cdots\} \qquad A_i = B_i \vee (A_i = C \wedge B_i = X)\ (\text{for } i = 1, \ldots, k)}{x_1{:}A_1, \ldots, x_k{:}A_k \vdash^{p + \texttt{KCons}(k)}_{0} c\ \langle x_1, \ldots, x_k\rangle : C \mid \emptyset} \quad (\text{Constr})$$

The dual to the above rule is the Case rule; the only point where credits associated with data can be released again. This is because this is the only point where we know about the actual constructor that is referenced by a variable, i.e. where we know whether a variable of a list type refers to a non-empty list, etc.

$$\frac{\begin{array}{c} c \in \mathsf{Constrs} \qquad \Gamma, y_1{:}B_1[A/X], \ldots, y_k{:}B_k[A/X] \vdash^{q_t}_{q'_t} e_1 : C \mid \psi_t \\ A = \mu X.\{\cdots \mid c : (p, \langle B_1, \ldots, B_k\rangle) \mid \cdots\} \qquad \Gamma, x{:}A \vdash^{q_f}_{q'_f} e_2 : C \mid \psi_f \\ \psi = \left\{ \begin{array}{ll} p + q = q_t + \texttt{KCaseT}(k) & q'_t = q' + \texttt{KCaseT}'(k) \\ q = q_f + \texttt{KCaseF}(k) & q'_f = q' + \texttt{KCaseF}'(k) \end{array} \right\} \end{array}}{\Gamma, x{:}A \vdash^{q}_{q'} \texttt{case}\ x\ \texttt{of}\ c\ \langle y_1, \ldots y_k\rangle\ \texttt{->}\ e_1 \mid e_2 : C \mid \psi \cup \psi_t \cup \psi_f} \quad (\text{Case})$$

Let-bindings. The two rules for let-expressions are the only ones that thread credits sequentially through the sub-rules. As in the operational semantics rules, the type rule for `LET ... IN` is identical to that below, except in replacing `KLet1`, `KLet2`, `KLet3` with `KLET1`, `KLET2`, `KLET3`, respectively. Note that we use a comma for the disjoint union of contexts throughout, hence duplicated uses of variables must be introduced through the Share rule, described in the next paragraph.

$$\frac{\Gamma \vdash^{q_1}_{q'_1} e_1 : A_1 \mid \psi_1 \qquad \Delta, x{:}A_1 \vdash^{q_2}_{q'_2} e_2 : A_2 \mid \psi_2 \qquad \psi_0 = \{\, q_1 = q - \texttt{KLet1} \quad q_2 = q'_1 - \texttt{KLet2} \quad q' = q'_2 - \texttt{KLet3} \,\}}{\Gamma, \Delta \vdash^{q}_{q'} \texttt{let}\ x = e_1\ \texttt{in}\ e_2\ :\ A_2 \mid \psi_0 \cup \psi_1 \cup \psi_2} \quad (\text{Let})$$

Substructural rules. We use explicit substructural type rules. Apart from simplifying proofs, the Share rule makes multiple uses of a variable explicit. Unlike in a strictly linear type system, variables can be used several times. However, the types of all occurrences must "add up" in such a way that the total credit associated with all occurrences is no larger than the credit initially associated with the variable. It is the job of the Share rule to track multiple occurrences, and it is the job of the $\curlyvee$-function to apportion credits.

$$\frac{\Gamma, x{:}B \vdash^{q}_{q'} e : C \mid \phi \qquad \psi \vdash A <: B}{\Gamma, x{:}A \vdash^{q}_{q'} e : C \mid \phi \cup \psi} \ (\text{Supertype}) \qquad \frac{\Gamma \vdash^{q}_{q'} e : D \mid \phi \qquad \psi \vdash D <: C}{\Gamma \vdash^{q}_{q'} e : C \mid \phi \cup \psi} \ (\text{Subtype})$$

$$\frac{\Gamma \vdash^{p}_{p'} e : A \mid \psi \quad \phi \Rightarrow \psi \cup \{q \geq p, q - p \geq q' - p'\}}{\Gamma \vdash^{q}_{q'} e : A \mid \phi} \text{(RELAX)} \qquad \frac{\Gamma \vdash^{q}_{q'} e : C \mid \psi}{\Gamma, x{:}A \vdash^{q}_{q'} e : C \mid \phi} \text{(WEAK)}$$

$$\frac{\Gamma, x{:}A_1, y{:}A_2 \vdash^{q}_{q'} e : C \mid \phi}{\Gamma, z{:}A \vdash^{q}_{q'} e[z/x, z/y] : C \mid \phi \cup \curlyvee(A \,|\, A_1, A_2)} \text{(SHARE)}$$

The ternary function $\curlyvee(A\,|B, C)$ is only defined for structurally-identical type-triples which differ in at most the names of resource variables. It returns a set of constraints that enforce the property that each resource variable in A is equal to the sum of its counterparts in B and C. The crucial property of this function is expressed in Lemma 4. For example,

$$A = \mu X.\{\texttt{Nil}{:}(a,\langle\rangle) \,|\, \texttt{Cons}{:}(d,\langle \mathsf{int}, X\rangle)\} \quad B = \mu X.\{\texttt{Nil}{:}(b,\langle\rangle) \,|\, \texttt{Cons}{:}(e,\langle \mathsf{int}, X\rangle)\}$$
$$C = \mu X.\{\texttt{Nil}{:}(c,\langle\rangle) \,|\, \texttt{Cons}{:}(f,\langle \mathsf{int}, X\rangle)\} \quad \curlyvee(A\,|B, C) = \{a = b + c, d = e + f\}$$

Subtyping. The type rules for subtyping depend on another inductively defined relation $\xi \vdash A <: B$ between two types A and B, relative to constraint set ξ. For any fixed constraint set ξ, the relation is both *reflexive* and *transitive*.

$$\frac{}{\xi \vdash A <: A} \qquad \frac{\text{for all } i \text{ holds } \xi \Rightarrow \{p_i \geq q_i\} \text{ and } \xi \vdash \overrightarrow{A_i} <: \overrightarrow{B_i}}{\xi \vdash \mu X.\{\cdots \,|\, c_i{:}(p_i, \overrightarrow{A_i}) \,|\, \cdots\} <: \mu X.\{\cdots \,|\, c_i{:}(q_i, \overrightarrow{B_i}) \,|\, \cdots\}}$$

$$\frac{\xi \Rightarrow \{p \leq q\,,\, p' \geq q'\} \qquad \xi \vdash \overrightarrow{B} <: \overrightarrow{A} \qquad \xi \vdash C <: D}{\xi \vdash \overrightarrow{A} \xrightarrow[p']{p} C <: \overrightarrow{B} \xrightarrow[q']{q} D}$$

The inference itself follows straightforwardly from these type rules. First, a standard typing derivation is constructed, and each type occurrence is annotated with fresh resource variables. The standard typing derivation is then traversed *once* to gather all the constraints. Since we found this easier to implement, substructural rules have been amalgamated with the other typing rules. Because all types have been annotated with fresh resource variables, subtyping is required throughout. Subtyping simply generates the necessary inequalities between corresponding resource variables, and will always succeed, since it is only permitted between types that differ at most in their resource annotations. Likewise, the RELAX rule is applied at each step, using the minimal constraints shown in the rule. (However, inequalities are turned into equalities using explicit slack variables, in order to minimise wasted credits.) The WEAK and SHARE rule are applied based on the free variables of the subterms.

In the final step, the constraints that have been gathered are fed to an LP-solver [2]. Any solution that is found is presented to the user in the form of an annotated type and a human-readable closed cost formula. In practice, we have found that these constraints can be easily solved by a standard LP-solver running on a typical laptop or desktop computer, partly because of their structure [11]. Since only a single pass over the program code is needed to construct these constraints, this leads to a highly efficient analysis.

5 Soundness of the Analysis

We now *sketch* the important steps for proving the main theorem. We first formalise the notion of a "well-formed" machine state, which simply says that for each variable, the type assigned by the typing context agrees with the actual value found in the heap location assigned to that variable by the environment. This is an essential invariant for our soundness proof.

Definition 1. *A memory configuration consisting of heap* $\mathcal{H}$ *and stack* $\mathcal{V}$ *is* well-formed *with respect to context* Γ *and valuation* v*, written* $\mathcal{H}\models_v\mathcal{V}:\Gamma$*, if and only if* $\mathcal{H}\models_v\mathcal{V}(x):\Gamma(x)$ *can be derived for all variables* $x \in \Gamma$*.*

$$\frac{\mathcal{H}(\ell) = (\mathsf{int}, \mathsf{n}) \qquad \mathsf{n} \in \mathbb{Z}}{\mathcal{H}\models_v \ell : \mathsf{int}} \qquad \frac{\mathcal{H}\models_v \ell : A \qquad \exists \phi \,.\, v \Leftarrow \phi \wedge \phi \vdash A <: B}{\mathcal{H}\models_v \ell : B}$$

$$\frac{\mathcal{H}(\ell) = (\mathsf{constr}_c, \ell_1, \dots, \ell_k) \quad \forall i \in \{1, \dots, k\} \,.\, \mathcal{H}\models_v \ell_i : B_i}{\mathcal{H}\models_v \ell : \mu X.\{\cdots \mid c : (q, \langle B_1, \dots, B_k\rangle) \mid \cdots\}}$$

It is obvious that evaluation must maintain a well-formed memory configuration.

Lemma 1. *If* $\mathcal{H}\models_v\mathcal{V}:\Gamma$ *and* $\mathcal{V},\mathcal{H} \vdash e \rightsquigarrow \ell, \mathcal{H}'$ *then also* $\mathcal{H}'\models_v\mathcal{V}:\Gamma$*.*

We remark that one might wish to prove a stronger statement to the effect that the result ℓ of the valuation is also well-formed given that the expression e was typeable. Unfortunately such a statement cannot be proven on its own and must necessarily be interwoven in Theorem 1.

We now formally define how credits are associated with runtime values, following our intuitive description from the previous section.

Definition 2. *If* $\mathcal{H}\models_v\ell : A$ *holds, then* $\Phi^v_{\mathcal{H}}(\ell{:}A)$ *denotes the number of credits associated with location* ℓ *for type* A *in heap* $\mathcal{H}$ *under valuation* v*. This value is always zero, except when* A *is a recursive datatype in which case it is recursively defined by*

$$\Phi^v_{\mathcal{H}}(\ell{:}A) = v(q) + \sum_i \Phi^v_{\mathcal{H}}(\ell_i{:}B_i[A/X])$$

when $A = \mu X.\{\cdots \mid c{:}(q, \langle B_1, \dots, B_k\rangle) \mid \cdots\}$ *and* $\mathcal{H}(\ell) = (\mathsf{constr}_c, \ell_1, \dots, \ell_k)$*. We extend to contexts by* $\Phi^v_{\mathcal{H}}(\mathcal{V} : \Gamma) = \sum_{x \in \mathrm{dom}(\Gamma)} \Phi^v_{\mathcal{H}}\big(\mathcal{V}(x){:}v(\Gamma(x))\big)$

Subsumption cannot increase the number of associated credits.

Lemma 2. *If* $\mathcal{H}\models_v\ell{:}A$ *and* $\phi \vdash A <: B$ *holds and* v *is a valuation satisfying* ϕ*, then* $\Phi^v_{\mathcal{H}}(\ell{:}A) \geq \Phi^v_{\mathcal{H}}(\ell{:}B)$

If a reference is duplicated, then the type of each duplicate must be a subtype of the original type.

Lemma 3. *If* $\curlyvee(A \,|\, B, C) = \phi$ *holds then also* $\phi \vdash A <: B$ *and* $\phi \vdash A <: C$*.*

The number of credits attached to any value of a certain type is always linearly shared between the two types introduced by sharing. In other words, the overall amount of available credits does not increase by using Share.

Lemma 4. *If the judgements* $\mathcal{H}\vDash_v \ell{:}A$ *and* $\curlyvee(A\,|\,B, C) = \phi$ *hold and* v *satisfies the constraint set* ϕ *then* $\Phi^v_{\mathcal{H}}(\ell{:}A) = \Phi^v_{\mathcal{H}}(\ell{:}B) + \Phi^v_{\mathcal{H}}(\ell{:}C)$. *Moreover, for* $A = B$ *and* $A = C$, *it follows that* $\Phi^v_{\mathcal{H}}(\ell{:}A) = 0$ *also holds.*

We can now formulate the main theorem (described intuitively in Section 4).

Theorem 1 (Soundness). *Fix a well-typed Schopenhauer program. Let* $r \in \mathbb{Q}^+$ *be fixed, but arbitrary. If the following statements hold*

$$\Gamma \vdash^{q}_{q'} e{:}A \mid \phi \tag{5.1}$$

$$\mathcal{V}, \mathcal{H} \vdash e \rightsquigarrow \ell, \mathcal{H}' \tag{5.2}$$

$$v : \mathsf{CV} \to \mathbb{Q}^+, \text{ satisfying } \phi \tag{5.3}$$

$$\mathcal{H}\vDash_v \mathcal{V}{:}v(\Gamma) \tag{5.4}$$

then for all $m \in \mathbb{N}$ *such that*

$$m \geq v(q) + \Phi^v_{\mathcal{H}}\big(\mathcal{V} : v(\Gamma)\big) + r \tag{5.5}$$

there exists $m' \in \mathbb{N}$ *satisfying*

$$\mathcal{V}, \mathcal{H} \vdash^{m}_{m'} e \rightsquigarrow \ell, \mathcal{H}' \tag{5.6}$$

$$m' \geq v(q') + \Phi^v_{\mathcal{H}'}\big(\ell{:}v(A)\big) + r \tag{5.7}$$

$$\mathcal{H}'\vDash_v \ell{:}v(A) \tag{5.8}$$

The proof is by induction on the lengths of the derivations of (5.2) and (5.1) ordered lexicographically, with the derivation of the evaluation taking priority over the typing derivation. This is required since an induction on the length of the typing derivation alone would fail for the case of function application, which increases the length of the typing derivation. On the other hand, the length of the derivation for the term evaluation never increases, but may remain unchanged where the final step of the typing derivation was obtained by a substructural rule. In these cases, the length of the typing derivation does decrease, allowing an induction over lexicographically ordered lengths of both derivations.

The proof is complex, but unsurprising for most rules. The arbitrary value r is required to "hide" excess credits when applying the induction hypothesis for subexpressions, which leaves those credits untouched. We show one case to provide some flavour of the overall proof:

$\rightsquigarrow$ CASE SUCCEED: By the induction hypothesis, we obtain for all $m_0 \geq v(q_t) + \Phi^v_{\mathcal{H}}(\mathcal{K}_i{:}B_i[A/X]) + \Phi^v_{\mathcal{H}}(\mathcal{V}{:}\Gamma) + r$ a suitable $m'_0 \geq v(q'_t) + \Phi^v_{\mathcal{H}}(\ell{:}C) + r$ such that e_1 evaluates under the annotated operational semantics with m_0 and m'_0. Observe that we have $\Phi^v_{\mathcal{H}}(\mathcal{K}{:}A) = v(p) + \sum_i \Phi^v_{\mathcal{H}}(\mathcal{K}_i{:}B_i[A/X])$ and $v(p) + v(q) = v(q_t) + \mathtt{KCaseT}(k)$ and $v(q'_t) = v(q') + \mathtt{KCaseT}'(k)$. Therefore $m = m_0 + \mathtt{KCaseT}(k) \geq v(q) + v(p) + \Phi^v_{\mathcal{H}}(\mathcal{K}_i{:}B_i[A/X]) + \Phi^v_{\mathcal{H}}(\mathcal{V}{:}\Gamma) + r = v(q) + \Phi^v_{\mathcal{H}}(\mathcal{K}{:}A) + \Phi^v_{\mathcal{H}}(\mathcal{V}{:}\Gamma) + r$ and $m' = m'_0 - \mathtt{KCaseT}'(k) \geq val(q') + \Phi^v_{\mathcal{H}}(\ell{:}C) + r$ as required.

Table 1. Table of Resource Constants for Stack, Heap and Time

Constant	Stack	Heap	WCET[2]	Constant	Stack	Heap	WCET[2]
KmkInt	1	2	83	KCaseF(k)	0	0	205
KpushVar	1	0	39	KCaseF′(k)	0	0	$56 + \text{RET}$
Kcall(k)	$4 + k$	0	142	KLet1	1	0	142
Kcall′(k)	$-(4 + k)$	0	$53 + \text{RET}$	KLet2	0	0	0
KCons(k)	$1 - k$	$2 + k$	$107 + 54k$	KLet3	-1	0	$3 + \text{RET}$
KCaseT(k)	$k - 1$	0	$301 + 80k$	KLET1	0	0	0
KCaseT′(k)	$-k$	0	$65 + \text{RET}$	KLET2	0	0	0
				KLET3	0	0	0

Table 2. Measurement and Analysis Results for Tree-Flattening

	N = 1			N = 2			N = 3			N = 4			N = 5		
	Heap	Stack	Time	Heap	Stack	Time	Heap	Stack	Time	Heap	Stack	Time	Heap	Stack	Time
revApp															
Analysis	14	25	2440	24	26	3596	34	27	4752	44	28	5908	54	29	7064
Measured	14	24	1762	24	24	2745	34	24	3725	44	24	4707	54	24	5687
Ratio	1	1.04	1.39	1	1.08	1.31	1	1.13	1.27	1	1.17	1.26	1	1.21	1.24
flatten															
Analysis	17	24	3311	34	34	6189	51	44	9067	68	54	11945	85	64	14823
Measured	17	24	2484	34	33	4372	51	43	6260	68	43	8148	85	43	10036
Ratio	1	1.00	1.33	1	1.03	1.42	1	1.02	1.45	1	1.26	1.47	1	1.49	1.48

6 Example Cost Analysis Results

In this section, we compare the bounds inferred by our analysis with concrete measurements for one operational model. Heap and stack results were obtained by instrumenting the generated code. Time measurements were obtained from unmodified code on a 32MHz Renesas M32C/85U embedded micro-controller with 32kB RAM. The cost parameters used for this operational model are shown in Table 1. The time metrics were obtained by applying AbsInt GmbH's **aiT** tool [8] to the compiled code of individual abstract machine instructions.

Our first example is a simple tree-flattening function and its auxiliary function, reverse-append. The *heap space consumption* inferred by our analysis is encoded as the following annotated type

```
SCHOPENHAUER typing for HumeHeapBoxed:
0, (tree[Leaf<10>:int|Node:#,#]) -(2/0)-> list[C:int,#|N] ,0
```

which reads, "for a given tree with l leaves, the heap consumption is $10l + 2$." Table 2 compares analysis and measurement results. As test input, we use

[2] Returns are performed through a fixed size table. On the Renesas M32C/85U this is compiled to a series of branches and the WCET therefore depends on the number of calling points in the program. We have $\text{RET} = \max(116, 51 + 15 \cdot (\#\text{ReturnLabels}))$.

balanced trees with $N = 1 \ldots 5$ leaves. Heap prediction is an exact match for the measured results. Stack prediction follows a linear bound over-estimating actual costs, which are logarithmic in general, using a tail-recursive reverse function. This linear bound is due to the design of our analysis, which cannot infer re-use of stack space in all cases (Campbell has described an extension to our approach [4] that may improve this). The predicted time costs are between 33% and 48% higher than the measured worst-cases.

6.1 Control Application: Inverted Pendulum

Our next example is an inverted pendulum controller. This implements a simple, real-time control engineering problem. A pendulum is hinged upright at the end of a rotating arm. Both rotary joints are equipped with angular sensors, which are the inputs for the controller (arm angle θ and pendulum angle α). The controller should produce as its output the electric potential for the motor that rotates the arm in such a way that the pendulum remains in an upright position.

The Hume code comprises about 180 lines of code, which are translated into about 800 lines of Schopenhauer code for analysis. The results for heap and stack usage (upper part of Table 3) show exact matches in both cases. For time we have measured the best-case (36118), worst-case (47635) and average number of clock cycles (42222) required to process the controlling loop over 6000 iterations during an actual run, where the Renesas M32C/85U actually controlled the inverted pendulum. Compared to the worst-case execution time (WCET) bound given by our automated analysis (63678) we have a margin of 33.7% between the predicted WCET and the worst measured run. The hard real-time constraint on this application is that the pendulum controller can only be made stable with a loop time of less than about 10ms. The measured loop time is 1.488ms, while our predicted loop time would be 1.989ms, showing that our controller is guaranteed to be fast enough to successfully control the pendulum under all circumstances.

6.2 Control Application: Biquadratic Filter

Our final control application is a second-order recursive linear filter, a biquadratic filter, so named because the transfer function is a ratio of two quadratic polynomials. It is commonly used in audio work and can be used to implement low-pass, high-pass, band-pass and notch filters. Well-known algorithms exist for computing filter coefficients from the desired gain, centre frequency and sample rate [14].

The lower part of Table 3 compares analysis results against measured costs for the components of the biquadratic filter. For heap, we obtain exact bounds for all but one box. For stack, we find a close match of the bounds with the measured values (within 12% units). For time, however, the bounds are significantly worse than the measured values. This is mainly due to the heavy use of floating-point operations in this application, which are implemented in software on the Renesas M32C/85U. This means that the WCET bounds for the primitive operations in the analysis cost table are already very slack.

Table 3. Comparison of Results for Pendulum and Biquad Filter Applications

Box	Analysis			Measured			Ratio		
	Heap	Stack	Time	Heap	Stack	Time	Heap	Stack	Time
pendulum									
control	299	93	63678	299	93	47635	1.00	1.00	1.34
biquad									
biquad	33	32	10330	33	32	5848	1.00	1.00	1.77
compute_filter	73	62	26392	73	59	13176	1.00	1.05	2.00
compute_params	40	38	47307	40	34	16107	1.00	1.12	2.94
scale_in	14	15	3919	10	15	1844	1.40	1.00	2.13
scale_out	33	33	16044	33	33	5920	1.00	1.00	2.71

The critical path through the system comprises the `scale_in`, `biquad` and `scale_out` boxes. If we sum their bounds, we obtain a total of 30293 clock cycles, or 947μs. This gives us a sample rate of about 1.056kHz, obviously well short of audio sampling rates of about 48kHz. However, this is a concrete guarantee for the application, and it tells us at an early stage, *without any measurement*, that the hardware we are using is not fast enough for real-time audio processing. The heap and stack bounds confirm, however, that we can fit static and dynamic memory on the board. The components are executed sequentially, so the largest component governs the dynamic memory for the entire system: this is 73 *heap* + 62 *stack* cells for the `compute_filter` box, or a maximum of 540 bytes of memory, well within our design maximum of 32kB.

One distinctive feature of our analysis is that it attributes costs to individual data type constructors. Therefore, our bounds are not only size-dependent, as would be expected, but more generally data-dependent. For a worst-case execution time analysis of `compute_filter`, we produce the following explanation:

```
Worst-case Time-units required to compute box compute_filter once:
  359 + 9374*X1 + 16659*X2 + 16123*X3 + 14570*X4     where
         X1 = one if 1. wire is live, zero if the wire is void
         X2 = number of "BPF" nodes at 1. position
         X3 = number of "HPF" nodes at 1. position
         X4 = number of "LPF" nodes at 1. position
```

In particular, since `BPF`, `HPF` and `LPF` are elements of an enumeration type, selecting a band pass, high pass or low pass filter, respectively, we know that only one of the three costs attached to these constructors (16659, 16123 or 14570) will apply. Furthermore, in the case where a null filter is selected, by providing `NULLF` as input, none of these three costs applies and the time bound for this case is, therefore, 9733 clock cycles. Being data-dependent, this parametrised bound is more accurate than the worst-case bound specified in Table 3, where we take the worst-case over all constructors to derive a value of 26392 clock cycles.

7 Related Work

While there has been significant interest in the use of amortised analysis for resource usage, in contrast to the work presented in this paper, none of this work considers multiple resources, none of the work has studied worst-case execution time, and none of it covers arbitrary recursive data structures. In particular, a notable difference to Tarjan's seminal work [17] (in addition to the fact that we perform automatic inference) is that credits are associated on a *per-reference* basis and not on the basis of the pure data layout in the memory. Okasaki [15] resorted to the use of *lazy evaluation* to solve this problem. In contrast, our per-reference credits can be directly applied to strict evaluation.

Hofmann and Jost were the first to develop an *automatic* amortised analysis for heap consumption [11], exploiting a difference metric similar to that used by Crary and Weirich [7] (the latter, however, only *check* bounds, and do not *infer* them, as we do). Hofmann and Jost have extended their method to cover a comprehensive subset of Java, including imperative updates, inheritance and type casts [12]. Shkaravska et al. subsequently considered heap consumption inference for first-order polymorphic lists, and are currently studying extensions to non-linear bounds [16]. Finally, Campbell [4] has developed the ideas of depth-based and temporary credit uses to give better results for stack usage.

A related idea is that of *sized types* [13], which express bounds on data structure sizes, and are attached to types in the same way as our *weights*. The difference to our work is that sized types express bounds on the size of the underlying data structure, whereas our weights are factors of the corresponding sizes, which may remain unknown. The original work on sized types was limited to type checking, but subsequent work has developed inference mechanisms [5,18].

A number of authors have recently studied analyses for heap usage. Albert et al. [1] present a fully automatic, live heap-space analysis for an object-oriented bytecode language with a scoped-memory manager. Most notably it is not restricted to a certain complexity class, and produces a closed-form upper bound function over the size of the input. However, unlike our system, data-dependencies cannot be expressed. Braberman et al. [3] infer polynomial bounds on the live heap usage for a Java-like language with automatic memory management. However, unlike our system, they do not cover general recursive methods. Finally, Chin et al. [6] present a heap and a stack analysis for a low-level (assembler) language with explicit (de-)allocation, which is also restricted to linear bounds.

8 Conclusions and Further Work

By developing a new type-based analysis, we have been able to automatically infer linear bounds on real-time, heap and stack costs for strict functional programs with algebraic data-types. The use of *amortised costs* allows us to determine a *provable* upper bound on the overall resource cost of running a program, by attaching numerical annotations to constructors. Thus, our analysis is not just size-dependent but also data-dependent. We have extended previous work on the inference of amortised costs [11] by considering arbitrary (recursive) data structures and by constructing a generic treatment of resource usage through our resource tables. In this way, we are able to separate the mechanics of our approach from the operational semantics that applies to the usage of a given resource. Previous work [10,11,12,18] has been restricted to the treatment of a single resource type, and usually also to list homomorphisms. For all programs studied here, we determine very tight bounds on both heap and stack usage. Our results show that the bounds we infer for worst-case execution times can be within 33.7% of the measured costs. However, in some degenerate cases they can be significantly higher (in some cases due to the use of *software* floating-point operations whose time behaviour can be difficult to analyse effectively).

We are currently experimenting with a number of further extensions. We have developed a working prototype implementation dealing with higher-order functions with flexible cost annotations and partial application (`http://www.embounded.org/software/cost/cost.cgi`). The corresponding (and extensive) theoretical proof is still, however, in preparation. This implementation also deals with many useful extended language constructs, such as optimised conditionals for a boolean base type, pattern-matches having multiple cases, multiple let-definitions, etc. Most of these extensions are theoretically straightforward, and in the interest of brevity, we have therefore excluded them from this paper.

We now intend to study how to improve our time results, to determine how to extend our work to non-linear bounds, and to determine whether sized types can be effectively combined with amortised analysis. We are also working to extend our study of worst-case execution time so that it covers other interesting embedded systems architectures, e.g. the Freescale MPC555 for automotive applications. Since this has a hardware floating-point unit, we anticipate that the issues we have experienced with software floating-point operations on the Renesas M32C/85U will no longer be a concern on this new architecture.

Acknowledgements

We thank Hugo Simões and our anonymous reviewers for their useful comments, and Christoph Herrmann for performing measurements on the Renesas architecture. This work is supported by EU Framework VI grants IST-510255 (EmBounded) and IST-15905 (Mobius); and by EPSRC grant EP/F030657/1 (Islay).

References

1. Albert, E., Genaim, S., Gómez-Zamalloa, M.: Live Heap Space Analysis for Languages with Garbage Collection. In: Proc. ISMM 2009: Intl. Symp. on Memory Management, Dublin, Ireland, June 2009, pp. 129–138. ACM, New York (2009)
2. Berkelaar, M., Eikland, K., Notebaert, P.: lp_solve: Open source (mixed-integer) linear programming system. GNU LGPL (Lesser General Public Licence), `http://lpsolve.sourceforge.net/5.5`

3. Braberman, V., Fernández, F., Garbervetsky, D., Yovine, S.: Parametric Prediction of Heap Memory Requirements. In: Proc. ISMM 2008: Intl. Symp. on Memory Management, Tucson, USA, June 2008, pp. 141–150. ACM, New York (2008)
4. Campbell, B.: Amortised Memory Analysis Using the Depth of Data Structures. In: Castagna, G. (ed.) ESOP 2009. LNCS, vol. 5502, pp. 190–204. Springer, Heidelberg (2009)
5. Chin, W.-N., Khoo, S.-C.: Calculating Sized Types. Higher-Order and Symbolic Computing 14(2,3), 261–300 (2001)
6. Chin, W.-N., Nguyen, H., Popeea, C., Qin, S.: Analysing Memory Resource Bounds for Low-Level Programs. In: Proc. ISMM 2008: Intl. Symp. on Memory Management, Tucson, USA, June 2008, pp. 151–160. ACM, New York (2008)
7. Crary, K., Weirich, S.: Resource Bound Certification. In: Proc. POPL 2000: ACM Symp. on Principles of Prog. Langs., Boston, USA, January 2000, pp. 184–198. ACM, New York (2000)
8. Ferdinand, C., Martin, F., Wilhelm, R., Alt, M.: Cache Behavior Prediction by Abstract Interpretation. Science of Comp. Prog. 35(2), 163–189 (1999)
9. Hammond, K., Michaelson, G.: Hume: a Domain-Specific Language for Real-Time Embedded Systems. In: Pfenning, F., Smaragdakis, Y. (eds.) GPCE 2003. LNCS, vol. 2830, pp. 37–56. Springer, Heidelberg (2003)
10. Hofmann, M.: A Type System for Bounded Space and Functional In-Place Update. Nordic Journal of Computing 7(4), 258–289 (Winter 2000)
11. Hofmann, M., Jost, S.: Static Prediction of Heap Space Usage for First-Order Functional Programs. In: Proc. POPL 2003: ACM Symp. on Principles of Prog. Langs., New Orleans, USA, January 2003, pp. 185–197. ACM, New York (2003)
12. Hofmann, M., Jost, S.: Type-Based Amortised Heap-Space Analysis. In: Sestoft, P. (ed.) ESOP 2006. LNCS, vol. 3924, pp. 22–37. Springer, Heidelberg (2006)
13. Hughes, R., Pareto, L., Sabry, A.: Proving the Correctness of Reactive Systems Using Sized Types. In: Proc. POPL 1996: ACM Symp. on Principles of Prog. Langs, St. Petersburg Beach, USA, January 1996, pp. 410–423. ACM, New York (1996)
14. Kuo, S.M., Lee, B.H., Tian, W.: Real-Time Digital Signal Processing: Implementations and Applications, 2nd edn., April 2006. Wiley, Chichester (2006)
15. Okasaki, C.: Purely Functional Data Structures. Cambridge University Press, Cambridge (1998)
16. Shkaravska, O., van Kesteren, R., van Eekelen, M.: Polynomial Size Analysis of First-Order Functions. In: Della Rocca, S.R. (ed.) TLCA 2007. LNCS, vol. 4583, pp. 351–365. Springer, Heidelberg (2007)
17. Tarjan, R.E.: Amortized Computational Complexity. SIAM Journal on Algebraic and Discrete Methods 6(2), 306–318 (1985)
18. Vasconcelos, P., Hammond, K.: Inferring Cost Equations for Recursive, Polymorphic and Higher-Order Functional Programs. In: Trinder, P., Michaelson, G.J., Peña, R. (eds.) IFL 2003. LNCS, vol. 3145, pp. 86–101. Springer, Heidelberg (2004)

Field-Sensitive Value Analysis by Field-Insensitive Analysis

Elvira Albert[1], Puri Arenas[1], Samir Genaim[1], and Germán Puebla[2]

[1] DSIC, Complutense University of Madrid (UCM), Spain
[2] CLIP, DLSIIS, Technical University of Madrid (UPM), Spain

Abstract. Shared and mutable data-structures pose major problems in static analysis and most analyzers are unable to keep track of the values of *numeric variables* stored in the heap. In this paper, we first identify sufficient conditions under which heap allocated numeric variables in object oriented programs (i.e., numeric fields) can be handled as non-heap allocated variables. Then, we present a static analysis to infer which numeric fields satisfy these conditions at the level of (sequential) *bytecode*. This allows instrumenting the code with *ghost* variables which make such numeric fields observable to any field-insensitive value analysis. Our experimental results in termination analysis show that we greatly enlarge the class of analyzable programs with a reasonable overhead.

1 Introduction

Static analyses which approximate the value of numeric variables have a large application field which includes its use for invariant generation, for finding ranking functions [15] which bound the number of iterations of loops in cost analysis, etc. Most existing *value* analyses are only applicable to numeric variables which satisfy two conditions: (1) all occurrences of a variable refer to the same memory location, and (2) memory locations can only be modified using the corresponding variable. Some notable exceptions are [8,11,10]. In general, the conditions above are not satisfied when numeric variables are stored in shared mutable data structures such as the heap. Condition (1) does not hold because memory locations (numeric variables) are accessed using reference variables, whose value can change during the execution. Condition (2) does not hold because a memory location can be modified using different references which are aliases and point to such memory location.

Example 1. Consider the following loop where *size* is a field of integer type:
while $(x.f.size > 0)$ $\{i{=}i{+}y.size; \quad x.f.size{=}x.f.size{-}1;\}$
This loop terminates in sequential execution because $x.f.size$ decreases at each iteration and, for any initial value of $x.f.size$, there are only a finite number of values which $x.f.size$ can take before reaching zero. Unfortunately, applying standard value analyses on numeric fields can produce wrong results, and further conditions are required. E.g., if we add the instruction $x{=}x.next$; within the loop body, the memory location pointed to by $x.f$ changes, invalidating Condition 1. Also, if we add $y.size{+}{+}$; as $x.f$ and y may be aliases, Condition 2 is false. □

A. Cavalcanti and D. Dams (Eds.): FM 2009, LNCS 5850, pp. 370–386, 2009.

This paper presents a novel approach for approximating the value of *numeric fields* in object-oriented programs which greatly improves the precision over existing field-insensitive value analyses while introducing a reasonable overhead. Our approach is developed for object-oriented *bytecode*, i.e., code compiled for *virtual machines* such as the Java virtual machine [9] or .NET, and consists of the following steps: (1) partition the program to be analyzed into *scopes*, (2) identify *trackable* numeric fields which meet the above conditions and hence can be safely handled by field-insensitive value analysis, (3) transform the program by introducing local *ghost* variables whose values represent the values of the corresponding numeric fields, and (4) analyze the transformed program scope by scope using existing field-insensitive value analysis. This allows reusing the large body of work devoted to numerical static analysis: polyhedra [7], intervals [6], octagons [12], etc.

Example 2. Consider the loop in Ex. 1, with a single scope. There are three program points where a numeric field with signature *size* is accessed for reading and one where it is accessed for writing. In this paper, we develop a *Reference Constancy Analysis* (RCA for short) which is able to infer that the references used in all four accesses are *constant* in the sense that, in all iterations of the loop, such references do not change their value. For brevity, in the rest of the paper we say that an access is constant to indicate that the reference used in the corresponding program point is constant. Our analysis also provides a symbolic representation of such values. This allows determining that the two read accesses and the write access through $x.f.size$ not only are constant but also they have the same value in the three different program points. This is sufficient for guaranteeing Condition 1 above. Besides, since in the loop there are no other write accesses using the signature *size*, Condition 2 above is also guaranteed. Thus, we can safely introduce a ghost variable, which becomes local variable v, and corresponds to the value of the numeric field $x.f.size$ in all three program points. As regards the read access $y.size$, RCA is able to prove that it is constant. However, Condition (2) cannot be proved since by looking at the loop alone it is not possible to know whether $x.f$ and y are aliases. Therefore no ghost variable can be introduced for $y.size$. The transformed loop is as follows:

$v = x.f.size$; *while* $(v{>}0)$ $\{i{=}i{+}y.size;\quad x.f.size{=}x.f.size\text{-}1;\quad v{=}v\text{-}1;\}$

Read accesses to $x.f.size$ are replaced by equivalent accesses to the ghost variable v. For write accesses, we keep the original access and replicate it using the corresponding ghost variable. This is because there may be aliases for $x.f.size$ outside the loop which may need the value of the original numeric field. A standard value analysis can now infer that v decreases, which guarantees termination. □

2 The Bytecode Language in Rule-Based Form

Since reasoning about bytecode programs is complicated, it is customary to formalize analyses on intermediate representations of the bytecode (e.g., [18]). We consider a simplified form of the rule-based *recursive* language of [2]. A *bytecode program* consists of a set of *procedures* and classes. A procedure p with k input arguments $\bar{x}{=}x_1,\ldots,x_k$ and m output arguments $\bar{y}{=}y_1,\ldots,y_m$ is defined by one or more *guarded rules*. Without loss of generality, we assume that there are no two procedures with the same name and different number of arguments. Though Java bytecode methods only have one output argument, we allow multiple output arguments since, as discussed in Sec. 4, our program transformation may introduce additional output arguments. Rules are defined as:

$$\begin{array}{ll} rule ::= p(\langle\bar{x}\rangle,\langle\bar{y}\rangle) \leftarrow g, b_1,\ldots,b_t & g ::= \mathsf{true} \mid bexp_1\ op\ bexp_2 \mid \mathsf{type}(x,c) \\ b ::= x{:=}exp \mid x{:=}\mathsf{new}\ c \mid x{:=}y.f \mid x.f{:=}y \mid q(\langle\bar{x}\rangle,\langle\bar{y}\rangle) & \\ bexp ::= x \mid \mathsf{null} \mid n & exp ::= bexp \mid x{-}y \mid x{+}y \mid x{*}y \mid x/y \\ op ::= > \mid < \mid \leq \mid \geq \mid = \mid \neq & \end{array}$$

where $p(\langle\bar{x}\rangle,\langle\bar{y}\rangle)$ is the *head* of the rule; g its guard, i.e., necessary conditions for the rule to be applicable; $b_1,\ldots,b_t$ the body of the rule; n an integer; x and y variables; f a field signature (i.e., globally unique), and $q(\langle\bar{x}\rangle,\langle\bar{y}\rangle)$ a procedure call (by value). We often do not write guards which are true. The language supports class definition, object creation, field manipulation, and type comparison through the instruction $\mathsf{type}(x,c)$, which succeeds if the runtime class of x is exactly c. A class c is a finite set of typed field names, where the type can be integer or a class name. The key features of this language are: (1) *recursion* is the only iteration mechanism, (2) *guards* are the only form of conditional, (3) there is no operand stack, (4) objects can be seen as records, and the behaviour induced by dynamic dispatch is compiled into *dispatch* blocks guarded by type checks, and (5) rules may have *multiple* return values. The translation from (Java) bytecode to the rule-based form is performed in two steps. First, a *control flow graph* (CFG) is built. Second, a *rule* is defined for each block and the operand stack is *flattened* by considering its elements as local variables [2].

We now introduce some terminology used to define an *operational semantics* for rule-based bytecode. An *activation record* is of the form $\langle p, bc, tv\rangle$, where p is a procedure name, bc is a possibly empty sequence of instructions and tv a variable mapping. Executions proceed between *configurations* of the form $A;h$, where A is a stack of activation records (which grows leftward) and h is the *heap*, i.e., a partial mapping from an infinite set of *memory locations* to *objects*. We use $h(r)$ to denote the object referred to by r in h and $h[r\mapsto o]$ to indicate the result of updating the heap h by making $h(r) = o$. An object o is a pair consisting of the object class tag and a mapping from field names to values which is consistent with the types of the fields. We use $o.f$ or $o(f)$ to refer to the value of the field f in the object o, and $o[f{\mapsto}v]$ to set the value of $o.f$ to v. The operational semantics is quite standard and consists of the following rules:

$$(1)\quad \frac{b \equiv x{:=}exp,\quad v = eval(exp, tv)}{\langle p, b{\cdot}bc, tv\rangle{\cdot}A; h \rightsquigarrow \langle p, bc, tv[x\mapsto v]\rangle{\cdot}A; h}$$

$$(2)\quad \frac{b \equiv x{:=}\mathsf{new}\ c,\quad o{=}\mathsf{newobject}(c),\quad r{\notin}dom(h)}{\langle p, b{\cdot}bc, tv\rangle{\cdot}A; h \rightsquigarrow \langle p, bc, tv[x\mapsto r]\rangle{\cdot}A; h[r\mapsto o]}$$

$$(3)\quad \frac{b \equiv x{:=}y.f,\quad tv(y)\in \mathrm{dom}(h),\quad o = h(tv(y))}{\langle p, b{\cdot}bc, tv\rangle{\cdot}A; h \rightsquigarrow \langle p, bc, tv[x\mapsto o.f]\rangle{\cdot}A; h}$$

$$(4)\quad \frac{b \equiv x.f{:=}y,\quad r = tv(x)\in \mathrm{dom}(h),\quad o = h(r)}{\langle p, b{\cdot}bc, tv\rangle{\cdot}A; h \rightsquigarrow \langle p, bc, tv\rangle{\cdot}A; h[r\mapsto o[f\mapsto tv(y)]]}$$

$$(5)\ \frac{\begin{array}{c} b \equiv q(\langle\bar{x}\rangle, \langle\bar{y}\rangle),\ \text{there is a program rule } q(\langle\bar{x}'\rangle, \langle\bar{y}'\rangle) \leftarrow g, b_1, \cdots, b_t \\ \text{such that } tv' = newenv(q),\ \forall i.tv'(x_i') = tv(x_i),\ eval(g, tv') = true \end{array}}{\langle p, b{\cdot}bc, tv\rangle{\cdot}A; h \rightsquigarrow \langle q, b_1 \cdot \ldots \cdot b_t, tv'\rangle{\cdot}\langle p[\bar{y}, \bar{y}'], bc, tv\rangle{\cdot}A; h}$$

$$(6)\ \frac{}{\langle q, \epsilon, tv\rangle{\cdot}\langle p[\bar{y}, \bar{y}'], bc, tv'\rangle{\cdot}A; h \rightsquigarrow \langle p, bc, tv'[\bar{y} \mapsto tv(\bar{y}')]\rangle{\cdot}A; h}$$

Intuitively, rule (1) accounts for all rules in the bytecode semantics which perform operations on variables. The evaluation $eval(exp, tv)$ returns the evaluation of the arithmetic or Boolean expression exp for the values of the corresponding variables from tv in the standard way, and for reference variables, it returns the reference. Rules (2), (3) and (4) deal with objects. We assume that newobject(c) creates a new object of class c and initializes its fields to either 0 or null, depending on their types. Rule (5) (resp., (6)) corresponds to calling (resp., returning from) a procedure. The notation $p[\bar{y}, \bar{y}']$ records the association between the formal and actual return variables. It is assumed that $newenv$ creates a new mapping of local variables for the corresponding method, where each variable is initialized as newobject does. Guards in different rules for the same procedure are always mutually exclusive. Execution is thus deterministic. An execution starts from an *initial configuration* $\langle start, p(\langle\bar{x}\rangle, \langle\bar{y}\rangle), tv\rangle; h$ and ends in a *final configuration* $\langle start, \epsilon, tv'\rangle; h'$ where $start$ is a marker for the initial entry which is guaranteed not to coincide with any procedure name, tv and h are initialized to suitable initial values, and tv' and h' include the final values. Program executions can be represented as *traces* $C_0 \rightsquigarrow C_1 \rightsquigarrow \cdots \rightsquigarrow C_\omega$, where C_ω is a final configuration. We use $C \rightsquigarrow^* C'$ to denote that the execution starting from C reaches C' in a finite number of steps. Non terminating executions have infinite traces.

Example 3. Consider the following rule-based form and bytecode (inside its CFG) corresponding to the method in Ex. 1 plus a final *return i*; instruction:

(1) $loop(\langle x, y, i\rangle, \langle r\rangle) \leftarrow$
  $s_0{:=}x$,
  ① $s_0{:=}s_0.f$,
  ② $s_0{:=}s_0.size$,
  $loop_c(\langle x, y, i, s_0\rangle, \langle r\rangle)$.

(2) $loop_c(\langle x, y, i, s_0\rangle, \langle r\rangle) \leftarrow$
  $\mathbf{s_0 \le 0}, s_0{:=}i, r{:=}s_0$.

(3) $loop_c(\langle x, y, i, s_0\rangle, \langle r\rangle) \leftarrow$
  $\mathbf{s_0 > 0}, s_0{:=}i, s_1{:=}y$,
  ③ $s_1{:=}s_1.size$,
  $s_0{:=}s_0{+}s_1, i{:=}s_0, s_0{:=}x$,
  ④ $s_0{:=}s_0.f,\ s_1{:=}s_0$
  ⑤ $s_1{:=}s_1.size$,
  $s_2{:=}1, s_1{:=}s_1{-}s_2$,
  ⑥ $s_0.size{:=}s_1, loop(\langle x, y, i\rangle, \langle r\rangle)$.

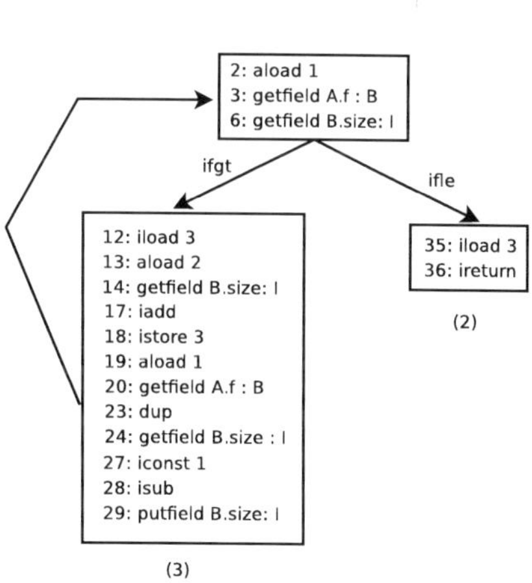

Variable names of the form s_i indicate that they originate from stack positions. Each block in the CFG is translated into a rule. The conditions on the edges become guards for the corresponding rules. Bytecode instructions are converted to a new representation. E.g., in the rule for block (2), the guard $\mathbf{s_0 \leq 0}$ corresponds to the condition ifle and iload 3 (3 refers to the third local variable i) is converted to $s_0{:=}i$. Instruction $s_1{:=}s_0$ corresponds to dup. Numbered circles are program point markers introduced for later reference. A is a class with a field of type B, and B is a class with an integer field. □

3 Reference Constancy Analysis

We present a *reference constancy analysis*, which aims at identifying reference variables which are constant at certain program points. The *program points* considered are the union of the program points of all program rules. All program points are made unique by numbering the program rules. The k-th program rule $p(\langle\bar{x}\rangle, \langle\bar{y}\rangle) \leftarrow g, b_1^k, \ldots, b_t^k$ has $t+1$ program points. The first one, $(k, 0)$, after the execution of the guard g and before the execution of b_1, then $(k, 1)$ between the execution of b_1 and b_2, until (k, t) after the execution of b_t. The analysis receives as input a program P and a procedure name p, which we refer to as *entry*. For any configuration $C = \langle q, b_i^k \cdot bc, tv\rangle \cdot A; h$ which is not initial, the program point to which C corresponds is $(k, i-1)$. Given a program P, we denote by $RF(P)$ (resp. $NF(P)$) the set of reference (resp. numeric) field signatures declared in P.

Definition 1 (access path function). *An* access path function *for a program P and an entry p is a syntactic construction of the form $l_j.f_1 \ldots f_n$, with $f_i \in RF(P)$ for $i = 1, \ldots, n$ and it represents a partial function from initial configurations to references. Given an initial configuration $C = \langle start, p(\langle\bar{x}\rangle, \langle\bar{y}\rangle), tv\rangle; h$ we define $l_j.f_1 \ldots f_n(C) \equiv h(\cdots(h(h(tv(l_j))(f_1))(f_2))\cdots)(f_n)$.*

Essentially, for determining the value of an access path in an initial configuration, we use the variable table and heap at such configuration in order to dereference w.r.t. the reference variable and reference fields in the access path. This function is undefined at paths that traverse objects which have not been allocated in the heap. Otherwise, it either returns a memory location in dom(h) or the value null. Equivalent notions have been defined for other languages (see, e.g. [1]).

Definition 2 (constant reference variable). *A reference variable z is* constant *at a program point (k, i) in a program P for an entry p w.r.t. the access path function $l_j.f_1 \ldots f_n$ if $\forall C \leadsto^* C'$ such that C is an initial configuration and $C' = \langle q, b_{i+1}^k \cdot bc, tv'\rangle \cdot A; h'$, we have $tv'(z) = l_j.f_1 \ldots f_n(C)$.*

Intuitively, a reference is constant w.r.t. an access path $l_j.f_1 \ldots f_n$ in a program point if, starting the execution from any initial configuration C, whenever we reach a configuration C' which corresponds to such program point, the reference always has the same value $l_j.f_1 \ldots f_n(C)$. Note that if execution reaches C' then $l_j.f_1 \ldots f_n(C)$ is defined since otherwise we must have attempted to dereference a null reference or a dangling pointer. In either case, the derivation would stop.

The idea behind RCA is similar in spirit to that of the classical numeric constant propagation analysis [6]. However, an important feature of RCA is that

either $\phi_1(x) = \phi_2(x)$ or $\phi_2(x) = \ell_{\mathsf{any}}$. We define $\langle\phi_1, \theta_1\rangle \sqcup_{as} \langle\phi_2, \theta_2\rangle = \langle\phi, \theta_1 \cap \theta_2\rangle$ s.t. $\phi(x) = \phi_1(x) \sqcup_{as} \phi_2(x)$. AS_d is the lattice $\langle AS, \top_{as}, \bot_{as}, \sqcup_{as}, \sqsubseteq_{as}\rangle$ where AS is the set of abstract states, $\top_{as}$ is the top of the lattice which is equal to $\langle\phi, \emptyset\rangle$ s.t $\forall x \in \mathcal{V}.\phi(x) = \ell_{\mathsf{any}}$, and $\bot_{as}$ is the bottom.

RCA assigns an abstract state from AS to each program point by relying on the transfer function $\tau : Instr \times AS \mapsto AS$ depicted in the following table:

b	$\tau(b, \langle\phi, \theta\rangle)$	*conditions*	b	$\tau(b, \langle\phi, \theta\rangle)$	*conditions*
(1) $x{:=}y.f$	$\langle\phi[x \mapsto \ell], \theta\rangle$	$f \in RF(P)$	(6) $x{:=}\mathsf{null}$	$\langle\phi[x \mapsto \ell_{\mathsf{null}}], \theta\rangle$	
(2) $x.f{:=}y$	$\langle\phi, \theta\backslash\{f\}\rangle$	$f \in RF(P)$	(7) $x{:=}exp$	$\langle\phi[x \mapsto \ell_{\mathsf{num}}], \theta\rangle$	$exp \not\equiv \mathsf{null}$
(3) $x{:=}y$	$\langle\phi[x \mapsto \phi(y)], \theta\rangle$		(8) $x \neq \mathsf{null}$	$\bot_{as}$	$\phi(x){=}\ell_{\mathsf{null}}$
(4) $x{:=}y.f$	$\langle\phi[x \mapsto \ell_{\mathsf{num}}], \theta\rangle$	$f \in NF(P)$	(9) $x.f{:=}y$	$\langle\phi, \theta\rangle$	$f{\in}NF(P)$
(5) $x{:=}$new c	$\langle\phi[x \mapsto \ell_{\mathsf{any}}], \theta\rangle$		(10) *otherwise*	$\langle\phi, \theta\rangle$	

where in (1) ℓ is defined as: *if* $f \in \theta$ *and* $\phi(y) \neq \ell_{any}$ *then* $\ell = \phi(y).f$ *else* $\ell = \ell_{any}$ and *Instr* denotes the set of all possible instructions that can appear in the body of a rule. Note that $\tau(b, \bot_{as}) = \bot_{as}$. In (1), when a reference variable x is assigned the value of a (reference) field, the transfer function updates the access path of x accordingly. In (2), when a reference field with signature f is assigned a value, f is eliminated from θ, since we can no longer guarantee that fields with the f signature preserve their initial value. Note that if in a subsequent program point, a reference variable x is assigned a field with the f signature, then the access path for x becomes ℓ_{any} in rule (1). This is needed to guarantee correctness w.r.t. Condition 1 in Sec. 1. In (3), assignments between variables are handled by just assigning their access paths as well. This allows capturing equality of access paths: if the analysis computes the same access path function ℓ for two reference variables x and y then x and y refer to the same memory location or they are both null. Although this notion is related to aliasing, note that we do not propagate aliasing information among scopes, but rather we concentrate on computing aliasing information which is guaranteed to hold regardless of the contents of the heap at the initial configuration. This allows analyzing scopes separately. In (4) and (7) numeric variables are abstracted to ℓ_{num}. They will be the target of the subsequent value analysis performed after instrumentation. In (5), when a new object is created in a fresh memory location r which is associated to a reference variable x, x is given ℓ_{any} as access path, as r does not exist in the heap at the initial configuration. In (8), if the abstract state tells us that a variable x definitely has the value null and we encounter a guard which checks that x is not null then such guard is guaranteed to fail and the rest of the rule will not be executed. This is captured by the abstract state $\bot_{as}$ which represents unreachable configurations. The remaining instructions do not alter reference constancy information. The transfer function is used to define a set of data-flow equations, whose least solution provides the reference constancy information. Below, $\bar{\exists}\bar{w}$ denotes the projection on $\bar{w}$ (i.e., eliminates all variables not in $\bar{w}$).

Definition 4 (RCA). *Given a program P and an entry p, the set of reference constancy equations of P w.r.t. p, denoted E_P^p (or E_P or E when it is clear from the context), is defined as follows:*

either $\phi_1(x) = \phi_2(x)$ or $\phi_2(x) = \ell_{\mathsf{any}}$. We define $\langle\phi_1, \theta_1\rangle \sqcup_{as} \langle\phi_2, \theta_2\rangle = \langle\phi, \theta_1 \cap \theta_2\rangle$ s.t. $\phi(x) = \phi_1(x) \sqcup_{as} \phi_2(x)$. AS_d is the lattice $\langle AS, \top_{as}, \bot_{as}, \sqcup_{as}, \sqsubseteq_{as}\rangle$ where AS is the set of abstract states, $\top_{as}$ is the top of the lattice which is equal to $\langle\phi, \emptyset\rangle$ s.t $\forall x \in \mathcal{V}.\phi(x) = \ell_{\mathsf{any}}$, and $\bot_{as}$ is the bottom.

RCA assigns an abstract state from AS to each program point by relying on the transfer function $\tau : \mathit{Instr} \times AS \mapsto AS$ depicted in the following table:

b	$\tau(b, \langle\phi, \theta\rangle)$	*conditions*	b	$\tau(b, \langle\phi, \theta\rangle)$	*conditions*
(1) $x{:=}y.f$	$\langle\phi[x \mapsto \ell], \theta\rangle$	$f \in RF(P)$	(6) $x{:=}\mathsf{null}$	$\langle\phi[x \mapsto \ell_{\mathsf{null}}], \theta\rangle$	
(2) $x.f{:=}y$	$\langle\phi, \theta\backslash\{f\}]\rangle$	$f \in RF(P)$	(7) $x{:=}exp$	$\langle\phi[x \mapsto \ell_{\mathsf{num}}], \theta\rangle$	$exp{\not\equiv}\mathsf{null}$
(3) $x{:=}y$	$\langle\phi[x \mapsto \phi(y)], \theta\rangle$		(8) $x \neq \mathsf{null}$	$\bot_{as}$	$\phi(x){=}\ell_{\mathsf{null}}$
(4) $x{:=}y.f$	$\langle\phi[x \mapsto \ell_{\mathsf{num}}], \theta\rangle$	$f \in NF(P)$	(9) $x.f{:=}y$	$\langle\phi, \theta\rangle$	$f{\in}NF(P)$
(5) $x{:=}\mathsf{new}\ c$	$\langle\phi[x \mapsto \ell_{\mathsf{any}}], \theta\rangle$		(10) *otherwise*	$\langle\phi, \theta\rangle$	

where in (1) ℓ is defined as: *if* $f \in \theta$ *and* $\phi(y) \neq \ell_{any}$ *then* $\ell = \phi(y).f$ *else* $\ell = \ell_{any}$ and *Instr* denotes the set of all possible instructions that can appear in the body of a rule. Note that $\tau(b, \bot_{as}) = \bot_{as}$. In (1), when a reference variable x is assigned the value of a (reference) field, the transfer function updates the access path of x accordingly. In (2), when a reference field with signature f is assigned a value, f is eliminated from θ, since we can no longer guarantee that fields with the f signature preserve their initial value. Note that if in a subsequent program point, a reference variable x is assigned a field with the f signature, then the access path for x becomes ℓ_{any} in rule (1). This is needed to guarantee correctness w.r.t. Condition 1 in Sec. 1. In (3), assignments between variables are handled by just assigning their access paths as well. This allows capturing equality of access paths: if the analysis computes the same access path function ℓ for two reference variables x and y then x and y refer to the same memory location or they are both null. Although this notion is related to aliasing, note that we do not propagate aliasing information among scopes, but rather we concentrate on computing aliasing information which is guaranteed to hold regardless of the contents of the heap at the initial configuration. This allows analyzing scopes separately. In (4) and (7) numeric variables are abstracted to ℓ_{num}. They will be the target of the subsequent value analysis performed after instrumentation. In (5), when a new object is created in a fresh memory location r which is associated to a reference variable x, x is given ℓ_{any} as access path, as r does not exist in the heap at the initial configuration. In (8), if the abstract state tells us that a variable x definitely has the value null and we encounter a guard which checks that x is not null then such guard is guaranteed to fail and the rest of the rule will not be executed. This is captured by the abstract state $\bot_{as}$ which represents unreachable configurations. The remaining instructions do not alter reference constancy information. The transfer function is used to define a set of data-flow equations, whose least solution provides the reference constancy information. Below, $\bar{\exists}\bar{w}$ denotes the projection on $\bar{w}$ (i.e., eliminates all variables not in $\bar{w}$).

Definition 4 (RCA). *Given a program P and an entry p, the set of reference constancy equations of P w.r.t. p, denoted E_P^p (or E_P or E when it is clear from the context), is defined as follows:*

1. *The entry p contributes the equation $p_{\downarrow}(\bar{x}) = \langle \phi, \theta \rangle$ where ϕ maps each reference variable x_i to a symbolic reference l_i and numeric variables to ℓ_{num}, and $\theta = RF(P)$;*
2. *Each rule $R^k \equiv p(\langle \bar{x} \rangle, \langle \bar{y} \rangle) \leftarrow g, b_1^k, \ldots, b_n^k \in P$, s.t. $\bar{z} = vars(R)$, contributes:*
   (a) *an initial equation $e_0^k(\bar{z}) = \tau(g, \mathsf{init}(p_{\downarrow}(\bar{x}), \bar{z} \setminus \bar{x}))$ such that $\mathsf{init}(\langle \phi, \theta \rangle, \bar{v}) = \langle \phi[v_i \mapsto \ell], \theta \rangle$, where $\ell = \ell_{null}$ if v_i is a reference variable, otherwise $\ell = \ell_{num}$;*
   (b) *for each b_j^k:*
      i. *if b_j^k is an instruction, we generate $e_j^k(\bar{z}) = \tau(b_j^k, e_{j-1}^k(\bar{z}))$;*
      ii. *if b_j^k is a call of the form $q(\langle \bar{w} \rangle, \langle \bar{s} \rangle)$, we generate $q_{\downarrow}(\bar{w}) = \bar{\exists} \bar{w}.e_{j-1}^k(\bar{z})$ and $e_j^k(\bar{z}) = \mathsf{extend}(e_{j-1}^k(\bar{z}), q_{\uparrow}(\bar{s}))$ s.t. $\mathsf{extend}(\langle \phi_1, \theta_1 \rangle, \langle \phi_2, \theta_2 \rangle) = \langle \phi_1[s_i \mapsto \phi_2(s_i)], \theta_1 \cap \theta_2 \rangle$ for $s_i \in \mathrm{dom}(\phi_2)$;*
   (c) *a final equation $p_{\uparrow}(\bar{y}) = \bar{\exists} \bar{y}.e_n^k(\bar{z})$.* □

Point 1 above indicates that on entry to $p(\bar{x})$ each x_i trivially holds its initial value l_i and all reference field signatures are constant. Point 2 traverses all rules in P. In Point 2a, we initialize the value of all variables in R^k which are not input arguments, which results in equation $e_0^k(\bar{z})$. Point 2(b)i states that if we have an instruction b_i^k, information for the next program point $e_i^k(\bar{z})$ can simply be obtained as $\tau(b_i^k, e_{i-1}^k(\bar{z}))$. Point 2(b)ii states that if b_i^k is a call $q(\bar{w}, \bar{s})$ then: the first equation declares a call $q_{\downarrow}(\bar{w})$ using $e_{i-1}^k(\bar{z})$ as initial input values, the second one uses the exit information of q, namely $q_{\uparrow}(\bar{s})$, together with the previously computed $e_{i-1}^k(\bar{z})$ in order to generate the analysis information at the next program point $e_i^k(\bar{x})$. In point 2c, we obtain information about the exit state for p, denoted $p_{\uparrow}(\bar{y})$, by removing all non-output variables from the information at the last program point in R^k, i.e., $e_n^k(\bar{z})$.

Once the set of equations E_P^p is generated, the analysis results are obtained by computing the least solution of E_P^p, which assigns an abstract element $\langle \phi, \theta \rangle \in AS$ to each equation. This can be done by bottom-up iterations, where we start from an initial solution $\perp_{as}$ for all equations and, then, at each iteration we use the results from the previous iteration in order to obtain a new solution for E_P^p. To ensure termination, new abstract states are merged with previous states using $\sqcup_{as}$ such that if a variable takes two different access paths, it becomes ℓ_{any}. As customary, $\sqcup_{as}$ merges the analysis results obtained for the different rules defining a procedure. The least solution of E_P^p over AS_d is denoted $I(E_P^p)$.

Example 5. Let *loop* be the entry of the program in Ex. 3. The initial equation for *loop* is $loop_{\downarrow}(x, y, i) = \langle \{x \mapsto l_1, y \mapsto l_2, i \mapsto \ell_{\mathsf{num}}\}, \{f\} \rangle$. The equations contributed by rule 1, where $\bar{z} = \{x, y, i, s_0, r\}$, $\bar{w} = \{x, y, i, s_0\}$ and $\bar{w}' = \{x, y, i\}$ are shown at the end of the example. The fixed point computation proceeds as follows. From $loop_{\downarrow}(\bar{w}')$ we generate e_0^1, which adds the initial values for s_0 and r. Then e_0^1 is used to learn the information for e_1^1 and so on. Note the change in value of s_0 in equations e_1^1 and e_2^1. Once we learn the information for e_3^1, we declare that we have a call to procedure $loop_c$. This is done by equation $loop_{c\downarrow}(\bar{w})$, which in turn activates (in the next iteration) the computation for the equations for $loop_c$ (rules 2 and 3). In each iteration, the new information is merged with that of the previous iterations using $\sqcup_{as}$. Column "analysis results" shows the information obtained once a fixpoint has been reached.

rule 1	analysis result
$e_0^1(\bar{z}){=}\tau(\mathsf{true}, \mathsf{init}(loop_{\downarrow}(\bar{w}'), \{s_0, r\}))$	$\langle\{x{\mapsto}l_1, y{\mapsto}l_2, s_0{\mapsto}\ell_{\mathsf{null}}, i{\mapsto}\ell_{\mathsf{num}}, r{\mapsto}\ell_{\mathsf{num}}\}, \{f\}\rangle$
$e_1^1(\bar{z}){=}\tau(s_0{:=}x, e_0^1(\bar{z}))$	$\langle\{x{\mapsto}l_1, y{\mapsto}l_2, \underline{s_0{\mapsto}l_1}, i{\mapsto}\ell_{\mathsf{num}}, r{\mapsto}\ell_{\mathsf{num}}\}, \{f\}\rangle$
$e_2^1(\bar{z}){=}\tau(s_0{:=}s_0.f, e_1^1(\bar{z}))$	$\langle\{x{\mapsto}l_1, y{\mapsto}l_2, \underline{s_0{\mapsto}l_1.f}, i{\mapsto}\ell_{\mathsf{num}}, r{\mapsto}\ell_{\mathsf{num}}\}, \{f\}\rangle$
$e_3^1(\bar{z}){=}\tau(s_0{:=}s_0.size, e_2^1(\bar{z}))$	$\langle\{x{\mapsto}l_1, y{\mapsto}l_2, s_0{\mapsto}\ell_{\mathsf{num}}, i{\mapsto}\ell_{\mathsf{num}}, r{\mapsto}\ell_{\mathsf{num}}\}, \{f\}\rangle$
$loop_{c\downarrow}(\bar{w}){=}\bar{\exists}\bar{w}.e_3^1(\bar{z})$	$\langle\{x{\mapsto}l_1, y{\mapsto}l_2, s_0{\mapsto}\ell_{\mathsf{num}}, i{\mapsto}\ell_{\mathsf{num}}\}, \{f\}\rangle$
$e_4^1(\bar{z}){=}\mathsf{extend}(e_3^1(\bar{z}), loop_{c\uparrow}(r))$	$\langle\{x{\mapsto}l_1, y{\mapsto}l_2, s_0{\mapsto}\ell_{\mathsf{num}}, i{\mapsto}\ell_{\mathsf{num}}, r{\mapsto}\ell_{\mathsf{num}}\}, \{f\}\rangle$
$loop_{\uparrow}(r){=}\bar{\exists}r.e_4^1(\bar{z})$	$\langle\{r{\mapsto}\ell_{\mathsf{num}}\}, \{f\}\rangle$

3.2 Compositional Reference Constancy Analysis

We now present a *compositional* RCA which can be used for analyzing different parts of the program, i.e., scopes, separately.

Example 6. Consider the program ⓐ in Ex. 4. It is similar to the one in Ex. 3, but we introduce two auxiliary methods *getSize* and *setSize* defined, resp., as follows: "*int getSize()*{*return this.size;*}" and "*void setSize(int n)*{*this.size=n;*}" and whose rule-based forms are, "$getSize(\langle this\rangle, \langle r\rangle){\leftarrow}s_0{:=}this, s_0{:=}s_0.size, r{:=}s_0$" and "$setSize(\langle this, n\rangle, \langle\rangle){\leftarrow}s_0{:=}this, s_1{:=}n, s_0.size{:=}s_1$", respectively. Now, the read accesses to field *size* (at program points ②, ③, and ⑤) are replaced by calls to *getSize* and the write access at program point ⑥ by a call to *setSize*. Note that now, in the whole program, instead of three, we only have one read access ($s_0{:=}s_0.size$, in the body of *getSize*) to the *size* field. Unfortunately, s_0 is not constant at that program point, as it sometimes has the value y (when calling from program point ③) and sometimes $x.f$ (when calling from program points ② and ⑤). Instead of giving up, compositional analysis should let us analyze *getSize* separately and infer that s_0 is constant within each call to *getSize*. □

The first step for achieving compositionality is to split the program P into scopes $S_1, \ldots, S_n$ by partitioning the procedures (and therefore rules) in P into groups such that there are no mutual calls (directly or indirectly) between any two different groups. Therefore, the strongly connected components (or SCCs) of the program are the smallest scopes we should consider. For the sake of simplicity, we assume that each scope S has a single entry p. This is not a restriction, as we can repeat the analysis for each entry separately. Scopes are analyzed in a reverse topological order. Since there are no cycles among scopes, when analyzing a scope S, we have already analyzed all scopes reachable from S.

The only change required in the analysis presented in Sect. 3.1 is to modify the transfer function in order to handle calls to procedures defined in external scopes. Let $q(\langle\bar{w}\rangle, \langle\bar{s}\rangle)$ be a call to a procedure defined in $S' \neq S$ for which we have computed $q_{\uparrow}(\bar{s}) = \langle\phi', \theta'\rangle \in I(E^q_{S'})$. To avoid variable renamings, we assume that such answer $q_{\uparrow}$ is returned with the same variable names. Now, we define the transfer function for this call as $\tau(q(\langle\bar{w}\rangle, \langle\bar{s}\rangle), \langle\phi, \theta\rangle) = \langle\phi'', \theta''\rangle$ where:

(1) $\theta'' = \theta \cap \theta'$;

(2) we distinguish three kinds of variables to define ϕ'':
(2.1) $\forall z \in \text{dom}(\phi) \setminus \bar{s}$, we have $\phi''(z) = \phi(z)$; otherwise
(2.2) $\forall z \in \text{dom}(\phi)$ which is numeric, $\phi''(z) = \ell_{\mathsf{num}}$; otherwise
(2.3) $\forall s_k \in \bar{s}$ if $\phi'(s_k) = l_j.f_1 \ldots f_n \wedge \{f_1, \ldots, f_n\} \subseteq \theta \wedge \phi(w_j) \neq \ell_{\mathsf{any}}$ then $\phi''(s_k) = \phi(w_j).f_1 \ldots f_n$, else $\phi''(s_k) = \ell_{\mathsf{any}}$.

Intuitively, field updates that might occur in the execution of q are learned in (1). Variables which are not output variables of q (2.1) are not affected by this step. In point (2.2), output numeric variables become ℓ_{num}. In (2.3), the answer for reference output variables of q is *renamed* to use them in this calling context. For this, we need to use the access paths computed for the input variables to perform the renaming on the output variables. We require that the involved field signatures are in θ and that the access path for w_j is not ℓ_{any}.

Example 7. We now split the program in Ex. 6 in three scopes: $S_1 = \{getSize\}$, $S_2 = \{setSize\}$ and $S_3 = \{loop, loop_c\}$. The analysis of S_1 results in $getSize_{\uparrow}(r) = \langle\{r \mapsto \ell_{\mathsf{num}}\}, \{f\}\rangle \in I(E_{S_1})$. The analysis of S_3 generates $E^{loop}_{S_3}$, which is as the one in Ex. 5 except for the equation that refers to the *size* field. In particular, equation $e^1_4(\bar{z})$ is replaced by: $e^1_4(\bar{z}) = \tau(getSize(\langle s_0\rangle, \langle s_0\rangle), e^1_3(\bar{z}))$. It results in the same value for e^1_4 as in Ex. 5, i.e., compositional analysis allows considering *size* constant in *getSize* without losing accuracy when composing the results. Thus, as for the program in Ex. 3, we conclude that in the calls to $getSize(\langle this\rangle, \langle r\rangle)$, *this* has the value $l_1.f$ at program points ②,⑤ and the value l_2 at ③. Reasoning similarly, we get that for the call to $setSize(\langle this, n\rangle, \langle\rangle)$, variable *this* always has the value $l_1.f$ at program point ⑥. □

Theorem 1 (soundness). *Let S be a scope and p be an entry. For any equation $e^k_i(\bar{x}) = \langle\phi, \theta\rangle \in I(E^p_S)$ and variable $z \in dom(\phi)$, if $\phi(z) = l_j.f_1 \ldots f_n$, then z is constant w.r.t. $l_j.f_1 \ldots f_n$ at program point (k, i).* □

Our method is parametric w.r.t. the choice of scopes. As a rule of thumb, the larger scopes are, the more context information we can propagate in the subsequent value analysis, but the less likely that numeric field accesses can be considered trackable. As motivated above, scopes should not be larger than methods, unless they are mutually recursive. For cost and termination, defining the scopes by first computing the SCCs and then grouping non-recursive SCCs that form a chain (consecutive SCCs in topological order) works well in practice.

4 An Instrumentation for Tracking Numeric Fields

We now identify sufficient conditions for instrumenting the program by adding *ghost* variables which correspond to the value of numeric fields. As for RCA, we define the instrumentation in a compositional way, guided by a set of scopes.

4.1 Finding Trackable Numeric Fields

Given an instruction b^k_j and a reference variable y, we use $acc\_path(y, b^k_j) = \ell$ as a shortcut for $e^k_{j-1}(\bar{x}) = \langle\phi, \theta\rangle \in I(E_S) \wedge \phi(y) = \ell$. We use S^* to refer to the union of S and all other scopes reachable from S. Given a scope S and a numeric field signature f, the set of *read access paths* for f in S, denoted $R(S, f)$, is the set of access paths of all variables y used for reading (i.e., instructions of the form $x{:=}y.f$) a field with the f signature in S^*. $R^+(S, f)$ denotes the set of access paths that originate from read accesses in S, and $R^*(S, f)$ those which originate from read accesses in $S^*\backslash\{S\}$. Thus, $R(S, f) = R^+(S, f) \cup R^*(S, f)$ where:

$$R^+(S, f) = \{acc\_path(y, b_j^k) \mid b_j^k \equiv x{:=}y.f \in S\}$$

$$R^*(S, f) = \left\{\ell' \left| \begin{array}{l} b_j^k \equiv q(\langle\bar{x}\rangle, \langle\bar{y}\rangle) \in S, \quad q \in S' \neq S, \quad \ell \in R(S', f) \\ \text{if } \ell = l_h.p \text{ then } \ell' = acc\_path(x_h, b_{j-1}^k).p \text{ else } \ell' = \ell_{\mathsf{any}} \end{array} \right.\right\}$$

In $R^+(S, f)$, for each access $x{:=}y.f$, we add the access path that the analysis has computed for y. Computing the read access paths for a scope S requires computing the read access paths for all other scopes in S^*. Since scopes subsume SCCs, read access paths can be computed in reverse topological order without iterating. For each call $q(\langle\bar{x}\rangle, \langle\bar{y}\rangle)$ such that q is the entry of scope S', we take $R(S', f)$ and rename it according to the calling context. This requires renaming each l_h using the access path of x_h at b_{j-1}^k. The set of write access paths for f in S, denoted $W(S, f)$, is computed in a similar way by just considering the access path of all variables y in instructions of the form $y.f{:=}x$, instead of $x{:=}y.f$.

Example 8. Following Ex. 7, the set $R^+(S_1, \mathit{size}) = \{l_1\}$, due to the instruction $s_0 = s_0.size$, and $R^*(S_1, \mathit{size}) = \emptyset$, since S_1 does not have calls to other scopes. $R^+(S_2, \mathit{size}) = R^*(S_2, \mathit{size}) = \emptyset$ since no read accesses to the field *size* occur in *setSize*. Also, $R^+(S_3, \mathit{size}) = \emptyset$, since S_3 does not access *size* directly, but $R^*(S_3, \mathit{size}) = \{l_1.f, l_2\}$. Note that $l_1.f$ originates from program point ② and ⑤ and l_2 from program point ③. Finally, $W(S_1, \mathit{size}) = \emptyset$, $W(S_2, \mathit{size}) = \{l_1\}$ and $W(S_3, \mathit{size}) = \{l_1.f\}$, where $l_1.f$ originates from program point ⑥. □

Definition 5 (trackable numeric field signature). *Given a scope S from a program P and a numeric field signature $f \in NF(P)$, f is* trackable *in scope S if (1) f is trackable in all scopes in $S^*\backslash\{S\}$ and one of the following conditions holds: (2) $W(S, f) = \emptyset$; or (3) $W(S, f) = \{\ell\}$ and ℓ is of the form $l_j.f_1 \ldots f_n$.*

Condition (1) is required in order to have a sound transformation, as we cannot track accesses which are not trackable in transitively reachable scopes. Then, Condition (2) refers to scenarios where we do not have any write access to f, like example ⓑ. In such case, the value of numeric fields read through (possibly) different access paths will be stored in different ghost variables. Condition (3) requires that all write accesses are done through the same path, like examples ⓐ, ⓒ (inner loop) and ⓔ. This is the reason why the field accesses in the examples ⓓ and ⓕ are not trackable. An essential point is that, though it is allowed to have read accesses to f through access paths different from ℓ, they cannot be tracked. This is the case in the read access $y.size$ in example ⓔ.

4.2 Instrumenting Trackable Numeric Fields

The following transformation describes how to instrument a scope S with ghost variables for the different trackable uses of a numeric field f:

1. If f is not trackable go to 4
2. **Add Arguments:** each head or call $p(\langle\bar{x}\rangle, \langle\bar{y}\rangle)$ such that $p \in S$ is converted to $p(\langle\bar{x}\cdot\bar{v}_r\rangle, \langle\bar{y}\cdot\bar{v}_w\rangle)$ with $\bar{v}_w = \{v_{\ell.f} \mid \ell \in W(S,f)\}$ and
   (a) if $W(S,f) = \emptyset$ then $\bar{v}_r = \{v_{\ell.f} \mid \ell \neq \ell_{\mathsf{any}} \in R(S,f)\}$
   (b) if $W(S,f) = \{\ell\}$ then if $\ell \in R(S,f)$ then $\bar{v}_r = \{v_{\ell.f}\}$ else $\bar{v}_r = \emptyset$
3. **Replicate Field Accesses:**
   (a) each $b_j^k \equiv y.f{:=}x \in S$ produces a subsequent assignment $v_{\ell.f}{:=}x$, if $acc\_path(y, b_j^k) = \ell$
   (b) each $b_j^k \equiv x{:=}y.f \in S$ produces a subsequent assignment $x{:=}v_{\ell.f}$, if $acc\_path(y, b_j^k) = \ell \neq \ell_{\mathsf{any}} \wedge W(S,f) \subseteq \{\ell\}$
4. **Handle External Calls:** Let $b_j^k \equiv q(\bar{x}, \bar{y}) \in S$ be an external call, and $q(\langle\bar{x}'\cdot\bar{v}'_r\rangle, \langle\bar{y}'\cdot\bar{v}'_w\rangle)$ be the head of the definition of q after transforming its corresponding scope. The call is translated to $q(\langle\bar{x}\cdot\bar{v}_r\rangle, \langle\bar{y}\cdot\bar{v}_w\rangle)$ where, given a variable $v'_\ell \in \bar{v}'_r \cup \bar{v}'_w$ with $\ell = l_h.f_1 \ldots f_n.f$, its corresponding variable v_m is:
   (a) if $acc\_path(x_h, b_{j-1}^k) = \ell_{\mathsf{any}}$ or f is not trackable in S, then $v_m = *$;
   (b) otherwise, $m = acc\_path(x_h, b_{j-1}^k).f_1 \ldots f_n.f$.

The scopes in a program are instrumented in a reverse topological order. For simplicity, in the presentation, a scope S is instrumented iteratively, once for each field in $NF(P)$. However, in the implementation, each scope is instrumented just once, simultaneously for all field signatures. The key features in our instrumentation are: (i) Ghost variables have names of the form $v_{l.f}$, where l is an access path function and f a numeric field. (ii) If the field access is not trackable in the current scope, then it is not safe to propagate the value of numeric fields to/from external calls. To handle this, we use the mark '$*$' which, at the input, should be interpreted as a random integer and, at the output, it indicates that we should ignore the corresponding output value when we return from a call. This syntax can be easily supported by modifying rules 5 and 6 in the semantics, and treating it in value analysis is straightforward. (iii) When there are updates to a field signature, we can only track read accesses which refer to the same access path function used for the updates (see explanation of condition 3 in Def. 5).

Intuitively, each step in the instrumentation of a scope S w.r.t. a field signature f is: (1) If f is not trackable in S, we only need to instrument external calls (step 4a) by ignoring the value of ghost variables. E.g., when we instrument the calling scope to the loop in example ⓑ, we cannot track the value of the field $x.f$. (2) Input and output ghost variables are added as follows. For output ghost variables, the definition of trackable ensures that there is at most one access path in the write set. For the input ones, if there are no write accesses, we can track all their possible read uses (step 2a); otherwise, we can only track the accesses through the same access path (step 2b), hence we have at most one variable. The same arguments are also added to internal calls. (3) We replicate field accesses with accesses to its corresponding ghost variable. The condition $W(S,f) \subseteq \{\ell\}$ takes care of issue (iii) above. (4) For calls to other scopes, it is guaranteed that they have been already instrumented. We have to look up at the reference constancy information to find out which ghost variables we must use in the calling context, step 4b. In step 4a, if the field is not trackable or its access path is not constant, it is not safe to track its value.

Example 9. We first transform S_1 in Ex. 7 w.r.t. *size*. Recall that $R(S_1, size) = \{l_1\}$ and $W(S_1, size) = \emptyset$. Thus, we add an input variable v_1 for the ghost variable $v_{l_1.size}$, resulting in: " $getSize(\langle this, \underline{v_1}\rangle, \langle r\rangle) \leftarrow s_0{:=}this, \underline{s_0{:=}v_1}, r{:=}s_0$". Note that we have replaced the read access statement $s_0{=}s_0.size$ by $s_0{=}v_1$, which reads the ghost variable v_1. Similarly, the transformation of S_2 w.r.t. *size* generates the rule: "$setSize(\langle this, n\rangle, \langle v_1\rangle) \leftarrow s_0{:=}this, s_1{:=}n, s_0.size{:=}s_1, \underline{v_1{:=}s_1}$", where now v_1 is an output value which stores the modification of $v_{l_1.size}$. Note that the write access $s_0.size{:=}s_1$ is replicated using variable v_1, which results in the additional statement $v_1{:=}s_1$. This corresponds to the intuition shown in the instrumentation of the Java code in Sec. 1, though it is more sophisticated as we have an inter-procedural transformation which allows multiple output variables. Hence, it could not be directly done in the original Java program. The instrumented version of rules (1), (2) and (3) of S_3 is:

(1) $loop(\langle x, y, i, \underline{v_1}\rangle, \langle r, \underline{v_1}\rangle) \leftarrow$
$s_0{:=}x, s_0{:=}s_0.f,$
$getSize(\langle s_0, \underline{v_1}\rangle, \langle s_0\rangle),$
$loop_c(\langle x, y, i, s_0, \underline{v_1}\rangle, \langle r, \underline{v_1}\rangle).$

(2) $loop_c(\langle x, y, i, s_0, \underline{v_1}\rangle, \langle r, \underline{v_1}\rangle) \leftarrow$
$\mathbf{s_0 \leq 0}, s_0{:=}i, r{:=}s_0.$

(3) $loop_c(\langle x, y, i, s_0, \underline{v_1}\rangle, \langle r, \underline{v_1}\rangle) \leftarrow$
$\mathbf{s_0 > 0}, s_0{:=}i, s_1{:=}y, getSize(\langle s_1, *\rangle, \langle s_1\rangle),$
$s_0{:=}s_0 + s_1, i{:=}s_0, s_0{:=}x, s_0{:=}s_0.f,$
$s_1{:=}s_0, getSize(\langle s_1, \underline{v_1}\rangle, \langle s_1\rangle),$
$s_2{:=}1, s_1{:=}s_1 - s_2, setSize(\langle s_0, s_1\rangle, \langle \underline{v_1}\rangle),$
$loop(\langle this, x, y, i, \underline{v_1}\rangle, \langle r, \underline{v_1}\rangle).$

Since the write set is $\{l_1.f\}$, only one variable v_1 can be added for the read access $l_1.f$ (i.e., ghost variable $v_{l_1.f.size}$) and we cannot track the one corresponding to the read access l_2 (step 2b). An important point is that, in the calls to *getSize*, we use either v_1 or $*$ depending on the access path of the first argument, computed in step 4b. Field-insensitive value analysis of the instrumented program is now able to infer that v_1 (i.e., $x.f.size$) is decreasing and has 0 as lower limit. This is due to the fact that, for $getSize(\langle this, v_1\rangle, \langle r\rangle)$, field-insensitive value analysis can now infer that $r = v_1$ (which corresponds to *this.size*) and for $setSize(\langle this, n\rangle, \langle v_1\rangle)$ it infers that v_1 decreases by one. Cost and termination analyses hence succeed to bound the number of loop iterations by the ranking function v_1. □

The following theorem guarantees that we can safely use the instrumented program for value analysis instead of the original one.

Theorem 2. *Let P be a program, P_F be its instrumentation for $NF(P)$, and $C = \langle start, p(\langle \bar{x}\rangle, \langle \bar{y}\rangle), tv\rangle; h$ an initial configuration. If there is a trace t of the form $C \leadsto_P^n C_n$ then there exists a trace t' of the form $C' \leadsto_{P_F}^m C_m$ s.t. $C'{=}\langle start, p(\langle \bar{x} \cdot \bar{*}\rangle, \langle \bar{y} \cdot \bar{*}\rangle),\ tv\rangle; h;\ m \geq n$; s.t. if we remove all ghost variables and states that originate from the instrumentation from t', we obtain t.* □

Even though the instrumented program may have non-deterministic behaviour due to ghost variables whose values are unknown ('$*$'), this does not introduce a loss of precision w.r.t. field-insensitive value analysis, since such unknowns correspond to numeric fields which are also unknown in field-insensitive analysis.

5 Experiments in the COSTA System

COSTA [2] is a static analyzer able to prove termination and obtain upper bounds on resource usage for a relatively large class of Java bytecode programs. We have integrated our method in COSTA as a pre-process to the existing field-insensitive value analysis. In order to assess its practicality on realistic programs, we have tried to infer termination of all the loops which contain numeric field accesses in their guards for all classes in the subpackages of "`java`" of the Sun's implementation of J2SE 1.4.2. In total, we have found 133 methods which contain loops of this form, which we have taken as entries. COSTA has an application extraction algorithm (or class analysis) which pulls methods transitively used from each entry. COSTA failed to analyze 11 methods because when analyzing context-independently, it is required to analyze more methods than it can handle.

Bench.	**Ru**	$\mathbf{L}_n$	$\mathbf{R}_s$	$\mathbf{R}_i$	$\mathbf{T}_{rca}$	$\mathbf{T}_{tr}$	$\mathbf{T}_{gh}$	$\mathbf{T}_i$	$\mathbf{T}_s$	**SD**
lang	315	13	13	0	0.12	0.01	0.02	3.33	5.47	1.64
util	685	24	24	0	0.58	7.88	4.90	20.21	39.36	1.95
beans	90	3	3	0	0.05	0.00	0.00	1.42	1.65	1.16
math	662	15	12	1	0.22	0.18	0.17	7.84	9.84	1.26
text	1743	24	20	1	0.79	0.34	0.37	37.33	141.04	3.78
awt	4524	90	87	0	2.44	7.56	7.59	98.56	248.49	2.52
io	716	6	5	2	0.61	0.49	0.27	17.79	23.94	1.35
security	58	1	1	0	0.03	0.01	0.00	0.90	0.98	1.09
total	8793	176	165	4	4.84	16.47	13.32	187.38	470.77	2.51

The above table shows our experimental results for the 122 methods which COSTA can handle which belong to the packages whose name appears in the first column. For each package, we provide the size of the code to be analyzed, given as number of rules (**Ru**), the number of loops ($\mathbf{L}_n$) analyzed in each package which contain numeric field accesses in their guards. The column $\mathbf{R}_s$ shows the number of loops involving numeric guards for which COSTA has been able to find a ranking function using our proposed approach to field-sensitive analysis. Column $\mathbf{R}_i$ shows the same for field-insensitive analysis. It can be observed that, before applying our technique, COSTA could prove termination of only 4 of the 176 loops. In those 4 loops it is possible to prove termination using a field-insensitive analyzer because, for example, termination is guaranteed by reaching exceptional states. When we apply our approach to field-sensitive analysis, we prove termination of 165 of the 176 loops. It is also worth mentioning that only in 3 loops we fail to prove termination because the numeric field in the guard is not trackable (in particular, the reference is not constant). In the other 8 loops, though the fields are trackable, we failed due to limitations of the underlying termination techniques used in COSTA, and which are not related to our approach. In most cases, the problem is that the termination condition does not depend on the size of the data structure, but rather on the particular value stored at some location within the data structure, and also to the use of linear arithmetic operations.

The next set of columns evaluate time efficiency. The experiments have been performed on an Intel Core 2 Quad Q9300 at 2.5GHz with 1.95GB of RAM, running Linux 2.6.27-11. Analysis times are shown in seconds. The time of the RCA is shown in $\mathbf{T}_{rca}$. Columns $\mathbf{T}_{tr}$ and $\mathbf{T}_{gh}$ show, resp., the times to infer the trackability condition and to instrument the program with ghost variables. We have observed that the examples which require more time to infer trackability always involve a high number of numeric fields and thus the transformation also has to consider a high number of ghost variables. The total analysis time of the field-sensitive analysis, which includes the previous three columns is in $\mathbf{T}_s$. The field-insensitive analysis time is shown in $\mathbf{T}_i$. Finally, the **SD** column shows the slowdown introduced by field-sensitive analysis. The total overhead is 2.51. We argue that our results are quite positive since the overhead introduced is reasonable in return for the quite significant accuracy gains obtained.

6 Conclusions and Related Work

This paper proposes, to the best of our knowledge, the first static analysis to support *numeric fields* in cost and termination analysis of object-oriented bytecode. A complementary analysis for *reference fields* is [17]. Traditionally, existing approaches to reason on shared mutable data structures either track all possible updates of fields (endangering efficiency) or abstract all field updates into a single element (sacrificing accuracy). Our work does not fall into either category, as it does not track all field updates but rather only those which behave like non heap-allocated variables. Miné's [11] value analysis for C takes a different approach by enriching the abstract domain to make the analysis field-sensitive. His motivation is different from ours, such analysis is developed to improve points-to analysis in the presence of pointer arithmetics. We argue that our approach is sufficiently precise for context-independent analysis as required by important applications of value analysis such as termination analysis, while introducing a reasonable overhead. Also, [4] enriches a numeric abstract domain with alien expressions (field accesses). Without additional information, such as our RCA, this domain would be rather limited (imprecise) for bytecode. The notion of `restricted` variables used in [1] for C programs is related to our notion of reference constancy. However, [1] imposes more restrictive conditions, namely it avoids global pointers to be used locally and local copies to escape from the local context and, thus, it does not imply our reference constancy condition. In general, more accurate aliasing analysis (see [1] and its references) can be used to improve the precision of our analysis when computing the read and write sets, but at a higher performance cost and, besides, such further precision might not be required in practice for analyzing subprograms context-independently. Must-aliasing (aliases at program points) does not imply constancy of references, since the values of two variables might but still alias at the program point of interest. However, infering transitive relations of must-aliasing, i.e., between variables at different program points might enable the inference of constancy information, but this results in a much more expensive analysis than ours. Our work shares its motivation with the evolving field of *local reasoning* [14], such as separation logic [16] and regional logic [3] which provide expressive frameworks to reason about programs with shared mutable data structures. While our goals are more restricted, our technique has the advantage of allowing fully automatic inference.

Acknowledgments. This work was funded in part by the Information Society Technologies program of the European Commission, Future and Emerging Technologies under the IST-15905 *MOBIUS* and IST-231620 *HATS* projects, by the Spanish Ministry of Education (MEC) under the TIN-2005-09207 *MERIT*, TIN-2008-05624 *DOVES* and HI2008-0153 (Acción Integrada) projects, and the Madrid Regional Government under the S-0505/TIC/0407 *PROMESAS* project.

References

1. Aiken, A., Foster, J.S., Kodumal, J., Terauchi, T.: Checking and inferring local non-aliasing. In: Proc.of PDLI 2003, pp. 129–140. ACM, New York (2003)
2. Albert, E., Arenas, P., Codish, M., Genaim, S., Puebla, G., Zanardini, D.: Termination Analysis of Java Bytecode. In: Barthe, G., de Boer, F.S. (eds.) FMOODS 2008. LNCS, vol. 5051, pp. 2–18. Springer, Heidelberg (2008)
3. Banerjee, A., Naumann, D., Rosenberg, S.: Regional logic for local reasoning about global invariants. In: Vitek, J. (ed.) ECOOP 2008. LNCS, vol. 5142, pp. 387–411. Springer, Heidelberg (2008)
4. Chang, B.-Y.E., Leino, K.R.M.: Abstract interpretation with alien expressions and heap structures. In: Cousot, R. (ed.) VMCAI 2005. LNCS, vol. 3385, pp. 147–163. Springer, Heidelberg (2005)
5. Codish, M., Taboch, C.: A semantic basis for the termination analysis of logic programs. J. Log. Program. 41(1), 103–123 (1999)
6. Cousot, P., Cousot, R.: Abstract Interpretation: a Unified Lattice Model for Static Analysis of Programs by Construction or Approximation of Fixpoints. In: POPL 1977, pp. 238–252. ACM, New York (1977)
7. Cousot, P., Halbwachs, N.: Automatic discovery of linear restraints among variables of a program. In: Proc. POPL. ACM, New York (1978)
8. Deutsch, A.: Interprocedural may-alias analysis for pointers: Beyond k-limiting. In: PLDI, pp. 230–241 (1994)
9. Lindholm, T., Yellin, F.: The Java Virtual Machine Specification. Addison-Wesley, Reading (1996)
10. Logozzo, F.: Cibai: An abstract interpretation-based static analyzer for modular analysis and verification of java classes. In: Cook, B., Podelski, A. (eds.) VMCAI 2007. LNCS, vol. 4349, pp. 283–298. Springer, Heidelberg (2007)
11. Miné, A.: Field-sensitive value analysis of embedded c programs with union types and pointer arithmetics. In: LCTES (2006)
12. Miné, A.: The octagon abstract domain. Higher-Order and Symbolic Computation 19(1), 31–100 (2006)
13. Nielson, F., Nielson, H.R., Hankin, C.: Principles of Program Analysis, 2nd edn. Springer, Heidelberg (2005)

14. O'Hearn, P.W., Reynolds, J.C., Yang, H.: Local Reasoning about Programs that Alter Data Structures. In: Fribourg, L. (ed.) CSL 2001 and EACSL 2001. LNCS, vol. 2142, p. 1. Springer, Heidelberg (2001)
15. Podelski, A., Rybalchenko, A.: A complete method for the synthesis of linear ranking functions. In: Steffen, B., Levi, G. (eds.) VMCAI 2004. LNCS, vol. 2937, pp. 239–251. Springer, Heidelberg (2004)
16. Reynolds, J.C.: Separation Logic: A Logic for Shared Mutable Data Structures. In: LICS, pp. 55–74 (2002)
17. Spoto, F., Hill, P., Payet, E.: Path-length analysis of object-oriented programs. In: EAAI 2006. ENTCS. Elsevier, Amsterdam (2006)
18. Vallee-Rai, R., Hendren, L., Sundaresan, V., Lam, P., Gagnon, E., Co, P.: Soot - a Java optimization framework. In: CASCON 1999, pp. 125–135 (1999)

Making Temporal Logic Calculational: A Tool for Unification and Discovery

Raymond Boute

INTEC, Ghent University, Belgium
Boute@intec.UGent.be
http://www.funmath.be

Abstract. In temporal logic, calculational proofs beyond simple cases are often seen as challenging. The situation is reversed by making temporal logic calculational, yielding shorter and clearer proofs than traditional ones, and serving as a (mental) tool for unification and discovery. A side-effect of unifying theories is easier access by practicians. The starting point is a simple generic (software tool independent) Functional Temporal Calculus (FTC). Specific temporal logics are then captured via *endosemantic functions*. This concept reflects tacit conventions throughout mathematics and, once identified, is general and useful. FTC also yields a reasoning style that helps *discovering* theorems by calculation rather than just proving given facts. This is illustrated by deriving various theorems, most related to liveness issues in TLA$^+$, and finding strengthenings of known results. Educational issues are addressed in passing.

1 Introduction and Overview

1.1 Motivation and Choice of Topic

Calculational proofs. Lamport observes [27, p. 99] that, in temporal logic, proof by calculation beyond simple cases becomes challenging. We show how to reverse the situation by making temporal logic amenable to the calculational style, turning it into a (mental, conceptual) tool for unification and discovery. Still, there are also broader concerns deserving some further elaboration.

Diversity versus disparity. In [2] and a companion tutorial "Why formal verification remains on the fringes of commercial development", Arvind stresses that no single model, technique or tool can cover all needs of systems design. Diversity is an evident fact conceptually, but accepting it is hampered by needless disparity in the formulation of models and methods in the literature and the presentation (notation, paradigm) of tools. Even the underlying theories are often stated as special logics, outside the mainstream of mathematics, and miss the directness and elegance engineers appreciate in algebra and calculus [31]. The more mature fields yield diversity in modeling (e.g., electrical, mechanical) without disparity.

In formal methods as well, mathematics is the most powerful intellectual tool, so "hiding the math" is not as helpful as is often suggested. Habrias et al. rightly

A. Cavalcanti and D. Dams (Eds.): FM 2009, LNCS 5850, pp. 387–402, 2009.

warn that tool use without awareness is the ruin of formal specification [22]. In analysis, pitfalls are notorious [34]. Since software is discrete, one might think the pitfalls are less subtle, but this is risky: even simple programs can be difficult to get right, as shown by Bentley's historical notes on binary search [5].

Moreover, "hiding the math" keeps tool users ignorant of major opportunities, especially in reasoning about systems requirements and realizations (e.g., programs). For instance, the link between informal and formal description, traditionally the weak link, can be made strong by formalizing various informal views and formally exploring their relationships [12]. Even using different notations can be advantageous if captured by a unifying framework [10] for reasoning. Again diversity is an asset, and mathematics can offer it without causing disparity.

Improving accessibility for practicians. Given the preceding remarks, wide use of formal methods in industry is best served by a constant supply of well-prepared students [12]. Yet, this is still a long-term option, since curriculum design lags behind insights in formal methods [35]. Meanwhile we should attempt lowering the threshold formal methods still represent in practice, but without sacrificing the safety and effectiveness that only mathematics can provide for tool users.

So, rather than "hiding the math", we aim at making it very accessible. Reconciling this goal with the need for diversity is possible by unifying theories. For programming theories, one unifying approach is due to Hoare and Jifeng [24].

The calculational semantics approach is arguably more accessible [11] as its style matches common engineering mathematics and its scope is broader. The main unifying element is a functional predicate calculus [10], allowing engineers to calculate with predicates and quantifiers ($\forall$, $\exists$) as fluently as taught with derivatives and integrals. As expected, reasoning is calculational, the style also advocated by Dijkstra [15], Gries [20,21] and others. The other element, generic functionals [9], supports unification with classical signals and systems modeling, together with the point-free style so convenient in computing science [1,9,30].

This is a rather wide program, but here we focus on a more restricted topic.

Choice of topic: model checking and temporal logic. Model checking [3,14,26,27] is a convenient method for verifying systems with automated tools. Apparently, it makes the task easy for the user: given a formal system description and a condition to be satisfied, the tool either confirms success or yields a counterexample. This has made model checking one of the most popular formal methods.

This simplicity of use is deceptive. Formalizing the description as well as the condition requires essentially mathematical aptitudes. Indeed, the conditions are typically expressed by temporal formulas, which are not very intuitive, as also noted by Lamport [27]. This can be alleviated by *patterns* [17,18,19], i.e. given temporal formulas "known" to express some property of interest. Such an approach is used in the Bandera project [4,19] for concurrent Java software.

However, *no predefined collection of patterns is complete* for practical application, and the tool user must be able to design new ones. Clarifying the intuitive meaning of patterns, exploring the relationship between them and designing new ones, is again most conveniently done using mathematics [8].

Rationale: proper formality as a tool for discovery. Insular logics have fostered the common belief that formality and intuition poorly match. By contrast, functional predicate calculus was found to be an asset for intuition, even developing it when exploring new domains. Calculational semantics [11] is an example.

This paper extends such benefits to model checking by a temporal calculus that is very accessible, helps discovery and develops intuition. In deriving the calculation rules, extensions of basic notions arise, such as *strengthened weak induction*. In illustrating applications, temporal calculations become simpler than classical proofs [27] and yield stronger results without prior knowledge.

1.2 Overview

Section 2 discusses style choices and presents a generic temporal calculus (FTC). Section 3 captures TLA$^+$ calculationally, facilitates reading by pruning repetitive parts, and derives some basic theorems for illustration. Section 4 illustrates calculational temporal reasoning by application to patterns about liveness issues.

2 Style Issues in Temporal Calculi and in General

2.1 From Temporal Logics to Temporal Calculi

Most formulations of temporal logic [28] follow the usual style of formal logic in presenting it as a separate language with axioms, and defines models via semantic functions in a metalanguage. This is suitable to study metamathematical issues.

For introducing temporal logic to the practicing engineer, it is helpful casting them into a calculus with the smooth algebraic flavor so appreciated in classical mathematics, as just another theory in the common framework. A simple approach is viewing temporal operators as an algebra of functions on (infinite) sequences. Here so-called *linear time* is assumed; branching time has slightly different rules, but derivable similarly using trees instead of sequences [3,33].

Here we briefly mention some other work on unifying frameworks for temporal logics. An abstract algebra approach based on Galois connections is *Temporal Algebra* [37], whereas *correspondence theory* takes a modal logics viewpoint [36]. A predicative semantics approach using *generic composition* is found in [13].

Our approach differs by its more concrete basis. Starting from the model rather than pure axioms reflects the systems view (model given, various aspects requiring various formalisms) as opposed to the pure formal logic view (single formalism, perhaps various models), as further discussed in [6,7]. In the analysis and design of patterns, the model is the domain of discourse anyway. Moreover, in this manner the usual temporal logic axioms [28] can still be cast into textually identical theorems [6], so calculations can have the same abstract flavor.

Different styles are possible, also depending on other desiderata.

Indeed, to support awareness when using a model checking tool, the calculus should match the tool's language. We illustrate later how to do this for TLA$^+$.

Yet, it is also conceptually helpful to start with a very elementary form of temporal calculus that captures the common concepts independently of tools. The derived results are easily 're-used' in designing calculi for specific tools.

2.2 A Purely Functional 'Bare Bones' Temporal Calculus (FTC)

a. Principle and operator definitions A very basic temporal calculus is obtained by defining temporal operators as predicate transformers, the predicates of interest pertaining to system behaviors (infinite sequences of system states).

Formally, let $\mathbf{S}$ be the state space (instantaneous values). *Behaviors* (infinite sequences) are functions of type $\mathbb{N} \to \mathbf{S}$, also written $\mathbf{S}^\infty$. The predicates of interest are Boolean-valued functions over $\mathbf{S}^\infty$, hence of type $\mathsf{BP} := \mathbf{S}^\infty \to \mathbb{B}$.

Logical operators of FTC are just pointwise extensions of the usual propositional operators: for any infix operator $\star$ (say, $\wedge$, $\vee$, $\Rightarrow$, $\equiv$) and any β in $\mathbf{S}^\infty$,

$$(P \star Q)\,\beta \equiv P\,\beta \star Q\,\beta \quad . \tag{1}$$

Propositional operators of type $\mathbb{B}^2 \to \mathbb{B}$ (for $\wedge$, $\vee$, $\Rightarrow$, $\equiv$) or $\mathbb{B} \to \mathbb{B}$ (for $\neg$) are thereby overloaded to type $\mathsf{BP}^2 \to \mathsf{BP}$ or $\mathsf{BP} \to \mathsf{BP}$ ("predicate transformers"). The extension can be made explicit if desired [9], but it is unambiguous here.

Temporal operators of FTC are predicate transformers of type $\mathsf{BP} \to \mathsf{BP}$, e.g.,

$$\bigcirc \quad (\text{"next"}) \quad \text{defined by} \quad \bigcirc P\,\beta \equiv P\,(\sigma\,\beta) \tag{2}$$

$$\Box \quad (\text{"henceforth"}) \quad \text{defined by} \quad \Box P\,\beta \equiv \forall\, n\,{:}\,\mathbb{N}\,.\,P\,(\sigma^n\,\beta) \tag{3}$$

$$\Diamond \quad (\text{"eventually"}) \quad \text{defined by} \quad \Diamond P\,\beta \equiv \exists\, n\,{:}\,\mathbb{N}\,.\,P\,(\sigma^n\,\beta) \tag{4}$$

As usual in functional formalisms, $f\,x\,y$ is read $(f\,x)\,y$, so $\Box P\,\beta = (\Box P)\,\beta$. Also, σ is the *shift* operator defined on any sequence s by $\sigma\,s\,m = s\,(m+1)$. Informally: σ drops the first symbol, e.g., $\sigma\,(a,b,c,d) = b,c,d$. The n-th power of a function is n-fold composition: $f^0\,x = x$ and $f^{n+1}\,x = f\,(f^n\,x)$ inductively.

By these definitions, FTC reduces temporal reasoning to predicate calculus.

Convention. As in functional predicate calculus, $\forall\,P$ expresses that predicate P is satisfied by all elements in its domain [10]. However, to highlight analogy with expressions of the form $\vdash \varphi$ in typical temporal logics [28], we define $\vdash$ for predicates P in BP by $\vdash P \equiv \forall\,P$. In pointwise form, $\vdash P \equiv \forall\,\beta\,{:}\,\mathbf{S}^\infty\,.\,P\,\beta$.

Aside: in formal logic, $\vdash$ is usually a metasymbol for "theoremhood". Adopting $\vdash$ within the language, as done here, adds flexibility for elucidating analogies and paradigm shifts. Also, to the "working mathematician" *provability* and *validity* are tantamount. Lamport [27, p. 92] simply states *"A temporal theorem is a temporal formula that is satisfied by all behaviors"*. For dealing with language and tool design technicalities, the usual sharper distinctions can be useful.

b. Illustration: deriving point-free theorems in FTC By *point-free* style we mean avoiding references to domain elements of functions [1,9,30]. Here the domain elements are the behaviors, typically referenced by a variable β (of type $\mathbf{S}^\infty$).

The point-free style allows writing formulas looking formally identical to the metatheorems and axioms of typical temporal logics [28].

The first stage in building this collection is deriving formulas by predicate calculus and getting rid of the variable β along the way. The second stage is using only point-free formulas already obtained, as a matter of style.

To convey the flavor, here are a few first-stage examples, chosen assuming minimal knowledge of predicate calculus, yet each yielding something interesting.

Example A: showing $\vdash (\Box P) \equiv \vdash P$.

$$\begin{array}{lll}
\vdash (\Box P) & \equiv \langle \text{Definition } \vdash \rangle & \forall \beta : \mathbf{S}^\infty . \Box P \beta \\
& \equiv \langle \text{Definition } \Box \rangle & \forall \beta : \mathbf{S}^\infty . \forall n : \mathbb{N} . P (\sigma^n \beta) \qquad (*) \\
(*) & \Rightarrow \langle \text{Inst. } n := 0 \rangle & \forall \beta : \mathbf{S}^\infty . P (\sigma^0 \beta) \\
& \equiv \langle f^0 x = x \rangle & \forall \beta : \mathbf{S}^\infty . P \beta \\
& \equiv \langle \text{Definition } \vdash \rangle & \vdash P \\
(*) & \Leftarrow \langle \text{Inst. } \beta' := \sigma^n \beta \rangle & \forall \beta : \mathbf{S}^\infty . \forall n : \mathbb{N} . \forall \beta' : \mathbf{S}^\infty . P \beta' \\
& \equiv \langle \text{Definition } \vdash \rangle & \forall \beta : \mathbf{S}^\infty . \forall n : \mathbb{N} . \vdash P \\
& \Leftarrow \langle \text{Const. pred.} \rangle & \vdash P \quad .
\end{array}$$

Gourmets may replace this 'ping-pong' proof by an equational one using domain change [10] under $f : \mathbf{S}^\infty \times \mathbb{N} \to \mathbf{S}^\infty$ with $f(\beta, n) = \sigma^n \beta$, noting Range $f = \mathbf{S}^\infty$.

Example B, "temporal instantiation": $\Box P \Rightarrow P$. Here is a detailed proof:

$$\begin{array}{lll}
\vdash (\Box P \Rightarrow P) & \equiv \langle \text{Definition } \vdash \rangle & \forall \beta : \mathbf{S}^\infty . (\Box P \Rightarrow P) \beta \\
& \equiv \langle \text{Pointw. ext. (1)} \rangle & \forall \beta : \mathbf{S}^\infty . \Box P \beta \Rightarrow P \beta \\
& \equiv \langle \text{Definition } \Box \rangle & \forall \beta : \mathbf{S}^\infty . \forall (n : \mathbb{N} . P (\sigma^n \beta)) \Rightarrow P \beta \\
& \equiv \langle f^0 x = x \rangle & \forall \beta : \mathbf{S}^\infty . \forall (n : \mathbb{N} . P (\sigma^n \beta)) \Rightarrow P (\sigma^0 \beta) \\
& \equiv \langle \text{Instant., } n := 0 \rangle & \forall \beta : \mathbf{S}^\infty . 1 \\
& \equiv \langle \text{Const. pred.} \rangle & 1 \quad . \quad \text{Note: WLOG, truth values are 0, 1.}
\end{array}$$

Note: $P \Rightarrow \Box P$, is not a theorem (try $\beta\, n = n$ and $P \beta \equiv \beta\, 0 = 0$).

Remark. Proofs can be compacted by noting that proving $\vdash P$ amounts to proving $P \beta$ for arbitrary β. For the $\Box P \Rightarrow P$ example, the calculation is

$$\begin{array}{lll}
\Box P \beta & \equiv \langle \text{Definition } \Box \rangle & \forall n : \mathbb{N} . P (\sigma^n \beta) \\
& \Rightarrow \langle \text{Inst. } n := 0 \rangle & P (\sigma^0 \beta) \\
& \equiv \langle \text{Definition } f^n \rangle & P \beta \quad ,
\end{array}$$

which shows $\Box P \beta \Rightarrow P \beta$ and hence, by pointwise extension (1), $(\Box P \Rightarrow P) \beta$.

Example C: induction. This example is chosen because it involves a nice generalization of the *weak induction principle* over natural numbers (WIN). A typical form of WIN is the following: for any predicate $Q : \mathbb{N} \to \mathbb{B}$,

$$\forall (n : \mathbb{N} . Q\, n \Rightarrow Q (n+1)) \Rightarrow (Q\, 0 \Rightarrow \forall m : \mathbb{N} . Q\, m) \quad . \tag{5}$$

The converse does not hold (try $Q\, n \equiv n = 1$). However, let us calculate

$$\begin{array}{lll}
\forall n : \mathbb{N} . Q\, n \Rightarrow Q (n+1) & & \\
\quad \equiv \langle \text{Dom. ch. } f := n, m : \mathbb{N}^2 . n + m \rangle & \forall n, m : \mathbb{N}^2 . Q (n+m) \Rightarrow Q (n+m+1) \\
\quad \equiv \langle \text{Nesting, } \sigma^n s\, m = s (n+m) \rangle & \forall n : \mathbb{N} . \forall m : \mathbb{N} . \sigma^n Q\, m \Rightarrow \sigma^n Q (m+1) \\
\quad \Rightarrow \langle \text{WIN (5) with } Q := \sigma^n Q \rangle & \forall n : \mathbb{N} . \sigma^n Q\, 0 \Rightarrow \forall m : \mathbb{N} . \sigma^n Q\, m \\
\quad \equiv \langle \text{Definition } \sigma \rangle & \forall n : \mathbb{N} . Q\, n \Rightarrow \forall m : \mathbb{N} . Q (n+m) \;;
\end{array}$$

$$\begin{aligned}&\forall\, n\!:\!\mathbb{N}\,.\,Q\,n \Rightarrow \forall\, m\!:\!\mathbb{N}\,.\,Q\,(n+m)\\ &\quad\Rightarrow \langle\text{Inst. with } m := 1\rangle\ \forall\, n\!:\!\mathbb{N}\,.\,Q\,n \Rightarrow Q\,(n+1)\ .\end{aligned}$$

The result is a *strengthened weak induction principle* over $\mathbb{N}$ (SWIN):

$$\forall\,(n\!:\!\mathbb{N}\,.\,Q\,n \Rightarrow Q\,(n+1)) \equiv \forall\,(n\!:\!\mathbb{N}\,.\,Q\,n \Rightarrow \forall\, m\!:\!\mathbb{N}\,.\,Q\,(n+m))\quad , \tag{6}$$

from which WIN (5) is easily recovered by instantiating the r.h.s. with $n := 0$.

SWIN also yields a temporal counterpart in FTC by calculating

$$\begin{aligned}
&\Box(P \Rightarrow \bigcirc P)\,\beta\\
&\equiv\quad \langle\text{Definition } \Box\rangle \quad \forall\, n\!:\!\mathbb{N}\,.\,(P \Rightarrow \bigcirc P)\,(\sigma^n\beta)\\
&\equiv\quad \langle\text{Pointw. ext. (1)}\rangle \quad \forall\, n\!:\!\mathbb{N}\,.\,P\,(\sigma^n\beta) \Rightarrow \bigcirc P\,(\sigma^n\beta)\\
&\equiv\quad \langle\text{Definition } \bigcirc\rangle \quad \forall\, n\!:\!\mathbb{N}\,.\,P\,(\sigma^n\beta) \Rightarrow P\,(\sigma\,(\sigma^n\beta))\\
&\equiv\quad \langle f\,(f^n x) = f^{n+1}x\rangle \quad \forall\, n\!:\!\mathbb{N}\,.\,P\,(\sigma^n\beta) \Rightarrow P\,(\sigma^{n+1}\beta)\\
&\equiv\quad \langle(6)\text{ with } Q\,n \equiv P\,(\sigma^n\beta)\rangle \quad \forall\, n\!:\!\mathbb{N}\,.\,P\,(\sigma^n\beta) \Rightarrow \forall\, m\!:\!\mathbb{N}\,.\,P\,(\sigma^{n+m}\beta)\\
&\equiv\quad \langle f^{n+m}x = f^m(f^n x)\rangle \quad \forall\, n\!:\!\mathbb{N}\,.\,P\,(\sigma^n\beta) \Rightarrow \forall\, m\!:\!\mathbb{N}\,.\,P\,(\sigma^m(\sigma^n\beta))\\
&\equiv\quad \langle\text{Definition } \Box\rangle \quad \forall\, n\!:\!\mathbb{N}\,.\,P\,(\sigma^n\beta) \Rightarrow \Box P\,(\sigma^n\beta)\\
&\equiv\quad \langle\text{Pointw. ext. (1)}\rangle \quad \forall\, n\!:\!\mathbb{N}\,.\,(P \Rightarrow \Box P)\,(\sigma^n\beta)\\
&\equiv\quad \langle\text{Definition } \Box\rangle \quad \Box(P \Rightarrow \Box P)\,\beta\ .
\end{aligned}$$

Hence $\Box(P \Rightarrow \bigcirc P) = \Box(P \Rightarrow \Box P)$ by function equality (note [9]: $f = g \equiv \mathcal{D}\,f = \mathcal{D}\,g \wedge \forall\, x\!:\!\mathcal{D}\,f\,.\,f\,x = g\,x$ where $\mathcal{D}\,f$ = domain f). This is the *strengthened (weak) temporal induction* principle (STI); in temporal theorem style:

$$\vdash (\Box(P \Rightarrow \bigcirc P) \equiv \Box(P \Rightarrow \Box P))\quad . \tag{7}$$

Example D, "infinitely often". Writing $\Box\Diamond\varphi$ is typical in specifications to express that a formula φ is satisfied "infinitely often". Note that this is a model-centric statement. More importantly, it is nearly always given without justification, perhaps assuming the intuitive interpretation "no matter how often φ has already happened, it will again". So a formal proof is all the more revealing.

In mathematics, the usual characterization of finiteness is by correspondence to the set of the first n natural numbers for some n, or even a subset thereof. Adopting this characterization, expressing that a general (i.e., non-temporal) predicate Q is satisfied for finitely many argument values is achieved by

$$\mathsf{Fin}\,Q \equiv \exists\, n\!:\!\mathbb{N}\,.\,\exists\, f\!:\!\mathbb{N}_{<n} \rightarrow \mathcal{D}\,Q\,.\,(\mathcal{D}\,Q)_Q \subseteq \mathcal{R}\,f\quad . \tag{8}$$

Note: S_Q is the set of elements in set S satisfying Q, and $\mathcal{R}\,f$ is the range of f.

Infiniteness is just the negation of finiteness, so we define $\exists_\infty\, Q \equiv \neg(\mathsf{Fin}\,Q)$ for any predicate Q. Specializing to predicates on natural numbers ($\mathcal{D}\,Q = \mathbb{N}$) allows showing that $\exists_\infty\, Q \equiv \forall\, n\!:\!\mathbb{N}\,.\,\exists\, m\!:\!\mathbb{N}\,.\,Q\,(m+n)$. The proof is quite instructive, but, being pure predicate calculus [10], not elaborated here.

It simply follows that, for any temporal predicate P in BP and any β in $\mathbf{S}^\infty$,

$$\Box(\Diamond\, P)\,\beta \equiv \exists_\infty\, n\!:\!\mathbb{N}\,.\,P\,(\sigma^n\beta)\quad . \tag{9}$$

This formally proves that $\Box(\Diamond P)$ is indeed equivalent to P being satisfied "infinitely often" according to the common mathematical characterization.

Example E, distributivity(-like) properties An important batch is

Distribut. $\Box/\wedge$: $\Box(P \wedge Q) \equiv \Box P \wedge \Box Q$ Dual: $\Diamond(P \vee Q) \equiv \Diamond P \vee \Diamond Q$
Dispatch. $\Diamond/\wedge$: $\Diamond(P \wedge Q) \Rightarrow \Diamond P \wedge \Diamond Q$ Dual: $\Box(P \vee Q) \Leftarrow \Box P \vee \Box Q$
Equal predic.: $\Box(P \equiv Q) \Rightarrow (\Box P \equiv \Box Q)$ Also: $\Box(P \equiv Q) \Rightarrow (\Diamond P \equiv \Diamond Q)$
Weaker predic.: $\Box(P \Rightarrow Q) \Rightarrow \Box P \Rightarrow \Box Q$ Also: $\Box(P \Rightarrow Q) \Rightarrow \Diamond P \Rightarrow \Diamond Q$

These are similar to certain properties in functional predicate calculus [10]. A noteworthy addition is $\exists_\infty(P \vee Q) \equiv \exists_\infty P \vee \exists_\infty Q$ for general predicates P and Q satisfying $\mathcal{D}\,P = \mathcal{D}\,Q$. For temporal predicates P and Q in BP, this yields $\Box(\Diamond(P \vee Q)) \equiv \Box(\Diamond P) \vee \Box(\Diamond Q)$; dual: $\Diamond(\Box(P \wedge Q)) \equiv \Diamond(\Box P) \wedge \Diamond(\Box Q)$.

We conclude this subsection with two important observations.

(a) FTC is entirely formulated within functional predicate calculus, without a separate temporal logic language. The operators are predicate transformers.

(b) FTC captures the essence of temporal logic (shown for linear temporal logic; branching logics can be handled analogously). It can thereby serve as an archetype for studying existing temporal logics, an issue addressed next.

2.3 Adapting the Style to Capture Various Existing Temporal Logics

FTC is functional whereas existing temporal logics are essentially expressional.

Note that terminology in the computing literature is often somewhat confusing, referring to "functions" and "predicates" when "expressions" and "propositions" (boolean expressions) respectively would be more appropriate to keep distinctions clear as outlined, for instance, by Gries and Schneider [21]. A classical misnomer is "the function $f(x)$ ('effovex')" to mean "the function f". Specifically in program semantics, "predicate transformer" is often confused with "proposition transformer". For instance, in the weakest precondition formula

$$wp(\texttt{x := x + 3})(x > 7) = x > 4 \quad ,$$

"$x > 7$" and "$x > 4$" have the form of propositions (boolean expressions).

Dijkstra and Scholten [16] avoid this discrepancy by considering program variables as functions over the state, and all arithmetic, relational and logical operators as implicitly extended pointwise to structures. Then "$x > 7$" and "$x > 4$" are indeed predicates and $wp(\texttt{x := x + 3})$ is a predicate transformer.

Whereas implicit extension to structures is viable in a specific context (program semantics), it is too restrictive in general mathematics, where extensions are better made explicit [9]. So a wider context requires a different approach.

Viewing "$wp(\texttt{x := x + 3})(x > 7)$" as a "normal" mathematical expression leads to errors right from the start, as Leibniz's principle [21] would yield

$$x > 7 \Rightarrow wp(\texttt{x := x + 3})(x > 7) = wp(\texttt{x := x + 3})\,1 \quad \text{(WRONG!)} \quad .$$

Our solution consists in viewing $wp(\texttt{x := x + 3})$ as a function that takes its argument (say, $x > 7$) as *purely syntactic*, yet its result (say, $x > 4$) as a normal mathematical expression unless, of course, it is again in a syntactic argument position, as in composing *wps*. Hence, for instance, it is correct to write

$$x > 5 \Rightarrow wp(\texttt{x := x + 3})(x > 7) \quad .$$

We call such functions *endosemantic*. Whereas typical semantic functions (meaning functions mapping syntax to denotations) are used only at the meta-level, endosemantic functions are adopted within the language (of mathematics).

To remove the impression that this is a new concept requiring (much) further explanation, note that we introduce the term "endosemantic" just for discussing explicitly some familiar tacit conventions throughout mathematics.

Substitution, for instance, is basically an endosemantic function. Indeed, adopting here the notation from Gries and Schneider [21],

$$(x + y)[x, y := y, x] \;=\; y + x$$

holds syntactically, by the definition of $[x, y := y, x]$. Yet, by the same token, in

$$(x + y)[x, y := y, x] \;=\; x + y$$

the left-hand side evaluates syntactically to $y + x$, but the complete equality is read within the language of mathematics as expressing commutativity of $+$.

A quite different example is the Fourier transform. In purely functional style,

$$\mathcal{F}\, f\, \omega \;=\; \int_{-\infty}^{+\infty} e^{-j\cdot\omega\cdot t} \cdot f(t) \cdot dt \quad . \tag{10}$$

Here variable bindings are systematic as in functional formalisms [10] and hence FTC. By contrast, in the traditional math/engineering textbook formulation

$$\mathcal{F}\,\{f(t)\} \;=\; \int_{-\infty}^{+\infty} e^{-j\cdot\omega\cdot t} \cdot f(t) \cdot dt \tag{11}$$

the same conventions would consider t free on the left and ω free on the right, making (11) nonsensical. However, we can salvage (11) by defining $\mathcal{F}$ as an endosemantic function taking an expression φ as a syntactic argument:

$$\mathcal{F}\,\{\varphi\} \;=\; \int_{-\infty}^{+\infty} e^{-j\cdot\omega\cdot t} \cdot \varphi \cdot dt \quad . \tag{12}$$

As a matter of bookkeeping, the variable names are assumed as given in the context, e.g., φ is assumed an "expression in t" (i.e., possibly containing t free). The images are expressions in ω. This salvages classical transform notations like

$$\mathcal{F}\,\{e^{-a\cdot t} \cdot h(t)\} \;=\; \frac{1}{a + j \cdot \omega} \quad ,$$

where $h(t)$ is the Heaviside unit step.

Temporal logics are captured by mapping temporal formulas (expressions) φ to predicates (functions) on $\mathbf{S}^\infty$ using an endosemantic function $\mathcal{M}$, as in $\mathcal{M}\,\varphi\,\beta$. However, adopting the symbol $\models$ (normally a metalevel symbol) for that purpose and writing $\beta \models \varphi$ rather than $\mathcal{M}\,\varphi\,\beta$ yields convenient visual correspondence with common notations.

The next section illustrates this approach in detail for TLA$^+$.

3 Capturing TLA$^+$ and Making Proof Rules Calculational

As an example, we chose Lamport's Temporal Logic of Actions [27] or TLA$^+$, and show how the aforementioned approach captures it as TCA. Since [27] is readily available on the web, no detailed account of TLA$^+$ is necessary here.

3.1 Basic Definitions for the *Temporal Calculus of Actions* (TCA)

Types For talking about functions, it is convenient to have their types at hand.

Although TLA$^+$ is untyped, types for the variables follow from an initial state and a next state specification. Moreover, as in [27], a well-structured specification is documented by a *type invariant* stating types explicitly. Hence in the sequel we pretend that variables have been declared with a type.

Let $T : I \to T$ be the family of types for the variables in the specification. The index set I is for bookkeeping, and can be tuned to the desired style. Then the state space is $\mathbf{S} := \times T$, a Cartesian product [10]. Behaviors have type $\mathbf{S}^\infty$.

We assume that basic arithmetic, relational and logical operators are available on these types (no details needed), and categorize expressions as follows.

$\mathcal{E}$ state expressions	$\mathcal{B}$ state propositions
$\mathcal{E}'$ transition expressions	$\mathcal{A}$ transition propositions, called "*actions*"
$\mathcal{X}$ temporal expressions	$\mathcal{F}$ temporal propositions ("*temporal formulas*")

In state expressions, state variables occur unprimed, in transition expressions they can also be primed, and in temporal expressions temporal operators (see below) can occur, so $\mathcal{E} \subset \mathcal{E}' \subset \mathcal{X}$. Propositions are boolean-valued expressions.

Conventions. Substituting an expression d for variable v in expression e is written $e[v := d]$ as in [21], or as $e[^v_d$. For multiple substitution, d and v can be tuples (of the same length), for instance, $(y + x)[^{x,y}_{z\cdot y, a\cdot x} = a \cdot x + z \cdot y$.

As in [11], s is a syntactic shorthand that stands in all bindings and mathematical expressions for the tuple formed by all state variable names in some fixed order (e.g., as declared). The tuple of the names of the variables as syntactic elements is written $\underset{\sim}{s}$. The set of variables is then $\mathcal{V} := \mathcal{R}\,\underset{\sim}{s}$ and we let $I := \mathcal{D}\,\underset{\sim}{s}$. So, for n state variables, the state space $\mathbf{S}$ is a set of n-tuples. Furthermore, for any expression e, we write e' for $e[^s_{s'}$, noting also that $s' = s[^s_{s'}$.

Example: given the declaration VARIABLE $num : \mathbb{Z}; cond : \mathbb{B}$, then $\mathbf{S} := \mathbb{Z} \times \mathbb{B}$ and s literally stands for $num, cond$, e.g., $\forall\, s : \mathbf{S} \,.\, p$ stands for $\forall\,(num, cond) : \mathbf{S} \,.\, p$.

Operators. In the tables, the leftmost colomns describe the syntax via the syntactic categories. The rightmost columns give translation into common notation.

a. Action operators

$\_ \cdot \_ : \mathcal{A} \times \mathcal{A} \to \mathcal{A}$	$a \cdot b \equiv \exists\, t : \mathbf{S} \,.\, a[^{s'}_t \wedge b[^s_t$
$[\_]_\_ : \mathcal{A} \times \mathcal{E} \to \mathcal{A}$	$[a]_e \equiv a \vee e = e'$
$\langle\_\rangle_\_ : \mathcal{A} \times \mathcal{E} \to \mathcal{A}$	$\langle a\rangle_e \equiv a \wedge e \neq e'$
UNCHANGED $: \mathcal{E} \to \mathcal{A}$	UNCHANGED $e \equiv e = e'$
ENABLED $: \mathcal{A} \to \mathcal{B}$	ENABLED $a \equiv \exists\, s' : \mathbf{S} \,.\, a$

b. Temporal operators are characterized using the endosemantic function $\models$, defined recursively on the structure of expressions. In view of $\mathcal{E} \subset \mathcal{E}' \subset \mathcal{X}$, the recursion basis are the state and transition expressions e in $\mathcal{E}$ and $\mathcal{E}'$, for which

$$\beta \models e \;=\; e[^{s,s'}_{\beta\,0,\beta\,1} \quad .$$

Note: for state expressions, $e[^{s,s'}_{\beta\,0,\beta\,1} = e[^{s}_{\beta\,0}$ since primed variables are absent.

For temporal expressions (in $\mathcal{X}$) and formulas (in $\mathcal{F}$).

$$\begin{array}{lll}
\bigcirc : \mathcal{X} \to \mathcal{X} & \beta \models \bigcirc\, e \;=\; \sigma\, \beta \models e & (\bigcirc \text{ does not appear in TLA}^+) \\
\square : \mathcal{F} \to \mathcal{F} & \beta \models \square\, \varphi \equiv \forall\, n : \mathbb{N} \,.\, \sigma^n\, \beta \models \varphi & \\
\diamond : \mathcal{F} \to \mathcal{F} & \beta \models \diamond\, \varphi \equiv \exists\, n : \mathbb{N} \,.\, \sigma^n\, \beta \models \varphi & \\
\boldsymbol{\forall}_{_} : \mathcal{V} \to \mathcal{F} \to \mathcal{F} & \beta \models \boldsymbol{\forall}_v\, \varphi \equiv \forall\, \gamma : \mathbf{S}^{\infty}_{\models \varphi} \,.\, (\natural\, \gamma)^{\mathsf{T}}_{\neq i} = (\natural\, \beta)^{\mathsf{T}}_{\neq i} & \text{where } i = \underset{\sim}{s}^{-}\, v \\
\boldsymbol{\exists}_{_} : \mathcal{V} \to \mathcal{F} \to \mathcal{F} & \beta \models \boldsymbol{\exists}_v\, \varphi \equiv \exists\, \gamma : \mathbf{S}^{\infty}_{\models \varphi} \,.\, (\natural\, \gamma)^{\mathsf{T}}_{\neq i} = (\natural\, \beta)^{\mathsf{T}}_{\neq i} & \text{where } i = \underset{\sim}{s}^{-}\, v
\end{array}$$

The temporal quantifiers $\boldsymbol{\forall}$ and $\boldsymbol{\exists}$ are mentioned for completeness only and may be safely skipped. The rather terse notation uses generic operators from [9], and for the *compacting operator* $\natural$ removing successive duplicates (stuttering),

$$\natural\, \beta \;=\; +\!\!+\, n : \mathcal{D}\, \beta \,.\, (n > 0 \wedge \beta\, (n-1) = \beta\, n)\, ?\, \varepsilon \mid \tau\, (\beta\, n) \quad , \tag{13}$$

where $+\!\!+$ is catenation, ε the empty sequence and $\tau\, e$ the sequence of just e.

Boolean combinations of temporal formulas are defined by distributivity:

$$\begin{array}{ll}
\beta \models \neg\, \varphi \equiv \neg\, (\beta \models \varphi) & \beta \models \forall\, (x : X \,.\, \varphi) \equiv \forall\, x : X \,.\, \beta \models \varphi \\
\beta \models (\varphi \star \psi) \equiv \beta \models \varphi \,\star\, \beta \models \psi & \beta \models \exists\, (x : X \,.\, \varphi) \equiv \exists\, x : X \,.\, \beta \models \varphi
\end{array} \tag{14}$$

Here $\star$ is any infix logical operator in $\{\Rightarrow, \equiv, \not\equiv, \oplus, \wedge, \vee\}$.

At the left-hand sides of the equivalences, $\star$, $\neg$, $\forall$, $\exists$ are TCA/TLA$^+$ operators, and at the right-hand side they are the "normal" logical operators. Risk of confusion is minor, since the calculation rules will be fully analogous. Because temporal formulas appear only syntactically, we can adopt the syntax of the target language, e.g., for optional parentheses, $\square\diamond\varphi$ stands for $\square\, (\diamond\, \varphi)$ etc.

3.2 Calculational Reasoning in TCA/TLA$^+$

Introduction. For any φ, the partial application $\models\!\varphi$ is a predicate of type BP. This differs from FTC predicates only in using postfix notation (β stands before $\models\!\varphi$ in $\beta \models \varphi$, but after P in $P\,\beta$). Up to this lexical detail, all calculation rules are inherited from FTC.

The $\vdash$ operator from is adapted (or overloaded) to temporal formulas φ by

$$\vdash \varphi \equiv \forall\, \beta : \mathbf{S}^{\infty} \,.\, \beta \models \varphi \quad . \tag{15}$$

Hence $\vdash \varphi$ expresses the fact that φ is a (temporal) theorem in Lamport's sense.

A *(temporal) tautology* is a (temporal) theorem containing only arbitrary formulas, which can be instantiated by specific ones as desired.

"Proving φ" then means "proving $\vdash \varphi$" but, as for FTC, expanding $\vdash \varphi$ in pointwise form according to (15) is necessary only in proving the basic theorems.

A calculational style for TCA/TLA$^+$ First, all calculations from FTC are inherited. It suffices replacing $P\,\beta$ by $\beta \models \varphi$ and, when desired, removing optional parentheses, e.g., duality $\Diamond P \equiv \neg(\Box(\neg P))$ becomes $\Diamond\varphi \equiv \neg\Box\neg\varphi$.

Basic tautologies are named correspondingly, again (as in FTC) borrowing the terminology from similar rules in general predicate calculus [10], for instance

$$\Box(\varphi \wedge \psi) \equiv \Box\varphi \wedge \Box\psi \quad \text{(Dist. }\Box/\wedge) \qquad \Box(\varphi \vee \psi) \Leftarrow \Box\varphi \vee \Box\psi \quad \text{(Coll. }\Box/\vee)$$
$$\Diamond(\varphi \vee \psi) \equiv \Diamond\varphi \vee \Diamond\psi \quad \text{(Dist. }\Diamond/\vee) \qquad \Diamond(\varphi \wedge \psi) \Rightarrow \Diamond\varphi \wedge \Diamond\psi \quad \text{(Disp. }\Diamond/\wedge).$$

We also recall the extra equational distributivity rules due to the underlying model (behaviors) and based on properties of the natural numbers, e.g.,

$$\Box\Diamond(\varphi \vee \psi) \equiv \Box\Diamond\varphi \vee \Box\Diamond\psi \quad \text{(Dist. }\Box\Diamond/\vee)$$
$$\Diamond\Box(\varphi \wedge \psi) \equiv \Diamond\Box\varphi \wedge \Diamond\Box\psi \quad \text{(Dist. }\Diamond\Box/\wedge).$$

Rules for "equal/weaker predicates", e.g., $\forall(P \mathrel{\widehat{\Rightarrow}} Q) \Rightarrow \forall P \Rightarrow \forall Q$ (WKP\∀) from general predicate calculus [10] and rule $\Box(P \Rightarrow Q) \Rightarrow \Box P \Rightarrow \Box Q$ (WKP\□) from FTC are renamed with "formula", as in $\Box(\varphi \Rightarrow \psi) \Rightarrow \Box\varphi \Rightarrow \Box\psi$ (WKF\□).

Even when calculating directly with $\beta \models \varphi$, the remark after *Example B* in section 2.2 shows how to omit repetitive parts, such as the prelude "We calculate, for arbitrary $\beta : \mathbf{S}^\infty$," and the postlude "Hence $\beta \models \varphi \star \beta \models \psi$ which yields $\vdash(\varphi \star \psi)$", where $\star$ is implication or equivalence as in the calculation chain.

Finally, we establish a calculational style *within* TCA/TLA$^+$ as follows. Thus far, all steps in all derivations were linked by propositional equivalences and implications, and β appeared explicitly. However, after deriving the □/◇-related tautologies, further calculations typically contain (only) steps of the form

$$\begin{aligned} \beta \models \varphi \quad &\Rightarrow \langle \text{Justification for } \beta \models \varphi \Rightarrow \beta \models \psi \rangle \quad \beta \models \psi \\ \beta \models \varphi \quad &\equiv \langle \text{Justification for } \beta \models \varphi \equiv \beta \models \psi \rangle \quad \beta \models \psi \;. \end{aligned}$$

The justifications can be temporal tautologies of the form $\varphi \Rightarrow \psi$ or $\varphi \equiv \psi$, since these can be instantiated for $\beta : \mathbf{S}^\infty$ using (15). There are more tautologies than just □/◇-related ones. Every rule from propositional calculus yields a temporal tautology by substituting $\beta \models \varphi$, $\beta \models \psi$ etc. for p, q etc., distributivity (14) for every operator to bring $\beta \models$ in front, and generalization for $\forall$.

As $\beta \models$ appears in every line in the same position, we omit it as a matter of convention, linking the steps by temporal equivalences and implications.

All these observations are illustrated in the following calculation, yielding the interesting modus ponens-like property $\Diamond\Box\varphi \wedge \Diamond\Box(\varphi \Rightarrow \psi) \Rightarrow \Diamond\Box\psi$.

$$\begin{aligned} \Diamond\Box\varphi \wedge \Diamond\Box(\varphi \Rightarrow \psi) \;&\equiv \langle \text{Dist. } \Diamond\Box/\wedge \rangle\; \Diamond\Box(\varphi \wedge (\varphi \Rightarrow \psi)) \\ &\equiv \langle \text{MP equiv.} \rangle\; \Diamond\Box(\varphi \wedge \psi) \\ &\equiv \langle \text{Dist. } \Diamond\Box/\wedge \rangle\; \Diamond\Box\varphi \wedge \Diamond\Box\psi \\ &\Rightarrow \langle \text{Weakening} \rangle\; \Diamond\Box\psi \;. \end{aligned}$$

Rule ⟨MP equiv.⟩ is "Modus Ponens as an equivalence": $\varphi \wedge (\varphi \Rightarrow \psi) \equiv \varphi \wedge \psi$. The redundancy is to obtain $\Diamond\Box\varphi \wedge \Diamond\Box(\varphi \Rightarrow \psi) \equiv \Diamond\Box\varphi \wedge \Diamond\Box\psi$ in passing.

Calculation is now fully *within* TCA. When possible, we use this style as it reduces writing, makes patterns conspicuous, and raises the abstraction level.

4 Applications to Liveness and Fairness in TLA$^+$

This section is an extended chain of examples about patterns related to liveness and fairness. The patterns are taken from Chapter 8 in *Specifying Systems* [27], which is readily available on the web. We show how TCA yields significantly simpler proofs and how the theorems themselves are *discovered* by calculation, sometimes even in a stronger form. Formulas are labeled as in the cited reference.

From [27, pp. 97–98], we quote the following equivalent patterns for "weak fairness", denoted $\mathrm{WF}_v\,(A)$. The motivation is discussed in the cited reference.

$$\Box(\Box\,\text{ENABLED}\,\langle A\rangle_v \Rightarrow \Diamond\,\langle A\rangle_v) \tag{8.7}$$
$$\Box\Diamond\,(\neg\,(\text{ENABLED}\,\langle A\rangle_v) \vee \Box\Diamond\,\langle A\rangle_v \tag{8.8}$$
$$\Diamond\Box\,(\text{ENABLED}\,\langle A\rangle_v) \Rightarrow \Box\Diamond\,\langle A\rangle_v \tag{8.9}$$

These will be the basis for the following calculational TCA/TLA$^+$-derivations.

Application example A. The motivation of (8.7) in [27, page 97] went via the intermediate form $\Box(\text{ENABLED}\,\langle A\rangle_v \Rightarrow \Diamond\,\langle A\rangle_v)$, later giving rise [27, page 99] to the question under which condition this form is equivalent to (8.7).

The answer in [27, page 99] is given in the form of a theorem:

$$\Box(E \Rightarrow \Box E \vee \Diamond A) \;\Rightarrow\; (\Box(E \Rightarrow \Diamond A) \equiv \Box(\Box E \Rightarrow \Diamond A)) \quad . \tag{8.11}$$

Formula (8.11) was designated as "complicated" and unfavorable to a proof by calculation (not to be confused with the technical term "calculational proof", which is not used in [27]), and a classical proof taking about one page was given.

Here follows a calculational derivation, which differs from a proof in the sense that the desired condition is *discovered* without knowing it in advance.

$$\begin{aligned}
\Box(E \Rightarrow \Diamond A) \equiv \Box(\Box E \Rightarrow \Diamond A) &\Leftarrow \langle\text{Equal form.}\backslash\Box\rangle\; \Box(E \Rightarrow \Diamond A \equiv \Box E \Rightarrow \Diamond A)\\
&\equiv \langle\text{RSDist.} \Rightarrow\backslash\equiv\rangle\; \Box(\neg\,(E \equiv \Box E) \Rightarrow \Diamond A)\\
&\equiv \langle\text{Inst. } \Box\varphi \Rightarrow \varphi\rangle\; \Box(\neg\,(E \Rightarrow \Box E) \Rightarrow \Diamond A)\\
&\equiv \langle\text{From} \Rightarrow \text{to} \vee\rangle\; \Box((E \Rightarrow \Box E) \vee \Diamond A)\\
&\equiv \langle\text{From} \Rightarrow \text{to} \vee\rangle\; \Box(\neg\, E \vee \Box E \vee \Diamond A)\\
&\equiv \langle\text{From} \vee \text{to} \Rightarrow\rangle\; \Box(E \Rightarrow \Box E \vee \Diamond A)
\end{aligned}$$

Application example B. In [27, page 101 ff.] the question is asked when separate fairness conditions can be combined in a single one, more specifically, *When can $WF_v(A) \wedge WF_v(B)$ be written as $WF_v(A \vee B)$?*

The answer in [27, page 102] is given in the form of a theorem:

$$\mathit{DR1} \wedge \mathit{DR2} \;\Rightarrow\; (\mathit{WF}_v(A) \wedge \mathit{WF}_v(B) \;\equiv\; \mathit{WF}_v(A \vee B)) \quad , \tag{8.20}$$
$$\text{where } \mathit{DR1} \triangleq \Box(\text{ENABLED}\,\langle A\rangle_v \Rightarrow \Box\neg\,\text{ENABLED}\langle B\rangle_v \vee \Diamond\,\langle A\rangle_v)$$
$$\mathit{DR2} \triangleq \Box(\text{ENABLED}\,\langle B\rangle_v \Rightarrow \Box\neg\,\text{ENABLED}\langle A\rangle_v \vee \Diamond\,\langle B\rangle_v)$$

The classical proof in [27, page 102 ff.] takes two and a half pages. It uses contradiction, which also requires knowing the result. Here we proceed calculationally, and by discovery, which happens to yield a stronger result along the way.

To avoid clutter in formulas and calculations, we introduce W defined by the following equivalent expressions for $\mathrm{W}\,A$, from which to choose as convenient.

$$\Box(\Box\mathrm{E}\,A \Rightarrow \Diamond A)\ (8.7') \quad \Box\Diamond\neg\mathrm{E}\,A \vee \Box\Diamond A\ (8.8') \quad \Diamond\Box\mathrm{E}\,A \Rightarrow \Box\Diamond A\ (8.9')$$

Obviously $WF_v(A) \equiv \mathrm{W}\langle A\rangle_v$. Note also that E and $\langle\ \rangle_v$ distribute over $\vee$.

The central question is when $WF_v(A \vee B)$ captures $WF_v(A) \wedge WF_v(B)$. Hence we investigate $\mathrm{W}\,(A \vee B) \Rightarrow \mathrm{W}\,A \wedge \mathrm{W}\,B$ by calculating

$$\begin{array}{ll}
& \mathrm{W}\,(A \vee B) \Rightarrow \mathrm{W}\,A \\
\equiv & \langle \text{Definition W (8.9')} \rangle\ (\Diamond\Box\mathrm{E}\,(A \vee B) \Rightarrow \Box\Diamond(A \vee B)) \Rightarrow \Diamond\Box\mathrm{E}\,A \Rightarrow \Box\Diamond A \\
\equiv & \langle \text{Shunt} \Rightarrow\text{, dist. E}/\vee \rangle\ \Diamond\Box\mathrm{E}\,A \Rightarrow (\Diamond\Box(\mathrm{E}\,A \vee \mathrm{E}\,B) \Rightarrow \Box\Diamond(A \vee B)) \Rightarrow \Box\Diamond A \\
\equiv & \langle \varphi \Rightarrow \varphi \vee \psi\text{, WKF} \rangle\ \Diamond\Box\mathrm{E}\,A \Rightarrow \Box\Diamond(A \vee B) \Rightarrow \Box\Diamond A \\
\equiv & \langle \text{Distributiv. } \Box\Diamond/\vee \rangle\ \Diamond\Box\mathrm{E}\,A \Rightarrow \Box\Diamond A \vee \Box\Diamond B \Rightarrow \Box\Diamond A \\
\equiv & \langle \varphi \vee \psi \Rightarrow \varphi \equiv \psi \Rightarrow \varphi \rangle\ \Diamond\Box\mathrm{E}\,A \Rightarrow \Box\Diamond B \Rightarrow \Box\Diamond A \\
\equiv & \langle \text{Shunt} \Rightarrow\text{, def. W)} \rangle\ \Box\Diamond B \Rightarrow \mathrm{W}\,A \qquad (*)
\end{array}$$

Hence $\mathrm{W}\,(A \vee B) \Rightarrow \mathrm{W}\,A \wedge \mathrm{W}\,B \ \equiv\ (\Box\Diamond B \Rightarrow \mathrm{W}\,A) \wedge (\Box\Diamond A \Rightarrow \mathrm{W}\,B)$.

The r.h.s. is sufficient for $\mathrm{W}\,(A \vee B) \Rightarrow \mathrm{W}\,A \wedge \mathrm{W}\,B$ but also necessary and hence the weakest condition possible. Hence the essential goal is amply met.

Just for completeness, we investigate $\mathrm{W}\,A \wedge \mathrm{W}\,B \Rightarrow \mathrm{W}\,(A \vee B)$ by calculating

$$\begin{array}{ll}
& \mathrm{W}\,A \Rightarrow \mathrm{W}\,B \Rightarrow \mathrm{W}\,(A \vee B) \\
\equiv & \langle \text{Def. W (8.7')} \rangle\ \Box(\Box\mathrm{E}\,A \Rightarrow \Diamond A) \Rightarrow \Box(\Box\mathrm{E}\,B \Rightarrow \Diamond B) \Rightarrow \Box(\Box\mathrm{E}\,(A \vee B) \Rightarrow \Diamond(A \vee B)) \\
\Leftarrow & \langle \text{WQF reverse} \rangle\ \Box((\Box\mathrm{E}\,A \Rightarrow \Diamond A) \Rightarrow (\Box\mathrm{E}\,B \Rightarrow \Diamond B) \Rightarrow \Box\mathrm{E}\,(A \vee B) \Rightarrow \Diamond(A \vee B)) \\
\equiv & \langle \text{Shunting} \Rightarrow \rangle\ \Box(\Box\mathrm{E}\,(A \vee B) \Rightarrow (\Box\mathrm{E}\,A \Rightarrow \Diamond A) \Rightarrow (\Box\mathrm{E}\,B \Rightarrow \Diamond B) \Rightarrow \Diamond(A \vee B)) \\
\equiv & \langle \text{Distrib. } \Diamond/\vee \rangle\ \Box(\Box\mathrm{E}\,(A \vee B) \Rightarrow (\Box\mathrm{E}\,A \Rightarrow \Diamond A) \Rightarrow (\Box\mathrm{E}\,B \Rightarrow \Diamond B) \Rightarrow \Diamond A \vee \Diamond B) \\
\equiv & \langle \text{Lemma A} \rangle\ \Box(\Box\mathrm{E}\,(A \vee B) \Rightarrow \Box\mathrm{E}\,A \vee \Diamond A \vee \Box\mathrm{E}\,B \vee \Diamond B) \\
\equiv & \langle \text{Distrib. E}/\vee \rangle\ \Box(\Box(\mathrm{E}\,A \vee \mathrm{E}\,B) \Rightarrow \Box\mathrm{E}\,A \vee \Diamond A \vee \Box\mathrm{E}\,B \vee \Diamond B) \\
\Leftarrow & \langle \text{Lemma C} \rangle\ \Box(\Box(\mathrm{E}\,A \vee \mathrm{E}\,B) \Rightarrow \Box\mathrm{E}\neg B \vee \Diamond A \vee \Box\mathrm{E}\neg A \vee \Diamond B) \\
\Leftarrow & \langle \text{Inst. } \Box\varphi \Rightarrow \varphi \rangle\ \Box(\mathrm{E}\,A \vee \mathrm{E}\,B \Rightarrow \Box\neg\mathrm{E}\,B \vee \Diamond A \vee \Box\neg\mathrm{E}\,A \vee \Diamond B) \\
\Leftarrow & \langle \text{Lemma B} \rangle\ \Box((\mathrm{E}\,A \Rightarrow \Box\neg\mathrm{E}\,B \vee \Diamond A) \wedge (\mathrm{E}\,B \Rightarrow \Box\neg\mathrm{E}\,A \vee \Diamond B)) \\
\equiv & \langle \text{Distrib. } \Box/\wedge \rangle\ \Box(\mathrm{E}\,A \Rightarrow \Box\neg\mathrm{E}\,B \vee \Diamond A) \wedge \Box(\mathrm{E}\,B \Rightarrow \Box\neg\mathrm{E}\,A \vee \Diamond B) \\
\equiv & \langle \text{Def. D below} \rangle\ \mathrm{D}\,(A, B) \wedge \mathrm{D}\,(B, A) \quad .
\end{array}$$

Lemma C is $\Box(\varphi \vee \psi) \Rightarrow \Box\neg\varphi \Rightarrow \Box\psi$. Lemmata A and B are just propositional:

Lemma A. $(p \Rightarrow p') \Rightarrow (q \Rightarrow q') \Rightarrow p' \vee q' \equiv p \vee p' \vee q \vee q'$

Lemma B. $(p \Rightarrow p') \wedge (q \Rightarrow q') \Rightarrow (p \vee q) \Rightarrow (p' \vee q')$

The definition we introduce for D to abbreviate the last line in the calculation is

$\mathrm{D}(A, B) \equiv \Box(\mathrm{E}\,A \Rightarrow \Box\neg\mathrm{E}\,B \vee \Diamond A)$.

Clearly, $DR1 \equiv \mathrm{D}(\langle A\rangle_v, \langle B\rangle_v)$ and similarly $DR2 \equiv \mathrm{D}(\langle B\rangle_v, \langle A\rangle_v)$.

Let us finally check the relationship with $(*)$ by calculating

$$
\begin{array}{rcll}
\Box\Diamond B \Rightarrow \mathrm{W}\, A & \equiv & \langle \text{Definition W (8.7')} \rangle & \Box\Diamond B \Rightarrow \Box(\Box \mathrm{E}\, A \Rightarrow \Diamond A) \\
& \Leftarrow & \langle \text{WQF in reverse} \rangle & \Box(\Diamond B \Rightarrow \Box \mathrm{E}\, A \Rightarrow \Diamond A) \\
& \Leftarrow & \langle \text{WQF rev., } B \Rightarrow \mathrm{E}\, B \rangle & \Box(\Diamond \mathrm{E}\, B \Rightarrow \Box \mathrm{E}\, A \Rightarrow \Diamond A) \\
& \Leftarrow & \langle \text{WQF rev., } \Box\varphi \Rightarrow \varphi \rangle & \Box(\Diamond \mathrm{E}\, B \Rightarrow \mathrm{E}\, A \Rightarrow \Diamond A) \\
& \equiv & \langle \text{Shunting } \Rightarrow \rangle & \Box(\mathrm{E}\, A \Rightarrow \Diamond \mathrm{E}\, B \Rightarrow \Diamond A) \\
& \equiv & \langle \text{From } \Rightarrow \text{ to } \vee \rangle & \Box(\mathrm{E}\, A \Rightarrow \neg \Diamond \mathrm{E}\, B \vee \Diamond A) \\
& \equiv & \langle \text{Duality } \Box/\Diamond \rangle & \Box(\mathrm{E}\, A \Rightarrow \Box \neg \mathrm{E}\, B \vee \Diamond A) \\
& \equiv & \langle \text{Definition D} \rangle & \mathrm{D}\,(A, B) \quad .
\end{array}
$$

5 Conclusions

In general, systems design requires diversity without the distraction and overhead of disparity. This is best achieved by offering the designer unified mathematical theories, with suitably lowered threshold to improve acessibility in practice.

Specifically, awareness in the use of model checking requires a higher mathematical standard than often suggested when advocating the use of automated tools. For accessibility, we have made the "user-friendliness" of the calculational style available in temporal reasoning. Unifying the various tool- or language-dependent temporal logics is made possible by a generic form (FTC), which is pure predicate calculus. Specific logics are then captured by endosemantic functions in a very direct and simple way, illustrated in detail for TLA$^+$.

Note that Lamport's *Specifying Systems* [27] concentrates on writing specifications. Proofs are considered in one chapter only, since introducing a temporal proof style (as in [28]) and meeting more proof obligations would have doubled the size of the book. Yet, not surprisingly, the proofs given concern patterns.

Formal reasoning about patterns keeps the complexity of temporal specifications manageable and within the grasp of intuition. The calculational approach makes this easier, and even supports discovery by newcomers in the field.

Still, when using this approach in an educational setting, it must be remembered that predicate calculus clearly remains a prerequisite, but this is amply compensated by its very wide usefulness.

References

1. Aarts, C., Backhouse, R., Hoogendijk, P., Voermans, E., van der Woude, J.: A Relational Theory of Data Types. Lecture notes, Eindhoven University of Technology (1992)
2. Arvind, Dave, N., Katelman, M.: Getting Formal Verification into Design Flow. In: Cuellar, J., Maibaum, T., Sere, K. (eds.) FM 2008. LNCS, vol. 5014, pp. 12–32. Springer, Heidelberg (2008)
3. Baier, C., Katoen, J.-P.: Principles of Model Checking. The MIT Press, Cambridge (2008)

4. Bandera Home Page, http://bandera.projects.cis.ksu.edu/
5. Bentley, J.: Programming Pearls. Addison-Wesley, Reading (2000) [10th printing, 2005]
6. Boute, R.: A calculus for reasoning about temporal phenomena. In: Proc. NGI-SION Symposium, April 1986, vol. 4, pp. 405–411 (1986)
7. Boute, R.: On the shortcomings of the axiomatic approach as presently used in Computer Science. In: CompEuro 1988. Design: Concepts, Methods and Tools, April 1988, pp. 184–193 (1988)
8. Boute, R., Verlinde, H.: Functionals for the Semantic Specification of Temporal Formulas for Model Checking. In: König, H., Heiner, M., Wolisz, A. (eds.) FORTE 2003, BTU Cottbus CS Reports, Brandenburg University of Technology, pp. 23–28 (2003)
9. Boute, R.: Concrete Generic Functionals: Principles, Design and Applications. In: Gibbons, J., Jeuring, J. (eds.) Generic Programming, pp. 89–119. Kluwer, Dordrecht (2003)
10. Boute, R.: Functional declarative language design and predicate calculus: a practical approach. ACM TOPLAS 27(5), 988–1047 (2005)
11. Boute, R.: Calculational semantics: deriving programming theories from equations by functional predicate calculus. ACM TOPLAS 28(4), 747–793 (2006)
12. Boute, R.: Using Domain-Independent Problems for Introducing Formal Methods. In: Misra, J., Nipkow, T., Sekerinski, E. (eds.) FM 2006. LNCS, vol. 4085, pp. 316–331. Springer, Heidelberg (2006)
13. Chen, Y., Liu, Z.: Integrating Temporal Logics. In: Boiten, E.A., Derrick, J., Smith, G.P. (eds.) IFM 2004. LNCS, vol. 2999, pp. 402–420. Springer, Heidelberg (2004)
14. Clarke, E.M., Grumberg, O., Peled, D.A.: Model Checking. The MIT Press, Cambridge (2000)
15. Dijkstra, E.W.: How Computing Science created a new mathematical style. EWD 1073 (1990), http://www.cs.utexas.edu/users/EWD/ewd10xx/EWD1073.PDF
16. Dijkstra, E.W., Scholten, C.S.: Predicate Calculus and Program Semantics. Springer, Heidelberg (1990)
17. Dwyer, M.B., Avrunin, G.S., Corbett, J.C.: Property Specification Patterns for Finite-State Specification. In: Ardis, M. (ed.) Proc. FMSP 1998, Second Workshop on Formal Methods in Software Practice, Clearwater Beach, FL, March 1998, pp. 7–15 (1998)
18. Dwyer, M.B., Avrunin, G.S., Corbett, J.C.: Patterns in Property Specification for Finite-State Specification. In: Proc. Twenty-First Intl. Conf. on Software Engineering, Los Angeles, May 1999, pp. 411–420 (1999)
19. Dwyer, M.B., Hatcliff, J.: Bandera Temporal Specification Patterns. In: ETAPS 2002 (Grenoble) and SMF 2002, Bertinoro (2002) (tutorial presentation), http://www.cis.ksu.edu/~santos/bandera/Talks/SFM02/02-SFM-Patterns.ppt
20. Gries, D.: Improving the curriculum through the teaching of calculation and discrimination. Communications of the ACM 34(3), 45–55 (1991)
21. Gries, D., Schneider, F.B. (eds.): A Logical Approach to Discrete Math. Springer, Heidelberg (1993)
22. Habrias, H., Faucou, S.: Linking Paradigms, Semi-formal and Formal Notations. In: Dean, C.N., Boute, R.T. (eds.) TFM 2004. LNCS, vol. 3294, pp. 166–184. Springer, Heidelberg (2004)
23. Henderson, P.B.: Mathematical Reasoning in Software Engineering Education. Comm. ACM 46(9), 45–50 (2003)
24. Hoare, C.A.R., Jifeng, H.: Unifying Theories of Programming. Prentice-Hall, Englewood Cliffs (1998)

25. Holloway, M.: Why engineers should consider formal methods. In: Proc. 16th. Digital Avionics Systems Conference (October 1997), `http://citeseerx.ist.psu.edu/viewdoc/summary?doi=10.1.1.50.5654`
26. Holzmann, G.J.: The SPIN model checker: Primer and Reference Manual. Addison Wesley, Reading (2004)
27. Lamport, L.: Specifying Systems: The TLA^+ Language and Tools for Hardware and Software Engineers. Pearson Education Inc., London (2002)
28. Manna, Z., Pnueli, A.: The Temporal Logic of Reactive and Concurrent Systems: Specification. Springer, New York (1992)
29. Manna, Z., Pnueli, A.: The Temporal Logic of Reactive and Concurrent Systems: Safety. Springer, Heidelberg (1995)
30. Oliveira, J.N.: Extended Static Checking by Calculation using the Pointfree Transform. In: Bove, A., Barbosa, L.S., Pardo, A., Pinto, J.S. (eds.) Language Engineering and Rigorous Software Development: LerNet ALFA Summer School 2008. LNCS, vol. 5520, pp. 195–251. Springer, Heidelberg (2009)
31. Parnas, D.L.: Education for computing professionals. IEEE Computer 23(1), 17–22 (1990)
32. Parnas, D.L.: Predicate Logic for Software Engineering. IEEE Trans. SWE 19(9), 856–862 (1993)
33. Pnueli, A.: Linear and branching structures in the semantics and logics of reactive systems. In: Brauer, W. (ed.) ICALP 1985. LNCS, vol. 194, pp. 15–32. Springer, Heidelberg (1985)
34. Thomas, G.B., Weir, M.D., Hass, J., Giordano, F.R.: Thomas's Calculus, 11th edn. Addison Wesley, Reading (2004)
35. Tucker, A.B., Kelemen, C.F., Bruce, K.B.: Our Curriculum Has Become Math-Phobic! ACM SIGCSEB, SIGCSE Bulletin 33 (2001), `http://citeseer.ist.psu.edu/tucker01our.html`
36. van Benthem, J.: Correspondence Theory. In: Gabbay, D., Guenthner, F. (eds.) Handbook of Philosophical Logic, 2nd edn., vol. 3, pp. 325–408. Kluwer, Dordrecht (2001)
37. von Karger, B.: Temporal Algebra. Mathematical Structures in Computer Science 8(3), 277–320 (1998)

A Tableau for CTL*

Mark Reynolds

The University of Western Australia, Perth, Australia
mark@csse.uwa.edu.au

Abstract. We present a sound, complete and relatively straightforward tableau method for deciding valid formulas in the propositional version of computation tree logic CTL*. This is the first such tableau.

CTL* is an exceptionally important temporal logic with applications from hardware design to agent reasoning but there is no easy automated reasoning approach to CTL*. The tableau here is a traditional tree-shaped or top-down style tableau and affords the possibility of reasonably quick decisions on the satisfiability of sufficiently short formulas and construction of models for them. Handling looping is subtle.

1 Introduction

CTL*, or full computation tree logic, was introduced in [9] to extend both the simple branching logic, CTL, of [2], and the linear temporal logic, PLTL of [15].

The language of CTL*, which is a propositional temporal language, is built recursively from the atomic propositions using the next X and until U operators of PLTL, and the universal path switching modality A of CTL as well as classical connectives. This language is appropriate for describing properties of all paths of states through a transition structure, or applications which can be modelled as such. This standard semantics for CTL* is called the semantics over R-generable models.

The main uses of CTL* in computer science are for developing and checking the correctness of complex reactive systems [10] and as a basis of more complex modal languages for reasoning about multi-agent systems [18]. CTL* is also used widely as a framework for comparing other languages more appropriate for specific reasoning tasks of this type. See the description in [4]. These include the purely linear and purely branching sub-languages.

Validity of formulas of CTL* is known to be decidable. This was proved in [9]. The specific form of some linear automata is used in [8] to give decision procedure of deterministic double exponential time complexity in the length of the formula. This agrees with the lower bound found in [26].

As with other temporal logics and despite these conclusive results, the search for other reasoning methods has been a major undertaking. Even for the basic task of deciding validity (or dually satisfiability) of a CTL* formula, there is interest in finding approaches which are more straightfoward, or more traditional, or more amenable to human understanding, or yield meaningful intermediate steps, etc. See, for example, the Hilbert-style axiomatization for CTL* in [19].

A. Cavalcanti and D. Dams (Eds.): FM 2009, LNCS 5850, pp. 403–418, 2009.

Tableaux are a popular style of reasoning technique and there has been a substantial amount of work on applying them to temporal logics: see [12] and [22] for surveys. They can be presented in an intuitive way, they are often suitable for automated reasoning and it is often not hard to prove complexity results for their use. It is also often the case that tableau procedures can quickly build models of satisfiable formulas even though the worst case performance is bad. Tableaux were first used for modal logics in [13] and [11] and there has been much work since on tableaux for temporal logics [27,5,6,23].

Despite all the interest in tableaux for temporal logic and for reasoning with CTL*, a tableau approach to CTL* has been a long standing open problem. Tableau-style elements do appear in the somewhat intricate CTL* model-checking systems in [1], [14] and [17] but model-checking is a distinct task from deciding validity. Model-checkers are given a formula and a structure and they check whether the given formula holds of the given system: useful for the verification of implementations. Validity deciders can be used to model-check but model-checkers can not in general decide validity: model-checking is an "easier" or less computationally complex reasoning task. In [24] there is a tableau system for model-checking with predicate CTL*. In [17] there is a complete deductive system for model-checking formulas in predicate CTL* and some of the derivation steps look similar to tableau-building steps.

There is a tableau for a related logic called "bundled" CTL* or BCTL* in [20]. BCTL* uses the same language as CTL* but has more satisfiable formulas and is easier to reason with (as discussed in [20]).

There are good reasons to try to devise a not too complicated tableau-style system for deciding validity in CTL*. Even though there is the seriously inconvenient double exponential lower bound on the complexity, there are reasons to believe that experienced tableau practitioners will be able to use a range of techniques to make fast implementations capable of delivering results for a wide range of practical reasoning problems. A general CTL* tableau can be the basis for searching for more practical sublanguages, and for assisting with human-guided derivations on bigger tasks. It can be the basis of proofs of correctness for alternative reasoning techniques like resolution or rewrite systems. It may assist with model-checking and program synthesis tasks. It may be extended to cope with some predicate reasoning.

The tableau construction we describe for CTL* is of the tree, or top-down, form. To decide the validity of ϕ, we build a tree with the nodes built from sets of formulas from a finite closure set defined from ϕ. A novel aspect is the fact that the nodes in the tableau are labelled with sets of sets of formulas. We use certain sets of formulas called hues, and then put together sets of hues called colours. This notation reflects some similar ideas in the CTL* axiomatic completeness proof in [19]. The proof of correctness is an interesting mixture of techniques from linear and branching temporal logic, and it has some subtleties.

The approach here is significantly modified from that for BCTL* given in [20] as that paper presents a bottom-up, or graph-based, tableau system and for

BCTL* we do not need any mechanism to check for loops, repetition and an important limit closure property (which we do not discuss here).

With CTL* in this paper, on the other hand, issues of looping become complex and are of paramount importance. We will see that there are two types of looping. There is good looping which allows us to put up-links in our tableau tree and help make a finite structure: we give a practical subroutine for checking quickly when this can happen. But there are also bad loops in the form of repetitive branch construction: the same colours coming up again and again along ever lengthening branches without the ability to loop those branches back on themselves. These turn out to be very subtle to deal with and we are only able to give some preliminary results on mechanisms for tackling repetition. This short paper side steps the issue of repetition and just puts a simple but grossly impractical bound on the length of branches allowed.

In section 2 we give a formal definition of CTL* and then see some example formulas in section 3. In section 4 we describe some of the mechanisms underlying the tableau and the following section 5 gives a loop checking algorithm. Section 6 presents the tableau definition and its soundness. An example tableau is set out in section 7. The next section sketches completeness. We briefy describe a prototype implementation before, in the conclusion, we mention some preliminary work on speeding up the tableau construction by preventing repetitive branch construction.

A long version of the paper [21] has full details of the intricate proofs.

2 Syntax and Sematics

CTL*, sometimes called the *full computational tree logic*, can be presented in different ways. The language of CTL* is presented here with what is called the logic of R-generable sets of paths on transition structures: this is the standard CTL* logic. We fix a countable set $\mathcal{L}$ of atomic propositions.

Definition 1. *A* transition frame *is a pair* (S, R) *where:*
S *is the non-empty set of* states
R *is a total binary relation* $\subseteq S \times S$
i.e. for every $s \in S$*, there is some* $t \in S$ *such that* $(s, t) \in R$.

Formulas are defined along infinite (i.e. ω-long) sequences of states. A *fullpath* in (S, R) is an infinite sequence $\langle s_0, s_1, s_2, ...\rangle$ of states such that for each i, $(s_i, s_{i+1}) \in R$. For the fullpath $\sigma = \langle s_0, s_1, s_2, ...\rangle$, and any $i \geq 0$, we write σ_i for the state s_i and $\sigma_{\geq i}$ for the fullpath $\langle s_i, s_{i+1}, s_{i+2}, ...\rangle$.

CTL* semantics is defined with respect to the set of all possible fullpaths.

Formulas of CTL* are evaluated in *transition structures*:

Definition 2. *A* (transition) structure *is a triple* $M = (S, R, g)$ *where:*
(S, R) *is a transition frame;*
$g : S \to \wp(\mathcal{L})$ *is a labelling of the states with sets of atoms.*

The formulas of CTL* are built from the atomic propositions in $\mathcal{L}$ recursively using classical connectives $\neg$ and $\wedge$ as well as the temporal connectives X, U and A: if α and β are formulas then so are $X\alpha$, $\alpha U\beta$ and $A\alpha$. As well as the standard classical abbreviations, **true**, $\vee$, $\rightarrow$, $\leftrightarrow$, we have linear time abbreviations $F\alpha \equiv \mathbf{true}U\alpha$ and $G\alpha \equiv \neg F\neg\alpha$, and we have the path switching modal diamond $E\alpha \equiv \neg A\neg\alpha$.

Truth of formulas is evaluated at fullpaths in structures. We write $M, \sigma \models \alpha$ iff the formula α is true at the fullpath σ in the structure $M = (S, R, g)$. This is defined recursively by:

$M, \sigma \models p$ iff $p \in g(\sigma_0)$, for any $p \in \mathcal{L}$
$M, \sigma \models \neg\alpha$ iff $M, \sigma \not\models \alpha$
$M, \sigma \models \alpha \wedge \beta$ iff $M, \sigma \models \alpha$ and $M, \sigma \models \beta$
$M, \sigma \models X\alpha$ iff $M, \sigma_{\geq 1} \models \alpha$
$M, \sigma \models \alpha U\beta$ iff there is some $i \geq 0$ such that $M, \sigma_{\geq i} \models \beta$ and for each j, if $0 \leq j < i$ then $M, \sigma_{\geq j} \models \alpha$
$M, \sigma \models A\alpha$ iff for all fullpaths σ' such that $\sigma_0 = \sigma'_0$ we have $M, \sigma' \models \alpha$

We say that α is *valid* in CTL*, and write $\models \alpha$, iff for all transition structures M, for all fullpaths σ in M, we have $M, \sigma \models \alpha$. α is *satisfiable* iff $\not\models \neg\alpha$.

3 Examples of CTL*

In this section we will give a taste of the kinds of properties expressible in CTL* and the issues which our decision procedure will have to deal with. We do this by listing a range of simple example CTL* formulas: their respective negations are also all useful examples to consider.

In helps our discussion to mention briefly the related logic BCTL* [20]. The two logics use the same language but BCTL* only considers a certain fixed set or *bundle* of fullpaths in the semantics. See [20] for details. It is much easier to reason with BCTL* but it is not a logic with many practical uses. If a formula is valid in BCTL* then it will also be valid in CTL* (but not vice versa).

Valid formulas of CTL* and of BCTL* appear in axiom systems for BCTL* in [25] and for CTL* in [19]. They include all the valid formulas of PLTL such as $\theta_1 = G(p \rightarrow q) \rightarrow (Gp \rightarrow Gq)$, $\theta_2 = Gp \rightarrow (p \wedge Xp \wedge XGp)$, $\theta_3 = (pUq) \leftrightarrow (q \vee (p \wedge X(pUq)))$ and $\theta_4 = (pUq) \rightarrow Fq$. There are also S5 axioms such as $\theta_5 = p \rightarrow AEp$ and $\theta_6 = Ap \rightarrow AAp$. The main interaction between the path switching and the linear time modalties is the valid formula $\theta_7 = AXp \rightarrow XAp$. There is also a special axiom saying that atomic propositions only depend on states: $\theta_8 = p \rightarrow Ap$ (for atom p).

Some more interesting valid formulas of CTL* are:

$$\theta_9 = E(pU(E(pUq))) \rightarrow E(pUq)$$
$$\theta_{10} = (AG(p \rightarrow qUr) \wedge qUp) \rightarrow qUr$$
$$\theta_{11} = G(EFp \rightarrow XFEFp) \rightarrow (EFp \rightarrow GFEFp).$$

The reader can verify the validity of these examples using semantic arguments.

Three interesting examples of formulas which are valid in CTL* but not valid in BCTL* are: $\theta_{12} = AG(p \rightarrow EXp) \rightarrow (p \rightarrow EGp)$,

$$\theta_{13} = AG(Ep \rightarrow EX((Eq)U(Ep))) \rightarrow (Ep \rightarrow EG((Eq)U(Ep))),$$
$$\theta_{14} = (AG(p \rightarrow EXr) \wedge AG(r \rightarrow EXp)) \rightarrow (p \rightarrow EG(Fp \wedge Fr)).$$

These come from [20] where they are related to the so-called *limit closure property* of CTL*.

The next three examples are not valid in CTL* nor valid in BCTL* but they are satisfiable in both CTL* and BCTL* They are $\theta_{15} = p$, $\theta_{16} = p \wedge Xp \wedge F\neg p$,

$$\begin{aligned}\theta_{17} = {} & AG(p \leftrightarrow X\neg p) \wedge AG(p \rightarrow \neg q) \wedge AG(p \rightarrow \neg r) \\ & \wedge AG(q \rightarrow \neg r) \wedge E(Fq \wedge Fr), \text{ and} \\ \theta_{18} = {} & AG(EXp \wedge EX\neg p) \wedge AG(Gp \vee (\neg r)U(r \wedge \neg p)).\end{aligned}$$

4 Preliminaries

Most of the work on temporal tableaux involves a move away from the traditional tree-shaped tableau building process of other modal logics. The standard approach for temporal logics is to start with a graph and repeatedly prune away nodes, according to certain removal rules, until there is nothing more to remove (success) or some failure condition is detected ([27,6]).

We return to the tree shape for CTL*.

We want to use a tableau approach to decide validity of a formula in CTL*. We will start with a formula ϕ and determine whether ϕ is satisfiable in CTL* or not. To decide validity we will simply determine satisfiabilty of the negation.

As in the usual tree-style tableau processes, we can non-deterministically build a tree from root to successors and backtrack on our choices if there is no way to continue building. So we have conditions for a successful termination.

The main difference here is that the nodes in our tree will be labelled with sets of sets of formulas rather than just sets of formulas. Obviously there is a risk of getting a very large tree to deal with.

From the closure set for ϕ, which is just the subformulas and their negations, we will define a certain set of subsets of the closure set called the *hues* of ϕ. The *colours* of ϕ will be certain sets of hues of ϕ. The nodes in our tableau tree will each be labelled with one colour. Whether a given colour can label a successor node will be determined by certain conditions on the formulas in the hues in the label colours on the successor and the parent.

Fix the formula ϕ whose satisfiability we are interested in.

Definition 3 (closure set). *The* closure set *for* ϕ *is* $\mathbf{cl}\phi = \{\psi, \neg\psi | \psi \leq \phi\}$*: its subformulas and their negations.*

Definition 4 (MPC). $a \subseteq \mathbf{cl}\phi$ *is* maximaly propositionally consistent (MPC) *iff for all* $\alpha, \beta \in \mathbf{cl}\phi$,
M1) if $\beta = \neg\alpha$ *then* ($\beta \in a$ *iff* $\alpha \notin a$)*; and*
M2) if $\alpha \wedge \beta \in \mathbf{cl}\phi$ *then* ($\alpha \wedge \beta \in a$ *iff both* $\alpha \in a$ *and* $\beta \in a$).

A hue is supposed to (approximately) capture a set of formulas which could all hold together of one fullpath.

Definition 5 (Hue). *$a \subseteq \mathbf{cl}\phi$ is a* hue *for ϕ iff all these conditions hold:*
H1) a is MPC;
H2) if $\alpha U \beta \in a$ and $\beta \notin a$ then $\alpha \in a$;
H3) if $\alpha U \beta \in \mathbf{cl}\phi \setminus a$ then $\beta \notin a$;
H4) if $A\alpha \in a$ then $\alpha \in a$.

For example, if $\phi = \neg\theta_{12}$ then

$$\begin{aligned}
&h38 = \{\neg(AG(p \to EXp) \to (p \to EGp)), (AG(p \to EXp) \wedge \neg(p \to EGp)),\\
&AG(p \to EXp), G(p \to EXp), \mathbf{true}, \neg\neg(p \to EXp),\\
&(p \to EXp), p, \neg\neg EXp, EXp, \neg\neg Xp, Xp,\\
&\neg(p \to EGp), (p \wedge \neg EGp), \neg EGp, A\neg Gp, \neg Gp, F\neg p, \neg\neg p\}
\end{aligned}$$

is a hue (which we will revisit later as $h38$ in an example tableau in section 7). To check that it is a hue involves some simple syntactic checks. For example, checking H2, we see that $\mathbf{true}U\neg p = F\neg p$ is in the hue but $\neg p$ is not. Thus **true** should be in the hue and it is. The careful reader might notice that although this satisfies the definition of a hue, it is not actually exactly the set of formulas satisfied by any fullpath in any model. It turns out to be unsatisfiable but that is beyond the simple syntactic checks to determine.

Another, very slightly different hue which we will look at in a moment is $h37$ which is the same as $h38$ except that it contains $\neg Xp$ instead of Xp and $\neg\neg Xp$.

Let H_ϕ be the set of hues of ϕ.

The usual temporal successor relation plays a role in determining allowed steps in the tableau. The relation r_X is put between hues a and b if a fullpath σ satisfying a could have a one-step suffix $\sigma_{\geq 1}$ satisfying b:

Definition 6 (r_X). *For hues a and b, we say that $a \; r_X \; b$ iff the following four conditions all hold:*
R1) $X\alpha \in a$ implies $\alpha \in b$.
R2) $\neg X\alpha \in a$ implies $\neg\alpha \in b$.
R3) $\alpha U \beta \in a$ and $\neg\beta \in a$ implies $\alpha U \beta \in b$.
R4) $\neg(\alpha U \beta) \in a$ and $\alpha \in a$ implies $\neg(\alpha U \beta) \in b$.

For example, the reader can check $h38 \; r_X \; h38$, $h38 \; r_X \; h37$ but $h37 \not r_X h38$.

The next relation aims to tell whether two hues could correspond to fullpaths starting at the same state. We just need the hues to agree on atoms and on universal path quantified formulas:

Definition 7 (r_A). *For hues a and b, put $a \; r_A \; b$ iff the following two conditions both hold:*
A1) $A\alpha \in a$ iff $A\alpha \in b$; and
A2) for all $p \in \mathcal{L}$, $p \in a$ iff $p \in b$

The reader can check that this is an equivalence relation on hues and that, for example, $h37 \; r_A \; h38$.

Now we move up from the level of hues to the level of colours. Could a set of hues be exactly the hues corresponding to all the fullpaths starting at a particular state? We would need each pair of hues to satisfy r_A but we would also need hues to be in the set to witness all the existential path quatifications:

Definition 8 (Colour). *Non-empty $c \subseteq H_\phi$ is a* colour *(of ϕ) iff the following two conditions hold. For all $a, b \in c$,*
C1) $a \; r_A \; b$
C2) if $a \in c$ and $\neg A\alpha \in a$ then there is $b \in c$ such that $\neg\alpha \in b$.

The set $\{h37, h38\}$, for example, is a colour. The formula $EXp = \neg A \neg Xp \in h37$ but $Xp \in h38$ witnesses the existential path quantification. Thus $\{h37\}$ is not a colour.

Let C_ϕ be the set of colours of ϕ.

We define a successor relation R_X between colours. It is defined in terms of r_X between the component hues and is supposed to approximately capture the successor relation between nodes in terms of the colours which they exhibit. Note that colours will in general have a non-singleton range of successors.

Definition 9 (R_X). *For all $c, d \in C_\phi$, put $c \; R_X \; d$ iff for all $b \in d$ there is $a \in c$ such that $a \; r_X \; b$.*

As an example, $\{h37, h38\} \; R_X \; \{h37, h38\}$ as the reader can check.

It is worth noting that colours and hues can be found in actual transition structures. We will need these concepts in our completeness proof.

Definition 10 (actual hues and colours). *Suppose (S, R, g) is a transition structure. If σ is a fullpath through (S, R) then we say that the* actual *(ϕ-)* hue *of σ in (S, R, g) is $h = \{\alpha \in \mathbf{cl}\phi | (S, R, g), \sigma \models \alpha\}$.*

If $s \in S$ then the set of all actual hues of all fullpaths through (S, R) starting at s is called the actual *(ϕ-)* colour *of s in (S, R, g).*

Building branches node by node in our tree-shaped tableaux will be straightforward using the mechanisms of colours and hues. The top three nodes in the later Figure 3, for example, shows the start of a tableau for $\neg\theta_{12}$. The root node is coloured $\{h37, h38\}$ with $\phi = \neg\theta_{12} \in h37$. As the root label has two hues there are two successor nodes ordered left to right. Both successor label colours are in the R_X relation to the root colour. Further, the left has a hue which is in the r_X relation to $h37$ and the right has a hue which is in the r_X relation to $h38$.

Tableaux can be built node by node. This can be done quickly by guessing successor hues and extending them to colours. The challenges for us will be to do with looping and repetition.

In our tableaux there will be "good looping" and "bad looping". Good looping will be when we discover that an ancestor of a node can serve as the successor of that node. Our tableaux will stray from being strictly tree-shaped in that they will allow us to loop up from nodes to their ancestors. This will be a way of making a finite model which nevertheless has infinite fullpaths. There will be subtle conditions determining when we are alowed to loop up in this way.

"Bad looping" on the other hand will be when we determine that we have extended a branch in a certain way which exhibits too much repetition with no allowed loops back up, and so no prospect of terminating this development in a successful and finite way. We will refer to this as repetition rather than looping. Again, there will be subtle rules to determine when we have such repetition. This allows us to stop constructing a branch and backtrack to a previous choice, or fail in a finite way.

As mentioned, in this paper we will use a simple but not particularly efficient method for terminating the development of repetitive branches. A better method would allow us to report unsatisfiable formulas earlier. It would also allow us to stop making unneccessarily long variations of branches which could be successful and shorter: thus it would help us report satisfiability earlier.

The simple method we will just use is imposing a branch length bound based on a function which bounds the size of minimal finite models of a formula in terms of the length of the formula.

Theorem 1 ([9]). *There is a function N from $\mathbb{N}$ to $\mathbb{N}$ such that if CTL* formula ϕ of length $|\phi|$ is satisfiable then it has a finite model with at most $N(|\phi|)$ states.*

The "small model" result sketched in [9] describes (but not explicitly) a function of triple exponential complexity in the length of the formula. However, later work sketched in [16] allows us to conclude that there is also a double exponential function (see [21]).

To proceed, choose any such function N which bounds the size of a minimal finite model of any satisfiable CTL* formula in terms of the length of the formula. In our tableau, we actual use a slightly bigger function to bound the allowed length of branches, namely

Definition 11. *The bound on the length of branches allowed in tableaux will be $M(n) = 2n.2^n.N(n)$ in terms of the length n of the input formula.*

The tableaux we construct will be roughly tree-shaped albeit the traditional upside down tree with a root at the top: predecessors and ancestors above, successors and descendants below. However, we will allow up-links from a node to one of its ancestors. Each node will be labelled with a colour, with the hues ordered and, unless it is a leaf, it will have one (ordered) successor for each hue.

First, in Figure 1, we define a structure with this basic format and then we add a couple of extra conditions to define a tableau.

It is worth noting here that condition PT7, which relates the colour label at one node with the label of any of it successors, is the essence of the tableau. Along with PT10, this is effectively a tableau construction rule. For any given colour there are only a limited set of other colours which lie in the R_X relation to the given colour, and they can be constructed in a straightforward way (from the formulas in the label of the given node): although we do not have space to spell out the corresponding tradional tableau rules here.

Definition 13 (tableau path). *σ is a* path *through (T, s, z), iff it is a sequence of nodes from T, with length $|\sigma| \leq \omega$, proceeding such that for each $j < |\sigma|$, there is some $i < |s_{\sigma_j}|$ such that $\sigma_{j+1} = s_{\sigma_j}(i)$*

Definition 12 (COPT). *A* Coloured Ordered Pseudo-Tree for ϕ *is a tuple* (T, s, z) *such that:*

PT1) T *is a set (of* nodes*), with one,* $\mathbf{root}_T \in T$*, called the* root*;*
PT2) *each node* $t \in T$ *has a finite number* $|s_t|$ *of* successors*,*
$\{s_t(0), s_t(1), ..., s_t(|s_t| - 1)\} \subseteq T$ *(*leaf nodes *have no successors);*
PT3) *each node* $t \in T$ *has a unique finite sequence of distinct nodes*
$t_0 = \mathbf{root}_T, t_1, t_2, ..., t_k = t$,
called the ancestors of t*, such that each* t_{i+1} *is a successor of* t_i
PT4) *for each* $t \in T$*, for each* $i < |s_t|$*, either* t *is the parent of* $s_t(i)$ *or* $s_t(i)$ *is an ancestor of* t*;*
PT5) $z : T \to C_\phi$ *is the* colouring*;*
PT6) *for each* $t \in T$*,* z_t *is a map enumerating the hues in* $z(t)$ *in some order;*
PT7) *for each* $t \in T$*, for each* $i < |s_t|$*,* $z(t)\ R_X\ z(s_t(i))$*;*
PT8) $\phi \in z_{\mathbf{root}_T}(0)$*;*
PT9) *for each* $t \in T$*, either* $|s_t| = 0$ *or there are* $|s_t| > 0$ *hues in* $z(t)$*;*
PT10) *for all* $t \in T$*, for all* $i < |s_t|$*,* $(z_t(i))\ r_X\ (z_{s_t(i)}(0))$*.*

Fig. 1. Definintion of a COPT

Definition 14 (tableau fullpath). *A path* σ *is a* fullpath *through* (T, s, z)*, iff it only ends at a leaf node, if it ends at all: i.e. if* $|\sigma| = n < \omega$ *then* σ_{n-1} *is a leaf node.*

The idea of eventualities in hues which need to be fulfilled will be important in our proof:

Definition 15 (Eventuality). $\beta \in \mathbf{cl}\phi$ *is an* eventuality *in hue* h *iff* $\alpha U \beta \in h$*.*

At various places in our proofs we will need to find hue threads, i.e. sequences of hues which lie within sequences of coloured nodes. In this subsection we introduce some tools for dealing with such a situation.

For the rest of this section, suppose that (T, s, z) is a COPT for ϕ.

Definition 16 (Hue thread). *Suppose* σ *is a path through* (T, s, z)*. A* hue thread *through* σ *is a sequence* η *of hues such that* $|\eta| = |\sigma|$*, for each* $j < |\eta|$*,* $\eta_j \in z(\sigma_j)$ *and for each* $j < |\eta| - 1$*,* $\eta_j\ r_X\ \eta_{j+1}$*.*

Definition 17 (Fulfilling hue thread). *Suppose* σ *is a path through* (T, s, z) *and* η *is a hue thread through* σ*. We say that* η *is* fulfilling *iff either* $|\sigma| < \omega$ *or* $|\sigma| = \omega$ *and all the eventualities in each* η_i *are witnessed by some later* η_j*; i.e. if* $\alpha U \beta \in \eta_i$ *then there is* $j \geq i$ *such that* $\beta \in \eta_j$*.*

The predecessor hue aspect of the definition of the successor relation R_X between colours of nodes PT7, ensures, by definition of R_X, that any hue in any colour has an r_X predecessor in any predecessor colour. In fact, it is unique as we now show. This enables us to *traceback* threads of hues backwards along paths.

Lemma 1. *If* u *is a successor of* t *in a COPT* (T, s, z) *and* $h \in z(u)$ *then there is a unique hue* $h' \in z(t)$ *such that* $h'\ r_X\ h$*.*

By iteratively tracing predecessor hues backwards from a leaf node, it is easy to see that any finite path has a hue thread:

Lemma 2. *Each path σ through (T, s, z) has at least one hue thread.*

Note that if two hue threads (of the same path) agree at any index then they must agree at all lesser indices all the way back to zero. This is because of (iterated application of) the traceback property lemma 1. It follows that:

Lemma 3. *Each path σ through (T, s, z) has only a finite number of hue threads.*

The following condition is rather non-algorithmic in its presentation. In the next section below we give some details of a model-checking style algorithm which we show determines whether this condition holds amongst other things.

Definition 18 (Fullpaths fulfilled). *We say that a COPT (T, s, z) has* fullpaths fulfilled *iff for every fullpath σ through (T, s, z), there is a fulfilling hue thread through σ.*

Notice that property PT10 puts a special significance on the initial hue in each colour label. This, along with the next condition, helps us ensure that each hue actually has a fullpath witnessing it. Note that the NTP is easy to check computationally.

Definition 19 (The nominated thread property). *We say that a COPT (T, s, z) has the* nominated thread property *(NTP) iff the following holds. Suppose $t \in T$, $0 < |s_t|$, $s_t(0)$ is an ancestor of t and that $t_0 = s_t(0), t_1, ..., t_k = t$ is a non-repeating sequence with each $t_{j+1} = s_{t_j}(0)$. Let σ be the fullpath $\langle t_0, t_1, ..., t_k, t_0, t_1, ..., t_k, t_0, t_1, ...\rangle$. Then $\langle z_{t_0}(0), z_{t_1}(0), ..., z_{t_k}(0), z_{t_0}(0), ...\rangle$ is a fulfilling hue thread for σ.*

5 How to Check That Labels Are Grounded

The condition of labels being grounded (LG) is the most important extra condition which we are putting on COPTs in order to allow them to be a tableau. Roughly, this means that the colour labels of nodes make sense in terms of the fullpaths which pass through them. This notion is intimately connected with the idea that all fullpaths looping around in our tableau must have corresponding sequences of hues which have their eventualities fulfilled. If a tableau search algorithm tries to add a new up-link to a tableau and finds that LG fails then it will know that the up-link should not be added.

We have invented a model-checking style procedure for doing this. The procedure is somewhat complicated to describe but is a straightforward polynomial-time algorithm looping around a few times to collect sets of sets of formulas from **cl**ϕ for each node.

Given a ϕ-tableau (T, s, z) we think of (T, s, z) as representing a different CTL* structure $(T, s, z)*$ called *the hypothetical structure* of (T, s, z) based on assuming that each leaf t in (T, s, z) is joined to a separate sub-structure which validates its label $z(t)$.

This structure $(T, s, z)*$ will have slightly specialised semantics for evaluating CTL* formulas. We also use a special definition of fullpaths. A fullpath σ through $(T, s, z)*$ is either 1) a normal ω-long fullpath through (T, s, z); or 2) a finite fullpath through (T, s, z) ending at a leaf t along with one of the hues $\text{end}(\sigma)$ from $z(t)$.

We write $M, \sigma \models \alpha$ iff the formula α is true of the fullpath σ in the structure $M = (T, s, z)*$. This is defined recursively by (uninteresting clauses omitted):

$M, \sigma \models p$ iff atom p is in some hue in $z(\sigma_0)$;
$M, \sigma \models X\alpha$ iff either σ_0 is not a leaf and $M, \sigma_{\geq 1} \models \alpha$
or σ_0 is a leaf and $X\alpha \in \text{end}(\sigma)$
$M, \sigma \models \alpha U \beta$ iff either there is some $i \geq 0$ such that $M, \sigma_{\geq i} \models \beta$
and for each j, if $0 \leq j < i$ then $M, \sigma_{\geq j} \models \alpha$
or there is some $i \geq 0$ such that σ_i is a leaf and
$\alpha U \beta \in \text{end}(\sigma)$ and for each j, if $0 \leq j < i$ then $M, \sigma_{\geq j} \models \alpha$

In the long version of this paper [21], we present the algorithm (LG), which we can not even sketch here. LG is essentially trying to determine what hues of the hypothetical structure exist at each node. It proceeds by adding more and more complex formulas (from $\mathbf{cl}(\phi)$) to its sets of hues and working out what new hues can be realised by fullpaths.

Careful examination of the LG algorithm in some detailed lemmas, allows us to conclude:

Lemma 4. *The LG algorithm determines exactly the colours of nodes in the hypothetical model.*

Definition 20. *The* hue of σ *through* $(T, s, z)*$ *is* $\{\alpha \in \mathbf{cl}(\phi) | (T, s, z)*, \sigma \models \alpha\}$.

The hypothetical *colour of a node t in (T, s, z) is the colour ($\in C_\phi$) being the set of hues of fullpaths through $(T, s, z)*$ which start at t.*

Definition 21 (LG). *COPT (T, s, z) has its* labels grounded *iff the hypothetical colour of each node t matches its label colour $z(t)$.*

6 The Tableau

Definition 22. *A* ϕ-tableau *is a finite COPT such that:*
LG) labels are grounded;
NTP) the nominated thread property holds;
BB) no node has more than $M(|\phi|)$ ancestors (see definition 11 for M).
It is a successful *tableau iff it has no leaves.*

A tableau algorithm or decision procedure here is any systematic way of finding from all tableaux for ϕ whether there is a successful one or not. There are clearly only finitely many tableaux for any particular ϕ so we don't need to be more prescriptive here about any particular algorithm.

It must be emphasized, however, that the very specific forms of the R_X relationship between one colour and any successor colour means that in fact, as we build a tableau (i.e. a COPT), there are only a very limited number of choices for successor colours. Furthermore, these choices can be determined efficiently and constructively from the formulas in the label of a node. Thus, this is no blind, "generate and test" algorithm. The unsophisticated implementation described in [21] is fast enough to be almost immediate on a wide range of interesting formulas as long as they do not contain much more than 50 symbols.

In this definition of tableau we have guaranteed termination of any reasonable tableau construction algorithm by putting a simple but excessive bound on the length of branches. This allows us to conclude failure in a finite time and to also abbreviate the search for successful tableaux.

Our work on the LG algorithm above actually takes us very close to the soundess result for the tableau. We can show that when there are no leaves then at the final stage of LG we have determined the standard colours of nodes in the corresponding standard model. As we have ϕ itself in a hue in a label we have soundness:

Lemma 5 (Soundness). *If ϕ has a successful tableau then it is satisfiable.*

7 A Tableau Example

Consider the example $\theta_{-12} = \neg\theta_{12} = \neg(AG(p \to EXp) \to (p \to EGp))$.

This formula is not satisfiable in CTL* as it is the negation of a validity.

The formula has length 30 and we find it has 39 hues and 258 colours. For convenience, we can label the hues $h1, h2, ..., h39$. Some of the important contents of some of the most interesting hues are listed in Figure 2.

Hue	Contents
h28	$\{\neg p, \neg Xp, EXp, F\neg p, A\neg Gp, \theta_{12}, AG(p \to EXp), p \to EGp, ...\}$
h30	$\{\neg p, Xp, EXp, F\neg p, A\neg Gp, \theta_{12}, AG(p \to EXp), p \to EGp, ...\}$
h34	$\{p, \neg Xp, EXp, F\neg p, EGp, \neg\theta_{12}, AG(p \to EXp), \neg(p \to EGp), ...\}$
h35	$\{p, Xp, EXp, Gp, EGp, \neg\theta_{12}, AG(p \to EXp), \neg(p \to EGp), ...\}$
h36	$\{p, Xp, EXp, F\neg p, EGp, \neg\theta_{12}, AG(p \to EXp), \neg(p \to EGp), ...\}$
h37	$\{p, \neg Xp, EXp, F\neg p, A\neg Gp, \neg\theta_{12}, AG(p \to EXp), \neg(p \to EGp), ...\}$
h38	$\{p, Xp, EXp, F\neg p, A\neg Gp, \neg\theta_{12}, AG(p \to EXp), \neg(p \to EGp), ...\}$

Fig. 2. θ_{-12}: some contents of some hues

The construction of a tableau for θ_{-12} can easily lead to very large graphs. The implementation by the author, produces a graph like that in Figure 3 at a certain stage. Only the first eleven nodes labeled $n0, n1, ..., n10$ are considered here. Their respective colours can be gleaned from examining the labels on edges in the tree in Figure 3: The edge labels in the diagram of the respective successor

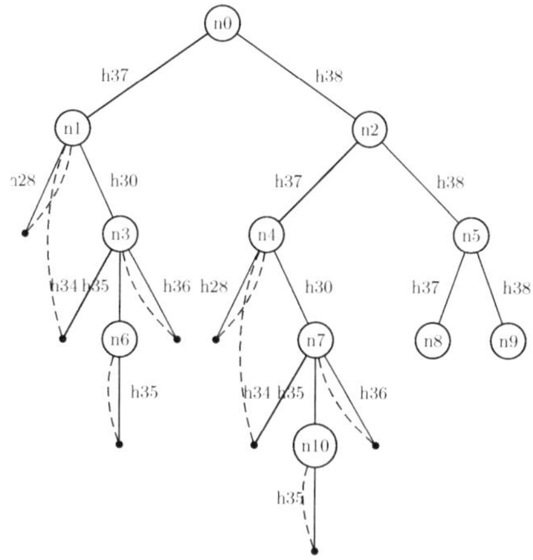

Fig. 3. A Partial Tableau for θ_{-12}

nodes, list the hues in the colour of the parent. Thus, $n0$, for example, is coloured with $\{h37, h38\}$.

In Figure 3 we show the nodes $n0, ..., n10$ in the tree starting from the root at the top. Successor relations are given in solid lines in left to right order across the page. The successor edges are labeled with that hue of the parent which requires their presence. Dashed lines indicate an up-link heading up to its destination. So, for example, the first successor of $n3$ is actually its parent $n1$, and there is a hue in the colour of $n1$ which is a successor hue of the first hue $h34$ in the colour of $n3$. The tableau can continue below $n8$ and $n9$. In fact, the sequence $n0, n2, n5, n9, ...$, of nodes which are all the same colour $\{h37, h38\}$ could continue indefinately if there was no limit on the length of branches.

The interested reader can check that we can not put an up-link in the tableau instead of this branch: for example, an up-link from $n2$ to itself (instead of having $n5$) would contradict the LG property as it would produce a fullpath satisfying Gp and that formula is in neither $h37$ nor $h38$.

However, we do have a limit on the length of branches and that eventually causes this tableau construction for θ_{-12} to fail. There is no successful tableau for θ_{-12}.

8 Completeness

In this section we give a high-level overview of the proof that if a model exists for ϕ then a successful tableau exists for ϕ. Say $(S, R, g), \sigma^0 \models \phi$ where (S, R, g) is any labelled transition structure and σ^0 is any fullpath through (S, R). We may assume that S has at most $N(|\phi|)$ elements.

We first show that there is a structure (T, s, z) which is like a tableau for ϕ but does not necessarily obey the bound BB on the length of branches: in fact, it will be a tree with infinitely many nodes. There will be no up-links but we still need to check that some conditions like label groundedness and nominated threading hold on infinite paths.

We simply work by induction to unwind (S, R, g) one node (i.e. state) at a time, but only introducing as many successors as there are hues in the actual colour at each node. There are some extra properties to obtain and a map w which allow us to keep track of the relationship between nodes in (S, R, g) and the unwinding.

In the next few stages of the construction, we change (T, s, z) with w so that nodes x with descendant y say, on the same branch which agree under w (i.e. x and y both map back from T to $w(x) = w(y)$, the same original state in S) are counted as "repeated" nodes and we replace the subtree rooted at the lower node y by a new up-link from y's parent back up to the original node x.

First we deal with leftmost branches which need special attention due to the nominated thread property: they need to witness all eventualities in initial hues. Other branches are dealt with later in a similar but easier process.

At this stage some of our finite loops may be too long to fit into the required bound on branch length. To solve this problem we now identify pairs of nodes along these paths which define an interval which can be cut out from the tableau. Basically, the bound is long enough that we can see all witnesses and be guaranteed of passing through nodes with the same w image again. We make cuts between such matching nodes when the interval in between does not add a new witness.

The construction sketched above allows us to conclude:

Lemma 6. *If a CTL* formula is satisfiable then it has a successful tableau.*

Thus any algorithm which systematically searches through all possible ϕ-tableaux for a successful one will thus eventually find one for ϕ.

9 Implementation

Implementation of a CTL* tableau search is relatively straightforward although it is a sizeable undertaking. A (Java) prototype implementation written by the author shows that for many interesting, albeit relatively small formulas, results can be obtained quickly despite the double exponential theoretical bounds. There are some preliminary results reported in [21].

We can only summarize the results briefly here. Apart from five cases where the computations do not halt in a reasonable time (say a few minutes), all answers given on the 18 example formulas and their negations are correct.

Amongst these 36 formulas of maximum length 56, the implementation generally gives the correct answer very quickly after less than ten tableau construction steps (including backtracking). Models of satifiable formulas amongst these examples, which are constructed by the implementation have less than ten states.

Setting the program an unsatisfiable formula which involves a lot of different colours generally causes it to take a long time. For example, $\neg\theta_{12}$ has 258 colours while $\neg\theta_{14}$ has over 2^{80} colours! The program does not halt on these.

10 Ongoing and Future Work

We have provided a sound and complete tableau system for the propositional full computational tree logic CTL*. This is the first such. It is also simple to implement [21].

Even though there is an existing decision procedure for CTL* (based on automata) there are many potential uses of new tableaux systems for CTL*. We can often extract counter-models and formal proofs from tableaux. They could be a base for developing, or proving correctness of, other techniques such as resolution or term rewriting. They may give indications of simpler more reasonable sub-languages. Tableaux help manual proofs of validity. They can be extended to help with reasoning in the predicate case, for example for software verification.

Although this tableau approach is usable in interesting ways already there is much work to do to make more practical use of this. In ongoing work described in [21] a reasonably general and quite usable repetition mechanism is proposed and proved correct.

Worst case performance is necessarily bad (at least double exponential) because of the complexity of the decision problem but there is great potential for vast improvements in running times in general or on certain classes of formulas. Nevertheless, even a naive implementation of the tableau procedure by the author is able to quickly decide some interesting non-trivial formulas and provide models for satisfiable formulas [21].

The first task is to have a general and efficient repetition detection mechanism. This needs to be developed and proved correct to replace the wasteful but simple bound based on maximum size of model for formulas of certain input length.

We have not mentioned directions for other improvements in this paper but important tasks include making use of preprocessing of relationships between hues, or at least remembering properties such as which ones do not have successor hues. Developing ways of reasoning ahead with partially determined colours and hues will also be useful.

References

1. Bhat, G., Cleaveland, R., Grumberg, O.: Efficient On-the-Fly Model Checking for CTL*. In: LICS 1995, pp. 388–397. IEEE Computer Society Press, Los Alamitos (1995)
2. Clarke, E., Emerson, E.: Synthesis of synchronization skeletons for branching time temporal logic. In: Engeler, E. (ed.) Logic of Programs 1979. LNCS, vol. 125, pp. 52–71. Springer, Heidelberg (1981)
3. Emerson, E.: Alternative semantics for temporal logic. Th. C. Sci. 26, 121–130 (1983)
4. Emerson, E.: Automated temporal reasoning for reactive systems. In: Moller, F., Birtwistle, G. (eds.) Logics for Concurrency. LNCS, vol. 1043, pp. 41–101. Springer, Heidelberg (1996)
5. Emerson, E., Clarke, E.C.: Using branching time temporal logic to synthesise synchronisation skeletons. Sci. of Computer Programming 2 (1982)

6. Emerson, E., Halpern, J.: Decision procedures and expressiveness in the temporal logic of branching time. J. Comp. and Sys. Sci. 30(1), 1–24 (1985)
7. Emerson, E., Halpern, J.: 'Sometimes' and 'not never' revisited: on branching versus linear time. J. ACM 33 (1986)
8. Emerson, E., Jutla, C.: Complexity of tree automata and modal logics of programs. In: 29th IEEE Foundations of Computer Science, Proceedings. IEEE, Los Alamitos (1988)
9. Emerson, E., Sistla, A.: Deciding full branching time logic. Information and Control 61, 175–201 (1984)
10. Emerson, E.A.: Temporal and modal logic. In: van Leeuwen, J. (ed.) Handbook of Theoretical Computer Science, vol. B. Elsevier, Amsterdam (1990)
11. Fitting, M.: Proof methods for modal and intuitionistic logics. Reidel, Dordrecht (1983)
12. Goré, R.: Tableau methods for modal and temporal logics. In: D'Agostino, M., et al. (eds.) Handbook of Tableau Methods, pp. 297–396. Kluwer, Dordrecht (1999)
13. Hughes, G., Cresswell, M.: An Intro. to Modal Logic. Methuen, London (1968)
14. Kupferman, O., Vardi, M., Wolper, P.: An automata-theoretic approach to branching-time model checking. J. ACM 47, 312–360 (2000)
15. Pnueli, A.: The temporal logic of programs. In: Proc. 18th Symposium on Foundations of Computer Science, Providence, RI, pp. 46–57 (1977)
16. Pnueli, A., Rosner, R.: On the synthesis of a reactive module. In: Proc. 16th Symposium of Principles of Programming Languages, pp. 179–190. ACM, New York (1989)
17. Pnueli, A., Kesten, Y.: A deductive proof system for CTL*. In: Brim, L., Jančar, P., Křetínský, M., Kucera, A. (eds.) CONCUR 2002. LNCS, vol. 2421, pp. 24–40. Springer, Heidelberg (2002)
18. Rao, A.S., Georgeff, M.P.: Modelling rational agents within a BDI-Architecture. In: Fikes, R., Sandewall, E. (eds.) Proceedings of the Second International Conference on Principles of Knowledge Representation and Reasoning, KR 1991, Cambridge, MA, pp. 473–484 (1991)
19. Reynolds, M.: An axiomatization of full computation tree logic. J. Symbolic Logic 66(3), 1011–1057 (2001)
20. Reynolds, M.: A tableau for bundled CTL*. J. Logic and Comp. 17, 117–132 (2007)
21. Reynolds, M.: A tableau for CTL*, long version. Tech. report, UWA (January 2009), http://www.csse.uwa.edu.au/~mark/research/Online/StarTab.html
22. Reynolds, M., Dixon, C.: Theorem-proving for discrete temporal logic. In: Fisher, M., Gabbay, D., Vila, L. (eds.) Handbook of Temporal Reasoning in Artificial Intelligence, pp. 279–314. Elsevier, Amsterdam (2005)
23. Schwendimann, S.: A new one-pass tableau calculus for PLTL. In: de Swart, H. (ed.) TABLEAUX 1998. LNCS (LNAI), vol. 1397, pp. 277–291. Springer, Heidelberg (1998)
24. Sprenger, C.: Deductive Local Model Checking. PhD thesis, Swiss Federal Institute of Technology, Lausanne, Switzerland (2000)
25. Stirling, C.: Modal and temporal logics. In: Abramsky, S., Gabbay, D., Maibaum, T. (eds.) H'book of Logic in Comp. Sci., OUP, vol. 2, pp. 477–563 (1992)
26. Vardi, M., Stockmeyer, L.: Improved upper and lower bounds for modal logics of programs. In: 17th ACM Symp. on Th. of Comp., pp. 240–251. ACM, New York (1985)
27. Wolper, P.: The tableau method for temporal logic: an overview. Logique et Analyse 28, 110–111 (1985)

Certifiable Specification and Verification of C Programs

Christoph Lüth and Dennis Walter

Deutsches Forschungszentrum für Künstliche Intelligenz
Bremen, Germany
Christoph.Lueth@dfki.de, Dennis.Walter@dfki.de

Abstract. A novel approach to the specification and verification of C programs through an annotation language that is a mixture between JML and the language of Isabelle/HOL is proposed. This yields three benefits: specifications are concise and close to the underlying mathematical model; existing Isabelle theories can be reused; and the leap of faith from specification language to encoding in a logic is small. This is of particular relevance for software certification, and verification in application areas such as robotics.

1 Introduction

Software verification is used to many ends, and each end has its own means. In this paper, we present an approach for the specification and verification of mathematically-oriented C programs in the context of software certification, where correctness and reliability of the verification process are a major concern. Therefore we emphasise trustworthiness and correctness, by reduction to a proof in a trusted theorem prover (in our case, Isabelle/HOL), such that the only leap of faith required is the embedding of the semantics of the programming language into the prover, and the actual definition of correctness.

To ensure consistency between specification and program code, we annotate the source code with specifications of its intended behaviour, but instead of extending the programming language with specification constructs (as in JML or ACSL [1,2]), we use the higher-order logic of the underlying prover, extended by convenient ways to relate to values of the program state. In our application domain, safety software in robotics[1], programs live in a fairly rich application domain, involving in particular concepts from geometry such as points, lines, or convex polygons. Using the prover's native higher-order language, specifications become concise and easy to read, since these concepts lend themselves well to higher-order formalisation. Moreover, we can use Isabelle's rich libraries.

The actual correctness proofs follow previous work [3,4,5]: we encode the programming language and its semantics into the theorem prover, define a semantic way of when a specification is satisfied, and show the verification rules as theorems. Verification conditions are generated (and proven) in Isabelle. However,

[1] `http://www.sams-project.org/`

A. Cavalcanti and D. Dams (Eds.): FM 2009, LNCS 5850, pp. 419–434, 2009.

Supported	Not supported
Addresses of local objects (via &)	Casts to and from **void** *
Pointer offsets and subtraction	Function pointers
sizeof operator	**switch**, **goto**, **continue**
Function calls in expressions	Arbitrary side effects

Fig. 1. A state maps base locations to types and sequences of scalar values

some work is necessary to scale this up for realistic programs: one has to make sure the proof state remains manageable, and we have to provide a modular way to verify each function separately. Hence, our main contribution is an approach which allows comprehensible, concise specifications of C programs in a rich problem domain, together with a well-defined, rational verification process, by tight integration of programming language and theorem prover.

The paper is structured as follows: Sec. 2 describes the semantic foundations, such as the supported C language subset, its denotational semantics, the semantic notion of specification, satisfiability, and how it is proven. Sec. 3 introduces the novel hybrid specification language we annotate program functions with, followed by an account on how programs are formally verified, given in Sec. 4. We look at related work and conclude in Sec. 5.

2 Semantic Foundations

Overall, our model is a text-book semantics as found in e.g. [6]. Its distinctive features are a deep embedding of a (subset of) the C language, to which we give a deterministic denotational semantics as a mapping from states to states, and a shallow embedding of functions.

2.1 The Low-Level State Model

The *state* represents a program's memory. Abstractly, it is a map from locations *Loc* to values *Val*. In contrast to the usual memory model as a stack of local variables and a heap containing allocated objects, we use a flat model where all objects are given a *base location*. An *object* is defined in the C standard as a "region of storage [...], the contents of which can represent values" [7, 3.14]. We represent it as a sequences of *scalar* values [7], modelled as partial functions from $\mathbb{N}$ to *Val*. Scalar values are integer and floating-point numbers—which we model as unbounded integers and reals—and references, $Val = Int + Real + Ref$, where a reference is a location or undefined (the null pointer) $Ref = Loc + 1$. Fig. 1 depicts the structure of the state space.

Concretely, a state is then a finite partial function $\Sigma : BaseLoc \rightharpoonup (Type \times (\mathbb{N} \rightharpoonup Val))$ mapping base locations to representations of objects and their (runtime) type *Type*. To access scalar values (possibly inside structures or arrays) we use *locations*, which are pairs $Loc = BaseLoc \times \mathbb{N}$. Thus, locations represent addresses. They allow a limited form of arithmetic, as defined in the standard:

Supported	Not supported
Addresses of local objects (via &)	Casts to and from **void** *
Pointer offsets and subtraction	Function pointers
sizeof operator	**switch**, **goto**, **continue**
Function calls in expressions	Arbitrary side effects

Fig. 2. Summary of supported and unsupported language features

we can add and subtract the offsets of locations sharing the same base location. (A simplifying assumption here is that all scalar values have the same size.) Our model precludes the use of structured values in expressions, so they cannot occur as arguments to assignment or functions. The basic operations on states are reading, writing, allocation and deallocation:

$$read: Loc \to \Sigma \to Val \quad update: Loc \to Val \to \Sigma \to \Sigma$$
$$fresh\text{-}loc: \Sigma \to BaseLoc \quad extend, dealloc: BaseLoc \to \Sigma \to \Sigma$$

The *fresh-loc* operator returns a base location that is not yet used. Deallocation is currently used for local variables on function exit; *malloc* and *free* could easily be supported by our model as well. State updates always succeed, i.e. at the state level we do not perform type checks, array bounds checks or pointer validity checks. Sanity checks are instead inserted into the semantics of pointer dereferencing and array access.

We do not follow the split heap approach [8] literally, but recover the needed inequalities through appropriate lemmas on field and array access. This keeps the state model reasonably close to the C standard.

2.2 Modelled Language Subset

We support a subset of the language given by the MISRA programming guidelines [9] (Fig. 2). Prominent features include those which are heavily used in our application domain: arbitrary nesting of structures and arrays, limited form of address arithmetic, function calls in expressions, and an &-operator that can be used on both global and local objects. Fig. 3 shows excerpts of the datatypes modelling the language. An external front-end parses the actual C source code into the Isabelle datatypes, and also performs static checks for type correctness, and conformance to our language subset, including the MISRA guidelines.

A rather drastic simplification from a theoretical point of view is the exclusion of recursive functions by the guidelines [9, Rule 16.2]. This allows us to give semantics to functions without the need for an explicit fixed-point operator.

Since expressions can have side-effects, evaluation order would be important. However, [9, Rule 12.2] requires that an expression must yield the same value under every evaluation order. We check this on the syntactic level in the front end, by ruling out problematic expressions such as (x= 2)/x−−, but allowing

$$
\begin{array}{rcl}
\textit{basic-type} & ::= & \textbf{int} \mid \textbf{double} \mid \textbf{void} \\
\textit{type} & ::= & \textit{basic-type} \\
& \mid & * \ \textit{type} \\
& \mid & \textbf{struct} \ \textit{id} \ (\textit{id} \times \textit{type}) \ \textit{list} \\
& \mid & \textit{type} \ [\textit{Nat}] \\
\\
\textit{stmt} & ::= & \textbf{while} \ \textit{expr} \ \{ * \ \textit{stmt} \} \\
& \mid & \textit{lval} = \textit{expr} \\
& \mid & \textit{id} \ (\textit{expr list})_{\mathsf{stmt}} \\
& \mid & \textit{stmt}; \ \textit{stmt} \mid \ldots \\
\\
\textit{id} & ::= & \textit{String} \\
\textit{arith-op} & ::= & + \mid - \mid * \mid \ldots \\
\textit{comp-op} & ::= & == \mid \mathrm{!=} \mid < \mid \ldots
\end{array}
\qquad
\begin{array}{rcl}
\textit{lval} & ::= & \textit{id}_{\textit{type}} \\
& \mid & \textit{ref-expr}[\textit{int-expr}]_{\textit{type}} \\
& \mid & \textit{lval}.\textit{id}_{\textit{type}} \\
& \mid & * \ \textit{ref-expr}_{\textit{type}} \\
\textit{ref-expr} & ::= & \textbf{NULL} \\
& \mid & \textit{lval} \\
& \mid & \& \ \textit{lval} \\
& \mid & \textit{id} \ (\textit{expr list})_{\mathsf{ref}} \\
\textit{int-expr} & = & \textit{Int} \\
& \mid & \textit{lval} \\
& \mid & \textit{int-expr comp-op int-expr} \\
& \mid & \textit{int-expr arith-op int-expr} \\
& \mid & \textit{id} \ (\textit{expr list})_{\mathsf{int}} \mid \ldots \\
\textit{expr} & = & \textit{int-expr} \mid \textit{double-expr} \mid \textit{ref-expr}
\end{array}
$$

Fig. 3. The datatypes of the deep C embedding (abridged). Names of datatypes are denoted *in italics*, and constructors written in concrete syntax. Note how we annotate lvalues with their type, such that we can compute necessary state offsets easily.

calls to side-effect free functions. As we only consider MISRA-conformant programs, it is adequate to fix the evaluation order, proceeding from left to right for both function argument lists and expression trees.

2.3 Denotational Semantics

Our semantics is deterministic and identifies all kinds of faults like invalid memory access, non-termination, or division by zero as complete failure. We use the overloaded semantic brackets $[\![-]\!]$ for all semantic functions, which assign a meaning to each of the datatypes modelling programs, amongst them

$$[\![\mathit{stmt}]\!] : \Gamma \to \Sigma \rightharpoonup 1 \times \Sigma \qquad [\![\mathit{expr}]\!] : \Gamma \to \Sigma \rightharpoonup \mathit{Val} \times \Sigma \qquad [\![\mathit{lval}]\!] : \Gamma \to \Sigma \rightharpoonup \mathit{Ref} \times \Sigma$$

where Γ is an environment which maps identifiers to locations. Note that in the presence of pointers, the evaluation of an lvalue (e.g. $*\mathsf{x}$) depends on the state. State transformers are composed with the Kleisli composition [10] (where α and β are type variables) $\gg= : (\Sigma \rightharpoonup \alpha \times \Sigma) \to (\alpha \to \Sigma \rightharpoonup \beta \times \Sigma) \to \Sigma \rightharpoonup \beta \times \Sigma$ which passes the result tuple of the first argument into the second function. The semantic function for an assignment evaluates the lvalue l to a location m, then the rvalue e side to a value v, and uses *update* to change the state:

$$[\![l = e]\!]\Gamma \stackrel{def}{=} [\![l]\!]\Gamma \gg= \lambda m.\ [\![e]\!]\Gamma \gg= \lambda v.\ \mathit{update}\ m\ v$$

The conditional statement and iteration are interpreted by corresponding operations on state transformers. A bounded iteration operator models the unfolding of the loop at most n times, and the semantics of iteration is the least number of unfoldings to make the loop condition false, if it exists, and undefined otherwise.

We consider the idealisation of machine integers to mathematical integers a sensible separation of concerns, as the absence of under-/overflow can in many practical cases be proven by means of abstract interpretation [11], and using modular arithmetic makes interactive verification unbearably cumbersome. Modelling floating-point numbers as real numbers ignores the issue of numerical precision. For the time being, we simply do not treat it formally.

2.4 Modelling Functions

Functions are modelled as HOL functions. The semantic function of a C function with n parameters takes n values, and returns a state transformer:

$$[\![\mathsf{type}\ \mathsf{id}(x_1,\ldots,x_n)\ \mathsf{block}]\!] : \Gamma \to \mathit{Val}^n \to \Sigma \rightharpoonup \mathit{Val} \times \Sigma$$

Both parameters and local declarations are translated into state extensions, and the new locations added to the environment, but parameters are initialised with the argument values, and are visible in the pre- and postconditions of the function. Ignoring specifications — which are also included in the full environment — the environment Γ maps variables to their allocated base location, and function identifiers to their semantics:

$$\Gamma \cong (\mathit{Id} \rightharpoonup \mathit{BaseLoc}) \times (\mathit{Id} \rightharpoonup (\mathit{Val}^n \to \Sigma \rightharpoonup \mathit{Val} \times \Sigma))$$

When calling a function f, we evaluate the n argument values, look up its value in the environment, written as $\Gamma\,!\,f$, and call the resulting state transformer:

$$[\![\mathsf{f}(\mathsf{args})]\!]\Gamma \stackrel{def}{=} [\![\mathsf{args}]\!]\Gamma \gg= (\Gamma\,!\,\mathsf{f})$$

2.5 Specifications

Semantically, we consider specifications to be state predicates. In the classic total Hoare calculus, a specification for a program p consists of a precondition P and a postcondition Q, written $[P]p[Q]$. In our typed setting, the precondition is a state predicate $P : \Sigma \to \mathit{bool}$, the program is a state transformer $p : \Sigma \rightharpoonup \alpha \times \Sigma$, and the postcondition a predicate over the state and the result of the program, $Q : \alpha \times \Sigma \to \mathit{bool}$. The specification is satisfied by p if each state satisfying P is mapped to one satisfying Q:

$$\begin{aligned} &\models : (\Sigma \to \mathit{bool}) \to (\Sigma \rightharpoonup \alpha \times \Sigma) \to (\alpha \times \Sigma \to \mathit{bool}) \to \mathit{bool} \\ &\models [P]\,p\,[Q] \stackrel{def}{=} \forall S.\ P\ S \longrightarrow \mathit{def}(p\ S) \wedge Q(p\ S) \end{aligned}$$

To show that a program satisfies a specification, we introduce a *syntactic* notion of satisfiability for each datatype in Fig. 3, which is defined in terms of the semantic notion (shown here for expressions and statements)

$$\begin{aligned} &\vdash_e : \Gamma \to (\Sigma \to \mathit{bool}) \to \mathit{expr} \to (\mathit{Val} \times \Sigma \to \mathit{bool}) \to \mathit{bool} \\ &\vdash_s : \Gamma \to (\Sigma \to \mathit{bool}) \to \mathit{stmt} \to (1 \times \Sigma \to \mathit{bool}) \to \mathit{bool} \end{aligned}$$

$$\Gamma \vdash_e [P]\ e\ [Q] \stackrel{def}{=} \models [P]\,[\![e]\!]\Gamma\,[Q] \qquad \Gamma \vdash_s [P]\ s\ [Q] \stackrel{def}{=} \models [P]\,[\![s]\!]\Gamma\,[Q]$$

2.6 Modular Verification

In order to handle realistic programs, verification needs to be modular, i.e. we want to verify each function in the program separately and use only its specification during the verification of its callers. Further, we want to keep the specification of each function *local* to its direct effects. For simple imperative languages, this is achieved by *frame rules* [12]. The presence of pointers complicates the situation as possible aliasing forces these rules to become inelegant and complex. Our solution is to make changes to the state possibly caused by a function (semantically, a state transformer) part of the specification. Recall that the state is essentially a finite map. We restrict a state S to a set of locations L by a restriction operation $S\upharpoonright_L$, and define the *modifies* predicate for two states S, T and a set of locations Λ which holds if S and T agree everywhere except for Λ:

$$S \simeq_\Lambda T \stackrel{def}{=} S\upharpoonright_{\neg\Lambda} = T\upharpoonright_{\neg\Lambda} .$$

We extend the notion of satisfaction by a *modification set*, which contains the only locations this state transformer may change, thus effectively integrating the frame rule into the notion of satisfaction.

$$\begin{aligned}
&\models : \mathit{Loc\ set} \to (\Sigma \to \mathit{bool}) \to (\Sigma \rightharpoonup \alpha \times \Sigma) \to (\alpha \times \Sigma \to \mathit{bool}) \to \mathit{bool}\\
&\Lambda \models [P]\, p\, [Q] \stackrel{def}{=} \forall S.\ P\ S \longrightarrow \mathit{def}(p\ S) \wedge Q(p\ S) \wedge S \simeq_\Lambda (p\ S)\\
&\vdash_s : \mathit{Loc\ set} \to \Gamma \to (\Sigma \to \mathit{bool}) \to \mathit{stmt} \to (1 \times \Sigma \to \mathit{bool}) \to \mathit{bool}\\
&\Lambda, \Gamma \vdash_s [P]\ s\ [Q] \stackrel{def}{=} \Lambda \models [P]\, [\![s]\!]\Gamma\, [Q]
\end{aligned}$$

The syntactic proof rules integrate checks that only locations in the modification set are modified. Sec. 4.2 gives further details, and an example (Fig. 7).

3 Program Specifications with Isabelle

Programs are specified through *annotations* embedded in the source code in specially marked comments (beginning with `/*@`, as in JML or ACSL). This way, annotated programs can be processed by any compiler without modifications. Annotations can occur before function declarations, where they take the form of *function specifications*, and inside functions in front of loops, where they serve as *loop specifications*, which play a technical rôle in that they allow automatic generation of verification conditions. A function specification consists of a precondition (`@requires`), a postcondition (`@ensures`) which relates the state before entry into the function (the *pre-state*) to the state after the function has returned (*post-state*), and a modification set (`@modifies`). Loop specifications consist of an invariant (`@invariant`), a variant (`@variant`; a measure function on program states, mapping program states to $\mathbb{N}$ given an appropriate C expression) ensuring termination of the loop, and an optional modification set; Fig. 4 gives an example. We first explore the design rationale before delving into the technicalities.

```
/*@ @modifies a[0:len], *res @*/
void avg(int *a, int len, double *res) {
  int i;
  /*@ @modifies i, *res, a[0:len]
      @variant len - i                @*/
  for (i=0; i<len; ++i) { *res += a[i]; a[i] = 0; }
  *res /= len;
  }
```

Fig. 4. Annotated function demonstrating features as found in e.g. JML

3.1 Design Rationale

Our aim is to specify and verify program modules for the domain of safety-relevant robotics and automation. Functions in these programs often represent mathematical operations. They range from simple vector operations (scalar product, transformations) over computing the convex hull of a point set to the approximation of the behaviour of a moving object. The data structures these operations work upon is rather restricted. For simplicity and memory safety, they tend to be static; dynamic objects are sparse. In many cases, these data types are structurally just tuples and sequences of real numbers and integers.

In contrast to their representations, the objects of interest in the mathematical domain are not necessarily discrete and finite. They include time-dependent functions, areas, polygons etc. Therefore, to obtain the desired degree of abstraction and detail in function specifications, an expressive, mathematically oriented language is required. Fundamental concepts like real numbers, sets, geometric transformations, but also concepts from analysis like derivations, integrals or limits should be easily definable or preferably predefined. Moreover, for the actual verification, a plethora of lemmas about these operations and their interaction will be needed. Also, for readability, the language should be syntactically flexible (e.g. support infix notation), and have a larger glyph set than 7-bit ASCII.

Finally, we do not expect to be able to prove the domain-related parts of program specifications automatically, by calling provers like Z3 [13] or CVC3 [14], despite the impressive advances these tools have made. For the interactive proof work it is then a real benefit if only one formal language needs to be understood.

These considerations led to the decision to directly use Isabelle as the specification language for state predicates as used in pre-/postconditions and invariants, in contrast to JML and ACSL, where extensions of the programming language are used in specifications. However, we need a way to refer to the program state, and in particular the value of variables in the specifications, and further there are technical specifications like ranges of array indices or validity of pointers, that are best written down in the C syntax. This resulted in a hybrid approach, where Isabelle and an extension of the C syntax can be combined by a quote/antiquote-mechanism, combining the best of both worlds.

3.2 The Specification Language

State predicates are boolean expressions over atomic formulas, formed by the operators &&, ||, !, --> (implication) and <-> (equivalence), and the quantifiers **forall** T i; P and **exists** T i; P. An atomic formula is one of the following: *(i)* a side-effect free C expression of integer type (with a valuation of 0 denoting *false* and anything else *true*), which may additionally contain bound variables introduced by the quantifiers above, the operator **old**(e) referring to the value of expression e in the pre-state, and the special symbol **result** which refers to the function's return value; *(ii)* a pointer predicate; or *(iii)* a quotation.

Pointer predicates use keywords to state common properties of pointers. These are **valid**(p) (expressing validity of a pointer), **array**(a, n) (array a has at least n elements), and **separated**(a, m, b, n) (the memory areas denoted by a[0:m] and b[0:n] are fully disjoint arrays).

Quotations are the means to embed Isabelle terms of type *bool* into specifications, e.g. to formulate the domain-related parts of a specification. A quotation consists of an arbitrary Isabelle term enclosed in ${...}. Reference to the program state within quoted Isabelle terms is made possible via *anti-quotations*, which allow expressions in C syntax to be spliced into a quotation. Anti-quotations are syntactically enclosed in '{...}. Intuitively, an anti-quoted C expression is interpreted by its semantic value (Sec. 2.3). As an example, using the predefined Isabelle functions *cmod* and *Complex*, ${cmod (Complex '{x+1} '{y}) < c} expresses that the complex number $(x+1)+iy$ has a modulus below c, where x and y are program variables of floating-point type. As a shorthand, for identifiers one may write 'x for '{x}, and $x for ${x}.

3.3 Translation to Isabelle

In contrast to programs, specifications are embedded shallowly as Isabelle functions, where the translation from the specification language to Isabelle is performed by the front-end. Preconditions P, postconditions Q and invariants I are translated to Isabelle functions of types

$$P : \Gamma \to \Sigma \to \mathit{Val}^n \to \mathit{bool} \qquad I : \Gamma \to \Sigma \to \mathit{bool}$$
$$Q : \Gamma \to (\Sigma \times \mathit{Val} \times \Sigma) \to \mathit{Val}^n \to \mathit{bool}$$

Note that the denotation of a modification set can also depend on the pre-state, e.g. to specify that *x is changed when passing a pointer x to a function. Modification sets are given the semantics $[\![\mathsf{mlist}]\!] : \Gamma \to \Sigma \to \mathit{Loc\ set}$, and the front-end simply outputs the modification set as a value of the datatype *mlist*.

The translation is performed by a collection of operations $\{\#, \#_l, \#_r, \#_i, \#_d\}$ on the abstract syntax of specification terms, for predicates, locations and the expression types. We only sketch the translation of preconditions, as the others are analogous. The generated Isabelle term for a precondition *Pre* will have form

$$\lambda\ \Gamma\ \Sigma\ (v_1, \ldots, v_n) \bullet \#(\mathit{Pre}) \qquad (1)$$

$$
\begin{array}{llcl}
\textit{Predicates:} & \#(\mathsf{A}\ \&\&\ \mathsf{B}) & \stackrel{def}{=} & (\#(\mathsf{A}) \wedge \#(\mathsf{B})) \\
& \#(\backslash\mathbf{valid}(\mathsf{p})) & \stackrel{def}{=} & (valid\_ptr\ \Sigma\ ([\![\mathsf{p}]\!]\ \Gamma\ \Sigma)) \\
& \#(\backslash\mathbf{array}(\mathsf{p},\ \mathsf{n})) & \stackrel{def}{=} & (valid\_arr\ \Sigma\ ([\![\mathsf{p}]\!]\ \Gamma\ \Sigma)\ ([\![\mathsf{n}]\!]\ \Gamma\ \Sigma)) \\
& \#(\mathsf{E1} < \mathsf{E2}) & \stackrel{def}{=} & \#_x(\mathsf{E1}) < \#_x(\mathsf{E2}) \quad (x \in \{l, d\}) \\
& \#(\$\{s_1\ `\{\mathsf{a1}\}\ s_2\ `\{\mathsf{a2}\} \cdots s_k\ \}) & \stackrel{def}{=} & (s_1\ \#_{x_1}(\mathsf{a1})\ s_2\ \#_{x_2}(\mathsf{a2}) \cdots s_k) \\
& & & \quad (x_i \in \{l, r, i, d\}) \\
\textit{Expressions:} & \#_x(\mathsf{E1} + \mathsf{E2}) & \stackrel{def}{=} & \#_x(\mathsf{E1}) + \#_x(\mathsf{E2}) \quad (x \in \{l, d\}) \\
& \#_i(\ \mathsf{lval}\ ) & \stackrel{def}{=} & int\,(read\ \#_l(\mathsf{lval})\ \Sigma) \\
& \#_l(\ \mathsf{lval}\ [\mathsf{e}]) & \stackrel{def}{=} & array\text{-}acc\ \#_l(\ \mathsf{lval}\ )\ \#_i(\mathsf{e}) \\
& \#_i(\$\mathsf{a}) & \stackrel{def}{=} & a
\end{array}
$$

Fig. 5. Rules for the translation from abstract to Isabelle syntax

The translation operation # generates the *body* of the lambda term (1). This means we translate state predicates in the implicit context of an environment Γ, the pre-state Σ and function argument values v_i. We cannot define this translation within Isabelle in terms of the semantic functions $[\![\cdot]\!]$, since Isabelle code may appear in quotations, and antiquotations may refer back to bound variables introduced in quotations, but the translation via # resembles the defined expression semantics on the quotation-free part of a specification term.

Fig. 5 shows representative translation rules. The logical connectives are directly translated to their Isabelle equivalents. For each pointer predicate there is an Isabelle counterpart with the additional arguments Γ and Σ; e.g. *valid_ptr* interprets **valid**. Since the arguments to pointer predicates are unextended C expressions, we can use the semantic function to interpret the abstract syntax in Isabelle. Quotations are output verbatim, except for anti-quotations, the translation of which is spliced into the quotation on the point of occurrence. The translation of expressions behaves like the respective semantic function, but outputs references to bound Isabelle variables ($a) by their name ($a$).

3.4 Representation Functions

A *representation function* maps objects represented implicitly in the state to their explicit denotation. For example, in the specification stating that the sum of the elements of a vector p.v is less than δ: ${ *sum* (*Vec* Σ `{p.v} `{p.vlen}) $< \delta$} the function $Vec :: \Sigma \to Loc \to int \to int\ list$ is a representation function, yielding a list as the denotation for a vector represented implicitly by an array p.v and its length p.vlen. Representation functions always refer to the state Σ, a location, and a tuple of C scalar values (of type Val^n). As they occur frequently, our language provides *representation anti-quotations* to express them easily: a representation function $R : \Sigma \to Loc \to Val^N \to \alpha$ can be refered to inside a quotation as ^R{x_0, x_1, .., x_N}, where the x_i are C lvalues. Fig. 6 shows a matrix inversion operation specified using representation anti-quotations.

```
/*@
  @requires \valid(m) && \valid(inv) &&
     ${ invertible ^Matrix{m} }
  @modifies *inv
  @ensures \result != -1 -->
     ${ ^Matrix{m} * ^Matrix{inv} = (1 :: mat3) }
  @*/
int invert_transform(const matrix3 *m, matrix3 *inv);
```

Fig. 6. Example specification: matrix inversion. m and inv are not required to be distinct. The specification assumes that a type of 3×3 matrices *mat3* and a constant $Matrix : \Sigma \to Loc \to mat3$ are defined in Isabelle. *1* is an overloaded constant, used here for the type *mat3*.

An alternative to using representation functions in our setting would be to develop a component-based state model that can be used in specifications directly (as in [5]). In our opinion, no state model can be conceived that is generic, yet makes it comfortable to directly work with representations of C values as provided by that model. In particular, this would require that all domain theorems are formulated in terms of the state model, which is unrealistic. Further, not all objects can be referenced as lvalues (in particular, there is no expression evaluating to a whole array).

4 Generating Verification Conditions

In this section we describe how specifications are translated to theorems in Isabelle, how these theorem are proven, and what automatic support we provide.

4.1 Translation to Correctness Propositions

All translated annotation elements given for a function specification are composed to form a proposition whose validity entails that the function at hand (call it f) satisfies its specification. This proposition basically is a Hoare triple as of Sec. 2.6. To be exact, it states that under the assumption that *all functions called by* f do satisfy their specification, execution of f in an arbitrary pre-state satisfying the precondition will, for all possible arguments of the right type and arity, *(1)* terminate, *(2)* not alter objects except those mentioned in the modification set, *(3)* not access arrays outside their bounds, *(4)* not dereference invalid (or **NULL**) pointers, *(5)* not perform a division by zero, and *(6)* end in a state that together with the pre-state satisfies the postcondition. Note that this proposition is formulated over the semantic interpretation of a C function, in which we abstract the numeric types. It is therefore possible to write code that will verify, but display unwanted behaviour in practice, by combining floating-point arithmetic and pointer manipulation.[2] We argue, however, that this kind of interplay is not common in applications, and can be avoided by other means.

Formally, the correctness proposition is as follows. Consider the specification

```
/*@ @requires Pre    @modifies mlist    @ensures Post @*/
int f(double x)
```

Let Γ be an appropriate environment which contains the relevant global variables and specifications of f's callees; further let *arg_types p a* express that the list of actual parameters *a* matches the formal parameter list *p* w.r.t. their types. Then the specification gets translated to the following Isabelle proposition:

$$\begin{array}{l} \forall\ \Lambda\ args\ S_1 \bullet \Lambda = [\![\mathsf{mlist}]\!]\ \Gamma\ S_1 \wedge arg\_types\ [\mathsf{x}]\ args \longrightarrow \\ \qquad \Lambda, \Gamma \vdash_f [\lambda S.\ S = S_1 \wedge \#(\mathsf{Pre})\ \Gamma\ S\ [\mathsf{x}]]\, \mathit{f(double\ x)} \\ \qquad\qquad [\lambda(r, S).\ \#(\mathsf{Post})\ \Gamma\ (S_1, r, S)\ [\mathsf{x}]] \end{array} \quad (2)$$

4.2 Program Proof Rules

To derive verification conditions for a concrete program and specification, we perform a backwards proof. Starting with proposition (2), we match the corresponding rule on the current state. By reducing the program term, we build up the postcondition. For this, there has to be at least one rule for each constructor of the datatypes representing the language, and the rules have to be formulated in such a way that the postcondition of the conclusion is a single variable, so it can match on any postcondition. The proof is performed by an Isabelle tactic that transforms the initial proof obligation (2) into a single *intermediate verification condition* (iVC) by applying proof rules that subsequently reduce the program term to purely logical expressions. In total, we have $\sim$ 80 rules for function definitions, local declarations, blocks, statements, expressions and all constituent parts of these. Fig. 7 shows three of the rules.

As usual, the rules are best read from bottom to top. Rule (IntLVal) reduces an lvalue integer expression (whose value is an integer) to the lvalue itself (whose value is the location of the integer). This is done by reflecting the action of reading a location within the predicate: the postcondition Q expecting the integer value becomes ($\lambda lv\ S \bullet \mathbf{let}\ iv = read\_int\ lv\ S\ \mathbf{in}\ Q\ iv\ S$), which expects a location, reads it as an integer, binds that value to an intermediate variable iv and then passes iv to Q. The let-binding avoids a blowup in predicate size and keeps the number of read operations in predicates small.

[2] The following code snippet will cause a segmentation fault on an IA-32 system, but is verifiable since `i <= 10000 && d > 0` is an invariant in the semantic interpretation.

```
int i = 0; int * p = &i; double d = 1.0;
while (i++ < 10000) d /= 2.0;
if (d <= 0) p = NULL;
*p = 0;
```

$$\frac{\Lambda, \Gamma \vdash_{lv} [P]\ \mathsf{lval}\ [\lambda lv\ S \bullet \textbf{let}\ iv = (read\_int\ lv\ S)\ \textbf{in}\ Q\ iv\ S]}{\Lambda, \Gamma \vdash_i [P]\ \mathsf{lval}\ [Q]} \quad \text{(IntLVal)}$$

$$\frac{\begin{array}{c}\forall l \bullet (\Lambda, \Gamma \vdash_e [R\ l]\ \mathsf{t}\ [\lambda a\ S \bullet \textbf{let}\ T = update\ l\ a\ S\ \textbf{in}\ Q\ T]) \\ \Lambda, \Gamma \vdash_{lv} [P]\ \mathsf{lv}\ [\lambda l\ S \bullet R\ l\ S \wedge l \in \Lambda]\end{array}}{\Lambda, \Gamma \vdash_s [P]\ \mathsf{lv} = \mathsf{t}\ [Q]} \quad \text{(Assign)}$$

$$\frac{\begin{array}{l}\forall \Lambda'\ S\ N \bullet\ \ \Lambda' = [\![\mathsf{mlist}]\!]\ \Gamma\ S \longrightarrow \\ \qquad (\Lambda', \Gamma \vdash_s [J\ \Lambda'\ S\ N]\ \mathsf{c}\ [\lambda T \bullet invar\ \Gamma\ T \wedge [\![\mathsf{var}]\!]\ \Gamma\ T < N] \wedge \\ \qquad \Lambda', \Gamma \vdash_b [K\ \Lambda'\ S\ N]\ \mathsf{b}\ [\lambda b\ T \bullet (b \longrightarrow J\ \Lambda'\ S\ N\ T) \wedge (\neg b \longrightarrow F\ T)])\end{array}}{\begin{array}{l}\Lambda, \Gamma \vdash_s [\lambda S \bullet \textbf{let}\ M = [\![\mathsf{mlist}]\!]\ \Gamma\ S\ \textbf{in} \\ \qquad\qquad (invar\ \Gamma\ S \wedge M \subseteq \Lambda \wedge \\ \qquad\qquad (\forall T \bullet S \simeq_M T \longrightarrow invar\ \Gamma\ T \longrightarrow K\ M\ S\ ([\![\mathsf{var}]\!]\ \Gamma\ T)\ T))] \\ \qquad \mathsf{while\ b\ c\ (loopanno}\ invar\ \mathsf{mlist\ var)} \\ \qquad [F]\end{array}} \quad \text{(WhileTotal)}$$

Fig. 7. Proof rules for integer lvalues, assignments and while statements

Since our pre- and postconditions are boolean-valued functions, we cannot use substitution to reflect assignments in predicates. Instead, we explicitly modify the program state. Rule (Assign) shows this: to prove an assignment with postcondition Q, we evaluate the lvalue we assign to (in the second premiss), showing it is a modifiable location ($l \in \Lambda$). We then evaluate the expression t (in the first premiss); the updated state is bound to an auxiliary variable T, which is passed to Q. This is equivalent to substitution: we create the predicate stating that updating the state at lv with t yields a state satisfying Q. The state predicate R is both the precondition of the first premiss and the postcondition of the second, thus logically connecting Q and P in the conclusion.

We shall only illustrate the rule for loops (WhileTotal) here. It demonstrates that proof rules for real program verification are a little more complex than what idealised textbook variants might suggest, and shows why it is useful to be able to prove the rules formally correct, making a manual correctness inspection of rules like these unnecessary. The precondition of the conclusion requires that the annotated invariant *invar* holds; that the annotated set of modifiable locations, M, is a subset of the modifiable location set Λ in the context; and that in each state T with $S \simeq_M T$ we may infer K from the invariant. We want to show that F holds after execution of the while statement. This holds given two premises. The first premiss states that an arbitrary run of the body in a state satisfying J re-establishes the invariant *invar*. The second premiss states that after evaluation of the condition b under the precondition K we either obtain F directly — for the case where b evaluates to *false* – or we end in a state satisfying some intermediate predicate J, if b evaluates to *true*. Both premises are formulated in the context of the annotated modification set mlist, instead of the context Λ of the loop itself, ensuring the loop body only modifies locations as annotated in the loop specification. Termination of the loop is also ensured, employing the annotated variant var; without going into details, the rule encodes the requirement that the variant, interpreted as a natural number, strictly decreases in each iteration.

Weakened weakening through modification sets. Modification sets introduce the essential property of *framing* (see Sec. 2.6), which shows up in what we call *weakened weakening*. In the conclusion of rule (WhileTotal) we weaken the invariant, roughly: $\forall T \bullet S \simeq_M T \longrightarrow \mathit{invar}\ T \longrightarrow K\,T$. This is essentially the statement that the invariant implies the weakest precondition of the loop body w.r.t. the invariant itself, K. We do not need to be able to do this for *any* state, but only for those states T with $S \simeq_M T$. Thus, facts about S can be used in proving the weakening, since these are also valid for the quantified states T if they are independent of the locations M. E. g., if the loop is the first statement of the function to be verified, then we know the function's precondition holds in S. The invariant therefore only needs to specify those properties that concern locations in M, which is exactly the desired framing property.

4.3 Reduction to Domain-Related and Program Safety VCs

The iVC is a single logical expression whose validity ensures program correctness. This expression is simplified through a set of tactics which ultimately yield verification conditions of three kinds, which then need to be proven interactively. The first ones are domain-related VCs, e.g. that a function specified to compute the inverse of an affine transform actually does so. The second ones are program safety VCs that could not automatically be proven. These are comprised of non-trivial array bounds checks, where the array is indexed in other ways than by an iteration variable, pointer dereferencing checks and checks for division by zero. Since pointer arithmetic is hardly used in mathematical operations, the safety of pointer dereferencing can be proven automatically by the tactics in most cases. The third kind of VC is concerned with modification sets; these VCs demand that only the specified locations have been modified. The only VCs of this kind that cannot be proved fully automatically are, again, those involving non-trivial array indexing. These are seldom and mostly easy to prove manually, since an assumption about the validity of the relevant array access will be available due to an earlier proof of that fact.

There are three main technical features of these tactics worth mentioning. *(1)* Thanks to the structure of the iVC, where every intermediate value and state is let-bound, we can avoid a combinatorial explosion in the size and number of VCs, similar to [15], because complex expressions do not occur repeatedly. *(2)* Concerning aliasing, we have proven ~ 100 lemmas about our state model that allow to exploit a restricted property of the split heap model [8], namely that structure fields with different names cannot be aliased for properly aligned structures. (a−>f and b−>g always denote different locations for valid pointers a and b). This eliminates many unnecessary VCs that would normally arise in a basic state model like ours. *(3)* Finally, properties of representation functions are known to the simplification tactics, such that, e. g., an update on a **struct** Point in the code is reflected by an associated update on the model point in the VC. Likewise, equalities such as $R\,(\mathit{update}\,l\,v\,\Sigma)\,m = R\,\Sigma\,m$, expressing that the R-representation at location m is independent of updates at l (with appropriate conditions on m and l, of course) are built into the tactics.

```
/*@ @requires \separated(ps, len, rs, rs_len)
  && \separated(qs, len, rs, rs_len)
  && len <= rs_len && -$pi/2 <= alpha && alpha <= $pi/2
 @modifies rs[0:len].x, rs[0:len].y
 @ensures (\result == OK) -->
 ${ ALL (s::real). (ALL i. 0 <= i & i < 'len -->
     arc_end s 'alpha ^Point{ps[$i]} = ^Point{qs[$i]}) -->
 (ALL i. 0 <= i & i < 'len -->
   arc s 'alpha ^Point{ps[$i]} <= convex_hull
    {^Point{ps[$i]},^Point{rs[$i]},^Point{qs[$i]}})
  } @*/
status archull(double alpha, vec2d *ps, vec2d *qs, int32 len,
               vec2d *rs, int32 rs_len );
```

Fig. 8. Example specification: the `archull` function

4.4 Example: Verification at Work

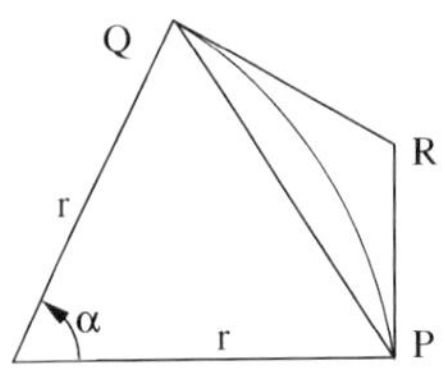

Fig. 9. The arc hull

Fig. 8 shows the specification of a function archull which calculates convex hulls of arcs. Each arc is given by its endpoints P_i and Q_i and the opening angle α of the corresponding circle segment which uniquely determines the radius r. The convex hull is constructed with the intersection point R_i of the tangents through P_i and Q_i, see Fig. 9. This is a typical function of medium complexity, which mixes domain-related and technical requirements. The function takes an array of start- and endpoints, and a single angle α, and stores the R_i in a result array.

The function is about 40 lines of C code, with calls to five other functions. The translated Isabelle theory is about 500 lines. Our tactic reduces this function to 4 domain-related proof obligations, 8 technical and program safety obligations, and 10 pointer-validity obligations (which are proven automatically).[3]

5 Related Work and Conclusion

This paper has presented an approach to the verification of C programs in the context of software certification in the area of mobile robotics. Its distinctive features are a deep embedding of a subset of C into Isabelle, and specification by annotation in a language directly based on Isabelle's higher-order language.

Closely related approaches such as Frama-C [17], Caduceus [3] or JML have a comparatively weak, essentially first-order specification language, which in turn can be used with many prover backends. In contrast, we have an expressive,

[3] The relevant Isabelle theories are provided at `http://www.informatik.uni-bremen.de/~cxl/sources/fm09.tgz`; a public release of the tool will be made avaibable at `http://www.sams-project.org/`

higher-order language, geared towards a specific prover. We believe the added expressivity of higher-order logic compensates for the loss of versatility. By that we appeal to both conciseness of specifications (hence readability) and logical expressivity. We cannot imagine how one would give a functional specification of, e.g., geometric algorithms in pure first-order logic. Another difference is the direct embedding of the programming language, as opposed to using an intermediate language such as Simpl [5] or Why [3]. Thus, we have to rely less on the transformations performed by a syntactical front-end, increasing confidence in the correctness of the verification process.

There is other work using theorem provers (including Isabelle) to verify C programs in different application domains, such as the L4 Verified project [18] verifying an operating system kernel, Verisoft [19] concerned with comprehensive verification (from the hardware to applications, including a verified compiler), etc. The different application domains emphasize that there must be different tools for different application scenarios [20] as each have their own requirements. Moreover, it makes a big difference whether verification is used for external certification, debugging or quality assurance. For example, model-checkers are far more useful for debugging (e.g. [21]) than for certification.

Refinement calculi like VDM and Z are close to our approach concerning the rich mathematical language used. However, we do not follow a refinement approach, although this is feasible in Isabelle. Instead, the concrete source code that will run on the real system comes under formal scrutiny, which is particularly relevant for safety-critical systems.

A denotational semantics (as opposed to an operational one, which captures the C standard more closely [22]) has not only the advantage of easier verification of the proof rules, but we can also use the denotations in the specification.

Our framework can presently handle C functions of medium length. The limiting factor is the size of the proof state produced during the generation of the verification conditions, which is—as usual for verification condition generators—exponential in the number of sequential conditional branches and linear for other program constructs. Care has been taken to keep the number of generated VCs small. A join construct helps to keep the exponentional growth incurred from conditionals in check. To be able to verify longer functions, one breaks them down into smaller components. Presently, the framework consists of the frontend, which is 14 kloc of Haskell (including a checker for MISRA conformance), and the Isabelle backend. This contains 30 theories with a total of 1150 theorems. The tactical support is 1700 lines of SML code. Using the prover language for specification has the further advantage that it allows a comprehensive formal approach, from domain modelling down to the code in one formalism [16].

The approach has been presented to the certification authority (TÜV Süd), and preliminarily approved. The final presentation of the project results is scheduled for October 2009. The current experience is positive. The design of the specification language has been validated in the weekly code and specification reviews within the project, where researchers with no previous exposure to formal methods and Isabelle were able to grasp specifications such as Fig. 8 quickly.

References

1. Chalin, P., Kiniry, J.R., Leavens, G.T., Poll, E.: Beyond assertions: Advanced specification and verification with JML and ESC/Java2. In: de Boer, F.S., Bonsangue, M.M., Graf, S., de Roever, W.-P. (eds.) FMCO 2005. LNCS, vol. 4111, pp. 342–363. Springer, Heidelberg (2006)
2. Baudin, P., Filliâtre, J.C., Marché, C., Monate, B., Moy, Y., Prevosto, V.: ACSL: ANSI C specification language. (October 2008), Preliminary design, version 1.4, `http://frama-c.cea.fr/download/acsl_1.4.pdf`
3. Filliâtre, J.C., Marché, C.: The Why/Krakatoa/Caduceus platform for deductive program verification. In: Damm, W., Hermanns, H. (eds.) CAV 2007. LNCS, vol. 4590, pp. 173–177. Springer, Heidelberg (2007)
4. Nipkow, T.: Hoare logics in Isabelle/HOL. In: Schwichtenberg, H., Steinbrüggen, R. (eds.) Proof and System-Reliability, pp. 341–367. Kluwer, Dordrecht (2002)
5. Schirmer, N.: Verification of Sequential Imperative Programs in Isabelle/HOL. PhD thesis, Technische Universität München (2006)
6. Winskel, G.: The Formal Semantics of Programming Languages. Foundations of Computing Series. MIT Press, Cambridge (1993)
7. Programming languages — C. ISO/IEC Standard 9899:1999(E), 2nd edn. (1999)
8. Bornat, R.: Proving pointer programs in Hoare logic. In: Backhouse, R., Oliveira, J.N. (eds.) MPC 2000. LNCS, vol. 1837, pp. 102–126. Springer, Heidelberg (2000)
9. MISRA-C: 2004. Guidelines for the use of the C language in critical systems (2004)
10. Moggi, E.: Notions of computation and monads. Information and Computation 93(1), 55–92 (1991)
11. Blanchet, B., Cousot, P., Cousot, R., Feret, J., Mauborgne, L., Miné, A., Monniaux, D., Rival, X.: A static analyzer for large safety-critical software. In: Proc. PLDI 2003, San Diego, California, USA, pp. 196–207. ACM Press, New York (2003)
12. Borgida, A., Mylopoulos, J., Reiter, R.: On the frame problem in procedure specifications. IEEE Transactions on Software Engineering 21(10), 785–798 (1995)
13. de Moura, L., Bjørner, N.: Z3: An efficient SMT solver. In: Ramakrishnan, C.R., Rehof, J. (eds.) TACAS 2008. LNCS, vol. 4963, pp. 337–340. Springer, Heidelberg (2008)
14. Barrett, C., Tinelli, C.: CVC3. In: Damm, W., Hermanns, H. (eds.) CAV 2007. LNCS, vol. 4590, pp. 298–302. Springer, Heidelberg (2007)
15. Flanagan, C., Saxe, J.B.: Avoiding exponential explosion: generating compact verification conditions. In: Proc. POPL 2001, pp. 193–205. ACM Press, New York (2001)
16. Frese, U., Hausmann, D., Lüth, C., Täubig, H., Walter, D.: The importance of being formal. In: Hungar, H. (ed.) Int. Workshop on the Certification of Safety-Critical Software Controlled Systems, SafeCert 2008. To appear in Electronic Notes in Theoretical Computer Science (2008)
17. Frama-C (2008), `http://frama-c.cea.fr/`
18. Heiser, G., Elphinstone, K., Kuz, I., Klein, G., Petters, S.M.: Towards trustworthy computing systems: Taking microkernels to the next level. ACM Operating Systems Review 41(4), 3–11 (2007)
19. The VeriSoft project, `http://www.verisoft.de/`
20. van Lamsweerde, A.: Formal specification: a roadmap. In: ICSE 2000: Proc. of the Conference on The Future of Software Engineering, pp. 147–159. ACM, New York (2000)
21. Ball, T., Millstein, T., Rajamani, S.K.: Polymorphic predicate abstraction. ACM TOPLAS 27(2), 314–343 (2005)
22. Norrish, M.: C Formalised in HOL. PhD thesis, University of Cambridge (1998)

Formal Reasoning about Expectation Properties for Continuous Random Variables

Osman Hasan[1], Naeem Abbasi[1], Behzad Akbarpour[1], Sofiène Tahar[1], and Reza Akbarpour[2]

[1] ECE Department, Concordia University, Montreal, QC, Canada
{o_hasan,n_ab,behzad,tahar}@ece.concordia.ca
[2] Imaging Research Laboratories, Robarts Research Institute, London, ON, Canada
rakbarpour@robarts.ca

Abstract. Expectation (average) properties of continuous random variables are widely used to judge performance characteristics in engineering and physical sciences. This paper presents an infrastructure that can be used to formally reason about expectation properties of most of the continuous random variables in a theorem prover. Starting from the relatively complex higher-order-logic definition of expectation, based on Lebesgue integration, we formally verify key expectation properties that allow us to reason about expectation of a continuous random variable in terms of simple arithmetic operations. In order to illustrate the practical effectiveness and utilization of our approach, we also present the formal verification of expectation properties of the commonly used continuous random variables: Uniform, Triangular and Exponential.

1 Introduction

Probabilistic analysis is a tool of fundamental importance to virtually all scientists and engineers as they often have to deal with systems that exhibit random or unpredictable elements. Traditionally, computer simulation techniques [6] are used to perform probabilistic analysis. However, they provide less accurate results and cannot handle large-scale problems due to their enormous processing time requirements. Due to the recent increase in the usage of hardware and software systems in safety-critical applications, such as medicine and transportation, the precision and accuracy of their analysis has become imperative. Therefore, simulation should not be relied upon for the analysis of such systems.

To overcome the above mentioned limitations, it has been recently proposed to conduct probabilistic analysis of systems in a higher-order-logic theorem prover [11]. The main idea behind this approach is to formally specify the behavior of systems, with random or unpredictable components, in higher-order logic, while representing the random components as formalized random variables. The probabilistic and statistical properties of random variables are then used to formally reason about systems characteristics, such as downtime, availability, number of failures, capacity, and cost, in a theorem prover. The analysis carried out in this

A. Cavalcanti and D. Dams (Eds.): FM 2009, LNCS 5850, pp. 435–450, 2009.

way is free from any approximation issues or flaws due to the mathematical nature of the models and the inherent soundness of the theorem proving approach. The milestones achieved so far, in this endeavor of developing a complete theorem proving based probabilistic analysis framework that is capable of analyzing any hardware or software system, include the formalization of probability theory [15], the ability to formalize discrete and continuous random variables and verify their probabilistic properties [15,11] and the ability to verify statistical properties of discrete random variables [11]. Whereas, to the best of our knowledge, the formal reasoning about statistical properties regarding continuous random variables has not been tackled in the open literature so far.

In this paper, as a first step towards filling the above mentioned gap, we present an infrastructure that allows us to formally reason about the expectation properties of most of the commonly used continuous random variables in a higher-order-logic theorem prover. Expectation plays a major role in decision making as it tends to summarize the probability distribution characteristics of a random variable in a single number. Thus, the contribution of this paper paves the way to formally analyze many engineering and physical science systems with continuous random components in a theorem prover. Some of the interesting examples include the performance analysis of *computer arithmetic systems* like floating-point arithmetic [19], where the Uniform random variable can be used to model the roundoff error, algorithms that utilize continuous random variables, such as the *Balls and Bins with feedback* [16] and network protocols by modeling the request arrival rates by the exponential random variables.

The most commonly used definition of expectation, for a continuous random variable X, is the probability density-weighted integral over the real line [16].

$$E[X] = \int_{-\infty}^{+\infty} x f(x) dx \tag{1}$$

The function f in the above equation represents the probability density function (PDF) of X and the integral is the well-known Reimann integral. The above definition is only limited to continuous random variables that have a well-defined PDF. A more general, but not so commonly used, definition of expectation for a random variable X, defined on a probability space (Ω, Σ, P) [7], is as follows:

$$E[X] = \int_{\Omega} X dP \tag{2}$$

This definition utilizes the Lebesgue integral and is general enough to cater for both discrete and continuous random variables. The reason behind its limited usage in the probabilistic analysis domain is the complexity of solving the Lebesgue integral, which takes its foundations from the measure theory that most engineers and computer scientists are not familiar with.

The obvious advantage of using Equation (1) is the user familiarity with Reimann integral that facilitates the reasoning process regarding the expectation properties in the theorem proving based probabilistic analysis approach. On the other hand, it requires extended real numbers, $\overline{\mathbb{R}} = \mathbb{R} \cup \{-\infty, +\infty\}$, whereas all the foundational work regarding theorem proving based probabilistic analysis has been built upon the standard real numbers $\mathbb{R}$, formalized by Harrison [10]. Thus, the formalization of the expectation definition, given in Equation (1), and making it compatible with the available formal probabilistic analysis infrastructure would require creating a new data type $\overline{\mathbb{R}}$, and re-verifying the already proven results in a theorem prover for this new data-type, which is a considerable amount of work. Now, the expectation definition, given in Equation (2), does not involve extended real numbers, as it accommodates infinite limits without any ad-hoc devices due to the inherent nature of the Lebesgue integral. It also offers a more general solution. The limitation, however, is the compromise on the interactive reasoning effort, as it is not a straightforward task for a user to build on this definition to formally verify the expectation of a random variable.

In this paper, we address the above mentioned limitation of using Lebesgue integration for defining expectation. Starting from Equation (2), we mainly utilize the properties of the Lebesgue integral to formally verify two simplified expressions for the expectation. The first one is for the case when the random variable X is bounded in the positive interval $[a, b]$

$$E[X] = \lim_{n\to\infty}\left[\sum_{i=0}^{2^n-1} a + \frac{i}{2^n}(b-a)P\left\{a + \frac{i}{2^n}(b-a) \le X < a + \frac{i+1}{2^n}(b-a)\right\}\right] \tag{3}$$

and the second one is for an unbounded positive random variable [7].

$$E[X] = \lim_{n\to\infty}\left[\sum_{i=0}^{n2^n-1} \frac{i}{2^n}P\left\{\frac{i}{2^n} \le X < \frac{i+1}{2^n}\right\} + nP(X \ge n)\right] \tag{4}$$

Both of the above expressions do not involve any concepts from Lebesgue integration theory and are based on the well-known arithmetic operations like summation, limit of a real sequence, etc. Thus, users can simply utilize them, instead of Equation (2), to reason about the expectation properties of their random variables and gain the benefits of the original Lebesgue based definition. It is also important to note that we have a different expression for the bounded case in order to facilitate the formal reasoning about the probability term, which becomes very challenging to reason about if the unbounded expectation equation is used for a bounded random variable.

To demonstrate the effectiveness of the above expressions, we utilize them for the formal verification of the expected values for the commonly used continuous random variables Uniform, Triangular and Exponential. Besides being illustrative examples, these results can be essentially utilized in conducting the formal performance analysis of many system that utilize these random variables.

The work described in this paper is done using the HOL theorem prover [8], which is based on higher-order logic. The main motivation behind this choice is the fact that most of the work that we build upon is developed in HOL, such as the formalization of the real number theory [10], probability theory [15], continuous random variables [11] and Lebesgue integration [4]. Though, it is important to note here that the ideas presented in this paper are not specific to the HOL theorem prover and can be adapted to any other higher-order-logic theorem prover as well, such as Isabelle, Coq or PVS.

The rest of the paper is organized as follows: Section 2 provides a review of related work. Then, in Section 3, we present some foundations regarding higher-order-logic based probabilistic analysis approach, such as the formalization of probability theory, random variables and Lebesgue integration. Next, Section 4 outlines the formal proof details regarding Equations (3) and (4). We utilize these theorems to illustrate the formal reasoning process regarding the expectation properties of the above mentioned three continuous random variables in Section 5. In Section 6, we present the formal probabilistic analysis of rounding error in floating-point numbers, in order to demonstrate the usefulness of our results in the domain of probabilistic analysis. Finally, Section 7 concludes the paper.

2 Related Work

Early foundations of probabilistic analysis in a higher-order-logic theorem prover were laid down by Nędzusiak [17] and Bialas [3] when they proposed a formalization of measure and probability theories in higher-order logic. Hurd [15] implemented their work and developed a framework for the verification of probabilistic algorithms in the HOL theorem prover. Random variables are basically probabilistic algorithms and thus can be formalized and verified, based on their probability distribution properties, using the methodology proposed in [15]. In fact, building upon Hurd's formalization, most of the commonly used discrete [15] and continuous [11] random variables have been formalized. The above mentioned formalization of probability theory has also been used to formally reason about statistical properties, such as expectation and variance, of discrete random variables [11]. Due to the fact that the discrete random variables can only attain a countable number of values, the expectation in this case has been formally defined using a summation rather than integration. Obviously such a definition cannot be used with continuous random variables, which have an uncountable range. The probabilistic analysis foundations, mentioned above, have been successfully used to conduct precise probabilistic analysis of many systems, such as computation algorithms [15,11], real-time systems [11], communication protocols [13], wireless systems [14], and hardware components [12].

As mentioned in the last section, Lebesgue integration is the core concept in the definition of expectation. Richter [18] formalized a significant portion of the Lebesgue integration theory in higher-order logic using Isabelle/HOL. But, this formalization can only handle functions that map subsets of real numbers to real numbers. This limitation somewhat restricts the usage of this formalization to define the expectation, where the function that needs to be integrated is the random variable that in its most general form maps the subsets of an arbitrary sample space to real numbers. More recently, Coble [4] formalized the Lebesgue integration theory in HOL. This formalization overcomes the limitation of Richter's work as it allows integration over functions that are measurable from a space of any arbitrary data-type to any subset of the real numbers. Coble's formalization of the Lebesgue integral has been used to formally define expectation of a random variable [4]. But in this formalization, some theorems have been verified under the assumption that measurable sets have to be equal to the power set of the sample space. This fact restricts Coble's formalization for sample spaces that do not contain any non-measurable subsets. Whereas, this condition is not satisfied for sample spaces for continuous random variables. Daumas *et. al.* [5] have also formalized some Lebesgue integration theory in the PVS theorem prover. The authors claim to have formally defined expectation based on this formalization, but no details were given in [5]. Moreover, to the best of our knowledge, no information regarding the utilization of this definition to formally reason about the expectation of continuous random variables has been provided in this work, which is the main contribution of our paper.

In this paper, we extend the measure theoretic formalization infrastructure, based on the works, presented in [15,11], available in the HOL theorem prover, with the ability to formally reason about expectation properties of *continuous random variables*. This would be a novelty that to the best of our knowledge has not been presented in the open literature so far. The main motivation behind using the measure theoretic approach instead of the one proposed by Audebaud [2] is to be able to utilize the Lebesgue integral, which has a foundational relationship with the measure theory. We utilize the Lebesgue integral formalization, presented in [4], for our work because it is available in the HOL theorem prover and is thus compatible with the other theories [15,11] that we build upon. Though, we make it general enough to tackle sample spaces for continuous random variables as well.

3 Preliminaries

In this section, we provide an overview of the higher-order-logic formalizations of probability theory, continuous random variables and Lebesgue integration theory. The intent is to introduce the main ideas along with some notation that is going to be used later in this paper.

3.1 Probability Theory and Random Variables in HOL

A *measure space* is defined as a triple (Ω, Σ, μ), where Ω is a set, called the *sample space*, Σ represents a σ-algebra of subsets of Ω and the subsets are usually referred to as *measurable sets*, and μ is a *measure* with domain Σ [7]. A *probability space* is a measure space (Ω, Σ, P) such that the measure, referred to as the probability and denoted by P, of the sample space is 1.

Hurd [15] formalized some measure theory to define a measure space as a pair (Σ, μ). Whereas the sample space, on which this pair is defined, is implicitly implied from the higher-order-logic definitions to be equal to the universal set of the appropriate data-type. Building upon this formalization, the probability space was also defined in HOL as a pair $(\mathcal{E}, \mathbb{P})$, where the domain of $\mathbb{P}$ is the set

$\mathcal{E}$, which is a set of subsets of infinite Boolean sequences $\mathbb{B}^\infty$. Both $\mathbb{P}$ and $\mathcal{E}$ are defined using the Carathéodory's Extension theorem, which ensures that $\mathcal{E}$ is a σ-algebra: closed under complements and countable unions.

Now, a random variable, which is one of the core concepts in probabilistic analysis, is fundamentally a probabilistic function and thus can be modeled in higher-order logic as a deterministic function, which accepts the infinite Boolean sequence as an argument. These deterministic functions make random choices based on the result of popping the top most bit in the infinite Boolean sequence and may pop as many random bits as they need for their computation. When the functions terminate, they return the result along with the remaining portion of the infinite Boolean sequence to be used by other programs. Thus, a random variable which takes a parameter of type α and ranges over values of type β can be represented in HOL by the function $\mathcal{F}$.

$$\mathcal{F} : \alpha \rightarrow B^\infty \rightarrow \beta \times B^\infty$$

As an example, consider the Bernoulli($\frac{1}{2}$) random variable that returns 1 or 0 with equal probability $\frac{1}{2}$. It can be formalized in HOL as follows

```
⊢ bit = (λs. if shd s then 1 else 0, stl s)
```

It accepts an infinite Boolean sequence, where `shd` and `stl` are the sequence equivalents of the list operation *'head'* and *'tail'*. The formalized $\mathbb{P}$ and $\mathcal{E}$ can be used to verify the basic laws of probability as well as probabilistic properties regarding random variables in the HOL theorem prover. For example:

$$\vdash \mathbb{P}\ \{\mathtt{s}\ \mid\ \mathtt{fst}\ (\mathtt{bit}\ \mathtt{s})\ =\ 1\}\ =\ \tfrac{1}{2}$$

where the HOL function `fst` selects the first component of a pair and $\{x|C(x)\}$ represents a set of all x that satisfy the condition C. It is important to note here that, since the probability measure $\mathbb{P}$ is only defined on sets in $\mathcal{E}$, it is absolutely necessary to verify that the set that appears in a probabilistic property is in $\mathcal{E}$ before we can formally verify that property in HOL. For the above example, this condition translates to the verification of $\{\mathtt{s}\ \mid\ \mathtt{fst}\ (\mathtt{bit}\ \mathtt{s})\ =\ 1\} \in \mathcal{E}$.

The above approach has been successfully used to formalize and verify most of the commonly used discrete random variables [15]. The sampling algorithms for discrete random variables are either guaranteed to terminate or satisfy probabilistic termination, meaning that the probability that the algorithm terminates is 1. On the other hand, the formalization of continuous random variables involves non-terminating algorithms and hence require a different approach than discrete random variables.

Building upon the above mentioned probability theory framework, an approach for the formalization of continuous random variables has been presented in [11]. The main idea is based on the concept of the Inverse Transform Method (ITM) [6], according to which, the random variable X, for any continuous cumulative distribution function (CDF) F, can be defined as $X = F^{-1}(U)$, where F^{-1} is the inverse function of F, and U represents the Standard Uniform random

Table 1. Continuous Random Variables in HOL

Distribution	CDF	Formalized Random Variable
Uniform(a,b)	0 if $x \leq a$; $\frac{x-a}{b-a}$ if $a < x \leq b$; 1 if $b < x$.	$\vdash \forall s\ l.\ uniform\_rv\ a\ b\ s\ =$ $(b-a)(std\_unif\_rv\ s) + a$
Triangular$(0,a)$	0 if $x \leq 0$; $(\frac{2}{a}(x - \frac{x^2}{2a}))$ if $x < a$; 1 if $a \leq x$.	$\vdash \forall s\ a\ .\ triangular\_rv\ l\ s\ =$ $a(1 - \sqrt{1 - std\_unif\_rv\ s})$
Exponential(l)	0 if $x \leq 0$; $1 - e^{-lx}$ if $0 < x$.	$\vdash \forall s\ l.\ exp\_rv\ l\ s\ =$ $-\frac{1}{l}ln(1 - std\_unif\_rv\ s)$

variable. The formal proof of this proposition is based on the CDF characteristic of the Standard Uniform random variable and some of the CDF properties [11]. ITM allows us to formalize any continuous random variable, which has a well-defined CDF, in terms of a formalized Standard Uniform random variable (`std_unif_rv`). Based on this approach, the CDFs and higher-order-logic definitions of three continuous random variables are given in Table 1 [11]. In this paper, we will utilize formally verified expressions, corresponding to Equations (3) and (4), to verify the expectation relations for these random variables in Section 5.

3.2 Lebesgue Integration in HOL

Lebesgue integration is based on the concept of measure and is defined for a class of functions called *measurable functions*, which are well-behaved functions between measurable spaces. Coble [4] formalized the Lebesgue integration theory in HOL based on a generalized measure space $(S, \mathbb{S}, \lambda)$. It is important to note here that, unlike Hurd's formalization of the measure space, we do have the flexibility to choose any sample space S in this case. The higher-order-logic definition of the Lebesgue integral utilizes the concepts of *indicator function* and *positive simple-function* [7]. The indicator function is defined as follows for a set A

$$\mathbb{I}_A(a) = \begin{cases} 1 & \text{if } a \in A; \\ 0 & \text{otherwise.} \end{cases} \tag{5}$$

Whereas, a function g is said to be a positive simple-function for the measure space $(S, \mathbb{S}, \lambda)$ iff it can be expressed as follows

$$g = \sum_{i=0}^{n} c_i \mathbb{I}_{a_i} \tag{6}$$

where c_i is a sequence of positive real values and a_i is a sequence of disjoint measurable sets such that $\bigcup_{i=0}^{n} a_i$ forms a partition of S. Now the integral for such a positive-simple function g can be defined as follows.

$$\int_S g \, d\lambda = \sum_{i=0}^{n} c_i(\lambda a_i) \tag{7}$$

The next step towards the formal definition of the Lebesgue integral is to define the integral for a positive function f that is measurable from $(S, \mathbb{S})$ to $(S', \mathbb{S}')$

$$\int_S f \, d\lambda = sup\left\{\int_S g d\lambda \;\middle|\; (\forall x.g(x) \leq f(x))\right\} \tag{8}$$

where g is a positive-simple function w.r.t the measure space $(S, \mathbb{S}, \lambda)$.

The Lebesgue integral of a real-valued measurable function from $(S, \mathbb{S})$ to $(S', \mathbb{S}')$ can now be formalized in terms of Equation (8) as follows

$$\int_S f \, d\lambda = \int_S f^+ \, d\lambda - \int_S f^- \, d\lambda \tag{9}$$

where $f(x) = f^+(x) - f^-(x)$ and f^+ and f^- are the positive and negative portions of f, respectively, and are both positive functions. It is also important to note that the integral of f is well-defined iff both f^+ and f^- are measurable from $(S, \mathbb{S})$ to $(S', \mathbb{S}')$ and their integrals do not both diverge to infinity.

Besides the formalization of the above definitions, many useful properties regarding the Lebesgue integral have also been verified in [4] as higher-order-logic theorems. For example, we utilize the following convergence of a positive measurable function to the Lebesgue integral property.

$$(\forall x \in S.(\forall n \; x.f_n(x) \leq f(x)) \wedge \left(\lim_{n\to\infty} f_n(x) = f(x)\right) \wedge \left(\lim_{n\to\infty} \int_S f_n \, d\lambda = r\right) \Rightarrow \int_S f \, d\lambda = r \tag{10}$$

The function f, in the above equation, is a positive real-valued function that is measurable from $(S, \mathcal{P}(S))$ to $(S', \mathcal{P}(S'))$, where $\mathcal{P}(A)$ denotes the power set of the set A. Whereas, the sequence f_n is a monotonically increasing sequence of positive simple-functions. It is important to note here that this theorem and many others in Coble's work [4] have been verified for the case when the measurable sets $\mathbb{S}$ is equal to the power set of the sample space S. This restricts the usage of these theorems to sample spaces for which all possible subsets are measurable. This condition is not satisfied for sample spaces that are used to model continuous random variables.

4 Verification of Expectation Relations

In this section, we utilize the probability and Lebesgue integration theories, described in the previous section, to formally verify the expectation relations for the bounded and unbounded random variables, given in Equations (3) and (4), respectively.

The first step in this regard is to formally define the expectation in terms of the Lebesgue integral. For this purpose, we utilize the definition of Lebesgue integral, given in Equation (9), as follows:

Definition 1. *Expectation of a Random Variable*

$\vdash \forall$ f. expec $(\mathcal{U}, \mathcal{E}, \mathbb{P})$ f = $\int_{\mathcal{U}}$ f d$\mathbb{P}$

The function expec accepts a probability space, $(\mathcal{U}, \mathcal{E}, \mathbb{P})$, and a random variable f that maps infinite Boolean sequences to real numbers. It is important to note that by using Hurd's formalization of the probability space $(\mathcal{U}, \mathcal{E}, \mathbb{P})$, where $\mathcal{U}$ represents the universal set of all Boolean sequences, as outlined in Section 3, we can utilize the above definition to reason about expectation of random variables formalized in [15,11]. Though, we had to generalize the Lebesgue integration theorems, proposed in Coble's work [4]. Since, the existing theorems are based on the assumption $\mathbb{S} = \mathcal{P}(S)$, which is not true for our probability space $(\mathcal{U}, \mathcal{E}, \mathbb{P})$, where the power set of the set of all Boolean sequences do contain non-measurable sets as has been formally verified in [15]. Our more generalized version of these theorems are based on the assumption that $\mathbb{S} = \{x | (x \in \mathcal{P}(S)) \wedge (x \ is \ measurable)\}$, which is obviously true for our probability space $(\mathcal{U}, \mathcal{E}, \mathbb{P})$.

4.1 Bounded Random Variables

The expectation property, given in Equation (3), can be expressed as a higher-order-logic theorem using Definition 1 as follows:

Theorem 1. *Expectation of Bounded Random Variables*

$$\vdash \forall \text{ a b f. } (0 \leq \text{a}) \wedge (\text{a} < \text{b}) \wedge (\forall \text{ s. a} \leq \text{f s} \leq \text{b}) \wedge$$
$$(\forall \text{ x y. x} < \text{y} \Rightarrow \{\text{s} \mid \text{x} \leq \text{f s} < \text{y}\} \in \mathcal{E}) \Rightarrow$$
$$\Bigg(\text{expec } (\mathcal{U}, \mathcal{E}, \mathbb{P}) \text{ f} =$$
$$\lim_{n \to \infty} \left[\sum_{i=0}^{2^n - 1} (\text{a} + \tfrac{\text{i}}{2^n}(\text{b} - \text{a}))\mathbb{P}\left\{\text{s} \;\middle|\; \text{a} + \tfrac{\text{i}}{2^n}(\text{b} - \text{a}) \leq \text{f s} < \text{a} + \tfrac{\text{i+1}}{2^n}(\text{b} - \text{a})\right\}\right]\Bigg)$$

The first three assumptions ensure that the random variable f is bounded in the positive interval $[a, b]$. Whereas, the fourth assumption ensures that the set involved in this verification is measurable.

In order to utilize any definition or property of Lebesgue integration theory with the above theorem, we first need to show that the triple $(\mathcal{U}, \mathcal{E}, \mathbb{P})$ is a measure space with a positive measure. We verified these conditions based on the corresponding theorems available in Hurd's formalization of the probability space $(\mathcal{E}, \mathbb{P})$ along with the definition of measure in [4] under the given assumptions.

Since our random variable f is a positive-valued real number, we do not have the term involving the f^- term in the Lebesgue integral definition and thus, for this specific case, Equations (8) and (9) become equivalent. This allows us to use the convergence of a positive measurable function to the Lebesgue integral property, given in Equation (10), to reason about Theorem 1. Using Modus Ponens (MP) rule, we can split the proof goal of Theorem 1 to the following five subgoals, corresponding to the monotonicity and positive simple-function requirement on f_n and the three assumptions of Equation (10):

$$\texttt{mono\_increasing}\left[\sum_{\texttt{i}=0}^{2^{\texttt{n}}-1}(\texttt{a}+\frac{\texttt{i}}{2^{\texttt{n}}}(\texttt{b}-\texttt{a}))\mathbb{I}_{\left\{\texttt{s}\ \middle|\ \texttt{a}+\frac{\texttt{i}}{2^{\texttt{n}}}(\texttt{b}-\texttt{a})\leq\texttt{f s}<\texttt{a}+\frac{\texttt{i}+1}{2^{\texttt{n}}}(\texttt{b}-\texttt{a})\right\}}(\texttt{x})\right] \tag{11}$$

$$\begin{gathered}\left(\forall\texttt{i}.(\texttt{i}<2^{\texttt{n}})\Rightarrow\left\{\texttt{s}\ \middle|\ \texttt{a}+\frac{\texttt{i}}{2^{\texttt{n}}}(\texttt{b}-\texttt{a})\leq\texttt{f s}<\texttt{a}+\frac{\texttt{i}+1}{2^{\texttt{n}}}(\texttt{b}-\texttt{a})\right\}\in\mathcal{E}\right)\wedge\\ \left(\forall\texttt{i}.0\leq\texttt{a}+\frac{\texttt{i}}{2^{\texttt{n}}}(\texttt{b}-\texttt{a})\right)\wedge\left(\texttt{FINITE}\{\texttt{i}|\texttt{i}<2^{\texttt{n}}\}\right)\end{gathered} \tag{12}$$

$$\left[\sum_{\texttt{i}=0}^{2^{\texttt{n}}-1}(\texttt{a}+\frac{\texttt{i}}{2^{\texttt{n}}}(\texttt{b}-\texttt{a}))\mathbb{I}_{\left\{\texttt{s}\ \middle|\ \texttt{a}+\frac{\texttt{i}}{2^{\texttt{n}}}(\texttt{b}-\texttt{a})\leq\texttt{f s}<\texttt{a}+\frac{\texttt{i}+1}{2^{\texttt{n}}}(\texttt{b}-\texttt{a})\right\}}(\texttt{x})\right]\leq\texttt{f}(\texttt{x}) \tag{13}$$

$$\lim_{\texttt{n}\to\infty}\left[\sum_{\texttt{i}=0}^{2^{\texttt{n}}-1}(\texttt{a}+\frac{\texttt{i}}{2^{\texttt{n}}}(\texttt{b}-\texttt{a}))\mathbb{I}_{\left\{\texttt{s}\ \middle|\ \texttt{a}+\frac{\texttt{i}}{2^{\texttt{n}}}(\texttt{b}-\texttt{a})\leq\texttt{f s}<\texttt{a}+\frac{\texttt{i}+1}{2^{\texttt{n}}}(\texttt{b}-\texttt{a})\right\}}(\texttt{x})\right]=\texttt{f}(\texttt{x}) \tag{14}$$

$$\exists\texttt{y}.\lim_{\texttt{n}\to\infty}\left[\sum_{\texttt{i}=0}^{2^{\texttt{n}}-1}(\texttt{a}+\frac{\texttt{i}}{2^{\texttt{n}}}\texttt{b}-\texttt{a})\mathbb{P}\left\{\texttt{s}\ \middle|\ \texttt{a}+\frac{\texttt{i}}{2^{\texttt{n}}}\texttt{b}-\texttt{a}\leq\texttt{fs}<\texttt{a}+\frac{\texttt{i}+1}{2^{\texttt{n}}}\texttt{b}-\texttt{a}\right\}\right]=\texttt{y} \tag{15}$$

The monotonically increasing property in the first subgoal is verified based on the facts that (1) the indicator function is 1 in only one interval or for one particular value of i and (2) as the argument of the sequence increases, i.e., n, the intervals become finer and thus the resulting value of the sequence increasingly gets closer to the value of $f\ x$. The second subgoal corresponds to the pre-conditions for the positive simple-function function f_n and consists of three subgoals. These three subgoals are discharged based on the fourth assumption of Theorem 1, arithmetic reasoning and set theory principles, respectively. The third subgoal is true as there is only one i, say i', for which the real value of $f\ x$ falls in the interval $[a+\frac{i}{2^n}(b-a), a+\frac{i+1}{2^n}(b-a))$ out of the 2^n possible values for i. Thus the indicator function is 1 for this particular i only and 0 otherwise, meaning that the summation is equal to $(a+\frac{i'}{2^n}(b-a))$. Now, substituting this value for the summation in the third subgoal along with the fact that $f\ x$ lies in the interval $[a+\frac{i'}{2^n}(b-a), a+\frac{i'+1}{2^n}(b-a))$ leads to its verification. The fourth subgoal is discharged based on reasoning similar to the previous subgoal, the monotonicity of the given sequence and the definition of the limit of a real sequence. Finally, the real sequence in the fifth subgoal is verified to be convergent by verifying that it is monotonic and that the probability term in the sequence is non-zero for only one particular value of i. The sequence thus has an upper bound b since the value of i is always less than 2^n and the maximum value for the probability term is 1. The verification of these five subgoals also concludes the verification of Theorem 1.

4.2 Unbounded Random Variables

The expectation property, given in Equation (4), can be expressed as a higher-order-logic theorem using Definition 1 as follows:

Theorem 2. *Expectation of Unbounded Random Variables*

$$\vdash \forall \texttt{ f. } (\forall \texttt{ s. } 0 \leq \texttt{f s}) \wedge (\forall \texttt{ x. } \{\texttt{s} \mid \texttt{f s} \geq \texttt{x}\} \in \mathcal{E})$$
$$(\forall \texttt{ x y. x} < \texttt{y} \Rightarrow \{\texttt{s} \mid \texttt{x} \leq \texttt{f s} < \texttt{y}\} \in \mathcal{E}) \Rightarrow$$
$$\Bigg(\texttt{expec } (\mathcal{U}, \mathcal{E}, \mathbb{P}) \texttt{ f} =$$
$$\lim_{\texttt{n} \to \infty} \left[\sum_{\texttt{i}=0}^{\texttt{n}2^{\texttt{n}}-1} \left(\tfrac{\texttt{i}}{2^{\texttt{n}}}\right) \mathbb{P}\left\{\texttt{s} \;\middle|\; \tfrac{\texttt{i}}{2^{\texttt{n}}} \leq \texttt{f s} < \tfrac{\texttt{i}+1}{2^{\texttt{n}}}\right\} + \texttt{n}\mathbb{P}\left\{\texttt{s} \;\middle|\; \texttt{f s} \geq \texttt{ n}\right\}\right]\Bigg)$$

The first assumption ensures that the random variable f is positive. The second and third guarantee that the sets that arise in this verification are measurable events. The summation range has been extended to $[0, n2^n - 1]$ so that the first probability term in the above theorem covers the interval $[0, n)$. While, the second probability term covers the rest of the positive unbounded interval.

The verification steps for Theorem 2 are very similar to the ones for Theorem 1. The major step is to split this goal into subgoals using Equation (10). These subgoals are then verified using arithmetic reasoning, set theory principles and the fact that the events in the two probability terms of the proof goal are disjoint, which means that one of the probability term is always equal to 0.

Our verification results matched the paper-and-pencil analysis counterpart for Theorem 2, which is available in [7], and confirmed the correctness of Theorem 1, which we had worked out ourselves and were not able to find it in any published texts. Besides checking for correctness for these mathematical relationships, the major motivation behind their verification is to utilize them to reason about the expected values of continuous random variables and thus in turn use these results for conducting formal probabilistic analysis of systems.

5 Expectation of Continuous Random Variables

To illustrate the effectiveness of the expectation relations, proved in the previous section, we now utilize them to verify the expectation of three continuous random variables, i.e., Uniform, Triangular and Exponential.

5.1 Uniform Random Variable

The expectation relation for the continuous Uniform random variable bounded in the interval $[a, b]$ can be formalized as follows:

Theorem 3. *Expectation of the Uniform(a,b) Random Variable*

$\vdash \forall$ a b. (0 $\leq$ a) $\wedge$ (a $<$ b) $\Rightarrow$
(expec $(\mathcal{U}, \mathcal{E}, \mathbb{P})$ (uniform_rv a b) = $\frac{a+b}{2}$)

In order to utilize Theorem 1 to reason about the correctness of the above theorem, we first verify that the Uniform random variable satisfies all pre-conditions, given in Theorem 1, based on the theorems given in [11]. Next, we rewrite the probability term in Theorem 1, using the CDF for the Uniform random variable, given in Table 1, to simplify our proof goal as follows:

$$\lim_{n\to\infty}\left[\sum_{i=0}^{2^n-1}\left(a+\frac{i}{2^n}(b-a)\right)\left(\frac{a+\frac{i+1}{2^n}(b-a)-a}{b-a}-\frac{a+\frac{i}{2^n}(b-a)-a}{b-a}\right)\right]=\frac{a+b}{2} \tag{16}$$

The above subgoal can now be discharged using arithmetic reasoning, along with the properties of summation of a real sequence and the limit of a real sequence. This also concludes the verification of Theorem 3.

5.2 Triangular Random Variable

The expectation relation for the continuous Triangular random variable bounded in the interval $[0, b]$ can be formalized as follows:

Theorem 4. *Expectation of the Triangular(b) Random Variable*

$\vdash \forall$ b. (0 $<$ b) $\Rightarrow$ (expec $(\mathcal{U}, \mathcal{E}, \mathbb{P})$ (triangular_rv b) = $\frac{b}{3}$)

The verification steps are similar to the ones for Theorem 3 and are primarily based on Theorem 1 and the CDF of the Triangular random variable.

5.3 Exponential Random Variable

The expectation for the continuous Exponential random variable, which is unbounded at the upper end, i.e., defined in $[0, \infty)$, can be formalized as follows:

Theorem 5. *Expectation of the Exponential(l) Random Variable*

$\vdash \forall$ a. (0 $<$ a) $\Rightarrow$ (expec $(\mathcal{U}, \mathcal{E}, \mathbb{P})$ (exp_rv a) = $\frac{1}{a}$)

Due to its unbounded nature, we use Theorem 2 to reason about the expectation of Exponential random variable. Now, after rewriting the probability term and some arithmetic simplification, we get the following subgoal:

$$\lim_{n\to\infty}\left[\left(1-e^{-\frac{a}{2^n}}\right)\left(\sum_{i=0}^{n2^n-1}\frac{i}{2^n}e^{-a\frac{i}{2^n}}\right)+ne^{-an}\right]=\frac{1}{a} \tag{17}$$

which can be broken into the following two subgoals.

$$\lim_{n \to \infty} \left(ne^{-an}\right) = 0 \tag{18}$$

$$\lim_{n \to \infty} \left[\left(\frac{1 - e^{-\frac{a}{2^n}}}{2^n} \right) \left(\sum_{i=0}^{n2^n - 1} i(e^{-\frac{a}{2^n}})^i \right) \right] = \frac{1}{a} \tag{19}$$

We proceed with the verification of the first subgoal by rewriting the exponential term e^{-an} as $(1 + x)^{-n}$, where $x > 0$. Next, we verify that the term $(1 + x)^n$ is greater than $1 + nx + \frac{1}{2}n(n - 1)x^2$, for all values of n, as the latter represents a truncated form of its Binomial expansion. This fact leads us to verify that the value of the real sequence $(\lambda n.n(1 + x)^{-n})$ will be less than the real sequence $(\lambda n.n(\frac{1}{2}n(n - 1)x^2)^{-1})$ for all values of n. This reasoning allows us to discharge the first subgoal, given in Equation (18), as the limit value of the real sequence $(\lambda n.n(\frac{1}{2}n(n - 1)x^2)^{-1}) = (\lambda n.\frac{2}{x^2(n-1)})$ is 0.

In order to simplify the verification of the second subgoal, given in Equation (19), we first evaluate the summation term by verifying the summation of a finite arithmetic-geometric series in HOL.

$$\sum_{k=0}^{n} kq^k = \frac{q}{(1 - q)^2}(1 - q^n) - \frac{nq^{n+1}}{1 - q} \tag{20}$$

The above relationship allows us to rewrite the second subgoal as follows:

$$\lim_{n \to \infty} \left(\frac{e^{-\frac{a}{2^n}}(1 - e^{-an})}{2^n(1 - e^{-\frac{a}{2^n}})} - ne^{-an} \right) = \frac{1}{a} \tag{21}$$

Now, Equation (18) and the already proved fact that the limit value of the real sequence $(\lambda n.e^{-1n})$ is 0 allows us to simplify the above subgoal as follows.

$$\lim_{n \to \infty} \left(\frac{e^{-\frac{a}{2^n}}}{2^n(1 - e^{-\frac{a}{2^n}})} \right) = \frac{1}{a} \tag{22}$$

We reason about the correctness of the above limit by first evaluating the following limit relationship.

$$\lim_{x \to 0} \left(\frac{xe^{-ax}}{(1 - e^{-ax})} \right) = \frac{1}{a} \tag{23}$$

The proof of the above equation is primarily based on the L'Hopital's Rule, which we also verified in HOL as part of this project. Now, the variable x in Equation (23) can be specialized to $\frac{1}{2^n}$. This expression along with the definitions of limit of a real sequence and the limit of a function when its arguments approaches a real value leads to the verification of the remaining subgoal, given in Equation (22). This also concludes the proof of Theorem 5.

The verification of the above three expectation properties does not involve any reasoning based on the Lebesgue integral. As a consequence, the verification process, which just took around 80 man hours with approximately 3500 lines of

HOL code, was very straightforward and quick in comparison to the verification of Theorems 1 and 2, which took around 350 man-hours and approximately 5000 lines. This clearly demonstrates the strength of our work, which is to provide the ability to build upon Theorems 1 and 2 and reduce the interactive reasoning efforts regarding the expectation properties of continuous random variables. Also, our theorems are quite general and can be built upon to reason about expected values of many other random variables as well, such as the Rayleigh and Pareto.

6 Round-Off Error in Floating-Point Representation

Algorithms involving floating-point numbers are extensively used these days in almost all digital equipment ranging from computer and digital processing to telecommunication systems. Due to their complexity and wide spread usage in safety critical domains, formal methods are generally preferred over traditional testing to ensure correctness of floating-point algorithms. A classical work in this regard is Harrison's error analysis of floating-point arithmetic in higher-order logic [9]. Harrison presents a formalization of floating point numbers, verification of upper bounds on the error in representing a real number with floating-point system and the error in floating-point arithmetic operations. Even though this analysis is very useful in identifying the worst case conditions, it doest not reflect upon the typical or average errors. In fact, the assumed worst case conditions rarely occur in practice. So the error analysis, based under these worst-case conditions can improperly suggest that the performance of the algorithm is poor.

In paper-and-pencil analyses, probabilistic techniques are thus utilized in the error analysis of floating-point algorithms [19]. The main idea behind this probabilistic approach is to model the error in a single floating-point number by an appropriate random variable and utilize this information to judge the expected value of error while representing a real number in floating-point system. This expected value of error can then be used to find the expected value of error in different floating-point arithmetic operations.

The above mentioned probabilistic analysis involves reasoning about the expectation value of a continuous random variable, since the error between a real number and its corresponding floating-point representation is continuous in nature. Thus, our proposed infrastructure can be directly utilized to conduct such analysis, something that to the best of our knowledge was not possible before.

We built upon Harrison's error bounds for floating-point representations of *big* ($|x| \in [2^k, 2^{k+1})$, *small* ($|x| \in [\frac{1}{2^{k+1}}, \frac{1}{2^k}] : k < 126$), and *tiny* ($|x| \in [0, \frac{1}{2^{126}}]$) real numbers [9]. The error is defined as the difference between the real value of the floating-point representation and the actual value of the corresponding real number ($\texttt{error(x)} = \texttt{float(x)} - \texttt{x}$), with round-to-nearest rounding mode. Based on this definition, upper bounds on the absolute value of error are verified to be equal to $\frac{2^k}{2^{24}}$, $\frac{1}{2^{k+1}2^{24}}$ and $\frac{1}{2^{150}}$, for the three cases above, respectively.

Assuming any value of error to be equally likely [19], we constructed formal probabilistic models for representing the above mentioned rounding errors using Uniform random variables defined in the intervals $[0, \frac{2^k}{2^{24}}]$, $[0, \frac{1}{2^{k+1}2^{24}}]$ and

$[0, \frac{1}{2^{150}}]$, respectively. Theorem 3 was then used to verify the expectation values of these floating-point errors using the HOL theorem prover.

Theorem 6. *Expectation of Floating-Point Errors*

$$\vdash \forall \text{ k x. } \left(\texttt{expec(uniform\_rv 0 } \frac{2^k}{2^{24}}\texttt{)} = \frac{2^{k-1}}{2^{24}}\right) \wedge \left(\texttt{expec(uniform\_rv 0 } \frac{1}{2^{k+1}2^{24}}\texttt{)} = \frac{1}{2^{k+1}2^{25}}\right) \wedge \left(\texttt{expec(uniform\_rv 0 } \frac{1}{2^{150}}\texttt{)} = \frac{1}{2^{151}}\right)$$

The above theorem plays a pivotal role in the statistical error analysis of floating-point arithmetic. Based on these average values of error in a single floating-point number, the average errors in floating point operations, like addition, subtraction and multiplication, that involve multiple floating-point numbers, can be evaluated. Similarly, this information can be further utilized in conducting the statistical error analysis of basic digital signal processing (DSP) systems by building on top of the DSP verification framework in HOL [1], which as of now does not include any probabilistic and statistical considerations.

7 Conclusions

In this paper, we have presented an infrastructure to reason about expectation properties of continuous random variables using a higher-order-logic theorem prover. This capability allows us to conduct formal statistical analysis of systems with continuous random components, a novelty, which is not supported by most of the existing probabilistic analysis tools.

We built upon a formalized Lebesgue integration theory to define expectation and based on this definition we verified two alternate expectation relations. These relations do not involve any concepts from the mathematically complex Lebesgue integration theory and thus facilitate reasoning about expected values of continuous random variables significantly. We utilized these relations to verify the expected values of the extensively used continuous random variables Uniform, Triangular and Exponential. To the best of our knowledge, this is the first time that the formal reasoning about the expectation of these continuous random variables has been presented in a higher-order-logic theorem prover.

Our formally verified expectation relations are valid for discrete random variables as well, due to the generic nature of the Lebesgue integral. In fact, we plan to link these relations to the summation based definition of expectation [11] in order to come up with a unified reasoning framework for both discrete and continuous random variables. Also, the presented results can be extended to be used for random variables that are not positive functions, since the Lebesgue integral allows integration over negative functions, as can be observed from Equation (9). Other interesting future research directions, that benefit from this work, include the formal reasoning frameworks for variance properties and tail distribution bounds and the ability to reason about statistical properties of systems that involve multiple continuous random variables.

References

1. Akbarpour, B., Tahar, S.: An Approach for the Formal Verification of DSP Designs using Theorem Proving. IEEE Transactions on CAD of Integrated Circuits and Systems 25(8), 1141–1457 (2006)
2. Audebaud, P., Paulin-Mohring, C.: Proofs of Randomized Algorithms in Coq. In: Uustalu, T. (ed.) MPC 2006. LNCS, vol. 4014, pp. 49–68. Springer, Heidelberg (2006)
3. Bialas, J.: The σ-Additive Measure Theory. J. of Formalized Mathematics 2 (1990)
4. Coble, A.: On Probability, Measure, and Integration in HOL4. Technical Report, Computing Laboratory, University of Cambridge, UK (2009), `http://www.srcf.ucam.org/~arc54/techreport.pdf`
5. Daumas, M., Martin-Dorel, E., Lester, D., Truffert, A.: Stochastic Formal Correctness of Numerical Allgorithms. In: First NASA Formal Methods Symposium, pp. 136–145 (2009)
6. Devroye, L.: Non-Uniform Random Variate Generation. Springer, Heidelberg (1986)
7. Galambos, J.: Advanced Probability Theory. Marcel Dekker Inc., New York (1995)
8. Gordon, M.J.C., Melham, T.F.: Introduction to HOL: A Theorem Proving Environment for Higher-Order Logic. Cambridge University Press, Cambridge (1993)
9. Harrison, J.: Floating Point Verification in HOL Light: The Exponential Function. Technical Report 428, Computing Laboratory, University of Cambridge, UK (1997)
10. Harrison, J.: Theorem Proving with the Real Numbers. Springer, Heidelberg (1998)
11. Hasan, O.: Formal Probabilistic Analysis using Theorem Proving. PhD Thesis, Concordia University, Montreal, QC, Canada (2008)
12. Hasan, O., Abbasi, N., Tahar, S.: Formal Probabilistic Analysis of Stuck-at Faults in Reconfigurable Memory Arrays. In: Leuschel, M., Wehrheim, H. (eds.) IFM 2009. LNCS, vol. 5423, pp. 277–291. Springer, Heidelberg (2009)
13. Hasan, O., Tahar, S.: Performance Analysis of ARQ Protocols using a Theorem Prover. In: Proc. International Symposium on Performance Analysis of Systems and Software, pp. 85–94. IEEE Computer Society, Los Alamitos (2008)
14. Hasan, O., Tahar, S.: Performance Analysis of Wireless Systems using Theorem Proving. In: Proc. First International Workshop on Formal Methods for Wireless Systems, Toronto, ON, Canada, pp. 3–18 (2008)
15. Hurd, J.: Formal Verification of Probabilistic Algorithms. PhD Thesis, University of Cambridge, Cambridge, UK (2002)
16. Mitzenmacher, M., Upfal, E.: Probability and Computing. Cambridge University Press, Cambridge (2005)
17. Nedzusiak, A.: σ-fields and Probability. J. of Formalized Mathematics 1 (1989)
18. Richter, S.: Formalizing Integration Theory, with an Application to Probabilistic Algorithms. Diploma Thesis, Technische Universität München, Department of Informatics, Germany (2003)
19. Widrow, B.: Statistical Analysis of Amplitude-quantized Sampled Data Systems. AIEE Trans. (Applications and Industry) 81, 555–568 (1961)

The Denotational Semantics of slotted-Circus*

Paweł Gancarski and Andrew Butterfield

Trinity College Dublin
Andrew.Butterfield@cs.tcd.ie

Abstract. This paper describes a complete denotational semantics, in the UTP framework, of *slotted-Circus*, a generic framework for reasoning about discrete timed/synchronously clocked systems. The key result presented here is a comprehensive semantics of the entire language that addresses various semantics issues that have been uncovered, whilst laying foundations for future extensions, particularly towards prioritized choice.

1 Introduction

1.1 Circus and slotted-Circus

The formal notation *Circus* is a unification of Z and CSP, and has been given a UTP semantics [OCW09]. A *Circus* text describes behaviour as a collection of actions, which are a combination of processes with mutable state. However, apart from event sequencing, there is no notion of time in *Circus*. A timed version of *Circus* (*Circus* Time Action or CTA) has been explored [SH02, She06] that introduces the notion of discrete time-slots in which sequences of events occur. The semantics of CTA has been developed using UTP, and there we find a two-level notion of history: the top-level views history as a sequence of time-slots; whilst the bottom-level records a history of events within a given slot.

Our interest in hardware compilation languages such as Handel-C [Cel02] led to a development of semantic theories based on the notion of time-slots in CTA, but with much more structure ("microslots") to the events within the timeslots [BW05]. Looking for a way to formally link *Circus* as a specification language to Handel-C as an implementation language, and given that CTA was a step in this direction, we decided to explore a UTP semantics for Handel-C.

As the Handel-C semantics had three levels of complexity, each supporting a larger range of language features, it was decided to develop a generic theory (called *slotted-Circus*), with time-slots whose bottom-level contents could be parameterised, as simple traces, or multisets of events, or as one of the three successively more complex "micro-slot" structures [BSW07]. That paper discussed a number of fundamental issues that had to be addressed, most regarding healthiness conditions. More recent work [GBW09] looked at subtleties involving communication and state update.

* This research was supported by a grant from Science Foundation Ireland, as well as partial support from Lero, the Irish Software Engineering Research Centre.

A. Cavalcanti and D. Dams (Eds.): FM 2009, LNCS 5850, pp. 451–466, 2009.

Another reason for using UTP was that it will allow us, in the future, to explore refinement links to other specification/programming languages also treated using the UTP framework.

This paper describes a complete denotational semantics, in the UTP framework, of *slotted-Circus*, finishing off earlier work. The key contribution here, apart from the completion, is an understanding of the key role played by refusals in the theory, particularly with respect to the semantics of hiding.

1.2 UTP: General Principles

Theories in UTP are expressed as second-order predicates[1] over a pre-defined collection of free observation variables, referred to as the *alphabet* of the theory. The predicates are generally used to describe a relation between a before-state and an after-state, the latter typically characterised by dashed versions of the observation variables. A predicate whose free variables are all undashed, referring only to the before-state, is called a *condition*. So for example, the program below on the left could be described by the predicate on the right:

$$\texttt{f} := \texttt{f} * \texttt{x};\ \texttt{x} := \texttt{x} - 1 \qquad\qquad f' = f * x \wedge x' = x - 1$$

Here logical variables f and f' denote the before- and after-values of the program variable `f`. We note that UTP follows the key principle that "programs are predicates" [Hoa85b] and so does not distinguish between the syntax of some language and its semantics as alphabetised predicates. In practise, we also need auxiliary logical variables to capture other aspects of a programs behaviour. For example, in a theory of simple imperative programming, we might use ok and ok' to model respectively the successful start and termination of a program. Our above example would then have its full semantics as follows:

$$ok \Rightarrow (\, ok' \wedge f' = f * x \wedge x' = x - 1\,)$$

A given theory is characterised by its alphabet, and a series of *healthiness conditions* that constrain the valid assertions that predicates may make. A healthiness condition is a property of a predicate that distinguishes sensible predicates from nonsense. So, for example the following predicate is clearly nonsense under our intended interpretation:

$$\neg\, ok \wedge ok'$$

It asserts that a program has not been started, but yet has terminated! It can be ruled out by the following healthiness condition (which yields false for the above predicate):

$$P = (ok \Rightarrow P)$$

Note that healthiness conditions should not be confused with ordinary conditions (predicates with only before-variables).

[1] Most definitions are in fact 1st-order, but we need 2nd-order in order to handle the notion of "healthiness", and recursion.

$$
\begin{array}{rcl}
\mathsf{Action} & ::= & \mathit{Skip} \mid \mathit{Stop} \mid \mathit{Chaos} \mid \mathit{Wait}\ \mathsf{t} \\
& \mid & \mathsf{Comm} \rightarrow \mathsf{Action} \mid \mathsf{Action} \sqcap \mathsf{Action} \mid \mathsf{Action} \,\Box\, \mathsf{Action} \\
& \mid & \mathsf{Action} \,[\![\, \mathsf{VS} \mid \mathsf{CS} \mid \mathsf{VS} \,]\!]\, \mathsf{Action} \mid \mathsf{Action} \setminus \mathsf{CS} \mid \mu\, \mathsf{Name} \bullet F(\mathsf{Name}) \\
& \mid & \mathsf{Name}^{+} := \mathsf{Expr}^{+} \mid \mathsf{Action}\, ;\ \mathsf{Action} \mid \mathsf{Action} \lhd \mathsf{Expr} \rhd \mathsf{Action} \mid \mathsf{Expr} * \mathsf{Action} \\
\mathsf{Comm} & ::= & \mathsf{Name.Expr} \mid \mathsf{Name!Expr} \mid \mathsf{Name?Name} \\
\mathsf{Expr} & ::= & \text{expression} \\
\mathsf{t} & ::= & \text{positive integer valued expression} \\
\mathsf{Name} & ::= & \text{channel or variable names} \\
\mathsf{CS} & ::= & \text{channel name sets} \\
\mathsf{VS} & ::= & \text{variable sets}
\end{array}
$$

Fig. 1. Slotted-*Circus* Syntax

1.3 Structure and Focus

The main technical emphasis of this paper is on the details of the semantics definitions of the language constructs, to ensure that the desired laws can be verified. We first present the syntax §2, generic framework §3, and healthiness conditions §4. We then discuss semantics §5 in some detail, and present some laws with a sketch of the proof of one of interest §6. We finish by mentioning related §7 and future §8 work, and concluding §9.

2 Syntax

The syntax of Slotted-*Circus* is similar to that of *Circus*, and a subset, relevant to this paper, is shown in Figure 1. The notation X^+ denotes a sequence of one of more X. We assume an appropriate syntax for describing expressions and their types, subject only to the proviso that at least booleans and non-negative integers are included.

The basic actions *Skip*, *Stop*, *Chaos*, as well as event prefix ($e \rightarrow A$) and hiding ($A \setminus H$) are similar to the corresponding CSP behaviours [Hoa85a, Sch00], while we also introduce variable assignmement (:=). Actions can be combined with internal ($\sqcap$) or external ($\Box$) choice, sequential composition (;), parallel composition ($[\![\_ \mid \_ \mid \_]\!]$), or conditional choice ($\lhd c \rhd$). Iteration can be described explicitly ($*$), or defined recursively ($\mu\, \_ \bullet \_$). The key construct related to time-slots, and hence not part of *Circus*, is *Wait* t which denotes an action that simply waits for t time-slots to elapse, and then terminates.

As an example we present a simple one-shot "factorial server" (Fig. 2) that waits for a request (channel *freq*) containing a natural number n, and then computes its factorial, exploiting parallelism where possible, finally returning the result as a response message (channel *fresp*). The server has the timing of a Handel-C program, where each assignment and channel communication takes a full time-slot (a.k.a. "clock-cycle"). A run of the server showing communication events, state variable changes, and the passage of time-slots is shown in

$$FS \mathrel{\widehat{=}} freq?n \rightarrow Wait\,1\,;\ \ FCOMP\,;\ \ fresp!f \rightarrow Wait\,1$$
$$FCOMP \mathrel{\widehat{=}} f := 1\,;\ \ Wait\,1\,;$$
$$(n > 1) * ((f := n * f\,;\ \ Wait1) \mathbin{[\![} \{f\} \mid \emptyset \mid \{n\} \mathbin{]\!]} (n := n - 1\,;\ \ Wait1))$$

Fig. 2. Factorial Server

Slot	1	2	3	4	5	6	7	8	9
Event	–	*freq*.4	–	–	–	–	–	–	*fresp*.24
Var:n	–	4	4	3	2	1	1	1	1
Var:f	–	–	1	4	12	24	24	24	24

Fig. 3. Factorial Server Run

Figure 3. Here we wait one slot for a request to compute 4!, and the client looks for the result two slots after it becomes available.

3 Generic Slot-Theory

Both the semantics of Handel-C [BW05] and the timed extension to *Circus* called "Circus Timed Actions (CTA)" [SH02, She06] have in common the fact that the models involve a sequence of "slots" that capture the behaviour of the system between successive clock ticks. In [BSW07] a comprehensive account is given of a generic UTP framework that captures the common aspects of these semantic models. The reason for developing a generic slot theory is that the way that events are recorded within a slot in CTA and Handel-C differ, with the latter semantics itself having three distinct variants. Here we provide a summary of the key concepts involved.

Although we are modelling a "discrete-time" theory, it has to be stressed that we can allow events to be ordered within a time-slot, albeit without timestamps at a finer granularity. The key concept is of a system governed by a global clock, and each slot models all that happens in-between two consecutive clock ticks. A slot contains information about the events that occurred during one time slot ("history") as well as the events being refused at that point. In CTA, a history is just a sequence ("trace") of events in the order in which they occurred during a slot. So the following example shows a run of CTA where events a and b both occur at least once in some order in every second time-slot:

$$\langle\langle\rangle, \langle a, b\rangle, \langle\rangle, \langle b, a, a\rangle, \langle\rangle, \langle b, a\rangle, \langle\rangle, \ldots\rangle$$

In the multi-set action (MSA) variant, we ignore event ordering within slots, viewing history as a bag of events, so the above example appears as

$$\langle\{\}, \{a \mapsto 1, b \mapsto 1\}, \{\}, \{a \mapsto 2, b \mapsto 1\}, \{\}, \{a \mapsto 1, b \mapsto 1\}, \{\}, \ldots\rangle$$

In fact with each slot we not only record an event history of some form but also the events being refused during a time-slot. So if we have an event type E and a history type constructor $\mathcal{H}$, then the type of slots is defined as:

$$\mathcal{S} \mathrel{\widehat{=}} \mathcal{H}\, E \times \mathbb{P}\, E$$

Essentially we now have a semantic domain that is parametric in the choice of $\mathcal{H}$ (plus some supporting definitions). We then build up event observations as "slotted-sequences", which are non-empty sequences of slots. The presence of clock-ticks in the history is denoted by the adjacency of two slots, so a slot-sequence of length $n + 1$ describes a situation in which the clock has ticked n times. The CTA example above can now be written in full, assuming that neither a nor b are refused during slots when they don't occur, but are refused at the end of the slot in which they do occur:

$$\langle (\langle\rangle, \emptyset), (\langle a, b\rangle, \{a, b\}), (\langle\rangle, \emptyset), (\langle b, a, a\rangle, \{a, b\}), (\langle\rangle, \emptyset), (\langle b, a\rangle, \{a, b\}), (\langle\rangle, \emptyset), \ldots\rangle$$

We can now describe the observational variables of our generic UTP theory:

$ok : \mathbb{B}$ —True if the process is stable, *i.e.*, not diverging.
$wait : \mathbb{B}$ —True if the process is waiting, *i.e.*, not terminated.
$state : Var \nrightarrow Value$ —An environment giving the current values of slotted-*Circus* variables
$slots : \mathcal{S}^+$: —A non-empty sequence of slots recording the timed event behaviour of the system.

The variables *ok*, *wait* play the same role as the in the reactive systems theory in [HH98, Chp. 8], while *state* follows the trend in [SH02] of grouping all the program variables under one observational variable, to simplify the presentation of the theory. We need to be very clear about the distinction between events and program variables — events denote visible communication actions used for synchronisation and/or to transfer data, whilst program variables are considered global in this paper, and the *state* component tracks their values as the program executes. In particular, the action of assigning to a variable updates *state*, but is not an event, and so is not recorded in *slots*.

In order to give the generic semantics of the language, we need, in addition to $\mathcal{H}$, to have definitions supplied of operations on such histories, that satisfy key properties. For example, we need to know what an empty history looks like, and how to concatenate histories, so that concatenation is associative, with the empty history as the identity element. Other operations to be defined include a history prefix relation, history subtraction, event hiding in histories, and event synchronisation between histories running in parallel — all satisfying a key set of laws — see [BSW07] for details.

Given the definition of $\mathcal{H}$, and the associated functions and relations, we need to lift many of these to work with slots and slot-sequences (see Fig. 4). Relation *EqvTrace*(*tr*, *slots*), asserts that *tr*, an event sequence, is compatible with the history in *slots*, ignoring time and refusals. Function *Refs* extracts refusals from

$$\begin{aligned} EqvTrace &: E^* \leftrightarrow \mathcal{S}^+ \\ Refs &: \mathcal{S}^+ \rightarrow (\mathbb{P}\, E)^+ \\ \preccurlyeq, \cong &: \mathcal{S}^+ \leftrightarrow \mathcal{S}^+ \\ \sharp, \setminus\!\!\setminus &: \mathcal{S}^+ \times \mathcal{S}^+ \nrightarrow \mathcal{S}^+ \\ SSync &: \mathbb{P}\, E \rightarrow \mathcal{S}^+ \times \mathcal{S}^+ \rightarrow \mathcal{S}^+ \\ SHide &: SLOT \times \mathbb{P}\, E \rightarrow \mathcal{S} \end{aligned}$$

Fig. 4. Slot-Sequence Functions/Relations

slot-sequences. The relations $\preccurlyeq$ and $\cong$ denote prefixing and equivalence of slot-sequences respectively — in this case equivalence is almost equality, except that the refusals in the last slot are ignored. Operations $\sharp$ and $\setminus\!\!\setminus$ denote slot concatenation and subtraction respectively — analogously to sequences, $\setminus\!\!\setminus$ is only defined if its second argument is a $\preccurlyeq$-prefix of its first. The key point to note here is that in the result of $s_1 \sharp s_2$, the last slot of s_1 is merged with the first slot of s_2. Function $SSync(c)(s_1, s_2)$ shows the effect of forcing the histories of s_1 and s_2 to synchronise on the events in set c, while $SHide(s, H)$ gives a slot were events in H are hidden (removed).

4 Healthiness Conditions

Healthiness conditions are characterised by idempotent predicate transformers, with a healthy predicate being a fixed point of such a transformer. The healthiness conditions we introduce here for slotted-*Circus* parallel some of those in [HH98, Chp. 8] for general reactive systems, namely **R1**, **R2**, **R3**, **CSP1** and **CSP2**. Here we shall only consider **R3**, **CSP1,2** in detail as they are explicitly invoked. **R1** and **R2** deal with the infeasibility of time travel and (direct) memory of past events, and are well covered elsewhere, and satisfied by all definitions we present in any case. The reactive conditions are aggregated as **R**, defined as the composition of **R1**–**3**.

The healthiness condition **R3** is one associated with all "reactive" systems in the UTP, covering process-algebras like ACP, CSP, and CCS.

$$\begin{aligned} \mathbf{R3}(P) &\mathrel{\widehat{=}} I\!\!I \lhd wait \rhd P \\ I\!\!I &\mathrel{\widehat{=}} DIV \vee ok' \wedge wait' = wait \wedge slots' = slots \\ DIV &\mathrel{\widehat{=}} \neg\, ok \wedge slots \preccurlyeq slots' \end{aligned}$$

R3 deals with the situation when a process has not actually started to run, because a prior process has yet to terminate, characterised by $wait = \text{TRUE}$. In this case the action of a yet-to-be started process should simply be to do nothing, an action we call "reactive-skip" ($I\!\!I$). Reactive skip has two behavioural modes: if started in an unstable state (i.e the prior computation is diverging), then all it guarantees is that the slots may get extended somehow; otherwise it stays stable, and leaves most other observations unchanged.

Conditions **CSP1** and **CSP2** In [HH98, Chp. 8] there are five of these presented, but for our purposes it suffices to consider only the first two.

A process is **CSP1** healthy if *all* it asserts, when started in an unstable state (due to some serious earlier failure), is that the event history may be extended:

$$\mathbf{CSP1}(P) \mathrel{\widehat=} P \lor \neg\, ok \land slots \preccurlyeq slots'$$

Healthiness condition **R1** simply states that we can never undo past events, but **CSP1** deals with behaviour in a particular starting condition — it says that if ok is false, then the only thing we can assert is that events may happen in accordance with **R1**.

A process predicate is **CSP2** healthy if it does not mandate instability, so if true with $ok' = False$, it is also true with $ok' = True$, all other observation variables being unchanged.

$$\mathbf{CSP2}(P) \mathrel{\widehat=} P;\ (ok \Rightarrow ok') \land wait' = wait \land slots' = slots \land state' = state \tag{1}$$

The effect of post-composing P with $(ok \Rightarrow ok') \land \ldots$ is remove any assertion of $\neg\, ok'$, so for example calculation shows that $\mathbf{CSP2}(P \land \neg\, ok') = P$ whereas by contrast $\mathbf{CSP}(P \land ok') = P \land ok'$.

5 Slotted Semantics

The language constructs of sequential composition, internal and conditional choice, iteration all have the same semantics as in standard UTP:

$$\begin{aligned} P;\ Q &\mathrel{\widehat=} \exists\, obs_m \bullet P[obs_m/obs'] \land Q[obs_m/obs] \\ P \sqcap Q &\mathrel{\widehat=} P \lor Q \\ P \lhd c \rhd Q &\mathrel{\widehat=} c \land P \lor \neg\, c \land Q \\ c * P &\mathrel{\widehat=} \mu\, L \bullet (P;\ L) \lhd c \rhd Skip \end{aligned}$$

Recursion $(\mu\, X \bullet F(X))$ is defined as the least fixed-point of F w.r.t to the refinement ordering (reverse implication), and obs is shorthand for all the observational variables.

5.1 Semantic Building Blocks

We define the semantics of *slotted-Circus* in terms of a number of basic building-blocks, largely to do with events and communication, that we now describe. This building blocks are all **R1**-,**R2**-healthy, but in general will not satisfy **R3** or the CSP healthiness conditions in themselves— they are intended to be used in constructions that do.

First we provide a predicate $NOEVTS$ that describes a situation that allows time to pass ($\#slots' > \#slots$) but disallows the occurrence of any events:

$$NOEVTS \mathrel{\widehat=} EqvTrace(\langle\rangle, slots' \smallsetminus slots)$$

It asserts that if we take the difference between before- and after-slots, then this will only be equivalent to the empty list $\langle\rangle$, which requires that every slot must contain an empty history component. A CTA example of this might be (r_i are arbitrary refusals):

$$slots' \setminus\!\setminus slots = \langle(\langle\rangle, r_1), (\langle\rangle, r_2), (\langle\rangle, r_3), (\langle\rangle, r_4)\rangle$$

Another very useful predicate asserts that a given set of events (E) have occurred, but that the clock has not yet ticked:

$$\begin{aligned} & EVTSNOW(E) \\ & \mathrel{\widehat=} \exists\, tt \bullet elems(tt) = E \land EqvTrace(tt, slots' \setminus\!\setminus slots) \land \#slots = \#slots' \end{aligned}$$

We are describing a situation where events occur in the first, and to date only time slot. We can find a trace tt equivalent to the observed slots, whose elements are the events in E, and where the before- and after-slots are of the same length, signifying that no clock tick has occurred. In CTA, this might be (r an arbitrary refusals, $E = \{a, b\}$):

$$slots' \setminus\!\setminus slots = \langle(\langle a, b, a\rangle, r)\rangle$$

In some situations, we want to describe events that occur immediately (in the first slot), as described by the predicate *IMMEVTS*:

$$IMMEVTS \mathrel{\widehat=} \exists\, E \bullet E \neq \emptyset \land EVTSNOW(E) \;;\; slots \preccurlyeq slots'$$

We require the existence of a non-empty sets of events that occur "now" (i.e. in the first time-slot), followed by an arbitrary extension of slots.

5.2 Semantics of Basic Actions

We now give the semantics of the basic actions, construct by construct.

$$Chaos \mathrel{\widehat=} \mathbf{R}(\mathbf{true})$$

The worst possible action in *slotted-Circus* is *Chaos*. It is the most unpredictable healthy process, and bottom of the refinement lattice.

$$Stop \mathrel{\widehat=} \mathbf{CSP1}(\mathbf{R3}(ok' \land wait' \land NOEVTS))$$

Action *Stop* has deadlocked — is stable, never terminates and never performs any event.

$$Skip \mathrel{\widehat=} \mathbf{R3}(\mathbf{CSP1}(state = state' \land \neg wait' \land ok' \land slots \cong slots'))$$

Action *Skip* terminates immediately in a stable state, without performing any events. In keeping with the CSP definition, *Skip* ignores the refusals of any preceding process, hence the use of slot-equivalence rather than slot-equality here.

$$\begin{aligned} &Wait\ t \mathrel{\widehat=} \mathbf{CSP1}(\mathbf{R3}(ok' \wedge del(t) \wedge NOEVTS)) \\ &\ del(t) \mathrel{\widehat=} (\#slots' - \#slots < t) \lhd wait' \rhd (\#slots' - \#slots = t \wedge state' = state) \end{aligned}$$

The action that introduces explicit timed behavior is $Wait\ t$. It never performs any events and has only two possible behaviors. The first one is to wait for t clock ticks, the second to terminate when the right time is reached.

$$x := e \mathrel{\widehat=} \mathbf{CSP1}\left(\mathbf{R3}\left(\begin{array}{l} ok' \wedge \neg wait' \wedge slots \cong slots' \\ \wedge\ state' = state \oplus \{x \mapsto val(e, state)\}\end{array}\right)\right)$$

Assignment is performed immediately, and for that reason is very similar to *Skip* — stable termination with no events or passing time observed. Valuation function *val* evaluates an expression given an environment. A key point to keep in mind here is that state-changes are recorded in the *state* variable and are not regarded as "events". The *state* here is globally visible — there are provisions in UTP and *Circus* for delimiting variable visibility but these are beyond the scope of this paper.

$$comm \rightarrow A \mathrel{\widehat=} (comm \rightarrow Skip);\ A$$

Unlike in CSP/CCS, an input communication binds an input value to a program variable, rather than the free occurrences of that name in the following process, so, for example, the input communication $c?x \rightarrow Skip$ ends by assigning the communicated value to the variable x. This allows us to treat the action $comm \rightarrow Skip$ as a basic building block and define more general prefixes in terms of it. We distinguish two basic behaviors of the prefix action: waiting for communication and performing it.

$$\begin{aligned} WTC(c) &\mathrel{\widehat=} POSS(c) \wedge NOEVTS \\ POSS(c) &\mathrel{\widehat=} c \notin \bigcup Refs(slots' \setminus\setminus slots) \\ TRMC(c) &\mathrel{\widehat=} EVTSNOW\{c\} \end{aligned}$$

While waiting for communication (WTC) we allow time to pass but we perform no events. We also inform the environment that we are ready to perform the specified event, by not refusing it (here *Refs* returns the refusals in each slot as a list). When we finally perform an event and terminate ($TRMC$) we have to make sure that the event is noted in the trace model. We also have to ensure that the specified event was not refused during the time-slots before the event occurred. For that reason we define the behavior of performing an event as $WTC(c);\ TRMC(c)$. We assemble all of this to get the following definition of prefix, noting in passing a key point that program variable state information is only propagated once the prefix action has terminated.

$$c \rightarrow Skip \mathrel{\widehat=} \mathbf{CSP1}\left(ok' \wedge \mathbf{R3}\left(WTC(c) \lhd wait' \rhd \left(\begin{array}{l} state' = state\ \wedge \\ WTC(c);\ TRMC(c)\end{array}\right)\right)\right)$$

The prefix action is also used to define channel-based communication. As per the usual CSP convention, sending a value is defined as performing an event - *channelName.value*, whilst receiving is defined as an external choice over all possible values allowable on a channel followed by assignment of the received value to the target variable. If we assume that channel c carries values of type $T = \{k_1, k_2, \ldots\}$, then

$$c!e \rightarrow Skip \mathrel{\widehat{=}} c.e \rightarrow Skip$$
$$c?x \rightarrow Skip \mathrel{\widehat{=}} \mathop{\Box}_{k:T} \bullet (c.k \rightarrow Skip;\ x := k)$$

Here $\Box_{k:T} \bullet P(x)$ is shorthand for $P(k_1) \Box P(k_2) \Box \ldots$.

5.3 Semantics of Composite Actions

External choice ($A \Box B$) allows external events to determine which action runs, so for example if we have $(a \rightarrow A) \Box (b \rightarrow B)$, then, if the environment performs a, we see that event occur, followed by an execution of action A. Unfortunately the very simple definition[2] of external choice proposed in [HH98], no longer suffices, as we may have to wait for several clock-ticks before an external event arises that resolves the choice.

$$A \Box B \mathrel{\widehat{=}} \mathbf{CSP2}(\, Stop \wedge A \wedge B \ \vee\ Choice(A, B) \ \vee\ Choice(B, A)\,)$$
$$Choice(C, R) \mathrel{\widehat{=}} C \wedge \left(R \wedge NOEVTS;\ \begin{pmatrix} IMMEVTS \vee \\ slots \cong slots' \wedge (\neg wait' \vee \neg ok') \end{pmatrix} \right)$$

Predicate $Choice(C, R)$ describes the circumstances where action C has been chosen, whilst R has been refused, which occurs in situation where R has performed no events. We capture these cases as follows: conjoin R with $NOEVTS$, and follow it sequentially with some "end"-condition E. All of this is conjoined with C to give

$$C \wedge (R \wedge NOEVTS;\ E)$$

i.e an execution of C consistent with R having done no events, and then ending in the situation described by E.

Now we can characterise three possible cases were C either: (i) performs an event after a delay: $E = IMMEVTS$; (ii) terminates without performing any events: $E = slots \cong slots' \wedge \neg wait'$ or (iii) diverges but performs no event: $E = slots \cong slots' \wedge \neg ok'$.

The parallel composition $A \llbracket s_A \mid \{\!|\ cs\ |\!\} \mid s_B \rrbracket B$ runs A and B in lock-step parallel (clock ticks at same time for both), with both actions required to synchronise on any channels mentioned in cs. Both actions run on local copies of the variables and are only allowed to modify those variables in their disjoint permission sets (s_A for A, s_B for B). The construct terminates when both actions have terminated — if one ends early then its behaviour is padded out with empty

---

[2] $A \Box B \mathrel{\widehat{=}} A \wedge B \lhd Stop \rhd A \vee B$.

slots. If s_A and s_B overlap, or A (B) assigns or inputs into variables not in s_A (s_B), then the construct is ill-formed. At present, we do not consider shared-write access to variables as constituting a healthy or well-formed process. The reason for this restriction is that reasoning about parallel processes with global shared variables is a complex business [WH02]. There is of course scope for investigating more liberal forms of parallel composition, but that is left for future work.

The definition of parallel composition (for well-formed compositions) is large but conceptually straightforward:

$$\begin{aligned} A \llbracket s_A \mid \{\!|\, cs \,|\!\} \mid s_B \rrbracket B \mathrel{\widehat=} \exists\, obs_A, obs_B \bullet\ & A[obs_A/obs'] \wedge B[obs_B/obs'] \wedge \\ & ok' = ok_A \wedge ok_B \wedge \\ & wait' = (wait_A \vee wait_B) \wedge \\ & ValidMerge(cs)(slots, slots', slots_A, slots_B) \wedge \\ & (wait_A \Rightarrow \sharp slots_A \geq \sharp slots_B) \wedge \\ & (wait_B \Rightarrow \sharp slots_A \leq \sharp slots_B) \wedge \\ & (\neg wait' \Rightarrow state' = (state_A - s_B) \oplus (state_B - s_A)) \end{aligned}$$

Both actions are running on local copies of observation variables $A[obs_A/obs'] \wedge B[obs_B/obs']$ and the outcome is determined as an appropriate merge of these: The composition is stable if both A and B are, and is waiting if either action is. The resulting slots are a valid merge of compatible slot-sequences from each action. If an action is still waiting for events then it has seen at least as many clock ticks as the other process (which may have terminated). When the whole construct has terminated, the final $state'$ value is determined by merging the changes from each side.

$$ValidMerge : \mathbb{P}\, E \rightarrow ((\mathcal{S}\ E)^+)^4 \rightarrow \mathbb{B}$$

$$ValidMerge(cs)(s, s', s0, s_1) \mathrel{\widehat=} (s' \setminus\!\setminus s) \in TSync(cs)(s0 \setminus\!\setminus s), (s_1 \setminus\!\setminus s))$$

Merging the traces of parallel actions is captured by a predicate ($ValidMerge$) that asserts that the final slots execution ($slots' \setminus\!\setminus slots$) is a member of all the valid ways in which the two actions slots can be merged, taking the synchronisation sets cs into account ($TSync$). The $TSync$ function returns all the possible fusings of two slot-sequences, slot-by-slot, with individual slots merged using $SSync$, the history-specific synchronisation parameter (see Fig 4). If one slot sequence is shorter than the other, then the shortest is padded out with null slots.

Our semantics, and that of CTA, differs here from that of timed-CSP [Sch00]. There $Skip$ need not terminate immediately, but can delay, so facilitating the following law:

$$(a \rightarrow Skip \parallel Skip) = a \rightarrow Skip$$

The same law holds for *slotted-Circus*, even though $Skip$ terminates immediately, because the singleton slots-sequence for the righthand $Skip$ is padded out by the definition of parallel, to match that of the lefthand action as it waits for, and eventually performs the event a.

$$A \setminus H \mathrel{\widehat=} \mathbf{R3}\left(\begin{array}{l} \exists\, s' \bullet A[s'/slots'] \wedge \\ \qquad slots' \setminus\!\setminus slots = map(SHide(H))(s' \setminus\!\setminus slots) \\ \qquad \wedge\ H \subseteq \bigcap Refs(s' \setminus\!\setminus slots) \end{array}\right) ; Skip$$

$$\begin{aligned} \mathit{Wait}\ n \,\Box\, \mathit{Wait}\ n+m &= \mathit{Wait}\ n \\ (\mathit{Skip} \,\Box\, (\mathit{Wait}\ n;\ P)) &= \mathit{Skip}, \quad n>0 \\ (c \rightarrow P) \,\Box\, (\mathit{Wait}\ n;\ (c \rightarrow P)) &= (c \rightarrow P) \\ \mathit{Stop} \,\Box\, A &= A \\ (c \rightarrow \mathit{Skip}) \setminus \{c\} &= \mathit{Skip} \end{aligned}$$

Fig. 5. (Some) Laws of slotted-*Circus*

The hiding operator $A \setminus H$ denotes an execution of action A, but with any events in event-set H hidden. The last assertion above about H and $\mathit{Refs}(\ldots)$ is implied by the definition of *SHide*, but is useful for proofs to have stated explicitly here. It has the effect of forcing a key properting of hiding, namely that of *maximal progress*, i.e. hidden events occur as soon as they are enabled. Without this semantic feature the following undesirable law would hold:

$$(a \rightarrow \mathit{Skip}) \setminus \{a\} = \mathit{Wait}\,0 \sqcap \mathit{Wait}\,1 \sqcap \ldots \sqcap \mathit{Wait}\ n \sqcap \ldots$$

This law is undesirable because it makes the performance of a single hidden event followed by termination equal to a wait for an arbitrary number of clock cycles — effectively a weak form of livelock. By forcing hidden events to be refused during every slot, we prevent them from waiting for a clock-tick, because the definition of prefix action requires events not to be refused when waiting. This results in the desired law, namely

$$(a \rightarrow \mathit{Skip}) \setminus \{a\} = \mathit{Skip}$$

At the end we add *Skip* to unconstrain the refusals set of the last slot.

6 Laws

The language constructs displayed here obey a wide range of laws, many of which have been described elsewhere [HH98, WC01, SH02, She06] for those constructs that slotted-*Circus* shares with other related languages like CSP or *Circus*(e.g. non-deterministic choice, sequential composition, conditional, guards, *STOP*, *SKIP*). Here we simply indicate (Fig.5) some of the laws that are peculiar to slotted-*Circus*, or whose proof was a challenge. The first law is a consequent of the fact that external choice treats termination as an "event" that can resolve an external choice. The proof of the latter two laws forced a lot of the design of the details of the semantic model described here. The definition of external choice and the its properties lead to the discovery of the state visibility issue addressed in [GBW09]. The last law vindicates the semantic choice (used here, in CTA, and Timed-CSP) that entangles refusals up with the individual slots, rather than keeping them seperate from the event history, as in the *Failures* model of CSP [Ros97].

The proof of $(c \rightarrow \mathit{Skip}) \setminus \{c\} = \mathit{Skip}$ was long and difficult, based on a large range of properties from the very top level (healthiness conditions and circus specific actions), to a very low level, that of a single slot. The whole proof is roughly sixteen pages and for that reason we leave it to a technical report [BG09]. What makes this law special is that interaction between hiding and communication is the only place where refusals influence the behavior of the action and is actually responsible for a set of accepted traces. This can been seen by considering the following lemma which forms the core of the proof:

$$\begin{aligned}&(WTC(c);\ TRMC(c)) \land c \in \bigcap Refs(slots' \setminus\setminus slots)\\ =\ &TRMC(c) \land c \in \bigcap Refs(slots' \setminus\setminus slots)\end{aligned}$$

Predicate $WTC(c);\ TRMC(c)$ is a part of the prefix definition which describes a situation where the action waited (for zero or more clock ticks) to perform c, and then did so. During the waiting period, c was not being refused. By contrast, the predicate $c \in \bigcap Refs(slots' \setminus\setminus slots)$ comes from the definition of hiding and requires that c be refused during any slots that have occurred. The only observations that satisfy both these requirements are ones where no clock ticks occur and communication is immediate, i.e $TRMC(C)$.

7 Related Work

In addition to the work done on state-rich reactive processes in UTP [OCW09] there has been attention paid to merging state and concurrency by others. The implementors of occam [SGS95] had to deal with the integration of state with its concurrency aspects, those being derived from CSP. An early integration of state and concurrency was the work on joining Object-Z and CSP [SD01], which was then followed up with real-time extensions [Smi02]. However these languages are very much at the specification level, with no explicit notion of assignment or global shared variables, as Object-Z schemas are interpreted as message-passing objects, so the concerns of this paper do not arise. The work on unifying CSP and B [But00] looks at linking the process of CSP with the actions of B. However while it converts CSP-like descriptions of behaviour into B state-machines, it has concept, at the CSP level of assignment to variables. Taking the denotational semantics of CSP and merging it with the algebraic semantics of CASL has resulting in a "data-rich' process algebra called CSP-CASL [Rog06]. Here the richness of CASL datatypes is made available for use as the types of values transmitted over communications channels. However there is no notion of state update through assignment in the theory.

A UTP semantics for Timed Communicating Object-Z (TCOZ [MD00]) is given in [QDC03]. The theory presented there has a communication component which is a variant of He and Sherif's CTA [SH02], with a richer notion of event that differentiates between interprocess communication, and the interaction of the environment with sensors and actuators. Like the CTA semantics, it embeds **R3** into the definition of sequential composition, and defines communication to only assert the state is unchanged when communications has completed. Again "active objects" in TCOZ have their variable-state encapsulated. However TCOZ has an asynchronous interface mechanism of sensors and actuators, with the actuators linking a local variable to a global one. This mechanism can be used for internal communication as well as with the external environment.

8 Future Work

In [BSW07] we described a number of different ways to instantiate event histories within a time-slot, including:

- $\mathcal{CTA}$: histories are just events sequences (essentially the CTA theory [She06]).
- $\mathcal{MSA}$: histories are multisets or bags, so ordering within a slot is irrelevant
- $\mathcal{SCSP}$: histories are simple event sets — however these fails to satisfy the required laws on which the theory depends.

An important aspect that has yet to be covered is what distinguishes the various instantiations from one another, i.e. how do the laws of $\mathcal{CTA}$ differ from those of $\mathcal{MSA}$, for instance. We know for example that the following is not a law of $\mathcal{MSA}$, but does apply in $\mathcal{CTA}$:

$$(a \rightarrow b \rightarrow P) \parallel (b \rightarrow a \rightarrow P) = Stop$$

In $\mathcal{MSA}$ the deadlock can be avoided if both a and b occur in the same time-slot.

Another key concept, which has guided the precise form of the definition of external choice, is that of modelling priority among choices, which makes sense in a slotted-theory because we have a deadline (next clock-tick) against which any priority resolution scheme can operate. We plan to explore schemes to give semantic support to prioritised choice by appropriate modifications to the external choice definition. Interestingly, early indications are that a notion of priority will work in the $\mathcal{MSA}$ instantiation, but not the $\mathcal{CTA}$ incarnation !

Also worthy of exploration are the details of the behaviour of the Galois links [HH98, Chp 4] between different instances of slotted-*Circus*, and between those and standard *Circus*. These details will provide a framework for a comprehensive refinement calculus linking all these reactive theories together. The goal is a scheme whereby *Circus* is a specification language and *slotted-Circus* is a refinement stage, on the way to a hardware implementation.

9 Conclusions

A denotational semantics for *slotted-Circus* has been presented, backed up by a techreport giving fuller details[BG09]. The general layers of the theory have been shown along with higher level building blocks used for defining the semantics. The key result presented here is a comprehensive semantics of the entire language that addresses various semantics issues that have been uncovered whilst laying foundations for future extensions, particularly towards prioritized choice.

A disadvantage of UTP is that some of the key proofs can be quite long and involved, as seen in the discussion regarding the hiding law. However, UTP also brings certain key advantages, which for our purposes outweigh this disadvantage:

- We are involved in a program of semantics unification — in this case bringing together *Circus*(itself a Z/CSP fusion), with related timed languages that combine both state and concurrency with message passing (CTA, Handel-C).
- Whilst standalone semantic models for each of the above are simpler, connecting them together formally is not.
- UTP is a common semantics foundation framework that supports both the merging of theories and the formal linking of them: given a predicate linking the observations of two different theories, the derivation of a galois connection putting them together in a refinement relationship is almost automatic [HH98, pp40–41]

The pain of developing formal models of languages, already well understood and formalised by other means, is, in our opinion, rewarded by the ease with which their formal interrelationships can then be explored.

Finally, the need to explicitly identify healthiness conditions, rather than have them emerge implicitly from the structure of a tailored semantic domain, seems to us to provide key comparative insights into the nature of languages under study.

The large amount of hand-proving involved has thrown the need for tool-support into sharp relief. This is exacerbated by the additional complexity that arises once time is added to the theory.

Acknowledgements. We would like to thank Jim Woodcock and his colleagues for many fruitful discussions on various aspects of this work.

References

[BG09] Butterfield, A., Gancarski, P.: Slotted-Circus: A generic UTP framework for discretely-timed circus. Technical Report TCD-CS-09-32, School of Computer Science & Statistic Trinity College Dublin, Trinity College, Dublin 2, Ireland (July 2009), `https://www.cs.tcd.ie/publications/tech-reports/reports.09/TCD-CS-2009-32.pdf`

[BSW07] Butterfield, A., Sherif, A., Woodcock, J.: Slotted-*circus*: A UTP-family of reactive theories. In: Davies, J., Gibbons, J. (eds.) IFM 2007. LNCS, vol. 4591, pp. 75–97. Springer, Heidelberg (2007)

[But00] Butler, M.J.: csp2b: A practical approach to combining csp and b. Formal Aspects of Computing 12, 182–196 (2000)

[BW05] Butterfield, A., Woodcock, J.: Prialt in Handel-C: an operational semantics. International Journal on Software Tools for Technology Transfer (STTT) 7(3), 248–267 (2005)

[Cel02] Celoxica Ltd. Handel-C Language Reference Manual, v3.0 (2002), `http://www.celoxica.com`

[GBW09] Gancarski, P., Butterfield, A., Woodcock, J.: State visibility and communication in unifying theories of programming. In: Chin, W.-N., Qin, S. (eds.) 3rd IEEE International Symposium on Theoretical Aspects of Software Engineering, pp. 47–54. IEEE Computer Society, Los Alamitos (2009)

[HH98] Hoare, C.A.R., He, J.: Unifying Theories of Programming. Series in Computer Science. Prentice Hall, Englewood Cliffs (1998), `http://www.unifyingtheories.org`

[Hoa85a] Hoare, C.A.R.: Communicating Sequential Processes. Intl. Series in Computer Science. Prentice Hall, Englewood Cliffs (1985)

[Hoa85b] Hoare, C.A.R.: Programs are predicates. In: Proc. of a discussion meeting of the Royal Society of London on Mathematical logic and programming languages, pp. 141–155. Prentice-Hall, Inc., Englewood Cliffs (1985)

[MD00] Mahony, B.P., Dong, J.S.: Timed communicating object Z. IEEE Trans. Software Eng. 26(2), 150–177 (2000)

[OCW09] Oliveira, M., Cavalcanti, A., Woodcock, J.: A UTP semantics for circus. Formal Asp. Comput. 21(1-2), 3–32 (2009)

[QDC03] Qin, S., Dong, J.S., Chin, W.-N.: A semantic foundation for TCOZ in unifying theories of programming. In: Araki, K., Gnesi, S., Mandrioli, D. (eds.) FME 2003. LNCS, vol. 2805, pp. 321–340. Springer, Heidelberg (2003)

[Rog06] Roggenbach, M.: CSP-CASL - A new integration of process algebra and algebraic specification. Theor. Comput. Sci. 354(1), 42–71 (2006)

[Ros97] Roscoe, A.W.: The Theory and Practice of Concurrency. international series in computer science. Prentice Hall, Englewood Cliffs (1997)

[Sch00] Schneider, S.: Concurrent and Real-time Systems — The CSP Approach. Wiley, Chichester (2000)

[SD01] Smith, G., Derrick, J.: Specification, refinement and verification of concurrent systems-an integration of object-Z and CSP. Formal Methods in System Design 18(3), 249–284 (2001)

[SGS95] SGS-THOMSON Microelectronics Limited. occam 2.1 reference manual, May 12 (1995)

[SH02] Sherif, A., He, J.: Towards a time model for circus. In: George, C.W., Miao, H. (eds.) ICFEM 2002. LNCS, vol. 2495, pp. 613–624. Springer, Heidelberg (2002)

[She06] Sherif, A.: A Framework for Specification and Validation of Real Time Systems using Circus Action. Ph.d. thesis, Universidade Federale de Pernambuco, Recife, Brazil (January 2006)

[Smi02] Smith, G.: An integration of real-time object-Z and CSP for specifying concurrent real-time systems. In: Butler, M., Petre, L., Sere, K. (eds.) IFM 2002. LNCS, vol. 2335, pp. 267–285. Springer, Heidelberg (2002)

[WC01] Woodcock, J., Cavalcanti, A.: *Circus*: a concurrent refinement language. Technical report, University of Kent at Canterbury (October 2001)

[WH02] Woodcock, J., Hughes, A.P.: Unifying theories of parallel programming. In: George, C.W., Miao, H. (eds.) ICFEM 2002. LNCS, vol. 2495, pp. 24–37. Springer, Heidelberg (2002)

Unifying Probability with Nondeterminism

Yifeng Chen[1] and J. W. Sanders[2]

[1] HCST Key Lab at School of EECS, Peking University, China
[2] International Institute for Software Technology, UNU, Macao

Abstract. Early support for reasoning about probabilistic system behaviour replaced nondeterminism with probabilism. Only relatively recently have formalisms been studied that combine the two, and hence facilitate reasoning about probabilistic systems at levels of abstraction more general than code. Such studies have revealed an unsuspected subtlety in the interaction between nondeterministic and probabilistic choices that can be summarised: the demon resolving the nondeterministic choice has memory of previous state changes, whilst the probabilistic choice is made spontaneously. As a result, assignments to distinct variables need no longer commute. This paper introduces a model with explicit control of the length of the demon's memory. It does so by expanding the standard (initial-final) state view of computation to incorporate a third state, the 'original' state which checkpoints the most recent nondeterministic choice. That enables a nondeterministic choice to be made on the basis of only certain past probabilistic choices and so facilitates independent nondeterministic combinations to be chosen against just those. Sound laws are presented and used to analyse first an example in which no new behaviour should result, and second one that lies beyond the scope of traditional models.

1 Introduction

Models of sequential systems that account for both (demonic) nondeterministic and probabilistic choice are necessary in order to reason about system behaviour at levels of abstraction more general than code. They find use, for example, in the top-down incremental derivation of implementations that have been unpopular since Dijkstra introduced them in the *wp* setting. However the interaction between the two forms of choice turned out to be more subtle than was at first supposed. Here is a representataive example [4]: for programs A and B, let $A \sqcap B$ and $A \;{}_{\frac{1}{2}}\!\oplus\; B$ denote their nondeterministic and fair probabilistic choices respectively; in the latter case, the result is equally likely to be A or B. Then, using standard notation for assignment,

$$\begin{array}{l}(x := 0 \sqcap x := 1) \fatsemi (y := 0 \;{}_{\frac{1}{2}}\!\oplus\; y := 1) \neq \\ (y := 0 \;{}_{\frac{1}{2}}\!\oplus\; y := 1) \fatsemi (x := 0 \sqcap x := 1) .\end{array} \tag{1}$$

Indeed, the probabilistic choice on the left is made *after* a value is assigned to x by the nondeterministic choice. Thus the probability of guaranteeing the

A. Cavalcanti and D. Dams (Eds.): FM 2009, LNCS 5850, pp. 467–482, 2009.

condition $x = y$ is 1/2. But the right-hand program behaves more nondeterministically: the nondeterministic choice can observe, and so exploit, the preceding probabilistic choice, so that in the worst case it may keep ensuring $x \neq y$; thus the probability of guaranteeing $x = y$ is reduced to 0. In the presence of both probability and nondeterminism, disjoint assignments no longer commute!

Of course in standard sequential programming, disjoint assignments commute as a result of the two distributivity laws:

$$\begin{aligned} (B \sqcap C) \mathbin{;} A &= (B \mathbin{;} A) \sqcap (C \mathbin{;} A) \\ A \mathbin{;} (B \sqcap C) &= (A \mathbin{;} B) \sqcap (A \mathbin{;} C). \end{aligned}$$

It is the second that fails in probabilistic programming. That feature of probabilistic systems has been used to good effect in modelling information flow (for example [1,9] will be discussed in Section 4). But 'unadulterated' nondeterminism has been found to be too strong, so that weaker versions have been considered. For instance, complementing [9], a restricted form of choice able to read only certain declared variables has been considered in [12]. Here we adopt a different approach and curtail the demons's memory. With little effort modifications are possible to make the demon prescient, if that is required, or to have more complex memory (see Section 5).

We consider probability, as has become standard, in the guise of a binary combinator $A \,{}_p\!\oplus\, B$ that chooses program A with probability p and B with the deficit probability $(1{-}p)$. That suffices to express known probabilistic algorithms and to reason about a moderately broad range of probabilistic behaviour [8]. It is shown there that Dijsktra's guarded-command language augmented with ${}_p\!\oplus$ provides a remarkably simple uniform notation facilitating the simultaneous treatment of functional and probabilistic behaviour. So with almost no extra complexity, probabilistic behaviour need not be handled by a 'second pass', but all at once with the consideration of input/output behaviour.

Two models of probability and nondeterminism have been developed in which the revised laws are sound: an expectation-transformer model [8] corresponding to the predicate-transformer model of standard programming, and a distributional model [8], corresponding to the standard binary-relational model. In the transformer model, each computation is modelled by transforming a random variable over final states (seen as an expectation) to the (pointwise) greatest expected value over initial states that can be guaranteed by executing the computation with 'reward' the post random variable. In the distributional model, each computation is seen as transforming an initial state to a set of distributions over final states (though in this paper we prefer to make it a relation between distributions). The distributional model is embedded in the transformer model by a Galois connection [8]. In the distributional model where nondeterminism is union, if sequential composition were to be the usual sequential composition of relations then equality would hold in (1). Thus the definition of sequential composition is more sophisticated in [4]. In common sequential programming, a relational composition $(S \mathbin{;} T)$ relates the final state of S and the initial state of T, reflecting the sequential state changes. The sequential composition of [4], however, also relates the initial state (distribution) of S with the final state of

T. Note this difference remains even when the state-distribution transformers are lifted to distribution transformers.

Here we follow the alternative of using the standard relational definition of sequential composition but a slightly more sophisticated definition of nondeterminism. We start from the observation that nondeterministic choices made after a sequential composition may be correlated with what happened well before. Thus we introduce a model of computation that enables a 'nondeterministic log' to be maintained and a 'nondeterministic checkpoint' to be taken to reset the log. The state from which the log extends is called the 'original' state of the computation; and we consider distributions over final state. A nondeterministic choice is resolved by reference to the log. But when the log is reset, original and current states coincide and there is no history for the demon to work from; the result is 'nondeterministically closed'. A computation then becomes a relation between such distributions. Three novel aspects of the model are:

1. each program construct is able to observe not only current state but also some original state, allowing sequential composition to be defined succinctly as a simple relational composition;
2. nondeterministic choice is separated into two operators: one binary operator $\oplus$ that arbitrarily combines probabilistic outcomes of two programs without the 'demonic' ability to act against previous probabilistic choices and another unary operator $\Box$ that performs the demonic act; such separation opens the door to include multiple nondeterministic choices with different backward-looking abilities;
3. the above two aspects explicitly reveal the interaction between probability and nondeterminism, and allow a (generalised) assignment to take into account observation of the original state, and 'angelically' act against a previous (demonic) nondeterministic choice, effectively achieving a kind of compensation.

In Section 2 the new model is described and sound laws presented. Proofs are largely routine using relational or predicate calculus. Section 3 contains a discussion of (1) to demonstrate that the new model preserves its properties; it then discusses the well-known Monty-Hall puzzle, and discusses a variant not able to be handled by previous models.

2 A Relational Model for Probabilistic Programming

In this section we introduce the notion of 'original state' and probability distributions that depend on original states. The semantic model supports seven basic commands. Healthiness conditions are introduced and sound algebraic laws are identified and used to transform programs into a normal form.

2.1 Distributions

Let $S = (V \to C)$ be the (finite) set of all states, each a mapping from program variables (denoted $x, y, \cdots, z$) to constants. Let $r, s, t, s_0, \cdots$ denote individual states. A (conditional) *probability distribution* is a function: $h : S \to (S \to [0,1])$ whose first argument s denotes the *original state* and second argument denotes the *current state*. Let $\mathbb{H}$ denote the set of such distributions, with members $h, h_0, h_1, \cdots$. Distributions are partially ordered: $h_1 \leqslant h_2$ iff $h_1.s.t \leqslant h_2.s.t$ for all $s, t \in S$.

A *well-formed* distribution d satisfies: from any original state s, the total probability of all current states is at most 1: $\sum_t d.s.t \leqslant 1$. Let $\mathbb{D}$ denote the set of well-formed distributions, with members $d, d_0, d_1, \cdots$. A well-formed distribution is a probability distribution over current states conditional on a specific original state. A well-formed distribution satisfying $d.s.t = p$ records that if the *original state* is s, then the probability of *reaching this point* of the program in a *current state* t is p. Thus the final distribution of a nonterminating program may have total probability less than 1. A *functional distribution* f is a well-formed distribution and $f.s.t$ is either 0 or 1 for all s and t. For example, the delta distribution δ is functional and yields probability 1 when the current state equals the original state: $\delta.s.t = 1$ iff $s = t$. Let $\mathbb{F}$ denote the set of functional distributions. We have $\mathbb{F} \subseteq \mathbb{D} \subseteq \mathbb{H}$.

For program reasoning, we adopt convenient notation. Suppose $V = \{x, y\}$; then $\langle x+y, x-y \rangle$ denotes a functional distribution indicating that the variables x and y have been updated to $x+y$ and $x-y$ respectively since the original state. The functional distribution $\langle x, y \rangle$, on the other hand, corresponds to the delta function in this context.

A *uniform distribution* u is a probability distribution such that for all t_1 and t_2 we have $u.s.t_1 = u.s.t_2$. Let $\mathbb{U}$ denote the set, with members $u, u_0, u_1, \cdots$. A *constant distribution* is uniform and for all s_1 and s_2, it satisfies $u.s_1.t = u.s_2.t$. Let $\mathbb{C}$ denote the set of constant distributions. For example, $1 \in \mathbb{C}$: for all states $1.s.t = 1$. We have $\mathbb{C} \subseteq \mathbb{U} \subseteq \mathbb{H}$. Symmetrically, a *current distribution* v is a probability distribution that is unchanged for every original state. Let $\mathbb{V}$ denote the set of current distributions, with members $v, v_0, \cdots$; then $\mathbb{C} \subseteq \mathbb{V} \subseteq \mathbb{H}$.

A *boolean distribution* b is such that for all s and t, the probability $b.s.t$ is either 0 or 1. Let $\mathbb{B}$ denote the set of boolean distributions, with members $b, b_0, b_1, \cdots$. Functional distributions are singleton boolean distributions which may depend on the original state. Evidently, $\mathbb{F} \subseteq \mathbb{B} \subseteq \mathbb{H}$.

We will use a notation $[S_0]$ where $S_0 \subseteq S$ to denote a boolean condition independent of the original state: $[S_0].s.t = 1 \;=\; (t \in S_0)$. For example, $[x = 1 \wedge y = 2]$ is equal to functional distribution $\langle 1, 2 \rangle$, and $[x = y]$ denotes the distribution such that $b.s.t = 1$ iff $t(x) = t(y)$ and $b.s.t = 0$ otherwise, and $[x = y] = \langle 0, 0 \rangle + \langle 1, 1 \rangle$. We have $[S_0] \in \mathbb{V}$.

2.2 Operations on Distributions

The *inner product* (over current states from every original state) between a well-formed distribution and a distribution is defined: $(d \cdot h).s.t \;\widehat{=}\; \sum_r d.s.r \times h.s.r$. The result distribution is always uniform. For example, the inner product $d \cdot [x = y]$ represents the total probability of the current states that satisfy $x = y$ from each original state.

The *linear combination* of two distributions h_1 and h_2 by a factor (uniform) distribution u is defined: $(h_1\ {}_u\!\oplus\ h_2).s.t\ \widehat{=}\ h_1.s.t * u.s.t\ +\ h_2.s.t * (1 - u.s.t)$. This definition allows the choosing factors (probabilities) to depend on original states. The *convex combination* $(d_1\ {}_u\!\oplus\ d_2)$ of two well-formed distributions by a uniform factor u is also well-formed. Inner product distributes over convex combination: $(d_1\ {}_u\!\oplus\ d_2) \cdot h = (d_1 \cdot h)\ {}_u\!\oplus\ (d_2 \cdot h)$.

The *state update* of a well-formed distribution by a program expression $e : S \to (S \to S)$ is defined: $(d \dagger e).s.t\ \widehat{=}\ \sum_{r:e(s,r)=t} d.s.r$. From any original state (*i.e.* the first argument), the probability of a final state is the total probability of the initial states mapped into the final state. The result of an update is always well-formed. Assignments with program expressions that depend on the original state can be applied to perform backward compensation (see Section 3). The *current-state composition* $(e_1 \circ e_2)$ of two expressions is defined: $(e_1 \circ e_2)(s,t)\ \widehat{=}\ e_1(s, e_2(s,t))$ (see its use in Law 1(3)). Two consecutive state updates correspond to the current-state composition of the expressions: $(d \dagger e_1) \dagger e_2 = d \dagger (e_2 \circ e_1)$. A similar composition for distribution and program expression is defined: $(h \circ e).s.t\ \widehat{=}\ h.s.e(s,t)$ (see its use in Law 2(5)). State update distributes over convex combination: $(d_1\ {}_u\!\oplus\ d_2) \dagger e = (d_1 \dagger e)\ {}_u\!\oplus\ (d_2 \dagger e)$. A useful equation relating inner product, state update and current-state composition is: $(d \dagger e) \cdot h = d \cdot (h \circ e)$.

The *convolution composition* between a well-formed distribution d and a distribution h is defined: $(d \otimes h).s.t\ \widehat{=}\ \sum_r d.s.r \times h.r.t$ (like matrix product it is associative). This composition represents the conditional probabilities in correspondence with the original states. It is easy to check that the result is always well-formed, and if h is uniform so is the result. The delta distribution δ is the unit of $\otimes$. In general, convolution does not distribute over probabilistic choice for well-formed distributions, although the distributivity does hold in special cases when the first argument of convolution is a functional distribution, the factor function on the right is a current distribution, or the factor function on the left is uniform:

$$\begin{aligned} f \otimes (d_1\ {}_h\!\oplus\ d_2) &= (f \otimes d_1)\ {}_h\!\oplus\ (f \otimes d_2) \\ d \otimes (d_1\ {}_v\!\oplus\ d_2) &= (d \otimes d_1)\ {}_v\!\oplus\ (d \otimes d_2) \\ (d_1\ {}_u\!\oplus\ d_2) \otimes d &= (d_1 \otimes d)\ {}_u\!\oplus\ (d_2 \otimes d). \end{aligned}$$

2.3 The Semantic Model

A computation is represented by a relation $A(d, d')$ between an initial (well-formed) distribution d and a final (well-formed) distribution d'. The initial (or final) distribution represents the probability distribution over the initial (or final) states conditional on the probabilistic choice taken back in the original state. The basic commands are defined as follows.

Abort $\perp$, representing nontermination, is the most nondeterministic computation and may end up in any final distribution from every initial distribution. The *assignment* $t := e(s,t)$ uses a program expression e to modify the state according to the initial state t and the original state s. The probability of a final state is the sum probabilities of the initial states mapped to it, all dependent on the original states. The final distribution may contain as much probability for nontermination as the initial distribution. *Skip* $\amalg = (t := t)$ (or alternatively $\amalg = (d' \geqslant d)$), is the unit of sequential composition. We adopt the view that if a computation, with a certain probability, does not terminate, then within that probability, its behaviour is chaotic: it may be in any state or may be in no state. Technically, the final distribution is always upwards-closed.

$$
\begin{array}{lcl}
\bot & \widehat{=} & \mathit{true} \\
t := e & \widehat{=} & d' \geqslant d \dagger e \\
A \mathbin{;} B & \widehat{=} & \exists d_0 \cdot A(d, d_0) \wedge B(d_0, d') \\
A \;{}_h\!\oplus\; B & \widehat{=} & \exists d_1, d_2 \cdot A(d, d_1) \wedge B(d, d_2) \wedge d' \geqslant d_1 \;{}_{d \cdot h}\!\oplus\; d_2 \\
A \oplus B & \widehat{=} & \bigcup_h \; A \;{}_h\!\oplus\; B \\
\Box(A) & \widehat{=} & \exists d_0 \cdot A(\delta,\, d_0) \;\wedge\; d' \geqslant d \otimes d_0 \\
\mu F & \widehat{=} & \bigcup \{\, A \mid A \subseteq F(A) \,\}
\end{array}
$$

Sequential composition $A \mathbin{;} B$ equates, and hides, the final distribution of A and the initial distribution of B. *Probabilistic choice* $A \;{}_h\!\oplus\; B$ with a choosing distribution h linearly combines the result distributions from A and B. *Open nondeterministic choice* $A \oplus B$ applies the universal union of convex combinations (with arbitrary choosing distributions) between relations. Note that finite union of relations, violating convexity closure, is not closed in the semantics, but open nondeterminism is. *Nondeterministic closure* $\Box(A)$ resets the initial state of A to be the original state; it is achieved with the delta distribution δ. The results from all possible initial states are recorded in d_0, representing how the final distributions depend on the initial states. The result distribution is convoluted with the initial distribution d to reflect the influence of the probability distribution of initial states. The definition of closure illustrates how a computation can take advantage of the history (as far back as the beginning of the nearest closure). *Recursion* is defined as the weakest (or largest) fixpoint μF where $F = F(X)$ is a program context that maps each relation X to another relation $F(X)$.

A derived command, the backward-looking nondeterministic choice $A \sqcap B \;\widehat{=}\; \Box(A \oplus B)$, corresponds to that of the standard probabilistic models and performs arbitrary convex combinations against the state at the beginning. Section 3.1 will show how this allows nondeterminism to act against the original probabilistic choices. *Binary conditional* that chooses A if b is true and otherwise B is a special case of probabilistic choice, equalling $A \;{}_b\!\oplus\; B$ where b is a boolean distribution. Note that both assignment and binary conditional may depend on original states. Their combined uses can support more sophisticated forms of compensation (see Section 3.2).

2.4 Healthiness Conditions

Healthiness conditions can be viewed as imposed properties that yield desirable laws. The total probability (over initial states) from each original state is at most 1. When it is less than 1, the deficiency represents the probability of nontermination. A principle of the unifying approach [5] and other totally-correct models is to assume that if the computation has not started then the computation becomes chaotic. In our probabilistic model, this is ensured by a healthiness condition: $A = (d=0 \vee A)$. Another healthiness condition ensures that if the computation may not terminate, the final distribution is chaotic for the probability of nontermination: $A = (A \mathbin{;} \text{II})$. Note that II itself also satisfies the first healthiness condition. Symmetrically, as a healthiness condition, skip is the left unit of sequential composition: $A = (\text{II} \mathbin{;} A)$. This ensures that for a specific final distribution, the possible initial distributions are downwards-closed. Arbitrary convex combinations of the final distributions (independently) from each initial state are closed (*i.e.* idempotence of $\oplus$): $A = (A \oplus A)$. This healthiness condition ensures idempotence of probabilistic choice in Law 2(1). In this paper, we assume that all computations are feasible (*i.e.* free of miracles) so that from any initial distribution, there exists some final distribution: $(A \mathbin{;} \bot) = \bot$. The fixpoint of our model uses Tarski's fixpoint theory and hence does not require the healthiness condition of Cauchy closure for continuity.

A specification A is called *nondeterministically closed* if $A = \square(A)$. Such a computation does not depend on original states. An assignment $t := e$ is closed if $e = e(t)$ does not depend on the original state s. A probabilistic choice $A \,{}_h\!\oplus\, B$ is closed if $h \in \mathbb{V}$ does not depend on the original state. Open nondeterminism $A \oplus B$ and sequential composition $A \mathbin{;} B$ are closed if both arguments are closed. Standard probabilistic programming corresponds to the sub-theory of nondeterministically closed specifications in the new model. Open specifications are useful if there exists some implementation mechanism (*e.g.* using a log file) that allows a computation to compensate against nondeterministic damage of undesirable errors in the past.

2.5 Algebraic Laws and Normal Form

The algebraic laws of this section are semantically sound. Law 1(1) and (2) are direct results of the healthiness conditions:

Law 1. (1) $\bot \mathbin{;} A = \bot = A \mathbin{;} \bot$ (2) $\text{II} \mathbin{;} A = A = A \mathbin{;} \text{II}$
(3) $t := e_1 \mathbin{;} t := e_2 = t := e_2 \circ e_1$.

The following laws identify expected properties of probabilistic choice:

Law 2
(1) $A \,{}_h\!\oplus\, A = A$ (2) $A \,{}_h\!\oplus\, B = B \,{}_{1-h}\!\oplus\, A$
(3) $(A \,{}_h\!\oplus\, B) \,{}_{h'}\!\oplus\, C = A \,{}_{hh'}\!\oplus\, (B \,{}_{h''}\!\oplus\, C)$ *where* $h'' = h'(1-h)/(1-hh')$, $h < 1$
(4) $(A \,{}_h\!\oplus\, B) \mathbin{;} C = (A \mathbin{;} C) \,{}_h\!\oplus\, (B \mathbin{;} C)$
(5) $t := e \mathbin{;} (A \,{}_h\!\oplus\, B) = (t := e \mathbin{;} A) \,{}_{h\circ e}\!\oplus\, (t := e \mathbin{;} B)$.

Pure nondeterministic choice $\oplus$ is similar to nondeterminism in the (non-probabilistic) sequential model. In particular, it satisfies right distributivity for sequential composition, which does not hold in previous probabilistic models, suggesting that the operator does not exploit history:

Law 3. (1) *The composition* $\oplus$ *is idempotent, commutative and associative.*
(2) *Sequential composition is associative and distributes over* $\oplus$.
(3) *The probabilistic choice* ${}_h\oplus$ *distributes over* $\oplus$.

Abort and skip are fixpoints of nondeterministic closure, which forces the current state to coincide with the original state for the assignment:

Law 4. (1) $\Box(\bot) = \bot$ (2) $\Box(\amalg) = \amalg$
(3) $\Box(t := e(s,t)) = t := e(t,t)$.

A nondeterministic closure resets the original state to be the initial state of its argument. Thus adjacent closures have the same effect as one closure. Closure distributes over convex combination with a current choosing distribution. If the second half of a sequential composition in a closure is closed, the outer closure can be decomposed into two closures in a sequential composition:

Law 5
(1) $\Box(A \,;\, B) = \Box(\Box(A) \,;\, B)$ (2) $\Box(A \,{}_h\oplus\, B) = \Box(\Box(A) \,{}_h\oplus\, B)$
(3) $\Box(A \oplus B) = \Box(\Box(A) \oplus B)$ (4) $\Box(A \,{}_v\oplus\, B) = \Box(A) \,{}_v\oplus\, \Box(B)$
(5) $\Box(A \,;\, \Box(B)) = \Box(A) \,;\, \Box(B)$.

The proof for Law 5(5) is included to illustrate the semantic reasoning style.

Proof. For all well-formed distributions d and d',

$[\Box(A \,;\, \Box(B))](d, d')$

$\Leftrightarrow$ definitions

$\exists d_0, d_1, d_2 \cdot A(\delta, d_1) \wedge B(\delta, d_2) \wedge [\Box(B)](d_1, d_0) \wedge d_0 = d_1 \otimes d_2 \wedge d' = d \otimes d_0$

$\Leftrightarrow$ predicate calculus

$\exists d_1, d_2 \cdot A(\delta, d_1) \wedge B(\delta, d_2) \wedge d' = d \otimes (d_1 \otimes d_2)$

$\Leftrightarrow$ associativity

$\exists d_1, d_2 \cdot A(\delta, d_1) \wedge B(\delta, d_2) \wedge d' = (d \otimes d_1) \otimes d_2$

$\Leftrightarrow$ predicate calculus

$\exists d_0, d_1, d_2 \cdot A(\delta, d_1) \wedge B(\delta, d_2) \wedge$
$[\Box(A)](d, d_0) \wedge d_0 = d \otimes d_1 \wedge [\Box(B)](d_0, d') \wedge d' = d_0 \otimes d_2$

$\Leftrightarrow$ definitions

$[\Box(A \,;\, \Box(B))](d, d')$.

Thus the two programs correspond to the same relation. □

Two usual laws hold for the weakest fixpoint operator:

Law 6. (1) $F(\mu F) = \mu F$ (1) *if* $A \subseteq F(A)$ *then* $A \subseteq \mu F$.

A program is called *finite* if it consists of only abort $\bot$, closed assignment $t := e(t)$, sequential composition, closed probabilistic choice $A \,{}_v\oplus\, B$, open nondeterminism $\oplus$ and nondeterministic closure $\Box$. A finite program is equal to $\bot$, $\amalg$ or can be written as:

$$\bigoplus_i \bigoplus_{j, v_{ij}} (t := e_{ij}(t,t) \,;\, \Box(N_{ij}))$$

where each N_{ij} is a program in normal form and for any i, we assume $\sum_j v_{ij} = 1$. Here we are using a collective form of probabilistic choices under which $A \;{}_v\!\oplus\; B$ is represented as $\bigoplus_{i,v_i} A_i$ where $i=1,2$, $v_1 = v$, $v_2 = 1-v$, $A_1 = A$ and $A_2 = B$. Adjacent probabilistic choices can be aggregated using Law 2(3). The following syntax represents the normal form formally.

Theorem 1. *Every finite program is semantically equal to a program in the following normal form* $\mathbf{N}$*:*

$$\begin{aligned} \mathbf{N} &::= \mathbf{M} \mid \mathbf{N} \oplus \mathbf{N} \\ \mathbf{M} &::= \bot \mid \amalg \mid (t := e(t) \,\text{;}\, \Box(\mathbf{N})) \mid \mathbf{M} \;{}_v\!\oplus\; \mathbf{M}. \end{aligned}$$

Proof. Notice that every program $M \in \mathbf{M}$ is closed according to Law 4(3) and Law 5(5).

1. Primitives are already in normal form: $\bot$, $t := e(t) \in \mathbf{N}$.
2. For two finite programs $N, N' \in \mathbf{N}$, their sequential composition $(N \,\text{;}\, N')$ can be reduced to normal form, because by induction:
   (a) If N is a primitive, $(N \,\text{;}\, N')$ is reducible according to Law 2(5) and Law 3(2).
   (b) Assume all $(N_i \,\text{;}\, N')$ are reducible. Then for $M, M' \in \mathbf{M}$ such that $M = \bigoplus_{i,v_i} (t := e_i \,\text{;}\, \Box(N_i))$ and $M' = \bigoplus_{j,v'_j} (t := e'_j \,\text{;}\, \Box(N'_j))$, according to Law 2(4), we have $(M \,\text{;}\, M') = \bigoplus_{i,v_i} (t := e_i \,\text{;}\, \Box(N_i) \,\text{;}\, M') = \bigoplus_{i,v_i} (t := e_i \,\text{;}\, \Box(N_i \,\text{;}\, M')) \in \mathbf{N}$. Thus in general $N = \bigoplus_i M_i$ and $N' = \bigoplus_j M'_j$, and $(N \,\text{;}\, N') = \bigoplus_{ij} (M_i \,\text{;}\, M'_j) \in \mathbf{N}$.
3. According to Law5(4), for all $M, M' \in \mathbf{M}$, we have $(M \;{}_v\!\oplus\; M') \in \mathbf{M}$. Thus for finite programs $N, N' \in \mathbf{N}$, their probabilistic choice is reducible: $(N \;{}_v\!\oplus\; N') = \bigoplus_{ij} (M_i \,\text{;}\, M'_j) \in \mathbf{N}$.
4. Obviously $(N \oplus N') \in \mathbf{N}$ for all $N, N' \in \mathbf{N}$.
5. If $N \in \mathbf{N}$, then $\Box(N) = \bigoplus_{i=1}^{1} \bigoplus_{j=1,v_1}^{1} (\amalg \,\text{;}\, \Box(N)) \in \mathbf{N}$ where $v_1 = 1$.

Thus every finite program can be transformed to normal form using just the laws, which are themselves sound in the semantic model. □

2.6 Program Verification

An assertion can be regarded as a predicate of a single distribution variable d. It is therefore more convenient to use a set of well-formed distributions to represent an assertion. If A is a program and $\mathbb{P}$, $\mathbb{Q} \subseteq \mathbb{D}$ are subsets of well-formed distributions, then annotation $(\mathbb{P} \;\; A \;\; \mathbb{Q}) \;\widehat{=}\; \forall d, d' \cdot (d \in \mathbb{P} \wedge A(d, d') \Rightarrow d' \in \mathbb{Q})$ states that if the computation A starts from an initial distribution in $\mathbb{P}$, then the final distributions that it yields lie in $\mathbb{Q}$. As our model is relational, if all assertions $\mathbb{P} \in \mathcal{P}$ and $\mathbb{Q} \in \mathcal{Q}$ in some set clusters satisfy $(\mathbb{P} \;\; A \;\; \mathbb{Q})$, so does their universal union: $(\bigcup \mathcal{P} \;\; A \;\; \bigcup \mathcal{Q})$.

3 Two Case Studies

In this section, we consider two case studies. In the first we revisit (1) and show that the new semantic model distinguishes the two sides, just like previous models; it illustrates the style of reasoning with the model. The second case study illustrates how the properties of realistic probabilistic programs are treated. The Monty-Hall problem is introduced and modified in a manner that demonstrates the power of the model.

3.1 The Example Mentioned in Introduction

Example (1) was originally studied in [4]. The difference between the two seemingly equal programs is due, semantically, to the fact that open nondeterministic choice can make different probabilistic choices from different original states. All commands normally share the same original state, but a nondeterministic closure can alter this and reset the original state, allowing the computation within the closure to act against the recorded probabilistic choice in the original state. We consider both informal and formal versions.

Let $V = \{ x, y \}$ be the set of all program variables whose values are boolean: $C = \{ 0, 1 \}$. To distinguish the two programs, we simply need to show that from some initial distribution (*i.e.* $\langle 0,0 \rangle$), the two programs may yield different sets of final distributions. The functional distribution $\langle 0,0 \rangle$ denotes that the probability is 1 for $x = 0$ and $y = 0$ regardless of original state.

We first consider the program on the left. The nondeterministic closure resets the distribution with the delta distribution $\langle x,y \rangle$, equating the current state to the original state. The open nondeterministic choice performs convex combination with an arbitrary factor distribution u between the results $\langle 0,y \rangle$ and $\langle 1,y \rangle$ of the assignments $x := 0$ and $x := 1$. The result of arbitrary convex combination is convoluted with the functional initial distribution. Convolution distributes over the convex combination. The effect is equivalent to choosing between $\langle 0,0 \rangle$ and $\langle 1,0 \rangle$ with an arbitrary constant factor. The fair probabilistic choice combines the result distributions with equal probability. For any constant factor, the overall probability for $x = y$ is always 1/2. Formally,

$$
\begin{array}{l}
\{ \langle 0,0 \rangle \} \\
\square \; \{ \langle x,y \rangle \} \\
\quad x := 0 \quad \{ \langle 0,y \rangle \} \quad \oplus \quad x := 1 \quad \{ \langle 1,y \rangle \} \\
\quad \{ \langle 0,y \rangle \; {}_u\!\oplus \; \langle 1,y \rangle \mid u \in \mathbb{U} \} \\
\{ \langle 0,0 \rangle \otimes (\langle 0,0 \rangle \; {}_u\!\oplus \; \langle 1,0 \rangle) \mid u \in \mathbb{U} \} \\
\{ \langle 0,0 \rangle \; {}_c\!\oplus \; \langle 1,0 \rangle \mid c \in \mathbb{C} \} \\
y := 0 \; {}_{\frac{1}{2}}\!\oplus \; y := 1 \\
\left\{ (\langle 0,0 \rangle \; {}_c\!\oplus \; \langle 1,0 \rangle) \; {}_{\frac{1}{2}}\!\oplus \; (\langle 0,1 \rangle \; {}_c\!\oplus \; \langle 1,1 \rangle) \mid c \in \mathbb{C} \right\} \\
\{ d \mid d \cdot [x = y] \; = \; c/2 + (1-c)/2 \; = \; 1/2 \}.
\end{array}
$$

The annotation for the probabilistic choice requires the universal union rule of Section 2.6 and:

$$\begin{array}{l}\{\,\langle 0,y\rangle\ {}_c\!\oplus\ \langle 1,y\rangle\,\}\\ \quad y:=0\quad \{\,\langle 0,0\rangle\ {}_c\!\oplus\ \langle 1,0\rangle\,\}\quad {}_{\frac{1}{2}}\!\oplus\quad y:=1\quad \{\,\langle 0,1\rangle\ {}_c\!\oplus\ \langle 1,1\rangle\,\}\\ \{\,(\langle 0,0\rangle\ {}_c\!\oplus\ \langle 1,0\rangle)\ {}_{\frac{1}{2}}\!\oplus\ (\langle 0,1\rangle\ {}_c\!\oplus\ \langle 1,1\rangle)\,\}.\end{array}$$

On the right-hand side of Example (1), the distribution before the nondeterministic choice has equal probability for distributions $\langle 0,0\rangle$ and $\langle 0,1\rangle$. That means the arbitrary uniform factor u's values at two original states $(0,0)$ and $(0,1)$ are exploited for convex combination in the subsequent nondeterminism. So no non-zero probability for $x=y$ can be *guaranteed*. Formally,

$$\begin{array}{l}\{\,\langle 0,0\rangle\,\}\quad y:=0\ {}_{\frac{1}{2}}\!\oplus\ y:=1\quad \left\{\,\langle 0,0\rangle\ {}_{\frac{1}{2}}\!\oplus\ \langle 0,1\rangle\,\right\}\\ \sqsupseteq\ \{\,\langle x,y\rangle\,\}\\ \qquad x:=0\quad \{\,\langle 0,y\rangle\,\}\quad \oplus\quad x:=1\quad \{\,\langle 1,y\rangle\,\}\\ \quad \{\,\langle 0,y\rangle\ {}_u\!\oplus\ \langle 1,y\rangle\ \mid\ u\in\mathbb{U}\,\}\\ \left\{\,(\langle 0,0\rangle\ {}_{\frac{1}{2}}\!\oplus\ \langle 0,1\rangle)\otimes(\langle 0,y\rangle\ {}_u\!\oplus\ \langle 1,y\rangle)\ \mid\ u\in\mathbb{U}\,\right\}\\ \left\{\,(\langle 0,0\rangle\ {}_{c_1}\!\oplus\ \langle 1,1\rangle)\ {}_{\frac{1}{2}}\!\oplus\ (\langle 1,0\rangle\ {}_{c_2}\!\oplus\ \langle 1,1\rangle)\ \mid\ c_1,c_2\in\mathbb{C}\,\right\}\\ \left\{\,d\ \mid\ d\cdot[x=y]=c_1\ {}_{\frac{1}{2}}\!\oplus\ (1-c_2),\ c_1,c_2\in\mathbb{C}\,\right\}.\end{array}$$

3.2 The Monty-Hall Problem

This case study illustrates how the nondeterministic demon and the computation can both benefit from the extra information recorded in the original state. The last variation of the case study is not captured by previous models.

The famous Monty-Hall puzzle (in this context, from [8]) describes a game show with a host, a contestant and three closed doors: one of them hides a car, which the contestant wishes to win, whilst the other two hide goats, which the contestant intends to avoid. The contestant begins by choosing a door, but it is not opened immediately. Instead, the host opens a door different from the one just chosen by the contestant and then offers the contestant the option of switching choices to one of the other two unopened doors. Contrary to common perception that the chance of winning the car is unchanged by whether or not the contestant switches, the correct move is to switch, and it doubles the overall chance from 1/3 (independent initial right choice among three) to 2/3 (initial wrong choice to be corrected with the host's assistance).

This puzzle and its solution involve both probability and nondeterminism. Let the variable x denote the host's initial choice (in program HC) of the door (number 1, 2 or 3) for the car, which is completely unknown to the contestant:

$$HC\ \widehat{=}\ x:=1\sqcap(x:=2\sqcap x:=3).$$

The variable y denotes the contestant's choice. The contestant, with no knowledge of the position of the car, chooses fairly among the three:

$$PC \;\widehat{=}\; y := 1 \;{}_{\frac{1}{3}}\!\oplus\; (y := 2 \;{}_{\frac{1}{2}}\!\oplus\; y := 3).$$

Note that this is one possible strategy for the contestant, and a program may well adopt a different (and possibly bad) strategy. The contestant's only knowledge is that the host chooses the door before the contestant's initial choice, and that the host is not prescient. The host's subsequent door opening (denoted with variable z) depends on the contestant's initial choice. If the choice is right, then the host chooses one of the two remaining goat doors; otherwise, the host chooses the only remaining goat door:

$$HC1 \;\widehat{=}\; (z := goat_1(x) \sqcap z := goat_2(x)) \;{}_{[x=y]}\!\oplus\; z := goat(x, y)$$

where the function $goat_1(x)$ returns the smaller door number other than x, $goat_2(x)$ returns the larger number, and $goat(x, y)$, defined only when $x \neq y$, returns the only other number. For example, $goat_2(2) = 3$ and $goat(1, 2) = 3$. The contestant's second choice results either in stay $ST \;\widehat{=}\; \mathrm{II}$ or switch $SW \;\widehat{=}\; y := goat(y, z)$. The game corresponds to the computation:

$$HC \,;\, PC \,;\, HC1 \,;\, ?\,.$$

A routine calculation guarantees probability 1/3 if the question mark is replaced by ST but 2/3 if that is replaced by SW. Note that the position of the car must not depend on the contestant's initial choice. The host's placement of the car *after* the contestant's choice is:

$$PC \,;\, HC \,;\, HC1 \,;\, ?\,.$$

It is *unknown* whether the (nondeterministic) host places the car against or for the contestant's interests, or indeed chooses neutrally. As a result, no matter what the contestant does in the end, the strategy cannot guarantee even a small probability of success. That phenomenon is modelled correctly by both this and previous models.

Now consider a less honest host who, though setting the car before the contestant, has detected the contestant's tendency to switch. He secretely tries to move the car to the door of the contestant's first choice with probability 1/3 (no move if the contestant is right):

$$HC2 \;\widehat{=}\; (x := y \;{}_{\frac{1}{3}}\!\oplus\; \mathrm{II}).$$

The host performs this dishonest act after opening a door but before the contestant's final choice:

$$HC \,;\, PC \,;\, HC1 \,;\, HC2 \,;\, ?\,.$$

Now the probability of initial correctness and staying with the original choice is increased to $1/3 + (2/3 \times 1/3) = 5/9$, while the probability of success for switching drops to 4/9.

However, an alert contestant decides to stay whenever he detects any noise of car movement (*i.e.* detecting a change of state; we assume that the host is not devious enough to move the car around behind the same door) but to switch otherwise:

$$AC \ \widehat{=}\ SW \ _{\delta}\!\oplus\ ST.$$

The contestant performs that scrutiny by comparing the *original state*, immediately after the host opens a door, with the *current state* before the final decision:

$$HC \ ⨾\ PC \ ⨾\ HC1 \ ⨾\ \Box(HC2 \ ⨾\ AC)\,.$$

The car moves with probability $2/3 \times 1/3 = 2/9$ when the contestant's initial choice was wrong. It is always favourable for the contestant to stay after detecting noise. Switching yields probability $2/3{\times}2/3 = 4/9$ of success for the contestant's unswitched initial wrong choice (greater than the success probability $1/3$ for staying). The overall probability of success of AC is $2/9 + 4/9 = 2/3$. Formally:

$\{\,\langle 1,1,1\rangle\,\}$
$\Box\Box\,\{\,\langle x,y,z\rangle\,\}$ Host's choice
$\quad x := 1 \oplus (x := 2 \oplus x := 3)\ ⨾$
$\{\,\langle 1,1,1\rangle \ _{c_1}\!\oplus (\langle 2,1,1\rangle \ _{c_2}\!\oplus \langle 3,1,1\rangle) \mid c_1, c_2, \in \mathbb{C}\,\}$
$y := 1 \ _{\frac{1}{3}}\!\oplus (y := 2 \ _{\frac{1}{2}}\!\oplus y := 3)\ ⨾$ Player's choice
$\{\, d \mid d \cdot [x = y] = 1/3\,\}$
$(z := goat_1(x) \sqcap z := goat_2(x)) \ _{[x=y]}\!\oplus\ z := goat(x,y)\ ⨾$ Host opens a door
$\{\, d \mid d \cdot [x = y] = 1/3 \wedge d \cdot [y \neq x = goat(y,z)] = 2/3\,\}$
$\Box\,\{\,\langle x,y,z\rangle\,\}$
$\quad x := y \ _{\frac{1}{3}}\!\oplus\ \text{II}\ ⨾$ Car move
$\quad \left\{\, \langle y,y,z\rangle \ _{\frac{1}{3}}\!\oplus \langle x,y,z\rangle \,\right\}$
$\quad y := goat(y,z) \ _{\delta}\!\oplus\ \text{II}$ Alert contestant's choice
$\left\{\, d \mid d \cdot [x = y] = \frac{2}{3} \times \frac{1}{3} + \frac{2}{3} \times \frac{2}{3} = 2/3 \,\right\}.$

4 Related Work

This work is most closely related to the distributional model of He *et al.* [4] which appeared more than two decades after Rabin's demonstration [11] of the remarkable effectiveness of probabilistic algorithms. The obvious difference is that in our model distributions are conditional (depending on two states rather than just one). That has an interesting consequence for the definition of sequential composition. In [4] the definition is complicated by having to take the average over each intermediate distribution in the composition; our definition is simply composition of binary relations as a result of our use of conditional distributions. That makes our definition more properly 'relational' in the style of UTP [5]. Rabin's paper was followed more closely by a succession of interesting probabilistic algorithms and of logics to facilitate model checking of probabilistic properties. For example Hansson and Jonsson [3] incorporate both time and probability. However in most of that work (demonic) nondeterminism is *replaced* by probabilism.

Our interest is in semantic models and (sound) laws for the top-down incremental derivation of an implementation from its specification. That requires nondeterminism (seen as arising from specification and modelling) *as well as* probabilism. McIver and Morgan's textbook [8] provides the fundamentals and indicates how a theory in the Dijkstra-Hoare style unfolds. It also contains Galois connections relating He *et al.*'s distributional model to the relational and predicate-transformer models of nonprobabilistic sequential programs and to the expectation-transformer model of probabilistic (nondeterministic) programs.

In order to handle original states we have adopted the view standard in mathematics but less so in computation where it has great relevance—that a conditional probability $P(A|B)$ may be used to update knowledge about $P(A)$ (for example by Bayes's formula) in the light of further, in our case sequentially provided, information. The idea of using conditional probabilities for a semantics of probabilistic programs, is not new. Incisive use of it has been made, notably, by Panangaden [10] and Ying [17]. Pananganden makes a convincing case that conditional probability distributions are the counterpart—in general—of 'probabilistic relations'. His treatment is aimed at the more general continuous case, but his insights apply here. It would be interesting to calculate his duality starting from our (nonstandard) state-based model to see what transformer model results; also to apply, to the model proposed here, the ideas captured in those extensions to 'probabilistic' predicates or relations, both at the level of the types of our semantics and in the monadic setting. Ying, on the other hand, uses conditional probability as the basis for a semantics of guarded-command-like programs with angelic choice and (of course) demonic choice but without recursion, iteration or explicit probabilistic choice that has the strength to support a refinement calculus. His models extend the distributional and expectation transformer models, by considering instead probabilistic predicates. As a result his semantics makes finer distinctions between programs and he is able to introduce a refinement relation that is probabilistic rather than Boolean in nature.

Varacca and Winskel [16] give an elegant analysis of how the monads for probability and nondeterminism might be combined. They contrast the distributive combination of the two (used, for instance, by Mislove *et al.* [7]) with their combination after modifying the probabilistic monad to contain only affine identities (hence ensuring the result can be lifted to the power set).

As indicated by our treatment of the Monty Hall problem and its variations, a framework incorporating probability and nondeterminism addresses issues of secrecy and information flow. Most closely related to our approach in that direction is the work of Morgan [9]. Whilst our nondeterminism has limited memory, his has limited vision, since program state is separated into visible and hidden parts; but then his novel refinement relation becomes the primary tool (whilst we retain the standard equivalence connecting nondeterminism and refinement:

$P \sqsubseteq Q$ iff $P = P \sqcap Q$). Morgan's approach is demonstrated on Chaum's 'Dining Cryptographers' and Rivest's 'Oblivious Transfer'. Pananganden's work mentioned above also provides an approach to the analysis of information flow in security protocols; see for instance [1] which contains further references.

There is a very much greater literature devoted to the difficult topic of probability in reactive and parallel programs. See [14] for a survey to 2004, in the setting of probabilistic automata. Inevitably some of those contributions are relevant to the sequential case. Typically there demonic nondeterminism is viewed as freedom to be exploited by a scheduler [13]. Whilst true as far is that is able to be exploited in the sequential case (for 'scheduler' read 'implementer'), here it is not the overriding consideration, which is the interaction between probabilistic choice and sequential composition. Focusing on that, the sequential case might be viewed as a convenient starting point for a later study of reactive nondeterministic and probabilistic computation, in which the interaction between nondeterminism and probability is studied without the concerns of deadlock, divergence and so on. Contributions to the reactive case that will no doubt be influential due to the combination of nondeterminism and probability include the work of Mislove *et al.* [7] and Tix *et al.* [15] which construct models of process algebra with nondeterminism and probability, as a solution to a domain equation using the Plotkin powerdomain. Also the probabilistic automata of Segala [13] embody important principles. As theories for reactive probabilistic systems account largely for the various forms of 'process testing', they appear currently to be surprisingly divergent from those for sequential probabilistic systems.

5 Conclusion and Further Work

This paper has introduced a relational probabilistic model containing both probabilistic choice and nondeterministic choice. The standard demonic nondeterministic choice is decomposed into two operators: one that performs convex closure and the other that performs nondeterministic closure. The introduction of original states and consequent use of conditional probability distributions help to relate sequential specifications with some past state, whilst at the same time ensuring that sequential composition remains relational.

That clarifies what nondeterminism really does, and facilitates further generalisations. One such is to allow commands, like assignment and probabilistic choice, to observe original state. That allows a later computation to perform compensation back to the starting point of the closest nondeterministic closure. Another possibility is to strengthen the manner in which a nondeterministic choice can exploit further history by introducing more original states; then an open nondeterministic choice can act against the probabilistic choices at several points set by nested nondeterministic closures. Such generalisations become possible only after we explicitly reveal what nondeterministic choices really do and they have, as we have seen, important application beyond the realm of probabilistic programs (for example in the design of security protocols, where the adversary can be regarded as nondeterministic if it is unknown whether it can observe certain information and take advantage of the observation).

Sequential composition of programs has been modelled as composition of binary relations, but at the expense of a mild complexity in the semantics. In the distributional model, the reverse is the case: the definition of sequential composition requires imposition of healthiness conditions. As a result, our version may prove easier in the so-far-unachieved goal of unifying probabilism with other programming constructs in the style of *Unifying Theories of Programming*, [5].

References

1. Chatzikokolakis, K., Palamidessi, C., Panangaden, P.: On the Bayes risk in information-hiding protocols. In: Proceedings of the 20th IEEE Computer Security Foundations, pp. 341–354. IEEE Computer Society, Los Alamitos (2007)
2. Fernandez, L., Piron, R.: Should She Switch? A Game Theoretic Analysis of the Monty Hall Problem. Mathematics Magizine 72(3), 214–217 (1999)
3. Hansson, H., Jonsson, B.: A logic for reasoning about time and reliability. Formal Aspects of Computing 6(5), 512–535 (1994)
4. He, J., Seidel, K., McIver, A.K.: Probabilistic models for the guarded command language. Science of Computer Programming 28(2), 171–192 (1997)
5. Hoare, C.A.R., He, J.: Unifying Theories of Programming. Prentice Hall, Englewood Cliffs (1998)
6. McIver, A.K., Morgan, C.C.: Abstraction, Refinement and Proof for Probabilistic Systems. Monographs in Computer Science. Springer, Heidelberg (2005)
7. Mislove, M., Ouaknine, J., Worrell, J.: Axioms for probability and nondeterminism. ENTCS 96, 7–28 (2004)
8. Morgan, C.C., McIver, A.K., Seidel, K.: Probabilistic Predicate Transformers. ACM TOPLAS 18(3), 325–353 (1996)
9. Morgan, C.C.: The shadow knows: Refinement of ignorance in sequential programs. In: Uustalu, T. (ed.) MPC 2006. LNCS, vol. 4014, pp. 359–378. Springer, Heidelberg (2006)
10. Pananganden, P.: Probabilistic relations. In: Baier, C., Huth, M., Kwiatkowska, M.Z., Ryan, M. (eds.) PROBMIV 1998, pp. 59–74 (1998)
11. Rabin, M.O.: Probabilistic algorithms. In: Traub, J.F. (ed.) Algorithms and Complexity: New Directions and Recent Results, pp. 21–39. Academic Press, London (1976)
12. Robinson, D., Morgan, C.C.: Restricted Demonic Choice for Modular Probabilistic Programs. In: ESSLI PLRC Workshop 1998 (1998)
13. Segala, R., Lynch, N.: Probabilistic simulations for probabilistic processes. In: Jonsson, B., Parrow, J. (eds.) CONCUR 1994. LNCS, vol. 836, pp. 1–43. Springer, Heidelberg (1994)
14. Sokolova, A., de Vink, E.: Probabilistic automata: system types, parallel composition and comparison. In: Baier, C., Haverkort, B.R., Hermanns, H., Katoen, J.-P., Siegle, M. (eds.) Validation of Stochastic Systems. LNCS, vol. 2925, pp. 1–43. Springer, Heidelberg (2004)
15. Tix, R., Keimel, K., Plotkin, G.: Semantic domains for combining probability and non-determinism. ENTCS 222, 3–99 (2009)
16. Varacca, D., Winskel, G.: Distributing probability over non-determinism. Mathematical Structures in Computer Science 16(1), 87–113 (2006)
17. Ying, M.: Reasoning about probabilistic sequential programs in a probabilistic logic. Acta Informatica 39, 315–389 (2003)

Towards an Operational Semantics for Alloy

Theophilos Giannakopoulos[1], Daniel J. Dougherty[1], Kathi Fisler[1], and Shriram Krishnamurthi[2]

[1] Department of Computer Science, WPI
[2] Computer Science Department, Brown University

Abstract. The Alloy modeling language has a mathematically rigorous denotational semantics based on relational algebra. Alloy specifications often represent operations on a state, suggesting a transition-system semantics. Because Alloy does not intrinsically provide a notion of state, however, this interpretation is only implicit in the relational-algebra semantics underlying the Alloy Analyzer.

In this paper we demonstrate the subtlety of representing state in Alloy specifications. We formalize a natural notion of transition semantics for state-based specifications and show examples of specifications in this class for which analysis based on relational algebra can induce false confidence in designs. We characterize the class of facts that guarantees that Alloy's analysis is sound for state-transition systems, and offer a sufficient syntactic condition for membership in this class. We offer some practical evaluation of the utility of this syntactic discipline and show how it provides a foundation for program synthesis from Alloy.

1 Introduction

Alloy [1], a popular relational modeling language, provides a syntax reminiscent of class-based programming languages, and its semantics is essentially equivalent to first-order logic with transitive closure. The language is accompanied by an Analyzer; this explores whether a specification has models through compilation into SAT problems and checking for satisfiability. Users can employ a graphical browser to explore instances of models and counter-examples to claims.

Though Alloy relations are powerful enough to encompass many common modeling techniques, Alloy does not have a native executable or machine model. For instance, the Alloy book says:

> *Typically an instance represents a state, or a pair of states (corresponding to execution of an operation), or a execution trace. The language has no built-in notion of state machines, however, ...*
> —*Software Abstractions* [1, page 258]

This is in contrast to B [2] and Z [3], for each of which a notion of state machine is built into the language. Alloy's flexibility is one of its main selling points: it supports a variety of idioms. However, this means the user of Alloy must always be vigilant: they must first choose an idiom and then ensure that they are constantly faithful to it. The language itself does not provide any special support for encoding or checking conformance to specific idioms. Furthermore, failure to adhere is punished not explicitly

A. Cavalcanti and D. Dams (Eds.): FM 2009, LNCS 5850, pp. 483–498, 2009.

but implicitly: in the best case through unexpected outcomes, and in the worst case by incorrect decisions based on the Analyzer's output.

Our first contribution is to show that representing state in Alloy specifications is more subtle than it appears at first glance. We present what might seem to be the obvious operational semantics, the one that a designer would intuit based on the descriptions in, for instance, the Alloy book. But we show that this fails: there are specifications in this class that are very naturally viewed as representing executions whose logical (Alloy) semantics is not faithful to the operational semantics. The consequences of this misalignment are drastic: there are situations in which the Alloy Analyzer will unavoidably fail to report invalid assertions about the code and situations in which the Analyzer will give the designer spurious simulations of specified operations that cannot in fact be implemented.[1]

Based on this analysis, we offer a proposal to rectify the situation. Concretely, we give a characterization of the class of facts for which we can guarantee that Alloy's analysis is sound for state-transition systems, and we offer a sufficient syntactic condition on the form of facts that guarantees that they are in this class.[2]

Experienced Alloy users might argue that they would not be stumped by these examples (though in our experience, even expert Alloy users do not immediately spot the problems). One shouldn't, however, have to be an expert to use a tool safely. We identify the difficulties and explain why things go wrong, and most importantly prescribe a discipline which, if followed, ensures that specifications will not go wrong. We give a precise definition of a state-based modeling idiom with accompanying guarantees, obeying the discipline "satisfiability iff implementability".

Specifications of stateful systems are useful in their own right, and they would be especially useful if they can support not only analysis but also synthesis of executable code. A synthesizer must, however, maintain a sound relationship between transition system specifications and the executable code it produces. This is especially interesting to us due to our prior work on Alchemy [4], a synthesizer that generates executable libraries over databases from Alloy specifications. Our observations while designing Alchemy about the difficulties of pinning down the meaning of stateful specifications inspired this work. But it should be stressed that the problem of reconciling the denotational and operational semantics of a language like Alloy is of fundamental importance to analysis itself, and is independent of any attempt at automatic code generation.

Contributions To summarize:

- we formalize a natural way to extract transition-system executions from relational-algebra instances;
- we show examples of specifications in this class for which analysis based on relational algebra can induce false confidence in designs;

[1] It is important to note that these are mismatches relative to the *semantics* of Alloy [1, Appendix C] and independent of the bounded-scope used by the Analyzer.

[2] *Facts* are statements used to eliminate invalid models—and hence always true in the resulting models—whereas *assertions* are statements that may be true or false.

- we characterize of the class of facts that guarantees that Alloy's analysis is sound for state-transition systems and offer a sufficient syntactic condition for ensuring this behavior; and
- we offer some practical evaluation of the utility of this syntactic discipline.

A by-product of these contributions is a firm foundation for establishing correctness of a synthesizer for state-based specifications [4,5].

2 Examples

We use a series of examples to illustrate the potential pitfalls in analysis and modelling of specifications with both relational and stateful interpretations. Figure 1 shows a sample Alloy specification. Signatures define domains and relations over domains: this example defines two domains (*State* and *Data*) and a relation *lastUsed* that maps each element of *State* to an element of *Data* (the domains are treated as unary relations): such a collection of domains and relations determines an *instance*, or for emphasis, a *relational algebra instance*. Facts capture closed formulas that must hold of every instance of the domains and relations specified through signatures. A common idiom for stateful specifications uses predicates to model operations over pre- and post-instances of some state object (a prime conventionally connotes the post-state): this example contains an operation *updateLastUsed* that caches the last datum accessed.

We are interested here in examples in which the Alloy Analyzer (which enforces the relational semantics) yields results that contradict stateful interpretations of the example. The Analyzer supports two kinds of analysis: simulation (running a predicate to obtain a satisfying instance) and checking (verifying that an assertion is valid of all instances). Both are important: as Jackson notes [6, page 4], simulation catches errors of overconstraint, while checking detects underconstraint. The soundness of both forms is essential to Alloy's contributions: quoting Jackson [op cit., page 16], "The analysis is guaranteed to be sound, in the sense that a model returned will indeed be a model. There are therefore no false alarms, and samples are always legitimate (and demonstrate consistency of the invariant or operation)".

In the context of stateful interpretations, simulating a predicate (such as *updateLastUsed* from Figure 1) should correspond to the execution of some code that induces the effect of the predicate (updating the cache). Notions of satisfiability and implementability for predicates are therefore at the heart of our explorations. While formal definitions are given later (Section 3), for now we rely on the following informal characterizations. Let p be a predicate (for example *updateLastUsed* in Figure 1) in a specification $\mathcal{A}$; p has a set of parameters (for example s, s', and d in *updateLastUsed*) and a *body* (the remainder of the predicate text). We say that p is *satisfiable* if there is a relational algebra model of the facts of the specification and a binding of the parameters to values such that the body of p holds. We say that p is *implementable* if, when viewed as a procedure, it can be realized as a transition—between nodes bound to s and s'—in a transition system in which each node is an instance satisfying the facts.

Suppose we ask the Alloy Analyzer to check the *newStamp* assertion of Figure 1. This assertion is not valid: there is nothing in the specification as written that requires

```
sig State {lastUsed : Data}
sig Data {stamp : Clock}
sig Clock {}

// remembering a new most recently used value
pred updateLastUsed [s, s' : State, d : Data] {
    s'.lastUsed = d and s.lastUsed != d}

// statically inconsistent with updateLastUsed
fact storeOne {#lastUsed = 1}

// not valid
assert newStamp { all s, s' : State| all d : Data |
    updateLastUsed [s,s',d] implies s'.d.stamp != s.d.stamp}
```

Fig. 1. An Alloy specification that is implementable but not satisfiable

stamps to be fresh. But rather than generate a countermodel to the assertion, the Analyzer will report that *newStamp* "may be valid." Since the Analyzer always works with a bounded domain size it is properly modest in suggesting validity. But in fact the Analyzer cannot find a countermodel for *newStamp* even in principle. The problem is that the *updateLastUsed* predicate is unsatisfiable. Thus, since no instance satisfies the antecedent of the implication in *newStamp*, the assertion is in fact valid.

Why is *updateLastUsed* not satisfiable? At first glance, it seems to be an entirely reasonable predicate specification. And indeed the natural implementation of this specification seems to obey the predicate body as well as the *storeOne* fact, which expresses the constraint that exactly one item should be cached via *lastUsed*: each call to *updateLastUsed* replaces the value of *lastUsed* in the current state. Unfortunately, the specification as written is not satisfiable because the *storeOne* fact captures more than the author intended. Under the Alloy semantics, the fact constrains instances to a total of one *lastUsed* value across *all* states, not *per* state. Indeed, the effect of writing *#lastUsed = 1* is to constrain Alloy models of this specification to conflate what are really two distinct states (pre and post), whereas in an imperative implementation only one is ever active at a time. (If the author had written *#lastUsed* = 1 as a "signature fact", that is, within the paragraph declaring *State*, then under the Alloy semantics this constraint would be treated as syntactic sugar for the constraint that for all States *s*, *s.lastUsed* has one item. The above scenario would arise if an author mistakenly moved a signature fact into a standalone fact.) This highlights the first pitfall to using the Analyzer to reason about a stateful system:

> **False confidence in assertion-checking:** the Analyzer cannot generate countermodels for invalid assertions about implementable predicates that are unsatisfiable under the facts.

Figure 2 shows a richer model of caches, in which each state contains a cache that maps keys to data. Keys are unique within each state. Adding a cache entry with a new key

```
sig State {cache : set Key → Data}
sig Key {}
sig Data {}

fact cacheKeysUnique {
    all s : State | no k : Key | #s.cache[k] > 1}

// cache d under a key that is not used in s
pred addEntryNewKey [s, s' : State, d : Data] {
    some k : Key | no s.cache[k] and
    s'.cache = s.cache + k→d}

fact oddCached {#cache = 1 or #cache = 3 or #cache = 5}
```

Fig. 2. An Alloy specification that is satisfiable but not implementable

inserts a datum into the cache using a key that was unused in the previous state. To limit the cache size, the specification author includes a fact that the number of cache lines must always be a small odd number (we use concrete numbers in light of Alloy's domain-size restrictions). Under Alloy's semantics, this predicate is satisfiable. It is not, however, implementable: using the *addEntryNewKey* operation, the number of cache lines will alternate between being odd and even in successive states. The fact, then, is not an invariant in the implementation. This illustrates another pitfall when reasoning about stateful specifications:

> **False confidence in simulation:** a design can include a predicate that cannot—in the context of the stated facts—correspond to any transition at all, yet this impossibility will go undetected by the analysis, in the sense that the Analyzer will build a satisfying instance without complaint.

These two examples exploit a similar problem: the Alloy specification includes a fact on the full model, rather than just facts on individual states. If the specification happens to talk about multiple points in time, special care must be taken to separate them. Imperative interpretations, in contrast, view only a single state at a time. In effect, the implementation views facts at a different level of granularity than the specification.

The lack of alignment between implementability and satisfiability under conventional relational algebra semantics exposes potentially serious problems for lightweight formal methods. Implementability without satisfiability implies that designers cannot reason about their designs through their specifications (once a model is unsatisfiable, the designer does not get useful feedback about its other properties). Satisfiability without implementability implies that assertions verified about the model might not hold of an actual implementation, so the verification effort has been wasted.

3 Transition Semantics

In order to formalize (and address) the problems with assertion checking over unimplementable predicates, we need a transition-system semantics for relational specifications, as well as characterizations of relational specifications for which those semantics yield meaningful results.

An Alloy *specification* $\mathcal{A} = (Sigs, Facts, Preds)$ is given by a set of signatures, facts, and predicates. It will be convenient to assume that all constraints on signatures are expressed as elements of *Facts* (this is without loss of generality).

The signature and facts in a specification provide the setting and constraints under which predicates and assertions are explored.

3.1 State-Based Frameworks

In a state-based modeling setting the most typical use of facts is to express state invariants, and this will be reflected in the semantics we define. But facts are not *necessarily* state-invariants: a naturally-occurring example is the use of trace constraints. For example one might impose the constraint that certain properties hold in the initial state of a system (such a property is not an invariant) or the constraint that all transitions must be an operation specified by one of the predicates (such a property is not a property of individual states).

So a transition system must obey two different kinds of constraints: local constraints on the states, and global constraints across states. We recognize this distinction in the following definition.

Definition 1. *An Alloy* framework $\mathcal{F} = (Sigs, Facts, Inv)$ *is given by a set of signatures, a set of facts, and a distinguished subset of the facts, the "state invariant" facts.*

This designation of certain facts as state invariants is not part of the Alloy language definition. So for each Alloy specification the semantics we develop in this paper is parametrized by the author's intentions as to which constraints in the set *Facts* are to be treated as invariants.

Our work on Alchemy [4] shows that identifying the updates required by relational specifications is the key challenge to interpreting Alloy specifications statefully. In particular, the relational semantics of arbitrary terms over the pre- and post-state atoms in predicates allow substantial leeway in how to perform an update. This work aligns relational and stateful interpretations using some restrictions on signatures and facts. These require some terminology:

Fix a distinguished signature, which we will call *State*. We call an Alloy relational type *immutable* if it has no occurrences of the *State* signature.

Definition 2. *An Alloy framework is a* state-based framework *if the type of each declared relation name is either immutable or is a sum of types of the form* $State \rightarrow A_1 \rightarrow \cdots \rightarrow A_n$ *where each* A_i *is immutable.*

The restriction that the *State* signature be the leftmost sig occurring is a matter of notational convenience; the essential requirement is that no relation name have more than one occurrence of *State*. For a formal treatment of the notion of type of a relation name see Edwards et al. [7].

Trace-based reasoning over states is typically done in the context of the Alloy *util/ordering* module: if the specification orders the *State* with this module then the functions *first*, *next*, and *last* are available. In this case the types of these functions violate the conditions in Definition 2. But such specifications are still considered "state-based" since *first, last,* and *next* are not "declared" in the specification. Indeed the semantics of these functions will be hard-wired into the transition semantics below.

For the rest of the paper we assume that all specifications are state-based.

3.2 Transition Systems

We base our operational semantics on transition systems. In anticipation of the use of the *util/ordering* module, we define ordered transition systems.

To avoid subtleties having to do with underlying data models we take the states in our transition systems to be relational algebras precisely of the sort that the Alloy Analyzer constructs; these can be viewed as database instances. In this case the transitions between states are the obvious database updates transforming one state to another.

If we are to think of the individual instances as each representing one state of the application we should certainly expect that each of the instances has a unique atom in the extension of the *State* signature name. And if we take seriously the notion that the *State* signature is supposed to capture the data that changes, we should require that the extensions of the immutable relation names should be the same in each state. This motivates the notion of a *coherent* set of instances, a set of instances comprising the set of nodes in a transition system.

Definition 3. *A set $\mathcal{Q}$ of instances is said to be* coherent *if*

- *each immutable relation name r has the same interpretation in each instance: $\forall I, I' \in \mathcal{Q} \,.\, I(r) = I'(r)$,*
- *each instance has a unique atom in the State signature: $\forall I \in \mathcal{Q}. |I(State)| = 1$, and*
- *no two instances have the same state atom: if $I \neq I'$ then $I(State) \neq I'(State)$.*

We do not assume that the set $\mathcal{Q}$ is finite in this definition.

Definition 4. *Let $\mathcal{F} = (Sigs, Facts, Inv)$ be a framework. A* transition system *$\mathcal{T}$ over the signatures of $\mathcal{F}$ is a pair $\langle Q, \delta \rangle$, where Q is a coherent set of relational algebra instances whose signature is given by Sigs, and $\delta \subseteq Q \times Q$ is a transition relation.*

$\mathcal{T}$ is an ordered transition system *if it has a designated linear ordering next on states and distinguished first and last states.*

Note that in the definition above we have not insisted that $\mathcal{T}$ obey the constraints imposed by the facts of $\mathcal{F}$. In fact we need to do some work to make sense of that notion, since transition systems are not themselves relational algebras, and so do not come equipped with a way to evaluate relational algebra expressions and formulas. The result of this work will be Definition 7.

We turn to the task of defining how to interpret expressions and formulas over $\mathcal{F}$ in a transition system. To do so we use a natural construction that allows us to treat a finite transition system as a single relational-algebra instance.

Definition 5 (Merging). *Let $\mathcal{Q}$ be a finite coherent set of instances. The instance $\sqcup\mathcal{Q}$ is given by setting, for each relation name r,*

$$\sqcup\mathcal{Q}(r) = \bigcup\{I(r) \mid I \in \mathcal{Q}\}$$

When $\mathcal{T} = (\mathcal{Q}, \delta)$ is a transition system it will be convenient to write $\sqcup\mathcal{T}$ for $\sqcup\mathcal{Q}$.

Observe that the notion of merging is well-defined only by virtue of our assumption that the instances in question are coherent. (Indeed, we note that the "$\bigcup$" in Definition 5 is somewhat of a red herring for immutable relations, since they have the same value in each instance of Q.)

Definition 6. *Let $\mathcal{T} = (Q, \delta)$ be a transition system.*

The value $\mathcal{T}(e)$ of an expression e is the set of tuples that is the value of e in the relational algebra $\sqcup\mathcal{T}$.

Say that sentence σ is true in $\mathcal{T}$, written $\mathcal{T} \models_{TS} \sigma$ if σ is true in $\sqcup\mathcal{T}$ in the ordinary relational algebra sense, that is, if $\mathcal{T} \models_{RA} \sigma$

We are now ready for the key definition for the transition-system semantics of a state-based framework, the notion of a *transition system for framework $\mathcal{F}$*.

Definition 7. *Let $\mathcal{F} = (Sigs, Facts, Inv)$ be a framework. A* transition system for $\mathcal{F}$ *is a transition system $\mathcal{T}$ over the signatures of $\mathcal{F}$ such that*

- *each node I satisfies each fact in Inv, and*
- *$\sqcup\mathcal{T}$ satisfies each fact not in Inv.*

If $\mathcal{F}$ includes an ordering on State then we require that $\mathcal{T}$ be an ordered transition system.

Definition 7 highlights the distinction between the facts that are intended to be viewed as state invariants and those that play the role of global constraints on the system. Assertions and the bodies of predicates that define operations must obviously be able to make reference to more than one state and so must be evaluated globally, that is, over the merge of the nodes as described in Definition 5.

The Transition Semantics of Predicates. For those predicates written in order to define operations we may define their transition-system semantics as follows.

The meaning of a predicate p is a *set* of transitions because p can be applied to different nodes, with different bindings of the parameters, of course, but also because predicates typically underspecify actions: different implementations of a predicate can yield different outcomes I' on the same input I. These should all be considered acceptable as long as the relation between pre- and post-states is described by the predicate.

Definition 8. *Fix an Alloy framework $\mathcal{F}$, and let p be a predicate over $\mathcal{F}$ with the property that p has among its parameters exactly two variables `s` and `s'` of type State. Let $\mathcal{T}$ be a transition system for $\mathcal{F}$. The meaning $[\![p]\!]^{\mathcal{T}}$ of p in $\mathcal{T}$ is the set of triples $\langle I, I', \eta \rangle$ such that*

- *η maps the parameters of p into the set of atoms of I (which equals the set of atoms of I'), mapping the unprimed State parameter to the State-atom of I and the primed State parameter to the State-atom of I';*
- *$\sqcup\{I, I'\}$ makes the body of p true under the environment η.*

We say that predicate p is implementable *if there exists a transition system $\mathcal{T}$ for $\mathcal{F}$ such that $[\![p]\!]^{TS} \neq \emptyset$.*

Our definition of "implementable" might appear odd at first glance. One might initially expect that an implementable predicate be defined as one for which there exists code that carries any I to an I' such that (I, I') makes the body of p true. Further consideration suggests that that is too much to ask: we should only insist that our code behave properly on nodes I that satisfy the pre-conditions of the predicate. But that won't work either, since there is no well-defined notion of "pre-condition" in an Alloy specification: in the rich language of Alloy predicates primed and unprimed elements mix freely within expressions and formulas. In this light the definition of "implementable" above seems to be the most restrictive reading that encompasses the intuitively implementable operation specifications.

3.3 Transition Systems from Instances

Having developed an "abstract" general notion of transition system for a framework the obvious question presents itself: what is the relationship of this class of structures to the relational algebra instances that are the foundation of Alloy?

The relationship is straightforward. In a natural way we can extract transition systems from relational algebra instances, formalizing the mental construction that Alloy users do whenever they are confronted with an instance for an analysis constraint in a state-based framework.

An instance that is intended to capture a transition typically has two atoms in the extension of the *State* signature and we read off the pre- and post-instances by projecting over these two atoms. Similarly for an instance modeling a trace: we think of each state atom in the instance as being an index into the part of the instance relevant to a particular transition-system node. (This is exactly what the standard Alloy visualization does, if one were to select a projection on *State*.) The next definition formalizes this intuition. It is convenient for our purposes to do this operation while retaining the state-atom, so it corresponds to an ordinary database join.

Definition 9 (Localizing). *Let I be an instance for a state-based specification and let $a \in I(State)$. The instance I_a is defined by*

- $I_a(r) = I(r)$ *when r is an immutable relation name;*
- $I_a(r) = a \bowtie I(r)$ *when r is a mutable relation name.*

Here $\bowtie$ is standard database join, so that $a \bowtie I(r)$ is the set of tuples in $I(r)$ whose entry in the State-column is a.

So any instance yields a transition system. What about the converse? We have seen in Definition 5 how to merge a transition system to obtain an instance; it remains to observe that merging and localization interact smoothly.

Lemma 10. *Merging and localizing are mutual inverses. That is,*

- *merging undoes localization: if I is an instance with $I(State) = \{a_j \mid j \in J\}$ then $\sqcup\{I_{a_j} \mid j \in J\} = I$;*
- *localization undoes merging: If Q is a finite coherent set of instances, then the set of instances obtained by localizing $\sqcup Q$ is Q: $\{(\sqcup Q)_a \mid a \in (\sqcup Q)(State)\} = Q$.*

It would, however, be a mistake to conclude from Lemma 10 that transition systems can be identified with relational-algebra instances. The central point is that *there is no reason to expect facts to be preserved* by merging or by localizing. And the facts that are viewed by the designer as state invariants are in consequence treated specially by our semantics: see Definition 7.

Example. Consider the relations in Figure 1. An Alloy instance would have this form:

$$\begin{array}{|rl|}\hline \mathit{State} = & \{\mathrm{s0}, \mathrm{s1}, \ldots\} \\ \mathit{Data} = & \{\mathrm{d0}, \mathrm{d1}, \ldots\} \\ \mathit{Clock} = & \{\mathrm{t0}, \mathrm{t1}, \ldots\} \\ \mathit{lastUsed} = & \{(\mathrm{s0}, \mathrm{d0}), (\mathrm{s1}, \mathrm{d1}), \ldots\} \\ \mathit{stamp} = & \{(\mathrm{d0}, \mathrm{t0}), (\mathrm{d1}, \mathrm{t1}), \ldots\} \\ \hline \end{array}$$

When this instance is systematically localized at the values in *State* we get a family of instances—

$$\begin{array}{|rl|}\hline \mathit{State} = & \{\mathrm{s0}\} \\ \mathit{Data} = & \{\mathrm{d0}, \mathrm{d1}, \ldots\} \\ \mathit{Clock} = & \{\mathrm{t0}, \mathrm{t1}, \ldots\} \\ \mathit{lastUsed} = & \{(\mathrm{s0}, \mathrm{d0})\} \\ \mathit{stamp} = & \{(\mathrm{d0}, \mathrm{t0}), (\mathrm{d1}, \mathrm{t1}), \ldots\} \\ \hline \end{array} \quad \begin{array}{|rl|}\hline \mathit{State} = & \{\mathrm{s1}\} \\ \mathit{Data} = & \{\mathrm{d0}, \mathrm{d1}, \ldots\} \\ \mathit{Clock} = & \{\mathrm{t0}, \mathrm{t1}, \ldots\} \\ \mathit{lastUsed} = & \{(\mathrm{s1}, \mathrm{d1})\} \\ \mathit{stamp} = & \{(\mathrm{d0}, \mathrm{t0}), (\mathrm{d1}, \mathrm{t1}), \ldots\} \\ \hline \end{array} \quad \ldots$$

—which form the nodes in a transition system.

4 Achieving Confidence in Analysis

The notions of localization and merging shed light on the examples from Section 2. Consider the specification in Figure 1. We observed that the predicate *updateLastUsed* was intuitively implementable; it is not hard to see that it is indeed implementable in the sense of Definition 8. But the predicate is not satisfiable. We understood intuitively that the source of the difficulty is the fact *storeOne*; now we can make the precise observation that *the fact storeOne is not preserved under merging*.

Next consider the specification in Figure 2. We observed that the predicate *addEntryNewKey* was (intuitively) not implementable; indeed it is not implementable in the sense of Definition 8. But the predicate is not satisfiable. This time the reason is the fact *oddCached*; this fact precludes implementation. Now we note that *the fact oddCached is not preserved under localization*.

These phenomena are perfectly general, as we summarize here.

Theorem 11. *Let $\mathcal{F} = (Sigs, Facts, Inv)$ be a framework.*

1. *The following are equivalent:*
   - *The sentences in Inv are preserved by arbitrary merging;*
   - *Every implementable predicate over $\mathcal{F}$ is satisfiable.*
2. *The following are equivalent:*
   - *The sentences in Inv are preserved by arbitrary localization.*
   - *Every satisfiable predicate over $\mathcal{F}$ is implementable.*

We have noted that the mismatch between satisfiability and implementability manifests itself in practical terms as an obstacle to having confidence in constraint-solving analyses. Specifically, confidence in assertions-checking arises precisely when countermodels to assertions in the relational algebra semantics encode countermodels in the transition semantics. This in turn means that validity in the transition system semantics implies validity in the relational algebra semantics. Dually, confidence in simulation (of predicates) arises from a guarantee that a relational algebra instance of a predicate does indeed correspond to a transition.

The next definition and result formalize these remarks.

Definition 12. *Let $\mathcal{F}$ be a framework and σ a sentence.*

- *We write $\mathcal{F} \models_{RA} \sigma$ to mean that σ holds in every relational algebra instance for $\mathcal{F}$.*
- *We write $\mathcal{F} \models_{TS} \sigma$ to mean that σ holds in every transition system over $\mathcal{F}$, in the sense of Definition 6.*

Then to say we can have confidence in assertions-checking in a framework $\mathcal{F}$ is to say that for any σ, $\mathcal{F} \models_{TS} \sigma$ implies $\mathcal{F} \models_{RA} \sigma$. To say we can have confidence in simulation in a framework $\mathcal{F}$ is to say that for any σ, $\mathcal{F} \models_{RA} \sigma$ implies $\mathcal{F} \models_{TS} \sigma$.

Proposition 13. *Let $\mathcal{F} = (Sigs, Facts, Inv)$ be a framework.*

1. *The following are equivalent:*
   - *the sentences in Facts are preserved by arbitrary merging.*
   - *for any σ, $\mathcal{F} \models_{TS} \sigma$ implies $\mathcal{F} \models_{RA} \sigma$. (We can have confidence in assertions-checking.)*
2. *The following are equivalent:*
   - *the sentences in Facts are preserved by arbitrary localization.*
   - *for any σ, $\mathcal{F} \models_{RA} \sigma$ implies $\mathcal{F} \models_{TS} \sigma$. (We can have confidence in predicate simulation.)*

A Sufficient Condition for Reliable Analysis

It may be illuminating to identify the preservation of properties under localization and merging as being at the heart of sound analysis, but since they are described in semantic terms they do not in themselves provide much guidance to the specification author. We next present a simple syntactic criterion that ensures that analysis can be trusted.

The difficulties explored in this paper all arise from the following dichotomy: certain expressions and formulas are naturally interpreted *in individual states* from the point of view of the implementer yet are interpreted *globally* by Alloy. The latter condition occurs because all states relevant to a formula being modeled are encoded into each individual Alloy instance.

Observe that for an immutable relation name r, the meanings of r in the various nodes of $\mathcal{T}$ are identical since Q is coherent. On the other hand, the interpretation mutable relations will of course vary across nodes. As a consequence, if e is an expression involving mutable relations, the value of e computed at a particular node I in $\mathcal{T}$ will in general be different from the "global" value $\mathcal{T}(e)$, and similarly for formulas. There is no surprise here, but this points to the need for care in defining the semantics of predicates and assertions since these typically involve formulas explicitly referring to more than one state. Indeed, it might suggest that our device of defining semantics in $\mathcal{T}$ in terms of standard semantics in $\sqcup\mathcal{T}$ does not capture intended usage.

These considerations motivate the next definition.

Definition 14 (Absoluteness). *Let e be an expression with at most a single State variable s occurring (more than one occurrence of s is permitted). Say that e is* absolute *if the following holds for every transition system* $\mathcal{T}$. *Let I be the unique node of* $\mathcal{T}$ *such that* $I(State) = \mathcal{T}(s)$; *then*

$$\mathcal{T}(e) = I(e)$$

So the meaning of an absolute expression survives the pun of viewing a relational algebra instance as representing a fragment of a transition system. Next we give a sufficient condition for expressions to be absolute, and a sufficient condition for facts to be preserved and reflected by the passage from instances to transition systems.

Definition 15 (State-bound expressions). *A* state-bound expression *is one for which every occurrence of a mutable relation name r is within the scope of some state variable s: that is, for each occurrence of r there is a subterm of the form* $s.f$ *such that r is a subterm occurrence of* f.

A sentence σ *is a* state-bound sentence *if*

- *every expression occurring in* σ *is a state-bound expression, and*
- *either* σ *has no occurrence of State variables, or is of the form all s: State . B with s the only State variable possibly occurring in B.*

For example, in Figure 2, the occurrence of *s.cache* in the fact *cacheKeysUnique* is state-bound; but the occurrence of *cache* in the fact *oddCached* is not state-bound. Of course, an expression involving only immutable relations is automatically state-bound.

Theorem 16. *State-bound expressions with at most one state-variable are absolute.*

State-bound facts are preserved by localizing and by merging.

As an immediate consequence of Proposition 13 and Theorem 16 we obtain the following sufficient condition for achieving confidence in both assertions-checking and simulation.

Corollary 17. *Let* $\mathcal{F}$ *be a framework whose associated set of facts is state-bound. Then a predicate is satisfiable if and only if it is implementable.*

Constraints in Predicate Bodies. Our results have so far constrained the form of facts, but not of predicates. This is perhaps surprising, as stateful predicate specifications often contain clauses that seem similar to facts (such as those capturing pre-conditions, post-conditions, or framing conditions). If is therefore natural to ask what happens if a predicate body violates our state-bound discipline. The answer is interesting, and sheds some additional light on the nature of the transition system semantics we have defined.

As a concrete example, let us revisit the *updateLastUsed* predicate from Figure 1, but with the problematic fact "inlined" into the body of the predicate.

// *remembering a new most recently used value*
pred *updateLastUsed* [*s*, *s*' : *State*, *d* : *Data*] {
  #*lastUsed* = 1 **and**
  s'.*lastUsed* = *d* **and** *s*.*lastUsed* != *d*}

This predicate poses no problems in assertions-checking or in the relationship between satisfiability and implementability. With the constraint that *lastUsed* is a singleton, the *updateLastUsed* predicate becomes unimplementable as well as unsatisfiable. This is a consequence of interpreting the predicate body using relational semantics over the merge of the individual states. As the inlined fact will never be true in any merged instance, the predicate is not satisfiable in any transition system. Although this may seem odd, it is consistent with the observations made in the discussion prior to Definition 6.

A similar analysis applies to the situation where a non-state-bound sentence that is not preserved under localization is used in a predicate body.

5 Advice to Alloy Users

Our results identify a subset of (or idiom over) Alloy specifications that capture transition systems without sacrificing accuracy of analysis in the relational semantics. Alloy users who wish to write such specifications should adopt two concrete guidelines:

1. Facts intended to capture state invariants must be preserved under localization and merging. Writing such facts either as signature constraints on the *State* signature or as state-bound sentences (Definition 15) ensures this.
2. Relations that are intended to be mutable (in an implementation) must be declared within the *State* signature.

Violating these rules can yield unreliable results from simulation or assertions-checking relative to the transition semantics defined in this paper.

As an example of these guidelines, imagine a designer trying to model a simple social networking application. The model captures each person's friends, as well as the members of the social network using two signatures:

sig *Person* {*friends* : **set** *Person*}
sig *SocNetwork* {*members* : **set** *Person*}

The designer proposes the following predicate to capture making one person (*p2*) a new friend of another (*p1*) (where & denotes intersection and + denotes union):

pred *makefriends* (*s*, *s*' : *SocNetwork*, *p1*, *p2* : *Person*) {
  p2 **not in** *p1*.*friends* **and**
  (*s*'.*members*) & *p1*.*friends* =
  (*s*.*members*) & *p1*.*friends* + *p2*}

This predicate violates guideline 2: the predicate is trying to update the *friends* relation, but that relation is not a component of the *SocNetwork* signature (which provides the *State* signature for this model). Instead, the designer should write the model as

sig *Person* {}
sig *SocNetwork* {*members* : **set** *Person*,
  friends : *Person* → *Person*}

pred *makefriends* (*s*, *s'* : *SocNetwork*, *p1*, *p2* : *Person*) {
  p2 **not in** *s.friends.p1* **and**
  s'.friends[*p1*] = *s.friends*[*p1*] + *p2*}

This example also helps illustrates a subtlety in guideline 1. Imagine adding the constraint that all friends are also members. The guideline (specifically, Definition 15) suggests writing this fact as *forall s: State — s.friends in s.members*, rather than the logically equivalent, and admittedly simpler, *friends in members*. Given the equivalence, the latter form is also preserved under localization and merging, despite the syntactic mismatch. This reflects the syntactic nature of guideline 1. In practice, we have not found this difference to be a problem, as discussed in the next section.

6 Validation: From Semantics to Synthesis

Until now, we have presented an idiomatic sub-language of Alloy for which we can define a coherent operational semantics. We now discuss two practical issues: usability in the sense of expressiveness for specification, and the potential for synthesis.

Usability. While usability can be hard to evaluate in an unbiased manner, we can at least ask whether existing specifications fall within the idiom defined here. In addition to several small and synthetic specifications, we are aware of at least two large specifications that fall within this language. The first is a specification of the access-control and execution behavior of Continue [8], a conference management application in use by several actual conferences (`continue2.cs.brown.edu`). Though Continue is coauthored by the fourth author, the specification was written by students unrelated to the project several years before the present research. Despite this, their specification nicely falls entirely within our subset (with all facts treated as state invariants).

The second such specification is for a new collaborative, Web-based programming environment that is under construction. That specification also has several diverse elements: operations for content creation, sharing, hiding, rating, commenting, and so forth. Again, the author of the specification was working entirely independently of this research and was unaware of it. That specification has one fact, of the form —forall x:X exists s:State ...—, that falls outside our subset. We interviewed the author to learn that this fact was included *only* to constrain the space of models to improve performance of the Analyzer; it does not capture a constraint of the logical model (and thus would not be required for code synthesis).

Synthesis. These specifications can also be processed by the Alchemy synthesizer. It cannot be re-used as a black-box, however, because the operational behavior of Alchemy is overly broad; for instance, given the specification

sig *State* $\{r : A\}$
sig B $\{t : A\}$
pred p $\{s.r$ **in** $s'.r + B.t\}$

Alchemy would be free to modify —t— (as we discuss in section 7). By restricting the operations Alchemy can generate, we can therefore obtain a synthesizer for specifications in the language of this paper whose generated code behaves consistently with the semantics defined here. Furthermore, Alchemy already produces systems with reasonable performance, at least for prototyping purposes [4]; by restricting the space of synthesized operations, we would be further improving its performance.

7 Related Work

We can view our work as providing an *adequate* semantics for Alloy. The notion of adequacy is usually credited to Plotkin's seminal work on the treatment of LCF as a programming language [9]. In our case, adequacy is a relationship between the denotational world of models and analysis, and the operational world of the implementation.

DynAlloy [10] originates, as does our work, from the observation that Alloy has only an "implicit" notion of operational semantics. Their response is different: they add another primitive notion, that of *actions,* to the language, together with a way of making partial correctness assertions. The emphasis in the DynAlloy work is on expressiveness of, and analysis of specifications in, their expanded language. In contrast, our focus is on the semantics of the common state-based idiom as expressed in pure Alloy.

Massoni, Gheyi and Borba [11] address the question of "conformance" between object-models and programs. They define a notion of "syntactic coupling" (defined in the PVS language) that relates object models with representations of run-time heaps. The main goal is to define and reason about the correctness of refactorings; the emphasis is on preservation of data properties expressed in the specification. They do not analyze the way that Alloy predicates induce operations on data.

Three of the present authors, with Yoo, introduced the Alchemy [4] program synthesizer for Alloy. Due to the lack of a crisp operational interpretation of Alloy, Alchemy relies on ad hoc syntactic criteria to determine the specification author's intent with respect to state changes. In contrast, this paper presents a precise operational characterization, providing a more rigorous formal footing for Alchemy.

Several efforts have tried to relate proofs to running programs. Bates and Constable [12] initiated a significant research program on the extraction of computational context, in the form of programs, from constructive proofs. This effort continues in popular proof assistants such as Coq [13]. Of course Alloy has no notion of proof structure. Nevertheless, we share their desire to have the executable code behave consistently with the outcome of any static analysis.

Our work can be seen as a result toward software synthesis, an effort initiated by Green [14] and Waldinger and Lee [15] and summarized by Rich and Waters [16]. Our prior work [4] discusses in detail the relationship between our approach and others.

Acknowledgments. We are grateful to Daniel Jackson for several helpful and detailed conversations about this work, including comments on several drafts of this paper. Michael Butler provided helpful information about the B method. This research is partially supported by the NSF.

References

1. Jackson, D.: Software Abstractions. MIT Press, Cambridge (2006)
2. Abrial, J.R.: The B-Book: Assigning Programs to Meanings. Cambridge University Press, Cambridge (1996)
3. Spivey, J.M.: The Z Notation: A Reference Manual, 2nd edn. Prentice Hall, Englewood Cliffs (1992)
4. Krishnamurthi, S., Dougherty, D.J., Fisler, K., Yoo, D.: Alchemy: Transmuting base alloy specifications into implementations. In: ACM SIGSOFT International Symposium on the Foundations of Software Engineering (2008)
5. Dougherty, D.J.: An improved algorithm for generating database transactions from relational algebra specifications. In: International Workshop on Rule-Based Programming (2009)
6. Jackson, D.: Alloy: a lightweight object modelling notation. ACM Transactions on Software Engineering and Methodology 11(2), 256–290 (2002)
7. Edwards, J., Jackson, D., Torlak, E.: A type system for object models. In: ACM SIGSOFT International Symposium on the Foundations of Software Engineering (2004)
8. Krishnamurthi, S., Hopkins, P.W., McCarthy, J.A., Graunke, P.T., Pettyjohn, G., Felleisen, M.: Implementation and use of the PLT Scheme web server. Higher-Order and Symbolic Computation 20(4), 431–460 (2007)
9. Plotkin, G.D.: LCF considered as a programming language. Theoretical Computer Science, 223–255 (1977)
10. Frias, M.F., López Pombo, C.G., Galeotti, J.P., Aguirre, N.M.: Efficient analysis of DynAlloy specifications. ACM Transactions on Software Engineering and Methodology 17(1) (December 2007)
11. Massoni, T., Gheyi, R., Borba, P.: A framework for establishing formal conformance between object models and object-oriented programs. Electronic Notes in Theoretical Computer Science 195, 189–209 (2008)
12. Bates, J.L., Constable, R.L.: Proofs as programs. ACM Transactions on Programming Languages and Systems 7(1), 113–136 (1985)
13. The Coq development team: The Coq proof assistant reference manual. LogiCal Project, Version 8.0 (2004)
14. Green, C.C.: Application of theorem proving to problem solving. In: International Joint Conference on Artificial Intelligence (1969)
15. Waldinger, R.J., Lee, R.C.T.: PROW: A step toward automatic program writing. In: International Joint Conference on Artificial Intelligence (1969)
16. Rich, C., Waters, R.C.: Automatic programming: Myths and prospects. IEEE Computer 21(8), 40–51 (1988)

A Robust Semantics Hides Fewer Errors

Steve Reeves and David Streader

Department of Computer Science, University of Waikato, Hamilton, New Zealand
{stever,dstr}@cs.waikato.ac.nz

Abstract. In this paper we explore how formal models are interpreted and to what degree meaning is captured in the formal semantics and to what degree it remains in the informal interpretation of the semantics. By applying a robust approach to the definition of refinement and semantics, favoured by the event-based community, to state-based theory we are able to move some aspects from the informal interpretation into the formal semantics.

1 Introduction

As engineers proud of our reputations and our subject we want aeroplanes to fly and banks to be trustworthy. As engineers we want real systems to function in the way we have specified them and for there to be no unpleasant surprises. But with increasing complexity we, like members of all other engineering disciplines, are forced to fall back on mathematics to help us achieve this. Mathematics offers us the ability to unambiguously communicate requirements and offers us proof as a basis for a formal notion of correctness. But mathematics works only with formal models, so we might be able to prove a refinement relation exists between abstract and concrete versions of a model at a formal level, but the models at that level have to reflect the actual, informal world and its requirements and implementations. Thus we have a gap that we must narrow as far as we can:

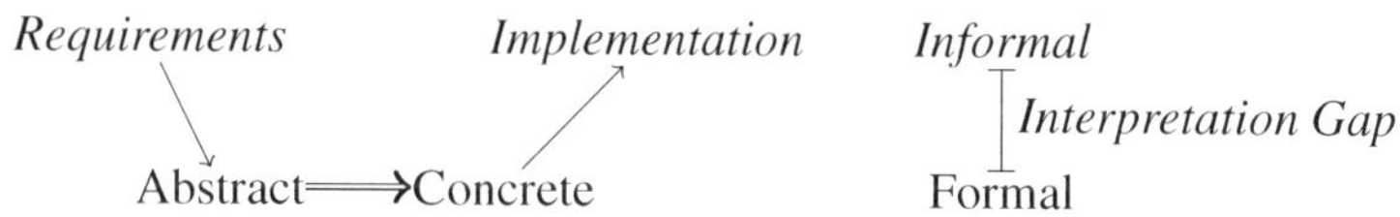

To an engineer formality without interpretation is useless. Engineers must pay close attention to how to interpret formal models if they wish to stop planes falling out of the sky and other unwanted events from occurring in the actual but *informal* world around us.

Consider this 13th century Sufi teaching story [1]:

> Once, a man found Mulla Nasruddin searching for something on the ground outside his house. On being asked, Nasruddin replied that he was looking for his key. The man also joined in the search and in due course asked Mulla: "Where exactly did you drop it?"
> Mulla answered: "In my house."
> "Then why are you looking here?" the man asked.
> "There is more light here than in my house," replied Mulla.

A. Cavalcanti and D. Dams (Eds.): FM 2009, LNCS 5850, pp. 499–515, 2009.

Theoreticians design languages and methodologies that, when successful, illuminate a path so engineers can construct reliable working software. But occasionally both theoreticians and engineers need to spend time looking not in the bright light of the formal theory but in the shadowy world of its interpretation. The problem with interpretations is that by their very nature they are to a greater or lesser extent informal since they must always have informal components which "connect" with the actual world. Thus we can completely formally prove nothing about interpretations, no matter that it is important to make the correct interpretation and for interpretations to seem natural to the engineer.

Of course, what we do is to compile actual world collections of properties that we want our system to have and properties that we want it not to have, represent these (i.e. build a model) in our formal world and try to prove that the properties, so represented, that we want to hold do hold, and those that we do not want to hold do not hold. The more properties we can compile, and the more we can prove hold or do not hold, the more confidence we can have that our formalisation reflects the actual, informal world. Thus the model is justified through experiments in the informal world, that is experiments on the program and the requirements. For any realistically large or complex system, this process can never be completed; the best we can do is make it as complete as possible.

In this paper we are interested in writing specifications and then constructing implementations that satisfy them. The formal construction of a more concrete specification from a more abstract one we will call a *refinement step*. Given that the very reason for writing the specification is to construct implementations that satisfy it we believe that it is very natural for the semantics of a specification to be *intimately* connected to the semantics of refinement (and not just share some common formal basis). This is true for many event-based formal methodologies: in CSP failures semantics is intimately related to failures refinement. Failures refinement is not always satisfactory when non-terminating processes are considered. Consequently failures/divergences refinement [2], NDFD refinement [3] and CFFD refinement [3] have been defined, but in each case not only is a new refinement defined but also a new semantics is defined.

In some state-based formal methods the same semantics are defined (partial relations) but with several distinct refinement preorders [4,5,6]. Although there is nothing wrong with this state-based approach we will argue that it leaves some of the meaning of operations out of the formal semantics and may cause some difficulties.

Our approach will be to use a general parameterised framework, taken from [7,8], where this intimate relation between semantics and refinement is a central idea and explore what effect it can have on a state-based formal method.

We are all familiar with mathematicians writing down terms that describe actual things and via (formal) reasoning drawing conclusions (other terms) from the original terms. It is the engineer who has the responsibility to interpret the terms and decide whether the formal reasoning steps correctly reflect the informal world. We can help the engineers by defining a semantics for the terms that is closer to the engineers' understanding of the world around them. Subsequently engineers only need think about the semantics rather than the terms. This works well as long as the correct semantics (and reasoning) is chosen.

Next we give a simple example to illustrate how easy it is to use the wrong semantics and how considering the formal model alone cannot clarify the situation.

1.1 Example

As the truth of a statement is ascertained by the construction of a valid proof, reasoning about the proof of statements should be reliable. By reasoning about what can be proved we are going to offer a rigorous but informal argument that the following formal statement FS *is invalid*.

From assumption $(Pa \wedge Pb) \rightarrow R$ we can show $(Pa \rightarrow R) \vee (Pb \rightarrow R)$ **FS**

Informal Argument: The assumption is that from a proof of $Pa \wedge Pb$ we can construct a proof of R. But this does not necessarily mean that we can construct a proof of R just from a proof of Pa or construct a proof of R just from a proof of Pb. This is clearly true as knowing either Pa or Pb is to know less that to know both Pa and Pb and there is at least the possibility that the truth of both Pa and Pb were needed in the construction of the proof of R.

But despite this (hopefully) convincing informal argument we can provide a formal proof that from $(Pa \wedge Pb) \rightarrow R$ we can indeed show $(Pa \rightarrow R) \vee (Pb \rightarrow R)$.

1.	$(Pa \wedge Pb) \rightarrow R$	
2.	$\neg((Pa \rightarrow R) \vee (Pb \rightarrow R))$	Ass
3.	$\neg((\neg Pa \vee R) \vee (\neg Pb \vee R))$	$Def \rightarrow .2$
4.	$Pa \wedge \neg R \wedge Pb \wedge \neg R$	$DeMorgan, \neg E$
5.	$\neg(Pa \wedge Pb) \vee R$	$Def \rightarrow .1$
6.	$\neg(Pa \wedge Pb)$	Ass
7.	$\perp$	$From - 4, 6$
8.	R	Ass
9.	$\perp$	$From - 4, 8$
10.	$\perp$	$\vee E, 5, 6, 7, 8, 9$
11.	$(Pa \rightarrow R) \vee (Pb \rightarrow R)$	$Cont, 2, 10$

What has gone wrong?

1.2 Explanation

The first mistake in Section 1.1 is the assumption that the interpretation of formal statements is both obvious and universally agreed upon. Indeed the statement **FS** can be given a classical or a constructive [9,10] interpretation.

With a constructive interpretation the informal argument is indeed correct. And the formal argument is incorrect as it is based upon classical logic. But if, as is common, the statement is given a classical logic interpretation then the mistake was made before the informal argument was constructed and indeed before the formal statement was given. The very first two sentences of Section 1.1 are mistaken. Classical logic is a logic of *truth* (or at least truth as formalised by truth-table semantics). It is constructive logic that is a logic of *proof* and hence choosing to base the argument on what can be *proved* is a mistake, as it makes use of the wrong semantics. Hence any informal argument based on proof cannot be said to relate to a classical interpretation of any formal statement.

In particular the previously given informal argument does not relate to the classical interpretation of **FS**.

As using the semantics can so easily lead us astray it might be tempting to avoid it, but this is not always very practical. To reason syntactically that one statement cannot be proved from another would require reasoning about all proofs, which is not easy to do. In such situations it is usual to reason about a semantics and appeal to a soundness and completeness result. This example illustrates that:

1. reasoning with semantics can be very helpful;
2. it is important to select the correct semantics; and
3. an apparently innocent change to the semantics, in the example the change is from *truth* to *proof*, can have disastrous effects.

One of the worst aspects of such "mistakes" is that they cannot be found by considering the formal arguments alone.

Naturally if changing the semantics is difficult then one solution is simply not to do it. But as illustrated later (Section 6) semantics are often changed even by theoreticians. It is useful to engineers and theoreticians alike to have different ways to safely interpret formal statements and choose the most appropriate interpretation for a given situation.

Here we are interested in the refinement of specifications and it is very clear from the many definitions in the literature that there is certainly no one universally agreed upon definition of refinement or indeed one interpretation of what refinement means.

We will next look at how an engineer might informally interpret the statement that A is a refinement of C and provide some answers to the question: what use is a formal refinement to an engineer?

2 Interpretation and Robustness of Refinement

We are interested in refinement, that is in the formal transformation of an abstract specification into a more concrete specification.

Before we give our formalisation of refinement we look at three informal interpretations of refinement each based on an associated interpretation of a specification. Each of these different interpretations may be of use to the engineer in different situations.

Refinement interpreted as preservation of guarantee, $\mathsf{A} \sqsubseteq_p \mathsf{C}$. Under this interpretation a specification is interpreted as a *guarantee* that "if the entity is used in the prescribed way then one of the prescribed observable behaviours will be seen and nothing else". Then we have the following natural informal notion of refinement, which appears in many places in the literature [6,4,5,11,12,13]

> The entity C is a refinement of a more abstract entity A when no user of A could observe if they were given C in place of A, which is to say that nothing they observe of C would suggest that they were not observing A, so the guarantee given with A is preserved.

Refinement interpreted as implication, $\mathsf{A} \sqsubseteq_\rightarrow \mathsf{C}$. Under this interpretation a specification is interpreted as an assertion about the behaviour of an entity (formalised naturally as a logical term $I_{\rightarrow}(\mathsf{A})$) [14]. A refinement relation holds between entities C and A if and only if the behaviours asserted by the interpretation of C satisfy the interpretation of A, formalised by $\mathsf{A} \sqsubseteq_{\rightarrow} \mathsf{C}$ iff $I_{\rightarrow}(\mathsf{C}) \rightarrow I_{\rightarrow}(\mathsf{A})$.

Refinement interpreted as subset of implementations, $\mathsf{A} \sqsubseteq_i \mathsf{C}$. Under this interpretation a specification is given by the set of its implementations. A concrete specification is a refinement of a more abstract specification if and only if the implementations satisfying the concrete specification are a subset of the implementations satisfying the abstract specification.

Definition 1. *Two interpretations of refinement $\sqsubseteq_x$ and $\sqsubseteq_y$ are called consistent if and only if for all entities* A *and* C $(\mathsf{A} \sqsubseteq_x \mathsf{C}) \leftrightarrow (\mathsf{A} \sqsubseteq_y \mathsf{C})$.

Definition 2. *The more consistent interpretations a definition of refinement has the more robust is the definition.*

In what follows, we advocate robustness both because it is useful to have different ways to interpret the same intuition and because we believe errors with the semantics of refinement are less likely to occur given a robust definition characterising the intuition.

We also see that, in the three sorts of refinement listed above, the refinement preorder characterises the semantics of a specification, and vice versa. This is another way in which a definition of refinement and a semantics of specifications can both be regarded as very robust, and intimately connected.

The idea that refinement and specification should characterise each other is not a new idea, nor is the usefulness of having more than one semantics. In the event-based world it would seem strange to use failures semantics and not use failures refinement, although it would be possible to do this.

In the event-based literature the definition of refinement frequently characterises the denotational semantics and hence it is not uncommon to use the definition of refinement to define the meaning or denotation of the operational semantics. This has been so popular an approach that a survey of over 150 different semantics, all based on different definitions of refinement, can be found in [15,16].

In the state-based literature this approach is not so common, but what is common is to define the semantics of an operation as a partial relation. Then different definitions of refinement, based on different interpretations of the partial relations, can be given without changing the semantics. In Section 6 we will discuss some consequences of this approach that could be avoided by using a semantic definition that, as in event-based approaches, is closely related to a robust definition of refinement.

3 A Robust Interpretation of Refinement

This section gives an outline of a formal definition of refinement and three consistent interpretations that follow from it (for further details see [7,8]).

Our first step towards formalising refinement is to decide what the user can observe, so we make some assumptions. In practice we are interested in reasoning about and refining small entities (modules) which are combined to make a larger entity. Thus we model an entity E as existing in some context X (the rest of the larger whole) interacting on the set of actions Act. All E's actions interact with X at the E-X interface (see Figure 1). X and U interact at a different interface and on a disjoint set of actions. We model the observer as a *passive* user U that is a third entity that observes or interacts with X, but neither blocks the X actions nor interferes with E-X communication.

We will give formal general definitions of refinement with explicit parameters representing both Ξ, the contexts in which entities will be placed, and O, an observation function from entities to sets of traces from $\wp(\mathbb{O})$ (of event names or states), where each trace $tr \in \mathbb{O}$ is a potential observation.

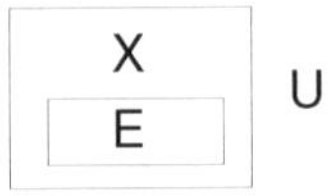

Fig. 1. Entity, conteXt and User and their interfaces

This general theory can be made more concrete by instantiating its parameters defining : one, how we represent our entities; two, the sets of contexts Ξ; and three, the observation function O from entities to sets of traces.

This instantiation of the general theory results in what we call a *special theory*. It has been shown ([17]) that some of the classic theories of operations, abstract data types (ADT) and processes that appear in the literature are special theories of the general theory given here.

3.1 Refinement Interpreted as Preservation of Guarantee

Definition 3. *Let Ξ be a set of contexts each of which the entities* A *and* C *can communicate privately with, and let O be a function which returns a set of traces, each trace being what a user observes of an execution. Then*[1]

$$\mathsf{A} \sqsubseteq_{\Xi,O} \mathsf{C} \triangleq \forall x \in \Xi. O([\mathsf{C}]_x) \subseteq O([\mathsf{A}]_x)$$

3.2 Refinement as Implication

It is easy to see that we can give entities in our general theory a relational semantics. We are not the first to use relations as a semantics for a diverse range of models: indeed Hoare and He in their Unifying Theories of Programming (UTP, [14]) do just this. The main difference between this work and others is that we motivate our relational semantics by defining a consistent testing semantics.

Definition 4. *Let Ξ be a set of contexts each of which the entity* A *can communicate privately with, and O be a function which returns a set of traces, each trace being a sequence of snap-shots that a user might observe of an execution. The relational semantics of an entity* A *is a subset of $\Xi \times \mathbb{O}$. Let*

$$\mathsf{A}_{\Xi,O}(x,o) \triangleq x \in \Xi \wedge o \in O([\mathsf{A}]_x)$$

then

$$[\![\mathsf{A}]\!]_{\Xi,O} \triangleq \{(x,o) | \mathsf{A}_{\Xi,O}(x,o)\}$$

[1] $[\mathsf{E}]_x$ denotes the execution of entity E in context x.

Refinement is now the subset relation between relations or implication between the predicates that define them. When Ξ and O are fixed and obvious from context we will omit them. For any entities A and C let

$$\mathsf{A} \sqsubseteq_{\rightarrow,\Xi,O} \mathsf{C} \triangleq \mathsf{C}_{\Xi,O} \rightarrow \mathsf{A}_{\Xi,O} \qquad \mathsf{A} \sqsubseteq_{\subseteq,\Xi,O} \mathsf{C} \triangleq [\![\mathsf{C}]\!]_{\Xi,O} \subseteq [\![\mathsf{A}]\!]_{\Xi,O}$$

then we have our first consistency result:

$$\mathsf{A} \sqsubseteq_{\Xi,O} \mathsf{C} \Leftrightarrow \mathsf{A} \sqsubseteq_{\subseteq,\Xi,O} \mathsf{C} \Leftrightarrow \mathsf{A} \sqsubseteq_{\rightarrow,\Xi,O} \mathsf{C}$$

3.3 Refinement as Subset of Implementation

Given that refinement is frequently characterised as the reduction of non-determinism and that software is currently run on deterministic computers we will define what it means to be deterministic in our general model.

Definition 5. *An entity* A *is deterministic iff its relational semantics is a function:*

$$Det_{\Xi,O}(\mathsf{A}) \triangleq (x,o) \in [\![\mathsf{A}]\!]_{\Xi,O} \wedge (x,p) \in [\![\mathsf{A}]\!]_{\Xi,O} \Rightarrow o = p$$

We now say that *implementations are deterministic entities* and so we can define the semantics of an entity A to be the set of implementations that satisfy it:

$$[\![\mathsf{A}]\!]_{I,\Xi,O} \triangleq \{\mathsf{I} \in I | Det_{\Xi,O}(\mathsf{I}) \wedge [\![\mathsf{I}]\!]_{\Xi,O} \subseteq [\![\mathsf{A}]\!]_{\Xi,O}\}$$

and then for any entities A and C:

$$\mathsf{A} \sqsubseteq_{I,\Xi,O} \mathsf{C} \triangleq [\![\mathsf{C}]\!]_{I,\Xi,O} \subseteq [\![\mathsf{A}]\!]_{I,\Xi,O}$$

Using this we recreate the relational semantics of the entity by taking the union of the functions and see our second consistency result:

$$\mathsf{A} \sqsubseteq_{I,\Xi,O} \mathsf{C} \Leftrightarrow \mathsf{A} \sqsubseteq_{\Xi,O} \mathsf{C}$$

4 Interfaces

In this section we will show why both contexts and users are needed to define refinement by demonstrating situations where two different types of interfaces are needed: a *transactional* interface between entities and contexts and an *interactive* interface between contexts and users.

We will refer to an interface as *transactional* if interaction (including observation) occurs at no more than two distinct points: initialisation and finalisation of the entity. If termination is successful then there may be distinct snap-shots that could be taken at finalisation, but if termination is unsuccessful then no final snap-shot is taken and all that can be inferred is that the entity fails to terminate.

An example of an entity with transactional interaction is a program that accepts a parameter when called and returns a value when it terminates. Clearly if the program fails to terminate no value can be returned.

In contrast we refer to an interface as *interactive* when interaction can occur at many points throughout the execution. Hence with interactive interfaces more than one snapshot can be taken prior to termination and even prior to non-termination.

An example of an interactive entity is a coffee machine. To obtain two cups of coffee the user first inserts a coin, then pushes the appropriate button and takes the first cup of coffee. But if after inserting a second coin the vending machine now "fails to terminate" by not producing a second cup of coffee the previously successful interactions mean that what has been observed cannot be represented by noting non-termination alone. (We still have our first cup of coffee!)

5 Abstract Data Type Refinement

With entities being abstract data types, contexts being the programs that use the ADTs (by using, calling, the operations the ADT provides) and users being the users of the program, we must have an interactive ADT/program interface. But the definition of refinement is sensitive to the type of program/user interface (see [7] for details).

A computational method for deciding whether data refinement holds between ADTs is problematic as the definition of data refinement involves quantification over all programs (usually an infinite collection). But the classic Hoare, He and Saunders result [18] uses retrieve or simulation relations between the state spaces of the two ADTs to define a forward or backward simulation between them. Usefully, the simulations are quantified only over all operations (a finite collection) in the ADTs, and it is proved that they are sound and jointly complete with respect to refinement. Thus the Hoare, He and Saunders guarantee is that if A is a forward or backward simulation of C then any observation that can be made of any program using C could have been made of the same program using A.

The Hoare, He and Saunders proof is based on the operations having a relational semantics and the behaviour of the program under consideration being defined by relational composition of the relational semantics of individual operations. The proof makes no restriction on the relations used to model the operations and to define the retrieve or simulation relation.

Partial relations are open to a variety of interpretations, the angelic and demonic interpretations (see Refinement Calculus [19]) and the distinct interpretations from [5,6,4] that we will discuss.

For example, let $D \triangleq \{a, b\}$ be a state space of two states and take an operation P where $[\![\mathsf{P}]\!] \subseteq D \times D$ and define the semantics of P by $[\![\mathsf{P}]\!] \triangleq \{(a, a)\}$. This specification can be considered either as requiring a partially correct implementation: when an implementation of P is started from state a then if it terminates it will terminate in state a; or as requiring a totally correct implementation: when an implementation of operation P is started from state a then it will terminate and it will terminate in state a. In addition the implementation's behaviour from state b could be interpreted as undefined or as blocked.

We need to be wary of using the sequential composition of partial relations since as Spivey pointed out modelling sequential composition of operations as the relational composition of partial relations has a meaning that *"differs from the meaning that would be natural in a programming language"*, Spivey [20, p136].

For example let $[\![\mathsf{O}]\!] \triangleq \{(a,a),(a,b)\}$ and $[\![\mathsf{P}]\!] \triangleq \{(a,a)\}$ and let $[\![\mathsf{O};\mathsf{P}]\!] \triangleq [\![\mathsf{O}]\!];[\![\mathsf{P}]\!]$. Spivey's problem can be seen by considering $[\![\mathsf{O};\mathsf{P}]\!] = \{(a,a)\}$ and asking what has happened when an implementation of O terminates in state b.

It is easy to see that modelling the relational semantics of a sequence of operations as the relational composition of the relational semantics of the individual operations, as in the Hoare, He and Saunders paper, is consistent with a partial correctness interpretation and with a demonic total correctness interpretation but not consistent with an angelic total correctness interpretation.

6 Semantic Changes: The Benign and the Problematic

In the state-based world Z, B and Event B use partial relations as their operational semantics. Thus Z, B and Event B formal models are of interest to us as they possess a formal operational semantics and yet are, by design, open to a variety of interpretations.

This has the desirable consequence of allowing these methods to be flexible in that they can be used in a wide range of situations, though this opens up the possibility that problems, of the kind discussed in Section 1, might be introduced.

Experts in Z know only too well that, given some common interpretations of Z, to use Z safely (avoiding the problems discussed in Section 5) you need to restrict how it is used to a particular (informal) methodology, a good example of which is the informal methodology followed in [5].

One of B's semantics for operations is give by (rel, pre) where rel is a relation between states and pre is a subset of states interpreted as an explicit precondition. From [13, pp. 296, 297 Property 6.4.1] we can see that the domain of rel defines the set of states on which operation is feasible. From the predicate definition of the application of an operation, from a state in which the operation is infeasible anything can be established and hence any invariant can be invalidated. Since one of the proof obligations required by B refinement is the preservation of the machine invariant by initialisation and all operations, we know that infeasible states are never reached. Hence Spivey's problem can be ignored as it is safe to consider the relational semantics of the operations over only the reachable, hence feasible, states, which are all in $dom(rel)$.

The toolkits of both B and Event B compute forward simulation, which is shown to imply their definitions of refinement. Although the definition of B refinement is essentially the same as data refinement found elsewhere [5, 19, 4, 6] the definition of Event B refinement [21] is based on what is called a simulation relation in [4], so it is not based on data refinement. Spivey's problem is avoided in B by using a set and relation semantics, but in Event B by using simulation in place of data refinement.

6.1 Data Types or Processes

Woodcock and Davies' definition of data refinement in [5] is that taken from [18] and applied to ADTs with operations that are interpreted as undefined outside of precondition, which some call contractual. Although using Z, with its partial relation semantics, they define data refinement while using a total correctness interpretation of the relational semantics. They have achieved this by changing the semantics of operations from Z partial relations to a lifted totalised semantics prior to computing data refinement. Another view is that the semantics has not changed and the transformation to total relations is just a step in the computation of refinement. Whatever your view, the transformation exists. For ease of discussion we will refer to it as a transformation of the semantics.

The engineer must therefore bear in mind that the Hoare, He and Saunders guarantee applied to the data types in [5] is based on operations with a total relation semantics due to the transformation of the semantics, not on Z's "official" partial relation semantics.

In [5, Table 16.1] value passing operations are modelled by winding the input values into a sequence initialised at the start of the program execution and the output values wound into a sequence to be observed. In addition another set of rules [5, Table 16.2] is defined in which input and output occurs and can be seen at each step.

In our terminology there is, therefore, a change in the program/user interface from transactional to interactive, and thus a change in the definition of refinement. Because we advocate using robust definitions of refinement where refinement can be used to define the semantics, we choose to view this change of refinement as a second transformation in the semantics. However, this is benign, as the two sets of rules are to the best of our knowledge equivalent.

Subsequently, Bolton and Davies' definition of data refinement in [6] is also that taken from [18] but is applied to ADTs with operations that are interpreted as blocked or guarded outside of precondition, which some call behavioural. They go on to make similar semantic transformations to those in [5]. But this time the second semantic transformation, that of changing the program/user interface from transactional to interactive, results in a subtly different refinement relation, singleton failures refinement, for which backward simulation *is not sound* [22]. One of the difficulties is that having made the apparently benign transformation in the semantics the lack of soundness cannot be discovered simply by looking at the formality. Just as in our example Section 1.1, looking at the formal proof alone will not reveal any errors.

6.2 Relational Semantics or Logical Semantics

The initial semantic transformation in Section 6.1 replaces partial relations with lifted total relations. The logical or axiomatic approach provides an alternative to using a transformation because it keeps the partial relation semantics but defines sets of axioms to characterise refinement.

Which semantics, the relational or logical, was used was regarded as unimportant as any refinement based on the logical definition was also, it was assumed, a refinement based on the relational definition.

But recently Boiten and Derrick have shown [23] a key result: the completeness of forward and backward simulation with respect to data refinement fails to hold for operations that are blocked outside of precondition when their semantics is given in the logical style, although it still holds for the relational-style semantics [22]. Further, using a *restricted* simulation relation, a soundness and completeness result can be re-established [22] for singleton failures refinement. This again shows us that an apparently innocent change in semantics can have unforeseen consequences.

If we regard Z's semantics as given by partial relations (where outside of precondition a specification is necessarily silent about what happens due to the partiality), yet use an axiomatic or logical definition of refinement, based for example on "undefined outside of precondition", then we have a semantics that is silent about what happens outside of precondition but a definition of refinement that is not silent about what happens outside of precondition. We can view this as saying that the definition of refinement extends the semantics with additional meaning, not found in the semantics (in this case the additional meaning defines the behaviour outside of the precondition).

It is now not clear if the meaning of the specification is given by the semantics or by the definition of refinement. If the meaning is given by the semantics then why use this definition of refinement that is based on a different meaning? If the meaning is given by refinement then why not formalise this in the semantics?

A way to make the formal model more robust would be, as we have advocated, to change the semantics to keep it "consistent" with the definition of refinement.

6.3 Conclusions

There is, of course, nothing wrong with the semantics of Z or B. But care is needed in interpreting Z and B. Z officially has a partial relational semantics but different people interpret this semantics differently and define different refinement relations. So are the different meanings formalised by the different refinement relations or is the official Z semantics now to be replaced (by the total relation version)? From the previous two sections and our example in Section 1.1 we conclude that understanding or interpreting formal models to the extent required to prevent failure of real (software) systems is far from easy. Apparently innocent changes to the semantic model can very easily introduce errors that are hard to detect even by theoreticians. Despite the difficulty of designing safe, useful theoretical frameworks we still need to give engineers greater freedom in how they develop software.

7 Stepwise Design

To design reliable complex systems that are open to human understanding we need both simple and intuitive high-level descriptions that clearly reflect the required behaviour and detailed low-level descriptions that an implementation can be clearly seen to satisfy.

If we tried to specify everything down to the last detail early in the design process we would fail to see any clear, big picture. Consequently we wish to add detail in a stepwise fashion through out the design process. But we wish to avoid leaving informal any essential methodological restrictions, so we wish to follow the design of B and formalise, as much as we can, any essential methodology.

7.1 Stepwise Semantics

The advantage of basing a wide variety of semantic models all on one common semantics is that we can uniformly define some operations, such as parallel composition, choice, event hiding, recursion on the semantics and then, with some effort, lift these definitions to the more detailed semantic models. For example, [15,16] referred to earlier, needs *one* definition of parallel composition not 150 definitions (one for each refinement they look at).

We advocate the following steps towards a target semantics.

Step 1. Any formal statement is written using some well-defined syntax. For example, let there be terms T_{Σ} constructed from some signature $\Sigma \triangleq \{\oplus\} \cup \mathsf{Act}$, where Act is a set of actions of interest, and $\mathsf{Act} \subseteq \mathsf{A}$, where A is the set of all possible actions, and $\oplus$ is an in-fixed binary operator $\oplus \in \mathsf{A} \times \mathsf{A} \rightarrow \mathsf{A}$.

To be of use to an engineer this must have some interpretation in the informal world where they work and do their designing. Such an interpretation I_{Sy} of terms in our example language is very flexible in as much as the terms can be interpreted as representing any entity from a set of things with a binary operation on this set. This syntax puts no further restrictions on what interpretations can be made.

We can reduce the flexibility in the way the terms can be interpreted by specifying a formal semantics for them. So, continuing our example, let us define the formal semantics of an action a to be a relation $[\![\mathsf{a}]\!] \subseteq S \times S$ over some set S, $[\![\mathsf{Act}]\!] \triangleq \{[\![\mathsf{a}]\!] | \mathsf{a} \in \mathsf{Act}\}$ and the semantics of the binary operator to be set union $[\![\oplus]\!] \triangleq \cup$.

From the semantic interpretation we can infer an equation: $[\![\mathsf{a} \oplus \mathsf{a}]\!] = [\![\mathsf{a}]\!]$. So now the valid interpretations are restricted to a subset of the valid interpretations given by I_{Sy}, namely by eliminating those that do not obey the equation.

We will write I_{Sem} for the standard and obvious informal interpretation of S as some set of states, a in Act as being an operation which moves between states and $[\![\mathsf{a}]\!]$ as the state-to-state relational semantics of the operation a. I_{Sem} is a valid interpretation for this more restricted semantics. And of course I_{Sem} talks about less of the informal world than I_{Sy} did, as our diagram suggests.

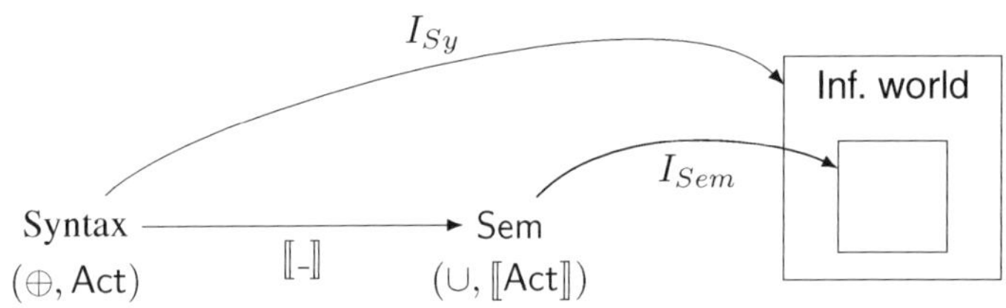

Let I_A and $I_C.[\![\text{-}]\!]$ be informal mappings from some formal domain D to the real world. We will refer to I_C as an I-refinement of I_A when for all d in D, $I_C([\![d]\!])$ is a subset of $I_A(d)$.

We have used some English here rather than using only mathematical notation to remind the reader that this has to be an informal definition (the informal world is involved), but from now we will rely on the reader to remember that all interpretations are an informal mapping into the informal ("real") world. Clearly in our example $I_{Sem}([\![d]\!])$ is a subset of $I_{Sy}(d)$ and hence I_{Sem} is an I-refinement of I_{Sy}.

To help make intuitions more robust we require that:

1. interpretations are homomorphic, e.g. $I_{Sy}(\mathsf{a} \oplus \mathsf{b}) \triangleq I_{Sy}(\mathsf{a})I_{Sy}(\oplus)I_{Sy}(\mathsf{b})$ and $I_{Sem}(\mathsf{a} \oplus \mathsf{b}) \triangleq I_{Sem}(\mathsf{a})I_{Sem}(\oplus)I_{Sem}(\mathsf{b})$

2. so are semantic mappings, $[\![\_]\!]$ the semantics of a term is given by the semantics of its components, e.g. $[\![\mathsf{a} \oplus \mathsf{b}]\!] \triangleq [\![\mathsf{a}]\!][\![\oplus]\!][\![\mathsf{b}]\!]$
3. informal intuitions are preserved, $I_{Sy}(\oplus) = I_{Sem}([\![\oplus]\!])$

Step 2. Let us extend our example and assume that $[\![\mathsf{a}]\!] = \{(1,1)\}$ and the state space is given by $S = \{1,2\}$. This relational semantics can be interpreted in several different ways, see Section 5 for four distinct interpretations.

Just as we refined how we interpret the syntax by defining the semantics of the terms we can also refine how we interpret the initial semantics Sem by defining a meaning (second semantics, Sem_2) for the initial semantics. In our example we can define how to lift and totalise the initial partial relation semantics. Lifting adds $\perp$ to S to give $S_\perp$ and operations now have $S_\perp \times S_\perp$ relational semantics and $\perp$ on the left of the relation is interpreted as the operation fails to start and on the right of the relation it is interpreted as the operation fails to terminate[2]. How we totalise the relation formalises the interpretation we wish to give it.

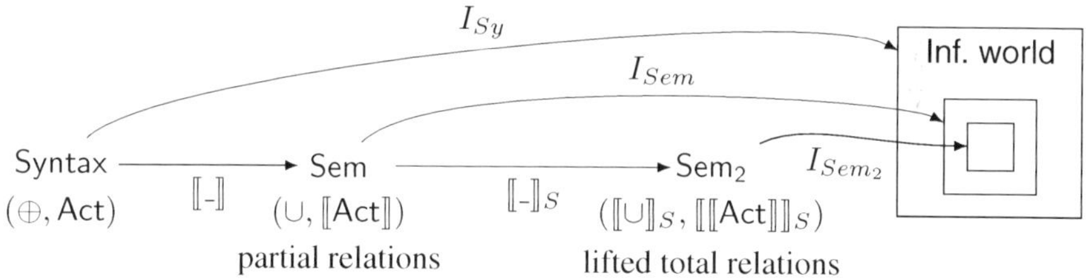

Interpreting $[\![\mathsf{a}]\!] = \{(1,1)\}$ as blocked (guarded) outside of precondition and requiring a totally correct implementation (so it must terminate from state 1) we map all, and only, states outside of the precondition to $\perp$ and only to $\perp$. Thus we have $[\![\{(1,1)\}]\!]_S = \{(1,1),(2,\perp),(\perp,\perp)\}$.

In our example the meaning of the partial relation semantics has been formalised by the application of a semantic function $[\![\_]\!]_S$ that lifts and makes total the partial relations. Of course we do not need to go through the intermediate semantics (partial relations) we could simply use a mapping $[\![[\![\_]\!]]\!]_S$ from the syntax to the new semantics. The advantage of using an intermediate semantics is that mathematical definitions and results can be established for the initial, or intermediate, semantics and this used to establish similar results for a whole range of more detailed semantics.

Because care is needed to make sure that intuitions at a high level of abstraction, for example with partial relation semantics $[\![\_]\!]$, transfer correctly to a less abstract level, for example for the lifted totalised semantics $[\![\_]\!]_S$ we advocate keeping to the three points raised at the end of step 1.

7.2 Refining Interpretations

Applying stepwise design to one of our robust interpretations of a high-level refinement, as defined in Section 3, can be done by including an explicit refinement operator $\sqsubseteq_H$

[2] For details of how to interpret the usual pre-state/post-state relations as relations between contexts and observation traces (time ordered sequence of snap-shots) see [7,22] and for details of how to extend this interpretation to cover lifted relations $S_\perp \times S_\perp$ see [22].

in the signature of our terms in the definition of our syntax in step 1. This allows us to talk about refinement at some level of abstraction, or equivalently gives a theory of refinement at some level of abstraction. We can now interpret this theory as a distinct further theory based at another level of abstraction. We will often use this method to view the original refinement in the original theory as taking place at a high-level of abstraction and the further theory given by the interpretation of the high-level theory as giving us a lower-level theory with its own lower-level refinement, which we will call $\sqsubseteq_L$ (see [8] for more details). This interpretation between theories is formalised by defining two semantic mappings. We use a semantic mapping $[\![\_]\!]_v$ to interpret, or *embed*, high-level entities $\mathsf{E_H}$ as low-level entities $\mathsf{E_L}$ and a separate semantic mapping vA to interpret, or *embed*, low-level entities as high-level entities. When they form a Galois connection we call such pairs of semantic mappings a *vertical refinement*, denoted by $\sqsubseteq_v$.

In Section 3.2 we have refinement as implication and we can view the context and observation function pair from that section as defining a logical theory and then apply the well-known reading of Galois connections as theory transformations between two theories, one at a high level based on $(\Xi_\mathsf{H}, O_\mathsf{H})$ and the other at a lower level based on $(\Xi_\mathsf{L}, O_\mathsf{L})$. Galois connections thus provide a very strict design step between theories and preserve many features of the theories including union, subset (which we use to define refinement), and fixed points. For our purposes all we need consider are simple Galois connections that capture a *silent outside of frame* intuition. Let the range of O_H be $\mathbb{O}_\mathsf{H}$ and $\Xi_\mathsf{H} \times \mathbb{O}_\mathsf{H}$ be the high-level *frame*. Subset refinement where $\mathsf{E_H} \sqsubseteq_\subseteq \mathsf{E_L}$ implies $(\Xi_\mathsf{H} \times \mathbb{O}_\mathsf{H}) \subseteq (\Xi_\mathsf{L} \times \mathbb{O}_\mathsf{L})$ and $[\![\mathsf{E_H}]\!]_{\Xi_\mathsf{H}, O_\mathsf{H}}$ is the same as $[\![\mathsf{E_L}]\!]_{\Xi_\mathsf{L}, O_\mathsf{L}}$ restricted to the high-level frame. We note that we can use *silent outside of frame* to give yet another valid interpretation to partial relational semantics.

The embedding refinement where $[\![\_]\!]_i$ is an embedding of the high-level frame in the low-level frame and $\mathsf{E_H} \sqsubseteq_i \mathsf{E_L}$ implies $[\![(\Xi_\mathsf{H} \times \mathbb{O}_\mathsf{H})]\!]_i \subseteq (\Xi_\mathsf{L} \times \mathbb{O}_\mathsf{L})$ and $[\![[\![\mathsf{E_H}]\!]_{\Xi_\mathsf{H}, O_\mathsf{H}}]\!]_i$ is the same as $[\![\mathsf{E_L}]\!]_{\Xi_\mathsf{L}, O_\mathsf{L}}$ restricted to the high-level frame.

The simple version of vertical refinement with subset or embedding morphisms is able to introduce nondeterminism, outside of frame, unlike one of our refinements defined in Section 3 which never introduces nondeterminism. Nevertheless, we call it a refinement because it offers an engineer a simple guarantee: that any behaviour of the low-level (concrete) specification that lies within the frame is a behaviour of the high-level (abstract) specification.

We consider an example when entities are operations and snapshots are evaluations (given by lists of bindings between angled brackets), that is variable-to-value mappings. Let variable vi be a real (in $\mathbb{R}$) in an abstract operation Op specifying correct behaviour, and

$$\Xi_\mathsf{H} = \{< vi \mapsto x > \mid x \in \mathbb{R}\}$$

$$O_\mathsf{H}(\mathsf{Op}) = \{(< vi \mapsto x >, < vi \mapsto y >) \mid x, y \in \mathbb{R} \wedge (y = x^2 \vee y = x)\}$$

(the pairs here are pre/post condition pairs of valuations). To introduce the error behaviour we refine H into the more concrete L by adding the Boolean vb (in $\mathbb{B}$) and

$$\Xi_\mathsf{L} = \{< vi \mapsto x, vb \mapsto a > \mid x \in \mathbb{R} \wedge a \in \mathbb{B}\}$$

$$O_{\mathsf{L}}([\![\mathsf{Op}]\!]_v) = \{(< vi \mapsto x, vb \mapsto a >, < vi \mapsto y, vb \mapsto b >) \mid x, y \in \mathbb{R} \wedge a, b \in \mathbb{B} \wedge$$
$$(((y = x^2 \vee y = x) \wedge b = true \wedge a = true) \vee (b = false \vee a = false))\}$$

The vertical semantic mapping $[\![\_]\!]_v$ is the obvious embedding of the abstract state into the concrete state when $vb \mapsto true$, the interesting point being that vertical refinement introduces nondeterminism, albeit outside the abstract frame, and $[\![\_]\!]_v$ tells us that the behaviour of the concrete operation only behaves like the abstract specification when vb remains $true$.

What happens to Spivey's problem and the lack of monotonicity when we use robust definitions of refinement and semantics? We are not attempting to offer a magic solution to these problems because we believe there are none, but assume we start with a robust definition of semantics and refinement where the semantics are partial relations. Recall that fixing the refinement fixes the semantics, so if we change the refinement to formalise the behaviour outside the precondition, e.g to being undefined, or to being guarded, then we are forced to change the semantics. We can do this by constructing a Galois connection between two theories. This is where our approach insulates us from relying on informal methodology as we now explain.

Let operation Op have partial relation semantics R_{Op}. Thus for Op we have contexts $\Xi_{\mathsf{Op}} = dom(\mathsf{R}_{\mathsf{Op}})$ and observations $\{(a, b) \mid a \in dom(\mathsf{R}_{\mathsf{Op}}) \wedge b \in ran(\mathsf{R}_{\mathsf{Op}})\}$. This will be true for all our operations, so different operations exist on different layers, or in different theories $(\Xi_{\mathsf{Op}}, O_{\mathsf{Op}})$.

The only formal way we define to reason about operations in different theories is, where possible, to embed one theory in another. Thus only after this has been done for all operations and all operations exist in the same theory or layer, and so all operations are defined over the same domain, can our robust refinements from Section 3 or sequential composition being applied.

What we have ended up with is a very familiar two-step approach: first, reason about partial relations (in their own theories) and avoid refinement and sequencing; and, secondly, only when these partial relations have been used to build total relations (by embedding them all in the same theory) do we apply refinement and sequencing.

We make no claim for novelty here as it can argued that it appears in the B tool kit, in the informal methodology of [5] and even in Dijkstra's early work [24]. What is new is that we have a very abstract framework that can be applied to operations with a wide variety of semantics and informal interpretations. Finally, this section could just have easily been applied to examples that are ADTs or processes.

8 Conclusion

The use of robust definitions of semantics and refinement as favoured in the event-based literature has been used as the basis for a state-based approach that keeps track of what is in the formal model and what remains to be interpreted informally. We advocate three broad principles: define refinement and the semantics of specifications to be robust; even small changes to a formal semantics should be checked formally; in stepwise design the semantic mappings should respect how specifications are composed by their operators, so the semantics of a term is built from the semantics of its components, and our informal intuitions are preserved. By following these principles we have interpreted partial relations as silent outside of frame and only if we consider operations that are all total on some domain have we been able to proceed by formal stepwise development.

Acknowledgements

Thanks are due to the four referees and the programme committee for FM 2009 for their very helpful, challenging and thought-provoking comments, questions and ideas.

References

1. Clarke, A.: The Fabulous Adventures of Nasruddin Hoja. Ta-Ha Publishers Ltd., UK (2001)
2. Roscoe, A.: The Theory and Practice of Concurrency. Prentice Hall International Series in Computer Science (1997)
3. Valmari, A., Tienari, M.: Compositional Failure-based Semantics Models for Basic LOTOS. Formal Aspects of Computing 7, 440–468 (1995)
4. de Roever, W.P., Engelhardt, K.: Data Refinement: Model oriented proof methods and their comparison. Cambridge Tracts in Theoretical Computer Science, vol. 47. Cambridge University Press, Cambridge (1998)
5. Woodcock, J., Davies, J.: Using Z: Specification, Refinement and Proof. Prentice Hall, Englewood Cliffs (1996)
6. Bolton, C., Davies, J.: A singleton failures semantics for communicating sequential processes. Formal Aspects of Computing 18, 181–210 (2006)
7. Reeves, S., Streader, D.: General refinement, part one: interfaces, determinism and special refinement. In: Proceedings of Refine 2008. ENTCS (2008)
8. Reeves, S., Streader, D.: General refinement, part two: flexible refinement. In: Proceedings of Refine 2008. ENTCS (2008)
9. Troelstra, A.S.: From constructivism to computer science. Theor. Comput. Sci. 211, 233–252 (1999)
10. Bridges, D., Reeves, S.: Constructive Mathematics in Theory and Programming Practice. Philosophia Mathematica 7, 65–104 (1999)
11. Derrick, J., Boiten, E.: Relational concurrent refinement. Formal Aspects of Computing 15, 182–214 (2003)
12. Derrick, J., Boiten, E.: Refinement in Z and Object-Z: Foundations and Advanced Applications. In: Formal Approaches to Computing and Information Technology. Springer, Heidelberg (2001)
13. Abrial, J.R.: The B-book: assigning programs to meanings. Cambridge University Press, New York (1996)
14. Hoare, C., Jifeng, H.: Unifying Theories of Programming. International Series in Computer Science. Prentice Hall, Englewood Cliffs (1998)
15. van Glabbeek, R.J.: Linear Time-Branching Time Spectrum I. In: Baeten, J.C.M., Klop, J.W. (eds.) CONCUR 1990. LNCS, vol. 458, pp. 278–297. Springer, Heidelberg (1990)
16. van Glabbeek, R.J.: The Linear Time - Branching Time Spectrum II. In: Best, E. (ed.) CONCUR 1993. LNCS, vol. 715, pp. 66–81. Springer, Heidelberg (1993)
17. Reeves, S., Streader, D.: State- and Event-based refinement. Technical report, University of Waikato (2006), `http://hdl.handle.net/10289/54`

18. He, J., Hoare, C.A.R., Sanders, J.W.: Data refinement refined. In: Robinet, B., Wilhelm, R. (eds.) ESOP 1986. LNCS, vol. 213, pp. 187–196. Springer, Heidelberg (1986)
19. Back, R.J.J., Wright, J.V.: Refinement Calculus: A Systematic Introduction. Springer-Verlag New York, Inc., Secaucus (1998)
20. Spivey, J.M.: The Z notation: A reference manual, 2nd edn. Prentice-Hall International series in computer science. Prentice Hall, Englewood Cliffs (1992)
21. Metayer, C., Abrial, J.R., Voisin, L.: Event-B language. RODIN Project Deliverable D7 (2005)
22. Reeves, S., Streader, D.: Guarded operations, Refinement and Simulation. Technical report, University of Waikato (2009), http://hdl.handle.net/10289/2196
23. Boiten, E., Derrick, J.: Incompleteness of relational simulations in the blocking paradigm. Draft (2008)
24. Dijkstra, E.W.: A Discipline of Programming. Prentice Hall, Englewood Cliffs (1976)

Analysis of a Clock Synchronization Protocol for Wireless Sensor Networks*

Faranak Heidarian**, Julien Schmaltz, and Frits Vaandrager

Institute for Computing and Information Sciences
Radboud University Nijmegen
P.O. Box 9010, 6500 GL Nijmegen, The Netherlands
{F.Heidarian,J.Schmaltz,F.Vaandrager}@cs.ru.nl

Abstract. We study a clock synchronization protocol for the Chess WSN. First, we model the protocol as a network of timed automata and verify various instances using the Uppaal model checker. Next, we present a full parametric analysis of the protocol for the special case of cliques (networks with full connectivity), that is, we give constraints on the parameters that are both necessary and sufficient for correctness. These results have been checked using the proof assistant Isabelle. Finally, we present a negative result for the special case of line topologies: for any instantiation of the parameters, the protocol will eventually fail if the network grows. This result suggests a variation of the fundamental result of Fan and Lynch on gradient clock synchronization, where the synchronization eventually fails as the network diameter grows, for a setting with logical clocks whose value may also decrease.

Keywords: industrial application, clock synchronization, timed automata, model checking, theorem proving, wireless sensor networks.

1 Introduction

Wireless sensor networks (WSNs) consist of potentially thousands of autonomous devices that communicate via radio and use sensors to cooperatively monitor physical or environmental conditions, such as temperature, sound or motion, at different locations. WSNs have numerous exciting applications, ranging from monitoring of dikes to smart kindergartens, and from forest fire detection to monitoring of the Matterhorn. It is an active research area with numerous workshops and conferences arranged each year.

The Dutch company Chess is currently developing a WSN architecture using an epidemic (gossip) communication model [15]. Gossiping in distributed systems refers to the repeated probabilistic exchange of information between two

* Research supported by the European Community's Seventh Framework Programme under grant agreement no 214755 (QUASIMODO). A preliminary version of the model presented in this paper appeared in [14].

** Research supported by NWO/EW project 612.064.610 Abstraction Refinement for Timed Systems (ARTS).

A. Cavalcanti and D. Dams (Eds.): FM 2009, LNCS 5850, pp. 516–531, 2009.

members [8,6]. The effect is that information can spread within a group just as it would in real life. Their simplicity, robustness and flexibility make gossip based algorithms attractive for data dissemination and aggregation in wireless sensor networks. However, formal analysis of gossip algorithms is a challenging research problem [2]. The Chess WSN currently distinguishes three protocol layers: the *Medium Access Control (MAC) layer*, which is responsible for regulating the access to the wireless shared channel,the intermediate *Gossip layer*, which is responsible for insertion of new messages, forwarding of current messages and deletion of old messages, and the *Application layer*, which has the business logic that interprets messages and may generate new messages. In our research we focus on the MAC layer of the Chess WSN. Characteristics of the other layers influence the design decisions for the MAC layer. For instance, the redundant nature of the Gossip layer justifies occasional message loss in the MAC layer.

The MAC layer uses a Time Division Multiple Access (TDMA) protocol. Time is divided in fixed length *frames*, and each frame is subdivided into *slots* (see Figure 1). Slots can be either *active* or *idle*. During active slots, a node is either

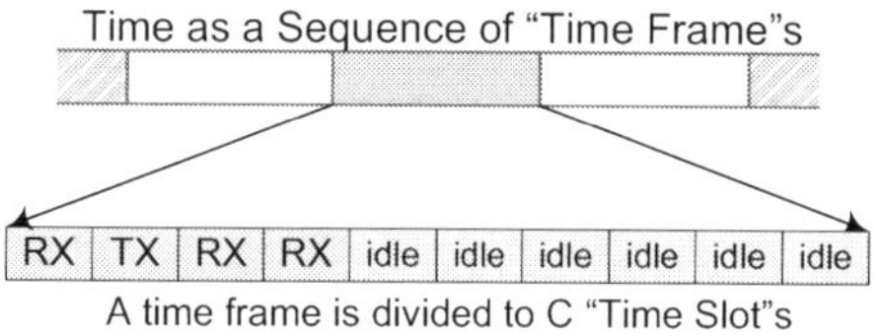

Fig. 1. The structure of a time frame

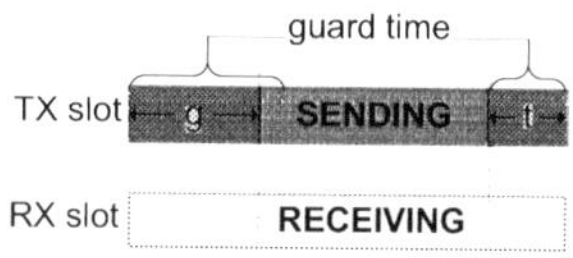

Fig. 2. TX and RX slots

listening for incoming messages from neighboring nodes ("*RX*") or it is sending a message ("*TX*"). During idle slots a node is switched to energy saving mode. These are battery operated devices with an expected uninterrupted field deployment of several years. Hence, energy efficiency is a major concern in the design of WSNs, the number of active slots is typically much smaller than the total number of slots (less than 1% in the current implementation [15]). The active slots are placed in one contiguous sequence which currently is placed at the beginning of the frame. A node can only transmit a message once per time frame in its TX slot. The MAC protocol takes care that neighboring nodes have different TX slots.

One of the greatest challenges in the design of the MAC layer is to find suitable mechanisms for clock synchronization: we must ensure that whenever some node is sending all its neighbors are listening. In this paper, we study clock synchronization in the Chess WSN. Each wireless sensor node comes equipped with a low-cost 32 KHz crystal oscillator that drives an internal clock that is used to determine the start and end of each slot. This may cause the TDMA time slot boundaries to drift and thus lead to situations in which nodes get out of sync. To overcome this problem, the notion of *guard time* is introduced: at the beginning of its TX slot, a sender, ready with its transmission, waits a certain

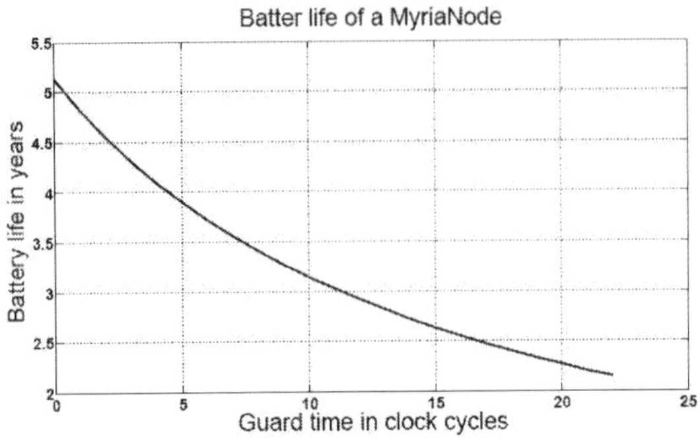

Fig. 3. Battery life as a function of guard time

amount of time for the receiver to be ready to receive messages, and it also waits for some time period at the end of its TX slot (see Figure 2). In the current implementation, each slot consists of 29 clock cycles, out of which 18 cycles are used as guard time. Assegei [1] calculated how the battery life of a wireless sensor node is influenced by the guard time. Figure 3, taken from [1], summarizes these results. Clearly, it is of vital importance to reduce the guard time as much as possible, since this directly affects the battery life, which is a key characteristics of WSNs. Reduction of the guard time is possible if the hardware clocks are properly synchronized.

Many clock synchronization protocols have been proposed for WSNs. In most of these protocols, clocks are synchronized to an accurate real-time standard like Universal Coordinated Time (UTC). We refer to [18] for an overview of this type of protocols. However, these protocols are based on the exchange of time stamp messages, and for the Chess WSN this creates an unacceptable computation and communication overhead. It is possible to come up with more efficient algorithms since for the MAC layer a weak form of clock synchronization suffices: a node only needs to be synchronized to its immediate neighbors, not to faraway nodes or to UTC. Fan and Lynch [7] study the *gradient clock synchronization (GCS)* problem, in which the difference between any two network nodes' clocks must be bounded from above by a non-decreasing function. Thus nearby nodes must be closely synchronized but faraway nodes are allowed to be more loosely synchronized. In the approach of [7], nodes compute logical clock values based on their hardware clocks and message exchanges, and the goal is to synchronize the nodes' logical clocks as closely as possible, while satisfying certain validity conditions. Logical clocks have been introduced by Lamport [9] to totally order the events in a distributed system. A key property of Lamport's logical clocks is that they never run backwards: their value can only increase. In fact, Fan and Lynch [7] assume that the rate of increase of each node's logical clock is at least $\frac{1}{2}$, at all times. Also Meier and Thiele [11], who adapt the work of Fan and Lynch to the setting of wireless sensor networks, make this assumption, but then Pussente and Barbosa [13] assume this rate to be at least $\frac{1}{\mathsf{D}}$, where D is the network diameter. For certain applications of WSNs it is important to have Lamport style logical clocks. For example, if two sensor nodes observe a moving object, then logical clocks allow one to establish the object's direction by determining which node observed the object first [11]. However, for the MAC layer there is no need to compute a total order on events: we only need to ensure that whenever one node is sending all neighbors are listening. If we are willing to set back clocks now and then, we obtain even more efficient clock synchronization protocols.

The current implementation of the Chess WSN uses *Median*, an extension of an algorithm proposed by Tjoa et al [19]. The idea is that in every frame each node computes its phase error to any of its direct neighbors. After the last active slot, each node adjust their clock by the median of the phase error of their immediate neighbors. Assegei [1] points out that the performance of the Median algorithm decreases if the network becomes more dynamic, and proposes a variation of this algorithm that uses Kalman filters. In this paper, we use formal methods to analyze another variation of the Chess algorithm in which a node adjusts its clock whenever a message arrives. Advantages of this algorithm are (a) unlike the Median approach and its variants we need almost no guard time at the end of a sending slot (2 clock ticks suffice instead of 9 ticks in the current implementation), and (b) the computational overhead becomes essentially zero. However, robustness of our algorithm still needs to be explored further.

In Section 2, we model the algorithm using timed automata. Section 3 describes the use of the timed automata model checker UPPAAL[4,3] to analyze WSNs with full connectivity. We verify various instances and identify three different scenarios that may lead to situations where the network is out of sync, Section 4 presents a full parametric analysis of the protocol for cliques (networks with a connection between every pair of nodes), that is, we give constraints on the parameters that are both necessary and sufficient for correctness. We have checked our results using the proof assistent Isabelle [12]. Section 5 presents some result for the special case of line topologies: for any instantiation of the parameters, the protocol will eventually fail if the network grows. This result suggests a variation of the fundamental result of Fan and Lynch [7] on gradient clock synchronization for a setting with logical clocks whose value may also decrease. Section 6, finally, discusses related work and draws conclusions. UPPAAL models and proofs for our paper are available at `http://www.ita.cs.ru.nl/publications/papers/fvaan/HSV09/`.

2 Uppaal Model

In this section, we describe the UPPAAL model that we constructed of the Chess protocol. For a detailed account of the timed automata model checking tool UPPAAL, we refer to [4,3] and to `http://www.uppaal.com`.

We assume a finite, fixed set of wireless nodes $\mathsf{Nodes} = \{0, \ldots, \mathsf{N}-1\}$. The behavior of an individual node $i \in \mathsf{Nodes}$ is described by three timed automata **Clock**(i) (Section 2.1), **WSN**(i) (Section 2.2) and **Synchronizer**(i)

(Section 2.3). Automaton **Clock**(i) models the hardware clock of node i, the **WSN**(i) automaton takes care of sending messages, and the **Synchronizer**(i) automaton resynchronizes the hardware clock of i upon receipt of a message. The complete protocol is modeled as a network that consists of timed automata **Clock**(i), **WSN**(i) and **Synchronizer**(i), for each $i \in \mathsf{Nodes}$.

Table 1 lists the parameters that are used in the model (constants in UPPAAL terminology), together with some basic constraints. The domain of all parameters is the set of natural numbers.

Table 1. Protocol parameters

Parameter	Description	Constraints
N	number of nodes	$0 < \mathsf{N}$
C	number of slots in a time frame	$0 < \mathsf{C}$
n	number of active slots in a time frame	$0 < \mathsf{n} \leq \mathsf{C}$
tsn[i]	TX slot number for node $i \in \mathsf{Nodes}$	$0 \leq \mathsf{tsn}[i] < \mathsf{n}$
$\mathsf{k_0}$	number of clock ticks in a time slot	$0 < \mathsf{k_0}$
g	guard time	$0 < \mathsf{g}$
t	tail time	$0 < \mathsf{g}$, $\mathsf{g} + \mathsf{t} + 2 \leq \mathsf{k_0}$
min	minimal time between two clock ticks	$0 < \mathsf{min}$
max	maximal time between two clock ticks	$\mathsf{min} \leq \mathsf{max}$

2.1 Clock

Timed automaton **Clock**(i) (Fig. 4) models behavior of the hardware clock of node i. It has a single location and a single transition. It comes equipped with a local clock variable x, which is initially 0, that is used to measure the time between clock ticks. Whenever x reaches the value min, the automaton enables an action tick[i]!. Broadcast channel tick[i] is used to synchronize all activities within node i. The tick[i]! event must occur before x has reached value max. Then x is reset to 0 and the (integer) value of i's hardware clock clk[i] is incremented by 1. For convenience and in order to enable model checking, we reset the hardware clock after $\mathsf{k_0}$ ticks, that is, the clock takes integer values modulo $\mathsf{k_0}$ (we use UPPAAL's modulo operator %). This is not an essential modeling assumption and we can easily change this.

2.2 Wireless Sensor Node

The **WSN**(i) automaton, displayed in Figure 6, is the most important automaton in our model. It has three locations and four transitions. The automaton uses an integer variable csn[i], initially 0, to record its current slot number. The automaton stays in initial location WAIT until the current slot number of i equals the TX slot number of i ($\mathsf{csn}[i] = \mathsf{tsn}[i]$) and the gth clock tick in this slot occurs. It then jumps to location GO_SEND. This is an urgent location that is left immediately via a start_message[i]!-transition to location SENDING. Broadcast

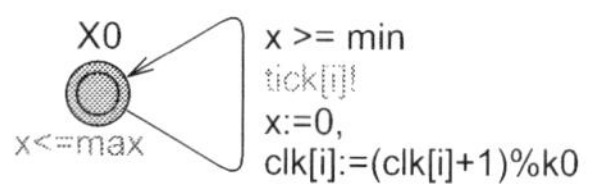

Fig. 4. Clock(i)

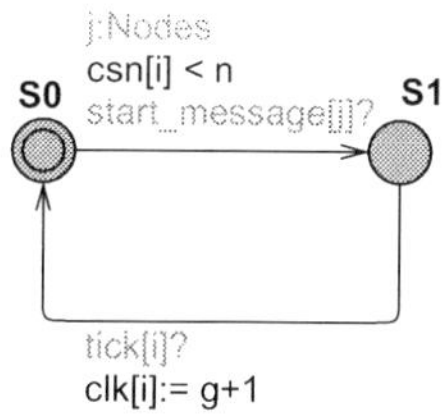

Fig. 5. Synchronizer(i)

channel start_message[i] is used to inform all neigboring nodes that a new message transmission has started. The automaton stays in location SENDING until the start of the tail interval, that is, until the $(\mathsf{k_0} - \mathsf{t})^{th}$ tick in the current slot, and then jumps back to location WAIT. At the end of each slot, i.e., when the $\mathsf{k_0}^{th}$ tick occurs, the automaton increments its current slot number (modulo C).

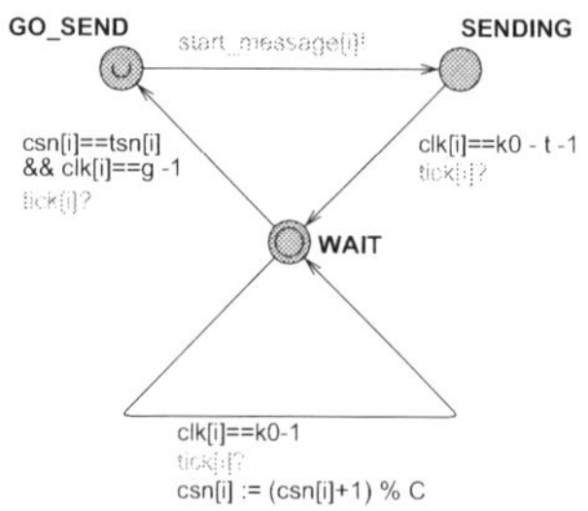

Fig. 6. WSN(i)

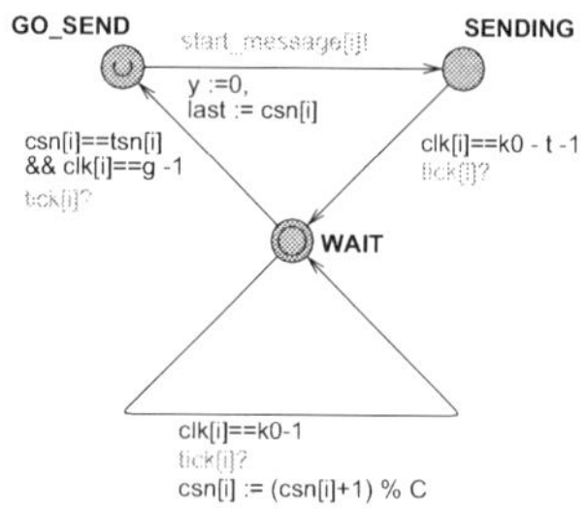

Fig. 7. WSN(i) with history variables

2.3 Synchronizer

The **Synchronizer**(i) automaton (Fig. 5) is the last component of our model. It performs the role of the clock synchronizer in the TDMA protocol. The automaton has two locations and two transitions. The automaton waits in its initial location S0 until some node j starts to transmit a new message, that is, until a start_message[j]? event occurs. We use the UPPAAL select statement to nondeterministically select j. The automaton then moves to location S1, provided node i is active (csn[i] $<$ n). Remember that at the moment when the start_message[j]? event occurs, the hardware clock of node j, clk[j], has value g. Therefore, node i resets its own hardware clock clk[i] to g$+1$ upon occurrence of the first clock tick following the start_message[j]? event. The automaton then returns to its initial location S0.

Note that in our model there is no delay between sending and receipt of messages. Following [11], we assume delay uncertainties to be negligible, and we therefore eliminate the delays themselves from our analysis. When communication is infrequent, this is reasonable since the impact of clock drift dominates over the influence of delay uncertainties.

Automaton **Synchronizer**(i) (Fig. 4) has no constraint on the value of j, that is, we assume that node i can receive messages from all other nodes in the network. Hence the network has full connectivity. It is easy to generalize our model to a setting without full connectivity by adding a guard $\mathsf{neighbor}(i,j)$ to the transition from S0 to S1 that indicates that i is a direct neighbor of j.[1] For networks with full connectivity, we assume that all nodes have unique TX slot numbers:

$$(\forall i,j \in \mathsf{Nodes})(\mathsf{tsn}[i] = \mathsf{tsn}[j] \;\Rightarrow\; i = j).$$

For networks that are not fully connected, this assumption can be relaxed to the requirement that neighboring nodes have distinct TX slot numbers.

3 Uppaal Analysis Results

A wireless sensor network is called *synchronized* if whenever a node is sending all neighboring nodes have the same slot number as the sending node. For networks with full connectivity this means that all nodes in the network agree on the current slot. We obtain the following formal definition of correctness.

Definition 1. *A network with full connectivity is* synchronized *if and only if for all reachable states*

$$(\forall i,j \in \mathsf{Nodes})(\mathsf{SENDING}_i \;\Rightarrow\; \mathsf{csn}[i] = \mathsf{csn}[j]).$$

Our objective is to find necessary and sufficient constraints on the system parameters that ensure that a network with full connectivity is synchronized. To this end, we assign different values to the parameters of the model and use UPPAAL to verify the property of Definition 1. Based on the outcomes (and in particular the counterexamples generated by UPPAAL) we try to derive general constraints. For networks with up to 4 nodes, UPPAAL is able to explore the state space within a few seconds.

It turns out that there are essentially three different scenarios that may lead to a state in which the network is not synchronized. In order to describe these scenarios at an abstract level, we need a bit of notation.

Let $s \in \{0,\ldots,\mathsf{C}-1\}$ be a slot. Then s is a *transmitting* slot, notation $\mathsf{TX}(s)$, if there is some node i that is transmitting in s, that is,

$$\mathsf{TX}(s) \quad\Leftrightarrow\quad (\exists i \in \mathsf{Nodes})(\mathsf{tsn}[i] = s).$$

We let $\mathsf{PREV}(s)$ denote the nearest transmitting slot that precedes s (cyclically). Formally, function $\mathsf{PREV} : \{0,\ldots,\mathsf{C}-1\} \rightarrow \{0,\ldots,\mathsf{C}-1\}$ is defined by

$$\mathsf{PREV}((s+1)\%\mathsf{C}) \;=\; \begin{cases} s & \text{if } \mathsf{TX}(s) \\ \mathsf{PREV}(s) & \text{otherwise} \end{cases} \tag{1}$$

[1] The $\mathsf{neighbor}(i,j)$ predicate does not have to be symmetric. In a wireless sensor network it may occur that i can receive messages from j, but not vice versa.

We write $\mathsf{D}(s)$ to denote the number of slots visited when going from $\mathsf{PREV}(s)$ to s, that is, $\mathsf{D}(s) = (s - \mathsf{PREV}(s))\%C$. We define $\mathsf{M} = \max_s \mathsf{D}(s)$ to be the maximal distance between transmitting slots. As we will see, M plays a key role in defining correctness.

3.1 Scenario 1: Fast Sender - Slow Receiver

In the first error scenario, a sending node is proceeding maximally fast whereas a receiving node runs maximally slow. The sender can then start with the transmission of a message while the receiver is still in an earlier slot. The scenario is illustrated in Figure 8. It starts when the fast and the slow node receive a

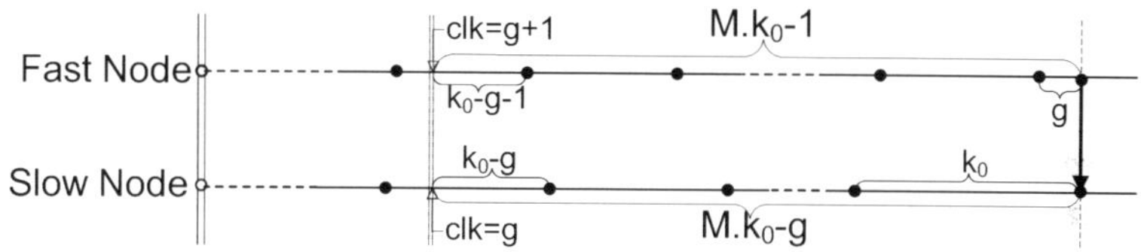

Fig. 8. Scenario 1: Fast Sender - Slow Receiver

synchronization message. Immediately following receipt of this message (at the same point in time), the hardware clock of fast node ticks and the synchronizer resets this clock to $\mathsf{g} + 1$. Now, in the worst case, it may take $\mathsf{M} \cdot \mathsf{k_0} - 1$ ticks before the fast node is in its TX slot with its hardware clock equal to g. Since the hardware clock of the fast node ticks maximally fast, the length of the corresponding time interval is $(\mathsf{M} \cdot \mathsf{k_0} - 1) \cdot \mathsf{min}$. The slow node will reach the TX slot of the fast node after $\mathsf{M} \cdot \mathsf{k_0} - \mathsf{g}$ ticks. With a clock that ticks maximally slow, this may take $(\mathsf{M} \cdot \mathsf{k_0} - \mathsf{g}) \cdot \mathsf{max}$ time. To prevent the fast node from starting transmission before the slow node has moved to the same slot, we must have:

$$(\mathsf{M} \cdot \mathsf{k_0} - \mathsf{g}) \cdot \mathsf{max} < (\mathsf{M} \cdot \mathsf{k_0} - 1) \cdot \mathsf{min} \tag{2}$$

Rather than the lower bound min and the upper bound max on the time between clock ticks, we sometimes find it convenient to consider the ratio

$$\rho = \frac{\mathsf{min}}{\mathsf{max}}$$

Since $0 < \mathsf{min} \leq \mathsf{max}$, it follows that ρ is contained in the interval $(0, 1]$. The following elementary lemma turns out to be quite useful.

Lemma 1. *Constraint (2) is equivalent to* $\mathsf{g} > (1 - \rho) \cdot \mathsf{M} \cdot \mathsf{k_0} + \rho$.

This implies that the worst case scenario occurs when the distance between TX slots is maximal: if the constraint holds for M it also holds when we replace M by a smaller value.

Example 1 (The Chess implementation). Constraint (2) allows us to infer a lower bound on the guard time g. In the current implementation of the protocol by Chess [15], a quartz crystal oscillator is used with a clock drift rate θ of at most 20 ppm (parts per million). This means that

$$\rho = \frac{1-\theta}{1+\theta} = \frac{1-20\cdot 10^{-6}}{1+20\cdot 10^{-6}} \approx 0,99996$$

In the Chess implementation, one time frame lasts for about 1 second. It consists of $\mathsf{C} = 1129$ slots and each slot consists of $\mathsf{k_0} = 29$ clock ticks. The number of active slots is small ($\mathsf{n} = 10$). A typical value for M is $\mathsf{C} - \mathsf{n} = 1119$. Hence

$$\mathsf{g} > (1-\rho)\cdot \mathsf{M}\cdot \mathsf{k_0} + \rho \approx 0,00004\cdot 1119\cdot 29 + 0,99996 = 2.298$$

Thus, according to our theoretical model, a value of $\mathsf{g} = 3$ should suffice. Chess actually uses a guard time of 9. Of course one should realize here that our model is overly simplified and, for instance, does not take into account (uncertainty in) message delays and partial connectivity. We will see that these restrictions greatly influence the minimal guard time.

3.2 Scenario 2: Fast Receiver - Slow Sender - before Transmission

In the second scenario, a receiving node runs maximally fast whereas a sending node proceeds maximally slow. The receiving node already leaves the slot in which it should receive a message from the sender before the sender has even started transmission. This scenario is illustrated in Figure 9. It when the fast

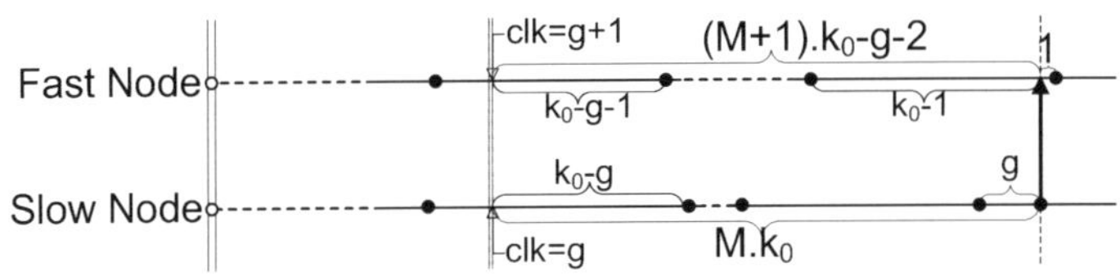

Fig. 9. Scenario 2: Fast Receiver - Slow Sender - before transmission

and the slow node receive a synchronization message. But now the node that has to send the next message runs maximally slow. It sends this message after $\mathsf{M}\cdot\mathsf{k_0}$ ticks have occurred, which takes $\mathsf{M}\cdot\mathsf{k_0}\cdot\mathsf{max}$ time. Meanwhile, the fast node has made maximal progress: immediately after receipt of the first synchronization message (at the same point in time), the hardware clock of the fast node ticks and the synchronizer resets this clock to $\mathsf{g}+1$. Already after $(\mathsf{k_0}-\mathsf{g}-1)\cdot\mathsf{min}$ time the node proceeds to the next slot. Another $(\mathsf{M}\cdot\mathsf{k_0}-1)\cdot\mathsf{min}$ time units later the fast node sets its clock to $\mathsf{k_0}-1$ and is about to leave the slot in which the slow node will send a message. If the slow node starts transmission after this point it is too late: after the next clock tick the fast node will increment its slot counter and the network is no longer synchronized. In order to exclude the second scenario, the following constraint must hold:

$$\mathsf{M} \cdot \mathsf{k_0} \cdot \mathsf{max} < ((\mathsf{M}+1) \cdot \mathsf{k_0} - \mathsf{g} - 2) \cdot \mathsf{min} \tag{3}$$

Also this constraint can be rewritten:

Lemma 2. *Constraint (3) is equivalent to* $\mathsf{g} < (1 - \frac{1}{\rho}) \cdot \mathsf{M} \cdot \mathsf{k_0} + \mathsf{k_0} - 2$.

Thus constraint (3) imposes an upper bound on guard time g. Since in practice one will always try to minimize the guard time in order to save energy, this constraint is only of theoretical interest. If we fill in the values of Example 1, we obtain $\mathsf{g} < 25.8$, which is close to the slot length $\mathsf{k_0} = 29$.

3.3 Scenario 3: Fast Receiver - Slow Sender - during Transmission

Our third scenario concerns a fast receiver and a slow sender. The receiver moves to a new slot while the sender is still transmitting a message. Figure 10 illustrates the scenario. As usual, the hardware clock of the fast node is set to $\mathsf{g}+1$ immediately after receipt of the synchronization message.

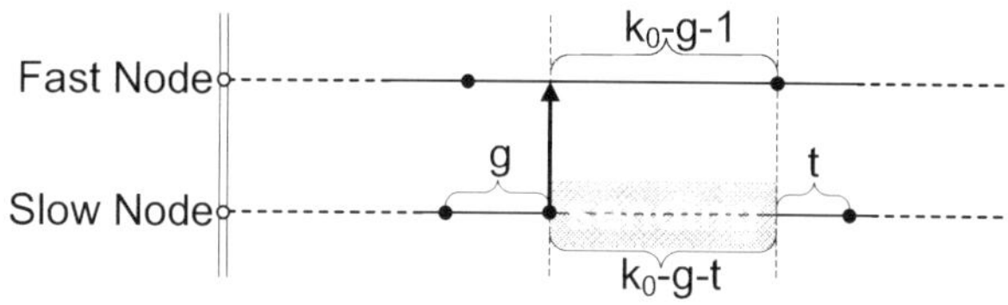

Fig. 10. Scenario 3: Fast Receiver- Slow Sender - during transmission

To exclude this scenario, the following condition should be satisfied:

$$(\mathsf{k_0} - \mathsf{g} - \mathsf{t}) \cdot \mathsf{max} < (\mathsf{k_0} - \mathsf{g} - 1) \cdot \mathsf{min} \tag{4}$$

Essentially, constraint (4) provides a lower bound on t: to rule out the scenario in Fig. 10, the sender should wait long enough before proceeding to the next slot.

Lemma 3. *Constraint (4) is equivalent to* $\mathsf{t} > (1 - \rho)(\mathsf{k_0} - \mathsf{g}) + \rho$.

If we fill in the values of Example 1 with g set to 3, we obtain $\mathsf{t} > 1.001$. Hence a value of $\mathsf{t} = 2$ should suffice. For the simple case of a static network with full connectivity and no uncertainty in message delays, we only need to reserve 5 clock cycles for guard and tail time together. In Section 5, we will see that for different network topologies indeed much larger values are required.

4 Proving Sufficiency of the Constraints

In this section, We outline our proof that the three constrains derived in Section 3 are sufficient to ensure synchronization in networks with full connectivity. We start our proof by stating some elementary invariants.

Lemma 4. *For any network with full connectivity the following invariant assertions hold, for all reachable states and for all* $i \in \mathsf{Nodes}$*:*

$$0 \leq \mathsf{x}_i \leq \mathsf{max} \tag{5}$$
$$0 \leq \mathsf{clk}[i] < \mathsf{k_0} \tag{6}$$
$$0 \leq \mathsf{csn}[i] < \mathsf{C} \tag{7}$$
$$\mathsf{GO\_SEND}_i \Rightarrow \mathsf{x}_i = 0 \tag{8}$$
$$\mathsf{GO\_SEND}_i \Rightarrow \mathsf{csn}[i] = \mathsf{tsn}[i] \tag{9}$$
$$\mathsf{GO\_SEND}_i \Rightarrow \mathsf{clk}[i] \in \{\mathsf{g}, \mathsf{g}+1\} \tag{10}$$
$$\mathsf{SENDING}_i \Rightarrow \mathsf{csn}[i] = \mathsf{tsn}]i] \tag{11}$$
$$\mathsf{SENDING}_i \Rightarrow \mathsf{g} \leq \mathsf{clk}[i] < \mathsf{k_0} - \mathsf{t} \tag{12}$$

Invariants (5), (6) and (7) assert that the state variables indeed take values in their intended domains: clock variables stay within the (real-valued) range $[0, \mathsf{max}]$, hardware clocks stay within the integer range $[0, \mathsf{k_0})$, and current slot numbers stay within the integer range $[0, \mathsf{C})$. Invariants (8)-(12) directly follow from the definitions of the automata in the network. For invariant (10), observe that since the tick?-transition from WAIT to GO_SEND may synchronize with the tick?-transition from S1 to S0, the value of $\mathsf{clk}[i]$ in $\mathsf{GO\_SEND}_i$ is potentially $\mathsf{g}+1$.

To be able to state more interesting invariants, we introduce two auxiliary global history (or ghost) variables. Clock y records the time that has elapsed since the last synchronization message (or the beginning of the protocol). Variable last records the last slot in which a synchronization message has been sent (initially $\mathsf{last} = -1$). Figure 7 shows the version of the $\mathbf{WSN}(i)$ automaton obtained after adding these variables. The only change is that upon occurrence of a synchronization $\mathsf{start\_message}[i]!$ clock y is reset to 0 and variable last is reset to $\mathsf{csn}[i]$.

We first state a few basic invariants which restrict the values of the new variables.

Lemma 5. *For any network with full connectivity the following invariant assertions hold, for all reachable states and for all* $i \in \mathsf{Nodes}$*:*

$$0 \leq \mathsf{y} \tag{13}$$
$$-1 \leq \mathsf{last} < \mathsf{C} \tag{14}$$
$$\mathsf{S1}_i \Rightarrow \mathsf{y} \leq \mathsf{x}_i \tag{15}$$
$$\mathsf{last} = -1 \Rightarrow \mathsf{S0}_i \tag{16}$$

Invariant (13) says that y is always nonnegative and invariant (14) says that last takes values in the integer domain $[-1, \mathsf{C}-1)$. If the system is in $\mathsf{S1}_i$ then a synchronization occurred after the last clock tick (invariant (15)), and if the system is in $\mathsf{S0}_i$ then no synchronization occurred yet (invariant (16)).

The key idea behind our correctness proof is that, given the local state of some node i and the value of last, we can compute the number $c(i)$ of ticks of i's hardware clock that has occurred since the last synchronization. Since we know the minimal and maximal clock speeds, we can then derive an interval that contains the value of y, the amount of real-time that has elapsed since the last synchronization. Next, given the value of y, we can compute an interval that contains the value of $c(j)$, for arbitrary node j. Once we know the value of $c(j)$, this gives us some information about the local state of node j. Through these correspondences, we are able to infer that if node i is sending the slot number of i and j must be equal.

Formally, for $i \in \mathsf{Nodes}$, the state function $c(i)$ is defined by

$$
\begin{aligned}
c(i) = \ &\textbf{if } \mathsf{last} = -1 \textbf{ then } \mathsf{clk}[i] \textbf{ else}\\
&\qquad \textbf{if } \mathsf{S1}_i \textbf{ then } 0 \textbf{ else}\\
&\qquad\qquad ((\mathsf{csn}[i] - \mathsf{last})\%\mathsf{C}) \cdot \mathsf{k_0} + \mathsf{clk}[i] - \mathsf{g}\\
&\qquad \textbf{fi}\\
&\textbf{fi}
\end{aligned}
$$

If there has been no synchronization yet ($\mathsf{last} = -1$) then $c(i)$ is just equal to the hardware clock $\mathsf{clk}[i]$. If the synchronizer is in location $\mathsf{S1}_i$, then we know that there has been no tick since the last synchronization, so $c(i)$ is set to 0. Otherwise, $c(i)$ is $\mathsf{k_0}$ times the number of slots since the last synchronization, incremented by the number of ticks in the current slot, minus g to take into account that the hardware clock has been reset to $\mathsf{g}+1$ after the last synchronization.

We can now state the main invariant result from this section.

Theorem 1. *Assume constraints (2), (3) and (4) hold. Then for any network with full connectivity the following invariant assertions hold, for all reachable states and for all* $i, j \in \mathsf{Nodes}$*:*

$$\mathsf{y} \leq c(i) \cdot \mathsf{max} + \mathsf{x}_i \tag{17}$$

$$c(i) > 0 \Rightarrow \mathsf{y} \geq (c(i) - 1) \cdot \mathsf{min} + \mathsf{x}_i \tag{18}$$

$$\mathsf{csn}[i] = \mathsf{tsn}[i] \wedge (\mathsf{clk}[i] < \mathsf{g} \vee \mathsf{GO\_SEND}_i) \Rightarrow \mathsf{last} \neq \mathsf{csn}[i] \tag{19}$$

$$\mathsf{csn}[i] = \mathsf{tsn}[i] \wedge \mathsf{clk}[i] = \mathsf{g} \Rightarrow (\mathsf{GO\_SEND}_i \vee \mathsf{SENDING}_i) \tag{20}$$

$$\mathsf{csn}[i] = \mathsf{tsn}[i] \wedge \mathsf{clk}[i] > \mathsf{g} \Rightarrow \mathsf{last} = \mathsf{csn}[i] \tag{21}$$

$$\mathsf{SENDING}_i \Rightarrow \mathsf{csn}[i] = \mathsf{csn}[j] = \mathsf{last} \tag{22}$$

$$\mathsf{GO\_SEND}_i \Rightarrow \mathsf{csn}[i] = \mathsf{csn}[j] \wedge \mathsf{clk}[i] = \mathsf{g} \tag{23}$$

$$\mathsf{last} \neq -1 \wedge \mathsf{last} \neq \mathsf{PREV}(\mathsf{csn}[i]) \Rightarrow (\mathsf{TX}(\mathsf{csn}[i]) \wedge \mathsf{last} = \mathsf{csn}[i]) \tag{24}$$

$$\mathsf{TX}(\mathsf{csn}[i]) \wedge \mathsf{clk}[i] = \mathsf{k_0} - 1 \Rightarrow \mathsf{last} = \mathsf{csn}[i] \tag{25}$$

$$\mathsf{S1}_i \Rightarrow \mathsf{clk}[i] < \mathsf{k}_0 - 1 \wedge \mathsf{last} = \mathsf{csn}[i] \quad (26)$$

$$c(i) \geq 0 \quad (27)$$

$$\mathsf{last} = -1 \Rightarrow \mathsf{csn}[i] = 0 \quad (28)$$

Proof. By induction, using the auxiliary invariants from Lemma's 4 and 5. The manual proof is about 14 pages long.

Invariants (17) and (18) are the key invariants that relate the values of $c(i)$ and y. Invariant (22) implies that the network is synchronized. This is the key correctness property we are interested in. All the other invariants in Theorem 1 are auxiliary assertions, needed to make the invariant inductive.

5 Line Topologies

The line topology has the minimum connectivity. The number of clock synchronization events per time frame is the least possible value for all (connected) topologies. To maintain synchronization, we need more accurate hardware clocks and a larger guard time. We assert that for a fixed value of the guard time, the network fails to synchronize if one keeps increasing the number of nodes. We claim that for a line network of size N, guard time g should be at least N.

To reduce the state space of the UPPAAL analysis, we consider only networks with perfect clocks, in which clock drift is zero. In UPPAAL concurrent events are non-deterministically ordered. Depending on this choice, clock misalignment and loss of synchronization are possible.

Figure 11 shows a scenario extracted from a UPPAAL counter-example. This scenario shows that for a network of size N the guard time cannot be $\mathsf{N} - 1$.

The scenario consists of two "staircases". One "fast" staircase has stairs with the minimum width, where the sender transmits the synchronization signal immediately before the receiver experiences a tick event and the receiver resets its clock counter to $g + 1$ in no time as the transitions are urgent, while the other "slow" staircase has stairs with the maximum width, where the sender transmits the synchronization signal immediately after the receiver experienced a tick event, so the receiver should wait a the duration of a tick before resetting its clock counter to $g + 1$. The staircases start from the same point, viz. when node number 1,the second node, tries to send messages to its neighbors, nodes 0 and 2. After $\mathsf{N} - 1$ steps, which takes a guard time period, the two staircases join again when node $\mathsf{N} - 2$ tries to communicate with node $\mathsf{N} - 1$. At that point, node $\mathsf{N} - 2$ has gone through g time units since its previous synchronization and is about to send a message to node $\mathsf{N} - 1$. On the other hand, node $\mathsf{N} - 1$ is about to make a clock tick and enter its new time slot, which is convenient for receiving the message from its neighbor. Synchronization is lost when node $\mathsf{N} - 2$ starts sending before node $\mathsf{N} - 1$ ticks.

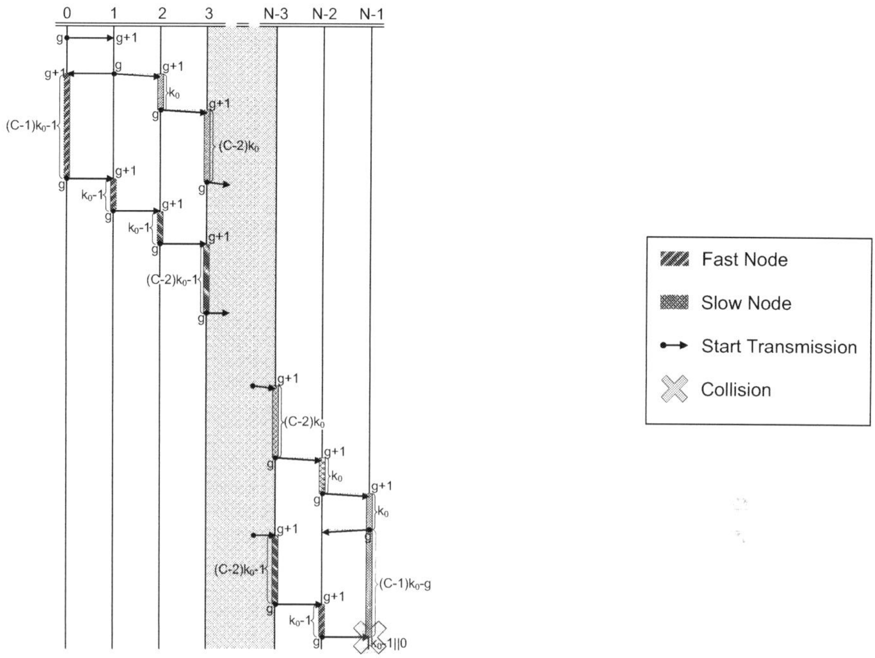

Fig. 11. An error scenario for line topologies

6 Conclusions and Related Work

Using timed automata model checking, we discovered some interesting error scenarios for line topologies: for any instantiation of the parameters, the protocol will eventually fail if the network grows. We believe that this error scenario is generic and may serve as a basis for a variation of the fundamental result of Fan and Lynch [7], reasserted by Locher and Wattenhofer [10], on gradient clock synchronization in a setting with logical clocks whose value may also decrease. We also succeeded in presenting a parametric verification for the very restrictive case of cliques (network with full connectivity). We used model checking to find the key error scenarios that underly the parameter constraints for correctness, and theorem proving to check the correctness of our manual invariant proof. In practical applications of WSNs, cliques rarely occur and therefore our results should primarily be seen as a first step towards a correctness proof for arbitrary and dynamically changing network topologies. Nevertheless, these results could give us an upper bound on allowable clock drift of a generic WSN.

The use of simulations will be essential for providing additional insight into the robustness and usefulness of our algorithm, also because occasional flaws of the MAC layer protocol may be resolved by the redundancy of the gossip layer. However, we believe simulation techniques will not be able to produce worst case counterexamples, such as the example of Figure 11 that was produced by the model checker UPPAAL.

Methodologically, the approach of this paper is similar to our study of the Biphase Mark Protocol [21], which also uses UPPAAL to analyze instances of the protocol and a theorem prover for the full parametric analysis. Theorem provers have been frequently and successfully applied for the analysis of clock synchronization protocols, see for instance [16,17]. An interesting research challenge is to synthesize (or prove the correctness of) the parameter constraints for the Chess protocol fully automatically. Recently, some approaches have been presented by which, for instance, the (parametric) Biphase Mark Protocol can be verified fully automatically [5,20]. However, we think these approaches are not powerful enough (yet) to handle the Chess protocol.

Acknowledgement. Many thanks to Frits van der Wateren, Marcel Verhoef and Bert Bos from Chess for explaining their WSN algorithms to us.

References

1. Assegei, F.A.: Decentralized frame synchronization of a TDMA-based wireless sensor network. Master's thesis, Eindhoven University of Technology, Department of Electrical Engineering (2008)
2. Bakhshi, R., Bonnet, F., Fokkink, W., Haverkort, B.: Formal analysis techniques for gossiping protocols. SIGOPS Oper. Syst. Rev. 41(5), 28–36 (2007)
3. Behrmann, G., David, A., Larsen, K.G., Håkansson, J., Pettersson, P., Yi, W., Hendriks, M.: Uppaal 4.0. In: Third International Conference on the Quantitative Evaluation of SysTems (QEST 2006), Riverside, CA, USA, September 11-14, pp. 125–126. IEEE Computer Society, Los Alamitos (2006)
4. Behrmann, G., David, A., Larsen, K.G.: A tutorial on Uppaal. In: Bernardo, M., Corradini, F. (eds.) SFM-RT 2004. LNCS, vol. 3185, pp. 200–236. Springer, Heidelberg (2004)
5. Brown, G.M., Pike, L.: Easy parameterized verification of biphase mark and 8n1 protocols. In: Hermanns, H., Palsberg, J. (eds.) TACAS 2006. LNCS, vol. 3920, pp. 58–72. Springer, Heidelberg (2006)
6. Demers, A., Greene, D., Hauser, C., Irish, W., Larson, J., Shenker, S., Sturgis, H., Swinehart, D., Terry, D.: Epidemic algorithms for replicated database maintenance. In: PODC 1987: Proceedings of the sixth annual ACM Symposium on Principles of distributed computing, pp. 1–12. ACM, New York (1987)
7. Fan, R., Lynch, N.A.: Gradient clock synchronization. Distributed Computing 18(4), 255–266 (2006)
8. Kermarrec, A.-M., van Steen, M.: Gossiping in distributed systems. SIGOPS Oper. Syst. Rev. 41(5), 2–7 (2007)
9. Lamport, L.: Time, clocks and the ordering of events in distributed systems. Communications of the ACM 21(7), 558–564 (1978)
10. Locher, T., Wattenhofer, R.: Oblivious gradient clock synchronization. In: Dolev, S. (ed.) DISC 2006. LNCS, vol. 4167, pp. 520–533. Springer, Heidelberg (2006)
11. Meier, L., Thiele, L.: Gradient clock synchronization in sensor networks. Technical Report 219, Computer Engineering and Networks Lab., ETH Zurich (2005)

12. Nipkow, T., Paulson, L.C., Wenzel, M.: Isabelle/HOL - A Proof Assistant for Higher-Order Logic. LNCS, vol. 2283. Springer, Heidelberg (2002)
13. Pussente, R.M., Barbosa, V.C.: An algorithm for clock synchronization with the gradient property in sensor networks. Parallel and Distributed Computing 69, 261–265 (2009)
14. QUASIMODO. Case studies: Models, Deliverable 5.5 from the FP7 ICT STREP project 214755 (QUASIMODO) (January 2009)
15. QUASIMODO. Preliminary description of case studies, Deliverable 5.2 from the FP7 ICT STREP project 214755 (QUASIMODO) (January 2009)
16. Rushby, J.: A formally verified algorithm for clock synchronization under a hybrid fault model. In: PODC 1994: Thirteenth annual ACM symposium on Principles of distributed computing, pp. 304–313. ACM, New York (1994)
17. Schmaltz, J.: A formal model of clock domain crossing and automated verification of time-triggered hardware. In: Baumgartner, J., Sheeran, M. (eds.) Formal methods in computer aided design, pp. 223–230. IEEE Computer Society, Los Alamitos (2007)
18. Sundararaman, B., Buy, U., Kshemkalyani, A.D.: Clock synchronization for wireless sensor networks: a survey. Ad Hoc Networks 3(3), 281–323 (2005)
19. Tjoa, R., Chee, K.L., Sivaprasad, P.K., Rao, S.V., Lim, J.G.: Clock drift reduction for relative time slot tdma-based sensor networks. In: Proceedings of the 15th IEEE International Symposium on Personal, Indoor and Mobile Radio Communications (PIMRC 2004), September 2004, pp. 1042–1047 (2004)
20. Umeno, S.: Event order abstraction for parametric real-time system verification. In: EMSOFT, pp. 1–10. ACM, New York (2008)
21. Vaandrager, F.W., de Groot, A.L.: Analysis of a biphase mark protocol with Uppaal and PVS. Formal Asp. Comput. 18(4), 433–458 (2006)

Formal Verification of Avionics Software Products

Jean Souyris[1], Virginie Wiels[2], David Delmas[1], and Hervé Delseny[1]

[1] Airbus France S.A.S.
316, route de Bayonne
31060 TOULOUSE Cedex 9, France
[2] Onera / DTIM*
2 avenue E. Belin, BP 74025
31055 Toulouse cedex, France
jean.souyris@airbus.com, Virginie.Wiels@onera.fr,
david.delmas@airbus.com, herve.delseny@airbus.com

Abstract. This paper relates an industrial experience in the field of formal verification of avionics software products. Ten years ago we presented our very first technological research results in [18]. What was just an idea plus some experimental results at that time is now an industrial reality. Indeed, since 2001, Airbus has been integrating several tool supported formal verification techniques into the development process of avionics software products. Just like all aspects of such processes, the use of formal verification techniques must comply with DO-178B [9] objectives and Airbus has been a pioneer in this domain.

Keywords: avionics software, safety, development process, verification, formal verification, Abstract Interpretation, static analysis.

1 Introduction

Industrial context. Avionics software products in onboard computers are major components of the systems of an aircraft. Such software products are developed according to very stringent rules imposed by the DO-178B standard. Of course verification, although being one activity among others, is the heaviest task of the development of an avionics software product. Verification, as defined by DO-178B, is performed by reviews, analyses or tests. The first two ones are purely intellectual while the latter basically consists in executing the program to be verified and in checking whether the results of this execution are those expected.

Airbus technological research in Formal Verification. The above mentioned verification means constituted the state of the art at the time DO-178B was written. During the last decade, new verification techniques coming from research in Computer Science have become usable in the industry of critical embedded software. These techniques are formal and are usually categorized as follows: Abstract Interpretation based static analysis, theorem proving and model-checking.

* Onera is the French aerospace lab and is working with Airbus on methods and certification aspects of formal verification.

A. Cavalcanti and D. Dams (Eds.): FM 2009, LNCS 5850, pp. 532–546, 2009.

Transfer to operational teams. Since 2001, Airbus has been transferring formal verification tools – and associated methods of use – to its teams who develop avionics software. The first set of tools to be transferred have been: Caveat [18], aiT [12] and Stackanalyzer [23] . They are all used for achieving some DO-178B verification objective. This means that they have been *qualified* in the sense of this standard.

The aim of this paper is to show how the development of avionics software could benefit from formal verification techniques far beyond their first use mentioned just above. This paper is based on the synthesis of ongoing technological research work at Airbus, in close cooperation with academic and industrial labs. The various aspects of this research are handled – or have been handled – in the context of the following past or ongoing research projects: DAEDALUS [5], ASTREE [1], THESEE [24], CAT [2], U3CAT [25], ASBAPROD (French civilian aviation project), ES_PASS [11].

Structure of the paper. Section 2 is a quick overview of the development and verification process of a DO-178B conforming avionics product. In section 3, the formal verification technologies used by Airbus are presented, whether already used industrially or close to be. Sections 4 and 5 show what development activities it is possible to base on the use of the tools introduced in section 3, and what are possible development processes including these activities. Considerations about the compliance of these new processes to DO-178B and, beyond, to DO-178C (the standard being defined) are discussed in section 6. Section 7 concludes and introduces future work.

2 DO-178B Compliant Development Process of an Avionics Software Product

The development of avionics software products has to conform to the DO-178B [9] standard. DO-178B does not prescribe a specific development process, it identifies important steps inside a development process and defines objectives for each of these steps. DO-178B distinguishes the development processes from "integral" processes that are meant to ensure correctness control and confidence of the software life cycle processes and their outputs. The verification process is part of the integral processes. In this section, we give an overview of the development and verification processes.

2.1 Development Processes

Four processes are identified:

- The software requirements process develops High Level Requirements (HLR) from the outputs of the system process;
- The software design process develops Low Level Requirements (LLR) and Software Architecture from the HLR;
- The software coding process develops source code from the software architecture and the LLR;
- The software integration process loads executable object code into the target hardware for hardware/software integration.

Each of the above mentioned processeses is a step towards the actual software product, Figure 1 presents the different steps.

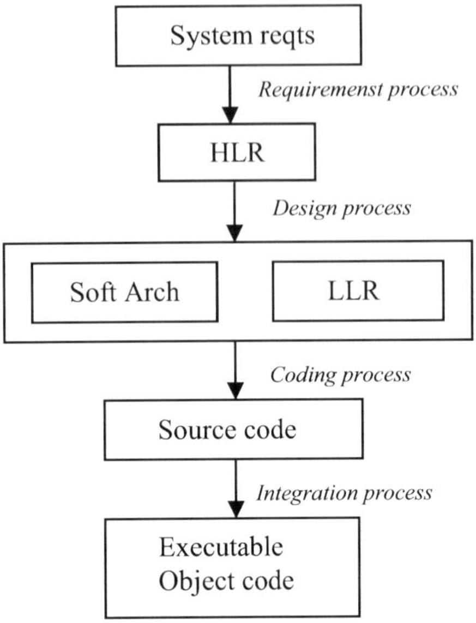

Fig. 1. DO-178B development processes

So far, for the software products it develops, Airbus has been defining the Low Level Requirements as being applied to design entities that are later implemented in the form of modules and functions of the programming language (C, most of the time) in a one-to-one manner. The way those design entities collaborate in order to implement the High Level Requirements is first defined during the software architecture phase.

2.2 Verification Process

The results of all activities[1] of the development must be verified. Detailed objectives are defined for each step of the development, typically some objectives are defined on the output of a development process itself and also on the compliance of this output to the input of the process that produced it. For example, Figure 2 presents the objectives related to LLR. Arrows are labeled with verification objectives; the loop arrow on LLR means the objectives only concern LLR while the arrow between LLR and HLR means that objectives address relationships between LLR and HLR.

On one hand, LLR shall be accurate and consistent, compatible with the target computer, verifiable, conform to requirements standards, and they shall ensure algorithm accuracy. On the other hand, LLR shall be compliant and traceable to HLR.

Verification means identified by DO-178B are reviews, analyses and test. Reviews provide a qualitative assessment of correctness. Analyses provide repeatable assessment of correctness. Reviews and analyses are used for all the verification objectives regarding HLR, LLR, software architecture and source code. Test is used to verify

[1] We use the terms activity and process, a process is a set of activities.

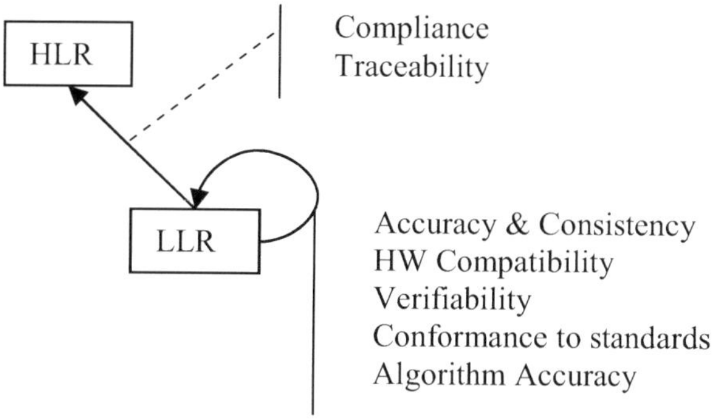

Fig. 2. Verification objectives associated to LLR

that the executable object is compliant with LLR and HLR. Test is always based on the requirements (functional test) and shall include normal range and robustness cases. A structural coverage analysis is performed to ensure that the software has been tested enough (different coverage criteria are used depending on the criticality level of the software).

3 Formal Verification Technologies Applicable to Avionics Programs

In this section, we briefly present the two kinds of formal techniques used for the verification of avionics programs (deductive methods and Abstract Interpretation based static analysis) and we describe the associated tools.

3.1 Deductive Methods

The first kind of formal technique we consider for the verification of programs is deductive proof based on Hoare logic [15], and the computation of Dijkstra's weakest precondition predicate transformer [8]. The objective is to prove user defined properties on a given program. Properties must be formally expressed in logic. This technique proceeds in two steps:

- computation of the verification conditions: post-conditions (properties that should hold after the execution of the program) are defined, this first step analyses the program and computes the conditions that must hold for these post-conditions to be verified;
- proof of the verification conditions: a theorem prover is used to prove the conditions computed before.

The first step is completely automated, the second step usually requires interaction with the user, but automation can be improved by the definition of specific heuristics.

Several tools exist for different programming languages (mostly C and java). The tools considered in this paper are Caveat and Frama-C [14].

3.2 Abstract Interpretation Based Static Analysis

The second kind of techniques is techniques based on Abstract Interpretation [4]. The principle of Abstract interpretation is the construction of a sound approximation of the semantics of programs. A specific approximation is generated for each particular property being analysed. Abstract interpretation is a completely automated technique. It may produce so called "false positives" (errors that can occur on the approximation of the program that has been computed, but cannot occur on the real program). The challenge is thus to be able to build a precise enough approximation in order to have as few false positives as possible. This usually implies a specialisation of the technique with respect to the analysed programs.

The Abstract Interpretation based tools considered in this paper are Astrée [3], aiT [12], Stackanalyzer [23] and Fluctuat [6].

3.3 Tools

We only present briefly the tools, the use of tools in the Airbus process will be described in section 4.

Caveat [18] is the first formal verification tool that Airbus has been using in development (since 2002). Caveat analyses C programs (with some restrictions in terms of language constructs) and has its own specification (or property) language based on first order logic.

Caveat proposes two main functionalities:

- data and control flow analysis;
- proof of user-specified properties.

Data and control flows analyses are fully automatic on the set of C modules given to Caveat.

Proof of user-specified properties is in general not automatic. For completing a proof or understanding why it cannot be completed, the user can use Caveat Interactive Predicate Transformer. This interactive part of the tool takes a first order logic formula as input that the user can handle in order to prove it equivalent to *true* or to understand that it is not possible. Each predicate transformation is performed under the control of the tool.

Frama-C [14] is a toolbox that aims at analysing C programs. It is extensible by means of plug-ins. A plug-in implements a specific analysis and can exchange data with other plug-ins or with the core of Frama-C thanks to a common specification language called ACSL.

Examples of existing plug-ins are:

- Abstract Interpretation based value analysis;
- Slicing;
- Weakest Precondition (WP) computation whose proof obligations are given to the WHY platform of provers.

It must be noticed that the development of simple but useful plug-ins is accessible to industrial Frama-C users.

Whereas Frama-C mixes several techniques coming from research in Computer Science, the following tools are all based on Abstract Interpretation.

Astrée [3] analyses – a subset of - C programs on which it aims at proving the absence of Run-Time Errors (RTE). Since it has been designed in the context of the Abstract Interpretation theory [13], it might produce *false alarms*, also called *false positives*, due to the abstraction of the concrete semantics of the analysed program. In order to make it industrially usable on safety-critical programs, Astrée had to be specialized for a family of programs. This has been made for control-command synchronous programs produced from SCADE (or SAO, SCADE ancestor) models. The result is that Astrée precision is very high (almost zero *false positives*) when analysing programs that belong to the family for which it has been specialized. Scalability is also very good, i.e., 500,000 lines of code are analysed successfully within a timescale compatible with industrial development constraints.

aiT [12] analyses a program in its binary form for computing an upper bound of the Worst Case Execution Time (WCET) of the program tasks. This static analyser contributes to proving that the timing constraints assigned to a program are met. Indeed all kinds of schedulability analyses take the WCET of the tasks of the system as input. Because the execution time of a piece of code also depends on the hardware on which it is intended to be executed, aiT includes a model of the target processor and its associated memory controller. Whereas the drawback of abstraction is the *false positive* in the case of an Abstract Interpretation based static analyser dealing with RTE, the counterpart for aiT is the overestimation of the WCET (upper bound).

Stackanalyzer [23] analyses a program in its binary form for computing an upper bound of the amount of memory actually used by the program task stack. This static analysis contributes to proving that no execution of the program will cause a stack overflow.

Fluctuat [6]. Whereas in mathematics the set of real numbers is infinite, the set of floating-point numbers is finite, be it float, double, etc. So, during the float operations performed by a program, rounding errors affect the results. This might lead to a significant difference between a floating-point value and the real one that should have been computed. Furthermore, a calculus scheme might be stable in the real arithmetic and become instable in the floating-point arithmetic. With respect to this problem, Fluctuat analyses C programs – note that there is a Fluctuat for a specific assembly language (TMS320C33 processor) – for computing safe ranges for:

- The floating-point values the variables still alive at the end of the program may have;
- The error between the floating point value and the real one that should have been computed if operations were in the real numbers, for each variable still alive at the end of the program.

Fluctuat does not only compute these ranges, it also allows the user to find the origin of imprecisions in its code. Problems like lacks of precision, instability, sensitivity are detected by this static analyser.

Certified compilation. There are various approaches for proving that a program in its binary (or assembly) form is semantically equivalent to the source program (in C, for instance) from which it has been compiled. Two of them are being considered: the

Translation validation [19] and the Certified compiler [17]. The first one consists in proving that after each production of a binary file, this executable program is semantically equivalent to the input source program (e.g., in C files). This is a kind of validator separated from the compiler. The second selected approach, i.e., the Certified compiler, consists in developing a compiler formally and proving once and for all that it produces target programs semantically equivalent to source programs.

Certified compilation is of utmost importance in itself, especially for safety-critical software products. It is also natural to consider it when formal verification is performed on source programs. Indeed, a bug of a compiler might lead to produce a code on which some proof of a property made on the source code does not longer hold.

4 Development Process Activities Based on the Use of Formal Techniques

4.1 Operational Use of Formal Methods

Unit Proof [10, 21]. Within the development process of the most safety-critical avionics programs, the unit verification technique is used for achieving DO-178B objectives related to the verification of the executable code with respect to the Low Level Requirements, the classical technique being the Unit Tests. Since 2002, a formal approach to Unit Verification is also used industrially: Unit Proof. The tool used for this activity is Caveat (see section 3.3). Basically, it consists in:

- Writing formal Low Level Requirements in Caveat property language during the detailed design activity of the development process;
- Once a C module has been written during the coding activity, the formal requirements of this C module and the module itself are given to Caveat for proving. This activity is performed for each C function of each C module. When a C function is called by the one being proved it is stubbed according to a sound technique.

Worst Case Execution Time analysis [22]. In real-time systems, computing correct values is not enough. Indeed, the program must also compute these values in due time in order to remain synchronised with the physical environment. The scheduling of the most critical avionics real-time programs is an *off-line scheduling*. This means that the serialisation (single processor) of the various program tasks is performed at design time, leading to a fixed interleaving of these tasks. In this context, schedulability analysis boils down to the safe computation of an upper bound of the Worst Case Execution Time of the program tasks, almost exclusively. This computation is performed with aiT (see section 3.3).

Maximum stack usage computation. The amount of memory given to a task of an avionics program is determined statically when the program is built. If any task stack of a program actually requires more memory than what has been allocated statically, a stack overflow exception is raised during execution. In order to avoid this serious problem, a safe upper bound of each stack of the program must be computed. With these figures, the computation a safe upper bound of the total amount of memory used for stacks is performed, by means of an analysis that takes into account some mechanisms such as interrupt tasks or Operating System calls.

4.2 Envisaged Use of Formal Methods

Integration Proof. The kind of defects that are covered by the Unit Proof technique does not include the ones that arise when a C function calls another one with a wrong interpretation of the service provided by the latter. Let us call this sort of bugs "design bugs" since they are introduced during the activity which aims at defining the interfaces between the future C functions.

Integration Proof is being elaborated in the frame of the research project ASBAPROD and can be defined as an extension of the Unit Proof technique. Indeed, instead of considering C functions individually, Integration Proof deals with sub-trees of the program call tree. Let us consider an example. Suppose four C functions: f(), g(), h() and i(), f() being the entry point of a call-tree (sub-tree of the whole program call-tree) containing the other C functions. Whereas the Unit Proof technique aims at proving that f (), g(), h() and i() satisfy their individual formal requirements without taking into account the semantics of their callees (the C functions they call), the goal of Integration Proof technique is to prove that the formal requirements of function f() are satisfied by taking into account the semantics of all C functions contained in "its" call-tree. The relevant design entities are bigger than the ones considered in Unit Proof but smaller than the whole program. The reason why we did not move from the proof of each C function individually to the proof of the whole – sequential – program made of these C functions is the fact that we want to keep a great automatic proof rate, for obvious industrial reasons. It is a design-time issue to define these intermediate-level entities in such a way that their further proof is as automatic as possible.

Proof of absence of Run-Time error [7, 20]. The underlying notion has been presented in several academic papers, such as [3, §2]: "*The absence of runtime errors is the implicit specification that there is no violation of the C norm (e.g., array index of bounds), no implementation-specific undefined behaviours (e.g., floating-point division by zero), no violation of the programming guidelines (e.g., arithmetic operators on short variables should not overflow the range* `[-32768,32767]` *although, on the specific platform, the result can be well-defined through modular arithmetic).*"

This includes checking that no floating-point overflow can occur, as suggested by DO-178B. So far, this need has been addressed through a combination of design and coding guidelines, testing activities and source code reviews. Today, the ASTRÉE static analyzer makes it possible to perform sound global proofs of absence of run-time errors on complete applications. The analysis process is highly automatic, especially when dealing with Airbus large control programs, generated from SCADE models.

Quality of floating-point calculus [6]. Freedom from run-time errors is not enough when dealing with complex control programs that make massive use of floating-point arithmetic. The accuracy of computations has to be addressed also, as requested by DO-178B. The usual way to deal with this issue is to conduct:

- a set of dedicated test cases on real hardware;
- intellectual analyses of the numerical precision of all floating-point operations. The goal is to check that the program parts using floating-point arithmetic can only generate negligible rounding errors, and cannot propagate errors on inputs (sensitivity analysis). Such an activity is both time-consuming and error-prone.

Today, the FLUCTUAT static analyser enables us to automate the latter activity in a sound and precise way for libraries of widely-used basic operators of control programs. Besides, this tool can also be used to assess the numerical accuracy of some critical system-level functions, through static analyses of the C code generated from limited sets of SCADE nodes.

Certified compilation. As stated in section 2, the development of an avionics program is made of four basic steps to which verification activities are applied. One step being the production of the object code from the source code by compilation (and production of the absolute binary code), it is natural to think about checking that this step does not introduce bugs. In the "traditional" development process (see section 2), an important verification activity consists in testing the program against its Low Level requirements and, later on, against its High Level Requirements, by execution on the real target (or on a very representative hardware). This verification covers the compiler outputs. With the use of formal verification techniques that apply to source code, the compiler outputs are not included in what is verified; the risk being that proofs made on the source code no longer hold on the binary code. This almost new activity will be supported by the use of either a "Certified" compiler [17] or by a validator [19] in order to prove that source and binary programs are semantically equivalent (see section 3.3).

4.3 Lessons Learnt and Deployment Aspects

We will give here some quantitative data for the techniques that have been deployed operationally at Airbus.

- Stack Analyzer is used on all the embedded software products developed by Airbus teams, on more than 10 projects for A380 and A400M aircrafts. All software developers use it, no specific training is necessary.
- AiT is used on approximately 6 projects and more are on the way. All software developers use it, without specific training, there is one specialised engineer who has more specific knowledge, is responsible for the tuning of the tools and can be consulted for advice by the other engineers. It is important to note that this specialist is not a formal method specialist, but a specialist of execution time estimation.
- Unit proof is deployed on three projects and necessitates a specific three-day training.

In the course of experimenting formal techniques, Airbus has defined five criteria for the choice of the techniques and the conditions of their operational use. These criteria are given and explained below.

- Soundness: the technique used has to be sound, i.e. it does not say a property is true if it might not be true.
- Applicability to the code that will be embedded onboard the aircraft: no specific model has to be developed to perform the verification, it is done directly on the code.
- Usability by "normal" engineers on "normal" computers: formal verification is performed on the computers that are used for software development (no need for super computers) and by the engineers (no need for formal method gurus).
- Ability to optimise an existing industrial process: formal techniques must bring better performances than classical methods.
- Certifiability: the objective is to get certification credits for the use of formal methods.

The three techniques that have been deployed operationally meet these five criteria. Moreover, in some cases, formal methods are the only way to keep the same rigor in verification and have an acceptable precision. For example, for stack analysis and worst case execution time computation, classical methods lead to safe but much overestimated results (because of the complexity of the software), formal tools provide better results that allow an optimisation of hardware resources. Finally, formal methods are used if they are automated. The experimental phase is used to augment automation (by defining proof heuristics for proof techniques or code annotations for abstract interpretation based techniques), deployment of the technique is done when sufficient automation is reached. Automation brings high efficiency to the maintenance phase, verification can indeed be redone very easily.

The operational deployment of several formal techniques necessarily modifies the verification process and more generally the development process. The next section will present foreseen evolution of the processes.

5 Towards Product-Based Assurance

5.1 Process and Product Based Assurances

In the Process based Assurance, the confidence in the fact that any execution of the software product conforms to the system specification for that product is obtained by the strict observance of DO-178B development process rules. It is the whole development process that allows to get reasonable confidence in the software product. In other words, if a software product is developed by performing the activities prescribed by DO-178B successfully it will be considered as "good for flight" by the regulation authorities. The main reason why DO-178B emphasizes the quality of the development process is that classical verification techniques do not make it possible to prove the absence of software errors.

In the product based assurance, the confidence is obtained by making sure that the software product has the required characteristics (or properties). The most ambitious goal would be to have a set of formal requirements of the program to develop which specify all aspects of the program execution, and to be able to prove that all possible executions of the binary program satisfy these requirements. If it was possible, this would prove that there is no software error.

5.2 Formal Verification Activities and Product Based Assurance

Executability. By this term we refer to the ability of the program to have well defined behaviours with respect to:

- The "ISO/IEC 9899:1999 (E)" standard (including IEEE 754 standard [16]);
- Specific coding and code generation rules;
- Timing constraints;
- Numerical precision constraints;
- Synchronisation / communication mechanisms.

It must be noticed that without proving the above properties, any proof of user defined requirements (see below) by partial formal verification techniques might be invalidated by some undefined behaviour. Therefore, whenever a formal verification technique not covering the detection of undefined behaviours is used, additional activities must be performed, either based on tools or on intellectual analyses.

Formally proving the executability of a program is the basic kind of Product based assurance. Furthermore, most of the tools mentioned in section 3 are able to analyse whole applications.

Proof of user-defined requirements. So far, there is no cost-effective industrial technique able to verify that whole avionics C programs satisfy their user-defined requirements formally. As stated in section 4, Unit Proof and Integration Proof techniques aim at such formal verification but on program pieces taken individually. The fact that the pieces considered in the Integration Proof technique are bigger than the ones of the Unit Proof technique leads to a better coverage but cannot stand for a formal verification of the whole application with respect to its High Level Requirements.

Nevertheless, we can look at the program pieces which are formally verified as intermediate software products, each of them being specified formally, and then consider such verifications as an application of the Product based assurance paradigm within the development process (Process based assurance).

Certified compilation. As stated in section 4.2, evidences that proofs performed at source code level still hold on the executable program is mandatory. This is another way of saying that in the Product based assurance, the actual software product is the executable program.

5.3 Mix of Formal Verification and Tests

Checking real program executions on real hardware will always be required by DO-178. The basic reason for that is the activity called software/hardware integration.

Beyond this reason, one must also take into account that the huge test campaigns performed on the real hardware during the "traditional" avionics software development process also allow to detect hardware defects. Indeed, most of the time, especially for flight control functions, both hardware and software are developed almost from scratch when a new aircraft is developed. This means that software tests on the real – new – hardware contribute to achieve hardware maturity earlier.

This second reason makes the reduction of the amount of tests an issue. It is clear that the test amount will not be reduced down to the sole software / integration tests.

Therefore, a trade-off between tool-aided formal verification and testing will have to be set, which combines the main advantages of both kinds of techniques, i.e., the automation and good coverage on the one hand, maximal representativity of the tests by execution on the hardware, on the other hand.

5.4 Development Processes Including Some Product Based Assurance

A "traditional" DO-178B conforming process could use static analysers to replace or strengthen some intellectual analyses in order to prove executability (see above). Since some static analysers deal with source code, one must trust the compilation in order to get sure that proofs still hold on the binary code.

Another way of improvement is to introduce Unit Proof technique (see section 4) for formal verification of the source code against its Low Level Requirements. One can also introduce Integration Proof technique (see section 4) for formal verification of the source code against its Low Level Requirements. In both cases, certified compilation is a way to secure the formal verification process.

Actually, there are many ways to introduce formal verification techniques in an avionics development process. An important criterion of such an introduction is whether a "certification credit" is based on the use of a technique or not. So far, Airbus has always been introducing formal verification techniques from which a certification credit has been derived. Nevertheless, it might be the case that some formal verification technique could be used for debugging rather than for achieving some DO-178 objective.

6 Certification Aspects

In this section, we will highlight the specificities of the certification process when formal methods are used for part of the verification. We consider certification with respect to DO-178B, the current software certification standard for avionics software. DO-178 is currently being updated by a dedicated international working group, version C of the standard should be available in 2010, we will end the section with a brief presentation of the current proposal regarding formal methods.

Several cases exist for what concerns certification:

- Formal techniques are used in places where reviews or analyses were used previously to reach the same verification objective. In that case formal methods are simply an alternative means to reach the objective, the main difference being that formal techniques are implemented by a tool and so this tool must be qualified with respect to DO-178B rules for the qualification of verification tools. More information on qualification of tools is given in subsection 6.1.
- Formal techniques replace verifications that were previously done by test.

- A first difference that occurs is that the verification is thus done on the source code instead of the object code. To reach the same level of confidence than with test, complementary analyses must be performed to ensure that the properties that are verified on source code are still satisfied by the object code (this can be done using formal methods also, see the work on certified compilation in section 3).
- The most complex case for certification is the unit or integration proof case, where formal methods are used to verify properties of a C program and replace unit test or integration test. The issue here is the coverage of the verification with respect to the c code. This issue is discussed in subsection 6.2.

6.1 Qualification of Tools

DO-178B distinguishes two kinds of tools: development tools that have an effect on the code being produced (for example code generators) and verification tools that are used to verify some properties on the code (but cannot insert errors). Formal methods tools have to be qualified as verification tools. It must be shown that the tool complies with its operational requirements under normal operational conditions. In practice, it means that a set of representative cases will be defined and it will be checked that the tool provides the expected results for these cases. Stackanalyzer, aiT and Caveat have been qualified as verification tools. No specific requirements are defined for formal method tools in DO-178B, but it might change in version C of the standard where the current proposal is to add objectives targeted for this kind of tools.

6.2 Coverage

When test is used to verify a function against its requirements, a set of requirement-based test cases are defined and executed. A functional coverage analysis is performed to ensure that test cases have been defined for every requirement and a structural coverage analysis is performed to ensure that all the code has been covered and that there is no dead code (for level A software, the most critical one, 100% MC/DC [13] is required). When formal proof is used to verify a C function against a set of properties, it ensures an exhaustive coverage for a given property, but it must also be demonstrated that the set of properties that has been defined covers all the behaviours of the code.

In the case of the unit proof, the argument provided to the certification authorities was based on a demonstration that the set of properties was complete (demonstration using formal proof and reviews). In the case of integration proof, the argument is still the object of research. The general issue that will have to be solved is to be able to measure the coverage of the code obtained by formal verification, and in some cases to be able to mix it with a coverage obtained by test in order to argument the complete coverage of code for certification authorities.

6.3 DO-178C

The update of DO-178 will leave the core of the standard mostly unchanged but will propose several technical supplements dealing with the use of specific techniques such as object-oriented languages or formal methods, a technical supplement on tools is also expected. The current draft of the formal method technical supplement defines what formal methods are, gives criteria for such methods, explains how and under which conditions formal methods can be used to reach DO-178 verification objectives at each step. For verification objectives on the executable object code, it replaces the testing objectives by more generic verification objectives, some testing is still required but some objectives can also be reached using formal methods.

7 Conclusion and Future Work

In this paper it has been shown how formal verification techniques can be used in the development process of avionics software products.

The authors are convinced that the story is far from being finished and that more and more formal verification techniques will be used in the future, as tools become available for industrial use. These techniques are the only way to face the dramatic increase of software complexity, especially when safety is at stake. Technological research is therefore continued in the following three areas: Computer Science research, by means of collaboration with labs, contribution to the development of tools and definition of methods of use.

Regulation aspects are a crucial issue for the industrial use of formal methods, the authors are working on means to conform to the standards but also on evolution of standards in the hope to facilitate future use of formal techniques.

Acknowledgements. The authors warmly thank Famantanantsoa Randimbivololona for his careful reading of this paper.

References

1. The ASTREE project (Analyse Statique de logiciels Temps-REel Embarqués). RNTL (2003), `http://www.di.ens.fr/~cousot/projets/ASTREE/`
2. The CAT project (C analysis toolbox). RNTL (2005)
3. Cousot, P., Cousot, R., Feret, J., Mauborgne, L., Miné, A., Monniaux, D., Rival, X.: The ASTRÉE analyser. In: Sagiv, M. (ed.) ESOP 2005. LNCS, vol. 3444, pp. 21–30. Springer, Heidelberg (2005)
4. Cousot, P., Cousot, R.: Basic Concepts of Abstract Interpretation. In: Jacquard, R. (ed.) Building the Information Society, pp. 359–366. Kluwer Academic Publishers, Dordrecht (2004)
5. DAEDALUS project. IST-1999-20527 of the european IST Programme of the Fifth Framework Programme (FP5) on the « validation of software components embedded in future generation critical concurrent systems by exhaustive semantic-based static analysis and abstract testing methods based on abstract interpretation » (DAEDALUS lasted from October 1st, 2000 to September 30th 2002)
6. Delmas, D., Goubault, E., Putot, S., Souyris, J., Tekkal, K., Védrine, F.: Towards an industrial use of FLUCTUAT on safety-critical avionics software. In: Alpuente, M., Cook, B., Joubert, C. (eds.) FMICS 2009. LNCS, vol. 5825, pp. 53–69. Springer, Heidelberg (2009)

7. Delmas, D., Souyris, J.: ASTRÉE: From research to industry. In: Riis Nielson, H., Filé, G. (eds.) SAS 2007. LNCS, vol. 4634, pp. 437–451. Springer, Heidelberg (2007)
8. Dijkstra, E.W.: A discipline of programming; automatic Computation. Prentice Hall Int., Englewood Cliffs (1976)
9. DO-178B/ED-12B. Software Considerations in Airborne Systems and Equipment Certification. RTCA/EUROCAE (1992)
10. Duprat, S., Souyris, J., Favre-Félix, D.: Formal verification workbench for avionics software. In: SIA (ed.) European Congress ERTS 2006 (European Real Time Software). R-2006-01-2A2 (2006)
11. ES_PASS project. ITEA 2 06042 (October 2007), `http://www.itea2.org/public/project_leaflets/ES_PASS_profile_oct-07.pdf`
12. Ferdinand, C., Heckmann, R., Langenbach, M., Martin, F., Schmidt, M., Theiling, H., Thesing, S., Wilhelm, R.: Reliable and precise WCET determination for a real life processor. In: Henzinger, T.A., Kirsch, C.M. (eds.) EMSOFT 2001. LNCS, vol. 2211, pp. 469–485. Springer, Heidelberg (2001)
13. Hayhurst, K.J., Veerhusen, D.S., Chilenski, J.J., Rierson, L.K.: A practical tutorial on Modified Condition/Decision Coverage. NASA/TM-2001-210876 (2001)
14. Frama-C, `http://frama-c.cea.fr/`
15. Hoare, C.A.R.: An axiomatic basis for computer programming. Communication of the ACM 12(10) (October 1969)
16. The Institute of Electrical and Inc Electronics Engineers. IEEE standard for binary floating-point arithmetic. Technical Report ANSI/IEEE Std 745. IEEE Computer Society, Los Alamitos (1985)
17. Leroy, X.: The Compcert verified compiler, software and commented proof (August 2008), `http://compcert.inria.fr/`
18. Randimbivololona, F., Souyris, J., Baudin, P., Pacalet, A., Raguideau, J., Schoen, D.: Applying Formal Proof Techniques to Avionics Software: A Pragmatic Approach. In: Woodcock, J.C.P., Davies, J., Wing, J.M. (eds.) FM 1999. LNCS, vol. 1709, pp. 1798–1815. Springer, Heidelberg (1999)
19. Rival, X.: Symbolic Transfer Functions-based Approaches to Certified Compilation. In: 31st Symposium on Principles of Programming Languages (POPL 2004), Venice. ACM, New York (2004)
20. Souyris, J., Delmas, D.: Experimental assessment of astrée on safety-critical avionics software. In: Saglietti, F., Oster, N. (eds.) SAFECOMP 2007. LNCS, vol. 4680, pp. 479–490. Springer, Heidelberg (2007)
21. Souyris, J., Favre-Felix, D.: Proof of properties in avionics. In: IFIP Congress Topical Sessions 2004, pp. 527–536 (2004)
22. Souyris, J., Le Pavec, E., Himbert, G., Jégu, V., Borios, G., Heckmann, R.: Computing the worst case execution time of an avionics program by abstract interpretation. In: 5th Intl. Workshop on Worst-Case Execution Time (WCET) Analysis, pp. 21–24 (2005)
23. Stackanalyzer, `http://www.absint.com/stackanalyzer/`
24. Projet 2005 THÉSÉE du RNTL (Réseau National des Technologies Logicielles) de l'ANR
25. Projet 2008 U3CAT de l'Agence nationale de la recherche (ANR)

Formal Verification of Curved Flight Collision Avoidance Maneuvers: A Case Study*

André Platzer and Edmund M. Clarke

Computer Science Department, Carnegie Mellon University, Pittsburgh, PA

Abstract. Aircraft collision avoidance maneuvers are important and complex applications. Curved flight exhibits nontrivial continuous behavior. In combination with the control choices during air traffic maneuvers, this yields hybrid systems with challenging interactions of discrete and continuous dynamics. As a case study illustrating the use of a new proof assistant for a logic for nonlinear hybrid systems, we analyze collision freedom of roundabout maneuvers in air traffic control, where appropriate curved flight, good timing, and compatible maneuvering are crucial for guaranteeing safe spatial separation of aircraft throughout their flight. We show that formal verification of hybrid systems can scale to curved flight maneuvers required in aircraft control applications. We introduce a fully flyable variant of the roundabout collision avoidance maneuver and verify safety properties by compositional verification.

1 Introduction

In air traffic control, collision avoidance maneuvers [1,2,3,4] are used to resolve conflicting flight paths that arise during free flight. See Fig. 1 for a series of increasingly more realistic—yet also more complicated—aircraft collision avoidance maneuvers. Fig. 1c shows a malfunctioning collision avoidance attempt. Collision avoidance maneuvers are a "last resort" for resolving air traffic conflicts that could lead to collisions. They are important whenever conflicts have not been detected by the pilots during free flight or by the flight directors of the Air Route Traffic Control Centers. Consequently, complicated online trajectory prediction or maneuver planning may no longer be feasible in the short time that remains for resolving the conflict. In the tragic 2002 mid-flight collision in Überlingen, the aircraft collided tens of seconds after the on-board traffic alert and collision avoidance system TCAS signalled a traffic alert. Thus, for safe aircraft control we need particularly reliable reactions with maneuvers whose correctness has been established previously by a thorough offline analysis. To ensure correct functioning of aircraft collision avoidance maneuvers under all circumstances, the temporal evolution of the aircraft in space must be analyzed carefully together with the effects that maneuvering control decisions have on

* This research was supported by DFG SFB/TR 14 AVACS, NASA NNG05GF84H, Berkman Faculty Award, CMU-GM CRL GM9100096UMA, NSF CCR-0411152, CCF-0429120, CCF-0541245, SRC 2008TJ1860, and AFRO 18727S3.

A. Cavalcanti and D. Dams (Eds.): FM 2009, LNCS 5850, pp. 547–562, 2009.

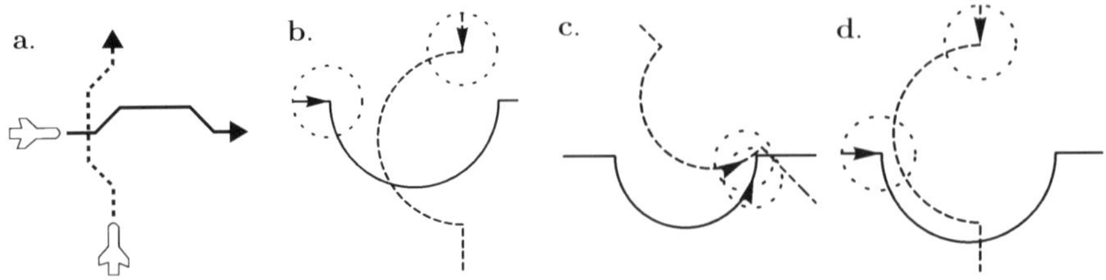

Fig. 1. Evolution of collision avoidance maneuvers in air traffic control

their dynamics. This results in complicated superpositions of physical system dynamics with control, which is an example of what is called hybrid system [5].

Several numerical [1,6,7,8,4] or optimization-based [6,7,9,4] approaches have been proposed for air traffic control. It is difficult to give sound formal verification results for these approaches due to errors in numerical computations or implicit definition of maneuvers in terms of complicated optimization processes. Formal verification is important to avoid collisions, see Fig. 1c. Formal results have been given by geometrical reasoning [2,3,10,11] in PVS. Yet, one still has to prove by other techniques that the hybrid dynamics of a flight controller actually follows the geometrical shapes. In contrast, we verify the hybrid system dynamics directly using a formally sound approach (assuming sound elementary decision procedures), consider curved flight, and achieve better automation.

Control Challenges. Because of the complicated spatio-temporal movement of aircraft, their maneuvers are challenging for verification. Unlike in ground transportation, braking and waiting is not an option to resolve conflicts. Consequently, aircraft maneuvers have to be coordinated such that the aircraft always respect minimal and maximal lateral and angular speed constraints yet always remain safely separated. Further, angular velocity for curving is the primary means of control, because changes in thrust and linear speed are less efficient for aircraft.

Technical Challenges. Complexities in analysis of aircraft maneuvers manifest most prominently in difficulties with analysing hybrid systems for flight equations. General solutions of flight equations involve trigonometric functions that depend on the angular velocity ω and the orientation of the aircraft in space. For straight line flight ($\omega = 0$), the movement in space is just linear so that classical analysis techniques can be used [5]. These include pure straight line maneuvers [1,12,2,3,4]; see, e.g., Fig. 1a. They have to assume instant turns for heading changes of the aircraft between multiple straight line segments. Instant turns, however, are impossible in midflight, because they are *not flyable*: Aircraft cannot suddenly change their flight direction from 0 to 45 degrees discontinuously. They need to follow a smooth curve instead, in which they slowly steer towards the desired direction by adjusting the angular velocity ω appropriately. Moreover, the area required by maneuvers for which instant turns could possibly be understood as adequately close approximations of properly curved flight is huge. Curved flight is thus an inherent part of real aircraft control.

During curved flight, the angular velocity ω is non-zero. For $\omega \neq 0$, flight equations have transcendental solutions, which generally fall into undecidable classes of arithmetics; see [13]. Consequently, maneuvers with curves, like in Fig. 1b–1d, are more realistic but also substantially more complicated for verification than straight line maneuvers like that in Fig. 1a. We have recently developed a *sound* verification algorithm that works with differential invariants [14] instead of solutions of differential equations to address this arithmetic. Now we show how a fully curved maneuver can be verified by extending our work [14].

In this paper, we introduce and verify the *fully flyable tangential roundabout maneuver (FTRM)*. It refines the non-flyable tangential roundabout maneuver (NTRM) from Fig. 1d, which has discontinuities at the entry and exit points of roundabouts, to a fully flyable curved maneuver. Unlike most previously proposed maneuvers [1,7,12,2,15,3,4], FTRM does not have non-flyable instant turns. It is flyable and smoothly curved. Unlike other approaches emphasizing the importance of flyability [6], we give formal verification results.

Contribution. Our main contribution is to show that reality in model design and coverage in formal verification are no longer incompatible desires even for applications as complex as aircraft maneuvers. As a case study illustrating the use of differential dynamic logic for hybrid systems [16], we demonstrate how tricky and nonlinear dynamics can be verified with our verification algorithm [14] in our verification tool KeYmaera. We introduce a fully curved flight maneuver and verify its hybrid dynamics formally. In contrast to previous approaches, we handle curved flight, hybrid dynamics, and produce formal proofs with almost complete automation. Manual effort is still needed to simplify arithmetical complexity and modularize the proof appropriately. We further illustrate the resulting verification conditions for the respective parts of the maneuver. Finally, we identify the most difficult steps during the verification and present new transformations to handle the enormous computational complexity. To reduce complexity, we still use some of the simplifications assumed in related work, e.g., synchronous maneuvering (i.e. aircraft make simultaneous maneuver choices).

Related Work. Lafferriere et al. [17] gave important decidability results for hybrid systems with some classes of linear continuous dynamics but only random discrete resets. These results do not apply to air traffic maneuvers, because they have non-trivial resets: the aircraft's position does not just jump randomly when switching modes but, rather, systematically according to the maneuver.

Tomlin et al. [1] analyze competitive aircraft maneuvers game-theoretically using numerical approximations of partial differential equations. As a solution, they propose roundabout maneuvers and give bounded-time verification results for straight-line approximations (Fig. 1a). We verify curved roundabouts with a sound symbolic approach that avoids approximation errors.

Flyability has been identified as one of the major challenges in Košecká et al. [6], where planning based on superposition of potential fields has been used to resolve air traffic conflicts. This planning does not guarantee flyability but, rather, defaults to classical vertical altitude changes whenever a nonflyable path is detected. The resulting maneuver has not yet been verified. The planning approach has been pursued by Bicchi and Pallottino [7] with numerical simulations.

Numerical simulation algorithms approximating discrete-time Markov Chain approximations of aircraft behavior have been proposed by Hu et al. [8]. They approximate bounded-time probabilistic reachable sets for one initial state. We consider hybrid systems combining discrete control choices and continuous dynamics instead of uncontrolled, probabilistic continuous dynamics.

Hwang et al. [4] have presented a straight-line aircraft conflict avoidance maneuver that involves optimization over complicated trigonometric computations, and validate it using random numerical simulation and informal arguments.

The work of Dowek et al. [2] and Galdino et al. [3] is probably closest to ours. They consider straight-line maneuvers and formalize geometrical proofs in PVS.

Attempts to Model Check discretizations of roundabout maneuvers [12,15] indicated avoidance of orthogonal collisions (Fig. 1b). Counterexamples found by our Model Checker in previous work show that collision avoidance does not extend to other initial flight paths of the classical roundabout (Fig. 1c).

Pallottino et al. [18] have presented a spatially distributed pattern for multiple roundabout circles at different positions. They reason manually about desirable properties of the system and estimate probabilistic results as in [8]. Pallottino et al. thus take a view that is complementary to ours: they determine the global compatibility of multiple roundabouts while assuming correct functioning within each local roundabout. We verify that the actual hybrid dynamics of each local roundabout is collision free. Generalizing our approach to a spatial pattern of verified local roundabouts could be interesting future work.

Similarly, the work by Umeno and Lynch [11,10] is complementary to ours. They consider real-time properties of airport protocols using Timed I/O Automata. We are interested in proving local properties of the actual hybrid system.

Our approach has a very different focus than other complementary work:

- Our maneuver directly involves curved flight unlike [1,8,2,3,4,11,10]. This makes our maneuver more realistic but much more difficult to analyze.
- Unlike [6,8,4], we do not give results for a finite (sometimes small) number of initial flight positions (simulation). Instead, we verify uncountably many initial states and give unbounded-time horizon verification results.
- Unlike [1,6,7,8,9,4], we use symbolic instead of numerical computation so that numerical and floating point errors cannot cause soundness problems.
- Unlike [7,12,8,2,3,4,11,10], we analyze hybrid system dynamics directly.
- Unlike [6,1,7,8,4,12,18] we produce formal, deductive proofs. Further unlike the formal proofs in [2,3,11,10], our verification is much more automatic.
- In [2,3,4,11,10], it remains to be proven that the hybrid dynamics and flight equations follow the geometrical thoughts. In contrast, our approach directly works for the hybrid flight dynamics. We illustrate verification results graphically to help understand them, but the figures do not prove anything.

– Unlike [19], we consider collision avoidance maneuvers, not just detection.
– Unlike [7,9], we do not guarantee optimality of the resulting maneuver.

2 Background: Differential Dynamic Logic

Hybrid Programs. We use a *hybrid program* (HP) notation [16] for hybrid systems that include hybrid automata (HA) [5]. Each discrete and continuous transition corresponds to a sequence of statements, with a nondeterministic choice ($\cup$) between these transitions. Line 2 in Fig. 2 represents a continuous transition in a simplistic altitude controller. It tests (denoted by $?q = up$) if the current location q is up, and then follows a differential equation $z' = 1$ restricted to invariant region $z \leq 9$ (conjunction $z' = 1 \wedge z \leq 9$). Line 3 tests guard $z \geq 5$ when in state up, resets z by a discrete assignment, and then changes location q to $down$. The * at the end indicates that the transitions of a HA repeat indefinitely. We will build HP directly, which gives more natural programs than HA-translation.

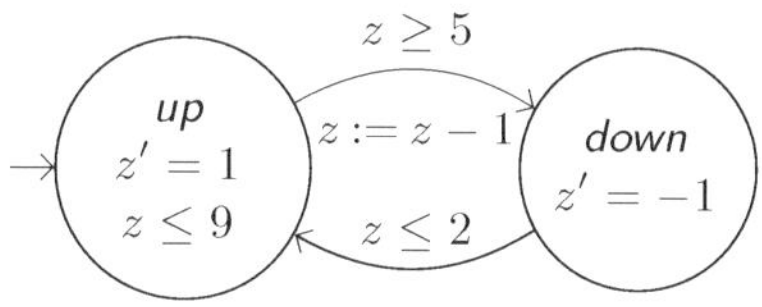

$$
\begin{array}{l}
q := up; \quad /^*\ \textit{initial location is up}\ ^*/ \\
(\quad (?q = up; \quad z' = 1 \wedge z \leq 9) \\
\cup\ (?q = up \wedge z \geq 5; \quad z := z - 1; \quad q := down) \\
\cup\ (?q = down; \quad z' = -1) \\
\cup\ (?q = down \wedge z \leq 2; \quad q := up; \quad ?z \leq 9))^*
\end{array}
$$

Fig. 2. Hybrid automaton vs. hybrid program (simplistic altitude control)

As *terms* we allow polynomials over $\mathbb{Q}$ with variables in a set V. *Hybrid programs (HP)* are built with the statements in Table 1. The effect of $x := \theta$ is an instantaneous discrete jump assigning θ to x. Instead, $x := *$ randomly assigns *any* real value to x by a nondeterministic choice. During a continuous evolution $x_1' = \theta_1 \wedge \ldots \wedge x_n' = \theta_n \wedge \chi$ with terms θ_i, all conjuncts need to hold. Its effect is a continuous transition controlled by the differential equation

Table 1. Statements and (informal) effects of hybrid programs (HP)

notation	statement	effect
$x := \theta$	discrete assignment	assigns term θ to variable $x \in V$
$x := *$	nondet. assignment	assigns any real value to $x \in V$
$x_1' = \theta_1 \wedge \ldots$ $\ldots \wedge x_n' = \theta_n \wedge \chi$	continuous evolution	diff. equations for $x_i \in V$ and terms θ_i, with formula χ as evolution domain
$?\chi$	state check	test formula χ at current state
$\alpha; \beta$	seq. composition	HP β starts after HP α finishes
$\alpha \cup \beta$	nondet. choice	choice between alternatives HP α or β
α^*	nondet. repetition	repeats HP α n-times for any $n \in \mathbb{N}$
$do\, \alpha\ until\ \chi$	evolve until	evolve HP α until χ holds

$x_1' = \theta_1, \ldots, x_n' = \theta_n$ that always satisfies the arithmetic constraint χ (thus remains in the region described by χ). This directly corresponds to a continuous evolution mode of a HA. The effect of state check $?\chi$ is a *skip* (i.e., no change) if χ is true in the current state and that of *abort*, otherwise. Non-deterministic choice $\alpha \cup \beta$ expresses alternatives in the behavior of the hybrid system. Sequential composition $\alpha; \beta$ expresses a behavior in which β starts after α finishes (β never starts if α continues indefinitely). Non-deterministic repetition α^*, repeats α an arbitrary number of times ($\geq$0). The operation *do* α *until* χ expresses that the system follows α exactly until condition χ is true.

Formulas of d$\mathcal{L}$. To express and combine correctness properties of HP, we use a verification logic for HP: The *differential dynamic logic* d$\mathcal{L}$ [16] is an extension of first-order logic over the reals with modal formulas like $[\alpha]\phi$, which is true iff all states reachable by following the transitions of HP α satisfy property ϕ (*safety*). Reachability properties are expressible using the dual modality $\langle\alpha\rangle\phi$, which is true iff there is a state satisfying ϕ that α can reach from its initial state. *Formulas of* d$\mathcal{L}$ are defined by the following grammar, where θ_1, θ_2 are terms, $\sim \in \{=, \leq, <, \geq, >\}$, ϕ, ψ are formulas, $x \in V$, and α is an HP (Table 1):

$$\text{Formula} ::= \theta_1 \sim \theta_2 \mid \neg\phi \mid \phi \wedge \psi \mid \phi \vee \psi \mid \phi \rightarrow \psi \mid \forall x\, \phi \mid \exists x\, \phi \mid [\alpha]\phi \mid \langle\alpha\rangle\phi \ .$$

A Hoare-triple $\{\psi\}\alpha\{\phi\}$ can be expressed as $\psi \rightarrow [\alpha]\phi$, which is true iff all states reachable by HP α satisfy ϕ when starting from an initial state that satisfies ψ.

3 Curved Flight in Roundabout Maneuvers

3.1 Flight Dynamics

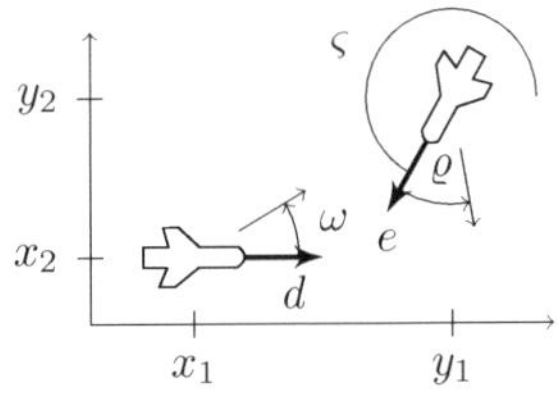

Fig. 3. Aircraft flight

The parameters of two aircraft at (planar) position $x = (x_1, x_2)$ and $y = (y_1, y_2)$ in $\mathbb{R}^2$ flying in directions $d = (d_1, d_2) \in \mathbb{R}^2$ and $e = (e_1, e_2)$ are illustrated in Fig. 3. Their dynamics is determined by their angular speeds $\omega, \varrho \in \mathbb{R}$ and linear velocity vectors d and e, which describe both the linear velocity $\|d\| := \sqrt{d_1^2 + d_2^2}$ and orientation of the aircraft in space. Roundabout maneuvers are horizontal collision avoidance maneuvers so that, like [1,12,9,15,18,3,4], we simplify to planar positions. We denote the flight equations for the aircraft at x and y with angular velocities ω, ϱ by $\mathcal{F}(\omega)$ and $\mathcal{G}(\varrho)$ respectively, see [1,13]:

$$[x' = d \quad d' = \omega d^{\perp}] \qquad (\mathcal{F}(\omega)) \qquad [y' = e \quad e' = \varrho e^{\perp}] \qquad (\mathcal{G}(\varrho))$$

There $d^{\perp} := (-d_2, d_1)$ is the *orthogonal complement* of vector d. Differential equations $\mathcal{F}(\omega)$ express that x is moving in direction d, which is rotating with angular velocity ω, i.e., evolves orthogonal to d. Equations $\mathcal{G}(\varrho)$ are similar for y, e and ϱ. In safe flight configurations, aircraft respect protected zone p. That is, they are separated by at least distance p, i.e., the state satisfies formula $\mathcal{S}(p)$:

$$\mathcal{S}(p) \equiv \|x - y\|^2 \geq p^2 \equiv (x_1 - y_1)^2 + (x_2 - y_2)^2 \geq p^2 \quad \text{for } p \in \mathbb{R} \qquad (1)$$

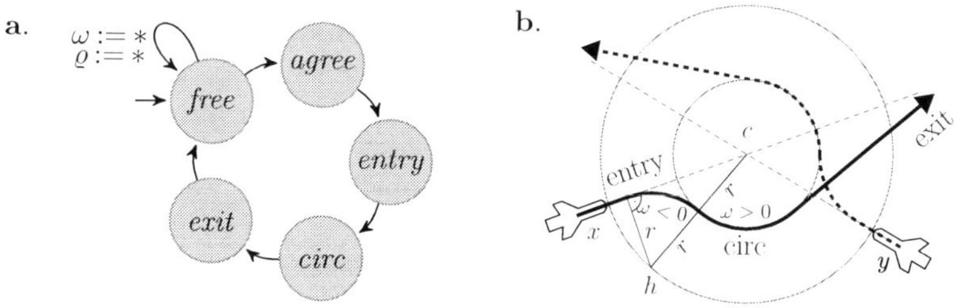

Fig. 4. Protocol cycle and construction of flyable roundabout maneuver

Like all other parameters, we treat p purely symbolically without a specific value. In practice, horizontal separation should be $\geq$5mi, vertical separation $\geq$1000ft.

3.2 Roundabout Maneuver Overview

FTRM consists of the phases in the protocol cycle in Fig. 4a which correspond to the marked flight phases in Fig. 4b. During free flight, the aircraft move without restriction by repeatedly choosing arbitrary new angular velocities ω and ϱ respectively (as indicated by the self loop at *free* in Fig. 4a). When the aircraft come too close to one another, they agree on a roundabout maneuver by negotiating a compatible roundabout center $c = (c_1, c_2)$ in coordination phase *agree* by communication. Next, the aircraft approach the roundabout circle in a right curve with $\omega < 0$ (*entry* mode) according to Fig. 4b, and reach a tangential position around center c. During the *circ* mode, the aircraft follow the circular roundabout maneuver around the agreed center c with a left curve of common angular velocity $\omega > 0$. Finally, the aircraft leave the roundabout in cruise mode ($\omega = 0$) in their original direction (*exit*) and enter free flight again when they have reached sufficient distance (the protocol cycle repeats as necessary).

3.3 Compositional Verification Plan

For verifying safety properties and collision avoidance of FTRM, we decompose the verification problem and pursue the following overall verification plan:

AC1 *Tangential roundabout maneuver cycle*: We prove that the protected zones of aircraft are safely separated at all times during the whole maneuver (including repetitive collision avoidance maneuver initiation and including multiple aircraft) with a simplified but not yet flyable entry operation $entry_n$. Subsequently, we refine this verification result to a flyable maneuver by verifying that we can replace $entry_n$ with its flyable variant *entry*.

AC2 *Bounded control choices for aircraft velocities*: We show that linear speeds remain unchanged during the whole maneuver (the aircraft do not stall).

AC3 *Flyable entry*: We prove that the simplified $entry_n$ procedure can be replaced by a flyable curve *entry* reaching the same position as $entry_n$.

AC4 *Bounded entry duration*: Flyable *entry* procedure succeeds in bounded time, i.e., aircraft reach the roundabout circle in some bounded time $\leq T$.

AC5 *Safe entry separation*: Most importantly, we prove that the protected zones of aircraft are still respected during the flyable entry procedure.

AC6 *Successful negotiation*: We prove that the negotiation phase (*agree*) satisfies the respective requirements of multiple aircraft simultaneously.

AC7 *Safe exit separation*: We show that, for its bounded duration, the exit procedure cannot produce collisions and that the initial *far separation* for free flight is reached again so that the FTRM cycle repeats safely.

This plan modularizes the proof and allows us to identify the respective safety constraints imposed by the various maneuver phases successively. We present details of these verification tasks in the sequel and summarize the respective verification results into a joint safety property of FTRM in Section 5. The proof and formulation for **AC2** is a simple variation of **AC1** and will not be discussed.

3.4 Tangential Roundabout Maneuver Cycles (AC1)

First, we analyze roundabouts with a simplified instant entry procedure and without an exit procedure (**AC1**), i.e., the non-flyable NTRM depicted in Fig. 1d. We refine this maneuver and its verification to the flyable FTRM afterwards.

Modular Correctness of Tangential Roundabout Cycles. We verify that NTRM safely avoids collisions, i.e., the aircraft always maintain a safe distance $\geq p$ during the curved flight in roundabout. In addition, these results show that arbitrary repetitions of the protocol cycle are always safe when, as a first step, we simplify the entry maneuver. The NTRM model and property are summarized in Fig. 5.

$$
\begin{aligned}
\psi &\equiv \mathcal{S}(p) \rightarrow [\mathit{NTRM}]\,\mathcal{S}(p)\\
\mathit{NTRM} &\equiv (\mathit{free};\ \mathit{agree};\ \mathit{entry}_n;\ \mathit{circ})^*\\
\mathit{free} &\equiv (\omega := *;\ \varrho := *;\ \mathcal{F}(\omega) \wedge \mathcal{G}(\varrho) \wedge \mathcal{S}(p))^*\\
\mathit{agree} &\equiv \omega := *;\ c := *\\
\mathit{entry}_n &\equiv d := \omega(x-c)^{\perp};\ \ e := \omega(y-c)^{\perp}\\
\mathit{circ} &\equiv \mathcal{F}(\omega) \wedge \mathcal{G}(\omega)
\end{aligned}
$$

Fig. 5. Nonflyable tangential roundabout collision avoidance maneuver NTRM

The simplified flight controller in Fig. 5 performs collision avoidance maneuvers by tangential roundabouts and repeats these maneuvers any number of times as needed. During each cycle of the loop of *NTRM*, the aircraft first perform arbitrary free flight (*free*) by choosing arbitrary new angular velocities ω and ϱ (repeatedly as indicated by the loop in *free*). Aircraft only fly freely while they are safely separated, which is expressed by constraint $\mathcal{S}(p)$ in the differential equation for *free*. Then the aircraft agree on an arbitrary roundabout center c and angular velocity ω (*agree*). We model this communication by nondeterministic assignments to the shared variables ω, c. Refinements include all negotiation processes that reach an agreement on common ω, c in bounded time. Next, they perform the simplified non-flyable entry procedure ($entry_n$) with instant turns (Fig. 1d). This operation identifies the goal state that *entry* needs to reach:

$$\mathcal{R} \equiv d = \omega(x-c)^{\perp} \wedge e = \omega(y-c)^{\perp} \tag{2}$$

It expresses that, at the positions x and y, respectively, the directions d and e are tangential to the roundabout circle at center c and angular velocity ω; see Fig. 6. Finally, the roundabout maneuver itself is carried out in *circ*. The collision avoidance roundabouts can be left again by repeating the loop and entering arbitrary free flight at any time. When further conflicts occur during free flight, the controller in Fig. 5 again enters roundabout conflict resolution maneuvers.

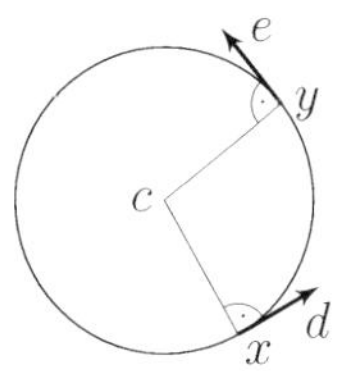

Fig. 6. $\mathcal{R}$

Multiple Aircraft. We prove separation for up to 5 aircraft participating in the roundabout at the same time. There, the safety property is mutual collision avoidance, i.e., each aircraft has a safe distance $\geq p$ to every other aircraft, which yields a quadratic number of separation properties that have to be verified. This quadratic increase in the size of the property that actually needs to be proven for a safe roundabout of n aircraft and the increased dimension of the underlying continuous state space increase verification times. Also see [13].

3.5 Flyable Entry Procedures (AC3)

For property **AC3** in Section 3.3, we generalize the verification results about NTRM with simplified entry procedures (Fig. 1d) to FTRM (Fig. 4b) by replacing the non-flyable $entry_n$ procedure with flyable curves (called *entry*). This turns the non-flyable NTRM into the flyable FTRM maneuver.

Flyable Entry Properties. A flyable entry maneuver that follows the smooth entry curve from Fig. 4b is constructed according to Fig. 7a and specified formally as:

$$(r\omega)^2 = \|d\|^2 \wedge \|x-c\| = \sqrt{3}r \wedge \exists\lambda\geq 0\,(x+\lambda d = c) \wedge \|h-c\| = 2r \wedge d = -\omega(x-h)^{\perp}$$
$$\rightarrow [\mathcal{F}(-\omega) \wedge \|x-c\| \geq r]\left(\|x-c\| \leq r \rightarrow d = \omega(x-c)^{\perp}\right) \tag{3}$$

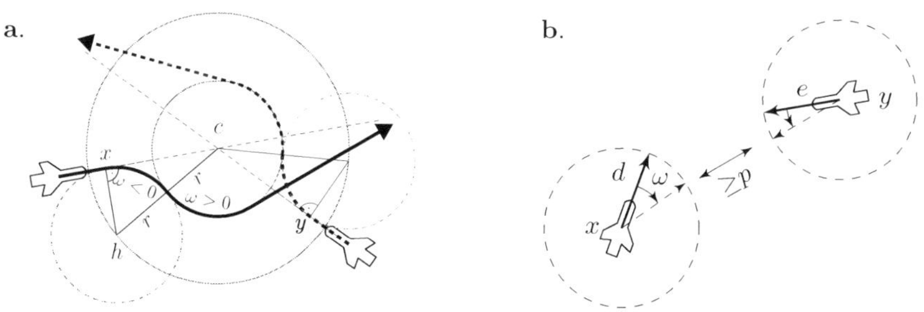

Fig. 7. Flyable entry maneuver: characteristics and separation

The assumptions in (3) express that r is the radius corresponding to speed $\|d\|$ and angular velocity ω ($(r\omega)^2 = \|d\|^2$) and that *entry* starts with distance $\sqrt{3}r$ to c heading towards c ($\exists\lambda{\geq}0\,(x + \lambda d = c)$). For the construction of the maneuver and positioning in space, we use the auxiliary anchor point $h \in \mathbb{R}^2$ identified in Fig. 7a and line 1 of (3). It is positioned relative to the roundabout center c and the x position at the start of the entry curve (i.e., with x at the right angle indicated in Fig. 7a). The entry curve around h is similar to the roundabout curve around c. Formally, h is characterized by distance r to x, distance $2r$ to c ($\|h - c\| = 2r$) and, further, vector $x - h$ is orthogonal to d and obeys the relative orientation of the curve belonging to $-\omega$ (hence $d = -\omega(x - h)^\perp$). The property in (3) specifies that the tangential goal configuration (2) around c is reached by a flyable curve when waiting until aircraft x and center c have distance r, because the domain restriction of the dynamics is $\|x - c\| \geq r$ (line 2) and the postcondition assumes $\|x - c\| \leq r$, which imply $\|x - c\| = r$. The feasibility of choosing anchor point h can be shown by proving an existence property; see [13].

Spatial Symmetry Reduction. The property in (3) can be verified in a simplified version. We use a new *spatial symmetry reduction* to simplify property (3) computationally. We exploit symmetries to reduce the spatial dimension by fixing variables. Without loss of generality, we recenter the coordinate system with c at position 0. Further, we can assume aircraft x comes from the left by changing the orientation of the coordinate system. Finally, we assume, without loss of generality, linear speed 1 (by rescaling units appropriately). Observe that we *cannot* fix a value for both the linear speed and the angular velocity, because the units are interdependent. In other words, if we fix the linear speed, we need to consider all angular velocities in order to verify the maneuver for each possible radius r of the roundabout maneuver (and corresponding ω). The x position resulting from these symmetry reductions can be determined easily by Pythagoras theorem (i.e., $(2r)^2 = r^2 + x_1^2$ for the triangle enclosed by h, x, c in Fig. 7a):

$$x = (\sqrt{(2r)^2 - r^2}, 0) = (\sqrt{3}r, 0) \ . \tag{4}$$

3.6 Bounded Entry Duration (AC4)

As the first step for showing that the entry procedure finally succeeds at goal (2) and maintains a safe distance all the time, we show that *entry* succeeds in bounded time and cannot take arbitrarily long to succeed (**AC4** in Section 3.3).

By a simple consequence of (3), the entry procedure follows a circular motion around anchor point h, see Fig. 7a. That is, when r is the radius belonging to angular velocity ω and linear speed $\|d\|$, the property $\|x - h\| = r$ is an invariant of *entry*; see [13]. By **AC2**, which can be proven easily, the speed $\|d\|$ is constant during the *entry* procedure. Thus, the aircraft proceeds with nonzero minimum progress rate $\|d\|$ around the circle. The flight duration for a full circle of radius r around h at constant linear speed $\|d\|$ is $\frac{2\pi r}{\|d\|}$, because its arc length is $2\pi r$. From the trigonometric identities underlying equation (4), we can read off that the aircraft completes a $\frac{\pi}{3} = 60°$ arc, see Fig. 7a. Hence, the maximum duration T

of the *entry* procedure is: $T := \frac{1}{6} \cdot \frac{2\pi r}{\|d\|} = \frac{\pi r}{3\|d\|}$ Instead of π, which is not definable in first-order real arithmetic, we can use any overapproximation, e.g., 3.15.

3.7 Safe Entry Separation (AC5)

In Section 3.5, we have shown that the simplified $entry_n$ procedure from NTRM can be replaced by a flyable *entry* maneuver that meets the requirements of approaching tangentially for each aircraft. Unlike in instant turns ($entry_n$), we have to show that the flyable entry maneuvers of multiple aircraft do not produce mutually conflicting flight paths, i.e., spatial separation of all aircraft is maintained during the entry of multiple aircraft (**AC5**). See Fig. 8 for multiple aircraft FTRM where separation is important.

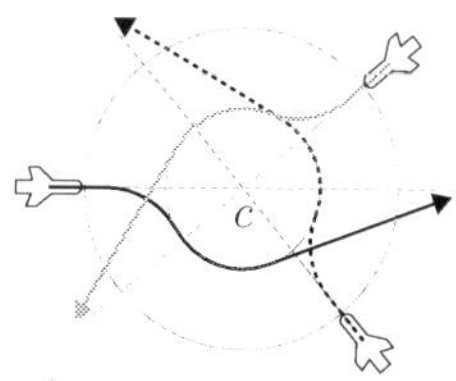

Fig. 8. Multiple aircraft

Bounded Overapproximation. We show that entry separation is a consequence of the bounded speed (**AC2**) and bounded duration (**AC4**) of the flyable entry procedure when initiating the negotiation phase *agree* with sufficient distance. We prove that, when following bounded speed for a bounded duration, aircraft only come closer by a bounded distance. Let b denote the overall speed bound during FTRM according to **AC2** and let T be the time bound for the duration of the entry procedure due to **AC4**. We overapproximate the actual behavior during the *entry* phase by arbitrary curved flight (see Fig. 7b). When the *entry* procedure is initiated with sufficient distance $\sqrt{2}(p + 2bT)$, the protected zone $p \geq 0$ will still be respected after the 2 aircraft follow *any* curved flight (including the actual choices during the *entry* phase and subsequent *circ* phase) with speed $\|d\| \leq b$ and $\|e\| \leq b$ up to $T \geq 0$ time units (see Fig. 7b):

$$\|x - y\| \geq \sqrt{2}(p + 2bT) \land p \geq 0 \land \|d\|^2 \leq \|e\|^2 \leq b^2 \land b \geq 0 \land T \geq 0 \\ \rightarrow [entry]\,(\|x - y\| \geq p) \quad (5)$$

In [13], we show that this property follows from the more general fact that aircraft only make limited progress in bounded time from some initial point z when starting with bounded speeds (even when changing ω arbitrarily):

$$x = z \land \|d\|^2 \leq b^2 \land b \geq 0 \rightarrow [\tau := 0;\ \mathcal{F}(\omega) \land \tau' = 1]\,(\|x - z\|_\infty \leq \tau b) \quad (6)$$

The maximum distance $\|x - z\|_\infty$ from z depends on clock τ and bound b. To reduce the polynomial degree and the verification complexity, we overapproximate distances from quadratic Euclidean norm $\|\cdot\|$ in terms of linearly definable supremum norm $\|\cdot\|_\infty$, instead, which is $\|x\|_\infty \leq c \equiv -c \leq x_1 \leq c \land -c \leq x_2 \leq c$.

Far Separation. By combining the estimation of the entry duration (3.6) at speed $\|d\| = b$ with the entry separation property (5), we determine the following magnitude as the *far separation* f, i.e., the initial distance guaranteeing that the *FTRM* protocol can be repeated safely in case new collision avoidance is needed:

$$f := \sqrt{2}(p + 2bT) = \sqrt{2}\left(p + \frac{2}{3}\pi r\right) \quad (7)$$

4 Synchronization of Roundabout Maneuvers

Following our verification plan in Section 3.3, we show that the various actions of multiple aircraft can be synchronized appropriately to ensure safety of the maneuver. We analyze the negotiation phase and compatible exit procedures.

4.1 Successful Negotiation (AC6)

For negotiation to succeed (**AC6**), we have to show that there is a common choice of the roundabout center c and angular velocity ω (or radius r) so that multiple participating aircraft can satisfy the local requirements of their respective entry procedures simultaneously, i.e., of the property (3) for **AC3**.

We prove that all corresponding choices of *agree* satisfy the mutual requirements of multiple aircraft simultaneously. As one possible option among others: when choosing roundabout center c as the simultaneous intersection (intersection $x + \lambda d = y + \lambda e$ after time λ) of the flight paths of the aircraft at x and y, the choices for c, r, ω are compatible for multiple aircraft; see Fig. 9a:

$$\begin{aligned}&\lambda > 0 \land x + \lambda d = y + \lambda e \land \|d\| = \|e\| \rightarrow\\&[c := x + \lambda d;\ r := *;\ ?\|x - c\| = \sqrt{3}r;\ ?\|y - c\| = \sqrt{3}r;\ \omega := *;\ ?(r\omega)^2 = \|d\|^2]\\&\qquad(\|x - c\| = \sqrt{3}r \land \lambda \geq 0 \land x + \lambda d = c \land \|y - c\| = \sqrt{3}r \land y + \lambda e = c) \quad (8)\end{aligned}$$

The tests in the dynamics ensure that the *entry* curve starts when x, y and c have appropriate distance $\sqrt{3}r$ identified in Section 3 and that r is the radius belonging to angular velocity ω and linear speed $\|d\|$. This property expresses that, for aircraft heading towards the simultaneous intersection of their flight paths with speed $\|d\| = \|e\|$ (line 1), the intersection of the linear flight paths (line 2) is a safe choice for c satisfying the joint requirements (line 3) identified in Section 3. For an analysis of far separation during negotiation and of the feasibility of these choices, see[13]. Other choices of c, ω than Fig. 9a are possible for asymmetric initial positions of aircraft, but computationally more involved.

4.2 Safe Exit Separation (AC7)

NTRM (Fig. 1d) does not need an exit procedure for safety, because the maneuver repeats when further air traffic conflicts arise. For FTRM, instead, we

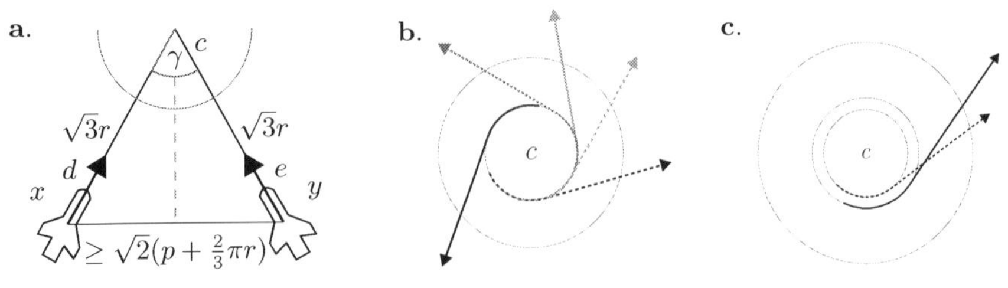

Fig. 9. Separation of negotiation and good and bad exit procedure separation

need to show that the exit procedure produces safe flight paths until the aircraft are sufficiently separated: When repeating the FTRM maneuver, the *entry* procedure needs far separation (7) not just distance p for safety, see Fig. 4b.

Safe Separation. If the aircraft enter simultaneously, they can exit simultaneously. For **AC7**, we first show that aircraft that exit simultaneously (from tangential positions of the roundabout circle) always respect their protected zones:

$$\mathcal{R} \wedge \|x - y\|^2 \geq p^2 \rightarrow [x' = d \wedge y' = e] \left(\|x - y\|^2 \geq p^2\right) \tag{9}$$

Thus, safely separated aircraft exiting simultaneously along straight lines from tangential positions ($\mathcal{R}$ by eqn. 2) of a roundabout always remain safely separated. We prove an overapproximation: exit rays (Fig. 9b–9c) are separated [13].

Far Separation. Aircraft reach arbitrary separation when following the exit procedure long enough. Using overapproximation Fig. 9b, we prove that—due to different exit directions $d \neq e$—the exit procedure will finally separate the aircraft arbitrarily far (starting from tangential configuration (2) of the roundabout):

$$\mathcal{R} \wedge d \neq e \rightarrow \forall a \, \langle x' = d \wedge y' = e \rangle \left(\|x - y\|^2 > a^2\right) \tag{10}$$

5 Flyable Tangential Roundabout Maneuver

We combine the results about the individual phases of flyable roundabouts into a full model of FTRM that inherits safety modularly. We collect the maneuver phases according to the protocol cycle of Fig. 4 and take care to ensure that the safety prerequisites are met, as identified for the respective phases in Section 3-4.

One possible instance of FTRM is the HP in Fig. 10, which is composed of previously illustrated parts of the maneuver. The technical construction and protocol cycle of the entry procedure have already been illustrated in Fig. 4. In FTRM, Π denotes the synchronous parallel product. By communication, FTRM operates synchronously, i.e., all aircraft make simultaneous mode changes [4].

$$\begin{aligned}
\psi &\equiv \|d\| = \|e\| \wedge r > 0 \wedge \mathcal{S}(f) \rightarrow [FTRM^*]\mathcal{S}(p)\\
\mathcal{C} &\equiv \|x - c\| = \sqrt{3}r \wedge \exists \lambda{\geq}0\,(x + \lambda d = c) \wedge \|y - c\| = \sqrt{3}r \wedge \exists \lambda{\geq}0\,(y + \lambda e = c)\\
FTRM &\equiv \mathit{free}^*;\;\; \mathit{agree};\;\; \Pi(\mathit{entry};\; \mathit{circ};\; \mathit{exit})\\
\mathit{free} &\equiv \omega := *;\;\; \varrho := *;\;\; \mathcal{F}(\omega) \wedge \mathcal{G}(\varrho) \wedge \mathcal{S}(f)\\
\mathit{agree} &\equiv c := *;\;\; r := *;\;\; ?(\mathcal{C} \wedge r > 0);\;\; ?\mathcal{S}(f);\\
&\qquad \omega := *;\;\; ?(r\omega)^2 = \|d\|^2;\;\; x_0 := x; d_0 := d; y_0 := y; e_0 := e\\
\mathit{entry} &\equiv \mathit{do}\,\mathcal{F}(-\omega)\;\mathit{until}\;\|x - c\|^2 = r^2\\
\mathit{circ} &\equiv \mathit{do}\,\mathcal{F}(\omega)\;\mathit{until}\;\exists \lambda{\geq}0\,\exists \mu{>}0\,(x + \lambda d = x_0 + \mu d_0)\\
\mathit{exit} &\equiv \mathcal{F}(0);\;\; ?\mathcal{S}(f)
\end{aligned}$$

Fig. 10. Flight control with flyable tangential roundabout collision avoidance

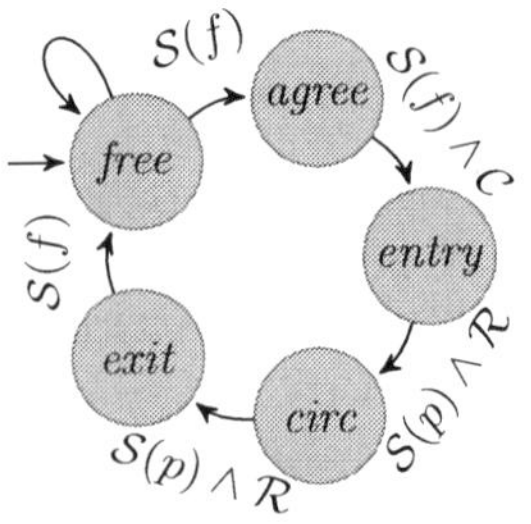

Decomposed property of system dynamics	See
$\mathcal{S}(f) \rightarrow [free]\,\mathcal{S}(f)$	Fig. 5
$\mathcal{S}(f) \rightarrow [agree](\mathcal{S}(f) \wedge \mathcal{C})$	(8), [13]
$\mathcal{C} \wedge \mathcal{S}(f) \rightarrow [entry]\,\mathcal{S}(p)$	(5)
$\mathcal{C} \wedge \mathcal{S}(f) \rightarrow [entry]\,\mathcal{R}$	(3)
$\mathcal{R} \wedge \mathcal{S}(p) \rightarrow [circ](\mathcal{S}(p) \wedge \mathcal{R})$	Fig. 5
$\mathcal{R} \wedge \mathcal{S}(p) \rightarrow [exit]\,\mathcal{S}(p)$	(9)
$\mathcal{R} \wedge \mathcal{S}(p) \rightarrow [exit]\,\mathcal{S}(f)$	(9), (10)

Fig. 11. Composing verification for flyable tangential roundabout maneuvers

Consequently, the parallel product $\Pi(entry; circ; exit)$ of HP simplifies to the conjunction of the respective differential equations in the various modes and can be defined easily: $(entry_x \wedge entry_y)$; $(circ_x \wedge circ_y)$; $(exit_x \wedge exit_y)$ where $entry_x$ is the entry procedure of the aircraft at position x (likewise for more aircraft).

To verify this maneuver, we split the proof into the modular properties that we have already shown previously following the verification plan from Section 3.3. Formally, we split the system at its sequential compositions, giving the subproperties depicted in Fig. 11. Formula $\mathcal{R}$ is due to equation (2) and $\mathcal{S}(p)$ by (1).

By combining the results about the FTRM flight phases as summarized in Fig. 11, we conclude that FTRM avoids collisions safely. The modular proof structure in Fig. 11 still holds when replacing any part of the maneuver with a different choice that still satisfies the specification, e.g., for different entry procedures that still succeed in tangential configuration $\mathcal{R}$ within bounded time. This includes roundabouts with *asymmetric positions*, i.e., where the initial distance to c can be different, and with *near conflicts*, where the flight paths do not intersect in one point but in a larger critical region [4]. Most notably, the separation proof in Section 3.7 tolerates asymmetric distances to c (Fig. 7b).

Theorem 1 (Safety property of flyable tangential roundabouts). *FTRM is collision free, i.e., the collision avoidance property ψ in Fig. 10 is valid. Furthermore any variation of FTRM with a modified entry procedure that safely reaches tangential configuration $\mathcal{R}$ in some bounded time T is safe. That is if the following formula holds, saying that, until time T, the aircraft have safe distance p and will have reached configuration $\mathcal{R}$ at time T, where τ is a clock:*

$$\mathcal{S}(f) \rightarrow [\tau := 0;\ entry \wedge \tau' = 1]\big((\tau \leq T \rightarrow \mathcal{S}(p)) \wedge (\tau = T \rightarrow \mathcal{R})\big) .$$

6 Experimental Results

Table 2 summarizes experimental results obtained using the tool KeYmaera on a 2.6GHz AMD Opteron with 4GB memory; we use different proof search settings than in [14]. Rows marked with $*$ indicate a property where simplifications like symmetry reduction have been used to reduce the computational complexity. Table 2 shows that even aircraft maneuvers with challenging hybrid curve

Table 2. Experimental results for air traffic control (see [13] for details)

Case study	See	Time(s)	Memory(MB)	Steps	Dimension
tangential roundabout	2 aircraft	10.4	6.8	197	13
tangential roundabout	3 aircraft	253.6	7.2	342	18
tangential roundabout	4 aircraft	382.9	10.2	520	23
tangential roundabout	5 aircraft	1882.9	39.1	735	28
bounded maneuver speed	**AC2**	0.5	6.3	14	4
flyable roundabout entry*	(3)	10.1	9.6	132	8
flyable entry feasible*	[13]	104.5	87.9	16	10
flyable entry circular	[13]	3.2	7.6	81	5
limited entry progress	(6)	1.9	6.5	60	8
entry separation	[13]	140.1	20.1	512	16
mutual negotiation successful	(8)	0.8	6.4	60	12
mutual negotiation feasible*	[13]	7.5	23.8	21	11
mutual far negotiation	[13]	2.4	8.1	67	14
simultaneous exit separation*	[13]	4.3	12.9	44	9
different exit directions	[13]	3.1	11.1	42	11

dynamics can be verified formally. Memory consumption of quantifier elimination is shown in Table 2, excluding the front-end. The dimension of the continuous state space and number of automatic proof steps are indicated. Except for simple help in the proof of one property, the proofs for Table 2 are automatic.

7 Summary

We have analyzed complex air traffic control applications. Real aircraft can only follow sufficiently smooth flyable curves. Hence, mathematical maneuvers that require instant turns give physically impossible conflict resolution advice. We have developed a new collision avoidance maneuver with smooth, fully flyable curves. Despite its complicated dynamics and maneuvering, we have verified collision avoidance in this flyable tangential roundabout maneuver formally using our verification algorithm for a logic of hybrid systems. Because of the intricate spatio-temporal movement of aircraft in curved roundabouts, some of the properties require intricate arithmetic, which we handled by symmetry reduction and degree-based reductions. The proof is automatic except for modularization and arithmetical simplifications to overcome the computational complexity.

While the flyable roundabout maneuver is a highly nontrivial and challenging study, we still use modeling assumptions that should be relaxed in future work, e.g., synchronous, symmetric conflict resolution. Further generalizations include different varying cruise speeds, disturbances or new aircraft. The proof structure behind Theorem 1 is already sufficiently general, but the computational complexity high. It would be interesting future work to see if the informal robustness studies of Hwang et al. [4] can be carried over to a formal verification result.

Acknowledgements. We would like to thank the anonymous referees for their helpful comments and César Muñoz for his feedback.

References

1. Tomlin, C., Pappas, G.J., Sastry, S.: Conflict resolution for air traffic management. IEEE T. Automat. Contr. 43(4), 509–521 (1998)
2. Dowek, G., Muñoz, C., Carreño, V.A.: Provably safe coordinated strategy for distributed conflict resolution. In: AIAA-2005-6047 (2005)
3. Galdino, A.L., Muñoz, C., Ayala-Rincón, M.: Formal verification of an optimal air traffic conflict resolution and recovery algorithm. In: Leivant, D., de Queiroz, R. (eds.) WoLLIC 2007. LNCS, vol. 4576, pp. 177–188. Springer, Heidelberg (2007)
4. Hwang, I., Kim, J., Tomlin, C.: Protocol-based conflict resolution for air traffic control. Air Traffic Control Quarterly 15(1), 1–34 (2007)
5. Henzinger, T.A.: The theory of hybrid automata. In: LICS, pp. 278–292. IEEE, Los Alamitos (1996)
6. Košecká, J., Tomlin, C., Pappas, G., Sastry, S.: 2-1/2D conflict resolution maneuvers for ATMS. In: CDC, Tampa, FL, USA, vol. 3, pp. 2650–2655 (1998)
7. Bicchi, A., Pallottino, L.: On optimal cooperative conflict resolution for air traffic management systems. IEEE Trans. ITS 1(4), 221–231 (2000)
8. Hu, J., Prandini, M., Sastry, S.: Probabilistic safety analysis in three-dimensional aircraft flight. In: CDC, vol. 5, pp. 5335–5340 (2003)
9. Hu, J., Prandini, M., Sastry, S.: Optimal coordinated motions of multiple agents moving on a plane. SIAM Journal on Control and Optimization 42, 637–668 (2003)
10. Umeno, S., Lynch, N.A.: Proving safety properties of an aircraft landing protocol using I/O automata and the PVS theorem prover. In: Misra, J., Nipkow, T., Sekerinski, E. (eds.) FM 2006. LNCS, vol. 4085, pp. 64–80. Springer, Heidelberg (2006)
11. Umeno, S., Lynch, N.A.: Safety verification of an aircraft landing protocol: A refinement approach. In: Bemporad, A., Bicchi, A., Buttazzo, G. (eds.) HSCC 2007. LNCS, vol. 4416, pp. 557–572. Springer, Heidelberg (2007)
12. Massink, M., Francesco, N.D.: Modelling free flight with collision avoidance. In: Andler, S.F., Offutt, J. (eds.) ICECCS, pp. 270–280. IEEE, Los Alamitos (2001)
13. Platzer, A., Clarke, E.M.: Formal verification of curved flight collision avoidance maneuvers: A case study. Technical Report CMU-CS-09-147, School of Computer Science, Carnegie Mellon University, Pittsburgh, PA (2009)
14. Platzer, A., Clarke, E.M.: Computing differential invariants of hybrid systems as fixedpoints. Form. Methods Syst. Des. (2009); In: Gupta, A., Malik, S. (eds.) CAV 2008. LNCS, vol. 5123, pp. 176–189. Springer, Heidelberg (2008)
15. Damm, W., Pinto, G., Ratschan, S.: Guaranteed termination in the verification of LTL properties of non-linear robust discrete time hybrid systems. In: Peled, D.A., Tsay, Y.-K. (eds.) ATVA 2005. LNCS, vol. 3707, pp. 99–113. Springer, Heidelberg (2005)
16. Platzer, A.: Differential dynamic logic for hybrid systems. J. Autom. Reasoning 41(2), 143–189 (2008)
17. Lafferriere, G., Pappas, G.J., Yovine, S.: A new class of decidable hybrid systems. In: Vaandrager, F.W., van Schuppen, J.H. (eds.) HSCC 1999. LNCS, vol. 1569, pp. 137–151. Springer, Heidelberg (1999)
18. Pallottino, L., Scordio, V.G., Frazzoli, E., Bicchi, A.: Decentralized cooperative policy for conflict resolution in multi-vehicle systems. IEEE Trans. on Robotics 23(6), 1170–1183 (2007)
19. Muñoz, C., Carreño, V., Dowek, G., Butler, R.W.: Formal verification of conflict detection algorithms. STTT 4(3), 371–380 (2003)

Connecting UML and VDM++ with Open Tool Support

Kenneth Lausdahl, Hans Kristian Agerlund Lintrup, and Peter Gorm Larsen

Aarhus School of Engineering, Denmark
kenneth@lausdahl.com, hlintrup@gmail.com, pgl@iha.dk

Abstract. Most formal method notations are text based, while tools used in industry often use graphical notations, such as UML. This paper demonstrates how the power of both approaches can be combined by providing the automatic translation of VDM++ models to and from UML. The translation is implemented as a plugin for the popular Eclipse development environment by the open-source Overture initiative. Both UML class diagrams and sequence diagrams can be translated, the latter enabling the novel ability to link with the combinatorial test facility of Overture.

1 Introduction

Currently, UML is the most popular abstract notation for describing software systems in industry. Thus, by automatically linking VDM and UML, VDM can be made available to a wider range of developers. This paper describes how an automatic connection between these two notations has been established [1]. The tool support resulting from this work enables both a classical connection to UML Class Diagrams (CDs) as well as a novel connection from UML Sequence Diagrams (SDs) to a new part of VDM++. The tool presented in this paper is part of the Overture open source project [2] linking to and from Enterprise Architect [3] (EA). The EA tool has been chosen in preference to other available products for two main reasons: It has excellent import and export functionality with the XMI represention of UML diagrams; and EA supports several new UML2 constructs, e.g. the n-ary association.

Conversions between formal languages and UML have been attempted several times in the past (e.g. [4,5,6,7,8,9]). A connection between VDM++ and UML CDs was developed as a part of VDMTools [10,11], but this only supports version 1.4 of UML whereas the work presented here extends that to version 2 of UML. In addition, this new research covers a novel connection to UML SDs. This connection exploits a recent extension of VDM++ for combinatorial testing using traces resembling regular expressions [12,13]. This means that SDs can be used as test sequence descriptions that can subsequently be executed automatically in VDM++.

Section 2 of this paper presents the basics of VDM++ and UML necessary to understand the selected translation rules presented in the rest of the paper. Section 3 provides an overview of the architecture of the tool support. Section 4 demonstrates the transformations between VDM++ and UML CDs. Section 5 illustrates the corresponding transformations with SDs. Section 6 provides examples illustrating the CD rules on extracts of the transformation between VDM++ and UML at VDM++ level. Finally, section 7 compares this work with related work and section 8 rounds off the paper with concluding remarks, including future work.

A. Cavalcanti and D. Dams (Eds.): FM 2009, LNCS 5850, pp. 563–578, 2009.

2 VDM++ and UML

VDM is a well-established formal method that uses a group of formal modelling languages, each supporting different forms of system specification. VDM++ [14] extends the ISO standardised VDM-SL [15] with features for object-oriented modelling and concurrency. An object-oriented model in VDM++ is composed of *class* specifications which may be linked by single or multiple *inheritance*. The internals of each class definition are similar to those of a regular VDM-SL model except that the visibility of each definition is controlled using *access modifiers* (public, protected and private). Each object's state consists of typed *instance variables*. *Operations* are able to access such instance variables whereas *functions* are pure in the sense that they cannot access or modify the state. Both functions and operations have a *signature* that describes the types of the parameters and return value. VDM++ classes may be active or passive. Active classes represent entities that have their own thread of control.

In order to automate the testing process, VDM++ contains a traces notation enabling the definition of different sequences of function/operation calls that one would like to have tested exhaustively [13]. These traces can use constructs for repetition, alternatives and trace bindings over finite sets. In a sense this is similar to model checking limitations, except that in VDM this is done with real and not symbolic values. However, errors in test cases are filtered away so other test cases starting with the same failed call sequence will be skipped automatically. The combinatorial testing feature is inspired by the TOBIAS tool [16,17].

VDMTools [10,11] provides a linking interface between VDM++ and the IBM Rational Rose[1] UML tool[2]. However, this tool support was developed when UML version 1.4 [18] was current. In this work we examine to what extent it is possible to take advantage of the new features in UML 2.0 [19].

The Unified Modeling Language (UML) is a semi-formal visual language for modeling object-oriented systems at a certain level of abstraction. It is widely used in the field of software engineering and is standardised by OMG [19]. UML is good for presenting and discussing models due to its visual capabilities, i.e. different structural and behavioral views of a system. Of the different views, CDs and SDs are of particular interest to our work. A CD is a structural or static view which provides a means of presenting classes and their relation to each other. Some of the main features are the visualization of classes, attributes, operations and associations between classes. An SD is a behavioral (dynamic) view which provides features for presenting interactions between instances of objects in a system e.g. showing how one instance of a class interacts with another at runtime.

3 Transformation Overview

The transformation between VDM++ and UML is performed at an abstract level, and specified using VDM++ itself in a bootstrapping fashion [20]. An Abstract Syntax Tree (AST) is specified for both VDM++ and UML. A transformation is then specified in

[1] Now known as the IBM Technical Developer.

[2] In recent years, XMI support for JUDE and Enterprise Architect has been added.

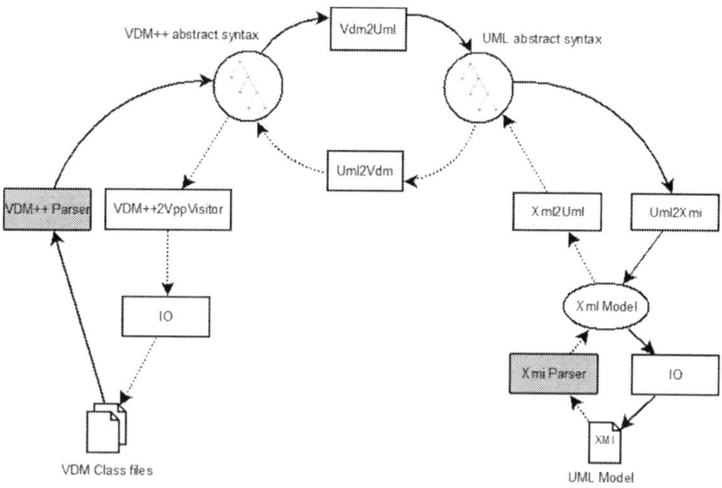

Fig. 1. Overview of components involved in the VDM++ and UML transformation process

VDM++ to accomplish the transformation between the two abstract representations. Fig. 1 gives an overview of the architecture of the transformation. The gray boxes denote Java implementations whereas all other boxes are specified in VDM++ and subsequently automatically converted to Java using VDMTool's support for automatic generation of Java code. Starting with a VDM model, it is first parsed to populate the VDM++ AST which is then transformed to a UML AST equivalent. The UML AST must then be de-parsed to the XML Metadata Interchange (XMI) format in order to be integrated with UML modeling tools. The dotted arrows in Fig. 1 shows transformation from UML to VDM++ whereas the solid arrows show the transformation from VDM++ to UML.

The XML Metadata Interchange (XMI) is a standard for exchanging meta data information via Extensible Markup Language (XML). It can be used for any meta model that can be expressed in the Object Management Group (OMG) Meta-Object Facility (MOF). XMI is standardized by the OMG [21]. XMI is widely used to exchange UML models by UML modeling tools.

The modelling of data in XMI is split into two parts: an *abstract* model and a *concrete* model, which is the vision of OMG. The abstract model represents the semantic information (e.g. UML class definitions) and it is an instance of an arbitrary MOF-based modeling language, such as UML. The concrete model represents the visual diagrams, such as SDs in UML. The Diagram Interchange [22] (XMI[DI]) is a standard specifying how visual diagrams should be specified.

There are several incompatibilities between different tool vendors' implementations XMI for UML. At the diagram interchange level the standard is almost nonexistent, and there are multiple incompatibilities between abstract models. Unfortunately this means that the goal of XMI, i.e. to enable the free interchange of UML models, is rarely possible. Moreover the new XMI 2.1 standard is even less widespread which limits the interchange of models even further.

4 Transformations for UML Class Diagrams

The static structure representation offered by a UML CD is largely conceptually compatible with VDM++ models. This includes concepts such as classes, inheritance, associations and multiplicities which all have a one-to-one relationship between UML and VDM++ making it possible to move both ways. However, only the static structure of a VDM model can be efficiently transformed to UML. VDM++ has a well-defined semantics for determining properties about a model, e.g. using pre- and post-conditions. Such elements are awkward to display in a visual UML model, because they can only be expressed in text. It would be possible to transform such bodies to OCL in UML and give the user access to the relevant definitions via a UML tool, but with the disadvantage of having to do a lot of navigation to access the definitions. This could be easily be done for a subset of VDM++ but OCL has a number of limitations that would increase the complexity of the mapping and make the bi-directional transformation harder to understand for the user. This can easily be reconsidered at a later stage if the analysis tools of such OCL expressions are improved.

A UML CD consists of classes connected by associations or generalizations to form a coherent system. Similarly, VDM++ classes constituting a VDM++ model are related by instance variables and inheritance. Fig. 2 show a CD which is generated automatically from a corresponding VDM++ model. The `Train` class, for example, would correspond to the VDM++ class shown below.

```
class Train is subclass of Vehicle
instance variables

passengers : map int to Passenger;
capacity   : nat := 345

thread
...
end Train
```

Note how the **`is subclass of`** clause corresponds to the inheritance arrow in the UML CD. Similarly, the `capacity` instance variable is represented as an attribute of the `Train` class. However, the instance variable `passengers` is more complex and is thus represented as a qualified association (it is a **`map`**) to the `Passenger` class.

4.1 UML 2 Class Diagrams

The building blocks of UML CDs have not changed radically since version 1.x, when VDMTools was released with its model transformation tool, Rose-VDM++ Link, supporting UML 1.4. However, the Rose-VDM++ Link left out a number of features of VDM, which have been captured by our tool. Also, the remaining features have all been examined and updated to comply with UML 2. In particular, this work has the ability to transform the following types, none of which is present in Rose-VDM++ Link:

1. Union types as constrained associations.
2. Product types as n-ary associations.
3. Active classes.

As well as explaining basic transformations, the subsection below explains how selected VDM constructs from the list above are related to a UML CD counterpart by one or more transformation rules. In total 17 such transformation rules have been defined for the mapping to CDs and here we will show 4 of these.

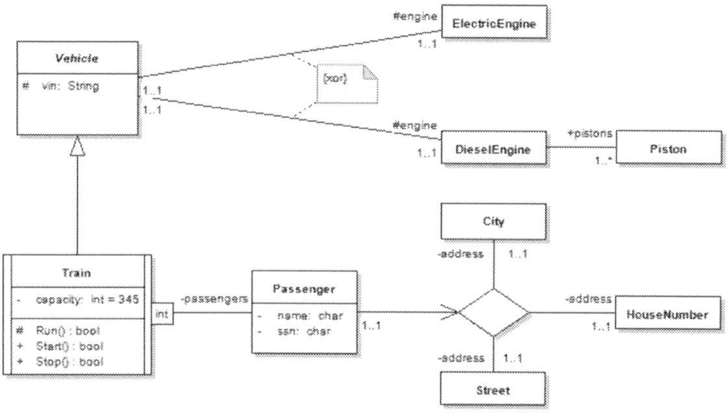

Fig. 2. Class diagram for a hypothetical case of a software system

4.2 Transformation Rules

In this paper we present a subset of the transformation rules to illustrate the principles underlying the transformation. The rules are both formulated in natural language and specified in VDM++. For space reasons only the natural language version of the rules is included. A reference to the full VDM++ specification for each rule is supplied in the text.

Each transformation rule describes how to move from a VDM construct to a UML equivalent. The phrase *meta class* refers to classes in the UML meta model, which defines all possible constituents of a UML model. For example, an instance of the meta class `Association` corresponds to the UML model construct *association*.

Transformation Rule 1
A VDM class with the keyword **`is subclass of`** followed by class-names is mapped as a sequence of superclass-names in the inheriting class. Notice that this approach is a simplification and that it does not comply with the UML specification. To comply with the specification, the UML meta-class `Generalization`, with the attributes `general` and `specific` referencing the superclass and subclass, respectively, should have been used. In this context, more than one subclass results in more than one instance of `Generalization`.

VDM supports single and multiple inheritance which is supported in the same way in UML. In fig. 2 it can be seen that the class `Train` inherits from the `Vehicle` class. The array in the UML diagram specifies which class is the base class. The corresponding VDM specification can be seen in listing 1 where the **is subclass of** key word is used to specify inheritance.

```
class Train is subclass of Vehicle
  ...
end Train

class Vehicle
...
end Vehicle
```

Listing 1. Inheritance between `Train` and `Vehicle`

In fact this transformation rule, along with all the others, has been formalised in VDM itself. The relevant operation dealing with inheritance is:

```
public build_Class : IOmlClass ==> IUmlClass
build_Class(c) ==
 (let name = c.getIdentifier(),
      inh  = if c.hasInheritanceClause()
             then c.getInheritanceClause()
             else nil,
...
      supers = getSuperClasses(inh)
 in
   return new UmlClass(name, ..., supers, ...);
```

where the `getSuperClasses` function is defined as:

```
public getSuperClasses : [IOmlInheritanceClause] ->
                          seq of IUmlClassNameType
getSuperClasses(inh) ==
  if inh = nil
  then []
  else let list = inh.getIdentifierList()
       in
         [new UmlClassNameType(list(i))
         | i in set inds list];
```

For space reasons, the remaining VDM specifications of the transformations have been left out of this article.

Transformation Rule 2
A union type is mapped as the meta-class `Association` between the owning class and the types specified in the union type. The resulting associations are decorated with a textual constraint {xor}. The constraint is an instance of the meta-class `Constraint`.

A VDM union type is a union of values from different types [14]. UML offers the meta class `Constraint` to represent a restriction stated in natural language, or in a language with a well defined semantics. Fig. 2 illustrates this rule with the {`xor`} constraint between `ElectricEngine` and `DieselEngine`. The rule states that the type constituents of a union type are mapped as separate UML classes (regardless of whether they are simple or constructed types). This is equivalent to the following VDM++ definition:

```
class Vehicle
...
instance variables

protected engine : DieselEngine | ElectricEngine;

end Vechicle
```

Transformation Rule 3
A VDM product type maps to:

- **3 a:** The UML meta-class `Class` if it is declared as a data type.
- **3 b:** The UML meta-class `Association` if it is not defined as a type (i.e. it is anonymous).

Each association-end that represents an entry in the product type is named according to the product type. The types constituting the product type are sorted alphabetically according to the name of the types used in the product type.

A product type is a composite structure, consisting of tuples of values. Since UML does not have an ordering for an N-ary association this construct is complicated to move to or from VDM++ because an ordering is required in a product type at the VDM level. A product type is shown in fig. 2 for the `address` instance variable in the `Passenger` class. If the product type had been declared as a type and thus used explicitly, the data type name would figure as a class in the UML CD. The `Passenger` class represented in VDM is shown below.

```
class Passenger

instance variables
name : seq of char;
ssn  : seq of char;
address : City * HouseNumber * Street;

end Passenger
```

The first statement of rule 3 explains that an explicitly declared product type is transformed as an ordinary UML class, named according to the data type definition. The second statement explains that an implicitly declared product type is transformed as a UML association linking each product type constituent. Because of the alphabetic sorting of the elements of a product type the mapping will only be bi-directional if the elements are sorted in the original VDM model. Otherwise the mapping of CDs is bi-directional.

Transformation Rule 4
A VDM class with a **thread** compartment is mapped as the UML meta-class `Class` with the meta-attribute `isActive` set to **true**.

A VDM class with a **thread** block has an independent thread of control. It corresponds to an active class in UML, exemplified in fig. 2 as the active class `Train`. In UML CDs, active classes are denoted by the extra vertical bars on each side of the class (in earlier versions of UML it was denoted by a bold line for the box of a class).

Fig. 2 also shows how the relationship **map** is represented as an association with a qualifier of type **int**. The association with a multiplicity of `0..*` at the target class `Piston` indicates a set type definition inside the `DieselEngine` class.

The access modifiers of class attributes are shown as prepended `'-'`, denoting private visibility. Also, notice that the attributes of class `Passenger` are not shown as separate classes, because of their simple data type, **char**.

5 Transformations for UML Sequence Diagrams

The primary transformation direction chosen in this work is to transform UML SDs to VDM++ trace definitions, since it is considered to have the greatest value. By transforming an SD into a trace definition, a trace can be seen both textually or visually. In this section the focus will be to present a subset of the rules to enable this transformation. The rules will be specified in such a way that a round-trip between VDM++ and UML is possible [13].

5.1 VDM++ Trace Definitions

A new VDM++ definition block has been introduced for trace definitions. The listing below shows an ordinary VDM++ class `Stack` followed by another class, `UseStack`, which has a **traces** block containing trace definitions. Each trace definition is given a name which is separated from its body by a colon. The body of a trace definition is similar to a regular expression for identifying sequences of function/operation calls on different instances of classes. It is possible to introduce bindings (also with looseness that is expanded to all possible combinations), alternatives (using the | operator) and repeat patterns (using different kinds of repeat patterns). Tool support exists for automatic test case generation using combinatorial testing principles.

5.2 UML 2 Sequence Diagrams

UML 2 SDs are intended to present a dynamic interaction between objects of a system. SDs show a collection of scenarios illustrating how the flow of control between different instances of classes evolves. The vertical line below each instance displayed at the top

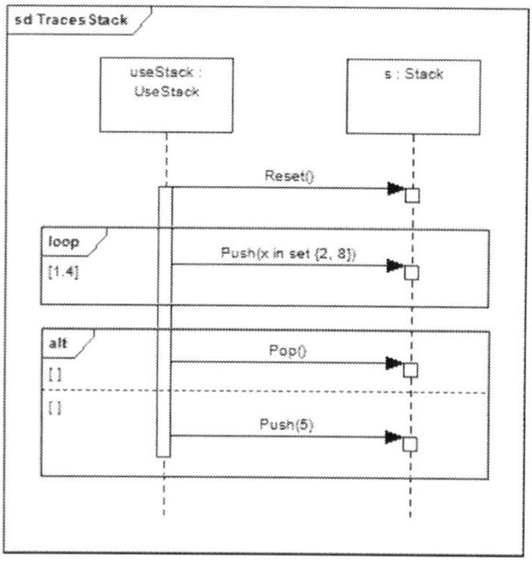

Fig. 3. A SD showing a simplified trace definition

of an SD indicates a lifeline. The horizontal arrows stemming from the lifeline indicate interactions with other lifelines. An arrow going from such a lifeline indicates a call of an operation named above the line with its parameters. An operation call on the same instance is showed as an arrow originating from and arriving at the same lifeline.

A significant improvement made to SDs in UML 2 is the ability to express procedural logic and the ability to nest fragments to an unlimited degree. Most important is the ability to express repetitions and alternatives using the **loop** and **alt** constructs, respectively. Both of these constructs may also be nested.

5.3 Sequence Diagrams and Trace Definitions

A UML SD visually represents a sequence of executions. As an example, fig. 3 shows the message calls `Reset`, `Push` and `Pop` which can be directly related to the application of these operations:

```
class Stack
... The usual kinds of basic Stack definitions
end Stack
class UseStack
instance variables
  stack : Stack := new Stack();
traces
 TS: stack.Reset() ;
     let x in set {2,8} in stack.Push(x){1,4};
     (stack.Push(9) | stack.Pop())
end UseStack
```

Traces like this will expand to 16 test cases (each being a sequence of operation calls):

```
TC1: stack.Reset();stack.Push(2);stack.Push(9)
TC2: stack.Reset();stack.Push(8);stack.Push(8);stack.Pop()
... 14 more
```

5.4 Transformation Rules

In order to combine SDs and VDM++ trace definitions, essential similarities must be found and described. The SD shown in fig. 3 is used to relate SDs' constructs to VDM++ trace definitions.

Transformation Rule 5
The class in which the trace is placed is the one from which all `Messages` in an SD originates.
An interaction transformation is only possible if all `Messages` originate from a single `Lifeline` (e.g. an instance of `UseStack` above).

Rule 5 describes that an SD must have one `LifeLine` from which all messages originate, since the object represented by this lifeline will be the class containing the trace definitions. This can be statically determined and if the limitation is not satisfied, a VDM++ trace definition cannot be derived.

Transformation Rule 6
The method name in a trace apply expression is transformed from the `Operation` property of the meta class `CallEvent` and the variable on which the method should be executed is transformed from the `LifeLine` at the receive end of the message, where a message object is linking it to a `LifeLine` representing the object. The arguments are directly transformed from the meta class `Message`.

Rule 6 describes that for every message in an SD, a function/operation call on an object will occur in a VDM++ trace. In relation to Fig. 3 this rule corresponds to the horizontal lines between `UseStack` and `s`.

Transformation Rule 7
The repeat pattern of an apply expression is transformed from the `Interaction-Constraint` of an `Operand` contained in a `CombinedFragment` where the `InteractionOperator` equals **`loop`**. The constraint of the `Operand` holding the message specifies how the repeat pattern should be set:

Table 1: Transformation rules for VDM++ constructs modelling collections

Constraint (Guard)	RepeatPattern				
	a*	a+	a?	a{x}	a{x,y}
`minint`	0	1	0	x	x
`maxint`	*	*	1	x	y

Rule 7 is one of the most important features of the trace definitions since it describes the constructs of a trace definition which makes it possible to create a large number of test cases with minimum effort. A combined fragment, shown in Fig. 3 as a labelled box (loop) covering both lifelines, shows how a trace definition calling `Push` should be repeated. To enable the transformation between UML and VDM++ a constraint is added to the combined fragment specifying the exact repeat pattern of all the messages within the fragment.

6 Examples of the VDM++/UML Transformations

To illustrate the usage of the UML transformation described in this paper the UML transformation specification itself can be transformed by the final implementation of the transformation as a Java program. In fig. 4 a class diagram can be seen which is a subset of the classes generated by the UML transformation. The figure shows a class diagram of the interface classes of from the UML AST. The specification is quite large; it consists of around 600 classes divided between the VDM language specification AST (OML), the UML AST and the actual transformation. In total the specification consists of around 6.900 lines of VDM excluding the VDM AST where, 3.400 of the lines are automatically generated from the UML AST VDM-SL type hierarchy which only consists of only 212 lines. When the model is code generated to Java the it has a size of more than 20.000 lines excluding parsing/deparsing and graphical user interface integration. A complete transformation from the UML VDM specification to a UML XMI file can be performed in around 3.5 sec, handling all 600 classes and the 6.900 lines plus around 17.000 lines for the VDM AST. The same time applies for transformations in both directions measured with a Intel(R) Core(TM) 2 CPU T7200 and 4 GB of RAM, running Microsoft Windows Vista SP2 32-bit with Java 1.6.0.12.

In the following subsections the transformation rules described in section 4 will be illustrated by small extracts from the VDM to UML transformation specification.

6.1 Generalization

The generalization rule 1 describes that VDM and UML support the same ways of using inheritance: both single and multiple inheritance is possible in both VDM and UML.

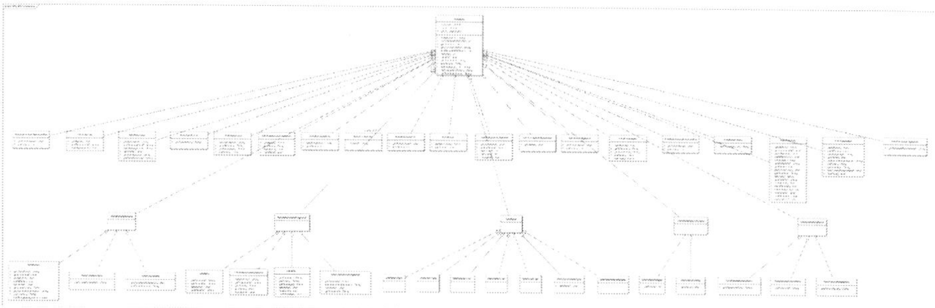

Fig. 4. Class diagram for the interfaces of the UML AST used in the transformation

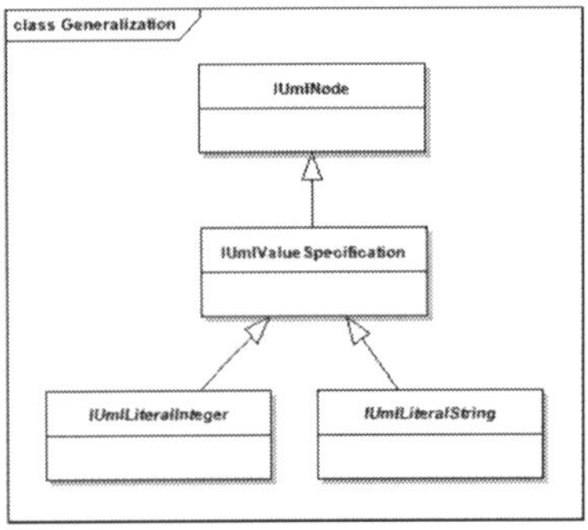

Fig. 5. Zoom of fig. 4 showing the class diagram with inheritance of value specifications

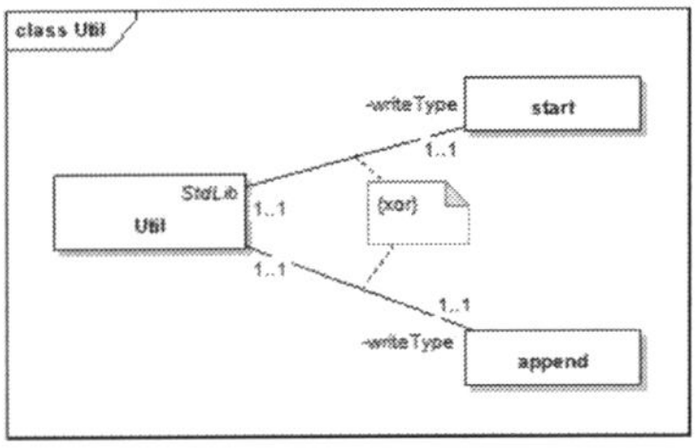

Fig. 6. A class diagram showing the `Util` class of the UML transformation with a constraint association

In fig. 5 a small sub part of fig. 4 is selected to show how the interface classes used in the UML AST are transformed from VDM classes to UML classes shown in a class diagram.

6.2 Union Types

The transformation of a union type in VDM will only be visible on a class diagram if a class has an instance variable or value of a union type. A union type is transformed into a constraint association where the constraint denotes an `xor` as described in rule 2. In fig. 6 the `Util` class, used to provide functionality for storage, is shown where the private instance variable describing the current `writeType` states if the current file should be appended or a new one created. The corresponding VDM model showing an extract of the `Util` class is shown in listing 2.

```
class Util is subclass of StdLib
instance variables

 static writeType : Append | Start :=  new Start();
  ...
end Util
```

Listing 2. VDM specification of the Util class

6.3 Product Types

The transformation of a product type will only be visible in a class diagram if used as an instance variable or a value inside a VDM class. A product type can hold a number of fields of individual types without having to name the elements. In fig. 7 a small extract of the `Vdm2Uml` class is shown. This is used for the abstract transformation between the VDM AST and UML AST. The class contains an instance variable which holds the model elements while they are being constructed until they are ready for further processing by the XMI mechanism.

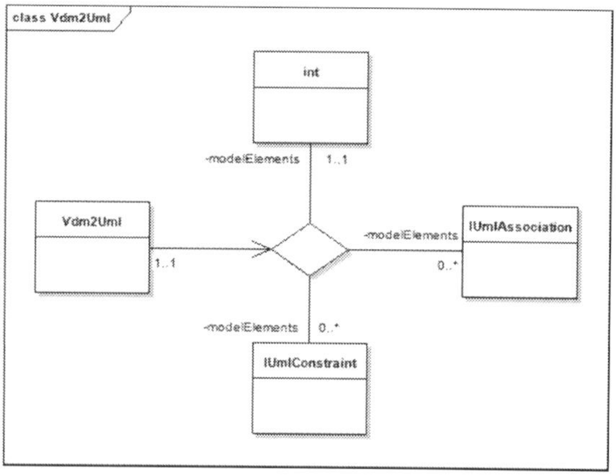

Fig. 7. The VDM specification class for the abstract transformation from VDM to UML showing a product type instance variable which holds the model elements which is being constructed

In listing 3 a sub part of the `Vdm2Uml` class is shown to illustrate how the product type is specified in VDM. The ordering matters in VDM since a product type is indexed with a number like in an array. A guide line is needed to describe how the associations would be mapped to VDM as seen in fig. 7. This is specified in rule 3 where it is stated that an N-ary association will be mapped so all associations are sorted by name.

```
class Vdm2Uml
instance variables

modelElements :
            int *                          -- runningElementId
            set of IUmlAssociation *       -- Associations
            set of IUmlConstraint;         -- Constraints
  ...
end Vdm2Uml
```

Listing 3. Extract from the `Vdm2Uml` class with a product type holding the model elements

7 Related Work

The idea of combining formal and informal languages to exploit the best of both worlds has been investigated by others before [4,5,6,7,8,9,23]. Common to these is the mapping between a formal method (Alloy, B, Z, Z++, VDM++) and the UML CDs which provides a static view. Most of these focus on a one-way translation from UML CDs to a formal notation. B and Z lack the basic notions of the object-oriented paradigm, thus they would not be able to make the same kind of bidirectional mapping that has been shown in this paper. Regarding UML CDs this work is similar to VDMTools [9] with a few improvements such as those from transformation rule 2, 3 and 4.

Connections to other parts of UML have been considered in the context of transformation between formal and informal models. UML Sequence diagrams and state machines have also been the subject of model transformations [6]. To enable such a transformation, rules must be stated before an actual transformation can take place. The specification of such rules is critical and is often not explicitly defined [4]. These rules can be specified in a formal way and proved as in [7], where they proved 80 per cent of the rules specified in B by isabelle/HOL. In this work the rules are formalised using VDM++ and validated using traditional testing techniques. In the UML community there exists a lot of work on the UML testing profile [24]. This also includes subsets of UML making use of OCL for model based testing [25]. However, we are not aware of any other work that uses UML diagrams as input for test automation.

8 Concluding Remarks and Further Work

This paper has described how a bi-directional translation between UML and VDM++ can be established. The tool support resulting from this work enables both a classical connection to UML Class Diagrams (CDs) as well as a novel connection from UML Sequence Diagrams (SDs) to a new part of VDM++ meant for test automation using combinatorial testing principles. The Overture tools including the UML connection are freely available and will be demonstarted at the FM'09 conference.

The transformation between UML and VDM++ is bidirectional and it is itself specified in VDM++. A few limitations exists for the transformation between UML and VDM++. The VDM++ model for this transformation has been largely left out of this paper for space reasons but the full model is available in [1]. The informal explanation for a subset of the rules have been presented in the paper.

At the moment the SD transformation is only available from UML to VDM++ but it is anticipated that the transformation in the opposite direction will be trivial to implement. It is also expected that UML SDs will be used to display logfiles from executions of VDM++ models. The current transformation is not able to cope with incremental changes both at the UML and VDM++ levels. It will be extended with merge functionality similar to that of VDMTools. Research investigating whether more general SDs can be transformed into a collection of trace definitions is planned. It is also anticipated that it will be expanded with support for UML 2 state machine diagrams. Finally it is our hope that it will be possible to extend the tool to be compatible with more UML tools. However, experience has demonstrated that the different tool vendors do not adhere to the XMI standard thus impeding the development of a tool supporting a wider range of UML tools (see also [26]).

Acknowledgements. We would like to thank the anonymous referees and Nick Battle and Hugo Macedo for valuable feedback and assistance with this work.

References

1. Lausdahl, K., Lintrup, H.K.: Coupling Overture to MDA and UML. Master's thesis, Aarhus University/Engineering College of Aarhus (December 2008)
2. Overture-Core-Team: Overture Web site (2007), `http://www.overturetool.org`
3. SparxSystems: Enterprise architect 7.1 Modeling & Design Tools for your Enterprise, `http://www.sparxsystems.com.au/`
4. Kim, S.K., Burger, D., Carrington, D.: An MDA Approach Towards Integrating Formal and Informal Modelling Languages. In: Fitzgerald, J.S., Hayes, I.J., Tarlecki, A. (eds.) FM 2005. LNCS, vol. 3582, pp. 448–464. Springer, Heidelberg (2005)
5. Snook, C., Butler, M.: UML-B: Formal modeling and design aided by UML. ACM Trans. Softw. Eng. Methodol. 15(1), 92–122 (2006)
6. Dascalu, S., Hitchcock, P.: An Approach to Integrating Semi-formal and Formal Notations in Software Specification. In: SAC 2002, pp. 1014–1020. ACM, New York (2002)
7. Laleau, R.: On the Interest of Combining UML with the B Formal Method for the Specification of Database Applications. In: ICEIS, pp. 56–63 (2000)
8. Fekih, H., Ayed, L.J.B., Merz, S.: Transformation of B Specifications into UML Class Diagrams and State Machines. In: Proceedings of the 2006 ACM symposium on Applied computing, pp. 1840–1844. ACM, New York (2006)
9. The-VDM-Tool-Group: The Rose-VDM++ Link. Technical report, CSK Systems (January 2008)
10. Elmstrøm, R., Larsen, P.G., Lassen, P.B.: The IFAD VDM-SL Toolbox: A Practical Approach to Formal Specifications. ACM SIGPLAN Notices 29(9), 77–80 (1994)
11. Fitzgerald, J., Larsen, P.G., Sahara, S.: VDMTools: Advances in Support for Formal Modeling in VDM. SIGPLAN Notices 43(2), 3–11 (2008)
12. Santos, A.S.: VDM++ Test Automation Support. Master's thesis, Minho University with exchange to Engineering College of Arhus (July 2008)
13. Larsen, P.G., Lausdahl, K., Battle, N.: Combinatorial Testing for VDM++ (July 2009) (submitted for publication)
14. Fitzgerald, J., Larsen, P.G., Mukherjee, P., Plat, N., Verhoef, M.: Validated Designs for Object–oriented Systems. Springer, New York (2005)
15. Fitzgerald, J., Larsen, P.G.: Modelling Systems – Practical Tools and Techniques in Software Development, 2nd edn. Cambridge University Press, Cambridge (2009)
16. Ledru, Y., du Bousquet, L., Maury, O., Bontron, P.: Filtering TOBIAS Combinatorial Test Suites. In: Wermelinger, M., Margaria-Steffen, T. (eds.) FASE 2004. LNCS, vol. 2984, pp. 281–294. Springer, Heidelberg (2004)
17. Ledru, Y., du Bousquet, L.: An Executable Formal Specification of a Test Generator. In: Automated Software Engineering 2006. IEEE, Los Alamitos (2006)
18. OMG: Unified modeling language specification version 1.4.2. Technical report (2005); This specification is also available from ISO as ISO/IEC 19501, formal/05-04-01, `http://www.omg.org/spec/UML/ISO/19501/PDF/`

19. OMG: Unified modeling language: Superstructure (August 2005), http://www.uml.org
20. Larsen, P.G.: Ten Years of Historical Development: "Bootstrapping" VDMTools. Journal of Universal Computer Science 7(8), 692–709 (2001)
21. OMG: Unified Modeling Language UML, OMG (2008); OMG Formally Released Versions of UML and ISO Released Versions of UML, http://www.omg.org/spec/UML/
22. OMG: Diagram interchange v1.0 (2004); version 1.0, formal/06-04-04, http://www.omg.org/cgi-bin/doc?formal/06-04-04
23. Idani, A., Ledru, Y.: Object oriented concepts identification from formal B specifications. Formal Methods System Design 30(3), 217–232 (2007)
24. Baker, P., Dai, Z.R., Grabowski, J., Haugen, O., Schieferdecker, I., Williams, C.: Model Driven Testing – Using the UML Testing Profile. Springer, Heidelberg (2008)
25. Bouquet, F., Grandpierre, C., Legeard, B., Peureux, F., Vacelet, N., Utting, M.: A subset of precise UML for model-based testing. In: A-MOST 2007: Proceedings of the 3rd international workshop on Advances in model-based testing, pp. 95–104. ACM, New York (2007)
26. Hooman, J., Kugler, H., Ober, I., Votintseva, A., Yushtein, Y.: Supporting UML-based Development of Embedded Systems by Formal Techniques. Software and Systems Modeling 7(2), 131–155 (2008)

Language and Tool Support for Class and State Machine Refinement in UML-B*

Mar Yah Said, Michael Butler, and Colin Snook

ECS, University of Southampton, Southampton, SO17 1BJ, UK
(mys05r,mjb,cfs)@ecs.soton.ac.uk

Abstract. UML-B is a 'UML-like' graphical front end for Event-B that provides support for object-oriented modelling concepts. In particular, UML-B supports class diagrams and state machines, concepts that are not explicitly supported in plain Event-B. In Event-B, refinement is used to relate system models at different abstraction levels. The same abstraction-refinement concepts can also be applied in UML-B. This paper introduces the notions of refined classes and refined state machines to enable refinement of classes and state machines in UML-B. Together with these notions, a technique for moving an event between classes to facilitate abstraction is also introduced. Our work makes explicit the structures of class and state machine refinement in UML-B. The UML-B drawing tool and Event-B translator are extended to support the new refinement concepts. A case study of an auto teller machine (ATM) is presented to demonstrate application and effectiveness of refined classes and refined state machines.

Keywords: Visual modelling languages, Formal specification, UML, Event-B, Refinement.

1 Introduction

UML-B [1] is a graphical formal modelling notation that has some resemblance with UML [2,3] and is based on Event-B [4] which is a new variant of classical B [8]. UML-B supports class diagrams and state machines, concepts that are not explicitly supported in plain Event-B. The UML-B notation is supported by the UML-B tool which is a plug-in feature for the Rodin Event-B verification tool [6,11]. The UML-B tool generates Event-B models corresponding to a UML-B development and the Rodin tool is then used to discharge proof obligations associated with the generated Event-B models. As detailed in [12], our motivations for developing UML-B are twofold. Firstly, in our experience industrial users find the UML-like language and tool appealing. Secondly, UML-B provides additional complementary structuring of Event-B models in the form of classes and state machines.

A development in classical B or Event-B is performed through refinement. Refinement [8,9] is a technique which is used to relate the abstract model of a software system to another model that is more concrete while maintaining the properties of the abstract

* This work has been presented at the IM_FMT 2009 workshop of the IFM2009 conference, Dusseldorf, Germany on 16 February 2009.

A. Cavalcanti and D. Dams (Eds.): FM 2009, LNCS 5850, pp. 579–595, 2009.

model. Refinement is an important technique for managing the complexity of a system being developed.

At the most abstract level of a refinement-based development, it is usual to specify invariants that define the properties of the system being modelled. These invariants must be preserved by all the events of the model. Each refinement step will add further invariants relating the abstract model and the refined model (gluing invariants). In Event-B, both state and events may be refined. This is achieved by extending the list of state variables (possibly suppressing some of them) and by replacing each abstract event by corresponding concrete events.

There are two main differences between Event-B and classical B with regards to refinement of events. In Event-B, several events may refine an abstract event whereas in classical B, only one event can refine an abstract event. The other difference is that in Event-B, we may have new events that refine *skip* whereas in classical B, this is not allowed. Another difference between classical B and Event-B is that Event-B distinguishes between contexts and machines. A context contains definitions and properties of types and constants. A machine contains state variables, invariants and events that update the variables. A machine may see several contexts.

UML-B incorporates the Event-B machine construct and a single UML-B machine may contain multiple classes and multiple state machines. Previously, UML-B supported machine refinement (a refinement relationship between UML-B machines) but had no support for refinement of classes or state machines (which are nested within UML-B machines). The work reported here enriches UML-B to support class and state machine refinement. The main contributions of our work are introducing notions of refined classes and inherited attributes which are described in Section 3 and notions of refined state machines and refined states which are described in Section 4. The other contribution is introducing a technique of event movement in Section 5. A further contribution is that we have implemented the UML-B extensions in the UML-B tool. In this work we focus on safety-preserving refinement and do not deal with liveness.

Section 3 describes class refinement using the notion of refined classes and inherited attributes which includes techniques for adding new classes and adding new attributes and associations to refined classes in a refinement. Section 4 describes state machine refinement and a technique for elaborating refined states into sub-states and the transitions elaboration technique. Section 5 describes a technique for moving class events of an abstract machine to a refined class or a new class in a refinement.

Before the technical details of the contributions are describes, we give some background on UML-B and the generated Event-B in Section 2 that outlines the existing relevant features of UML-B. Section 6 presents the ATM case study using the refinement techniques describes in Sections 3, 4 and 5. Section 7 concludes the paper.

2 Background of UML-B and Generated Event-B

UML-B provides four kind of diagrams. They are package, context, class and state machine diagrams. A package diagram is a top-level diagram that shows the structure and relationships between components (machines and contexts) in a project. A context is described in a context diagram which is similar to a class diagram but has only constant data and structured types. A machine is specified by a class diagram and state machine diagram(s) representing data structures that may be changed by events or transitions. Events may be attached to classes in a class diagram. Events can also be represented by the transitions in a state machine diagram. Further descriptions focus on the class and state machine diagrams as the rest of the sections mostly concerns these. The semantics of a UML-B model is given by the Event-B generated by the UML-B tool according to a set of translation rules.

A class diagram may contain classes. Each class may have attributes, associations, events and state machines. An attribute defines a data value of an instance of a class. An association is a special case of an attribute that defines a relationships between two classes. Events and state machines may modify some or all the attributes of any class. Each UML-B context gives rise to an Event-B context (i.e., the UML-B tool generates a corresponding Event-B context). Each UML-B machine gives rise to both an implicit Event-B context and an Event-B machine. The implicit context is used to define types for the classes and states in the UML-B machine. In the generated Event-B machine, classes, class attributes and associations become variables. Events and transitions in classes and state machines become events in the generated Event-B machine.

Fig. 1 contains screenshots from the UML-B tool showing an example of a package diagram that contains machine **M1** (a) which has a class diagram (b) containing classes

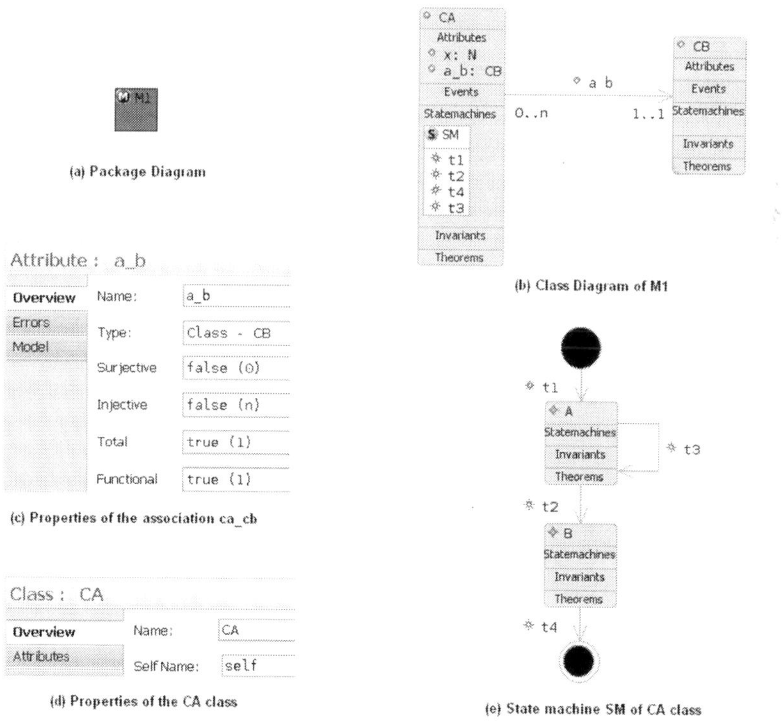

Fig. 1. Package diagram and the UML-B specification of the Abstract Machine M1

CA and CB. These classes give rise to the sets CA_SET and CB_SET in the generated Event-B implicit context. In the generated Event-B machine the classes CA and CB give rise to variables. The class CA consists of the attribute x of type $\mathbb{N}$ and also the association a_b of type CB. The multiplicity property for the association a_b shown in Fig. 1(c) specifies a many-to-one relationship (i.e., total function). A full explanation of association multiplicity may be found in [12]. The attributes x and a_b give rise to variables in the generated Event-B machine.

For each class, attribute and association, a type invariant will be generated in the Event-B machine. For example, the class CA corresponds to the type invariant which specifies that CA is a subset of CA_SET ($CA \in \mathbb{P}\ (CA\_SET)$). Attribute x corresponds to the type invariant $x \in CA \rightarrow \mathbb{N}$ that specifies x is defined for all CA. Each class has a self name property with a default value *self*, i.e., the default identifier that represents an instance of a class (which may be changed by the modeller). The self name property of the class CA is shown in Fig. 1(d). A class may have events and for each event, its parameters, guards and actions can be defined explicitly as properties. μB (micro B) notation [12] that borrows from the Event-B notation is used for textual guards and actions. μB uses an object-oriented style dot notation to show ownership of entities, i.e., attributes and associations, by classes. Variables used in an expression can represent owned features using the dot notation. For example, *i.x* refers to the value of the variable x which belongs to instance i. Another example of this will be presented later (Fig. 5).

Attached to the class CA is its state machine, SM, listing its four transitions *t1*, *t2*, *t3* and *t4*. The state machine SM in Fig. 1(e) shows its two states, A and B and the transitions. The solid circle is the initial state, whereas, the solid circle with an outer circle is the final state. The translation to Event-B for a state machine can either be a disjoint sets representation or state function representation. These two styles are introduced in [10] and they are supported in the UML-B tool. UML-B allows modellers to switch between these two representations.

For a disjoint sets representation, a disjoint sets of CA are introduced as variables as follows:

$$A \in \mathbb{P}(CA)$$
$$B \in \mathbb{P}(CA)$$
$$A \cap B = \varnothing$$

That is, variable A represents the set of instances of CA that are in the state A and similarly for B. For a state function representation, a variable SM (i.e., the state machine belonging to the class CA) is introduced representing a function mapping CA to an enumerated set of states, SM_STATES as follows:

$$SM\_STATES = \{A,B\}$$
$$SM \in CA \longrightarrow SM\_STATES$$

That is, SM maps each instance of CA to its state. In this paper, the translation to Event-B is described using the disjoint sets representation. The generated Event-B machine for **M1** is shown in the Rodin screenshot of Fig. 2. Each Event-B statement is preceded by its label which describes its purpose. For example, *CA.type* is a label for the Event-B statement $CA \in \mathbb{P}\ (CA\_SET)$. The states A and B of SM state machine represent variables of type *CA* (i.e., the state machine owner). An instance of CA changes its state when a transition fires. For the states, an additional invariant stating that they

```
INVARIANTS
  CA.type   :   CA ∈ ℙ (CA_SET)
  CB.type   :   CB ∈ ℙ (CB_SET)
  x.type   :   x ∈ CA → N
  a_b.type   :   a_b ∈ CA → CB
  A.type   :   A ∈ ℙ (CA)
  B.type   :   B ∈ ℙ (CA)
  disjointStates B,A   :   B ∩ A = ∅
EVENTS
t1   ≙
ANY
  self // constructed instance of class CA
WHERE
  self.type   :   self ∈ CA_SET \ CA
THEN
  SM_enterState_A   :   A = A ∪ {self}
  CA_constructor   :   CA = CA ∪ {self}
END
t2   ≙
ANY
  self // contextual instance of class CA
WHERE
  self.type   :   self ∈ CA
  SM_isin_A   :   self ∈ A
THEN
  SM_enterState_B   :   B = B ∪ {self}
  SM_leaveState_A   :   A = A \ {self}
END
```

```
EVENTS
t3   ≙
ANY
  self //   contextual instance of class CA
WHERE
  self.type   :   self ∈ CA
  SM_isin_A   :   self ∈ A
THEN
  skip
END

t4   ≙
ANY
  self //   contextual instance of class CA
WHERE
  self.type   :   self ∈ CA
  SM_isin_B   :   self ∈ B
THEN
  SM_leaveState_B   :   B = B \ {self}
  CA_destructor   :   CA = CA \ {self}
  CA.a_b_destructor   :   a_b = {self} ⩤ a_b
  CA.x_destructor   :   x = {self} ⩤ x
END
```

Fig. 2. Generated Event-B specification of M1

are disjoint is generated (i.e., $A \cap B = \varnothing$). For each transition there is a guard that specifies an instance source state (labelled as *.._isin_..*) and actions that specify its target state (labeled as *.._enterState_..*) and its departure from the current state (labelled as *.._leaveState_..*). The parameter, *self*, indicates an instance of a class. A transition from an initial state such as *t1*, defines a constructor for the class. The translation of *t1* selects an unused instance and adds it to the set of *CA* (labelled *self.type*). A transition to a final state such as *t4* is a destructor which removes an instance from current instances and from the domain of all the class variables. The transition *t3* is a self loop transition which does not changes state. In the generated Event-B the event *t3* has a guard that specifies its source state but with a skip action i.e., not changing state. Invariants and theorems (assertions requiring proofs) can be attached to classes or states and become part of the Event-B machine. A full explanation and examples of these is in [1].

3 Refinement of Classes in UML-B

In this section, the refinement techniques concerning the notion of refined classes and inherited attributes are described.

The motivation for refined classes and inherited attributes come from performing refinement in Event-B. The notion of refined classes and inherited attributes in UML-B reflect the refinement of variables in Event-B. A refined class is one that refines a more abstract class and an inherited attribute is one that inherits an attribute of the abstract class. A notion of refined classes is needed in UML-B because some elements of an abstract UML-B model need to be retained by the refinement.

In Event-B refinement, a machine that refines a more abstract machine may keep variables of an abstract machine, may drop some of the variables and may introduce new variables. In UML-B refinement, a machine that refines a more abstract machine may contain refined classes where each refined class refines a class of its abstract machine (i.e., keeps variables of its abstract machine). In UML-B refinement, a machine may drop some of refined classes (i.e., drop some variables). Also in UML-B refinement, a machine may introduce new classes (i.e., new variables) in a class diagram.

In UML-B refinement, a refined class may inherit attributes of its abstract class (i.e., keeps variables of its abstract machine). A refined class may drop some of the attributes of its abstract class (i.e., drop some variables of its abstract machine) and a refined class may introduce new attributes (i.e., new variables). The following schematic table illustrates a refined class that inherits and drops abstract attributes and introduces new attributes. The table lists the attributes for class `C` and a refined class `C`. Class `C` contains attributes *a1*, *a2* and *a3*. In refinement, the refined class `C` inherits attributes *a1* and *a2*, drops attribute *a3* and has new attributes *a4* and *a5*. In the generated Event-B machine, both a class and a refined class give rise to variables. A type invariant is generated for an abstract class i.e., Class `C` but not for a refined class because its type is already defined in the abstract Event-B machine. Similarly both the inherited attributes and new attributes give rise to variables and a type invariant is generated for each new attribute but not for the inherited attributes.

Class C	**Refined Class C**
a1	a1 (*inherited*)
a2	a2 (*inherited*)
a3	a4 (*new*)
	a5 (*new*)

We describe here a simple example of performing refinement in UML-B using the notion of refined classes and inherited attributes. Fig. 3(a) shows an example of a package diagram that manages a refinement relationship between machines. The package diagram shows that machine **M2** refines machine **M1** (of Fig. 1). The class diagram of **M2** is shown in Fig. 3(b) where it consists of refined classes `CA` and `CB` refining the classes `CA` and `CB` of **M1** respectively. The refined class `CA` inherits attribute *x* and association *a_b*. The refined class `CB` has a new association *cb_cc*. Machine **M2** has a new class, `CC` which gives rise to a new set (*CC_SET*) in the generated Event-B implicit context. In the generated Event-B machine for machine **M2**, the variables `CA`, `CB`, `x` and `a_b` are retained. The machine **M2** has new variables `CC` and `cb_cc` with their type invariants $CC \in \mathbb{P}\,(CC\_SET)$ and $cb\_cc \in CB \rightarrow CC$ respectively.

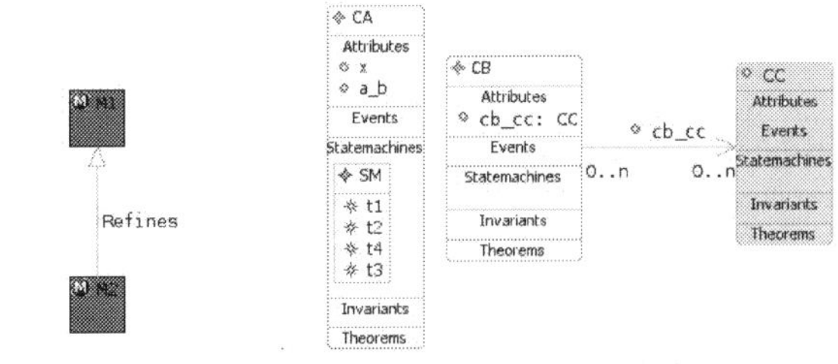

(a) Package Diagram (b) Class Diagram of M2

Fig. 3. Package diagram and Class Diagram of Machine M2

In Event-B refinement, a machine must provide a refinement of each abstract event. This can be either one or many event(s) refining one abstract event. New events may be introduced in a refinement. Similarly, in UML-B refinement, at least one concrete event must refine each abstract event and new events may be introduced. These concrete events can either be attached to a refined (or a new) class or a state machine of a refined (or a new) class. In UML-B refinement, we can also define additional invariants and theorems by attaching them to refined classes and states that reflect adding invariants and theorems in Event-B refinement.

4 Refinement of State Machines in UML-B

In this section, the refinement techniques concerning the notion of refined state machines and refined states are described. The motivation for refined state machines and

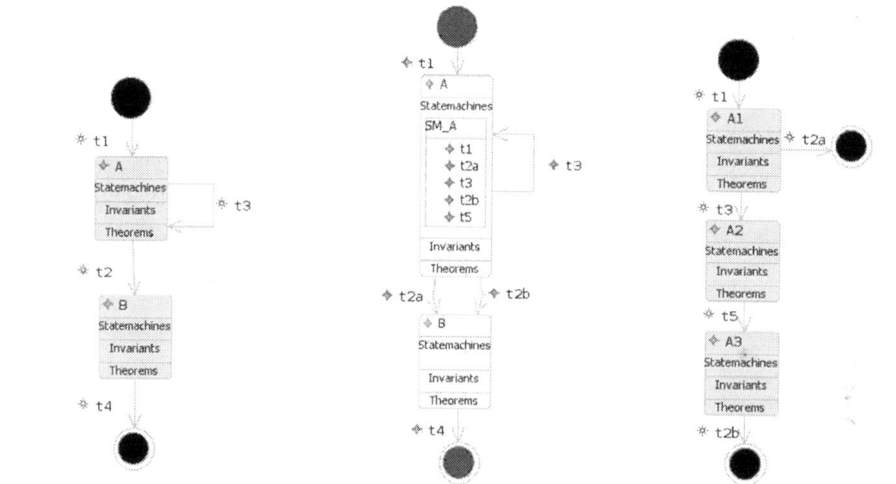

(a) State machine SM of class CA of M1

(b) Refined state machine SM of M2 refining SM of M1

(c) State machine SM_A of refined state machine SM

Fig. 4. Refinement of State machine (machine M2 refines machine M1)

refined states come from combining the state machine hierarchy in UML-B with refinement in Event-B. The essential concept is that state machines are refined by elaborating an abstract state with nested sub-states. A refined state machine is one that refines a more abstract state machine and a refined state is one that refines a more abstract state.

In UML-B refinement, a machine may contain refined state machines and refined states. We describe first an example of performing refinement in UML-B using the notion of refined state machines and refined states. We will then describe the general rules. Fig. 4 shows an example of a state machine refinement. The refined class `CA` of **M2** (Fig. 3(b)) has a refined state machine `SM` (Fig. 4(b)) refining the state machine `SM` of **M1** (Fig. 4(a)). The states of refined state machine `SM` are refined state `A` and refined state B refining state A and state B of **M1**. The refined state machine SM contains the transitions *t1*, *t2a*, *t2b*, *t3* and *t4* which refine the corresponding abstract transitions of machine **M1**. In Fig. 4(b), the abstract transition *t2* is replaced with transitions *t2a* and *t2b* which refine the abstract transition *t2* of machine **M1**. This refinement of a state machine reflects refinement in Event-B where many events can refine one abstract event. The transitions *t2a* and *t2b* have different source sub-states (i.e., representing different guards in Event-B) which are defined in the nested state machine SM_A.

The nested state machine SM_A (Fig. 4(c)) elaborates the refined state A (Fig. 4(b)) of **M2**. The nested state machine, SM_A has three states A1, A2 and A3. The transitions *t1*, *t2a*, *t2b* and *t3* in the nested state machine SM_A are labelled the same as the incoming and outgoing transitions of the refined state A. The same labels indicates that the transition *t1* of the state machine SM_A is the transition *t1* of the refined state machine SM and similarly for *t2a*, *t2b* and *t3*. The transition *t1* of the nested state machine SM_A in Fig. 4(c) elaborates the incoming transition *t1* of the refined super-state A. This means, in the refinement, the target state of the transition *t1* is the sub-state A1. The transitions *t2a* and *t2b* of the nested state machine SM_A elaborate the outgoing transition *t2a* and *t2b* of the refined super-state A. In Fig. 4(b) we do not see a distinction between transitions *t2a* and *t2b*. In Fig. 4(c) we can see a distinction: *t2a* has sub-state A1 as a source while *t2b* has A3 as a source. The transition *t3* of the nested state machine SM_A elaborates the self loop transition of the refined super-state A specifying its source state as the state A1 and its target state as A2. In the nested state machine SM_A, the transition *t5* is a new transition representing a new event in the generated Event-B machine.

In the generated Event-B machine, type invariants are created for all sub-states, where their types are their super-state, for example $A1 \in \mathbb{P}\ (A)$ is a type invariant for the state A1. An additional invariant is generated to specify that all sub-states constitute their super-state. For example, A = A1 ∪ A2 ∪ A3. Other generated invariants are a number of disjointness invariants specifying that all sub-states are disjoint.

In the next paragraphs, we give a general definition of state machine refinement based on the example given above. A refined state machine refines a more abstract state machine. The structure of a refined state machine is an elaboration of the structure of its abstraction in two possible ways:

- Each transition is replaced by one or more transitions.
- An abstract state may be elaborated by a nested state machine (see below).

In the given example, we used the techniques of state elaboration and transition elaboration. In UML-B refinement, a refined state may be elaborated to sub-states contained in a nested state machine forming a state machine hierarchy. State elaboration enables more transitions to be added to a nested state machine. Some of these transitions elaborate the incoming and outgoing transitions of the refined super-state. Some of these transitions are new transitions (i.e, reflects introducing new events in Event-B refinement).

In UML-B, nested state machines are modelled in separate state machine diagrams from their parent state machine diagrams. Therefore, the transition elaboration technique is needed so that transitions in a nested state machine can elaborate the incoming and outgoing transitions of the super-state. In a nested state machine, a transition with an initial source state elaborates at most one incoming transition to the super-state and a transition with a final target state elaborates at most one outgoing transition from the super-state. Our experience is that having separate diagrams for nested state machines scales better than embedding them directly in a single diagram. A single diagram can result in scalability problems when there are many levels of state machine hierarchy and a nested state machine has many states. On the other hand, it can be useful to see at least one level of nesting in a single diagram. We will investigate this in future.

An abstract state may have a self loop transition. In UML-B refinement, while the state is elaborated into sub-states, the self loop transition may be elaborated as one of the transitions between any two of the sub-states. The elaborated transition defines the state changes from a sub-state to another sub-state when the transition fires. When refining a self loop transition, the occurrence of the transition can either be many times or can be restricted to once. Restriction to once means removing looping behaviour and this is a valid refinement since we focus on preserving safety, not liveness, in our current work.

5 Event Movement

This section describes the technique of moving a class event in UML-B refinement. There are two methods of moving a class event in a refinement, these are (1) move to a refined class as a transition of a state machine and (2) move to a new class in a refinement either as a class event or a transition in a state machine. Method (1) does not need any new UML-B language feature. However, method (2) creates a motivation for the need to be able to change the default *self* name in UML-B.

We describe both methods by giving first an example of an abstract machine in which a refinement is based upon. Figure 5(a) shows a class CA with attribute *x* and event *ev1*. Figure 5(b) shows the properties of the event *ev1* showing its parameter *y*, a guard and an action. The action is defined using μB notation and uses a default identifier *self*, i.e., the self name property which represents an instance of a class CA. The self name property becomes a parameter of the *ev1* event in the corresponding Event-B machine.

For method (1), in a refinement, the class event of the abstract machine may be moved to a state machine of the refined class CA as a transition *ev1* between the states A1 and A2. In the generated Event-B machine for the event *ev1*, an additional guard specifying the current state A1 for the event to take place ($self \in A1$) and also additional actions specifying an instance move to the state A2 ($A2 := A2 \cup \{self\}$) and

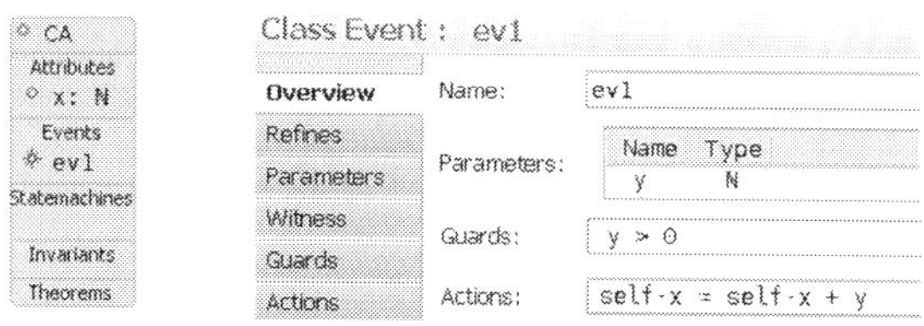

(a) Class CA (a) Properties of event ev1

Fig. 5. Example of the UML-B specification of an abstract machine

an action specifying an instance leaves the current state A1 ($A1 := A1 \setminus \{self\}$) are generated. The effect of this refinement is to constrain when the event occur.

For method (2), in a refinement, a class event may be moved to a new class as a class event or as a transition in a state machine. We describe here the event movement technique when a class event is move to a new class as a transition in a state machine. Assume that the UML-B specification in Fig. 6 is a refinement of the abstract machine in Fig. 5. In the refinement, a new class CC is introduced and event *ev1* is moved to the class CC (Fig. 6(a)). The event *ev1* become a transition between the states C1 and C2 of state machine CCsm (Fig. 6(c)).

The self name property of the class CC is changed to *selfCC* from the default *self* (Figure 6(b)). This change is necessary to avoid conflicts with the default *self* name of the refined class CA. In a class event or a transition refining an abstract class event, a parameter whose type is the abstract class is introduced to replace a *self* parameter of the abstract class. For example, a parameter *ca*, of type CA is added to the *ev1* transition as shown in the property view in the Figure 6(d). A witness property is defined for the transition *ev1* which specifies that *ca* in the refinement level represents *self* of its abstract level (i.e., *ca* = *self*).

The witness property is adapted from Event-B. In Event-B, a witness is used when replacing a parameter of an abstract event with a different parameter in a concrete event in the refinement. The witness is defined by a predicate involving the abstract parameter.

Section 6 of the ATM case study will demonstrate the usefulness of moving events from one class to another in refinement. In the first refinement of the ATM case study, the *withdraw* event of the Account class is moved to the ATM class as a transition in a state machine of the class ATM.

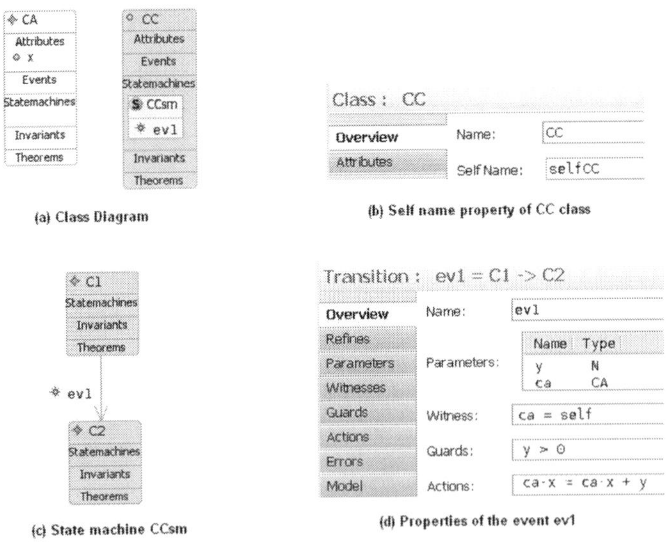

Fig. 6. Example of the UML-B refinement for the second method

6 ATM Case Study

A case study based on an auto teller machine (ATM) was undertaken to validate the extension of UML-B with regards to the notion of refined classes and refined state machines. An ATM is a machine that allows bank customers to do some of the banking transactions 24 hours per day. It allows bank customers to perform a range of functions, including withdraw cash, check account balance and print mini-statements. In order to perform these functions through an ATM, bank customers need to use their ATM cards which are provided to them by the bank. The case study focused on the requirements for the cash withdrawal and check balance functions. There are seven levels for the ATM UML-B development. These machines are linked by a refinement relationship. We described in details the first three levels and described briefly the other four levels. The summary for the first three machine level is as follows:

Abstract machine (ATM_A): Models bank accounts and operations on accounts.
First Refinement (ATM_R1): Introduces the ATMs and ATM cards.
Second Refinement (ATM_R2): Introduces an explicit validation transition for cards and splits withdrawal into a bank transition and an ATM transition.

The package diagram in Fig. 7 shows a refinement relationship between the machines.

Fig. 7. ATM Package Diagram

Fig. 8 shows a UML-B specification of the ATM abstract machine. The abstract machine consists of a class `Account` (8(a)) with its attribute *bal* and four events namely, *createAccount*, *deposit*, *withdraw* and *checkBalance*. The *Account* class represents the set of accounts that currently exist in the system. The attribute *bal* represents the balance of an account. The *withdraw* event has one added parameter, *am* of type natural number. The parameter is shown in the property view in Fig. 8(b) including the guard and action. *self* is the self name property defined for the class `Account`. The *withdraw* event can only occur if the amount, *am*, is less than or equal to the balance in the account. The *withdraw* event will result in decreasing the balance of the account by *am* amount.

The first refinement of the ATM model introduces two new classes which are `ATM` and `Card` which represent the sets of ATMs and ATM cards respectively. The UML-B specification is shown in Fig. 9. The class diagram (Fig. 9(a)) of `ATM_R1` contains the new classes and a refined class `Account` refining the `Account` class of **ATM_A**. The class `ATM` has an association *atm_card* with the class `Card`. The class `Card` has an association *card_account* with the refined class `Account`. The refined class inherits the *bal* attribute and refines the two events, namely, *createAccount* and *deposit* of `ATM_A`. The other two events namely, *withdraw* and *checkBalance* are moved to the new class `ATM` in this refinement level as transitions in the state machine `ATM_SM` of the class ATM. At the abstract level (Fig. 8), we specify the effect of a withdrawal on the account

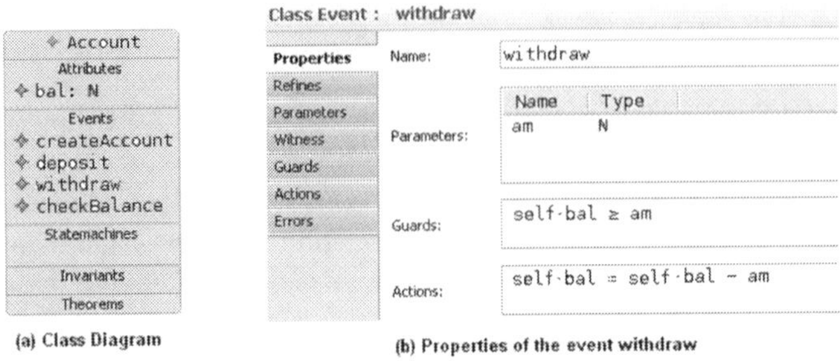

Fig. 8. UML-B specification of ATM abstract machine

balance. In the refinement (Fig. 9), we further specify that the withdrawal takes place via an ATM. At the abstract level it is natural to specify the withdrawal as an event of the Account class while in the refinement it is natural to specify it as an event of the ATM class.

The state machine `ATM_SM` in Fig. 9(b) partitions the behaviour of an ATM into either an *idle* state, (i.e., not being used/not active) or *active_atm* state (i.e., is being used). An ATM changes its state when it is triggered by a transition. The *create* transition creates a new instance of an ATM and sets its state as *idle*. The *insertCard* transition can occur when an ATM is in the *idle* state and the card inserted is a valid ATM card. When it occurs it changes an ATM state from *idle* to *active_atm*. The *ejectCard* transition changes an ATM state from *active_atm* to *idle*. While an ATM is in *active_atm* state, an ATM user can use it for withdrawal or checking an account balance (i.e., *checkBalance* transition). The *withdrawOK* transition represents a successful withdrawal transaction, whereas, the *withdrawFail* transition represents a failure possibly because the withdrawal amount exceeds the account balance. The transitions *withdrawOK* and *checkBalance* refine the abstract event *withdraw* and *checkBalance* respectively. The transitions *insertCard*, *ejectCard* and *withdrawFail* are new events.

Fig. 9(c) shows the properties of the *withdrawOK* transition with the parameters, witness, guards and action. The witness specifies that the parameter *ac* represents the *self* parameter of the abstract *withdraw* event. In this refinement, the guards are strengthened so that the *withdrawOK* transition can only occur when an ATM card is inserted ($selfATM \in dom(atm\_card)$) and the card in the ATM is a valid card for the account whose balance is being modified ($selfATM.atm\_card = c$ and $c.card\_account = ac$). Fig. 9(d) shows the refines property of the *withdrawOK* transition.

The second refinement models an explicit validation transition for cards and splits withdrawal and balance check into a bank transition and an ATM transition. This is achieved by elaborating the *active_atm* state into sub-states. The class diagram of machine **ATM_R2** contains three refined classes refining the classes `Account`, `ATM` and `Card` of **ATM_R1**. An attribute *atm_cash*, which represents the amount of cash stored in an ATM is added to the refined class `ATM`. A new class `Pin` is introduced which represents a set of ATM PIN numbers. The refined class `Card` has an association *card_pin*

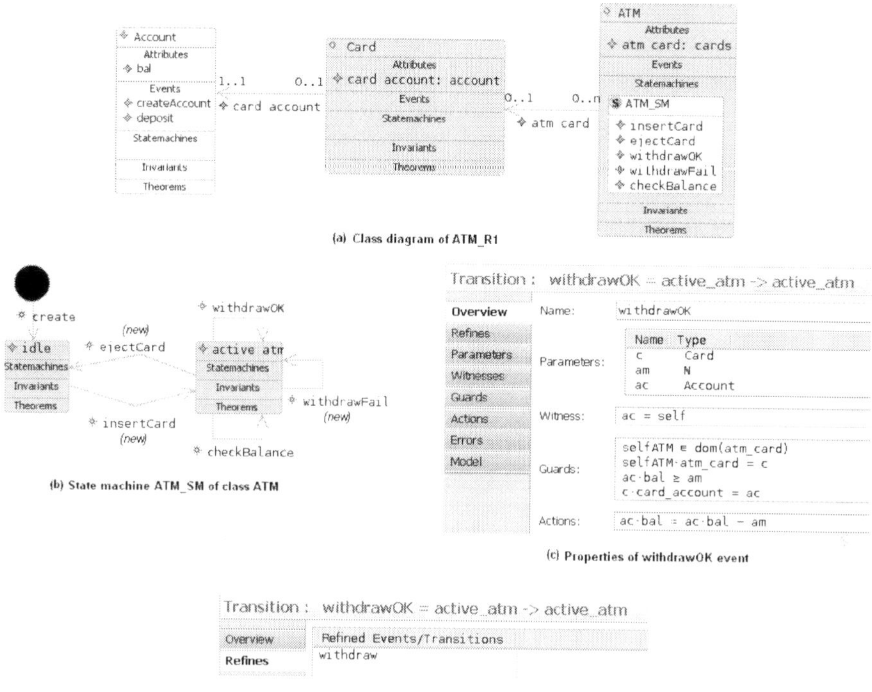

(a) Class diagram of ATM_R1

(b) State machine ATM_SM of class ATM

(c) Properties of withdrawOK event

(d) Refines property of withdrawOK event

Fig. 9. UML-B specification of ATM First Refinement

with the class Pin.The refined class ATM contains refined state machine ATM_SM which contains two refined states refining the states *idle* and *active_atm* of **ATM_R1** (Fig. 10(a)). The transitions *ejectCard1*, *ejectCard2*, *ejectCard3* and *ejectCard4* refine the abstract transition *ejectCard*. The transitions *insertCard*, *withdrawOK*, *withdrawFail* and *checkBalance* refine their corresponding abstract transitions in **ATM_R1**.

A new state machine named active_atm_SM is added to the refined state *active_atm* of **ATM_R2** and it contains five sub-states, namely, *validating*, *invalidCard*, *transOption*, *performedTrans* and *endTrans* (Fig. 10(b)). The state machine has a transition *insertCard* which elaborates the incoming transition to the refined super-state active_atm. The outgoing transitions *ejectCard1*, *ejectCard2*, *ejectCard3* and *ejectCard4* from the states *invalidCard*, *transOption*, *performedBankTrans* and *endTrans* respectively elaborate the outgoing transitions of the refined super-state *active_atm*. The transitions *withdrawOK*, *withdrawFail* and *checkBalance* elaborate the self loop transitions of the refined super-state *active_atm*. The transitions *validateCardOK*, *validateCardFail*, *withdrawATM* and *checkBalATM* are new transitions.

The third refinement models the request and response communication between the ATMs and the bank. The fourth refinement models the send and receive events of the request and response communication between ATMs and the bank. In third and fourth refinement, nested state machines are added to the ATM state machine forming four

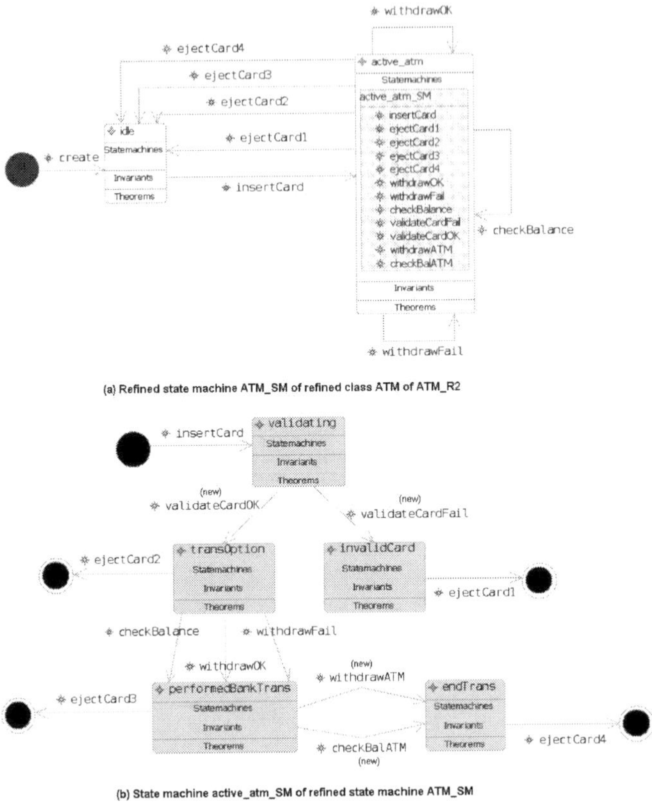

Fig. 10. UML-B specification of ATM Second Refinement

levels of nested state state machines. The fifth refinement introduces a form of communication between ATMs and the bank using message passing via two channels per ATM. The sixth refinement merged the channel pairs into single channel.

The state machine refinement in the second, third and fourth refinements introduced additional levels in the state machine nesting hierarchy. This supports a form of modular reasoning, since refinement invariants are only required for the states that are being elaborated, so it localizes proof effort.

All the models for the ATM development were constructed using the UML-B tool and corresponding Event-B machines were generated. All the proof obligations (POs) for the seven machines were generated and proved using the Rodin tool provers [6]. The total number of proof obligations (POs) is 962 in which all of them are proved automatically. The POs for each machine are: **ATM_A**:5, **ATM_R1**:35, **ATM_R2**:169, **ATM_R3**:156, **ATM_R4**:186, **ATM_R5**:358 and **ATM_R6**:53.

7 Conclusions

We have introduced notions of refined class and refined state machine for UML-B. We used these to described the following five refinement techniques:

- Add new attributes and associations to a refined class
- Add new classes in a refinement
- State elaboration
- Transition elaboration
- Move event to a refined class or a new class in a refinement

We extended the UML-B tool to support these new techniques.

UML-B enhances classical UML-B [12] which is a profile of UML that defines a subset and specialisation of UML. Classical UML-B is based on classical B rather than Event-B and it has restricted support for refinement. Some of the techniques used here (state elaboration, transition elaboration) were previously introduced by Snook and Walden [13] for classical UML-B. However, we provide a more precise definition of refined state machine and we provide tool support based on UML-B giving a different modeling visualization from the UML diagram symbols used in [13]. We also introduce class refinement techniques, which are not with dealt in [13]. In [14], a process for refinement involving the application of patterns that are based on the techniques introduced in [13] is suggested.

The techniques of adding new attributes and associations to a class and adding new classes to a class diagram have been introduced in informal way for refinement of UML class diagram [16] but no formal notation nor formal refinement concept is used. Templates are introduced for attributes and associations to specify the translation of model elements to low level design and implementation. Also, the technique of state elaboration has been introduced in a refinement of UML state diagram [15] again without a formal notion of refinement. Simons [21] has presented a theory of compatible object refinement based on several proposed state-chart refinements that includes state elaboration.

There is much work on combining UML with formal notations and we now outline some of this. However, unlike our work, none of this work supports refinement in UML to the best of our knowledge. Lano, Clark and Androutsopoulos [17] present the translation of UML-RSDS into classical B. The constraint language used is OCL whereas we use μB. Idani, Ledru and Bert [18] have investigated the reverse in which they proposed an approach and tool support for the construction of UML diagrams from B specifications. Ledang and Souquiéres have introduced an approach for modelling the communication between UML state charts in B in [23]. Other work on the integration of UML and B are in [22,24] as outlined in [12]. Integration work of UML with Z has been investigated in [20]. In this work, class diagrams, state machines and the UML-RT structure diagrams are translated to CSP-OZ (an integrated formal method) specifications. In [19], a framework called UML + Z for building, analysing and refining models based on UML and Z is introduced. In [25], a transformation rules from VDM++ into UML class diagram and sequence diagram have been investigated.

We have presented the use of the above listed techniques in the ATM case study which was modelled using the UML-B tool. The Rodin tool was used to generate and prove the proof obligations. The approach of elaborating states with sub-states in refinement supports an incremental refinement approach. The hierarchical structure of nested state machines also supports modular reasoning by localising the invariants required for refinement proofs into the relevant state and its substates. An archive of UML-B development for the ATM case study can be uploaded[1]. Currently, we are working on the extensions to UML-B to support decomposition. We believe that the result of our research will be a methodology of refinement in UML-B which will assists modelling in UML-B.

Acknowledgements. This material is based upon work supported by the DEPLOY Project, which is an FP7 Integrated Project supported by European Commission (Grant N 214158). The first author is funded by the Malaysian Government, IPTA Academic Training Scheme and University Putra Malaysia (UPM).

References

1. Snook, C., Butler, M.: UML-B and Event-B: An Integration of Languages and Tools. In: The IASTED International Conference on Software Engineering (2008)
2. Object Management Group. Introduction to OMG's Unified Modelling Language (UML) (2007) (Date Last Accessed: 25/1/08)
3. Rumbaugh, J., Booch, G., Jacobson, I.: The Unified Modelling Language User Guide. Addison Wesley, Reading (1999)
4. Metayer, C., Abrial, J.R., Voisin, L.: Event-B Language. Technical Report Deliverable 3.2, EU Project IST-511599 - RODIN (2005), `http://rodin.cs.ncl.ac.uk/deliverables/D7.pdf` (Date Last Accessed: 25/1/08)
5. Rigorous Open Development Environment for Complex Systems (RODIN) - IST 511599, `http://rodin.cs.ncl.ac.uk/` (Date Last Accessed: 25/1/08)
6. Abrial, J.R., Butler, M., Hallerstede, S., Voisin, L.: An Open Extensible Tool Environment for Event-B. In: Liu, Z., He, J. (eds.) ICFEM 2006. LNCS, vol. 4260, pp. 588–605. Springer, Heidelberg (2006)
7. Evans, N., Butler, M.: A Proposal For Records in Event-B. In: Misra, J., Nipkow, T., Sekerinski, E. (eds.) FM 2006. LNCS, vol. 4085, pp. 221–235. Springer, Heidelberg (2006)
8. Abrial, J.: The B-Book: Assigning Programs to Meanings. Cambridge University Press, Cambridge (1996)
9. Abrial, R., Hallerstede, S.: Refinement, Decomposition and Instantiation of Discrete Models: Application to Event-B. Journal Fundamentae Informatica 77, 1–28 (2007)
10. Butler, M., Yadav, D.: An Incremental Development of the Mondex System in Event-B. Journal Formal Aspects of Computing 20(1), 61–77 (2008)
11. Butler, M., Hallerstede, S.: The Rodin Formal Modelling Tool. In: BCS-FACS Christmas 2007 Meeting, Formal Methods In Industry, London (2007)
12. Snook, C., Butler, M.: UML-B: Formal Modelling and Design Aided by UML. ACM Transactions on Software Engineering and Methodology 15, 92–122 (2006)
13. Snook, C., Walden, M.: Refinement of Statemachines Using Event B Semantics. In: Julliand, J., Kouchnarenko, O. (eds.) B 2007. LNCS, vol. 4355, pp. 171–185. Springer, Heidelberg (2006)

[1] http://deploy-eprints.ecs.soton.ac.uk/95/

14. Plaska, M., Walden, M., Snook, C.: Documenting the Progress of the System Development. In: Proc. of Workshop on Methods, Models and Tools for Fault Tolerance (2007)
15. OMG: UML 2.1.2 Superstructure Specification (2007), http://www.omg.org/cgi-bin/docs/formal/2007-11-02.pdf
16. Bergner, K., Rausch, A., Sihling, M., Vilbig, A.: Structuring and Refinement of Class Diagrams. In: Proc. of the 32nd Annual Hawaii International Conference, vol. Track 6 (1999)
17. Lano, K., Clark, D., Androutsopoulos, K.: UML to B: Formal Verification of Object Oriented Models. In: Boiten, E.A., Derrick, J., Smith, G.P. (eds.) IFM 2004. LNCS, vol. 2999, pp. 187–206. Springer, Heidelberg (2004)
18. Idani, A., Ledru, L., Bert, D.: Derivation of UML Class Diagrams as Static Views of Formal B Developments. In: Lau, K.-K., Banach, R. (eds.) ICFEM 2005. LNCS, vol. 3785, pp. 37–51. Springer, Heidelberg (2005)
19. Amálio, N., Polack, F., Stepney, S.: UML + Z: Augmenting UML with Z. In: Frappier, M., Habrias, H. (eds.) Software Specification Methods: an Overview Using a Case Study, new edn. Hermes Science Publishing (2006)
20. Moller, M., Olderog, E., Rasch, H., Wehrheim, H.: Linking CSP-OZ with UML and Java: A Case Study. In: Boiten, E.A., Derrick, J., Smith, G.P. (eds.) IFM 2004. LNCS, vol. 2999, pp. 267–286. Springer, Heidelberg (2004)
21. Simons, A.J.H.: A Theory of Regression Testing for Behaviourally Compatible Object Types: Research Articles. Journal Softw. Test. Verif. Reliab. 16(3), 133–156 (2006)
22. Facon, P., Laleau, R., Nguyen, H.P.: Mapping Object Diagrams into B Specifications. In: Methods Integration Workshop, Electronic Workshops in Computing (eWiC). Springer, Heidelberg (1996)
23. Ledang, H., Souquiéres, J.: Contributions for Modelling UML State-Charts in B. In: Butler, M., Petre, L., Sere, K. (eds.) IFM 2002. LNCS, vol. 2335, pp. 109–127. Springer, Heidelberg (2002)
24. Sekerinski, E.: Graphical Design of Reactive systems. In: Bert, D. (ed.) B 1998. LNCS, vol. 1393, pp. 182–197. Springer, Heidelberg (1998)
25. Lausdahl, K.G., Lintrup, H.K.A., Larsen, P.G.: Coupling Overture to MDA and UML. Master Thesis (2008)

Dynamic Classes: Modular Asynchronous Evolution of Distributed Concurrent Objects*

Einar Broch Johnsen[1], Marcel Kyas[2], and Ingrid Chieh Yu[1]

[1] Department of Informatics, University of Oslo, Norway
{einarj,ingridcy}@ifi.uio.no
[2] Department of Computer Science, Freie Universität Berlin, Germany
marcel.kyas@fu-berlin-de

Abstract. Many long-lived and distributed systems must remain available yet evolve over time, due to, e.g., bugfixes, feature extensions, or changing user requirements. To facilitate such changes, formal methods can help in modeling and analyzing runtime software evolution. This paper presents an executable object-oriented modeling language which supports runtime software evolution. The language, based on Creol, targets distributed systems by active objects, asynchronous method calls, and futures. A dynamic class construct is proposed in this setting, providing an asynchronous and modular upgrade mechanism. At runtime, class redefinitions gradually upgrade existing instances of a class and of its subclasses. An upgrade may depend on previous upgrades of other classes. For asynchronous runtime upgrades, the static picture may differ from the actual runtime system. An operational semantics and a type and effect system are given for the language. The type analysis of an upgrade infers and collects dependencies on previous upgrades. These dependencies are exploited as runtime constraints to ensure type safety.

1 Introduction

Many long-lived distributed systems require continuous system availability, but still need to change their code due to bugfixes as well as new, improved, or redundant functionality. Examples of such systems are found in, e.g., financial transactions, aeronautics and space missions, biomedical sensors, and telephony and Internet services. For these systems, code changes must happen at runtime. In large distributed systems, runtime updates need to be applied in an asynchronous and modular manner, and propagate gradually through the distributed system. A challenge for software upgrade systems is to balance flexibility, robustness, and user-friendliness. An appropriate upgrade system should propagate upgrades automatically, provide means to control *when* components are upgraded, and ensure the availability of system services during the upgrade [1,20]. In order

* This research is partly funded by the EU projects IST-33826 CREDO: Modeling and Analysis of Evolutionary Structures for Distributed Services (`http://credo.cwi.nl`) and FP7-231620 HATS: Highly Adaptable and Trustworthy Software using Formal Methods (`http://www.hats-project.eu`).

A. Cavalcanti and D. Dams (Eds.): FM 2009, LNCS 5850, pp. 596–611, 2009.

to ensure that upgrades are correct and result in foreseen changes, formal models and analysis methods for runtime software evolution are needed.

This paper presents a modeling language which supports the runtime evolution of distributed object-oriented systems. The language extends Creol [17], an executable formalism in which distributed concurrent objects communicate by asynchronous method calls and futures [7,8,22], with *dynamic class operations*. These may introduce new functionality and interfaces for classes, change data structures and implementations for existing functionality, and remove legacy code. Dynamic class operations provide a *modular* form of software evolution because upgrades to a class C apply to all existing instances of C and of its subclasses. Compared to previous approaches [6,13,18,19], our approach supports the gradual upgrade of active objects and upgrade operations propagate asynchronously through the system. It is a challenge for formal methods to reason about the runtime evolution of distributed systems. This paper focuses on ensuring type safety at runtime as class definitions evolve.

An operational semantics and type system for dynamic class operations are introduced and integrated with the semantics and type system of Creol. Creol is type-safe in the sense that runtime type errors do not occur for well-typed programs; in particular, method binding always succeeds. We show that well-typed dynamic class operations maintain this property. As classes gradually evolve, a type-safe upgrade of one class may require that an upgrade of another class has already been applied; e.g., when new code contains calls to methods introduced in a previous upgrade. Upgrades may be arbitrarily delayed in the asynchronous setting, so upgrades injected into the system in one order may be applied in another. This causes a discrepancy between the static system view, as provided by a typing environment for dynamic class operations, and the situation at runtime. We develop a type and effects system [2] to analyze dynamic class upgrades and to automatically infer and collect dependencies between class upgrades. Thus, the dependencies of an upgrade operation need not be provided by the modeler. A characterizing feature of our approach is that the dependencies inferred during type analysis are imposed as constraints on the applicability of a particular upgrade at runtime. This may delay certain upgrade operations at runtime to ensure that execution remains type safe. This paper presents the proposed dynamic class operations for a kernel language, but the approach is supported in the complete Creol language. The type system and operational semantics of this paper have been implemented and integrated with Creol's execution platform.

Paper overview. Sect. 2 presents the kernel language, its type system, and semantics. Sect. 3 provides an example of dynamic class upgrades. Sect. 4 introduces operations for dynamic class upgrades, their type system, and semantics. Sect. 5 discusses related work, and Sect. 6 concludes the paper.

2 A Language for Distributed Concurrent Objects

Consider a kernel language for distributed concurrent objects, similar to, e.g., Featherweight Java [15]. The language targets distributed systems by supporting asynchronous method calls and futures (i.e., returns from asynchronous calls). In contrast to Java each concurrent object encapsulates its state; i.e., all external manipulation of the object state is through calls to the object's methods. In addition, objects execute concurrently: each object has a processor which executes the processes of that object. Processes in different objects execute in parallel. A process corresponds to the activation of a method. Only one process may be active in an object at a time; the other processes in the object are *suspended.* We distinguish between *blocking* a process and *releasing* a process. Blocking is used for synchronization and stops the execution of the process, but does not let a suspended process resume. Releasing a process suspends the execution of that process and lets a suspended process resume. Thus, if a process is blocked there is no execution in the object, if it is released another process in the object may execute. Although processes need not terminate, the execution of several processes may be combined using *release points* within method bodies. At a release point, the active process may be released and a suspended process may resume.

Method calls are asynchronous and the result of a call is stored in a future, which may be read or polled. Return values are accessed by need; i.e., the execution blocks if attempting to read from a future without a return value. In contrast, polling a future never blocks. The scheduling of processes at release points is influenced by await-statements with Boolean guards, including the polling of futures. If a guard evaluates to false, the process is released. Only a process whose guard evaluates to true may resume execution. Remark that release points make it straightforward to combine active (i.e., nonterminating) and reactive processes in an object. Thus, an object may behave both as a client and as a server while abstracting from the exact interleaving of these roles.

The behavior of an object may depend on its context of interaction; we let object variables (references) be typed by *interfaces.* These contain method signatures and provide context-dependent encapsulation, as different sets of methods may be available through different interfaces. Variables typed by different interfaces may refer to the same object. A class *implements* an interface I if its instances may be typed by I. A class may implement several interfaces and different classes may provide different implementations of the same interface. Reasoning control is ensured by substitutability at the level of interfaces: *an object supporting an interface I may be replaced by another object supporting I or a subinterface of I* in a context depending on I. This substitutability is reflected in the semantics by the fact that late binding applies to all external method calls, as the runtime class of the object reference is not in general statically known.

The *syntax* is given in Fig. 1. We emphasize the differences with Java. A program P is a list of interface and class definitions, followed by a method body. To illustrate the generality of the dynamic class construct, a class may inherit from a list of superclasses (possibly just Object), extending these with additional fields $\overline{f}$ and methods $\overline{M}$. *Expressions* e are standard apart from the asynchronous method call $e!m(\overline{e})$ and the (blocking) read operation v.get. *Statements* s are standard apart from release points await g and release. *Guards* g are conjunctions of Boolean expressions b and polling operations $v?$ on futures v. When the guard

$$
\begin{array}{llll}
P & ::= \overline{D}\ \overline{L}\ \{\overline{T\ x}; sr\} & D & ::= \textsf{interface}\ I\ \textsf{extends}\ \overline{I}\ \{\overline{M_s}\} \\
sr & ::= s; \textsf{return}\ e & L & ::= \textsf{class}\ C\ \textsf{extends}\ \overline{C}\ \textsf{implements}\ \overline{I}\ \{\overline{T\ f}; \overline{M}\} \\
v & ::= f \mid x & M & ::= M_s\{\overline{T\ x}; sr\} \\
b & ::= \textsf{true} \mid \textsf{false} \mid v & e & ::= v \mid \textsf{new}\ C(\,) \mid e.\textsf{get} \mid e!m(\overline{e}) \mid \textsf{null} \\
T & ::= I \mid \textsf{bool} \mid \textsf{fut}(T) & s & ::= v := e \mid \textsf{await}\ g \mid \textsf{skip} \mid s; s \mid \textsf{if}\ g\ \textsf{then}\ s\ \textsf{fi} \mid \textsf{release} \\
M_s & ::= T\ m\ (\overline{T\ x}) & g & ::= b \mid v? \mid g \wedge g
\end{array}
$$

Fig. 1. The language syntax. Variables v are fields (f) or local variables (x), C is a class name, and I an interface name.

in an await statement evaluates to false, the statement gets preceded by a release, otherwise it becomes a skip. The release statement suspends the active process.

2.1 Typing

Type analysis is done by a type and effect system [2] in the context of a *mapping family*, defined as follows: Let n be a name, d a declaration, $i \in I$ a mapping index, and $[n \mapsto_i d]$ the binding of n to d indexed by i. A *mapping family* Γ is built from the empty mapping family $\emptyset$ and indexed bindings by the constructor $+$. The *extraction* of an indexed mapping Γ_i from Γ is defined by $\emptyset_i = \varepsilon$ and $(\Gamma + [n \mapsto_{i'} d])_i = \textbf{if}\ (i = i')\ \textbf{then}\ \Gamma_i + [n \mapsto_i d]\ \textbf{else}\ \Gamma_i$. The *application* for the indexed mapping Γ_i, is $\varepsilon(n) = \bot$, and $(\Gamma_i + [n \mapsto_i d])(n') = \textbf{if}\ (n = n')\ \textbf{then}\ d\ \textbf{else}\ \Gamma_i(n')$.

The typing context uses four indexes; the mappings $\Gamma_{\mathcal{I}}$ and $\Gamma_{\mathcal{C}}$ map interface and class names to interface and class declarations, and Γ_v maps program variable names to types. In the absence of class upgrades, $\Gamma_{\mathcal{I}}$ and $\Gamma_{\mathcal{C}}$ correspond to *static tables.* The subtype relation $T_1 \preceq T_2$ is defined by interface inheritance. Only declarations extend Γ_v. Some auxiliary functions are defined on a mapping family Γ. The field declarations in a class C and its superclasses are collected by $attr(C, \Gamma)$ and $implements(C, I, \Gamma)$ matches signatures for methods declared in an interface I to those in C (to check that C provides bodies for the declarations of I). We assume for simplicity that variable declarations $\overline{T\ x}$ are well-typed and denote by $[\overline{x} \mapsto_v \overline{T}]$ the associated mapping (built from the bindings $[x \mapsto_v T]$).

Finally, there is a mapping of *dependencies* $\Gamma_d : \textsf{Dep} \rightarrow \textsf{Set}[\textsf{Dep}]$, where the type Dep consist of pairs of class names and natural numbers. An upgrade of a class C can be uniquely identified by a natural number; e.g., $\langle C, 5\rangle$ represents the fifth upgrade of C. Elements in $\Gamma_d(\langle C, u\rangle)$ will represent classes on which an upgrade u of a class C depends; these dependencies are inferred from the current class table by the type analysis, and exploited for dynamic classes in Sect. 4.

The type rules are given in Fig. 2. Judgments have the form $\Gamma \vdash e : T\,\langle\Sigma\rangle$ and $\Gamma \vdash s\,\langle\Sigma\rangle$, where Γ is the typing environment and $\Sigma : \textsf{Set}[\textsf{Dep}]$ the effect. To simplify the presentation, we assume that method declarations in interfaces are unique and well-typed and omit the analysis of interfaces. Furthermore, the (straightforward) definitions of auxiliary functions on Γ are omitted.

The rules (Poll) and (Get) for operations on futures convert types from T to fut(T). Let *interfaces*($\Gamma_{\mathcal{C}}(C)$) denote the interfaces of C as declared in $\Gamma_{\mathcal{C}}$. Rule (New) shows the connection between the type of the variable and the interfaces

$$\text{(Poll)}\ \frac{\Gamma \vdash v : \mathsf{fut}(T)\ \langle\Sigma\rangle}{\Gamma \vdash v? : \mathsf{bool}\ \langle\Sigma\rangle} \qquad \text{(Get)}\ \frac{\Gamma \vdash v : \mathsf{fut}(T)\ \langle\Sigma\rangle}{\Gamma \vdash v.\mathsf{get} : T\ \langle\Sigma\rangle} \qquad \text{(New)}\ \frac{\exists T' \in interfaces(\Gamma_C(C)) \cdot T' \preceq T}{\Gamma \vdash \mathsf{new}\ C(\,) : T\ \langle(C, curr(C,\Gamma))\rangle} \qquad \text{(Skip)}\ \frac{}{\Gamma \vdash \mathsf{skip}}$$

$$\text{(IntCall)}\ \frac{\Gamma \vdash \overline{e} : \overline{T}\ \langle\Sigma\rangle \quad \exists C \in matchint(m, \overline{T} \to T', \Gamma_v(\mathsf{this}), \Gamma_C)}{\Gamma \vdash \mathsf{this}!m(\overline{e}) : \mathsf{fut}(T')\ \langle\Sigma \cup (C, curr(C,\Gamma))\rangle} \qquad \text{(ExtCall)}\ \frac{\Gamma \vdash \overline{e} : \overline{T}\ \langle\Sigma_1\rangle \quad \Gamma \vdash e : I\ \langle\Sigma_2\rangle \quad matchext(m, \overline{T} \to T', I, \Gamma_{\mathcal{I}})}{\Gamma \vdash e!m(\overline{e}) : \mathsf{fut}(T')\ \langle\Sigma_1 \cup \Sigma_2\rangle} \qquad \text{(Null)}\ \frac{I \in dom(\Gamma_{\mathcal{I}})}{\Gamma \vdash \mathsf{null} : I}$$

$$\text{(Var)}\ \frac{\Gamma(v) = T}{\Gamma \vdash v : T\ \langle[\![v]\!]\rangle} \qquad \text{(Assign)}\ \frac{\Gamma \vdash e : T'\ \langle\Sigma\rangle \qquad T' \preceq \Gamma_v(v)}{\Gamma \vdash v := e\ \langle[\![v]\!] \cup \Sigma\rangle} \qquad \text{(And)}\ \frac{\Gamma \vdash g_1 : \mathsf{bool}\ \langle\Sigma_1\rangle \quad \Gamma \vdash g_2 : \mathsf{bool}\ \langle\Sigma_2\rangle}{\Gamma \vdash g_1 \wedge g_2 : \mathsf{bool}\ \langle\Sigma_1 \cup \Sigma_2\rangle}$$

$$\text{(Await)}\ \frac{\Gamma \vdash g : \mathsf{bool}\ \langle\Sigma\rangle}{\Gamma \vdash \mathsf{await}\ g\ \langle\Sigma\rangle} \qquad \text{(Release)}\ \frac{}{\Gamma \vdash \mathsf{release}} \qquad \text{(Composition)}\ \frac{\Gamma \vdash s\ \langle\Sigma_1\rangle \quad \Gamma \vdash s'\ \langle\Sigma_2\rangle}{\Gamma \vdash s; s'\ \langle\Sigma_1 \cup \Sigma_2\rangle} \qquad \text{(Conditional)}\ \frac{\Gamma \vdash b : \mathsf{bool}\ \langle\Sigma_1\rangle \quad \Gamma \vdash s\ \langle\Sigma_2\rangle}{\Gamma \vdash \mathsf{if}\ b\ \mathsf{then}\ s\ \mathsf{fi}\ \langle\Sigma_1 \cup \Sigma_2\rangle}$$

$$\text{(Method)}\ \frac{\Gamma' = \Gamma + [\overline{x} \mapsto_v \overline{T}] + [\overline{x'} \mapsto_v \overline{T'}] \qquad \Gamma' \vdash e : T'\ \langle\Sigma_1\rangle \quad \Gamma' \vdash s\ \langle\Sigma_2\rangle}{\Gamma \vdash T'\ m\ (\overline{T\ x})\{\overline{T'\ x'}; s; \mathsf{return}\ e\}\ \langle\Sigma_1 \cup \Sigma_2\rangle} \qquad \text{(Program)}\ \frac{\Gamma + [\overline{x} \mapsto_v \overline{T}] \vdash s \qquad \forall L \in \overline{L} \cdot \Gamma_{\mathcal{I}} + \Gamma_{\mathcal{C}} + \Gamma_d^L \vdash L}{\Gamma_{\mathcal{I}} + \Gamma_{\mathcal{C}} + \bigcup_{L \in \overline{L}} \Gamma_d^L \vdash \overline{L}\ \{\overline{T\ x}; s; \mathsf{return}\ true\}}$$

$$\text{(Class)}\ \frac{\forall M \in \overline{M} \cdot \Gamma + [\mathsf{this} \mapsto_v C] + [attr(C,\Gamma)] \vdash M\ \langle\Sigma^M\rangle \qquad \forall I \in \overline{I} \cdot implements(C, I, \Gamma)}{\Gamma + [\langle C, 0\rangle \mapsto_d \bigcup_{M \in \overline{M}} \Sigma^M] \vdash \mathsf{class}\ C\ \mathsf{extends}\ \overline{C}\ \mathsf{implements}\ \overline{I}\ \{\overline{T\ f}; \overline{M}\}}$$

Fig. 2. The type and effect system. Judgments for the Boolean constants true and false are similar to (Release). We omit empty effects; e.g., $\Gamma \vdash e\ \langle\emptyset\rangle$ is written $\Gamma \vdash e$.

of the class; the typing of a class instance depends on the context. The function $curr(C, \Gamma)$ identifies the current version number of a class C. In (IntCall) the auxiliary predicate *matchint*, given a method name, signature, and class, checks that an internal invocation may be bound in the class mapping. Similarly, in (ExtCall), *matchext* checks that the interface of the callee can bind the external call. Any interface can type null in (Null). For a variable v, let $[\![v]\!]$: Dep denote the class in which v is declared and its version number (which is easily retrieved from the typing environment). The effect of the analysis of expressions and guards is a set of dependencies to versions of the current class and its superclasses.

In rule (Method), local declarations extend the typing environment used for statements in the method body. The dependencies from different statements are accumulated in (Composition). The effect of the analysis of a method is the set of all dependencies from the body of the method. In (Class), this is bound to the class name, the context is extended with fields, and each method is typechecked. For each method M in rule (Class), the dependencies of M are stored in the effect Σ^M. Thus, Γ_d maps the dependencies of the initial version of C to the dependencies accumulated from the type analysis of the class; i.e., $\langle C, 0\rangle \mapsto_d \bigcup_{M \in \overline{M}} \Sigma^M$. In (Program), a program is type checked in the context $\Gamma_{\mathcal{I}} + \Gamma_{\mathcal{C}}$. Here, Γ_d^L denotes the dependency mapping derived for class L in the program.

$$\begin{array}{rl} \mathit{config} ::= & \epsilon \mid \mathit{class} \mid \mathit{object} \mid \mathit{msg} \mid \mathit{config}\ \mathit{config} \\ \mathit{class} ::= & (C\#n, \mathit{vs}, \mathit{impl}, \mathit{inh}, \mathit{ob}, \mathit{fds}, \mathit{mtds}) \\ \mathit{object} ::= & (o, \mathit{pv}, \mathit{processQ}, \mathit{fds}, \mathit{active}) \\ \mathit{processQ} ::= & \epsilon \mid \mathit{process} \mid \mathit{processQ}\ \mathit{processQ} \\ \mathit{msg} ::= & (\mathit{fid}, \mathit{mc}, \mathit{mode}, \mathit{val}) \mid (\mathit{bind}, \overline{C}, \mathit{fid}, \mathit{mc}) \\ & \mid (\mathit{bound}, o, \mathit{process}) \\ \mathit{process} ::= & (\mathit{fds}, \mathit{sr}) \mid \mathsf{error} \end{array} \qquad \begin{array}{rl} o ::= & (\mathit{oid}, C\#n) \\ \mathit{fds} ::= & \overline{T\ v\ \mathit{val}} \\ \mathit{active} ::= & \mathit{process} \mid \mathsf{idle} \\ \mathit{mc} ::= & \mathit{oid}.m(\overline{\mathit{val}}) \\ \mathit{val} ::= & \mathit{oid} \mid \mathit{fid} \mid \mathsf{null} \mid b \\ \mathit{mtd} ::= & T\ m(\overline{T\ x})\{\mathit{process}\} \\ \mathit{mtds} ::= & \epsilon \mid \mathit{mtd} \mid \mathit{mtds}\ \mathit{mtds} \end{array}$$

Fig. 3. Syntax for runtime configurations; *oid* and *fid* are object and future identifiers

2.2 Context-Reduction Semantics

The semantics is given by a small-step reduction relation on *configurations* of objects, classes, and futures (see Fig. 3). To accommodate upgrades in Sect. 4, stage and version numbers are introduced in the semantics. A *class* has an id (i.e., a name and a *stage number* n: Nat, which changes when the class or one of its superclasses is upgraded), a *version number* vs: Nat (which changes only when the class itself is upgraded), a list of interfaces, a list of superclasses, a set of object ids, a set of fields with default values, and a set of methods. Default values for types are given by a function *default* (e.g., $\mathit{default}(I) = \mathsf{null}$, $\mathit{default}(\mathsf{bool}) = \mathsf{false}$, and $\mathit{default}(!T) = \mathsf{null}$). An *object* has an id *oid*, a class with a stage number $C\sharp n$, a process version set $pv : \mathsf{Set}[\mathit{fid} \times \mathsf{Nat}]$, a queue pq of suspended processes, fields *fds*, and an active process. In an object o, pv tracks the stage of the class for (pending) method activations on o: these may be either internal calls or incoming requests. The idle process indicates that no method is active in the object and error that method binding has failed. A *future* $(\mathit{fid}, \mathit{mc}, \mathit{mode}, \mathit{val})$ captures the state of a method call: initially *sleeping*, then *active*, and finally, it becomes *completed* and stores the result from the call. Let $\mathit{mode} \in \{\mathsf{s}, \mathsf{a}, \mathsf{c}\}$ represent these states. The *initial configuration* of a program $\overline{L}\ \{\overline{T\ x}; sr\}$ has classes and one object $(o, \emptyset, \epsilon, \epsilon, (\overline{T\ x\ \mathit{default}(T)}), sr)$.

Reduction takes the form of a relation $\mathit{config} \to \mathit{config}'$. The main rules are given in Fig. 4. The context reduction semantics decomposes a statement into a reduction context and a redex, and reduces the redex [12]. *Reduction contexts* are method bodies M, statements S, expressions E, and guards G with a single hole denoted by $\bullet$:

$$\begin{array}{ll} M ::= \bullet \mid S; \mathsf{return}\ e \mid \mathsf{return}\ E & S ::= \bullet \mid v := E \mid S; s \mid \mathsf{if}\ G\ \mathsf{then}\ s_1\ \mathsf{fi} \\ E ::= \bullet \mid E.\mathsf{get} \mid E!m(\overline{e}) \mid \mathit{oid}!m(\overline{\mathit{val}}, E, \overline{e}) & G ::= \bullet \mid E? \mid G \wedge g \mid b \wedge G \end{array}$$

Redexes reduce in their respective contexts; i.e., body-redexes in M, stat-redexes in S, expr-redexes in E, and guard-redexes in G. Redexes are defined as follows:

$$\begin{array}{ll} \mathit{body\text{-}redexes} & ::= \mathsf{return}\ \mathit{val} \\ \mathit{stat\text{-}redexes} & ::= x := \mathit{val} \mid f := \mathit{val} \mid \mathsf{await}\ g \mid \mathsf{skip}; s \mid \mathsf{if}\ b\ \mathsf{then}\ s\ \mathsf{else}\ s\ \mathsf{fi} \mid \mathsf{release} \\ \mathit{expr\text{-}redexes} & ::= x \mid f \mid \mathit{fid}.\mathsf{get} \mid \mathit{oid}!m(\overline{\mathit{val}}) \mid \mathsf{new}\ C() \\ \mathit{guard\text{-}redexes} & ::= \mathit{fid}? \mid b \wedge g \end{array}$$

Filling the hole of a context M with a redex r is denoted $M[r]$. Before evaluating the expression e in the method body $s; \mathsf{return}\ e$, the body will be reduced to $\mathsf{skip}; \mathsf{return}\ e$. For simplicity, we elide the skip and write just $\mathsf{return}\ e$.

(Red-Call1)
$$\frac{oid \neq \mathsf{this} \qquad \mathit{fid} \text{ is fresh}}{\begin{array}{c}(o, pv, pq, fds, (l, M[oid!m(\overline{val})])) \\ \rightarrow (o, pv, pq, fds, (l, M[\mathit{fid}])) \\ (\mathit{fid}, oid.m(\overline{val}), \mathsf{s}, \mathsf{null})\end{array}}$$

(Red-Call2)
$$\frac{\mathit{fid} \text{ is fresh}}{\begin{array}{c}((oid, C\#n), pv, pq, fds, (l, M[\mathsf{this}!m(\overline{val})])) \\ \rightarrow ((oid, C\#n), pv \cup \{(\mathit{fid}, n)\}, pq, fds, (l, M[\mathit{fid}])) \\ (\mathit{fid}, oid.m(\overline{val}), \mathsf{s}, \mathsf{null})\end{array}}$$

(Red-New)
$$\frac{oid \text{ is fresh} \qquad fds'' = attr(C\#n)}{\begin{array}{l}(o, pv, pq, fds, (l, M[\mathsf{new}\ C()]))\ (C\#n, vs, impl, inh, ob, fds', mtds) \\ \rightarrow (o, pv, pq, fds, (l, M[oid]))\ (C\#n, vs, impl, inh, (ob \cup \{oid\}), fds', mtds) \\ \quad ((oid, C\#n), \epsilon, \epsilon, fds'', (\epsilon, \mathsf{skip}))\end{array}}$$

(Red-Poll)
$$\frac{b = (m \equiv \mathsf{c})}{\begin{array}{c}(o, pv, pq, fds, (l, M[\mathit{fid}?]))\ (\mathit{fid}, mc, m, val) \\ \rightarrow (o, pv, pq, fds, (l, M[b]))\ (\mathit{fid}, mc, m, val)\end{array}}$$

(Red-Await)
$$\begin{array}{l}(o, pv, pq, fds, (l, M[\mathsf{await}\ g])) \\ \rightarrow (o, pv, pq, fds, (l, M[\mathsf{if}\ g\ \mathsf{then} \\ \qquad \mathsf{skip\ else\ release};\ \mathsf{await}\ g\ \mathsf{fi}]))\end{array}$$

(Red-Bound)
$$\begin{array}{c}((oid, C), pv, pq, fds, \mathsf{idle}) \\ (bound, oid, process) \\ \rightarrow ((oid, C), pv, pq :: process, fds, \mathsf{idle})\end{array}$$

(Red-Release)
$$\begin{array}{c}(o, pv, pq, fds, (l, M[\mathsf{release}])) \\ \rightarrow (o, pv, pq :: (l, M[\mathsf{skip}]), fds, \mathsf{idle})\end{array}$$

(Red-Return)
$$\frac{l(\mathsf{destiny}) = \mathit{fid} \qquad pv' = pv \setminus \{(\mathit{fid}, n)\}}{\begin{array}{c}(o, pv, pq, fds, (l, \mathsf{return}\ val : T))\ (\mathit{fid}, oid.m(\overline{val}), \mathsf{a}, \mathsf{null}) \\ \rightarrow (o, pv', pq, fds, \mathsf{idle})\ (\mathit{fid}, oid.m(\overline{val}), \mathsf{c}, val)\end{array}}$$

(Red-Reschedule)
$$\begin{array}{c}(o, pv, p :: pq, fds, \mathsf{idle}) \\ \rightarrow (o, pv, pq, fds, p)\end{array}$$

(Red-Bind1)
$$\begin{array}{l}((oid, C\#n), pv, pq, fds, p)\ (\mathit{fid}, oid.m(\overline{val}), \mathsf{s}, \mathsf{null}) \\ \rightarrow ((oid, C\#n), pv \cup \{(\mathit{fid}, n)\}, pq, fds, p) \\ \quad (\mathit{fid}, oid.m(\overline{val}), \mathsf{a}, \mathsf{null})\ (bind, C\#n, \mathit{fid}, oid.m(\overline{val}))\end{array}$$

(Red-Get)
$$\begin{array}{l}(o, pv, pq, fds, (l, M[\mathit{fid}.\mathsf{get}])) \\ (\mathit{fid}, mc, \mathsf{c}, val) \\ \rightarrow (o, pv, pq, fds, (l, M[val]))\end{array}$$

(Red-Bind2)
$$\frac{lookup(m(\overline{val}), sig(m(\overline{val}), \mathit{fid}), \mathit{fid}, mtds) = \mathsf{error}}{\begin{array}{l}(bind, (C\#n; \overline{cid}), \mathit{fid}, oid.m(\overline{val}))(C\#n', vs, impl, inh, ob, fds, mtds) \rightarrow \\ (bind, (\overline{inh}; \overline{cid}), \mathit{fid}, oid.m(\overline{val}))\ (C\#n', vs, impl, inh, ob, fds, mtds)\end{array}}$$

(Red-Context)
$$\frac{config \rightarrow config'}{\begin{array}{c}config\ config'' \\ \rightarrow config'\ config''\end{array}}$$

(Red-Bind4)
$$\frac{\begin{array}{c}process \neq \mathsf{error} \qquad n \leq n' \\ lookup(m(\overline{val}), sig(m(\overline{val}), \mathit{fid}), \mathit{fid}, mtds) = process\end{array}}{\begin{array}{l}(bind, C\#n; \overline{cid}, \mathit{fid}, oid.m(\overline{val}))\ (C\#n', vs, impl, inh, ob, fds, mtds) \\ \rightarrow (bound, oid, process)\ (C\#n', vs, impl, inh, ob, fds, mtds)\end{array}}$$

(Red-Bind3)
$$\begin{array}{c}(bind, \varepsilon, \mathit{fid}, oid.m(\overline{val})) \\ \rightarrow (bound, oid, \mathsf{error})\end{array}$$

Fig. 4. The context reduction semantics

Expressions and guards. In (Red-Call1) and (Red-Call2), external and internal asynchronous calls add a sleeping future to the configuration, returning its id to the caller. Note that an internal call extends the process version set with a pair consisting of the new future and the current stage number. This is because the asynchronous call to an internal method creates an obligation for the object to keep this method available until the call has been executed. In (Red-Get), a read on a future variable in the active process only reduces if the corresponding future is in completed mode. Otherwise, the process is blocked. In (Red-New), a new instance of a class C is introduced into the configuration (with fields collected from C and its superclasses using $attr(C)$). In (RED-POLL), a future variable is polled to see if a call has been executed.

Release and rescheduling. Guards determine whether a process should be released. In (RED-AWAIT), a process at a release point proceeds if its guard is true and releases otherwise. When a process is released, its guard is reused to reschedule the process. When an active process is released in (RED-RELEASE) or terminates, it is replaced by the idle process, which allows a process from the process queue to be scheduled for execution in (RED-RESCHEDULE).

Method invocation, binding, and return. A method call results in an activation on the callee's process queue. As the call is asynchronous, there is a delay between the call and its activation, represented by the sleeping mode of a future. After the call, (RED-BIND1) creates a bind request to the callee's class and the future changes its mode to active, preventing multiple activations. Note that the bind request extends the process version set with a pair consisting of the new future and the current stage number of the object, similar to an invocation for an internal call. The process version set influences the applicability of upgrades, delaying those upgrades that may introduce errors into the nonterminated processes. (RED-BIND2) traverses the implicit inheritance tree until binding fails in (RED-BIND3) or succeeds in (RED-BIND4). Successful binding results in a *bound* message to the callee, which is loaded into the process queue in (RED-BOUND). When the process terminates, the result is stored by (RED-RETURN) in the future identified by the destiny variable. This future changes its mode to completed and the active process becomes idle. When a process terminates, its return value is placed in the associated future and the future id is removed from the process version set pv by (RED-RETURN). Finally, (RED-CONTEXT) reduces subconfigurations.

Adapting the type system to runtime configurations, we let $\Delta \vdash_R config$ ok denote that *config* is well-typed. The initial state of a well-typed program is well-typed, and type soundness can be established for the type system and reduction semantics of this paper (the details of the proof are given in [16]):

Theorem 1. *If* $\Delta \vdash_R config$ ok *and* $config \to config'$*, then there is an extension* Δ' *of* Δ *such that* $\Delta' \vdash_R config'$ ok.

3 Example of Dynamic Class Extensions

Let an interface Account provide basic banking services; e.g., depositing money and receiving the balance for an account. Class BankAccount implements Account; an internal method increaseBalance is called by method deposit. The comment *V:0* indicates that this is class version 0.

```
class BankAccount implements Account {                              -- V:0
  Nat bal:=0;
  Bool increaseBalance (Nat sum) { bal := bal + sum; return true }
  Nat balance ( ) { return bal }
  Bool deposit (Nat sum) { return this!increaseBalance(sum) }}
```

By *dynamically extending* the class with new methods transfer and withdraw, money can be transferred to a receiver account or withdrawn. To log transactions, a general method modifyBalance will modify the balance of the account and log the transaction:

```
class BankAccount implements Account {                                      -- V:1
  Nat bal:=0; Log l;
  Nat modifyBalance (Int sum) {Nat w; w := 0; l:= new Log(); bal := bal + sum;
    l.addlog(this, sum); if sum < 0 then w := -sum fi; return w }
  Bool increaseBalance(Nat sum) {bal := bal + sum; return true }
  Nat balance ( ) { return bal }
  Bool deposit (Nat sum) { fut⟨Nat⟩ w; w:=this!modifyBalance(sum); return true }
  Nat withdraw (Nat sum ) { await sum ≤ bal; return this!modifyBalance(-sum) }
  Bool transfer (Nat sum, Account acc) { fut⟨Nat⟩ w; await sum ≤ bal;
    w:=this!modifyBalance(-sum); return acc!deposit(w.get()) }}
```

Here, the class is extended with a new field l, new methods modifyBalance, withdraw, and transfer. Furthermore, deposit is redefined to use the internal method modifyBalance. (Remark that allowing asynchronous calls as statements in the language would remove the need for the future w in deposit.) However, the new methods withdraw and transfer are only known internally in the class. To *export* them the class is extended with a new interface TransferAcc with appropriate signatures for transfer and withdraw, after which transfer and withdraw may be invoked on pointers typed by TransferAcc. If we can type check that BankAccount implements TransferAcc, it is type-safe to bind a pointer typed by TransferAcc to an instance of BankAccount and call transfer and withdraw on this object:

```
class BankAccount implements Account, TransferAcc {                         -- V:2
  Nat bal:=0; Log l;
  Nat modifyBalance (Int sum) { Nat w; w := 0; l:= new Log(); bal := bal + sum;
    l.addlog(this, sum); if sum < 0 then w := -sum fi; return w }
  Bool increaseBalance(Nat sum) {bal := bal + sum; return true }
  Nat balance ( ) { return bal }
  Bool deposit (Nat sum) { fut⟨Nat⟩ w; w:=this!modifyBalance(sum); return true }
  Nat withdraw (Nat sum ) { await sum ≤ bal; return this!modifyBalance(-sum) }
  Bool transfer (Nat sum, Account acc) { fut⟨Nat⟩ w; await sum ≤ bal;
    w:=this!modifyBalance(-sum); return acc!deposit(w.get()) }}
```

As increaseBalance is now redundant, we *dynamically simplify* BankAccount by removing it. After the upgrades, the initial class definition has been replaced by

```
class BankAccount implements Account, TransferAcc {                         -- V:3
  Nat bal:=0; Log l;
  Nat modifyBalance (Int sum) { Nat w; w := 0; l:= new Log(); bal := bal + sum;
    l.addlog(this, sum); if sum < 0 then w := -sum fi; return w }
  Nat balance ( ) { return bal }
  Bool deposit (Nat sum) { fut⟨Nat⟩ w; w:=this!modifyBalance(sum); return true }
  Nat withdraw (Nat sum ) { await sum ≤ bal; return this!modifyBalance(-sum) }
  Bool transfer (Nat sum, Account acc) { fut⟨Nat⟩ w; await sum ≤ bal;
    w:=this!modifyBalance(-sum); return acc!deposit(w.get()) }}
```

These dynamic upgrades are here realized by three upgrade messages added to the running system: upgrading BankAccount with the redefinition of deposit and the new methods modifyBalance, withdraw and transfer; exporting new functionality by extending BankAccount with the TransferAcc interface; and removing the redundant method increaseBalance. A type-safe introduction of these upgrades in a distributed system requires a combination of type checking and careful timing at runtime. Adding the new interface requires the presence of methods withdraw and transfer, so the first upgrade of BankAccount must already have occurred. Moreover, the class of I must implement Log. There are similar dependencies for removing increaseBalance: the redefinition of deposit must occur before the class simplification, otherwise method binding may fail. Similarly, we must ensure that the old definition of deposit is not a process in any runtime object.

4 Dynamic Classes

Software evolution in a running system may be perceived as a series of operations injected into the system, which modify the classes and the class hierarchy. An upgrade U is any dynamic class operation, as given by the following syntax:

$$\begin{array}{ll} U ::= \mathsf{new\text{-}class}\ C\ \mathsf{extends}\ \overline{C}\ \mathsf{implements}\ \overline{I}\ \{\overline{T\ f}; \overline{M}\} & \mid \mathsf{new\text{-}interface}\ I\ \mathsf{extends}\ \overline{I}\ \{\overline{M_s}\} \\ \quad\mid \mathsf{update}\ C\ \mathsf{extends}\ \overline{C}\ \mathsf{implements}\ \overline{I}\ \{\overline{T\ f}; \overline{M}\} & \mid \mathsf{simplify}\ C\ \mathsf{retract}\ \overline{C}\ \{\overline{T\ f}; \overline{M}\} \end{array}$$

A *class addition* adds the representation of the new class to the system, an *interface addition* extends the type system, a *class update* extends an existing class with new fields and methods and redefines existing methods in the class, and a *class simplification* removes redundant superclasses, fields, and methods from an existing class. Upgrades propagate asynchronously at runtime. They first change classes, then subclasses, and eventually the objects of those classes.

4.1 Typing of Dynamic Classes

Dynamic class operations are type checked in a sequence of typing environments $\Gamma^0, \Gamma^1, \ldots$, which extend each other; Γ^0 is the typing environment for the original program and Γ^i the current static view of the system. We describe the construction of Γ^{i+1} for the next well-typed upgrade U. The type system for judgments $\Gamma^{i+1} \vdash U$ is shown in Fig. 5, extending the system in Fig. 2. For simplicity, we omit the analysis of new-interface and focus on class updates. We assume that new interfaces are well-typed and that $\Gamma^i_{\mathcal{I}}$ are correctly extended for each update. (As before, we omit the straightforward analysis of superinterfaces and method signatures.) Rule (New-Class) for class additions requires a fresh name, type checks like a class in the original program, and extends $\Gamma^i_{\mathcal{C}}$. Remark that the version number of the new class is different from that of the program's original classes. This reflects the fact that the new class may depend on other dynamic changes to the system. For a new class, we remove the dependency to the class itself; i.e., $(C, 0)$ is removed from the dependency mapping.

Rule (Class-Extend) for the extension of a class C obeys a substitutability discipline captured by the predicate *refines*$(\overline{M}, \overline{M}_1)$; if $M \in \overline{M}$ redefines $M_1 \in \overline{M}_1$, the signature of M must be a subtype of the signature of M_1. The extended class replaces the definition of C in $\Gamma^i_{\mathcal{C}}$ by the binding Γ'. When retrieving the old version of the class from $\Gamma^i_{\mathcal{C}}$, we represent the class compactly as a tuple

$$\frac{\begin{array}{c}C \notin dom(\Gamma^i_C) \quad \Gamma' = [C \mapsto_C (\overline{I}, \overline{C}, \overline{T\ f}, \overline{M})] \quad \forall I \in \overline{I} \cdot implements(C, I, \Gamma + \Gamma') \\ \forall M \in \overline{M} \ \cdot \ \Gamma^i + \Gamma' + [\mathsf{this} \mapsto_v C] + [attr(C, \Gamma^i + \Gamma')] \vdash M \ \langle \Sigma^M \rangle\end{array}}{\Gamma^i + \Gamma' + [\langle C, 1\rangle \mapsto_d \bigcup_{M \in \overline{M}} \Sigma^M \setminus \{(C, 0)\}] \vdash \mathsf{new\text{-}class}\ C\ \mathsf{extends}\ \overline{C}\ \mathsf{implements}\ \overline{I}\ \{\overline{T\ f}; \overline{M}\}} \ (\textsc{New-Class})$$

$$\frac{\begin{array}{c}\Gamma^i_C(C) = (\overline{I_1}, \overline{C_1}, \overline{T_1\ f_1}, \overline{M_1}) \quad \Gamma' = [C \mapsto_C (\overline{I_1}; \overline{I}, \overline{C_1}; \overline{C}, \overline{T_1\ f_1}; \overline{T\ f}, (\overline{M_1} \oplus \overline{M}))] \\ vs = curr(C, \Gamma^i_d) \quad refines(\overline{M}, \overline{M_1}) \quad \forall I \in \overline{I} \cdot implements(C, I, \Gamma^i + \Gamma') \\ \forall M \in \overline{M} \ \cdot \ \Gamma^i + \Gamma' + [\mathsf{this} \mapsto_v C] + [attr(C, \Gamma^i + \Gamma')] \vdash M \ \langle \Sigma^M \rangle\end{array}}{\Gamma^i + \Gamma' + [\langle C, vs+1\rangle \mapsto_d \bigcup_{M \in \overline{M}} \Sigma^M \cup \{(C, vs)\}] \vdash \mathsf{update}\ C\ \mathsf{extends}\ \overline{C}\ \mathsf{implements}\ \overline{I}\ \{\overline{T\ f}; \overline{M}\}} \ (\textsc{Class-Extend})$$

$$\frac{\begin{array}{c}\Gamma^i_C(C) = (\overline{I_1}, \overline{C_1}, \overline{T_1\ f_1}, \overline{M_1}) \quad \Gamma' = [C \mapsto_C (\overline{I_1}, (\overline{C_1} \setminus \overline{C}), (\overline{T_1\ f_1} \setminus \overline{T\ f}), (\overline{M_1} \setminus \overline{M}))] \\ \overline{D} = \{C\} \cup below(C, \Gamma^i_C)\} \quad dep = \bigcup_{D \in \overline{D}} \{(D, curr(D, \Gamma^i_d))\} \quad vs = curr(C, \Gamma^i_d) \\ \forall D \in \overline{D} \cdot \Gamma^i + \Gamma' + [\mathsf{this} \mapsto_v D] + [attr(D, \Gamma^i + \Gamma')] \vdash (\Gamma^i_C + \Gamma')(D).mtds \\ \forall D \in \overline{D} \wedge \ \forall I \in \Gamma^i_C(D).impl \cdot implements(D, I, \Gamma^i + \Gamma')\end{array}}{\Gamma^i + \Gamma' + [\langle C, vs+1\rangle \mapsto_d dep \cup \{(C, vs)\}] \vdash \mathsf{simplify}\ C\ \mathsf{retract}\ \overline{C}\ \{\overline{T\ f}; \overline{M}\}} \ (\textsc{Class-Simplify})$$

Fig. 5. The type system for dynamic class extensions. Judgments have the form $\Gamma^{i+1} \vdash U$, where Γ^i is the current typing environment before the operation U.

and we denote by $\overline{M_1} \oplus \overline{M}$ the union operation which retains methods in $\overline{M}$ in case of name conflicts. The function $curr(C, \Gamma^i_d)$ identifies the current version number of a class C by inspecting the dependency mapping. The new features of the class extension are type checked in a similar way as rule (Class) and the resulting dependencies, accumulated by the type analysis of methods, are bound to the new version $curr(C, \Gamma^i_d) + 1$ of the class in Γ^{i+1}_d. Moreover, in order to ensure that multiple upgrades to the same class occur in a correct order, the current version of the class is also included in this mapping.

In rule (Class-Simplify), which removes features from a class C, the simplification is restricted to superclasses, fields, and methods which are not statically needed in Γ^i. To verify this requirement, it is necessary to type check the new version of the class as well as its subclasses, identified by the function $below(C, \Gamma^i_C)$, in the updated typing environment Γ^{i+1}. The dependencies of the simplification operation are the current versions of the subclasses and of the class itself. As effects are not needed for the construction of the dependency mapping (the simplification only affects subclasses), for brevity, we elide the effects of methods and denote by $\Gamma(C).mtds$ and $\Gamma(C).impl$ the methods and interfaces of a class C and type check each single method and interface similar to rule (Class).

In the asynchronous setting of distributed concurrent objects, upgrades may be delayed and even bypass each other. Hence, the system reflected by the current typing environment Γ^i may differ considerably from the running system. To ensure that the execution is type safe, we exploit the dependency mapping of Γ^i to impose constraints on the applicability of the i'th upgrade at runtime. The constraints ensure that if one upgrade depends on another, they will be applied in the correct order, otherwise, they may be applied in any order, or in parallel.

$$\textsc{(Dep)}\quad \frac{hd \in \{new, ext\} \qquad vs \geq n}{\begin{array}{l}(hd, C, impl, inh, fds, mtds, ((C', n) \cup dep))\\ \quad (C'\#n', vs, impl', inh', ob, fds', mtds')\\ \rightarrow (hd, C, impl, inh, fds, mtds, dep)\\ \quad (C'\#n', vs, impl', inh', ob, fds', mtds')\end{array}}$$

$$\textsc{(New-Class)}\quad \begin{array}{l}(new, C, impl, inh, fds, mtds, \emptyset)\\ \rightarrow (C\#1, 1, impl, inh, \epsilon, fds, mtds)\end{array}$$

$$\textsc{(Dep-Simplify)}\quad \frac{\begin{array}{c}dep = (C', n) \cup dep' \qquad vs \geq n\\ odep' = odep \cup \{(o, C'\#n') | o \in ob\}\end{array}}{\begin{array}{l}(simp, C, inh, fds, mtds, dep, odep)\\ (C'\#n', vs, impl, inh', ob, fds', mtds')\\ \rightarrow (simp, C, inh, fds, mtds, dep', odep'\})\\ (C'\#n', vs, impl, inh', ob, fds', mtds')\end{array}}$$

$$\textsc{(Dep-Object)}\quad \frac{\begin{array}{c}oldest(pv) \geq n'\\ odep = \{(oid, C'\#n')\} \cup odep'\end{array}}{\begin{array}{l}(simp, C, inh, fds, mtds, dep, odep)\\ \quad ((oid, C'\#n), pv, pq, fds, active)\\ \rightarrow (simp, C, inh, fds, mtds, dep, odep')\\ \quad ((oid, C'\#n), pv, pq, fds, active)\end{array}}$$

$$\textsc{(Extend-Class)}\quad \begin{array}{l}(ext, C, impl, inh, fds, mtds, \emptyset)\\ \quad (C\#n, vs, impl', inh', ob, fds', mtds')\\ \rightarrow (C\#(n+1), vs+1, impl'; impl,\\ \quad inh'; inh, ob, fds'; fds, mtds' \oplus mtds)\end{array}$$

$$\textsc{(Simplify-Class)}\quad \begin{array}{l}(simp, C, inh, fds, mtds, \emptyset, \emptyset)\\ \quad (C\#n, vs, impl, inh', ob, fds', mtds')\\ \rightarrow (C\#(n+1), vs+1, impl, inh' \setminus inh,\\ \quad ob, fds' \setminus fds, mtds' \setminus mtds)\end{array}$$

$$\textsc{(Class-Inh)}\quad \frac{n'' > n'}{\begin{array}{l}(C'\#n'', vs', impl', inh', ob', fds', mtds')\\ (C\#n, vs, impl, (\overline{cid}; C'\#n'; \overline{cid}'), ob, fds, mtds)\\ \rightharpoonup (C'\#n'', vs', impl', inh', ob', fds', mtds')\\ (C\#n+1, vs, impl, (\overline{cid}; C'\#n''; \overline{cid}'), ob, fds, mtds)\end{array}}$$

$$\textsc{(Red-Context2)}\quad \frac{config \rightharpoonup config'}{\begin{array}{l}config\ config''\\ \rightharpoonup config'\ config''\end{array}}$$

$$\textsc{(Obj-State)}\quad \frac{n' > n \quad fds' = transf(fds, attr(C))}{\begin{array}{l}((oid, C\#n), pv, pq, fds, \mathsf{idle})\\ (C\#n', vs, impl, inh, ob, fds, mtds)\\ \rightharpoonup ((oid, C\#n'), pv, pq, fds', \mathsf{idle})\\ (C\#n', vs, impl, inh, ob, fds, mtds)\end{array}}$$

$$\textsc{(Upgrade)}\quad config \xrightarrow{upg} config\ upg$$

$$\textsc{(Red)}\quad \frac{\begin{array}{c}config_1 \rightharpoonup ! config_1'\\ config_1' \rightarrow config_2\end{array}}{config_1 \longrightarrow_{up} config_2}$$

Fig. 6. The context reduction semantics for class upgrades

4.2 Semantics for Dynamic Classes

We extend the runtime syntax of Figure 3 with upgrade messages as follows:

$$\begin{array}{llr}upg ::= & (new, C, impl, inh, fds, mtds, dep) \,|\, (ext, C, impl, inh, fds, mtds, dep) & dep ::= \overline{(C, n)}\\ | & (simp, C, inh, fds, mtds, dep, odep) \,|\, \ldots & odep ::= \overline{(o, C\#n)}\end{array}$$

An upgrade message for a new class or class extension has a class name C, a list *impl* of interfaces, a list *inh* of superclasses, a list *fds* of new fields, a set *mtds* of new (or redefined) methods, and a set *dep* of constraints to classes in the runtime system. For class simplification, *inh*, *fds* and *mtds* are the superclasses, fields and methods to be removed, respectively. For simplification, applicability not only depends on class constraints but also propagates to the state of runtime objects, as there may exist processes in or communication between objects in the runtime environment that uses fields or methods to be removed. Thus, in addition to class constraints, a class simplification message includes a set *odep* of constraints on objects, which is initially empty but gradually extended during the verification of class constraints. If a message injected into the runtime configuration is well-typed in Γ^i, then *dep* is $\Gamma^i_d(\langle C, curr(C, \Gamma^i_d)\rangle)$. Thus, the static dependencies of the current upgrade are introduced into the runtime configuration.

The semantics for dynamic class operations extends the reduction system of Fig. 4 with the rules given in Fig. 6. A reduction step in the extended system takes the form $config_1 \longrightarrow_{up} config_2$ in (Red), where $config_1 \rightharpoonup ! config_1'$ reduces $config_1$ to *normal form* by the relation $\rightharpoonup$, which consists of the two rules (Class-Inh) and (Obj-State), before the relation $\rightarrow$ applies. The $\rightharpoonup$ relation abstracts from locking disciplines that would otherwise be needed, as explained below.

Dynamic class operations are initiated by injecting a message *upg* into the configuration by (Upgrade). For the *extension* of a class C, this message is $(ext, C, impl, inh, fds, mtds, dep)$ which cannot be applied unless the constraints in *dep* are satisfied, checked by (Dep). Thus, the upgrade is delayed at runtime until other upgrades have been applied. When the constraints are satisfied, the superclasses, fields, and methods of the runtime class definition are extended and the stage and version numbers increased in (Extend-Class). (For the operator $\oplus$, see Sect. 4.1.) Similarly, (New-Class) creates a new runtime class when the constraints are satisfied. For the *simplification* of a class C, the message is $(simp, C, inh, fds, mtds, dep, \emptyset)$. When verifying class constraints in (Dep-Simplify), the set *ob* of instances of a class is used for stage constraints in *odep*. These are checked in (Dep-Object). To guarantee that an object is of stage n, we must ensure that all processes stemming from older versions of the class have completed and that there are no pending calls from such processes to local methods (which could be scheduled for removal). Rule (Dep-Object) compares stage constraints to the *oldest* stage number in the object's process version set *pv*. When no unsatisfied dependencies remain, the simplification can be applied in (Simplify-Class).

Updating the object state. When an object's class or superclass has been upgraded, the object's state must be updated *before* new code is allowed to execute. New instances of a class automatically get the new fields, but the upgrade of existing instances must be closely controlled; errors may occur if new or redefined methods, which rely on fields that are not yet available in the object, were executed. With recursive or nonterminating methods objects cannot generally be expected to reach a state without pending processes. Consequently, it is too restrictive to wait for the completion of all processes before applying an upgrade. However, objects may reach *quiescent* states when the processor has been released and before any pending process has been activated. Quiescent states are those in which the active process is idle. Any object which does not deadlock will eventually reach a quiescent state. In our language, nonterminating activity is defined by recursion, which ensures at least one quiescent state in each cycle.

Class upgrades propagate to objects in two steps. When a class C is upgraded in (Extend-Class) or (Simplify-Class), both its stage and version numbers increase. In order to notify objects of this change, the stage change propagates in rule (Class-Inh) to the subclasses of C, and the subclasses recursively increment their stage numbers. Since this notification is given priority, the object gets an upgrade the next time it interacts with a class in rule (Red-Bind4). Before the new process is activated, the active process must become idle, in which case (Obj-State) applies. The *transf* function returns the new state, retaining the values of old fields.

The reduction $\longrightarrow_{up}$ in (Red) reduces a subconfiguration by $\rightharpoonup$ to its normal form before a $\rightarrow$ rewrite, simulating locking the object. Thus, the use of the $\rightharpoonup$ relation abstracts from two locking disciplines; one to deny access to classes for *bind* messages while (Class-Inh) is applicable and the other to delay processing *bind* messages from a callee by an upgraded class until the callee's state has been updated. A class may be upgraded several times before the object reaches a quiescent state, so the object may miss some upgrades. However a single state update suffices to ensure that the object, once upgraded, is a complete instance of the present version of its class. Extending Theorem 1, type soundness holds for the dynamic class system (the details of the proof are given in [16]):

Theorem 2 (Subject reduction). *Let P be a well-typed program with initial configuration init and let $U_1, \ldots, U_n$ be a series of well-typed dynamic class operations with runtime representation upg_i for U_i. If init $\longrightarrow_{up}$config and upg_{i+1} is injected in the runtime configuration after upg_i for all $i < n$, then there is a typing context Δ such that $\Delta \vdash_R$ config* ok.

Proof (sketch). The proof is by induction over the number of reduction steps and then by cases. We show that injecting upg_i maintains the well-typedness of the configuration. Furthermore, we show that the dependencies provided by the static analysis enforce an ordering of upgrades such that new definitions give well-typed configurations. Especially, existing processes as well as new processes and fields in runtime objects are well-typed after the possible reductions.

5 Related Work

For many modern distributed applications, system availability during reconfiguration is crucial. Among dynamic or online upgrade solutions, version control systems aim at modular evolution; some keep multiple co-existing versions of a class or schema [3, 4, 5, 11, 13, 14], others apply a global update or "hot-swapping" [1, 6, 18, 19]. The approaches differ for active behavior, which may be disallowed [6, 13, 18, 19], delayed [1], or supported [14, 21]. Hjálmtýsson and Gray [14] propose proxy classes and reference indirection for C++, with multiple versions of each class. Old instances are not upgraded, so their activity is not interrupted. Existing approaches for Java, using proxies [19] or modifying the Java virtual machine [18], use global upgrade and do not apply to active objects.

Automatic upgrades by lazy global update has been proposed for distributed objects [1] and persistent object stores [6], in which instances of upgraded classes are upgraded, but inheritance and (nonterminating) active code are not addressed, limiting the effect and modularity of the class upgrade. Remark that the use of recursion instead of loops in our approach guarantees that all non-blocked processes will eventually reach a quiescent state. In [6] the ordering of upgrades is serialized and in [18] invalid upgrades raise exceptions.

It is interesting to apply formal techniques to systems for software evolution. Formalizations of runtime upgrade mechanisms are less studied, but exist for imperative [21], functional [4], and object-oriented [5] languages. In a recent upgrade system for (sequential) C [21], type-safe updates of type declarations and procedures may occur at annotated points identified by static analysis. However, the approach is synchronous as upgrades which cannot be applied immediately will fail. Closer to our work, UpgradeJ [5] uses an incremental type system in which class versions are only typechecked once. Our type system is incremental in this sense for new classes and class extensions, but class simplification requires rechecking the subclasses of the modified class. In contrast to our work, UpgradeJ is synchronous and uses explicit upgrade statements in programs. Upgrades only affect the class hierarchy and not running objects. Multiple versions of a class will coexist and the programmer must explicitly refer to the different class versions in the code. Compared to previous work by the authors [23], dynamic classes allow much more flexible runtime upgrades, including simplification operations which necessitate additional runtime overhead, yet the type system has been simplified. However, we do not support the removal of interfaces from classes. This would increase the runtime overhead significantly, as all objects with fields typed by that particular interface would need to be inspected.

6 Conclusion

This paper presents a kernel language for distributed concurrent objects in which programs may evolve at runtime by means of dynamic class operations. The granularity of this mechanism for reprogramming fits well with object orientation and it is modular as a single upgrade may affect a large number of running objects. The mechanism does not impose any particular requirements on the developers of initial applications and provides a fairly flexible mechanism for program evolution. It supports not only the addition of new interfaces and classes to running programs, but also the extension, redefinition, and simplification of existing classes. The dynamic class operations proposed in this paper integrate naturally with the concurrency model adapted in the Creol language and a prototype implementation has been integrated with Creol's execution platform.

The paper presents a type and effect system for dynamic class operations. A characteristic feature of our approach is that the type analysis identifies dependencies between different upgrades which are exploited at runtime to impose constraints on the runtime applicability of a particular upgrade in the asynchronous distributed setting, and suffice to guarantee type soundness. We currently investigate the application of other formal methods to dynamic class operations. In particular, lazy behavioral subtyping [9] seems applicable in order to extend the scope of object-oriented program logics to runtime program evolution.

References

1. Ajmani, S., Liskov, B., Shrira, L.: Modular software upgrades for distributed systems. In: Thomas, D. (ed.) ECOOP 2006. LNCS, vol. 4067, pp. 452–476. Springer, Heidelberg (2006)

2. Amtoft, T., Nielson, F., Nielson, H.R.: Type and Effect Systems: Behaviours for Concurrency. Imperial College Press (1999)
3. Armstrong, J.: Programming Erlang: Software for a Concurrent World. Pragmatic Bookshelf (2007)
4. Bierman, G., Hicks, M., Sewell, P., Stoyle, G.: Formalizing dynamic software updating. In: Proc. 2nd Intl. Workshop on Unanticipated Software Evolution (2003)
5. Bierman, G., Parkinson, M., Noble, J.: UpgradeJ: Incremental typechecking for class upgrades. In: Vitek, J. (ed.) ECOOP 2008. LNCS, vol. 5142, pp. 235–259. Springer, Heidelberg (2008)
6. Boyapati, C., Liskov, B., Shrira, L., Moh, C.-H., Richman, S.: Lazy modular upgrades in persistent object stores. In: Proc. OOPSLA 2003, pp. 403–417. ACM Press, New York (2003)
7. Caromel, D., Henrio, L.: A Theory of Distributed Object. Springer, Heidelberg (2005)
8. de Boer, F.S., Clarke, D., Johnsen, E.B.: A complete guide to the future. In: De Nicola, R. (ed.) ESOP 2007. LNCS, vol. 4421, pp. 316–330. Springer, Heidelberg (2007)
9. Dovland, J., Johnsen, E.B., Owe, O., Steffen, M.: Lazy behavioral subtyping. In: Cuellar, J., Maibaum, T., Sere, K. (eds.) FM 2008. LNCS, vol. 5014, pp. 52–67. Springer, Heidelberg (2008)
10. Drossopoulou, S., Damiani, F., Dezani-Ciancaglini, M., Giannini, P.: More dynamic object re-classification: $\text{Fickle}_{\text{II}}$. ACM TOPLAS 24(2), 153–191 (2002)
11. Duggan, D.: Type-Based hot swapping of running modules. In: Norris, C., Fenwick, J.J.B. (eds.) Proc. 6th Intl. Conf. on Functional Programming (ICFP 2001). ACM SIGPLAN notices, vol. 36(10), pp. 62–73. ACM Press, New York (2001)
12. Felleisen, M., Hieb, R.: The revised report on the syntactic theories of sequential control and state. Theor. Comp. Sci. 103(2), 235–271 (1992)
13. Gupta, D., Jalote, P., Barua, G.: A formal framework for on-line software version change. IEEE Trans. Software Eng. 22(2), 120–131 (1996)
14. Hjálmtýsson, G., Gray, R.S.: Dynamic C++ classes: A lightweight mechanism to update code in a running program. In: Proc. USENIX Tech. Conf. (May 1998)
15. Igarashi, A., Pierce, B.C., Wadler, P.: Featherweight Java: a minimal core calculus for Java and GJ. ACM TOPLAS 23(3), 396–450 (2001)
16. Johnsen, E.B., Kyas, M., Yu, I.C.: Dynamic classes: Modular asynchronous evolution of distributed concurrent objects. Research Report 383, Dept. of Informatics, Univ. of Oslo, Norway (May 2009)
17. Johnsen, E.B., Owe, O.: An asynchronous communication model for distributed concurrent objects. Software and Systems Modeling 6(1), 35–58 (2007)
18. Malabarba, S., Pandey, R., Gragg, J., Barr, E., Barnes, J.F.: Runtime support for type-safe dynamic Java classes. In: Bertino, E. (ed.) ECOOP 2000. LNCS, vol. 1850, pp. 337–361. Springer, Heidelberg (2000)
19. Orso, A., Rao, A., Harrold, M.J.: A technique for dynamic updating of Java software. In: Proc. Intl. Conf. on Software Maintenance (ICSM 2002), pp. 649–658. IEEE Computer Society Press, Los Alamitos (2002)
20. Soules, C.A.N., et al.: System support for online reconfiguration. In: Proc. USENIX Tech. Conf., pp. 141–154 (2003)
21. Stoyle, G., Hicks, M., Bierman, G., Sewell, P., Neamtiu, I.: Mutatis Mutandis: Safe and predictable dynamic software updating. ACM TOPLAS 29(4), 22 (2007)
22. Welc, A., Jagannathan, S., Hosking, A.: Safe futures for Java. In: Proc. OOPSLA 2005, pp. 439–453. ACM Press, New York (2005)
23. Yu, I.C., Johnsen, E.B., Owe, O.: Type-safe runtime class upgrades in Creol. In: Gorrieri, R., Wehrheim, H. (eds.) FMOODS 2006. LNCS, vol. 4037, pp. 202–217. Springer, Heidelberg (2006)

Abstract Object Creation in Dynamic Logic*

To Be or Not to Be Created

Wolfgang Ahrendt[1], Frank S. de Boer[2], and Immo Grabe[2,3]

[1] Chalmers University, Göteborg, Sweden
[2] CWI, Amsterdam, The Netherlands
[3] Christian-Albrechts-University Kiel, Germany

Abstract. In this paper we give a representation of a weakest precondition calculus for abstract object creation in dynamic logic, the logic underlying the KeY theorem prover. This representation allows to both specify and verify properties of objects at the abstraction level of the (object-oriented) programming language. Objects which are not (yet) created never play any role, neither in the specification nor in the verification of properties. Further, we show how to symbolically execute abstract object creation.

1 Introduction

In object-oriented programming languages like Java, objects can be dynamically created by the constructor methods provided by their class. This high-level way of object creation abstracts from the underlying representation of objects and the implementation of object creation. At the abstraction level of the programming language, objects are described as instances of their classes, i.e., the classes provide the only operations which can be performed on objects. Moreover, these operations can only be performed on the created objects, the objects not (yet) created do not exist and therefore can also not be referred to by any programming construct. For practical purposes it is important to be able to specify and verify properties of objects at the abstraction level of the programming language. Specification languages like the Java Modeling Language (JML) [10] and the Object Constraint Language (OCL) [12] abstract from the underlying representation of objects. In [6] a Hoare logic is presented to verify properties of an object-oriented programming language at the abstraction level of the programming language itself. This Hoare logic is based on a weakest precondition calculus for object creation which abstracts from the implementation of object creation.

In this paper we give a representation of a weakest precondition calculus for abstract object creation in dynamic logic, the logic underlying the KeY theorem

* This work has been supported by the EU-projects IST-33826 *Credo: Modelling and analysis of evolutionary structures for distributed services.* (`http://credo.cwi.nl`) and ICT-2007-3 *HATS: Highly Adaptable and Trustworthy Software using Formal Methods.* (`http://www.cse.chalmers.se/research/hats/`).

A. Cavalcanti and D. Dams (Eds.): FM 2009, LNCS 5850, pp. 612–627, 2009.

prover [3]. This representation allows to both specify and verify properties of objects at the abstraction level of the programming language. Objects which are not (yet) created never play any role, neither in the specification nor in the verification of properties.

The generalization of Hoare logic to dynamic logic is of particular interest because it allows for the specification of properties of dynamic object structures which cannot be expressed in first-order logic, like reachability. In Hoare logic such properties require quantification over (finite) sequences or recursively defined predicates in the specification language which seriously complicates both the weakest precondition calculus and the underlying logic. In dynamic logic we can restrict to first-order quantification and use the modalities to express for example reachability properties.

An interesting consequence of the abstraction level of the specification language studied in this paper is the *dynamic scope* of the quantification over objects because it is restricted to the created objects and as such is also affected by object creation. However, we show that the standard logic of first-order quantification also applies in the presence of (object) quantifiers with a dynamic scope.

Further, we show how to symbolically execute abstract object creation in KeY. In general, symbolic execution in KeY accumulates in a simultaneous substitution the assignments generated by a computation. This accumulation involves a pre-processing of the substitution which in general simplifies its actual application. However, we cannot simply accumulate abstract object creation because its side-effects can only be processed by the actual application of the corresponding substitution. We show how to solve this problem by the introduction of fresh logical variables which are used as temporary place holders for the newly created objects. The use of these place holders together with the fact that we can always anticipate object creation allows to symbolically execute abstract object creation.

Related Work

Most formalisations of object-oriented programs, like embeddings into the logic of higher-order theorem provers PVS [14] and Isabelle [9], or dynamic logic as employed in the KeY theorem prover, use an explicit representation of objects. Object creation is then formalized in terms of the information about which objects are in fact created. Such an explicit representation of objects additionally requires an axiomatization of certain consistency requirements, e.g., the global invariant that the values of the fields of created objects only refer to created objects. These requirements pervade the correctness proofs with the basic case distinction between "to be or not to be created" and adds considerably to the length of the proofs, as we will illustrate in Section 5.

The contribution of this paper is the formalization of object creation in dynamic logic which abstracts from an explicit representation of objects and the corresponding implementation of object creation. Proofs in this formalization only refer to created objects and as such are not pervaded by irrelevant implementation details.

Outline

In Section 2 we introduce a dynamic logic for a simple WHILE-language with object creation. This language allows us to focus on object creation. We present the axiomatization of the language in terms of the sequent calculus given in Section 3. Please observe that this calculus can be extended to other programming constructs of existing object-oriented languages like Java as described in [5]. With the calculus at hand symbolic execution of programs is described in Section 4. After a discussion of the state of the art in symbolic execution with respect to object creation and a look into the expressiveness of our approach in Section 5 we conclude with Section 6.

2 Dynamic Logic

To focus on the abstract object creation we restrict ourselves to a simple WHILE-language as our object-oriented programming language. The language contains data of three types Object, Integer, and Boolean. In [5] Becker and Platzer present a similar dynamic logic for Java Card called ODL. ODL covers the type system of Java. Besides the type system, dynamic dispatch, side-effects of expressions, and exception handling are presented in terms of program transformations. However ODL models object creation in terms of an explicit representation of objects. To obtain a logic covering Java that follows our theory of abstract object creation this representation can be replaced by our theory or our theory can be extended analogous to [5].

2.1 Syntax

We assume the sets F of fields and GVar of global variables to be given. Fields are the instance variables of objects. We assume a partitioning of GVar into a set PVar of program variables and a set LVar of logical variables. Logical variables do not change during program execution, i.e. there are no assignments to logical variables. They are used to express invariant properties and for (first-order) quantification. All fields and variables are typed. As mentioned before we restrict to the types Object, Integer, and Boolean. We omit explicit declarations. We have the following grammar for statements and expressions:

$$\begin{array}{ll} s ::= \mathsf{while}\ e\ \mathsf{do}\ s\ \mathsf{od} \mid \mathsf{if}\ e_1\ \mathsf{then}\ s_2\ \mathsf{else}\ s_3\ \mathsf{fi} \mid s_1; s_2 \mid \mathsf{skip} \mid & \\ \quad u := \mathsf{new} \mid e_1.x := e_2 \mid u := e & \text{statements} \\ e ::= u \mid e.x \mid \mathsf{null} \mid e_1 = e_2 \mid \mathsf{if}\ e_1\ \mathsf{then}\ e_2\ \mathsf{else}\ e_3\ \mathsf{fi} \mid f(e_1, ..., e_n) & \text{expressions} \end{array}$$

The statement while denotes the usual looping. Conditional branching is denoted by if–then–else. The condition for both looping and branching is given by a Boolean expression. A semicolon denotes sequential composition. By skip we denote the empty statement. Object creation is denoted by $u :=$ new, where u is a program variable. An assignment to a program variable is denoted by $u := e$. A dot denotes dereferencing, i.e., $e_1.x := e_2$ denotes an assignment to the field x of the object referenced by e_1. For technical convenience only we do not have assignments $e.x := \mathsf{new}$. In order to separate object creation from the aliasing problem we reason about such assignments in terms of the statement $u := \mathsf{new}; e.x := u$, where u is a fresh program variable.

The expression null of type Object denotes the undefined reference. The Boolean expression $e_1 = e_2$ denotes the test for equality between the values of the expressions e_1 and e_2, e.g., e_1 and e_2 refer to the same object in case e_1 and e_2 are variables of type Object. A conditional expression is denoted by if–then–else. The function $f(e_1, ..., e_n)$ denotes an arithmetic or Boolean operation of arity n. We assume every statement and expression to be well-typed. It is important to note that object expressions, i.e., expressions of type Object, can only be compared for equality, dereferenced, or appear as argument of a conditional expression.

Formulas. Dynamic logic (DL) is a variant of *modal logic*. Different parts of a formula are evaluated in different worlds (states), which vary in the interpretation of, in our case, program variables and fields. DL extends full first-order logic with two additional (mix-fix) operators: $\langle\,.\,\rangle\,.$ (diamond) and $[\,.\,]\,.$ (box). In both cases, the first argument is a *program* (fragment), whereas the second argument is another DL formula. A formula $\langle p\rangle\phi$ is true in a state s if execution of p terminates when started in s and results in a state where ϕ is true. As for the other operator, a formula $[p]\phi$ is true in a state s if execution of p, when started in s, does *either* not terminate *or* results in a state where ϕ is true. In other words, the difference between the operators is the one between total and partial correctness.[1] DL is closed under all logical connectives. For instance, the formula $\forall\, l.\,(\langle p\rangle\; (l = u) \;\leftrightarrow\; \langle q\rangle\; (l = u))$ states equivalence of p and q w.r.t. the program variable u.

An example formula involving object creation is $\forall l.\langle u := \mathsf{new}\rangle\neg(u = l)$. It states that every new object indeed is new because the logical variable l ranges over all the objects that exist *before* the object creation $u := \mathsf{new}$. Consequently, after the execution of $u := \mathsf{new}$ we have that the new object is not equal to any object that already existed before, i.e., $\neg(u = l)$, when l refers to an "old" object. Note that the formula $\langle u := \mathsf{new}\rangle\forall l.\neg(u = l)$ has a completely different meaning. In fact the formula is false (cf. Section 3.3). These examples also illustrate a further advantage of DL over Hoare logic: the presence of explicit quantifiers in both formulas make clearer the difference in meaning.

All major program logics (Hoare logic, wp calculus, DL) have in common that the resolving of assignments requires substitutions in the formula, in one way or the other. In the KeY approach, the effect of substitutions is delayed, by having *explicit substitutions* in the logic, called *'updates'*. In this paper, elementary updates have the form $u := \mathsf{new}$, $e_1.x := e_2$, or $u := e$. Updates are brought

[1] Just as in standard modal logic, the diamond resp. box operators quantify existentially resp. universally over states (reached by the program). In case of deterministic programs, however, the only difference between the two is whether termination is claimed or not.

into the logic via the update modality $\{\,.\,\}\,.$, connecting arbitrary updates with arbitrary formulas, like in $0 < v \rightarrow \{u := v\}\, 0 < u$.

A full account of KeY style DL is found in [4].

2.2 Semantics

To define the semantics of our DL we assume given an arbitrary (infinite) set O of *object identities*, with typical element o. We define null itself to be an element of O, i.e., the value of the expression null is null itself. By $dom(T)$ we denote the domain of values of type T, e.g., $dom(\text{Object}) = O$.

States. A state $\Sigma = (\sigma, \tau)$ is a pair consisting of a heap σ and an environment τ. The heap σ is a partial function such that $\sigma(o)$ for every $o \in O$, if defined, denotes the internal state of object o. That is, the value of a field x of an object o, for which $\sigma(o)$ is defined, is given by $\sigma(o)(x) \in dom(T)$. The domain $dom(\sigma)$ of objects that exist in a heap σ is given by the set of objects o for which $\sigma(o)$ is defined. In order to describe unbounded object creation we require the domain of a heap to be finite.

The environment τ assigns values to the global variables. The value of a variable v is given by $\tau(v)$.

We require every state $\Sigma = (\sigma, \tau)$ to be consistent, i.e.,

- $\mathsf{null} \in dom(\sigma)$,
- $\sigma(o)(x) \in dom(\sigma)$ for every $o \in dom(\sigma)$ and field x of type Object,
- $\tau(v) \in dom(\sigma)$ for every global variable v of type Object.

In words, null is an existing object, the fields of type Object of existing objects refer to existing objects and all global variables of type Object refer to existing objects.

Semantics of Expressions and Statements. The semantics of an expression e of type T is a partial function $[\![e]\!] : \Sigma \rightharpoonup dom(T)$. As an example, if $[\![e]\!]$ is defined and does not evaluate to null then

$$[\![e.x]\!](\sigma, \tau) = \sigma([\![e]\!](\sigma, \tau))(x),$$

otherwise $[\![e.x]\!]$ is undefined. For a general treatment of failures we assume given a predicate $def(e)$ which defines the conditions under which the expression e is defined. For example, we have that $def(u.x) \equiv \neg(u = \mathsf{null})$.

The semantics of a statement s is a partial function $[\![s]\!] : \Sigma \rightharpoonup \Sigma$. We focus on the semantics of object creation. In order to formally describe the initialisation of newly created objects, we first introduce for each type T an initial value of type T, i.e., $init_{\text{Object}} = \mathsf{null}$, $init_{\text{Integer}} = 0$, and $init_{\text{Boolean}} = \mathsf{false}$. We define *init* to be the initial state, i.e., the state that assigns to each field x of type T its initial value $init_T$. For the selection of a new object we use a choice function ν on heaps to get a fresh object, i.e., $\nu(\sigma) \notin dom(\sigma)$.

We now define

$$[\![u := \mathsf{new}]\!](\sigma, \tau) = (\sigma[o := init], \tau[u := o]),$$

where $o = \nu(\sigma)$. The heap $\sigma[o := init]$ assigns the local state *init* to the new object o and the environment $\tau[u := o]$ assigns this object to the program variable u.

Semantics of Formulas. A formula ϕ in dynamic logic is valid if $\Sigma \models \phi$ holds for every consistent state Σ. For a logical variable l of type Object, we have the following semantics of universal quantification

$$(\sigma, \tau) \models \forall l.\phi \text{ iff for all } o \in dom(\sigma) : (\sigma, \tau[l := o]) \models \phi,$$

where the consistency of $(\sigma, \tau[l := o])$ implies that the object o exists in σ. Consequently, quantification is restricted to the existing objects. Note that null is always included in the scope of the quantification (i.e., the scope of the quantification is non-empty).

Returning to the above example, we have

$$\begin{array}{l}(\sigma, \tau) \models \forall l.\langle u := \mathsf{new}\rangle\neg(u = l)\\ \text{iff}\\ (\sigma, \tau[l := o]) \models \langle u := \mathsf{new}\rangle\neg(u = l)\end{array}$$

for all $o \in dom(\sigma)$. Let $o' = \nu(\sigma)$. By the semantics of the diamond modality of dynamic logic and the above semantics of object creation we conclude that

$$\begin{array}{l}(\sigma, \tau[l := o]) \models \langle u := \mathsf{new}\rangle\neg(u = l)\\ \text{iff}\\ (\sigma[o' := init], \tau[l := o]) \models \neg(u = l)\\ \text{iff}\\ o \neq o'\end{array}$$

Note that since $o' \notin dom(\sigma)$ by definition of $\nu(\sigma)$ indeed $o \neq o'$ for all $o \in dom(\sigma)$.

3 Axiomatization

In this section, we introduce a proof system for dynamic logic with object creation which abstracts from the explicit representation of objects in the semantics defined above. As a consequence the rules of the proof system are purely defined in terms of the logic itself and do not refer to the semantics. It is characteristic for dynamic logic, in contrast to Hoare logic or weakest precondition calculi, that program reasoning is fully interleaved with first-order logic reasoning, because diamond, box or update modalities can appear both outside and inside the logical connectives and quantifiers. It is therefore important to realise that in the following proof rules, ϕ, ψ and alike, match *any* formula of our logic, possibly containing programs or updates.

3.1 Sequent Calculus

We follow [5,3] in presenting the proof system for dynamic logic as a sequent calculus. A sequent is a pair of sets of formulas (each formula closed for logical variables) written as $\phi_1, ..., \phi_m \vdash \psi_1, ..., \psi_n$. The intuitive meaning is that, given all of $\phi_1, ..., \phi_m$ hold, at least one of $\psi_1, ..., \psi_n$ must hold. We use capital Greek letters to denote (possibly empty) sets of formulas. For instance, by $\Gamma \vdash \phi \rightarrow \psi, \Delta$ we mean a sequent containing at least an implication formula on the right side. Sequent calculus rules always have one sequent as conclusion and zero, one or many sequents as premises:

$$\frac{\Gamma_1 \vdash \Delta_1 \;\ldots\; \Gamma_n \vdash \Delta_n}{\Gamma \vdash \Delta}$$

Semantically, a rule states that the validity of all n premises implies the validity of the conclusion ("top-down"). Operationally, rules are applied bottom-up, reducing the provability of the conclusion to the provability of the premises, starting from the initial sequent to be proved. Rules with no premise close the current proof branch. In Fig. 1 we present some of the rules dealing with propositional connectives and quantifiers (see [8] for the full set). We omit the rules for the left hand side, the rules to deal with negation and the rule to cover conditional expressions. $\phi[l/e]$ denotes standard substitution of l with e in ϕ.

$$\mathsf{impRight}\ \frac{\Gamma, \phi \vdash \psi, \Delta}{\Gamma \vdash \phi \rightarrow \psi, \Delta} \qquad \mathsf{andRight}\ \frac{\Gamma \vdash \phi, \Delta \qquad \Gamma \vdash \psi, \Delta}{\Gamma \vdash \phi \wedge \psi, \Delta}$$

$$\mathsf{allRight}\ \frac{\Gamma \vdash \phi[l/c], \Delta}{\Gamma \vdash \forall l.\phi, \Delta} \quad \text{with } c \text{ a new constant} \qquad \mathsf{allLeft}\ \frac{\Gamma, \forall l.\phi, \phi[l/e] \vdash \Delta}{\Gamma, \forall l.\phi \vdash \Delta} \quad \text{with } e \text{ an expression}$$

$$\mathsf{close}\ \frac{}{\Gamma, \phi \vdash \phi, \Delta} \qquad \mathsf{ind}\ \frac{\Gamma \vdash \phi[l/0], \Delta \qquad \Gamma \vdash \forall l.(\phi \rightarrow \phi[l/l+1]), \Delta}{\Gamma \vdash \forall l.\phi, \Delta} \quad \text{with } l \text{ of type Integer}$$

Fig. 1. Some first-order rules

When it comes to the rules dealing with programs, most of them are not sensitive to the side of the sequent and can moreover be applied to subformulas even. For instance, $\langle s_1; s_2 \rangle \phi$ can be split up into $\langle s_1 \rangle \langle s_2 \rangle \phi$ regardless of where it occurs. For that we introduce the following syntax

$$\frac{\lfloor \phi' \rfloor}{\lfloor \phi \rfloor}$$

for a schema rule where the premise is constructed from the conclusion via replacing an occurrence of ϕ by ϕ'.

In Fig. 2 we present the rules dealing with statements. The schematic modality $\llparenthesis\cdot\rrparenthesis$ can be instantiated with both $[\cdot]$ and $\langle\cdot\rangle$, though consistently within a single rule application. The extension of these rules with the predicate *def*(e) to reason about failures is standard and therefore omitted.

$$\text{split}\ \frac{\lfloor \llparenthesis s_1\rrparenthesis\llparenthesis s_2\rrparenthesis\phi \rfloor}{\lfloor \llparenthesis s_1; s_2\rrparenthesis\phi \rfloor} \qquad \text{if}\ \frac{\lfloor (e \rightarrow \llparenthesis s_1\rrparenthesis\phi) \wedge (\neg e \rightarrow \llparenthesis s_2\rrparenthesis\phi) \rfloor}{\lfloor \llparenthesis \mathsf{if}\ e\ \mathsf{then}\ s_1\ \mathsf{else}\ s_2\ \mathsf{fi}\rrparenthesis\phi \rfloor}$$

$$\text{unwind}\ \frac{\lfloor \llparenthesis \mathsf{if}\ e\ \mathsf{then}\ s; \mathsf{while}\ e\ \mathsf{do}\ s\ \mathsf{od}\ \mathsf{else}\ \mathsf{skip}\ \mathsf{fi}\rrparenthesis\phi \rfloor}{\lfloor \llparenthesis \mathsf{while}\ e\ \mathsf{do}\ s\ \mathsf{od}\rrparenthesis\phi \rfloor}$$

$$\text{assignVar}\ \frac{\lfloor \{u := e\}\phi \rfloor}{\lfloor \llparenthesis u := e\rrparenthesis\phi \rfloor} \qquad \text{assignField}\ \frac{\lfloor \{e_1.x := e_2\}\phi \rfloor}{\lfloor \llparenthesis e_1.x := e_2\rrparenthesis\phi \rfloor}$$

$$\text{createObj}\ \frac{\lfloor \{u := \mathsf{new}\}\phi \rfloor}{\lfloor \llparenthesis u := \mathsf{new}\rrparenthesis\phi \rfloor}$$

Fig. 2. Dynamic logic rules

Total correctness formulas of the form $\langle \mathsf{while} \ldots\rangle\phi$ are proved by first applying the induction rule ind (possibly after generalising the formula) and applying the unwind rule within the induction step. For space reasons, we omit the invariant rule dealing with formulas of the form $[\mathsf{while} \ldots]\phi$ (see [5,4]).

3.2 Application of General Updates

Updates are essentially delayed substitutions.[2] They are resolved by application to the succeeding formula, e.g., $\{u := e\}(u > 0)$ leads to $e > 0$. Update application is only allowed on formulas *not* starting with either a diamond, box or update modality. The last restriction is dropped for symbolic execution, see Section 4.

We now define update application on formulas in terms of a rewrite relation $\{\mathcal{U}\}\phi \leadsto \phi'$ on formulas. As a technical vehicle, we extend the update operator to expressions, such that $\{\mathcal{U}\}e$ is an expression, for all updates $\mathcal{U}$ and expressions e. Accordingly, the rewrite relation $\leadsto$ carries over to such expressions: $\{\mathcal{U}\}e \leadsto e'$.

Fig. 3 defines $\leadsto$ for all standard cases (see also [13,3]). The symbol $\mathcal{U}$ matches all updates, whereas $\mathcal{U}_{nc}$ ('*non-creating*') excludes the form $u := \mathsf{new}$. Furthermore, Lit is the set of literals of all types, in our context $\{\mathsf{null}, \mathsf{true}, \mathsf{false}\} \cup \{\ldots, -1, 0, 1, \ldots\}$. (Recall LVar is the set of logical variables.)

[2] The benefit of delaying substitutions in the context of symbolic execution is illustrated in Section 4.

$$\frac{\{\mathcal{U}\}\phi_1 * \{\mathcal{U}\}\phi_2 \rightsquigarrow \phi'}{\{\mathcal{U}\}(\phi_1 * \phi_2) \rightsquigarrow \phi'} \quad \text{with } * \in \{\wedge, \vee, \rightarrow\}$$

$$\frac{\neg\{\mathcal{U}\}\phi \rightsquigarrow \phi'}{\{\mathcal{U}\}(\neg\phi) \rightsquigarrow \phi'}$$

$$\frac{Q\, l.\, \{\mathcal{U}_{nc}\}\phi \rightsquigarrow \phi'}{\{\mathcal{U}_{nc}\}(Q\, l.\, \phi) \rightsquigarrow \phi'} \quad \text{with } Q \in \{\forall, \exists\},\ l \text{ not in } \mathcal{U}_{nc}$$

$$\{\mathcal{U}\}\alpha \rightsquigarrow \alpha \quad \text{with } \alpha \in \text{LVar} \cup \text{Lit}$$

$$\frac{\{\mathcal{U}_{nc}\}e_1 = \{\mathcal{U}_{nc}\}e_2 \rightsquigarrow e'}{\{\mathcal{U}_{nc}\}(e_1 = e_2) \rightsquigarrow e'}$$

$$\frac{f(\{\mathcal{U}\}e_1, ..., \{\mathcal{U}\}e_n) \rightsquigarrow e'}{\{\mathcal{U}\}f(e_1, ..., e_n) \rightsquigarrow e'}$$

$$\frac{(\{u := e_1\}e_2).x \rightsquigarrow e'}{\{u := e_1\}(e_2.x) \rightsquigarrow e'}$$

$$\frac{(\{e.x := e_1\}e_2).y \rightsquigarrow e'}{\{e.x := e_1\}(e_2.y) \rightsquigarrow e'} \quad x, y \text{ different fields}$$

$$\{u_1 := e\}u_2 \rightsquigarrow u_2 \quad u_1, u_2 \text{ different variables}$$

$$\{u := e\}u \rightsquigarrow e$$

$$\frac{\mathsf{if}\ (\{e.x := e_1\}e_2) = e\ \mathsf{then}\ e_1\ \mathsf{else}\ (\{e.x := e_1\}e_2).x\ \mathsf{fi} \rightsquigarrow e'}{\{e.x := e_1\}(e_2.x) \rightsquigarrow e'}$$

Fig. 3. Update Application, standard cases

The aliasing analysis performed by the last rule is the motivation to add conditional expressions to our language. Object creation of the form $u := \mathsf{new}$ is only covered as far as it behaves like any other update. The cases where object creation makes a difference are discussed separately in Section 3.3. The relation $\rightsquigarrow$ is defined in a big-step manner, such that updates are resolved completely in a single $\rightsquigarrow$ step.

Note that $\rightsquigarrow$ is not defined for formulas of the form $\{\mathcal{U}\}\langle s\rangle\phi$, $\{\mathcal{U}\}[s]\phi$ or $\{\mathcal{U}\}\{\mathcal{U}'\}\phi$, i.e., they are not subject to update application. We return to formulas with nested updates, like $\{\mathcal{U}\}\{\mathcal{U}'\}\phi$, in Section 4.

The following rule links the rewrite relation $\rightsquigarrow$ with the sequent calculus:

$$\mathsf{applyUpd}\ \frac{\lfloor \phi' \rfloor}{\lfloor \{\mathcal{U}\}\phi \rfloor} \quad \text{with } \{\mathcal{U}\}\phi \rightsquigarrow \phi'$$

3.3 Contextual Application of Object Creation

To define update application on $\{u := \mathsf{new}\}e$, simple substitution is not sufficient, i.e., replacing u in e by some expression, because we cannot refer to the newly created object in the state prior to its creation. However, since object expressions can only be compared for equality, or dereferenced, and do not appear as arguments of any other function, we define update application by a contextual analysis of the occurrences of u in e.

We define application of $u := \mathsf{new}$ inductively. Some cases are already covered in Section 3.2, Fig. 3 (the rules dealing with unrestricted $\mathcal{U}$). The other cases are discussed in the following.

If u_1, u_2 are different variables, then

$$\{u_1 := \mathsf{new}\}u_2 \rightsquigarrow u_2$$

Since the fields of a newly created object are initialised we have

$$\{u := \mathsf{new}\}u.x \rightsquigarrow init_T$$

where T is the type of x.

If e is neither u nor a conditional expression then

$$\frac{(\{u := \mathsf{new}\}e).x \rightsquigarrow e'}{\{u := \mathsf{new}\}(e.x) \rightsquigarrow e'}$$

Otherwise, if e is a conditional expression then

$$\frac{\mathsf{if}\ \{u := \mathsf{new}\}b\ \mathsf{then}\ \{u := \mathsf{new}\}(e_1.x)\ \mathsf{else}\ \{u := \mathsf{new}\}(e_2.x)\ \mathsf{fi} \rightsquigarrow e'}{\{u := \mathsf{new}\}(\mathsf{if}\ b\ \mathsf{then}\ e_1\ \mathsf{else}\ e_2\ \mathsf{fi}\ .x) \rightsquigarrow e'}$$

Note that we use here the valid equation:
$\mathsf{if}\ b\ \mathsf{then}\ e_1\ \mathsf{else}\ e_2\ \mathsf{fi}\ .x = \mathsf{if}\ b\ \mathsf{then}\ e_1.x\ \mathsf{else}\ e_2.x\ \mathsf{fi}$.

The only other possible context of u is that of an equality $e = e'$. We distinguish the following cases.

If neither e nor e' is u or a conditional expression then they cannot refer to the newly created object and we define[3]

$$\frac{(\{u := \mathsf{new}\}e) = (\{u := \mathsf{new}\}e') \rightsquigarrow e''}{\{u := \mathsf{new}\}(e = e') \rightsquigarrow e''}$$

If e is u and e' is neither u nor a conditional expression (or vice versa) then after $u := \mathsf{new}$ the expressions e and e' cannot denote the same object (because one of them refers to the newly created object and the other one refers to an already existing object) and so we define

$$\{u := \mathsf{new}\}(e = e') \rightsquigarrow \mathsf{false}$$

On the other hand if both the expressions e and e' equal u we obviously have

$$\{u := \mathsf{new}\}(e = e') \rightsquigarrow \mathsf{true}$$

If e is a conditional expression of the form $\mathsf{if}\ b\ \mathsf{then}\ e_1\ \mathsf{else}\ e_2\ \mathsf{fi}$ then

$$\frac{\mathsf{if}\ \{u := \mathsf{new}\}b\ \mathsf{then}\ \{u := \mathsf{new}\}(e_1 = e')\ \mathsf{else}\ \{u := \mathsf{new}\}(e_2 = e')\ \mathsf{fi} \rightsquigarrow e''}{\{u := \mathsf{new}\}(e = e') \rightsquigarrow e''}$$

And similarly for $e' = e$. Note that we use here the valid equation:
$(\mathsf{if}\ b\ \mathsf{then}\ e_1\ \mathsf{else}\ e_2\ \mathsf{fi} = e') = \mathsf{if}\ b\ \mathsf{then}\ e_1 = e'\ \mathsf{else}\ e_2 = e'\ \mathsf{fi}$

Since object expressions can only be compared for equality, dereferenced or appear as argument of a conditional expression, it is easy to see that for every boolean expression e there exists an expression e' such that $\{u := \mathsf{new}\}e \rightsquigarrow e'$.

The following lemma states the semantic correctness of the rewrite relation $\{u := \mathsf{new}\}e \rightsquigarrow e'$: The value of e' in the state *before* the assignment $u := \mathsf{new}$ equals the value of e *after* the assignment.

[3] To see why the shifting inwards of $\{u := \mathsf{new}\}$ is necessary, consider the case $\{u := \mathsf{new}\}(u.x = u.x)$.

Lemma 1
If $\{u := \mathsf{new}\}e \rightsquigarrow e'$ *and* $[\![u := \mathsf{new}]\!](\Sigma) = \Sigma'$ *then* $[\![e']\!](\Sigma) = [\![e]\!](\Sigma')$.

The proof of this lemma involves a further elaboration of proofs given in [2].

Now we define the rewriting of $\{u := \mathsf{new}\}\phi$, where ϕ is a first-order formula in predicate logic (which does not contain modalities). The rules for this generalization are standard. We present a rule for quantification as an example:

$$\frac{(\{u := \mathsf{new}\}\phi[l/u]) \wedge \forall l.(\{u := \mathsf{new}\}\phi) \rightsquigarrow \psi}{\{u := \mathsf{new}\}\forall l.\phi \rightsquigarrow \psi}$$

where l is a logical variable. This rewrite rule takes care of the *changing scope* of the quantified variable l by distinguishing the following cases: p holds for the new object is expressed by the first conjunct $\{u := \mathsf{new}\}\phi[l/u]$ which is obtained by application of the update to $\phi[l/u]$ and p holds for all 'old' objects is expressed by the second conjunct $\forall l.(\{u := \mathsf{new}\}\phi)$.

As an example, we derive $\{u := \mathsf{new}\}\forall l.\neg(u = l) \rightsquigarrow \neg(\mathsf{true}) \wedge \forall l.\neg\,\mathsf{false}$:

$$\dfrac{\dfrac{\{u := \mathsf{new}\}(u = u) \rightsquigarrow \mathsf{true}}{\{u := \mathsf{new}\}\neg(u = u) \rightsquigarrow \neg(\mathsf{true})} \quad \dfrac{\dfrac{\{u := \mathsf{new}\}(u = l) \rightsquigarrow \mathsf{false}}{\{u := \mathsf{new}\}\neg(u = l) \rightsquigarrow \neg\,\mathsf{false}}}{\forall l.\{u := \mathsf{new}\}\neg(u = l) \rightsquigarrow \forall l.\neg\,\mathsf{false}}}{\dfrac{\{u := \mathsf{new}\}\neg(u = u) \wedge \forall l.\{u := \mathsf{new}\}\neg(u = l) \rightsquigarrow \neg(\mathsf{true}) \wedge \forall l.\neg\,\mathsf{false}}{\{u := \mathsf{new}\}\forall l.\neg(u = l) \rightsquigarrow \neg(\mathsf{true}) \wedge \forall l.\neg\,\mathsf{false}}}$$

The resulting formula is equivalent to false. We use this to prove the formula $\langle u := \mathsf{new}\rangle\forall l.\neg(u = l)$, which states that u is different from all objects existing *after* the update (including u itself), invalid. In fact we have the following derivation for $\neg\langle u := \mathsf{new}\rangle\forall l.\neg(u = l)$.

$$\begin{array}{ll}
\mathsf{closeTrue} & \overline{} \\
 & \forall l.\neg\,\mathsf{false} \vdash \mathsf{true} \\
\mathsf{notLeft} & \overline{\neg(\mathsf{true}), \forall l.\neg\,\mathsf{false} \vdash} \\
\mathsf{andLeft} & \overline{\neg(\mathsf{true}) \wedge \forall l.\neg\,\mathsf{false} \vdash} \\
\mathsf{applyUpd} & \overline{\{u := \mathsf{new}\}\forall l.\neg(u = l) \vdash} \\
\mathsf{assignVar} & \overline{\langle u := \mathsf{new}\rangle\forall l.\neg(u = l)) \vdash} \\
\mathsf{notRight} & \overline{\vdash \neg\langle u := \mathsf{new}\rangle\forall l.\neg(u = l)}
\end{array}$$

On the other hand, we have the following derivation of

$$\forall l.\langle u := \mathsf{new}\rangle\neg(u = l)$$

which expresses in an abstract and natural way that u indeed is a new object different from objects existing *before* the update.

$$\begin{array}{ll}
\mathsf{closeFalse} & \overline{} \\
 & \mathsf{false} \vdash \\
\mathsf{notRight} & \overline{\vdash \neg\,\mathsf{false}} \\
\mathsf{applyUpd} & \overline{\vdash \{u := \mathsf{new}\}\neg(u = c)} \\
\mathsf{assignVar} & \overline{\vdash \langle u := \mathsf{new}\rangle\neg(u = c)} \\
\mathsf{allRight} & \overline{\vdash \forall l.(\langle u := \mathsf{new}\rangle\neg(u = l))}
\end{array}$$

The second example shows that the standard rules for quantification apply to the quantification over the existing objects.

4 Symbolic Execution

4.1 Simultaneous Updates for Symbolic State Representation

The proof system presented so far allows for classical backwards reasoning, in a weakest precondition manner. We now generalise the notion of updates, to allow for the *accumulation* of substitutions, thereby delaying their application. In particular, this can be done in a *forward manner*, giving the proofs a *symbolic execution* nature. We illustrate this principle by example, in Fig. 4.

$$
\begin{array}{rc}
\mathsf{close} & \overline{\phantom{u < v \vdash u < v}} \\
 & u < v \vdash u < v \\
\mathsf{applyUpd} & \overline{u < v \vdash \{w := u \,|\, u := v \,|\, v := u\} v < u} \\
\mathsf{mergeUpd} & \overline{u < v \vdash \{w := u \,|\, u := v\}\{v := w\} v < u} \\
\mathsf{assignVar} & \overline{u < v \vdash \{w := u \,|\, u := v\}\langle v := w \rangle v < u} \\
\mathsf{mergeUpd} & \overline{u < v \vdash \{w := u\}\{u := v\}\langle v := w \rangle v < u} \\
\mathsf{split, assignVar} & \overline{u < v \vdash \{w := u\}\langle u := v; v := w \rangle v < u} \\
\mathsf{split, assignVar} & \overline{u < v \vdash \langle w := u; u := v; v := w \rangle v < u}
\end{array}
$$

Fig. 4. Symbolic execution style proof

The first application of the update rule mergeUpd introduces what is called the simultaneous update $w := u \,|\, u := v$. After applying the second mergeUpd, note that the w from the inner update was turned into a u in the simultaneous update. This is achieved by *applying* the outer update to the inner one:

$$
\mathsf{mergeUpd}\ \frac{\lfloor \{\mathcal{U}_1 \,|\, \ldots \,|\mathcal{U}_n \,|\mathcal{U}'\}\phi \rfloor}{\lfloor \{\mathcal{U}_1 \,|\, \ldots \,|\mathcal{U}_n\}\{U\}\phi \rfloor}
$$
$$
\text{with } \{\mathcal{U}_1 \,|\, \ldots \,|\mathcal{U}_n\}\mathcal{U} \leadsto \mathcal{U}'
$$

For this, we need to extend the rewrite relation $\leadsto$ towards defining application of updates to updates:

$$
\frac{u := \{\mathcal{U}_{nc}\}e \leadsto \mathcal{U}'}{\{\mathcal{U}_{nc}\}(u := e) \leadsto \mathcal{U}'} \qquad \frac{(\{\mathcal{U}_{nc}\}e_1).x := \{\mathcal{U}_{nc}\}e_2 \leadsto \mathcal{U}'}{\{\mathcal{U}_{nc}\}(e_1.x := e_2) \leadsto \mathcal{U}'}
$$

What remains is the definition of the application of simultaneous updates to *expressions*. For space reasons, we will not include the full definition here, but only one interesting special case, where two left-hand sides both write the field x which is accessed in $e.x$.

$$
\frac{\mathsf{if}\ ((\mathcal{U}e_2) = e)\ \mathsf{then}\ e_2'\ \mathsf{else}\ \mathsf{if}\ ((\mathcal{U}e_1) = e)\ \mathsf{then}\ e_1'\ \mathsf{else}\ \mathcal{U}(e).x\ \mathsf{fi}\ \mathsf{fi} \leadsto e'}{\mathcal{U}(e.x) \leadsto e'}
$$
$$
\text{with } \mathcal{U} = \{e_1.x := e_1' \,|\, e_2.x := e_2'\}
$$

This already illustrates two principles: a recursive alias analysis has to be performed on all left-hand sides, and moreover, in case of a clash, the rightmost update will 'win'. The latter is exactly what reflects the destructive semantics of imperative programming. Most cases are, however, much simpler. Most of the time, it is sufficient to think of an application of a simultaneous update as an application of a standard substitution (of more than one variable). For a full account on simultaneous updates, see [13].

The idea to use simultaneous updates for symbolic execution was developed in the KeY project [3], and turned out to be a powerful concept for the validation of real world (Java) programs. A simultaneous update forms a representation of the symbolic state which is reached by "executing" the program in the proof up to the current proof node. The program is "executed" in a forward manner, avoiding the backwards execution of (pure) weakest precondition calculi, thereby achieving better readability of proofs. The simultaneous update is only applied to the post-condition as a final, single step. The KeY tool uses these updates not only for verification, but also for test case generation with high code based coverage [7] and for symbolic debugging.

4.2 Symbolic Execution and Abstract Object Creation

A motivation to choose the setting of dynamic logic with updates is to allow for abstract object creation in symbolic execution style verification. To do so, we have to answer the question of how symbolic execution and abstract object creation can be combined. The problem is that there is no natural way of merging object creation $\{u := new\}$ with other updates. Consider, for instance, the following formulas, only the first of which is valid.

$$\langle u := \mathsf{new}; v := u\rangle(u = v) \qquad\qquad \langle u := \mathsf{new}; v := \mathsf{new}\rangle(u = v)$$

Symbolic execution generates the following formulas:

$$\{u := \mathsf{new}\}\{v := u\}(u = v) \qquad\qquad \{u := \mathsf{new}\}\{v := \mathsf{new}\}(u = v)$$

Merging the updates naively results in both cases in:

$$\{u := \mathsf{new} \mid v := \mathsf{new}\}(u = v)$$

Whichever semantics one gives to a simultaneous update with two object creations, the formula cannot be both valid and invalid.

The proposed solution is twofold: not to merge an object creation with other updates at all, but to create a second reference to the new object, to be used for merging. For this, we introduce a *fresh* auxiliary variable to store the newly created object, and generate *two* updates according to the following rule:

$$\mathsf{createObj}\ \frac{\lfloor \{a := \mathsf{new}\}\{u := a\}\phi \rfloor}{\lfloor \langle u = \mathsf{new}\rangle\phi \rfloor}$$
with a a fresh program variable

The inner update $\{u := v\}$ can be merged with other updates resulting from the analysis of ϕ. The next point to address is the "disruption" of the symbolic state, caused by object creation being unable to merge with their "neighbours", thereby strictly separating state changes happening before and after object creation. The key idea to overcome this is to gradually move all object creations to the very front (as if all objects were allocated up front) and perform standard symbolic execution on the remaining updates. We achieve this by the following rule:

$$\mathsf{pullCreation}\ \frac{\lfloor \{u := \mathsf{new}\}\mathcal{U}_{nc}\phi \rfloor}{\lfloor \mathcal{U}_{nc}\{u := \mathsf{new}\}\phi \rfloor}$$
$$\text{with } u \text{ not appearing in } \mathcal{U}_{nc}$$

We illustrate symbolic execution with abstract object creation by an example.

$$\begin{array}{rc}
\mathsf{notRight, closeFalse} & \\ \hline
 & \vdash \neg \mathsf{false} \\
\mathsf{applyUpd} & \\ \hline
 & \vdash \{a := \mathsf{new}\}\neg(v = a) \\
\mathsf{applyUpd} & \\ \hline
 & \vdash \{a := \mathsf{new}\}\{u := v \,|\, v := a \,|\, w := u\}\neg(w = v) \\
\mathsf{mergeUpd} & \\ \hline
 & \vdash \{a := \mathsf{new}\}\{u := v \,|\, v := a\}\{w := u\}\neg(w = v) \\
\mathsf{mergeUpd, assignVar} & \\ \hline
 & \vdash \{a := \mathsf{new}\}\{u := v\}\{v := a\}\langle w := u\rangle\neg(w = v) \\
\mathsf{pullCreation} & \\ \hline
 & \vdash \{u := v\}\{a := \mathsf{new}\}\{v := a\}\langle w := u\rangle\neg(w = v) \\
\mathsf{split, createObj} & \\ \hline
 & \vdash \{u := v\}\langle v := \mathsf{new};\, w := u\rangle\neg(w = v) \\
\mathsf{split, assignVar} & \\ \hline
 & \vdash \langle u := v;\, v := \mathsf{new};\, w := u\rangle\neg(w = v)
\end{array}$$

5 Discussion

5.1 Object Creation vs. Object Activation

Proof systems for object-oriented languages([1]) usually achieve the uniqueness of objects via an injective mapping, here called obj, from the natural numbers to object identities. Only the object identities $\mathsf{obj}(i)$ up to a maximum index i are considered to stand for actually created objects. In each state, the successor of this maximum index is stored in a ghost variable, here called next. (In case of Java, next would be a `static` field, for each class). Object creation increases the value of next, which conceptually is more an activation than a creation. Quantifiers cover the entire co-domain of obj, including "not yet created" objects. In order to restrict a certain property ϕ to the "created" objects, the following pattern is used: $\forall l.(\psi \rightarrow \phi)$, where ψ restricts to the created objects. Formulas of the form $\exists n.\,(n < \mathsf{next} \wedge \mathsf{obj}(n) = l)$ are the approach taken in ODL[5]. To avoid the extra quantifier, ghost instance variable of boolean type, here called created, can be used to indicate for each object whether or not it has already been "created" [4]. In this case we set the created status of the "new" object (identified by next) and increase next. The assertion $\forall n.(\mathsf{obj}(n).\mathsf{created} \leftrightarrow n < \mathsf{next})$ retains the relation between the created status and the object counter next on the level of the proofs. In both case, we need further assertions to state that fields of created objects always refer to created objects.

$$
\begin{array}{ll}
\text{close} & \overline{} \\
 & c.\mathsf{cr}, \mathsf{obj}(\mathsf{next}) = c \vdash c.\mathsf{cr} \\
\text{equality} & \overline{c.\mathsf{cr}, \mathsf{obj}(\mathsf{next}) = c \vdash \mathsf{obj}(\mathsf{next}).\mathsf{cr}} \\
\text{notLeft} & \overline{\neg\mathsf{obj}(\mathsf{next}).\mathsf{cr}, c.\mathsf{cr}, \mathsf{obj}(\mathsf{next}) = c \vdash} \\
\text{(2 rules)} & \overline{(\mathsf{obj}(\mathsf{next}).\mathsf{cr} \leftrightarrow \mathsf{next} < \mathsf{next}), c.\mathsf{cr}, \mathsf{obj}(\mathsf{next}) = c \vdash} \\
\text{allLeft} & \overline{\forall n.(\mathsf{obj}(n).\mathsf{cr} \leftrightarrow n < \mathsf{next}), c.\mathsf{cr}, \mathsf{obj}(\mathsf{next}) = c \vdash} \\
\text{assumption(1)} & \overline{c.\mathsf{cr}, \mathsf{obj}(\mathsf{next}) = c \vdash} \\
\text{notRight} & \overline{c.\mathsf{cr} \vdash \neg(\mathsf{obj}(\mathsf{next}) = c)} \\
\text{applyUpd} & \overline{c.\mathsf{cr} \vdash \{u := \mathsf{obj}(\mathsf{next}) \mid \mathsf{obj}(\mathsf{next}).\mathsf{cr} := \mathsf{true} \mid \mathsf{next} := \mathsf{next}+1\}\neg(u = c)} \\
\text{createObj} & \overline{c.\mathsf{cr} \vdash \langle u := \mathsf{new}\rangle\neg(u = c)} \\
\text{impRight} & \overline{\vdash c.\mathsf{cr} \rightarrow \langle u := \mathsf{new}\rangle\neg(u = c)} \\
\text{allRight} & \overline{\vdash \forall l.\, (l.\mathsf{cr} \rightarrow \langle u := \mathsf{new}\rangle\neg(u = l))}
\end{array}
$$

Fig. 5. Object activation style proof

To state in this setting that a new object indeed is new we need to argument the formula introduced in Section 3, i.e. $\forall l.\, (l.\mathsf{created} \rightarrow \langle u := \mathsf{new}\rangle\neg(u = l))$. In fact the formula in Section 3 is not valid in this setting. An object activation style proof of this is given in Fig. 5 (abbreviating $\mathsf{created}$ by cr). Many steps in this proof are caused by the particular details of the explicit representation of objects and the simulation of object creation by object activation.

5.2 Expressiveness

Many interesting properties of dynamic object structures, like reachability in dynamic linked data structures, cannot be expressed in first-order predicate logic. There are approaches to simulate reachability by an overapproximation of the reachable states [11]. In first-order dynamic logic however we can use the modalities to express such properties. For example, if a linked list is given in terms of a field *next* and the data is stored in a field *data* then the following formula in dynamic logic states that the object denoted by v is reachable from the object denoted by u:

$$\langle \mathsf{while}\ u \neq v\ \mathsf{do}\ u := u.next\ \mathsf{od}\rangle(\mathsf{true})$$

Note that in DL such formulas can be used to express properties themselves.

6 Conclusion

In this paper we gave a representation of a weakest precondition calculus for abstract object creation in dynamic logic and the KeY theorem prover. Abstract object creation is formalized in terms of an inductively defined rewrite relation. The standard sequent calculus for dynamic logic is extended with a schema rule which allows to substitute formulas in sequents and thus provides a general mechanism to import for example specific rewrite relations. The resulting logic abstracts from an explicit representation of objects and the corresponding implementation of object creation. As such it abstracts from irrelevant implementation details which in general complicate proofs. Moreover, it treats the dynamic scope of quantified object variables in a standard manner. Finally, we have shown how to symbolically execute abstract object creation in KeY.

Currently, we are implementing and extending the toy language to other programming constructs of object-oriented languages like Java.

References

1. Abadi, M., Leino, K.R.M.: A logic of object-oriented programs. In: Bidoit, M., Dauchet, M. (eds.) CAAP 1997, FASE 1997, and TAPSOFT 1997. LNCS, vol. 1214, pp. 682–696. Springer, Heidelberg (1997)
2. America, P., de Boer, F.S.: Reasoning about dynamically evolving process structures. Formal Asp. Comput. 6(3), 269–316 (1994)
3. Beckert, B., Hähnle, R., Schmitt, P.H. (eds.): Verification of Object-Oriented Software. LNCS (LNAI), vol. 4334. Springer, Heidelberg (2007)
4. Beckert, B., Klebanov, V., Schlager, S.: Dynamic Logic. In: Beckert, B., et al. (eds.) [3], pp. 69–177
5. Beckert, B., Platzer, A.: Dynamic Logic with Non-rigid Functions. In: Furbach, U., Shankar, N. (eds.) IJCAR 2006. LNCS (LNAI), vol. 4130, pp. 266–280. Springer, Heidelberg (2006)
6. de Boer, F.S.: A WP-calculus for OO. In: Thomas, W. (ed.) FOSSACS 1999. LNCS, vol. 1578, pp. 135–149. Springer, Heidelberg (1999)
7. Engel, C., Hähnle, R.: Generating Unit Tests from Formal Proofs. In: Gurevich, Y., Meyer, B. (eds.) TAP 2007. LNCS, vol. 4454, pp. 169–188. Springer, Heidelberg (2007)
8. Giese, M.: First-Order Logic. In: Beckert, B., et al (ed.) [3], pp. 21–68
9. Klein, G., Nipkow, T.: A machine-checked model for a Java-like language, virtual machine, and compiler. Transactions on Programming Languages and Systems 28(4), 619–695 (2006)
10. Leavens, G.T., Leino, K.R.M., Poll, E., Ruby, C., Jacobs, B.: JML: notations and tools supporting detailed design in Java. In: OOPSLA 2000 Companion, pp. 105–106. ACM, New York (2000)
11. Lev-Ami, T., Immerman, N., Reps, T.W., Sagiv, S., Srivastava, S., Yorsh, G.: Simulating Reachability Using First-Order Logic with Applications to Verification of Linked Data Structures. In: Nieuwenhuis, R. (ed.) CADE 2005. LNCS (LNAI), vol. 3632, pp. 99–115. Springer, Heidelberg (2005)
12. Object Modeling Group. Object Constraint Language Specification, version 2.0 (2005)
13. Rümmer, P.: Sequential, Parallel, and Quantified Updates of First-Order Structures. In: Hermann, M., Voronkov, A. (eds.) LPAR 2006. LNCS (LNAI), vol. 4246, pp. 422–436. Springer, Heidelberg (2006)
14. van den Berg, J., Jacobs, B.: The LOOP Compiler for Java and JML. In: Margaria, T., Yi, W. (eds.) TACAS 2001. LNCS, vol. 2031, pp. 299–312. Springer, Heidelberg (2001)

Reasoning about Memory Layouts

Holger Gast

Wilhelm-Schickard-Institut für Informatik
University of Tübingen
gast@informatik.uni-tuebingen.de

Abstract. Verification methods for memory-manipulating C programs need to address not only well-typed programs that respect invariants such as the split heap memory model, but also programs that access through pointers arbitrary memory objects such as local variables, single struct fields, or arrays slices. We present a logic for memory layouts that covers these applications and show how proof obligations arising during the verification can be discharged automatically using the layouts.

1 Introduction

Verification methods of programs that manipulate the heap necessarily formalize and reason about the memory layout: each access to the memory generates the proof obligation that the accessed region is allocated, and the influence of writes on the validity of assertions needs to be determined by considering the possible aliasing between pointers. The required reasoning has been automated successfully for Burstall's split heap memory model, which in particular is expressive enough for object-oriented programming languages (e.g. [1,2]). Single objects as well as sets of objects are supported by current reasoning technology (e.g. [3]).

Burstall's memory model assumes that all pointers are object references and objects with different references do not overlap. It is therefore too imprecise for many C programs, and the employed reasoning techniques do not scale directly to more precise memory models [4]. Unfortunately, the excluded "low-level" usage is not confined to a few border cases, but is well within the range of idiomatic C code. A few examples from the current Linux kernel, which are deliberately taken from different modules, will illustrate the point.

Data structures throughout the kernel are, for instance, protected by mutexes. The following functions (from `mutex.c`) acquire and release mutexes.

```
void mutex_lock(struct mutex *lock);
void mutex_unlock(struct mutex *lock);
```

The mutexes, i.e. memory objects of type `struct mutex`, are allocated in various ways. In `socket.c`, for instance, global mutexes protect the (global) `ioctl` settings. Calls like `mutex_lock(&br_ioctl_mutex)` are thus distributed throughout the module. But mutexes also protect `inodes` (defined in `fs.h`):

```
struct inode { ... struct mutex i_mutex; ... }   (1)
```

A. Cavalcanti and D. Dams (Eds.): FM 2009, LNCS 5850, pp. 628–643, 2009.

Locking such an `inode` involves passing a pointer to a struct member:

```
mutex_lock(&inode->i_mutex);
```
(2)

Furthermore, it is common to pass pointers to local variables and also to fields within local variables (from `hrtimer.c`, where `struct hrtimer_sleeper t;`):

```
hrtimer_init_on_stack(&t.timer, /*... */);
```
(3)

Also elements from local arrays are passed by reference (from `compat.h`, where `struct timespec tv[2];`):

```
if (get_compat_timespec(&tv[0], &t[0])) { ... }
```
(4)

Indeed, these examples do not represent particularly "low-level" kernel code. Similar idioms are presented in manuals and textbooks as the established best practice.

The common challenge in these examples is that the specifications of the called functions do not foresee these particular uses, but are formulated with respect to the passed pointers alone — they are small specifications [5]. To verify the calls, it is necessary to reason about the layout of the data structures and their components, and to derive frame axioms for the remaining data structures.

This paper's contribution is a method for automatic reasoning about the above situations within Hoare logic. We provide a language for expressing layouts and a logic and proof method for refining and re-interpreting layouts. The approach is flexible in that it supports user-defined layout components and user-provided refinements and re-interpretations. This contribution is thus complementary to the work presented in [6], where unfoldings were left as future work. The treatment of layouts is also independent of the specific Hoare logic used; instead, it solves proof obligations which generally arise in Hoare logics.

The development presented in this paper is mechanized in Isabelle/HOL to ensure its soundness. We also use Isabelle/HOL as an example verification environment, and the presented proof strategies are implemented as ML tactics to establish their utility. However, a second perspective is possible: the theorems that are used for verification can be seen as a first-order axiomatization of the introduced layout constants and operators. In this perspective, HOL serves as a meta-logic in which these theorems are proven (see [7] for a similar discussion). We will emphasize this connection throughout the presentation.

Organization of the Paper. Section 2 analyzes the proof obligations about memory layouts arising in Hoare logics and summarizes the main concepts from [6]. Section 3 gives a framework for reasoning about memory layouts that covers both refinements and re-interpretations. Section 4 shows that the framework can solve the introductory examples. Section 5 surveys related work. Section 6 concludes.

2 Memory-Related Proof Obligations in the Hoare Logic

This section summarizes the considered programming language and Hoare logic. It then examines the proof obligations resulting from the use of a low-level memory model and introduces our formalization of memory layouts. For brevity, the presentation elides the less important definitions from [6].

2.1 Language and Hoare Logic

The language that we consider is inspired by Norrish's detailed analysis of C [8]. Its expressions include the usual primitive arithmetic operations, pointer dereferencing, and side-effecting operators, as well as pointer arithmetic and an address operator applicable to arbitrary l-values (i.e. memory objects). As statements, we support if, while, return, blocks with local variable declarations, and the execution of expressions. The syntax is the same as in C.

We use a standard big-step operational semantics. Compared with [8], we introduce mainly two simplifications with the purpose of focussing on memory-related aspects: first, expressions are executed left-to-right and side-effects are committed to memory immediately. Second, there is no distinction between allocated and initialized memory (cf. [8, Sec. 3.1.2] for both).

The memory model is captured by the following Isabelle/HOL type, where addr is a type isomorphic to 32-bit words [9]. ("⇒" denotes total functions.)

```
record memory =
  m-dom   :: "addr set"
  m-cnt   :: "addr ⇒ byte"
  m-valid :: "bool"
```

A memory state's *domain* and *content* together define a partial function from the allocated addresses to their content. The *history variable* m-valid designates whether any illegal accesses have occurred during the execution [10]. The operational semantics accesses memory only through the functions fetch and store, which transfer byte representations of values from and to memory. These functions set m-valid to false if unallocated addresses are manipulated.

```
fetch :: "addr ⇒ nat ⇒ memory ⇒ byte list × memory"
store :: "addr ⇒ byte list ⇒ memory ⇒ memory"
```

Execution is defined relative to a context, given by the following record type, which contains the definitions of struct types, functions, and local variables ("⇀" denotes partial functions; ty is the datatype representing the language types).

```
record ctx =
  ctx-structs :: "string ⇀ struct-def"
  ctx-prog    :: "string ⇀ func"
  ctx-vars    :: "string ⇀ addr × ty"
```

Note that this memory model does not make a structural distinction between local variables and the heap. In particular, it is possible to apply the address operator and pointer arithmetic for accessing local variables.

We use a Hoare logic for fault-avoiding partial correctness. The rules are forward-style and generalize Floyd's assignment axiom [6]. The treatment of recursive functions and auxiliary variables are based on Schirmer's presentation [11]. Side-effecting expressions are handled using Kowaltowski's approach [12]. For the purposes of the present paper, only the memory-related proof obligations are important. They are analyzed subsequently.

2.2 Formalizing Layouts

Memory layouts are usually perceived as recursively nested objects (e.g. [10,13]), which suggests a formalization by a grammar (or equivalently an algebraic data type). This approach has, however, the drawback that it fixes the set of possible memory layouts. The examples in Section 1, on the other hand, suggest that different views on a single memory state may be necessary. We therefore use a shallow embedding of memory layouts into HOL, i.e. we define HOL constants and functions that capture the memory region covered by a layout. The central notion is therefore that of a *cover*, which describes a region by comprehension:

$$\mathsf{cover} = \text{"}\mathsf{addr\ set} \Rightarrow \mathsf{bool}\text{"}$$

All covers mentioned subsequently will be *well-formed* in the sense that they accept a single address set or none at all. It is then straightforward to define raw memory regions, and the regions occupied by some typed value, or a variable, and by arrays.[1]

$$\begin{array}{ll}
\mathsf{block\ a\ n} & \equiv \lambda \mathsf{S}.\ \mathsf{S} = \{\mathsf{a} \mathinner{..<} \mathsf{a} \oplus \mathsf{n}\} \wedge \mathsf{a} \leq \mathsf{a} \oplus \mathsf{n} \\
\mathsf{typed\text{-}block}\ \Gamma\ \mathsf{a\ t} & \equiv \lambda \mathsf{S}.\ \mathsf{block\ a\ (of\text{-}nat\ (sz\text{-}of\text{-}ty}\ \Gamma\ \mathsf{t}))\ \mathsf{S} \wedge \mathsf{is\text{-}small\text{-}type}\ \Gamma\ \mathsf{t} \\
\mathsf{var\text{-}block}\ \Gamma\ \mathsf{v} & \equiv \mathsf{typed\text{-}block}\ \Gamma\ (\mathsf{addr\text{-}of}\ \Gamma\ \mathsf{v})\ (\mathsf{type\text{-}of}\ \Gamma\ \mathsf{v}) \\
\mathsf{array}\ \Gamma\ \mathsf{t\ p\ i\ j} & \equiv \lambda \mathsf{S}.\ \mathsf{S} = \{\ \mathsf{p} \oplus[\Gamma,\mathsf{t}]\ \mathsf{i} \mathinner{..<} \mathsf{p} \oplus[\Gamma,\mathsf{t}]\ \mathsf{j}\ \} \wedge 0 \leq_s \mathsf{i} \wedge \mathsf{i} \leq_s \mathsf{j}\ \wedge \\
& \quad \mathsf{p} \oplus[\Gamma,\mathsf{t}]\ \mathsf{i} \leq \mathsf{p} \oplus[\Gamma,\mathsf{t}]\ \mathsf{j} \wedge \mathsf{unat\ j} * (\mathsf{sz\text{-}of\text{-}ty}\ \Gamma\ \mathsf{t}) \leq \mathsf{unat\ max\text{-}word}
\end{array}$$

The covers $\mathsf{block\ a\ n}$ and $\mathsf{array}\ \Gamma\ \mathsf{t\ p\ i\ j}$ thus describe continuous regions of addresses. The side-conditions exclude overflows in the address arithmetic. The remaining two constants introduce typed views on blocks. Composite structures are expressed using the following disjointness combinator for covers:

$$\mathsf{A} \parallel \mathsf{B} \equiv \lambda \mathsf{S}.\ \exists \mathsf{S1\ S2}.\ \mathsf{A\ S1} \wedge \mathsf{B\ S2} \wedge \mathsf{S} = \mathsf{S1} \cup \mathsf{S2} \wedge \mathsf{S1} \cap \mathsf{S2} = \{\}$$

Subsequently, a *layout block* is a cover given by a defined constant, as opposed to being constructed by the disjointness combinator.

As an example, a variable p (of type int*), and the region it refers to would be formalized as follows (double quotes surround strings; to-ptr converts the byte representation of the pointer into an address; rdv reads the byte representation of the value stored in a variable)):

$$\mathsf{var\text{-}block}\ \Gamma\ \text{"p"} \parallel \mathsf{typed\text{-}block}\ \Gamma\ (\mathsf{to\text{-}ptr}\ (\mathsf{rdv}\ \Gamma\ \text{"p"}))\ \mathsf{int}$$

In a first-order setting, the type cover would be taken as primitive. The introduced constants then become first-order functions and they are used in first-order axioms about layouts, as shown subsequently.

[1] sz-of-ty, addr-of, and type-of look up information on types and variables; of-nat and unat convert between `nat` and `word` [9]; is-small-type asserts that the size of a type can be represented in 32 bits; max-word is the the largest 32-bit word. λ denotes a function; $\{\mathsf{a} \mathinner{..<} \mathsf{b}\}$ is the Isabelle/HOL notation for the interval $[a, b)$; relations $\leq_s$ and $<_s$ are signed comparison on words [9], $\oplus$ is raw address arithmetic, pointer arithmetic $\oplus[\Gamma,\mathsf{t}]$ uses a type and the definition context.

2.3 Normal Form of Assertions

The essence of lightweight separation [6] is that the user simply specifies the memory layout in addition to a first-order (or higher-order) assertion about the memory content. The memory layout is captured by covers, using the following *covered* predicate (read "M is covered by A"):

$\mathsf{M} \blacktriangleright \mathsf{A} \equiv \mathsf{m\text{-}valid}\ \mathsf{M}\ \wedge\ \mathsf{A}\ (\mathsf{m\text{-}dom}\ \mathsf{M})$

For an assertion P about the content, the normal form of assertions is therefore:

$$\lambda \Gamma\, \mathsf{M}.\ \exists x_1 \ldots x_n.\ \mathsf{M} \blacktriangleright \mathsf{A} \wedge \mathsf{P}\, \Gamma\, \mathsf{M}\, x_1 \ldots x_n \qquad (5)$$

The variables $x_1 \ldots x_n$ name intermediate results encountered during expression evaluation as usual in forward-style Hoare logics. In post-conditions of expressions, the result v would be an additional parameter [12]. In a first-order setting, Γ, M, and possibly v would be allowed to occur free in A and P.

2.4 Proof Obligations on Allocatedness

Since the Hoare logic is fault-avoiding, any memory access generates the proof obligation that the region is allocated. This condition is captured by the *allocated* predicate (read "A is allocated in M", where A is a cover and M a memory state):

$\mathsf{M} \rhd \mathsf{A} \equiv \mathsf{m\text{-}valid}\ \mathsf{M}\ \wedge\ (\exists \mathsf{S}.\ \mathsf{S} \subseteq \mathsf{m\text{-}dom}\ \mathsf{M}\ \wedge\ \mathsf{A}\ \mathsf{S})$

In the rule for dereference expressions *e, for instance, let P be the post-condition of the evaluation of e. Following [12], it is a predicate on the current context Γ, the memory state M after the possibly side-effecting execution of e, and the computed result v. The necessary proof obligation is:

$$\forall \Gamma\ \mathsf{M}\ \mathsf{v}.\ \mathsf{P}\ \Gamma\ \mathsf{M}\ \mathsf{v} \longrightarrow \mathsf{M} \rhd \mathsf{typed\text{-}block}\ \Gamma\ (\mathsf{to\text{-}ptr}\ \mathsf{v})\ \mathsf{t} \qquad (6)$$

By construction of the Hoare rules, P will be in normal form and the allocatedness can be determined from the layout given in P. The *subcover* relation captures just the necessary inclusion of the covered regions:

$\mathsf{A} \preceq \mathsf{B} \equiv \forall \mathsf{S}.\ \mathsf{B}\ \mathsf{S} \longrightarrow (\exists \mathsf{S'}.\ \mathsf{S'} \subseteq \mathsf{S}\ \wedge\ \mathsf{A}\ \mathsf{S'})$

The following theorem is then used to reduce (6) to a proof about layouts alone.

$$\frac{\mathsf{M} \blacktriangleright \mathsf{A} \qquad \mathsf{B} \preceq \mathsf{A}}{\mathsf{M} \rhd \mathsf{B}} \qquad (7)$$

2.5 Side-Conditions in Memory Layouts

Memory layouts usually include tacit assumptions about the involved addresses. The C standard prescribes, for instance, that an allocated block consists of a sequence of increasing addresses, which motivates the side-condition excluding overflows in the address arithmetic in the definition of block and array (Section 2.2). For the purposes of verification, these assumptions constitute invariants. Including them into the definitions of cover constants facilitates automatic reasoning, since theorems about the constants have fewer premises. The definition of a cover constant c with parameters $x_1 \ldots x_n$ therefore usually has the following form (where the $x_1 \ldots x_n$, but not the covered region S, occur in P).

$$c\, x_1 \ldots x_n \;\equiv\; \lambda S.\; S = \cdots \wedge P\, x_1 \ldots x_n$$

To express that the side-conditions hold, the covered region itself is immaterial. We say that a cover is *valid* if it covers some memory region; from the validity, it can be deduced that the side-conditions are satisfied.

$$\mathsf{is\text{-}valid\ A} \;\equiv\; \exists \mathsf{S}.\ \mathsf{A\ S}$$

It is obviously possible to derive validity from a given memory layout by means of the subcover relation; furthermore, the subcover relation itself preserves validity.

$$\frac{\mathsf{M} \blacktriangleright \mathsf{A} \qquad \mathsf{B} \preceq \mathsf{A}}{\mathsf{is\text{-}valid\ B}} \qquad\qquad \frac{\mathsf{is\text{-}valid\ A} \qquad \mathsf{B} \preceq \mathsf{A}}{\mathsf{is\text{-}valid\ B}} \tag{8}$$

With the interpretation of side-conditions as invariants, an is-valid statement should be read as "the side-conditions hold". In Section 3, this reading explains how side-conditions are maintained through unfoldings.

2.6 Side-Effects, Disjointness, and Aliasing

Side-effects in the semantics are formalized in Hoare rules by syntactic manipulations of assertions. Suppose, for instance, that a command c performs some side-effect f on the memory, i.e. for the pre-state M, the post-state is f M. In a higher-order setting, the Hoare rule can be given directly (cf. [11, Figure 3.1]):

$$\vdash \{\, \lambda \Gamma M.\; Q\, \Gamma\, (f\, M)\,\}\; c\; \{\, Q\,\}$$

In a first-order verification environment, the β-reduction is replaced by a syntactic substitution, as in Hoare's assignment axiom.

We prefer to use a forward-style Hoare logic in order to emulate the reasoning possible in separation logic [5,7]. Here, Floyd's assignment axiom can be generalized by introducing *inverse operators* [6]. Let F be a function such that F M (f M) = M, i.e. F undoes the effect of f by replacing a specific region by the content from its first argument. The forward-style Hoare rule for command c is then obtained by existentially quantifying over the previous memory state M':

$$\vdash \{\, \mathsf{P}\,\}\; \mathsf{c}\; \{\, \lambda \Gamma\, \mathsf{M}.\ \exists \mathsf{M'}.\ \mathsf{P}\ \Gamma\ (\mathsf{F\ M'\ M}) \wedge \mathsf{Q}\ \Gamma\ \mathsf{M}\,\}$$

The assertion Q expresses the result of f, such as a particular region now containing a particular value. Again, in a first-order system, the verification condition generator would apply a syntactic substitution.

In both cases, therefore, the "current" memory state M in some assertion P is replaced by a modified state (g M), where g is either the effect itself or its inverse operator. In both cases, the goal must be to remove the operator g in order to retrieve an assertion about the "current" state M itself.

To illustrate the point, suppose f is the operator store a v M which writes the byte-representation of value v at address a in M. Suppose then that precondition

P contains the assertion to-int (rdv Γ "x" M) $>$ 0, which reads the content of variable "x" and interprets the byte-representation as an integer. The postcondition would be to-int (rdv Γ "x" (STORE a (length v) M' M)) $>$ 0 instead. Intuitively, this assertion reads: "*before* the side-effect, x contained a positive value".

We thus wish to simplify terms of the form mac (mop M), where mac is a *memory accessor* like rdv Γ x and mop is a *memory operator* like STORE a (length v) M'. We capture the behaviour of memory accessors and operators abstractly by the following constants (where the predicates eqv-inside and eqv-outside assert that their memory arguments are the same inside and outside, respectively, a region covered by A).

$$\begin{aligned} \text{accesses mac M A} &\equiv \forall \text{M'}.\ \text{eqv-inside A M M'} \longrightarrow \text{mac M} = \text{mac M'} \\ \text{modifies mop M A} &\equiv \text{eqv-outside A M (mop M)} \end{aligned}$$

Theorem (9) then allows the desired simplification to take place. Premises 1 and 2 are properties of the involved accessor and modifier constants. Premises 3 and 4 are solved automatically, since all covers we use are well-formed.

$$\frac{\begin{array}{c}\text{is-valid B} \longrightarrow \text{accesses mac M B} \\ \text{is-valid A} \longrightarrow \text{modifies mop M A} \\ \text{wf-cover A} \quad \text{wf-cover B} \\ \text{M} \blacktriangleright \text{C} \qquad \text{A} \parallel \text{B} \preceq \text{C}\end{array}}{\text{mac (mop M)} = \text{mac M}} \tag{9}$$

In a first-order setting, the verification condition generator would use (9) to pre-generate rewrite rules by solving the premises 1–4 with provided theorems.

2.7 Function Calls

The specification of functions introduces the frame inference problem (e.g. [7]): it must be possible to infer from the specification which parts of the memory remain unmodified. As the examples in Section 1 show, no reasonable restriction can be placed on the memory objects that can be passed by reference. Our solution is to introduce a constant frame which asserts that a memory region given by a cover R has not been modified between the states M and M'.

$$\text{frame R M M'} \equiv \text{wf-cover R} \wedge \text{eqv-inside R M M'}$$

A function specification then consists of the pre- and post-conditions of the form

$$\begin{aligned} &\text{M} \blacktriangleright \text{A} \parallel \text{R} \wedge \text{frame R M0 M} \wedge \text{P} \\ &\text{M} \blacktriangleright \text{B} \parallel \text{R} \wedge \text{frame R M0 M} \wedge \text{Q} \end{aligned}$$

where A and B capture the memory parts directly manipulated by the function and R and M0 are auxiliary variables.

The pre-condition of the function call must then imply the function's precondition. For a pre-condition $\exists x_1 \ldots x_n.$ M $\blacktriangleright$ C $\wedge$ P', the proof obligation becomes:

$$\forall x_1 \ldots x_n\,.\ \text{M} \blacktriangleright \text{C} \wedge \text{P'} \longrightarrow \text{M} \blacktriangleright \text{A} \parallel \text{?R} \wedge \text{frame ?R ?M0 M} \wedge \text{P}$$

Here the auxiliary variables have become unknowns ?R and ?M0 that can be instantiated (cf. [11, Sec. 3.1.1]). The reasoning task is expressed by theorem (10): we need to rewrite the cover C suitably, assuming that its invariants hold.

$$\frac{\text{M} \blacktriangleright \text{C} \qquad \text{is-valid C} \longrightarrow \text{C} = \text{A}}{\text{M} \blacktriangleright \text{A}} \tag{10}$$

3 A Framework for Reasoning about Memory Layouts

Section 2 has identified the memory-related proof obligations arising in Hoare logics and has reduced them to subcover and equality relations between (first-order) covers. However, the challenges from Section 1 remain: in each of these examples, the manipulated memory parts are not directly given in the specified layout; instead, the layout must first be refined and re-interpreted. This section presents a matching framework for general *unfoldings* of memory layouts.

3.1 Unfoldings of Layouts

In the following examples, we use the syntax supported by our Isabelle/HOL implementation: a variable block for x is written «x» and a typed block at p with type t is rendered as «p:t»; «:t» alone denotes type t. Context arguments, rdv, to-ptr, etc. are inserted by translation functions [14, Sec. 8.6].

In the example (2), then, the local variable `inode` points to a record containing a mutex object, while the called function expects the mutex object alone. The required equality in (10) becomes:

«inode» || «inode : struct inode» = «&inode->i_mutex : struct mutex» || ?R

The task is to unfold «inode : struct inode» into the constituent fields to expose the mutex. The examples (3) and (4) do, indeed, not introduce any new complications, because Hoare logic and memory layouts treat heap- and stack-allocated memory objects in the same way. The required equality for (3) is

«t» = «&t.timer : struct hrtimer» || ?R

In the final example (4), the only difference is that the variable `tv` is of type `struct timespec[2]`, i.e. contains an array rather than a struct:

«tv» = «&tv[0]: struct timespec» || ?R

The automated reasoning support must thus be able to re-write memory layouts on the fly. The unfolding rules used in our framework are of the form:

$$\frac{\mathsf{P}_1 \ldots \mathsf{P}_n}{\text{is-valid A} \longrightarrow \mathsf{A} = \mathsf{B}_1 \parallel \cdots \parallel \mathsf{B}_m} \qquad (11)$$

Whenever the premises $\mathsf{P}_1 \ldots \mathsf{P}_n$ hold, the layout A can be refined into layout $\mathsf{B}_1 \parallel \cdots \parallel \mathsf{B}_m$. In the case $m = 1$, the unfolding is, in fact, a re-interpretation of layout block A. Note also how the side-conditions associated with A (Section 2.5) are available during the unfolding — the framework will apply the rule only in corresponding situations. The invariants associated with A therefore need not be repeated in the premises $\mathsf{P}_1 \ldots \mathsf{P}_n$. If a theorem does not depend on the validity of A, it can omit the implication in the conclusion.

As a first example, variables can be re-interpreted as typed blocks by (12). When the program takes the address of a variable, the automated reasoning will apply the theorem correspondingly.

$$\frac{\text{a} = \text{addr-of } \Gamma \text{ v} \qquad \text{t} = \text{type-of } \Gamma \text{ v}}{\text{var-block } \Gamma \text{ v} = \text{typed-block } \Gamma \text{ a t}} \qquad (12)$$

By (13), unfolding rules can also be used to prove subcover relations as needed for allocatedness (7) and disjointness (9) proofs.

$$\frac{\text{is-valid A} \longrightarrow \text{A} = \text{B}}{\text{B} \preceq \text{A}} \tag{13}$$

By reflexivity of the equality and subcover relations and the following theorems, unfoldings can be applied anywhere within a nested layout:

$$\frac{\begin{array}{c}\text{is-valid A} \longrightarrow \text{A} = \text{A'};\\ \text{is-valid B} \longrightarrow \text{B} = \text{B'}\end{array}}{\text{is-valid (A} \parallel \text{B)} \longrightarrow \text{A} \parallel \text{B} = \text{A'} \parallel \text{B'}} \qquad \frac{\text{A} \preceq \text{A'} \quad \text{B} \preceq \text{B'}}{\text{A} \parallel \text{B} \preceq \text{A'} \parallel \text{B'}} \tag{14}$$

In principle, the examples from Section 1 can be solved using the above theorems and the unfolding rules for special data structures from Section 4. For restricted assertion languages, a brute-force unfolding with all possible rules is viable [7]. For first-order (or higher-order) assertions, we develop a two-step proof search. For a given proof obligation $\mathsf{B} \preceq \mathsf{A}$ or is-valid $\mathsf{A} \longrightarrow \mathsf{A} = \mathsf{B}$, it first *locates* all elementary blocks from B in A and then *unfolds* A to expose the blocks B, using the information gathered in the first step during the second.

3.2 Locating Memory Blocks

The proof obligations to be treated have the form $\mathsf{B}_1 \parallel \cdots \parallel \mathsf{B}_m \preceq \mathsf{A}_1 \parallel \cdots \parallel \mathsf{A}_n$ or is-valid$(\mathsf{A}_1 \parallel \cdots \parallel \mathsf{A}_n) \longrightarrow \mathsf{A}_1 \parallel \cdots \parallel \mathsf{A}_n = \mathsf{B}_1 \parallel \cdots \parallel \mathsf{B}_m$. For the proof search, it is useful to consider the blocks $\{\mathsf{B}_1 \ldots \mathsf{B}_m\}$ as a multiset by associativity and commutativity of disjointness. By abuse of notation, we will therefore write $\{\mathsf{B}_1 \ldots \mathsf{B}_m\} \preceq \mathsf{A}$ for layout blocks $\mathsf{B}_1 \ldots \mathsf{B}_m$ and cover A. The location phase enriches this notation further with a justification of the subcover relation. In our Isabelle/HOL implementation of the proof search, this information is kept in ML data structures; for using a first-order prover, it can be encoded in terms.

The justification for a subcover relation $\mathsf{B}_k \preceq \mathsf{A}$ (for $k \in [1, m]$) consists in unfolding A in particular positions. Positions are denoted by *paths* in $(L|R)^*$ (for "left" and "right"; the empty path is ε, concatenation is written $p \cdot q$; the sub-layout of A at p is $A{\downarrow_p}$). Since unfoldings can occur recursively, the enriched notation is:

$$\{(\mathsf{B}_k, p_{k0}, ((u_{k1}, p_{k1}) \ldots (u_{km_k}, p_{km_k})))\}_{k=1}^{m} \preceq \mathsf{A} \tag{15}$$

The reading, to be defined formally in Section 3.3, is: for each k, the block B_k is found inside A by first following path p_{k0}, then applying unfolding rule u_{k1} (using (13)), then following p_{k1}, and proceeding in this manner until all unfoldings and paths have been exhausted. Note that for each application of an unfolding rule u_{kj}, its premises need to be proven (see (11)).

We now show that justifications can be computed efficiently. The central idea is to prepare in advance a set S for subcover justifications of all possible combinations of a given set of unfolding rules. The process starts with the trivial justification $\{(A, \varepsilon, \varepsilon)\} \preceq A$, which captures the reflexivity of the subcover relation. Then, for any $(\{(C, \varepsilon, J)\} \preceq D) \in S$ and unfolding step u of the form (11), where $\sigma C = \sigma A$ for some σ, i.e. C unifies with A, we insert for $k = 1 \ldots m$ into S a new justification

$$\{(\sigma \mathsf{B}_k, \epsilon, ((\sigma u, p_k), \sigma J))\} \preceq \sigma D$$

The application of substitution σ here is defined by its application to all occurring terms and theorems. The path p_k is the path to B_k on the right-hand side in (11). Note that these justifications are sound by lemmata (16).

$$\mathsf{C} \preceq \mathsf{C} \parallel \mathsf{D} \qquad \mathsf{D} \preceq \mathsf{C} \parallel \mathsf{D} \tag{16}$$

If this saturation process terminates with a set S, then by construction $B \preceq A$ can be proven by the given unfolding rules iff there is some path p_0, substitution σ, and justification $(\{(B', \varepsilon, J)\} \preceq A') \in S$ such that $B = \sigma B'$ and $A\downarrow_{p_0} = \sigma A'$. The resulting justification is then $\{(B, p_0, \sigma J)\} \preceq A$.

To solve the proof obligations given at the beginning of this section efficiently, just apply this step to all pairs A_i and B_j. A term index is used to identify possible justifications. The desired result (15) is found.

Remark 1. The generation phase might fail to terminate. This is, in particular, the case for recursive, linked data structures such as lists or trees, whose structural unfoldings can be applied several times in a row. The termination argument for the only approach handling such unfoldings relies on a restricted form of assertions that is not sufficient for full functional verification [7]. We therefore leave the question as future work.

Remark 2. If the unfoldings are not deterministic, a block B_j might be located in A_i by several justifications. (However, by definition of disjointness, it cannot be located in a different $\mathsf{A}_{i'}$.) In the subsequent presentation, we assume that a single justification has been computed; if ambiguities arise, they are resolved by iteration through the possible solutions.

3.3 Computing Unfoldings

The result of the location phase is of the form $\{(\mathsf{B}_k, p_{0k}, J_k)\}_{k=1}^m \preceq \mathsf{A}$: it captures precisely where the $\mathsf{B}_1 \ldots \mathsf{B}_m$ are located inside layout A. To compute the actual unfolding equality, it is sufficient to follow the justifications $\{(p_{0k}, J_k)\}_{k=1}^m$ in a recursive process. We give the process in the form of inference rules for a judgement

$$\{(\mathsf{B}_k, p_{0k}, J_k) | P\, k\} \rightsquigarrow \textsf{is-valid}\ \mathsf{A} \longrightarrow \mathsf{A} = \mathsf{B}$$

where P selects a subset of $[1, m)$ and the result $\textsf{is-valid}\ \mathsf{A} \longrightarrow \mathsf{A} = \mathsf{B}$ is a theorem. The recursion base consists in a single B_k being actually found:

$$\{(\mathsf{B}_k, \varepsilon, \varepsilon)\} \rightsquigarrow \textsf{is-valid}\ \mathsf{B}_k \longrightarrow \mathsf{B}_k = \mathsf{B}_k \tag{17}$$

The first recursion step computes the unfoldings of two disjoint sub-multisets of the B_k using theorem (14).

$$\frac{\begin{array}{l}\{(\mathsf{B}_k, p'_{0k}, J_k) | P\,k \wedge p_{0k} = L \cdot p'_{0k}\} \rightsquigarrow \textsf{is-valid A} \longrightarrow \textsf{A} = \textsf{B} \\ \{(\mathsf{B}_k, p'_{0k}, J_k) | P\,k \wedge p_{0k} = R \cdot p'_{0k}\} \rightsquigarrow \textsf{is-valid A'} \longrightarrow \textsf{A'} = \textsf{B'} \\ \forall k. P\,k \longrightarrow p_{0k} \neq \varepsilon\end{array}}{\{(\mathsf{B}_k, p_{0k}, J_k) | P\,k\} \rightsquigarrow \textsf{is-valid (A} \parallel \textsf{A')} \longrightarrow \textsf{A} \parallel \textsf{A'} = \textsf{B} \parallel \textsf{B'}} \quad (18)$$

Finally, if the paths in the justification have been exhausted, an unfolding takes place. We denote by $u(A)$ the application of the unfolding rule of the form (11) to a term A, which yields the unfolded layout. At this point the premises of step u need to be proven.[2] Note how the local paths p_k become the new paths in the justification.

$$\frac{\{(\mathsf{B}_k, p_k, J_k) | P\,k\} \rightsquigarrow \textsf{is-valid}\ u(\mathsf{A}) \longrightarrow u(\mathsf{A}) = \mathsf{B}}{\{(\mathsf{B}_k, \varepsilon, (u, p_k) \cdot J_k) | P\,k\} \rightsquigarrow \textsf{is-valid A} \longrightarrow \textsf{A} = \textsf{B}} \quad (19)$$

Remark 3. Since (18) and (19) apply only to judgments of specific forms, the completeness of this procedure must be discussed. Consider therefore a justification $\{(\mathsf{B}_k, p_k, J_k) | P\} \preceq A$ where A is a layout block and the B_k can be proven disjoint by the given unfolding rules. If the multiset is a singleton, rule (17) applies. Next, since the blocks B_k can be proven disjoint, either all p_k must be non-empty, in which case (18) applies, or they are all empty. (Otherwise, there would be some k and k' with $\mathsf{B}_{k'} \preceq \mathsf{B}_k$, contradicting disjointness.) In this latter case, (19) applies with some common unfolding rule u, since we can assume that the justifications have been selected correspondingly by Remark 2.

The process of unfolding a memory layout is thus made deterministic by employing the information gathered in the location phase.

3.4 Unfolding On-Demand

The above presentation of the proof search assumes that unfolding rules have the static form (11). This is, however, too restrictive in general: locating a set of array elements and array slices in a given array would require "guessing" a suitable split of the index range in advance (see Section 4.2). The problem is solved by lazy computation of unfoldings. The unfolding rules are used only in two places: to generate the subcover theorems for the location phase by (13) and to compute the unfolding in (19). The first use can be removed if the subcover theorems are given directly. When the unfolding rule is required in (19), more information is available in the form of the proven premises of (11). We therefore apply a standard strategy (e.g. [14, Sec. 10.2.5]): when (19) is applied, an ML function is called with the current judgment. The function returns both the unfolding rule u and the paths p_k for each of the blocks in the left-hand side. Unfoldings in this way are computed lazily, on-demand.

[2] Note that the same premises have been proven during the location phase. In the ML implementation, we keep the proven premises as Isabelle theorems.

4 Applications

The framework from Section 3 supports automatic reasoning about a wide range of unfoldings of memory layouts. In this section, we apply it to examples derived from Section 1 by giving specific unfolding rules. For brevity, we can only show prototypical examples that focus on the main considerations of the paper.

4.1 Struct Types

The layout of a struct type is given with its type definition. It consists of the struct's fields, possibly separated by padding to ensure alignment of the fields' data. Since it can be added straightforwardly, we neglect padding for brevity. Using auxiliary constants field-off and field-ty, which determine the offset and type of a field in a given struct type, we can define a new cover for a single field:

$$\text{field-block}\ \Gamma\ \text{p t f} \equiv \text{typed-block}\ \Gamma\ (\text{p} \oplus (\text{of-nat}\ (\text{field-off}\ \Gamma\ \text{t f})))\ (\text{field-ty}\ \Gamma\ \text{t f})$$

For a list of fields, their joined layout is then given by a recursive function:

$$\begin{aligned} \text{fields-cover}\ \Gamma\ \text{t a}\ [] &= \text{Empty} \\ \text{fields-cover}\ \Gamma\ \text{t a}\ ((\text{f,ty})\ \#\ \text{fs}) &= \text{field-block}\ \Gamma\ \text{a t f}\ \|\ \text{fields-cover}\ \Gamma\ \text{t a fs} \end{aligned}$$

With these preliminary definitions, we can prove a general unfolding theorem for struct types. Its premise captures that type t is a defined struct in the context Γ.

$$\frac{\text{wf-struct}\ \Gamma\ \text{t}}{\text{typed-block}\ \Gamma\ \text{a t} = \text{fields-cover}\ \Gamma\ \text{t a}\ (\text{struct-fields}\ \Gamma\ \text{t})} \tag{20}$$

For a specific struct type such as struct point { int x; int y; }, the special rule (21) can be generated from (20) directly. Here point-known Γ captures, again, that the definition of struct point is present in context Γ.

$$\frac{\text{point-known}\ \Gamma}{\begin{aligned}\text{typed-block}\ \Gamma\ \text{a (struct point)} = {} & \text{field-block}\ \Gamma\ \text{a (struct point) "x"}\ \| \\ & \text{field-block}\ \Gamma\ \text{a (struct point) "y"}\end{aligned}} \tag{21}$$

The re-interpretation of a local variable of struct type as a memory object is given by the unfolding step (12). Together with (21), the challenges of the introductory examples can be solved. Suppose, for instance, a function void set(int *p, int i) sets *p to i. Its precondition requires a layout M ▶ «p : int» ‖ R, the postcondition asserts that *p = i and R is framed, i.e. not modified. We can then verify the following triple automatically (where struct point s; and int i; are local variables; «s.x» is expanded to reading field x from struct variable s).

⊢ { M ▶ «s» ‖ «i» ∧ point-known Γ ∧ P «s. x» i }
 set(&s.y, 1);
 { M ▶ «s» ‖ «i» ∧ point-known Γ ∧ P «s. x» i ∧ «s. y» = 1 }

For the function call, the given layout is unfolded to reveal the field-block for s.y and to show that the remainder R of the memory consists of the field-block for s.x and the local variable i. Note that the higher-order predicate P represents an arbitrary further assertion about s.x and i, independently of its actual structure.

This example covers usage (3) directly. It also shows the simpler usage (2) to be supported, where the variable-block re-interpretation (12) can be omitted.

4.2 Arrays

The unfolding of arrays poses the problem that the necessary refinement of the layout cannot be determined in advance, because it depends on the actual slices and elements that need to be revealed. Unfoldings are therefore computed lazily (Section 3.4) and explicit subcover theorems are used in the location phase:[3] (22) and (23) allow the prover to locate slices and elements, and (27) re-interprets an array element as a typed block, thus enabling access by pointer arithmetic.

$$\frac{\mathsf{i} \leq_s \mathsf{i'} \quad \mathsf{i'} <_s \mathsf{j'} \quad \mathsf{j'} \leq_s \mathsf{j}}{\mathsf{array}\ \Gamma\ \mathsf{t\ a\ i'\ j'} \preceq \mathsf{array}\ \Gamma\ \mathsf{t\ a\ i\ j}} \tag{22}$$

$$\frac{\mathsf{i} \leq_s \mathsf{j} \quad \mathsf{j} <_s \mathsf{k}}{\mathsf{array\text{-}elem}\ \Gamma\ \mathsf{t\ a\ j} \preceq \mathsf{array}\ \Gamma\ \mathsf{t\ a\ i\ k}} \tag{23}$$

$$\frac{\mathsf{p} = \mathsf{a} \oplus [\Gamma,\mathsf{t}]\ \mathsf{j}}{\mathsf{array\text{-}elem}\ \Gamma\ \mathsf{t\ a\ j} = \mathsf{typed\text{-}block}\ \Gamma\ \mathsf{p\ t}} \tag{24}$$

With these rules, the location phase can associate layout blocks with a given array, proving the premises in the process. When the actual unfolding is required, an ML function is called to compute an unfolding rule tailored to the situation. Towards that end, it determines the relative order of the indices from the proven premises and uses the theorems (25) and (26).

$$\frac{\mathsf{i} \leq_s \mathsf{j} \quad \mathsf{j} \leq_s \mathsf{k}}{\mathsf{array}\ \Gamma\ \mathsf{t\ a\ i\ k} = \mathsf{array}\ \Gamma\ \mathsf{t\ a\ i\ j} \parallel \mathsf{array}\ \Gamma\ \mathsf{t\ a\ j\ k}} \tag{25}$$

$$\mathsf{is\text{-}valid}(\mathsf{array}\ \Gamma\ \mathsf{t\ a\ j\ (j{+}1)}) \longrightarrow \mathsf{array}\ \Gamma\ \mathsf{t\ a\ j\ (j{+}1)} = \mathsf{array\text{-}elem}\ \Gamma\ \mathsf{t\ a\ j} \tag{26}$$

Theorem (26) is of particular interest, because it crucially uses the invariants associated with the single-element array. An array element is simply a typed-block (see (24)) which does not contain all invariants of arrays (Section 2.2).

Arrays in local variables, which have type Array t n with constant size n and element type t, are found by the following rule (27), which is applied after (12).

$$\mathsf{is\text{-}valid}\ (\mathsf{typed\text{-}block}\ \Gamma\ \mathsf{a}\ (\mathsf{Array\ t\ n})) \longrightarrow \mathsf{typed\text{-}block}\ \Gamma\ \mathsf{a}\ (\mathsf{Array\ t\ n}) = \mathsf{array}\ \Gamma\ \mathsf{t\ a\ 0\ n} \tag{27}$$

Again, this unfolding relies on the validity of the typed block to establish the side-conditions of the array from the well-formedness of the Array type.

With these unfoldings, the last introductory challenge (4) can be resolved. Here, a local variable int a[16]; is allocated and some assertion about its first i elements is given. It can is then proven automatically that setting a[i] does not influence that assertion, as stated in the following triple.

$$\begin{array}{l} \vdash \{\mathsf{M} \blacktriangleright «\mathsf{i}» \parallel «\mathsf{a}» \wedge 0 \leq_s \mathsf{i} \wedge \mathsf{i} <_s 16 \wedge (\forall\, \mathsf{k}. 0 \leq_s \mathsf{k} \wedge \mathsf{k} <_s \mathsf{i} \longrightarrow «\mathsf{a[k]}» = 0)\} \\ \quad \mathsf{a[i]} = 1; \\ \quad \{\mathsf{M} \blacktriangleright «\mathsf{i}» \parallel «\mathsf{a}» \wedge 0 \leq_s \mathsf{i} \wedge \mathsf{i} <_s 16 \wedge (\forall\, \mathsf{k}. 0 \leq_s \mathsf{k} \wedge \mathsf{k} <_s \mathsf{i} \longrightarrow «\mathsf{a[k]}» = 0)\} \end{array}$$

This example shows also that our method goes beyond automated fragments of separation logic [7,15] in handling local assumptions on quantified variables.

[3] The implementation never applies the same rule twice in a row, which prevents non-termination with (22).

A final example demonstrates the flexibility of the presented framework. Suppose the function void memcpy(char *src, char *dst, int n) copies memory byte-wise. Its precondition demands that the source and destination arrays are allocated:

$$\mathsf{M} \blacktriangleright \mathsf{array}\ \Gamma\ «\mathsf{:char}»\ \mathsf{src}\ 0\ \mathsf{n}\ \|\ \mathsf{array}\ \Gamma\ «\mathsf{:char}»\ \mathsf{dst}\ 0\ \mathsf{n}\ \|\ \mathsf{R}$$

Its post-condition asserts the same layout, that the elements of src have been copied to dst, and that only the dst array has been modified, such that any assertions about src and R continue to hold.

$$\begin{array}{l} \mathsf{M} \blacktriangleright \mathsf{array}\ \Gamma\ «\mathsf{:char}»\ \mathsf{src}\ 0\ \mathsf{n}\ \|\ \mathsf{array}\ \Gamma\ «\mathsf{:char}»\ \mathsf{dst}\ 0\ \mathsf{n}\ \|\ \mathsf{R}\ \wedge \\ \quad \mathsf{array\text{-}elems}\ \Gamma\ «\mathsf{:char}»\ \mathsf{src}\ 0\ \mathsf{n}\ \mathsf{M} = \mathsf{array\text{-}elems}\ \Gamma\ «\mathsf{:char}»\ \mathsf{dst}\ 0\ \mathsf{n}\ \mathsf{M}\ \wedge \\ \quad \mathsf{frame}\ (\mathsf{R}\ \|\ \mathsf{array}\ \Gamma\ «\mathsf{:char}»\ \mathsf{src}\ 0\ \mathsf{n})\ \mathsf{M0}\ \mathsf{M} \end{array}$$

Then, we can implement a low-level string concatenation. We prove the following triple in a variable context int m; int n; char *a; char *b; char *dst;.

$$\begin{array}{l} \vdash \{\ \mathsf{M} \blacktriangleright «\mathsf{a}» \ \|\ «\mathsf{n}» \ \|\ «\mathsf{b}» \ \|\ «\mathsf{m}» \ \|\ «\mathsf{dst}» \ \| \\ \qquad \mathsf{array}\ \Gamma\ «\mathsf{:char}»\ \mathsf{a}\ 0\ \mathsf{n}\ \|\ \mathsf{array}\ \Gamma\ «\mathsf{:char}»\ \mathsf{b}\ 0\ \mathsf{m}\ \|\ \mathsf{array}\ \Gamma\ «\mathsf{:char}»\ \mathsf{dst}\ 0\ (\mathsf{n}+\mathsf{m})\ \wedge \\ \quad\ \ \mathsf{array\text{-}elems}\ \Gamma\ «\mathsf{:char}»\ \mathsf{a}\ 0\ \mathsf{n}\ \mathsf{M} = \mathsf{A}\ \wedge\ \mathsf{array\text{-}elems}\ \Gamma\ «\mathsf{:char}»\ \mathsf{b}\ 0\ \mathsf{m}\ \mathsf{M} = \mathsf{B}\ \} \\ \quad \mathsf{memcpy(a,dst,n);} \\ \quad \mathsf{memcpy(b,dst + n,m);} \\ \ \ \{\ \mathsf{array\text{-}elems}\ \Gamma\ «\mathsf{:char}»\ \mathsf{dst}\ 0\ (\mathsf{n}+\mathsf{m})\ \mathsf{M} = (\mathsf{A}\ @\ \mathsf{B})\ \} \end{array}$$

In the second call, the precondition of memcpy mentions an array starting at index 0, while the actual argument is a slice starting at n. The re-interpretation (28) shifts a given array slice to begin at index 0.

$$\frac{\mathsf{b} = \mathsf{a} \oplus [\Gamma,\mathsf{t}]\ \mathsf{i} \qquad \mathsf{m} = \mathsf{n}\ \text{-}\ \mathsf{i}}{\mathsf{is\text{-}valid}\ (\mathsf{array}\ \Gamma\ \mathsf{t}\ \mathsf{a}\ \mathsf{i}\ \mathsf{n}) \longrightarrow \mathsf{array}\ \Gamma\ \mathsf{t}\ \mathsf{a}\ \mathsf{i}\ \mathsf{n} = \mathsf{array}\ \Gamma\ \mathsf{t}\ \mathsf{b}\ 0\ \mathsf{m}} \tag{28}$$

5 Related Work

The problem of proving the disjointness of memory regions has recently attracted much attention in connection with the verification of object-oriented programs. Kassios [16] proposes to express the memory region occupied by an object's representation as an additional specification variable. The disjointness of the regions, hence the independence of assertions from particular memory operations, can then be asserted without breaking encapsulation. The approach has been implemented by several authors [3,1]. The work addresses Burstall's memory model and uses direct pointer comparisons throughout. It does therefore not scale directly to more low-level memory models. Greve [17] proposes to express the memory region occupied by data structures by functions with the intention of proving disjointness of modified memory regions. Neither of these approaches addresses the problems of re-interpretation and structural refinement of memory layouts beyond the field-level access encompassed by Burstall's model.

Automatic unfoldings of memory layouts are supported by the Smallfoot [7] tool. It is based on a restricted form of separation logic that is suitable for expressing shape invariants of data structures. Recently, Tuerk [15] has shown that some assertions of the content of data structures can be be handled in parallel with their structure. The unfolding mechanism in both works relies on the fact that all assertions give rise to finitely many unfoldings, such that an undirected search is possible. Tuerk uses [18] to cover call-by-reference with entire local variables, but not with more general memory objects.

Tuch [10] applies separation logic to structured data types. In particular, he develops a theory for struct types in C. The automatic reasoning provided is limited: a specialized tactic allows the user to fold and unfold struct definitions as needed. Neither arrays nor references to local variables are supported. Cohen et al. [13] establish a typed memory model over untyped C memory states by expressing the additional disjointness invariants using a ghost variable. Special statements `split` and `join` in the language serve to manipulate the layout. The approach handles structs and is extensible to bit-fields and arrays. The frame inference problem for functions is not discussed.

6 Conclusion

We have presented a method for automatic reasoning about memory layouts in a flexible and extensible manner. A small language of layouts allows memory-related proof obligations arising in Hoare logics to be formulated succinctly. The actual elements of layouts are not fixed, but can be defined as needed: local variables, blocks accessed by pointers, structs, and arrays are readily formalized. Our reasoning framework supports a general notion of unfoldings of memory elements. Unfoldings comprise both structural refinements and re-interpretations of layout blocks. Structs and arrays can thus be split automatically into their constituent elements as needed, and local variables can be interpreted as memory objects, which allows them to be accessed by pointers in arbitrary ways. Introducing a new unfolding generally requires nothing more than proving an unfolding equality theorem about a cover constant. Using the flexibility, it is possible to verify idiomatic usages of C that are not currently covered by other verification methodologies.

The presented method is suitable for reasoning about a low-level, byte-addressed memory model. The key insight is to encode invariants about memory layouts into the definition of layout constants, and to propagate the invariants through unfoldings. As an illustration, the theory reduces reasoning about arrays to proving inequalities between indices without further side-conditions; overflows in the address arithmetic are excluded by the invariants associated with arrays.

Three future directions of the work appear promising. The first one is to apply standard first-order reasoners rather than specialized ML tactics. Even though the theory is developed in Isabelle/HOL to ensure soundness, first-order theorems are sufficient for the actual verification. A second direction is the verification of low-level programs using pointer-casts. The re-interpretations necessary when using casts can be expressed as unfolding theorems handled by the framework. Finally, the developed logic of memory layouts is largely independent of the employed Hoare logic. It would therefore be interesting to integrate the reasoning with an existing verification condition generator.

References

1. Smans, J., Jacobs, B., Piessens, F., Schulte, W.: An automatic verifier for Java-like programs based on dynamic frames. In: Fiadeiro, J.L., Inverardi, P. (eds.) FASE 2008. LNCS, vol. 4961, pp. 261–275. Springer, Heidelberg (2008)
2. Filliâtre, J.C., Marché, C.: The Why/Krakatoa/Caduceus platform for deductive program verification. In: Damm, W., Hermanns, H. (eds.) CAV 2007. LNCS, vol. 4590, pp. 173–177. Springer, Heidelberg (2007)
3. Banerjee, A., Barnett, M., Naumann, D.A.: Boogie Meets Regions: A Verification Experience Report. In: Shankar, N., Woodcock, J. (eds.) VSTTE 2008. LNCS, vol. 5295, pp. 177–191. Springer, Heidelberg (2008)
4. Rakamarić, Z., Hu, A.J.: A scalable memory model for low-level code. In: Jones, N.D., Müller-Olm, M. (eds.) VMCAI 2009. LNCS, vol. 5403, pp. 290–304. Springer, Heidelberg (2009)
5. O'Hearn, P.W., Reynolds, J.C., Yang, H.: Local reasoning about programs that alter data structures. In: Fribourg, L. (ed.) CSL 2001 and EACSL 2001. LNCS, vol. 2142, pp. 1–19. Springer, Heidelberg (2001)
6. Gast, H.: Lightweight separation. In: Mohamed, O.A., Muñoz, C., Tahar, S. (eds.) TPHOLs 2008. LNCS, vol. 5170, pp. 199–214. Springer, Heidelberg (2008)
7. Berdine, J., Calcagno, C., O'Hearn, P.W.: Smallfoot: Modular automatic assertion checking with separation logic. In: de Boer, F.S., Bonsangue, M.M., Graf, S., de Roever, W.-P. (eds.) FMCO 2005. LNCS, vol. 4111, pp. 115–137. Springer, Heidelberg (2006)
8. Norrish, M.: C formalised in HOL. PhD thesis, University of Cambridge, Technical Report UCAM-CL-TR-453 (1998)
9. Dawson, J.E.: Isabelle theories for machine words. In: Seventh International Workshop on Automated Verification of Critical Systems (AVOCS 2007). ENTCS (2007)
10. Tuch, H.: Structured types and separation logic. In: 3rd International Workshop on Systems Software Verification, SSV (2008)
11. Schirmer, N.: Verification of Sequential Imperative Programs in Isabelle/HOL. PhD thesis, Technische Universität München (2005)
12. Kowaltowski, T.: Axiomatic aproach to side effects and general jumps. Acta Informatica 7, 357–360 (1977)
13. Cohen, E., Moskal, M., Schulte, W., Tobies, S.: A precise yet efficient memory model for C. In: 4th International Workshop on Systems Software Verification (SSV). ENTCS (2009)
14. Paulson, L.C.: Isabelle – A Generic Theorem Prover. LNCS, vol. 828. Springer, Heidelberg (1994)
15. Tuerk, T.: A formalisation of Smallfoot in HOL. In: Berghofer, S., et al. (eds.) TPHOLs 2009. LNCS, vol. 5674, pp. 465–484. Springer, Heidelberg (2009)
16. Kassios, I.T.: Dynamic frames: Support for framing, dependencies and sharing without restrictions. In: Misra, J., Nipkow, T., Sekerinski, E. (eds.) FM 2006. LNCS, vol. 4085, pp. 268–283. Springer, Heidelberg (2006)
17. Greve, D.: Scalable normalization for heap manipulating functions. In: International Workshop on the ACL2 Theorem Prover and its Applications (2007)
18. Parkinson, M., Bornat, R., Calcagno, C.: Variables as resource in Hoare logics. In: LICS 2006: Proceedings of the 21st Annual IEEE Symposium on Logic in Computer Science, Washington, DC, USA, pp. 137–146. IEEE Computer Society, Los Alamitos (2006)

A Smooth Combination of Linear and Herbrand Equalities for Polynomial Time Must-Alias Analysis

Helmut Seidl[1], Vesal Vojdani[1,*], and Varmo Vene[2,*]

[1] Lehrstuhl für Informatik II, Technische Universität München
Boltzmannstraße 3, D-85748 Garching b. München, Germany
{seidl,vojdanig}@in.tum.de
[2] Deptartment of Computer Science, University of Tartu,
J. Liivi 2, EE-50409 Tartu, Estonia
varmo@cs.ut.ee

Abstract. We present a new domain for analyzing *must*-equalities between address expressions. The domain is a smooth combination of Herbrand and affine equalities which enables us to describe field accesses and array indexing. While the full combination of uninterpreted functions with affine arithmetics results in intractable assertion checking algorithms, our restricted domain allows us to construct an analysis of address *must*-equalities that runs in polynomial time. We indicate how this analysis can be applied to infer access patterns in programs manipulating arrays and structs.

1 Introduction

Consistent correlations between memory locations used by a program lies at the heart of many safety properties. In order to verify absence of data races in multi-threaded programs, accesses to memory locations need to be correlated with locks that guard them. In a language with pointer variables, correlating address expressions requires knowing when two expressions *must* alias, i.e., evaluate to the same memory location. In general, techniques for verifying the correct use of interface methods (e.g., [1]) can be refined with must-alias information to check that calls in a syntactically correct sequence consistently refer to the right data elements: a sequence such as $\mathsf{open}(e_1)$; ...; $\mathsf{close}(e_2)$; e.g., should access the same file handle when referring to the address expressions e_1 and e_2.

More recently, program-specific correlations have been studied: the length of a list is, perhaps, maintained in a separate variable which is thus semantically correlated. Lu et al. [11] apply statistical techniques to detect plausible multi-variable correlations of this kind. Their methods, although successful in detecting real bugs, are flow-insensitive and essentially syntactic; hence not ideal for formal verification. As the precise control flow as well as equalities between variables in

* Partially supported by the Estonian Science Foundation under grant no. 6713.

A. Cavalcanti and D. Dams (Eds.): FM 2009, LNCS 5850, pp. 644–659, 2009.

the program are ignored, syntactically similar expressions may not represent the same *semantic* correlation, while syntactically different expressions could very well be correlated. In order to enable sound inference of semantic correlations between addresses, we propose a novel analysis of *must-equalities*.

Our analysis is able to interprocedurally relate address expressions which use array indexing and field selection in structs. An access to a nested struct consists in the base address of the data element followed by sequences of selectors, such as $A.person.name$. Two such expressions are definitely equivalent if they are *textually identical*. This corresponds to the *Herbrand* interpretation of the binary operator "." and the selector labels. In order to deal with arrays as well, we enhance this base domain by affine expressions for indexed accesses. Two index expressions are equivalent iff they are equivalent w.r.t. the *arithmetic interpretation*. We show that the resulting combination of theories allows to infer *all* valid address equalities in polynomial time.

This is in stark contrast to previous work on assertion checking over the domains of uninterpreted functions and linear arithmetic. Detecting affine equalities in programs was pioneered by Karr [9]. This algorithm was extended to the inter-procedural case by Müller-Olm and Seidl [13]. A long line of research has provided methods for intra-procedurally detecting Herbrand equalities precisely [3, 10, 12, 22] — while the inter-procedural case still remains unsolved. A precise analysis algorithm is known for *functions* without side effects [16] and for arbitrary procedures if only unary operator symbols are considered [6].

When it comes to combining affine and Herbrand equalities, the basic approach is inspired by methods of combining decision procedures [18]. However, Gulwani and Tiwari [4] have shown that assertion checking over the full combined domain is coNP-hard. Hence, they subsequently present a highly expressive domain that allows sound analysis of pointer arithmetic and recursive data-structures in the style of Deutsch [2], but their algorithm is no longer complete w.r.t. their chosen abstraction [5]. Our domain construction, based on a sufficiently restricted subclass of Herbrand terms carefully enhanced with fragments of linear arithmetic, enables sound and complete analysis in polynomial time.

2 The Programming Model

One key abstraction on which our method relies is that we only track the values of **int** variables and pointers. Thus, we ignore the values stored in arrays or structs. To simplify our setting, we make the additional assumption that the tracked variables themselves are never accessed indirectly through pointers; a common coding practice when developing safety-critical code [8]. Programs to be analyzed are modeled by systems of flow graphs as in Figure 1.

Let $\mathbf{X} = \{\mathbf{x}_1, \ldots, \mathbf{x}_k\}$ denote the set of **int**-variables and $\mathbf{A} = \{\mathbf{a}_1, \ldots, \mathbf{a}_m\}$ the set of pointer variables used by the program. For the moment, we assume all variables to be global, but we will present methods for local variables in Section 7. In addition, we assume that we are given a set of names $\mathcal{C}$ denoting the global static data-structures of the program. Each of these data-structures is built up

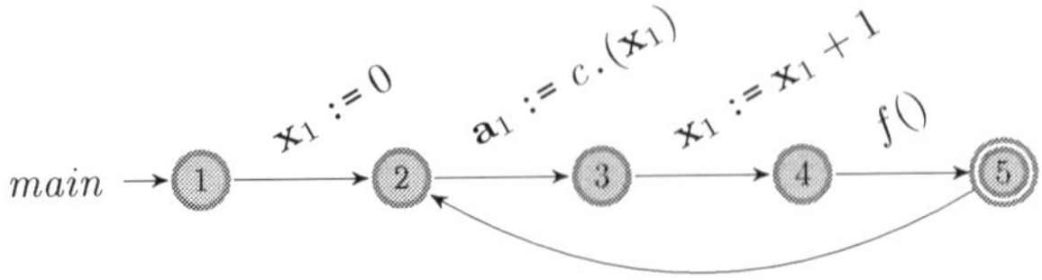

Fig. 1. Example flow-graph for a *main*-function

by forming structs and arrays from a set of base types, such as **int**, **float** or **mutex**. In the presence of dynamic memory allocation, we infer must-equality relationships between pointer variables while also relying on may-alias pointer analysis, as further explained in Section 8; until then, we only deal with static data structures.

As we are only interested in assignments to integer and pointer variables, the set of statements Stmt at edges of programs in our model consists of:

- Affine assignments of the form $\mathbf{x}_j := t_0 + \sum_{i=1}^{k} t_i\mathbf{x}_i$ (with $t_i \in \mathbb{Z}$ and $\mathbf{x}_i \in \mathbf{X}$).
- Address assignments of the form $\mathbf{a}_j := adr$ where adr is an address expression possibly involving variables from $\mathbf{X}$ and $\mathbf{A}$ in a way we will specify below.
- Non-deterministic assignments, $\mathbf{x}_j := ?$ and $\mathbf{a}_j := ?$, which are used to abstract assignments that our analysis cannot handle.

With $\mathcal{C}$ denoting the set of global variable names, an address expressions adr is constructed from constants $B \in \mathcal{C}$ and address variables $\mathbf{a}_i$ according to the grammar:

$$adr \ ::= \ B \mid \mathbf{a}_i \mid adr\,.\,b \mid adr\,.\,(l)$$

where b is a field selector and l is an index expression of the form $l \equiv t_0 + t_1\mathbf{x}_1 + \ldots + t_1\mathbf{x}_k$. We assume that address expressions are *well-typed*. In particular, a selector b can only be applied to an address expression denoting a pointer to a struct with component b; likewise, only a pointer to an array can be indexed.

A *program* comprises a finite set Proc of *procedure names*. Execution starts with a call to the distinguished procedure $main \in$ Proc. Each procedure $q \in$ Proc is given through a *control flow graph* $G_q = (N_q, E_q, e_q, r_q)$ which consists of a set N_q of *program points*; a set of edges $E_q \subseteq N_q \times (\mathsf{Stmt} \cup \mathsf{Proc}) \times N_q$ annotated with assignments or procedure calls; a special *entry point* $e_q \in N_q$; and a special *return point* $r_q \in N_q$. We assume here that the program points of different procedures are disjoint.

Every address pointing somewhere into the global data-structures can be uniquely represented by an expression $B.s_1.\ldots.s_r$ where B is the base address of a global data-structure and each s_i is either a field selector or an array index in $\mathbb{Z}$. Since we consider addresses in fixed global data-structures only, the length r is bounded by some global constant d. Let $\mathcal{A}$ denote the set of all these addresses. Since we ignore the values stored in the global data-structures, a program state can be represented by a pair $\langle x, a\rangle$ where $x \in \mathbb{Z}^k$ and $a \in \mathcal{A}^m$ describe the values of the **int** variables and the address variables, respectively. We denote the set of all states by $\mathbb{S} = \mathbb{Z}^k \times \mathcal{A}^m$. Throughout this paper, we use k and m to denote the number of the (global) integer and address variables, and we use d to denote the maximal depth of data structures!

For an affine combination $t = t_0 + t_1\mathbf{x}_1 + \ldots + t_k\mathbf{x}_k$ and a state $\sigma = \langle x, a\rangle$, we write $[\![t]\!]\sigma$ for the value $t_0 + t_1x_1 + \ldots + t_kx_k \in \mathbb{Z}$. Likewise, for an address expression *adr* we write $[\![adr]\!]\sigma$ to denote the address obtained from *adr* by *substituting* the address variables in *adr* (if there are any) with their values in σ and by *evaluating* all affine index expressions w.r.t. the values of the **int**-variables in σ. Thus, the semantics of assignments for *sets* of states S is defined by:

$$[\![\mathbf{x}_j := t]\!]S = \{\langle (x_1, \ldots, x_{j-1}, [\![t]\!]\langle x, a\rangle, x_{j+1}, \ldots, x_k), a\rangle \mid \langle x, a\rangle \in S\} \qquad (1)$$
$$[\![\mathbf{x}_j :=?]\!]S = \{\langle (x_1, \ldots, x_{j-1}, z, x_{j+1}, \ldots, x_k), a\rangle \mid \langle x, a\rangle \in S, z \in \mathbb{Z}\} \qquad (2)$$

$$[\![\mathbf{a}_j := adr]\!]S = \{\langle x, (a_1, \ldots, a_{j-1}, [\![adr]\!]\langle x, a\rangle, a_{j+1}, \ldots, a_k)\rangle \mid \langle x, a\rangle \in S\} \quad (3)$$
$$[\![\mathbf{a}_j :=?]\!]S = \{\big\langle x, (a_1, \ldots, a_{j-1}, a'_j, a_{j+1} \ldots, a_k)\big\rangle \mid \langle x, a\rangle \in S, \quad (4)$$
$$a'_j \in \mathcal{A} \text{ of appropriate type}\}$$

Every program execution π can be considered as a transformation $[\![\pi]\!] : 2^{\mathbb{S}} \to 2^{\mathbb{S}}$ of the set of states before the execution into the set of states after the execution. Here, we find it convenient to define the semantics as the transformation $\mathbf{R}[u] : 2^{\mathbb{S}} \to 2^{\mathbb{S}}$ that describes which program states can be attained at program point u when program execution starts in a given set of states. Given the transformation $\mathbf{R}[u]$, we can recover the *collecting semantics* of u, i.e., the set of all program states possibly attained during program execution when reaching u, as the set $\mathbf{R}[u](\mathbb{S})$.

In order to define the transformations $\mathbf{R}$, we additionally consider for every procedure q, the transformation of a set of program states before a call to q into the set of program states after the call. In order to determine this transformation, we introduce for every program point u of q, the auxiliary transformation $\mathbf{S}[u]$ which collects the transformation induced by the executions from u to the end point r_q of q at the same level, i.e., all recursive calls on its path towards the end of the procedure have returned. Then, the transformation of q is given by $\mathbf{S}[e_q]$ for the start point e_q of q, and we have:

[S1]	$\mathbf{S}[r_q]$	$\supseteq \mathsf{Id}$	
[S2]	$\mathbf{S}[u]$	$\supseteq \mathbf{S}[v] \circ [\![s]\!]$	if (u, s, v) is an assignment edge
[S3]	$\mathbf{S}[u]$	$\supseteq \mathbf{S}[v] \circ \mathbf{S}[e_q]$	if (u, q, v) is a call edge

[R0]	$\mathbf{R}[e_{main}]$	$\supseteq \mathsf{Id}$	
[R1]	$\mathbf{R}[e_q]$	$\supseteq \mathbf{R}[u]$	if $(u, q, \_)$ is a call edge
[R2]	$\mathbf{R}[v]$	$\supseteq [\![s]\!] \circ \mathbf{R}[u]$	if (u, s, v) is an assignment edge
[R3]	$\mathbf{R}[v]$	$\supseteq \mathbf{S}[e_q] \circ \mathbf{R}[u]$	if (u, q, v) is a call edge

Here, the ordering "$\supseteq$" on transformers $f, g : 2^{\mathbb{S}} \to 2^{\mathbb{S}}$ is defined by $f \supseteq g$ iff for every set of states S, $f(S) \supseteq g(S)$.

3 Address Equalities

Our goal is to detect equalities between address expressions. In order to do so, we additionally need to track affine equalities between **int** variables. An affine equality is an assertion $t_0 + t_1\mathbf{x}_1 + \ldots + t_k\mathbf{x}_k \doteq 0$ for $t_0, \ldots, t_k \in \mathbb{Q}$. An address equality is an assertion of the form: $adr \doteq adr'$ of address expressions adr, adr'. Here, "$\doteq$" serves as a formal equality symbol. A program state σ *satisfies* the affine equality $t \doteq 0$ iff the left-hand side evaluates to zero: $[\![t]\!]\sigma = 0$. Likewise, the state σ satisfies the address equality $adr \doteq adr'$ iff $[\![adr]\!]\sigma = [\![adr']\!]\sigma$. This means that we consider the Herbrand interpretation for the operator "." as well as for base addresses and field selectors, but use an arithmetic interpretation for index expressions. The latter allows us to identify semantically equal index expressions, such as $\mathbf{x}_1 + 5 + 2\mathbf{x}_1$ and $5 + 3\mathbf{x}_1$.

The state σ satisfies a finite conjunction E of affine and address equalities iff σ satisfies every equality in E. In this case, we write $\sigma \models E$. Likewise for a set S of states, we write $S \models E$ iff $\sigma \models E$ for all $\sigma \in S$. The conjunction E is *valid* at a program point u, if E is satisfied by all states possible at u, i.e., $\mathbf{R}[u] \models E$.

Example 1. In the program from Figure 1, we are interested in the equalities which hold at program point 4. The set of states possible at this point is given by $\mathbf{R}[4] = \{\langle n, c\,.\,(n-1)\rangle \mid n > 0\}$, and thus the equality $\mathbf{a}_1 \doteq c\,.\,(-1 + \mathbf{x}_1)$ is valid at this program point. □

Given this notion of satisfiability, we say that a conjunction of equalities E implies another conjunction of equalities E', iff for all states $\sigma \in \mathbb{S}$, $\sigma \models E$ implies $\sigma \models E'$. Thus, the conjunctions of address and affine equalities can be ordered by implication "$\Rightarrow$". The greatest element $\top$ w.r.t. this ordering is the empty conjunction or true, as it is satisfied by all states. The bottom element $\bot$ in the ordering is false, denoting an unsatisfiable conjunction of equalities.

Consider a finite conjunction E with affine equalities $t_{i0} + t_{i1}\mathbf{x}_1 + \ldots + t_{ik}\mathbf{x}_k \doteq 0$, $i = 1, \ldots, h$. Assume that the conjunction E is satisfiable. Then, we say that it is in *canonical form* iff the following conditions are satisfied:

1. the affine equalities — more precisely, the corresponding coefficient matrix (t_{ij}) — is in row echelon form;[1]
2. the left-hand sides in the address equalities of E are pairwise distinct variables; and
3. no variable that is on the left-hand side of an address equality in E occurs in any of the right-hand sides.

By these restrictions, any conjunction in canonical form comprises at most k affine equalities as well as at most m address equalities.

Example 2. Take the conjunction $(\mathbf{a}_1\,.\,d \doteq c\,.\,(2\mathbf{x}_1)\,.\,d) \wedge (\mathbf{a}_1\,.\,m \doteq c\,.\,(\mathbf{x}_1)\,.\,m)$. An equivalent conjunction in canonical form is $(\mathbf{a}_1 \doteq c\,.\,(2\mathbf{x}_1)) \wedge (\mathbf{x}_1 \doteq 0)$. □

[1] A matrix is said to be in row echelon form if all zero rows are at the bottom, the leading entry of each non-zero row except the first occurs to the right of the leading entry of the previous row, and the leading entry of any non-zero row is 1.

Lemma 1. *For every finite conjunction of equalities E, a finite conjunction in canonical form which is equivalent to E can be constructed in polynomial time.*

Proof. Assume that the conjunction is of the form $E = E_a \wedge E_x$ where E_a is a conjunction of address equalities and E_x is a conjunction of affine equalities. We proceed in three steps. First, we replace every index expression t occurring in the conjunction E_a with the expression $\mathbf{x}_t$ for a fresh variable $\mathbf{x}_t$. Let E'_a denote the resulting conjunction of address equalities.

In the second step, we compute a most general unifier σ for E'_a w.r.t. the Herbrand interpretation. If unification succeeds, then due to the specific form of address expressions, the substitution σ will map each auxiliary variable $\mathbf{x}_t$ either to a field selector or to another auxiliary variable $\mathbf{x}_{t'}$. If there exists an $\mathbf{x}_t$, such that $\sigma(\mathbf{x}_t)$ is a field selector, then the conjunctions are inconsistent and the whole conjunction is equivalent to false.

Otherwise, let E'_x denote the conjunction of all equalities $t_1 - t_2 \doteq 0$ for which the corresponding auxiliaries $\mathbf{x}_{t_i}$ were unified, i.e., $\sigma(\mathbf{x}_{t_1}) = \sigma(\mathbf{x}_{t_2})$. Then E_a is equivalent to the conjunction of E'_x with $E''_a = \bigwedge_i (\mathbf{a}_i \doteq adr_i)$ where the address expressions adr_i are obtained from $\sigma(\mathbf{a}_i)$ by substituting back the affine index expressions t for the auxiliary variables $\mathbf{x}_t$.

Thus, a canonical form of the conjunction E is given by $E''_a \wedge E''_x$, where E''_x is the echelon form for the conjunction $E_x \wedge E'_x$. Using a linear unification algorithm [19] for computing σ, we conclude that the canonical form of E can be computed in time $\mathcal{O}((|E_x| + |E'_x|) \cdot k^2) = \mathcal{O}((s + r \cdot d) \cdot k^2)$ if E consists of s affine equalities and r address equalities. □

Note that we give the complexity estimates in this paper under the uniform cost measure, i.e., we assume a constant cost for arithmetic operations.

Lemma 2. *Assume E is a satisfiable conjunction of equalities in canonical form with k* **int***-variables, and addresses of length at most d. Then the following holds:*

1. *For every affine combination t, $E \Rightarrow (t \doteq 0)$ can be decided in time $\mathcal{O}(k^2)$.*
2. *For every address expression adr, $E \Rightarrow (\mathbf{a}_i \doteq adr)$ can be decided in time $\mathcal{O}(d \cdot k^2)$.*

Proof. As the first statement is immediate from linear algebra, we only prove the second. Let us assume that $adr \equiv A.s_1.\dots.s_h$, i.e., adr does not contain an address variable. Then the implication holds iff E contains an equality $\mathbf{a}_i \doteq A.s'_1.\dots.s'_h$, and for each $\lambda = 1, \dots, h$, the access expressions s_λ and s'_λ are equal under E: either both s_λ and s'_λ are field selectors and identical, or both s_λ and s'_λ are index expressions and $E \Rightarrow (s_\lambda - s'_\lambda \doteq 0)$.

Now assume that $adr \equiv \mathbf{a}_j.s_1.\dots.s_h$ for some address variable $\mathbf{a}_j$. Unless $adr \equiv \mathbf{a}_i$, the implication can only hold if E also contains an equality for $\mathbf{a}_i$. Moreover, this equality is of the form $\mathbf{a}_i \doteq a.s'_1.\dots.s'_{h+l}$ for some $l \geq 0$ where a is either an address constant A or an address variable $\mathbf{a}_r$. Then the implication holds iff E also contains an equality $\mathbf{a}_j \doteq a.s''_1.\dots.s''_l$ where for $\lambda = 1, \dots, l$, the accesses s'_λ and s''_λ are equal under E, and for $\lambda = l+1, \dots, h$, the accesses s'_λ and

$s_{\lambda-l}$ are equal under E. Assuming that the address equality in E for particular address variables can be retrieved in constant time, at most d affine equalities must be checked for subsumption by E — giving us the stated complexity bound. $\square$

Thus, both logical implication and equivalence between satisfiable conjunctions E, E' in canonical form can be decided in time $\mathcal{O}((m^2 \cdot d + k) \cdot k^2)$.

Let $\mathbb{E}$ denote the set of equivalence classes of finite conjunctions ordered by implication. The greatest lower bound of (the equivalence classes of) two conjunctions $E, E' \in \mathbb{E}$ is (the equivalence class containing) the conjunction of all the equalities in E and E'. The partial order $\mathbb{E}$ thus is a complete lattice — given that all descending chains are finite.

Corollary 1. *Every chain $E_0 \Rightarrow \ldots \Rightarrow E_p$ of pairwise inequivalent conjunctions E_j using k* **int** *variables and m address variables has length $p \leq m + k + 1$.*

This follows because any two inequivalent conjunctions E_i and E_j have counterparts in canonical form, E'_i and E'_j, respectively. The implication $E'_i \Rightarrow E'_j$ can only hold, if E'_i contains strictly more equalities than E'_j. Therefore, all chains in the lattice will eventually stabilize after at most $m + k + 1$ steps.

In summary, we have proven that the set of equivalence classes of conjunctions of address equalities ordered with implication $(\mathbb{E}, \Rightarrow)$ is a complete lattice.

4 Weakest Pre-conditions

Our approach to computing all valid equalities is based on an effective weakest pre-condition computation. For a conjunction of equalities E, the weakest pre-condition for an assignment and a non-deterministic assignment is given by substitution and universal quantification, respectively:

$$[\![\mathbf{x}_i := t]\!]^\top(E) = E[t/\mathbf{x}_i] \qquad [\![\mathbf{a}_i := a]\!]^\top(E) = E[a/\mathbf{a}_i]$$
$$[\![\mathbf{x}_i := ?]\!]^\top(E) = \forall\, \mathbf{x}_i.\, E \qquad [\![\mathbf{a}_i := ?]\!]^\top(E) = \forall\, \mathbf{a}_i.\, E$$

While our domain is closed under substitution, it does not directly support universal quantification. We are rescued by the fact that in the sub-domain of linear arithmetic, determining the weakest pre-condition for a non-deterministic assignment to an **int** variable $\mathbf{x}_i$, it suffices to consider the conjunction of the weakest pre-conditions of the assignments $\mathbf{x}_i := 0$ and $\mathbf{x}_i := 1$ [13]. On the other hand, $\forall\, \mathbf{a}_i.\, E$ for a conjunction E in canonical form involving the address variable $\mathbf{a}_i$ is necessarily false, if $\mathbf{a}_i$ can range over at least two addresses [16]. For simplicity of presentation, let us assume there are no singleton types. Thus, the weakest pre-conditions for non-deterministic assignments can be simplified:

$$[\![\mathbf{x}_i := ?]\!]^\top(E) = E[0/\mathbf{x}_i] \wedge E[1/\mathbf{x}_i]$$
$$[\![\mathbf{a}_i := ?]\!]^\top(E) = \begin{cases} \mathsf{false} & \text{if } \mathbf{a}_i \text{ occurs in } E \\ E & \text{otherwise} \end{cases}$$

Note that these results do not hold for the general combination of linear arithmetic with uninterpreted functions.

We now set up a constraint system to characterize the weakest pre-condition *transformers* $\mathbf{R}^\top[v]$, which transform conjunctions of equalities at the program point v into the weakest pre-condition for their validity at *program start*. The constraint system uses auxiliary transformers $\mathbf{S}^\top[v]$, which transform the post-condition of a procedure q into the weakest pre-condition at the program point v of the same procedure q.

$$
\begin{array}{llll}
[\mathrm{S1}^\top] & \mathbf{S}^\top[r_q] & \Rightarrow \mathsf{Id} & \\
[\mathrm{S2}^\top] & \mathbf{S}^\top[u] & \Rightarrow [\![s]\!]^\top \circ \mathbf{S}^\top[v] & (u,s,v) \text{ an assignment edge} \\
[\mathrm{S3}^\top] & \mathbf{S}^\top[u] & \Rightarrow \mathbf{S}^\top[e_q] \circ \mathbf{S}^\top[v] & (u,q,v) \text{ a call edge}
\end{array}
$$

$$
\begin{array}{llll}
[\mathrm{R0}^\top] & \mathbf{R}^\top[e_{main}] & \Rightarrow \mathsf{Id} & \\
[\mathrm{R1}^\top] & \mathbf{R}^\top[e_q] & \Rightarrow \mathbf{R}^\top[u] & (u,q,\_) \text{ a call edge} \\
[\mathrm{R2}^\top] & \mathbf{R}^\top[v] & \Rightarrow \mathbf{R}^\top[u] \circ [\![s]\!]^\top & (u,s,v) \text{ an assignment edge} \\
[\mathrm{R3}^\top] & \mathbf{R}^\top[v] & \Rightarrow \mathbf{R}^\top[u] \circ \mathbf{S}^\top[e_q] & (u,q,v) \text{ a call edge}
\end{array}
$$

Here, the ordering "$\Rightarrow$" on transformers $f, g \colon \mathbb{E} \to \mathbb{E}$ is defined by $f \Rightarrow g$ iff for all conjunctions of equalities E, $f(E) \Rightarrow g(E)$. The greatest solution to the system will be the weakest pre-condition transformers. We state this as a theorem.

Theorem 1. *For every program point u, set of states $S \subseteq \mathbb{S}$, and conjunction of equalities $E \in \mathbb{E}$,*

$$\mathbf{S}[u](S) \models E \iff S \models \mathbf{S}^\top[u](E) \quad \textit{and} \quad \mathbf{R}[u](\mathbb{S}) \models E \iff \mathbf{R}^\top[u](E) = \mathsf{true}$$

Proof. The identity and weakest pre-condition transformers for individual edges are defined in a standard way. Relating the least fixed point of the system $\mathbf{S}$ with the greatest fixed point of the system $\mathbf{S}^\top$, we are only required to show that the following conditions are satisfied:

$$
\begin{aligned}
f(S) \cup g(S) \models E &\iff S \models f^\top(E) \wedge g^\top(E) \\
(f \circ g)(S) \models E &\iff S \models (g^\top \circ f^\top)(E).
\end{aligned}
$$

These follow from the properties of weakest pre-condition transformers. The second equivalence follows from an analogous fixed-point induction and the fact that $\mathbb{S} \models E$ only if $\mathsf{true} \Rightarrow E$. □

Example 3. In our example program, the weakest predicate transformers for program points 2, 3 and 4 are given by the constraints:

$$
\begin{array}{ll}
\mathbf{R}^\top[2] \Rightarrow [0/\mathbf{x}_1] & \mathbf{R}^\top[2] \Rightarrow \mathbf{R}^\top[4] \\
\mathbf{R}^\top[3] \Rightarrow \mathbf{R}^\top[2] \circ [c\,.(\mathbf{x}_1)/\mathbf{a}_1] & \mathbf{R}^\top[4] \Rightarrow \mathbf{R}^\top[3] \circ [\mathbf{x}_1 + 1/\mathbf{x}_1]
\end{array}
$$

Using methods described below, we find that $\mathbf{R}^\top[2]$ maps the post-condition $\mathbf{a}_1 \doteq c\,.(-1 + \mathbf{x}_1)$ to the pre-condition $\mathbf{a}_1 \doteq c\,.(-1)$. □

Solving such constraint systems requires effective computation of function comparisons, greatest lower bounds and compositions. Thus, we need an finite and effective representation of these predicate transformers.

5 Finite Representation

Inspired by order-theory, let us call single address equalities $\mathbf{a}_i \doteq adr$ and affine equalities $t \doteq 0$ *atomic*. Let $\mathbb{E}_A$ denote the set of atomic equalities. According to Lemma 1, every conjunction has a canonical form, which is a conjunction of atomic equalities. Hence, every transformer $f\colon \mathbb{E} \to \mathbb{E}$, which is completely distributive, i.e., preserves true and distributes over conjunctions, is uniquely determined by its restriction $f|_{\mathbb{E}_A}$ to atomic equalities.

This observation, though, does not provide yet a finite representation of weakest pre-condition transformers, since the number of single equalities is still infinite. The second idea, therefore, is not to track weakest pre-conditions for each equality separately, but to consider *generic equalities*. Every generic equality serves as a template which covers a range of equalities of similar form simultaneously.

In order to infer weakest pre-conditions for all affine equalities, we consider the generic post-condition $p \equiv \mathbf{p}_0 + \mathbf{p}_1\mathbf{x}_1 + \cdots + \mathbf{p}_k\mathbf{x}_k \doteq 0$, where $\mathbf{p}_0, \ldots, \mathbf{p}_k$ are fresh variables not occurring in the program. The weakest pre-conditions for p can be represented as conjunctions of equalities

$$\sum_{i=0}^{k} c_{i0}\mathbf{p}_i + \sum_{i=0}^{k}\sum_{j=1}^{k} c_{ij}\mathbf{p}_i\mathbf{x}_j \doteq 0 \tag{5}$$

for constants $c_{ij} \in \mathbb{Q}$.

Example 4. Since our running example has just one **int** variable, the generic affine post-condition is is $e_{\mathit{aff}} \equiv \mathbf{p}_0 + \mathbf{p}_1\mathbf{x}_1 \doteq 0$. The parametric pre-condition for e_{aff} w.r.t. the assignment $\mathbf{x}_1 := \mathbf{x}_1 + 1$ is then $\mathbf{p}_0 + \mathbf{p}_1 + \mathbf{p}_1\mathbf{x}_1 \doteq 0$. □

A generic address post-condition is of the form $\mathbf{a}_i \doteq a\,.\,s_1\,.\,\ldots\,.\,s_r$ (for some $r \leq d$) where a is either an address constant in $\mathcal{C}$ or another address variable in $\mathbf{A}$, and each s_l is either a field name or an indexing pattern $\mathbf{p}_{l0} + \mathbf{p}_{l1}\mathbf{x}_1 + \cdots + \mathbf{p}_{lk}\mathbf{x}_k$. Weakest pre-conditions for such a generic address post-condition will be conjunctions of parametric affine equalities and parametric address equalities. The generic coefficients to be considered in the parametric affine equalities now are elements from the set $\mathbf{P}_r = \{\mathbf{p}_{li} \mid l \in [1,r], i \in [0,k]\}$. Thus, the affine equalities are of the form:

$$c_{000} + \sum_{j=1}^{k} c_{00j}\mathbf{x}_j + \sum_{l=1}^{r}\sum_{i=0}^{k} c_{li0}\mathbf{p}_{li} + \sum_{l=1}^{r}\sum_{i=0}^{k}\sum_{j=1}^{k} c_{lij}\mathbf{p}_{li}\mathbf{x}_j \doteq 0 \tag{6}$$

for constants $c_{lij} \in \mathbb{Q}$. Also, the parametric address equalities will be address equalities where index expressions are of the same form as left-hand sides in (6).

Example 5. For the address variable $\mathbf{a}_1$, a generic post-condition is of the form $e_{adr} \equiv \mathbf{a}_1 \doteq c.(\mathbf{p}_{10} + \mathbf{p}_{11}\mathbf{x}_1)$. The parametric pre-condition for e_{adr} w.r.t. the assignment $\mathbf{a}_1 := c.(\mathbf{x}_1)$ is given by $c.(\mathbf{x}_1) \doteq c.(\mathbf{p}_{10} + \mathbf{p}_{11}\mathbf{x}_1)$, whose canonical form is $-\mathbf{x}_1 + \mathbf{p}_{10} + \mathbf{p}_{11}\mathbf{x}_1 \doteq 0$. □

The conjunction of parametric equalities forms a lattice $\mathbb{E}_d$, which has the same structure as the lattice $\mathbb{E}$ – except that the set of **int** variables is now extended with the set of parameters $\mathbf{p}_{l0}$ and products $\mathbf{p}_{li}\mathbf{x}_j$ of parameters and **int** variables. The height of the complete lattice $\mathbb{E}_d$ therefore is bounded by $\mathcal{O}(d \cdot k^2 + m)$.

In our application, generic post-conditions suffice to arrive at a finite specification of weakest pre-condition transformers. Let T denote the set of well-typed generic address equalities. Then the set T is finite and of cardinality $\mathcal{O}(m^2 \cdot t \cdot d)$, where t is the maximal size, i.e., number of fields, of a global data structure's type. This set T is *complete* in the sense that for any concrete atomic equality $e \in \mathbb{E}_A$, there exists a substitution $\sigma \colon \mathbf{P}_d \to \mathbb{Q}$ and a generic post-condition $e' \in T$ such that $e = e'\sigma$. Any function $f \colon T \to \mathbb{E}_d$ can be extended to a completely distributive function $\mathsf{ext}(f) \colon \mathbb{E} \to \mathbb{E}$ defined by $(\mathsf{ext}(f))(e) = (f(e'))\sigma$ for all atomic equalities $e = e'\sigma$ (e' is a generic equality, σ a substitution).

We now show that the weakest predicate transformers that occur in our constraint system can indeed be obtained as extensions of functions from $T \to \mathbb{E}_d$. In order to do so, we set up a new constraint system $\mathbf{R}^\sharp$ over functions from $T \to \mathbb{E}_d$. This is obtained from the constraint system $\mathbf{R}^\top$ by replacing all operations by their parametric counterparts. Thus, implication "$\Rightarrow^\sharp$" and greatest lower bounds $\wedge^\sharp$ are now defined according to the domain $\mathbb{E}_d$. Also, the transfer functions for assignments are lifted to parametric equalities. It remains to define composition $\circ^\sharp$ for functions $f^\sharp, g^\sharp \colon T \to \mathbb{E}_d$.

First, we observe that every parametric equality can be obtained from one of the generic post-conditions by a transformation σ of the parameters. Therefore assume that e' is a generic post-condition and $g^\sharp(e') = e_1 \wedge \cdots \wedge e_r$ where $e_l = e'_l\sigma_l$ for generic post-conditions e'_l and linear transformations σ_l. Then we define

$$(f^\sharp \circ^\sharp g^\sharp)(e') = (f^\sharp(e'_1))\sigma_1 \wedge \cdots \wedge (f^\sharp(e'_r))\sigma_r \,.$$

If e' is the generic affine equality, this amounts to computing the canonical form of a conjunction of $\mathcal{O}(k^4)$ parametric equalities. If e' is a generic address equality, the canonical form must be computed for a conjunction of $\mathcal{O}(m^2)$ parametric address equalities and $\mathcal{O}(d^2k^4)$ parametric affine equalities whose normalization may at worst consume time $\mathcal{O}(m^2 \cdot d^4 \cdot k^8)$.

Example 6. Let $f = [\![\mathbf{x}_1 := ?]\!]^\top$ and $g = [\![\mathbf{a}_1 := c.(\mathbf{x}_1)]\!]^\top$. We then compute the composition $(f \circ g)(e_{adr})$ as follows:

$$\begin{aligned}(f \circ g)(e_{adr}) &= f(-\mathbf{x}_1 + \mathbf{p}_{10} + \mathbf{p}_{11}\mathbf{x}_1 \doteq 0) \\ &= (f(e_{aff}))\,\sigma \quad \text{for } \sigma = [\mathbf{p}_{10}/\mathbf{p}_0, (-1 + \mathbf{p}_{11})/\mathbf{p}_1] \\ &= ((\mathbf{p}_0 \doteq 0) \wedge (\mathbf{p}_0 + \mathbf{p}_1 \doteq 0))\sigma \\ &= ((\mathbf{p}_0 \doteq 0) \wedge (\mathbf{p}_1 \doteq 0))\,\sigma = (\mathbf{p}_{10} \doteq 0) \wedge (-1 + \mathbf{p}_{11} \doteq 0)\end{aligned}$$

This computation occurs during the analysis of our running example, because the while-loop has the same effect as the non-deterministic assignment of f. □

Theorem 2. *For any program point* u, $\mathbf{R}^{\top}[u] = \mathsf{ext}\,(\mathbf{R}^{\sharp}[u])$.

Proof. We proceed by fixpoint induction. A crucial step is to show that not only "$\wedge$", but also composition commutes with ext, i.e., that

$$\mathsf{ext}\,(f) \circ \mathsf{ext}\,(g) = \mathsf{ext}\,(f \circ^{\sharp} g)$$

To see that, we calculate:

$$\begin{aligned}(\mathsf{ext}\,(f) \circ \mathsf{ext}\,(g))(e'\sigma) &= \mathsf{ext}\,(f)(\mathsf{ext}\,(g)(e'\sigma) &&= \mathsf{ext}\,(f)(g(e'))\sigma)\\ &= \mathsf{ext}\,(f)((\textstyle\bigwedge e'_i\sigma_i)\sigma) &&= \mathsf{ext}\,(f)(\textstyle\bigwedge e'_i(\sigma_i\sigma))\\ &= \textstyle\bigwedge(f(e'_i))(\sigma_i\sigma) &&= (\textstyle\bigwedge(f(e'_i))\sigma_i)\sigma\\ &= ((f \circ^{\sharp} g)(e'))\sigma &&= (\mathsf{ext}\,(f \circ^{\sharp} g))(e'\sigma)\end{aligned}$$

where $g(e') = \bigwedge e'_i\sigma_i$ as above. □

Example 7. We can now compute the solution to the constraint system by fixpoint iteration starting from true. The computation stabilizes after three iterations, giving the following pre-conditions for the address post-condition:

$$\begin{aligned}\mathbf{R}^{\top}[2](e_{adr}) &= (\mathbf{a}_1 \doteq c.(\mathbf{p}_{10})) \wedge (\mathbf{p}_{10} + \mathbf{p}_{11} \doteq 0) \wedge (-1 + \mathbf{p}_{11} \doteq 0)\\ \mathbf{R}^{\top}[3](e_{adr}) &= (\mathbf{p}_{10} \doteq 0) \wedge (-1 + \mathbf{p}_{11} \doteq 0)\\ \mathbf{R}^{\top}[4](e_{adr}) &= (\mathbf{p}_{10} + \mathbf{p}_{11} \doteq 0) \wedge (-1 + \mathbf{p}_{11} \doteq 0)\end{aligned}$$

For the affine post-condition e_{aff}, the pre-condition $(\mathbf{p}_0 \doteq 0) \wedge (\mathbf{p}_1 \doteq 0)$ is obtained, meaning no non-trivial affine equalities hold at these points. □

6 Computing All Valid Equalities

Given the weakest pre-condition transformer $\mathbf{R}^{\top}[v]$ for program point v, computing all equalities which are valid at v then boils down to solving a suitable inhomogeneous system of equations. We have:

Theorem 3. *The equalities that hold at each program point can be computed in polynomial time.*

Proof. Let e' denote a generic post-condition and $e = e'\sigma$ an atomic equality for some substitution σ of the parameters occurring in e'. By Theorem 1, e holds at program point u iff $\mathbf{R}^{\top}[u](e) = \mathsf{true}$, which, by Theorem 2, means that $(\mathbf{R}^{\sharp}[u](e'))\sigma = \mathsf{true}$. The latter means that $\mathbf{R}^{\sharp}[u](e')$ does not contain nontrivial address equalities, but is a conjunction of at most $\mathcal{O}(d \cdot k^2)$ affine equalities $t \doteq 0$ where $t\sigma \doteq 0$ is valid for all values $x \in \mathbb{Z}^k$.

Assume that $\mathbf{p}'_1, \ldots, \mathbf{p}'_r$ are the parameters occurring in t, the affine combination t is of the form: $t \equiv c_{00} + \sum_{i=1}^{k}(c_{0i} + \sum_{l=1}^{r} c_{li}\mathbf{p}'_l)\,\mathbf{x}_i$ for suitable $c_{li} \in \mathbb{Q}$. Then $t\sigma \doteq 0$ is valid for all values $x \in \mathbb{Z}^k$ iff $c_{00} = 0$ and σ is a solution of each of the equations $c_{0i} + \sum_{l=1}^{r} c_{li}\mathbf{p}'_l \doteq 0$ $(i = 1, \ldots, k)$. We conclude that finding all substitutions σ such that $e'\sigma$ is valid at program point u can be reduced to solving a system of $\mathcal{O}(k \cdot d \cdot k^2) = \mathcal{O}(d \cdot k^3)$ inhomogeneous equations over $\mathbb{Q}$ where the number of unknowns is bounded by $d \cdot (k+1)$. The latter task can be done with a polynomial number of arithmetic operations. By repeating this procedure for every possible generic post-condition, we obtain a finite representation of all equalities which are valid at program point u. □

Example 8. As we saw in Example 7, at all points in the loop the parametric pre-condition for e_{aff} has $\mathbf{p}_0 = \mathbf{p}_1 = 0$ as its solution. The parametric pre-condition for the generic post-condition e_{adr}, on the other hand, is given by:

$$\mathbf{R}^\top[4](\mathbf{a}_1 \doteq c.(\mathbf{p}_{10} + \mathbf{p}_{11}\mathbf{x}_1)) \;=\; (\mathbf{p}_{10} + \mathbf{p}_{11} \doteq 0) \wedge (-1 + \mathbf{p}_{11} \doteq 0)$$

As no **int**-variables $\mathbf{x}_i$ are involved here, this pre-condition is true iff $\mathbf{p}_{11} = 1$ and $\mathbf{p}_{10} = -1$. Therefore, the only non-trivial equality which holds at program point 4 is $\mathbf{a}_1 \doteq c.(-1 + \mathbf{x}_1)$. □

To summarize, the set of all equalities, which hold at a given program point, can be compactly represented by a polynomially sized set of triples $\langle e, \sigma, V\rangle$ — each consisting of a generic post-condition e together with one particular solution for the conjunction of parametric affine pre-conditions of e and a basis V of the vector space of solutions of the corresponding homogeneous system. Assuming that the basis V is in (column) echelon form, we can determine if a given equality holds at a certain program point in time $\mathcal{O}(d^2 \cdot k^2)$.

7 Local Variables

All program variables have so far been considered *global*. Along the lines of [15], we now extend the analysis to possibly recursive programs with local variables as well. From the k integer variables, we consider the first $k' \leq k$ variables $\mathbf{x}_1, \ldots, \mathbf{x}_{k'}$ as local and the remaining ones as global. Similarly for pointers, the first $m' \leq m$ variables $\mathbf{a}_1, \ldots, \mathbf{a}_{m'}$ denote local variables while the remaining ones denote global pointer variables.

For passing of parameters, we adopt w.l.o.g. the convention that *all* locals of the caller are passed by value into the locals of the callee. This enables us to reason about equalities involving local variables of the caller.

We extend the concrete semantics with an extra operator H which transforms the effect of a procedure body into the effect of a procedure call:

$$\begin{aligned}\mathsf{H}(f)(S) = \{\langle (x_1, \ldots, x_{k'}, x'_{k'+1}, \ldots, x'_k), (a_1, \ldots, a_{m'}, a'_{m'+1}, \ldots, a'_m)\rangle \mid \\ \langle x, a\rangle \in S, \langle x', a'\rangle \in f(\{\langle x, a\rangle\})\}\end{aligned}$$

The constraint system for computing weakest pre-conditions of procedure calls is modified accordingly by introducing the operator $\mathsf{H}^\top$:

$$\begin{array}{lll}
[\mathrm{S1}^\top] & \mathbf{S}^\top[r_q] \Rightarrow \mathsf{Id} & \\
[\mathrm{S2}^\top] & \mathbf{S}^\top[u] \;\Rightarrow [\![s]\!]^\top \circ \mathbf{S}^\top[v] & (u, s, v) \text{ an assignment edge} \\
[\mathrm{S3}^\top] & \mathbf{S}^\top[u] \;\Rightarrow \mathsf{H}^\top(\mathbf{S}^\top[e_q]) \circ \mathbf{S}^\top[v] & (u, q, v) \text{ a call edge}
\end{array}$$

Here, the operator H^{T} must be defined such that statement 1 of Theorem 1 holds for the new constraint system. Given the concrete transformer f of a procedure and the corresponding weakest pre-condition transformer f^{T}, the following condition must hold for all sets of states S and conjunctions of equalities E:

$$\mathsf{H}(f)(S) \models E \iff S \models \mathsf{H}^{\mathsf{T}}(f^{\mathsf{T}})(E)$$

Consider an arbitrary post-condition E for a procedure call to f. This post-condition may not only speak about globals, but also about locals of the caller as well as any local variable further down in the call-stack. All these locals, however, are inaccessible during the execution of the procedure f and thus can temporarily be considered as *constants*. In order to deal with these temporary constants, we introduce place holders $\bullet_\tau$ for every possible type of local pointer variables a_j or constant addresses.

Accordingly, we consider the following set of parametric post-conditions E':

$$\begin{array}{llll} (1) & \mathbf{a}_i \doteq \mathbf{a}_j \,.\, s & (2) & \mathbf{a}_i \doteq \bullet_\tau \,.\, s \\ (3) & \bullet_\tau \doteq \mathbf{a}_i \,.\, s & (4) & \bullet_{\tau_1} \doteq \bullet_{\tau_2} \,.\, s \end{array}$$

for global pointer variables a_i, a_j and type-compatible parametric sequences of selectors s, where each parametric index is of the form $\mathbf{p}_{l0} + \mathbf{p}_{l(k'+1)}\mathbf{x}_{k'+1} + \cdots + \mathbf{p}_{lk}\mathbf{x}_k$. Furthermore, we consider the parametric affine post-condition:

$$(5) \qquad \mathbf{p}_0 + \mathbf{p}_{k'+1}\mathbf{x}_{k'+1} + \cdots + \mathbf{p}_k\mathbf{x}_k \doteq 0$$

for global variables $\mathbf{x}_{k'+1}, \ldots, \mathbf{x}_k$. Assume now that we are given the weakest pre-conditions $f^{\mathsf{T}}(E')$ of the called procedure for all these post-conditions E' speaking about global variables (and perhaps $\bullet_\tau$).

We now define the weakest pre-condition $\mathsf{H}^{\mathsf{T}}(f^{\mathsf{T}})(E)$. In each case, we decompose $E = E'\sigma$ for a generic post-condition E' of one of the types (1) through (5) and a suitable substitution σ. Then, we define

$$\mathsf{H}^{\mathsf{T}}(f^{\mathsf{T}})(E) = (f^{\mathsf{T}}(E'))\sigma\,.$$

It only remains to explain the decomposition of E. We first consider a post-condition E of the form $\mathbf{a}_i \doteq \mathbf{a}_j \,.\, s$ for global variables $\mathbf{a}_i, \mathbf{a}_j$. Then E' is of the parametric post-condition of format (1). For every index expression $s_l = t_0 + t_1\mathbf{x}_1 + \cdots + t_k\mathbf{x}_k$ in s, σ maps p_{l0} to the affine combination consisting of t_0 together with all occurring multiples of locals, i.e., to $t_0 + t_1\mathbf{x}_1 + \cdots + t_{k'}\mathbf{x}_{k'}$.

If E is of the form $\mathbf{a}_i \doteq X \,.\, s$ where $\mathbf{a}_i$ is a global variable and X either is a local of the caller, a constant address or a place holder $\bullet_\tau$ all of the type τ, we choose E' of the parametric format (2) and σ is constructed as before, but moreover maps the place holder $\bullet_\tau$ in E' to X.

The case where E is of the form $X \doteq \mathbf{a}_i \,.\, s$ is treated analogously. In case where E is of the form $X_1 \doteq X_2 \,.\, s$ and each X_i is a local of the caller, constant address or place holder, then we choose the appropriate generic post-condition E' now of type (4). The substitution σ treats index expressions as before, but now maps $\bullet_{\tau_1}$ to X_1 and $\bullet_{\tau_2}$ to X_2.

Finally, if E is an affine equality $t_0 + t_1\mathbf{x}_1 + \cdots + t_k\mathbf{x}_k \doteq 0$, then we choose E' to be of format (5) where the substitution σ maps p_0 to $t_0 + t_1\mathbf{x}_1 + \cdots + t_{k'}\mathbf{x}_{k'}$, and p_i to t_i for $i > k'$.

Example 9. Consider the post-condition $\mathbf{a}_1 \doteq \mathbf{a}_2 . (\mathbf{p}_{10} + \mathbf{p}_{11}\mathbf{x}_1 + \mathbf{p}_{12}\mathbf{x}_2)$, where $\mathbf{a}_1$, $\mathbf{a}_2$, and $\mathbf{x}_1$ are local, but $\mathbf{x}_2$ is global and may be changed during the procedure call. Assume that the callee only performs the statement $\mathbf{x}_2 := ?$. Since the post-condition is of the type (4), we compute the pre-condition as follows:

$$\begin{aligned}&[\![\mathbf{x}_2 \doteq ?]\!]^\top(\bullet_{\tau_1} \doteq \bullet_2 . (\mathbf{p}_{10} + \mathbf{p}_{12}\mathbf{x}_2)) = \\ &\quad(\bullet_{\tau_1} \doteq \bullet_2 . (\mathbf{p}_{10})) \wedge (\bullet_{\tau_1} \doteq \bullet_2 . (\mathbf{p}_{10} + \mathbf{p}_{21})) = (\bullet_{\tau_1} \doteq \bullet_2 . (\mathbf{p}_{10})) \wedge (\mathbf{p}_{21} \doteq 0)\end{aligned}$$

To obtain the weakest pre-condition of $\mathbf{a}_1 \doteq \mathbf{a}_2 . (\mathbf{p}_{10} + \mathbf{p}_{11}\mathbf{x}_1 + \mathbf{p}_{12}\mathbf{x}_2)$, we apply the substitution σ, which maps $\mathbf{p}_{10}$ to $\mathbf{p}_{10} + \mathbf{p}_{11}\mathbf{x}_1$ and replaces the place-holders with the local address variables: $\mathbf{a}_1 \doteq \mathbf{a}_2 . (\mathbf{p}_{10} + \mathbf{p}_{11}\mathbf{x}_1) \wedge \mathbf{p}_{21} \doteq 0$. □

The second part of our analysis applies the weakest pre-condition transformers of procedures, as defined through the first part of the constraint system, to construct a constraint system for the weakest pre-condition transformers for post-conditions at program points v:

$$\begin{array}{llll}[\mathrm{R0}^\top] & \mathbf{R}^\top[e_{main}] & \Rightarrow \mathsf{Id} & \\ [\mathrm{R1}^\top] & \mathbf{R}^\top[e_q] & \Rightarrow \mathbf{R}^\top[u] & (u, q, \_) \text{ a call edge} \\ [\mathrm{R2}^\top] & \mathbf{R}^\top[v] & \Rightarrow \mathbf{R}^\top[u] \circ [\![s]\!]^\top & (u, s, v) \text{ an assignment edge} \\ [\mathrm{R3}^\top] & \mathbf{R}^\top[v] & \Rightarrow \mathbf{R}^\top[u] \circ \mathsf{H}^\top(\mathbf{S}^\top[e_q]) & (u, q, v) \text{ a call edge}\end{array}$$

This time, however, the post-conditions for the weakest pre-condition transformer $\mathbf{R}^\top[v]$ for a program point of a procedure f need not use $\bullet$-variables to refer to variables deeper down in the call-stack. Instead, they may refer to the *locals* of f. Accordingly, occurring transformers are described by their weakest pre-conditions for the generic affine post-condition together with the generic address post-conditions $\mathbf{a}_i \doteq \mathbf{a}_j . s$ for local or global address variables a_i, a_j and suitable selector sequences s.

8 Example Application: Race Detection

One common approach to data race analysis is to ensure the following condition for every pair of accesses in the program: if the two access expressions *may* alias, then the acquired lock expressions *must* alias [17]. We ensure this condition by inferring access correlations using the must-equality analysis and associating these correlations with may-alias equivalence classes, as we will illustrate through the following example.

Example 10. Assume the address variables $\mathbf{a}_{acc}$ and $\mathbf{a}_{lock}$ represent an access expression and a lock expression that need to be correlated, and our must-alias analysis provides the following information:

$$(\mathbf{a}_{acc} \doteq \mathbf{a}_1 . data . (\mathbf{x}_1)) \wedge (\mathbf{a}_{lock} \doteq \mathbf{a}_1 . mutex . (\mathbf{x}_1))$$

These equalities imply that the access to the data array of the structure pointed to by $\mathbf{a}_1$ is protected by a corresponding element in the mutex array. □

The access pattern we can infer in the above example depends on the information we have about $\mathbf{a}_1$. If the analysis can infer that $\mathbf{a}_1$ is definitely equal to some statically allocated structure c, a pattern for access to the elements of c is obtained. Otherwise, may-alias analysis [7] is called upon to divide the set of all pointer variables into equivalence classes. The simplest such approach, which suffices for some applications [11], equates all pointers of the same type. Then our method allows to infer access patterns for data structures of a given type. A more refined analysis distinguishes heap objects depending also on their allocation sites, in which case our analysis derives more refined patterns.

Note that must-equality information complements may-aliasing by ensuring that $\mathbf{a}_{acc}$ and $\mathbf{a}_{lock}$ are referring to the *same object* within the equivalence class of $\mathbf{a}_1$. This is crucial in order to verify per-element locking schemes, where each element in, e.g., a linked list has its own lock. Pratikakis et al. [20] describe a technique based on existentially typed label-flow to address this issue with the aid of programmer annotations; must-equality information allows one to infer per-element correlations automatically.

9 Conclusion

We have presented a must-alias analysis which infers all equalities between address expressions and can be proven to be valid w.r.t. the chosen abstraction. In this abstraction, conditional branching is replaced with non-deterministic branching and pointers stored in the shared data-structures are not tracked. We indicated how these equalities can be used to infer correlations between locks and accesses. Our analysis infers relevant must-equality information also for dynamically allocated data which combined with may-alias information allows one to infer access patterns. A variant of this approach has been implemented in the Goblint data race analyzer [23] and also extended by an accompanying may-alias analysis [21].

For simplicity, we have assumed that index expressions are evaluated over the integral domain $\mathbb{Z}$. Instead, we could have chosen $\mathbb{Z}_{2^w}$, i.e., integers modulo a suitable power of 2, by replacing the linear algebra methods for vector spaces of affine equalities with the corresponding methods for modules over the principal ideal ring $\mathbb{Z}_{2^w}$ [14]. However, if the programs to be analyzed only employ simple forms of index expressions, it might be sufficient to replace tracking of affine equalities with tracking of variable equalities alone [15].

References

1. Chakrabarti, A., de Alfaro, L., Henzinger, T., Jurdziński, M., Mang, F.: Interface compatibility checking for software modules. In: Brinksma, E., Larsen, K.G. (eds.) CAV 2002. LNCS, vol. 2404, pp. 428–663. Springer, Heidelberg (2002)
2. Deutsch, A.: Interprocedural may-alias analysis for pointers: beyond k-limiting. In: PLDI 1994, pp. 230–241. ACM Press, New York (1994)

3. Gulwani, S., Necula, G.C.: A polynomial-time algorithm for global value numbering. In: Giacobazzi, R. (ed.) SAS 2004. LNCS, vol. 3148, pp. 212–227. Springer, Heidelberg (2004)
4. Gulwani, S., Tiwari, A.: Assertion checking over combined abstraction of linear arithmetic and uninterpreted functions. In: Sestoft, P. (ed.) ESOP 2006. LNCS, vol. 3924, pp. 279–293. Springer, Heidelberg (2006)
5. Gulwani, S., Tiwari, A.: An abstract domain for analyzing heap-manipulating low-level software. In: Damm, W., Hermanns, H. (eds.) CAV 2007. LNCS, vol. 4590, pp. 379–392. Springer, Heidelberg (2007)
6. Gulwani, S., Tiwari, A.: Computing procedure summaries for interprocedural analysis. In: De Nicola, R. (ed.) ESOP 2007. LNCS, vol. 4421, pp. 253–267. Springer, Heidelberg (2007)
7. Hind, M., Burke, M., Carini, P., Choi, J.-D.: Interprocedural pointer alias analysis. ACM Trans. Prog. Lang. Syst. 21(4), 848–894 (1999)
8. Holzmann, G.J.: The power of ten: Rules for developing safety critical code. IEEE Computer 39(6), 95–97 (2006)
9. Karr, M.: Affine relationships among variables of a program. Acta Informatica 6(2), 133–151 (1976)
10. Kildall, G.A.: A unified approach to global program optimization. In: POPL 1973, pp. 194–206. ACM Press, New York (1973)
11. Lu, S., Park, S., Hu, C., Ma, X., Jiang, W., Li, Z., Popa, R.A., Zhou, Y.: MUVI: automatically inferring multi-variable access correlations and detecting related semantic and concurrency bugs. In: SOSP 2007, pp. 103–116. ACM Press, New York (2007)
12. Müller-Olm, M., Rüthing, O., Seidl, H.: Checking Herbrand equalities and beyond. In: Cousot, R. (ed.) VMCAI 2005. LNCS, vol. 3385, pp. 79–96. Springer, Heidelberg (2005)
13. Müller-Olm, M., Seidl, H.: Precise interprocedural analysis through linear algebra. In: POPL 2004, pp. 330–341. ACM Press, New York (2004)
14. Müller-Olm, M., Seidl, H.: Analysis of modular arithmetic. ACM Trans. Prog. Lang. Syst. 29(5) (2007)
15. Müller-Olm, M., Seidl, H.: Upper adjoints for fast inter-procedural variable equalities. In: Drossopoulou, S. (ed.) ESOP 2008. LNCS, vol. 4960, pp. 178–192. Springer, Heidelberg (2008)
16. Müller-Olm, M., Seidl, H., Steffen, B.: Interprocedural Herbrand equalities. In: Sagiv, M. (ed.) ESOP 2005. LNCS, vol. 3444, pp. 31–45. Springer, Heidelberg (2005)
17. Naik, M., Aiken, A.: Conditional must not aliasing for static race detection. In: POPL 2007, pp. 327–338. ACM Press, New York (2007)
18. Nelson, G., Oppen, D.C.: Simplification by cooperating decision procedures. ACM Trans. Prog. Lang. Syst. 1(2), 245–257 (1979)
19. Paterson, M., Wegman, M.N.: Linear unification. In: STOC 1976, pp. 181–186. ACM Press, New York (1976)
20. Pratikakis, P., Foster, J.S., Hicks, M.: Existential label flow inference via CFL reachability. In: Yi, K. (ed.) SAS 2006. LNCS, vol. 4134, pp. 88–106. Springer, Heidelberg (2006)
21. Seidl, H., Vojdani, V.: Region analysis for race detection. In: SAS 2009. LNCS, vol. 5673, pp. 171–187. Springer, Heidelberg (2009)
22. Steffen, B., Knoop, J., Rüthing, O.: The value flow graph: A program representation for optimal program transformations. In: Jones, N.D. (ed.) ESOP 1990. LNCS, vol. 432, pp. 232–247. Springer, Heidelberg (1990)
23. Vojdani, V., Vene, V.: Goblint: Path-sensitive data race analysis. Annales Univ. Sci. Budapest., Sect. Comp. 30, 141–155 (2009)

On the Complexity of Synthesizing Relaxed and Graceful Bounded-Time 2-Phase Recovery*

Borzoo Bonakdarpour[1] and Sandeep S. Kulkarni[2]

[1] VERIMAG
Centre Équation
2 ave de Vinage
38610, Gières, France
borzoo@imag.fr

[2] Department of Computer Science and Engineering
Michigan State University
East Lansing, MI 48824, USA
sandeep@cse.msu.edu

Abstract. The problem of enforcing bounded-time 2-phase recovery in real-time programs is often necessitated by conflict between fault-tolerance requirements and timing constraints. In this paper, we address the problem of synthesizing two types of 2-phase recovery: relaxed and graceful. Intuitively, relaxed 2-phase recovery requires that in the presence of faults, the program recovers to an *acceptable* behavior within some time θ and recovers to *ideal* behavior within time δ. And, graceful 2-phase recovery allows us to capture a requirement that the time to recover from faults is proportional to the perturbation caused by that fault. We show that the problem of synthesizing relaxed bounded-time 2-phase recovery is NP-complete although a similar problem of graceful 2-phase recovery can be solved in polynomial-time both in the size of the input program's region graph. Finally, based on the results in this paper, we argue that the requirement of intermediate *recording* of a fault before reaching legitimate states can increase the complexity of adding fault-tolerance substantially.

Keywords: Fault-tolerance, Real-time, Bounded-time recovery, Phased recovery, Program synthesis, Program transformation.

1 Introduction

Achieving correctness is perhaps the most important aspect of using formal methods in design and development of computing systems. Such correctness turns out to be a fundamental element in gaining assurance about reliability and robustness of safety/mission critical embedded systems. These systems are often

* This work is partially sponsored by the COMBEST European project, NSF CAREER CCR-0092724, and ONR Grant N00014-01-1-0744.

A. Cavalcanti and D. Dams (Eds.): FM 2009, LNCS 5850, pp. 660–675, 2009.

real-time due to their controlling duties and integrated with physical processes in hostile environments. Hence, *time-predictability* and *fault-tolerance* are two desirable features of programs that operate in such systems. However, these features have conflicting natures, making achieving and reasoning about their correctness fairly complex.

One way to deal with this complexity is to design automated synthesis and revision algorithms that build programs that are correct-by-construction. Algorithmic synthesis of programs in the presence of an adversary has mostly been addressed in the context of timed controller synthesis (e.g., [12,14,4,5]) and game theory (e.g., [13,15]). In controller synthesis (respectively, game theory), program and *fault* transitions can be modeled as controllable and uncontrollable actions (respectively, in terms of two players). In both approaches, the objective is to restrict the actions of a *plant* or *player* at each state through synthesizing a *controller* or a *wining strategy*, such that the behavior of the entire system always meets some safety and/or reachability conditions. However, the notion of dependability and in particular fault-tolerance requires other functionalities that are not typically addressed in controller synthesis and game theory. For instance, fault-tolerance is concerned with *bounded-time recovery*, where a program returns to its normal behavior when its state is perturbed due to the occurrence of faults. In this context, a recovery mechanism is normally *added* to a program so that it reacts to faults properly.

Although synthesis algorithms are known to be intractable, it has been shown that their complexity can be overcome through:

- focusing on safety and liveness properties typically used in specifying systems rather than considering any arbitrary specification,
- rigorous complexity analysis for each class of properties to identify bottlenecks,
- devising intelligent heuristics that address complexity bottlenecks, and
- exploiting efficient implementation techniques.

By applying these principles, we have been able to synthesize distributed fault-tolerant programs with reachable states of size 10^{60} and beyond [9,11], even though the worst case complexity (NP-completeness in the state space) initially seemed to be unfeasible to cope with in practice. In case of real-time dependable systems, however, the problem is more complex, because of conflicting nature of requirements and high complexity of decision procedures simultaneously.

In this paper, we focus on one aspect of the conflict between real-time constraints and fault-tolerance requirements. In particular, the fault-tolerance requirement of the program may require that eventually the program recovers to its legitimate states from where its subsequent behavior is *ideal*, i.e., one that could occur in the absence of faults. Also, the real-time constraints may require that the recovery to the ideal behavior be achieved quickly. When satisfying both these requirements is not feasible, one approach is to ensure that the program recovers quickly to an *acceptable* behavior and eventually recovers to its *ideal* behavior. The recovery requirements for *acceptable* and *ideal* behavior can be specified in terms of a set of states Q and S respectively. Thus, the requirements for a real-time fault-tolerant system can be viewed as a *2-phase recovery*, where the program eventually reaches Q within some time θ and eventually reaches S in some time δ.

There are different variations for such 2-phase recovery problem. The scenario discussed above can be expressed in terms of constraints of the form $(\neg S \mapsto_{\leq\theta} Q)$ and $(Q \mapsto_{\leq\delta} S)$, i.e., starting from any state in $\neg S$, the program first recovers to Q (acceptable behavior) in time θ and subsequently from each state in Q, it recovers to states in S (ideal behavior) in time δ. We denote this variation as strict 2-phase recovery.

Another variation is $(\neg S \mapsto_{\leq\theta} (Q - S))$ and $(Q \mapsto_{\leq\delta} S)$, i.e., the program first recovers to $(Q - S)$ in time θ and subsequently from each state in Q, it recovers to S in time δ. We denote this variation as ordered-strict 2-phase recovery. One motivation for such a requirement is that we first *record* the occurrence of the fault before ideal behavior can resume. Thus, the program behavior while *recording* the fault (e.g., notifying the user) is strictly different from its ideal behavior.

Third possible variation is $(\neg S \mapsto_{\leq\theta} Q)$ and $(\neg S \mapsto_{\leq\delta} S)$, i.e., the program recovers to Q (acceptable behavior) in time θ and it recovers to states in S (ideal behavior) in time δ. We denote this variation as relaxed 2-phase recovery. One motivation for such requirements is to provide a tradeoff for the designer. In particular, if one can obtain a quick recovery to Q, then one can utilize the remaining time budget in recovering to S. Observe that such tradeoff is not possible in strict 2-phase recovery.

Fourth possible variation is $(Q \mapsto_{\leq\delta} S)$ and $(\neg S \mapsto_{\leq\theta} S)$, i.e., if the program is perturbed to Q, then it recovers to S in time δ and if the program is perturbed to any state, then it recovers to a state in S in time θ. We denote this variation as graceful 2-phase recovery. One motivation for such requirements is a scenario where (1) faults that perturb the program to Q only are more common and, hence, a quick recovery (small δ) is desirable in restoring the ideal behavior, and (2) faults that perturb the program to $\neg Q$ are rare and, hence, slow recovery (large θ) is permissible.

In [10], we introduced the notion of bounded-time 2-phase recovery in a general sense. We also addressed the complexity of synthesizing fault-tolerant real-time programs that mask the occurrence of faults and provide strict and ordered-strict 2-phase recovery. In this paper, we focus on synthesis of relaxed and graceful 2-phase recovery. The main contributions of the paper are as follows:

- We formally define and classify different types of bounded-time 2-phase recovery in the context of fault-tolerant real-time programs.
- Regarding synthesizing relaxed 2-phase recovery, we show that
  - the general problem is NP-complete,
  - the problem can be solved in polynomial-time, if $S \subseteq Q$ and it is required that Q be closed, i.e., the program cannot begin in a state in Q and reach a state outside Q, and
  - the problem remains NP-complete, if $S \subseteq Q$ but Q is not required to be closed.

- Regarding synthesizing graceful 2-phase recovery, we show that the problem can always be solved in polynomial-time.

We emphasize that all complexity results are in the size of the input program's region graph.

Organization of the Paper. The rest of the paper is organized as follows. Section 2 is dedicated to define real-time programs and specifications. In Section 3, we formally define the different variations of 2-phase recovery. In Section 4, we define the problem statement for synthesizing 2-phase recovery. Section 5 presents our results on the complexity of synthesis of relaxed and graceful 2-phase recovery. Finally, we conclude in Section 6.

2 Real-Time Programs and Specifications

2.1 Real-Time Program

In our framework, real-time programs are specified in terms of their state space and their transitions [3,2]. Let $V = \{v_1, v_2 \cdots v_n\}$, $n \geq 1$, be a finite set of *discrete variables* and $X = \{x_1, x_2 \cdots x_m\}$, $m \geq 1$, be a finite set of *clock variables*. Each discrete variable v_i, $1 \leq i \leq n$, is associated with a finite *domain* D_i of values. Each clock variable x_j, $1 \leq j \leq m$, ranges over nonnegative real numbers (denoted $\mathbb{R}_{\geq 0}$). A *location* is a function that maps discrete variables to a value from their respective domain. A *clock constraint* over the set X of clock variables is a Boolean combination of formulae of the form $x \preceq c$ or $x - y \preceq c$, where $x, y \in X$, $c \in \mathbb{Z}_{\geq 0}$, and $\preceq$ is either $<$ or $\leq$. We denote the set of all clock constraints over X by $\Phi(X)$. A *clock valuation* is a function $\nu : X \rightarrow \mathbb{R}_{\geq 0}$ that assigns a real value to each clock variable.

For $\tau \in \mathbb{R}_{\geq 0}$, we write $\nu + \tau$ to denote $\nu(x) + \tau$ for every clock variable x in X. Also, for $\lambda \subseteq X$, $\nu[\lambda := 0]$ denotes the clock valuation that assigns 0 to each $x \in \lambda$ and agrees with ν over the rest of the clock variables in X. A *state* (denoted σ) is a pair (s, ν), where s is a location and ν is a clock valuation for X. Let u be a (discrete or clock) variable and σ be a state. We denote the value of u in state σ by $u(\sigma)$. A *transition* is an ordered pair (σ_0, σ_1), where σ_0 and σ_1 are two states. Transitions are classified into two types:

- *Immediate transitions:* $(s_0, \nu) \rightarrow (s_1, \nu[\lambda := 0])$, where s_0 and s_1 are two locations, ν is a clock valuation, and λ is a set of clock variables, where $\lambda \subseteq X$.
- *Delay transitions:* $(s, \nu) \rightarrow (s, \nu + \delta)$, where s is a location, ν is a clock valuation, and $\delta \in \mathbb{R}_{\geq 0}$ is a *time duration*. Note that a delay transition only advances time and does not change the location. We denote a delay transition of duration δ at state σ by (σ, δ).

Thus, if ψ is a set of transitions, we let ψ^s and ψ^d denote the set of immediate and delay transitions in ψ, respectively.

Definition 1 (real-time program). A *real-time program* $\mathcal{P}$ is a tuple $\langle S_{\mathcal{P}}, \psi_{\mathcal{P}} \rangle$, where $S_{\mathcal{P}}$ is the *state space* (i.e., the set of all possible states), and $\psi_{\mathcal{P}}$ is a set of transitions such that $\psi_{\mathcal{P}} \subseteq S_{\mathcal{P}} \times S_{\mathcal{P}}$. ∎

Definition 2 (state predicate). Let $\mathcal{P} = \langle S_{\mathcal{P}}, \psi_{\mathcal{P}} \rangle$ be a real-time program. A *state predicate* S of program $\mathcal{P}$ is any subset of $S_{\mathcal{P}}$, such that if φ is a constraint involving clock variables in X, where $S \Rightarrow \varphi$, then $\varphi \in \Phi(X)$, i.e., clock variables are only compared with nonnegative integers. ∎

By *closure* of a state predicate S in a set $\psi_{\mathcal{P}}$ of transitions, we mean that (1) if an immediate transition originates in S then it must terminate in S, and (2) if a delay transition with duration δ originates in S then it must remain in S continuously, i.e., intermediate states where the delay is in interval $(0, \delta]$ are all in S.

Definition 3 (closure). A state predicate S is *closed* in program $\mathcal{P} = \langle S_{\mathcal{P}}, \psi_{\mathcal{P}} \rangle$ (or briefly $\psi_{\mathcal{P}}$) iff

$$(\forall (\sigma_0, \sigma_1) \in \psi^s_{\mathcal{P}} \; : \; ((\sigma_0 \in S) \Rightarrow (\sigma_1 \in S))) \;\; \wedge$$
$$(\forall (\sigma, \delta) \in \psi^d_{\mathcal{P}} \; : \; ((\sigma \in S) \Rightarrow \forall \epsilon \mid ((\epsilon \in \mathbb{R}_{\geq 0}) \; \wedge \; (\epsilon \leq \delta)) \; : \; \sigma + \epsilon \in S)). \;\blacksquare$$

Definition 4 (computation). A *computation* of $\mathcal{P} = \langle S_{\mathcal{P}}, \psi_{\mathcal{P}} \rangle$ (or briefly $\psi_{\mathcal{P}}$) is a finite or infinite timed state sequence of the form:

$$\overline{\sigma} = (\sigma_0, \tau_0) \rightarrow (\sigma_1, \tau_1) \rightarrow \cdots$$

if the following conditions are satisfied: (1) $\forall j \in \mathbb{Z}_{\geq 0} : (\sigma_j, \sigma_{j+1}) \in \psi_{\mathcal{P}}$, (2) if $\overline{\sigma}$ reaches a terminating state σ_f where there does not exist a state σ such that $(\sigma_f, \sigma) \in \psi^s_{\mathcal{P}}$, then we let $\overline{\sigma}$ stutter at σ_f, but advance time indefinitely, and (3) the sequence $\tau_0, \tau_1, \cdots$ (called the *global time*), where $\tau_i \in \mathbb{R}_{\geq 0}$ for all $i \in \mathbb{Z}_{\geq 0}$, satisfies the following constraints:

1. *(monotonicity)* for all $i \in \mathbb{Z}_{\geq 0}$, $\tau_i \leq \tau_{i+1}$,
2. *(divergence)* if $\overline{\sigma}$ is infinite, for all $t \in \mathbb{R}_{\geq 0}$, there exists $j \in \mathbb{Z}_{\geq 0}$ such that $\tau_j \geq t$, and
3. *(consistency)* for all $i \in \mathbb{Z}_{\geq 0}$, (1) if (σ_i, σ_{i+1}) is a delay transition (σ_i, δ) in $\psi^d_{\mathcal{P}}$ then $\tau_{i+1} - \tau_i = \delta$, and (2) if (σ_i, σ_{i+1}) is an immediate transition in $\psi^s_{\mathcal{P}}$ then $\tau_i = \tau_{i+1}$. ∎

We distinguish between a *terminating* computation and a *deadlocked* finite computation. Precisely, when a computation $\overline{\sigma}$ terminates in state σ_f, we include the delay transitions (σ_f, δ) in $\psi^d_{\mathcal{P}}$ for all $\delta \in \mathbb{R}_{\geq 0}$, i.e., $\overline{\sigma}$ can be extended to an infinite computation by advancing time arbitrarily. On the other hand, if there exists a state σ_d, such that there is no outgoing (delay or immediate) transition from σ_d then σ_d is a *deadlock state*.

2.2 Specification

Let $\mathcal{P} = \langle S_\mathcal{P}, \psi_\mathcal{P} \rangle$ be a program. A *specification* (or *property*), denoted *SPEC*, for $\mathcal{P}$ is a set of infinite computations of the form $(\sigma_0, \tau_0) \rightarrow (\sigma_1, \tau_1) \rightarrow \cdots$ where $\sigma_i \in S_\mathcal{P}$ for all $i \in \mathbb{Z}_{\geq 0}$. Following Alpern and Schneider [1] and Henzinger [17], we require that all computations in *SPEC* satisfy time-monotonicity and divergence. We now define what it means for a program to satisfy a specification.

Definition 5 (satisfies). Let $\mathcal{P} = \langle S_\mathcal{P}, \psi_\mathcal{P} \rangle$ be a program, S be a state predicate, and *SPEC* be a specification for $\mathcal{P}$. We write $\mathcal{P} \models_S SPEC$ and say that $\mathcal{P}$ *satisfies SPEC from* S iff (1) S is closed in $\psi_\mathcal{P}$, and (2) every computation of $\mathcal{P}$ that starts from S is in *SPEC*. ∎

Definition 6 (invariant). Let $\mathcal{P} = \langle S_\mathcal{P}, \psi_\mathcal{P} \rangle$ be a program, S be a state predicate, and *SPEC* be a specification for $\mathcal{P}$. If $\mathcal{P} \models_S SPEC$ and $S \neq \{\}$, we say that S is an *invariant of* $\mathcal{P}$ *for SPEC*. ∎

Whenever the specification is clear from the context, we will omit it; thus, "S is an invariant of $\mathcal{P}$" abbreviates "S is an invariant of $\mathcal{P}$ for *SPEC*". Note that Definition 5 introduces the notion of satisfaction with respect to infinite computations. In case of finite computations, we characterize them by determining whether they can be extended to an infinite computation in the specification.

Definition 7 (maintains). We say that program $\mathcal{P}$ *maintains SPEC* from S iff (1) S is closed in $\psi_\mathcal{P}$, and (2) for all computation prefixes $\overline{\alpha}$ of $\mathcal{P}$ that start in S, there exists a computation suffix $\overline{\beta}$ such that $\overline{\alpha}\overline{\beta} \in SPEC$. We say that $\mathcal{P}$ *violates SPEC* from S iff it is not the case that $\mathcal{P}$ maintains *SPEC* from S. ∎

We note that if $\mathcal{P}$ satisfies *SPEC* from S then $\mathcal{P}$ maintains *SPEC* from S as well, but the reverse direction does not always hold. We, in particular, introduce the notion of *maintains* for computations that a (fault-intolerant) program cannot produce, but the computation can be extended to one that is in *SPEC* by adding *recovery* computation suffixes, i.e., $\overline{\alpha}$ may be a computation prefix that leaves S, but $\overline{\beta}$ brings the program back to S (see Section 3 for details).

Specifying timing constraints. In order to express time-related behaviors of real-time programs (e.g., deadlines and recovery time), we focus on a standard property typically used in real-time computing known as the *bounded response property*. A bounded response property, denoted $P \mapsto_{\leq \delta} Q$ where P and Q are two state predicates and $\delta \in \mathbb{Z}_{\geq 0}$, is the set of all computations $(\sigma_0, \tau_0) \rightarrow (\sigma_1, \tau_1) \rightarrow \cdots$ in which, for all $i \geq 0$, if $\sigma_i \in P$ then there exists j, $j \geq i$, such that (1) $\sigma_j \in Q$, and (2) $\tau_j - \tau_i \leq \delta$, i.e., it is always the case that a state in P is followed by a state in Q within δ time units.

The specifications considered in this paper are an intersection of a *safety* specification and a *liveness* specification [1,17]. In this paper, we consider a special case where safety specification is characterized by a set of bad immediate transitions and a set of bounded response properties.

Definition 8 (safety specification). Let $SPEC$ be a specification. The *safety specification* of $SPEC$ is the union of the sets $SPEC_{\overline{bt}}$ and $SPEC_{\overline{br}}$ defined as follows:

1. *(timing-independent safety)* Let $SPEC_{bt}$ be a set of immediate *bad transitions*. We denote the specification whose computations have no transition in $SPEC_{bt}$ by $SPEC_{\overline{bt}}$.
2. *(timing constraints)* We denote $SPEC_{\overline{br}}$ by the conjunction $\bigwedge_{i=0}^{m}(P_i \mapsto_{\leq \delta_i} Q_i)$, for state predicates P_i and Q_i, and, response times δ_i. ∎

Throughout the paper, $SPEC_{\overline{br}}$ is meant to prescribe how a program should carry out bounded-time phased recovery to its normal behavior after the occurrence of faults. We formally define the notion of recovery in Section 3.

Definition 9 (liveness specification). A liveness specification of $SPEC$ is a set of computations that meets the following condition: for each finite computation $\overline{\alpha}$, there exists a computation $\overline{\beta}$ such that $\overline{\alpha}\overline{\beta} \in SPEC$. ∎

Remark 1. In our synthesis problem in Section 4, we begin with an initial program that satisfies its specification (including the liveness specification). We will show that our synthesis techniques *preserve* the liveness specification. Hence, the liveness specification need not be specified explicitly. ∎

3 Fault Model and Fault-Tolerance

3.1 Fault Model

The faults that a program is subject to are systematically represented by transitions. A class of *faults* f for program $\mathcal{P} = \langle S_\mathcal{P}, \psi_\mathcal{P} \rangle$ is a subset of *immediate* and *delay* transitions of the set $S_\mathcal{P} \times S_\mathcal{P}$. We use $\psi_\mathcal{P}[]f$ to denote the transitions obtained by taking the union of the transitions in $\psi_\mathcal{P}$ and the transitions in f. We emphasize that such representation is possible for different types of faults (e.g., stuck-at, crash, fail-stop, timing, performance, Byzantine, message loss, etc.), nature of the faults (permanent, transient, or intermittent), or the ability of the program to observe the effects of the faults.

Definition 10 (fault-span). We say that a state predicate T is an f-span (read as *fault-span*) of $\mathcal{P} = \langle S_\mathcal{P}, \psi_\mathcal{P} \rangle$ from S iff the following conditions are satisfied: (1) $S \subseteq T$, and (2) T is closed in $\psi_\mathcal{P}[]f$. ∎

Observe that for all computations of $\mathcal{P} = \langle S_\mathcal{P}, \psi_\mathcal{P} \rangle$ that start from states where S is true, T is a boundary in the state space of $\mathcal{P}$ up to which (but not beyond which) the state of $\mathcal{P}$ may be perturbed by the occurrence of the transitions in f. Subsequently, as we defined the computations of $\mathcal{P}$, one can define computations of program $\mathcal{P}$ in the presence of faults f by simply substituting $\psi_\mathcal{P}$ with $\psi_\mathcal{P}[]f$ in Definition 4.

3.2 Phased Recovery and Fault-Tolerance

Now, we define the different types of 2-phase recovery properties discussed in Section 1.

Definition 11 (2-phase recovery). Let $\mathcal{P} = \langle S_\mathcal{P}, \psi_\mathcal{P} \rangle$ be a real-time program with invariant S, Q be an arbitrary *intermediate recovery predicate*, f be a set of faults, and $SPEC$ be a specification (as defined in Definitions 8 and 9). We say that $\mathcal{P}$ *provides* (ordered-strict, strict, relaxed or graceful) 2-phase recovery from S and Q with recovery times $\delta, \theta \in \mathbb{Z}_{\geq 0}$, respectively, iff $\langle S_\mathcal{P}, \psi_\mathcal{P}[]f \rangle$ maintains $SPEC_{\overline{br}} \equiv (\neg S \mapsto_{\leq \theta} Q_1) \ \wedge \ (Q_2 \mapsto_{\leq \delta} S)$ from S, where, depending upon the type of the desired 2-phase recovery, Q_1 and Q_2 are instantiated as follows:

	ordered-strict	strict	relaxed	graceful
Q_1	$Q - S$	Q	Q	S
Q_2	Q	Q	$\neg S$	Q

We call θ and δ *intermediate recovery time* and *recovery time*, respectively. ∎

Definition 12 (fault-tolerance). Let $\mathcal{P} = \langle S_\mathcal{P}, \psi_\mathcal{P} \rangle$ be a real-time program with invariant S, f be a set of faults, and $SPEC$ be a specification as defined in Definitions 8 and 9. We say that $\mathcal{P}$ is *f-tolerant to SPEC from S*, iff (1) $\mathcal{P} \models_S SPEC$, and (2) there exists T such that T is an f-span of $\mathcal{P}$ from S and $\langle S_\mathcal{P}, \psi_\mathcal{P}[]f \rangle$ maintains $SPEC$ from T. ∎

Notation. Whenever the specification $SPEC$ and the invariant S are clear from the context, we omit them; thus, "f-tolerant" abbreviates "f-tolerant to $SPEC$ from S".

4 Problem Statement

Given are a fault-intolerant real-time program $\mathcal{P} = \langle S_\mathcal{P}, \psi_\mathcal{P} \rangle$, its invariant S, a set f of faults, and a specification $SPEC$ such that $\mathcal{P} \models_S SPEC$. Our goal is to synthesize a real-time program $\mathcal{P}' = \langle S_{\mathcal{P}'}, \psi_{\mathcal{P}'} \rangle$ with invariant S' such that $\mathcal{P}'$ is f-tolerant to $SPEC$ from S'. We require that our synthesis methods obtain $\mathcal{P}'$ from $\mathcal{P}$ by *adding fault-tolerance* to $\mathcal{P}$ without introducing new behaviors in the absence of faults. To this end, we first define the notion of *projection*. Projection of a set $\psi_\mathcal{P}$ of transitions on state predicate S consists of immediate transitions of $\psi^s_\mathcal{P}$ that start in S and end in S, and delay transitions of $\psi^d_\mathcal{P}$ that start and remain in S continuously.

Definition 13 (projection). *Projection* of a set ψ of transitions on a state predicate S (denoted $\psi|S$) is the following set of transitions:

$$\psi|S = \{(\sigma_0, \sigma_1) \in \psi^s \mid \sigma_0, \sigma_1 \in S\} \ \cup$$
$$\{(\sigma, \delta) \in \psi^d \mid \sigma \in S \ \wedge \ (\forall \epsilon \mid ((\epsilon \in \mathbb{R}_{\geq 0}) \ \wedge \ (\epsilon \leq \delta)) \ : \ \sigma + \epsilon \in S)\}. \ ∎$$

Since meeting timing constraints in the presence of faults requires time predictability, we let our synthesis methods incorporate a finite set Y of new clock variables. We denote the set of states obtained by abstracting the clock variables in Y from a state predicate U by $U\backslash Y$. Likewise, if ψ is a set of transitions, we denote the set of transitions obtained by abstracting the clock variables in Y by $\psi_{\mathcal{P}}\backslash Y$. Now, observe that in the absence of faults, if S' contains states that are not in S then $\mathcal{P}'$ may include computations that start outside S. Hence, we require that $(S'\backslash Y) \subseteq S$. Moreover, if $\psi'_{\mathcal{P}}|S'$ contains a transition that is not in $\psi_{\mathcal{P}}|S'$ then in the absence of faults, $\mathcal{P}'$ can exhibit computations that do not correspond to computations of $\mathcal{P}$. Therefore, we require that $(\psi_{\mathcal{P}'}\backslash Y)|(S'\backslash Y) \subseteq \psi_{\mathcal{P}}|(S'\backslash Y)$.

Problem Statement 1. Given a program $\mathcal{P} = \langle S_{\mathcal{P}}, \psi_{\mathcal{P}} \rangle$, invariant S, specification *SPEC*, and set f of faults such that $\mathcal{P} \models_S$ *SPEC*, identify $\mathcal{P}' = \langle S_{\mathcal{P}'}, \psi_{\mathcal{P}'} \rangle$ and S' such that:

- $(C1)$ $S_{\mathcal{P}'}\backslash Y = S_{\mathcal{P}}$, where Y is a finite set of new clock variables,
- $(C2)$ $(S'\backslash Y) \subseteq S$,
- $(C3)$ $(\psi_{\mathcal{P}'}\backslash Y) \mid (S'\backslash Y) \subseteq \psi_{\mathcal{P}}|(S'\backslash Y)$, and
- $(C4)$ $\mathcal{P}'$ is f-tolerant to *SPEC* from S'. ∎

Note that the above problem statement can be instantiated for all four types of 2-phase recovery. In this paper, we focus on relaxed and graceful 2-phase recovery. Hence, we instantiate the problem statement with these two types and whenever it is clear from the context, for brevity, we omit the instantiation.

Notice that conditions $C1..C3$ in Problem Statement 1 precisely express the notion of behavior restriction (also called *language inclusion*) used in controller synthesis and game theory. Moreover, constraint $C4$ implicitly implies that the synthesized program is not allowed to exhibit new finite computations, which is known as the *non-blocking* condition. It is easy to observe that unlike controller synthesis problems, our notion of *maintains* (cf. Definition 7) embedded in condition $C4$ allows the output program to exhibit recovery computations that input program does not have.

5 Synthesizing Relaxed and Graceful 2-Phase Recovery

In this section, first, in Subsection 5.1, we show that the problem of synthesizing relaxed 2-phase recovery is NP-complete. Then, in Subsection 5.2, we show that it can be solved in polynomial-time if Q is required to be closed in the synthesized program. Subsequently, we interpret this result and identify its effect in Subsection 5.3. We present our polynomial algorithm for graceful 2-phase recovery in Subsection 5.4. Finally, we consider whether there are other types of 2-phase recovery instances in Subsection 5.5.

5.1 Complexity of Synthesizing Relaxed 2-Phase Recovery

In this section, we show that, in general, the problem of synthesizing fault-tolerant real-time programs that provide relaxed 2-phase recovery is NP-complete in the size of locations of the given fault-intolerant real-time program.

Instance. A real-time program $\mathcal{P} = \langle S_\mathcal{P}, \psi_\mathcal{P} \rangle$ with invariant S, a set of faults f, and a specification $SPEC$, such that $\mathcal{P} \models_S SPEC$, where $SPEC_{\overline{br}} \equiv (\neg S \mapsto_{\leq \theta} Q) \wedge (\neg S \mapsto_{\leq \delta} S)$ for state predicate Q and $\delta, \theta \in \mathbb{Z}_{\geq 0}$.

The decision problem (R2P). Does there exist an f-tolerant program $\mathcal{P}' = \langle S_{\mathcal{P}'}, \psi_{\mathcal{P}'} \rangle$ with invariant S' such that $\mathcal{P}'$ and S' meet the constraints of Problem Statement 1 when instantiated with relaxed 2-phase recovery?

We show that the R2P problem is NP-complete by reducing the *2-path problem* [16,6] to R2P.

Theorem 1. *The problem of transforming a fault-intolerant real-time program into a fault-tolerant program that provides* relaxed *2-phased recovery is NP-complete in the size of locations of the fault-intolerant program.* ∎

Corollary 1. *The problem of transforming a fault-intolerant real-time program into a fault-tolerant program that provides* relaxed *2-phased recovery is NP-complete in the size of locations of the fault-intolerant program even if $S \subseteq Q$.* ∎

5.2 Synthesizing Relaxed 2-Phase Recovery with Closure of Q

In this section, we show that if the intermediate predicate Q is required to be closed in the synthesized program, then the problem of synthesizing relaxed 2-phase recovery can be solved in polynomial time in the size of the time-abstract bisimulation of the input program. Towards this end, we propose the algorithm Add_RelaxedPhasedRecovery .

Assumption 1. For simplicity of presentation, we assume that the number of fault occurrences in any computation is at most 1. Note that the proof of Theorem 1 is valid even with this assumption. In [8], we have shown that if multiple faults occur within a computation, for a given state, one can compute the maximum time required to reach a state predicate. ∎

Next, we describe our algorithm Add_RelaxedPhasedRecovery:

- (*Step 1: Initialization*). Using the technique described above from [2], we obtain the region graph, $R(\mathcal{P})$, for the input program by using the routine ConstructRegionGraph (Line 1). Vertices of $R(\mathcal{P})$ (denoted $S^r_\mathcal{P}$) are regions. Edges of $R(\mathcal{P})$ (denoted $\psi^r_\mathcal{P}$) are of the form $(s_0, \rho_0) \to (s_1, \rho_1)$ iff for some clock valuations $\nu_0 \in \rho_0$ and $\nu_1 \in \rho_1$, $(s_0, \nu_0) \to (s_1, \nu_1)$ is a transitions in $\psi_\mathcal{P}$. Likewise, we convert state predicates and sets of transitions into corresponding region predicates and sets of edges. For example, S^r denotes the region predicate obtained from input S, and it is obtained as $S^r = \{(s, \rho) \mid \exists (s, \nu) : ((s, \nu) \in S \ \wedge \ \nu \in \rho)\}$.

Algorithm 1. Add_RelaxedPhasedRecovery

Input: A real-time program $\mathcal{P} = \langle S_{\mathcal{P}}, \psi_{\mathcal{P}} \rangle$ with invariant S, fault transitions f, bad transitions $SPEC_{bt}$, and $SPEC_{\overline{br}} \equiv (\neg S \mapsto_{\leq \theta} Q) \wedge (\neg S \mapsto_{\leq \delta} S)$, where Q is an intermediate recovery predicate, such that $S \subseteq Q$.

Output: If successful, a fault-tolerant real-time program $\mathcal{P}' = \langle S_{\mathcal{P}'}, \psi_{\mathcal{P}'} \rangle$ and invariant S' such that $\langle S_{\mathcal{P}}, \psi'_{\mathcal{P}}[]f \rangle \models_{S'} SPEC_{\overline{br}}$ and Q is closed in $\psi_{\mathcal{P}'}$.

1: $\langle S^r_{\mathcal{P}}, \psi^r_{\mathcal{P}} \rangle,\ S^r_1,\ Q^r,\ f^r,\ SPEC^r_{bt} :=$ ConstructRegionGraph($\langle S_{\mathcal{P}}, \psi_{\mathcal{P}} \rangle$, S, Q, f, $SPEC_{bt}$);

2: $ms := \{r_0 \mid \exists r_1, r_2 \cdots r_n : (\forall j \mid 0 \leq j < n : (r_j, r_{j+1}) \in f^r) \wedge (r_{n-1}, r_n) \in SPEC^r_{bt}\}$;

3: $mt := \{(r_0, r_1) \in \psi^r_{\mathcal{P}} \mid (r_1 \in ms) \vee ((r_0, r_1) \in SPEC^r_{bt})\}$;

4: $T^r_1 := S^r_{\mathcal{P}} - ms$;

5: **repeat**

6: $\quad T^r_2,\ S^r_2 := T^r_1,\ S^r_1$;

7: $\quad \psi^r_{\mathcal{P}_1} := \psi^r_{\mathcal{P}}|S^r_1 \cup \{((s_0, \rho_0), (s_1, \rho_1)) \mid (s_0, \rho_0) \in (T^r_1 - Q^r) \wedge (s_1, \rho_1) \in T^r_1 \wedge$ $\exists \rho_2 \mid \rho_2$ is a time-successor of $\rho_0 : (\exists \lambda \subseteq X : \rho_1 = \rho_2[\lambda := 0])\} \cup$ $\{((s_0, \rho_0), (s_1, \rho_1)) \mid (s_0, \rho_0) \in (Q^r - S^r_1) \wedge (s_1, \rho_1) \in Q^r \wedge$ $\exists \rho_2 \mid \rho_2$ is a time-successor of $\rho_0 : (\exists \lambda \subseteq X : \rho_1 = \rho_2[\lambda := 0])\} - mt$;

8: $\quad \psi^r_{\mathcal{P}_1},\ ns :=$ Add_BoundedResponse($\langle S^r_{\mathcal{P}}, \psi^r_{\mathcal{P}_1} \rangle$, $Q^r - S^r$, S^r, δ);

9: $\quad T^r_1 := T^r_1 - ns$;

10: $\quad \psi^r_{\mathcal{P}_1},\ ns := \overline{transform}$ (Add_BoundedResponse($transform(\langle S^r_{\mathcal{P}}, \psi^r_{\mathcal{P}_1} \rangle)$, $T^r_1 - Q^r$, Q^r, θ));

11: $\quad T^r_1,\ Q^r := T^r_1 - ns,\ Q^r - ns$;

12: $\quad$ **while** $(\exists r_0, r_1 : r_0 \in T^r_1 \wedge r_1 \notin T^r_1 \wedge (r_0, r_1) \in f^r)$ **do**

13: $\qquad T^r_1 := T^r_1 - \{r_0\}$;

14: $\quad$ **end while**

15: $\quad$ **while** $(\exists r_0 \in (S^r_1 \cap T^r_1) : (\forall r_1 \mid (r_1 \neq r_0 \wedge r_1 \in S^r_1) : (r_0, r_1) \notin \psi^r_{\mathcal{P}_1}))$ **do**

16: $\qquad S^r_1 := S^r_1 - \{r_0\}$;

17: $\quad$ **end while**

18: $\quad$ **if** $(S^r_1 = \{\} \vee T^r_1 = \{\})$ **then**

19: $\qquad$ **print** `‘‘no solution to relaxed 2-phase recovery exists’’`; **exit**;

20: $\quad$ **end if**

21: **until** $(T_1 = T_2 \wedge S_1 = S_2)$

22: $\langle S_{\mathcal{P}'}, \psi_{\mathcal{P}'} \rangle,\ S', T' :=$ ConstructRealTimeProgram($\langle S^r_{\mathcal{P}}, \psi^r_{\mathcal{P}_1} \rangle$, S^r_1, T^r_1);

23: **return** $\langle S_{\mathcal{P}'}, \psi_{\mathcal{P}'} \rangle,\ S',\ T'$;

In order to ensure that the synthesized program does not violate timing-independent safety, we identify the set ms of regions from where a computation can violate $SPEC_{\overline{bt}}$ by the occurrence of faults alone (Line 2). Clearly, the program should not reach a region in ms. Hence, we remove (Line 4) ms from the region predicate T^r_1, which is used to compute the fault-span of the program being synthesized. The set of edges that should not be included in the synthesized program, mt, consists of edges that reach ms and the edges in $SPEC^r_{bt}$. These edges are removed while constructing the possible program transitions (Line 7).

– *(Step 2: Adding* $(Q \mapsto_{\leq \delta} S)$ *).* In this step, we first recompute the set $\psi_{\mathcal{P}_1}$ of program edges (Line 7) that could potentially be used during phased recovery in the synthesized program. Towards this end, we partition the edges based on their originating states: If an edge originates from a state in S^r_1 (estimated invariant of the synthesized program), then by constraint $C3$ of Problem Statement 1, the edge must be included in the original program. If the edge originates in a region in $Q^r_1 - S^r_1$ then due to closure requirement of Q, it must end in Q^r_1. And, if the edge originates in a region in $T^r_1 - Q^r_1$ then due to closure requirement of fault-span, it must end in T^r_1. Furthermore, the edges must meet the time monotonicity condition and not present in the set mt. It is straightforward to observe that the edges computed on Line 7 must be a superset of the edges in a program that satisfies constraints of Problem Statement 1.

We use the program constructed on Line 7 and invoke the procedure Add_BoundedResponse to add $(Q \mapsto_{\leq\delta} S)$. Add_BoundedResponse (from [7]) adds a clock variable, say t_1, which gets reset when $Q - S$ becomes true. It computes a shortest path from every region in $Q_1^r - S_1^r$ to some region in S_1^r. If the delay on this path is less than or equal to δ, it includes that path in the synthesized program. If the delay is more than δ then it includes the corresponding region in $Q_1^r - S_1^r$ in ns. It follows that regions in ns cannot be included in the synthesized program. Hence, we remove ns from T_1^r and Q^r on Lines 9 and 11, respectively. Add_BoundedResponse can also add additional paths whose length is larger than that of the shortest paths but less than δ. However, for relaxed 2-phase recovery, addition of such additional paths needs to be performed after adding the second timing constraint in Line 10.

- (*Step 3: Adding* $(\neg S \mapsto_{\leq\gamma} Q)$). For each region r in Q^r, we identify $wt(r)$ that denotes the length of the path from r to a region in S^r. Next, we add the property $(\neg S \mapsto_{\leq\gamma} Q)$, where the value of γ depends upon the exact state reached in Q. Since we need to ensure $(\neg S \mapsto_{\leq\theta} Q)$, γ must be less than θ. And, since we need to ensure $(\neg S \mapsto_{\leq\delta} S)$, the time to reach a region r in Q^r must be less than $\delta - wt(r)$.

  To achieve this with Add_BoundedResponse, we transform the given region graph by the function *transform*, where we replace each region r in Q^r by r_1 (that is outside Q^r) and r_2 (that is in Q^r) such that there is an edge from r_1 to r_2. All incoming edges from $T_1^r - Q^r$ to r now reach r_1. All other edges (edges reaching r from another state in Q^r and outgoing edges from r) are connected to r_2. The weight of the edge from r_1 to r_2 is set to $\max(0, \theta + wt(r) - \delta)$. Now, we call Add_BoundedResponse add $(T_1 - Q \mapsto_{\leq\theta} Q)$. Notice that the transformation of the region graph along with invocation of Add_BoundedResponse (Line 10) ensures that any computation of the synthesized program that that starts from a state σ_0 in $\neg S$ and reaches a state σ_1 in $Q - S$ within θ still has sufficient time to reach a state σ_2 in S such that the overall delay between σ_0 and σ_2 is less than δ. In other words, the output program will satisfy $(T_1 - Q \mapsto_{\leq\delta} S)$ no matter what path it takes to achieve 2-phase recovery. We now collapse region r_1 and r_2 (created by *transform*) to obtain region r. We use $\overline{transform}$ to denote such collapsing.

- (*Step 4: Repeat if needed or construct synthesized program*). Since we remove some regions from T_1^r, we ensure closure of T_1^r in f by the loop on Lines 12-14. Furthermore, due to constraint $C4$ of the problem statement, S_1^r cannot have deadlock regions from where there are no outgoing edges. Hence, on Lines 15-17, we remove such deadlocks. If this removal causes S_1^r or T_1^r to be an empty set then the algorithm declares failure (Line 19).

  Since removal of regions from S_1^r or T_1^r can potentially affect the bounded response properties added on Lines 8 and 10, Steps 2 and 3 may have to be repeated. If no regions are removed (i.e., we reach a fixpoint), then we construct the corresponding real-time program $\mathcal{P}' = \langle S_{\mathcal{P}'}, \psi_{\mathcal{P}'} \rangle$ on Line 22. Since the construction of the region graph is a bisimulation of the corresponding real-time program, such reverse transformation is possible.

Theorem 2. *The Algorithm Add_RelaxedPhasedRecovery is* sound, *i.e., the synthesized program satisfies the constraints of Problem Statement 1, and* complete, *i.e., the algorithm finds a fault-tolerant program provided one exists.* ∎

5.3 Interpretation of Closure of Q

One main observation from the results in Subsections 5.1 and 5.2 is that the requirement of 'closure of Q', where Q is the intermediate recovery predicate, appears to play a crucial role in reducing the complexity. Thus, one may pose questions on the intuitive implication of this requirement in practice. There are two ways of characterizing the intermediate recovery predicate:

- One characterization is that predicate Q identifies an acceptable behavior of the program. In this case, it is expected that once the program starts exhibiting acceptable behavior, it continues to exhibit acceptable (or ideal) behavior in future. In such a characterization, closure of Q is satisfied.
- Another characterization is that the predicate Q identifies a *special* behavior that does not occur in the absence of faults. This special behavior can include notification or recording of the fault, suspension of normal operation for a certain duration, etc. Thus, in such a characterization, the program reaches Q, then leaves Q and eventually starts exhibiting its ideal behavior. In such a characterization, closure of Q is not satisfied.

The results in this paper shows that the complexity of the former characterization is significantly less than the latter. In other words, requiring that faults be recorded causes a significant growth in the complexity.

5.4 Complexity of Synthesizing Graceful 2-Phase Recovery

We present a somewhat counter-intuitive result: a sound and complete solution to the Problem Statement 1 when instantiated for graceful 2-phase recovery. This algorithm also requires Assumption 1 from Subsection 5.2. Without loss of generality, we assume that $\delta \leq \theta$. If $\delta > \theta$, then graceful 2-phase recovery corresponds to the requirement $(\neg S \mapsto_{\leq \theta} S)$. We now describe the algorithm.

- (*Step 1: Initialization*). This step is identical to that in Algorithm 1 and it constructs the region graph $R(\mathcal{P})$.
- (*Step 2: Adding* $(Q \mapsto_{\leq \delta} S)$). In this step, we add recovery paths to $R(\mathcal{P})$ so that $R(\mathcal{P})$ satisfies $(Q \mapsto_{\leq \delta} S)$. The set of edges used in this step (Line 7) differs from the corresponding step in Add_RelaxedPhasedRecovery. In particular, if an edge originates in Q_1^r, it need not terminate in Q_1^r. This is due to the fact that Q is not necessarily closed in graceful 2-phase recovery. Thus, the transitions computed for $\psi_{\mathcal{P}_1}$ of program edges are as specified on Line 7.

Algorithm 2. Add_GracefulPhasedRecovery

Input: A real-time program $\mathcal{P} = \langle S_{\mathcal{P}}, \psi_{\mathcal{P}} \rangle$ with invariant S, fault transitions f, bad transitions $SPEC_{bt}$, and $SPEC_{\overline{br}} \equiv (\neg S \mapsto_{\leq \theta} S) \wedge (\neg Q \mapsto_{\leq \delta} S)$, where Q is an intermediate recovery predicate, such that $S \subseteq Q$.

Output: If successful, a fault-tolerant real-time program $\mathcal{P}' = \langle S_{\mathcal{P}'}, \psi_{\mathcal{P}'} \rangle$ and invariant S' such that $\langle S_{\mathcal{P}}, \psi'_{\mathcal{P}}[]f \rangle \models_{S'} SPEC_{\overline{br}}$.

// This algorithm is obtained by changing the following lines from Algorithm 1

7 : $\psi^r_{\mathcal{P}_1} := \psi^r_{\mathcal{P}} | S^r_1 \cup \{((s_0, \rho_0), (s_1, \rho_1)) \mid (s_0, \rho_0) \in (T^r_1 - S^r) \wedge (s_1, \rho_1) \in T^r_1 \wedge$
$\exists \rho_2 \mid \rho_2$ is a time-successor of $\rho_0 : (\exists \lambda \subseteq X : \rho_1 = \rho_2[\lambda := 0])\} - mt;$

10 : $\psi^r_{\mathcal{P}_1}, ns :=$ Add_BoundedResponse$((\langle S^r_{\mathcal{P}}, \psi^r_{\mathcal{P}_1} \rangle), T^r - S^r_1, S^r_1, \theta)$;

After adding recovery edges, we invoke the procedure Add_BoundedResponse (Line 8) with parameters $Q^r - S^r$, S^r, and δ to ensure that $R(\mathcal{P})$ indeed satisfies the bounded response property $Q \mapsto_{\leq \delta} S$. Since the value of ns returned by Add_BoundedResponse indicates that there does not exist a computation prefix that maintains the corresponding bounded response property from the regions in ns, in Line 9, the algorithm removes ns from T^r_1.

- (*Step 3: Adding* $(\neg S \mapsto_{\leq \theta} S)$). This task is achieved by calling Add_BoundedResponse, where from each state in $\neg S$, we add a shortest path from that state to a state in S. Note that the paths from states in Q have a delay of at most δ. If such a path does not exist from a state in Q then, in Step 2, that state would have been included in ns and, hence, removed from T^r_1. While the addition of the second bounded response property is possible for graceful 2-phase recovery, for reasons discussed after Theorem 3, it is not possible for relaxed 2-phase recovery.
- (*Step 4*). This step is identical to that in Algorithm 1.

Theorem 3. *The Algorithm Add_GracefulPhasedRecovery is sound and complete.* ∎

Next, we discuss the main the main reason that permits solution of graceful 2-phase recovery be in polynomial-time without closure of Q, but causes the addition of relaxed 2-phase recovery to be NP-complete. Observe that in Line 10 in Add_RelaxedPhasedRecovery, we added recovery paths from states in T_1 to states in Q. Without closure property of Q, the paths added for Add_RelaxedPhasedRecovery can create cycles with paths added from Q to S. Such cycles outside S prevent the program from recovering to the invariant predicate within the required timing constraint. To the contrary, in Line 10 in Add_GracefulPhasedRecovery, we added recovery paths from states in T_1 to states in S. These paths cannot create cycles with paths added from $Q - S$. Moreover, the paths also do not increase the delay in recovering from Q to S. For this reason, the problem of Add_GracefulPhasedRecovery could be solved in polynomial-time.

5.5 Other Types of 2-Phase Recovery

Let us consider Definition 11 closely. Interesting possible values for Q_1 are Q, S and $Q - S$ and interesting possible values for Q_2 are $\neg S$ and Q. Thus, the different combinations for 2-phase recovery are as shown in the table below.

	$Q_1 = Q$	$Q_1 = S$	$Q_1 = Q - S$
$Q_2 = Q$	strict	graceful	ordered-strict
$Q_2 = \neg S$	relaxed	single phase	ordered-relaxed

Of these, we showed that the problem of relaxed 2-phase recovery is NP-complete. It is straightforward to observe that this proof can be extended to show that synthesizing ordered-relaxed 2-phase recovery is also NP-complete. Moreover, in [10], we showed that the problems of synthesizing strict and ordered-strict 2-phase recovery are NP-complete. As mentioned in Subsection 5.4, one surprising result in this table, however, is that the problem of synthesizing graceful 2-phase recovery can be solved in polynomial-time.

6 Conclusion

In this paper, we focused on complexity analysis of synthesizing bounded-time 2-phase recovery. This type of recovery consists of two bounded response properties of the form: $(\neg S \mapsto_{\leq \theta} Q_1) \;\wedge\; (Q_2 \mapsto_{\leq \delta} S)$. We characterized S as an ideal behavior and $Q_{1,2}$ as acceptable intermediate behaviors during recovery. Each property expresses one phase of recovery within the respective time bounds θ and δ in a fault-tolerant real-time program. We formally defined different scenarios of 2-phased recovery, characterized their applications in real-world systems, and considered two types of them called relaxed (where $Q_1 = Q$ and $Q_2 = \neg S$) and graceful (where $Q_1 = S$ and $Q_2 = Q$). We showed that, in general, the problem of synthesizing relaxed 2-phase recovery is NP-complete. However, the problem can be solved in polynomial-time, if $S \subseteq Q$ and Q is closed in the synthesized program. We also found a surprising result that the problem of synthesizing graceful 2-phase recovery can be solved in polynomial-time even though all other variations are NP-complete. We emphasize that all complexities are in the size of the input program's region graph.

Based on the complexity analysis, we find that the problem of synthesizing relaxed 2-phase recovery is significantly simpler, if the intermediate recovery predicate Q is closed in the execution of the synthesized program. This result implies that if the intermediate recovery predicate is used for *recording* the fault, then the complexity of the corresponding problem is substantially higher than the case where the program quickly provides acceptable behavior.

One future research direction is to develop heuristics to cope with the NP-complete instances. Based on our experience with synthesizing distributed fault-tolerant programs [9,11], we believe that efficient implementation of such heuristics makes it possible to synthesize real programs in practice. Another research problem is to consider the case where a real-time program is subject to different classes of faults and a different type of tolerance is required for each fault class.

References

1. Alpern, B., Schneider, F.B.: Defining liveness. Information Processing Letters 21, 181–185 (1985)
2. Alur, R., Dill, D.: A theory of timed automata. Theoretical Computer Science 126(2), 183–235 (1994)
3. Alur, R., Henzinger, T.A.: Real-time system = discrete system + clock variables. International Journal on Software Tools for Technology Transfer 1(1-2), 86–109 (1997)
4. Asarin, E., Maler, O.: As soon as possible: Time optimal control for timed automata. In: Vaandrager, F.W., van Schuppen, J.H. (eds.) HSCC 1999. LNCS, vol. 1569, pp. 19–30. Springer, Heidelberg (1999)
5. Asarin, E., Maler, O., Pnueli, A., Sifakis, J.: Controller synthesis for timed automata. In: IFAC Symposium on System Structure and Control, pp. 469–474 (1998)
6. Bang-Jensen, J., Gutin, G.: Digraphs: Theory, Algorithms and Applications. Springer, Heidelberg (2002)
7. Bonakdarpour, B., Kulkarni, S.S.: Automated incremental synthesis of timed automata. In: Brim, L., Haverkort, B.R., Leucker, M., van de Pol, J. (eds.) FMICS 2006 and PDMC 2006. LNCS, vol. 4346, pp. 261–276. Springer, Heidelberg (2007)
8. Bonakdarpour, B., Kulkarni, S.S.: Incremental synthesis of fault-tolerant real-time programs. In: Datta, A.K., Gradinariu, M. (eds.) SSS 2006. LNCS, vol. 4280, pp. 122–136. Springer, Heidelberg (2006)
9. Bonakdarpour, B., Kulkarni, S.S.: Exploiting symbolic techniques in automated synthesis of distributed programs with large state space. In: IEEE International Conference on Distributed Computing Systems (ICDCS), pp. 3–10 (2007)
10. Bonakdarpour, B., Kulkarni, S.S.: Masking faults while providing bounded-time phased recovery. In: Cuellar, J., Maibaum, T., Sere, K. (eds.) FM 2008. LNCS, vol. 5014, pp. 374–389. Springer, Heidelberg (2008)
11. Bonakdarpour, B., Kulkarni, S.S.: SYCRAFT: A tool for synthesizing fault-tolerant distributed programs. In: van Breugel, F., Chechik, M. (eds.) CONCUR 2008. LNCS, vol. 5201, pp. 167–171. Springer, Heidelberg (2008)
12. Bouyer, P., D'Souza, D., Madhusudan, P., Petit, A.: Timed control with partial observability. In: Hunt Jr., W.A., Somenzi, F. (eds.) CAV 2003. LNCS, vol. 2725, pp. 180–192. Springer, Heidelberg (2003)
13. de Alfaro, L., Faella, M., Henzinger, T.A., Majumdar, R., Stoelinga, M.: The element of surprise in timed games. In: Amadio, R.M., Lugiez, D. (eds.) CONCUR 2003. LNCS, vol. 2761, pp. 144–158. Springer, Heidelberg (2003)
14. D'Souza, D., Madhusudan, P.: Timed control synthesis for external specifications. In: Alt, H., Ferreira, A. (eds.) STACS 2002. LNCS, vol. 2285, pp. 571–582. Springer, Heidelberg (2002)
15. Faella, M., LaTorre, S., Murano, A.: Dense real-time games. In: Logic in Computer Science (LICS), pp. 167–176 (2002)
16. Fortune, S., Hopcroft, J.E., Wyllie, J.: The directed subgraph homeomorphism problem. Theoretical Computer Science 10, 111–121 (1980)
17. Henzinger, T.A.: Sooner is safer than later. Information Processing Letters 43(3), 135–141 (1992)

Verifying Real-Time Systems against Scenario-Based Requirements

Kim G. Larsen, Shuhao Li, Brian Nielsen, and Saulius Pusinskas

Center for Embedded Software Systems (CISS)
Aalborg University
Selma Lagerlöfs Vej 300, DK-9220 Aalborg, Denmark
{kgl,li,bnielsen,saulius}@cs.aau.dk

Abstract. We propose an approach to automatic verification of real-time systems against scenario-based requirements. A real-time system is modeled as a network of Timed Automata (TA), and a scenario-based requirement is specified as a Live Sequence Chart (LSC). We define a trace-based semantics for a kernel subset of the LSC language. By equivalently translating an LSC chart into an observer TA and then non-intrusively composing this observer with the original system model, the problem of verifying a real-time system against a scenario-based requirement reduces to a classical real-time model checking problem. We show how this is accomplished in the context of the Uppaal model checker.

1 Introduction

A model checker typically needs two inputs: a model $\mathcal{M}$ characterizing the state-transition behaviors of a finite state concurrent system, and a temporal logic formula $\mathcal{P}$ specifying the properties of interest. For real-time model checkers such as Kronos [20] and Uppaal [3], $\mathcal{M}$ might be a network of Timed Automata (TA) [1], and $\mathcal{P}$ might be a formula of the TCTL logic [20] or a fragment of the CTL logic [3]. While the enhanced versions of TA are relatively expressive modeling formalisms, the TCTL or CTL logics appear to be property specification languages of only limited capability, intuitiveness, and convenience:

- The atomic propositions can only be state propositions, where messages (events) are not allowed to appear [20,3];
- There is no means for specifying non-trivial quantitative timing constraints (e.g., there is no time-bounded temporal operator like $\Diamond_{[1,3]}$) [3].

These limitations imply that straightforward characterizations of event synchronizations, causal relations, or scenarios such as "**if** process B sends message m_1 to process A, and C sends m_2 to D (in any order), **then** B **must** send m_3 to C within 1 to 3 time units" as a query in Kronos and Uppaal are not possible.

Essentially, the query languages of these model checkers describe only *intra*-process properties, i.e., whether all states ($\Box$) or at least one state ($\Diamond$) along all paths (A) or at least one path (E) of the individual processes or the product

A. Cavalcanti and D. Dams (Eds.): FM 2009, LNCS 5850, pp. 676–691, 2009.

process (i.e., the parallelly composed system model) satisfy some particular properties. In contrast, the *inter*-process properties describe how different processes interact, collaborate and cooperate via message or rendezvous synchronizations.

Live Sequence Chart (LSC) [11] is a visual formalism for scenario-based specification and programming. It extends the classical Message Sequence Charts (MSC) [13] by adding modalities[1]. The LSC language is unambiguous because it has strictly defined semantics, e.g., the executable (operational) semantics [11] and the trace-based semantics [7].

We envisage LSC as a nice complement to the intra-process property specification language of (real-time) model checkers in general and of Uppaal in particular:

- *Intuitiveness.* LSC has the necessary language constructs to describe a variety of causality and non-trivial scenarios. As a visual formalism, LSC is more intuitive in capturing scenario-based user requirements than the CTL fragment of Uppaal in its textual form;
- *Expressiveness.* It has been shown that a kernel subset [15] of LSC can be embedded into CTL*, *provided that* event occurrences can be used as atomic propositions [15]. This indicates that LSC cannot always be encoded as CTL*;
- *Counterexample display.* LSC provides the possibility of displaying counterexamples also in the requirement specifications.

In this paper we capture a scenario that is to be verified using an LSC chart. We obtain a behavior-equivalent observer TA from this chart by mapping the LSC cuts and discrete advancement steps to TA locations and edges, respectively. We let the observer TA spy on the relevant events of the original system via model instrumentation, semaphore locking, and parallel composition. In this way, the problem of verifying a real-time system against a scenario-based requirement will be reduced to a classical model checking problem in Uppaal.

1.1 Related Work

To model check real-time systems against complex properties or scenario-based requirements, various approaches have been proposed.

One solution is the observer automata approach [4], i.e., to construct a number of auxiliary TA to capture the scenario-based requirements, and then parallelly compose them with the original TA models. While this method can be practically useful [16], there are some limitations: (1) manual constructions of observer TA could be labor-intensive and error-prone. To be composed with the observer TA, the original system model may need to be modified; (2) the observer TA and the original system engage in normal channel synchronizations, thus specifying process interactions only *liberally* (i.e., no particular sending and receiving process

[1] The *existential* and *cold* (resp. *universal* and *hot*) modalities represent the provisional (resp. mandatory) requirements. For example, an existential (resp. universal) chart specifies restrictions over at least one satisfying (resp. all possible) system runs; a cold condition may be violated, whereas a hot one must be satisfied.

is specified for a message). In our verification framework, automatic construction of observers from LSC charts overcomes both problems.

Another line of research is first to capture the scenario-based requirements using the assume-guarantee style visual formalisms such as Triggered MSC [19], Template MSCs [10], or the even richer LSC [11], and then transform them into directly verifiable formalisms. In particular LSCs can be translated into Timed Büchi Automaton (TBA) [14], TA [17], temporal logic [14,12,15,8,6], or sequences of LSC elements [18], and the verification problem can be converted to a classical model checking problem [14], or solved directly [18].

In [14] an LSC chart is transformed into a TBA. To specify real-time requirements, timers [2,13] and timing annotations (or delayed intervals) [2] are added to the LSC charts. To enable the transformation, each location of the LSC chart is equipped with a discrete (integer) clock. Since timers can only express timing constraints within a *single* chart and within a *single* process, and delayed intervals can only express the minimal and maximal delays between two *consecutive* locations, these restrict the expression of timing constraints across processes and across charts. Our LSC charts use TA-like real-valued clock variables. This flavor of timing constraint agrees well with the original system model, and enables smooth translation of timing information into the observer TA, and seamless embedding of the observer TA into the Uppaal verification framework.

An LSC-to-TA translation has been proposed in [17], which inspires our current translation. Since we use LSC only as a property specification language, and not also as a modeling language [17], we define a clearer semantics, according to which there is no need to translate one LSC chart into multiple TA as in [17].

LSCs can also be translated into temporal logic formulas [12,15,8,6]. For the kernel subset of LSC in [15], it has been shown that existential charts can be expressed using the CTL logic, and universal charts can be expressed using (LTL$\cap$ CTL) [12,15]. Similar results are achieved in [8]. However, these methods do not handle explicit time in the charts, and the extraordinary size of the resulting formula limits the scale of the charts that can be translated and verified.

In [18] properties are extracted from LSCs as sequences of LSC elements, and algorithms have been developed to check whether these sequences are respected by the FSM computation graph of the TA model that is exported from Uppaal. However, simultaneous regions (simregions) in LSCs are used only to model broadcast communications, and conditions cannot be a part of simregions. Our notion of simregion uses the "[condition] [message]/[assignment]" pattern, thus enables smooth translation into a TA edge.

1.2 Contributions

The contributions of this paper include: (1) we define a kernel subset of the LSC language that is suitable for capturing scenario-based requirements of real-time systems, and define a trace-based semantics; (2) we propose a behavior-equivalent translation of an LSC chart into a TA; (3) we present a method of embedding the translated TA into Uppaal, thus encoding the problem of verifying systems against LSC requirements as a classical model checking problem.

2 Modeling and Specification of Real-Time Systems

In Uppaal, a real-time system is modeled as a network of TA. These TA communicate on shared global variables, or via handshaking on CCS-style synchronization channels. Standard constructs of TA include locations, edges, clock constraints, clock resets, and location invariants. In addition, Uppaal has a number of extensions [3] to the TA formalism such as urgent and committed locations[2], broadcast channels, data variables, variable constraints and updates, etc. Fig. 1(a)-1(d) give an example of a network of TA.

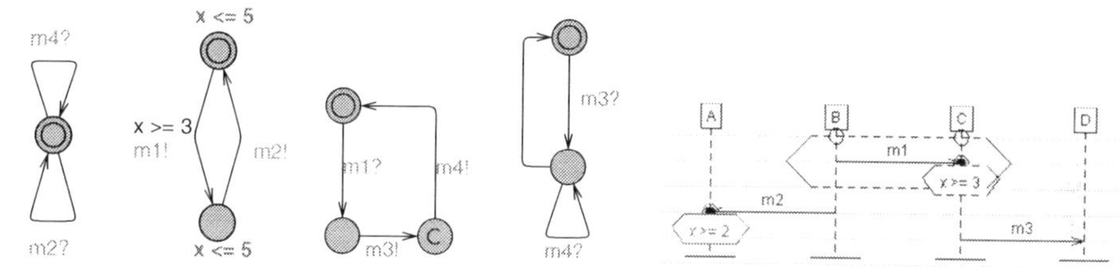

(a) TA A (b) TA B (c) TA C (d) TA D (e) LSC chart $\mathcal{L}$

Fig. 1. A real-time system model (network of TA) and its requirement (LSC chart)

Uppaal uses a fragment of the CTL logic as its property specification language. Atomic propositions can only be state propositions. Properties can be specified using a number of patterns: reachability ($\mathsf{E}\Diamond\phi$), safety ($\mathsf{A}\Box\phi$, $\mathsf{E}\Box\phi$), and liveness properties ($\mathsf{A}\Diamond\phi$, $\phi \leadsto \varphi$). In particular the *leads-to* or *response* property $\phi \leadsto \varphi$ is a shorthand for $\mathsf{A}\Box(\phi \Rightarrow \mathsf{A}\Diamond\varphi)$, meaning that whenever ϕ is satisfied, then eventually φ will be satisfied.

Although a lot of properties can be specified using these patterns, many others still cannot. Consider a user requirement on the TA in Fig. 1: **if** we observe that process B sends message m_1 to process C when clock x is no less than 3, **then** afterwards (and before m_1 can be observed again) we **must** observe that B sends m_2 to A when x is no less than 2, and C sends m_3 to D (in any order). Clearly, this scenario cannot be specified as a Uppaal CTL formula.

However, the above scenario requirement can be easily captured using Live Sequence Charts (Fig. 1(e)). For instance, the first block of diagrammatic elements $\{m_1, x \geq 3\}$ means that: when m_1 in the original model is observed, the clock value of x should be no less than 3 at that time. If this is the case, then the monitored execution continues; otherwise, it is a cold violation of the prechart[3].

[2] A *committed* location is a TA location where time is frozen, and the outgoing transitions have higher priority to be taken than those from non-committed ones.

[3] A universal chart can optionally contain a *prechart*, which specifies the scenario which, if successfully executed, forces the system to satisfy the scenario given in the actual chart body (the *main chart*).

3 From LSC to Uppaal Timed Automata

3.1 Live Sequence Chart

We consider the following LSC elements: instance, location, message, clock variable, condition, assignment, and simregion.

An LSC chart can have a role, a type, and an activation mode. In this paper we consider the role of *system property specification*, i.e., a monitored chart will just "listen to" the messages and read the clock variables in the original system models, but never emit messages or reset those clocks. We consider the *universal* type charts. Furthermore, we consider the *invariant* activation mode, i.e., the chart will be activated whenever a minimal event (i.e., an event that is minimal in the partial order induced by the chart) is matched, regardless of the state of the main chart.

Each LSC chart $\mathcal{L}$ describes a particular interaction scenario of a set I of processes (or instances, or agents). Along each instance line $i \in I$ there are a finite set of "positions" $pos(i) = \{0, 1, \ldots, p\_max_i\}$, which denote the possible points of communication and computation. We denote all *locations* of $\mathcal{L}$ as $L = \{\langle i,p \rangle | i \in I \ \wedge \ p \in pos(i)\}$.

Let Σ be the alphabet of messages (a.k.a. "channels" in Uppaal). A *message* $m = (\langle i,p \rangle, \sigma, \langle i',p' \rangle) \in L \times \Sigma \times L$ corresponds to instance i, while in position p, sending σ to instance i' at position p'. The (finite) set of all messages appearing in $\mathcal{L}$ are denoted as M. We call σ the message *label*. We say that i and i' are the source (src) and destination (dest) instances, respectively. Messages are assumed to be instantaneous (thus we use the terms *message* and *event* interchangeably). Furthermore, messages are assumed to be of *hot* temperature, i.e., they never get lost during transmission. This paper does not consider concurrent messages, thus each location can be the end point of at most one message in the chart.

Let the finite sets of real-valued *clock variables* (ranging over $\mathbb{R}_{\geq 0}$) of $\mathcal{L}$ and of the original system model $\mathcal{S}$ be $C_{\mathcal{L}}$ and $C_{\mathcal{S}}$, respectively. The set of readable clock variables in $\mathcal{L}$ will be $C = C_{\mathcal{L}} \cup C_{\mathcal{S}}$. Since $\mathcal{L}$ is a monitored chart, only clocks in $C_{\mathcal{L}}$ can be reset in the chart.

A *clock constraint* is of the form $x \bowtie n$ or $x - y \bowtie n$ where $x, y \in C$, $n \in \mathbb{Z}$, and $\bowtie \in \{<, \leq, =, \geq, >\}$. A *condition* is a finite conjunction of clock constraints. The set of conditions are denoted G. Conditions may be either hot or cold.

A *clock reset* is of the form $x := 0$ where $x \in C_{\mathcal{L}}$. An *assignment* a is a finite set of clock resets. For simplicity it is denoted as a set a of clocks to be reset. The set of all assignments is $A = 2^{C_{\mathcal{L}}}$.

When there is a message m sent from one instance i_1 to another instance i_2, the message anchoring point on i_1 or i_2 could be associated with a condition g and/or an assignment a. The condition g is a predicate which is evaluated immediately *after* the message has been observed, and the assignment is a reset of the clocks in a providing that g evaluates to true. The message, condition and assignment can be collectively viewed as an atomic step of LSC execution, i.e., they take place at the same time, hence the notion of *simultaneous region* (simregion), which is inspired by [14].

Definition 1 (simregion). *A* simregion *s is a set of LSC message, condition, and assignment, $s \subseteq (M \cup G \cup A)$, which satisfy the following requirements:*

- *non-emptiness: $\exists e \in (M \cup G \cup A). e \in s$;*
- *uniqueness: $\forall m, n \in M.(m \in s \land n \in s) \Rightarrow m = n$; (similarly for condition and assignment.)*
- *non-overlapping: for any two simregions s and s', we have $\forall e \in (M \cup G \cup A).(e \in s \land e \in s') \Rightarrow s = s'$.* □

We write a simregion as $s = \{m, g, a\}$, where m, g, and a represent the message, condition, and assignment, respectively. The set of all simregions is denoted $S \subseteq 2^{(M \cup G \cup A)}$.

A message spans across two instance lines. A condition spans across one or more instance lines. In a simregion, the message, condition and assignment (if any) have exactly one common anchoring point. If a simregion s has a message, then the condition and/or assignment (if any) of s anchor either at the message head, or at the message tail. If a simregion s has no message, then s consists of a condition test, or an assignment, or both of them combined and anchored together (possibly across multiple instance lines). In this case, s is called a *non-message* simregion. For such a simregion, we adopt the As-Soon-As-Possible (ASAP) semantics for its firing, i.e., the condition test (if any) will be evaluated immediately after the previous simregion.

Fig. 1(e) is an example LSC chart, where there are three simregions $s_1 = \{m_1, x \geq 3\}$, $s_2 = \{m_2, x \geq 2\}$, and $s_3 = \{m_3\}$.

3.2 Trace-Based Semantics

We define $\lambda : L \rightarrow S \cup \{nil\}$ as a labeling function. For location $l \in L$, if $\lambda(l) \in S$, then there is a simregion anchoring at l; if $\lambda(l) = nil$, then l represents an entry/exit point of the prechart(Pch)/main chart(Mch).

Locations of an LSC chart are partially ordered by the following rules:

- Along each instance line, if location l_1 is above l_2, then $l_1 \leq l_2$;
- All locations in the same simregion have the same order, $\forall s \in S, \forall l, l' \in L.(\lambda(l) = s) \land (\lambda(l') = s) \Rightarrow (l \leq l') \land (l' \leq l)$.

The partial order relation $\preccurlyeq \subseteq L \times L$ is defined as a transitive closure of $\leq$.

Definition 2 (cut). *A* cut *is a downward-closed set of locations that span across all the instance lines. Downward-closure means that if a location l is included in cut c, so are all of its preordered locations: $\forall c \subseteq L, \forall l, l' \in L.(l \in c \land l' \preccurlyeq l) \Rightarrow l' \in c$.* □

We define $loc : (S \cup 2^L) \rightarrow 2^L$ to map a simregion $s \in S$ to a set $loc(s)$ of locations that it anchors, and to map a cut $c \in 2^L$ to its *frontier* $loc(c)$, which is a set of locations that constitute the downward border line progressed so far.

Let $c \subseteq L$ be a cut, and $s \in S$ be a simregion that follows c immediately. A cut c' is an *s-successor* of c, denoted $c \xrightarrow{s} c'$, if c' is achieved by adding the set of locations that s anchors into c, or formally, $c \xrightarrow{s} c' \Leftrightarrow \forall l \in loc(s).(l \notin c) \wedge (c' = c \cup loc(s))$.

A cut c is *minimal* (denoted $\top$) if each location in c is a top location of some instance line, and c is *maximal* (denoted $\bot$) if the bottom locations of all instance lines are included in c. The frontiers of cuts $\top$ and $\bot$ do not contain simregion anchoring points. A minimal or maximal cut represents a compulsory synchronization for all involved instances. Thus the partial order relation $\preccurlyeq$ on L is extended as follows (and finally also extended to its transitive closure):

- All locations in the same minimal or maximal cut have the same order, $\forall c \in \{Pch.\top, Pch.\bot, Mch.\top, Mch.\bot\}.\forall l, l' \in loc(c).(l \preccurlyeq l') \wedge (l' \preccurlyeq l)$.

Specifically, we view the maximal cut of the prechart and the minimal cut of the main chart as the same cut, i.e., $Pch.\bot = Mch.\top$.

If cut c has $c' = Mch.\bot$ as its s-successor, then we override c' as $Pch.\top$ (if any) or $Mch.\top$, which represents the situation where a universal chart goes back to its initial state upon the successful completion of a round of monitoring.

For instance in Fig. 1(e), the possible cuts are: $\{\}$, $\{s_1\}$, $\{s_1, s_2\}$, $\{s_1, s_3\}$, $\{s_1, s_2, s_3\}$, where e.g. $\{s_1\}$ is a shorthand for the cut where simregion s_1 has been stepped over. Clearly, cuts $\{s_1, s_2\}$ and $\{s_1, s_3\}$ are the s_2-successor and s_3-successor of cut $\{s_1\}$, respectively.

Definition 3 (configuration). *A* configuration *of an LSC chart is a tuple (c, v), where c is a cut, and v maps each clock variable to a non-negative real number, $v : C_{\mathcal{L}} \to \mathbb{R}_{\geq 0}$.* □

For $d > 0$, notation $(v + d) : C_{\mathcal{L}} \to \mathbb{R}_{\geq 0}$ means that the function v is shifted by d such that $\forall x \in C_{\mathcal{L}}.v(x + d) = v(x) + d$.

A configuration at the minimal cut $\top$ with all clocks assigned their initial values (e.g., 0's) is called the *initial* configuration.

An assignment $a \in A$ can be viewed as a transformer for function v, thus $a(v)$ represents the new valuation after the assignment.

A configuration can be viewed as the "state" of an LSC chart. A universal chart starts from the initial configuration, advances from one configuration to a next one, until hot violation occurs, or until the chart arrives at the maximal cut and then starts all over again (i.e., to begin a next round execution).

There are three kinds of valid advancement steps between two configurations:

- *Synchronization step.* Given a chart configuration (c, v), and a simregion s which has a message m, and optionally a condition g, and/or an assignment a. There is a synchronization step $(c, v) \xrightarrow{m} (c', a(v))$ if, $c \xrightarrow{s} c'$ and $v \models g$;
- *Silent step.* Given a chart configuration (c, v), and a simregion s which optionally has a message m, and/or a condition g, and/or an assignment a. There is a silent step $(c, v) \xrightarrow{\tau} (c', a(v))$ if either
  - (*silent advancement*). $(\nexists m \in M.m \in s)$, and $v \models g$, and $c \xrightarrow{s} c'$; or
  - (*premature termination*). g.temp = cold, and $v \not\models g$, and $c' = Pch.\top$;

– *Time delay step.* Given a chart configuration (c, v). There is a time delay step $(c, v) \xrightarrow{d} (c, v+d)$ if there exists a simregion that follows cut c, and the clock constraints in its conditions (if any) will be satisfied after delay d, i.e., $\exists s = \{m, g, a\}.(v+d) \models g$.

Definition 4 (run). *A* run *of a universal LSC chart is a sequence of configurations* $(c_0, v_0) \cdot (c_1, v_1) \cdot \ldots$ *that are connected by the advancement steps, i.e.,* $\forall i \geq 0. \exists u_i \in (M \cup \{\tau\} \cup \mathbb{R}_{\geq 0}).(c_i, v_i) \xrightarrow{u_i} (c_{i+1}, v_{i+1})$. □

The transition relation $\rightarrow$ as mentioned above each time consumes only a single letter $u \in (M \cup \{\tau\} \cup \mathbb{R}_{\geq 0})$. We extend it to $\rightarrow^*$ such that it consumes a (finite or infinite) word $w \in (M \cup \{\tau\} \cup \mathbb{R}_{\geq 0})^* \cup (M \cup \{\tau\} \cup \mathbb{R}_{\geq 0})^\omega$.

Let Π be the alphabet of all possible advancement steps in the original system model, which subsumes $(M \cup \{\tau\} \cup \mathbb{R}_{\geq 0})$ and can in addition include other messages not ever appeared in M.

Definition 5 (satisfaction of a prechart/main chart). *A timed trace* $\gamma \in \Pi^* \cup \Pi^\omega$ satisfies *an LSC prechart or main chart* $\mathcal{C}$ *if its projection* $\gamma|_{(M \cup \{\tau\} \cup \mathbb{R}_{\geq 0})}$ *has a finite prefix* μ *which is the accepted word of a run that starts from the initial configuration and ends in a maximal cut configuration of* $\mathcal{C}$*, i.e.,* $\gamma \models \mathcal{C} \Leftrightarrow \exists \mu \in (M \cup \{\tau\} \cup \mathbb{R}_{\geq 0})^*, \xi \in (M \cup \{\tau\} \cup \mathbb{R}_{\geq 0})^* \cup (M \cup \{\tau\} \cup \mathbb{R}_{\geq 0})^\omega. (\gamma|_{(M \cup \{\tau\} \cup \mathbb{R}_{\geq 0})} = \mu \cdot \xi) \wedge \exists v'.(\top, v_0) \xrightarrow{\mu}{}^* (\bot, v')$. □

If a universal chart $\mathcal{L}$ has no prechart Pch, then it is treated as being satisfied by an empty word.

We define $\Vdash$ to denote that a finite trace $\gamma \in \Pi^*$ satisfies chart $\mathcal{C}$ *exactly*: $\gamma \Vdash \mathcal{C} \Leftrightarrow (\gamma \models \mathcal{C}) \wedge \forall \alpha, \mu, \beta \in \Pi^*.(\alpha \cdot \mu \cdot \beta = \gamma) \wedge (\alpha \neq \varepsilon \ \vee \ \beta \neq \varepsilon) \Rightarrow (\mu \not\models \mathcal{C})$.

Now we define the satisfaction relation for a full universal chart:

Definition 6 (satisfaction of universal LSC chart). *A timed trace* $\gamma \in \Pi^\omega$ satisfies *a universal chart* $\mathcal{L}$ *iff, whenever a finite subtrace of* γ *matches the prechart, then the main chart is matched immediately afterwards,* $\gamma \models \mathcal{L} \Leftrightarrow \forall \alpha, \mu \in \Pi^*, \beta \in \Pi^\omega.(\alpha \cdot \mu \cdot \beta = \gamma) \wedge (\mu \Vdash Pch) \Rightarrow \beta \models Mch$. □

A timed language $Lang \subseteq \Pi^\omega$ satisfies $\mathcal{L}$, denoted $Lang \models \mathcal{L}$, iff, $\forall \gamma \in Lang. \gamma \models \mathcal{L}$. Clearly, $Lang$ characterizes the system behaviors that respect $\mathcal{L}$.

For a network $\mathcal{S}$ of timed automata, we use $\mathcal{S} \vdash \mathcal{L}$ to denote that the timed traces (language) of $\mathcal{S}$ satisfy LSC $\mathcal{L}$.

3.3 LSC to TA Translation

For each LSC chart $\mathcal{L}$, we construct a Uppaal TA $O_{\mathcal{L}}$. The basic idea is that for each cut of the LSC, we assign a TA location in Uppaal; for each discrete advancement step (i.e., a simregion) that connects two consecutive cuts, we assign a TA edge. The translation is conducted incrementally based on the partial order relation $\preccurlyeq$.

3.3.1 Determining the Partial Order on LSC Simregions

By analyzing the graphical layout of the LSC chart, the partial order $\preccurlyeq$ on the set L of locations is determined according to the rules given in Section 3.2.

Since an advancement of a cut is caused by stepping over a simregion, the partial order $\preccurlyeq$ on L can thus be lifted to $\preccurlyeq'$ on $S \cup \{Pch.\top, Mch.\top, Mch.\bot\}$ as follows: $\forall s_1, s_2 \in (S \cup \{Pch.\top, Mch.\top, Mch.\bot\}).(s_1 \preccurlyeq' s_2 \Leftrightarrow \exists l_1 \in loc(s_1), l_2 \in loc(s_2).l_1 \preccurlyeq l_2)$.

For instance in Fig. 1(e), the partial order $\preccurlyeq'$ among the three simregions s_1 (middle), s_2 (left), and s_3 (right) is: $s_1 \preccurlyeq' s_2$, and $s_1 \preccurlyeq' s_3$.

3.3.2 Translating LSC Cut into TA Location

The initial cut of an LSC chart is the minimal cut $\top$ of the prechart (if any) or of the main chart (otherwise). While respecting $\preccurlyeq'$, the cut advances towards $Mch.\bot$ by stepping over simregions. Each time a simregion is stepped over, a new cut is reached.

If we view all the instances of an LSC chart collectively as a whole system, then a cut can be viewed as a "location" of the TA of this whole system. For the minimal cut of the prechart (if any) and the minimal and maximal cuts of the main chart, we assign the TA locations l_{pmin}, l_{min}, and l_{max}, respectively. Note that l_{max} is a committed location, which will be connected to l_{pmin} (if any) or l_{min} via an edge of internal action transition, meaning that a next round of monitoring will begin immediately. The l_{pmin}, l_{min}, and l_{max} locations are three mandatory synchronization points for all the instances in the chart.

Time can elapse while staying in an LSC cut just like in a TA location. Specifically, a cut that is followed by a non-message simregion corresponds to a committed TA location. In that cut time is frozen and cannot elapse.

Since there are only finitely many instances and finitely many simregions in an LSC chart, the number of cuts will also be finitely many.

3.3.3 Translating LSC Simregion into TA Edge

If s is a message-simregion, then we map the message, condition (if any) and assignment (if any) of s into one edge of the TA. See Fig. 2(a)-2(b).

Due to the restriction of Uppaal that broadcast channels cannot be guarded by timing constraints, in the TA of Fig. 2(b), m_1 cannot be simply treated as

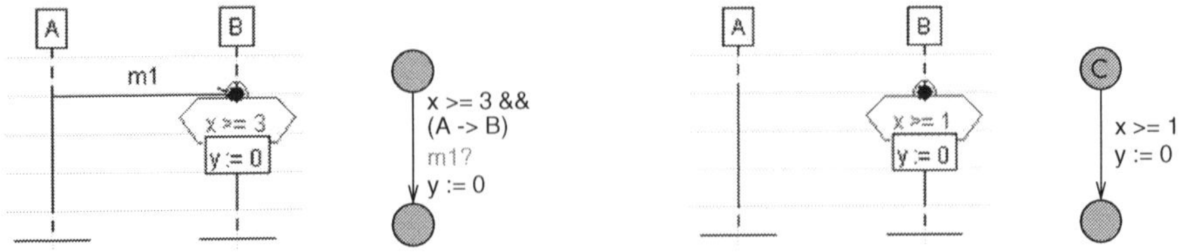

(a) A message-simregion (b) The TA edge (c) A non-msg. simregion (d) The TA edge

Fig. 2. From simregion to TA edge

a broadcast channel. Instead, some spying techniques will be adopted such that the translated TA will be notified of each message synchronization in the original system *immediately after* its occurrence (cf. Section 4.1).

In an LSC chart, a message m is sent from one particular instance to another one (e.g., from A to B). To preserve this sender/receiver information in the translated TA, the TA edge will be further guarded by the predicate $A \rightarrow B$ (shorthand for "$src = A$ && $dest = B$"). See Fig. 2(b).

If s is a non-message simregion, then the ASAP semantics is adopted. To enforce the ASAP semantics, the source location of the translated TA edge will be marked as a committed location. See Fig. 2(c)-2(d) for an example.

3.3.4 Incremental Construction of the TA

The LSC to TA translation is carried out incrementally. Assume that a TA location l has already been created for the current LSC cut (see Fig. 3(b), location l, and Fig. 3(a), cut $\{s_1\}$). Following that cut there could be a number of simregions that can be stepped over. Each of them should correspond to an outgoing edge from TA location l. Without loss of generality, we assume that there are two such immediately following simregions s_2 and s_3.

If s_2 and s_3 are both message-simregions (Fig. 3(a)), then the two new TA edges will be concatenated to location l. Let the two new edges be (l_1, l_2) and (l_3, l_4), respectively. Then l_1 and l_3 will be superposed on l. See Fig. 3(b).

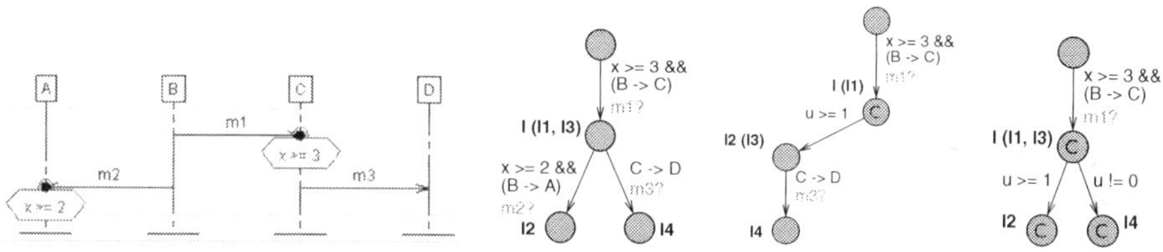

(a) The simregions (b) case #1 (c) case #2 (d) case #3

Fig. 3. TA edge construction for two subsequent simregions

If in Fig. 3(a) s_2 is replaced by a non-message simregion, then according to the ASAP semantics, the edge (l_1, l_2) will be executed immediately, and edge (l_3, l_4) will follow, but cannot be the other way around. When concatenating these two edges to the TA, we mark l_1 as a committed location, and superpose it on l. There is only one possible interleaving where edge (l_3, l_4) follows (l_1, l_2). See Fig. 3(c).

If in Fig. 3(a) s_2 and s_3 are both non-message simregions, then according to the ASAP semantics, both (l_1, l_2) and (l_3, l_4) will be executed immediately, therefore the executions will be interleaved. See Fig. 3(d).

3.3.5 Implicitly Allowed Behavior

In addition to the *explicitly* specified behaviors in the chart, there are also *implicitly* allowed behaviors that are due to: (1) unconstrained events, (2) cold violations, and (3) prechart pre-matching.

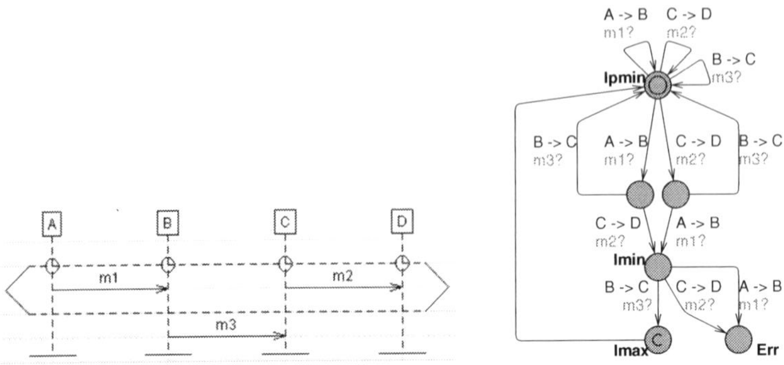

(a) An LSC chart (b) The translated TA

Fig. 4. Prechart matching

Let *Chan* be the set of channels of $\mathcal{S}$, and $Chan' \subseteq Chan$ be the set of channels of $\mathcal{L}$. Clearly, channels in $(Chan \backslash Chan')$ are not constrained by $\mathcal{L}$. For each message m whose label belongs to $(Chan \backslash Chan')$, we add an m?-labeled self-loop edge to each non-committed location l of the translated TA $O_{\mathcal{L}}$. For readability they are not shown in Fig. 4.

According to the LSC semantics, cold violations of prechart or main chart are not failures. Instead, they just bring the chart back to the minimal cut. To model this, for a cut c and each following simregion s that has a cold condition g, we add edges from the corresponding TA location l to l_{pmin} (if *Pch* exists) or l_{min} (otherwise) to correspond to the $\neg g$ conditions (of DNF form). Similarly, given a cut c in the prechart, for each message m that occurs in $\mathcal{L}$ but does not follow c immediately, we also add an m?-labeled edge (l, l_{pmin}). See Fig. 4.

According to the LSC semantics, under invariant mode the prechart will be continuously monitored. Thus for instance in Fig. 4(a), the sequence $m_1 \cdot m_1 \cdot m_2$ will match the prechart. To enforce this semantics, for each message m that appear in the chart, we add an m?-labeled self loop to location l_{pmin}.

3.3.6 Undesired Behavior

The construction of the TA so far considers only the legal (or admissible) behaviors. When the current configuration (c, v) is in the main chart, if an observed message m is not enabled at cut c, or the hot condition of the simregion that immediately follows c evaluates to false under v, then there will be a hot violation. In this case, we add a dead-end (sink) location Err in the TA, and for each such violation we add an edge to Err.

3.3.7 Complexity

Let the number of simregions appearing in $\mathcal{L}$ be n. In the worst case, the number of locations in the translated TA $O_{\mathcal{L}}$ is $2^n + 1$. This happens when $\mathcal{L}$ consists of only the prechart or the main chart, and the messages in $\mathcal{L}$ are totally unordered.

The number of outgoing edges from a location l of $O_{\mathcal{L}}$ depends on: (1) the number of unconstrained events, ue; (2) the number of the following simregions in the corresponding cut c of $\mathcal{L}$, fs; (3) the length of the condition (in case the condition evaluates to false), lc; and (4) the number of messages that cause violations of the chart, cv. Therefore, the number of outgoing edges from a TA location is at the level $O(ue + fs + lc + cv)$.

3.4 Equivalence of LSC and TA

Since all the clocks in the original system model $\mathcal{S}$ are also visible to the LSC chart $\mathcal{L}$, we extend the configuration of $\mathcal{L}$ from $C_{\mathcal{L}}$ to $C_{\mathcal{L}} \cup C_{\mathcal{S}}$.

If in the translated $O_{\mathcal{L}}$ we ignore the undesired and implicitly allowed behaviors, i.e., we ignore the edges that correspond to hot violations, unconstrained events, cold violations, and prechart pre-matching, then we have:

Lemma 1. *If a configuration (c, v) of $\mathcal{L}$ corresponds to a semantic state (l, v) of $O_{\mathcal{L}}$, then: (1) each simregion s that follows (c, v) in $\mathcal{L}$ uniquely corresponds to an outgoing edge (l, l') in $O_{\mathcal{L}}$, and (2) the target configuration (c', v') of s in $\mathcal{L}$ uniquely corresponds to the target semantic state (l', v') in $O_{\mathcal{L}}$.* □

Theorem 1. *For any trace tr in $O_{\mathcal{L}}$: $tr \models \mathcal{L} \Leftrightarrow (O_{\mathcal{L}}, tr) \models (l_{min} \leadsto l_{max})$.* □

Proofs of the lemmas and theorems can be found at the authors' webpages.

The prechart pre-matching mechanism does introduce undesired extra behaviors and non-determinacy. For instance in Fig. 4(b), $tr = m_1 \cdot m_2 \cdot m_1 \cdot m_2 \cdot m_3$ could be an accepted trace in $O_{\mathcal{L}}$. But since its prefix $tr' = m_1 \cdot m_2 \cdot m_1$ can be rejected, thus tr does not really satisfy $\mathcal{L}$. It coincides that the particular trace tr in the model $O_{\mathcal{L}}$ does not satisfy the property $(l_{min} \leadsto l_{max})$.

Theorem 1 indicates that $O_{\mathcal{L}}$ has exactly the same set of *legal* traces as $\mathcal{L}$.

4 Embedding into Uppaal

4.1 Synchronizing with the Original System

When composing $O_{\mathcal{L}}$ with $\mathcal{S}$, we want $O_{\mathcal{L}}$ to "observe" $\mathcal{S}$ in a *timely* and *non-intrusive* manner. To this end, for each channel $ch \in Chan$, we make the following modifications:

(1) In $\mathcal{S}$ (e.g., Fig. 5(a)-5(b)), for each edge (l_1, l_2) that is labeled with ch!, we add a committed location l'_1 and a cho!-labeled edge in between edge (l_1, l_2) and location l_2. Here cho is a dedicated fresh channel which aims to notify $O_{\mathcal{L}}$ of the occurrence of the ch-synchronization in $\mathcal{S}$. The location invariant (if any) of l_2 will be copied on to l'_1. Furthermore, we use a global boolean flag variable (or a binary semaphore) *mayFire* to further guard the ch-synchronization. This semaphore is initialized to true at system start. It is cleared immediately after the ch-synchronization in $\mathcal{S}$ is taken, and it is set again immediately after the cho-synchronization is taken. See Fig. 5(d).

(2) In $O_{\mathcal{L}}$, each synchronization label ch? is renamed to cho?. See Fig. 5(c), 5(e).

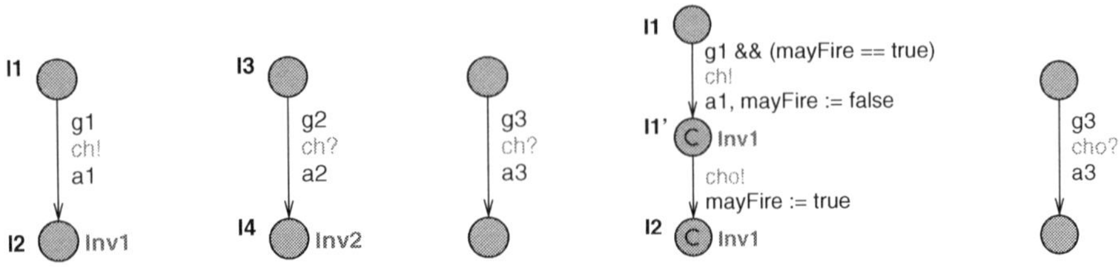

(a) emt. edge (b) recv. edge (c) obs. edge (d) mod. emt. edge (e) mod. obs. edge

Fig. 5. Edge modifications in the original system model $\mathcal{S}$ and the observer TA $O_{\mathcal{L}}$

If $\mathcal{L}$ has non-message simregions, then $O_{\mathcal{L}}$ has committed locations. If in a certain state both $O_{\mathcal{L}}$ and some TA in $\mathcal{S}$ are in committed locations (e.g., l_{m+1} in Fig. 6(c), l_2 in Fig. 6(a)), there will be a racing condition. But according to the ASAP semantics of $\mathcal{L}$, the (internal action) edge in $O_{\mathcal{L}}$ has higher priority. To this end, for each edge (l_i, l_{i+1}) in $O_{\mathcal{L}}$, if l_{i+1} is a committed location, then we add "$NxtCmt$:= true" to the assignment of the edge, otherwise we add "$NxtCmt$:= false". Here the global boolean flag variable (or semaphore) $NxtCmt$ denotes whether the observer TA will be in a committed location. This semaphore is initialized to false at system start. See Fig. 6(d). Accordingly, for each ch-labeled edge (l_i, l_{i+1}) in $\mathcal{S}$ where $ch \in Chan$ and l_i is a committed location, we add "$NxtCmt$ == false" to the condition of the edge, see Fig. 6(b).

Our method of composing the observer TA $O_{\mathcal{L}}$ with the original model $\mathcal{S}$ is similar to that of [9]. While their method works only when the target state of a communication action is not a committed location in the original model, in our method, due to the first locking mechanism (using *mayFire*), we have no restrictions on whether a location in $\mathcal{S}$ is a normal, urgent or committed one. Broadcast channels can be handled the same way as binary synchronization channels in our method. Furthermore, due to the second locking mechanism (using $NxtCmt$), we guarantee the enforcement of the ASAP semantics in $O_{\mathcal{L}}$.

Since our method involves only syntactic scanning and manipulations, the method is not expensive. For each $ch \in Chan$, we need to introduce a dedicated

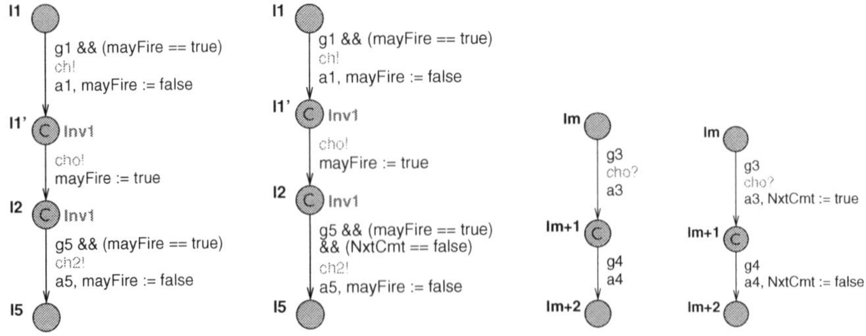

(a) emitting edge (b) modified emitting edge (c) in obs. TA (d) in modified obs. TA

Fig. 6. Edge modifications when there are committed locations in the obs. TA

fresh channel cho. For each occurrence of the emitting edge ch!, we need to introduce a fresh committed location in $\mathcal{S}$. Moreover, we need two global boolean flag variables ($mayFire$, $NxtCmt$) as the semaphores.

4.2 Verification Problem

After the modifications, the original system model $\mathcal{S}$ becomes $\mathcal{S}'$, and the observer TA $O_{\mathcal{L}}$ for chart $\mathcal{L}$ becomes $O'_{\mathcal{L}}$. Let the minimal and maximal cuts of the main chart of $\mathcal{L}$ correspond to locations l_{min} and l_{max} of $O'_{\mathcal{L}}$, respectively. Recall that the Uppaal "leads-to" property ($\phi \rightsquigarrow \varphi$) stands for $\mathsf{A}\Box(\phi \Rightarrow \mathsf{A}\Diamond\, \varphi)$, where ϕ, φ are state formulas.

Lemma 2. *If $O_{\mathcal{L}}$ has no committed location, and all $ch \in Chan$ are binary synchronization channels, then* $\mathcal{S} \models \mathcal{L} \Leftrightarrow (\mathcal{S}'||O'_{\mathcal{L}}) \models (l_{min} \rightsquigarrow l_{max})$. □

In a more general form, we have:

Theorem 2. $\mathcal{S} \models \mathcal{L} \Leftrightarrow (\mathcal{S}'||O'_{\mathcal{L}}) \models (l_{min} \rightsquigarrow l_{max})$. □

Theorem 2 indicates that the problem of checking whether a system model $\mathcal{S}$ satisfies an LSC requirement $\mathcal{L}$ can be equivalently transformed into a classical model checking problem ("ϕ leads-to φ") in Uppaal.

5 An Example

We put things together by using the example in Fig. 1. The original system $\mathcal{S}$ consists of timed automata A, B, C, and D, having channels m_1, m_2, m_3, m_4, and clock variable x. The scenario-based requirement $\mathcal{L}$ is given in Fig. 1(e).

After modifying $\mathcal{S}$ and the translated observer TA $O_{\mathcal{L}}$, we get the newly composed network of TA ($\mathcal{S}'||O'_{\mathcal{L}}$), see Fig. 7 and Fig. 8.

For this newly composed model, we check in Uppaal the property ($l_{min} \rightsquigarrow l_{max}$), and it turns out to be satisfied. This indicates that $\mathcal{S}$ does satisfy the requirements that are specified in $\mathcal{L}$.

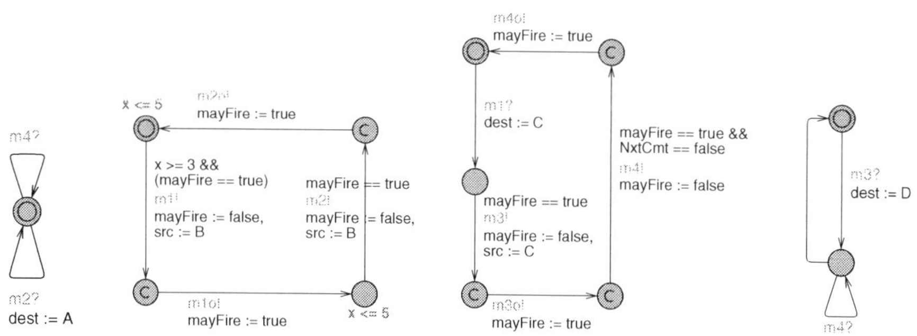

(a) TA A' (b) TA B' (c) TA C' (d) TA D'

Fig. 7. The modified model $\mathcal{S}'$ of the original system in Fig. 1(a)-1(d)

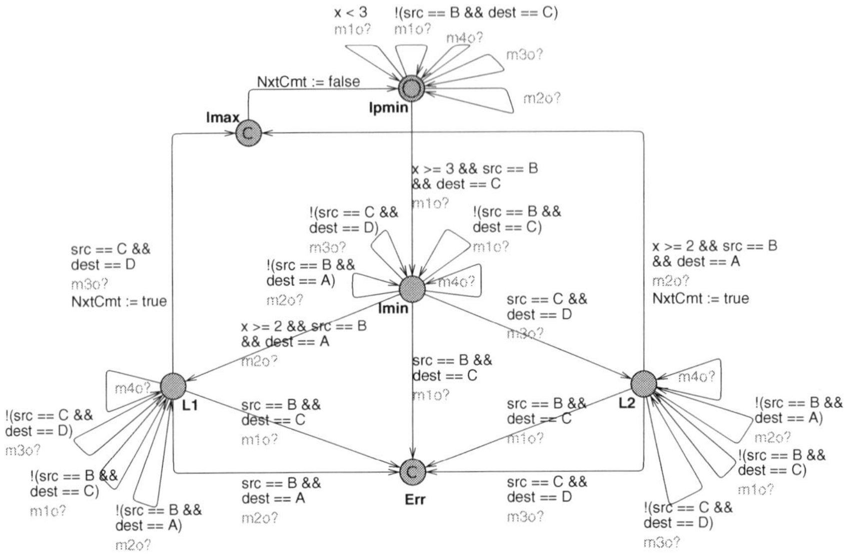

Fig. 8. The translated and modified observer TA $O'_{\mathcal{L}}$ of the chart in Fig. 1(e)

If in $\mathcal{L}$ the condition of m_2 is changed from $x \geq 2$ to e.g. $x \geq 4$, then the property will not be satisfied. There will be a counterexample, e.g., when $O'_{\mathcal{L}}$ has to synchronize on the channel m2o in location L2 of Fig. 8, but the value of clock x falls in $[3, 4)$, then it gets stuck there.

6 Conclusions

This paper deals with the verification of real-time systems against scenario-based requirements by using model transformation and event spying techniques. Since both the LSC to TA translation and the non-intrusive composing method are automatic steps, our approach can be fully automated.

Based on previous work [17], the translation algorithms in this paper have been implemented as a prototype LSC-to-TA translator, which has been integrated into the Uppaal GUI and verification server. Experiments with some non-trivial examples showed the effectiveness of this method and tool.

Future work includes: (1) empirical evaluations for studying the applicability and scalability of this approach; (2) to support the translations of more chart elements such as subchart, if-then-else structure, loop, forbidden and ignored event, co-region, symbolic instances, and other chart modes; (3) to consider multiple charts for system modeling as well as for property specification; (4) to specify interaction scenarios for timed game solving and controller synthesis.

Acknowledgements. We thank Sandie Balaguer and Alexandre David for (re-)implementing the translation algorithms and tool, and integrating them into Uppaal. This research has received funding from the EuropeanCommunity's Seventh Framework Programme under grant agreement no. 214755.

References

1. Alur, R., Dill, D.L.: A theory of timed automata. TCS 126, 183–235 (1994)
2. Alur, R., Holzmann, G.J., Peled, D.: An analyzer for message sequence charts. Software Concepts and Tools 17(2), 70–77 (1996)
3. Behrmann, G., David, A., Larsen, K.G.: A Tutorial on Uppaal. In: Bernardo, M., Corradini, F. (eds.) SFM-RT 2004. LNCS, vol. 3185, pp. 200–236. Springer, Heidelberg (2004)
4. Bengtsson, J., Yi, W.: Timed Automata: Semantics, Algorithms and Tools. In: Desel, J., Reisig, W., Rozenberg, G. (eds.) Lectures on Concurrency and Petri Nets. LNCS, vol. 3098, pp. 87–124. Springer, Heidelberg (2004)
5. Bontemps, Y.: Relating Inter-Agent and Intra-Agent Specifications: The Case of Live Sequence Charts. PhD thesis, University of Namur (2005)
6. Bontemps, Y., Schobbens, P.-Y.: The computational complexity of scenario-based agent verification and design. J. Applied Logic 5(2), 252–276 (2007)
7. Damm, W., Harel, D.: LSCs: Breathing Life into Message Sequence Charts. Formal Methods in System Design 19(1), 45–80 (2001)
8. Damm, W., Toben, T., Westphal, B.: On the Expressive Power of Live Sequence Charts. In: Reps, T., Sagiv, M., Bauer, J. (eds.) Wilhelm Festschrift. LNCS, vol. 4444, pp. 225–246. Springer, Heidelberg (2007)
9. Firley, T., Huhn, M., Diethers, K., Gehrke, T., Goltz, U.: Timed Sequence Diagrams and Tool-Based Analysis - A Case Study. In: France, R.B., Rumpe, B. (eds.) UML 1999. LNCS, vol. 1723, pp. 645–660. Springer, Heidelberg (1999)
10. Genest, B., Minea, M., Muscholl, A., Peled, D.: Specifying and Verifying Partial Order Properties Using Template MSCs. In: Walukiewicz, I. (ed.) FOSSACS 2004. LNCS, vol. 2987, pp. 195–210. Springer, Heidelberg (2004)
11. Harel, D., Marelly, R.: Come, Let's Play: Scenario-Based Programming Using LSCs and the Play-Engine. Springer, Heidelberg (2003)
12. Harel, D., Kugler, H.: Synthesizing State-Based Object Systems from LSC Specifications. Int. J. of Foundations of Computer Science 13(1), 5–51 (2002)
13. ITU: Z. 120 ITU-TS Recommendation Z.120: Message Sequence Chart 2000 (1999)
14. Klose, J., Wittke, H.: An Automata Based Interpretation of Live Sequence Charts. In: Margaria, T., Yi, W. (eds.) TACAS 2001. LNCS, vol. 2031, pp. 512–527. Springer, Heidelberg (2001)
15. Kugler, H., Harel, D., Pnueli, A., Lu, Y., Bontemps, Y.: Temporal Logic for Scenario-Based Specifications. In: Halbwachs, N., Zuck, L.D. (eds.) TACAS 2005. LNCS, vol. 3440, pp. 445–460. Springer, Heidelberg (2005)
16. Lahtinen, J.: Model checking timed safety instrumented systems. Research Report TKK-ICS-R3, Helsinki University of Technology, Espoo, Finland (2008)
17. Pusinskas, S.: From Live Sequence Charts to Uppaal. PhD thesis (forthcoming)
18. Rye-Andersen, J.G., Jensen, M.W., Goettler, R., Jakobsen, M.: PEEL: Property Extraction Engine for LSCs. Master thesis, Aalborg University (2004)
19. Sengupta, B., Cleaveland, R.: Triggered Message Sequence Charts. In: FSE (2002)
20. Yovine, S.: Kronos: A verification tool for real-time systems. STTT 1(1/2), 123–133 (1997)

Formal Specification of a Cardiac Pacing System

Artur Oliveira Gomes and Marcel Vinícius Medeiros Oliveira

Universidade Federal do Rio Grande do Norte – Brazil
artur.o.gomes@gmail.com, marcel@dimap.ufrn.br

Abstract. The International Grand Challenge project on Verified Software is a long-term research program involving people from all over the world and is aimed to stimulate the creation of new theories and tools to be applied on industrial-scale problems. One of the challenges proposed is to make a formal development of a cardiac pacemaker. In this paper, we present a formal specification of this system using the Z notation and also discuss our experience in building this formal model and the decisions made during the process.

Keywords: industrial applications, formal modelling, Z, pacemaker.

1 Introduction

The lack of formalism in most software developments raises difficulties in developing relatively low cost trustworthy software within a well-defined and controllable time frame. For decades, software failures have costed billions of dollars a year [17]. During this period, software have been delivered with restricted warranties of failures and errors, resulting in the well-known software crisis. For this reason, more rigourous approaches have been adopted in the development processes of safety-critical systems. These approaches offer a depth in the analysis of computing systems that would otherwise be impossible. The lack of tools were initially a problem in the adoption of these approaches. Nevertheless, formal methods and their tools have already reached a level of usability that could be applied even in industrial scale applications allowing software developers to provide more meaningful guarantees to their projects.

In 2005, Tony Hoare suggested the Verification Grand Challenge [8] that is aimed to stimulate many researchers around the world to create a verification toolkit assuring that a software system meets the user's needs. In this challenge, many application areas were proposed by the Verified Software Initiative [9]. During the last year, our group has been working on the pacemaker challenge [10], which consists of creating a formal model of a cardiac pacemaker based on the informal requirements given by Boston Scientific [3]. The motivation of this challenge is the high-security nature of the system: once implanted, any software failure could affect the patient's health adversely and also lead to death.

As part of the Verified Software Initiative, different groups must take the same challenges and use different formalisms in their solution. Because of our previous

A. Cavalcanti and D. Dams (Eds.): FM 2009, LNCS 5850, pp. 692–707, 2009.

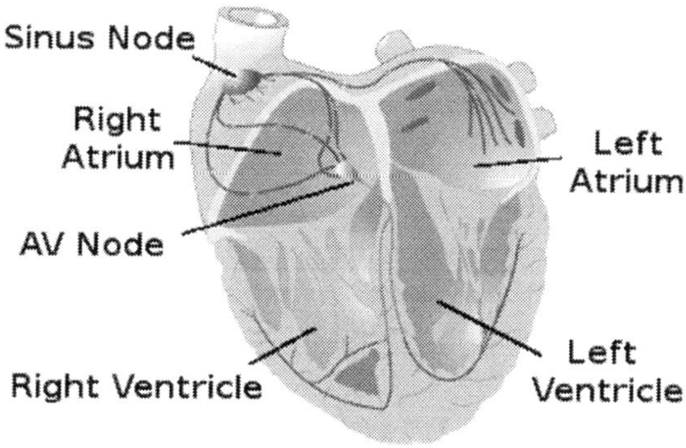

Fig. 1. Innerview of the human heart

experience on using the Z notation [16], we have taken it as the specification language to formally model the pacemaker. Besides, we also intend to validate that the formal specification satisfies the informal requirements. This can be achieved by using a theorem prover, like ProofPower-Z [13], to formulate proofs of specification-to-model correspondence for high-assurance secure systems like the one presented here.

In Section 2, we explain how the heart works and present an overview of the pacemaker. Section 3 presents the formalisation of the Pacemaker using Z. Finally, in Section 4, we discuss our results, along with directions for future work.

2 The Pacemaker

The contractions of the heart are made by electrical stimuli provided by cells specialised in producing electricity, the so-called pacemaker cells. They produce electricity by quickly changing their electrical charge from positive to negative and back. Signals arising in the Sinus node (Figure 1) stimulate the left and right atria to contract together and travel to the Atrioventricular node (AV node). After a delay (AV delay), the stimuli are conducted through fibers to the left and right ventricle, causing them to contract at the same time.

When working properly, the heart's electrical system automatically responds to the body's changing need for oxygen. However, sometimes the native pacemaker has difficulties to keep the correct pace; in these cases, a pacemaker (hereafter called as pacemaker or pulse generator) [15] is needed to restore the normal rhythm of the heart. A pacemaker is a medical device, powered by batteries, that uses electrical impulses to fix an abnormal rhythm of the heart rate. The pacemaker uses electrodes, called leads, which are in contact with the heart muscles, senses and stimulates them. Each heartbeat is monitored continuously and registered by the pacemaker. With the help of a built-in accelerometer, the pacemaker is able to detect when the patient is moving faster, by sensing the degree of vibration in the body. For example, it speeds up the heartbeat when climbing stairs and slows it down when you sleep. Also a Device Controller-Monitor (DCM) is used to communicate to the pacemaker allowing the cardiologist to program correct parameters, and to test and extract reports from the pacemaker.

For each patient, the cardiologist must define the correct pacing mode (Bradycardia Operating Mode) in the pacemaker. When the lead is implanted in the atrium or in the ventricle, a single chamber pacemaker is used. However, when leads are implanted in both chambers, atrium and ventricle, a dual chamber pacemaker is used. After programmed with the correct pacing mode, the pacemaker is able to sense the heart and to determine the interval of each pace. In combination with the pacing mode, the cardiologist must control a subset of the programmable parameters used to deliver the correct bradycardia therapy.

3 Formalization of the Pacemaker in Z

The overall state of the pacemaker is based on a Z state called *PulseGen* whose structure is illustrated in Figure 2. Many operations over that state were modelled according to its informal specification [10] and according to more detailed sources like [15]. The *PulseGen* state will be presented next along with many operations in order to illustrate our approach to the pacing and sensing modules. For conciseness, we assume some basic knowledge on the Z notation.

3.1 The *PulseGen* Components

The pacemaker is composed by programmable parameters, measured parameters, lead support, telemetry information, battery status information, implant data, event markers, accelerometer, a clock, and sensing and pacing modules. We start our approach by modelling the state of the pulse generator. We illustrate our model using following components of *PulseGen* state: the *PacingPulse* used to deliver pulses to the heart; the *SensingPulse* used to sense the heart; the *TimeSt* used as a clock; the *EventMarkers* used to control sensed and paced events; the *BatteryStatus* used to store information from the battery; and the *ProgrammableParameters* used in bradycardia operating modes to deliver pulses responding to sensed pulses. These components are necessary to construct the pacing and sensing modules presented here.

***PacingPulse* Component.** The component *PacingPulse*, presented below, is part of the pacing module, which is responsible to deliver pulses to the heart.

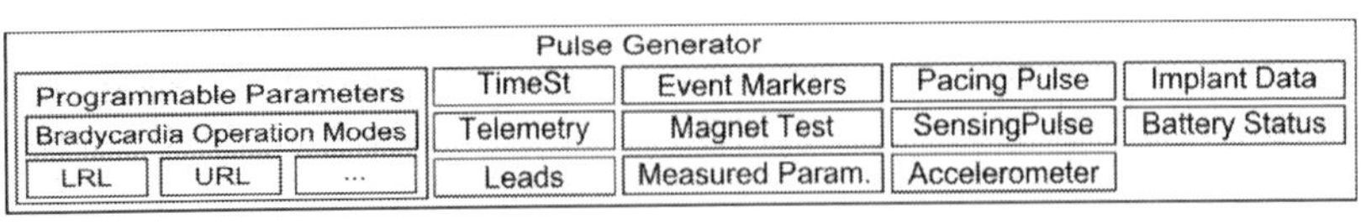

Fig. 2. Overview of the Pulse Generator state

Some of these parameters like pulse width and pulse amplitude of the atrium and the ventricle should be programmed by the cardiologist in order to give the heart the correct therapy. Moreover, *PacingPulse* keeps track of the last activity from the heart by using the state components *last_p_a_pulse* and *last_p_v_pulse* – *a* from atrium and *v* from ventricle – which are necessary to determine the delay between delivered pulses. The informal specification states that some of the bradycardia operation modes, discussed later in this paper, restricts the pulse generator to deliver pulses to ventricle only, atrial only or even to both chambers.

PacingPulse

$$paced\_a\_pulse\_width,\ paced\_a\_pulse\_amp,\ last\_p\_a\_pulse : \mathbb{R}$$
$$paced\_v\_pulse\_width,\ paced\_v\_pulse\_amp,\ last\_p\_v\_pulse : \mathbb{R}$$

***SensingPulse* Component.** On the other hand, the pulse generator must store information concerning the heart activity. It means that a *SensingPulse* component should be capable to store information like the cardiac cycles length, the sensing threshold (atrium and ventricle), the measurement of the pulse width and of the pulse amplitude for both chambers, and the last heart activity for both chambers. Furthermore, it also stores the current rate of the heartbeats. These information have to be regularly updated and used to decide if the heart failed and how the pulse generator should respond.

SensingPulse

$$card\_cycles\_l : \mathbb{R};\ current\_rate : \mathbb{N}$$
$$a\_sensing\_threshold,\ v\_sensing\_threshold : \mathbb{R}$$
$$sensed\_a\_pulse\_width,\ s\_v\_pulse\_w : \mathbb{R}$$
$$sensed\_a\_pulse\_amp,\ s\_v\_pulse\_amp : \mathbb{R}$$
$$last\_s\_a\_pulse,\ last\_s\_v\_pulse : \mathbb{R}$$

***TimeSt* Component.** A very important component used by sensing operations is *TimeSt*. It allows the pacemaker to keep all measurements of pulses coming from the heart that are detected by the leads. It is not very clear from Boston Scientific's document how timing should be dealt with. We represented *time* using a timestamp with discrete intervals of 1 ms. Using these intervals, our specification is able to cope with intervals between pulses, since the shortest interval takes much longer than this (around 300ms). Pulse data coming from the atrium and the ventricle are constantly updated by an operation and stored in the variables *a_curr_measurement* and *v_curr_measurement*.

TimeSt

$$time, a\_start\_time, v\_start\_time, a\_max, v\_max : \mathbb{R}$$
$$a\_delay, v\_delay, a\_curr\_measurement, v\_curr\_measurement : \mathbb{R}$$

There are three important moments during the measurement that should be taken into account: the time when any voltage has been sensed by the pacemaker in the atrium or in the ventricle (a_start_time and v_start_time); the maximal pulse amplitude that has been detected in the atrium or in the ventricle for each sensed pulse (a_max and v_max); and the time in which the pulse delay ends in the atrium or in the ventricle (a_delay and v_delay).

***BatteryStatus* Component.** The battery status is used to control the pacemaker's function. The battery is fully charged in the beginning of life (BOL). During its lifetime, it may be near a replacement, in which case it is considered Elective Replacement Near (ERN). These two first stages do not restrict any function of the pacemaker. When it is time to replace the battery (ERT), the pacemaker restricts its functions in order not to compromise the therapy. The last stage, elective replacement past (ERP), indicates that the replacement time has passed. We have modelled these values as the following Z free type.

$$BATT\_STATUS\_LEVEL ::= BOL \mid ERN \mid ERT \mid ERP$$

The variable $batt\_status\_level$ of the $BatteryStatus$ component indicates the current level of the battery life, as follows.

$$\begin{array}{|l} \hline BatteryStatus \\ \hline batt\_status\_level : BATT\_STATUS\_LEVEL \\ \hline \end{array}$$

Bradycardia Operating Modes. The pacemaker is able to apply 23 different programmed pacing modes or bradycardia operating modes. These modes have an important role in the pacemaker because they allow the pacemaker to deliver the correct therapy. Some of the bradycardia operating modes, however, are only able to sense the heartbeat, with no interference to the heart.

Our model of the bradycardia operating modes uses some free types that we describe in the sequel. First, we define the availability of the modes using the $SWITCH$ free type with two constants: ON and OFF. The chambers in which the bradycardia operating mode will sense and pace are defined using the free type $CHAMBERS$. Variables of this type can assume values according to the chambers that must be sensed and paced: C_NONE for no chambers; C_ATRIUM for the atrium only; $C\_VENTRICLE$ for the ventricle only; and C_DUAL for both the atrium and the ventricle. Finally, the way in which the bradycardia operating mode must respond to sensed events is modelled by the type $RESPONSE$: R_NONE for no response; $TRIGGERED$ for an indication that the heart is beating too slowly; $INHIBITED$ for an indication that the heart is beating at a proper rate; and $TRACKED$ for cases whether the pacemaker is able to decide the best response between $INHIBITED$ and $TRIGGERED$.

$$\begin{array}{l} SWITCH ::= ON \mid OFF \\ CHAMBERS ::= C\_NONE \mid C\_ATRIUM \mid C\_VENTRICLE \mid C\_DUAL \\ RESPONSE ::= R\_NONE \mid TRIGGERED \mid INHIBITED \mid TRACKED \end{array}$$

The schema BOM represents a bradycardia operation mode. It is composed of five variables: *switch*, *chambers_paced*, *chambers_sensed*, *response_to_sensing* and *rate_modulation*. The availability of the bradycardia operating mode is indicated by the variable *switch*. The variables *chambers_paced* and *chambers_sensed* inform which chambers, during the therapy, the pacemaker will pace and sense, respectively. The response that should be given to sensed pulses is stored in the variable *response_to_sensing*. Finally, the *rate_modulation* informs when the pacemaker uses an accelerometer to monitor the body's movement. The modes that use an accelerometer are named as rate-adaptive pacing modes.

$$\begin{array}{|l}
\textit{BOM} \\
\hline
switch : SWITCH;\ chambers_paced, chambers_sensed : CHAMBERS; \\
response_to_sensing : RESPONSE;\ rate_modulation : \mathbb{B} \\
\hline
\end{array}$$

By way of illustration we present the *VOO* bradycardia operation mode, a non-rate-adaptive mode, in which the pacemaker works without sensing the heart, and only paces the ventricle. According to the informal specification, all non-rate-adaptive modes, as *VOO*, are available during the entire battery life.

$$\begin{array}{|l}
\textit{VOO} \\
\hline
BOM;\ BatteryStatus \\
\hline
switch = ON \land rate_modulation = false \\
chambers_sensed = C_NONE \land response_to_sensing = R_NONE \\
chambers_paced = C_VENTRICLE \\
batt_status_level \in BOL \cup ERN \cup ERT \cup ERP \\
\hline
\end{array}$$

We have modelled further 22 operation modes like this. They belong to the set of all bradycardia operating modes, defined as the type *MODE* presented below, which used in the *BO_MODE* component of the *PulseGen* state.

$$MODE \mathrel{\widehat=} VOO \lor AOO \lor DOO \lor \ldots$$

The bradycardia operating mode (*BO_MODE*) component of the *PulseGen* state is presented below. The pacemaker therapy depends on the programmed bradycardia operation mode.

$$\begin{array}{|l}
\textit{BO_MODE} \\
\hline
bo_mode : MODE \\
\hline
\end{array}$$

***ProgrammableParameters* Component.** In the informal specification, a set of 26 programmable parameters is described. These parameters can be used by the cardiologist to set up the pacemaker according to each individual patient. The component *ProgrammableParameters* was modelled as the conjunction of each individual programmable parameter like *BO_MODE*.

$$ProgrammableParameters \mathrel{\widehat=} BO\_MODE \land LRL \land URL \land \ldots$$

This concludes the description of the *ProgrammableParameters*. We now turn our attention to the component that is responsible for the events markers.

***EventMarkers* Component.** The event markers are a report of how the pacemaker is responding to the heart. It makes it possible for the cardiologist to know if the pacemaker is delivering the correct pace. According to the informal specification, there are markers to atrial events, ventricle events, and markers for occurrences of abnormal activities between the heart and the pacemaker. In this paper, we use the ventricular markers to illustrate our approach to model the markers. A free type was defined in order to model occurrences of pacing events (*VP*) or sensing events (*VS*) in the ventricle, premature ventricular contraction (*PVC*) and noise indication (*TN*).

$$V\_MARKERS ::= VS \mid VP \mid PVC \mid TN$$

We modelled the real time ventricular markers (*RT_V_MARKERS*) as a sequence of tuples, illustrated below. Each tuple stores information on what event occurred, the actual pulse width and amplitude, as well as noise indication and the time that the event occurred. The only restriction is that no two event markers from the same chamber can occur at the same time. In the definition below, we use ProofPower-Z's notation $m1.5$ and $m2.5$ to denote the fifth element of the tuples, which represent the time of occurrence of $m1$ and $m2$, respectively.

$$\begin{array}{l} RT\_V\_MARKERS \mathrel{\widehat=} \\ \quad \{\, s : \mathrm{seq}\,\{\, marker : V\_MARKERS;\ width : \mathbb{R};\ amp : \mathbb{R}; \\ \qquad\qquad noise : \mathbb{R};\ time : \mathbb{R} \bullet (marker, width, amp, noise, time)\,\} \\ \quad\ \mid \forall i, j : \mathrm{dom}\, s \mid i \neq j \\ \qquad \bullet\ (\exists\, m1, m2 : \mathrm{ran}\, s \mid m1 = s(i) \land m2 = s(j) \bullet m1.5 \neq m2.5)\} \end{array}$$

Three of the four event markers available to the pacemaker were modelled. Atrial markers are generated for each event that occurs in the atrium. Similarly, ventricular markers are generated for events in the ventricle. Augmentation markers are generated simultaneously with atrial or ventricular markers, during atrial tachycardia response (*ATR*) or an post ventricular atrial refractory period extension (*PVARP-Ext*). Markers modifiers were not modelled due to difficulties to understand when these events occur.

$$\begin{array}{|l} \_\_ EventMarkers \_\_\_\_\_\_\_\_ \\ a\_marker : RT\_A\_MARKERS; \\ v\_marker : RT\_V\_MARKERS; \\ augmentation\_marker : RT\_AUGMENTATION\_MARKERS \\ \hline \end{array}$$

As a result of the absence of the event markers modifiers, we have not been able to model the following functionalities of the pacemaker: hysteresis pacing, which is used as a delay used for pulses coming from the heart before pacing pulses; rate smoothing, which is used to avoid sudden changes in the pacing rate; and sensor rate, which is used during rate-adaptive pacing modes to establish limits for pacing rates as a result of the rate-adaptive algorithm. We are currently looking for further sources of information that are capable to provide us with the answers needed (see Section 4).

3.2 The *PulseGen* State

The state of the pacemaker is modelled as *PulseGen* and contains all information concerning the pacemaker. The schema bellow is the composition of all components like *ProgrammableParameters*, *EventMarkers*, *PacingPulse*, *SensingPulse* and bradycardia operation modes. The *PulseGen* is also composed by others components that have not been presented here for the sake of conciseness[1]. For instance, we have omitted the specification of other components like *ImplantData*, which is able to store information concerning the implant like date and serial numbers, and *MagnetTest*, which stores information of the magnet test that is used to determine the device battery levels. These components and operations are not used in the pacing and sensing modules.

$$\begin{aligned} PulseGen \mathrel{\widehat{=}} & \ PacingPulse \land SensingPulse \land TimeSt \land Leads \\ & \land MeasuredParameters \land MagnetTest \land Accelerometer \\ & \land EventMarkers \land BatteryStatus \land ImplantData \\ & \land TelemetrySession \land ProgrammableParameters \end{aligned}$$

The *PulseGen* proved to be very large and complex, and as consequence, the industrial theorem prover we use, ProofPower, was not able to cope with the specification. The main problem was the time spent to load the specification. In order to overcome this problem, the ProofPower development team suggested us to use the following notation to formalise the pacemaker's overall state.

$$PG \mathrel{\widehat{=}} [PGcomp : PulseGen]$$

The system is modelled as a state with one component of type *PulseGen*. Using this approach, loading the state and the operations presented in the next section did not present any problems.

3.3 Operations on the Pacemaker

We modelled the pacemaker as the state *PG* presented above. The general approach to define any operation *Op* on this state is as follows.

$$\begin{array}{|l} \text{--- } Op \text{ ---} \\ \Xi PG \\ \hline \exists\, PulseGen;\ PulseGen' \\ \mid PGcomp = \theta PulseGen \land PGcomp' = \theta PulseGen' \bullet P \\ \hline \end{array}$$

[1] The pacemaker full specification can be downloaded from `http://www.consiste.dimap.ufrn.br/~artur/pacemaker/pacemaker-in-z.pdf`

The predicates P of the operation refer to $PulseGen$. For this reason, we use $PGcomp = \theta PulseGen \land PGcomp' = \theta PulseGen'$ to ensure that $PGcomp$ is the initial $PulseGen$ and $PGcomp'$ is the final $PulseGen'$. Obviously, operations that change the state work on ΔPG instead of ΞPG.

3.4 Time Notion in the Pacemaker

The pacing and sensing modules of the pulse generator update the state every millisecond. We model this increment by the operation below, *SetTimer*, that increments *time* in 1 ms.

$$
\begin{array}{l}
\textit{SetTimer} \\
\hline
\Delta PG \\
\hline
\exists\, PulseGen;\ PulseGen' \mid \\
\qquad PGcomp = \theta PulseGen \land PGcomp' = \theta PulseGen' \bullet \\
time' = time + real1 \land \\
\theta(PulseGen \setminus (time)) = \theta(PulseGen \setminus (time))' \\
\hline
\end{array}
$$

The predicate $\theta(PulseGen \setminus (time)) = \theta(PulseGen \setminus (time))'$ guarantees that only the variable *time* is changed in the state. This operation is used by the operation *BradTherapy* presented in Section 3.7.

3.5 Pacing Pulse Module

In our approach, operations of the pulse generator state were modelled as a disjunction of two operations, in which the first one – suffixed by *ok* – changes the state if its constraints are satisfied. On the other hand, the second operation – suffixed by *nok* – leaves the state unchanged when the operation constraints are not satisfied. Using this approach, we guarantee that our operations are total, avoiding undefinedness as much as possible.

The operation *SetMode* is used by the pulse generator to deliver pulses to the heart according to its bradycardia operation mode. The selection of the correct mode depends on the patient's needs and is up to the cardiologist. As an example, we present below the operation *SetVOO*.

$$SetVOO \mathrel{\widehat{=}} SetVOOok \lor SetVOOnok$$

In VOO mode, the pulse generator should output pulses between programmed intervals, known as the lower rate limit (*lower_rate_limit*). The precondition of this operation ensures that the bradycardia operation is VOO ($bo\_mode \in VOO$) and also that the operation is available in all stages of the battery life ($batt\_status\_level \in BOL \cup ERN \cup ERT \cup ERP$). Furthermore, the operation should only be invoked if, by adding the timestamp of the last delivered pulse to the ventricle (*last_p_v_pulse*) to the *lower_rate_limit* interval, we have the same value as the actual timestamp (*time*). On these conditions, the pacing module sets the pulse amplitude and width. The variable *v_pulse_amp_regulated* is a tuple whose first part is a *SWITCH* typed value and the second part is the amplitude value. The current timestamp is updated using the time of the last delivered pulse time ($last\_p\_v\_pulse' = time$). Finally, a new ventricular pulse (VP) marker is created to register the delivery of the pulse.

$$
\begin{array}{l}
\textbf{SetVOOok} \\
\Delta PG \\
\hline
\exists\, PulseGen;\ PulseGen' \mid \\
\quad PGcomp = \theta PulseGen \land PGcomp' = \theta PulseGen' \bullet \\
\quad bo\_mode \in VOO \land \\
\quad batt\_status\_level \in BOL \cup ERN \cup ERT \cup ERP \land \\
\quad last\_p\_v\_pulse + PulseWidth(lower\_rate\_limit) = time \land \\
\quad (time - last\_p\_v\_pulse) \geq PulseWidth(upper\_rate\_limit) \land \\
\quad paced\_v\_pulse\_amp' = v\_pulse\_amp\_regulated.2 \land \\
\quad paced\_v\_pulse\_width' = v\_pulse\_width \land \\
\quad last\_p\_v\_pulse' = time \land \\
\quad v\_marker' = \\
\qquad v\_marker \frown \langle (\, VP, v\_pulse\_amp\_regulated.2, \\
\qquad\qquad v\_pulse\_width, real\, 0,\ time\,)\rangle \land \\
\quad \theta(PulseGen \setminus (\, v\_marker,\ paced\_v\_pulse\_amp, \\
\qquad\qquad paced\_v\_pulse\_width,\ last\_p\_v\_pulse)\,)' = \\
\quad \theta(PulseGen \setminus (\, v\_marker,\ paced\_v\_pulse\_amp, \\
\qquad\qquad paced\_v\_pulse\_width,\ last\_p\_v\_pulse)\,) \\
\hline
\end{array}
$$

The operation *SetVOOnok* below guarantees that the state of the pulse generator remains unchanged if we have no output pulses delivered to the heart.

$$
\begin{array}{l}
\textbf{SetVOOnok} \\
\Delta PG \\
\hline
\exists\, PulseGen;\ PulseGen' \mid \\
\quad PGcomp = \theta PulseGen \land PGcomp' = \theta PulseGen' \bullet \\
\quad (bo\_mode \in VOO) \land \\
\quad batt\_status\_level \in BOL \cup ERN \cup ERT \cup ERP \land \\
\quad \neg\, (\, (last\_p\_v\_pulse + PulseWidth(lower\_rate\_limit)) = time \land \\
\qquad (time - last\_p\_v\_pulse) \geq PulseWidth(upper\_rate\_limit)\,) \land \\
\quad \theta(PulseGen)' = \theta(PulseGen) \\
\hline
\end{array}
$$

During the pacemaker's lifetime, only one bradycardia operation mode can be used at a time. The *SetMode* operation illustrated below is defined as the disjunction of all setting operations of each individual mode.

$$SetMode \mathrel{\widehat=} SetVOO \lor SetAOO \lor SetVVI \lor SetAAI \lor \ldots$$

This concludes the specification of the pacing pulse module. In the next section we present the specification of the module that is capable to sense pulses coming from the heart, the sensing module.

3.6 Sensing Module

The mechanism that measures the voltage of pulses coming from the heart was modelled as the operation *SensingModule*, which is composed by two operations: *VentricularMeasurement* and *AtrialMeasurement*.

$$SensingModule \mathrel{\widehat{=}} VentricularMeasurement \lor AtrialMeasurement$$

We only present the *VentricularMeasurement* operation, which is defined below as a disjunction of three operations. The specification of the *AtrialMeasurement* is similar and omitted here for conciseness.

$$VentricularMeasurement \mathrel{\widehat{=}} VentricleStart \lor VentricleMax \lor VentricleEnd$$

Each one of these operations is used in a specific moment during the measurement of sensed pulses. The first operation, *VentricleStart*, updates the pulse generator with the exact time in which the pulse coming from the ventricle starts. This pulse is detected if the current sensed voltage ($v\_curr\_measurement$) is strictly greater than the current value of the ventricle pulse (r_wave) and if there were no registered pulse activity ($r\_wave = real\,0$). In this case, the start time (v_start_time) is stored and r_wave is updated.

VentricleStart

$$\Delta PG$$

$$\begin{array}{l} \exists\, PulseGen;\ PulseGen' \mid \\ \quad PGcomp = \theta PulseGen \land PGcomp' = \theta PulseGen' \bullet \\ \quad (v\_curr\_measurement > r\_wave) \land r\_wave = real\,0 \land \\ \quad (r\_wave' = v\_curr\_measurement) \land v\_start\_time' = time \land \\ \quad \theta(PulseGen \setminus (r\_wave, v\_start\_time))' = \\ \qquad \theta(PulseGen \setminus (r\_wave, v\_start\_time)) \end{array}$$

The pacemaker should also store the higher measurement of the pulse detected. This task is achieved by the *VentricleMax* operation: while the current measurement is increasing ($v\_curr\_measurement > r\_wave$), the maximum voltage sensed in the ventricle (v_max) and the current value of r_wave are updated with the current measurement.

VentricleMax

$$\Delta PG$$

$$\begin{array}{l} \exists\, PulseGen;\ PulseGen' \mid \\ \quad PGcomp = \theta PulseGen \land PGcomp' = \theta PulseGen' \bullet \\ \quad v\_curr\_measurement > r\_wave \land \\ \quad v\_max' = v\_curr\_measurement \land \\ \quad r\_wave' = v\_curr\_measurement \land \\ \quad \theta(PulseGen \setminus (r\_wave, v\_max))' \\ \qquad = \theta(PulseGen \setminus (r\_wave, v\_max)) \end{array}$$

The last sensing operation, *VentricleEnd*, updates the time in which the current sensed pulse (v_delay) and the sensed pulse itself ends, when there is no activity ($v\_curr\_measurement = real\,0$).

$$
\begin{array}{l}
\textit{VentricleEnd} \\
\Delta PG \\
\hline
\exists\, PulseGen;\ PulseGen' \mid \\
\quad PGcomp = \theta PulseGen \wedge PGcomp' = \theta PulseGen' \bullet \\
\quad v\_curr\_measurement = real\,0 \wedge \\
\quad r\_wave' = v\_curr\_measurement \wedge v\_delay' = time \wedge \\
\quad \theta(PulseGen \setminus (r\_wave, v\_delay))' = \theta(PulseGen \setminus (r\_wave, v\_delay))
\end{array}
$$

The information stored is used to calculate the duration of the pulse sensed. This duration is used to determine the heartbeat rate as we discuss in the sequel.

Sensing Markers. We now turn our focus to the operations that create event markers, which correspond to heart activities. By way of illustration, we present the operation *VentricularSensedMarker*, which creates markers from ventricular sensed activities and updates the pulse generator with new information.

$$
\begin{array}{l}
\textit{VentricularSensedMarker} \\
\Delta PG \\
\hline
\exists\, v\_sense, v\_sense\_prev : V\_MKR\_ANN;\ a\_sense : A\_MKR\_ANN \\
\quad \mid a\_sense = last(a\_marker) \wedge v\_sense = last(v\_marker) \\
\quad\ \wedge\, v\_sense\_prev = last(front(v\_marker)) \\
\quad \bullet \exists\, PulseGen;\ PulseGen' \\
\qquad \mid PGcomp = \theta PulseGen \wedge PGcomp' = \theta PulseGen' \\
\qquad \bullet\ card\_cycles\_l' = (v\_sense.5 - v\_sense\_prev.5) \wedge \\
\qquad s\_v\_pulse\_w' = (delay - start\_time) \wedge \\
\qquad s\_v\_pulse\_amp' = v\_max \wedge last\_s\_v\_pulse' = start\_time \wedge \\
\qquad (((v\_sense.5 \leq a\_sense.5 \leq start\_time) \wedge \\
\qquad\quad (v\_marker' = v\_marker \frown \langle (VS, s\_v\_pulse\_w, \\
\qquad\qquad\qquad s\_v\_pulse\_amp, real\,0, last\_s\_v\_pulse)\rangle)) \\
\qquad\ \vee ((\neg(v\_sense.5 \leq a\_sense.5 \leq start\_time)) \wedge \\
\qquad\qquad v\_marker' = v\_marker \frown \langle (PVC, s\_v\_pulse\_w, \\
\qquad\qquad\qquad s\_v\_pulse\_amp, real\,0, last\_s\_v\_pulse)\rangle)) \wedge \\
\qquad \theta(PulseGen \setminus (v\_marker, s\_v\_pulse\_w, \\
\qquad\qquad\qquad s\_v\_pulse\_amp, last\_s\_v\_pulse))' \\
\qquad = \theta(PulseGen \setminus (v\_marker, s\_v\_pulse\_w, \\
\qquad\qquad\qquad s\_v\_pulse\_amp, last\_s\_v\_pulse))
\end{array}
$$

The cardiac cycle length, which is the delay between two consecutive pulses from the same chamber ($card\_cycles\_l' = (v\_sense.5 - v\_sense\_prev.5)$); ventricular pulse width, which is the time interval between the beginning of the sensed pulse and its end; ventricular pulse amplitude, which is the higher voltage sensed in the pulse ($s\_v\_pulse\_amp' = v\_max$); and the last sensed ventricular pulse, which is the start time of the sensed pulse ($last\_s\_v\_pulse' = v\_start\_time$). The ventricular markers are also updated with a new marker: if the pacemaker detected an atrial event after the previous ventricular event $((v\_sense.5 \leq a\_sense.5 \leq start\_time))$, we have a ventricular sensed pulse (VS); otherwise, we have a premature ventricular contraction (PVC).

The operation *SensingMarkers* interprets the data that was measured and creates the appropriate markers as discussed above.

$$SensingMarkers \mathrel{\widehat{=}} AtrialSensedMarker \lor VentricularSensedMarker \lor AugmentationMarker$$

Some other markers are also stored. For instance, the atrial tachycardia marker is caused by intermittent pulses faster than the natural heartbeat. Furthermore, the augmentation markers are created simultaneously with atrial and ventricle markers to store information concerning a PVC if no atrial activity occurred before the contraction. Finally, information about the atrial tachycardia response (ATR) like its starting time and duration period are also stored.

3.7 Pacing and Sensing Module: The Bradycardia Therapy

The *BradTherapy* operation models one cycle of the pacemaker's behaviour.

$$BradTherapy \mathrel{\widehat{=}} SetTimer \mathbin{;} SensingModule \mathbin{;} SensingMarkers \mathbin{;} SetMode$$

As a result of this operation, the *time* is incremented, the *SensingModule* measures the heart activities, the *SensingMarkers* analyzes these activities, and finally, *SetMode* responds to the heart needs accordingly (delivering pulses or skipping), depending on each programmed bradycardia operation mode. This concludes our specification of the pacemaker.

4 Conclusions

In this paper, we presented parts of a pacemaker specification, one of the challenges proposed by the Verified Software Initiative. This specification differs from the previous one [6] in that it includes new features of the pacemaker like event markers, restrictions on the parameter changes, and functionalities based on the battery level.

The specification was loaded in ProofPower-Z in less than two minutes, using a *Intel Core2 Duo* 2.4Ghz with 3Gb DDR2 RAM machine. Initially, however, ProofPower-Z presented a long delay to load our specification. The delay was caused by the extensive use of the schema calculus, which allows us to modularise the definition of the state of the *PulseGen*. Our system was represented a large conjunction of many different schemas, each of them corresponding to a component of the pacemaker. In the background, ProofPower-Z has to define the HOL types that represent the corresponding Z types. As a result, we have a background processing, whose complexity is exponential on the number of components. An alternative solution to the one we presented here is to eliminate some conjunctions of schemas by assembling these in a single schema. However, proofs would probably be more complex since the number of variables for that new component is much higher than the approach chosen. Furthermore, we would possibly loose the modularity of the proofs.

So far, we created over 250 schemas, including the pulse generator state and 149 operations. This amounts to over 4000 lines of Z specification in a 84 pages document. The current version of our specification covers over 95 percent of the entire informal specification.

The consistency of our specification has been partially checked through reasoning. So far, we have only focused in checking the consistency of the model; no validation experiments regarding safety conditions were performed yet. As part of our reasoning, we have proved that the initialisation of the system is a valid one and we have calculated the preconditions of the operations. The latter has been executed to guarantee that our intention to have total operations has been fulfilled. We have achieved the proof of the initialisation in parts. First, we proved the validity of the initialisation of each one of the *PulseGen*'s components. Finally, we proved, using a more general theorem that the initialisation of the whole system is valid. Proofs were quite simple, and achieved with few rewriting steps and the input of a few simple witnesses. For the same reasons, the calculi of the pre-conditions were also quite simple. In total, we have proved 46 theorems resulting in over 1291 lines of proof script.

The formal specification of the pacemaker proved to be a complex task and required an intensive research on the system's domain, whose understanding was the main problem. The informal specification [3] does not provide enough information for a software development team to construct a pacemaker system without any previous knowledge on basic cardiological information such as pacing modes, timing cycles, and event markers.

We have contacted experts from Boston Scientific many times to obtain a more detailed specification of some components originally presented in [10]. Unfortunately, some answers were not enough to formally specify parts of the system. As a consequence, few operations have not yet been modelled like the rate-adaptive algorithm, an specific algorithm that is used to recognise the body's movement and increase the frequency of pulses delivered. Another example of under-specification is the threshold test and event markers modifiers. For us, it is clear that researchers involved in this challenge must look for additional resources as cardiological books [4] and pacemaker guides [15], in order to understand the vast functionalities of the pacemaker system.

4.1 Related Work

Using VDM, colleagues from Newcastle University, Engineering College of Århus and Universidade do Minho [11] have developed a partial model of the pacemaker. Besides a *sequential* model of the pacemaker, Macedo *et. al* [11] also modelled a *concurrent* and a *distributed real-time* model of the pacemaker using VDM++ [5]. Their approach in the sequential model is similar to ours. Both use the notion of event sensing and reaction to specify the pacemaker operations. The pacemaker logs each event using markers that are used by the operations. The VDM's group modelled 8 of the 19 bradycardia operation modes including the corresponding programmable parameters. The inclusion of event markers on the *PulseGen* state allows us to create a model similar to the one proposed by them. Moreover, by adding an *Accelerometer* to the *PulseGen*, we are able to formally model the detection of human movement, allowing the pacemaker to operate in rate-adaptive bradycardia operation modes.

The sequential model of [11] has been validated through several tests like *absence of sensed pulses* and *outputted pulses at the correct time*. Some of these test cases have been re-used in the validation of their *concurrent* model and also their *distributed real-time* model. The extension of our model and their validation is in our research agenda as we discuss in the sequel.

4.2 Future Work

Our final aim is to create a prototype of the pacemaker that deals with the informal specification provided. Ideally, we would like to acquire the original hardware provided by Software Quality Research Labs. Due to budget restrictions, we will simulate the verified pacemaker on a Field Programmable Gate Array (FPGA). For that, we will refine our model into Handel-C [2] code using a refinement calculus like ZRC [1], and then, load the resulting program into a FPGA. An interesting piece of future work is to create some test scenarios to validate our system.

It is also in our agenda the extension of our model to to include concurrency using *Circus* [12], a combination of Z and CSP, and the derivation of the *Circus* specification into code using its refinement calculus and tool support [7]. Notions of real-time are also to be incorporated in our model in a later stage using *Circus*' timed version [14].

Acknowledgments

Jim Woodcock has originally proposed this challenge to our research group. The problem with the delay to load the specification has been solved with the help of Rob Arthan and Roger Jones. INES and CNPq partially supports the work of the authors: grants 550946/2007-1, 620132/2008-6, and 573964/2008-4.

References

1. Cavalcanti, A., Woodcock, J.: Zrc - a refinement calculus for z. Formal Aspects of Computing 10(3), 267–289 (1998)
2. Celoxica. Handel-C language reference manual, v3.0 (2002)
3. Boston Scientific Corporation. Altrua pacemaker system guide (2008)

4. Ellenbogen, K.A., Wood, M.A.: Cardiac Pacemakers and ICDs. Wiley-Blackwell (2005)
5. Fitzgerald, J.S., Tjell, S., Larsen, P.G., Verhoef, M.: Validation support for distributed real-time embedded systems in vdm++. In: HASE 2007: Proceedings of the 10th IEEE High Assurance Systems Engineering Symposium, Washington, DC, USA, pp. 331–340. IEEE Computer Society, Los Alamitos (2007)
6. Gomes, A.O., Oliveira, M.V.M.: Towards a formal development of a cardiac pacemaker. In: Brazilian Symposium on Formal Methods (SBMF)– Special Track Proceedings, Salvador, Brazil (2008)
7. Gurgel, A.C., Castro, C.G., Oliveira, M.V.M.: Tool support for the circus refinement calculus. In: Börger, E., Butler, M., Bowen, J.P., Boca, P. (eds.) ABZ 2008. LNCS, vol. 5238, p. 349. Springer, Heidelberg (2008)
8. Hoare, T.: The verifying compiler: A grand challenge for computing research. Journal of the ACM 50 (2003)
9. Hoare, T., Leavens, G.T., Misra, J., Shankar, N.: The verified software initiative: A manifesto (2007)
10. Software Quality Research Laboratory. Pacemaker System Specification (2007), `http://sqrl.mcmaster.ca/_SQRLDocuments/PACEMAKER.pdf`
11. Macedo, H.D., Larsen, P.G., Fitzgerald, J.: Incremental Development of a Distributed Real-Time Model of a Cardiac Pacing System Using VDM. In: Cuellar, J., Maibaum, T., Sere, K. (eds.) FM 2008. LNCS, vol. 5014, pp. 181–197. Springer, Heidelberg (2008)
12. Oliveira, M.V.M.: Formal Derivation of State-Rich Reactive Programs using Circus. PhD thesis, Department of Computer Science, University of York, YCST-2006/02 (2005)
13. Oliveira, M.V.M., Cavalcanti, A., Woodcock, J.: Unifying theories in proofpower-z. In: Formal Aspects of Computing (2007)
14. Sherif, A.: A Framework for Specification and Validation of Real-Time Systems using Circus Actions. PhD thesis, Center of Informatics - Federal University of Pernambuco, Brazil (2006)
15. Stroobandt, R., Barold, A.F.S.S.: Cardiac Pacemakers Step by Step – An Illustrated Guide. Blackwell Publishing Ltd., Malden (2003)
16. Woodcock, J.C.P., Davies, J.: Using Z–Specification, Refinement, and Proof. Prentice-Hall, Englewood Cliffs (1996)
17. Woodcock, J., Banach, R.: The verification grand challenge. J. UCS 13(5), 661–668 (2007)

Automated Property Verification for Large Scale B Models*

Michael Leuschel[1], Jérôme Falampin[2], Fabian Fritz[1], and Daniel Plagge[1]

[1] Institut für Informatik, Universität Düsseldorf
Universitätsstr. 1, D-40225 Düsseldorf
{leuschel,plagge}@cs.uni-duesseldorf.de
[2] Siemens Transportation Systems
150, avenue de la République, BP 101
92323 Châtillon Cedex, France

Abstract. In this paper we describe the successful application of the ProB validation tool on an industrial case study. The case study centres on the San Juan metro system installed by Siemens. The control software was developed and formally proven with B. However, the development contains certain assumptions about the actual rail network topology which have to be validated separately in order to ensure safe operation. For this task, Siemens has developed custom proof rules for AtelierB. AtelierB, however, was unable to deal with about 80 properties of the deployment (running out of memory). These properties thus had to be validated by hand at great expense (and they need to be revalidated whenever the rail network infrastructure changes).

In this paper we show how we were able to use ProB to validate all of the about 300 properties of the San Juan deployment, detecting exactly the same faults automatically in around 17 minutes that were manually uncovered in about one man-month. This achievement required the extension of the ProB kernel for large sets as well as an improved constraint propagation phase. We also outline some of the effort and features that were required in moving from a tool capable of dealing with medium-sized examples towards a tool able to deal with actual industrial specifications. Notably, a new parser and type checker had to be developed. We also touch upon the issue of validating ProB, so that it can be integrated into the SIL4 development chain at Siemens.

Keywords: B-Method, Model Checking, Constraint-Solving, Tools, Industrial Applications.

1 Background Industrial Application

Siemens Transportation Systems have been developing rail automation products using the B-method since 1998.[1] The best known example is obviously

* Part of this research has been EU funded FP7 project 214158: DEPLOY (Industrial deployment of advanced system engineering methods for high productivity and dependability).

[1] At that time Siemens Transportation Systems was named MTI (Matra Transport International).

A. Cavalcanti and D. Dams (Eds.): FM 2009, LNCS 5850, pp. 708–723, 2009.

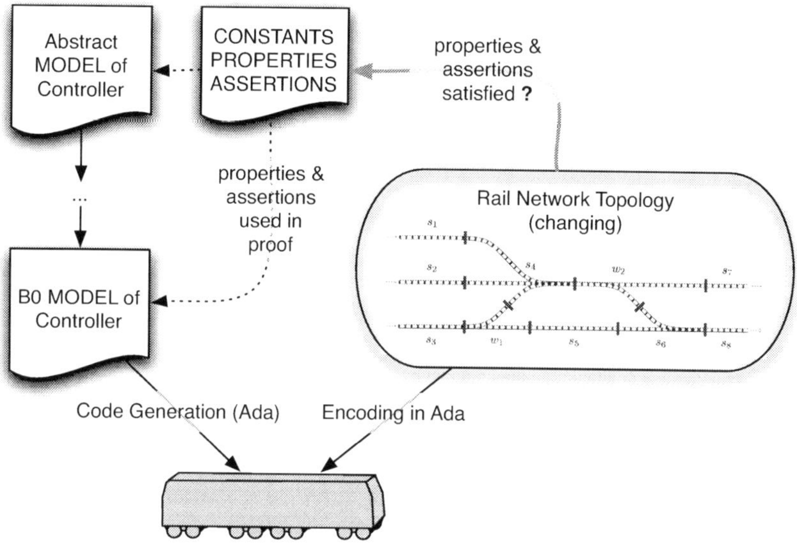

Fig. 1. Overview of the Constants Validity Problem

the software for the fully automatic driverless Line 14 of the Paris Métro, also called Météor (**Met**ro **e**st-**o**uest **r**apide) [4]. But since then, many other train control systems have been developed and installed worldwide by STS [7,3,9]. One particular development is in San Juan (Puerto Rico), which we will use as case study in this paper. The line consists of 16 stations, 37 trains and a length of 17.2 km, transporting 115,000 passengers per day. Several entities of Siemens produced various components of this huge project, such as the rolling stock and the electrification. STS developed the ATC (Automatic Control System) named SACEM (Système d'Aide à la Conduite, à l'Exploitation et à la Maintenance).

STS are successfully using the B-method and have over the years acquired considerable expertise in its application. STS use Atelier B [19], together with in-house developed automatic refinement tools. In this paper, we describe one aspect of the current development process which is far from optimal, namely the validation of properties of parameters only known at deployment time. The parameters are typically constants in the B model. Figure 1 gives an overview of this issue. Note, the figure is slightly simplified as there are actually two code generators and data redundancy check during execution. The track is divided into several sub-sections, each sub-section is controlled by a safety critical software. In order to avoid multiple developments, each software is made from a generic B-model and parameters that are specific to a sub-section. The proofs of the generic B-model rely on assumptions that formally describe the topology properties of the track. We therefore have to make sure that the parameters used for each sub-section actually verify the formal assumptions.

For example, in case of the San Juan development, about 300 assumptions were made.[2] It is vital that these assumptions are checked when the system is put in place, as well as whenever the rail network topology changes (e.g., due to line extension or addition or removal of certain track sections).

For this, Siemens Transportation Systems (STS) have developed the following approach:

1. The topology is extracted from the ADA program and encoded in B syntax, written into AtelierB definition files.
2. The relevant part of the B model is extracted and conjoined with the definition files containing the topology.
3. The properties and assertions[3] are proven with Atelier B, using custom proof rules and tactics.

There are two problems with this approach.

- If the proof of a property fails, the feedback of the prover is not very useful in locating the problem (and it may be unclear whether there actually is a problem with the topology or "simply" with the power of the prover).
- The constants are very large (relations with thousands of tuples) and the properties so complex (see Figure 2) that Atelier B quite often runs out of memory. For example, for the San Juan development, 80 properties (out of the 300) could not be checked by Atelier B.

The second point means that these properties have to be checked by hand (e.g., by creating huge spreadsheets on paper for the compatibility constraints of all possible itineraries). For the San Juan development, this meant about one man month of effort, which is likely to grow much further for larger developments such as [9].

The starting point of this paper was to try to automate this task, by using an alternative technology. Indeed, the ProB tool [13,15] has to be capable of dealing with B properties in order to animate and model check B models. The big question was, whether the technology would scale to deal with the industrial models and the large constants in this case study.

In Section 2 we elaborate on what had to be done to be able to parse and load large scale industrial B models into the ProB tool. In Section 3 we present the new constraint propagation algorithms and datastructures that were required to deal with the large sets and relations of the case study. The results of the case study itself are presented in Section 4, while in Section 5 we present how we plan to validate ProB for integration into the development cycle at Siemens. Finally, in Section 6 we present more related work, discussions and an outlook.

[2] Our model contains 226 properties and 147 assertions; some of the properties, however, are extracted from the ADA code and determine the network topology and other parameters.

[3] In B assertions are predicates which should follow from the properties.

```
cfg_ipart_cdv_dest_aig_i : t_nb_iti_partiel_par_acs --> t_nb_cdv_par_acs;

!(aa,bb).(aa : t_iti_partiel_acs &  bb : cfg_cdv_aig &
   aa |-> bb : t_iti_partiel_acs <| cfg_ipart_cdv_transit_dernier_i |> cfg_cdv_aig
    => bb : cfg_ipart_cdv_transit_liste_i[(cfg_ipart_cdv_transit_deb(aa)
                      .. cfg_ipart_cdv_transit_fin(aa))]);

cfg_ipart_pc1_adj_i~[{TRUE}] /\ cfg_ipart_pc2_adj_i~[{TRUE}] = {};

!(aa,bb).(aa : t_aig_acs & cfg_aig_cdv_encl_deb(aa) <= bb &
          bb <= cfg_aig_cdv_encl_fin(aa)
   => cfg_aig_cdv_encl_liste_i(bb) : t_cdv_acs);

!(aa).(aa : t_aig_acs
   => t_cdv_acs <| cfg_aig_cdv_encl_liste_i~ |>
   cfg_aig_cdv_encl_deb(aa)..cfg_aig_cdv_encl_fin(aa):t_cdv_acs +-> NATURAL);

cfg_canton_cdv_liste_i |> t_cdv_acs : seq(t_cdv_acs);

cfg_cdv_i~[{c_cdv_aig}] /\ cfg_cdv_i~[{c_cdv_block}] = {};

dom({aa,bb|aa : t_aig_acs & bb : t_cdv_acs &
     bb : cfg_aig_cdv_encl_liste_i[(cfg_aig_cdv_encl_deb(aa) ..
         cfg_aig_cdv_encl_fin(aa))]}) = t_aig_acs;

ran({aa,bb|aa : t_aig_acs & bb : t_cdv_acs &
     bb : cfg_aig_cdv_encl_liste_i[(cfg_aig_cdv_encl_deb(aa) ..
         cfg_aig_cdv_encl_fin(aa))]}) = cfg_cdv_i~[{c_cdv_aig}];
```

Fig. 2. A small selection of the assumptions about the constants of the San Juan topology

2 Parsing and Loading Industrial Specifications

First, it is vital that our tool is capable of dealing with the actual Atelier B syntax employed by STS. Whereas for small case studies it is feasible to adapt and slightly rewrite specifications, this is not an option here due to the size and complexity of the specification. Indeed, for the San Juan case study we received a folder containing 79 files with a total of over 23,000 lines of B.

Improved Parser. Initially, ProB [13,15] was built using the jbtools [20] parser. This parser was initially very useful to develop a tool that could handle a large subset of B. However, this parser does not support all of Atelier B's features. In particular, jbtools is missing support for DEFINITIONS with parameters, for certain Atelier B notations (tuples with commas rather than `|->`) as well as for definition files. This would have made a translation of the San Juan example (containing 24 definition files and making heavy usage of the unsupported features) near impossible. Unfortunately, jbtools was also difficult to maintain and extend.[4] This was mainly due to the fact that the grammar had to be made suitable for top-down predictive parsing using JavaCC, and that it used several pre- and post-passes to implement certain difficult features of B (such as the relational composition operator ';', which is also used for sequential

[4] We managed to somewhat extend the capabilities of jbtools concerning definitions with parameters, but we were not able to fully support them.

composition of substitutions), which also prevented the generation of a clean abstract syntax tree.

Thus, the first step towards making ProB suitable for industrial usage, was the development of a new parser. This parser was built with extensibility in mind, and now supports almost all of the Atelier B syntax. We used SableCC rather than JavaCC to develop the parser, which allowed us to use a cleaner and more readable grammar (as it did not have to be suitable for predictive top-down parsing) and to provide fully typed abstract syntax tree.

There are still a few minor differences with Atelier B syntax (which only required minimal changes to the model, basically adding a few parentheses). In fact, in some cases our parser is actually more powerful than the Atelier B variant (the Atelier B parser does not distinguish between expressions and predicates, while our parser does and as such requires less parentheses).

Improved Type Inference. In the previous version of ProB, the type inference was relatively limited, meaning that additional typing predicates had to be added with respect to Atelier B. Again, for a large industrial development this would have become a major hurdle. Hence, we have also implemented a complete type inference and checking algorithm for ProB, also making use of the source code locations provided by the new parser to precisely pinpoint type errors. The type inference algorithm is based upon Prolog unification, and as such is more powerful than Atelier B's type checker,[5] and we also type check the definitions. The machine structuring and visibility rules of B are now also checked by the type checker. The integration of this type checker also provides advantages in other contexts: indeed, we realised that many users (e.g., students) were using ProB without Atelier B or a similar tool for type checking. The new type checker also provides performance benefits to ProB, e.g., by disambiguating between Cartesian product and multiplication for example.

The scale of the specifications from STS also required a series of other efficiency improvements within ProB. For example, the abstract syntax tree of the main model takes 16.7 MB in Prolog form, which was highlighting several performance issues which did not arise in smaller models.

All in all, about eight man-months of effort went into these improvements, simply to ensure that our tool is capable of loading industrial-sized formal specifications. The development of the parser alone took 4-5 man months of effort.

One lesson of our paper is that it is important for academic tools to work directly on the full language used in industry. One should not underestimate this effort, but it is well worth it for the exploitation avenues opened up. Indeed, only in very rare circumstances can one expect industrialists to adapt their models to suit an academic tool.

In the next section we address the further issue of effectively dealing with the large data values manipulated upon by these specifications.

[5] It is even more powerful than the Rodin [1] type checker, often providing better error messages.

3 Checking Complicated Properties

The San Juan case study contains 142 constants, the two largest of which (cfg_ipart_pos_aig_direct_i, cfg_ipart_pos_aig_devie_i) contain 2324 tuples. Larger relations still can arise when evaluating the properties (e.g., by computing set union or set comprehensions).

The previous version of ProB represented sets (and thus relations) as Prolog lists. For example, the set $\{1,2\}$ would be represented as `[int(1),int(2)]`. This scheme allows to represent partial knowledge about a set (by partially instantiating the Prolog structure). E.g., after processing the predicates $card(s) = 2$ and $1 \in s$, ProB would obtain `[int(1),X]` as its internal representation for s (where `X` is an unbound Prolog variable).

However, this representation clearly breaks down with sets containing thousands or tens of thousands of elements. We need a datastructure that allows us to quickly determine whether something is an element of a set, and we also need to be able to efficiently update sets to implement the various B operations on sets and relations.

For this we have used an alternative representation for sets using AVL trees — self-balancing binary search trees with logarithmic lookup, insertion and deletion.

To get an idea of the performance, take a look at the following operation, coming from a B formalisation of the Sieve of Eratosthenes, where `numbers` was initialised to `2..limit` and where `cur=2`:

```
numbers := numbers - ran(%n.(n:cur..limit/cur|cur*n))
```

With limit=10,000 the previous version of ProB ran out of memory after about 2 minutes on a MacBook Pro with 2.33 GHz Core2 Duo processor and 3 GB of RAM. With the new datastructure this operation, involving the computation of a lambda expression, the range of it and a set difference, is now almost instantaneous (0.2 seconds). For limit = 100,000 it requires 2.1 seconds, for limit = 1,000,000 ProB requires about 21.9 seconds, and for limit = 10,000,000 ProB requires about 226.8 seconds. Figure 3 contains an log-log plot of the runtime for various values of `limit`, and clearly shows that ProB's operations scale quasi linearly with the size of the sets operated upon (as the slope of the runtime curve is one).

There is one caveat, however: this datastructure can (for the moment) only be used for fully determined values, as ordering is relevant to store and retrieve values in the AVL tree. For example, we cannot represent the term `[int(1),X]` from above as an AVL tree, as we do not know which value `X` will take on. Hence, for partially known values, the old-style list representation still has to be used. For efficiency, it is thus important to try to work with fully determined values as much as possible. For this we have improved the constraint propagation mechanism inside the ProB kernel. The previous version of ProB [15] basically had three constraint propagation phases: deterministic propagation, non-deterministic propagation and full enumeration. The new kernel now has a much more fine-grained constraint propagation, with arbitrary priorities. Every kernel computation gets a priority value, which is the estimated branching factor of that computation. A priority number of 1 corresponds to a deterministic

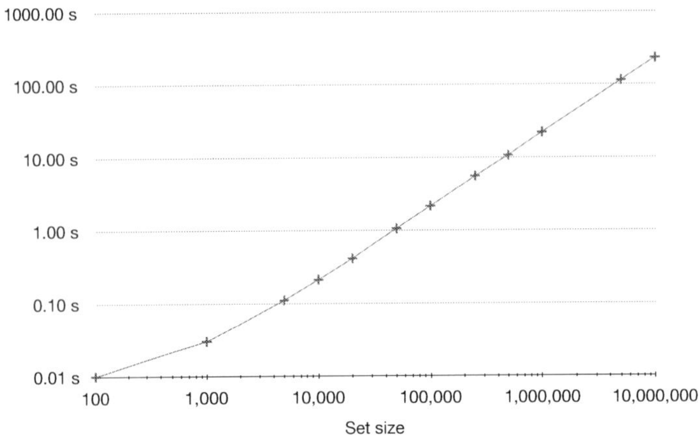

Fig. 3. Performance of the new ProB datastructure and operations on large sets

computation. For example, the kernel computation associated with, $x = z$ would have a priority value of 1 while $x \in \{1, 2, 3\}$ would have a priority value of 3. A value of 0 indicates that the computation will yield a fully determined value. At every step, the kernel chooses the computation with the lowest priority value.

Take for example the predicate `x:NAT +-> NAT & x={y|->2} & y=3`. Here, `y=3` (priority value 0) would actually be executed before `x={y|->2}`, and thus ensure that afterward a fully determined AVL-tree would be constructed for `x`. The check `x:NAT +-> NAT` is executed last, as it has the highest priority value.

Compared to the old approach, enumeration can now be mixed with other computations and may even occur before other computations if this is advantageous. Also, there is now a much more fine-grained selection among the non-deterministic computations. Take for example, the following predicate: `s1 = 9..100000 & s2 = 5..100000 & s3 = 1..10 & x:s1 & x:s2 & x:s3`. The old version of ProB would have executed `x:s1` before `x:s2` and `x:s3`. Now, `x:s3` is chosen first, as it has the smallest possible branching factor. As such, ProB very quickly finds the two solutions $x = 9$ and $x = 10$ of this predicate.

In summary, driven by the requirements of the industrial application, we have improved the scalability of the ProB kernel. This required the development of a new datastructure to represent and manipulate large sets and relations. A new, more fine grained constraint propagation algorithm was also required to ensure that this datastructure could actually be used in the industrial application.

4 The Case Study

As already mentioned, in order to evaluate the feasibility of using ProB for checking the topology properties, Siemens sent the STUPS team at the University of Düsseldorf the models for the San Juan case study on the 8th of July 2008. There were 23,000 lines of B spread over 79 files, two of which were to be analysed: a simpler model and a hard model. It then took us a while to understand the models and get them through our new parser, whose development was being finalised at that time.

On 14th of November 2008 we were able to animate and analyse the first model. This uncovered one error in the assertions. However, at that point it became apparent that a new datastructure would be needed to validate bigger models. At that point the developments described in Section 3 were undertaken. On the 8th of December 2008 we were finally able to animate and validate the complicated model. This revealed four errors.

Note that we (the STUPS team) were not told about the presence of errors in the models (they were not even hinted at by Siemens), and initially we believed that there was still a bug in ProB. Luckily, the errors were genuine and they were *exactly* the same errors that Siemens had uncovered themselves by manual inspection.

The manual inspection of the properties took Siemens several weeks (about a man month of effort). Checking the properties takes 4.15 seconds, and checking the assertions takes 1017.7 seconds (i.e., roughly 17 minutes) using ProB 1.3.0-final.4 on a MacBook Pro with 2.33 GHz Core2 Duo (see also Figure 4).

Note that all properties and assertions were checked twice, both positively and negatively, in order to detect undefined predicates (e.g., $0/0 = 1$ is undefined). We return to this issue in Section 5.

The four false formulas found by ProB are the following ones:

1. `ran(cfg_aig_cdv_encl) = cfg_cdv_aig`
2. `cfg_ipart_aig_tild_liste_i : t_liste_acs_2 --> t_nb_iti_partiel_par_acs`
3. ```
   dom(t_iti_partiel_acs <| cfg_ipart_cdv_dest_aig_i |> cfg_cdv_aig) \/
   dom(t_iti_partiel_acs <| cfg_ipart_cdv_dest_saig_i |> cfg_cdv_block)
   = t_iti_partiel_acs
   ```
4. ```
   ran(aa,bb|aa:t_aig_acs & bb:t_cdv_acs & bb:cfg_aig_cdv_encl_liste_i[
   (cfg_aig_cdv_encl_deb(aa)..cfg_aig_cdv_encl_fin(aa))]) =
   cfg_cdv_i~[c_cdv_aig]
   ```

Inspecting the Formulas. Once our tool has uncovered unexpected properties of a model, the user obviously wants to know more information about the exact source of the problem.

This was one problem in the Atelier B approach: when a proof fails it is very difficult to find out why the proof has failed, especially when large and complicated constants are present.

To address this issue, we have developed an algorithm to compute values of B expressions and the truth-values of B predicates, as well as all sub-expressions and sub-predicates. The whole is assembled into a graphical tree representation.

A graphical visualisation of the fourth false formula is shown in Figure 5. For each expression, we have two lines of text: the first indicates the type of the node, i.e., the top-level operator. The second line gives the value of evaluating the expression. For predicates, the situation is similar, except that there is a third line with the formula itself and that the nodes are coloured: true predicates are

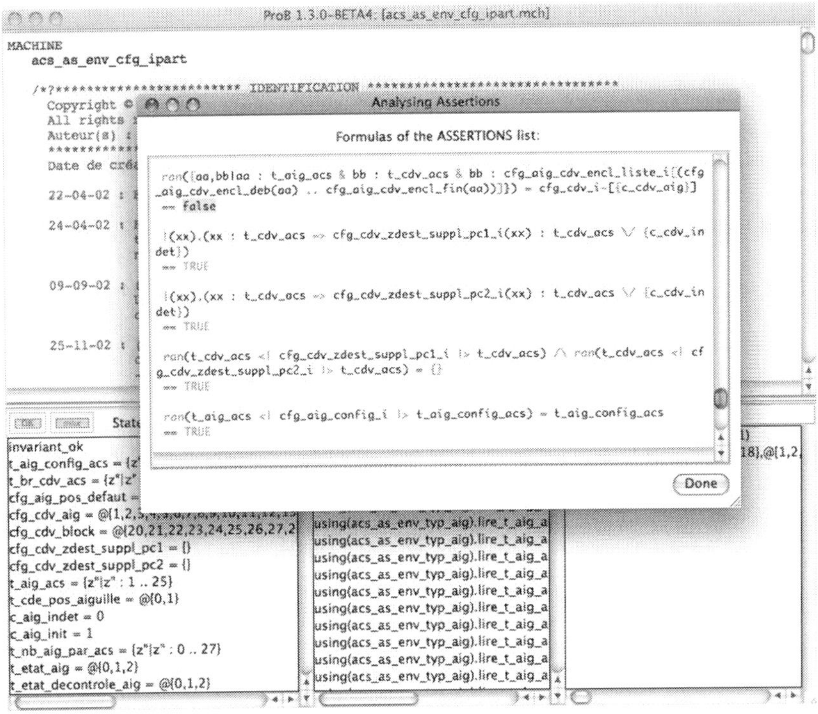

Fig. 4. Analysing the Assertions

green and false predicates are red. (An earlier version of the graphical viewer is described in [17].)

Note that the user can type custom predicates to further inspect the state of the specification. Thus, if the difference between the range expression and `cfg_cdv_i [c_cdv_aig]` is not sufficiently clear, one can evaluate the set difference between these two expressions. This is shown in Figure 6, where we can see that the number 19 is an element of `cfg_cdv_i [c_cdv_aig]` but not of the range expression.

In summary, the outcome of this case study was extremely positive: a man-month of effort has been replaced by 17 minutes computation on a laptop. Siemens are now planning to incorporate ProB into their development life cycle, and they are hoping to save a considerable amount of resources and money. For this, validation of the ProB tool is an important aspect, which we discuss in the next section.

5 Validation of ProB

In this case study, ProB was compared with Atelier B. For this specific use, the performances of ProB are far better than the performances of Atelier B, but

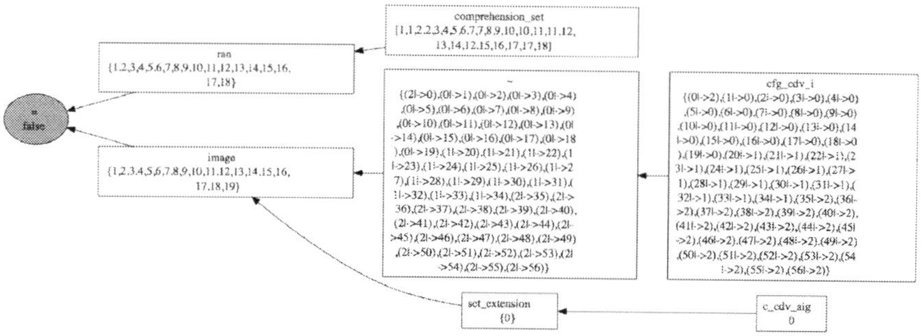

Fig. 5. Analysing the fourth false assertion

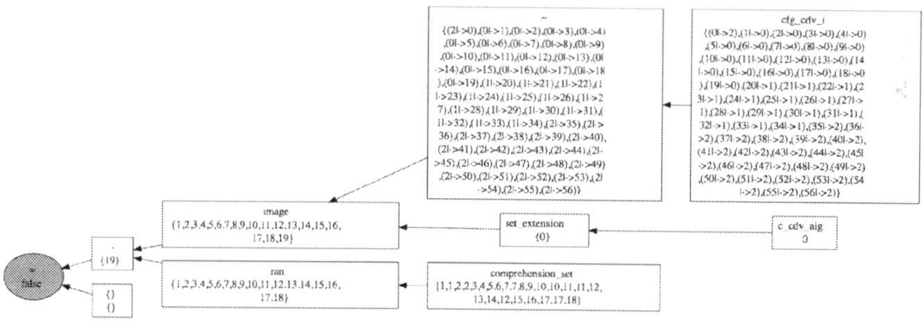

Fig. 6. Analysing a variation of the fourth false assertion

ProB is not yet qualified for use within a SIL 4 (the highest safety integrity level) development life cycle. If ProB evaluates an assumption to be true, Siemens would like to be able to rely on this result and not have to investigate the correctness of this assumption manually.

There are two ways this issue can be solved:

– Use a second, independently developed tool to validate the assumptions. One possibility would be Atelier B, but as we have already seen it is currently not capable to deal with the more complicated assumptions. Another possibility would be to use another animator, such as Brama [18] or AnimB. These tools were developed by different teams using very different programming languages and technology, and as such it would be a strong safety argument if both of these tools agreed upon the assumptions. This avenue is being investigated, but note that Brama and AnimB are much less developed as far as the constraint solving capabilities are concerned.[6] Hence, it is still unclear whether they can be used for the complicated properties under consideration.

[6] Both Brama and AnimB require all constants to be fully valued, AnimB for the moment is not capable of enumerating functions, etc.

– Validate ProB, at least those parts of ProB that have been used for checking the assumptions. We are undertaking this avenue, and provide some details in the remainder of this section.

The source code of ProB contains >40,000 lines of Prolog, >7,000 lines of Tcl/Tk, > 5,000 lines of C (for LTL and symmetry reduction), 1,216 lines of SableCC grammar along with 9,025 lines of Java for the parser (which are expanded by SableCC into 91,000 lines of Java).[7]

1. Unit Tests:
   ProB contains over a 1,000 unit tests at the Prolog level. For instance, these check the proper functioning of the various core predicates operating on B's datastructures. E.g., it is checked that $\{1\} \cup \{2\}$ evaluates to $\{1, 2\}$.
2. Run Time Checking:
   The Prolog code contains a monitoring module which — when turned on — will check pre- and post-conditions of certain predicate calls and also detect unexpected failures. This overcomes to some extent the fact that Prolog has no static typing.
3. Integration and Regression Tests:
   ProB contains over 180 regression tests which are made up of B models along with saved animation traces. These models are loaded, the saved animation trace replayed and the model is also run through the model checker. These tests have turned out to be extremely valuable in ensuring that a bug once fixed remains fixed. They are also very effective at uncovering errors in arbitrary parts of the system (e.g., the parser, type checker, the interpreter, the ProB kernel, ...).
4. Self-Model Check:
   With this approach we use ProB's model checker to check itself, in particular the ProB kernel and the B interpreter. The idea is to formulate a wide variety of mathematical laws and then use the model checker to ensure that no counter example to these laws can be found.
   Concretely, ProB now checks itself for over 500 mathematical laws. There are laws for booleans (39 laws), arithmetic laws (40 laws), laws for sets (81 laws), relations (189 laws), functions (73 laws) and sequences (61 laws), as well as some specific laws about integer ranges (24 laws) and the various basic integer sets (7 laws). Figure 7 contains some of these laws about functions. These tests have been very effective at uncovering errors in the ProB kernel and interpreter. So much so, that even two errors in the underlying SICStus Prolog compiler were uncovered via this approach.
5. Positive and Negative Evaluation:
   As already mentioned, all properties and assertions were checked twice, both positively and negatively. Indeed, ProB has two Prolog predicates to evaluate B predicates: one positive version which will succeed and enumerate solutions if the predicate is true and a negative version, which will succeed

[7] In addition, there are > 5,000 lines of Haskell code for the CSP parser and about 50,000 lines of Java code for the Rodin [1] plugin.

```
law1 ==  (dom(ff\/gg) = dom(ff) \/ dom(gg));
law2 ==  (ran(ff\/gg) = ran(ff) \/ ran(gg));
law3 ==  (dom(ff/\gg) <: dom(ff) /\ dom(gg));
law4 ==  (ran(ff/\gg) <: ran(ff) /\ ran(gg));
law5 ==  ( (ff \/ gg)~ = ff~ \/ gg~);
law6 ==  (dom((ff ; (gg~))) <: dom(ff));
...
law10 == (ff : setX >->> setY  <=>  (ff : setX >-> setY  &  ff~: setY >-> setX));
law11 == (ff : setX >+> setY  <=> (ff: setX +-> setY &
                 !(xx,yy).(xx:setX & yy:setX & xx/=yy & xx:dom(ff) &
               yy: dom(ff)  => ff(xx)/=ff(yy)))) ;
law12 == (ff : setX +->> setY  <=>  (ff: setX +-> setY &
                                    !yy.(yy:setY => yy: ran(ff))));
```

Fig. 7. A small selection of the laws about B functions

if the predicate is false and then enumerate solutions to the negation of the predicate. With these two predicates we can uncover undefined predicates:[8] if for a given B predicate both the positive and negative Prolog predicates fail then the formula is undefined. For example, the property `x = 2/y & y = x-x` over the constants `x` and `y` would be detected as being undefined, and would be visualised by our graphical formula viewer as in Figure 8 (yellow and orange parts are undefined).

In the context of validation, this approach has another advantage: for a formula to be classified as true the positive Prolog predicate must succeed *and* the negative Prolog predicate must fail, introducing a certain amount of redundancy (admittedly with common error modes). In fact, if both the positive and negative Prolog predicates would succeed for a particular B predicate then a bug in ProB would have been uncovered.

In order to complete the validation of ProB we are planning to do the following steps:

1. Validation of the parser (via pretty-printing and re-parsing and ensuring that a fixpoint is reached).
2. Validation of the type checker.
3. The development of a formal specification of core parts of ProB and its functionality.
4. An analysis of the statement coverage of the Prolog code via the above unit, integration and regression tests. In case the coverage is inadequate, the introduction of more tests to ensure satisfactory coverage at the Prolog level.
5. The development of a validation report, with description of ProB's functions, and a classification of functions into critical and non-critical, and a detailed description of the various techniques used to ensure proper functioning of ProB.

[8] Another reason for the existence of these two Prolog predicates is that Prolog's built-in negation is generally unsound and cannot be used to enumerate solutions in case of failure.

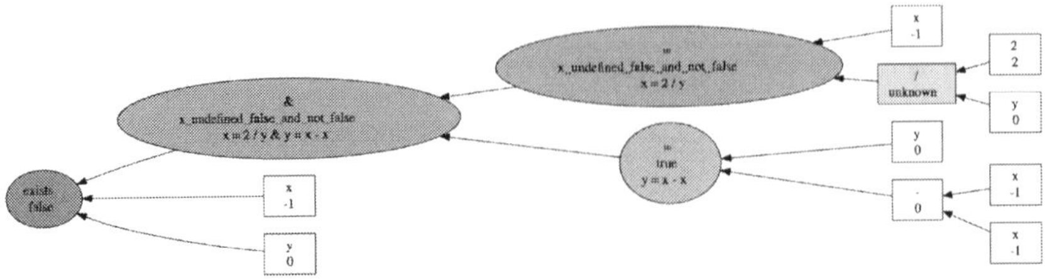

Fig. 8. Visualising an undefined property

6 More Related Work, Conclusion and Outlook

More Related Work. In addition to the already discussed approach using Atelier B and proof, and the animators Brama and AnimB we would like to mention the BZ-TT [12], a test generation tool for B and Z specifications. A specification is translated into constraints and the CLPS-B constraint solver [5] is used to find boundary values and to determine test sequences [2]. BZ-TT is now part of a commercial product named LEIRIOS Test Generator. The tool is focused on test generation; many of the features required for the Siemens case study are *not* supported by BZ-TT (e.g., set comprehensions, machine structuring, definitions and definition files, ...).

Alternative Approaches. We have been and still are investigating alternative approaches for scalable validation of models, complementing ProB's constraint solving approach.

One candidate was the bddbddb package [23], which provides a simple relational interface to binary decision diagrams and has been successfully used for scalable static analysis of imperative programs. However, we found out that for dealing with the B language, the operations provided by the bddbddb package were much too low level (everything has to be mapped to bit vectors), and we abandoned this avenue of research relatively quickly.

We are currently investigating using Kodkod [21] as an alternative engine to solve or evaluate complicated constraints. Kodkod provides a high-level interface to SAT-solvers, and is also at the heart of Alloy [10]. Indeed, for certain complicated constraints over first-order relations, Alloy can be much more efficient than ProB. However, it seems unlikely that Kodkod will be able to effectively deal with relations containing thousands or tens of thousands of elements, as it was not designed for this kind of task. Indeed, Alloy is based upon the "small scope hypothesis" [11], which evidently is not appropriate for the particular industrial application of formal methods in this paper. In our experience, Alloy and Kodkod do not seem to scale linearly with the size of sets and relations. For example, we reprogrammed the test from Figure 3 using Kodkod, and it is about two orders of magnitude slower than ProB for 1,000 elements and three orders of magnitude for 10,000 elements (363.2 s versus 0.21 s; see also the log-log plot in Figure 9 which indicates an exponential growth as the slope of the Kodkod

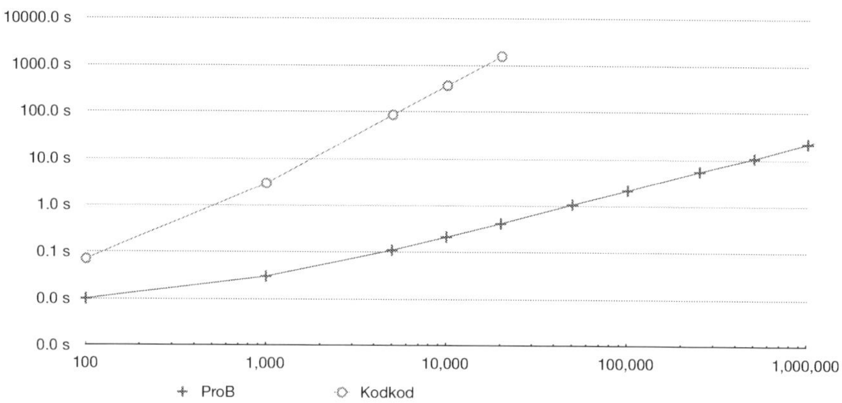

Fig. 9. Performance of the new ProB vs Kodkod on large sets

curve is > 1). In addition, the higher-order aspects of B would in all likelihood still have to be solved by ProB (Alloy and Kodkod only support first-order relations).

We are also investigating whether the SMT solver Yices [8] could be used to complement ProB's constraint solving engine. First experiments with SAL (which is based upon Yices) were only partially successful: some simple examples with arithmetic give big speedups, but for more complicated datastructures the translation to SAL breaks down (see also the translation from Z to SAL in [6] and the discussion about the performance compared to ProB in [16]). However, not all features of SAL are required and some useful features of Yices are not accessible via SAL. So, we plan to investigate this research direction further.

Conclusion and Outlook. In order to overcome the challenges of this case study, various research and development issues had to be addressed. We had to develop a new parser with an integrated type checker, and we had to devise a new datastructure for large sets and relations along with an improved constraint propagation algorithm. The result of this study shows that ProB is now capable of dealing with large scale industrial models and is more efficient than Atelier B for dealing with large data sets and complex properties. About a man month of effort has been replaced by 17 minutes of computation. Furthermore, ProB provides help in locating the faulty data when a property is not fulfilled. The latest version of ProB can therefore be used for debugging large industrial models.

In the future, Siemens plan to replace Atelier B by ProB for this specific use (data proof regarding formal properties). STS and the University of Düsseldorf will validate ProB in order to use it within the SIL4 development cycle at STS. We have described the necessary steps towards validation. In particular, we are using ProB's model checking capabilities to check ProB itself, which has amongst others uncovered two errors in the underlying Prolog compiler.

We also plan to work on even bigger specifications such as the model of the Canarsie line (the complete B model of which contains 273,000 lines of B [9], up from 100,000 lines for Météor [4]). As far as runtime is concerned, there is still a lot of leeway. In the San Juan case study 17 minutes were required on a two year old laptop to check all properties and assertions. The individual formulas could actually be easily split up amongst several computers and even several hours of runtime would still be acceptable for Siemens. As far as memory consumption is concerned, for one universally quantified property we were running very close to the available memory (3 GB). Luckily, we can compile ProB for a 64 bit system and we are also investigating the use ProB's symmetry reduction techniques [14,22] inside quantified formulas.

References

1. Abrial, J.-R., Butler, M., Hallerstede, S.: An open extensible tool environment for Event-B. In: Liu, Z., He, J. (eds.) ICFEM 2006. LNCS, vol. 4260, pp. 588–605. Springer, Heidelberg (2006)
2. Ambert, F., Bouquet, F., Chemin, S., Guenaud, S., Legeard, B., Peureux, F., Utting, M., Vacelet, N.: BZ-testing-tools: A tool-set for test generation from Z and B using constraint logic programming. In: Proceedings of FATES 2002, August 2002, pp. 105–120 (2002); Technical Report, INRIA
3. Badeau, F., Amelot, A.: Using B as a high level programming language in an industrial project: Roissy VAL. In: Treharne, H., King, S., Henson, M.C., Schneider, S. (eds.) ZB 2005. LNCS, vol. 3455, pp. 334–354. Springer, Heidelberg (2005)
4. Behm, P., Benoit, P., Faivre, A., Meynadier, J.-M.: Météor: A successful application of B in a large project. In: Wing, J.M., Woodcock, J.C.P., Davies, J. (eds.) FM 1999. LNCS, vol. 1708, pp. 369–387. Springer, Heidelberg (1999)
5. Bouquet, F., Legeard, B., Peureux, F.: CLPS-B - a constraint solver for B. In: Katoen, J.-P., Stevens, P. (eds.) TACAS 2002. LNCS, vol. 2280, pp. 188–204. Springer, Heidelberg (2002)
6. Derrick, J., North, S., Simons, T.: Issues in implementing a model checker for Z. In: Liu, Z., He, J. (eds.) ICFEM 2006. LNCS, vol. 4260, pp. 678–696. Springer, Heidelberg (2006)
7. Dollé, D., Essamé, D., Falampin, J.: B dans le tranport ferroviaire. L'expérience de Siemens Transportation Systems. Technique et Science Informatiques 22(1), 11–32 (2003)
8. Dutertre, B., de Moura, L.M.: A fast linear-arithmetic solver for DPLL(T). In: Ball, T., Jones, R.B. (eds.) CAV 2006. LNCS, vol. 4144, pp. 81–94. Springer, Heidelberg (2006)
9. Essamé, D., Dollé, D.: B in large-scale projects: The Canarsie line CBTC experience. In: Julliand, J., Kouchnarenko, O. (eds.) B 2007. LNCS, vol. 4355, pp. 252–254. Springer, Heidelberg (2006)
10. Jackson, D.: Alloy: A lightweight object modelling notation. ACM Transactions on Software Engineering and Methodology 11, 256–290 (2002)
11. Jackson, D.: Software Abstractions: Logic, Language and Analysis. MIT Press, Cambridge (2006)
12. Legeard, B., Peureux, F., Utting, M.: Automated boundary testing from Z and B. In: Eriksson, L.-H., Lindsay, P.A. (eds.) FME 2002. LNCS, vol. 2391, pp. 21–40. Springer, Heidelberg (2002)

13. Leuschel, M., Butler, M.: ProB: A model checker for B. In: Araki, K., Gnesi, S., Mandrioli, D. (eds.) FME 2003. LNCS, vol. 2805, pp. 855–874. Springer, Heidelberg (2003)
14. Leuschel, M., Butler, M., Spermann, C., Turner, E.: Symmetry reduction for B by permutation flooding. In: Julliand, J., Kouchnarenko, O. (eds.) B 2007. LNCS, vol. 4355, pp. 79–93. Springer, Heidelberg (2006)
15. Leuschel, M., Butler, M.J.: ProB: an automated analysis toolset for the B method. STTT 10(2), 185–203 (2008)
16. Leuschel, M., Plagge, D.: Seven at a stroke: LTL model checking for high-level specifications in B, Z, CSP, and more. In: Ameur, Y.A., Boniol, F., Wiels, V. (eds.) Proceedings Isola 2007. Revue des Nouvelles Technologies de l'Information, vol. RNTI-SM-1, pp. 73–84. Cépaduès-Éditions (2007)
17. Leuschel, M., Samia, M., Bendisposto, J., Luo, L.: Easy Graphical Animation and Formula Viewing for Teaching B. In: The B Method: from Research to Teaching, pp. 17–32 (2008)
18. Servat, T.: Brama: A new graphic animation tool for B models. In: Julliand, J., Kouchnarenko, O. (eds.) B 2007. LNCS, vol. 4355, pp. 274–276. Springer, Heidelberg (2006)
19. Steria, F.: Aix-en-Provence. Atelier B, User and Reference Manuals (1996), `http://www.atelierb.societe.com`
20. Tatibouet, B.: The jbtools package (2001), `http://lifc.univ-fcomte.fr/PEOPLE/tatibouet/JBTOOLS/BParser_en.html`
21. Torlak, E., Jackson, D.: Kodkod: A relational model finder. In: Grumberg, O., Huth, M. (eds.) TACAS 2007. LNCS, vol. 4424, pp. 632–647. Springer, Heidelberg (2007)
22. Turner, E., Leuschel, M., Spermann, C., Butler, M.: Symmetry reduced model checking for B. In: Proceedings Symposium TASE 2007, Shanghai, China, June 2007, pp. 25–34. IEEE, Los Alamitos (2007)
23. Whaley, J., Lam, M.S.: Cloning-based context-sensitive pointer alias analysis using binary decision diagrams. In: PLDI 2004: Proceedings of the ACM SIGPLAN 2004 conference on Programming language design and implementation, pp. 131–144. ACM Press, New York (2004)

Reduced Execution Semantics of MPI: From Theory to Practice★

Sarvani Vakkalanka, Anh Vo, Ganesh Gopalakrishnan, and Robert M. Kirby

School of Computing, University of Utah, Salt Lake City UT 84112, USA
http://www.cs.utah.edu/formal_verification

Abstract. There is growing need to develop formal verification tools for Message Passing Interface (MPI) programs to eliminate bugs such as deadlocks and local assertion violations. Of all approaches, dynamic verification is most practical for MPI. Since the number of interleavings of concurrent programs grow exponentially, we devise a dynamic interleaving reduction algorithm (*dynamic partial order reduction*, DPOR) tailor-made for MPI, called POE. The key contributions of this paper are: (i) a formal semantics that elucidates the complex dynamic semantics of MPI, and played an essential role in the design of the POE algorithm and the construction of the ISP tool, and (ii) a formal specification of our POE algorithm. We discuss how these ideas may help us build dynamic verifiers for other APIs, and summarize a dynamic verifier being designed for applications written using a recently proposed API for multi-core communication.

1 Introduction

It has been widely observed that exploiting concurrency *efficiently* and *correctly* is an issue of growing importance. Practical concurrent programs are written using various shared memory and message passing application programming interfaces (APIs). The execution semantics of these programs are governed largely by the API semantics, the compiler induced semantics, and the runtime (*e.g.*, scheduling, memory allocation) semantics. Therefore, it has been widely recognized that two popular forms of formal verification – namely *model based verification* and *static analysis* – can play only a supportive role, with dynamic verification [1] being the most practical *primary* approach for real-world concurrent programs. Except for debugging concurrent algorithms, model based verification would be prohibitively expensive – especially if it were to be employed to directly model the API semantics, the C semantics, or the runtime semantics. Similarly, static analysis methods cannot accurately predict the synchronizations and communications in programs where locks or message communicators are determined through complex synchronizations.

Dynamic verification tools take as their input the user code and a user provided test harness. Then, using customized scheduling algorithms, they enforce specific classes of concurrent schedules to occur. Such schedules are effective in hunting down bugs, and often are sufficient to provide important formal coverage guarantees. Dynamic verification tools almost always employ techniques such as dynamic partial order reduction (DPOR) [2,3], bounded preemption searching [4,5], or combinations of DPOR

★ Supported in part by Microsoft and NSF award CNS00509379.

A. Cavalcanti and D. Dams (Eds.): FM 2009, LNCS 5850, pp. 724–740, 2009.

and symmetry [6] reduction to prevent redundant state/interleaving explorations. While many such tools exists for verifying shared memory concurrent programs, there is a noticeable dearth of dynamic verification tools supporting the *scientific programming* community that employs the Message Passing Interface (MPI, [7]) API as their *lingua franca*. The importance of MPI is well known: it is employed in virtually all scientific explorations requiring parallelism, such as weather simulation, medical imaging, and earthquake modeling that are run on *expensive* supercomputers. Our group has developed the only formal dynamic verification tool for MPI programs currently in existence, called ISP [8,9,10,11,12]. As complete verification of MPI programs is infeasible, ISP focuses on detecting common errors in MPI programs such as deadlocks, assertion violations, and resource leaks. For these bug classes, ISP guarantees completeness of coverage under reasonable assumptions [8,9,10] that are almost always met in practice.

The main contributions of this paper are: (i) a simple and intuitive formal semantics for MPI that was developed hand-in-hand with the construction of ISP, and (ii) a rigorous description of the primary algorithm underlying ISP called "POE" (Partial Order avoiding Elusive Interleavings), which was sketched in [8]. This paper covers four MPI constructs in detail, highlighting the primary differences between our previous work [13,14] in which we wrote a reasonably comprehensive higher level reference semantics for about 150 MPI constructs in TLA+ [15]. We now highlight *why* dynamic verification of MPI programs is different from previous dynamic verification methods for shared memory programs. Then, beginning § 2, we elaborate on our formal semantics and formally describe the POE algorithm in § 3. In § 5, we sketch ongoing work, as well as our concluding remarks.

Challenges of Designing a Dynamic Verifier for MPI: MPI is inherently a low level notation, and the process of optimizing an MPI program increases the use of non-deterministic as well as asynchronous (non-blocking) MPI calls. In such programs, many MPI bugs remain latent, and surface when ported to a new MPI platform where the buffer allocations, node-to-node speeds, or MPI runtime scheduling policies may be different. ISP has been used with great success on many such programs of several thousands of lines of code such as ParMETIS [16] and MADRE [17], in addition to analyzing [18] almost all the examples from popular MPI textbooks such as [19], and has found numerous issues in these programs (*e.g.* [20]). We now list the challenges in developing a dynamic verifier that can handle such a range of programs, and is capable of running on ordinary laptop computers with acceptable runtimes.

Consider Figure 1 in which we employ *non-blocking sends* (`Isend`) and *non-blocking receives* (`Irecv`) – both typically used for efficiency. After issuing an `Isend`, the process can continue issuing subsequent statements that are in the delay slot

```
P1                      P2                      P3
---                     ---                     ---
Isend(to P3,d1,&h1);    Isend(to P3,d2,&h2);    Irecv(from ANY_SRC,x,&h3);
..delay slot..          ..delay slot..          ..delay slot..
Wait(h1);               Wait(h2);               Wait(h3);
                                                if(p(x)) then OK else BUG
```

Fig. 1. MPI Example Showing Need for Formalization

```
P1                          P2                          P3
---                         ---                         ---
Isend(to P3,d1,&h1);        Barrier();                  Irecv(from ANY_SRC,x,&h3);
Barrier();                  Isend(to P3,d2,&h2);        Barrier();
Wait(h1);                   Wait(h2);                   Wait(h3);
                                                        if(p(x)) then OK else BUG
```

Fig. 2. Augmented MPI Example Showing Need for MPI-specific DPOR

(the region from `Isend` till the following `Wait` or `Test`). Statements in the delay slot must not access the send/receive buffer. The same assumptions also apply to the `Irecv` call. The `Wait` detects whether the non-blocking operation has finished. Some MPI systems have enough memory that they can serve as temporary storage, absorbing the sent data and causing the `Wait` to return instantaneously; others will wait for the receiving process to come along and convey the data directly. Now in the first interleaving, it is possible that the MPI wildcard receive (receive from any sender, written '`MPI_Irecv(from MPI_ANY_SRC)`') of P3 matches P1. ISP must then replay the MPI program, ensuring that P2's send will match P3's receive (else, the data dependent bug may be missed). Now, in a dynamic verification tool for shared memory concurrent programs such as [5,3,2], one can force desired schedules simply by controlling the *issue order* of API calls. However, with MPI, if we *issued* the `Isend` of P1 followed by the wildcard `Irecv` of P3 and then issue the `Isend` of P2, we may still have P2's `Isend` race ahead (inside the MPI runtime) and *match* the `Irecv`. Thus, building a dynamic verifier for a complex API such as MPI requires a deep understanding of *the evolution states of each individual MPI call.* This understanding is the focus of the formal model proposed in this paper, where we show that each MPI call goes through four states: *issued* (notated as $\rhd$), *returned* ($\lhd$), *matched* ($\Diamond$), and *completed* ($\bullet$).

Figure 2 provides additional insights into the need for a focused formal semantics that guides implementations. All MPI processes must issue ($\rhd$) the Barrier call before it can be crossed; also no instruction after a barrier can be performed until all prior instructions have been issued (*but perhaps not matched,* $\Diamond$) in every process. Now suppose we want to replay the execution of this program so as to cause `Isend(to P3,d2,&h2)` in P2 to match P3's wildcard receive. Because of the MPI barrier semantics, we must issue `Isend(to P3,d1,&h1)` in P1 before we can issue `Isend(to P3,d2,&h2)` of P2. But now, all bets are off: the MPI runtime may again match `P1`'s call with `P3`. POE handles Figure 2 by first collecting, but deliberately not issuing the `Isend` and `Irecv` into the MPI runtime. Then ISP issues all the barrier calls into the MPI runtime. Thus, notice that we have issued the `Barrier` *before* issuing a statement prior to it! Our formal semantics helps us justify that this *out of order issue* of MPI commands is sound, as these commands are not related by the MPI *intra happens-before* [21] relation that is formally defined here.

After determining which `Isends` can match a wildcard receive, ISP dynamically rewrites `Recv(ANY_SRC)` to `Recv(from P1)` in one play and `Recv(from P2)` in the replay. This is to ensure that both these matches happen, *regardless of the speed of the cluster machine or the MPI library* on which the dynamic verification is occurring. In other words, the scheduler can "fire and forget" *dynamically determinized* MPI commands into the MPI runtime, knowing that they will match eventually. Such practical details of ISP are well described in [9]; this paper's focus is on a suitable formalization of MPI.

The formal semantics presented in this paper not only explicate the salient events (namely, $\triangleright$, $\triangleleft$, $\lozenge$, and $\bullet$) marking the progress of an MPI API call, but also formally define the intra process *happens-before* order that then allows us to schedule MPI actions in ISP. As opposed to our earlier formal specifications [13,14], our emphasis in this formalization has been to decide what to leave out, *i.e.*, focus on a few core MPI constructs, their constituent events, and the relationships between the events of various calls. Even so, we leave out many details of these constructs such as communicators, tags, etc., as our objective is to understand the happens-before relation *under a given set of communication matches*. Doing it all – *i.e.*, describing hundreds (of the total of over 300) MPI calls as well as all their event details and arguments – would be impractical and/or pointless. For example, even without revealing the event details, the work of [14] that covers about 150 MPI calls in detail occupies 192 printed (11-point font formatted) pages of TLA+. Another formal semantics for a small subset of MPI has recently been provided in [22]. It employs a fairly elaborate state machine to describe how MPI commands execute and interact with each other. One of the earliest MPI formal specifications was in [23]. These works do not meet our objectives of guiding the implementation of a dynamic verification tool.

Summary of Features of ISP: Since the rest of this paper is on the aforesaid formal semantics of MPI, we close off this section with a summary of ISP's practical nature. ISP is a practical push-button dynamic verifier for MPI programs that is available for download and study [24]. It has three GUIs that help debug large programs, one written in Java, the other using Visual Studio, and the third using Eclipse. While we characterize only four MPI constructs in-depth in this paper, we believe that we can similarly model the remaining 60 or so frequently used MPI calls currently supported by ISP. For example, the call `MPI_Send` can be regarded as `atomic{MPI_Isend;MPI_Wait}`. As reported earlier, ISP has handled many large real-world case studies with success, including ParMETIS [16], a parallel genome assembler mpiBLAST [25], and a large benchmark from Livermore called IRS [26]. On ParMETIS (a 14K LOC example), ISP's efficient dynamic partial order reduction algorithm POE produced only *one* interleaving, finishing in seconds on a laptop [9]. ISP handles all practical aspects of MPI including `ANY_SOURCE`, `ANY_TAG`, `WAIT_ANY`, `PROBE` and `IPROBE`, almost all collectives, as well as communicators. The engineering details of the dynamic scheduling control methods of ISP are reported in [10], and are not included here.

2 MPI Introduction

This section provides an overview of the four MPI functions `Isend` (S), `Irecv` (R), `Wait` (W), and `Barrier` (B), based on our understanding of the MPI standard [7], reading the MPI sources, and from past experiences [13,14]. Most MPI programs have two or more processes communicating through MPI functions. The MPI library is part of the **MPI runtime** and can be thought of as another process. All the processes have MPI process ids called ranks $\in Nat = \{0, 1, \ldots\}$ that range from $0 \ldots n-1$ for n processes. Every MPI function is in one of the following states:

issued (▷): The MPI function has been issued into the MPI runtime.

returned (◁): The MPI function has returned and the process that *issued* this function can continue executing.

matched (◇): Since most MPI functions usually work in a group (for example, a S from one process will be matched with a corresponding R from another process), an MPI function is considered *matched* when the MPI runtime is able to match the various MPI functions into a group which we call a *match-set*. Another example of a *match-set* is the one contributed to by a Barrier (B). All the function calls in the *match-set* will be considered as having attained the *matched* state.

complete (•): An MPI function can be considered to be complete according to the MPI process that issues the MPI function when all visible memory effects have occurred (*e.g.*, in case the MPI runtime has sufficient buffering, we can consider an `Isend` to complete when it has copied out the memory buffer into the runtime bufer). The completion condition is different for different MPI functions (*e.g.*, the `Irecv` matching the `Isend` may not have seen the data yet, but still `Isend` can complete on the send side).

An MPI function $F \in \{S, R, W, B\}$ in state $s \in \{\triangleright, \triangleleft, \diamond, \bullet\}$ will be denoted F^S. We use F_i to denote that F is invoked by process with rank i. Two distinct MPI functions $M \in \{S, R, W, B\}$ and $N \in \{S, R, W, B\}$ from the same process i will be denoted as $M_{i,j}$ and $N_{i,k}$ where j and $k \in Nat$ and $j \neq k$.

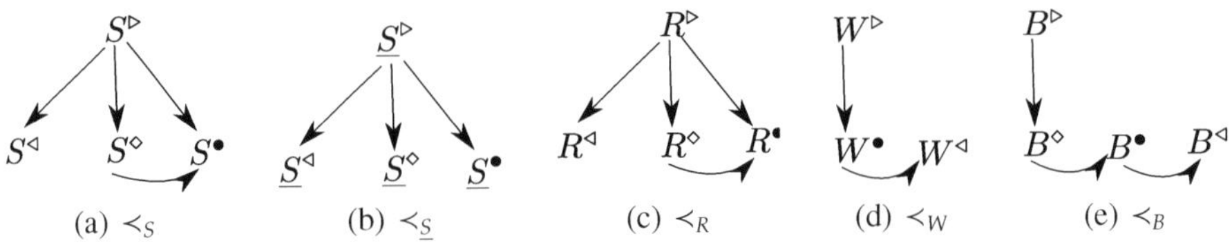

Fig. 3. Partial Orders of MPI function states

2.1 MPI Functions

MPI_Isend (S) is a non-blocking send that has the following simplified prototype:

```
Isend (int dest, Datatype buffer, Request &handle);
```

where `dest` is the destination process rank where the message is to be sent, `buffer` is the actual data payload that must be sent and `handle` is set by the MPI runtime and uniquely identifies the S in the MPI runtime. The function call *returns* immediately (non-blocking) while the actual send can happen at a later time. An S is considered *complete* by the process issuing it if the data from the buffer is copied out. The buffer can be either copied out into the MPI runtime provided buffer or to the buffer space of the MPI process receiving this message. Hence, if the MPI runtime has buffer available, the S can be *completed* immediately. Otherwise, the S can be completed only after it is *matched* with a matching R. It is illegal for the MPI process to re-use the send buffer before the send is *completed*. The completion of a send is detected by the process issuing it using `Wait` (W). We use $\underline{S}$ to denote a buffered send and S to denote a send with no runtime buffering. For a given send, we have a partial order ($<_{\underline{S}}$) of its state transition as follows:

- $\{S^{\triangleright} < S^{\triangleleft},\ S^{\triangleright} < S^{\Diamond},\ S^{\triangleright} < S^{\bullet}\}$.
- When the send cannot be buffered by the runtime we have $<_S = <_{\underline{S}} \cup \{S^{\Diamond} < S^{\bullet}\}$.

Figure 3(a) shows the partial order when the send is not buffered $<_S$ while Figure 3(b) shows the partial order when the send is buffered $<_{\underline{S}}$. The evolution of the state of each MPI operation according to these partial orders is caused by the processes issuing their operations and the MPI runtime advancing the state of the operations.

MPI_Irecv (R) is a non-blocking receive with the following prototype:

```
Irecv (int src, Datatype buffer, Request &handle);
```

where `src` is the rank of the process from where the message is to be received. The data is received into `buffer` and `handle` is returned by the MPI runtime which uniquely identifies the receive in the MPI runtime. The function call *returns* immediately and is considered *complete* when all the data is copied into `buffer`. It is illegal to re-use `buffer` before the receive completes. The completion of a receive is detected by the process using `Wait` (W). For a given R, we have a partial order ($<_R$) of its states as follows: $\{R^{\triangleright} < R^{\triangleleft},\ R^{\triangleright} < R^{\Diamond},\ R^{\triangleright} < R^{\bullet},\ R^{\Diamond} < R^{\bullet}\}$ shown in Figure 3(c).

MPI_Wait (W) is a blocking call and is used to detect the completion of a send or a receive and has the following prototype: `Wait(&handle)`, where `handle` is returned in a S or a R. The MPI runtime blocks the call to W until the send or receive is *complete*. The MPI runtime resources associated with the `handle` are freed when a W is invoked and `handle` is set to a special field called `REQUEST_NULL`. A W call with `handle` set to `REQUEST_NULL` is ignored by the MPI runtime. An S or R without an eventual W is considered as a resource leak. For a given W, we have the following partial order ($<_W$): $\{W^{\triangleright} < W^{\bullet},\ W^{\bullet} < W^{\triangleleft}\}$ as shown in Figure 3(d).

MPI_Barrier (B) is a blocking function and is used to synchronize MPI processes and has the following prototype `Barrier ()`. A process blocks after issuing the barrier until all the participating processes also issue their respective barriers. Note that unlike the traditional barriers used in threads where all the instructions before the thread barrier must also be complete when the barrier returns, the MPI B does not provide any such guarantees. An MPI B can be considered as a *weak fence* instruction. It is this behavior of MPI barriers that makes the traditional DPOR unsuitable for MPI (Figure 2). Given a B of a process, we have the following partial order ($<_B$): $\{B_{\triangleright} < B_{\Diamond} < B_{\bullet} < B_{\triangleleft}\}$ (shown in Figure 3(e)).

In addition to the above partial orders, we also have partial order rules for S; W and R; W (S may or may not be buffered) defined by providing the extra *coupling edges* between $<_S$ and $<_W$: $<_{SW} = \{S^{\bullet} < W^{\bullet}\}$, $<_{RW} = \{R^{\bullet} < W^{\bullet}\}$ As we show soon, this level of elucidation of MPI function states gives rise to an elegant formal semantics for it.

2.2 MPI Ordering Guarantees

We now describe various ordering guarantees for various MPI functions. These ordering guarantees provided by the MPI runtime according to the MPI standard define the order in which MPI program execution proceeds. We have already seen $<_S, <_{\underline{S}}, <_R <_W, <_B, <_{SW}, <_{RW}$ orders in Section 2.1 MPI also provides the following FIFO guarantees:

- For any two sends $S_{i,j}(l, \&h1)$, $S_{i,k}(l, \&h2)$, $j < k$ from the same process i targeting the same destination (l), the first send $S_{i,j}$ is *matched-before* the second send $S_{i,k}$. Note that this order is irrespective of the buffering status of the sends.
- For any two receives $R_{i,j}(l, \&h1)$, $R_{i,k}(l, \&h2)$ $j < k$ from the same process i receiving from the same source (l), the first receive is *matched-before* the second.
- For any two receives $R_{i,j}(*, \&h1)$, $R_{i,k}(l, \&h2)$, $j < k$ from the same process i, when the first receive $R_{i,j}$ can receive from any source (called wildcard receive and denoted as '*' henceforth), the first receive is always *matched-before* the second.

We call the above guarantees the *matches-before* ($\prec_{mb}$) ordering where
$\prec_{mb}= \{S^{\diamond}_{i,j}(l, \&h1) \prec S^{\diamond}_{i,k}(l, \&h2), R^{\diamond}_{i,j}(l, \&h1) \prec R^{\diamond}_{i,k}(l, \&h2), R^{\diamond}_{i,j}(*, \&h1) \prec R^{\diamond}_{i,k}(l, \&h2)\}$
Matches-before is a fundamental ordering relation in MPI. The MPI standard requires that two messages sent from process i towards process j must arrive in the same order (called *non-overtaking* in MPI). The role of matches-before is to constrain the order in which sends and receives match so as to guarantee non-overtaking. Notice that the sends and receives need only to be matched in order. However, since the completion is only detected by a W, the MPI standard does not enforce any order on the completion of the sends and receives leaving the choice to the MPI library implementation.

Finally, for blocking MPI functions like W and B, any following MPI functions can be issued only after the blocking call is complete. We call this the *fence-order* ($\prec_{fo}$). Given an MPI process barrier $B_{i,j}$ or $W_{i,j}$ and a following MPI function $F_{i,k}$ where $F \in \{S, R, W, B\}$ and ($j < k$), $\prec_{fo}= \{B^{\triangleleft}_{i,j} \prec F^{\triangleright}_{i,k}, W^{\triangleleft}_{i,j} \prec F^{\triangleright}_{i,k}\}$. In addition to the above orders we have the following issue order: For any two MPI function $M_{i,j}$ and $N_{i,k}$ where $M, N \in \{SR, B, W\}$ and $j < k$, we have $\prec_{io}= \{M^{\triangleright}_{i,j} \prec N^{\triangleright}_{i,j}\}$. The issue order precisely captures why B and W can block the issue of subsequent instructions.

Note that all the orders are defined on MPI functions within a process. We call the union of all the above orders the *mpi-intra-happens-before-order*, denoted as $\prec_{mhb}$.

Definition 1. MPI-Intra-Happens-Before-Order $\prec_{mhb} = \prec_S \cup \prec_{\underline{S}} \cup \prec_R \cup \prec_W \cup \prec_B \cup \prec_{SW} \cup \prec_{RW} \cup \prec_{mb} \cup \prec_{fo} \cup \prec_{io}$.

MPI-Intra-Happens-Before-Order defines the partial order of the salient MPI events observable at each MPI process.

2.3 Commit States

A commit state is a state that decides the fate of an MPI function. Since this happens to be when the MPI functions are matched, we call the $\diamond$ state of each MPI function its commit state. Hence, we consider the following states as commit states: *commit* = $\{S^{\diamond}, R^{\diamond}, B^{\diamond}\}$. Since W does not have a $\diamond$ state (this is because W is a local process operation), we do not consider W to have a commit state.

In this paper, we do not define the full semantics of how the local memory of an MPI program gets updated; should such a definition be desired, we would take the commit events, consider them occurring according to $\prec_{mhb}$, and define the state transition semantics for the process memories. These notions will help define the formal semantics of MPI in subsequent sections.

3 MPI Formal Semantics for Verification

In Section 3.1, *communication records* that model the MPI runtime state of each MPI operation are introduced. In Section 3.2, we show how the operations of the MPI runtime cause an *IntraHB* ordering among the communication records. This relation is obtained from the *mhb* relation defined earlier, except it is constructed over communication records and not MPI operations. We will then give transition rules that describe how MPI processes and their runtimes advance in their execution states. All this defines the *full* execution semantics of MPI. In Section 4.1, we present the POE algorithm elegantly by constraining the transition rules to fire in a certain priority order. It is well known that partial order reduction algorithms can be obtained by prioritizing transition systems in such a manner that a proper subset of executions (interleavings) is obtained. Section 4.2 provides soundness arguments.

3.1 Communication Records and Global State

Formalizing MPI requires the formalization of the processes and the runtime. We consider the MPI function invocations as *visible operations* [27] or simply *operations*, and any other operations performed by the processes as *invisible*. The MPI runtime helps advance the state of the process operations. We also assume that all `Isends` (S) considered are non-buffered (ones for which the system does not provide adequate buffering, to cause their matching W to return immediately). Section 4.4 deals with buffering.

The *PID* (MPI rank) of each of P processes ranges over $\{0,\ldots,P-1\}$. The MPI runtime is assigned PID $R \notin \{0,\ldots,P-1\}$. A process i's operations are are numbered $\{1,\ldots n_i\}$, where the first operation is `Init` and the n_i^{th} operation is `Finalize`, as required by the MPI standard (we suppress them). The jth operation executed by the ith MPI process is $p_{i,j}$, where operation $p \in \{S,R,B,W\}$. A state s of an MPI operation $p_{i,j}$ is denoted as $p^s_{i,j}$ where $s \in \{\triangleright,\triangleleft,\lozenge,\bullet\}$. We denote a send and its arguments as $S_{i,j}(l,h_{ij})$ where i is the rank of the processes issuing the send and j is the dynamic operation count of process i. l is the destination where the message is to be sent, *i.e.*, $l \in PID$ and h_{ij} is the send's handle. The wait corresponding to the send is $W_{i,k}(h_{ij})$ where $k > j$. `Irecv` (R) also follows similar notations, except that the source argument of R $l \in PID \cup \{*\}$, where $*$ is a wildcard receive. The set of all possible handles $H = \cup_{i \in PID}\, h_{\{i\} \times \{1\ldots n_i\}}$. A process that executes an MPI operation creates a single communication record in the MPI runtime, denoted by the **eight tuple** $cr = \langle pid, pc, op, src, dest, handle, match, state\rangle$, where $pid \in PID$, $\forall i \in PID, pc \in \{1,\ldots,n_i\}$, $op \in \{S,R,W,B\}$, $src \in PID \cup \{*\}$, $dest \in PID$, $handle \in H$, $match$ is a set of communication records that forms a match set with cr, and $state \in \{\triangleright,\triangleleft,\lozenge,\bullet\}$. We use $\perp$ for a communication record field when its value is undefined. For example, *src* is undefined for sends, while the *dest* field is undefined for recvs.

The communication record generated by $p_{i,j}$ is denoted by $c_{i,j}$, with its field f denoted $c_{i,j}.f$. Often, a communication record $c_{i,j}$ is considered synonymous with $p_{i,j}(\ldots)$ where $p \in \{S,B,W,R\}$. In fact, this connection is more than superficial: after it issues, the state of an MPI operation, as defined in Section 2, is defined by the state of the associated communication record. The dynamic state of the MPI program consists of the current set of communication records in the MPI runtime and the current PC (program

$$\mathbf{PS}^{\triangleright}: \frac{s:\langle l,C\rangle,\ \ p_{i,l_i} = S_{i,l_i}(j,\ h_{i,l_i})}{s':\langle l, C \cup \{\ \langle i, l_i, S, \bot, j, h_{i,l_i}, \bot, \triangleright\rangle\ \}\ \rangle} \qquad \mathbf{PR}^{\triangleright}: \frac{s:\langle l,C\rangle,\ \ p_{i,l_i} = R_{i,l_i}(j,\ h_{i,l_i})}{s':\langle l, C \cup \{\ \langle i, l_i, R, j, \bot, h_{i,l_i}, \bot, \triangleright\rangle\ \}\ \rangle}$$

$$\mathbf{PW}^{\triangleright}: \frac{s:\langle l,C\rangle,\ \ p_{i,l_i} = W_{i,l_i}(h_{i,j})}{s':\langle l, C \cup \{\ \langle i, l_i, W, \bot, \bot, h_{i,j}, \bot, \triangleright\rangle\ \}\ \rangle} \qquad \mathbf{PB}^{\triangleright}: \frac{s:\langle l,C\rangle,\ \ p_{i,l_i} = B_{i,l_i}}{\langle l, C \cup \{\ \langle i, l_i, B, \bot, \bot, \bot, \bot, \triangleright\rangle\ \}\ \rangle}$$

Fig. 4. MPI Process Transitions

counter) of the processes. Let C be the set of all possible communication records. The total state space of the system is: $\{1,\ldots,n_0\} \times \{1,\ldots,n_1\} \times \ldots \times \{1,\ldots,n_{P-1}\} \times 2^C$. The current state s is denoted as $\langle l, C\rangle$ where l is the tuple of all the current program counters. $l = \langle PC_0, PC_1, \ldots, PC_{P-1}\rangle$ where $PC_i \in \{1,\ldots n_i\}$ and C is the current set of communication records. l_i is used to access the program counter of process with rank i. $s.l$ is used to access the program counter tuple and $s.C$ is used to access the communication records in the current state.

3.2 Transition Systems

In this section we describe process transitions and runtime transitions that constitute our formal model for MPI.

Process Transitions: Figure 4 shows the process transitions for the four MPI functions that we have chosen to model. Since the processes *issue* the MPI functions into the MPI runtime, we annotate the name of each transition by $\triangleright$. $PS^{\triangleright}$ can be read as '**P**rocess-**S**end-Issue.' The state transition system shows the current state s on the top and the next state s' at the bottom. The initial state denoted by s_0 has l_i for every process i set to 1 and $C = \emptyset$. Every *issue* event results in the creation of a new communication record which is created and added to C in the next state s'. We describe the $PS^{\triangleright}$ transition in detail. For $PS^{\triangleright}$, the current state s is $\langle l, C\rangle$ and p_{i,l_i} denotes the MPI operation invoked by process i at the PC denoted by l_i. $S_{i,l_i}(j, h_{i,l_i})$ is the send being issued where j is the destination to which the message is to be sent. The transition creates a new communication record whose *pid* is i, *pc* is l_i, *op* is S, and *dest* is j. The *src* and *handle* fields are set to $\bot$. Finally, the state is set to $\triangleright$ denoting that the send is in the *issued* state. The rest of the transitions can be understood similarly.

MPI Runtime Transitions perform the actual message passing and synchronization operations. However, the transitions must obey the partial order rules described in Section 2. Given the set of communication records, we construct the *IntraHB* graph at every state s that follows from the $\prec_{mhb}$, as described now. The *IntraHB* relation helps define the MPI semantics, mainly by defining how MPI commands match.

Definition 2. *For a state $s = \langle l, C\rangle$, the graph s.IntraHB $= (V, E)$, where $V = s.C$. Further, for communication records $c_{i,j}$ and $c_{i,k}$, with $j < k$, $\langle c_{i,j}, c_{i,k}\rangle \in E$ iff one of these holds:*

- $c_{i,j}.op = c_{i,k}.op = S \wedge c_{i,j}.dest = c_{i,k}.dest$
- $c_{i,j}.op = c_{i,k}.op = R \wedge (c_{i,j}.src = * \vee c_{i,j}.src = c_{i,k}.src)$
- $c_{i,j}.op = S \wedge c_{i,k}.op = W \wedge c_{i,k}.handle = h_{ij}$
- $c_{i,j}.op = R \wedge c_{i,k}.op = W \wedge c_{i,k}.handle = h_{ij}$
- $c_{i,j}.op = B \vee c_{i,j}.op = W$

The edges between the communication records are added based on the partial orders defined in Section 2. It is called as an *IntraHB* (intra happens-before) graph since the edges are between the communication records within the process. $c_{i,j}$ and $c_{i,k}$ are two communication records of process i. The first condition in Definition 2 is to satisfy the ordering relation $S^{\Diamond}_{i,j}(l, h_{ij}) \prec S^{\Diamond}_{i,k}(l, h_{i,k})$. The second condition is to satisfy the ordering conditions $R^{\Diamond}_{i,j}(l, h_{i,j}) \prec R^{\Diamond}_{i,k}(l, h_{ik})$, and $R^{\Diamond}_{i,j}(*, h_{i,j}) \prec R^{\Diamond}_{i,k}(l, h_{ik})$. The third and fourth conditions satisfy the ordering conditions $S^{\bullet}_{i,j}(l, h_{ij}) \prec W^{\bullet}i, k(h_{ij})$ and $R^{\bullet}_{i,j}(l, h_{ij}) \prec W^{\bullet}i, k(h_{ij})$ respectively. The last condition is to satisfy the $\prec_{fo}$ (*fence-order*).

Definition 3. *For communication records $c_{i,j}$ and $c_{i,k}$ and state s, if $\langle c_{i,j}, c_{i,k}\rangle \in E$ where E is the second component of s.IntraHB, we refer to $c_{i,j}$ as an* **ancestor** *of $c_{i,k}$.*

Figure 6 defines the POE algorithm in terms of execution steps termed as *execute*. For any state s in this execution beginning with the initial program state s_0, we define the set $s.C_R$ associated with s to be those communication records that have crossed through their commit points. The update rule to obtain $s_i.C_R$ (the C_R set of the current state s_i) from $s_{i-1}.C_R$ (the C_R set of the previous state) is the following:

Definition 4. $s_0.C_R = \emptyset$, *and for all* $i > 0$, $s_i.C_R = s_{i-1}.C_R \cup \{c_{i,j} \in s_i.C \mid c_{i,j}.state = \Diamond\}$.

Since W's commit point is the same as completion, we do not add W to C_R and instead add it to C_{cpl}, where $s.C_{cpl}$ are the set of communication records that are *completed* by the MPI runtime. The completion criteria is different for different MPI functions as described in Section 2.

Definition 5. $s_i.C_{cpl} = s_{i-1}.C_{cpl} \cup \{c_{i,j} \in s_i.C \mid c_{i,j}.state = \bullet\}$.

Definition 6. *For a given state* $s = \langle l, c\rangle$ *let* $c_{i,k} \in s.C$ *and* $s.IntraCB = (V, E)$. *Define* $c_{i,k} \in C_{\downarrow}$ *iff for every* $c \in Ancestors(c_{i,k})$ *one of the following is true:*

- $c.op = S \wedge c_{i,k}.op = W \wedge c \in s.C_{cpl}$
- $c.op = R \wedge c_{i,k}.op = W \wedge c \in s.C_{cpl}$
- $c.op = S \wedge c_{i,k}.op = S \wedge c \in s.C_R$
- $c.op = R \wedge c_{i,k}.op = R \wedge c \in s.C_R$
- $c.op = B \wedge c \in s.C_{cpl}$
- $c.op = W \wedge c \in s.C_{cpl}$

$s.C_{\downarrow}$ is the set of communication records where all the ancestors of every communication records are either completed or matched (depending on the MPI operations), *i.e.*, the ancestors have crossed their commit points. Hence, $s.C_{\downarrow}$ is the set of communication records that can now be matched or completed without violating $\prec_{mhb}$. It must be noted that each of the condition in Definition 6 satisfies $\prec_{mhb}$. Our semantics, in effect, defines the set of all allowed executions of MPI programs.

We now define the MPI runtime transitions in Figure 5. We employ a convenient notational abbreviation introduced through a simple example:

- For a set s and an item x, let $s + x$ denote $s \cup \{x\}$.

$$\mathbf{RR}: \frac{s:\langle\, l, C\,\rangle,\ c_{x,i}, c_{y,j} \in s.C_{\downarrow},\ c_{x,i} = R_{x,i}(y, h_{x,i}),\quad c_{y,j} = S_{y,j}(x, h_{y,j}),\ y \in PID}{s' : \langle l, C : c_{x,i}[match \leftarrow @ + c_{y,j}, state \leftarrow \Diamond]\,\rangle}$$

$$\mathbf{RR*}: \frac{s:\langle\, l, C\,\rangle,\ c_{x,i}, c_{y,j} \in s.C_{\downarrow}, c_{x,i} = R_{x,i}(*, h_{x,i}),\quad c_{y,j}.op = S_{y,j}(x),\ y \in PID}{s' : \langle l, C : c_{x,i}[match \leftarrow @ + c_{y,j}, src \leftarrow y, state \leftarrow \Diamond]\rangle}$$

$$\mathbf{RS}: \frac{s:\langle\, l, C\,\rangle,\ c_{i,j} \in s.C_{\downarrow}, c_{k,l} \in s.C_{R},\ c_{i,j} = S_{i,j}(k, h_{i,j}),\quad c_{k,l} = R_{k,l}(i, h_{k,l}),\ c_{k,l}.match = \{c_{i,j}\}}{s' : \langle l, C : c_{i,j}[match \leftarrow @ + c_{k,l}, state \leftarrow \Diamond]\,\rangle}$$

$$\mathbf{RB}: \frac{s:\langle\, l, C\,\rangle,\ C_1 \subseteq s.C_{\downarrow},\ |\, C_1 \,|= P,\quad \forall c_{i,j} \in C_1 :\ c_{i,j} = B_{i,j}}{s' : \langle\, l, C : \forall c_{i,j} \in C_1\ :\ c_{i,j}[match \leftarrow @ + C_1, state \leftarrow \Diamond]\,\rangle}$$

$$\mathbf{RW}: \frac{s:\langle\, l, C\,\rangle,\ c_{i,k} \in s.C_{\downarrow},\ c_{i,k}.op = W}{s' : \langle\, C : c_{i,k}[state \leftarrow \bullet]\,\rangle} \qquad \mathbf{R\text{–}\bullet}: \frac{s:\langle\, l, C\,\rangle,\ c_{i,k} \in s.C_{R}, c_{i,k}.op = R/S/B}{s' : \langle\, l, C : c_{i,k}[state \leftarrow \bullet]\,\rangle}$$

$$\mathbf{RR}^{\lhd}: \frac{s:\langle\, l, C\,\rangle,\ c_{i,k} \in C,\ c_{i,k}.op = R}{s' : \langle\, l[l_i \leftarrow l_i + 1], C : c_{i,k}[state \leftarrow \lhd]\,\rangle} \qquad \mathbf{RS}^{\lhd}: \frac{s:\langle\, l, C\,\rangle,\ c_{i,k} \in C,\ c_{i,k}.op = S}{s' : \langle\, l[l_i \leftarrow l_i + 1], C : c_{i,k}[state \leftarrow \lhd]\,\rangle}$$

$$\mathbf{RW}^{\lhd}: \frac{s:\langle\, l, C\,\rangle,\ c_{i,k} \in s.C_{cpl},\ c_{i,k}.op = W}{s' : \langle\, l[l_i \leftarrow l_i + 1], C : c_{i,k}[state \leftarrow \lhd]\,\rangle} \qquad \mathbf{RB}^{\lhd}: \frac{s:\langle\, l, C\,\rangle,\ c_{i,k} \in s.C_{cpl},\ c_{i,k}.op = B}{s' : \langle\, l[l_i \leftarrow l_i + 1], C : c_{i,k}[state \leftarrow \lhd]\,\rangle}$$

Fig. 5. MPI Runtime Transitions

- Let $C : c_{x,i}[match \leftarrow @ + h_{y,j}]$ stand for "the set C except that the member $c_{x,i}$ in it has its match component updated by the addition of $h_{y,j}$" . Here, @ stands for $c_{x,i}.match$ (a notation inspired by TLA+).

RR (**R**untime-**R**eceive) transition matches a send and matching receive. In the current state $s = \langle l, C\rangle$, consider $c_{x,i}$ and $c_{y,j}$ such that both communication records are in $s.C_{\downarrow}$, *i.e.*, both the communication records are ready to be matched since all their ancestors have either been matched or completed. If $c_{x,i}$ is $R_{x,i}(y, h_{x,i}$ *i.e.* it is a receive trying to receive a message from process y and $c_{y,j}$ is $S_{y,j}(x, h_{y,j})$ is a send that matches the receive, then the send is matched with the receive which is the new state s' where $c_{x,i}$'s *match* is updated. Note that it is acceptable to update either the send or receive match. We just chose to show the runtime transition with a receive match being set. We could also have set both the send and receive matches at the same time. However, our attempt is to keep the MPI runtime as generic as possible to allow all possible sets of interleavings. Note that the receive is set to the $\Diamond$ state but not to the $\bullet$ state. This is because the receive buffer is still not filled with the sent data. This also allows any following receive to be matched and completed before $c_{x,i}$ itself is completed. In other words, as soon as a receive 'chooses its partner,' the following receive can choose its partner.

RR* (**R**untime-**R**eceive-wildcard) transition is similar to RR transition except that the *src* field of the receive which was a wildcard receive previously is now replaced by y which is the matching send process rank. This models 'dynamic source rewriting for wildcard receives, as was illustrated in Section 1. Strictly speaking, **RR*** is a *family* of transitions involving one receiver and its matching senders; we however choose to view it as a single transition for convenience.

RS (**R**untime-**S**end) transition is similar to RR transition except that the receive's *match* set is already populated with the send's communication record. The matching receive is searched in the $s.C_R$ set because a previously fired RR/RR* transition has set the receive to the $\Diamond$ state which, in effect, moves the receive into the C_R set. The matching receive is found by comparing the receive's *match* to the send's communication record. We only set the send's match field and move the send to the $\Diamond$ state to keep the runtime as generic as possible as described in RR transition.

RW (**R**untime-**W**ait) transition is in $s.C_\downarrow$ if its corresponding send or receive has been completed as described in Definition 6. Since the send (receive) is complete, the W can also be completed.

RB (**R**untime-**B**arrier) transition checks that the $C_1 \subseteq C_\downarrow$ where is C_1 has only barriers and the number of barriers is equal to P (number of MPI processes). That is, it checks that all the processes have issued their barriers. In that case, the barriers are moved to the $\Diamond$ state. The barriers are only moved to the $\Diamond$ state and not the $\bullet$ state even though there is no actual data to transfer. The reason for this is to seamlessly support other MPI collective functions like barriers that also have data to be transferred (e.g. `MPI_Bcast`). In such a case, the completion or the transfer of data can happen later. It can be seen that our runtime transitions can readily be applied to other MPI functions.

R-$^\bullet$ (**R**untime-any-help-complete) are the runtime transitions to complete any transitions that have been matched, *i.e.* are in C_R. The S, R and B that are matched can be moved to complete state. Note that there is a causal order between the RR(S/B)/RR* and RR(S/B)$^\bullet$ transitions for a specific send/receive/barrier.

The RS$^\bullet$ transition will be different from what is presented here *when the MPI runtime can buffer sends*. In that case, instead of checking that $c_{k,l} \in s.C_R$, we must check that $c_{k,l} \notin s.C_{cpl}$. Since the send is already completed (the send buffer is copied into the MPI runtime) when the send is buffered, it is already in the $s.C_{cpl}$ set. Because of this early copying of the send buffer, a buffered send need not be moved from state $\Diamond$ to $\bullet$. Hence, when trying to move a send from state $\Diamond$ to $\bullet$, we must first ensure that the send is not buffered *i.e.* the send is not yet completed.

RR$^\lhd$ (**R**untime-**R**eceive-return) and **RS$^\lhd$** (**R**untime-**S**end-return) transition increments the program counter and sets the state to $\lhd$. Note that the receive/send can return at any time irrespective of their current state because they are non-blocking operations.

RW$^\lhd$ (**R**untime-**W**ait-return) and (**R**untime-**B**arrier-return) **RB$^\lhd$** transitions also increment the PC and set the state to $\lhd$. However, note that there is a causal order from RW to RW$^\lhd$ and RB to RB$^\lhd$.

It can be easily verifed that the $\prec_{mhb}$ order is respected by all the transitions discussed in this section.

4 POE Algorithm

The reachable state space generated by firing the MPI transitions (both process and runtime) described in Section 3 describes the full reachable state space of a given MPI program. The POE algorithm is obtained by erecting a partial order (priority order)

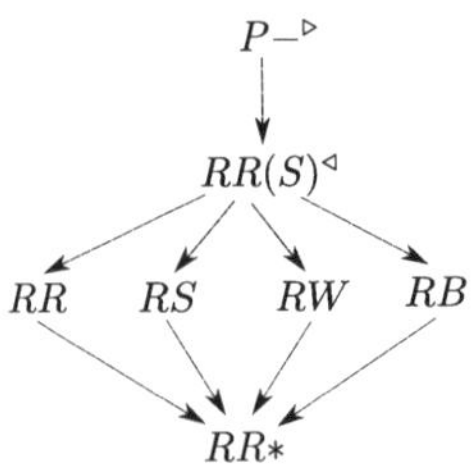


```
1: POE(s) {
2:   if (s is a final state) return;
3:   t = getHighestPriorityTrans(s);
4:   if (t is not an R* transition) {
5:     s' = execute(s,t); POE(s');
6:   } else {
7:     for all (t in R*TransitionsAtState(s)) {
8:       s' = execute(s,t); POE(s'); }}}}
```

Fig. 6. The Priority Order for getHighestPriorityTrans, and the POE_{MSE} algorithm

among the runtime transitions, as shown in Figure 6, where an arrow point from a higher priority transition to a lower priority transition.

In Figure 6, $P-^{\triangleright}$ stands for the process issue transitions (Notation: $P-$ abbreviates PS, PR, etc.) This means that all processes will first try to issue transitions through the $P-$ moves. When no such issue is possible, we can entertain the $R-$ moves (runtime transitions). The runtime transitions for send and receive return (namely $RR^{\triangleleft}$, $RS^{\triangleleft}$) are next in the priority order and have the same priority. This means that every send/receive issued immediately returns since the return transitions increment the program counter. The above two priorities also means that the POE algorithm lets each of the processes execute until they reach the blocking call (W or B) and then executes any runtime transitions. This is because there are no more process transitions available until the blocking calls complete and return. POE combines the RB and the corresponding $RB^{\triangleleft}$ transitions into a single RB transition. Similarly, RW and corresponding $RW^{\triangleleft}$ transitions are shown in Figure 6 as RW. Once the blocking calls, return, the processes all execute until they again reach their blocking points. The RS and RR transitions are the combined RS, corresponding $RS^{\bullet}$ and RR together with the corresponding $RR^{\bullet}$. The RR, RW, RS and RB transitions have the same priority. Finally, the $RR*$ ($RR*$ together with corresponding $RR^{\bullet}$) transition has the lowest priority. This means that the $RR*$ transition is only executed when there are no other transitions left. This was illustrated in Section 1 by postponing the wildcard receives till all senders were discovered, so that one can perform the maximally diverse extent of rewrites. The **for** loop on Line 7 shows that we will process even (seemingly) unrelated **RR*** transition families together. This is important for soundness, to ensure the C1 condition of [27, Chapter 10], as follows: firing one of the **RR*** transitions may enable a send transition that now matches another **RR*** transition. We now illustrate the working of POE algorithm on a simple example.

4.1 Illustration of POE

Consider the MPI program shown in Figure 7. The two sends $S_{0,1}$ and $S_{1,2}$ can match the wildcard receive $R_{2,1}$. The POE algorithm first executes the process transitions corresponding to $S_{0,1}$, $B_{1,1}$ and $R_{2,1}$. At this point, process P_2 gets blocked on the barrier call. However, the send and receive both return to now execute their $B_{0,2}$ and $B_{2,2}$ calls. At this point all the processes are blocked on their barrier calls and no more process transitions are available to be executed. Either RR* transition that matches $S_{0,1}$ to $R_{2,1}$ or RB transition that matches and returns the three barriers can be executed. Using the priority order, since the RB transition has a higher priority, the barriers get matched and return. The RR* transition is still not executed by the runtime. Since all the processes now return from their barriers, the processes start issuing new instructions, since the process transitions have a higher priority than the RR* transition. The $S_{1,2}$ is issued and the W operations of all the processes are issued. Since W is a blocking call, all the processed block at their W operations. At this point, the only transitions are the two RR* transitions where one transition matches $R_{2,1}$ with $S_{0,1}$ and the other matches $R_{2,1}$ with $S_{1,2}$. The POE algorithm executes one interleaving by matching $R_{2,1}$ with $S_{0,1}$ by re-writing the source of receive to 0. The interleaving also matches $R_{2,4}$ with $S_{1,2}$. It then re-starts the process and re-executes the interleaving this time by matching $R_{2,1}$ with $S_{1,2}$. But now, since $R_{2,1}$ is expecting a send from process 1 and there is no such send available, *the program deadlocks* which is detected by POE. The example illustrates how POE algorithm prioritizes the MPI transitions so that it is able to find all the matching transitions of a wildcard receive.

4.2 Proof of Correctness

Theorem 1. *Assuming non-buffered sends, POE finds all possible deadlocks.*

Proof. The only source of non-determinism is due to wildcard receives. To show that we detect all deadlocks, it is sufficient to prove that we detect all possible sends that can match a wildcard receive (*i.e.*, ample sets are correctly built according to C1, [27, Chapter 10]). We prove this by contradiction. Assume that there is a send S_i that can match the wildcard receive R_j under a native MPI program execution, but somehow, due to our priority ordering, is not matched by the POE algorithm. This means that when the RR* transition involving R_j is executed (matching another send, say $S_i^{'}$), the S_i is not yet issued (if it were issued, then the $RR*$ rule would have picked it). Also, since $RR*$ transition is of the lowest priority, this means that there are no other higher priority transitions that could meanwhile have been executed. Thus, in particular, S_i is blocked at a B or a W instruction of the process of S_i. But then, even a native execution could also not get past this B or W and provide a match to $RR*$.

4.3 Implementing POE

POE can be supported by any MPI-standard compliant MPI library. This is because ISP forwards MPI calls to the MPI runtime only when they are ready to match. One can consider ISP as an auxiliary runtime that uses the MPI runtime just to transport messages, and ensure the progress of the MPI processes. The priority order of POE has the run-time effect of reshuffling the MPI commands – but in a manner that does not violate *IntraHB*. Clearly, no one can be sure of the exact *IntraHB* intended by the original MPI designers or (tacitly) assumed by the scores of MPI users merely by reading [7] or studying particular MPI library code bases. However, there is sufficient evidence that we have indeed unearthed this *IntraHB* relation by the fact that we could effortlessly port ISP to run on three operating systems (Linux, MAC OS/X, and Windows), and on four MPI libraries (MPICH2, OpenMPI, Microsoft MPI, and MVAPICH MPI). Further engineering details of ISP are described in [9,10].

4.4 Send Buffering Issues

The POE algorithm works only when the sends do not have adequate (system-provided or user-provided) buffering. However, if sends can be buffered, it can miss deadlocks present in a program. Consider the MPI example shown in Figure 8.

P_0	P_1	P_2
$S_{0,1}(2,h_{01})$	$B_{1,1}$	$R_{2,1}(*,h_{21})$
$B_{0,2}$	$S_{1,2}(2,h_{12})$	$B_{2,2}$
$W_{0,3}(h_{01})$	$W_{1,3}(h_{12})$	$W_{2,3}(h_{21})$
		$R_{2,4}(1,h_{24})$
		$W_{2,5}(1,h_{25})$

Fig. 7. "Crooked" Barrier Example

P_0	P_1	P_2
$S_{0,1}(1,h_{01})$	$S_{1,1}(2,h_{11})$	$R_{2,1}(*,h_{21})$
$W_{0,2}(h_{01})$	$W_{1,2}(h_{11})$	$W_{2,2}(h_{21})$
$S_{0,3}(2,h_{03})$	$R_{1,3}(0,h_{13})$	$R_{2,3}(0,h_{23})$
$W_{0,4}(h_{03})$	$W_{1,4}(h_{13})$	$W_{2,4}(h_{23})$

Fig. 8. Buffering Sends and Deadlocks

When none of the sends are buffered, only $S_{1,1}$ can match the wildcard receive $R_{2,1}$ and there is no deadlock. However, when $S_{1,1}$ is buffered, the $W_{1,2}$ can complete even before the send is matched. This enabled the the $S_{0,1}$ and $R_{1,3}$ to match and since $S_{0,1}$ is matched, it can complete unblocking the $W_{0,2}$. Now, $S_{0,3}$ is issued and since the wildcard receive is not yet matched, it can be matched with $S_{0,3}$ and result in a deadlock since $R_{2,3}$ will not have a matching send. Note that this deadlock cannot happen when none of the sends are buffered. We call this the *slack inelastic property* [28] of MPI. One solution would be to buffer all the sends. However, this will mean that any deadlocks corresponding to non-buffered sends will not be detected by POE. Since buffer allocation is a dynamic property, our goal is to extend POE so that it can detect all forms of deadlocks. Currently, we are working on a slack independent error detection algorithm that improves upon POE.

5 Concluding Remarks

In this paper, we presented a formal semantics for a subset of four MPI operations. Our semantics first characterize the states through which each MPI function call go through. It then describes the MPI runtime transitions that help progress the issued MPI functions through their states. The crux of our definitions was the identification of the relations MPI Intra Happens Before ($\prec_{mhb}$) as well as the *IntraHB* graph. Basically these relations capture how MPI guarantees the non-overtaking property. Our definitions reveal the full generality of executions admitted by all MPI standard compliant libraries.

We take our formal semantic definitions and simply introduce a priority of firing of the MPI runtime rules. This gives our MPI-specific partial order reduction algorithm POE. We also have implemented our ISP tool by closely following our formal semantics.

The broader lessons from our work are that real world APIs such as MPI are really complex. Yet, by discovering the essential states through with each API call goes through, one can set up elegant state transition systems that then help guide reduction algorithms and implementations. Given the push towards multi-core CPUs and the general parallelism "feeding frenzy," many APIs are being defined by various groups. Our ideas may play a role in developing dynamic verification tools for these APIs also. This fact has been reaffirmed not only through ISP but through another line of recent work [29] on developing a dynamic formal verifier for applications written using the recently proposed Multi-core Communications API (MCAPI [30]).

References

1. Godefroid, P.: Model Checking for Programming Languages using Verisoft. In: POPL, pp. 174–186 (1997)
2. Flanagan, C., Godefroid, P.: Dynamic partial-order reduction for model checking software. In: POPL, pp. 110–121. ACM, New York (2005)
3. The Java Pathfinder, `http://javapathfinder.sourceforge.net`
4. Musuvathi, M., Qadeer, S.: Iterative context bounding for systematic testing of multithreaded programs. In: Proceedings of the ACM SIGPLAN Conference on Programming Language Design and Implementation (PLDI), pp. 446–455 (2007)
5. CHESS: Find and Reproduce Heisenbugs in Concurrent Programs, `http://research.microsoft.com/en-us/projects/chess/`
6. Yang, Y., Chen, X., Gopalakrishnan, G., Wang, C.: Automatic Discovery of Transition Symmetry in Multithreaded Programs using Dynamic Analysis. In: SPIN 2009, Grenoble (June 2009)
7. MPI Standard 2.1., `http://www.mpi-forum.org/docs/`
8. Vakkalanka, S., Gopalakrishnan, G., Kirby, R.M.: Dynamic verification of MPI programs with reductions in presence of split operations and relaxed orderings. In: Gupta, A., Malik, S. (eds.) CAV 2008. LNCS, vol. 5123, pp. 66–79. Springer, Heidelberg (2008)
9. Vo, A., Vakkalanka, S., DeLisi, M., Gopalakrishnan, G., Kirby, R.M., Thakur, R.: Formal verification of practical mpi programs. In: PPoPP 2009 (2009)
10. Vakkalanka, S., DeLisi, M., Gopalakrishnan, G., Kirby, R.M.: Scheduling considerations for building dynamic verification tools for MPI. In: PADTAD-VI 2008 (2008)
11. Vakkalanka, S., et al.: Static-analysis Assisted Dynamic Verification of MPI Waitany Programs (Poster Abstract). In: EuroPVM/MPI (September 2009) (accepted)
12. Vo, A., et al.: Sound and Efficient Dynamic Verification of MPI Programs with Probe Non-Determinism. In: Ropo, M., Westerholm, J., Dongarra, J. (eds.) EuroPCM/MPI 2009. LNCS, vol. 5759, pp. 271–281. Springer, Heidelberg (2009)
13. Palmer, R., DeLisi, M., Gopalakrishnan, G., Kirby, R.M.: An Approach to Formalization and Analysis of Message Passing Libraries. In: Leue, S., Merino, P. (eds.) FMICS 2007. LNCS, vol. 4916, pp. 164–181. Springer, Heidelberg (2008)
14. Li, G., et al.: Formal Specification of the MPI 2.0 Standard in TLA+. Under Submission, `http://www.cs.utah.edu/formal_verification/mpitla/`
15. Lamport, L.: Specifying Systems: The TLA Language and Tools. Addison-Wesley, Reading (2004)
16. Karypis, G., Kumar, V.: Parallel multilevel k-way partitioning scheme for irregular graphs. In: SuperComputing, SC (1996)
17. Siegel, S.F., Siegel, A.R.: MADRE: The Memory-Aware Data Redistribution Engine. In: Lastovetsky, A., Kechadi, T., Dongarra, J. (eds.) EuroPVM/MPI 2008. LNCS, vol. 5205, pp. 218–226. Springer, Heidelberg (2008)
18. Workshop on Exploiting Concurrency Efficiently and Correctly, Grenoble, Discussion of Challenge Problems (June 2009), `http://www.cs.utah.edu/ec2`

19. Pacheco, P.: Parallel Programming with MPI. Morgan Kaufmann, San Francisco (1996)
20. DeLisi, M.: Umpire Test Suite Results using ISP, http://www.cs.utah.edu/formal_verification/ISP_Tests/
21. Lamport, L.: Time Clocks, and the Ordering of Events in a Distributed System. Communications of the ACM 21(7), 558–564 (1978)
22. Siegel, S.F.: Efficient Verification of Halting Properties for MPI Programs with Wildcard Receives. In: VMCAI 2006, pp. 413–429 (2006)
23. Georgelin, P., Pierre, L., Nguyen, T.: A Formal Specification of the MPI Primitives and Communication Mechanisms. Rapport de Recherche LIM 1999-337, Marseille (October 1999)
24. http://www.cs.utah.edu/formal_verification/ISP-release/
25. mpiBLAST: Open-Source Parallel BLAST, http://www.mpiblast.org/
26. The IRS Benchmark Code, https://asc.llnl.gov/computing_resources/purple/archive/benchmarks/irs/
27. Clarke, E.M., Grumberg, O., Peled, D.: Model Checking. MIT Press, Cambridge (1999)
28. Martin, R., Manohar, A.: Slack Elasticity in Concurrent Computing. In: Jeuring, J. (ed.) MPC 1998. LNCS, vol. 1422, p. 272. Springer, Heidelberg (1998)
29. Sharma, S., Gopalakrishnan, G., Mercer, E., Holt, J.: MCC - A runtime verification tool for MCAPI user applications. In: FMCAD 2009, Austin (accepted, 2009)
30. The Multicore Communications API (MCAPI), http://www.multicore-association.org

A Metric Encoding for Bounded Model Checking*

Matteo Pradella[1], Angelo Morzenti[2], and Pierluigi San Pietro[2]

[1] CNR IEIIT-MI, Milano, Italy
[2] Dipartimento di Elettronica e Informazione, Politecnico di Milano, Italy
{pradella,morzenti,sanpietr}@elet.polimi.it

Abstract. In Bounded Model Checking, both the system model and the checked property are translated into a Boolean formula to be analyzed by a SAT-solver. We introduce a new encoding technique which is particularly optimized for managing quantitative future and past metric temporal operators, typically found in properties of hard real time systems. The encoding is simple and intuitive in principle, but it is made more complex by the presence, typical of the Bounded Model Checking technique, of backward and forward loops used to represent an ultimately periodic infinite domain by a finite structure. We report and comment on the new encoding technique and on an extensive set of experiments carried out to assess its feasibility and effectiveness.

Keywords: Bounded model checking, metric temporal logic.

1 Introduction

In Bounded Model Checking [1] a system under analysis is modeled as a finite-state transition system and a property to be checked is expressed as a formula in temporal logic. The model and the property are both suitably translated into boolean logic formulae, so that the model checking problem is expressed as an instance of a SAT problem, that can be solved efficiently thanks to the significant improvements that occurred in recent years in the technology of the SAT-solver tools [9,3]. Infinite, ultimately periodic temporal structures that assign a value to every element of the model alphabet are encoded through a finite set of boolean variables, and the cyclic structure of the time domain is encoded into a set of *loop selector variables* that mark the start and end points of the period. As it usually occurs in a model checking framework, a (bounded) model-checker tool can either prove a property or disprove it by exhibiting a counter example, thus providing means to support simulation, test case generation, etc.

In previous work [10], we introduced techniques for managing bi-infinite time in bounded model checking, thus allowing for a more simple and systematic use of past operators in Linear Temporal Logic. In [11,12], we took advantage of the fact that, in bounded model-checking, both the model and the formula to be checked are ultimately translated into boolean logic. This permits to provide the model not only as a state-transition system, but, alternatively, as a set of temporal logic formulae. We call this a *descriptive* model, as opposed to the term *operational* model used in case it consists of

* Work partially supported by the European Commission, Programme IDEAS-ERC, Project 227977-SMSCom.

A. Cavalcanti and D. Dams (Eds.): FM 2009, LNCS 5850, pp. 741–756, 2009.

a state-transition system. The descriptive model is much more readable and concise if the adopted logic includes past and metric temporal operators, allowing for a great flexibility in the degree of detail and abstraction that the designer can adopt in providing the system model. The model-checking problem is reduced to the problem of satisfiability for a boolean formula that encodes both the modeled system and its conjectured property to be verified, hence the name Bounded *Satisfiability* Checking that we adopted for this approach.

In this paper we take a further step to support efficient Bounded Satisfiability- and Bounded Model-checking by introducing a new encoding technique that is particularly efficient in case of temporal logic formulae that contain time constants having a high numerical value.

In previous approaches [2,10,11,12] the operators of temporal logic that express in a precise and quantitative way some timing constraints were encoded by (rather inefficiently) translating them into combinations of non-metric Linear Temporal Logic operators. For instance, the metric temporal logic formula $\Diamond_{=d}P$, which asserts that property P holds at d time units in the future (w.r.t the implicit present time at which the formula is asserted) would be translated into d nested applications of the LTL next-time operator, $\circ^d P$, and then encoded as a series of operator applications, with obvious overhead.

The new encoding for the metric operators translates the time constants in a way that makes the resulting boolean formula much more compact, and hence the verification carried out by the SAT solver-based tools may be significantly faster.

Thus our technique can be usefully applied to all cases where temporal logic formulae that embed important time constants are used. This is both the case of Bounded Satisfiability Checking, where the system model is expressed as a (typically quite large) set of metric temporal logic formulae, and also of more traditional Bounded Model Checking, when the model of the system under analysis is provided by means of a state transition system but one intends to check a hard real-time property with explicit, quantitatively stated timing constraints.

The paper is structured as follows. In Section 2 we provide background and motivations for our work. Section 3 introduces the new metric encoding and analyzes its main features and properties. Section 4 provides an assessment of the new encoding by reporting the experimental results obtained on a set of significant benchmark case studies. Finally, in Section 5 we draw conclusions.

2 Preliminaries

In this section, to make the paper more readable and self-contained, we provide background material on Metric Temporal Logic and bi-infinite time, on Boundel Model- and Satisfiability-Checking, and on the Zot toolkit.

2.1 A Metric Temporal Logic on Bi-infinite Time

We first recall here Linear Temporal Logic with past operators (PLTL), in the version introduced by Kamp [6], and next extend it with metric temporal operators.

Syntax of PLTL. The alphabet of PLTL includes: a finite set Ap of propositional letters; two propositional connectives $\neg, \vee$ (from which other traditional connectives such as $\top, \bot, \neg, \vee, \wedge, \rightarrow, \ldots$ may be defined); four temporal operators (from which other temporal operators can be derived): "until" $\mathcal{U}$, "next-time" $\circ$, "since" $\mathcal{S}$ and "past-time" (or Yesterday) , $\bullet$. Formulae are defined in the usual inductive way: a propositional letter $p \in Ap$ is a formula; $\neg\phi, \phi \vee \psi, \phi\mathcal{U}\psi, \circ\phi, \phi\mathcal{S}\psi, \bullet\phi$, where ϕ, ψ are formulae; nothing else is a formula.

The traditional "eventually" and "globally" operators may be defined as: $\Diamond\phi$ is $\top\mathcal{U}\phi$, $\Box\phi$ is $\neg\Diamond\neg\phi$. Their past counterparts are: $\blacklozenge\phi$ is $\top\mathcal{S}\phi$, $\blacksquare\phi$ is $\neg\blacklozenge\neg\phi$. Another useful operator for PLTL is "Always" $\mathcal{A}lw$, defined as $\mathcal{A}lw\ \phi := \Box\phi \wedge \blacksquare\phi$. The intended meaning of $\mathcal{A}lw\ \phi$ is that ϕ must hold in every instant in the future and in the past. Its dual is "Sometimes" $\mathcal{S}om\ \phi$ defined as $\neg\mathcal{A}lw\neg\phi$.

The dual operators of $\mathcal{U}$ and $\mathcal{S}$ are called "Release" $\mathcal{R}$ and "Trigger" $\mathcal{T}$, respectively. The definition of $\phi\mathcal{R}\psi$ is $\neg(\neg\phi\mathcal{U}\neg\psi)$, while $\phi\mathcal{T}\psi$ is $\neg(\neg\phi\mathcal{S}\neg\psi)$. They allow the convenient *positive normal form*: Formulae are in positive normal form if their alphabet is $\{\wedge, \vee, \mathcal{U}, \mathcal{R}, \circ, \mathcal{S}, \bullet, \mathcal{T}\} \cup Ap \cup \overline{Ap}$, where $\overline{Ap}$ is the set of formulae of the form $\neg p$ for $p \in Ap$. This form, where negations may only occur on atoms, is very convenient when defining encodings of PLTL into propositional logic. Every PLTL formula ϕ on the alphabet $\{\neg, \vee, \mathcal{U}, \circ, \mathcal{S}, \bullet\} \cup Ap$ may be transformed into an equivalent formula ϕ' in positive normal form.

For the sake of brevity, we also allow n-ary predicate letters (with $n \geq 1$) and the $\forall, \exists$ quantifiers as long as their domains are finite. Hence, one can write, e.g., formulae of the form: $\exists p\ \mathrm{gr}(p)$, with p ranging over $\{1, 2, 3\}$ as a shorthand for $\bigvee_{p\in\{1,2,3\}} \mathrm{gr}_p$.

Semantics of PLTL. In our past work [10], we have introduced a variant of bounded model checking where the underlying, ultimately periodic timing structure was not bounded to be infinite only in the future, but may extend indefinitely also towards the past, thus allowing for a simple and intuitive modeling of continuously functioning systems like monitoring and control devices. In [11], we investigated the performance of verification in many case studies, showing that tool performance on bi-infinite structures is comparable to that on mono-infinite ones. Hence adopting a bi-infinite notion of time does not impose very significant penalties to the efficiency of bounded model checking and bounded satisfiability checking. Therefore, in what follows, we present only the simpler bi-infinite semantics of PLTL. Each experiment of Section 4 use either bi-infinite time (when there are past operators) or mono-infinite time (typically, when there are only future operators).

A bi-infinite word S over alphabet 2^{Ap} (also called a $\mathbb{Z}$-word) is a function $S : \mathbb{Z} \longrightarrow 2^{Ap}$. Hence, each position j of S, denoted by S_j, is in 2^{Ap} for every j. Word S is also denoted as $\ldots S_{-1}S_0S_1\ldots$. The set of all bi-infinite words over 2^{Ap} is denoted by $(2^{Ap})^{\mathbb{Z}}$.

For all PLTL formulae ϕ, for all $S \in (2^{Ap})^{\mathbb{Z}}$, for all integer numbers i, the satisfaction relation $S, i \models \phi$ is defined as follows.

$$S, i \models p, \iff p \in S_i, \text{for } p \in Ap$$
$$S, i \models \neg\phi \iff S, i \not\models \phi$$

$S, i \models \phi \vee \psi \iff S, i \models \phi$ or $S, i \models \psi$
$S, i \models \circ\phi \iff S, i+1 \models \phi$
$S, i \models \phi\mathcal{U}\psi \iff \exists k \geq 0 \mid S, i+k \models \psi$, and $S, i+j \models \phi \; \forall 0 \leq j < k$
$S, i \models \bullet\phi \iff S, i-1 \models \phi$
$S, i \models \phi\mathcal{S}\psi \iff \exists k \geq 0 \mid S, i-k \models \psi$, and $S, i-j \models \phi \; \forall 0 \leq j < k$

Metric temporal operators. Metric operators are very convenient for modeling hard real time systems, with quantitative time constraints. The operators introduced in this section do not actually extend the expressive power of PLTL, but may lead to more succinct formulae. Their semantics is defined by a straightforward translation τ into PLTL.

Let $\sim \in \{\leq, =, \geq\}$), and c be a natural number. We consider here two metric operators, one in the future and one in the past: the bounded eventually $\Diamond_{\sim c}\phi$, and its past counterpart $\blacklozenge_{\sim c}\phi$. The semantics of the future operators is the following (the past versions are analogous):

$$\begin{array}{l}
\tau(\Diamond_{=0}\phi) := \phi \\
\tau(\Diamond_{=t}\phi) := \circ\tau(\Diamond_{=t-1}\phi), \text{for } t > 0 \\
\hline
\tau(\Diamond_{\leq 0}\phi) := \phi \\
\tau(\Diamond_{\leq t}\phi) := \phi \vee \circ\tau(\Diamond_{\leq t-1}\phi), \text{for } t > 0 \\
\hline
\tau(\Diamond_{\geq 0}\phi) := \Diamond\phi \\
\tau(\Diamond_{\geq t}\phi) := \circ\tau(\Diamond_{\geq t-1}\phi), \text{for } t > 0
\end{array}$$

Versions of the bounded operators with $\sim \in \{<, >\}$ may be introduced as a shorthand. For instance, $\Diamond_{>0}\phi$ stands for $\circ\Diamond_{\geq 0}\phi$. Other two dual operators are "bounded globally": $\Box_{\sim c}\phi$ is $\neg\Diamond_{\sim c}\neg\phi$, and its past counterpart is $\blacksquare_{\sim c}\phi$, which is defined as $\neg\blacklozenge_{\sim c}\neg\phi$. Other metric operators are the bounded versions of $\mathcal{U}, \mathcal{R}, \mathcal{S}, \mathcal{T}$ ((see e.g. [10]), which are typically defined as primitive in metric temporal logics, with the various $\Diamond$ operators above defined as derived. In our experience, however, $\Diamond$ operators above are much more common in specifications, therefore we chose to implement them as native in the metric encoding. The latter bounded operators are instead translated into PLTL without a native metric encoding. For instance, $\phi_1\mathcal{U}_{\leq t}\phi_2$ is defined by $\tau(\phi_1\mathcal{U}_{\leq 0}\phi_2) := \phi_2$, $\tau(\phi_1\mathcal{U}_{\leq t}\phi_2) := \phi_2 \vee (\phi_1 \wedge \circ\phi_1\mathcal{U}_{\leq t-1}\phi_2)$ for $t > 0$. Hence, all operators of metric temporal logic are supported, although not all bounded operators have an optimized definition.

2.2 The Zot Toolkit

Zot is an agile and easily extendible bounded model checker, which can be downloaded at http://home.dei.polimi.it/pradella/, together with the case studies and results described in Section 4. Zot provides a simple language to describe both descriptive and operational models, and to mix them freely. This is possible since both models are finally to be translated into boolean logic, to be fed to a SAT solver (Zot supports various SAT solvers, like MiniSat [3], and MiraXT [8]). The tool supports different logic languages through a multi-layered approach: its core uses PLTL, and on top of it a decidable predicative fragment of TRIO [4] is defined (essentially, equivalent to

Metric PLTL). An interesting feature of Zot is its ability to support different encodings of temporal logic as SAT problems by means of plugins. This approach encourages experimentation, as plugins are expected to be quite simple, compact (usually around 500 lines of code), easily modifiable, and extendible.

Zot offers two basic usage modalities:

1. *Bounded satisfiability checking (BSC)*: given as input a specification formula, the tool returns a (possibly empty) history (i.e., an execution trace of the specified system) which satisfies the specification. An empty history means that it is impossible to satisfy the specification.
2. *Bounded model checking (BMC)*: given as input an operational model of the system and a property, the tool returns a (possibly empty) history (i.e., an execution trace of the specified system) which satisfies it.

The provided output histories have temporal length $\leq k$, the bound *k* being chosen by the user, but may represent infinite behaviors thanks to the encoding techniques illustrated in Section 3. The BSC/BMC modalities can be used to check if a property $prop$ of the given specification $spec$ holds over every periodic behavior with period $\leq k$. In this case, the input file contains $spec \wedge \neg prop$, and, if $prop$ indeed holds, then the output history is empty. If this is not the case, the output history is a counterexample, explaining why $prop$ does not hold.

3 Encoding of Metric Temporal Logic

We describe next the encoding of PLTL formulae into boolean logic, whose result includes additional information on the finite structure over which a formula is interpreted, so that the resulting boolean formula is satisfied in the finite structure if and only if the original PLTL formula is satisfied in a (finite or possibly) infinite structure. For simplicity, we present a variant of the bi-infinite encoding originally published in [10], and then introduce metric operators on it. Indeed, when past operators are introduced over a mono-infinite structure (e.g., [2]), however, the encoding can be tricky to define, because of the asymmetric role of future and past: future operators do extend to infinity, while past operators only deal with a finite prefix. The reader may refer to [10], and [11] for a more thorough comparison between mono- and bi-infinite approaches to bounded model checking. The complete mono-infinite encoding can be found in the extended version of the present paper [13].

For brevity in the following we call state S_i the set of assignments of truth values to propositional variables at time i. The idea on which the encoding is based is graphically depicted in Figure 1. A ultimately periodic bi-infinite structure has a finite representation

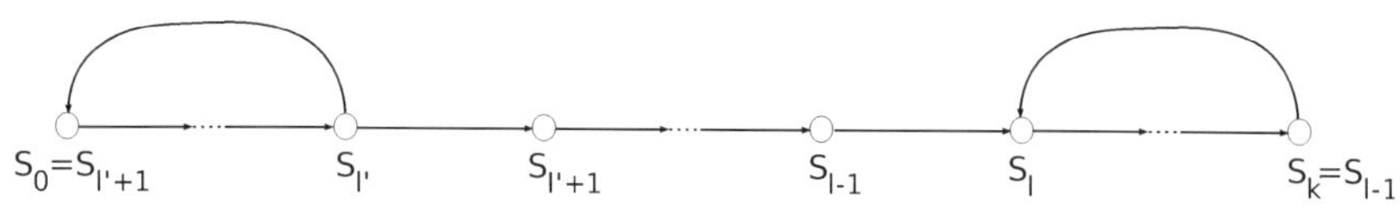

Fig. 1. A bi-infinite bounded path

that includes a non periodic portion, and two periodic portions (one towards the future, and one towards the past). The interpreter of the formula (in our case, the SAT solver), when it needs to evaluate a formula at a state beyond the last state S_k, will follow the "backward link" and consider the states S_l, S_{l+1}, ... as the states following S_k. Analogously, to evaluate a formula at a state precedent to the first state S_0, it will follow the "forward link" and consider the states S'_l, $S_{l'-1}$, ... as the states preceding S_0.

The encoding of the model (i.e. the operational description of the system, if any) is standard - see e.g. [2]. In the following we focus on the encoding of the logic part Φ of the system (or its properties).

Let Φ be a PLTL formula. Its semantics is given as a set of boolean constraints over the so called *formula variables*, i.e., fresh unconstrained propositional variables. There is a variable $|[\phi]|_i$ for each subformula ϕ of Φ and for each instant $0 \leq i \leq k+1$ (instant $k+1$, which is not explicitly shown in Figure 1, has a particular role in the encoding, as we will show next).

First, one needs to constrain the propositional operators in Φ. For instance, if $\phi_1 \wedge \phi_2$ is a subformula of Φ, then each variable $|[\phi_1 \wedge \phi_2]|_i$ must be equivalent to the conjunction of variables $|[\phi_1]|_i$ and $|[\phi_2]|_i$.

Propositional constraints, with p denoting a propositional symbol:

ϕ	$0 \leq i \leq k$
p	$\|[p]\|_i \iff p \in S_i$
$\neg p$	$\|[\neg p]\|_i \iff p \notin S_i$
$\phi_1 \wedge \phi_2$	$\|[\phi_1 \wedge \phi_2]\|_i \iff \|[\phi_1]\|_i \wedge \|[\phi_2]\|_i$
$\phi_1 \vee \phi_2$	$\|[\phi_1 \vee \phi_2]\|_i \iff \|[\phi_1]\|_i \vee \|[\phi_2]\|_i$

The following formulae define the basic temporal behavior of future PLTL operators, by using their traditional fixpoint characterizations.

Temporal subformulae constraints:

ϕ	$-1 \leq i \leq k$
$\circ\phi_1$	$\|[\circ\phi_1]\|_i \iff \|[\phi_1]\|_{i+1}$
$\phi_1\mathcal{U}\phi_2$	$\|[\phi_1\mathcal{U}\phi_2]\|_i \iff \|[\phi_2]\|_i \vee (\|[\phi_1]\|_i \wedge \|[\phi_1\mathcal{U}\phi_2]\|_{i+1})$
$\phi_1\mathcal{R}\phi_2$	$\|[\phi_1\mathcal{R}\phi_2]\|_i \iff \|[\phi_2]\|_i \wedge (\|[\phi_1]\|_i \vee \|[\phi_1\mathcal{R}\phi_2]\|_{i+1})$

(1)

ϕ	$0 \leq i \leq k+1$
$\bullet\phi_1$	$\|[\bullet\phi_1]\|_i \iff \|[\phi_1]\|_{i-1}$
$\phi_1\mathcal{S}\phi_2$	$\|[\phi_1\mathcal{S}\phi_2]\|_i \iff \|[\phi_2]\|_i \vee (\|[\phi_1]\|_i \wedge \|[\phi_1\mathcal{S}\phi_2]\|_{i-1})$
$\phi_1\mathcal{T}\phi_2$	$\|[\phi_1\mathcal{T}\phi_2]\|_i \iff \|[\phi_2]\|_i \wedge (\|[\phi_1]\|_i \vee \|[\phi_1\mathcal{T}\phi_2]\|_{i-1})$

Notice that such constraints do not consider the implicit eventualities that the definitions of $\mathcal{U}$ and $\mathcal{S}$ impose (they treat them as the "weak" until and since operators), nor consider loops in the time structure.

To deal with eventualities and loops, one has to encode an infinite structure into a finite one composed of $k+1$ states $S_0, S_1, \ldots S_k$. The "future" loop can be described by means of other $k+1$ fresh propositional variables $l_0, l_1, \ldots l_k$, called *loop selector variables*. At most one of these loop selector variables may be true. If l_i is true then state $S_{i-1} = S_k$, i.e., the bit vectors representing the state S_{i-1} are identical to those for state S_k. Further propositional variables, InLoop_i ($0 \leq i \leq k$) and LoopExists, respectively mean that position i is inside a loop and that a loop actually exists in the structure. Symmetrically, there are new loop selector variables l'_i to define the loop which goes towards the past, and the corresponding propositional letters InLoop'_i, and LoopEsists′.

The variables defining the loops are constrained by the following set of formulae.

Loop constraints:

Base	$\neg l_0 \wedge \neg\text{InLoop}_0 \wedge \neg l'_k \wedge \neg\text{InLoop}'_k$
$1 \leq i \leq k$	$(l_i \Rightarrow S_{i-1} = S_k) \wedge (\text{InLoop}_i \iff \text{InLoop}_{i-1} \vee l_i)$ $(\text{InLoop}_{i-1} \Rightarrow \neg l_i) \wedge (\text{LoopExists} \iff \text{InLoop}_k)$ $(l'_i \Rightarrow S_{i+1} = S_0) \wedge (\text{InLoop}'_i \iff \text{InLoop}'_{i+1} \vee l'_i)$ $(\text{InLoop}'_{i+1} \Rightarrow \neg l'_i) \wedge (\text{LoopExists}' \iff \text{InLoop}'_0)$

The above loop constraints state that the structure may have at most one loop in the future and at most one loop in the past. In the case of a cyclic structure, they allow the SAT solver to select nondeterministically exactly one of the (possibly) many loops.

To properly define eventualities, we need to introduce new propositional letters $\langle\langle\Diamond\phi_2\rangle\rangle_i$, for each $\phi_1\mathcal{U}\phi_2$ subformula of Φ, and for every $0 \leq i \leq k+1$. Analogously, we need to consider subformulae containing the operator $\mathcal{R}$, such as $\phi_1\mathcal{R}\phi_2$, by adding the new propositional letters $\langle\langle\Box\phi_2\rangle\rangle_i$. This is also symmetrically applied to $\mathcal{S}$ and $\mathcal{T}$, using $\blacklozenge, \blacksquare$. Then, constraints on these eventuality propositions are quite naturally stated as follows.

Eventuality constraints:

ϕ	Base
$\phi_1\mathcal{U}\phi_2$	$\neg\langle\langle\Diamond\phi_2\rangle\rangle_0 \wedge \big(\text{LoopExists} \Rightarrow \big(\lvert[\phi_1\mathcal{U}\phi_2]\rvert_k \Rightarrow \langle\langle\Diamond\phi_2\rangle\rangle_k\big)\big)$
$\phi_1\mathcal{R}\phi_2$	$\langle\langle\Box\phi_2\rangle\rangle_0 \wedge \big(\text{LoopExists} \Rightarrow \big(\lvert[\phi_1\mathcal{R}\phi_2]\rvert_k \Leftarrow \langle\langle\Box\phi_2\rangle\rangle_k\big)\big)$
$\phi_1\mathcal{S}\phi_2$	$\neg\langle\langle\blacklozenge\phi_2\rangle\rangle_k \wedge \big(\text{LoopExists}' \Rightarrow \big(\lvert[\phi_1\mathcal{S}\phi_2]\rvert_0 \Rightarrow \langle\langle\blacklozenge\phi_2\rangle\rangle_0\big)\big)$
$\phi_1\mathcal{T}\phi_2$	$\langle\langle\blacksquare\phi_2\rangle\rangle_k \wedge \big(\text{LoopExists}' \Rightarrow \big(\lvert[\phi_1\mathcal{T}\phi_2]\rvert_0 \Leftarrow \langle\langle\blacksquare\phi_2\rangle\rangle_0\big)\big)$

ϕ	$1 \leq i \leq k$
$\phi_1\mathcal{U}\phi_2$	$\langle\langle\Diamond\phi_2\rangle\rangle_i \iff \langle\langle\Diamond\phi_2\rangle\rangle_{i-1} \vee (\text{InLoop}_i \wedge \lvert[\phi_2]\rvert_i)$
$\phi_1\mathcal{R}\phi_2$	$\langle\langle\Box\phi_2\rangle\rangle_i \iff \langle\langle\Box\phi_2\rangle\rangle_{i-1} \wedge (\neg\text{InLoop}_i \vee \lvert[\phi_2]\rvert_i)$

ϕ	$0 \leq i \leq k-1$
$\phi_1\mathcal{S}\phi_2$	$\langle\langle\blacklozenge\phi_2\rangle\rangle_i \iff \langle\langle\blacklozenge\phi_2\rangle\rangle_{i+1} \vee \big(\text{InLoop}'_i \wedge \lvert[\phi_2]\rvert_i\big)$
$\phi_1\mathcal{T}\phi_2$	$\langle\langle\blacksquare\phi_2\rangle\rangle_i \iff \langle\langle\blacksquare\phi_2\rangle\rangle_{i+1} \wedge \big(\neg\text{InLoop}'_i \vee \lvert[\phi_2]\rvert_i\big)$

The formulae in the following table provide the constraints that must be included in the encoding, for any subformula ϕ, to account for the absence of a forward loop in the structure (the first line of the table states that if there is no loop nothing is true beyond the k-th state) or its presence (the second line states that if there is a loop at position i then state S_{k+1} and S_i are equivalent).

Last state constraints:

Base	$\neg\text{LoopExists} \Rightarrow \neg\lvert[\phi]\rvert_{k+1}$
$1 \leq i \leq k$	$l_i \Rightarrow (\lvert[\phi]\rvert_{k+1} \iff \lvert[\phi]\rvert_i)$

(2)

Then, symmetrically to the last state, we must define first state (i.e. 0 time) constraints (notice that in the bi-infinite encoding instant -1 has a symmetric role of instant $k+1$).

First state constraints:

$$\begin{array}{c|l} \text{Base} & \neg\text{LoopExists}' \Rightarrow \neg|[\phi]|_{-1} \\ \hline 0 \leq i \leq k-1 & l'_i \Rightarrow (|[\phi]|_{-1} \iff |[\phi]|_i) \end{array} \tag{3}$$

The complete encoding of Φ consists of the logical conjunction of all above components, together with $|[\Phi]|_0$ (i.e. Φ is evaluated only at instant 0).

3.1 Encoding of the Metric Operators

We present here the additional constraints one has to add to the previous encoding, to natively support metric operators. We actually implemented also a mono-infinite metric encoding in Zot, but for simplicity we are focusing here only on the bi-infinite one.

Notice that

$$\Diamond_{\leq t}\phi \iff \neg\Box_{\leq t}\neg\phi, \qquad \Diamond_{=t}\phi \iff \Box_{=t}\phi, \qquad \Diamond_{\geq t}\phi \iff \Diamond_{=t}\Diamond\phi$$

(the past versions are analogous). Hence, in the following we will not consider the $\Box_{=t}$, $\Diamond_{\geq t}$, $\Box_{\geq t}$ operators, and their past counterparts.

Ideally, with an *unbounded* time structure, the encoding of the metric operators should be the following one (considering only the future, as the past is symmetrical):

$$|[\Diamond_{=t}\phi]|_i \iff |[\phi]|_{i+t}, \qquad |[\Box_{\leq t}\phi]|_i \iff \bigwedge_{j=1}^{t} |[\phi]|_{i+j}$$

Unfortunately, the presence of a *bounded* time structure, in which bi-infinity is encoded through loops, makes the encoding less straightforward. With simple PLTL one refers at most to one instant in the future (or in the past) or to an eventuality. As the reader may notice in the foregoing encoding, this is still quite easy, also in the presence of loops. On the other hand, the presence of metric operators, affects the loop-based structure, as logic formulae can now refer to time instants well beyond a single future (or past) unrolling of the loop.

To represent the values of subformulae inside the future and past loops, we introduce new propositional variables, $\langle\langle \text{MF}(\cdot,\cdot)\rangle\rangle$ for the future-tense operators, and $\langle\langle \text{MP}(\cdot,\cdot)\rangle\rangle$ for the past ones. For instance, for $\Diamond_{=5}\psi$, we introduce $\langle\langle \text{MF}(\psi, j)\rangle\rangle$, $0 \leq j \leq 4$, where the propositions $\langle\langle \text{MF}(\psi, j)\rangle\rangle$ are used to represent the value of ψ j time units after the starting point of the future loop. This means that, if the future loop selector is at instant 18 (i.e. l_{18} holds), then $\langle\langle \text{MF}(\psi, 2)\rangle\rangle$ represents $|[\psi]|_{20}$ (i.e. ψ at instant 18+2). Analogously and symmetrically, $\langle\langle \text{MP}(\psi, j)\rangle\rangle$ are introduced for past operators with argument ψ, and represent the value of ψ j time units after the starting point of the past loop. That is, if the past loop selector is at instant 7 (i.e. l'_7), then $\langle\langle \text{MP}(\psi, 2)\rangle\rangle$ represents $|[\psi]|_{7-2}$.

The first constraints are introduced for any future or past metric formulae in Φ.

$$\begin{array}{c|c} \phi & 0 \leq j \leq t-1 \\ \hline \Diamond_{=t}\phi,\ \Box_{\leq t}\phi,\ \Diamond_{\leq t}\phi & \langle\langle \text{MF}(\phi, j)\rangle\rangle \iff \bigvee_{i=1}^{k} l_i \wedge |[\phi]|_{i+\text{mod}(j,k-i+1)} \\ \blacklozenge_{=t}\phi,\ \blacksquare_{\leq t}\phi,\ \blacklozenge_{\leq t}\phi & \langle\langle \text{MP}(\phi, j)\rangle\rangle \iff \bigvee_{i=0}^{k-1} l'_i \wedge |[\phi]|_{i-\text{mod}(j,i+1)} \end{array} \tag{4}$$

We now provide the encoding of every metric operator, composed of two parts: the first one defines it inside the bounded portion of the temporal structure (i.e. for instants i in $0 \leq i \leq k$), and the other one, based on *MF* and *MP*, for the loop portion.

$$
\begin{array}{c|c}
\phi & -1 \leq i \leq k \\
\hline
\Diamond_{=t}\phi & |[\Diamond_{=t}\phi]|_i \iff |[\phi]|_{i+t}, \text{ when } i+t \leq k \\
 & |[\Diamond_{=t}\phi]|_i \iff \langle\langle \text{MF}(\phi, t+i-k-1)\rangle\rangle, \text{ elsewhere} \\
\Box_{\leq t}\phi & \Box_{\leq t}\phi \iff \bigwedge_{j=1}^{\min(t,k-i)} |[\phi]|_{i+j} \wedge \bigwedge_{j=k+1-i}^{t} \langle\langle \text{MF}(\phi, i+j-k-1)\rangle\rangle \\
\Diamond_{\leq t}\phi & \Diamond_{\leq t}\phi \iff \bigvee_{j=1}^{\min(t,k-i)} |[\phi]|_{i+j} \vee \bigvee_{j=k+1-i}^{t} \langle\langle \text{MF}(\phi, i+j-k-1)\rangle\rangle
\end{array}
\tag{5}
$$

$$
\begin{array}{c|c}
\phi & 0 \leq i \leq k+1 \\
\hline
\blacklozenge_{=t}\phi & |[\blacklozenge_{=t}\phi]|_i \iff |[\phi]|_{i-t}, \text{ when } i \geq t \\
 & |[\blacklozenge_{=t}\phi]|_i \iff \langle\langle \text{MP}(\phi, t-i-1)\rangle\rangle, \text{ elsewhere} \\
\blacksquare_{\leq t}\phi & \blacksquare_{\leq t}\phi \iff \bigwedge_{j=1}^{\min(t,i)} |[\phi]|_{i-j} \wedge \bigwedge_{j=i+1}^{t} \langle\langle \text{MP}(\phi, i+j-1)\rangle\rangle \\
\blacklozenge_{\leq t}\phi & \blacklozenge_{\leq t}\phi \iff \bigvee_{j=1}^{\min(t,i)} |[\phi]|_{i-j} \vee \bigvee_{j=i+1}^{t} \langle\langle \text{MP}(\phi, i+j-1)\rangle\rangle
\end{array}
$$

The most complex part of the metric encoding is the one considering the behavior on the past loop of future operators, and on the future loop of the past operators. First, let us consider the behavior of future metric operators on the past loop.

$$
\begin{array}{c|c}
\phi & 0 \leq i \leq k-1 \\
\hline
\Diamond_{=t}\phi & l'_i \Rightarrow \left(\begin{array}{c} \bigwedge_{j=1}^{\min(t,k-i)} (|[\phi]|_{i+j} \iff |[\phi]|_{\text{mod}(j-1,i+1)}) \wedge \\ \bigwedge_{j=k-i+1}^{t} \left(\begin{array}{c} \langle\langle \text{MF}(\phi, i+j-k-1)\rangle\rangle \iff \\ |[\phi]|_{\text{mod}(j-1,i+1)} \end{array} \right) \end{array} \right) \\
\Box_{\leq t}\phi & \text{InLoop}'_i \Rightarrow \left(|[\Box_{\leq t}\phi]|_i \iff \left(\begin{array}{c} \bigwedge_{j=1}^{\min(k-i,t)} (\neg\text{InLoop}'_{i+j} \vee |[\phi]|_{i+j}) \wedge \\ \bigwedge_{j=0}^{\min(i,t-1)} (\text{InLoop}'_{\min(k,i+t-j)} \vee |[\phi]|_j) \end{array} \right) \right) \\
\Diamond_{\leq t}\phi & \text{InLoop}'_i \Rightarrow \left(|[\Diamond_{\leq t}\phi]|_i \iff \left(\begin{array}{c} \bigvee_{j=1}^{\min(k-i,t)} (\text{InLoop}'_{i+j} \wedge |[\phi]|_{i+j}) \vee \\ \bigvee_{j=0}^{\min(i,t-1)} (\neg\text{InLoop}'_{\min(k,i+t-j)} \wedge |[\phi]|_j) \end{array} \right) \right)
\end{array}
\tag{6}
$$

The main aspect to consider is the fact that, if l'_i (i.e. the past loop selector variable holds at instant i), then i has two possible successors: $i+1$ and 0. Therefore, if $\Diamond_{=4}\phi$ holds at i (which is inside the past loop), then ϕ must hold both at $i+4$, and at 3. This kind of constraint is captured by the upper formula for $\Diamond_{=t}\phi$, which relates the truth values of ϕ in instants outside of the past loop (i.e., $|[\phi]|_{i+j}$) with the instants inside (i.e., $|[\phi]|_{\text{mod}(j-1,i+1)}$ represents the value of ϕ at instants going from 0 to i, if l'_i holds).

Another aspect to consider is related to the size of the time constant used (i.e. t in this case). Indeed, if $i+t > k$, then we are considering the behavior of ϕ outside the bound $0..k$. This means that we need to consider the behavior of ϕ also in the future loop, hence we refer to $\langle\langle \text{MF}(\phi, i+j-k-1)\rangle\rangle$ (see the lower formula for $\Diamond_{=t}\phi$).

As far as $\Box_{\leq t}\phi$ is concerned, its behavior inside the past loop is in general expressed by two parts. The first one considers ϕ inside the past loop, starting from instant i and going forward, towards the right end of the loop (i.e. where l' holds, say i'). This situation is covered by the upper formula for $\Box_{\leq t}\phi$. If $i+t$ is still inside the past loop (i.e. $i+t \leq i'$), this suffices. If this is not the case, we must consider the remaining instants, going from $i'+1$ to $i+t$. Because we are considering the behavior *inside* the past loop, the instant after i' is 0, so we must translate instants outside of the loop (i.e. where $InLoop'$ does not hold), to instants going from 0 to $i + t - i' - 1$: in all these instants ϕ must hold. This constraint is given by the lower formula for $\Box_{\leq t}\phi$.

The encoding for the past operators is symmetrical, and is the following:

	$1 \leq i \leq k$
$\blacklozenge_{=t}\phi$	$l_i \Rightarrow \left(\begin{array}{c} \bigwedge_{j=2}^{\min(t,i)} (\lvert[\phi]\rvert_{i-j} \iff \lvert[\phi]\rvert_{k-\mathrm{mod}(j-1,k-i+1)}) \wedge \\ \bigwedge_{j=1+i}^{t} \left(\begin{array}{c} \langle\langle \mathrm{MP}(\phi, j-i-1) \rangle\rangle \iff \\ \lvert[\phi]\rvert_{k-\mathrm{mod}(j-1,k-i+1)} \end{array} \right) \end{array} \right)$
$\blacksquare_{\leq t}\phi$	$\mathrm{InLoop}_i \Rightarrow \left(\lvert[\blacksquare_{\leq t}\phi]\rvert_i \iff \left(\begin{array}{c} \bigwedge_{j=1}^{\min(i,t)} (\neg\mathrm{InLoop}_{i-j} \vee \lvert[\phi]\rvert_{i-j}) \wedge \\ \bigwedge_{j=0}^{\min(k-i,t-1)} (\mathrm{InLoop}_{\max(0,i-t+j)} \vee \lvert[\phi]\rvert_{k-j}) \end{array} \right) \right)$
$\blacklozenge_{\leq t}\phi$	$\mathrm{InLoop}_i \Rightarrow \left(\lvert[\blacklozenge_{\leq t}\phi]\rvert_i \iff \left(\begin{array}{c} \bigvee_{j=1}^{\min(i,t)} (\mathrm{InLoop}_{i-j} \wedge \lvert[\phi]\rvert_{i-j}) \vee \\ \bigvee_{j=0}^{\min(k-i,t-1)} (\neg\mathrm{InLoop}_{\max(0,i-t+j)} \wedge \lvert[\phi]\rvert_{k-j}) \end{array} \right) \right)$

The actual implementation of the metric encoding contains some optimizations, not reported here for the sake of brevity, like the re-use, whenever possible, of the various $\langle\langle \mathrm{MF}(\cdot,\cdot) \rangle\rangle$, and $\langle\langle \mathrm{MP}(\cdot,\cdot) \rangle\rangle$ propositional letters.

A first assessment of the encoding. The behavior of the new encoding has been first experimented on a very simple specification of a synchronous shift-register, where, at each clock tick, an input bit is shifted of one position to the right. A specification of this system can be described by the following formula:

$$Alw(in \leftrightarrow \Diamond_{=d} out)$$

where in is true when a bit enters the shift register, out is true when a bit "exits" the register after a delay $d > 0$ (a constant representing the number of memory bits in the register). The Zot toolkit has been applied to this simple specification, using the nonmetric, PLTL-only encoding of ([10]) and the new metric encoding.

The implemented nonmetric encoding is actually the one presented in the current section, without the metric part of Sub-section 3.1. In practice, this means that every metric temporal operator is translated into PLTL before applying the encoding, by means of its definition of Section 2.

The experimental results (with the same hardware and software setup described in Section 4.1) are graphically shown in Figure 2, where Gen represents the generation phase, i.e., the generation of a boolean formula in conjunctive normal form, starting from the above specification, and SAT represents the verification phase, performed by a SAT solver, with a bound $k = 400$ and various values of delay d (from 10 to 150). The first two upper diagrams show the time, in seconds, for Gen and SAT phases, using either a PLTL encoding or the metric encoding, as a function of delay d, while the third upper diagram shows the speedup, as a percentage of speed increase over the PLTL encoding, when using the metric encoding, again as a function of delay d. As one can see, the speedup obtained for both the Gen and SAT phases is proportional to delay d, and can be quite substantial (up to 250% for SAT and 300% for Gen phases). The three lower diagrams report, in a similar way, on the size of the generated boolean formula, in terms of the thousands of variables (Kvar) and clauses (Kcl): the reduction in the size

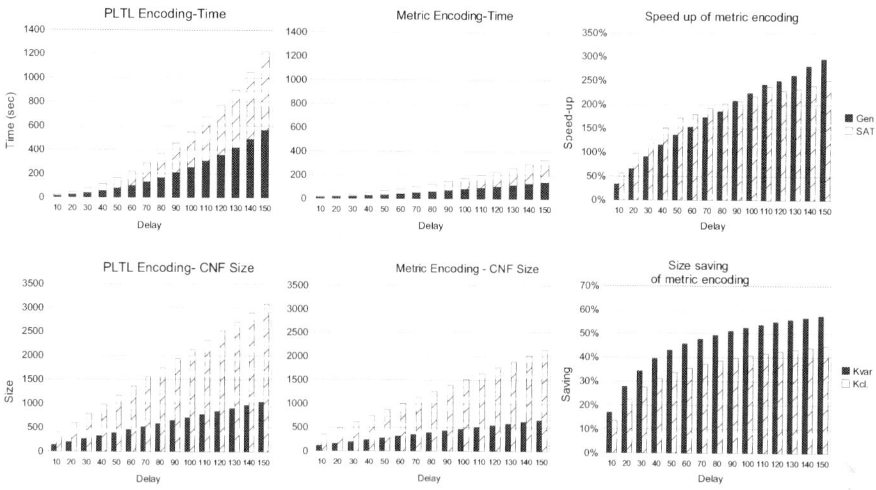

Fig. 2. Summary of experimental data for the synchronous version of a Shift Register

of the generated encoding increases with the value of d and tends to reach a stable value around 60%.

These results can be explained by comparing the two encodings. In general, if a formula ϕ contains a time constant, then the number of subformulae is much higher in the nonmetric enconding than in the metric one. For instance, in the above example, the non-metric encoding of $\Diamond_{=d}out$ is translated into d nested applications of the next-time operator, $\circ^d out$, hence there are $d+1$ subformulae, $\circ^i out$ for $0 \leq i \leq d$, while in the metric encoding of $\Diamond_{=d}out$ there are only two subformulae, $\Diamond_{=d}out$ itself and out. Concerning the number of generated boolean variables, this is much higher for the nonmetric encoding, due to the presence of a larger number of subformulae. Again with reference to the example, we have $(d+1)\cdot(k+2)$ subformula variables in the nonmetric case and $2\cdot(k+2)+2\cdot d$ variables for the metric encoding (of which $2\cdot(k+2)$ subformula variables and $2\cdot d$ MF and MP variables).

Regarding the size of the generated constraints, it is immediate to notice that propositional, eventuality and loop contraints have the same size, which is $O(k)$, in both encodings. The size of the remaining constraints is shown in the following table, where MF and MP constraints are those of type (4), (5), and (6) introduced for the metric encoding only.

e $O(d+k)$ (i.e., less than in the nonmetric case) variables and $O(d\cdot k)$ constraints, which is same as in the nonmetric case but with a smaller constant factor (in this case, 2 rather than 3). This is also clear from Fig. 2, where the size saving tends to a constant when d is large enough.

The analysis of the other metric temporal operators, $\Box_{\leq t}\phi$ and $\Diamond_{\leq t}\phi$, leads to similar conclusions.

4 Experimental Results

First we briefly describe the five case studies that we adopted for our experiments. For all of them we provide both a descriptive and an operational model. A complete archive with the files used for the experiments, and the details of the outcomes, can be found in the Zot web page at http://home.dei.polimi.it/pradella/.

Real-time allocator (RTA). This case study, described in [12], consists of a real-time allocator which serves a set of client processes, competing for a shared resource. The system numeric parameters are the number of processes n_p and the constants T_{req} within which the allocator must respond to the requests, and the maximum time T_{rel} that a process can keep the resource before releasing it. In our experiments, both a descriptive and an operational model were considered, using three processes, and with two different system settings for each version: a first one with $T_{rel} = T_{req} = 3$, and a second one with $T_{rel} = T_{req} = 10$. We first generated a simple run of the system (Property Sat); then we considered four hard real time properties, described in [12], called *Simple Fairness*, *Conditional Fairness*, *Precedence*, and *Suspend Fairness*. It is worth noticing that the formula specifying *Suspend Fairness* includes a relatively high time constant ($T_{rel} \cdot n_p$) and is therefore likely to benefit from the metric encoding. We adopted the bi-infinite encoding for this case study, which allowed to consider only regime behaviors, thus abstracting away system initialization.

Fischer's protocol (FP). FP [7] is a timed mutual exclusion algorithm that allows a number of timed processes to access a shared resource. We considered the system in two variants: one with 3 processes and a delay 5 t.u.; the other one with 4 processes and a delay of 10 t.u. We used the tool to check the safety property (i.e. it is never possible that two different processes enter their critical sections at the same time instant) and to generate a behavior in which there is always at least one alive process. We adopted the bi-infinite encoding, for reasons similar to those already explained for RTA case study.

Kernel Railway Crossing (KRC). This is a standard benchmark in real time systems verification [5], which we used and described in a previous work [12]. In our example we adopted a descriptive model and studied the KRC problem with two sets of time constants, allowing a high degree of nondeterminism on train behavior. In particular, the first set of constants was: $d_{Max} = 9$ and $d_{min} = 5$ t.u. for the maximum and minimum time for a train to reach the critical region, $h_{Max} = 6$ and $h_{min} = 3$ for the maximum and minimum time for a train to enter the critical region once it is first sensed, and $\gamma = 3$ for the movement of the bar from up to down and vice versa. The set of time constants for the second experiment was $d_{Max} = 19$, $d_{min} = 15$, $h_{Max} = 16$, $h_{min} = 13$, and $\gamma = 10$. For each of the two settings we proved both satisfiability of the specification (Sat) and the safety property, using a mono-infinite encoding.

Timer Reset Lamp (TRL). This is the Timer Reset Lamp first presented in [12], with three settings ($\Delta = 10$, $\Delta = 15$, and $\Delta = 20$) and two analyzed properties (the first one, that the lamp is never lighted for more than Δ t.u.: it is false, and the tool generates a counter-example; the second one, namely that the lamp can remain lighted for more than Δ t.u. only if the *ON* button is pushed twice within Δ t.u., is true). This system was analyzed with a bi-infinite encoding.

Asynchronous Shift Register (ASR). The simplest case study is an *asynchronous* version of the Shift Register example discussed in Section 3, where the shift does not occur at every tick of the clock, but only at a special, completely asynchronous *Shift* command. We consider two cases, with the number of bits $n = 16$ and $n = 24$, and we prove satisfiability of the specification and one timed property (if the *Shift* signal remains true for n time units (t.u.) then the value *In* which was inserted in the Shift register at the beginning of the time interval will appear at the opposite side of the register at the end of the time interval). This case study was analyzed with reference to a bi-infinite encoding.

4.1 Results

The experiments were run on a PC equipped with two XEON 5335 (Quadcore) processors at 2.0 Ghz, with 16 GB RAM, running under Gentoo X86-64 (2008.0). The SAT-solver was MiniSat. The experimental results are shown in Table 1. The suffix *-de* indicates analysis carried out on the descriptive version of the model, while *-op* is used for the operational version. The table reports, for various values of the bound k (30, 60, and 90), both Generation time, i.e., the time in seconds taken for building the encoding and transforming it into conjunctive normal form, and SAT time, i.e., the time in seconds taken by the SAT solver to answer. Only the timings of the metric version is reported, since the ones of the non-metric version can be obtained by the following speed up measures. Performance is gauged by providing three measures of speed up as a percentage of the time taken by the metric version (e.g., 0% means no speed-up, 100% means double speed, i.e., the encoding is twice as fast, etc.): $\frac{T_{\mathrm{PLTL}}-T_{\mathtt{metric}}}{T_{\mathtt{metric}}}$, where $T_{\mathtt{metric}}$ and T_{PLTL} represent the time taken by the metric and the PLTL encodings, respectively. The first measure shows the speed up in the generation phase, the second in SAT time and the third one in Total time (i.e., in the sum of Gen and SAT time). On average, the speed up is 42,2% for Gen and 62,2% for SAT, allowing for a 47,9% speed up in the total time. The best results give speed up of, respectively, 224%, 377% and 231%, while the worst results are -7%, -34% and -16%.

Speed up for SAT time appears to be more variable and less predictable than the one for Gen time, although often significantly larger. This is likely caused by the complex and involved ways in which the SAT algorithm is influenced by the numerical values of the k bound, of the time constants in the specification formulae and by their interaction, due to the heuristics that it incorporates. For instance, the speed up for Gen increases very regularly with the bound k, because of the smaller size of the formula to be generated, while SAT may vary unpredictably and significantly with the value of k (e.g., compare property op-P2 for TRL-10, when the speed up increases with k, and TRL-20, when the speed up actually decreases with k). A thorough discussion of these aspects is out of the scope of the present paper, also because they may change from one SAT-solver to another one.

Table 1. Summary of collected experimental data

Case	Property	Gen. (s): Metric			SAT (s): Metric			Gen. Speed-up			SAT Speed up			Total Speed-up		
		k=30	k=60	k=90	k=30	k=60	k=90	k=30	k=60	k=90	k=30	k=60	k=90	k=30	k=60	k=90
RTA-3-de	Sat	14,6	42,4	84,0	12,6	45,1	99,5	4%	2%	2%	2%	4%	1%	3%	3%	1%
	Simple	16,8	49,6	97,6	14,9	54,6	117,8	8%	8%	9%	11%	10%	11%	10%	9%	10%
	Cond	19,7	59,1	116,8	18,6	68,2	146,7	9%	9%	9%	14%	9%	20%	12%	9%	15%
	Prec	22,4	69,7	142,0	21,5	78,3	170,9	2%	−1%	−2%	1%	1%	5%	2%	0%	2%
	Suspend	18,5	55,3	109,3	19,6	64,2	145,1	28%	31%	33%	35%	38%	47%	31%	35%	41%
RTA-3-op	Sat	2,4	5,3	8,8	0,9	2,6	5,2	3%	9%	12%	2%	2%	2%	3%	6%	8%
	Simple	3,6	8,4	14,4	1,7	5,3	11,2	14%	24%	25%	39%	30%	24%	22%	26%	25%
	Cond	5,1	12,7	22,4	3,0	9,1	19,2	16%	25%	22%	27%	26%	32%	20%	26%	27%
	prec	6,6	17,1	31,3	4,0	13,9	29,2	0%	5%	1%	4%	−2%	−1%	1%	2%	0%
	suspend	4,7	11,2	19,7	3,2	11,1	21,4	49%	72%	75%	94%	58%	74%	67%	65%	75%
RTA-10-de	Sat	72,1	243,9	506,8	82,8	324,3	779,9	7%	3%	4%	4%	4%	−8%	5%	4%	−3%
	Simple	76,9	255,2	541,8	100,0	334,9	768,6	20%	18%	19%	23%	24%	−34%	22%	21%	−13%
	Cond	83,9	277,7	586,2	100,7	384,2	539,9	17%	17%	18%	27%	21%	−34%	22%	20%	−7%
	Prec	103,2	344,6	734,5	124,7	498,6	66,4	6%	4%	3%	5%	−2%	11%	6%	0%	4%
	Suspend	85,3	274,3	577,1	94,8	419,3	6294	53%	63%	62%	79%	57%	−23%	67%	60%	−16%
RTA-10-op	Sat	6,3	13,6	24,7	2,5	7,4	18,2	−1%	3%	1%	0%	0%	−6%	−1%	2%	−2%
	Simple	8,1	19,2	33,4	14,7	19,1	50,9	32%	40%	45%	12%	82%	18%	19%	61%	29%
	Cond	9,9	24,6	42,4	6,5	24,0	37,0	29%	36%	46%	44%	31%	63%	35%	33%	54%
	Prec	15,4	43,0	78,5	10,3	36,2	75,5	2%	−1%	5%	3%	1%	3%	2%	0%	4%
	Suspend	9,6	24,1	44,5	4,7	45,3	633,6	159%	196%	224%	377%	136%	88%	231%	157%	97%
FP-3-5-de	Sat	11,4	31,7	60,3	9,2	31,1	66,9	28%	33%	37%	39%	49%	51%	33%	41%	44%
	Safety	11,9	32,5	62,6	9,5	34,1	73,9	28%	33%	37%	42%	44%	50%	34%	39%	44%
FP-3-5-op	Sat	2,7	6,2	10,4	1,3	3,9	7,1	0%	−1%	0%	−1%	−3%	0%	0%	−2%	0%
	Safety	2,9	6,7	11,7	1,5	4,7	10,8	0%	−1%	0%	−3%	0%	0%	−1%	−1%	0%
FP-4-10-de	Sat	26,3	80,3	159,0	25,6	94,9	200,6	67%	74%	81%	95%	115%	102%	81%	96%	93%
	Safety	27,3	83,7	163,1	27,7	101,2	221,0	70%	71%	80%	87%	90%	89%	78%	82%	85%
FP-4-10-op	Sat	4,3	10,6	18,0	4,3	8,4	15,3	0%	−1%	−1%	0%	0%	0%	0%	−1%	0%
	Safety	4,8	11,6	19,9	4,1	14,9	27,1	−1%	−1%	−1%	0%	0%	−1%	−1%	0%	−1%
KRC-9-5-6-3-de	Sat	2,1	4,7	7,9	0,9	3,3	6,3	24%	30%	34%	57%	34%	80%	34%	32%	54%
	Safety	2,2	5,0	8,4	0,2	0,4	0,6	23%	29%	36%	26%	32%	38%	23%	29%	36%
KRC-9-5-6-3-op	Sat	1,4	3,0	4,8	0,5	1,3	2,9	−1%	−1%	−0%	0%	0%	1%	0%	−1%	0%
	Safety	1,5	3,2	5,5	0,1	0,2	0,3	−2%	−2%	−6%	0%	0%	−1%	−2%	−2%	−6%
KRC-19-15-16-13-de	Sat	2,4	5,4	9,1	1,0	3,4	6,4	102%	127%	149%	213%	231%	279%	135%	167%	202%
	Safety	2,5	5,7	9,6	0,2	0,4	0,7	95%	124%	146%	115%	145%	175%	96%	125%	148%
KRC-19-15-16-13-op	Sat	2,0	4,2	6,8	1,0	1,8	4,0	−1%	−1%	3%	−1%	−1%	−1%	−1%	−1%	1%
	Safety	2,0	4,4	7,1	0,1	0,3	0,4	−1%	0%	0%	2%	6%	0%	0%	0%	0%
TRL-10-de	p1	2,9	6,9	11,6	1,4	4,4	9,2	34%	39%	48%	61%	67%	70%	43%	50%	58%
	p2	3,1	8,0	13,7	2,1	8,5	12,5	49%	49%	61%	66%	60%	83%	56%	55%	71%
TRL-10-op	p1	1,1	2,3	3,6	0,3	0,9	1,7	35%	39%	47%	71%	68%	85%	43%	47%	59%
	p2	1,4	3,0	4,7	0,5	1,5	2,9	57%	61%	75%	105%	121%	253%	70%	81%	143%
TRL-15-de	p1	3,9	9,2	16,3	2,1	6,6	14,0	43%	56%	68%	71%	90%	87%	53%	70%	77%
	p2	4,3	10,9	18,3	2,6	12,2	31,0	68%	72%	90%	110%	97%	35%	84%	85%	55%
TRL-15-op	p1	1,1	2,4	3,7	0,3	0,9	1,6	63%	60%	69%	104%	117%	140%	72%	75%	91%
	p2	1,4	3,1	5,0	0,5	1,6	3,0	95%	107%	130%	186%	208%	242%	120%	141%	172%
TRL-20-de	p1	5,3	13,0	23,0	3,0	10,2	21,8	49%	69%	77%	91%	97%	99%	65%	81%	88%
	p2	5,7	14,4	26,5	3,6	15,7	46,9	77%	91%	100%	148%	166%	183%	104%	130%	153%
TRL-20-op	p1	1,4	3,1	5,1	0,4	1,1	2,1	67%	67%	64%	122%	145%	157%	79%	88%	92%
	p2	1,8	3,8	6,3	0,6	2,5	8,5	104%	134%	143%	242%	226%	84%	140%	170%	109%
ASR-24-de	Sat	11,3	31,3	59,4	14,6	31,4	67,9	3%	−1%	−1%	−4%	0%	−1%	−1%	0%	−1%
	Prop	12,7	33,8	64,0	9,8	34,4	78,5	22%	31%	35%	41%	38%	30%	31%	35%	32%
ASR-24-op	Sat	1,9	4,4	6,9	1,7	1,9	3,7	0%	−7%	−1%	−1%	−1%	−1%	0%	−5%	−1%
	Prop	2,5	5,9	9,4	1,0	3,2	5,7	68%	73%	92%	118%	125%	168%	83%	92%	121%
ASR-16-de	Sat	6,7	17,6	33,2	4,6	15,7	33,4	0%	2%	2%	0%	0%	0%	0%	1%	1%
	Prop	7,4	20,0	36,4	5,1	18,3	40,3	22%	25%	28%	34%	31%	27%	27%	28%	27%
ASR-16-op	Sat	1,4	3,0	5,0	0,7	1,3	2,4	−2%	7%	2%	3%	6%	3%	0%	6%	2%
	Prop	1,9	4,2	6,9	0,7	2,1	3,7	57%	67%	69%	94%	97%	131%	67%	77%	90%

It is easy to realize, as already noticed in Section 3 for the example of the synchronous shift register, that significant improvements are obtained, with the new metric encoding, for analysing Metric temporal logic properties with time constants having a fairly high numerical value. The larger the value, the larger the speed up. This is particularly clear for TRL, RTA and FP case studies.

The fact that the underlying model was descriptive or operational may have a significant impact on verification speed, but considering only the speed up the results are much more mixed. For instance, the operational versions of FP and KRC, although more efficient, had a worse speed up than their corresponding descriptive cases, while the reverse occurred for the operational versions of RTA, ASR and TRL. The only exception is for the Sat case, where no property is checked against the model, and hence no gain can be obtained for the operational model. A decrease in benefit for certain descriptive models may be caused by cases where subformulae in metric temporal logic with large time constants are combined with other non-metric subformulae.

The measure of the size of the generated formulae is not reported here, but it is worth pointing out that, thanks to the new metric encoding, the size may be reduced of 50% or more when there are high time constants and/or large k bounds. For instance, in case KRC-19-15-16-13-de (Safety) the number of clauses of the metric encoding is less than half of the nonmetric one, while in case FP-4-10-de (both sat and Safety), the metric encoding is around one third smaller.

5 Conclusions

In this paper, a new encoding technique of linear temporal logic into boolean logic is introduced, particularly optimized for managing quantitative future and past metric temporal operators. The encoding is simple and intuitive in principle, but it is made more complex by the presence, typical of the technique, of backward and forward loops used to represent an ultimately periodic infinite domain by a finite structure.

We have shown that, for formulae that include an explicit time constant, like e.g., $\Diamond_{=t}\phi$, the new metric encoding permits an improvement, in the size of the generated SAT formula and in the SAT solving time, that is proportional to the numerical value of the time constant. In practical examples, the overall performance improvement is limited by other components of the encoding algorithm that are not related with the value of the time constants (namely, those that encode the structure of the time domain, or the non-metric operators). Therefore, the gain in performance can be reduced in the less favorable cases in which the analyzed formula contains few or no metric temporal operators, or the numerical value of the time constants is quite limited.

An extensive set of experiments has been carried out to asses its feasibility and effectiveness for Bounded Model Checking (and Bounded Satisfiability Checking). Average speed up in SAT solving time was 62%. The experimental results show that the new metric encoding can successfully be applied when the property to analyze includes time constants with a fairly high numerical value.

Acknowledgements. We thank Davide Casiraghi for his valuable work on Zot's metric plugins.

References

1. Biere, A., Cimatti, A., Clarke, E., Zhu, Y.: Symbolic model checking without BDDs. In: Cleaveland, W.R. (ed.) TACAS 1999. LNCS, vol. 1579, pp. 193–207. Springer, Heidelberg (1999)
2. Biere, A., Heljanko, K., Junttila, T., Latvala, T., Schuppan, V.: Linear encodings of bounded LTL model checking. Logical Methods in Computer Science 2(5), 1–64 (2006)
3. Eén, N., Sörensson, N.: An extensible SAT-solver. In: Giunchiglia, E., Tacchella, A. (eds.) SAT 2003. LNCS, vol. 2919, pp. 502–518. Springer, Heidelberg (2004)
4. Ghezzi, C., Mandrioli, D., Morzenti, A.: TRIO: A logic language for executable specifications of real-time systems. Journal of Systems and Software 12(2), 107–123 (1990)
5. Heitmeyer, C., Mandrioli, D.: Formal Methods for Real-Time Computing. John Wiley & Sons, Inc., New York (1996)
6. Kamp, J.A.W.: Tense Logic and the Theory of Linear Order (Ph.D. thesis). University of California at Los Angeles (1968)
7. Lamport, L.: A fast mutual exclusion algorithm. ACM TOCS-Transactions On Computer Systems 5(1), 1–11 (1987)
8. Lewis, M., Schubert, T., Becker, B.: Multithreaded SAT solving. In: 12th Asia and South Pacific Design Automation Conference (2007)
9. Moskewicz, M.W., Madigan, C.F., Zhao, Y., Zhang, L., Malik, S.: Chaff: engineering an efficient SAT solver. In: DAC 2001: Proceedings of the 38th Conf. on Design automation, pp. 530–535. ACM Press, New York (2001)
10. Pradella, M., Morzenti, A., San Pietro, P.: The symmetry of the past and of the future: Bi-infinite time in the verification of temporal properties. In: Proc. of the 6th joint meeting of the European Software Engineering Conference and the ACM SIGSOFT Symposium on the Foundations of Software Engineering ESEC/FSE, Dubrovnik, Croatia (September 2007)
11. Pradella, M., Morzenti, A., San Pietro, P.: Benchmarking model- and satisfiability-checking on bi-infinite time. In: Fitzgerald, J.S., Haxthausen, A.E., Yenigun, H. (eds.) ICTAC 2008. LNCS, vol. 5160, pp. 290–304. Springer, Heidelberg (2008)
12. Pradella, M., Morzenti, A., San Pietro, P.: Refining real-time system specifications through bounded model- and satisfiability-checking. In: 23rd IEEE/ACM International Conference on Automated Software Engineering (ASE 2008), September 15-19, pp. 119–127 (2008)
13. Pradella, M., Morzenti, A., San Pietro, P.: A metric encoding for bounded model checking (extended version). ArXiv-CoRR, 0907.3085 (July 2009)

An Incremental Approach to Scope-Bounded Checking Using a Lightweight Formal Method

Danhua Shao, Sarfraz Khurshid, and Dewayne E. Perry

Department of Electrical and Computer Engineering
The University of Texas at Austin
Austin, TX 78712, USA
{dshao,khurshid,perry}@ece.utexas.edu

Abstract. We present a novel approach to optimize *scope-bounded* checking programs using a relational constraint solver. Given a program and its correctness specification, the traditional approach translates a bounded code segment of the *entire* program into a declarative formula and uses a constraint solver to search for any correctness violations. Scalability is a key issue with such approaches since for non-trivial programs the formulas are complex and represent a heavy workload that can choke the solvers. Our insight is that bounded code segments, which can be viewed as a *set* of (possible) execution paths, naturally lend to *incremental* checking through a *partitioning* of the set, where each partition represents a sub-set of paths. The partitions can be checked independently, and thus the problem of scope-bounded checking for the given program reduces to several sub-problems, where each sub-problem requires the constraint solver to check a less complex formula, thereby likely reducing the solver's overall workload. Experimental results show that our approach provides significant speed-ups over the traditional approach.

Keywords: Scope-bounded checking, Alloy, first-order logic, SAT, lightweight formal method, computation graph, white-box testing.

1 Introduction

Scope-bounded checking [1, 4, 5, 9, 11, 17], i.e., systematic checking for a bounded state-space, using off-the-shelf solvers [7, 21, 24], is becoming an increasingly popular methodology to software verification. The state-space is typically bounded using bounds (that are iteratively relaxed) on input size [1], and length of execution paths [9].

While existing approaches that use off-the-shelf solvers have been used effectively for finding bugs, scalability remains a challenging problem. These approaches have a basic limitation: they require translating the bounded code segment of the *entire* program into *one* input formula for the solver, which solves the complete formula. Due to the inherent complexity of typical analyses, many times solvers do not terminate in a desired amount of time. When a solver times out, e.g., fails to find a counterexample, typically there is no information about the likely correctness of the program checked or the coverage of the analysis completed.

This paper takes a *divide-and-solve* approach, where smaller segments of bounded code are translated and analyzed—even if the encoding or analysis of some segments

A. Cavalcanti and D. Dams (Eds.): FM 2009, LNCS 5850, pp. 757–772, 2009.

time out, other segments can still be analyzed to get useful results. Our insight is that bounded code segments, which can be viewed as a *set* of (possible) execution paths, naturally lend to *incremental* checking through a partitioning of the set, where each partition represents a sub-set of paths. The partitions can be checked independently, and thus the problem of scope-bounded checking for the given program reduces to several sub-problems, where each sub-problem requires the constraint solver to check a less complex formula, thereby likely reducing the solver's overall workload.

We develop our approach in the context of the Alloy tool-set [14]—a lightweight formal method—and the Java programming language. The Alloy specification language is a first-order logic based on sets and relations. The Alloy Analyzer [13] performs scope-bounded analysis for Alloy formulas using off-the-shelf SAT solvers.

Previous work [5, 6, 15, 29] developed translations for bounded execution fragments of Java code into Alloy's relational logic. Given a procedure *Proc* in Java and its pre-condition *Pre* and post-condition *Post* in Alloy, the following formula is solved [15, 29]:

$$Pre \wedge translate(\mathbf{Proc}) \wedge \neg Post$$

Given bounds on loop unrolling (and recursion depth), the *translate()* function translates the bounded code fragments of procedure *Proc* from Java into a first order logic formula. Using bounds on the number of objects of each class, the conjunction of *translate(Proc)* with *Pre* and *Post* is translated into a propositional formula. Then, a SAT solver is used to search solutions for the formula. A solution to this formula corresponds to a path in *Proc* that satisfies *Pre* but violates *Post*, i.e., a counterexample to the correctness property.

In our view, the bounded execution fragment of a program that is checked represents a set of possible execution paths. Before translating the fragment into relational logic, our approach implicitly partitions the set of paths using a partitioning *strategy* (Section 4), which splits the given program into several *sub*-programs—each representing a smaller bounded execution fragment—such that

$$path(\mathbf{Proc}) = \bigcup_{i=1}^{n} path(\mathbf{Sub}_i)$$

Function *path(p)* represents the set of paths for a bounded execution segment *p*. Sub_1, …, Sub_n are sub-programs corresponding to path partitioning. To check the procedure *Proc* against pre-condition *Pre* and post-condition *Post*, we translate bounded execution fragment of each sub-program into a first order logic formula and check correctness separately.

$$Pre \wedge translate(\mathbf{Proc}) \wedge \neg Post \Leftrightarrow$$

$$\{\mathbf{Pre} \wedge \mathbf{translate}(\mathbf{Sub}_1) \wedge \neg \mathbf{Post}\} \wedge .... \wedge \{\mathbf{Pre} \wedge \mathbf{translate}(Sub_n) \wedge \neg \mathbf{Post}\}$$

Thus, the problem of checking *Proc* is divided into sub-problems of checking smaller sub-programs, Sub_1, …, Sub_n. Since the control-flow in each sub-program is less complex than the entire procedure, we expect the sub-problems to represent easier SAT problems.

This paper makes the following contributions:

- *An incremental approach.* To check a program against specifications, we propose to divide the program into smaller sub-programs and check each of them individually with respect to the specification. Our approach uses path partitioning to reduce the workload to the backend constraint solver.
- *Implementation.* We implement our approach using the Forge framework [5] and KodKod model finder [28].
- *Evaluation.* Experiments using Java library code show that our approach can significantly reduce the checking time.

2 Example

This section presents a small example to illustrate our path partitioning and program splitting algorithm. Suppose we want to check the `contains()` method of class `IntList` in Figure 1 (a):

An object of `IntList` represents a singly-linked list. The `header` field points to the first node in the list. Objects of the inner class `Entry` represent list nodes. The `value` field represents the (primitive) integer data in a node. The *next* field points to the next node in the list. Figure 1 (b) shows an instance of `IntList`.

Consider checking the method `contains()`. Assume a bound on execution length of one loop unrolling. Figure 2 (a) shows the program and its *computation graph* [15] for this bound.

Our program splitting algorithm uses the computation graph and is *vertex-based*: Given a vertex in the computation graph, we split the graph into two sub-graphs—(1) *go-through* sub-graph and (2) *bypass* sub-graph. The go-through sub-graph has all the paths that go through the vertex and the bypass sub-graph has all the paths that bypass the vertex. Given the computation graph in Figure 2 (a), splitting based on vertex 11 generates the go-through sub-graph shown in Figure 2 (b) and the bypass sub-graph

```
public class IntList {
    private Entry header = null;
    private static class Entry {
        int value;
        Entry next;

        Entry (int value, Entry next){
            this.value = value;
            this.next = next;
        }
    };
    public boolean contains (int key) {
        Entry e = this.header;
        while ( e != null){
            if (e.value == key){
                return true;
            }
            e = e.next;
        }
        return false;
    }
}
```

(a)

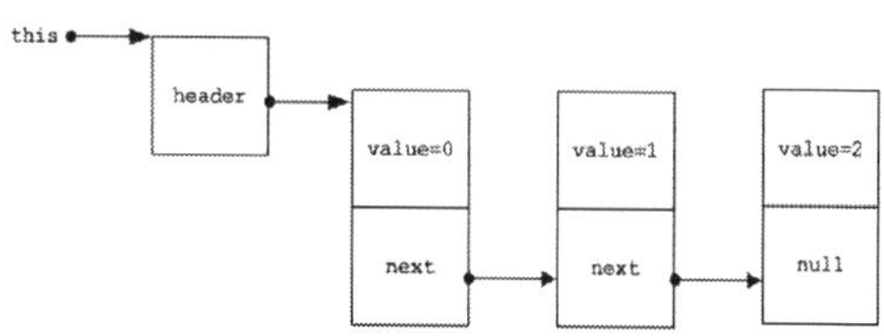

(b)

Fig. 1. Class `IntList` (`contains()` method and an instance)

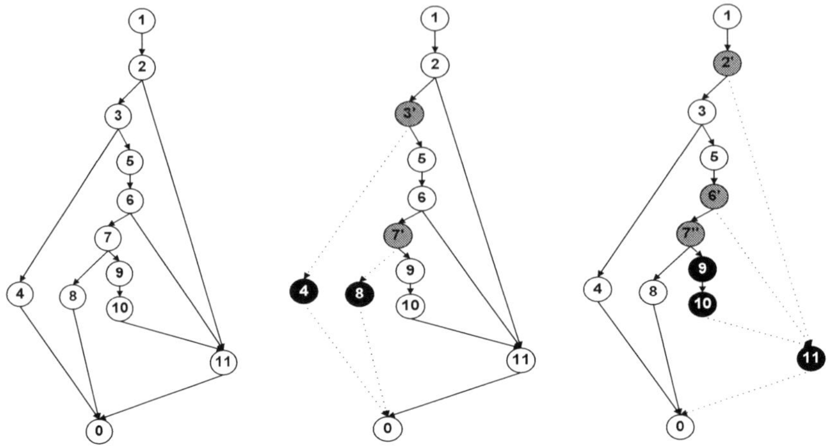

(a)

```
  public boolean
  constains(int key)
  {
1 : Entry e = this.header;
2 : if (e != null){
3 :  if (e.value == key){
4 :   return true;
    }
5 :  e = e.next;
6 :  if (e != null){
7 :   if (e.value == key){
8 :    return true;
     }
9 :   e = e.next;
    }
10:  assume(e == null);
   }
11: return false;
0 :}
```

(b)

```
  public boolean
  go-through(int key)
  {
1 : Entry e = this.header;
2 : if (e != null){
3': assume !(e.value==key);
4 :

5 :  e = e.next;
6 :  if (e != null){
7':  assume!(e.value==key);
8 :

9 :   e = e.next;
    }
10:  assume(e == null);
   }
11: return false;
0 :}
```

(c)

```
  public boolean
  bypass(int key)
  {
1 : Entry e = this.header;
2': assume(e != null);
3 : if (e.value == key){
4 :   return true;
    }
5 : e = e.next;
6': assume (e != null);
7'': assume(e.value == key);
8 : return true;

9 :

10:

11:
0 :}
```

Fig. 2. Splitting of program `contains()` based on Vertex 11. *Broken lines* in sub-graph indicate edges removed constructing this sub-program during splitting. *Gray nodes* in a sub-graph denote that a branch statement in original program has been transformed into an assume statement. In programs below computation graph, the corresponding statements are show in Italic. *Black nodes* denote the statements removed during splitting.

shown in Figure 2 (c). Thus the problem of checking the contains method using a bound of one loop unrolling is solved using two calls to SAT based on the two computation sub-graphs.

3 Background

The goal of our computation graph splitting algorithm is to optimize traditional bounded exhaustive checking of programs using constraints in relational logic. The traditional approach [5] [15] [29] translates the entire bounded Java code segment into one relational logic formula. The conjunction of the code formula and the negation of correctness specifications are passed to a relational logic constraint solver. Solutions are translated back to executions that violate the specification.

3.1 Relational Logic and SAT-Based Analysis

Traditional approaches use a subset of Alloy [14] as the relational logic for Java code translation. Alloy is a first-order declarative language based on *relations*. A relation is a collection of tuples of atoms. A relation can have any finite arity. A set is viewed as a unary relation, and a scalar is a singleton set.

In Alloy, *expressions* are formed by relations combined with a variety of operators. The standard set operators are union (+), intersection (&), difference (-). Unary relational operators are transpose (~), transitive closure (^), and reflexive transitive closure (*), which have their standard interpretation. Binary relational operators are join (.), product (->), and update (++).

Expression quantifiers turn an expression into a *formula*. The formula 'no e' is true when e denotes a relation containing no tuples. Similarly, 'some e', and 'one e' are true when e has some, and exactly one tuple respectively. Formulas can also be made with relational comparison operators: subset (in), equality (=) and inequality (!=). So 'e1 in e2' is true when every tuple in (the relation denoted by the expression) e1 is also a tuple of e2. Alloy provides the standard logical operators: conjunction (&&), disjunction (||), implication ($\Rightarrow$), bi-implication ($\Leftrightarrow$), and negation (!).

A *model* of an Alloy formula is an assignment of relational variables to sets of tuples built from a universe of atoms within a given *scope*. So Alloy Analyzer is a model finder for Alloy formula.

The Alloy Analyzer uses a *scope*, i.e., a bound on the universe of discourse, to perform *scope-bounded* analysis: the analyzer translates the given Alloy formula into a propositional satisfiability (SAT) formula (w.r.t. the given scope) and uses off-the-shelf SAT technology to solve the formula.

3.2 Java to Relational Logic Translation

A relational view of the program heap [15] allows translation of a Java program into an Alloy formula using three steps: (1) encode data, (2) encode control-flow, and (3) encode data-flow.

Encoding data builds a representation for classes, types, and variables. Each class or type is represented as a set, *domain*, which represents the set of object of this class or values of this type. Local variables and arguments are encoded as singleton sets. A field of a class is encoded as a binary, functional relation that maps from the class to the type of the field. For example, to translate the program in Figure 2 (a), we define four domains: List, Entry, integer, and boolean. Field header is a partial function from List to Entry, and field next is a partial function from Entry to Entry. Field value is a function from Entry to integer.

Data-flow is encoded as relational operations on sets and relations. Within an expression in a Java statement, field deference is encoded as relational join, and an update to a field is encoded as relational override. For a branch statement, predicates on variables or expressions are encoded as corresponding formulas with relational expressions. Method calls are encoded as formulas that abstract behavior of the callee methods.

Given a program, encoding control-flow is based on computation graph. Each edge ($v_i \rightarrow v_j$) in the computation graph is represented as a boolean variable $E_{i,j}$. True value of edge variable means the edge is taken. The control flow from one statement to its sequential statement another is viewed as relational implication. For example, code segment `{A; B; C;}` is translated to '$E_{A,B} \Rightarrow E_{B,C}$'. Control flow splits at a *branching* statement—the two branch edges are viewed as a relational disjunction. For each branch edge, a relational formula is generated according to the predicate. Only data that satisfied the relational formula can take this edge. In Figure 2 (a), control flow at vertex 3 is translated into '($E_{2,3} \Rightarrow E_{3,4}$ || $E_{3,5}$) and ($E_{3,4} \Rightarrow$ e.value = key) and ($E_{3,5} \Rightarrow$!(e.value = key))'. If the control flow takes `then` branch $E_{3,4}$, the constraint '($E_{3,4} \Rightarrow$ e.value = key)' should be satisfied. An `assume` statement is translated into the formula for its predicate. For example, at vertex 10 of Figure 2 (a), the control-flow is encoded as '($E_{10,3} \Rightarrow$ no e)'. This constraint restricts that this edge is taken only when `e` is `null`.

In our splitting algorithm, sub-graphs are constructed by removing branch-edges at selected branch statements. According to the translation scheme, a branch statement is equivalent to two assume statements with complementary predicates. So removing one branch can be implemented as transforming the branch statement into an assume statement. In Figure 2 (a), removing the `then` branch of vertex 3, branch statement '`if(e.value == key)`' will be transformed to 'assume !(e.value == key)'. Its relational logic translation is '($E_{2,3} \Rightarrow E_{3,4}$) and ($E_{3,5} \Rightarrow$!(e.value = key))'. The semantics of `else` branch is preserved after the transformation to an `assume` statement.

With encoding of data-flow and control-flow, the conjunction of all generated formulas is the formula for the code segment under analysis. A model to this code formula corresponds to a valid path of the code fragment.

4 Algorithm

The goal of our splitting algorithm is to divide the complexity of checking the program while preserving its semantics (w.r.t. to the given scope). This paper presents a *vertex-based* splitting algorithm. Splitting a program into two sub-programs partitions paths in the program based on a chosen vertex: one sub-program has all paths that go through the vertex and the other sub-program has all paths that bypass that vertex. Our vertex-based path splitting guarantees the consistency between the original program and sub-programs. For a heuristic measure of the complexity of checking, we propose to use the number of branches. Our strategy is selecting a vertex so that the number of branches in each of sub-programs is minimized.

Our approach checks a given program *p* as follows.

1. Translate *p* into *p'* where *p'* represents the *computation graph* [15] of *p*, i.e., the loops in *p* are unrolled and method calls in-lined to generate *p*;
2. Represent *p'* as a graph *CG* = (*V*, *E*) where *V* is a set of vertices such that each statement in *p'* has a corresponding vertex in *V*, and *E* is a set of edges such that each control-flow edge in *p'* has a corresponding edge in *E*. For each edge *e* = (*u*, *v*), *u*=*e.from*, and *v* = *e.to*;
3. Apply the splitting heuristic to determine a likely optimal splitting vertex *v*;

4. Split *CG* into two sub-graphs CG_1 and CG_2;
5. Recursively split CG_1 and CG_2 if needed;
6. Check the set of sub-programs corresponding to the final set of sub-graphs.

Recall a computation graph has one *Entry* vertex and one *Exit* vertex for the program. *Entry* has no predecessor and *Exit* has no successor. A vertex *v* representing a branch-statement has two successors: vertex *v.then* and vertex *v.else*. Vertices that do not represent branch-statements have only one successor, *v.next*. The computation graph of a program is a *DAG* (Directed Acyclic Graph). An *execution path* in the computation graph is a sequence of vertices from *Entry* to *Exit* through edges in *E*.

Definition. Given a CG = (V, E) and a set of edges S $\subset$ E,

then-branch-predecessor(*S*) =

{ *u* | *u*$\in$ V, *u* is a branch-statement, at least one edge in *S* is reachable from *u.then*, but no edge in *S* is reachable from *u.else*}

else-branch-predecessor(*S*) =

{ *u* | *u*$\in$ V, *u* is a branch, at least one edge in *S* is reachable from *u.else*, but no edge in *S* is reachable from *u.then*}

Sub-CG(S) = (*V*′, *E*′)

V′ = *V*, and

E′= *E* – {*e* | *e* $\in$ *E*, *e* = *u*→*u.else* if *u* is in *then-branch-predecessor*(*S*), or *e* = *u*→*u.then* if *u* is in *else-branch-predecessor*(*S*)} .

Theorem 1. Given a computation graph *CG*=(*V*, *E*) and a set of edges *S*$\subset$*E*, an execution path *p* visits at least one edge in *S* if and only if *p* is a path in *Sub-CG*(*S*) = (*V*′, *E*′).

Proof. *Sub-CG*(*S*) is a sub-graph of *CG* with fewer edges. An execution path in *CG* is still in *Sub-CG*(*S*) if and only if this path does not contain any edge in *E* - *E*′.

⇒ Assume that there is a path *p* in CG that visits an edge in S but is not in the sub-graph. Suppose *p* visits an edge $v_i \rightarrow v_j$ that has been removed. According to the definition of the sub-graph, none of the edge in *E* is reachable from $v_i \rightarrow v_j$, i.e., a contradiction.

⇐ Assume *p* is a path in *CG* that does not visit any edge in *S*. Let *P* = {*q* | *q* is a path of *CG*, *q* visits *S*}. Since *S* is not empty, *P* is not empty. For each path *q* in *P*, match *p* and *q* according to their vertex sequence. Let v_i be the last vertex in *p* that matches a vertex in P. v_i must be a branch vertex. Let edge $v_i \rightarrow v_j$ and edge $v_i \rightarrow v_j'$ be the two branches from v_i. Suppose edge $v_i \rightarrow v_j$ is in *p*. $v_i \rightarrow v_j$ cannot reach any edge in *S*. Since v_i is the last vertex-match with paths in *P*, $v_i \rightarrow v_j'$ can reach an edge in *S*. So $v_i \rightarrow v_j$ should be removed according to definition of *then-branch-predecessor* (*S*) or *else-branch-predecessor* (*S*). So any path that does not visit an edge in *S* will be removed from sub-graph. ■

Since the computation graph of the program is a DAG after loop unrolling, we can linearly order the vertices using a topological sort.

Given a computation graph *CG*, let *order* represent *topological-sort*(*CG*) such that *order*[*Exit*] =0; *order*[*Entry*] = *n*-1; and *n* is number of vertices in *CG*.

Definition. Let u be a vertex in CG. Define the set *go-through-edge*(u) = $\{e \mid e \in E, e.to = u\}$.

Theorem 2. Given a vertex u in CG, a path visits u if and only if the path visits an edge in *go-through-edge(u)* .

Proof. Since CG is a directed graph, all paths visiting vertex u will go through an edge whose end point is u. ■

Definition. Given a vertex u in CG, *bypass-edge*(u) = $\{e \mid e \in E$, order[$e.from$] > order[u] and order[$e.to$] < order[u]$\}$.

Theorem 3. Given a vertex u, a path p bypasses u if and only if p visits an edge in *bypass-edge(u).*

Proof. ⇒ Let path p: $v_0 \rightarrow v_1 \rightarrow v_2 \rightarrow \ldots \rightarrow v_m$ be a path in CG, v_0 = *Entry* and v_m = *Exit*. According to the topological sort, order[v_0] > order[v_1] > order[v_2] > … > order[v_m]. For vertex u, if $u \neq$ *Entry* and $u \neq$ *Exit*, then order[u] < order[*Entry*] and order[u] >order[*Exit*]. Since u is not in p, there must be two vertices v_i and v_j in p such that order[v_i] > order[u] and order[v_j] <order[u]. By definition, edge $v_i \rightarrow v_j$ is in *bypass-edge(u)* .

⇐ Let path p: $v_0 \rightarrow v_1 \rightarrow v_2 \rightarrow \ldots \rightarrow v_m$ be a path in CG, v_0 = *Entry* and v_m = *Exit*. Since p visits a path in *bypass-edge(u)* there exist an edge $v_i \rightarrow v_j$ such that order[v_i] > order[u] and order[v_j] <order[u]. According to the topological sort, order[v_k] > order[v_i] > order[u] if k < i, and order[v_k] < order[v_j] < order[u] if k>j. So path p can not visit u. ■

Theorem 4. Given a vertex u in CG, a path visits u if and only if the path is in *Sub-CG (go-through-edge(u))*.

Proof. Follows from Theorem 2 and Theorem 1. Since paths that visit u are the paths that visit *go-through-edge(u)* and paths that visit go-through-edge(u) are the paths in *Sub-CG(go-through-edge(u))*, therefore paths that visit u are the paths in *Sub-CG(go-through-edge(u)*. ■

Theorem 5. Given a vertex u in CG, a path bypasses u if and only if the path is in *Sub-CG(bypass-edge(u))*.

Proof. Follows from Theorem 3 and Theorem 1. Since paths that visit u are the paths that visit *bypass-edge(u)* and paths that visit *bypass-edge*(u) are the paths in *Sub-CG(bypass-edge(u))*, therefore paths that visit u are the paths in *Sub-CG (bypass-edge(u))*. ■

Algorithm
Figure 3 shows our splitting algorithm. The method *branches*() returns the branch vertices of a given computation graph. If one edge of a branch vertex has been removed in a sub-graph, this branch vertex will not be counted as a branch in that sub-graph.

```
List<CG> Split-CG(CG cg)
{
    List<CG> sub = new List<CG>();
    for (Vertex u : cg.vertices){
        branch1 = branches(Sub-CG(go-through-edge(u))).size();
        branch2 = branches(Sub-CG(bypass-edge(u))).size();
        split-complexity = max(branch1, branch2);
        if (split-complexity < current-complexity){
            v=u;
            current-complexity = split-complexity;
        }
    }
    sub.add(Sub-CG(go-through-edge(v)));
    sub.add(Sub-CG(bypass-edge(v)));
    return sub;
}
```

Fig. 3. Program splitting algorithm

To illustrate, consider the example form Section 2. The split-complexity of v_{11} can be calculated in the following steps:

1) For go-through sub-graph,
   go-through-edge(v_{11}) = { $v_2 \rightarrow v_{11}$, $v_6 \rightarrow v_{11}$, $v_{10} \rightarrow v_{11}$};
   branches(*Sub-CG*(*go-through-edge*(v_{11})))= {v_2, v_6};
2) For bypass sub-graph,
   bypass-edge(v_{11}) = { $v_3 \rightarrow v_4$, $v_7 \rightarrow v_8$)};
   branches(*Sub-CG*(*bypass-edge*(v_{11})))= {v_3};
3) For split-complexity,
   Split-complexity(v_{11}) = max {|{ v_2,v_6}|, |{v_3}|} = 2.

According to the definition of *Sub-CG*, some branch edges will be removed to construct a sub-graph. Given a branch, edge removing is implemented by transforming the branch statement into an **`assume`** statement. The semantic consistency of this transformation is discussed in the background section.

5 Experiments

To evaluate our approach, we compare performance of our sub-program-based *incremental* analysis and the traditional entire program analysis. We select the Forge tool-set [6] as the baseline, since it is the most recent implementation of the traditional approach from the Alloy group at MIT. We piggyback on Forge to implement our incremental approach.

Experimental evaluation is based on checking four procedures in Java library classes: `contains()` of `LinkedList` (a singly-linked acyclic list), `contains()` of `BinarySearchTree`, `add()` of `BinarySearchTree`, and `topologicalsort()` of `Graph` (directed acyclic graph).

In relational logic based bounded verification, the bound specifies the numbers of loop unrolling, scope, and bit-width—the number of bits used to represent an integer value. While translating integer into propositional logic, we set the bit-width to 4 in all the four experiments. *Scope* defines the maximum number of nodes in a list, tree, or graph. *Unrolling* specifies the number of unrollings for a loop body. For `contains()` of `LinkedList` and `contains()` of `BinarySearchTree`, we check them with fixed scope and varied unrolling. For add() of `BinarySearchTree`, and `topologicalsort()` of `Graph`, we check them with fixed unrolling and varied scope.

For each bound, we run our *incremental* analysis and the traditional entire program analysis to check a procedure against its *pre-condition* and *post-condition*, which represent the usual correctness properties including structural invariants. In incremental analysis, we did two round splitting and generated four sub-programs. While checking each sub-program, we record the checking time, number of branches, variables and clauses of CNF formula. The *total* time is the sum of the checking time of all sub-programs. For the traditional analysis, we similarly record the checking time, number of branches, variables and clauses of CNF formula. The speedup is the ratio of the checking time of the traditional analysis to the total checking time of our incremental analysis.

We ran experiments on a Dual-Core 1.8GHz AMD Opteron processor with 2 GB RAM. We selected MiniSAT as the SAT solver. We run each experiment three times and use the average as the final result. The results are showed in the tables that follow.

Table 1 and Table 2 show the performance comparison for different loop unrollings. Table 3 and Table 4 show the comparison for different scopes. Results from the four experiments showed that our splitting algorithm gave at least a 2.71X performance improvement over the traditional approach, whereas the maximum speed-up was 36.73X.

The results also show that our splitting algorithm scales better. As unrolling increasing from 5 to 8, speedup of checking `contains()` of `LinkedList` increases from 3.99X to 36.73X. As scope increasing from 4 to 7, speedup of checking add() of `BinarySearchTree` increases from 4.78X to 12.6X.

Table 1. `LinkedList.contains()` (bit-width = 4, scope = 8)

unrolling		sub0	sub1	sub2	sub3	total	entire	speedup
5	time (sec.)	2	1	82	1	86	343	3.99X
	# branch	1	2	2	2		10	
	# variable	4655	4149	4731	3969		4740	
	# clauses	10081	8353	10167	7563		14271	
6	time(sec.)	8	1	173	7	189	653	3.46X
	# branch	2	2	2	3		12	
	# variable	4911	4149	4985	4226		4996	
	# clauses	10945	8353	11031	8436		15213	
7	time(sec.)	66	1	428	3	498	4541	9.12X
	# branch	2	3	3	3		14	
	# variable	5165	4406	5242	4226		5252	
	# clauses	11809	9218	11904	8436		16155	
8	time(sec.)	179	1	359	44	583	21414	36.73X
	# branch	3	3	3	4		16	
	# variable	5422	4406	5496	4484		5508	
	# clauses	12674	9218	12768	9310		17097	

Table 2. `BinarySearchTree.contains()` (bit-width = 4, scope = 7)

unrolling		sub0	sub1	sub2	sub3	total	entire	speedup
4	time(sec.)	564	552	390	388	1894	6468	3.42X
	# branch	4	4	3	4		12	
	# variable	7776	7369	6961	6724		7808	
	# clauses	20734	19185	17635	16726		21193	
5	time(sec.)	1	2427	1745	301	4474	15015	3.36X
	# branch	7	7	5	4		15	
	# variable	8151	8151	7376	6724		8224	
	# clauses	22170	22178	19300	16726		22859	
6	time(sec.)	698	1879	546	936	4059	18982	4.68X
	# branch	7	5	5	6		18	
	# variable	8599	8192	7539	6976		8640	
	# clauses	23941	22400	19822	17861		24525	
7	time(sec.)	1	2535	2834	686	6056	28435	4.71X
	# branch	11	11	6	7		21	
	# variable	8975	8975	7784	7140		9056	
	# clauses	25386	25394	20850	18392		26191	
8	time(sec.)	794	1085	1289	623	3791	18703	4.94X
	# branch	13	13	7	7		24	
	# variable	9384	9384	7948	7140		9472	
	# clauses	26945	26953	21381	18392		27857	

The relative lower speedup in `contains()` of `BinarySearchTree` and `topologicalsort()` of `Graph` show a limitation of our approach. Compared with traditional approach which checks correctness against specifications only once, our *divide-and-solve* approach requires multiple correctness checking, one checking for one sub-program. In case the complexity of specification formula is much heavier than code formula, the benefit from dividing the code formula will be reduced largely by the overhead from multiple checking specification formulas. However, even with specification of complex data structure invariants, our approach still shows 5X speedup in `contains()` of `BinarySearchTree` with 8 unrollings and 7 nodes.

The results show that our splitting heuristic is effective at evenly splitting the branches. Moreover, the smaller number of variables and clauses for the incremental approach shows the workload to SAT has been effectively divided by splitting entire program into sub-programs using our approach.

Table 3. `BinarySearchTree.add()` (unrolling = 3, bit-width = 4)

scope		sub0	sub1	sub2	sub3	total	entire	speedup
4	time(sec.)	2	3	1	3	9	43	4.78X
	# branch	5	6	6	7		11	
	# variable	4878	5092	4692	5083		9686	
	# clauses	16132	17393	15079	17397		36929	
5	time(sec.)	13	15	3	9	40	249	6.23X
	# branch	5	6	6	7		11	
	# variable	6705	7038	6446	6653		12837	
	# clauses	22457	24308	20990	22973		49623	
6	time(sec.)	140	316	30	19	505	4339	8.59X
	# branch	5	6	6	7		11	
	# variable	8689	9161	8349	8340		16335	
	# clauses	29414	31943	27487	28965		63809	
7	time(sec.)	1675	6409	863	76	9023	109730	12.16X
	# branch	5	6	6	7		11	
	# variable	11030	11661	10601	10247		20380	
	# clauses	37703	40998	35270	35738		80187	

Table 4. `Graph.TopologicalSort` () (unrolling = 7, bit-width = 4)

scope		sub0	sub1	sub2	sub3	total	entire	speedup
7	time(sec.)	183	152	118	1	454	1436	3.16X
	# branch	1	1	1	1		7	
	# variable	269908	197682	125456	53230		269962	
	# clauses	1073479	785037	496595	208153		1084273	
8	time(sec.)	210	199	114	1	524	1422	2.71X
	# branch	1	1	1	1		7	
	# variable	299104	219070	139036	59002		299158	
	# clauses	1197974	875832	553690	231548		1210304	
9	time(sec.)	214	278	157	1	650	2113	3.25X
	# branch	1	1	1	1		7	

Table 4. *(continued)*

	# variable	357978	262236	166494	70752		358032	
	# clauses	1457783	1065867	673951	282035		1471649	
10	time(sec.)	357	255	187	2	801	2844	3.55X
	# branch	1	1	1	1		7	
	# variable	402696	295010	187324	79638		402750	
	# clauses	1659106	1212870	766634	320398		1674508	
11	time(sec.)	611	341	263	2	1217	3694	3.04X
	# branch	1	1	1	1		7	
	# variable	439783	322189	204595	87001		439837	
	# clauses	1829579	1337181	844783	352385		1846517	
12	time(sec.)	558	519	247	2	1326	4372	3.31X
	# branch	1	1	1	1		7	
	# variable	476935	349417	221899	94381		476989	
	# clauses	2003834	1464198	924562	384926		2022308	

6 Related Work

Our work is based on previous research [15] that models a heap-manipulating procedure using Alloy and finds counterexamples using SAT. Jackson et al. [15] proposed an approach to model complex data structures with relations and encode control flow, data flow, and frame conditions into relational formulas. Vaziri et al. [29] optimized the translation to boolean formulas by using a special encoding of functional relations. Dennis et al. [5] provided explicit facilities to specify imperative code with first-order relational logic and used an optimized relational model finder [28] as the backend constraint solver. Our algorithm can reduce the workload to the backend constraint solver by splitting the computation graph that underlies all these prior approaches and dividing the procedure into smaller sub-programs.

DynAlloy [8] is a promising approach that builds on Alloy to directly support sequencing of operations. We believe our incremental approach can optimize DynAlloy's solving too.

Bounded exhaustive checking, e.g., using TestEra [16] or Korat [1] can check programs that manipulate complex data structures. Testing, however, has a basic limitation that running a program against one input only checks the behavior for that input. In contrast, translating a code segment to a formula that is solved allows checking all (bounded) paths in that segment against all (bounded) inputs.

The recent advances in constraint solving technology have led to a rebirth of symbolic execution [17, 18]. Guiding symbolic execution using concrete executions is rapidly gaining popularity as a means of scaling it up in several recent frameworks, most notably DART [10], CUTE [26], and EXE [2]. While DART and EXE focus on properties of primitives and arrays to check for security holes (e.g., buffer overflows), CUTE has explored the use of white-box testing using preconditions, similar to Korat [1]. Symbolic/concrete execution can be viewed as an extreme case of our approach where each sub-program represents exactly one path in the original program. As the number of paths increases, the number of calls to the constraint solver increases in symbolic execution. Our approach is motivated by our quest to find a sweet spot between checking all paths at once (traditional approach) and each path one-by-one (symbolic/concrete execution).

Model checkers have traditionally focused on properties of control [12, 22]. Recent advances in software model checking [9, 30] have allowed checking properties of data. However, software model checkers typically require explicit checking of each execution path of the program under test.

Slicing techniques [27] have been used to reduce workload of bounded verification. Dolby et al. [6] and Saturn [31] perform slicing at the logic representation level. Millett et al. [23] slice Promela programs for SPIN model checker [12]. Visser et al. [30] and Corbett et al. [2] prune the parts that are not related to temporal constraints and slice at the source code level. Since slicing is based on constraints, the effectiveness depends on the properties to be checked. Statements that do not manipulate any relations in properties will not be translated into formula for checking. If constraints are so complex that all the relations show up, no statements will be pruned. Our program-splitting algorithm can still reduce workload to backend constraint solvers because our path partitioning algorithm is independent of constraints to be checked.

Sound static analyses, such as traditional shape analysis [25, 19] and recent variants [20], provide correctness guarantees for all inputs and all execution paths irrespective of a bound. However, they typically require additional user input in the form of additional predicates or loop invariants, which are not required for scope-bounded checking, which provides an under-approximation of the program under test.

7 Conclusions

Scalability is a key issue in *scope-bounded* checking. Traditional approaches translate the bounded code segment of the *entire* program into *one* input formula for the underlying solver, which solves the complete formula in one execution. For non-trivial programs, the formulas are complex and represent a heavy workload that can choke the solvers.

We propose a *divide-and-solve* approach, where smaller segments of bounded code are translated and analyzed. Given a vertex in the control-flow graph, we split the computation graph of the program into two sub-graphs: go-through sub-graph and bypass sub-graph. The go-through sub-graph has all the paths that go through the vertex and the bypass sub-graph has all the paths that bypass the vertex. Our vertex-based path partitioning can guarantee the semantic consistency between the original program and the sub-programs. We propose to use the number of branch statements as a heuristic to compute an analysis complexity metric of a program. To effectively divide the analysis complexity of a program, the heuristic selects a vertex so that the number of branch statements in each of sub-programs is minimized.

We evaluated our *divide-and-solve* approach by comparison with the traditional approach by checking four Java methods against pre-conditions and post-conditions defined in Alloy. The experimental results show that our approach provides significant speed-ups over the traditional approach.

The results also show other potential benefits of our program splitting algorithm. Because all sub-graphs are independent, they can be checked in parallel. Since our program splitting algorithm can effectively divide the workload, parallel checking the sub-programs would likely introduce significant speedups. Incremental compilation and solving are likely to provide further optimizations.

In ongoing work, we are exploring novel strategies for dividing the workload. We aim to leverage concepts from traditional dynamic and static analysis. For example, notions of code coverage in software testing lend to division strategies.

Acknowledgments

We thank Greg Dennis for his help on the Forge framework. This work was supported in part by NSF grants IIS-0438967, CCF-0702680, and CCF-0845628, and AFOSR grant FA9550-09-1-0351.

References

1. Boyapati, C., Khurshid, S., Marinov, D.: Korat: Automated Testing Based on Java Predicates. In: Proc. of ACM/SIGSOFT International Symposium on Software Testing and Analysis, ISSTA (2002)
2. Cadar, C., Ganesh, V., Pawlowski, P., Dill, D., Engler, D.: EXE: Automatically Generating Inputs of Death. In: Proc. of the 13th ACM Conference on Computer and Communications Security (CCS) (2006)
3. Corbett, J.C., Dwyer, M.B., Hatcliff, J., Laubach, S., Pasareanu, C.S., Robby, Zheng, H.: Bandera: extracting finite-state models from Java source code. In: Proc. of International Conference on Software Engineering, ICSE (2000)
4. Darga, P., Boyapati, C.: Efficient software model checking of data structure properties. In: Proc. of the International Conference on Object-Oriented Programming, Systems, Languages, and Applications, OOPSLA (2006)
5. Dennis, G., Chang, F.S.H., Jackson, D.: Modular verification of code with SAT. In: Proc. of the International Symposium on Software Testing and Analysis, ISSTA (2006)
6. Dolby, J., Vaziri, M., Tip, F.: Finding Bugs Efficiently with a SAT Solver. In: Proc. of the 6th joint meeting of the European Software Engineering Conference and the ACM SIGSOFT Symposium on the Foundations of Software Engineering, ESEC/FSE (2007)
7. Eén, N., Sörensson, N.: An extensible SAT solver. In: Giunchiglia, E., Tacchella, A. (eds.) SAT 2003. LNCS, vol. 2919, pp. 502–518. Springer, Heidelberg (2004)
8. Frias, M.F., Galeotti, J.P., López Pombo, C.G., Aguirre, N.M.: DynAlloy: upgrading alloy with actions. In: Proc. of International Conference on Software Engineering, ICSE (2005)
9. Godefroid, P.: Model Checking for Programming Languages using VeriSoft. In: Proc.of ACM Symposium on Principles of Programming Languages, POPL (1997)
10. Godefroid, P., Klarlund, N., Sen, K.: DART: Directed automated random testing. In: Proc. of ACM SIGPLAN conference on Programming language design and implementation, PLDI (2005)

11. Heitmeyer, C., James Kirby, J., Labaw, B., Archer, M., Bharadwaj, R.: Using abstraction and model checking to detect safety violations in requirements specifications. IEEE Transactions on Software Engineering 24(11), 927–948 (1998)
12. Holzmann, G.J.: The SPIN Model Checker: Primer and Reference Manual. Addison-Wesley, Reading (2004)
13. Jackson, D.: Automating first-order relational logic. In: Proc. of the International Symposium on Foundations of Software Engineering, FSE (2000)
14. Jackson, D.: Software Abstractions: logic, language, and analysis. MIT Press, Cambridge (2006)
15. Jackson, D., Vaziri, M.: Finding bugs with a constraint solver. In: Proc. of the International Symposium on Software Testing and Analysis, ISSTA (2000)
16. Khurshid, S., Marinov, D.: TestEra: Specification-based Testing of Java Programs Using SAT. Automated Software Engineering Journal 11(4) (October 2004)
17. Khurshid, S., Pasareanu, C., Visser, W.: Generalized Symbolic Execution for Model Checking and Testing. In: Garavel, H., Hatcliff, J. (eds.) TACAS 2003. LNCS, vol. 2619, pp. 553–568. Springer, Heidelberg (2003)
18. King, J.C.: Symbolic execution and program testing. Communications of the ACM 19(7) (July 1976)
19. Klarlund, N., Møller, A., Schwartzbach, M.I.: MONA implementation secrets. In: Yu, S., Păun, A. (eds.) CIAA 2000. LNCS, vol. 2088, p. 182. Springer, Heidelberg (2001)
20. Kuncak, V.: Modular Data Structure Verification. Ph.D. thesis, EECS Department, Massachusetts Institute of Technology (2007)
21. Leonardo, M., Bjørner, N.: Z3: An Efficient SMT Solver. In: Ramakrishnan, C.R., Rehof, J. (eds.) TACAS 2008. LNCS, vol. 4963, pp. 337–340. Springer, Heidelberg (2008)
22. McMillan, K.: Symbolic Model Checking. Kluwer Academic Publishers, Dordrecht (1993)
23. Millett, L.I., Teitelbaum, T.: Slicing Promela and its applications to model checking. In: Proc. of the 4th International SPIN Workshop (1998)
24. Moskewicz, M., Madigan, C., Zhao, Y., Zhang, L., Malik, S.: Chaff: Engineering an Efficient SAT Solver. In: Proc. of 39th Design Automation Conference, DAC (2001)
25. Sagiv, M., Reps, T., Wilhelm, R.: Parametric shape analysis via 3-valued logic. ACM Transactions on Programming Languages and Systems (TOPLAS) 24(3), 217–298 (2002)
26. Sen, K., Marinov, D., Agha, G.: CUTE: A concolic unit testing engine for C. In: Proc. of the 10th European software engineering conference held jointly with 13th ACM SIGSOFT international symposium on Foundations of software engineering, ESEC/FSE (2005)
27. Tip, F.: A survey of program slicing techniques. Journal of Programming Languages 3(3), 121–189 (1995)
28. Torlak, E., Jackson, D.: Kodkod: A Relational Model Finder. In: Grumberg, O., Huth, M. (eds.) TACAS 2007. LNCS, vol. 4424, pp. 632–647. Springer, Heidelberg (2007)
29. Vaziri, M., Jackson, D.: Checking properties of heap-manipulating procedures with a constraint solver. In: Garavel, H., Hatcliff, J. (eds.) TACAS 2003. LNCS, vol. 2619, pp. 505–520. Springer, Heidelberg (2003)
30. Visser, W., Havelund, K., Brat, G.P., Park, S., Lerda, F.: Model checking programs. In: Proc. of International Conference on Automated Software Engineering, ASE (2000)
31. Xie, Y., Aiken, A.: Saturn: A scalable framework for error detection using boolean satisfiability. ACM Transactions on Programming Languages and Systems (TOPLAS) 29(3) (2007)

Verifying Information Flow Control over Unbounded Processes

William R. Harris[1], Nicholas A. Kidd[1], Sagar Chaki[2], Somesh Jha[1], and Thomas Reps[1,3]

[1] University of Wisconsin
{wrharris,kidd,jha,reps}@cs.wisc.edu
[2] Soft. Eng. Inst., Carnegie Mellon University
chaki@sei.cmu.edu
[3] GrammaTech Inc.

Abstract. *Decentralized Information Flow Control* (DIFC) systems enable programmers to express a desired DIFC policy, and to have the policy enforced via a reference monitor that restricts interactions between system objects, such as processes and files. Past research on DIFC systems focused on the reference-monitor implementation, and assumed that the desired DIFC policy is correctly specified. The focus of this paper is an automatic technique to verify that an application, plus its calls to DIFC primitives, does indeed correctly implement a desired policy. We present an abstraction that allows a model checker to reason soundly about DIFC programs that manipulate potentially unbounded sets of processes, principals, and communication channels. We implemented our approach and evaluated it on a set of real-world programs.

1 Introduction

Decentralized Information Flow Control (DIFC) systems [1,2,3,4] allow application programmers to define their own DIFC policies, and then to have the policy enforced in the context of the entire operating system. To achieve this goal, DIFC systems maintain a mapping from OS objects (processes, files, etc.) to *labels*—sets of atomic elements called *tags*. Each process in the program creates tags, and gives other processes the ability to control the distribution of the process's data by collecting and discarding tags. The DIFC runtime system monitors all inter-process communication, deciding whether or not a requested data transfer is allowed based on the labels of system objects.

Example 1. Consider the diagram in Fig. 1 of a web server that handles sensitive information. A `Handler` process receives incoming HTTP requests, and spawns a new `Worker` process to service each request. The `Worker` code that services the request may not be available for static analysis, or may be untrusted. The programmer may wish to enforce a *non-interference policy* requiring that information pertaining to one request — and thus localized to one `Worker` process — should never flow to a different `Worker` process.

A. Cavalcanti and D. Dams (Eds.): FM 2009, LNCS 5850, pp. 773–789, 2009.

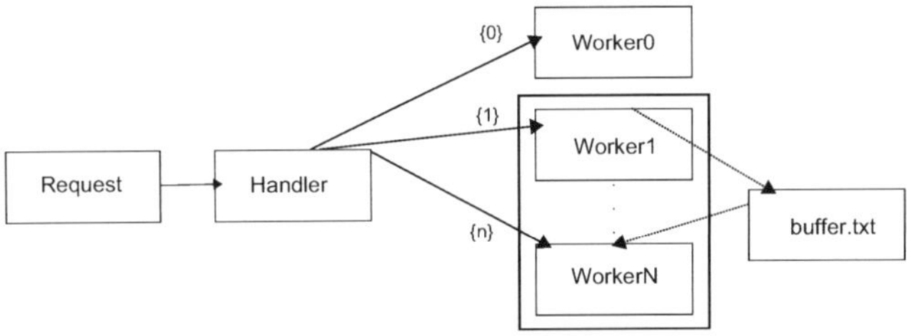

Fig. 1. An inter-process diagram of a typical web server

DIFC mechanisms are able to block any communication between OS objects. Thus, in addition to ensuring that the use of DIFC mechanisms implements a desired security policy, the programmer must also ensure that retrofitting an existing system with DIFC primitives does not negatively impact the system's functionality. In Ex. 1, the desired functionality is that the `Handler` must be able to communicate with each `Worker` at all times. An overly restrictive implementation could disallow such behaviors. Ex. 1 illustrates a tension between security and functionality: a naïve system that focuses solely on functionality allows information to flow between all entities; conversely, the leakage of information can be prevented in a way that cripples functionality.

Our goal is to develop an automatic method to ensure that security policies and application functionality are simultaneously satisfied. Our approach to this problem is to leverage progress in model checkers [5,6] that check concurrent programs against temporal logic properties (e.g., linear temporal logic). However, the translation from arbitrary, multiprocess systems to systems that can be reasoned about by model checkers poses key challenges due to potential unboundedness along multiple dimensions. In particular, the number of processes spawned, communication channels created, and label values used by the reference monitor are unbounded. However, current model checkers verify properties of models that use bounded sets of these entities. To resolve this issue, we propose a method of abstraction that generates a model that is a sound, and in practice precise, approximation of the original system in the sense that if a security or functionality property holds for the model, then the property holds for the original program. Our abstraction applies the technique of *random isolation* [6] to reason precisely about unbounded sets of similar program objects.

The contributions of this work are as follows:

1. We present a formulation of DIFC program execution in terms of transformations of logical structures. This formulation allows a natural method for abstracting DIFC programs to a bounded set of structures. It also permits DIFC properties of programs to be specified as formulas in first-order logic. To our knowledge, this is the first work on specifying a formal language for such policies.

2. We present a formulation of the principle of random isolation [6] in terms of logical structures. We then demonstrate that random isolation can be applied to allow DIFC properties to be checked more precisely.
3. We implemented a tool that simulates the abstraction of logical structures in C source code and then checks the abstraction using a predicate-abstraction-based model checker.
4. We applied the tool to check properties of several real-world programs. We automatically extracted models of modules of Apache [7], FlumeWiki [3], ClamAV [8], and OpenVPN [9] instrumented with our own label-manipulation code. Verification took a few minutes to less than 1.25 hours.

While there has been prior work [10,11] on the application of formal methods for checking properties of actual DIFC systems, our work is unique in providing a method for checking that an *application* satisfies a DIFC correctness property under the rules of a given DIFC system. Our techniques, together with the recent verification of the Flume reference-monitor implementation [11], provides the first system able to (i) verify that the program adheres to a specified DIFC policy, and (ii) verify that the policy is enforced by the DIFC implementation.

The rest of the paper is organized as follows: §2 describes Flume, an example DIFC system for which we check applications. §3 gives an informal overview of our techniques. §4 gives the technical description. §5 describes our experimental evaluation. §6 discusses related work.

2 A Flume Primer

Our formulation is based most closely on the Flume [3] DIFC system; however, our abstraction techniques should work with little modification for most DIFC systems. We briefly discuss the Flume datatypes and API functions provided by Flume, and direct the reader to [3] for a complete description.

- **Tags & Labels.** A *tag* is an atomic element created by the monitor at the request of a process. A *label* is a set of tags associated with an OS object.
- **Capabilities.** A *positive capability* t^+ allows a process to add tag t to the label of an OS object. A *negative capability* t^- allows a process to remove t.
- **Channels.** Processes are not allowed to create their own file descriptors. Instead, a process asks Flume for a new *channel*, and receives back a pair of *endpoints*. Endpoints may be passed to other processes, but may be claimed by at most *one* process, after which they are used like ordinary file descriptors.

For each process, Flume maintains a secrecy label, an integrity label, and a capability set. In this work, we only consider secrecy labels, and leave the modeling of integrity labels as a direction for future work. The monitor forbids a process p with label l_p to send data over endpoint e with label l_e unless $l_p \subseteq l_e$. Likewise, the monitor forbids a process p' to receive data from endpoint e' unless $l_{e'} \subseteq l_{p'}$. A Flume process may create another process by invoking the `spawn` command.

```
    void Handler() {
1.      Label lab;
2.      int data;
3.      while (*) {
4.          Request r = get_next_http_request();
5.          data = get_data(r);
7.          lab = create_tag();
8.          Endpoint e0, e1;
9.          create_channel(&e0, &e1);
10.         spawn("/usr/local/bin/Worker", {e1}, lab, {}, r);
11.         data = recv(claim_endpoint(e0)); }}
```

Fig. 2. Flume pseudocode for a server that enforces the same-origin policy

`spawn` takes as input (i) the path to a binary to execute, (ii) a set of endpoints that the new process may access from the beginning of execution, (iii) an initial label, (iv) and an initial capability set, which must be a subset of that of the spawning process. An example usage of `spawn` is given in Fig. 2.

Example 2. The pseudocode in Fig. 2 enforces non-interference between the `Worker` processes from Fig. 1. The `Handler` perpetually polls for a new HTTP request, and upon receiving one, it spawns a new `Worker` process. To do so, it (i) has Flume create a new tag, which it stores as a singleton label value in label-variable `lab` (line 7), (ii) has Flume create a new channel (line 9), and (iii) then launches the `Worker` process (line 10), setting its initial secrecy label to `lab`—not giving it the capability to add or remove the tag in `lab` (indicated by the {} argument)—and passing it one end of the channel to communicate with the `Handler`. Because the `Handler` does not give permission for other processes to add the tag in `lab`, no process other than the `Handler` or the new `Worker` can read information that flows from the new `Worker`.

3 Overview

The architecture of our system is depicted in Fig. 3. The analyzer takes as input a DIFC program and a DIFC policy. First, the program is (automatically) extended with instrumentation code that implements *random-isolation* semantics (§3.3). Next, *canonical abstraction* (§3.2) is performed on the rewritten program to generate a finite-data model. Finally, the model and the DIFC policy are given as input to the concurrent-software model checker Copper, which either verifies that the program adheres to the DIFC policy or produces a (potentially spurious) execution trace as a counterexample. We now illustrate each of these steps by means of examples.

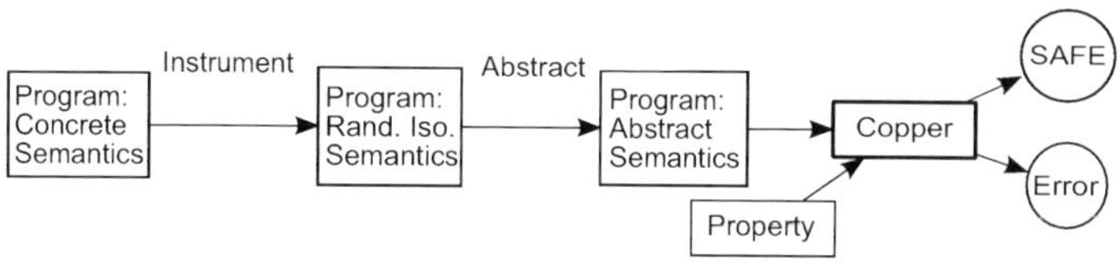

Fig. 3. System architecture

3.1 Concrete Semantics

Program states are represented using *first-order logical structures*, which consist of a collection of individuals, together with an interpretation for a finite *vocabulary* of finite-arity relation symbols. An *interpretation* is a truth-value assignment for each relation symbol and appropriate-arity tuple of individuals. For DIFC systems, these relations encode information such as:

1. "Label variable x does (or does not) contain tag t in its label."
2. "Process p has (or has not) sent information to process q."

Tab. 1 depicts structures as they are transformed by program statements. The convention used is that every boxed node represents a tag individual, and every circled node represents a label individual. The name of an individual may appear outside of the circle. An arrow from an identifier to a circle individual denotes that a particular unary relation holds for the individual, and an arrow between nodes denotes that a binary relation holds for the individuals. A dotted arrow indicates that it is unknown whether a given tuple of a relation does or does not hold, and the relationship is said to be *indefinite*. Otherwise, the relationship is said to be *definite* (i.e., definitely holds or definitely does not hold). A doubled box indicates a *summary* individual, which represents one or more concrete individuals in abstracted structures. The value of the unary relation iso is written inside the individuals in the diagrams for random-isolation semantics. A program statement transforms one structure to another, possibly by adding individuals to the structure or altering the values of relations. State properties are specified as logical formulas.

Example 3. The top row, left column of Tab. 1 gives an example of how one concrete state is transformed into the next state by execution of the statement `lab = create_tag()`. Suppose that the statement has been executed twice previously, introducing tag individuals t and u, where u is a member of the label m. This containment is encoded by a relation R_{Tag}, denoted in the figure by an arrow from m to t. The next execution of the statement creates a new tag v and relates the label m to v while ending the relationship between m and u.

3.2 Canonical Abstraction

Unbounded sets of concrete structures can be abstracted into bounded sets of abstract structures using canonical abstraction with respect to some set of unary

Table 1. Illustration of the standard and random-isolation semantics of the statement `lab := create_tag()` and their corresponding abstract semantics

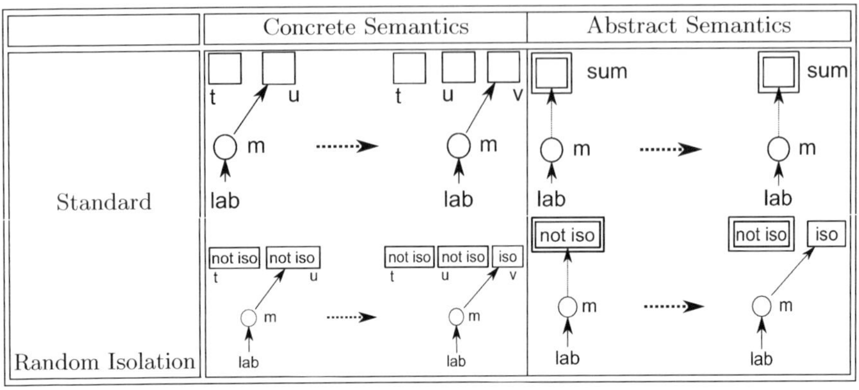

relations $\mathcal{A}$ [12]: each concrete structure S is mapped to an abstract structure $S^{\#}$ that has exactly one individual for each combination of unary relations in $\mathcal{A}$. If multiple concrete individuals that map to the same canonical individual yield different values in some relation $R \notin \mathcal{A}$, then the abstract structure records that the abstract individual may or may not be in the relation R.

Example 4. Consider the top row of Tab. 1. Assume that every tag created belongs to the same relations in $\mathcal{A}$. Thus all tag individuals will be mapped under canonical abstraction into a single abstract summary tag individual, sum. This can introduce imprecision. Suppose that in a concrete structure, $R_{Tag}(m, u)$ holds before the latest execution of `create_tag`, at which point it no longer holds and $R_{Tag}(m, v)$ holds. In the abstraction of this structure, tags t, u, and v are all represented by *sum*. Thus, after the second execution of the statement `create_tag`, sum represents all of label m's tags, but also represents tags that are not elements of m. This is reflected in Tab. 1 by a dotted arrow from the label m to the summary tag individual.

3.3 Random Isolation

Ex. 4 demonstrates that abstraction over the unary relations of a program state is insufficiently precise to prove interesting DIFC properties. We thus use random isolation [6] to reason about an individual from a set, and to generalize the properties proved about the individual object to a proof about all individuals in the set. Random isolation can be formulated as introducing a special unary relation iso in structures. When freshly allocated individuals are created and relations over individuals are updated, the invariant is maintained that iso holds for at most one individual. Furthermore, if iso ever holds for an individual u, then it must continue to hold for u for the remainder of the program's execution. The relation iso can be used to increase the precision of reasoning about an individual in an abstract structure.

Example 5. Consider the state transformation given in the bottom row, left column of Tab. 1. When the program is executed under random-isolation semantics, the call to `create_tag` non-deterministically chooses whether iso holds for the newly created tag. Tab. 1 illustrates the case in which the present call returns a tag for which iso does hold. Now consider the bottom row, right column of Tab. 1, in which the relations used to abstract program states include iso. There is now a definite relationship between the label and the most recently allocated tag. This definite relationship may allow for stronger claims to be made about a structure when properties of the structure are checked.

4 Formal Definition of Abstraction

4.1 Inputs

Subject Programs. To simplify the discussion, we assume a simple imperative language L_{Lab} in which programs are only able to manipulate DIFC labels, send and receive data over channels, and spawn new processes. The full grammar for such a language is given in [13]. The semantics of a program in L_{Lab} can be expressed by encoding program states as logical structures with interpretations in 2-valued logic. A 2-valued logical structure S is a pair $\langle U^S, \iota \rangle$, accompanied by a vocabulary of relations $\mathcal{P}$ and constants $\mathcal{C}$. The set U^S is the universe of individuals of S, and for $p \in \mathcal{P}$ of arity k and every tuple $(u_1, u_2, \ldots, u_k) \in (U^S)^k$, the interpretation ι maps $p(u_1, u_2, \ldots, u_k)$ to a truth value: 0 or 1. The interpretation ι also maps each constant in $\mathcal{C}$ to an individual.

Let $\mathcal{A} \subseteq \mathcal{P}$ be the set of unary *abstraction relations.* For a 2-valued structure S, S' is the *canonical abstraction* of S with respect to $\mathcal{A}$ if S' is a 3-valued structure in which each individual in the universe of S' corresponds to a valuation of the relations in $\mathcal{A}$. Each element in S then maps under an *embedding function* α to the element that represents its evaluation under the relations in $\mathcal{A}$. By construction, for $\alpha(u) \in U^{S'}$ and $R \in \mathcal{A}$, it is the case that $R(\alpha(u)) \in \{0, 1\}$. However, it may be the case that for some individual $u \in U^{S'}$, there exist $u_1, u_2 \in \alpha^{-1}(u)$ and a relation $p \in \mathcal{P}$ such that $p(\ldots, u_1, \ldots) = 0$ and $p(\ldots, u_2, \ldots) = 1$. It is then the case that $p(\ldots, u, \ldots) = 1/2$ where $1/2$ is a third truth value that indicates the absence of information, or uncertainty about the truth of a formula. The truth values are partially ordered by the precision ordering $\sqsubseteq$ defined as $0 \sqsubset 1/2$ and $1 \sqsubset 1/2$. Values 0 and 1 are called *definite* values; $1/2$ is called an *indefinite* value. If φ is a closed first-order logical formula, then let $[\![\varphi]\!]_2^S$ denote the 2-valued truth value of φ for a 2-valued structure S, and let $[\![\varphi]\!]_3^{S'}$ denote its 3-valued truth value for a 3-valued structure S'. For a more complete discussion of the semantics of 3-valued logic, see [12].

By the Embedding Theorem of Sagiv et al. [12], if S is a 2-valued structure, S' is the canonical abstraction of S with embedding function α, Z is an assignment that has a binding for every free variable in φ, and $[\![\varphi]\!]_3^{S'}(Z) \neq 1/2$, then it must be the case that $[\![\varphi]\!]_2^S(Z) = [\![\varphi]\!]_3^{S'}(\alpha \circ Z)$. In other words, any property that has a definite value in S' must have the same definite value in all S that abstract to S'.

In the context of label programs, individuals correspond to process identifiers, per-process variables, tags, channels, and endpoints. Relations encode the state of the program at a particular program point. The constants represent information about the currently executing program statement. Let $U^S = P \cup L \cup T \cup C \cup E$, where P is the set of process identifiers, M is the set of labels, T is the set of tags created during execution, C is the set of channels created during execution, and E is the set of endpoints created during execution.

We now consider a fragment of the relations and constants used in modeling. The complete sets of both the relations and constants are given in [13]:

- $\{\mathsf{isproc}(u), \mathsf{islabel}(u), \mathsf{istag}(u), \mathsf{ischannel}(u), \mathsf{isendp}(u)\}$ denote membership in each of the respective sets. These are the "sort" relations, denoted by Sorts. Each individual has exactly one sort.
- $R_x(u)$ is a unary relation that is true iff the label or endpoint u corresponds to program variable x.
- $R_P(u)$ is a unary relation that is true iff the process identified by u began execution at program point P.
- $R_{Tag}(u, t)$ is a binary relation that is true iff u is a label and t is a tag in the label of u.
- $R_{Chan}(e, c)$ is a binary relation that is true iff e is an endpoint of channel c.
- $R_{Owns}(p, u)$ is a binary relation that is true iff p is a process id and u is a label or endpoint that belongs to a variable local to p.
- $R_{Label}(u_1, u_2)$ is a binary relation that is true iff u_1 is a process identifier or an endpoint and u_2 is the label of u_1.
- For every set of entry points $\mathcal{G}$, there is a binary relation $R_{Flow:\mathcal{G}}(u_1, u_2)$ that is true iff u_1 and u_2 are process ids and there has been a flow of information from u_1 to u_2 only through processes whose entry points are in $\mathcal{G}$.
- $R_{Blocked}(p_1, p_2)$, a binary relation that is true iff p_1 and p_2 are process ids and there has been a flow of information from p_1 to p_2 that was blocked.

We consider the fragment of the vocabulary of constants $\mathcal{C} = \{\mathsf{cur}_p, \mathsf{cur}_{lab}, \mathsf{cur}_+, \mathsf{cur}_-, \mathsf{new}_t\}$. These denote the id, label, positive capability, and negative capability of the process that is to execute the next statement, along with the newest tag allocated. For a program with a process p designated as the first process to execute starting at program point P, the initial state of the program is the logical structure: $\langle \{p_{id}, p_{lab}, p_+, p_-\}, \iota \rangle$ where ι is defined such that each individual is in its sort relation, p_{id} is related to its entry point P, p_{id} is related to its label and capabilities, and the constants that denote the current process, its label, and its capabilities are mapped to p_{id}, p_{lab}, and p_+, p_- respectively.

To execute, the program non-deterministically picks a process, say q_{id}, and updates ι to map cur_{id}, cur_{lab}, cur_+, and cur_- to the id, label, and capabilities of q_{id}. The program then executes the next statement of process q_{id}. The statement transforms the relations over program state as described by the action schemas in [13]. We provide a few of the more interesting schemas in Fig. 4 as examples. For clarity in presenting the action schemas, we use the meta-syntax if φ_0 then φ_1 else φ_2 to represent the formula $(\varphi_0 \rightarrow \varphi_1) \wedge (\neg\varphi_0 \rightarrow \varphi_2)$. Additionally, we define $\mathsf{subset}(x, y)$ to be true iff the label x is a subset of the label y:

$$\mathsf{subset}(x, y) \equiv \forall t : R_{Tag}(x, t) \rightarrow R_{Tag}(y, t) \quad (1)$$

Along with transforming relations, some program statements have the additional effect of expanding the universe of individuals of the structure. In particular:

- `create_channel` adds new endpoint individuals u_{e0}, u_{e1} and a new channel individual u_c to the universe. It redefines the interpretation to add each of these individuals to the appropriate sort relations.
- `create_tag` adds a new tag individual u_t and similarly defines the interpretation to add this tag to its sort relation.
- `spawn` adds a new process id p_{id} and new labels p_{lab}, p_+, p_- that represent the label, positive capability, and negative capability of the process, respectively. It redefines the interpretation to add each of these individuals to their respective sorts.

Fig. 4 defines formally the action schema for the following two actions:

- `send(e);` attempts to send data from the current process to the channel that has `e` as an endpoint. The action potentially updates both the set of all flow-history relations and the blocked-flow relation. To update a flow-history relation $R_{Flow:\mathcal{G}}(u_1, u_2)$, the action checks if u_1 represents the id of the current process. If so, it takes f, the endpoint in u_1 to which the variable e maps, and checks if f is an endpoint of the channel u_2. If so, it checks if the label of u_1 is a subset of that of the endpoint of f and if so, adds (u_1, u_2) to the flow-history relation. Otherwise, the relation is unchanged.
  To update relation $R_{Blocked}(p_1, p_2)$, let f be the endpoint that belongs to u_1 and mapped by variable `e`. If f is an endpoint of a channel for which the other endpoint is owned by p_2, and the label of p_1 is not a subset of the label of f, then $R_{Blocked}(p_1, p_2)$ is updated. Otherwise, the relation is unchanged.
- `l := create_tag();` creates a new tag and stores it in the variable l. This updates the relation R_{Tag}. To update the value of the entry $R_{Tag}(u, t)$, the action checks if u represents a label belonging to the current process and if the variable l maps to u. If so, then $R_{Tag}(u, t)$ holds in the post-state if and only if t is the new tag. Otherwise, the relation R_{Tag} is unchanged.

Specifications. DIFC specifications can be stated as formulas in first-order logic. The following specifications are suitable for describing desired DIFC properties for programs written for DIFC systems.

- $\mathsf{NoFlowHistory}(P, Q, D) = \forall p, q : (R_P(p) \wedge R_Q(q) \wedge p \neq q) \rightarrow \neg R_{Flow:(\mathcal{G}-\{D\})}$ (p, q). For program points P, Q, D, this formula states that no process that begins execution at P should ever leak information to a different process that begins execution at Q unless it goes through a process in D. Intuitively, this can be viewed as a *security property*.

Statement	Update Formula
`send(e);`	$R'_{Flow:\mathcal{G}}(u_1, u_2) = \mathsf{isproc}(u_1) \wedge \mathsf{ischan}(u_2) \wedge (u_1 = cur_{id}$ $\wedge(\exists f, m : R_e(f) \wedge R_{Owns}(u_1, f)$ $\wedge R_{Chan}(f, u_2) \wedge R_{Label}(f, m)$ $\wedge\ (\exists s : R_{Flow:\mathcal{G}}(s, u_1))$ $\wedge\ \mathsf{subset}(cur_{lab}, m))) \vee R_{Flow:\mathcal{G}}(u_1, u_2)$ $R'_{Blocked}(p_1, p_2) = \mathsf{isproc}(p_1) \wedge \mathsf{isproc}(p_2) \wedge (u_1 = cur_{id}$ $\wedge(\exists c, f, g, m : R_{Owns}(f) \wedge R_e(f)$ $\wedge R_{Chan}(f, c) \wedge R_{Chan}(g, c)$ $\wedge R_{Owns}(p_2, g) \wedge R_{Label}(f, m)$ $\wedge\neg\mathsf{subset}(cur_{lab}, m)))$ $\vee R_{Blocked}(p_1, p_2)$
`l := create_tag();`	$R'_{Tag}(u, t) = \mathsf{islabel}(u) \wedge \mathsf{istag}(t)$ $\wedge$ if $R_{Owns}(\mathsf{cur}_{id}, u) \wedge R_l(u)$ then $t = \mathsf{new}_t$ else $R_{Tag}(u, t)$

Fig. 4. Example action schemas for statements in L_{Lab}. Post-state relations are denoted with primed variables. Each post-state tuple of a relation R is expressed in terms of values of pre-state tuples. Post-state relations that are the same as their pre-state counterparts are not shown above.

- $\mathsf{DefiniteSingleStepFlow}(P, Q) = \forall p, q : (R_P(p) \wedge R_Q(q)) \rightarrow \neg R_{Blocked}(p, q)$. For program points P and Q, this formula states that whenever a process that begins execution in P sends data to a process that begins execution in Q, then the information should not be blocked. Intuitively, this can be viewed as a *functionality property*.

Abstraction. The abstract semantics of a program in L_{Lab} can now be defined using 3-valued structures. Let P be a program in L_{Lab}, with a set of program variables $\mathcal{V}$ and a set of program points $\mathcal{L}$. To abstract the set of all concrete states of P, we let the set of abstraction relations $\mathcal{A}$ be $\mathcal{A} = \mathsf{Sorts} \cup \{R_x | x \in \mathcal{V}\} \cup \{R_P | P \in \mathcal{L}\}$.

By the Embedding Theorem [12], a sound abstract semantics is obtained by using exactly the same action schemas that define the concrete semantics, but interpreting them in 3-valued logic to obtain transformers of 3-valued structures.

4.2 Checking Properties Using Random Isolation

A simple example suffices to show that the canonical abstraction of a structure S based on the set of relations $\mathcal{A}$ is insufficiently precise to establish interesting DIFC properties of programs.

Example 6. Consider again the server illustrated in Fig. 1. In particular, consider a *concrete* state of the program with structure S in which n Worker processes have been spawned, each with a unique tag t_k for process k. In this setting, when a Worker with label u_i attempts to send data to a different Worker that can read data over a channel with an endpoint u_j where $i \neq j$, then $\mathsf{subset}(u_i, u_j) = 0$. Thus, no information can leak from one Worker to another. However, an analysis of the *abstract* states determines soundly, but imprecisely, that such a program might not uphold the specification $\mathsf{NoFlowHistory}(\mathsf{Worker}, \mathsf{Worker}, \emptyset)$. Let S' be the canonical abstraction of S based on $\mathcal{A}$. Under this abstraction, all tags in S are merged into a single abstract tag individual t in S'. Thus, for any process p, $R_{Tag}(p, t) = 1/2$, and subset yields $1/2$ when comparing the labels of any process and any endpoint. Thus, if a Worker attempts to send data over a channel used by another Worker, the analysis determines that the send *might* be successful and thus that data may be leaked between separate Worker processes.

Intuitively, the shortcoming in Ex. 6 arises because the abstraction collapses information about the tags of all processes into a single abstract individual. However, random isolation can prove a property for one tag individual t non-deterministically distinguished from the other tags, and then soundly infer that the property is true of all tags individuals. We first formalize this notion by stating and proving the principle of random isolation in terms of 3-valued logic. We then examine how the principle can be applied to DIFC program properties. The proof requires the following lemma:

Lemma 1. *Let $\varphi[x]$ be a formula that does not contain the relation* iso, *and in which x occurs free. Let S be a 2-valued structure. For $u \in U^S$, let ρ_u map S to a structure that is identical to S except that it contains a unary relation* iso *that holds only for element u. Let α perform canonical abstraction over the set of unary relations $\mathcal{A} \cup \{\mathsf{iso}\}$. Then*

$$[\![\forall x : \varphi[x]]\!]_2^S \sqsubseteq \bigsqcup_{u \in U^S} [\![\forall x : iso(x) \rightarrow \varphi[x]]\!]_3^{\alpha(\rho_u(S))}$$

Proof. See [13]. □

The benefits of random isolation stem from the following theorem, which shows that when checking a universally quantified formula $\forall x : \varphi[x]$, one only needs to check whether the weaker formula $\forall x : \mathsf{iso}(x) \rightarrow \varphi[x]$ holds.

Theorem 1. *For a program P, let $\mathcal{T}$ be the set of all logical structures that are reachable under the standard, concrete semantics of P, and let $\mathcal{U}$ be the set of all abstract 3-valued structures that are reachable under the 3-valued interpretation of the concrete semantics after the random-isolation transformation has been applied to P. Let $\varphi[x]$ be a formula that does not contain the relation* iso. *Then*

$$\bigsqcup_{S \in \mathcal{T}} [\![\forall x : \varphi[x]]\!]_2^S \sqsubseteq \bigsqcup_{S^\# \in \mathcal{U}} [\![\forall x : \mathsf{iso}(x) \rightarrow \varphi[x]]\!]_3^{S^\#} \quad (2)$$

Proof. Let $S \in \mathcal{T}$ be a state reachable in the execution of P. Let A be defined on a two-valued structure S as $A(S) = \bigcup_{u \in U^S} \{\alpha(\rho_u(S))\}$. By the soundness of the abstract semantics, it must be the case that for $S' \in A(S)$, there exists some $S^\# \in \mathcal{U}$ such that S' embeds into $S^\#$. Thus, by the Embedding Theorem [12],

$$\bigsqcup_{u \in U^S} [\![\forall x : \mathsf{iso}(x) \rightarrow \varphi(x)]\!]_3^{\alpha(\rho_u(S))} \sqsubseteq \bigsqcup_{S^\# \in \mathcal{U}} [\![\forall x : \mathsf{iso}(x) \rightarrow \varphi(x)]\!]_3^{S^\#}$$

and thus by Lem. 1, we have

$$[\![\forall x : \varphi(x)]\!]_2^S \sqsubseteq \bigsqcup_{S^\# \in \mathcal{U}} [\![\forall x : \mathsf{iso}(x) \rightarrow \varphi(x)]\!]_3^{S^\#}$$

Eqn. (2) follows from properties of $\sqcup$ and the soundness of the abstract semantics [12]. □

Example 7. Consider again the example of the server with code given in Fig. 2 checked against the specification $\mathsf{NoFlowHistory}(\mathsf{Worker}, \mathsf{Worker}, \emptyset)$. Let the server execute under random-isolation semantics with isolation relations isoproc and isotag. We want to verify that every state reachable by the program satisfies the formula $\mathsf{NoFlowHistory}(P, Q, D)$. Thm. 1 can be applied here in two ways:

1. One can introduce a unary relation isoproc that holds true for exactly one process id and then check

$$\forall p : \mathsf{isoproc}(p) \rightarrow \forall q : ((R_P(p) \wedge R_Q(q)) \rightarrow \neg R_{Flow:\mathcal{G}-\{\mathcal{D}\}}(p, q))$$

   Intuitively, this has the effect of checking only the isolated process to see if it can leak information.
2. Consider instances where a flow relation $R_{Flow:\mathcal{G}}$ is updated on a send from the isolated process. Information will only be allowed to flow from the sender if the label of the sender is a subset of the label of the endpoint. The code in Fig. 2 does not allow this to happen, but the abstraction of the (ordinary) concrete semantics fails to establish that the flow is definitely blocked (illustrated in Ex. 6).
   By Thm. 1, one can now introduce a unary relation isotag that holds for at most one tag and instead of checking subset as defined in Eqn. (1), check the formula: $\forall t : \mathsf{isotag}(t) \rightarrow (R_{Tag}(x, t) \rightarrow R_{Tag}(y, t))$. When the tag is in the sender's label, the abstract structure encodes the fact that the tag is held by exactly one process: the isolated sender. Thus the abstraction of the random-isolation semantics is able to establish that the flow is definitely blocked.

5 Experiments

There is an immediate correspondence between the operations defined in the grammar of L_{Lab} and the API of the DIFC system Flume. We took advantage of a close correspondence between abstraction via 3-valued logic and predicate abstraction (details can be found in [13]) and modeled the abstraction of the

Table 2. Results of model checking

Program	Size (LOC)	# Procs. (runtime)	Property	Result	Time
FlumeWiki	110	unbounded	Correct	safe	1h 9m 16s
			Interference	possible bug	37m 53s
Apache	596	unbounded	Correct	safe	1h 13m 27s
			Interference	possible bug	18m 30s
ClamAV	3427	2	Correct	safe	7m 55s
			NoRead	possible bug	3m 25s
			Export	possible bug	3m 25s
OpenVPN	29494	3	Correct	safe	2m 17s
			NoRead	possible bug	2m 52s
			Leak	possible bug	2m 53s

random-isolation semantics in C code via a source-to-source translation tool implemented with CIL [14], a front-end and analysis framework for C (see [13]). The tool takes as input a program written against the Flume API that may execute using bounded or unbounded sets of processes, tags, and endpoints. Our experiments demonstrate that information-flow policies for real-world programs used in related work [1,2,3,4] can often be expressed as logical formulas over structures that record DIFC state; that these policies can be checked quickly, and proofs or violations can be found for systems that execute using bounded sets of processes and tags; and that these policies can be checked precisely, albeit in significantly more time, using random isolation to find proofs or violations for programs that execute using unbounded processes and tags.

We applied the tool to three application modules—the request handler for FlumeWiki, the Apache multi-process module, and the scanner module of the ClamAV virus scanner—as well as the entire VPN client, OpenVPN. For each program, we first used the tool to verify that a correct implementation satisfied a given DIFC property. We then injected faults into the implementations that mimic potential mistakes by real programmers, and used the tool to identify executions that exhibited the resulting incorrect flow of information. The results are given in Fig. 2.

FlumeWiki. FlumeWiki [3] is a Wiki based on the MoinMoin Wiki engine [15], but redesigned and implemented using the Flume API to enforce desired DIFC properties. A simplification of the design architecture for FlumeWiki serves as the basis for the running example in Fig. 1. We focused on verifying the following properties:

- **Security:** Information from one `Worker` process should never reach another `Worker` process. Formally, $\mathsf{NoFlowHistory}(\mathsf{Worker}, \mathsf{Worker}, \emptyset)$.
- **Functionality:** A `Worker` process should always be able to send data to the `Handler` process. Formally, $\mathsf{DefiniteSingleStepFlow}(\mathsf{Worker}, \mathsf{Handler})$.

We created a buggy version ("Interference") by retaining the DIFC code that allocates a new tag for each process, but removing the code that initializes each new process with the tag. The results for both versions are presented in Fig. 2.

Apache. The Apache [7] web server modularizes implementations of policies for servicing requests. We analyzed the *preforking* module, which pre-emptively launches a set of worker processes, each with its own channel for receiving requests. We checked this module against the properties checked for FlumeWiki above. Because there was no preexisting Flume code for Apache, we wrote label-manipulation code by hand and then verified it automatically using our tool.

ClamAV. ClamAV [8] is a virus-detection tool that periodically scans the files of a user, checking for the presence of viruses by comparing the files against a database of virus signatures. We verified flow properties over the module that ClamAV uses to scan files marked as sensitive by a user. Our results demonstrate that we are able to express and check a policy, *export protection* (given below as the security property), that is significantly different from the policy checked for the server models above. The checked properties are as follows:

- **Security:** ClamAV should never be able to send private information out over the network. Formally, $\mathsf{NoFlowHistory}(\mathsf{Private}, \mathsf{Network}, \emptyset)$.
- **Functionality:** ClamAV should always be able to read data from private files. Formally, $\mathsf{DefiniteSingleStepFlow}(\mathsf{Private}, \mathsf{ClamAV})$.

Because there was no DIFC manipulation code in ClamAV, we implemented a "manager" module that initializes private files and ClamAV with DIFC labels, similar to the scenario described in [2]. We introduced a functionality bug ("NoRead") into the manager in which we did not initialize ClamAV with the tags needed to be able to read data from private files. We introduced a security bug ("Export") in which the handler accidentally gives ClamAV sufficient capabilities to export private data over the network.

OpenVPN. OpenVPN [9] is an open-source VPN client. As described in [2], because VPNs act as a bridge between networks on both sides of a firewall, they represent a serious security risk. Similar to ClamAV, OpenVPN is a program that manipulates sensitive data using a bounded number of processes. We checked OpenVPN against the following flow properties:

- **Security:** Information from a private network should never be able to reach an outside network unless it passes through OpenVPN. Conversely, data from the outside network should never reach the private network without going through OpenVPN. Formally, $\mathsf{NoFlowHistory}(\mathsf{Private}, \mathsf{Outside}, \mathsf{OpenVPN}) \wedge \mathsf{NoFlowHistory}(\mathsf{Outside}, \mathsf{Private}, \mathsf{OpenVPN})$.
- **Functionality:** OpenVPN should always be able to access data from both networks. Formally, $\mathsf{DefiniteSingleStepFlow}(\mathsf{Private}, \mathsf{OpenVPN}) \wedge \mathsf{DefiniteSingleStepFlow}(\mathsf{Outside}, \mathsf{OpenVPN})$.

Because there was no DIFC manipulation code in OpenVPN, we implemented a "manager" module that initializes the networks and OpenVPN with suitable labels and capabilities. We introduced a bug ("NoRead") in which the manager does not initialize OpenVPN with sufficient capabilities to read data from the networks. We introduced another bug ("Leak") in which the manager initializes the network sources with tag settings that allow some application other than OpenVPN to pass data from one network to the other. Our results indicate that the approach allows us to analyze properties over bounded processes for large-scale programs.

The analyzes of FlumeWiki and Apache take significantly longer than those of the other modules. We hypothesize that this is due to the fact that both of these modules may execute using unbounded sets of processes and tags, whereas the other modules do not. Their abstract models can thus frequently generate non-deterministic values, leading to the examination of many control-flow paths.

Limitations. Although the tool succeeded in proving or finding counterexamples for all properties that we specified, we do not claim that the tool can be applied successfully to all DIFC properties. For instance, our current methods cannot verify certain correctness properties for the full implementation of FlumeWiki [3], which maintains a database that relates users to their DIFC state, and checks and updates the database with each user action, because to do so would require an accurate model of the database. The extension of our formalism and implementation to handle such properties is left for future work.

6 Related Work

Much work has been done in developing interprocess information-flow systems, including the systems Asbestos [16], Hi-Star [2], and Flume [3]. While the mechanisms of these systems differ, they all provide powerful low-level mechanisms based on comparison over a partially ordered set of labels, with the goal of implementing interprocess data secrecy and integrity. Our approach can be viewed as a tool to provide application developers with assurance that code written for these systems adheres to a high-level security policy.

Logical structures have been used previously to model and analyze programs to check invariants, including heap properties [12] and safety properties of concurrent programs [17]. In this paper, we used the semantic machinery of first-order logic to justify the use of random isolation, which was introduced in [6] to check atomic-set serializability problems.

There has been previous work on static verification of information-flow systems. Multiple systems [18,19] have been proposed for reasoning about finite domains of security classes at the level of variables. These systems analyze information flow at a granularity that does not match that enforced by interprocess DIFC systems, and they do not aim to reason about concurrent processes.

The papers that are most closely related to our work are by Chaudhuri et al. [10] and Krohn and Turner [11]. The EON system of Chaudhuri et al. analyzes secrecy and integrity-control systems by modeling them in an expressive but decidable extension of Datalog and translating questions about the presence of an attack into a query. Although the authors analyze a model of an Asbestos web server, there is no discussion of how the model is extracted. Krohn and Turner [11] analyze the Flume system itself and formally prove a property of non-interference. In contrast, our approach focuses on automatically extracting and checking models of applications written for Flume and using abstraction and model checking. Our work concerns verifying a different portion of the system stack and can be viewed as directly complementing the analysis of Flume described in [11].

Guttman *et al.* [20] present a systematic way based on model checking to determine the information-flow security properties of systems running Security-Enhanced Linux. The goal of these researchers was to verify the policy. Our work reasons at the code level whether an application satisfies its security goal. Zhang *et al.* [21] describe an approach to the verification of LSM authorization-hook placement using CQUAL, a type-based static-analysis tool.

References

1. Efstathopoulos, P., Krohn, M., VanDeBogart, S., Frey, C., Ziegler, D., Kohler, E., Mazières, D., Kaashoek, F., Morris, R.: Labels and event processes in the Asbestos operating system. SIGOPS Oper. Syst. Rev. 39(5), 17–30 (2005)
2. Zeldovich, N., Boyd-Wickizer, S., Kohler, E., Mazières, D.: Making information flow explicit in HiStar. In: OSDI (2006)
3. Krohn, M., Yip, A., Brodsky, M., Cliffer, N., Kaashoek, M.F., Kohler, E., Morris, R.: Information flow control for standard os abstractions. In: SOSP (2007)
4. Conover, M.: Analysis of the Windows Vista Security Model. Technical report, Symantec Corporation (2008)
5. Chaki, S., Clarke, E., Groce, A., Ouaknine, J., Strichman, O., Yorav, K.: Efficient verification of sequential and concurrent C programs. Form. Methods Syst. Des. 25(2-3), 129–166 (2004)
6. Kidd, N.A., Reps, T.W., Dolby, J., Vaziri, M.: Finding concurrency-related bugs using random isolation. In: Jones, N.D., Müller-Olm, M. (eds.) VMCAI 2009. LNCS, vol. 5403, pp. 198–213. Springer, Heidelberg (2009)
7. Apache: Apache, `http://www.apache.org`
8. ClamAV: ClamAV, `http://www.clamav.net`
9. OpenVPN: OpenVPN, `http://www.openvpn.net`
10. Chaudhuri, A., Naldurg, P., Rajamani, S.K., Ramalingam, G., Velaga, L.: EON: Modeling and analyzing dynamic access control systems with logic programs. In: CCS (2008)
11. Krohn, M., Tromer, E.: Non-interference for a practical DIFC-based operating system. In: IEEE Symposium on Security and Privacy (2009)
12. Sagiv, M., Reps, T., Wilhelm, R.: Parametric shape analysis via 3-valued logic. ACM Trans. Program. Lang. Syst. 24(3), 217–298 (2002)
13. Harris, W.R., Kidd, N.A., Chaki, S., Jha, S., Reps, T.: Verifying information flow control over unbounded processes. Technical Report UW-CS-TR-1655, Univ. of Wisc (May 2009)
14. Necula, G., McPeak, S., Rahul, S., Weimer, W.: CIL: Intermediate language and tools for analysis and transformation of C programs (2002)

15. MoinMoin: The MoinMoin wiki engine (December 2006), `http://moinmoin.wikiwikiweb.de`
16. Vandebogart, S., Efstathopoulos, P., Kohler, E., Krohn, M., Frey, C., Ziegler, D., Kaashoek, F., Morris, R., Mazières, D.: Labels and Event Processes in the Asbestos Operating System. ACM Trans. Comput. Syst. 25(4), 11 (2007)
17. Yahav, E.: Verifying safety properties of concurrent java programs using 3-valued logic. In: POPL (2001)
18. Denning, D.E., Denning, P.J.: Certification of programs for secure information flow. Commun. ACM 20(7), 504–513 (1977)
19. Myers, A.C.: JFlow: practical mostly-static information flow control. In: POPL (1999)
20. Guttman, J.D., Herzog, A.L., Ramsdell, J.D., Skorupka, C.W.: Verifying Information-Flow Goals in Security-Enhanced Linux. Journal of Computer Security (2005)
21. Zhang, X., Edwards, A., Jaeger, T.: Using CQUAL for static analysis of authorization hook placement. In: USENIX Security Symposium, pp. 33–48 (2002)

Specification and Verification of Web Applications in Rewriting Logic*

María Alpuente[1], Demis Ballis[2], and Daniel Romero[1]

[1] Universidad Politécnica de Valencia,
Camino de Vera s/n, Apdo 22012, 46071 Valencia, Spain
{alpuente,dromero}@dsic.upv.es
[2] Dipartimento di Matematica e Informatica,
Via delle Scienze 206, 33100 Udine, Italy
demis@dimi.uniud.it

Abstract. This paper presents a Rewriting Logic framework that formalizes the interactions between Web servers and Web browsers through a communicating protocol abstracting HTTP. The proposed framework includes a scripting language that is powerful enough to model the dynamics of complex Web applications by encompassing the main features of the most popular Web scripting languages (e.g. PHP, ASP, Java Servlets). We also provide a detailed characterization of browser actions (e.g. forward/backward navigation, page refresh, and new window/tab openings) via rewrite rules, and show how our models can be naturally model-checked by using the Linear Temporal Logic of Rewriting (LTLR), which is a Linear Temporal Logic specifically designed for model-checking rewrite theories. Our formalization is particularly suitable for verification purposes, since it allows one to perform in-depth analyses of many subtle aspects related to Web interaction. Finally, the framework has been completely implemented in Maude, and we report on some successful experiments that we conducted by using the Maude LTLR model-checker.

1 Introduction

Over the past decades, the Web has evolved from being a static medium to a highly interactive one. Currently, a number of corporations (including book retailers, auction sites, travel reservation services, etc.) interact primarily through the Web by means of complex interfaces which combine static content with dynamic data produced "on-the-fly" by the execution of server-side scripts (e.g. Java servlets, Microsoft ASP.NET and PHP code). Typically, a Web application consists of a series of Web scripts whose execution may involve several

* This work has been partially supported by the EU (FEDER) and the Spanish MEC TIN2007-68093-C02-02 project, by the Universidad Politécnica de Valencia program PAID-06-07 (TACPAS), Generalitat Valenciana, under grant Emergentes GV/2009/024, and by the Italian MUR under grant RBIN04M8S8, FIRB project, Internationalization 2004. Daniel Romero is also supported by FPI–MEC grant BES–2008–004860.

A. Cavalcanti and D. Dams (Eds.): FM 2009, LNCS 5850, pp. 790–805, 2009.

interactions between a Web browser and a Web server. In a typical scenario, the browser/server interact by means of a particular "client-server" protocol in which the browser requests the execution of a script to the server, then the server executes the script, and it finally turns its output into a response that the browser can display. This execution model -albeit very simple- hides some subtle intricacies which may yield erroneous behaviors.

Actually, Web browsers support backward and forward navigation through Web application stages, and allow the user to open distinct (instances of) Web scripts in distinct windows/tabs which are run in parallel. Such browser actions may be potentially dangerous, since they can change the browser state without notifying the server, and may easily lead to errors or undesired responses. For instance, [1] reports on a frequent error, called the *multiple windows problem*, which typically happens when a user opens the windows for two items in an online store, and after clicking to buy on the one that was opened first, he frequently gets the second one being bought. Moreover, clicking refresh/forward/backward browser buttons may sometimes produce error messages, since such buttons were designed for navigating stateless Web pages, while navigation through Web applications may require multiple state changes. These problems have occurred frequently in many popular Web sites (e.g. Orbitz, Apple, Continental Airlines, Hertz car rentals, Microsoft, and Register.com) [2]. Finally, naïvely written Web scripts may allow security holes (e.g. unvalidated input errors, access control flaws, *etc.* [3]) producing undesired results that are difficult to debug.

Although the problems mentioned above are well known in the Web community, there is a limited number of tools supporting the automated analysis and verification of Web applications. The aim of this paper is to explore the application of formal methods to formal modeling and automatic verification of complex, real-size Web applications.

Our contribution. This paper presents the following original contributions.
- We define a fine-grained, operational semantics of Web applications based on a formal navigational model which is suitable for the verification of real, dynamic Web sites. Our model is formalized within the Rewriting Logic (RWL) framework [4], a rule-based, logical formalism particularly appropriate to modeling concurrent systems [5]. Specifically, we provide a rigorous rewrite theory which i) completely formalizes the interactions between multiple browsers and a Web server through a request/response protocol that supports the main features of the HyperText Transfer Protocol (HTTP); ii) models browsers actions such as refresh, forward/backward navigation, and window/tab openings; iii) supports a scripting language which abstracts the main common features (e.g. session data manipulation, data base interactions) of the most popular Web scripting languages. iv) formalizes *adaptive navigation* [6], that is, a navigational model in which page transitions may depend on user's data or previous computation states of the Web application.
- We also show how rewrite theories specifying Web application models can be model-checked using the *Linear Temporal Logic of Rewriting* (LTLR) [7,8]. The

LTLR allows us to specify properties at a very high level using RWL rules and hence can be smoothly integrated into our RWL framework.
- Finally, the verification framework has been implemented in Maude [9], a high-performance RWL language, which is equipped with a built-in model-checker for LTLR. By using our prototype, we conducted an experimental evaluation which demonstrates the usefulness of our approach.

To the best of our knowledge, this work represents the first attempt to provide a formal RWL verification environment for Web applications which allows one to verify several important classes of properties (e.g. reachability, security, authentication constraints, mutual exclusion, liveness, *etc.*) w.r.t. a *realistic* model of a Web application which includes detailed browser-server protocol interactions, browser navigation capabilities, and Web script evaluation.

Plan of the paper. The rest of the paper is organized as follows. Section 2 briefly recalls some essential notions about Rewriting Logic. Section 3 illustrates a general model for Web interactions which informally describes the navigation through Web applications using HTTP. In Section 4, we specify a rewrite theory formalizing the navigation model of Section 3. This model captures the interaction of the server with multiple browsers and fully supports the most common browser navigation features. In Section 5, we introduce LTLR, and we show how we can use it to formally verify Web applications. In Section 6, we discuss some related work and then we conclude.

2 Preliminaries

We assume some basic knowledge of term rewriting [10] and Rewriting Logic [5]. Let us first recall some fundamental notions which are relevant to this work. The static state structure as well as the dynamic behavior of a concurrent system can be formalized by a RWL specification encoding a *rewrite theory*. More specifically, a *rewrite theory* is a triple $\mathcal{R} = (\Sigma, E, R)$, where:
(**i**) (Σ, E) is an order-sorted equational theory equipped with a partial order $<$ modeling the usual subsort relation. Σ, which is called the *signature*, specifies the operators and sorts defining the type structure of $\mathcal{R}$, while E is a set of (possibly conditional) equational axioms which may include commutativity (comm), associativity (assoc) and unity (id). Intuitively, the sorts and operators contained in the signature Σ allow one to formalize system states as ground terms of a term algebra $\tau_{\Sigma,E}$ which is built upon Σ and E.
(**ii**) R defines a set of (possibly conditional) labeled rules of the form $(l : t \Rightarrow t' \text{ if } c)$ such that l is a label, t, t' are terms, and c is an optional boolean term representing the rule condition. Basically, rules in R specify general patterns modeling state transitions. In other words, R formalizes the dynamics of the considered system.

Variables may appear in both equational axioms and rules. By notation $x : S$, we denote that variable x has sort S. A *context* C is a term with a single hole, denoted by $[\,]$, which is used to indicate the location where a reduction occurs.

$C[t]$ is the result of placing t in the hole of C. A *substitution* σ is a finite mapping from variables to terms, and $t\sigma$ is the result of applying σ to term t.

The system evolves by applying the rules of the rewrite theory to the system states by means of *rewriting modulo* E, where E is the set of equational axioms. This is accomplished by means of *pattern matching modulo* E. More precisely, given an equational theory (Σ, E), a term t and a term t', we say that t *matches* t' *modulo* E (or that t *E-matches* t') via substitution σ if there exists a context C such that $C[t\sigma] =_E t'$, where $=_E$ is the congruence relation induced by the equational theory (Σ, E). Hence, given a rule $r = (l : t \Rightarrow t' \text{ if } c)$, and two ground terms s_1 and s_2 denoting two system states, we say that s_1 *rewrites* to s_2 modulo E via r (in symbols $s_1 \xrightarrow{r} s_2$), if there exists a substitution σ such that s_1 E-matches t via σ, $s_2 = C[t'\sigma]$ and $c\sigma$ holds (i.e. it is equal to *true* modulo E). A computation over $\mathcal{R}$ is a sequence of rewrites of the form $s_0 \xrightarrow{r_1} s_1 \ldots \xrightarrow{r_k} s_k$, with $r_1, \ldots, r_k \in R$, $s_0, \ldots, s_k \in \tau_{\Sigma,E}$.

3 A Navigation Model for Web Applications

A Web *application* is a collection of related Web pages, hosted by a Web server, containing Web scripts and links to other Web pages. A Web application is accessed using a Web browser which allows one to navigate through Web pages by clicking and following links.

Communication between the browser and the server is given through the HTTP protocol, which works following a *request-response* scheme. Basically, in the *request* phase, the browser submits a URL to the server containing the Web page P to be accessed, along with a string of input parameters (called the *query* string). Then, the server retrieves P and, if P contains a Web script α, it executes α w.r.t. the input data specified by the query string. According to the execution of α, the server defines the Web application *continuation* (that is, the next page P' to be sent to the browser), and *enables* the links in P' dynamically (*adaptive navigation*). Finally, in the *response* phase, the server delivers P' to the browser.

Since HTTP is a stateless protocol, the Web servers are coupled with a session management technique, which allows one to define Web application states via the notion of *session*, that is, global stores that can be accessed and updated by Web scripts during an established connection between a browser and the server.

The *navigation model* of a Web application can be graphically depicted at a very abstract level by using a graph-like structure as follows. Web pages are represented by nodes which may contain a Web script to be executed (α). Solid arrows connecting Web pages model navigation links which are labeled by a condition and a query string. Conditions provide a simple mechanism to implement a general form of adaptive navigation: specifically, a navigation link will be enabled (i.e. clickable) whenever the associated condition holds. The query string represents the input parameters which are sent to the Web server. Finally, dashed arrows model Web application continuations, that is, arcs pointing to Web pages which are automatically computed by Web script executions. Conditions labeling continuations allow us to model any possible evolution of the

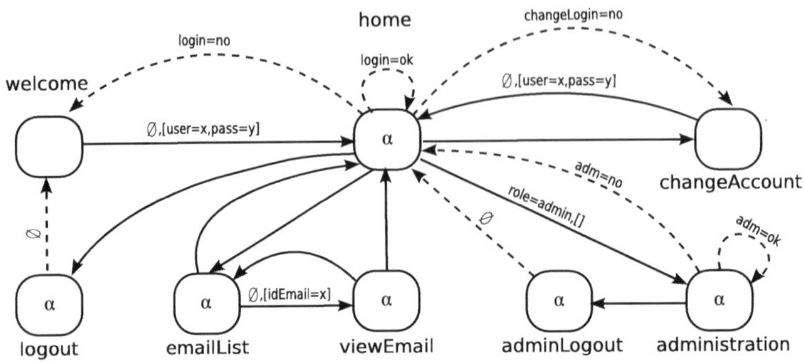

Fig. 1. The navigation model of a Webmail application

Web application of interest. Web application continuations as well as adaptive navigations are dynamically computed w.r.t. the current session (i.e. the current application state).

Example 1. Consider the navigation model given in Figure 1 representing a generic Webmail application which provides some typical functions such as login/logout features, email management, system administration capabilities, *etc.* The solid arrow between the welcome and the home page whose label is ∅,{user=x,pass=y} defines a navigation link which is always enabled and requires two input parameters. The home page has got two possible continuations (dashed arrows) login=ok and login=no. According to the user and pass values provided in the previous transition, only one of them is chosen. In the former case, the login succeeds and the home page is delivered to the browser, while in the latter case the login fails and the welcome page is sent back to the browser.

An example of adaptive navigation is provided by the navigation link connecting the home page to the administration page. In fact, navigation through that link is enabled only when the condition role=admin holds, that is, the role of the logged user is admin.

4 Formalizing the Navigation Model as a Rewrite Theory

In this section, we define a rewrite theory specifying a navigation model, which allows us to formalize the navigation through a Web application via a communicating protocol abstracting HTTP. The communication protocol includes the interaction of the server with multiple browsers as well as the browser navigation features. Our formalization of a Web application consists of the specifications of the following three components: the Web scripting language, the Web application structure, and the communication protocol.

The Web scripting language. We consider a scripting language which includes the main features of the most popular Web programming languages.

Basically, it extends an imperative programming language with some built-in primitives for reading/writing session data (getSession, setSession), accessing and updating a data base (selectDB, updateDB), capturing values contained in a query string sent by a browser (getQuery). The language is defined by means of an equational theory (Σ_s, E_s), whose signature Σ_s specifies the syntax as well as the type structure of the language, while E_s is a set of equations modeling the operational semantics of the language through the definition of an *evaluation* operator $[\![\_]\!]$: ScriptState $\rightarrow$ ScriptState, where ScriptState is defined by the operator

$$(\_,\_,\_,\_,\_) : (\mathsf{Script} \times \mathsf{PrivateMemory} \times \mathsf{Session} \times \mathsf{Query} \times \mathsf{DB}) \rightarrow \mathsf{ScriptState}$$

Roughly speaking, the operator $[\![\_]\!]$ takes as input a tuple $(\alpha, \mathsf{m}, \mathsf{s}, \mathsf{q}, \mathsf{db})$ representing a script α, a private memory m, a session s, a query string q and a data base db, and returns a new script state $(\mathsf{skip}, \mathsf{m}', \mathsf{s}', \mathsf{q}, \mathsf{db}')$ in which the script has been completely evaluated (i.e. it has been reduced to the skip statement) and the private memory, the session and the data base might have been changed because of the script evaluation. In our framework, sessions, private memories, query strings and data bases are modeled by sets of pairs id $=$ val, where id is an identifier whose value is represented by val. The full formalization of the operational semantics of our scripting language can be found in the technical report [11].

The Web application structure. The Web application structure is modeled by an equational theory (Σ_w, E_w) such that $(\Sigma_w, E_w) \supseteq (\Sigma_s, E_s)$. (Σ_w, E_w) contains a specific sort Soup [9] for modeling multisets (i.e. *soup* of elements whose operators are defined using commutativity, associativity and unity axioms) as follows:

$$\emptyset : \rightarrow \mathsf{Soup} \quad \text{(empty soup)}$$
$$\_,\_ : \mathsf{Soup} \times \mathsf{Soup} \rightarrow \mathsf{Soup}\ [\text{comm assoc Id} : \emptyset] \quad \text{(soup concatenation)}.$$

The structure of a Web page is defined with the following operators of (Σ_w, E_w)

$$(\_,\_,\{\_\},\{\_\}) : (\mathsf{PageName} \times \mathsf{Script} \times \mathsf{Continuation} \times \mathsf{Navigation}) \rightarrow \mathsf{Page}$$
$$(\_,\_) : (\mathsf{Condition} \times \mathsf{PageName}) \rightarrow \mathsf{Continuation}$$
$$\_,[\_] : (\mathsf{PageName} \times \mathsf{Query}) \rightarrow \mathsf{Url}$$
$$(\_,\_) : (\mathsf{Condition} \times \mathsf{Url}) \rightarrow \mathsf{Navigation}$$

where we enforce the following subsort relations Page $<$ Soup, Query $<$ Soup, Continuation $<$ Soup, Navigation $<$ Soup, Condition $<$ Soup. Each subsort relation S $<$ Soup allows us to automatically define soups of sort S.

Basically a Web page is a tuple $(\mathsf{n}, \alpha, \{\mathsf{cs}\}, \{\mathsf{ns}\}) \in \mathsf{Page}$ such that n is a name identifying the Web page, α is the Web script included in the page, cs represents a soup of possible continuations, and ns defines the navigation links occurring in the page. Each continuation appearing in $\{\mathsf{cs}\}$ is a term of the form $(\mathsf{cond}, \mathsf{n}')$, while each navigation link in ns is a term of the form $(\mathsf{cond}, \mathsf{n}', [\mathsf{q}_1, \ldots, \mathsf{q}_n])$. A condition is a term of the form $\{\mathsf{id}_1 = \mathsf{val}_1, \ldots, \mathsf{id}_k = \mathsf{val}_k\}$. Given a session s, we say that a continuation $(\mathsf{cond}, \mathsf{n}')$ is *enabled* in s, iff cond $\subseteq$ s, and a navigation link $(\mathsf{cond}, \mathsf{n}', [\mathsf{q}_1, \ldots, \mathsf{q}_n])$ is *enabled* in s iff cond $\subseteq$ s. A Web application is defined as a soup of Page elements defined by the operator $\langle\_\rangle$: Page $\rightarrow$ WebApplication.

Example 2. Consider again the Web application of Example 1. Its Web application structure can be defined as a soup of Web pages $\mathsf{wapp} = \langle \mathsf{p}_1, \mathsf{p}_2, \mathsf{p}_3, \mathsf{p}_4, \mathsf{p}_5, \mathsf{p}_6, \mathsf{p}_7, \mathsf{p}_8 \rangle$ as follows:

$$\begin{aligned}
\mathsf{p}_1 =&(\mathsf{welcome}, \mathsf{skip}, \{\emptyset\}, \{(\emptyset, \mathsf{home}, [\mathsf{user}, \mathsf{pass}])\})\\
\mathsf{p}_2 =&(\mathsf{home}, \alpha_{\mathsf{home}}, \{(\mathsf{login} = \mathsf{no}, \mathsf{welcome}), (\mathsf{changeLogin} = \mathsf{no}, \mathsf{changeAccount}),\\
&\qquad (\mathsf{login} = \mathsf{ok}, \mathsf{home})\},\\
&\quad \{(\emptyset, \mathsf{changeAccount}, [\emptyset]), (\mathsf{role} = \mathsf{admin}, \mathsf{administration}, [\emptyset])\\
&\quad (\emptyset, \mathsf{emailList}, [\emptyset]), (\emptyset, \mathsf{logout}, [\emptyset])\})\\
\mathsf{p}_3 =&(\mathsf{emailList}, \alpha_{\mathsf{emailList}}, \{\emptyset\}, \{(\emptyset, \mathsf{viewEmail}, [\mathsf{emailId}]), (\emptyset, \mathsf{home}, [\emptyset])\})\\
\mathsf{p}_4 =&(\mathsf{viewEmail}, \alpha_{\mathsf{viewEmail}}, \{\emptyset\}, \{(\emptyset, \mathsf{emailList}, [\emptyset]), (\emptyset, \mathsf{home}, [\emptyset])\})\\
\mathsf{p}_5 =&(\mathsf{changeAccount}, \mathsf{skip}, \{\emptyset\}, \{(\emptyset, \mathsf{home}, [\mathsf{user}, \mathsf{pass}])\})\\
\mathsf{p}_6 =&(\mathsf{administration}, \alpha_{\mathsf{admin}}, \{(\mathsf{adm} = \mathsf{no}, \mathsf{home}), (\mathsf{adm} = \mathsf{ok}, \mathsf{administration})\},\\
&\qquad \{\emptyset, \mathsf{adminLogout}, [\emptyset]\})\\
\mathsf{p}_7 =&(\mathsf{adminLogout}, \alpha_{\mathsf{adminLogout}}, \{(\emptyset, \mathsf{home})\}, \{\emptyset\})\\
\mathsf{p}_8 =&(\mathsf{logout}, \alpha_{\mathsf{logout}}, \{(\emptyset, \mathsf{welcome})\}, \{\emptyset\})
\end{aligned}$$

where the application Web scripts might be defined in the following way

$\alpha_{\mathsf{home}} =$

```
login := getSession("login") ;
if (login = null) then
  u := getQuery(user) ;
  p := getQuery(pass) ;
  p1 := selectDB(u) ;
  if (p = p1) then
    r := selectDB(u."-role") ;
    setSession("user", u) ;
    setSession("role", r) ;
    setSession("login", "ok")
  else
    setSession("login", "no") ;
    f := getSession("failed") ;
    if (f = 3) then
       setSession(forbid,"true") fi ;
    setSession("failed", f+1) ;
  fi  fi
```

$\alpha_{\mathsf{admin}} =$

```
u := getSession("user") ;
adm := selectDB("admPage") ;
if (adm = "free")∨(adm = u) then
   updateDB("admPage", u) ;
   setSession("adm", "ok")
else
   setSession("adm", "no")
fi
```

$\alpha_{\mathsf{emailList}} =$

```
u := getSession("user") ;
es := selectDB(u . "-email) ;
setSession("email-found", es)
```

$\alpha_{\mathsf{viewEmail}} =$

```
u := getSession("user") ;
id := getQuery(idEmail) ;
e := selectDB(id) ;
setSession("text-email", e)
```

$\alpha_{\mathsf{adminLogout}} =$ `updateDB("admPage", "free")` $\alpha_{\mathsf{logout}} =$ `clearSession`

The communication protocol. We define the communication protocol by means of a rewrite theory (Σ_p, E_p, R_p), where (Σ_p, E_p) is an equational theory formalizing the Web application states, and R_p is a set of rewrite rules specifying Web script evaluations and request/response protocol actions.

The equational theory (Σ_p, E_p). The theory is built on top of the equational theory (Σ_w, E_w) (i.e. $(\Sigma_p, E_p) \supseteq (\Sigma_w, E_w)$) and models, on the one hand, the entities into play (i.e. the Web server, the Web browser and the protocol messages); on the other hand, it provides a formal mechanism to evaluate enabled continuations as well as enabled adaptive navigations which may be generated "on-the-fly" by executing Web scripts. More formally, (Σ_p, E_p) includes the following operators.

$$\begin{aligned}
\mathsf{B}(_,_,_,\{_\},\{_\},_,_,_) &: (\mathsf{Id} \times \mathsf{Id} \times \mathsf{PageName} \times \mathsf{URL} \times \mathsf{Session} \times \mathsf{Message} \\
&\qquad \times \mathsf{History} \times \mathsf{Nat}) \rightarrow \mathsf{Browser} \\
\mathsf{S}(_,\{_\},\{_\},_,_) &: (\mathsf{WebApplication} \times \mathsf{BrowserSession} \times \mathsf{DB} \times \mathsf{Message} \\
&\qquad \times \mathsf{Message}) \rightarrow \mathsf{Server} \\
\mathsf{H}(_,\{_\},_) &: (\mathsf{PageName} \times \mathsf{URL} \times \mathsf{Message}) \rightarrow \mathsf{History} \\
\mathsf{B2S}(_,_,_,[_],_) &: (\mathsf{Id} \times \mathsf{Id} \times \mathsf{PageName} \times \mathsf{Query} \times \mathsf{Nat}) \rightarrow \mathsf{Message} \\
\mathsf{S2B}(_,_,_,\{_\},\{_\},_) &: (\mathsf{Id} \times \mathsf{Id} \times \mathsf{PageName} \times \mathsf{URL} \times \mathsf{Session} \times \mathsf{Nat}) \rightarrow \mathsf{Message} \\
\mathsf{BS}(_,\{_\}) &: (\mathsf{Id} \times \mathsf{Session}) \rightarrow \mathsf{BrowserSession} \\
_\|_\|_ &: (\mathsf{Browser} \times \mathsf{Message} \times \mathsf{Server}) \rightarrow \mathsf{WebState}
\end{aligned}$$

where we enforce the following subsort relations $\mathsf{History} < \mathsf{List}$, $\mathsf{URL} < \mathsf{Soup}$, $\mathsf{BrowserSession} < \mathsf{Soup}$, $\mathsf{Browser} < \mathsf{Soup}$, and $\mathsf{Message} < \mathsf{Queue}$[1].

We model a browser as a term of the form

$$\mathsf{B}(\mathsf{id_b}, \mathsf{id_t}, \mathsf{n}, \{\mathsf{url}_1, \ldots, \mathsf{url_l}\}, \{\mathsf{id}_1 = \mathsf{val}_1, \ldots, \mathsf{id_m} = \mathsf{val_m}\}, \mathsf{m}, \mathsf{h}, \mathsf{i})$$

where $\mathsf{id_b}$ is an identifier representing the browser; $\mathsf{id_t}$ is an identifier modeling an open tab of browser $\mathsf{id_b}$; n is the name of the Web page which is currently displayed on the Web browser; $\mathsf{url}_1, \ldots, \mathsf{url_l}$ represent the navigation links which appear in the Web page n; $\{\mathsf{id}_1 = \mathsf{val}_1, \ldots, \mathsf{id_m} = \mathsf{val_m}\}$ is the last session that the server has sent to the browser; m is the last message sent to the server; h is a bidirectional list recording the history of the visited Web pages; and i is an internal counter used to distinguish among several response messages generated by repeated refresh actions (e.g. if a user pressed twice the refresh button, only the second refresh is displayed in the browser window).

The server is formalized by using a term of the form

$$\mathsf{S}(\langle \mathsf{p}_1, \ldots, \mathsf{p_l}\rangle, \{\mathsf{BS}(\mathsf{id_{b1}}, \{\mathsf{s}_1\}), .., \mathsf{BS}(\mathsf{id_{bn}}, \{\mathsf{s_n}\})\}, \{\mathsf{db}\}, \mathsf{fifo_{req}}, \mathsf{fifo_{res}})$$

where $\langle \mathsf{p}_1, \ldots, \mathsf{p_l}\rangle$ defines the Web application currently in execution; $\mathsf{s_i} = \{\mathsf{id}_1 = \mathsf{val}_1, \ldots, \mathsf{id_m} = \mathsf{val_m}\}$ is the session that belongs to browser $\mathsf{id_{bi}}$, which is needed to keep track of the Web application state of each user; $\mathsf{db} = \{\mathsf{id}_1 = \mathsf{val}_1, \ldots, \mathsf{id_k} = \mathsf{val_k}\}$ specifies the data base hosted by the Web server; and $\mathsf{fifo_{req}}$,$\mathsf{fifo_{res}}$ are two queues of messages, which respectively model the request messages which still have to be processed by the server and the pending response messages that the server has still to send to the browsers.

We assume the existence of a bidirectional channel through which server and browser can communicate by message passing. In this context, terms of the form

$$\mathsf{B2S}(\mathsf{id_b}, \mathsf{id_t}, \mathsf{n}, [\mathsf{id}_1 = \mathsf{val}_1, \ldots, \mathsf{id_m} = \mathsf{val_m}], \mathsf{i})$$

model *request* messages, that is, messages sent from the browser $\mathsf{id_b}$ (and tab $\mathsf{id_t}$) to the server asking for the Web page n with query parameters $[\mathsf{id}_1 = \mathsf{val}_1, \ldots, \mathsf{id_m} = \mathsf{val_m}]$. Instead, terms of the form

$$\mathsf{S2B}(\mathsf{id_b}, \mathsf{id_t}, \mathsf{n}, \{\mathsf{url}_1, \ldots, \mathsf{url_l}\}, \{\mathsf{id}'_1 = \mathsf{val}'_1, \ldots, \mathsf{id}'_\mathsf{m} = \mathsf{val}'_\mathsf{m}\}, \mathsf{i})$$

[1] We represent a queue with elements $e_1, \ldots, e_n$ by $(e_1, \ldots, e_n)$, where e_1 is the first element of the queue.

model *response* messages, that is, messages sent from the server to the browser $\mathsf{id_b}$ (and tab $\mathsf{id_t}$) including the computed Web page n along with the navigation links $\{\mathsf{url}_1, \ldots, \mathsf{url}_l\}$ occurring in n, and the current session information[2].

Using the operators described so far, we can precisely formalize the notion of Web application state as a term of the form

$$\mathsf{br} \parallel \mathsf{m} \parallel \mathsf{sv}$$

where br is a soup of browsers, m is a channel modeled as a queue of messages, and sv is a server. Intuitively, a Web application state can be interpreted as a snapshot of the system capturing the current configurations of the browsers, the server and the channel.

The equational theory (Σ_p, E_p) also defines the operator

$$\mathsf{eval}(\_,\_,\_,\_) : \mathsf{WebApplication} \times \mathsf{Session} \times \mathsf{DB} \times \mathsf{Message} \rightarrow \mathsf{Session} \times \mathsf{DB} \times \mathsf{Message}$$

whose semantics is specified by means of E_p (see [11] for the precise formalization of eval). Given a Web application w, a session s, a data base db, and a request message $\mathsf{b2s} = \mathsf{B2S}(\mathsf{id_b}, \mathsf{id_t}, \mathsf{n}, [\mathsf{q}], \mathsf{k})$, $\mathsf{eval}(\mathsf{w}, \mathsf{s}, \mathsf{db}, \mathsf{b2s})$ generates a triple $(\mathsf{s}', \mathsf{db}', \mathsf{s2b})$ containing an updated session s', an updated data base db', and a response message $\mathsf{s2b} = \mathsf{S2B}(\mathsf{id_b}, \mathsf{id_t}, \mathsf{n}', \{\mathsf{url}_1, \ldots, \mathsf{url_m}\}, \mathsf{s}', \mathsf{k})$. Intuitively, the operator eval allows us to execute a Web script and dynamically determine (i) which Web page n' is generated by computing an enabled continuation, and (ii) which links of n' are enabled w.r.t. the current session.

The rewrite rule set R_p. It defines a collection of rewrite rules of the form $\mathsf{label} : \mathsf{WebState} \Rightarrow \mathsf{WebState}$ abstracting the standard request-response behavior of the HTTP protocol and the browser navigation features. First, we give the rules that formalize the HTTP protocol, and then the rules that correspond to the browser navigation features. More specifically, the HTTP protocol specifies the requests of multiple browsers, the script evaluations, and the server responses by means of the following rules.

$$\begin{aligned}\mathsf{ReqIni}:\ & \mathsf{B}(\underline{\mathsf{id_b}, \mathsf{id_t}, \mathsf{p_c}, \{(\mathsf{np}, [\mathsf{q}])}, \mathsf{urls}\}, \{\mathsf{s}\}, \mathsf{lm}, \mathsf{h}, \mathsf{i}), \mathsf{br} \parallel \mathsf{m} \parallel \mathsf{sv} \Rightarrow \\ & \qquad \mathsf{B}(\mathsf{id_b}, \mathsf{id_t}, \underline{\mathsf{emptyPage}}, \emptyset, \{\mathsf{s}\}, \underline{\mathsf{m_{idb,idt}}}, \underline{\mathsf{h_c}}, \mathsf{i}), \mathsf{br} \parallel (\mathsf{m}, \underline{\mathsf{m_{idb,idt}}}) \parallel \mathsf{sv}\end{aligned}$$

where $\mathsf{m_{idb,idt}} = \mathsf{B2S}(\mathsf{id_b}, \mathsf{id_t}, \mathsf{np}, [\mathsf{q}], \mathsf{i})$ and $\mathsf{h_c} = \mathsf{push}((\mathsf{p_c}, \{(\mathsf{np}, [\mathsf{q}]), \mathsf{urls}\}, \mathsf{m_{idb,idt}}), \mathsf{h})$

$$\begin{aligned}\mathsf{ReqFin}:\ & \mathsf{br} \parallel (\underline{\mathsf{m_{idb,idt}}}, \mathsf{m}) \parallel \mathsf{S}(\mathsf{w}, \{\mathsf{bs}\}, \{\mathsf{db}\}, \mathsf{fifo_{req}}, \mathsf{fifo_{res}}) \Rightarrow \\ & \qquad \mathsf{br} \parallel \mathsf{m} \parallel \mathsf{S}(\mathsf{w}, \{\mathsf{bs}\}, \{\mathsf{db}\}, (\mathsf{fifo_{req}}, \underline{\mathsf{m_{idb,idt}}}), \mathsf{fifo_{res}})\end{aligned}$$

where $\mathsf{m_{idb,idt}} = \mathsf{B2S}(\mathsf{id_b}, \mathsf{id_t}, \mathsf{np}, [\mathsf{q}], \mathsf{i})$

$$\begin{aligned}\mathsf{Evl}:\ & \mathsf{br} \parallel \mathsf{m} \parallel \mathsf{S}(\mathsf{w}, \{\mathsf{BS}\underline{(\mathsf{id_b}, \{\mathsf{s}\})}, \mathsf{bs}\}, \underline{\{\mathsf{db}\}, (\mathsf{m_{idb,idt}}}, \mathsf{fifo_{req}}), \mathsf{fifo_{res}}) \Rightarrow \\ & \qquad \mathsf{br} \parallel \mathsf{m} \parallel \mathsf{S}(\mathsf{w}, \{\mathsf{BS}(\mathsf{id_b}, \underline{\{\mathsf{s}'\}}), \mathsf{bs}\}, \underline{\{\mathsf{db}'\}}, \mathsf{fifo_{req}}, (\mathsf{fifo_{res}}, \underline{\mathsf{m}'}))\end{aligned}$$

where $(\mathsf{s}', \mathsf{db}', \mathsf{m}') = \mathsf{eval}(\mathsf{w}, \mathsf{s}, \mathsf{db}, \mathsf{m_{idb,idt}})$

---

[2] Session information is typically represented by HTTP *cookies*, which are textual data sent from the server to the browser to let the browser know the current application state.

$$\mathsf{ResIni}: \mathsf{br} \parallel \mathsf{m} \parallel \mathsf{S}(\mathsf{w}, \{\mathsf{bs}\}, \{\mathsf{db}\}, \mathsf{fifo_{req}}, \underline{(\mathsf{m_{idb,idt}}}, \mathsf{fifo_{res}})) \Rightarrow \mathsf{br} \parallel (\mathsf{m}, \underline{\mathsf{m_{idb,idt}}}) \parallel \mathsf{S}(\mathsf{w}, \{\mathsf{bs}\}, \{\mathsf{db}\}, \mathsf{fifo_{req}}, \mathsf{fifo_{res}})$$

$$\mathsf{ResFin}: \mathsf{B}(\underline{\mathsf{id_b}, \mathsf{id_t}}, \mathsf{emptyPage}, \emptyset, \{\mathsf{s}\}, \mathsf{lm}, \mathsf{h}, \underline{\mathsf{i}}), \mathsf{br} \parallel (\underline{\mathsf{S2B}((\mathsf{id_b}, \mathsf{id_t}, \mathsf{p'}, \mathsf{urls}, \{\mathsf{s'})\}, \mathsf{i})}, \mathsf{m}) \parallel \mathsf{sv} \Rightarrow \mathsf{B}(\mathsf{id_b}, \mathsf{id_t}, \underline{\mathsf{p'}, \mathsf{urls}, \{\mathsf{s'}\}}, \mathsf{lm}, \mathsf{h}, \mathsf{i}), \mathsf{br} \parallel \mathsf{m} \parallel \mathsf{sv}$$

where $\mathsf{id_b}, \mathsf{id_t} : \mathsf{Id}$, $\mathsf{br} : \mathsf{Browser}$, $\mathsf{sv} : \mathsf{Server}$, $\mathsf{urls} : \mathsf{URL}$, $\mathsf{i} : \mathsf{Nat}$, $\mathsf{q} : \mathsf{Query}$, $\mathsf{h} : \mathsf{History}$, $\mathsf{w} : \mathsf{WebApplication}$, $\mathsf{m}, \mathsf{m'}, \mathsf{m_{idb,idt}}, \mathsf{fifo_{req}}, \mathsf{fifo_{res}} : \mathsf{Message}$, $\mathsf{p_c}, \mathsf{p'}, \mathsf{np} : \mathsf{PageName}$, $\mathsf{s}, \mathsf{s'} : \mathsf{Session}$, and $\mathsf{bs} : \mathsf{BrowserSession}$ are variables.

Roughly speaking, the request phase is split into two parts, which are respectively formalized by rules ReqIni and ReqFin. Initially, when a browser with identifier $\mathsf{id_b}$ requests the navigation link $(\mathsf{np}, [\mathsf{q}])$ appearing in a Web page $\mathsf{p_c}$ of the tab $\mathsf{id_t}$, rule ReqIni is fired. The execution of ReqIni generates a request message $\mathsf{m_{idb,idt}}$ which is enqueued in the channel and saved in the browser as the last message sent. The history list is updated as well. Rule ReqFin simply dequeues the first request message $\mathsf{m_{idb,idt}}$ of the channel and inserts it into $\mathsf{fifo_{req}}$, which is the server queue containing pending requests. Rule Evl consumes the first request message $\mathsf{m_{idb,idt}}$ of the queue $\mathsf{fifo_{req}}$, evaluates the message w.r.t. the corresponding browser session $(\mathsf{id_b}, \{\mathsf{s}\})$, and generates the response message which is enqueued in $\mathsf{fifo_{res}}$, that is, the server queue containing the responses to be sent to the browsers. Finally, rules ResIni and ResFin implement the response phase. First, rule ResIni dequeues a response message from $\mathsf{fifo_{res}}$ and sends it to the channel m. Then, rule ResFin takes the first response message from the channel queue and sends it to the corresponding browser tab.

It is worth noting that the whole protocol semantics is elegantly defined by means of only five, high-level rewrite rules without making any implementation detail explicit. Implementation details are automatically managed by the rewriting logic engine (i.e. rewrite modulo equational theories). For instance, in the rule ReqIni, no tricky function is needed to select an arbitrary navigation link $(\mathsf{np}, [\mathsf{q}])$ from the URLs available in a Web page, since they are modeled as associative and commutative soups of elements (i.e. $\mathsf{URL} < \mathsf{Soup}$) and hence a single URL can be extracted from the soup by simply applying pattern matching modulo associativity and commutativity.

We formalize browser navigation features as follows.

$$\mathsf{Refresh}: \mathsf{B}(\mathsf{id_b}, \mathsf{id_t}, \mathsf{p_c}, \{\mathsf{urls}\}, \{\mathsf{s}\}, \underline{\mathsf{lm}}, \mathsf{h}, \mathsf{i}), \mathsf{br} \parallel \mathsf{m} \parallel \mathsf{sv} \Rightarrow \mathsf{B}(\mathsf{id_b}, \mathsf{id_t}, \mathsf{emptyPage}, \emptyset, \{\mathsf{s}\}, \underline{\mathsf{m_{idb,idt}}}, \mathsf{h}, \underline{\mathsf{i}+1}), \mathsf{br} \parallel (\mathsf{m}, \underline{\mathsf{m_{idb,idt}}}) \parallel \mathsf{sv}$$

where $\mathsf{lm} = \mathsf{B2S}(\mathsf{id_b}, \mathsf{id_t}, \mathsf{np}, \mathsf{q}, \mathsf{i})$ and $\mathsf{m_{idb,idt}} = \mathsf{B2S}(\mathsf{id_b}, \mathsf{id_t}, \mathsf{np}, \mathsf{q}, \mathsf{i}+1)$

$$\mathsf{OldMsg}: \mathsf{B}(\underline{\mathsf{id_b}, \mathsf{id_t}}, \mathsf{p_c}, \{\mathsf{urls}\}, \{\mathsf{s}\}, \mathsf{lm}, \mathsf{h}, \underline{\mathsf{i}}), \mathsf{br} \parallel (\underline{\mathsf{S2B}(\mathsf{id_b}, \mathsf{id_t}, \mathsf{p'}, \mathsf{urls'}, \{\mathsf{s'}\}, \mathsf{k})}, \mathsf{m}) \parallel \mathsf{sv} \Rightarrow \mathsf{B}(\mathsf{id_b}, \mathsf{id_t}, \mathsf{p_c}, \{\mathsf{urls}\}, \{\mathsf{s}\}, \mathsf{lm}, \mathsf{h}, \mathsf{i}), \mathsf{br} \parallel \mathsf{m} \parallel \mathsf{sv} \quad \text{if } \underline{\mathsf{i} \neq \mathsf{k}}$$

$$\mathsf{NewTab}: \mathsf{B}(\mathsf{id_b}, \mathsf{id_t}, \mathsf{p_c}, \{\mathsf{urls}\}, \{\mathsf{s}\}, \mathsf{lm}, \mathsf{h}, \mathsf{i}), \mathsf{br} \parallel \mathsf{m} \parallel \mathsf{sv} \Rightarrow \mathsf{B}(\mathsf{id_b}, \mathsf{id_t}, \mathsf{p_c}, \{\mathsf{urls}\}, \{\mathsf{s}\}, \mathsf{lm}, \mathsf{h}, \mathsf{i}), \underline{\mathsf{B}(\mathsf{id_b}, \mathsf{id_{nt}}, \mathsf{p_c}, \{\mathsf{urls}\}, \{\mathsf{s}\}, \emptyset, \emptyset, 0)}, \mathsf{br} \parallel \mathsf{m} \parallel \mathsf{sv}$$

where $\mathsf{id_{nt}}$ is a new fresh value of the sort Id.

$$\mathsf{Backward}: \mathsf{B}(\mathsf{id_b}, \mathsf{id_t}, \mathsf{p_c}, \{\mathsf{urls}\}, \{\mathsf{s}\}, \mathsf{lm}, \mathsf{h}, \mathsf{i}), \mathsf{br} \parallel \mathsf{m} \parallel \mathsf{sv} \Rightarrow \mathsf{B}(\mathsf{id_b}, \mathsf{id_t}, \underline{\mathsf{p_h}, \{\mathsf{urls_h}\}}, \{\mathsf{s}\}, \underline{\mathsf{lm_h}}, \mathsf{h}, \mathsf{i}), \mathsf{br} \parallel \mathsf{m} \parallel \mathsf{sv}$$

where $(\mathsf{p_h}, \{\mathsf{url_h}\}, \mathsf{lm_h}) = \mathsf{prev}(\mathsf{h})$

$$\mathsf{Forward}: \mathsf{B}(\mathsf{id_b}, \mathsf{id_t}, \mathsf{p_c}, \{\mathsf{urls}\}, \{\mathsf{s}\}, \mathsf{lm}, \mathsf{h}, \mathsf{i}), \mathsf{br} \parallel \mathsf{m} \parallel \mathsf{sv} \Rightarrow \mathsf{B}(\mathsf{id_b}, \mathsf{id_t}, \underline{\mathsf{p_h}, \{\mathsf{urls_h}\}}, \{\mathsf{s}\}, \underline{\mathsf{lm_h}}, \mathsf{h}, \mathsf{i}), \mathsf{br} \parallel \mathsf{m} \parallel \mathsf{sv}$$

where $(\mathsf{p_h}, \{\mathsf{urls_h}\}, \mathsf{lm_h}) = \mathsf{next}(\mathsf{h})$

where $\mathsf{id_b}, \mathsf{id_t}, \mathsf{id_{nt}} : \mathsf{Id}$, $\mathsf{br} : \mathsf{Browser}$, $\mathsf{sv} : \mathsf{Server}$, $\mathsf{urls}, \mathsf{url'}, \mathsf{urls_h} : \mathsf{URL}$, $\mathsf{q} : \mathsf{Query}$, $\mathsf{h} : \mathsf{History}$ $\mathsf{m}, \mathsf{lm}, \mathsf{lm_h}, \mathsf{m_{idb,idt}} : \mathsf{Message}$, $\mathsf{i}, \mathsf{k} : \mathsf{Nat}$, $\mathsf{p_c}, \mathsf{p'}, \mathsf{np}, \mathsf{p_h} : \mathsf{PageName}$, and $\mathsf{s}, \mathsf{s'} : \mathsf{Session}$ are variables.

Rules Refresh and OldMsg model the behavior of the refresh button of a browser. Rule Refresh applies when a page refresh is invoked. Basically, it first increments the browser internal counter, and then a new version of the last request message lm, containing the updated counter, is inserted into the channel queue. Note that the browser internal counter keeps track of the number of repeated refresh button clicks. Rule OldMsg is used to consume all the response messages in the channel, which might have been generated by repeated clicks of the refresh button, with the exception of the last one ($i = k$).

Finally, rules NewTab, Backward and Forward are quite intuitive: an application of NewTab simply generates a new Web application state containing a new fresh tab in the soup of browsers, while Backward (resp. Forward)) extracts from the history list the previous (resp. next) Web page and sets it as the current browser Web page.

It is worth noting that applications of rules in R_p might produce an infinite number of (reachable) Web application states. For instance, an infinite applications of rule newTab would produce an infinite number of Web application states, each of which represents a finite number of open tabs. Therefore, to make analysis and verification feasible, we set some restrictions in our prototypical implementation of the model to limit the number of reachable states (e.g. we fixed upper bounds on the length of the history list, on the number of tabs the user can open, *etc.*). An alternative approach that we plan to pursue in the future is to define a state abstraction by means of a suitable equational theory in the style of [12]. This would allow us to produce finite (and hence effective) descriptions of infinite state systems.

5 Model Checking Web Applications Using LTLR

The formal specification framework presented so far allows us to specify a number of subtle aspects of the Web application semantics which can be verified using model-checking techniques. To this respect, the Linear Temporal Logic of Rewriting (LTLR)[8] can be fruitfully employed to formalize properties which are either not expressible or difficult to express using other verification frameworks.

The Linear Temporal Logic of Rewriting. LTLR is a sublogic of the family of the Temporal Logics of Rewriting TLR* [8], which allows one to specify properties of a given rewrite theory in a simple and natural way. In particular, we chosen the "tandem" $LTLR/(\Sigma_p, E_p, R_p)$. In the following, we provide an intuitive explanation of the main features of LTLR; for a thorough discussion, please refer to [8].

LTLR extends the traditional Linear Temporal Logic (LTL) with *state predicates* (SP) and *spatial action patterns* (Π). A LTLR formulae w.r.t. SP and Π can be defined by means of the following BNF-like syntax:

$$\varphi ::= \delta \mid p \mid \neg\varphi \mid \varphi \vee \varphi \mid \varphi \wedge \varphi \mid \bigcirc \varphi \mid \varphi \mathcal{U} \varphi \mid \Diamond\varphi \mid \Box\varphi$$
$$\text{where } \delta \in SP, p \in \Pi, \text{ and } \varphi \in LTLR(SP, \Pi)$$

Since LTLR generalizes LTL, the modalities and semantic definitions are entirely similar to those for LTL (see, e.g., [13]). The key new addition is the semantics of spatial actions; the relation $R, (\pi, \gamma) \models \delta$ holds if and only if the proof term $\gamma(0)$ of a current computation is an instance of a spatial action pattern δ.

Let us illustrate the state predicates and the spatial action patterns by means of a rather intuitive example. Let (Σ_p, E_p, R_p) be the rewrite theory specified in Section 4, modeling the Web application states as terms $\mathsf{b}\|\mathsf{m}\|\mathsf{s}$ of sort WebState. Then, the state predicate $\mathsf{B}(\mathsf{ib_b}, \mathsf{id_t}, \mathsf{page}, \{\mathsf{urls}\}, \{\mathsf{s}\}, \mathsf{m}, \mathsf{h}, \mathsf{i})\|\mathsf{m}\|\mathsf{sv} \models \mathsf{curPage}(\mathsf{page}) = \mathsf{true}$ holds (i.e. evaluates to true) for each state such that page is the current Web page displayed in the browser. Besides, the spatial action pattern $\mathsf{ReqIni}(\mathsf{id_b}\backslash\mathsf{A})$ allows us to localize all the applications of the rule ReqIni where the rule's variable $\mathsf{id_b}$ are instantiated with A, that is, all ReqIni applications which refer to the browser with identifier A.

LTLR properties for Web Applications. This section shows the main advantages of coupling LTLR with Web applications specified via the rewrite theory (Σ_p, E_p, R_p).

Concise and parametric properties. As LTLR is a highly parametric logic, it allows one to define complex properties in a concise way by means of state predicates and spatial action patters. As an example, consider the Webmail application given in Example 1, along with the property *"Incorrect login info is allowed only 3 times, and then login is forbidden"*. This property might be formalized as the following standard LTL formula:

$$\Diamond(\mathsf{welcomeA}) \rightarrow \Diamond(\mathsf{welcomeA} \wedge \bigcirc(\neg(\mathsf{forbiddenA}) \vee (\mathsf{welcomeA} \wedge \bigcirc(\neg(\mathsf{forbiddenA}) \vee$$
$$(\mathsf{welcomeA} \wedge \bigcirc(\neg(\mathsf{forbiddenA}) \vee \bigcirc(\mathsf{forbiddenA} \wedge \Box(\neg\mathsf{welcomeA})))))))$$

where welcomeA and forbiddenA are atomic propositions respectively describing (i) user A is displaying the welcome page, and (ii) login is forbidden for user A. Although the property to be modeled is rather simple, the resulting LTL formula is textually large and demands a hard effort to be specified and verified.

Moreover, the complexity of the formula would rapidly grow when a higher number of login attempts was considered[3].

By using LTLR we can simply define a login property which is parametric w.r.t. the number of login attempts as follows. First of all, we define the state predicates: (*i*) curPage(id,pn), which holds when user id[4] is displaying Web page pn; (*ii*) failedAttempt(id,n), which holds when user id has performed n failed login attempts; (*iii*) userForbidden(id), which holds when a user is forbidden from logging on to the system. Formally,

$$\begin{aligned} \mathsf{B}(\mathsf{id},\mathsf{id_t},\underline{\mathsf{pn}},\{\mathsf{urls}\},\{\mathsf{s}\},\mathsf{lm},\mathsf{h},\mathsf{i}),\mathsf{br}\ \|\mathsf{m}\|\ \mathsf{sv} &\models \mathsf{curPage}(\mathsf{id},\mathsf{pn}) = \mathsf{true} \\ \mathsf{br}\,\|\,\mathsf{m}\,\|\,\mathsf{S}(\mathsf{w},\{\mathsf{BS}(\underline{(\mathsf{id},\{\mathsf{failed}=\mathsf{n}\})},\mathsf{bs}\},\{\mathsf{db}\},\mathsf{f_{req}},\mathsf{f_{res}}) &\models \mathsf{failedAttempt}(\mathsf{id},\mathsf{n}) = \mathsf{true} \\ \mathsf{br}\,\|\,\mathsf{m}\,\|\,\mathsf{S}(\mathsf{w},\{\mathsf{BS}(\underline{(\mathsf{id},\{\mathsf{forbid}=\mathsf{true}\})},\mathsf{bs}\},\{\mathsf{db}\},\mathsf{f_{req}},\mathsf{f_{res}}) &\models \mathsf{userForbidden}(\mathsf{id}) = \mathsf{true} \end{aligned}$$

Then, the security property mentioned above is elegantly formalized by means of the following LTLR formula

$$\Diamond(\mathsf{curPage}(\mathsf{A},\mathsf{welcome}) \wedge \bigcirc(\Diamond\mathsf{failedAttempt}(\mathsf{A},3))) \rightarrow \Box\mathsf{userForbidden}(\mathsf{A})$$

Observe that the previous formula can be easily modified to deal with a distinct number of login attempts —it is indeed sufficient to change the parameter counting the login attempts in the state predicate failedAttempt(A, 3). Besides, note that we can define state predicates (and more in general LTLR formulae) which depend on Web script evaluations. For instance, the predicate failedAttempt depends on the execution of the login script α_{home} which may or may not set the forbid value to true in the user's browser session.

Web script evaluation witnesses the "on-the-fly" capability of our framework which allows us to specify, in a natural way, suitable properties to check the behavior of the scripts.

Unreachability properties. Unreachability properties can be specified as LTLR formulae of the form $\Box\neg\langle\mathsf{State}\rangle$, where State is an unwanted state the system has not to reach. By using unreachability properties over the rewrite theory (Σ_p, E_p, R_p), we can detect very subtle instances of the *multiple windows problem* mentioned in Section 1.

Example 3. Consider again the Webmail application of Example 1. Assume that a user may interact with the application using two email accounts MA and MB. Let us consider a Web application state in which the user is logged in the home page with her account MA. Now, assume that the following sequence of actions is executed: (1) the user opens a new browser tab; (2) the user changes the account in one of the two open tabs and logs in using MB credentials; (3) the user accesses the emailList page from both tabs.

After applying the previous sequence of actions, one expects to see in the two open tabs the emails corresponding to the accounts MA and MB. However, the

[3] Try thinking of how to specify an LTL formula for a more flexible security policy permitting 10 login attempts.

[4] We assume that the browser identifier univocally identifies the user.

Webmail application of Example 1 displays the emails of MB in both tabs. This is basically caused by action (2) which makes the server override the browser session with MB data without notifying the state change to the tab associated with the MA account.

This unexpected behavior can be recognized by using the following LTLR unreachability formula $\Box\neg\,\mathsf{inconsistentState}$ where $\mathsf{inconsistentState}$ is a state predicate defined as:

$$\begin{array}{l} \mathsf{B}(\underline{\mathsf{id}}, \underline{\mathsf{idA}}, \mathsf{p_A}, \{\mathsf{urls_A}\}, \{\underline{(\mathsf{user} = \mathsf{MA})}, \mathsf{s_A}\}, \mathsf{lm_A}, \mathsf{h_A}, \mathsf{i_A}), \\ \mathsf{B}(\underline{\mathsf{id}}, \underline{\mathsf{idB}}, \mathsf{p_B}, \{\mathsf{urls_B}\}, \{\underline{(\mathsf{user} = \mathsf{MB})}, \mathsf{s_B}\}, \mathsf{lm_B}, \mathsf{h_B}, \mathsf{i_B}), \mathsf{br} \parallel \mathsf{m} \parallel \mathsf{sv} \\ \qquad\qquad\qquad\qquad \models \mathsf{inconsistentState} = \mathsf{true} \qquad \mathsf{if}(\mathsf{MA} \neq \mathsf{MB}) \end{array}$$

Roughly speaking, the property $\Box\neg\,\mathsf{inconsistentState}$ states that we do not want to reach a Web application state in which two browser tabs refer to distinct user sessions. If this happens, one of the two session is out-of-date and hence inconsistent.

Finally, it is worth noting that by means of LTLR formulae expressing unreachability statements, we can formalize an entire family of interesting properties such as:

- *mutual exclusion* (e.g. $\Box\neg(\mathsf{curPage}(\mathsf{A}, \mathsf{administration}) \wedge \mathsf{curPage}(\mathsf{B}, \mathsf{administration}))$),
- *link accessibility* (e.g. $\Box\neg\,\mathsf{curPage}(\mathsf{A}, \mathsf{PageNotFound})$),
- *security properties*, (e.g. $\Box\neg(\mathsf{curPage}(\mathsf{A}, \mathsf{home}) \wedge \mathsf{userForbidden}(\mathsf{A}))$).

Liveness through spatial actions. Liveness properties state that something good keeps happening in the system. In our framework, we can employ spatial actions to detect *good* rule applications. For example, consider the following property "*user* A *always succeeds to access her* home *page from the* welcome *page*". This amount to saying that, whenever the protocol rule ReqIni is applied to request the home page of user A, the browser will eventually display the home page of user A. This property can be specified by the following LTLR formula:

$$\Box([\mathsf{ReqIni}(\mathsf{Id_b}\backslash\mathsf{A}, \mathsf{p_c}\backslash\mathsf{welcome}, \mathsf{np}\backslash\mathsf{home})] \rightarrow \Diamond\mathsf{curPage}(\mathsf{A}, \mathsf{home}))$$

Implementation. The verification framework we presented has been implemented in a prototypical system, written in Maude [9], which is publicly available along with several examples at
`http://www.dsic.upv.es/~dromero/web-tlr.html`.

The prototype allows one to define Web application models as extended rewrite theories specified by means of Maude specifications. Then, specifications can be automatically verified using the Maude built-in operator `tlr check`[7] which supports model checking of rewrite theories w.r.t. LTLR. We tested the tool on several examples including all the examples presented in the paper. Preliminary experiments have demonstrated that the experimental system work very satisfactorily on several Web applications models. We are currently developing a Web interface for the tool. Moreover, as future work, we want to define a translator from Web applications written in a commercial language to our Web models.

6 Related Work and Conclusions

Web applications are complex software systems playing a primary role of primary importance nowadays. Not surprisingly, several works have previously addressed the modeling and verification of such systems. A variant of the μ-calculus (called constructive μ-calculus) is proposed in [14] which allows one to model-check connectivity properties over the *static* graph-structure of a Web system. However, this methodology does not support the verification of dynamic properties— e.g. reachability over Web pages generated by means of Web script execution.

Both Linear Temporal Logic (LTL) and Computational Tree Logic (CTL) have been used for the verification of dynamic Web applications. For instance, [15] and [16] support model-checking of LTL properties w.r.t. Web application models represented as Kripke structures. Similar methodologies have been developed in [17] and [18] to verify Web applications by using CTL formulae. All these model-checking approaches are based on coarse Web application models which are concerned neither with the communication protocol underlying the Web interactions nor the browser navigation features. Moreover, as shown in Section 5, CTL and LTL property specifications are very often textually large and hence difficult to formulate and understand. [6] presents a modeling and verification methodology that uses CTL and considers some basic adaptive navigation features. In constrast, our framework provides a complete formalization which supports more advanced adaptive navigation capabilities.

Finally, both [2] and [19] do provide accurate analyses of Web interactions which point out typical unexpected application behaviors which are essentially caused by the uncontrolled use of the browser navigation buttons as well as the shortcomings of HTTP. Their approach however is different from ours since it is based on defining a novel Web programming language which allows one to write safe Web applications: [2] exploits type checking techniques to ensure application correctness, whereas [19] adopts a semantic approach which is based on program continuations.

In this paper, we presented a detailed navigation model which accurately formalizes the behavior of Web applications by means of rewriting logic. The proposed model allows one to specify several critical aspects of Web applications such as concurrent Web interactions, browser navigation features and Web scripts evaluations in an elegant, high-level rewrite theory. We also coupled our formal specification with LTLR, which is a linear temporal logic designed to model-check rewrite theories. The verification framework we obtained allows us to specify and verify even sophisticated properties (e.g. the multiple windows problem) which are either not expressible or difficult to express within other verification frameworks. Finally, we developed a prototypical implementation and we conducted several experiments which demonstrated the practicality of our approach.

Model checking as a tool is widely used in both academia and industry. In order to improve the scalability of our technique, as future work we plan to look at the approach of encoding the model-checking problem into SAT, and the resulting question of determining the efficiency in Maude of different encodings.

References

1. Message, R., Mycroft, A.: Controlling Control Flow in Web Applications. Electronic Notes in Theoretical Computer Science 200(3), 119–131 (2008)
2. Graunke, P., Findler, R., Krishnamurthi, S., Felleisen, M.: Modeling Web Interactions. In: Degano, P. (ed.) ESOP 2003. LNCS, vol. 2618, pp. 238–252. Springer, Heidelberg (2003)
3. Open Web Application Security Project: Top ten security flaws, `http://www.owasp.org/index.php/OWASP_Top_Ten_Project`
4. Martí-Oliet, N., Meseguer, J.: Rewriting Logic: Roadmap and Bibliography. Theoretical Computer Science 285(2), 121–154 (2002)
5. Meseguer, J.: Conditional Rewriting Logic as a Unified Model of Concurrency. Theoretical Computer Science 96(1), 73–155 (1992)
6. Han, M., Hofmeister, C.: Modeling and Verification of Adaptive Navigation in Web Applications. In: 6th International Conference on Web Engineering, pp. 329–336. ACM, New York (2006)
7. Bae, K., Meseguer, J.: A Rewriting-Based Model Checker for the Linear Temporal Logic of Rewriting. ENTCS. Elsevier, Amsterdam (to appear)
8. Meseguer, J.: The Temporal Logic of Rewriting: A Gentle Introduction. In: Degano, P., De Nicola, R., Meseguer, J. (eds.) Concurrency, Graphs and Models. LNCS, vol. 5065, pp. 354–382. Springer, Heidelberg (2008)
9. Clavel, M., Durán, F., Eker, S., Lincoln, P., Martí-Oliet, N., Meseguer, J., Talcott, C.: All About Maude - A High-Performance Logical Framework. LNCS, vol. 4350. Springer, Heidelberg (2007)
10. TeReSe (ed.): Term Rewriting Systems. Cambridge University Press, Cambridge (2003)
11. Alpuente, M., Ballis, D., Romero, D.: A Rewriting Logic Framework for the Specification and the Analysis of Web Applications. Technical Report DSIC-II/01/09, Technical University of Valencia (2009), `http://www.dsic.upv.es/~dromero/web-tlr.html`
12. Meseguer, J., Palomino, M., Martí-Oliet, N.: Equational Abstractions. Theoretical Computer Science 403(2-3), 239–264 (2008)
13. Manna, Z., Pnueli, A.: The Temporal Logic of Reactive and Concurrent Systems. Springer, Heidelberg (1992)
14. Alfaro, L.: Model Checking the World Wide Web. In: Berry, G., Comon, H., Finkel, A. (eds.) CAV 2001. LNCS, vol. 2102, pp. 337–349. Springer, Heidelberg (2001)
15. Flores, S., Lucas, S., Villanueva, A.: Formal Verification of Websites. Electronic notes in Theoretical Computer Science 200(3), 103–118 (2008)
16. Haydar, M., Sahraoui, H., Petrenko, A.: Specification Patterns for Formal Web Verification. In: 8th International Conference on Web Engineering, pp. 240–246. IEEE Computer Society, Los Alamitos (2008)
17. Miao, H., Zeng, H.: Model Checking-based Verification of Web Application. In: 12th IEEE International Conference on Engineering Complex Computer Systems, pp. 47–55. IEEE Computer Society, Los Alamitos (2007)
18. Donini, F.M., Mongiello, M., Ruta, M., Totaro, R.: A Model Checking-based Method for Verifying Web Application Design. Electronic Notes in Theoretical Computer Science 151(2), 19–32 (2006)
19. Queinnec, C.: Continuations and Web Servers. Higher-Order and Symbolic Computation 17(4), 277–295 (2004)

Verifying the Microsoft Hyper-V Hypervisor with VCC

Dirk Leinenbach[1] and Thomas Santen[2]

[1] German Research Center for Artificial Intelligence (DFKI), Saarbrücken, Germany
dirk.leinenbach@dfki.de
[2] European Microsoft Innovation Center, Aachen, Germany
thomas.santen@microsoft.com

Abstract. VCC is an industrial-strength verification suite for the formal verification of concurrent, low-level C code. It is being developed by Microsoft Research, Redmond, and the European Microsoft Innovation Center, Aachen. The development is driven by two applications from the Verisoft XT[1] project: the Microsoft Hyper-V Hypervisor and SYSGO's PikeOS micro kernel.

This paper gives a brief overview on the Hypervisor with a special focus on verification related challenges this kind of low-level software poses. It discusses how the design of VCC addresses these challenges, and highlights some specific issues of the Hypervisor verification and how they can be solved with VCC.

1 The Microsoft Hypervisor

The development of VCC is driven by the verification of the Microsoft Hyper-V Hypervisor, which is an ongoing collaborative research project between the European Microsoft Innovation Center, Microsoft Research, the German Research Center for Artificial Intelligence, and Saarland University in the Verisoft XT project [1]. The Hypervisor is a relatively thin layer of software (100 KLOC of C, 5 KLOC of assembly) that runs directly on x64 hardware. The Hypervisor turns a single real multi-processor x64 machine with virtualization extensions into a number of virtual multi-processor x64 machines. These virtual machines include additional machine instructions (hypercalls) to create and manage other virtual machines.

The Hypervisor code is divided into two strata. The *kernel stratum* is a small multi-processor operating system, complete with hardware abstraction layer, kernel, memory manager, and scheduler (but no device drivers). The *virtualization stratum* runs in each thread an "application" that simulates an x64 machine without the virtualization features, but with some additional Hypervisor specific machine instructions. Simulation means that the observable effect of a machine instruction executed on the virtualized machine basically is the same as on the real machine.

For the most part, a virtual machine – also called a *guest* – is simulated by simply running the real hardware. However, guests – not necessarily knowing that they run under the Hypervisor – set up their own address translation on top of the Hypervisor's virtual address space. The Hypervisor needs to simulate the composition of these

[1] Work partially funded by the German Federal Ministry of Education and Research (BMBF) in the framework of the Verisoft XT project under grant 01 IS 07 008.

A. Cavalcanti and D. Dams (Eds.): FM 2009, LNCS 5850, pp. 806–809, 2009.

two layers of address translation in order to simulate the translation lookaside buffers (TLBs) of the virtual machines. To do this efficiently, the Hypervisor maintains *shadow page tables* (SPTs) which mimic the combined effect of both translation steps. TLB simulation is the most important factor in system performance. Thus, the Hypervisor uses a very complex and highly optimized SPT algorithm, which leverages the degrees of freedom given by the weak hardware TLB semantics.

The verification of a piece of software like the Hypervisor – which was not written with formal verification in mind – poses a number of challenges to a verification tool: (1) In an industrial process, developers and testers must drive the verification process. Thus, verification should be primarily driven by assertions stated at the level of code itself, rather than by guidance provided to interactive theorem provers. (2) The Hypervisor is written in C, which has only a weak, easily circumvented type system and explicit memory (de)allocation, so memory safety has to be explicitly verified. (3) The Hypervisor is a concurrent piece of software and makes heavy use of lock-free synchronization. In particular, address translations are gathered asynchronously and non-atomically (requiring multiple reads and writes to traverse the page tables), creating races in the SPT algorithm with guest system code that operates on the page tables. (4) A typical way to prove properties of a concurrent data type is to show that it simulates some simpler type. To keep annotations tightly integrated with the code, a way of proving concurrent simulation in the code itself is needed. (5) Part of the Hypervisor is written in assembly code. An integrated verification of C and assembly code is needed, which addresses the subtle interactions between the two and the implications on hardware resources.

2 VCC

VCC is geared towards sound verification of functional properties of low-level concurrent C code. An important goal is that the annotations will eventually be integrated into the codebase and maintained by the software developers, evolving along with the code. Thus, VCC embeds specifications and annotations (such as function contracts and type invariants) into the C code. Many of these annotations are similar to those found, e.g., in Spec# [2]. Using conditional compilation, the annotations are hidden from standard C compilers. VCC performs static modular analysis, in which each function is verified in isolation, using only the contracts of functions that it calls and invariants of types used in its code. First, VCC translates programs together with annotations into the Boogie language [3]. Then, the Boogie tool generates verification conditions and passes them to the first order theorem prover Z3 [4]. If Z3 is not able to verify the verification conditions, several diagnostic tools are available for convenient debugging of the program and the annotations.

Although C is not typesafe, most code in a well-written C system adheres to a strict type discipline. Taking advantage of this fact, VCC implements a Spec#-style object and ownership model. Objects may coincide with (pointers to) C structures, but also with sub-structures and arrays. System invariants guarantee that valid objects of the same type with different addresses do not overlap, so they behave like objects in a modern (typesafe) object oriented system. As in some other concurrency methodologies (e.g., [5]), the ownership model allows a thread to perform sequential writes only to data that it owns, and sequential reads only to data that it owns or can prove is not changing.

Type definitions can have type invariants, which are one- or two-state predicates on data, describing the properties of "valid" instances of the type, and how they can evolve from one system state to another.

In addition to contracts and invariants, VCC allows augmenting the operational code of a program with ghost (specification) data and code, which is seen only by the verifier. One application of ghost code is maintaining abstractions of operational data, e.g., representing a list as a set. Ghost code also establishes and maintains the ownership relations of objects and can provide existential witnesses to the first order prover.

VCC accommodates concurrent access to data that is marked as volatile even if the data is not owned by the current thread (using operations guaranteed to be atomic on the given platform), leveraging the observation that a correct concurrent program typically can only race on volatile data. Indeed VCC does not allow lock-free access to non-volatile data. Updates of volatile data are required to preserve invariants but are otherwise unconstrained. Volatile data is, e.g., used to implement locks [6].

Concurrent programs implicitly deal with chunks of knowledge about the shared state. For example, a program attempting to acquire a spin lock must "know" that the spin lock has been initialized and is still allocated [6]. But such knowledge is ephemeral – it could be broken concurrently by other threads – so passing knowledge to a function in the form of a precondition is too weak. Instead, VCC provides a special kind of ghost objects called *claims*. A claim is associated with a number of objects: it guarantees certain properties of those objects, in particular, that they stay allocated as long as a claim to them exists. A comprehensive overview of VCC can be found in [7].

3 Verifying the Hypervisor

Usually, the implementation correctness of a system is verified by proving a simulation theorem between the implementation and an abstract model. The simulation proof of the Hypervisor depends on a model / specification of the x64 processor architecture, which has been developed by Saarland University. The model is described in C, which allows us to combine code correctness proofs and proofs which refer to the processor model within a single tool, namely VCC.

The model of the processor core is implemented as a number of ghost functions operating on a ghost structure which represents the processor's state. In particular, there are ghost functions which specify the effect of executing individual x64 instructions. For components outside the processor core we cannot use a functional specification, because these components might change their state independently of the core: the TLB is allowed to cache new translations on its own initiative, the memory might be changed by other processor cores, and the state of the APIC may change due to interrupt requests from devices or other processor cores. Therefore, these components are specified by restricting their transitions with two-state invariants.

The x64 processor model is used in two places in the Hypervisor verification project. First, we use it for the low-level correctness proofs of the Hypervisor implementation, in particular for the verification of assembly code [8]. Second, the x64 model is used for the top-level specification of the Hypervisor, i.e., that the Hypervisor correctly simulates x64 machines for the guests. For each partition, the (volatile) ghost state for the top-level specification contains, among others, general information about the partition (privileges, IPC state), a set of x64 processor states, and the memory content. We use two-state invariants to specify the legal transitions of the top-level model. Most of the time, these two-state invariants correspond to the two-state invariants of the x64 model. However, we need additional invariants to specify the execution of Hyper-V specific instructions and hypercalls.

The equivalent of the aforementioned simulation proof in our setting is to enforce a coupling invariant between the (volatile) ghost state of the top-level model and the implementation state. Verifying this relation in VCC ensures that the implementation transitions are covered by corresponding *admissible* transitions of the top-level model.

As of July 2009, the Hypervisor verification is still ongoing. Data structure invariants are in place and the larger part of public interfaces is specified. Several hundred functions have been verified with VCC. We are confident that VCC is powerful enough to successfully verify all functions. The specifications provide a detailed documentation that is provably in sync with the code, which is an added value of the exercise in itself. The Hypervisor is part of a released product with very low defect density. Therefore, we did not expect to find many bugs in the code, and indeed less than a handful have been found during the verification process. All of them are very unlikely to let the Hypervisor fail in practical operation. Applying the now available technology early in the process of a product development could help to prevent defects and reduce the effort to meet high quality bars.

Acknowledgment. We thank the great team who contributed to this project!

References

1. Verisoft XT: The Verisoft XT project (2007), `http://www.verisoftxt.de`
2. Barnett, M., Leino, K.R.M., Schulte, W.: The Spec# programming system: An overview. In: Barthe, G., Burdy, L., Huisman, M., Lanet, J.-L., Muntean, T. (eds.) CASSIS 2004. LNCS, vol. 3362, pp. 49–69. Springer, Heidelberg (2005)
3. Barnett, M., Chang, B.Y.E., Deline, R., Jacobs, B., Leino, K.R.M.: Boogie: A modular reusable verifier for object-oriented programs. In: de Boer, F.S., Bonsangue, M.M., Graf, S., de Roever, W.-P. (eds.) FMCO 2005. LNCS, vol. 4111, pp. 364–387. Springer, Heidelberg (2006)
4. de Moura, L., Bjørner, N.: Z3: An efficient SMT solver. In: Ramakrishnan, C.R., Rehof, J. (eds.) TACAS 2008. LNCS, vol. 4963, pp. 337–340. Springer, Heidelberg (2008)
5. Jacobs, B., Piessens, F., Leino, K.R.M., Schulte, W.: Safe concurrency for aggregate objects with invariants. In: Aichernig, B.K., Beckert, B. (eds.) SEFM 2005, pp. 137–147. IEEE, Los Alamitos (2005)
6. Hillebrand, M.A., Leinenbach, D.C.: Formal verification of a reader-writer lock implementation in C. In: SSV 2009. ENTCS, Elsevier Science B.V., Amsterdam (2009), `http://www.verisoftxt.de/PublicationPage.html`
7. Cohen, E., Dahlweid, M., Hillebrand, M., Leinenbach, D., Moskal, M., Santen, T., Schulte, W., Tobies, S.: VCC: A practical system for verifying concurrent C. In: Urban, C. (ed.) TPHOLs 2009. LNCS, vol. 5674, pp. 1–22. Springer, Heidelberg (2009), `http://vcc.codeplex.com/`
8. Maus, S., Moskal, M., Schulte, W.: Vx86: x86 assembler simulated in C powered by automated theorem proving. In: Meseguer, J., Roşu, G. (eds.) AMAST 2008. LNCS, vol. 5140, pp. 284–298. Springer, Heidelberg (2008)

Industrial Practice in Formal Methods: A Review

J.C. Bicarregui[1], J.S Fitzgerald[2], P.G. Larsen[3], and J.C.P. Woodcock[4]

[1] STFC Rutherford Appleton Laboratory
Juan.Bicarregui@stfc.ac.uk
[2] Newcastle University
John.Fitzgerald@ncl.ac.uk
[3] Engineering College of Aarhus
pgl@iha.uk
[4] University of York
Jim.Woodcock@cs.york.ac.uk

Abstract. We examine the the industrial application of formal methods using data gathered in a review of 62 projects taking place over the last 25 years. The review suggests that formal methods are being applied in a wide range of application domains, with increasingly strong tool support. Significant challenges remain in providing usable tools that can be integrated into established development processes; in education and training; in taking formal methods from first use to second use, and in gathering and evidence to support informed selection of methods and tools.

1 Introduction

The successful transfer of formal methods technology into industrial practice has been a goal of researchers and practitioners for several decades. Indeed, by the early 1990s questions were being raised about whether formal methods could ever be viable in industrial settings. Several reviews in that decade [1,2,3,4] reported significant successes but also identified challenges to formal methods adoption including a lack of good tooling and objective evidence for the commercial benefits. Opinions diverged on whether formal methods were delivering hoped-for improvements in practice. Standards, tools, and education would "make or break" industrial adoption [5] and some saw a chasm between academics who "see formal methods as inevitable" and practitioners who "see formal methods as irrelevant" [6].

Following a decade of advances in both methods and tools, it seems appropriate to undertake a new review of industrial experience, including past as well as current projects, with the aim of developing an ongoing, updated resource using a consistent review format for each project. Here we present a short summary of the review, its findings, our observations and suggested challenges. We focus on aspects relevant to developers and users of industry-strength formal methods and tools. Further detail on the review can be found at [7,8].

A. Cavalcanti and D. Dams (Eds.): FM 2009, LNCS 5850, pp. 810–813, 2009.

2 A Review of Industrial Applications of Formal Methods

Using a structured questionnaire, data was collected on 62 industrial projects known from the literature, mailing lists, and personal experience to have employed formal techniques. Data on 56 of the projects were collected from individuals who had been involved and data on the remainder were gathered from the literature. This initial collection may be biased to those with whom we had the strongest contacts. However, the uniform way in which the data was collected does allow comparison between projects, and gives some insight into current practice. It should be stressed that the review is not a statistical survey and so does not form a basis for general inferences about formal methods applications.

The largest application domains were transport (16 projects) and the financial sector (12). Other major sectors were defence (9), telecommunications (7), and office and administration (5). Some 20% of responses indicated that the projects related to software development tools themselves, suggesting that developers are to some extent taking their own medicine. The most strongly represented application types were real-time (20), distributed (17), transaction processing (12) and high data volume (13). 30% of responses indicated that certification standards applied, notably IEC 61508, Common Criteria and UK Level E6 for IT Security Evaluation. Half of respondents estimated the size of the software: the split was roughly equal between 1–10, 10–100, and 100–1000 KLOC. Two projects are from the 1980s, 23 are from the 1990s and 37 are from 2000-2008.

Mild correlations were observed between techniques and software types, indicating higher than average use of model checking in consumer electronics and of inspection in transaction processing software. The use of model checking has increased greatly from 13% in the 1990s to 51% in the present decade. No significant change was apparent for proof, refinement, execution or test case generation.

Some 85% of responses indicated that project staff had prior formal methods experience. Of those reporting no previous expertise, half were in teams with mixed experience levels and half introducing techniques to a novice team. Over half the responses indicated that training had been given.

Respondents were asked to comment on the time, cost and quality implications. The effect on time was, on average, seen as beneficial: three times as many reported a reduction in time as reported an increase. Several projects noted increased time in the specification phase. Of those reporting on costs, five times as many projects reported reductions as reported an increase. 92% of projects reported enhanced quality compared to other techniques; none reported a decrease. Improvement was attributed to better fault detection (36%); improved design (12%), confidence in correctness (10%) and understanding (10%).

3 Observations and Challenges

Trends in Tooling. In spite of the observation in 1993 that tools are "neither necessary nor sufficient" [2], it is now almost inconceivable that an industrial application would proceed without tools. Nevertheless, one respondent saw tools as a potential source of rigidity:

> "...not having a tool allowed us to modify the notation ...to appeal to the target audience. This was crucial to the success of the project.... Had we been locked into an inflexible tool, the project would have failed."

Although tool capabilities have increased, almost all previous surveys and about a quarter of the responses in our review report a lack of "ruggedised" tools. Particular challenges include: support for human interaction in automated deduction, common formats for model interchange and analysis, the lack of support for tools offered on a "best efforts" basis and the need to integrate heterogeneous tools into tool chains. Expectations from tools are also high. One respondent commented:

> "...formal methods need to provide answers in seconds or minutes rather than days. ... model-checking has to be tightly integrated into the ... tools that developers are already using."

Tools usability was poorly rated by many respondents: "Tools don't lend themselves to use by mere mortals." Such comments challenge the community to ensure that potential industry users are communicating their requirements effectively to tools providers, and that the tools providers are responding by ensuring that usability is gaining adequate attention in tools research and development.

Evidence. Previous surveys have noted the lack of evidence to support adoption decisions [1] and appropriate cost models [2]. Only half the projects that we reviewed reported the cost consequences of using formal methods. Some cost data may be sensitive but nonetheless this suggests that pilot studies are not always gathering relevant evidence. In our view, the decision to adopt development technology is often risk-based and convincing evidence of the value of formal techniques in identifying defects can be at least as powerful as a quantitative cost argument. We conjecture that it would be more effective for methods and tools developers to emphasise the de-risking of the development process than to make cost arguments. Pilot applications should observe factors relevant to the needs of those making critical design decisions. This would suggest that the construction of a strong body of evidence showing the utility and ease of use of formal techniques is at least as high a priority as the gathering of more evidence on development costs.

Second Use. Responses to the review questionnaire suggest that the entry cost for formal methods is perceived as high, although the cost can drop dramatically on second use [9]. It is noticeable that very few published reports of formal methods applications describe second or subsequent use, though 75% of respondents in our study indicated that they will use similar methods again. This may be a lack of reporting, or it may represent a challenge to the community to secure and report on series of applications.

Skills and Psychological Barriers. Several responses identify psychological barriers to the use of formal techniques: "people like making things work; lack of early visible progress"; "many developers are 'builders' who do not want to specify everything"; "Barriers: formal methods people ... Too much emphasis on properties and refinement rather than actually constructing something".

Respondents also identified skills deficiencies as a major impediment to formal methods adoption. We do not believe that it is not possible to de-skill the verification process entirely, so the challenges remain of improving education/training and providing provide technology that is readily adopted by engineering teams, taking account of skills, psychology and even the social context.

4 Conclusions

Our review paints a picture in which a substantial range of application areas have been shown to benefit from formal modelling and verification technology. Some of the impediments identified a decade ago have been addressed, notably in the focussed use of methods supported by strong tools. Many challenges remain, particularly in ensuring tools' usability, integration into development processes, providing evidence to support second and subsequent use, and overcoming skills and other barriers to adoption. Initiatives such as the Verified Software Repository offer a basis for well-founded experiments that, it is to be hoped, will help to address these challenges in the next decade. We intend to continue with the collection of data regarding on industrial practice in formal methods[1] and intend to produce new survey reports at 5-year intervals.

Acknowledgements. We are grateful to all the contributors to our review and to the EU FP7 Integrated Project *Deploy* for support.

References

1. Austin, S., Parkin, G.: Formal methods: A survey. Technical report, National Physical Laboratory, Teddington, Middlesex, UK (March 1993)
2. Craigen, D., Gerhart, S., Ralston, T.: An International Survey of Industrial Applications of Formal Methods, vol. 2. U.S. National Institute of Standards and Technology, Computer Systems Laboratory (March 1993)
3. Clarke, E.M., Wing, J.M.: Formal methods: State of the art and future directions. ACM Computing Surveys 28(4), 626–643 (1996)
4. Bloomfield, R., Craigen, D.: Formal methods diffusion: Past lessons and future prospects. Technical Report D/167/6101, Adelard, London, UK (December 1999)
5. Hinchey, M.G., Bowen, J.P.: To formalize or not to formalize? IEEE Computer 29(4), 18–19 (1996)
6. Glass, R.L.: Formal methods are a surrogate for a more serious software concern. IEEE Computer 29(4), 19 (1996)
7. VSR: Verified Software Repository (2009), `http://vsr.sourceforge.net/fmsurvey.htm`
8. Woodcock, J., Larsen, P.G., Bicarregui, J., Fitzgerald, J.: Formal Methods: Practice and Experience. ACM Computing Surveys (in press, 2009)
9. Miller, S.P.: The industrial use of formal methods: Was Darwin right? In: 2nd IEEE Workshop on Industrial Strength Formal Specification Techniques, Boca Raton, FL, pp. 74–82. IEEE Computer Society, Los Alamitos (1998)

[1] Potential contributors are invited to contact the authors.

Model-Based GUI Testing Using UPPAAL at Novo Nordisk

Ulrik H. Hjort[2], Jacob Illum[1], Kim G. Larsen[1], Michael A. Petersen[2], and Arne Skou[1]

[1] Department of Computer Science, Aalborg University, Denmark
[2] Novo Nordisk A/S, Hillerød, Denmark

Abstract. This paper details a collaboration between Aalborg University and Novo Nordisk in developing an automatic model-based test generation tool for system testing of the graphical user interface of a medical device on an embedded platform. The tool takes as input an UML Statemachine model and generates a test suite satisfying some testing criterion, such as edge or state coverage, and converts the individual test case into a scripting language that can be automatically executed against the target. The tool has significantly reduced the time required for test construction and generation, and reduced the number of test scripts while increasing the coverage.

1 Introduction

Model-based development (MBD), [6], is a recent and very promising approach to industrial software development addressing the increasingly complex world of making correct and timely software. Although originally developed for general software systems, MBD has demonstrated great potential within embedded system and in particular safety critical systems for which failures after field deployment are unacceptable, either due to the catastrophic consequences of such failures or the impossibility of updating the software after deployment. MBD techniques address these problems by working with precise mathematical models of the software system and using these models for e.g., formal verification of correctness, automatic code generation, and/or automatic test generation.

The benefits from working with models are numerous: Models are easier to communicate and more precise than textual specifications; models allow for fast prototyping as models can be simulated effortlessly; correctness of the model can be established mathematically; with automatic code generation, manual labor is minimizes assuring faster time to market and less bugs.

The world of model checking has always been a strong proponent for building models and specifications for hardware and software systems and the research field is offering many methods for establishing model correctness. Recently, algorithms and methods from model checking have been extended to other types of model analysis such as automatic controller synthesis, [5,7], and optimal planning and scheduling, [1,3]. The latter turns out to be particularly applicable for

A. Cavalcanti and D. Dams (Eds.): FM 2009, LNCS 5850, pp. 814–818, 2009.

automatic test suite generation, as finding a smallest possible test suite satisfying some coverage criteria is, simply, a planning or scheduling problem.

In this paper, we describe the development of a tool chain for adapting model-based model checking, planning and scheduling techniques to the application of automatic test suite generation. The technology underlying the tool chain is provided by Aalborg University, who with their widely recognized model-checking tool UPPAAL, [2], has made numerous significant contribution to the field of model checking. The case for the tool chain is testing graphical user interfaces on an embedded platform and provided by the large Danish health care company Novo Nordisk A/S. Worldwide, Novo Nordisk employs more than 27,000 employees spread over 81 countries. Novo Nordisk is a world leader in diabetes care, but their business areas also stretch into haemostasis management, growth hormone therapy and hormone replacement therapy.

2 The UPPAAL Model Checker

UPPAAL is a tool for design, simulation and model checking (formal verification) of real-time systems modeled as networks of timed automata extended with discrete data types and user-defined functions. Based on more than a decade of research, UPPAAL provides very efficient algorithms and symbolic data structures for analyzing such models.

Since the release of UPPAAL in the mid-nineties, several variants have emerged, realizing the strength of both timed automata as a modeling language for real-time behavior and the efficiency of UPPAAL's symbolic model checking engine. The different variants are available from `http://www.uppaal.com`.

3 The Case Study: GUI Testing

The purpose of this collaborative work between Aalborg University and Novo Nordisk has been to develop a test generation tool for system testing of graphical user interfaces using the UPPAAL model checking tool.

The choice of UPPAAL as the engine for test generation is motivated by the groups solid knowledge of this particular tool, so, similar tools could have been selected. However, this particular project relies heavily upon optimization extensions of UPPAAL developed for solving planning and scheduling problems. In many ways, this approach is similar to that of Reactis, [4], and Smartesting, [8]. Furthermore, the Novo Nordisk is also exploring the use of UPPAAL for protocol verification, thus, reusing UPPAAL eliminates the introduction of more tools.

The company is developing the hardware and software of an embedded device for medical purposes. This device has a graphical user interface to receive instructions from and provide feedback to the user. The software department at Novo Nordisk has the assignment of system testing the GUI to determine whether all interactions work appropriately and that the expected information is displayed on the screen. The specification of the behavior is traditionally made

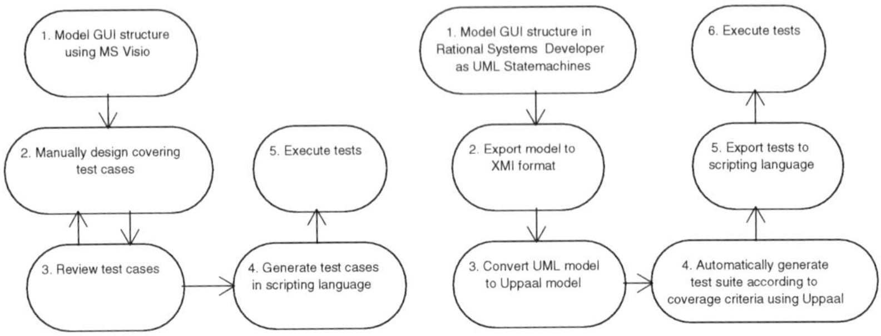

Fig. 1. Old (left) and new (right) testing process

in Microsoft Visio to provide a graphical representation that can be used in the review process as well as for implementation.

The process for the system testers is to look at the Visio drawings and manually generate a set of test cases that cover the behavior of the GUI and validate that the output is correct. These tests need to be reviewed and accepted, before they are finally converted to a scripting language that can automatically be executed against the platform. This process is depicted on the left of Figure 1.

This approach has a number of drawbacks, namely, that 1) manual creation of test cases is error prone and time consuming process (typically 30 days per GUI scenario model), 2) establishing whether the test cases do in fact cover the model is difficult, 3) changes to the model require the entire process to be repeated.

By introducing model-based testing in this process, we can alleviate these drawbacks by removing the manual task of test generation and test review, knowing that the output of the automatic process is mathematically guaranteed to cover the model. And finally, since the technology is fully automated, changes to the model are reflected in the test cases by the push of a button.

To ease the transition to model-based GUI specifications, we have chosen UML Statemachines as an input model since 1) UML is an establish standard familiar to most developers and thus requires minimal re-education, 2) Novo Nordisk has the software infrastructure in place to support the building of UML models, 3) the UML Statemachine notion is very similar to the current Visio models thus maintaining the current validation process.

To accommodate this choice, it has been necessary to adapt UPPAAL to accept UML Statemachine models. This has been accomplished by converting the XMI exchange format into UPPAAL models. The engines of UPPAAL and UPPAAL CORA are then applied to the models and used to generate a test suite with either edge or state coverage. The resulting test cases are, finally, converted into the scripting language that can be executed on the target. This new process is depicted to the right of Figure 1.

The variant of UML Statemachines that can be translated to UPPAAL is a subset of UML Statemachines allowing only some constructions extended with features from UPPAAL, such as variables and clocks. These elements are interpreted with UPPAAL semantics. Thus, the extension is not using a certain UML profile, however, this is a viable future avenue to explore. Omitted features from UML Statemachine include associating arbitrary activities as effects of transitions, allowing effects to only update variables and clocks.

4 Conclusion

Using the automated testing tool has reduced the time used on test construction from upwards of 30 days to 3 days spent modelling and then a few minutes on actual test generation. The benefits extend into the specification process, as the model structure is used for specifications and later refined with action code to allow for automatic test generation. This removes the process of keeping specifications and test models consistent, an otherwise tedious and error-prone process. Furthermore, the testing tool has decreased the number of test cases while at the same time increasing and guaranteeing full model coverage in terms of edge coverage. The automatically generated test scripts have uncovered a number of bugs in the software, even "difficult" bugs that can be hard to detect, since the test generation process makes no assumptions about how the system should be used; something testers have a tendency to do. The GUI models that have been constructed have approximately 200 states and 350 transitions, and test generation for the models takes around one minute.

The company has experienced that creating usable models for test generation requires time, however, once the model has been generated making changes, extensions, and doing maintenance is easy. Finally, the fact that specification changes are immediately reflected in the test suite has proved extremely helpful for bug detection.

In conclusion, the collaboration has been very successful and beneficial to both company and university. The project has proven that active research can result in a commercially usable tool within a few months. The ongoing work of this project has reached a state where the company has even requested continued support on the tool, since it has become an integrated part of the development process.

References

1. Behrmann, G., Brinksma, E., Hendriks, M., Mader, A.: Scheduling lacquer production by reachability analysis – a case study. In: Workshop on Parallel and Distributed Real-Time Systems 2005. IEEE Computer Society, Los Alamitos (2005)
2. Behrmann, G., David, A., Larsen, K.G.: A tutorial on UPPAAL. In: Bernardo, M., Corradini, F. (eds.) SFM-RT 2004. LNCS, vol. 3185, pp. 200–236. Springer, Heidelberg (2004)
3. Behrmann, G., Larsen, K.G., Rasmussen, J.I.: Optimal scheduling using priced timed automata. ACM SIGMETRICS Perform. Eval. Rev. 32(4), 34–40 (2005)
4. Reactis by Reactive Systems Inc. (July 2009), `http://www.reactive-systems.com`

5. Cassez, F., Jessen, J.J., Larsen, K.G., Raskin, J.-F., Reynier, P.-A.: Automatic synthesis of robust and optimal controllers - an industrial case study. In: HSCC. LNCS, vol. 5469, pp. 90–104. Springer, Heidelberg (2009)
6. Frankel, D.S. (ed.): Model Driven Architecture: Applying MDA to Enterprise Computing. John Wiley & Sons, Chichester (2003)
7. Jessen, J.J., Rasmussen, J.I., Larsen, K.G., David, A.: Guided controller synthesis for climate controller using UPPAAL TIGA. In: Raskin, J.-F., Thiagarajan, P.S. (eds.) FORMATS 2007. LNCS, vol. 4763, pp. 227–240. Springer, Heidelberg (2007)
8. Smartesting (July 2009), `http://www.smartesting.com`

Author Index

Abbasi, Naeem 435
Ahrendt, Wolfgang 612
Akbarpour, Behzad 435
Akbarpour, Reza 435
Albert, Elvira 370
Alpuente, María 790
Archer, Myla 173
Arenas, Puri 370

Ballis, Demis 790
Bicarregui, J.C. 810
Bonakdarpour, Borzoo 660
Bonzanni, Nicola 16
Boute, Raymond 387
Butler, Michael 579
Butterfield, Andrew 451

Chaki, Sagar 773
Chen, Wei 321
Chen, Yifeng 467
Clarke, Edmund M. 547

Daylight, Edgar G. 273
de Boer, Frank S. 612
Delmas, David 532
Delseny, Hervé 532
Derrick, John 305
Dong, Jin Song 123
Dougherty, Daniel J. 483

Eshuis, Rik 239

Falampin, Jérôme 708
Feenstra, K. Anton 16
Fisler, Kathi 483
Fitzgerald, J.S 810
Fokkink, Wan 16
Fritz, Fabian 708

Ganai, Malay 256
Gancarski, Paweł 451
Gast, Holger 628
Genaim, Samir 370
Giannakopoulos, Theophilos 483
Gomes, Artur Oliveira 692
Gopalakrishnan, Ganesh 724
Grabe, Immo 612
Groz, Roland 207
Guo, Qiang 305
Gupta, Aarti 256

Hammond, Kevin 354
Haneberg, Dominik 190
Harris, William R. 773
Hasan, Osman 435
Heidarian, Faranak 516
Heitmeyer, Constance 173
Hjort, Ulrik H. 814
Hoenicke, Jochen 338
Hofmann, Martin 354

Illum, Jacob 814

Jaffar, Joxan 72
Jeffords, Ralph 173
Jha, Somesh 773
Johnsen, Einar Broch 596
Jost, Steffen 354

Khurshid, Sarfraz 757
Kidd, Nicholas A. 773
Kirby, Robert M. 724
Kohlhase, Michael 223
Krepska, Elzbieta 16
Krishnamurthi, Shriram 483
Kulkarni, Sandeep S. 660
Kundu, Sudipta 256
Kyas, Marcel 596

Lang, Frédéric 157
Larsen, Kim G. 676, 814
Larsen, Peter Gorm 563, 810
Lausdahl, Kenneth 563
Leinenbach, Dirk 806
Leino, K. Rustan M. 338
Lemburg, Johannes 223
Leonard, Elizabeth 173
Leuschel, Michael 708
Li, Shuhao 676
Lintrup, Hans Kristian Agerlund 563

Liu, Shanshan 123
Liu, Yang 123, 321
Liu, Yanhong A. 321
Loidl, Hans-Wolfgang 354
Lüth, Christoph 419

Mateescu, Radu 157
McIver, Annabelle K. 41, 289
Meinicke, Larissa 41
Morgan, Carroll C. 41, 289
Morzenti, Angelo 741
Mota, Alexandre 140

Nielsen, Brian 676

O'Halloran, Colin 23
Oliveira, Marcel Vinícius Medeiros 692

Perry, Dewayne E. 757
Petersen, Michael A. 814
Plagge, Daniel 708
Platzer, André 547
Podelski, Andreas 338
Pradella, Matteo 741
Puebla, Germán 370
Pusinskas, Saulius 676

Rajamani, Sriram K. 33
Ramos, Rodrigo 140
Reeves, Steve 499
Reif, Wolfgang 190
Reps, Thomas 773
Reynolds, Mark 403
Romero, Daniel 790
Roychoudhury, Abhik 123

Said, Mar Yah 579
Sampaio, Augusto 140
Sanders, J.W. 467
San Pietro, Pierluigi 741
Santen, Thomas 806
Santosa, Andrew E. 72
Scaife, Norman 354
Schäf, Martin 338
Schellhorn, Gerhard 190
Schierl, Andreas 190
Schmaltz, Julien 516
Schröder, Lutz 223
Schrieb, Jonas 106
Schulz, Ewaryst 223
Seidl, Helmut 644
Shahbaz, Muzammil 207
Shao, Danhua 757
Shukla, Sandeep K. 273
Skou, Arne 814
Snook, Colin 579
Souyris, Jean 532
Streader, David 499
Sun, Jun 123, 321

Tahar, Sofiène 435
Tonetta, Stefano 89
Tschantz, Michael Carl 1

Vaandrager, Frits 516
Vakkalanka, Sarvani 724
Vene, Varmo 644
Vo, Anh 724
Vojdani, Vesal 644

Walkinshaw, Neil 305
Walter, Dennis 419
Wang, Chao 256
Wehrheim, Heike 106
Wiels, Virginie 532
Wies, Thomas 338
Wing, Jeannette M. 1
Wonisch, Daniel 106
Woodcock, J.C.P. 810

Yu, Ingrid Chieh 596

SPRINGER NATURE

GPSR Compliance

The European Union's (EU) General Product Safety Regulation (GPSR) is a set of rules that requires consumer products to be safe and our obligations to ensure this.

If you have any concerns about our products, you can contact us on ProductSafety@springernature.com

In case Publisher is established outside the EU, the EU authorized representative is:

Springer Nature Customer Service Center GmbH
Europaplatz 3
69115 Heidelberg, Germany

FSC
www.fsc.org
MIX
Papier | Fördert gute Waldnutzung
FSC® C083411

Kolibri 360 GmbH
Ferdinand-Jühlke-Straße 7
99095 Erfurt, Deutschland
produktsicherheit@kolibri360.de